THE PENGUIN DICTIONARY OF PSYCHOLOGY

Arthur S. Reber was born in 1940 in Philadelphia. He took his BA degree at the University of Pennsylvania in 1961 and his Ph.D. at Brown University in 1967.. He is currently Broeklundian Professor of Psychology at Brooklyn College and the Graduate Center of the City University of New York. He has also taught at the University of British Columbia, Canada, was a Fulbright Professor (1977–8) at the University of Innsbruck, Austria, and a Visiting Scholar at the University of North Wales in Bangor, UK. His published work includes several score papers in cognitive psychology, the psychology of language, developmental psychology, and such diverse areas as philosophical psychology, gambling and critiques of parapsychology. He is the author of *Implicit Learning and Tacit Knowledge* (Oxford University Press), *The New Gambler's Bible* (Three Rivers Press) and co-editor with D. Scarborough of *Toward a Psychology of Reading* (LEA Press).

THE PENGUIN DICTIONARY OF
PSYCHOLOGY

SECOND EDITION

ARTHUR S. REBER

PENGUIN BOOKS

PENGUIN BOOKS

Published by the Penguin Group
Penguin Books Ltd, 80 Strand, London WC2R 0RL, England
Penguin Putnam Inc., 375 Hudson Street, New York, New York 10014, USA
Penguin Books Australia Ltd, 250 Camberwell Road, Camberwell, Victoria 3124, Australia
Penguin Books Canada Ltd, 10 Alcorn Avenue, Toronto, Ontario, Canada M4V 3B2
Penguin Books India (P) Ltd, 11 Community Centre, Panchsheel Park, New Delhi – 110 017, India
Penguin Books (NZ) Ltd, Cnr Rosedale and Airborne Roads, Albany, Auckland, New Zealand
Penguin Books (South Africa) (Pty) Ltd, 24 Sturdee Avenue, Rosebank 2196, South Africa

Penguin Books Ltd, Registered Offices: 80 Strand, London WC2R 0RL, England

www.penguin.com

First published 1985
Published simultaneously by Viking
Second edition published 1995
11

Copyright © Arthur S. Reber, 1985, 1995
All rights reserved

The moral right of the author has been asserted

Set in 8½/9 Times Lasercomp
Typeset by Datix International Limited, Bungay, Suffolk
Printed in England by Clays Ltd, St Ives plc

To J R and Y R who,
each in their own way,
taught me the love of language

Contents

Acknowledgements

In the first edition of the Dictionary I asked for feedback from readers. Well, I am pleased to say I got it – some of it fairly pointed I might add. This edition is hence much improved by my colleagues who published reviews, wrote and on occasions called me to provide me with new terms, advice on terms to delete, and, most important, corrections to definitions that were either misleading, unclear, or in a few cases, outright wrong. So, my thanks go out to Rhianon Allen, Alan Auerbach, Charles Catania, Helen Ross, Myron Weiner, P. A. Young, and Carl Zuckerman for their input. Special thanks go to Bob Thompson, who went over the first edition with his usual care and thoughtfulness and made many helpful suggestions. My editors at Penguin, Ravi Mirchandani and Stefan McGrath, provided the right balance of nagging and support. Finally, as I did ten years ago, I want to thank Martin Richards of the University of Cambridge for coming out of 'editorial retirement' and functioning once again as general overseer of the project.

A.R.

Preface to First Edition

Dictionary writers incur certain obligations, the first of which is to provide the reader with a quick rundown on how the material is presented, what abbreviations are in use, what typesetting conventions have been employed and what notational formats are used. This obligation is fulfilled on page xviii. The second obligation is more delicate, to present the reader with a justification/rationalization of what has been wrought. That is the first task here. This dictionary is a little different from the standard list of words and their associated meanings and it is worth initially taking up a bit of space to give the reader some background information to explain how the volume came to be written, what my aims were in compiling it and why it has its occasionally eccentric style.

I began thinking about a work such as this some twenty years ago when I was a graduate student. Students were required to write a number of essays in areas of psychology that were often quite remote from those of their particular concentration, and the first problem we had to deal with was that sudden jolt produced by the jargon of a new area. It was with interest that I discovered that when a Piagetian developmentalist used the term *accommodation* it meant something rather different from what was intended by a social psychologist studying the actions of an individual in a group or a vision scientist examining changes in the lens of the eye, that *discrimination* meant one thing to a learning theorist and another to a psychologist writing on race relations, that Jung's *self* was an entity of a rather different sort than James's. And it was with even greater interest that I began to recognize that these differences, compelling as they were, often masked subtle but critical commonalities in meaning and patterns of usage.

When stuck, as I often was, I turned to existing reference works. I found most of the dictionaries I consulted, both within psychology proper as well as the more general, comprehensive works, to be of surprisingly little help. For the most part, they gave definitions using that 'zero-redundancy' style which typifies the reference work whose editors are desperately fighting length problems. In short, if I already had a pretty good hypothesis about what a term meant the dictionary could confirm or disconfirm it, but if I went as a child to find out how the term was actually used I often ended up more frustrated than when I began.

As the years went by I began making notes on terms, notes not so much on what exactly a given technical term meant but notes that reflected more how it was actually employed, what sorts of meanings were being functionally relayed by it, what connotations were associated with it, what pragmatic force it carried and how it was used (and abused) by various authors. In my mind I always thought of my ever-growing compendium of terms as my 'lexicon' (see here page 418) although, as it now turns out, my editors would have none of this. As far back as I can recall I have never been at a meeting, conference, colloquium or even just at my desk without a pocketful of 4- × 6-inch cards upon which I jot notes should a colleague, writer or speaker present me with a new term or a novel nuance on an old one. What you hold in your hand now is the product of roughly twenty years of note-taking and a frenzied three-year period during which my collection of over 20,000 cards was collated and all earlier versions of my 'lexicon' were edited and rewritten.

If you open to any random page you will see, alas, that most of the entries turned out to be rather mundane and very much like those to be found in any ordinary dictionary. After all, terms like *small group* or *T-maze* just don't have much in the way of subtlety about them. But terms like *language* and *emotion* do, and so do, surprisingly, *memory* and *self* and *unconscious*, and it is here that I do hope that my little volume can serve some useful function.

People (like my long-suffering editors) kept asking me things like, 'Who's this dictionary written for?' or 'What is the readership supposed to be here?' I honestly have never been able to supply them with a simple answer to these questions. I wrote this book for everyman, for the expert in one field who needs to know a term in a domain of our science that she or he is unfamiliar with, for the graduate student who like myself two decades back is frustrated by a new area and its terminological eccentricities, for the undergraduate student taking a first course in psychology who is told by the professor that the essence of the course is 'learning a new vocabulary,' and perhaps, most significantly, for the curious layman who wants to know just what a term means. It was also written for myself, a dedicated word maven who has always enjoyed thumbing through dictionaries and encyclopedias and who takes great pleasure in the playful use of the honored tongue of English kings. All other word-lovers are free to browse.

Finally, here, a few specifics on the form of this dictionary:

1. *Scope*. The primary concern was to cover psychology and psychiatry reasonably thoroughly and to include terms from other disciplines when they shared terminological overlap with these fields. Casting this kind of net can get pretty arbitrary at times and I have no doubt that good judgement failed me on more than a few occasions. As I mention below, I would appreciate having omissions called to my attention for future editions.

2. *Alphabetization*. Unless you have written or edited a work such as this you

cannot fully appreciate what a problem alphabetization can be. Where to list the terms in a reference work poses several difficulties when, as in this case, the majority of the terms are compounds made up of more than one word. For example, a term like *mixed transcortical aphasia* could legitimately be put under *mixed, transcortical* or *aphasia*, depending on whether one feels that the essential nature of the disorder is that it is mixed, transcortical or an aphasia. Most reference works of recent vintage have solved these problems by the simple device of adopting an 'absolute' alphabetizing rule in which every entry is listed under the alphabetic location of the term as it is encountered. Such a dictionary would enter *mixed transcortical aphasia* under *mixed*. The obvious advantage of this technique is that terms can be located easily and unambiguously – and writers and editors do not have to suffer over where to place a given term.

However, I have eschewed this easy way out, electing instead to use the 'key'- or 'head'-word technique whereby compound terms are listed on the basis of the most important word. In this work you will find *mixed transcortical aphasia* under *aphasia, mixed transcortical*, you will find *short-term memory* under *memory, short-term* and you will find *normal distribution* under *distribution, normal*. In a few cases this policy was carried out with a vengeance; see, e.g., *reinforcement, schedules of*.

The final decision to adopt this procedure was made on the basis that I like to snoop around in dictionaries and I like all my *aphasias* together so that I can compare them; I find the grouping of several dozen kinds of *memory* deeply informative since it reveals the manner in which various theorists have been thinking about them; and I like to be able to see the relationships between the many different kinds of *distributions* that have made their way into the psychologist's lexicon. When it is appropriate terms will, of course, follow normal alphabetization rules. A term like *factitious disorder* will be found under *factitious*, since this is the operative word, and *oral eroticism* will be found under *oral*, with all the other compounds based on this keyword. In any case, all compound terms are cross-listed under each of the individual words and, where possible, under all of the various synonyms, which should minimize confusion.

3. *Names.* Since this is a dictionary and not an encyclopedia, my preference was not to include short biographies of important people. However, again since it is a dictionary, it seemed reasonable to include eponymous terms. Entries will be, therefore, found for laws, principles, syndromes and the like that are named after individuals, and occasionally extensive entries are included for those whose fame is such that an adjectivized form of their name exists. Hence, there are entries for Freudian, Skinnerian, Pavlovian, Adlerian and so forth. Moreover, since many of the terms in this volume are the direct result of neologistic exercises of individual people and often the very sense of

a term cannot be dissociated from its coiner, it was often necessary to refer to the operative individual in the entry. A list of these persons, with a few simple facts about each, is printed at the end of the dictionary.

4. *Coverage.* The issue here was how completely to cover a term, how much information to provide in each definition. Most of the entries are relatively straightforward, for they present terms that are dealt with easily and coverage is short and (to that extent) sweet. However, many of the terms in psychology are not dealt with so easily; they require considerable discussion of their semantic nuances and characteristic manners of use. Perhaps not surprisingly, these typically are the most important terms in the field, the very ones that were the stimuli for this project in the first place. To deal with a term like *personality* or *mental retardation* or *perception* in a half dozen lines as some works do is to invite further confusion.

After considerable paring, I ended up with roughly 175 terms that required 'extensive' coverage ('extensive' is defined here as 200 words or more). These are terms that have (often unacknowledged) subtleties of usage or are controversial in their manner of usage or simply have meanings that are denotatively or connotatively complex. A list of them is printed on pages xix–xx.

5. *Style.* The writing of this book was, as much as was possible, a one-man affair. Having all the entries composed by a single author has a distinct virtue in that there is a certain measure of consistency, a kind of continuity in style and coverage that is not going to be found in a work in which one or more editors oversee the submissions of many different writers.

Despite being basically a reference work designed to provide working definitions of the terms of a field of scholarly endeavor, this book is shot through with a singular style for which I make no apologies. Many an entry was written with the ghost of Samuel Johnson whispering in my right ear and the spectre of Ambrose Bierce hissing in my left: I am often critical of the manner in which a term has been used, I frequently object to the particular set of connotations that have come to be associated with certain key phrases and I do, on occasions, go so far as to conjecture that the very conceptual foundations of a technical term render it unworthy of being included in the psychologist's lexicon. For some samples here, see the entries on *innovative therapies, intelligence, meaning, parapsychology, psychology* and *Rorschach test*.

I am not disturbed about offending the occasional sensibility in this manner. In large measure all I have done in these cases is to review and expose the excesses of my colleagues, past and present. However, I am much concerned about offending through error, misrepresentation or misinterpretation. Since this volume ultimately needs to reflect the terms as they are actually used in our protean science, it is important that it be accurate and comprehensive. It is here that the single-author format suffers most. Although I like to think of myself as a bit of a generalist, there have been times when I have felt more than a little unhappy with my state of ignorance. The approach I took in such cases was to compose an entry based on what I knew or could discover by reading and then ask one of my wiser and more knowledgeable colleagues to critique it for me. This turns out to be an interesting technique. It does get the job done in most cases and it lets you see who your friends are – it also gave me a brand-new way to characterize a good friend: someone who is kind enough to tell you in private that if you do what you indicate you are about to do you will make a fool out of yourself in public. Above I thanked those friends whose names I could recall. There must be literally hundreds of others who have been gently abused by me at a meeting or conference over the meaning of some arcane term. A general note of thanks goes out to all these nameless.

Finally here, let me put out a call for more friends. The plan is to revise this dictionary at irregular intervals and I ask readers who wish to to inform me about where I have lapsed or strayed from accuracy of meaning or pattern of usage. Simply send a note to either the publisher or, if preferred, to me directly at: Department of Psychology, Brooklyn College, The City University of New York, Brooklyn, New York, NY 11210, USA.

A.R.
Brooklyn, NY
November 21, 1984

Preface to Second Edition

When I began working on this edition I was struck, much to my surprise, by how much the language of psychology had changed in just ten years. While most of the classic terms are still about and still used in much the same way, there has been a subtle but most detectable drift not just in the terminology but in the very phraseology of the language of our field. Entries written back in the early 1980's that felt so modern and up-to-date then now often felt antiquated and stilted. I frequently found myself squirming at my own words, muttering to myself, 'No one talks that way in psychology any more.' I have tried to isolate these shifts and understand them, which has been no mean task. It is my sense that some four or five primary forces have been sculpting the language of our field in the past decade or so and contributing to these changes. Specifically,

– *The cognitive and neuroanatomical orientations.* The increased interest in these foci have led to the outright introduction of many new terms but also have contributed to distinct shifts in the meaning and usage patterns of old ones. The majority of the revisions in this edition were stimulated by the continued increasing interest in the cognitive approach to psychological science and in the growing search for physiological and neurological explanations of behavior. Here's a couple of examples: the old behaviorist term **connectionism**, which rated a mere three lines in the first edition, is now a major entry with a host of additional connotations reflecting its use in the cognitive sciences. A physiological staple **hippocampus** had to be completely rewritten and accompanied by a variety of anatomically and functionally related structures that weren't even mentioned in the first edition. And to give you a sense for the kinds of problems that can drive a lexicographer batty: the term **implicit memory** which was (according to a recent analysis of key words carried out by the American Psychological Society) the single most frequently cited term in psychology in the years from 1988 to 1992 was not even in the first edition! There are several hundreds of new and completely rewritten entries in the areas of cognition, neuroanatomy, and physiological psychology.

– *The extending boundaries of social psychology.* Social psychology has, in the past decade, broadened its scope considerably. Once concerned primarily with core concepts like attribution and achievement, it has become much more richly interwoven with the study of personality, developmental psychology, and the cognitive sciences. These extensions have been marked both by the introduction of new terms and by the emergence of subtle shifts in meaning in old terms. These changes represent the next most important source of revisions and additions.

– *The DSM-IIIR and IV and the ICD-10*. The first edition used the DSM-III and the ICD-9 as the touchstones for psychiatric terminology; this edition has had to take into account the changes in terminology and usage mandated by the new editions. The casual reader probably doesn't understand (nor really care, I suspect), but these new editions of the DSM and the ICD made my life miserable! The problem is that I couldn't simply toss out all the old terms and meanings and slip in the new. For one, these new 'official' nosologies have not yet filtered into the literature – at least not to the point where they have displaced the older terminology. Worse, students and researchers are still working with materials that were written using the old guidelines and need to have links created between them and the new. And even worse, to be perfectly honest, much of the new officially sanctioned terminology is awkward and stilted and I suspect that, independent of insurance forms and legal documents, it is going to be resisted by many professionals. In any event, I tried to deal with these problems by keeping many (although not all) of the clinical terms from the first edition, introducing the new terms and usage patterns from the DSM-IV and the ICD-10 and, where possible, identifying the common patterns of meaning and usage between the old and the new. My critics, I am sure, will let me know whether I succeeded here or not.

– *Tests and measurements*. To be quite frank, I thought the material dealing with psychometric instruments in the first edition was weak and I wanted to make appropriate revisions for this edition. The problem, however, is that there are just too many psychometric instruments about these days. A glance at any current text in psychological assessment is enough to make a lexicographer feel weak-kneed. To include every personality test, every device designed to measure intelligence, every neurological, developmental, cognitive, vocational, educational, additudinal, sensorimotor, and psychiatric instrument currently in use would double the size of this volume. There seemed only one simple way out of this conundrum: I decided to be pragmatic rather than comprehensive and to let popularity be my guide. Hence, in this edition I have entries only for some thirty or so of the most commonly used psychometric instruments. They include those most frequently used in practice and research and those that were referenced most often in the literature. As a result, many obscure and rarely used psychological tests included in the first edition have been dropped and several widely employed ones missing from that edition have been added. Admittedly my procedure here is arbitrary, but sometimes you just have to be arbitrary.

– *Simple linguistic drift.* A subtle but real linguistic drift properly accompanies every growing scientific field as new ideas and approaches gain a foothold and old ones lose their purchase. This is as it should be; if there wasn't a need for a new edition of a dictionary every ten years or so it would be a clear indictment of our field. But acknowledging change is not the same thing as dealing with it. The problem is that scientific fields progress in fits and starts and many hot, new topics quickly become cold and old. The nagging problem facing the lexicographer is just how many of the new terms that emerge during these local explosions of research on a new topic should be included. After all, the likely long-range prospects for most of these neologisms is pretty dim, and in any event, if I were to include them all, the dictionary would quickly become weighty, cumbersome, and too expensive. I finally decided to handle this problem in my usual egocentric fashion: I made guesses based on personal intuitions. I know this is not the optimum solution to the problem, but it was the only one I could think of – and certainly the easiest. When the third edition rolls around I will patch up errors in judgement (and, of course, replace them with new ones).

Then there is that biggie, what to do with 'old' terms, those that no longer have much lexicographic currency, especially given the pressures on length caused by all the new terms and new meanings of old ones? My decision here was to keep almost all of them, although to shorten the definitions in many cases. My reasoning took several forms. First, if things are going to keep changing so fast who knows when a term will be resuscitated (look at what happened to **connectionism**!). Second, just because a term is not being used much these days does not mean that someone won't still need to look it up – hopefully all of us, students and professionals alike, will always maintain a healthy respect for the past. Third, it seems to me that one of the functions of a dictionary like this one is that it needs to reflect the historical elements of the field as well as its current state. Fourth, I happen to like the nuances of some of these older terms; they often provide intriguing clues about historical issues in psychology and so I often kept a term just because I happen to like it. If you can't have fun doing lexicography you really shouldn't be doing it.

Finally, a few stylistic and editorial changes were made for this edition, as follows:

1. I eliminated cross-referenced terms where the cross-referencing seemed less than necessary. For example, in the first edition a term like **abuse, drug** was listed as a separate entry with the definition '➤ **drug abuse**.' Such entries have been dropped from this edition. Hence, to find a term, look it up under the alphabetic listing of the first word. This change does not affect the 'grouping'

of definitions under a major heading. That is, all of the different specialized kinds of memory will still be found under **memory**.

I should point out that this simple stylistic shift saved dozens and dozens of pages, allowing me to introduce many new terms and expand the definitions of many others without markedly increasing the length of the book. Alas, one can only pull off a trick like this once. I have no idea what I will do for the third edition.

2. The 'minor' phobias have been dropped from the dictionary proper. Instead they have placed in Appendix A, which begins on page 864. Part I of that appendix gives each specialized phobia and its phobic object, Part II provides the technical term for each phobic object. In the appendix you will also find a short editorial comment on phobias and terminology. Major phobias (e.g., **agoraphobia**) still have full definitions in the body of the dictionary.

3. Goaded by my friend Alan Auerbach, I had originally planned to introduce a pronunciation guide for unusual and frequently mispronounced terms. However, after much agonizing I decided against doing so. The reason is simple: dialectic variation. This book is sold in a variety of countries in which a wonderful array of standard dialects of English are spoken. It just struck me as arrogant to assume that one or another pronunciation was to be designated as the 'acceptable' one when common sense and cross-cultural sensitivities clearly show otherwise. If you are stuck on just how to pronounce a particular word, ask someone.

Once again, let me end with a request for help for the future. I have no doubt that, despite my best efforts and those of my editors, errors both of omission and commission have crept in. As before, I would appreciate being informed (gently, of course) of any such. I can still be contacted at Department of Psychology, Brooklyn College of CUNY, Brooklyn, NY 11210, USA.

A. R.
Brooklyn, NY
February 3, 1995

Abbreviations

abbrev.	abbreviat/ed, -ion	pl.	plural
adj.	adjective	sing.	singular
ant.	antonym	syn.	synonym
et seq.	and the following (entries)	var.	variant
lit.	literally	vb.	verb
n.	noun	➤	see
obs.	obsolete	➤➤	see also

Note. An asterisk (*) has been used in cross-references to indicate that the entry referred to should be looked up under the word following the asterisk. Thus, for example, the reference '➤ **spherical *aberration**' means that the reader should refer to the entry **aberration, spherical**.

List of Major Entries

The following list of terms contains those which are given extensive coverage in this volume. These are terms whose definition or manner of usage is complex and/or subtle and where some degree of detail is necessary. The note 'et seq.' here means that this term is followed by a large number of combined terms based on that one.

abnormal
abstract
acquired (et seq.)
addiction
Alzheimer's disease
anger
antipsychotic drugs
aggression (et seq.)
anxiety (et seq.)
apperception
assimilation (et seq.)
association (et seq.)
associationism
attitude
autism (et seq.)
automicity
barbiturates (et seq.)
basal ganglia
behavior (et seq.)
behaviorism
Cannabis sativa
category
chance
code
color vision, theories of
concept (et seq.)
concept formation and
    learning
conditioning (et seq.)
connectionism
consciousness
conservation
constitutional theory
contiguity principle
correlation (et seq.)

cranial nerves
décalage
definition
degrees of freedom
delusion (et seq.)
demand characteristics
dependence (et seq.)
determinism
development (et seq.)
diagnosis
Diagnostic and Statistical
    Manual
discrimination
disease
dogma
dominance (et seq.)
Down syndrome
ego (et seq.)
emotion (et seq.)
emotion, theories of
empathy
empiricism
environment
error (et seq.)
evolutionary theory
experiment (et seq.)
factor (et seq.)
factor analysis
fatigue
feedback
field theory
forced-choice
forgetting
Freudian
function

functionalism
generalization (et seq.)
genotype
Gestalt psychology
grammar (et seq.)
hearing, theories of
heredity-environment
    controversy
heritability
homosexuality
Hullian
hypnosis
hysteria
illusion
image
information
inhibition (et seq.)
innate
innovative therapies
instinct
intelligence (et seq.)
interference (et seq.)
interpretation
language (et seq.)
laterality
learning (et seq.)
love
maturation
meaning (et seq.)
mechanism
memory (et seq.)
mental (et seq.)
mental retardation (et
    seq.)
method, scientific

A

A 1. ➤ **amplitude** (2). **2.** ➤ **albedo**.

a-, an- Prefix meaning *from, away from, absent from*, etc.

abasement H. Murray's term for a need to surrender one's self or will to another, to atone for real or imagined shortcomings.

abasia Inability to walk owing to impairment in motor coordination. ➤ **astasia**.

abatement Generally, lessening or diminishing. Often used with respect to pain or the symptoms of a disease or disability.

abdominal reflex Contraction of the abdominal muscles when the overlying skin is stroked lightly.

abducens 1. The ➤ **abducent nerve**. **2.** Pertaining to movement away from the central plane of the body. ➤ **abduction**.

abducent nerve The VIth cranial nerve. It innervates the external rectus muscle in the eye which functions to rotate the eyeball outward.

abduction 1. Lateral movement of a limb away from the median plane of the body. Compare with ➤ **adduction**. **2.** C. S. Peirce's term for the cognitive process whereby hypotheses are generated on the basis of some known facts. Abduction, in Peirce's terms, was a fundamental component of creative thought.

abductor A muscle which, upon contraction, moves a limb away from the body. Compare with ➤ **adductor**.

aberration The act of wandering or straying from the normal course. The term enjoys wide currency and is used of the behavior of an intact organism as well as for biological structures, physical systems, instruments, etc.

aberration, chromatic Unequal refraction of light of different wavelengths as they pass through a lens producing a colored image.

aberration, mental A more-or-less nontechnical term used loosely for any mental disorder.

aberration, spherical Distortions of light waves passing through a lens produced either by the natural curvature of the lens or by irregularities in the curvature of the lens. Also called *diopteric aberration*.

abient Characterizing movement away from something. ant. ➤ **adient**.

ability The qualities, power, competence, faculties, proficiencies, dexterities, talents, etc. that enable one to perform a particular feat at a specified time. The essence of the term is that the person can perform this task *now*, no further training is needed. The main distinction thus is between ability and ➤ **aptitude**. Ability is an individual's potential to perform; aptitude is an individual's potential *for* performance, or the possibility of the individual being trained up to a specified level of ability. Intelligence tests, for example, are ability tests.

abiogenetic Pertaining to spontaneous genesis, the emergence of living forms from nonliving material, the process of the creation of life.

abiotic Not compatible with life.

ablation Removal of part of an organ. Usually refers to surgical removal. When the full organ or structure is removed, the term ➤ **extirpation** is generally used.

Abney's effect A perceptual phenomenon experienced when a large area is suddenly illuminated. Rather than appearing all at once, the light seems to come on first in the center of the patch and then spread to the edges. When extinguished, the edges disappear first, the center last.

abnormal Lit., any departure from the norm or the normal. The term is used variously to denote such things as purely quantitative deviations in statistical analyses and deviant behavior patterns of individuals. Although this latter reference has been the dominant one in psychology for a long time, there has been some reluctance recently on the part of clinicians and personality theorists to use it in this fashion. The difficulty stems from the tendency to have the boundaries of 'normalness' defined by a particular theory of personality. This has led to considerable difficulty. For example, within classical *psychoanalysis* homosexuality is classified as abnormal, within a *social learning theory* analysis it is not. Note that falling back on the original 'statistical' usage will not solve the problem and it will produce others; Einstein would of necessity be called abnormal. The years have layered onto this term too many value judgements and any of a number of synonyms are preferable: *maladaptive, maladjusted, deviant,* etc. Note that the tendency is to use these other terms with respect to the behavior of the individual under consideration, to evaluate it in terms of whether or not it is adaptive behavior for him or her, rather than as a cold label for the behavior itself or for any individual displaying it.

abnormal fixation ➤ **fixation, abnormal**.

abnormal psychology The branch of psychology concerned with abnormal behavior. Because of the difficulties with the term ➤ **abnormal**, many favor dropping this term from the psychologist's lexicon. Other terms offered as a replacement include *psychology of deviance, psychopathology* and *study of maladaptive behavior*.

abortion 1. Generally, the cessation or 'arrest' of any condition. 2. More specifically and commonly, the termination of a pregnancy prior to the point where the fetus is viable. The issue of viability is handled by some in terms of approximate length of gestation (i.e. between roughly the 20th and 25th weeks) and by others in terms of physical development (i.e. a fetus

of approximately 20 cm in length and weighing roughly 500 g). Ultimately, however, viability is going to be dependent to some extent on the development of medical technology. In Great Britain, for example, 24 weeks is by law the upper limit for abortions for 'social' reasons but there is no specific limit for abortions for 'medical' reasons.

abortion, spontaneous Any expelling of a premature fetus prior to the point of viability without any specific attempt on anyone's part to produce termination of the pregnancy.

aboulia ➤ **abulia**.

abreaction A psychoanalytic term used to describe the weakening or elimination of anxiety by the 'reliving' of the original tension-evoking experience. 'Reliving' can refer to an imaginal or emotional re-experience as well as to an actual one. ➤➤ **catharsis**.

abscissa The horizontal coordinate of a point in a plane Cartesian coordinate system. Commonly, although strictly speaking not correctly, the term is used for the x-axis. In standard notation, values of the *independent variable* are plotted on the abscissa. ➤➤ **axis; Cartesian coordinates**.

absence Momentary mental inattention, a short period during which consciousness is 'missing.' A common aspect of epilepsy, the individual typically has no memory of what transpired during the period. ➤ **amnesia;** ➤➤ **fugue**.

absolute 1 adj. Not *relative*, not varying, characterizing a thing that has intrinsic meaning or value independent of other data, events or considerations. 2 n. ➤ **cultural *absolute**.

absolute, cultural A ➤ **value** (2) that the members of a particular society or culture hold and which they believe to be universal, enduring and applicable to all societies and cultures and not merely their own.

absolute error ➤ **error, absolute**.

absolute limen ➤ **threshold**.

absolute pitch The ability to recognize

the pitch of any given tone and give its name. Also called *perfect pitch*.

absolute refractory period ➤ **refractory period, absolute**.

absolute scale ➤ **scale, absolute**.

absolute sensitivity An occasional synonym for *absolute threshold*. For discussion ➤ **threshold**.

absolute threshold ➤ **threshold**, especially (1).

absolute value ➤ **value, absolute**.

absolute zero ➤ **zero, absolute**.

absorption 1. In the study of sensory processes, the capture or taking in of chemical, electromagnetic or other physical stimuli by a receptor. For example, ➤ **spectral absorption**. 2. Preoccupation with a particular activity. The connotations here may be positive, in that one so absorbed is one whose attention is productively focused, or they may be negative in that such absorption may be viewed as a withdrawal from reality. vb. *absorb*.

absorption spectrum ➤ **spectral absorption; spectral sensitivity**.

abstinence syndrome A term occasionally used for the full range of physiological disturbances caused by the sudden withdrawal of a drug on which one has developed a physical dependence. ➤ **withdrawal**.

abstract 1 adj. From the Latin for *drawn away*. Most usages of the term focus on qualities of objects, events, phenomena, etc. which are considered separate or apart from the objects, events or phenomena themselves. Thus, an abstract idea is an intangible one considered apart from specific instances. For example, 'patriotism' is an abstract idea separate from particular patriotic people or events. Note that even when dealing with more concrete things an element of abstraction exists. 'Chair' can be regarded as somewhat less abstract than 'patriotism' although it still may represent an abstract class of chairs devoid of specific attributes. It is probably best to handle the term

itself abstractly, relating it to a general dimension that runs from abstract to concrete. ➤➤ **concept; prototype**. 2 vb. The same general notion is found here, i.e. the idea of *withdrawal*. To abstract is to extract and the cognitive processes involved are neither simple nor well understood. One may abstract a simple concept (e.g., 'red' as a property of many red things), an idealization (e.g., 'perfection' as an underlying prototype never found in reality but inducible from many non-perfect exemplars), a narrative (e.g., a simple paraphrase capturing the main ideas of a story), and so forth.

abstract ability A mental activity often taken as the hallmark of intellectual functioning; the ability to appreciate the ➤ **abstract** and/or symbolic aspects of situations.

abstract attitude A general type of cognitive functioning typified by voluntary shifting of mental set from situation to situation, moving from concrete to ➤ **abstract** as circumstances dictate, alternating from a focusing on a whole problem to concentrating on its parts, etc.

abstract idea (or **quality**) Any idea or quality which is *abstract* in the sense of being an element or symbol characteristic of a general conceptualization rather than of some particular or concrete instance. Presumably, all abstract ideas are inductions based upon the detection of common elements across many situations. ➤ **abstract** (1); ➤➤ **prototype; semantic *memory**.

abstract intelligence See discussions under ➤ **abstract** and ➤ **intelligence**.

abstraction 1. The cognitive process (about which little is known) whereby an abstract idea or concept is isolated from a number of exemplars. 2. The result of this process; the hypothesized mental representation of an abstract concept.

abstraction theory An umbrella term for a number of theories in *cognitive psychology* that argue that memory and knowledge systems are built up by a process whereby abstract information is extracted from the numerous specific episodes or instances that one experiences. For example, if a hairy, four-legged creature should walk into the room, these theorists would argue that you know it is a dog because it fits the deep abstract representation you have of the category 'dog.' Compare with ➤ **instance theory; prototype**.

abulia A reduction in ability to initiate actions and thoughts and a general indifference about the consequences of action. The term is properly reserved for truly pathological cases. var. *aboulia*.

abundancy motive Quite literally, the desire to attain an abundancy of things. A tendency to seek beyond simple satisfaction of needs that derive from deficiencies. ➤ **deficiency motive**.

abusability The term refers to the notion that some children seem to 'invite' abuse or maltreatment from their parents. Some factors which seem to contribute are excessive crying, physical handicaps, prematurity.

abusable child ➤ **abusability**.

abusing parent 1. Lit., a parent guilty of ➤ **child abuse**. 2. A label for a hypothetical personality type possessing a particular set of characteristics. In theory it is highly likely that a person of this type will become an abusing parent in sense 1. Research has failed to discover any clearcut personality traits which typify abusing parents other than the fact that they were likely to have been abused themselves as children.

ABX An experimental procedure in which the subject is presented with three stimuli on each trial and must decide whether the last (X) matches the first (A) or the second (B).

academic problem A loose term used to cover cases where a student is having academic problems in the absence of any disorder that might be responsible such as a learning or attentional disorder.

academic skills disorders Any of several disorders of childhood characterized by

impairment in academic function in school. Specific forms include *developmental* *arithmetic disorder*, *developmental* *expressive writing disorder*, and *developmental* *reading disorder*. Also called ➤ **learning disorders**.

acalculia Lit., the inability to perform simple arithmetic operations. Generally used to refer to the loss of such ability resulting from injury and not for cases resulting from simple ignorance or lack of schooling. See and compare with ➤ **developmental *arithmetic disorder**.

acatamathesia ➤ **akatamathesia**.

acathexis Lack of ➤ **cathexis**, lack of emotion toward something which is (unconsciously) of considerable importance.

acathisia ➤ **akathisia**.

acceleration Properly, the term refers not simply to increasing change in some variable, but to the *rate* of the increase in the change. Consider the following series of numbers where each represents, say, speed of a car in successive seconds: (a) 0, 3, 6, 9, 12; (b) 0, 3, 7, 12, 18; (c) 0, 3, 5, 6. Here series (a) represents *zero* or *uniform* acceleration – each increase is the same; (b) displays *positive* acceleration – each increase increases; and (c) is an example of *negative* acceleration – each increase decreases. Reversing these series would produce examples of equivalent *deceleration* functions. In psychology, a common use is in the description of learning curves in which the classical finding is the negatively accelerated curve with rapid early growth and a gradual leveling off.

accent 1. Emphasis; rhythm as marked by the accentuation of a series of words, tones, beats, etc. See here ➤ **stress** (2). 2. An individual's speech patterns in a language which reflect habits of pronunciation acquired in speaking either another language or another dialect of that language. Compare with ➤ **dialect**.

access In addition to the standard dictionary meanings, the term is often used metaphorically to refer to retrieval of information from memory. The term was borrowed from computer-sciences terminology and is used mostly, although not exclusively, in studies of human memory. It can be used for the process, as well as the actual fact, of recall.

accessible 1. Generally, available. 2. In studies of memory, retrievable, recallable. 3. In social psychology, open to personal interaction, not withdrawn.

accessory nerve Another name for the *spinal accessory cranial nerve*.

accident An event that was unforeseen and hence unpredicted, or whose causes are at present unknown. Usually the connotation is negative. See also discussion under ➤ **chance** for some philosophical issues which relate to the way these terms are used.

accidental error ➤ **error**.

accident prone A term loosely used to describe persons who display a somewhat higher than average rate of accidents. Such individuals may indeed contribute to their high accident rates by any number of conscious or unconscious reasons or they may simply be the unlucky ones at the tail of a frequency distribution.

acclimation Lit., adaptation or adjustment to a new climate. 'Climate' here is used loosely and can encompass simple repetition of a stimulus or the social and cultural milieu of a new country.

accommodation 1. Generally, any movement or adjustment either physical or psychological which is made in preparation for incoming stimuli. This is a very rich concept and there are several specific uses, as follows: 2. In vision, adjustment of the shape of the lens of the eye to compensate for the distance of the object of focus from the retina. 3. In Piaget's theory, the modification of internal schemes to fit a changing cognizance of reality. See here the accompanying concept, ➤ **assimilation** (4). 4. In sociology and social psychology, a process of social adjustment designed to maintain harmony within a group, or between antagonistic groups. The adjustment may take any of several forms including compromise, conciliation, arbitration or the simple mutual acceptance of a truce. The term is used here with respect to the behavior of single individuals as well as to that of a whole group or even a nation.

acculturation 1. With reference to children the term refers to the gradual acquisition of the behavior patterns of the surrounding culture, in particular the subculture within which they are raised. This basic notion is also embodied in the term ➤ **cultural transmission**. For more on it, ➤ **socialization** and **enculturation**. 2. Somewhat more broadly, the adoption or assimilation of cultural elements from another culture.

accuracy test Any test which emphasizes accuracy of performance independent of the time it takes to complete it. ➤ **power test**; compare with ➤ **speed test**.

acenesthesia Lit., the lack of common sensation. Hence, either: 1 a general lack of well-being or 2 a lack of normal sense concerning one's body.

acetophenazine One of the phenothiazine derivatives used as an antipsychotic drug.

acetylcholine (ACh) An excitatory ➤ **neurotransmitter** found in a variety of locations. It is the transmitter substance liberated at the neuromuscular junctions of all skeletal muscles; it is also the neurotransmitter in the ganglia of the ➤ **autonomic nervous system** and it functions to excite target organs of the post-ganglionic fibers of the parasympathetic division. It is found diffusely throughout the brain and concentrated specifically in neurons of the basal ganglia.

acetylcholinesterase (AChE) An enzyme produced by the post-synaptic membrane that destroys ➤ **acetylcholine** by breaking it into acetate and choline and thus stopping the post-synaptic potential.

ACh = ➤ **acetylcholine**.

AChE = ➤ **acetylcholinesterase**.

achieved role ➤ **role, achieved**.

achievement 1. Accomplishment, the attaining of a goal. 2. The goal itself. 3. ➤ **level of achievement**.

achievement age ➤ **age, achievement**.

achievement, level of The degree to which one has achieved on a standardized test. Used primarily in studies of education.

achievement motive 1. Generally, a personal motive manifested as a striving for success; quite literally, a motive to achieve, ➤ **need for achievement**. 2. In H. Murray's theory of personality, the term has a similar meaning but is conceptualized as entailing the notion of overcoming obstacles or tackling those things which are known to be difficult.

achievement test Any test designed to evaluate a person's current state of knowledge or skill. Contrast with ➤ **aptitude test**, which is designed to evaluate potentialities for achievement (ideally) independent of current knowledge.

achromat A person with ➤ **achromatopsia**.

achromatic 1. Lit., without color, in the sense of the dimensions of ➤ **hue** and ➤ **saturation**. Hence, the term refers to visual stimuli which are describable completely in terms of ➤ **brightness** in the black-white dimension. 2. Characteristic of a lens corrected to counterbalance *chromatic *aberration*.

achromatic color Any 'color' lacking in ➤ **hue** and ➤ **saturation**, one describable in terms of ➤ **brightness**, i.e. black and white.

achromatic interval 1. In vision, the interval between the absolute threshold for a monochromatic stimulus and the intensity level required for the observer to sense the hue of the given stimulus. 2. In ➤ **audition**, the analogous interval between the absolute threshold for a pure tone and the intensity level required for the sensing of the pitch of the presented tone.

achromatism 1. Colorlessness. 2. ➤ **achromatopsia**.

achromatopsia A condition wherein all visual experiences are *achromatic*, lacking in both ➤ **hue** and ➤ **saturation**. Many species are naturally achromatopic; however, when the condition occurs in humans it is usually called *total color blindness*. Such achromats are totally lacking in ➤ **cones** and, as one might expect, they see everything in shades of gray, are *photophobic* (highly sensitive to bright lights) and have poor visual acuity. var., *achromatopia*. ➤ **monochromatism**.

acid Street slang for *lysergic acid diethylamide* ➤ **(LSD-25)**.

acou-, acousia-, acousis- Prefixes meaning 'hearing.'

acoumeter ➤ **audiometer**.

acoustic Pertaining to sound, especially from the point of view of the physicist. Compare with ➤ **auditory**.

acoustic confusion Any 'confusion' (over which stimulus was presented) based upon acoustic factors. For example, hearing *bat* when the stimulus was *pat*. Compare with ➤ **semantic confusion**.

acoustic cue Any aspect of the acoustic signal in speech used to distinguish between phonetic elements. For example, ➤ **voice onset time** is an acoustic cue which distinguishes between the initial sounds in such words as 'tie' and 'die.'

acoustic filter Any device that selectively screens out ('filters') certain frequencies while permitting others to pass. ➤ **filter** and related entries.

acoustic generalization ➤ **generalization, acoustic**.

acoustic pressure The average force of a sound stimulus on an area (generally measured in ➤ **dynes**/cm^2). In *audition* the eardrum is the usual point of measurement.

acoustics 1. A branch of physics concerned with the study of the physical properties of sound. ➤ **psychoacoustics**. 2. The properties of a hall or room which affect the characteristics of the sounds heard.

acoustic spectrum A term occasionally and incorrectly used when ➤ **auditory spectrum** is meant.

acoustic store A hypothesized memory system whereby auditory (and perhaps even visual) inputs are stored in a form that reflects their acoustic properties. Contrast with ➤ **articulatory store**, in which the hypothesized mechanism is based on the motor system for producing sounds. ➤ **iconic**, **echoic** and **short-term *memory**.

acquiescence Generally, a tendency to agree with the viewpoint of others. Often used with the connotation that, if the source is an authority, the acquiescent person will tend toward agreement regardless of the nature of the content of the statement. ➤ **authoritarian personality**.

acquired Simply, *learned*. However, there are major problems associated with this term and its manner(s) of use. First, those behaviors which are learned are often presented in contrast with those which are considered innate. For instance, roller-skating is an acquired skill, bipedalism is not. However, it is manifestly clear that roller-skating is dependent upon particular genetic, species-specific characteristics which members of the species *Homo sapiens* have as part of their innate endowment; only a feeling of futility would reward attempts to have a fish acquire this skill. Moreover, bipedalism does not emerge in the absence of the proper conditions; Victor, the famous wild boy of Aveyron, locomoted on all fours when he was first discovered. Thus, when the term is used to mean 'learned' it is really being used to reflect the notion that the behavior so characterized seems to depend *primarily* upon critical experiential factors. Similar connotations accompany the term ➤ **innate**. Second, because of this notion that all behaviors have both genetic and environmental components, one cannot really speak of any particular behavior as being acquired or innate. Rather one must recognize (although most authors either miss this point or fail to be clear on it) that only *differences* between behaviors can be

legitimately referred to. Much of the dispute which has raged over the question of the innateness of intelligence hinges on this point. ➤➤ **heritability**.

acquired characteristic Quite literally, any *characteristic* which results from experience or environmental factors. As is pointed out in the previous entry, the term is properly used of environmentally produced *modifications* in structural characteristics or *differences* in behavioral characteristics.

acquired characteristics, inheritance of The doctrine which states that proficiencies and attributes with survival value acquired through effort and use during the lifetime of an organism are passed on genetically to succeeding generations. When put forward by the elaborately named French naturalist, Jean-Baptiste Pierre Antoine de Monet Lamarck, it was the first coherent theory of the process of evolution prior to the Darwinian theory of natural selection. Although there has been no convincing evidence to support the Lamarckian process, the concept itself seems to have some survival value. Darwin himself expressed a version of it and it has been revived in various guises by several modern biologists and psychologists, most notably Piaget. Most contemporary theorists, however, regard it as little more than a historical curiosity.

acquired discrimination of cues Quite literally, the process whereby two or more cues originally responded to as equivalent become functionally differentiated from each other as a result of differential reinforcement of responses made to each. Thus stated, the term is synonymous with the simple term ➤ **discrimination** (1); its interest and use derives from comparison with *acquired equivalence of cues*, whereby two or more cues which are potentially discriminable are rendered functionally equivalent to each other by reinforcing responses to them equally. The point of these contrasting operations is that questions of *discrimination* or *equivalence* are not to be answered absolutely but rather functionally.

acquired drive ➤ **drive, acquired**.

acquired dyslexia ➤ **dyslexia, acquired**.

acquired equivalence of cues ➤ **acquired discrimination of cues**.

acquisition 1. Generally, gaining, acquiring, incorporating, etc.; hence, a common and loose synonym for ➤ **learning**. As such, it is usually defined in operational terms as a change in a response measure and typically is used to refer to that portion of any learning process during which there is a consistent increase in responsiveness and the change has a certain permanence. Thus, phenomena such as ➤ **adaptation**, ➤ **habituation** and ➤ **sensitization** are generally outside the scope of acquired behaviors, even though they often produce a change in a response measure, since the change is of a temporary nature. For further discussion of these definitional boundaries ➤ **learning**. 2. Loosely, the process of acquiring or gaining something, or achieving something. This meaning is neutral with regard to the theoretical issues that accompany the use of meaning 1 and is expressed very broadly, e.g., the acquisition of a valued object, the acquisition of a complex skill, the acquisition of a language, etc. 3. Some authors use the term as a synonym for ➤ **maturation**. This is becoming rarer – happily so, since *learning* and *maturation* are often contrasted.

acquisition trial ➤ **trial, learning**.

acquisitiveness Loosely, a behavioral trait reflected by a tendency to possess or hoard things.

acro- Combining form from the Greek, meaning *extremity* or *topmost*. Used of the top of the head, hands, feet, fingers and toes, as well as to refer to heights.

acroanesthesia Loss of sensation in one or more extremities. var., *acroanaesthesia*.

acroesthesia Hypersensitivity in one or more extremities. var., *acroaesthesia*.

acromegaly Chronic disease caused by hyperfunctioning of cells in the anterior lobe of the pituitary gland resulting in an excess of growth hormone. Characteristic symptoms are elongated bones in the extremities, especially in the hands and feet and in the facial bones and the jaw.

acronym A pronounceable abbreviation of a multi-word term or phrase composed of the first letters of each word, e.g., WAT for Word Association Test, WISC for Wechsler Intelligence Scale for Children.

acroparesthesia ➤ **paresthesia** (numbness, itching or tingling) in the fingers and hands. var., *acroparaesthesia*.

act 1. n. Much has been written on this term over the decades. The only sensible meaning, in sum, is, simply, a ➤ **response** or a pattern of behavior. 2 n. Historically, ➤ **act psychology**. 3 vb. To respond.

ACTH ➤ **adrenocorticotrophic hormone**.

acting out 1. A rather irrational, impulsive display. This meaning is usually reserved for uncontrollable outbursts in problem children. 2. The display of feeling and emotion which has previously been inhibited. Here the term is used with a neutral or even positive connotation in that such self-expression is regarded as healthy and therapeutic. 3. A coping style in which the individual deals with conflict or stress by actions rather than by reflections or feelings.

action 1. Generally, the actual performance of some function, the occurrence of a process. 2. The result of such performance or occurrence. Usage is broad; the operations may be overt and obvious like walking or talking, where the connotation is that action is conscious and purposive, or they may be more covert and internal, like heart action, neural action potential or the action of a drug, from which these connotations are missing.

action current ➤ **action potential**.

action potential The term refers to the whole series of changes in electrical potential which occur when an impulse is propagated by a neuron. Strictly, the term refers

8

to the momentary difference in electrical potential between active and resting parts of an individual neuron while firing.

action research As originally conceptualized by K. Lewin, research carried out with the express purpose of achieving an understanding of phenomena that leads to practical applications and solutions of real world problems.

action-specific energy A term in classical ethological theory referring to a hypothetical well of energy assumed to be associated with a particular unlearned response. Immediately after the response is made the action-specific energy is very low; it recovers over time and, according to Lorenz's analysis, should the specific **sign-stimulus** (or **releaser**) not occur, the energy 'spills over' and ➤ **vacuum activity** or, in some situations, ➤ **displacement** (2) occurs.

activation Basically, preparing for action. The use of the term, however, is generally restricted to the activating effect of one internal organ upon another (e.g., *reticular activating system*). It is, therefore, not properly a synonym for either ➤ **arousal**, which is more often used in a general fashion, or ➤ **stimulation**, which is used to refer to 'activation' produced by external means.

activation theory of emotion ➤ **theories of** *emotion. This theory is more commonly referred to as the *arousal theory*.

active 1. Functioning, operational. 2. Characterizing a particular attitude or stance whereby one spontaneously initiates events and influences a situation. 3. Descriptive of a posture of control and initiative, particularly in sexual matters. See here ➤ **active and passive** for Freud's usage of the term and its opposite.

active analysis ➤ active *therapy.

active and passive Classical psychoanalysis assumed the existence of a polarized dimension of activity–passivity. The former was associated with masculinity, aggression, sadism and voyeurism; the latter with femininity, submissiveness,

masochism and exhibitionism. Moreover, Freud added the possibility that each of these 'natural' modes can be reversed to its opposite so that a masochistic male is viewed as one who has 'reversed' his sadistic instincts. The whole active–passive apparatus can certainly be viewed as a respectable starting-place for a general theory, although, as many have argued, it soon leads into absurdities, as in the not uncommon syndrome of a female who is characterized as one who 'actively pursues passive aims.'

active avoidance see the discussion under ➤ **avoidance**.

active therapy ➤ **therapy, active**.

active vocabulary ➤ **vocabulary, active**.

activity 1. A generic term safely applicable as a synonym for action, movement, behavior, mental process, physiological functions, etc. Because of its great generality, activity is usually bound up with a qualifying adjective, e.g., goal-directed activity, random activity, problem-solving activity, etc. 2. One of the three hypothesized universal dimensions of ➤ **semantic space** in C. Osgood's theory of word meaning. ➤➤ **semantic differential**.

activity analysis 1. Generally, the objective analysis of the various activities engaged in by a person. 2. In industrial/organizational psychology, an analysis of this kind carried out with respect to the job the individual is expected to do.

activity cage Any of a number of animal cages designed to record general activity. The simplest is a cage with a large rotating wheel in which the animal can run; a counter attached to the wheel records revolutions. A more sophisticated device, becoming popular, is a cage fixed with light beams and photoelectric cells which count 'interruptions' as the animal moves about.

activity cycle Lit., a cycle or rhythm in activity. Most organisms display activity cycles which can be traced to metabolic and hormonal cycles associated with hunger, thirst, sex, diurnal rhythms, etc.

activity drive A hypothesized drive introduced in an attempt to account for the fact that virtually all organisms display a fairly constant level of activity, which takes place in the absence of any (obvious) physiologically produced motivating drive state. ➤ **drive**.

activity inventory An objective listing ('inventory') of the various components ('activities') of a particular job; often included as part of a full *activity analysis*.

activity wheel ➤ **activity cage**.

act psychology A philosophical psychological system espoused originally by Franz Brentano. His position was formulated in opposition to the so-called 'content' focus of ➤ **structuralism** (1). Structuralists argued that the basic subject matter of psychology was the conscious content of mind, the act psychologists focused on the acts or processes of mind as the fundamental source of empirical data. As an empirical system it made few lasting contributions to psychology but it served an important historical role. It formulated the base for others such as the ➤ **Würzburg school** to build upon and provided many of the philosophical foundations that helped give rise to ➤ **functionalism**.

act, pure-stimulus A term introduced by Clark Hull to refer to any behavior that does not explicitly lead an organism toward a goal. A pure-stimulus act is one which sets up the proprioceptive stimuli necessary for the full instrumental response to take place.

actual conflict ➤ **conflict, actual**.

actual neurosis A term originally used by Freud to refer to a neurosis which resulted from the tension of real, 'actual' frustrations or real organic dysfunctions. It was later taken up by W. Reich and assumed by him to represent the basis of all neurosis.

acuity Generally, the capacity to discriminate fine detail; keenness of perception. The term is usually used with a quali-

fier to denote the specific form of acuity under consideration; when found unqualified it almost always refers to *visual *acuity*.

acuity, auditory **1.** Sensitivity of hearing with reference to the absolute threshold for detection of sounds of various frequencies. **2.** The ability to discriminate fine distinctions in sound stimuli. Meaning 2 more accurately captures the meaning of the base term ➤ **acuity** than does 1 although it is less common.

acuity grating A set of dark bars presented on a white background. By adjusting the distance between the bars until the *minimum separable* is achieved one gets an estimate of visual acuity.

acuity, sensory Generally, fineness or keenness of perception. An umbrella term which is used to cover the classic issues of sensory psychophysics; namely, detection and discrimination of stimuli. High sensory acuity means that stimuli of low intensity and/or short duration can be detected and that small differences between stimuli can be discriminated. ➤ **visual *acuity**.

acuity, stereoscopic A measure of visual acuity given as the minimum difference in depth (distance from the viewer) that can be perceived using both eyes.

acuity, vernier Visual acuity in which the measure of fine detail that can be perceived is given by the minimum amount of displacement between the top and bottom halves of a line that can just be detected.

acuity, visual The capacity to see fine details of objects in the visual field. Visual acuity is typically expressed by the number of degrees of visual arc subtended by the visual object that can just be seen or by the width of the object itself. In clinical practice standard displays are used (e.g., Snellen chart) and acuity is given by a ratio D'/D, where D' is the standard or normal viewing distance and D is the distance at which the object viewed would subtend an angle of 1 minute of arc. For example, 20/50 means that when 20 feet away the person can distinguish an object that would subtend 1 minute of arc were he or she standing 50 feet away; i.e. this person has poor visual acuity. Visual acuity is measured in a variety of ways, the most common being *recognition* (of which the above example using the Snellen chart is one), *resolution* (➤ acuity grating) and *localization* (➤ e.g, vernier *acuity and stereoscopic *acuity).

acupuncture A technique for producing regional anesthesia. Following ancient charts developed over centuries, largely by the Chinese, each region of the body is associated with a particular locale. Anesthesia is produced by inserting a long thin needle at the critical point and often either twirling it or passing a mild electric current through it. How and why acupuncture works (that is, how and why from the mechanistic viewpoint of the Western scientist) is not known and until recently the technique received very little attention from Western researchers. The most frequently cited hypothesis is that some form of neural blocking is involved whereby neural firing patterns set up by the needles block the transmission of the pain fibers in another region of the body.

acute 1. Generally, highly sensitive, extremely responsive. 2. Sharp, intense. ➤ acute *pain. 3. With respect to diseases or to the symptoms of a disease, sudden in onset and relatively short-lived. 4. With respect to experimental work in physiology, the term characterizes preparations which are short-term or temporary. Contrast (3) and (4) with ➤ chronic. A variety of diseases and syndromes often have an *acute* (3) stage which is of special significance; these are found under the alphabetical listing of the disease or syndrome itself.

acute brain disorder A cover term for any disability due to a reversible (hence, temporary) impairment of brain tissue.

acute pain ➤ pain, acute.

acute preparation ➤ preparation, acute.

acute schizophrenic episode ➤ schizophrenic episode, acute.

acute stress disorder ➤ post-traumatic stress disorder.

acute (drug) tolerance ➤ tolerance, acute.

adaptation 1. In experimental psychology, a change in the responsiveness or sensitivity of a sensory receptor or a sense organ which is temporary in nature. Generally speaking, increases in stimulation decrease sensitivity while decreases in stimulation increase sensitivity, and the term is applicable to both processes. This meaning is captured in a number of combined phrases where the particular stimulus dimension under consideration is specified; e.g., *chromatic* (or *spectral*) *adaptation, brightness adaptation, dark adaptation, phonetic adaptation,* etc. Only such phrases of which the intended meaning is not immediately apparent or of which important aspects need specifying are listed in this volume. Contrast this pattern of use with ➤ habituation and desensitization. 2. In social psychology and sociology, a shift in sociological or cultural disposition. Thus, one is said to 'adapt' to a new environment. 3. In evolutionary theory, any structural or behavioral change that has survival value.

adaptation, cross ➤ Adaptation (1) to all stimuli of a group after exposure to but one stimulus from that group. Cross adaptation is common in smell where adapting the subject to one odor will produce a diminution in sensitivity to a large variety of other odors.

adaptation level (AL) A neutral position on a sensory continuum; specifically, the level to which the sense organ has adapted. A full theory of sensory-context effects was built up around this notion by Harry Helson. Generally the theory maintains that the neutral, adapted background provides a standard against which new stimuli are perceived. Thus, for example, originally cool water may be made to feel warm if the subject first adapts to rather cold water. Although the theory

11

was designed with sensory processes in mind, it has been widely applied to fields far removed from simple sensory continua, particularly the study of attitudes and attitude change.

adaptation level theory   See the discussion under ➤ **adaptation level**.

adaptation, selective   Quite literally, adaptation that is selective. Thus, if a subject is presented repeatedly with a particular stimulus, ➤ **adaptation** (1) will occur and the subject will show a diminished sensitivity to that stimulus. If, however, the subject still displays a normal response to similar but discriminably different stimuli then one can say that selective adaptation has occurred.

adaptation syndrome   ➤ **general adaptation syndrome (GAS)**.

adaptation time   The length of time it takes for *adaptation* (1) to occur, i.e. the time from onset of stimulation to the point where no further changes in the sensory system occur.

adaptive   1. Functioning so as to facilitate adaptation. **2.** Appropriate, useful, aiding in adjustment. This term, particularly when used in the phrase *adaptive behavior*, has become increasingly common and many use it where terms such as *sane* and *normal* were once used. That is one who is 'sane' or 'normal' is one whose behavior is 'adaptive'. ➤➤ **maladaptive**.

adaptive behavior ➤ **adaptive**.

ADD ➤ **attention-deficit hyperactivity disorder**

ADDH ➤ **attention-deficit hyperactivity disorder**

addiction   Any psychological or physiological overdependence of an organism on a drug. Originally the term was used only for physiological dependencies where the drug had altered the biochemistry of the individual such that continued doses (often, of increasing size – ➤ **tolerance**) were required, as is the case with the opiates

and with alcohol. However, the line between purely physiological addiction and psychological dependence is far from clear and over the years the semantic realm of the term expanded. Even in the technical literature one can find gems like, 'the patient was addicted to chocolate cake'. The confusions attending such loose usage plus the definitional problems that emerged with the attempts of different governmental bodies to circumscribe the use of various illicit drugs led the World Health Organization to recommend recently that the term *dependence* be used, with proper qualifiers for cases where drugs are involved. ➤ **drug *dependence**, et seq.

additive mixture ➤ **color mixing**.

additive scale ➤ **scale, additive**.

address   The location in a computer where a particular piece of information is stored. The concept is useful in interpreting theories of *memory* where many models (particularly those represented as computer simulations) characterize the storage process as one of putting away information in an 'addressable store' for later retrieval with the implication that the recall process involves knowing how to find the location of the information. ➤➤ **content-addressable store**.

adduction   Movement of a limb or the eyes toward the median plane of the body. Compare with ➤ **abduction** (1).

adductor   A muscle which, upon contraction, moves a limb toward the median plane of the body. Compare with ➤ **abductor**.

A-delta fibers ➤ **free nerve endings**.

adenine   One of four nucleotide bases which make up both ➤ **deoxyribonucleic acid** and ➤ **ribonucleic acid**.

adenohypophysis ➤ **pituitary gland**.

adenosine triphosphate (ATP)   A molecule involved in cellular energy metabolism. When ATP is converted into adenosine diphosphate energy is released; when converted into ➤ **cyclic adenosine monophosphate** it serves as a messenger in the production of postsynaptic potentials.

adenylate cyclase An enzyme that converts ➤ adenosine triphosphate into ➤ cyclic adenosine monophosphate. It operates as part of the process of mediating the intracellular effects of many neurotransmitters and peptide hormones.

adequate sample ➤ sample, adequate.

adequate stimulus ➤ stimulus, adequate.

ADH Abbreviation for *antidiuretic hormone*. ➤ vasopressin.

ADHD ➤ attention-deficit hyperactivity disorder.

ad hoc From the Latin, meaning 'for this purpose.' Generally applied to any hypothesis or hypothetical explanation developed to explain a particular set of data that does not fit into an existing theoretical framework. An *ad hoc* hypothesis is one developed after the data have been collected.

adiadochokinesia ➤ dysdiadochokinesia.

adient Characterizing movement toward something. Contrast with ➤ abient.

adipocytes Lit., *fat cells*. Interest in these cells has increased recently because of the fact that obese people have more and larger adipocytes than those of normal weight.

adipose Fatty, pertaining to fat.

adipsia Lit., the absence of drinking; As a chronic syndrome it can be produced by lesions in the lateral hypothalamus.

adjective check list A self-inventory personality-assessment instrument consisting of 300 adjectives. The respondent simply checks those which are considered to be self-descriptive.

adjusting schedule ➤ schedules of *reinforcement.

adjustment **1.** Generally, the relationship that any organism establishes with respect to its environment. The term usually refers to social or psychological adjustment and when used in this sense it carries clear positive connotations, e.g., *well-adjusted*. The implication is that the individual is involved in a rich, ongoing process of developing his or her potential, reacting to and in turn changing the environment in a healthy, effective manner. On the other hand, a subtle, negative connotation of the term can be found. This is reflected by the semantic overlap that it has with the term ➤ conformity, with the implication that, in adjusting, the person has given up personal initiative. **2.** A state of complete equilibrium between an organism and its environment, a state wherein all needs are satisfied and all organismic functions are being carried out smoothly. **3.** In statistics, any procedure for correcting, weighting or reinterpreting data so as to be able to 'adjust' for unusual or atypical conditions.

adjustment disorder A general psychiatric category used for a maladaptive reaction to a stressful situation occurring soon (the criterion usually stated is three months) after the onset of the stressor. Put simply, the individual fails to adjust properly to the new conditions of his or her life. Such 'disorders' are quite common and usually temporary; either the stressor is removed or else the person finds a new mode of adaptation to the situation.

adjustment, method of ➤ methods of *scaling.

adjuvant Descriptive of supplementary therapeutic techniques. Psychotherapeutic drugs are often referred to as adjuvant procedures.

Adlerian Characterizing the theory and psychoanalytic practices put forward by Alfred Adler (1870–1937). Often referred to as *individual psychology*, the primary concept is that of *inferiority* and the crux of the human condition is assumed to be the struggle against feelings of inferiority be they conscious or unconscious, physical, psychological or social.

13

ad lib From the Latin *ad libitum*, meaning *without restriction*. It is generally used to refer to ad lib body weight, which is the weight approached by a fully mature organism given unlimited access to a balanced diet, i.e. one on ad lib feeding. Also called *free-feeding*. The term is also used in a variety of contexts where lack of restriction is the intended meaning.

adolescence The period of development marked at the beginning by the onset of puberty and at the end by the attainment of physiological or psychological maturity. It should be noted that the term is much less precise than it appears since both the onset of puberty and the attainment of maturity are effectively impossible to define or specify.

adrenal 1. Pertaining to the kidney. **2.** Pertaining to the ➤ **adrenal gland** and/or its secretions.

adrenal gland An endocrine gland located adjacent to and covering the upper part of the surface of the kidney. The inner *adrenal medulla*, composed of modified sympathetic ganglion cells, secretes ➤ **epinephrine** (*adrenalin*) and small amounts of ➤ **norepinephrine** (noradrenalin) and ➤ **dopamine**. The outer *adrenal cortex* arises, embryonically, from the urogenital mesoderm and produces several groups of hormones, the *glucocorticoids* (➤ **cortisol**; **cortisone**; **corticosterone**), the *mineralocorticoids* (➤ **aldosterone**) and various sex hormones including *androgens* (➤ **ketosteroid**), *estrogens* (➤ **estradiol**) and ➤ **progesterone**. Also called *suprarenal gland*.

adrenalin ➤**epinephrine.** Adrenalin comes from the Latin and means *toward the kidney*, which is where the adrenal gland is located. The contemporary use of *epinephrine* as the term of choice (it is from the Greek and means *on the kidney*) was spurred by the adoption of Adrenalin as a proprietary name by a drug company. It should be noted, however, that the adjectival form ➤ **adrenergic** is used uniformly. var., *adrenaline*.

adrenaline ➤ **adrenalin**.

adrenergic Characterizing neurons and neural fibers and pathways which, when stimulated, release ➤ **epinephrine** (*adrenalin*), It should be noted that while *epinephrine* is the preferred term for the substance itself, *adrenergic* is the preferred adjectival form. ➤ **adrenalin** for the reasons for this terminological peculiarity.

adreno- Combining form meaning *adrenal*.

adrenocorticotrophic hormone (ACTH) A hormone secreted by the anterior pituitary that functions in the growth and development of the adrenal cortex. It also plays a critical role in the continued functioning of the adrenal cortices by stimulating the production of glucocorticoids and has been implicated in suppressing the production of testosterone. Vars., *adrenocorticotropic hormone*, *corticotrophic hormone*.

adrenogenital syndrome A congenital defect in the adrenal cortices. The abnormality begins *in utero* and requires treatment soon after birth, failing which, in severe cases, death ensues from salt loss and dehydration. Affected females typically display ambiguous external genitalia; males are superficially normal in appearance. If untreated, in addition to the salt loss and dehydration, both sexes undergo rapid premature sexual development in the first years of life.

adrenosterone A weak ➤ **androgen** secreted by the adrenal cortices.

adult intelligence ➤ **intelligence, adult**.

adultomorphism Interpreting the behavior of a child from an adult point of view; an unwarranted attribution of adult characteristics, traits or processes to the child.

advantage by illness A general term used for the 'beneficial' aspects that accompany some mental disorders. The gain may be *primary* (or *paranosic*) in that a symptom may function to relieve immediate anxiety (e.g., the primary gain of claustrophobia is freedom from the anxiety that accompanies closed-in places) or it may be *second-*

ary (or *epinosic*) in that the disability serves as a device to avoid unpleasant duties (e.g., an agoraphobic who cannot leave home cannot be expected to hold down a job). Also called *gain by illness*. ➤➤ **flight into illness**.

adventitious reinforcement Reinforcement delivered independently of any response on the part of the subject. Despite the lack of a 'true' cause-and-effect relationship between the organism's responses and the received reinforcements, adventitious reinforcement can have a powerful effect upon behavior. ➤ e.g., **superstitious behavior.**'

-ae- Alternative spelling to *-e-* used in terms of Greek and Latin origin.

aerial perspective A fuzziness or loss of the clarity of distant objects caused by the atmosphere. The effect is produced by the loss of color and brightness contrast between the distant objects and the background. It is one of the monocular cues for depth perception.

aero- Combining form meaning *air* or *gas*.

aerobic Pertaining to or characteristic of organisms (or tissues) which require or are not destroyed by free oxygen.

aerobic exercise Any exercise designed to increase oxygen uptake in the body.

aerophagia Lit., air-eating. The gulping and swallowing of air.

aetiology ➤ **etiology**.

affect A general term used more-or-less interchangeably with various others such as *emotion, emotionality, feeling, mood,* etc. Historically, the term has had various, more specialized usages. At one point it was considered to be one of the three 'mental functions' along with cognition and volition. Later, Titchener used it as a label for the pleasantness–unpleasantness dimension of feeling. Contemporary usage is, however, very loose although the DSM–IV recommends that it be differentiated from ➤ **mood**, which is used for more pervasive and sustained emotional states. Distinguish from the verb *to affect*, where the accent is on the final syllable, and from ➤ **effect**.

affect, appropriateness of The extent to which an individual's emotional response to a particular situation is considered (from a 'normal' or 'acceptable' point of view) to be appropriate. Inappropriate affect is, generally speaking, the hallmark of all psychological or psychiatric disorders.

affect, displacement of The shifting (i.e. 'displacing') of feeling or emotion from the object or person toward which it was originally experienced on to another object or person.

affection 1. In some older writings, ➤ **affect. 2.** More commonly, a mild form of ➤ **love** (but see that term for the difficulties involved in meaning and usage).

affective Pertaining to or characteristic of ➤ **affect**.

affective attack A violent, highly emotional attack on one animal by another.

affective components In social psychology, those subjective feeling or mood states that accompany an attitude. The term is often used with the connotation that these states are the result of physiological actions.

affective disorder ➤ **mood disorders**.

affective fixation ➤ **fixation, affective**.

affective psychosis Loosely, any psychosis with severe disturbances in mood or feeling. The classic example is the *bipolar disorder*. ➤➤ **mood disorders**.

affective syndrome, organic ➤ **organic mood syndrome**.

afferent The term refers to the conduction of nerve impulses from the periphery (the sense organs) to or toward the central nervous system. Thus, *afferent pathways* are neural pathways that carry information from the receptors to the central nervous system. Contrast with ➤ **efferent**.

afferent code Loosely, the pattern of

neural action in the *afferent* (sensory) pathways. The term 'code' is used because these patterns are not simple (and only partly known). For example, increasing the intensity of a stimulus does not merely increase the number of neurons firing or the number of responses each makes, rather it results in a complex change in the overall pattern of firing at various locations in the nervous system.

affiliation The standard dictionary meaning here is appropriate for most uses in psychology: bringing into close contact or association. The connotation is always positive; affiliation is association with co-operation, companionship, even love. Several personality theorists, particularly Henry Murray, have hypothesized the existence of a basic human ➤ **need for affiliation**.

affordance In J. J. Gibson's theory of perception, the 'invitational' quality of a percept or an event. Thus, a part of the affordance of a hammer is its graspability, of a chair its sit-on-ability. In a sense, affordance refers to the intrinsic properties of items and events.

affricate A speech sound which, in simplest terms, is made up of a stop and a *fricative*, e.g., [ʃ] in *jaw* or [č] in *chair*.

a fortiori Latin for *with stronger reason* or, more loosely, *from firmer ground*. Used of a conclusion or inference that follows logically from an even more compelling chain of logic than one previously accepted as logically true.

afterdischarge Generally, any neural activity that continues after the stimulus that initiated it has been terminated.

aftereffect Generally, and quite literally, any effect of a stimulus that either exceeds in duration that of the stimulus itself or occurs after the stimulus has been removed.

afterimage A perceptual experience that occurs after the original source of stimulation has been removed. Afterimages (as the name implies) are most readily detected in the visual modality. Various forms of afterimages are known to exist, as the following entries detail.

afterimage, movement ➤ **motion aftereffect**

afterimage, negative Generally, an *afterimage* whose properties are antagonistic to those of the original stimulus. Although occasionally the term *complementary* is used for these afterimages (particularly when discussing color vision), there are doubts that they are true complements; e.g., the afterimages induced from short-wavelength stimuli (blues) are too red compared with the values obtained from color mixing to be true complements (see the various entries on ➤ **color vision**). Negative afterimages are relatively long lasting, particularly when compared with ➤ **positive *afterimages**.

afterimage, positive An *afterimage* seen immediately after the termination of a visual stimulus which has the same qualitative characteristics as the original. Positive afterimages are fleeting and are best observed when a very brief, very intense light is used and the eye has been thoroughly dark adapted. There are several different such images; ➤ **Hering afterimage, Hess image, Purkinje image**.

aftersensation Any sensory ➤ **aftereffect**; e.g., an ➤ **afterimage**.

agamogenesis 1. Asexual reproduction. **2.** Parthenogenesis.

age Unless used with a qualifying term (see following entries) this term should always be taken as the length of time since the birth of an organism, i.e, its ➤ **chronological *age**.

age, achievement A measure of achievement given as the average or 'normal' age at which that particular level of performance is reached. The term, although loosely used by many, is really only applicable when age norms have been established for the skills being assessed. Occasionally called *educational age* when school performance is under consideration.

age, anatomical Body development as assessed primarily by skeletal growth and ossification. The most common method is the degree of ossification of the carpal bones in the wrist. ➤ **carpal *age**.

age, basal On standardized tests, the highest age level at which *all* test items for that age are passed by an individual.

age, carpal Bone development as determined by the degree of ossification of the carpal (wrist) bones. It is the most common technique for assessing ➤ **anatomical *age**.

age, chronological (CA) Simply, ➤ **age**, i.e. time since birth. Note, however, that various notational systems are used to mark CA. In very young children up to approximately 3 or 4 years the CA is generally given strictly in months; from here until adolescence the figure is usually presented in years and months, denoted, for example, as 9-6, standing for 9 years and 6 months; after adolescence the months are generally considered negligible.

age, conception Age as measured from the (estimated) time of conception. Also called *gestational age*.

age, dental An assessment of dental development based upon the number of permanent teeth which have emerged at a particular chronological age relative to the norms for that age.

age, developmental 1. Very generally, any assessment of development expressed in terms of ➤ **age norms**. **2.** A composite assessment of development based upon a combined index of a variety of developmental indices. The term is also used by some authors to refer only to physical, sensory and motoric processes and not to the cognitive and intellectual. This distinction is inappropriate and fails to reflect the degree of interaction between these several functions.

age, educational Simply, the grade-level performance of a child as assessed by standardized tests. ➤ **achievement *age**.

age-equivalent The level or stage of development of any characteristic trait, skill, etc. expressed as relative to what is typical of the average at an equivalent age. For many important developmental variables like physical growth, intelligence, reading skills, etc., age-equivalent scales have been constructed which are used to reflect the level of development of an individual child relative to the norms in the population as a whole.

age-grade scaling The standardizing of educational materials by determining the norms for a population of children who are at the appropriate grade level for their age.

ageism A ➤ **prejudice** based on age, specifically one based on the fact that the individuals discriminated against are elderly.

age, maximal On standardized tests, the lowest age level at which all test items for that age are failed by an individual.

age, mental (MA) The level of intellectual development as measured by an ➤ **intelligence test**. In the normal case (i.e. the statistically average case) the MA is equal to the ➤ **chronological *age** (CA). The concept of a mental age is only meaningful when the testing procedures used are clearly specified and *age-equivalent* scales have been established; it is of little value when dealing with adults. ➤ **intelligence quotient**.

agenesis 1. Lack of reproductive capacity. **2.** Complete or partial failure of an organ or organ part to develop properly.

age norm 1. The average score on a standardized test observed in a large, representative sample of children at a particular age. **2.** The average age at which particular performances are expected to emerge. Note that the 'expectation' implied in meaning 2 is based upon the empirical scores from meaning 1.

agent Loosely and broadly, anything which produces an effect.

age, physiological A person's age, in terms of level of physiological development. Although there are no really clear criteria for making such measurements, some rough estimates can be provided on the basis of such factors as hormonal levels, glandular secretions, musculature, neural development, etc.

agerasia Vigorous, healthy appearance in a person of advanced years.

age ratio A ratio between the age at which the first of two standardized tests is given to a child and the age at which the second is administered. Since the predictive power of tests increases with increasing age and decreases with time between administrations the ratio serves as a rough estimate of the value of the test scores.

age scale An occasionally used, shortened form of *age-equivalent scale* (see discussion under ➤ **age-equivalent**).

age score A score on any standardized test expressed in terms of the age at which the average child achieves that score.

age, test A score on a test that has been standardized for various ages; one for which an ➤ **age-equivalent** scale exists.

ageusia Partial or complete loss of the sense of taste. Usually used with a qualifier to identify the locus of the dysfunction: *central ageusia* is due to a cerebral lesion; *conduction ageusia* to lesions in the afferent pathway; and *peripheral ageusia* to dysfunctions of the taste buds.

agglutination Lit., 'gluing together.' Hence: **1.** In physiology a term used in a variety of contexts in which substances (microorganisms, tissues, blood corpuscles, etc.) become clumped by mutual adhesion. **2.** In linguistics, a process whereby new words are formed by combining existing words.

aggression An extremely general term used for a wide variety of acts that involve attack, hostility, etc. Typically, it is used for such acts as can be assumed to be motivated by any of the following: (a) fear or frustration; (b) a desire to produce fear or flight in others; or (c) a tendency to push forward one's own ideas or inter-

ests. While this will do as a loose but acceptable definition, it barely touches on the nuances of usage in the psychological literature. Patterns of usage typically reflect some theoretical bias on the part of the writer. For example, ethologists treat it as an evolutionarily determined ('instinctive') pattern of reaction to specific stimuli such as invasion of territory or attack upon offspring; those with a Freudian orientation treat aggression as a conscious manifestation of Thanatos (the hypothesized death instinct); Adler's followers regard it as a display of the will to power, the desire to control others; those who tie together the notions of aggression and frustration define it as any response to a frustrating situation (➤ **frustration-aggression hypothesis** for a discussion); and social-learning theorists view aggressive acts as responses learned through observation and imitation of others and subsequent reinforcement for the behavior. The point to be emphasized here is that the concept plays a central role in many theoretical conceptions and, as is so often the case in the social sciences, usage follows theory and no mutually accepted definition can be found. Many combined phrases are also found; important ones follow.

aggression, altruistic Aggression that functions to protect others. ➤ **Maternal *aggression** is a good example. ➤ **altruism**.

aggression, angry Generally, the kind of aggression that most think of when the term *aggression* is used, i.e. aggression evoked by frustration or the thwarting of one's goals. Aggression induced by anger.

aggression, anticipatory **1.** A counterattack against a predator (➤ **predatory *aggression**). **2.** An aggressive reaction in defense of one's territory against an intruder. ➤ **territoriality**.

aggression, displaced Aggression directed at an organism or object that is not responsible for the factors which initially stimulated the aggressive behavior. In many cases simple contiguity is sufficient, i.e. the organism or object attacked was simply present when the attacker became aggressive. Other causes are more complex; a person or object may be attacked some time after the initial aggression-causing incident because they are 'safe' and are not likely to counterattack. The term is often used by clinicians as evidence of the action of the defense mechanism of ➤ **displacement**.

aggression, fear-induced Quite literally, aggressive action induced by extreme fear, as when a normally meek animal cornered by a predator suddenly turns on it and attacks.

aggression, induced Lit., aggression which has been 'induced.' The term is used primarily with respect to an experimental procedure developed for the study of aggressive behavior. An experimental animal is subjected to conditions of stress (usually unavoidable electric shock) in the presence of another animal or some neutral object. The stressed animal in such a situation will often aggress on the other animal or object. See here ➤ **displaced *aggression**.

aggression, instrumental 1. Aggressive actions which result from learning experiences; aggression which was acquired through the action of reinforced responding. **2.** An aggressive act that is a means to another end, e.g., shoving someone aside to get out of a room quickly.

aggression, interfemale Aggression between females of a species. Much less common than ➤ **intermale *aggression**, when it does occur it too appears to be dependent on testosterone.

aggression, intermale Aggression between the males of a species. It is observed in some species as the normal reaction of one adult male to any other unfamiliar adult male, in other species it is restricted to mating situations. In all cases, however, it is behavior that is intimately linked with the hormone testosterone; immature or castrated males do not display this pattern of aggression.

aggression, maternal Any attack-like response of a female when approaches or threatening gestures are made by another toward her offspring.

aggression, predatory Aggression against a natural prey. Note that many ethologists do not consider such behavior true aggression but rather a (necessarily violent) natural food-gathering response. As some have suggested, it is the unfortunate labeling of this behavior as a form of aggression which has contributed to much of the misunderstanding of the term, including misestimates of how widespread it is.

aggression, territorial Aggression that is specifically designed to protect one's territory and to defend it against intruders. Occasionally it occurs in anticipation of another violating one's territory; ➤ **anticipatory *aggression** (2). ➤➤ **territoriality**.

aggression, weaning A mild form of aggressive response by parents directed against their offspring who are showing resistance to being weaned. Although this is the literal and most common meaning, the term is also used more metaphorically to cover similarly mild attacks on overly dependent offspring independently of the weaning issue.

aggressive 1 adj. of ➤ **aggression**. Used here with all of the various connotative and theoretically colored meanings of that term. **2.** Vigorous and enthusiastic. This usage is common in medicine, where the phrase 'aggressive treatment' means using all available means to treat a condition. One will also occasionally see similar connotative references to 'aggressive problem solving,' 'aggressively friendly people,' etc. See here ➤ **aggressiveness** (2).

aggressiveness 1. Originally, displaying aggression. The tendency to engage in hostile, aggressive acts. By extension: **2.** Self-assertiveness; the tendency to work vigorously and perhaps ruthlessly toward the fulfillment of one's aims. **3.** The tendency to aim for social dominance, to control the actions and beliefs of others in a group. Note that depending upon the context the term can be made to carry either rather positive connotations or distinctly negative ones.

aging Growing old. The process of progressive change which occurs with the passage of time, independent of the vagaries of life, the assaults of disease and the random abuses of social living. Physiologically it is a progressive, irreversible process the underlying biochemical aspects of which are extremely complex and largely unknown. var., *ageing*.

agitated depression ➤ **depression, agitated**.

agitation Restlessness.

agitolalia ➤ **agitophasia**.

agitophasia Extremely rapid speech with slurring and omission of words. Also called *agitolalia*.

aglossia 1. Lit., lack of a tongue. 2. By extension, complete lack of articulate speech.

agnosia Lit., not knowing. Thus, a defect in recognition. Generally, an agnosic can sense objects and forms but is unable to consciously recognize and interpret their meaning. Agnosia is the result of neurological pathology and can be manifested in almost any perceptual/cognitive system. Various special forms follow, others are listed under their appropriate alphabetic listing (e.g., *prosopagnosia*).

agnosia, apperceptive An ➤ **agnosia** in which recognition failure is due to an impairment in visual perception. Such individuals fail to recognize objects normally because they do not see them properly. Contrast with ➤ **associative** *agnosia**.

agnosia, associative An ➤ **agnosia** in which recognition failure is due to factors other than the modality-specific deficits that cause *apperceptive *agnosia*. In associative agnosia the patient's percepts are, in H. L. Teuber's telling phrase, 'stripped of their meaning.'

agnosia, auditory Inability to recognize or interpret the meanings of spoken words.

agnosia, ideational Faulty recognition or interpretation of symbols.

agnosia, tactile Inability to recognize or interpret objects by touch. Also called *tactoagnosia* and *finger agnosia*.

agnosia, visual Inability to recognize or interpret objects in the visual field. Also called *optic agnosia*.

agonist 1. A muscle that contracts and operates in opposition to another, its antagonist; when bending the elbow, for example, the biceps is the agonist, the triceps the antagonist. See here ➤ **antagonistic muscles**. 2. Any drug that acts to enhance or facilitate the actions of another drug. An agonistic effect may be produced in any of several ways. The drug may mimic the effects of the other drug, it may act to interfere with the process of deactivation of the other drug, it may encourage retention of the drug by the body, etc. See and contrast with the various forms of ➤ **drug *antagonism**.

agoraphobia Generally, a fear of open spaces. Agoraphobia is the most commonly cited phobic disorder of those persons who seek psychiatric or psychological treatment. It has a variety of manifestations, the most common being a deep fear of being caught alone in some public place (indeed, this is regarded by some authorities as the defining feature of the disorder). When placed in threatening situations agoraphobics may experience panic attacks. ➤ **panic disorders**.

agrammatism The loss of grammatical speech. The patient usually has a full vocabulary but is incapable of ordering the words grammatically. Usually due to a cerebral disorder, it is sometimes a symptom of certain functional disorders.

agraphia Partial or complete loss of writing ability due to cerebral pathology. An analog of ➤ **motor *aphasia**. Several special forms are often noted but their meanings are obvious; e.g., *acoustic agraphia* is loss of ability to write what was heard, etc.

agrypnia An occasional synonym for ➤ **insomnia**.

a-ha experience A term used to describe the feeling that accompanies the moment of insight, that instant when the various disparate aspects of a problem-solving situation suddenly fit together to yield the solution.

ahedonia ➤ **anhedonia**.

ahistorical General term for any approach to behavior which stresses the role of contemporary circumstances and places little or no emphasis upon earlier events and circumstances as causes of present behaviors. *Behaviorism* is an example of an approach that leans toward the ahistorical, particularly when it is applied to clinical situations. Note, however, that no coherent psychological theory can take a totally ahistorical perspective; e.g. even a 'pure' behavior therapist usually needs some understanding of the conditions under which a particular maladaptive behavior pattern was acquired in order to develop a useful behavior modification program. Thus the term is used as a label to distinguish such approaches from those that are strongly historical, such as the classical psychoanalytic theories.

ahypnia ➤ **insomnia**.

ahypnosia ➤ **insomnia**.

AI ➤ **artificial intelligence**.

aim 1. A goal or goal state toward which behavior is orientated. This usage generally carries the connotation of volition; successful completion of a piece of work may be an aim, one may even speak of a rat's achieving the food at the end of a maze as an aim. Nonvoluntary, reflexive actions, even though they may accomplish some purpose, are not regarded as embodying aims. 2. A symbolic thought, an image or an idea that represents the end point of directed behavior. Here, aim is a mentalistic term and, unlike sense 1, is used to characterize the internal state of the organism and not the external environment. 3. In psychoanalytic theory, the

'end product' of behavior. The distinction is made here between the actual person, object, event or behavior which serves as the 'end product' in the outside world that the individual seeks (the so-called *external aim*) and the gratifying psychic state of the organism experienced when the external aim is achieved (the *internal aim*).

aim-inhibited A psychoanalytic term characterizing an action or a relationship in which there is no conscious recognition of the underlying motive or drive. The term is most commonly used for inhibitions of the erotic or sexual component in social relationships and friendships.

airsickness ➤ **motion sickness**.

air swallowing ➤ **aerophagia**.

akatamathesia 1. Generally, the loss of the ability to comprehend. 2. Specifically, the loss of the ability to understand spoken language. var., *acatamathesia*.

akathisia Inability or, more accurately, extreme unwillingness to sit down. The disorder is characterized by extreme restlessness and agitation and even the thought of sitting down causes anxiety. The syndrome is associated with some antipsychotic drugs and occurs as an occasional side effect of the phenothiazine derivatives. var., *acathisia*.

akinesia Partial or complete loss of motor control; usually used for voluntary muscle movements only.

akinesthesia Partial or complete loss of ➤ **kinesthesis**.

akinetic apraxia ➤ **apraxia, akinetic**.

AL ➤ **adaptation level**.

alallia Generally, loss of ability to speak. Some authors use the term only for *functional* disorders, reserving ➤ **aphasia** for those with organic origins; others use it more broadly to cover various syndromes due to psychic, anatomical and/or cerebral pathologies.

alarm reaction The first stage in the ➤ **general adaptation syndrome**.

albedo The reflectance of any surface; specifically, the percentage of light that is reflected by a surface measured against the total light falling on that surface.

albedo perception Quite literally, perceiving the ➤ **albedo**. That is, using the ratio of reflected light to incident light as the primary cue for perceiving the brightness of stimuli. Since the albedos of, say, a piece of chalk and a piece of coal will be the same as the incident illumination is increased or decreased, the perceived brightnesses of the two will remain constant. Hence, albedo perception is the basis of *brightness constancy*.

albinism A category of pigment disorders characterized by a less than normal production of melanin in the skin. Although the term is often used as though it represented a single syndrome, in reality over a dozen varieties have been identified. *Albino* is used to designate the individual with albinism. ·

albino ➤ **albinism**.

alcohol abuse A general label for any pathological syndrome associated with excessive alcohol use. A variety of characteristics is found in serious cases, including a daily need for alcohol, continuing consumption in the face of physical disorders which are exacerbated by alcohol, 'blackouts' or periods of amnesia, extended alcoholic 'binges' lasting several days, repeated but unsuccessful attempts to quit drinking, and overall mental and emotional deterioration. In modern psychiatric writings the term is used in a manner roughly equivalent with meaning (1) of the more common term ➤ **alcoholism**. It is classified as a *substance use disorder* ➤ **substance-related disorder**, although many of the complications that occur with extended abuse of alcohol (e.g., ➤ **alcohol amnestic disorder** and ➤ **alcohol withdrawal delirium**) are regarded as ➤ **organic mental disorders**.

alcohol amnestic disorder Memory impairment associated with prolonged, excessive consumption of alcohol. Also known as ➤ **Korsakoff's syndrome**. ➤➤ **amnestic syndrome**.

alcohol dependence Alcohol is a drug and the discussion under *drug *dependence* applies to this term.

alcohol hallucinosis A syndrome of vivid auditory hallucinations following the sudden cessation of alcohol intake after an extended history of alcohol abuse.

alcoholic 1 adj. Pertaining to alcohol. **2** n. One who has any of a variety of disorders associated with excessive alcohol consumption. See here ➤ **alcohol abuse**.

alcoholic dementia ➤ **Korsakoff's syndrome**.

alcoholic jealousy An irrational, paranoid-like jealousy often observed in cases of chronic alcohol abuse.

alcoholic psychosis A general term used to cover the serious, disabling outcome of excessive, chronic ➤ **alcohol abuse**.

alcohol intoxication A loose term used to cover any pattern of erratic, maladaptive behavior and impaired judgement resulting from consumption of alcohol. The criterion determining intoxication is usually arrived at on the basis of blood-alcohol levels and/or specific sensory and motor tests.

alcohol intoxication, idiosyncratic ➤ **Alcohol intoxication** with its accompanying change in mood and behavior following ingestion of an amount of alcohol too small to produce the condition in most people. Note that the DSM-IV no longer recognizes this as a separate disorder. Also called *pathological intoxication*.

alcoholism 1. The personality and behavioral syndrome characteristic of a person who abuses alcohol. ➤ **alcohol abuse**. **2.** The actual state or condition of one who habitually consumes excessive amounts of alcohol.

alcoholism, acute A severe case of alcohol intoxication. The 'acute' qualifier denotes that the term is applied to single, short-lived episodes. Compare with ➤ chronic *alcoholism.

alcoholism, chronic Long-term ➤ alcohol abuse.

alcohol withdrawal An organic mental disorder characterized by coarse tremor of the hands, eyelids and tongue, nausea, weakness, sweating, depressed mood, anxiety and irritability. It follows, usually within a few hours, of cessation of alcohol intake in an individual who has been drinking for several days or longer. This disorder is often called 'uncomplicated' to distinguish it from cases where *delirium* is one of the symptoms.

alcohol withdrawal delirium Delirium resulting from sudden cessation of alcohol intake following an extended period of alcohol abuse. Typically symptoms are hallucinations (usually visual), rapid and irregular heartbeat, agitation, tremors, sweating and high blood pressure. ➤➤ delirium tremens.

aldosterone A hormone produced by the adrenal cortices. It helps regulate metabolism by causing the retention of sodium by the kidneys.

alethia Lit. inability to forget. Perhaps, in its own way, a more debilitating disorder than might be supposed.

alexia Lit., without words. A language-related disability characterized by the partial or complete loss of the ability to identify the printed word. The disorder is often quite specific in that alexics do not have impairment of vision and can identify spoken words normally. Sometimes called *word blindness* and *visual aphasia*.

alexia, pure A rather crystallized form of ➤ alexia in which the patient can still write but cannot read; indeed, they cannot even read what they themselves have just written.

alexithymia A disruption in both affective and cognitive processes. It is not treated as a 'true' psychiatric syndrome but rather as a general characterization of a number of traits which are often seen together in a variety of disorders, including those with psychosomatic origins and some addictions and drug-dependency disorders. Typically the alexithymic person has relatively undifferentiated emotions and thinking tends to dwell excessively on the mundane.

alg(o)- Combining form meaning *pain*.

algedonic Relating to the pleasantness–unpleasantness or the pleasure–pain dimensions of experience.

algesia Of, or referring to, pain or the pain sense. Specifically, the capacity for the experiencing of pain. Occasionally used to denote a heightened sensitivity for pain, although most authors prefer *hyperesthesia* for this condition. var., *algesis*. ant., *analgesia*.

algesimeter Any device for measuring sensitivity to pain. A variety of such devices exists, ranging from the pressing of finely calibrated needles on the skin to the presentation of controlled amounts of radiant energy to a small spot on the skin. In all cases, the basic data are the subjects' reports of subjective experience.

algethesia The subjective experiencing of pain.

algethesis The sense of pain. However, to appreciate that there is more than a single sensory system involved in the experience of pain, ➤ pain et seq.

-algia Combining form meaning pain.

algolagnia Lit. pain-lust. Hence, the arousal of sexual feelings through pain. The term is occasionally used as a cover for both ➤ sadism and ➤ masochism.

algophilia Lit., a liking for pain. An occasional synonym for ➤ masochism.

algorithm A method or procedure for solving a particular problem that is guaranteed to lead, eventually, to the solution. In some instances usable algorithms exist such as those for performing long division, solving linear equations, etc. In many cases, however, they either do not exist (e.g., proving most mathematical theorems) or are so inefficient as to be of no practical value (e.g., finding the optimum move in a chess game). Contrast with ➤ **heuristic**, where the search for the solution is directed and not guaranteed.

ALI defense (ruling) The American Law Institute standard for the defense of legal insanity. It specifies that the individual's behavior must be a consequence of a mental disorder that rendered the person either (a) incapable of realizing the moral status and consequences of his or her actions or (b) incapable of controlling or inhibiting his or her own actions. Cases with a diagnosed ➤ **antisocial personality disorder** are specifically excluded. ➤➤ **insanity defense**.

alienation 1. Most contemporary usage reflects the standard dictionary meanings: a feeling of strangeness or separation from others; a sense of a lack of warm relations with others. **2.** Existentialists, however, have made the term a central construct in their psychology and appended a subtle but important meaning to the above. Rather than concentrate solely upon alienation of one human from others, they also stress the alienation of a person from him- or herself. This separation of the individual from the presumed 'real' or 'deeper' self is assumed to result from preoccupation with conformity, the wishes of others, the pressures from social institutions, and other 'outer-directed' motivations. **3.** An antiquated term for progressive insanity.

alienation, coefficient of A measure of the degree of departure of an empirical correlation from 1.0 (or perfect correlation). The coefficient, usually denoted as k, is given by $\sqrt{(1 - r^2)}$, where r is the observed correlation. As $r \to 1.0$, $k \to 1$. Hence, k can be used as a measure of prediction error of one variable in the correlation, given the known values of the other.

alienist An obsolescent term once common in forensic work for a physician (usually but not necessarily a psychiatrist) who can testify in court on the competence (or lack thereof) of persons who are parties to a legal case.

aliment A ➤ **Piagetian** term used to refer to a new object which a child incorporates into its existing schema. The root of the word is Latin and the literal meaning is nourishment or food. Piaget's use is metaphorical but intuitively appropriate.

alimentary canal (or **tract**) The system of organs comprising a tubular passage from mouth to anus that serves digestive functions. It includes the mouth, pharynx, esophagus, stomach, small and large intestines, and the rectum.

all- Prefix meaning different, other or alternative.

allachesthesia ➤ **allesthesia** (1).

allele (*al-leel*) One of the two (or more) different forms of a given gene. The term *allelemorph* is often used to mean the same thing and alleles are said to be in an *allelemorphic relationship* with each other.

allelotropia In vision, the apparent shifting in lateral position of an element in the visual field when a similar element is presented to a disparate position in the other eye. Also called *displacement*.

allesthesia 1. Generally, sensing the location of a touch stimulus at a point other than where the stimulus was actually applied. Also called *allachesthesia* and *allochesthesia*. **2.** Specifically, such a sensation referred from one limb to the other. Also called *allochiria* and *allocheiria*.

alliaceous Characteristic of a class of garlic-like odors.

alliesthesia Shifts in the pleasantness or unpleasantness of a stimulus depending on internal stimuli.

allo- Prefix meaning: **1.** Outside of or away from, often with the connotation of away from one's self. **2.** In linguistics, it denotes one member of a group of forms all of which taken together constitute a linguistic unit. See here ➤ **allomorph**, **allophone**.

allocator In social psychology, an individual who possesses the power to dispense rewards and punishments to others in his or her group. For more discussion of this basic concept and the use of related terms ➤ **social *power**.

allocentric Outside the self. Occasionally used of the senses of vision and audition.

allocheiria ➤ **allesthesia** (2).

allochesthesia ➤ **allesthesia** (1).

allochiria ➤ **allesthesia** (2).

allochthonous Characteristic of or referring to events originating from outside the organism or the self. Compare with ➤ **autochthonous**.

alloeroticism The focusing of sexuality toward others, the opposite of *autoeroticism*. var., *alloerotism*.

alloerotism ➤ **alloeroticism**.

allokinesis Movement on the opposite side of the body to that intended.

allomorph One of two or more linguistic forms that have the same meaning but differ in their form. For example, the prefixes *in-*, *il-*, *im-* and *ir-* are all allomorphic variations of a single morpheme meaning 'not' as in *invalid*, *illiterate*, *improper* and *irrespective*.

allomorphic 1. Generally, characteristic of or pertaining to the changing of the outward or superficial form of something while leaving the basic underlying character unchanged. 2. Specifically, characteristic of an ➤ **allomorph**.

allophone One of two or more elementary sounds in a particular language that differ in acoustic or articulatory properties but without conveying any difference in meaning. For example, the [p] in *pin* is accompanied by a distinct puff of air while the [p] in *spin* is not. Nevertheless speakers of English will treat them as the same sound; the acoustic difference does not signal a semantic distinction. These two

'p's' are said to be allophonic variations of the single ➤ **phoneme** /p/.

alloplasty 1. Generally, a process of adaptation whereby modifications in the outside world are made. Alloplastic changes are changes in the external environment. 2. In psychoanalysis, the process of adjusting to the outside world in which the libido turns from self toward environmental objects and persons. Contrast with ➤ **autoplasty**.

allopsychic Descriptive of psychic processes in which the primary reference point is in the external world; e.g., *projection* is considered to be an allopsychic process. Contrast with ➤ **autopsychic**.

all-or-none law 1. In neurophysiology, the principle that any neuron propagates its characteristic neural impulse at full strength or not at all. ➤ **rate law**. 2. In learning, the principle that associations either are formed completely on a single trial or are not formed at all. Contrast this usage with the notion expressed by the term ➤ **continuity theory**. ➤➤ **all-or-none *learning**.

all-or-none learning ➤ **learning, all-or-none**.

allotriophagy Lit., strange eating. ➤ e.g., **pica**.

allotropic Lit., other-directed. Characterizing persons who are not self-centered, who are concerned with the well-being of others.

all-trans retinal ➤ **rhodopsin**.

alogia 1. An occasional synonym for ➤ **aphasia**. 2. A condition marked by speech that is dramatically reduced in amount or content (or both). Here the patient isn't really aphasic but appears instead to be suffering from a thought disorder.

alopecia Baldness

alphabet Most simplistically, the sequence of symbols (A, B, C, . . .) used to express a language in written form. But buried beneath this simple notion, as the study of reading is beginning to make clear, is a sublime richness and depth.

Alphabets are, historically, the most recent of all writing systems (➤ **orthography**). Unlike others such as ➤ **semasiographies** and ➤ **logographies**, they operate by representing the sound pattern of the spoken language in visual form and thereby achieve maximum flexibility. Unlike ➤ **syllabaries**, which also represent sounds, however, alphabets code the underlying abstract phonemic elements of a language. Interestingly, the alphabet was invented but once, in ancient Greece as a derivation from the Phoenician syllabary, and *all* existing alphabetic writing systems share this single common ancestor. For more on this problem and the contemporary terminology ➤ **reading**.

alpha blocking A change in the alpha rhythm of an EEG (➤ **electroencephalogram**) resulting from any shift away from normal, waking, relaxation. Alpha rhythms may be 'blocked' (or inhibited) by the person orienting toward a stimulus such as a sound or light, by a state of apprehension or anxiety, or by a mental activity such as performing multiplication covertly.

alpha error ➤ **error (Type I and Type II)**.

alpha level ➤ **significance level**.

alpha male In ethology, a term used to designate the male at the top of a ➤ **dominance hierarchy** of a troop.

alpha motion ➤ **motion, alpha**.

alpha response In classical eyelid conditioning, a rapid, low-amplitude response that is assumed to be an unconditioned response that develops as a result of sensitization during training. Contrast with ➤ **beta response**.

alpha rhythm (or **wave**) The pattern of electrical activity of the brain characteristic of a normal, awake but relaxed person. The typical alpha wave is between, roughly, 8 and 12 Hz.

alt Abbreviation for alternative, alternate or alternating.

alter ego A nontechnical term for a person so close to oneself that he or she seems to be a 'second self.'

alternate forms ➤ **comparable *forms**.

alternate forms reliability ➤ **reliability, alternate forms**.

alternating personality ➤ **multiple personality**.

alternating perspective The shift in ➤ **perspective** that occurs when one fixates on a particular stimulus for a period of time. See the example of the Necker cube under ➤ **reversible *figure** to experience the effect.

alternating vision ➤ **vision, alternating**.

alternative hypothesis ➤ **null *hypothesis**.

alternative schedule ➤ **schedules of *reinforcement**.

altricial Pertaining to species helpless at birth and dependent on parental care for survival.

altruism 1. The elevation of the welfare, happiness, interests or even the survival of others above one's own. 2. Behaving so as to increase the safety, interests or life of others while simultaneously jeopardizing one's own. Sense 1 is the more general and more common; it denotes a principle as well as a practice. It is also the meaning favored in contemporary ethology although here the term is restricted to circumstances where the behavior benefits neither the individual nor his or her own direct offspring. This meaning introduces an interesting subtlety in that many species engage in what seem to be altruistic behaviors, although, from the ethological point of view, they are not. For example, in *kin-selection altruism* one acts in a manner that jeopardizes one's safety but protects or promotes that of one's own kin, hence the behavior is arguably in one's own interests in that it increases the likelihood of the survival of one's own genes. Similarly, in *reciprocal altruism* the actions are often based on the notion that today's giver of supportive acts will be tomorrow's receiver. Distinguish from ➤

helping behavior, in which there is no risk involved.

altruism, reciprocal R. Triver's term for what is best summed up by the Golden Rule: 'Do unto others as you would have them do unto you.' The term is used primarily in ➤ **sociobiology**, where a genetic basis for the behavior is the focus of the research. ➤➤ **altruism**.

altruistic aggression ➤ **aggression, altruistic**.

altruistic suicide ➤ **suicide, altruistic**.

alveolar A speech sound produced by placing the tip or blade of the tongue against the alveolar ridge, e.g., /t/in *tap*, /n/ in *nap*.

alveolar ridge The hard ridge of the upper gums just behind the upper teeth.

Alzheimer's disease A progressive form of dementia characterized by the gradual deterioration of intellectual abilities such as memory, judgement, and the capacity for abstract thought, and other higher level cortical functions as well as by changes in personality and behavior. It is of insidious onset, most commonly after age 65; cases of early onset (before age 50) are rare. In the early stages memory impairments and subtle personality changes may be the only symptoms; with progression to later stages the various cognitive and behavioral changes become apparent; in the terminal stages the patient becomes totally mute and inattentive and unable to care for him or herself. Although the atrophy of the brain and accompanying ➤ **amyloid plaques** that characterize the disease can sometimes be detected by a CAT-scan (➤ **computer assisted tomography**) or MRI (➤ **magnetic resonance imaging**), it is generally diagnosed by exclusion; that is, after all other possible causes for the mental deterioration have been excluded. Recent evidence suggests that the disorder has a genetic basis, particularly in cases of early onset.

amacrine cells Cells in the retina that link ganglion cells with the bipolar cells.

amaurosis Generally, complete loss of vision occurring with no evidence of any pathological condition in the eye itself. Various forms are noted and usually qualified so that the cause is apparent; e.g., *diabetic amaurosis, lead amaurosis*.

amaurotic (familial) idiocy A general term for a group of related, genetically transmitted diseases all of which are marked by retardation and vision deficits and produced by faulty metabolism.

amaurotic (familial) idiocy, infantile ➤ **Tay-Sach's disease**.

amazon From the Greek myth of a race of female warriors, a tall, muscular woman. The term is occasionally used, inaccurately, with the implication that such women are lesbians; there is no relationship between a woman's physical stature and her sexual preferences.

ambi- Prefix meaning *both*, usually with the connotation of equality of the two things under consideration; e.g., *ambidextrous*.

ambidextrous 1. Lit., equally skilled in the use of both hands. 2. More loosely, having no hand preference.

ambiguity Having two or more meanings or interpretations; a characteristic of a stimulus, statement or situation that permits more than one reading. In a very real sense all things are ambiguous to some extent. Typically, however, the context, one's previous learning, and general perceptual and cognitive factors constrain the situation so that one interpretation overwhelms the others that could possibly be made. Most of the interest in psychology has concerned stimulus situations where the constraints are loose enough for the potential multiple meanings to emerge, e.g., *projective tests, ambiguous figures*, etc.

ambiguity, tolerance of A dimension representing the degree to which one is able to tolerate lack of clarity in a situation or in a stimulus. To some extent no one is fond of being continuously confronted with ambiguous situations. However, this term is typically used as though it were an underlying personality dimension and the primary interest is in the pole of 'intolerance:' those persons who have a great deal of difficulty in tolerating even mildly ambiguous circumstances. Such individuals tend to react with anxiety and withdrawal from uncertain situations and such a pattern of behavior has been hypothesized to be an aspect of the *authoritarian personality*.

ambiguous figure ➤ **figure, ambiguous**.

ambisexual Characterizing that which displays no sex or gender dominance. The term is used most often to designate traits or characteristics which are found equally in both sexes. See here ➤ **sex differences**. Distinguish from ➤ **asexual**; ➤ **bisexual** (especially meaning 4).

ambivalence **1.** Having simultaneous, contrasting or mixed feelings about some person, object or idea. **2.** A tendency to 'flip-flop' one's feelings or attitudes about a person, object or idea. This sense presupposes sense 1. **3.** A state in which one is pulled in two mutually exclusive directions or toward two opposite goals. This meaning derived originally from K. Lewin's work in *field theory* and shows up most clearly in the research on behavioral reactions to various forms of ➤ **conflict**.

ambivalent/resistant attachment ➤ **attachment styles**.

ambivert One who achieves a balance between ➤ **introversion** and ➤ **extraversion**; such a person is said to tend toward *ambiversion*.

ambly- A combining form from the Greek meaning *dull*. Used generally to denote deficiency or dysfunction.

amblyacousia A general term for any hearing deficit.

amblyaphia A diminished sense of touch.

amblygeustia Dulled or deficient sense of taste.

amblyopia A non-organic, permanent vision loss, particularly spatial vision. It is typically caused by disorders that affect the degree of coordination between the two eyes such as different refractive errors in the two eyes, misalignment of the eyes, different degrees of *astigmatism*, or *strabismus*. In layman's terms, *lazy eye*.

ambulatory **1.** Able to walk. **2.** Not requiring confinement. These two uses do not necessarily entail each other and are used distinctly.

ameliorate To improve. Used particularly with respect to improvement in diseases, dysfunctions or other conditions.

amenorrhea Absence of menstrual period. Compare with ➤ **dysmenorrhea**.

amentia Generally, any serious mental deficiency. The term is rarely used today.

American College Testing Program (ACT) A test of academic potential in wide use in the United States. It is designed to aid in the evaluation of applicants to colleges and universities and is the primary competitor of the Scholastic Aptitude Test (SAT), the most widely used of these tests in North America. ACT consists of four sub-tests in English, mathematics, natural sciences and social sciences which are combined to produce a composite score. The tests are primarily achievement-oriented and were designed to evaluate how well students can apply already developed skills and acquired knowledge.

American Sign Language (ASL) The system of gestures, hand signals and finger spelling used by the deaf in North America (and other English-speaking locales). Also called *Ameslan*.

Ameslan A contraction for the *Ame*rican *Sign Lan*guage for the deaf.

Ames room A specially constructed room designed by the artist/psychologist Adelbert Ames which provides a striking demonstration of the cues for depth perception. The room is of distorted construction: three of the walls are actually trapezoidal and the ceiling slants markedly.

However, because of the use of the cues of shading, linear perspective and interposition, the room appears normal to an outside observer. Looking into the room produces many illusions: objects and persons appear distorted particularly in their apparent size, round objects seem to roll uphill, etc. ➤ **transactional theory (of perception)**, the point of view that Ames argued for.

ametropia General term for any refractive deficit in the eye, e.g., *hyperopia, myopia, astigmatism*.

amimia Partial or complete loss of the ability to express oneself with gestures or signs.

amine Any of a large group of organic compounds of nitrogen. The ones of primary interest in psychology are the ➤ **biogenic amines**.

amine transmitters ➤ **biogenic amines**.

amino acid Any of a large group of organic compounds marked by the presence of both an *amino group* and a *carboxyl group*. They are linked by peptide bonds to form proteins. Over 20 different amino acids are known to be necessary as sources of energy for proper metabolism and growth and several either are precursors of neurotransmitters or function as transmitter substances themselves. See here ➤ **gamma-amino butyric acid (GABA), glutamic acid, glycine**.

amino group A radical composed of two atoms of hydrogen and one of nitrogen.

amitriptyline A tricyclic compound used as an antidepressant. It functions as an agonist of serotonin by blocking its reuptake. Trade name, Elaril.

Ammon's horn ➤ **hippocampus**.

amnesia Generally, any partial or complete loss of memory. A number of specific forms of amnesia are recognized, each denoting a particular kind of deficit in memory; they are presented in the entries that follow. Note, however, that two basic distinctions enter into the classification

system that is currently in use. One has to do with whether the amnesic syndrome is 'physiological' and caused by some form of damage to brain tissue (the so-called ➤ **organic *amnesias**) or 'psychological' and caused by any of a variety of factors including alterations in the memorial code (e.g., ➤ **infantile *amnesia**) or neurotic reactions (e.g., *repressive amnesia*). The other has to do with temporal factors whereby the memory disability is intimately related to events that occurred at specific times. This classification system can be most easily appreciated by looking at the entries ➤ **retrograde *amnesia** and ➤ **anterograde *amnesia**. Also called *amnestic disorder*.

amnesia, anterograde Loss of memory for events and experiences occurring subsequent to the amnesia-causing trauma. In cases of complete anterograde amnesia the patient is incapable of forming new memories, although recall of material learned prior to the onset is largely unaffected. Compare with ➤ **retrograde *amnesia**.

amnesiac One suffering from ➤ **amnesia**. The shortened form *amnesic* is also found.

amnesia, dissociative An inability to recall important personal information resulting from a traumatic or stressful experience; despite appearing as a disorder of memory, it is regarded as a ➤ **dissociative disorder**.

amnesia, episodic A 'hole' in one's memory; loss of information for isolated events or episodes. Also called *lacunar amnesia* and *catathymic amnesia*.

amnesia, global Complete ➤ **amnesia** evidencing both *retrograde* and *anterograde* forms.

amnesia, infantile Loss of memory for events and experiences that occurred early in life, generally before the age of 2 or 3. Several theories have been put forward to explain this most intriguing finding. Psychoanalysts argue that it is due to ➤ **repression**; cognitivists maintain that the shift in encoding of memories that occurs with the emergence of language renders these early memories irretrievable; neuropsychologists point to the strong possibility that the neural mechanisms required for long-term memory may be functionally immature during the early years. If this last explanation turns out to be correct, the others will be redundant.

amnesia, organic A general label for any amnesia caused by physiological dysfunctions.

amnesia, post-encephalic Any ➤ amnesia that results from a viral infection, particularly one that affects the temporal lobes and the underlying limbic system. The most commonly implicated is the herpes simplex virus, which has an affinity for this area of the brain.

amnesia, post-traumatic Generally, any loss of memory following a traumatic experience. Note that *traumatic* here may be used either for physical injury or for a disturbing psychological experience. Hence, the term will be used to refer both to organic amnesias and to psychoneurotic amnesias, although the preferred and more commonly intended meaning is the organic.

amnesia, retrograde Loss of memory for events and experiences occurring in a (usually fairly short, circumscribed) period of time prior to the amnesia-causing trauma. Since retrograde amnesia often involves the inability to recall material once known, most memory researchers consider it to be a failure of the ability to retrieve or recall the information rather than a true loss of that information.

amnesia, source An inability to recall the source of information. The individual knows that he or she knows something but simply cannot recall where or how the knowledge was acquired. A classic case is reading a book and then some time later being unable to recall whether one read the book or saw the movie (or both). While source amnesia occurs as a neurological abnormaltity, in moderate form it is normal and ubiquitous. ➤ **source *memory.**

amnesia, temporal lobe An ➤ amnesia resulting from damage to neurological structures in the temporal lobes, specifically the *hippocampus*, the *amygdala* and related structures. It is marked by serious deficits in ➤ **long-term *memory** while often leaving ➤ **short-term *memory** and ➤ **implicit *memory** intact.

amnesia, transient global (TGA) A relatively short lived, although virtually complete amnesic episode. Most TGA's last only a few minutes (or hours at the most), a period during which the individual has virtually no memory. The syndrome is similar to amnesias of the Korsakoff's type (**Korsakoff's syndrome**) in that long-established memories are intact, only the recently learned is forgotten. TGA's are rare and seen with some head injuries, restricted blood supply to the brain, and occasionally with severe migraines.

amnesic (amnestic) Terms used to indicate pertinence to amnesia; the adjectival forms of **amnesia**. Also occasionally used for one suffering from *amnesia* although *amnesiac* is preferred.

amnesic aphasia ➤ aphasia, anomic.

amnesic apraxia ➤ apraxia, amnesic.

amnestic disorder ➤ amnesia.

amnestic syndrome Generally, severe impairment of memory usually affecting both the ability to learn new material (see here ➤ **short-term *memory**) as well as the ability to recall that which was learned in the past (➤**long-term *memory**). The term is a psychiatric/neurological diagnostic category for cases in which the impairment results from organic dysfunctions. The most common cause is thiamine deficiency, particularly that associated with chronic alcohol abuse.

amniocentesis A procedure in which a thin needle guided by ultrasound is inserted through the abdomen or via the vagina into the uterus of a pregnant woman. The fluid and cells withdrawn can then be analyzed for possible defects in the fetus. Many hereditary biochemical disorders can be identified by examining the extracted amniotic fluid. The sex of the unborn child can, of course, also be determined.

amok An acute, murderous frenzy. It is often considered a ➤ **culture-specific syndrome** particular to certain Malaysian groups; the term itself is borrowed from one of the Malaysian languages. However, the behavior seems to be rather more widespread than early classifiers suspected, although there is a suggestion that cultural values may make it more or less likely to occur – a truism which can be made for any culturally bounded behavior. var., *amuck*.

amphetamines A class of drugs including benzedrine, dexedrine and methedrine that act as central-nervous-system stimulants. Amphetamines suppress appetite, increase heart rate and blood pressure and, in larger doses, produce a feeling of euphoria and power. Therapeutically, they are used to alleviate depression, control appetite, relieve ➤ **narcolepsy** and, paradoxically, to control childhood ➤ **hyperkinesis**. Amphetamine abuse is common and chronic use leads to a model paranoid psychosis.

amphi- Prefix meaning *on both sides*, *at both ends* or *around*.

amphigenous inversion ➤ **bisexuality** (2 and 3).

ampho- Prefix meaning *both*.

amplitude 1. Generally, intensity, value, amount or extent of some thing. 2. More specifically, the maximum displacement of a periodic wave. This meaning is often expressed as *maximum amplitude* (symbol: A) to distinguish it from: 3. The average displacement of the wave, which is occasionally called *affective amplitude*. When the physical stimulus is highly controlled, as with a pure tone, then meanings 2 and 3 are equivalent.

amuck ➤ **amok**.

amusia Lit., loss of musical ability. Generally used for partial or complete inability to comprehend (*sensory amusia*) and/

or produce (*motor amusia*) music as a result of organic damage.

amygdala An almond-shaped neural structure composed of several nuclei and comprising part of the temporal lobe. It is classified as part of the ➤ **limbic system** and is intimately connected with the *hypothalamus*, *hippocampus*, the *cingulate gyrus* and the *septum*. It plays a significant role in emotional behavior and motivation, particularly aggressive behaviors, and, as part of the temporal lobe, apparently serves memory functions as well. Also (and more properly) called the *amygdaloid complex*.

amygdalotomy A form of psychosurgery in which amygdaloid fibers are severed. It has been used in cases of extreme uncontrollable violence. ➤ **psychosurgery** for discussion of this and other procedures.

amyloid plaques Abnormal protein coatings on nerve cells in the brain. They are found in the brains of patients with ➤ **Alzheimer's disease** and in individuals with ➤ **Down syndrome**.

ana- Prefix meaning *away from*, *back*, or *up*, *upper*.

anabolic Generally, promoting a buildup or restoration of a structure or body. Anabolic agents such as testosterone or similar steroids stimulate anabolism.

anabolic steroids ➤ **steroids**.

anabolism 1. Generally, the building up of a body structure. 2. The restorative phase of ➤ **metabolism**. Contrast with ➤ **catabolism**.

anaclisis Generally, reclining or leaning. Typically used to refer to an emotional dependency upon another. adj., *anaclitic*.

anaclitic depression R. Spitz's term used to characterize the severe and progressive depression found in infants who had lost their mothers and did not obtain a suitable substitute. Although the original usage of the term was linked closely to mothering in humans, recent research has shown that the syndrome is a general phenomenon and occurs in other species, particularly primates, when there is a dramatic lack of normal 'creature comfort' during early childhood. The connotations of the term have broadened to reflect these findings. ➤ **reactive attachment disorder**.

anaclitic identification A general tendency for identification with a parent who is supportive and nurturing.

anaclitic object choice A psychoanalytic term for the adult selection of a loved one who resembles closely or is modeled on one's own mother (or other adult upon whom one depended as a child).

anacusia Total deafness. vars., *anacousia, anacusis*.

anaerobic Pertaining to or characteristic of organisms (or tissues) which require, or are not destroyed by, an absence of free oxygen.

anaerobic exercise Exercise that is not dependent upon the use of breathed oxygen. Compare with ➤ **aerobic exercise**.

anaesthesia Common variant spelling of ➤ **anesthesia**.

anaglyph A picture printed in two complementary colors slightly offset from each other. When viewed through lenses of corresponding colors (one color to each eye) the effect is one of stereoscopic depth. This process is that used in the production of 3-D movies.

anaglyptoscope Device which shifts the angle of lighting on a test object, resulting in a reversal of areas of shadow and light. It is used to demonstrate the role of shadows in the perception of depth. var., *anaglyphoscope*.

anagogic From the Greek, meaning *leading up*, and hence pertaining to the spiritual or the ideal. Used by Jung to refer to the idealistic or moralistic aspects of unconscious thought.

anagram Any of several word problems based upon the rearranging of letters in words. There are many variations on the basic theme with the following three the most often used in psychological experiments: (a) the simple, *single solution* anagram, for which the subject is given a set of scrambled letters and required to find the word they spell (e.g., HIRAC – CHAIR); (b) the *word* anagram, for which the subject begins with a real word and must rearrange the letters to find another word (e.g., SHORE – HORSE); (c) the *multiple solution* anagram, for which the subject must find as many different words as possible using any or all of the letters in the initial word (e.g., there are several dozen words which can be formed using the letters in TEACHER).

anal Referring to the ➤ **anus**.

anal character An adult who compulsively displays characteristics which, according to psychoanalytic theory, are referrable to the ➤ **anal stage**. The *anal expulsive* character typically is said to be compulsively pliant, untidy, generous, etc.; the *anal retentive* to be obstinate, orderly, miserly, etc. Generally, the theory proposes that the anal character, whether it occurs in either of these two extreme forms or, more commonly, in a form which combines these traits, is an infantile ➤ **fixation** on the anal region and the anal functions.

analepsis From the Greek, meaning *taking up*; hence, restoration of health, recovery.

anal eroticism Sensual or sexual pleasure derived from the anus either by direct stimulation or by the sequences of behaviors associated with defecation. var., *anal erotism*.

anal expulsive (stage) Some psychoanalytic theorists hypothesize two distinct aspects to the ➤ **anal stage**, one characterized by anal expulsiveness, in which pleasure is derived from the passing of feces, and the other characterized by anal retentiveness, in which pleasure is associated with the withholding of feces. ➤➤ **anal character** for the personality types assumed by psychoanalytic theory to result from fixation at the anal stage.

analgesia Insensitivity to pain. Hence, any substance that serves to relieve pain is an *analgesic*. The term is also used for procedures which do not directly involve the introduction of a substance, e.g., *hypnotic analgesia* (➤ **hypnosis** for discussion).

anal impotence A psychoanalytic term for the inability to pass feces in the presence of other persons.

anal intercourse Sexual intercourse with the penis inserted in the anus. The term is used for hetero- and homosexual relations.

anality That part of libidinous energy associated with the anal region.

analog 1. Generally, a correspondence or a resemblance. A thing or event is said to be an analog of another if there is a coherent correspondence between their parts, functions, roles, etc. ➤ **analogy.** 2. Specifically, in biology, an organ or part similar in function to another but different in structure and origin; e.g., the wing of the bat is in an analogous relation to the wings of birds. Compare with structures which are ➤ **homologous**. var., *analogue*.

analogical reasoning Reasoning whereby decisions about objects, events or concepts depend upon perceived similarities in the relationships between pairs. ➤ **analogy** for further discussion.

analogies test A test in which a relationship between two terms is given and the person is required to complete an analogous relationship. Questions typically take the form: *A* is to *B* as *C* is to . . .; e.g., *fence* is to *field* as *frame* is to . . .?

analogue ➤ **analog**.

analogy Generally, likeness, similarity, correspondence. Specific usages include: 1. A description, argument or explanation based on systematic comparison of one thing with another, already known thing. Analogical reasoning so carried through is a useful *heuristic* for revealing corre-

spondences between things, but as a *logical* argument it fails to satisfy the principles necessary for proving the validity of a proposition. **2.** In biology, a correspondence in function between two organs or parts. ➤ **analog** (2).

anal retentive ➤ **anal expulsive**.

anal sadistic The term generally refers to any sadistic pleasure hypothesized to originate in the *anal stage*. It is argued by many psychoanalysts that such behavior derives from harsh punishment during toilet training. Some theorists have even hypothesized the existence of a separate ➤ **anal sadistic stage** in development.

anal sadistic stage (or **level** or **phase**) A stage in psychosexual development assumed by some psychoanalysts to be part of the anal stage but distinguishable as a distinct component by a focus upon *anal eroticism* and sadistic impulses toward the parents, who are the agents of toilet training.

anal stage (or level or phase) In psychoanalytic theory, the stage of psychosexual development marked by preoccupation with the anus and its functions. From the libidinal point of view, the stage is marked by the deriving of sensuous pleasure from anal stimulation and defecation; from the ego perspective the stage is characterized by the beginning of socialization, as indicated by control over the sphincter muscles. Note that two opposing tendencies are assumed to be operating here; ➤ **anal retentive** and **anal expulsive**.

anal triad In psychoanalytic theory, a hypothesized syndrome in which the three traits characteristic of the retentive variety of the *anal character* (compulsive orderliness, stinginess and obstinacy) are displayed.

analysand One undergoing analysis. According to most historians of the psychoanalytic movement this term was introduced because the medical students taking a psychoanalytic internship who routinely undergo analysis as part of their training objected to being called *patients*!

analysis **1.** Generally, the process of separating a 'thing' into its component parts or elementary qualities. The term is ubiquitous in all scientific disciplines and hence the 'thing' may be a mechanical, physical entity, a chemical or biological substance, a percept, an image, idea, emotion, etc. Because of its wide application the term is usually qualified so that the form or the theoretical motivation for the analysis is specified. Some of these qualified terms follow below, others are found under the appropriate alphabetical listing. **2.** The particular set of techniques and procedures used in the practice of ➤ **psychoanalysis**. This meaning is actually consonant with meaning 1; it is given separate listing merely because it occurs so frequently without qualification in the literature that it is sometimes taken as the dominant sense of the term. **3.** The outcome of either of the above two processes. The connotation here is that of *reductionism*; it is a process designed to reveal fundamental components . or root causes. Contrast with ➤ **synthesis**. adjs., *analytic*, *analytical*.

analysis by synthesis A phrase referring to a broad class of pattern-recognition schemes or, more accurately, a class of information-processing theories which seek to explain such elementary phenomena as the simple fact that yo· ca· un·er· ·ta·d t·e m·an·ng ·f t·is ·en·en·e e·en ·ho·gh ·ve·y t·ir· le·te· is ·is·in· fr·m t·e l·st ·ar·. Analysis-by-synthesis models operate on the assumption that humans possess a vast network of memories, strategies and schemata which enable them to evaluate inputs, anticipate incoming stimuli, form guesses based on context, exclude irrelevant kangaroo material, fill in missing features, etc. In short, 'synthesize' in order to 'analyze' the input. Such models have been used in studies of sensory psychology, psycholinguistics, thinking, reading, and cognition in general.

analysis, didactic The psychoanalysis that one who is training to become a psychoanalyst undergoes as part of the educational process.

analysis, lay Psychoanalysis carried out by a ➤ **lay analyst**.

analysis of covariance (ANCOVA) An extension of the ➤ **analysis of variance** used when there is improper control of one or more of the variables. The procedure allows for 'statistical control' of the uncontrolled variations so that normal analysis techniques may be carried out without distorting the results.

analysis of variance (ANOVA) A statistical method for making simultaneous comparisons between two or more means. An ANOVA yields a series of values (F values) which can be statistically tested to determine whether a significant relation exists between the experimental variables. ➤➤ **F-test**.

analyst **1.** Generally, a practitioner of ➤ analysis (2), i.e. a ➤ **psychoanalyst**. **2.** A follower of Jung's principles of ➤ **analytic psychology**.

analytic (or analytical) ➤ analysis.

analytic language Any language which tends to express grammatical relationships by the use of auxiliary words rather than inflections. Syntactic components are generally carried by word-order rules in such languages (of which English is an example). Compare with ➤ **synthetic language**.

analytic psychology **1.** Generally, the form of psychoanalysis put forward by Carl Jung. **2.** Occasionally, a label used for any approach to psychology that emphasizes the breaking down of phenomena into their component parts. var., *analytical psychology*.

anamnesis From the Greek, meaning *recall* or *recollection*. **1.** In general, recall or the ability to recall past events. **2.** In medicine, the personal case history of a disorder as provided by the patient. Originally the term was used specifically for the patient's statements concerning a particular disability and his or her considerations about important antecedents deemed relevant to it. Many others, particularly psychiatrists, use the term to encompass any and all aspects of the patient's medical history, including information other than that provided by the patient such as biographical data, reports from family, etc. Compare with ➤ catamnesis.

anandria Absence of normal male characteristics.

anankastia A general label for the condition in which an individual feels as though he or she is being forced to behave, think or feel in ways that go against their personal will. The notion of 'force' here is meant broadly and the term is used for a variety of conditions involving phobias, compulsions and obsessions. var., *anancastia.*

anankastic personality ➤ compulsive personality disorder and obsessive-compulsive disorder.

anaphia Loss of or diminution in the sense of touch.

anaphora A reference to something previously mentioned. An anaphoric word or anaphoric reference relates to another, antecedent, word or proposition. In 'Max is a millionaire, I want to be one too' *millionaire* is the antecedent, *one* is the anaphoric word.

anaphrodisia Condition of diminished or absent desire for sex.

anaphylaxis A state of hypersensitivity to a particular substance. Seen as a reaction to various drugs (e.g., penicillin) or other foreign substances (e.g., the toxin in a bee or wasp sting). The term is restricted to states of hypersensitivity which result from previous administration or injection of the substance. The primary symptoms are wheezing, extreme difficulty in breathing, chest constriction and occasionally convulsions.

anaphylaxis, psychological An extension of the meaning of anaphylaxis to cover psychological hypersensitivity resulting from a previous traumatic experience such that later presentation of the original circumstances causes deep psychological distress.

anarthria Partial or complete loss of articulate speech. Usually the term is used for disorders of articulation resulting from central-nervous-system lesions. Occasionally it may be used for those resulting from peripheral motor or muscular defects, although the preferred term for these latter syndromes is ➤ dysarthria.

anastasis A return to health.

anastomosis A general anatomical/neurological term for any direct communication or joining between two anatomical structures, organs, neural processes, tissues, etc.

anatomical age ➤ age, anatomical.

anchor (or anchorage) 1. A reference point or standard against which judgements take place; ➤ e.g., anchor point. 2. A foundation upon which a thing is built or to which it is attached.

anchoring A ➤ cognitive *heuristic in which decisions are made based on an initial 'anchor.' E.g., in a classic study, one group of people asked whether the chance of nuclear war was greater or less than 1% estimated it to be about 10%; another group asked if it was greater or less than 90% estimated it to be over 20%.

anchoring of ego The process of reaching the satisfying state of security and comfortableness with one's personal and physical surroundings.

anchor point(s) Reference point(s) or standard(s) used to provide an observer with subjective criteria against which future judgements can be made. Used in *category estimation* scaling, where the extremes of the stimulus dimension are given to the subject as anchor points, and in preference rankings, where the neutral point anchors the scale ranging from least preferred to most preferred.

ANCOVA ➤ analysis of covariance.

androgen Any of the male sex hormones responsible for the development of male sex characteristics. Androgens are secreted primarily by the testes and the adrenal cortices in the male and in small amounts by the ovaries in the female. ➤ e.g., **androstenedione**, **testosterone**.

androgen-insensitivity syndrome A congenital condition in which normal responsiveness to androgens is lacking. Such individuals are externally female since the developing fetus does respond to the small amounts of estrogen normally produced in males although they possess the Y male-sex chromosome. They are infertile and do not menstruate. Also called *testicular-feminizing syndrome*.

androgenization Lit., the process of becoming a male. The term specifically refers to the complex processes in the developing embryo initiated by exposure to androgens and resulting in the development of male sex organs.

androgyny From Greek *andros* (= man) and *gyne* (= female), the condition in which some male and some female characteristics are present in the same individual. The term is used with respect to both biological/physical and psychological/behavioral characteristics. In general, differentiated from ➤ **hermaphrodite** since, except in rare cases, a person displaying androgyny shows sexual differentiation and can be labelled as biologically male or female. Some authors restrict the use of the term to biological males who display physical or behavioral female characteristics, while reserving ➤ **gynandry** for biological females with male characteristics. Compare with ➤ **effeminate** and distinguish from ➤ **bisexual**.

androgyny scale ➤ Bem Sex Role Inventory.

android Resembling a male. Used both as a noun and an adjective.

andromania An occasional synonym for ➤ **nymphomania**.

androphile 1. One who exhibits an extreme affection for males. 2. Preferring man. This latter usage is generally restricted to various parasites.

-andro(s)- Combining forms from the Greek meaning *man*, *male* or *masculine*.

androstenedione A natural androgen found in both males and females produced mainly by the adrenal cortices and, to a lesser degree, by the gonads. Relatively weak as an androgen itself, it is the direct precursor of testosterone, the most powerful of the androgens.

anecdotal evidence Obviously, evidence which is anecdotal, i.e. casually observed and related like a narrative. Although generally regarded as unacceptable scientifically (how can one replicate an anecdote or verify it conclusively?) such evidence can often form the basis for further systematic experimentation.

anechoic Lit., free from echo. Anechoic chambers constructed with sound-absorbing walls have been very useful in many experiments on *audition*.

anemotropism An orienting response (➤ **tropism**) to air currents.

anencephalus A congenital deformity in which the brain has failed to develop.

anepia Inability to speak.

anergasia Generally, loss of function. Used of such dysfunctions as result from central-nervous-system lesions.

anergia Sluggishness, lack of energy.

anesthesia Generally, any partial or complete loss of sensitivity. Thus, an *anesthetic* is any chemical that induces anesthesia, generally by raising the threshold required for the neurons to respond. ➤➤ **analgesia**. var., *anaesthesia*.

anesthesia, glove A ➤ **functional disorder** involving loss of sensitivity in the hand and wrist. Since there is no combination of neural fibers which serve this area and no other, with these symptoms we have prima facie evidence of a psychogenic disorder. Similar syndromes affecting the lower extremities are known as *shoe* (or *foot*) *anesthesia* and *stocking anesthesia*.

anesthesia sexualis Lack of sexual responsiveness.

'angel dust' ➤ phencyclidine.

anger Very generally, a fairly strong emotional reaction which accompanies a variety of situations such as being physically restrained, being interfered with, having one's possessions removed, being attacked or threatened, etc. Anger is often defined (or, better, *identified*) by a collection of physical reactions, including particular facial grimaces and body positions characteristic of action in the autonomic nervous system, particularly the sympathetic division. In many species anger produces overt (or implicit) attack. As with many emotions anger is extremely difficult to define objectively. The problem is that it is a rather fuzzy concept and hedges into other emotional reactions of similar kind such as ➤ **animus**, **rage**, **hostility**, **hatred**, etc. See these, and other related entries, for discussions of the distinctions typically drawn. Note, however, that the question of the synonymity of anger and these other terms can only be answered by the context in which they are found and the author's theoretical orientation when using them. Although the preferred connotations of the term are those outlined above, many use the term in ways that overlap with the other terms.

angina 1. Generally, a feeling of suffocation, of being choked. 2. A disease of the pharynx characterized by attacks of choking. 3. *Angina pectoris*, a disease of the heart caused by insufficient blood supply; primary symptoms are intermittent attacks of severe chest pain with a sense of suffocating pressure.

anginophobia 1. Generally, a pathological fear of suffocation. 2. More specifically, an intense, compelling fear of an attack of *angina pectoris* (➤ **angina** 3). Many angina sufferers carry this additional psychic burden.

angio- Combining form meaning *vessel*. Used commonly for blood vessels but may also refer to that contained within a vessel such as a seed.

angiotensin ➤ renin.

angiotensinogen ➤ renin.

angry aggression ➤ aggression, angry.

Angst German for *anxiety*, *anguish* or *psychic pain*. 1. In the existential school, this mental turmoil is regarded as *the* fundamental reality of beings who come to realize the indeterminacy of things and who must confront life as a forum within which personal choice is essential and the responsibility for decisions made must be borne. 2. For its use in psychoanalysis, see the discussion under ➤ **pain** (3).

ångström unit The internationally accepted unit of measurement of wavelength given as one ten-millionth of a millimeter (or one ten-thousandth of a micron).

angular gyrus A gyrus (cerebral convolution) of the posterior portion of the parietal lobe. The left angular gyrus has been implicated in language functions, particularly reading.

anhedonia Condition marked by a general lack of interest in living, in the pleasures of life; a loss in the ability to enjoy things. It is regarded as a defining feature of ➤ **depression**. var., *ahedonia*.

anhypnia ➤ insomnia.

anhypnosis ➤ insomnia.

aniconia A lack of mental imagery. It has been suggested that the early behaviorist J. B. Watson was aniconic, a condition which may have contributed to his lack of sympathy for those who made imagery so important in their theories.

anima 1. Originally, the soul. 2. In the early writings of Carl Jung, one's inner being, that aspect of one's psyche in intimate association with one's unconscious. Compare here with his use of the term ➤ **persona**. 3. In Jung's later writings, the feminine archetype, which was differentiated from **animus**, the masculine archetype. In arguing for this essential bisexuality of all persons, Jung hypothesized that both components were present in both sexes.

animal magnetism Mesmer's term for the universal force through which hypnotic effects were hypothesized to be mediated. ➤ **hypnosis**.

animal psychology A loose term for either of the following: **1.** The study of psychological processes from a phylogenetic point of view, in which comparisons between the behavior of various species are the primary focus. See here ➤ **comparative psychology**. **2.** Any psychological investigation which uses animals as subjects.

animatism The belief that a kind of impersonal supernatural force exists in all things, animate or inanimate. Some anthropologists argue that it is a cultural precursor to **animism**.

animism **1.** Loosely, the belief that all things animate or inanimate, living or not living, possess a soul or other form of spiritual essence that transcends the physical forms. The term is used with several, more specific connotations in various areas, as follows: **2.** In anthropology, it is often argued that animism, as derived from the more primitive beliefs of ➤ **animatism**, represents the earliest form of religion. As a religious belief system, animism actually has a sophisticated panoply of spirits with specific powers and roles to play in the nature of things and persons. **3.** In developmental psychology, the term is used for early patterns of thought and speech in young children in which feelings, desires and beliefs of the child are invested in the non-human and the non-living. ➤ **anthropomorphism**. **4.** In various philosophical and psychological perspectives something akin to these notions is also found. A number of gentle euphemisms have been coined to denote these ideas since the above meanings have tarnished the term so that there is a distinct reluctance to use it to represent anything that one would want others to take seriously. See here ➤ **panpsychism**, ➤ **teleology** (especially 1) and ➤ **vitalism**.

animosity Intense and enduring hostility with the implication that the feelings are open and active.

animunculus Lit., the animal in the head.

Hence, the sketched representations of the body of an animal as projected on the somatosensory cortex. The equivalent to the ➤ **homunculus** (2).

animus **1.** An intense and enduring dislike. See here ➤ **anger, hostility** and related entries. **2.** In Jung's later writings, the unconscious masculine archetype in women. ➤ **anima** (3).

anion A negatively charged ion. ➤ **cation**

aniseikonia Dissimilarity in the size and shape of the two retinal images. var., *anisoiconia*.

anis(o)- Combining form denoting *unequal, dissimilar* or *nonsymmetrical*.

anisocoria A condition in which the diameters of the pupils are of unequal size.

anisoiconia ➤ **aniseikonia**.

anisometropia Unequal refractive power in the two eyes.

anisopia A general term for any inequality of vision in the two eyes.

anisotropia Lit., unequal in or when turning. Hence: **1.** Of a lens, the property of being differentially refractive when oriented in different directions. **2.** In perception, the shift in the apparent length of a line or rod when it is turned through space. ➤ e.g., **foreshortening**.

ankle clonus A repetitive contraction-relaxation of the ankle muscles. It is a common symptom of neurological diseases of the central nervous system.

ankylo- Combining form meaning stiffly bent or crooked, or characterizing a fusing of parts.

ankyloglossia A condition in which the membrane attached to the underside of the tongue is abnormally short and inflexible. Hence, tongue-tied.

ankylosis Generally, any abnormal fusing of the cartilage and bones of a joint resulting in stiffness and immobility.

Anlage In German, lit., a *laying on*. Hence: **1.** A primordial cluster of cells which forms the foundation for the development of an organ or part. **2.** By extension, a predisposing factor or condition which functions as the basis for the development of a mental process.

Anna O., the case of One of the first and most famous case studies in psychoanalysis. The patient known as 'Anna O.' (subsequently revealed to have been Bertha Pappenheim, who later in her life became a well-known and much respected humanitarian and social-relief worker) was originally diagnosed as an hysteric with functional limb paralysis and a tendency toward a multiple personality. She was treated by Josef Breuer and is frequently cited as the first demonstrated success of psychoanalytic therapy. The term 'talking cure' was actually coined by Anna to describe the cathartic outcome of working through her problems verbally.

annihilation anxiety Profound and disturbing anxiety that has loss of self and loss of identity at its core.

anniversary reaction A strong emotional reaction to an earlier event occurring at the same time of the year as the original event. Most commonly seen as a depressed state on the anniversary of some earlier tragedy such as the death of a loved one.

annoyer E. L. Thorndike's term for any stimulus possessing noxious or unpleasant properties. Defined operationally, an annoyer is any stimulus which an organism will learn to escape or avoid. Contrast with ➤ **satisfier**.

annulment A psychoanalytic term for the process through which painful, anxiety-provoking ideas and images are neutralized or 'annulled.' The standard theory maintains that annulment operates through the use of day-dreams, fantasies and the like. Compare with ➤ **repression**, wherein the assumption is that these painful ideas are removed from awareness entirely.

annulus Any ring-shaped structure. The term is used broadly to describe stimuli

with circular shapes, ring-like anatomical structures, etc. var., *anulus*.

anodyne Any pain-relieving agent, an analgesic.

anoesia Lacking the ability to comprehend or understand; idiocy. var., *anoia*.

anoetic From the Greek, meaning *unable to think*. Hence: **1.** Not relevant to cognition. Affects or emotions are sometimes called anoetic functions. **2.** Not relevant to or on the borderline of consciousness. Passive, implicit processing of information is occasionally referred to as anoetic processing.

anoia ➤ anoesia.

anomalous contour ➤ subjective *contour.

anomalous dichromatism (or **dichromacy**) ➤ dichromacy, anomalous.

anomalous sentence Any sentence that is syntactically correct but makes no (obvious) semantic sense. Perhaps the most famous is Chomsky's example, 'Colorless green ideas sleep furiously.'

anomalous stimulus ➤ stimulus, inadequate.

anomalous trichromatism (or **trichromacy**) ➤ trichromacy, anomalous.

anomaly Generally, any marked deviation from the norm or the expected. The usual connotation is the literal 'a-norm.' That is, characterizing something distinguishable from social or statistical norms without any implication of pathology or perversion. See discussion under ➤ **normal**.

anomia **1.** Partial or complete loss of the ability to recall names. The term is used in this manner only for aphasic and amnestic syndromes and not for the common condition endured by so many. **2.** Occasionally ➤ **anomie** (2), but this usage is not recommended.

anomic aphasia ➤ aphasia, anomic.

anomic suicide ➤ suicide, anomic.

anomie (or **anomy**) **1.** In a society or

group, a condition in which there is a breakdown of social structure, a general lack of social values and a dissolution of cultural norms. Anomie connotes confusion, disorganization and a collective insecurity and may occur in a number of conditions such as those following some catastrophe like an earthquake, a war or, less obviously, when large numbers of persons from rural backgrounds emigrate to urban centers where their original social values are rendered irrelevant yet assimilation is resisted by the urban society. **2.** A condition in which the members of a superficially well-organized society feel isolated and disconnected, resulting from an excessively specialized social structure which limits closeness and intimacy. This meaning is used to characterize the psychological state of many who live in highly developed, technological, urban societies. To prevent confusion, some writers use *anomie* for meaning 1 and *anomy* or *anomia* for 2. Anomy is a useful term here, anomia is not since it already has a very different meaning.

anomy See discussion under ➤ **anomie**.

anonymity The meaning in psychology is basically that of standard usage: any condition in which one's identity is unknown to others. The interest in the concept in the social sciences derives from considerable evidence that under such conditions people tend to behave in more immoral, unethical and even lethal ways than they ordinarily would. Compare with ➤ **deindividuation**.

anoopsia ➤ **anopsia** (1).

anopia **1.** A general term for defective vision. **2.** Lack of one or both eyes. **3.** ➤ **anopsia**.

anopsia **1.** A tendency for one or both eyes to turn upward. var., *anoopsia*. **2.** Failure of normal use of vision, resulting from strabismus, cataract or serious refractive errors.

anorchism Congenital lack of one or both testes.

anorectic Lacking in appetite. var., *anorectous*.

anorexia Lit., lacking in appetite. The term is most commonly used with respect to eating (➤ **anorexia nervosa**), although 'appetite' is occasionally extended to cover other desires such as sex (➤ **sexual *anorexia**).

anorexia nervosa An ➤ **eating disorder** characterized by intense fear of becoming obese, dramatic weight loss, obsessive concern with one's weight, disturbances of body image such that the patient 'feels fat' when of normal weight or even when emaciated, and in females, *amenorrhea*. The classic *anorexic* is young (rarely over 30), female (roughly 95% of all cases) and from a middle- or upper-class family. They frequently are described as 'model children.' The disorder is rather resistant to treatment and can have an unremitting course leading to death, although in the large majority of cases there is spontaneous full recovery. The term *anorexia*, which is often used as a shortened form of the syndrome, is actually somewhat mis leading here in that the real loss of appetite does not occur until late in the course of the disorder – at the outset the patient is typically hungry like anyone on a sharply reduced food-intake regimen.

anorexia, sexual A lack of appetite for sex, a loss of sexual desire.

anorgasmia A condition characterized by a total inability to achieve orgasm.

anorthopia **1.** Visual defect in which straight lines are not perceived as straight, the perception of symmetry and parallel stimuli being distorted. **2.** ➤ **strabismus.**

anorthoscopic Lit., abnormally viewed. The term is used to refer broadly to perception under unusual or highly artificial conditions.

anosmia General term for any deficiency in the sense of smell.

anosognosia **1.** An unwillingness or failure to recognise and deal with a deficiency or disease. **2.** A neurological disorder marked by an inability to recognize that one has a disorder. Fascinatingly, a brain injured patient may be completely blind as a result of the injury but have no conscious sense of his or her own blindness, or a hemiplegic patient may be completely unaware of his or her inability to use one arm and hand.

ANOVA ➤ **analysis of variance**.

anovulatory Lit., without ovulation. The term is used to characterize the necessarily infertile menstrual cycle that occurs when there is a failure of the ovary to release an egg.

anoxia A marked deficiency in the supply of oxygen to the body tissues.

ANS (or **ans**) ➤ **autonomic nervous system**.

ant- Prefix meaning *against, opposed to, counter to.* var., *anti-*.

Antabuse Brand name for the drug ➤ **disulfiram**.

antagonism Generally, a state of affairs between two processes, stimuli, structures or organisms such that their effects are in opposition to each other.

antagonism, drug Generally, a state of affairs resulting from an interaction between two drugs such that their joint effect is less than that of either drug taken alone. *Pharmacologic antagonism* results when one drug (the *antagonist*) prevents another drug (the *agonist*) from combining with its receptors. *Physiological antagonism* (or *functional antagonism*) occurs when two drugs have their effects upon different receptor sites but yield counter-balancing physiological effects. *Biochemical antagonism* refers to conditions in which one drug has an indirect inhibiting effect upon another; e.g., it may produce more rapid excretion of the substance from the body. *Chemical antagonism* is used for the circumstances when two drugs simply neutralize each other and yield an inactive substance.

antagonist Generally, an opponent. Any-

thing which operates in opposite fashion with respect to another thing (its ➤ **agonist**).

antagonistic Generally, having the property of counteracting, neutralizing or inhibiting the effects of something else. For the various special usages see the following entries and ➤ **antagonism** et seq. Compare with ➤ **synergic, synergistic**.

antagonistic color ➤ **complementary** *color*. ➤ **theories of** *color vision* for more detail.

antagonistic muscles Pairs of muscles that work in opposition: one muscle contracts a limb, the other extends it. When one muscle is flexed the other is relaxed; they never flex simultaneously. This coordinated functioning is called *reciprocal*. ➤ **extensor, flexor**.

ante- Prefix meaning *before*, either in time or in space.

antecedent 1. Generally, something which precedes a phenomenon in a manner which 'invites' the inference of causality. 2. In logic, the conditional or hypothetical proposition, the so-called 'if' clause. ➤ **consequent**.

antedating goal response, fractional ➤ **fractional antedating goal response**.

antedating response Generally, any anticipatory response; a response that occurs earlier in a sequence of responses than was originally learned.

anterior 1. In the temporal sense, to precede. 2. In the spatial sense, to be in front of. Contrast with ➤ **posterior**. Note that in anatomical terminology of upright species like *Homo sapiens, anterior* is frequently found as a synonym for *ventral* and *posterior* becomes a synonym for *dorsal*. 3. In phonetics, a distinctive feature for distinguishing the sounds of a language. Anterior sounds are produced toward the front of the mouth (e.g., *z* in 'zoo'), *nonanterior* are further back (e.g., *sh* in 'shoe').

anterior nuclei (of the thalamus) Collectively, the anterodorsal, anteromedial, and the anteroventral nuclei in the *thalamus*. Part of the ➤ **limbic system**, these nuclei receive input from the *hippocampus* and the mammillary bodies of the *hypothalamus* and project their axons to the *cingulate gyrus*.

anterior root ➤ spinal root.

anterior thalamic nuclei ➤ **anterior nuclei (of the thalamus)**.

antero- Combining form denoting *front, before, prior to*.

anterograde Extending forward in space or progressing forward in time.

anterograde amnesia ➤ **amnesia, anterograde**.

anterograde degeneration ➤ **degeneration** (1).

anterolateral system One of the two main ascending neural systems for somatic sensation (the other is the ➤ **dorsal column–medial lemniscal system**). Its pathways originate in cells of the dorsal horn, cross at the spinal level and ascend in lateral columns. They carry information about pain, temperature and some touch and function in perception, arousal and motor control.

anthropo- Combining form meaning *man* or *relating to man*.

anthropocentrism The point of view that *Homo sapiens* lies at the center of things. The species analog of *egocentrism*.

anthropoid Lit., in the form of a man. Used of the great apes.

anthropology Lit., the study of mankind. Depending upon who is doing the defining, anthropology may include archeology, linguistics, psychology, sociology and smatterings of biology, anatomy, genetics and comparative literature. Most practitioners tend to segment the discipline into ➤ **cultural *anthropology** and **physical *anthropology**.

anthropology, cultural The sub-discipline within anthropology concerned primarily with the study of ➤ **culture** and the complex social structures which make up communities, societies and nations. Originally the field focused upon nonliterate societies, particularly the non-Western, although this limitation no longer applies. In fact, the term itself is now used nearly synonymously with *social *anthropology*.

anthropology, physical The sub-discipline within anthropology concerned primarily with the study of man from a biological and evolutionary perspective. Strong focus is on measurement, classification and comparative analysis of various racial, geographical and ethnic groups, and the evolutionary relationships between these biological factors and the physical and cultural environments. Occasionally called *somatic anthropology*.

anthropology, social In Great Britain, the preferred synonym for ➤ **cultural *anthropology**.

anthropometry Lit., measurement of man. The area of ➤ **physical *anthropology** concerned with measuring and classifying the human physical form.

anthropomorphism Attributing human characteristics to lower organisms or inanimate objects. The anthropomorphic fallacy is most often committed by those unsophisticated in animal research. The tendency to say that a rat that is consuming a food pellet after a reinforced trial is 'enjoying itself' or that a cat receiving lateral hypothalamic stimulation is experiencing 'pleasure' is almost irresistible, but it can be misleading. One should be careful not to imbue non-humans with what may be species-specific human characteristics.

anthroponomy A term put forward some years ago by Walter S. Hunter as a replacement for *behaviorism*. Hunter was such a staunch behaviorist that he even once suggested that the term *psychology* be abandoned since its connotations were too mentalistic. He was not taken seriously in either case.

anthropophagy Cannibalism.

anthroposemiotics ➤ semiotics.

anti- Common prefix meaning *against, opposing, counteracting, reversing*.

antianxiety drugs An umbrella label for several classes of drugs that are prescribed for the reduction of anxiety. Included are the ➤ **benzodiazepines** such as **chlordiazepoxide** and **diazepam**, the muscle-relaxant derivative ➤ **meprobamate**, sedatives such as the ➤ **barbiturates**, and **buspirone**, which was first introduced as an ➤ **antipsychotic drug**. Currently the most useful and most often prescribed are the benzodiazepines. While these drugs are called antianxiety drugs (or *anxiolytics*), there is little evidence that they directly relieve anxiety. Rather their primary action is to produce muscle relaxation and sedation through central nervous system action. In some texts the term *minor *tranquilizers* may still be used to refer to these drugs. For reasons outlined under that term, it is no longer recommended.

antibodies Proteins that recognize the proteins that mark invading microorganisms (➤ **antigens**) and attack and kill them.

anticathexis Lit., against ➤ **cathexis**. Thus: **1.** An action that blocks cathexis, that prevents investment of psychic energy. **2.** An action that maintains the repression of a cathection. The process presumed to carry this out is the reversal of emotional 'charge,' turning love into hate or hate into love. Also called *countercathexis*.

anticholinergic Pertaining to a substance or agent which inhibits, impedes or blocks cholinergic action. That is, one which blocks impulses in the ➤ **cholinergic nerves**.

anticipation A preparatory mental set in which one is primed for the perception of a particular stimulus.

anticipation error ➤ **error, anticipation**.

anticipation method **1.** A technique for studying serial learning in which the subject is required to provide (anticipate) the next succeeding item of a list while viewing any particular item. **2.** A technique in verbal-learning experiments in which the subject is prompted when the proper response is not made quickly. The latter is also called *prompting method*.

anticipatory aggression ➤ **aggression, anticipatory**.

anticipatory regret ➤ **regret, anticipatory**.

anticipatory response Any response that precedes the stimulus designed to evoke or elicit it; any response that occurs before it should.

anticonformity The tendency to reject pressure to conform. Unlike ➤ **independence** (3), in which the connotation is that the person is motivated by personal beliefs and opinions different from those put forward by the group, anticonformity is reserved for cases where the individual reacts negatively to external pressures no matter what they are. Also called *counterconformity*.

anticonvulsants A general category of drugs used to control seizures in disorders such as epilepsy. Interestingly, some (e.g., *clonazepam, carbamazepine*) are also used prophylactically to prevent the mood swings of *bipolar disorder*.

antidepressant drugs A general pharmacological classification of drugs used in fairly severe depressive disorders. Three main groups of drugs are included, the ➤ **monoamine oxidase inhibitors**, the ➤ **tricyclic compounds**, and the serotonin re-uptake inhibitors. Some classification systems include the *amphetamines* as antidepressants, although they are more commonly grouped with the ➤ **stimulants**; others include ➤ **lithium** because of its use in the treatment of *bipolar disorder*.

antidiuretic hormone ➤ **vasopressin**.

antidromic (neural) conduction The passing of a neural impulse in the reverse direction, from axon to the dendrites.

antigens Protein markers that identify infectious microorganisms to the ➤ **immune system** allowing it to develop ➤ **antibodies**.

antihistamine Lit., any substance or agent which inhibits or blocks the effect of *histamine*. They are of some use in controlling rashes and allergic reactions caused by release of histamine and are helpful to sufferers from hayfever. They are also used occasionally as mild sedatives because they tend to produce drowsiness in most (but not all) persons.

anti-intraception A tendency to be opposed to that which is subjective, imaginative, humanistic. It is regarded as a characteristic of the ➤ **authoritarian personality**.

antimania drugs Drugs used for the treatment of *hypomania* and *bipolar disorder*. The drug of choice here is one of the *lithium* compounds. Note that while the common term is 'antimania' there is evidence that these drugs also help in preventing the depressive aspect of manic-depression.

antimetropia A condition in which the two eyes have differences in refractive power. To a certain extent everyone is antimetropic; the term, however, is reserved for cases where the differences are dramatic; e.g., one eye is myopic and the other hyperopic.

antimode The least frequent score in a distribution.

antinomy A logical contradiction or inconsistency of the most basic kind where two (or more) separate principles lead to mutually incompatible conclusions: both 'A' and 'not A' are implied as being true. See, and compare with, ➤ **paradox**.

antiobsessional drugs A group of drugs used to reduce the symptoms of ➤ **obsessive-compulsive disorders**. Included are ➤ **clomipramine**, **fluoxetine** and **fluvoxamine**. Interestingly, these drugs are all also used as antidepressants although their action here appears to be independent of their antidepressant effects; other antidepressants do not ameliorate the obsessive-compulsive symptoms.

antipraxia Characteristic of functions, processes or (in medicine) symptoms which are antagonistic to each other.

antipredator behavior A general term for a variety of devices which prey species have evolved for protecting themselves from predators. Among them are camouflage, group defense, evasion, repellent odors or tastes, and mimicry.

antipsychotic drugs An umbrella label for several categories of drugs that are prescribed in cases of psychotic disorders. Included are the ➤ **phenothiazines** and related ➤ **thioanthines**, the ➤ **butyrophenones**, the ➤ **indolones**, and the generally less effective ➤ **rauwolfia alkaloids**. Generally speaking all of these drugs function to alleviate symptoms; they do not cure the disorders for which are prescribed. They ameliorate the confused states, disturbed thinking and erratic *affect* of various psychoses and produce a general quietude, a slowing of responsiveness to external stimuli and a lessening of attentiveness without major changes in wakefulness or arousability. They also have a number of side-effects that can be troublesome, such as muscular disorders, tremors, dry mouth, hypotension, and various toxic allergic reactions. In this capacity, ➤ **tardive dyskinesia**. In some texts the term **major *tranquilizers** may still be used to refer to some of these drugs. For reasons outlined under that term, it is no longer recommended. Also known as *neuroleptics* (although see that term for nuances).

antisocial Descriptive of behavior which is disruptive and harmful (or potentially so) to the functioning of a group or society. Contrast with ➤ **asocial** and ➤ **prosocial**.

antisocial personality disorder A personality disorder marked by a history of irresponsible and antisocial behavior beginning in childhood or early adolescence (typically as a ➤ **conduct disorder**) and continuing into adulthood. Early manifestations include lying, stealing, fighting, vandalism, running away from home, and cruelty. In adulthood the general pattern continues, characterized by such factors as significant unemployment, failures to conform to social norms, property destruction, stealing, failure to honor financial obligations, reckless disregard for one's own or others' safety, incapacity to maintain enduring relationships, poor parenting, and a consistent disregard for the truth. Also noted as an important feature is a glibness accompanied by a lack of remorse and a lack of or lessened ability to feel guilty for one's actions. Other labels that have been used over the years to capture this syndrome include ➤ **psychopathic personality** and ➤ **sociopathic personality**.

antonym test A verbal test where the subject is given a word and must supply its antonym as quickly as possible.

anulus ➤ **annulus**.

anus The opening of the rectum, the lower outlet of the alimentary canal.

anvil = ➤ **incus**; ➤ **auditory** *ossicles.

anxiety **1.** Most generally, a vague, unpleasant emotional state with qualities of apprehension, dread, distress and uneasiness. Anxiety is often distinguished from ➤ **fear** in that an anxiety state is often (*usually* say some, *always* insist others) objectless, whereas fear assumes a specific feared object, person or event. **2.** In learning theory, the term is used to connote a secondary (or conditioned) drive which functions to motivate avoidance responding. Thus an avoidance response is assumed to be reinforced by a reduction in anxiety. **3.** In Freudian theory, anxiety is treated as 1, with the additional assumption that it acts as a signal that psychic danger would result were an unconscious wish to be realized or acted upon. See here ➤ *Angst*. **4.** In existential theory, the emotional accompaniment of the immediate awareness of the meaninglessness, incompleteness and chaotic nature of the world in which we live. There is an interesting temporal issue involved in these several uses. In the first two, anxiety is treated as a consequent emotion, a learned reaction which results from a particular state of affairs. In 3, it is regarded as an anticipatory reaction whose origins lie at the level of unconscious conflict. In 4, it has neither of these elements, being treated instead as a pure, immediate outcome of 'being-in-the-world.' There are many compound terms that are built on this one. Some follow, others are found under the alphabetic listing of the modifying term.

anxiety disorder A cover term for a variety of maladaptive syndromes which have severe anxiety as the dominant disturbance. Included are ➤ **generalized anxiety disorder**, ➤ **panic disorder**, ➤ **phobic disorder** and ➤ **post-traumatic-stress disorder**.

anxiety disorders of childhood or adolescence A general category of mental disorders occurring in childhood or adolescence all of which have inappropriate anxiety as the primary feature. Included are ➤ **avoidant disorder of childhood or adolescence**, ➤ **overanxious disorder** and ➤ **separation-anxiety disorder**.

anxiety equivalent A psychoanalytic term for the physical symptoms which substitute for conscious awareness of anxiety; e.g., racing heart, trembling, lightheadedness, sweating, rapid breathing, etc. The term is not used for these sympathetic reactions when the individual is conscious of being anxious.

anxiety fixation A psychoanalytic term for anxiety in later life which is hypothesized to derive from earlier experiences.

anxiety, free-floating The kind of vague, nebulous anxiety associated with the ➤ **generalized anxiety disorders**. Also called *neurotic anxiety*.

anxiety hierarchy A series of related situations (or acts, events or mental images of them) which are ranked according to their anxiety-involving properties for an individual. They are used in desensitization techniques in behavior therapy.

anxiety, moral In psychoanalysis, anxiety which derives from the prohibitions of the superego. Compare with ➤ **neurotic** *anxiety (2).

anxiety neurosis A subclass of anxiety disorders characterized by recurrent periods of intense anxiety. Usually included in this category are ➤ **panic disorders**, **generalized anxiety disorders** and **obsessive-compulsive disorders**. Also called *anxiety state*.

anxiety, neurotic 1. ➤ free-floating *anxiety 2. In psychoanalysis, anxiety that derives from id impulses. Used more or less synonymously with ➤ instinctual anxiety. Compare this meaning with ➤ moral *anxiety

anxiety object A psychoanalytic term for the object upon which one symbolically displaces anxiety originally caused by other factors.

anxiety, persecutory ➤ paranoid anxiety.

anxiety reaction ➤ generalized anxiety disorder.

anxiety-relief response A term coined by behavior therapists for a learned operant response which can be used to reduce or relieve feelings of anxiety. The technique is to associate the response (usually saying out loud or thinking a word like 'calm' or 'relax') with the cessation of a painful stimulus (like an electric shock). With the response now connected to a feeling of relief it can (at least in principle) be used in other anxious moments or circumstances.

anxiety state ➤ anxiety neurosis.

anxiety, tolerance of A loose term used for the extent to which an individual can put up with anxiety-provoking situations without having them adversely affect ability to function.

anxiolytic amnestic disorder ➤ sedative, hypnotic, or anxiolytic amnestic disorder.

anxiolytics ➤ antianxiety drugs.

anxiolytic withdrawal ➤ sedative, hypnotic, or anxiolytic withdrawal.

anxiolytic withdrawal delirium ➤ sedative, hypnotic, or anxiolytic withdrawal delirium.

apanthropy An aversion to society or human companionship.

apareunia Inability to have sexual intercourse. The term is used for organic, 'mechanical' problems such as vaginal obstructions.

apathy Indifference, unresponsiveness, displaying less interest or reactivity to a situation than would normally be expected. adj., *apathetic* or (occasionally) *apathic.*

aperiodic reinforcement (schedule) A general term for reinforcement which is irregular or intermittent; any ➤ schedule of *reinforcement other than continuous reinforcement is classified as *aperiodic.* Also called *intermittent reinforcement.*

aperture 1. Generally, an opening or orifice. 2. In any optical system, the opening through which light passes; e.g., the pupil of the eye.

Apgar score After Virginia Apgar, an American physician, a scaled score of a newborn's physical condition based on five measures (heart rate, respiration, muscle tone, color and reflexive responsiveness). Usually an Apgar score is taken one minute after birth and again four minutes later.

aphagia Lit., the absence of eating. A condition in which the organism ceases ingestion of solid foods, assumed to result from a lesion in the *lateral *hypothalamus.* Compare with ➤ hyperphagia and distinguish from ➤ anorexia nervosa.

aphakia Lensless. A condition in which the lens of the eye is missing or has been removed, as in the common treatment for cataracts. The aphakic eye sees blues more vividly and is more responsive to very short-wavelength light which is normally absorbed by the lens.

aphasia A general term covering any partial or complete loss of language abilities. The origins are always organic, namely a lesion in the brain. There are literally dozens of varieties of aphasia and the classification systems and the symptoms of each variety are constantly being revised. Some classification systems are based on the (presumed) cortical locale of of the lesion, others upon the general sensory and/or motor functions which are impaired and still others on the particular linguistic skills which are lost. There is, not surprisingly, little agreement on the synonymity of the various specialized terms which are in use. The entries which follow give the most commonly used terms and the synonyms which seem warranted for each.

aphasia, anomic An aphasia due presumably to lesions of the angular gyrus. The dominant symptom is a severe loss of the ability to name objects, i.e. lexical selection is badly impaired. Also known as *amnesic aphasia* and *nominal aphasia*.

aphasia, ataxic A general term for an aphasia characterized by loss of ability to articulate. Used similarly to ➤ **motor *aphasia**.

aphasia, auditory A form of aphasia in which the patient is unable to comprehend the meaning of spoken words. Also known as *word deafness* or *pure word deafness*, although these terms are misleading since the patient is not deaf. Of course, calling it an *aphasia* is also misleading since patients with the disorder are not aphasic and speak normally.

aphasia, Broca's A type of aphasia presumed to be due to damage to ➤ **Broca's area**. The aphasic who receives this diagnostic label typically produces little speech and that which is produced tends to be slow, very poorly articulated and generated with considerable effort. Usually function words, inflectional endings and other 'dispensable' elements are dropped, giving the speech a *telegraphic* quality. Interestingly, such patients can usually comprehend spoken and written language normally or nearly normally, although in the motor form writing is also impaired. Also called *motor aphasia, expressive aphasia* or, on occasion, *non-fluent aphasia*. See discussion under ➤ **motor *aphasia**.

aphasia, conduction An aphasia presumed to be due to lesions which interrupt the nerve fibers connecting Broca's and Wernicke's areas (➤ **arcuate fasciculus**). The typical symptom here is difficulty in repeating a sentence just heard, although frequently there is also impairment of coprehension and some difficulty in articulation.

aphasia, developmental A term occasionally and incorrectly used for any of the syndromes properly called ➤ **developmental language disorders**. Aphasia refers to *loss* of language; children in this category are those who fail to develop language properly.

aphasia, global A form of aphasia so named because language abilities are disrupted on a global scale. Generally presumed to be due to lesions in both Broca's and Wernicke's areas.

aphasia, mixed transcortical An aphasia caused by lesions involving the entire border zone of the frontal-parietal-occipital lobes. The language loss is usually total and the patient may only be capable of repeating words (*echolalia*) and show no other language competence. Also called, ambiguously, *isolation of speech syndrome*.

aphasia, motor A form of aphasia characterized by a partial or complete loss of the ability to produce articulate speech. Often, a particular variety of ➤ **Broca's *aphasia** is termed motor aphasia. In principle, motor aphasias result from lesions of cortical tissue responsible for the motor functions of speech and Broca's aphasias from lesions to Broca's area. However, the proximity of these areas in the brain makes such distinctions academic. ➤ **anarthria**, which is used more generally for disturbances in articulation.

aphasia, optic A neurological condition marked by an inability to name visually presented objects. The condition differs from associative aphasia in that the patient knows the meaning of the stimulus (i.e., he or she may mime putting on a boot when shown one) but cannot produce the name (i.e., say 'boot'). Also called *anomia*.

aphasia, syntactic A form of aphasia characterized by the loss of the ability to connect words properly so that the basic rules of syntax are adhered to. Also called *cataphasia*; see also, but distinguish from, ➤ **agrammatism**.

aphasia, transcortical A general label for

47

an aphasia caused by a lesion that is outside of the perisylvan language centers: that is, outside of Broca's and Wernicke's areas. There are several forms here, *mixed, motor* and *sensory*.

aphasia, transcortical motor A nonfluent aphasia similar in many respects to ➤ **Broca's *aphasia** with intact comprehension. The lesion, however, is anterior to Broca's area in the frontal lobe.

aphasia, transcortical sensory A fluent aphasia with dysfunctions of comprehension. The lesion is usually in the junction of the parietal, temporal and occipital lobes.

aphasia, traumatic A general term for any aphasia resulting from a head injury.

aphasia, Wernicke's A form of aphasia presumed to be due to lesions in ➤ **Wernicke's area**. Typically, a patient so classified tends to articulate normally, even fluently, but the speech tends to be 'empty,' without coherency and full of lexical selection and grammatical errors. Comprehension of both written and spoken language is also impaired as is the ability to repeat phrases. Also known as *receptive aphasia*, *sensory aphasia* and *fluent aphasia*.

aphemia Generally, loss of the ability to speak. May be used as a strict synonym for ➤ **motor *aphasia**; some authors use it more broadly to cover impairments which are *functional* in origin (i.e. non-organic). The former is preferred; the latter merely confusing.

aphonia Inability to produce the voiced speech sounds which use the larynx. Typically, the term is reserved for conditions which are not produced by brain lesions but due to any of a number of other factors, e.g., damage to peripheral nerves, laryngitis or functional disturbances.

aphoresis Lack of energy, weakness, poor endurance.

aphrasia Generally, inability (or refusal) to produce normal, fluent speech. The term is reserved for non-organic syndromes; contrast with ➤ **aphasia**.

aphrenia Lit., without mind. Used loosely in some older psychiatric writings for a loss of normal, conscious functioning.

aphrodisiac Generally, anything which stimulates sexual desire.

aphthenxia Generally, inability to speak owing to spasms in the muscles which control speech.

aplasia Generally, failure of an organ or body part to develop normally.

apnea Cessation of breathing. Typically temporary in nature and usually observed either immediately or soon after a period of heavy, deep breathing, which suggests that it is caused by reduction in stimulation of the respiratory center because of lowered carbon dioxide levels. Although associated with several diseases it is also observed in perfectly healthy individuals during deep sleep, particularly the aged and the very young. It is believed by many to be the cause of many crib deaths. ➤ **sudden infant death syndrome**. var., *apnoea*.

apnoea ➤ **apnea**.

apo- Prefix denoting *away* or *separate*.

apokamnosic Easily fatigued.

apolepsis Cessation of function, used generally.

apomorphine A morphine derivative which acts as a central-nervous-system depressant in ways similar to morphine. It also acts on the brain's vomiting center, making it an emetic, especially since when administered by injection it is not ejected with the vomit.

apopathic behavior A general term for any behavior influenced by or even requiring the presence of other persons, although not specifically directed at them. The classic examples are 'showing off' or 'putting on airs.'

apoplexy An acute, abrupt loss of consciousness and subsequent motor paralysis caused by brain hemorrhage, embolism or thrombosis.

a posteriori Latin for *from what comes after*. Used to describe an inductively developed hypothesis or argument, i.e. one developed by inferring cause from a known set of facts.

a posteriori fallacy The fallacious conclusion that some event B was caused by some other event A on the grounds that an after-the-fact analysis of one's data showed that B did indeed occur after A (*post hoc, ergo propter hoc,* after this, therefore because of this). This fallacy, like all others, is a logical one; A may really have caused B but a retrospective analysis is not sufficient to show this. The fallacy typically occurs when a researcher does a bit too much ➤ **data snooping**.

a posteriori tests Any statistical procedure that is introduced after the data have already been collected and examined. They are typically carried out because interesting trends have emerged in the data that call out for examination. ➤➤ **post hoc tests**.

apparatus 1. Most commonly in psychology, any device or instrument designed to facilitate running an experiment. **2.** In physiology, any group of organs, parts and tissues which are functionally coordinated. Here, qualifiers are always used, e.g., ➤ **vocal apparatus** refers to the full set of structures and organs for producing sounds.

apparent motion ➤ **motion, apparent**.

appeal 1. Any action which serves to stimulate emotions or desires in others. **2.** The underlying value or incentive contained in a message or action.

appearance-reality task A task used with young children designed to explore their understanding of reality. In this task a child is shown objects that appear to be one thing but are actually something else; e.g., a rock made of painted sponge, an egg made from chalk. ➤➤ **false-belief task**.

appeasement behavior In comparative studies and ethology, any behavior of an animal which terminates attack on it by another animal of the same species. See here ➤ **submission** (2).

apperception 1. In the original sense, dating back to Leibniz (1646–1716), it refers to a final, clear phase of perception where there is recognition, identification or comprehension of what has been perceived. Several other historically prominent philosophical and psychological theorists have used the term with slight variations on this basic meaning. **2.** For J. H. Herbart (1776–1841) it characterized what he considered the fundamental process of acquiring knowledge wherein the perceived qualities of a new object, event or idea are assimilated with and related to already existing knowledge. He used the term *apperceptive mass* for the previously acquired knowledge. In some form or another, this basic notion that learning and understanding depend upon recognizing relationships between new ideas and existing knowledge is axiomatic of nearly all educational theory and practice. **3.** W. Wundt (1832–1920) used the term in a somewhat similar fashion to refer to the active mental process of selecting and structuring internal experience, the focus of attention within the field of consciousness. The term is now rarely used in experimental psychology. However, the concepts underlying it are important and efforts to reintroduce them with a more modern, cognitive slant would be appreciated by many cognitive psychologists.

apperceptive agnosia ➤ **agnosia, apperceptive**.

apperceptive mass ➤ **apperception** (2).

appersonation A psychotic delusion in which one assumes the identity of another. Distinguish from the non-technical term **impersonation**, where there is no delusion on the part of the individual.

appestat A term occasionally used for the area(s) in the hypothalamus assumed to play an important role in the control of appetite.

appetite 1. The term comes directly from the Latin for a *longing for*. This sense is carried over into most uses in psychology. Generally, motivational systems which are called *appetitive* are those which are derived from normal physiological functioning, e.g., hunger, thirst, sex and the like. The occasional tendency to limit the term to food and eating is inaccurately restrictive. Moreover, much contemporary usage implicitly reflects the notion that appetites may be learned or modified through experience. One may speak of developing an appetite for unusual foods or uncommon sexual preferences. **2.** In some older writings, particularly those of McDougall's school of *hormic psychology*, an ➤ **instinct**. But see that term for difficulties in meaning and usage.

appetitive Pertaining to appetite. Often used to refer to *positive reinforcers* that are ingested. Thus a food reinforcer to a hungry organism is called an appetitive reinforcer ➤ **appetite** (1).

applied psychology An umbrella term used for all those sub-disciplines within psychology that seek: (a) to apply principles, discoveries and theories of psychology in practical ways in related areas such as education, industry, marketing, opinion polling, sport, etc.; and/or (b) to discover basic principles that can be so applied. There is a subtle difference between these two approaches; one basically exploits what is known, the other strives for additional knowledge and is motivated by the aim of practical application.

apport The hypothesized moving of an object to a particular place by paranormal means. ➤ **parapsychology** for further discussion on this and other similar 'phenomena.'

apprehension **1.** Etymologically the word derives from *prehension*, the act of seizing or of grasping. Hence, by extension, apprehension is the mental, conscious, 'grasping' of the nature of a stimulus or an event. Apprehension is generally treated as a rather primitive, immediate act (➤ **apprehension span**) and distinguished from ➤ **comprehension**, which involves more in the way of reflection and interpretation. **2.** By further extension, a vague fear or anxiousness about possible future occur-

rences. Here the notion is that one is 'seized' or 'enveloped' by a feeling of unease.

apprehension span The maximum number of objects or events that can be perceived in a single short exposure. It can be measured by having the subject report either the number of objects exposed or their identity. ➤ **attention span** and **subitize**.

apprehensiveness A relatively mild sense of anxiety about upcoming events, an uneasiness about future happenings.

approach–approach conflict ➤ **conflict, approach–approach**.

approach–avoidance conflict ➤ **conflict, approach–avoidance**.

approach gradient This term refers to the increased tendency to approach a desired goal as the organism gets closer to that goal. This gradient is assumed to be less steep than the *avoidance gradient*; that is, as one gets near them, positive goals do not increase in desirability as rapidly as negative goals increase in non-desirability. ➤ **conflict** et seq.

approach response Any 'movement' toward an object or goal. 'Movement' here may mean literal, physical movement toward a physical object or figurative, cognitive, affective movement toward a way of thinking or feeling about a person, idea, etc.

appropriateness of affect ➤ **affect, appropriateness of**.

approximation conditioning A synonym for ➤ **shaping**.

appurtenance A ➤ **Gestalt psychology** term for the characteristics of a perceptual field which mutually interact. Classic examples are ➤ **color contrast**, ➤ **foreshortening**, ➤ **Mach bands**.

apraxia From the Greek, meaning *without action*. Hence, partial or complete loss of the ability to perform purposive movements. The term is restricted to conditions resulting from cortical lesions in which there is no paralysis or loss of sensory function. Apraxia is a very general term; specific forms are given in the entries that follow. Note, however, that usage is often annoyingly inconsistent. What is given here as the meaning of *ideational apraxia*, for example, is occasionally the syndrome referred to by the term *ideomotor apraxia*. Let the reader beware. adj., *apraxic* (generally), *apractic* (occasionally).

apraxia, akinetic A form of apraxia characterized by an inability to carry out spontaneous movements.

apraxia, amnesic (or **amnestic**) A form of apraxia characterized by an inability to carry out a sequence of movements upon request. The problem in most cases so diagnosed is memorial; the patient cannot remember the instructions about later movements when the time comes to perform them.

apraxia, callosal A ➤ limb *apraxia caused by damage to the anterior *corpus callosum*.

apraxia, constructional An ➤ apraxia characterized by a deficit in the ability to draw pictures or objects or assemble objects from other elements such as building blocks. It is caused by lesions in the right hemisphere, usually the right parietal lobe.

apraxia, ideational Improper use of objects owing to an inability to identify them correctly or to conceptualize their appropriate functions.

apraxia, ideokinetic A form of apraxia characterized by an inability to carry out a series of ordered movements. The patient may be capable of performing each separate act but the sequential order is confused.

apraxia, ideomotor A form of apraxia characterized by an inability to execute a single, complex movement properly. The patient will perform inappropriate movements in the course of action.

apraxia, left parietal A ➤ limb *apraxia

caused by damage to the posterior lobe of the left hemisphere.

apraxia, limb ➤ Apraxia characterized by (a) movements of the wrong part of a limb, (b) incorrect movements of the right part of the limb, or (c) correct movements of the limb but in an inappropriate order. Occasionally the term *ideokinetic *apraxia* is used for symptoms (a) and (b) and *ideomotor *apraxia* for (c).

apraxia, motor A general term for any of several forms of apraxia involving an inability to carry out planned acts; e.g., ➤ ideomotor *apraxia and ➤ ideokinetic *apraxia.

apraxia, ocular An ➤ apraxia in which the patient is unable to maintain fixation; their eyes wander back and forth between objects.

apraxia, sympathetic A ➤ limb *apraxia caused by damage to the anterior lobe of the left hemisphere.

a priori Latin for *from what comes before*. Reasoning developed deductively as, for example, a hypothesis formed on the basis of definitions previously formed or principles previously assumed.

a priorism The doctrine that the mind comes equipped with ➤ innate ideas and that, as a result, genuine knowledge independent of experience is possible. Contrast with ➤ empiricism. var., *apriorism*.

a priori (or **planned**) **tests** A statistical procedure used in lieu of an overall significant analysis of variance allowing one to test for significance of individual comparisons. Such tests can, in principle, be used only when the experimental hypotheses indicate that particular effects can be expected to be manifested in the data independent of overall effects. Compare with ➤ a posteriori tests.

a priori validity ➤ validity, a priori.

aprosexia Inability to concentrate on things. The problem may result from sensory or mental deficiencies.

aprosodia A disorder of speech marked

51

by loss of the ability to use properly the various ➤ **prosodic features**, such as stress, tonal shifts, cadence and emotional gesturing. There is a suggestion that it is associated with lesions in the right (or nondominant) hemisphere.

aptitude Generally, potential for achievement. The term is used with the connotation that a person displays an aptitude for something by a measurable, present ability that is interpreted as indicating that one may make, with some confidence, a prediction that their performance will increase markedly with additional training. The reason for phrasing it in this convoluted fashion is that tests of aptitude are, in reality, tests of performance and interest; the distinction in usage comes from the notion of making a prediction about future achievements. ➤ **ability** and **achievement** for further discussion.

aptitude, special ➤ aptitude test.

aptitude test Generally, any test designed to measure potential for achievement. Various types of aptitude tests are often distinguished, namely *special*, *general* and *multiple*. Special-aptitude tests are those designed to measure potential for a restricted, single capacity like mechanical, clerical or musical aptitude. General-aptitude tests are broad-based tests designed to determine potential in relatively nonspecific domains; intelligence tests are general-aptitude tests. Multiple-aptitude tests are test batteries in which a number of factors are assessed. These classifications should be viewed pragmatically: special tests are only relatively special (e.g., the finger-dexterity test is a 'special' test for a specific aptitude but is clearly an aspect of a more general sensory/motor aptitude); and general tests are only relatively general (e.g., general intelligence tests are routinely factor-analyzed into more specific components such as verbal, quantitative, analytical, spatial, etc.). Multiple tests may, of course, be as 'special' or 'general' as the subtests which make up the full test battery.

aqueduct of Sylvius Canal in the mid-

brain going from the posterior end of the third ventricle to the fourth ventricle. Also called *cerebral aqueduct*.

aqueous humor The watery liquid in the anterior and posterior chambers of the eye between the cornea and the lens.

arachnoid membrane The web-like (hence the name) middle membrane covering the spinal cord and brain.

Arago phenomenon The relative insensitivity to light of the very center of the visual field at very low levels of illumination.

arational ➤ nonrational.

arborization Interlacing, branching. Used of nerve processes which display tree-like conformations.

arbor vitae Lit., tree of life. Used of: (1) the tree-like outline seen in longitudinal sections of the cerebellum; (2) the branching ridges of the cervix.

arche- Combining form meaning *beginning*, *onset*.

archetypal form ➤ primordial image.

archetype 1. Generally, an original model, the first formed, the primordial type. 2. In Jung's characterization of the psyche, the inherited, unconscious ideas and images that are the components of the ➤ **collective unconscious**. Although he hypothesized the existence of many archetypes, several were presumed to have evolved sufficiently to be treated as distinct systems; see e.g., ➤ **anima**, **animus**, **persona**, **self**(6), **shadow**.

Archimedes spiral A simple line drawing of a spiral. It is used in the study of ➤ **motion aftereffects**.

architectonic Systematic, well structured, orderly. Used primarily in neurophysiology to refer to the orderly structure of neural pathways and centers.

arc sine transformation A transformation which, when applied to data expressed in proportions, has the effect of minimizing differences between proportions near 0 and 1 and maximizing those near 0.5. Thus, the ➤ **standard *deviation** of two sample distributions of proportions are made more nearly equal permitting the use of *t tests* without violating assumptions concerning homogeneity of variance.

arcuate fasciculus A major fiber pathway connecting ➤ **Wernicke's area** ➤ with **Broca's area**. Damage to the neurons in the pathway leads to ➤ **conduction *aphasia**.

arcuate nucleus A hypothalamic nucleus containing the cells which produce the hypothalamic hormones. It is also the area where sensory nerves from the face and tongue terminate.

area The general dictionary meaning (circumscribed space, bounded domain) forms the conceptual basis for all specialized uses, namely: **1.** A region of the cerebral cortex which can be geographically, histologically, or functionally distinguished from surrounding regions; e.g., ➤ **Broca's area**. **2.** The region under the curve of a distribution; or, more specifically, the region under the curve as specified by any two points along the x-axis. This area so identified will contain a determinable number of cases (for frequency distributions) or determinable proportion of cases (for probability distributions). **3.** A field of study, e.g., the area of cognitive psychology.

area diagram A graphic method of presenting data in the form of a figure (most often a circle) divided in sections in which the size (area) of each is proportional to the quantity represented. The familiar 'pie' chart is a good example.

area postrema An area in the lower portion of the brain that is intimately involved in vomiting. Interestingly, the ➤ **blood-brain barrier** here is rather more permeable than most other places, allowing relatively easy access of toxins to the vomiting center so that the expulsion of the ingested poisons may be initiated.

area sampling ➤ **sampling, area**.

area under the curve ➤ **area** (2).

areola **1.** The pigmented area surrounding the nipple of the breast. **2.** The part of the iris immediately enclosing the pupil of the eye.

argot A formal term meaning slang. Specifically, a specialized slang which reflects the common and unique experiences of a particular group. Originally, argot was reserved for the language of criminal groups, now it is more widely used and references to the 'scientist's argot' are found. ➤ **jargon**.

argument constraints In linguistics, constraints imposed by the semantic entailments of verbs, adjectives, adverbs, etc., which must be satisfied for a phrase or sentence to make sense. For example, color names require that the 'argument' be a physical thing; a verb like 'think' requires that the agent be a sentient creature; an adverb like 'angrily' entails an actor capable of emotions, etc. Violations of these constraints yield anomalous sentences.

Argyll-Robertson pupil A dysfunctioning pupil in which the normal reflexive contraction to light is missing, although the pupil still contracts normally during accommodation. The symptom is common in syphilitic *locomotor ataxia* and various forms of paralysis.

aristogenics An occasional synonym for ➤ **eugenics**

Aristotelian Of or pertaining to the doctrines of the 4th-century BC Greek philosopher. Aristotle argued that man is a rational animal endowed with an innate capacity for attaining knowledge from sense perception and that knowledge is the result of deduction of universals and principles from perceptual information and not the 'recovering' of innate ideas, as Plato maintained. The term is also used to refer to Aristotle's methodology, which exhibits parallels to his psychological theory. He advocated the use of close observation and accurate classification of natural phenomena. Hence, the term is

53

often used as a synonym for *empirical*. However, Aristotle also formalized a system of deductive propositional logic and so the term is also frequently used to refer specifically to this particular form of logic. At the most general level, the term can be taken to indicate the principle of careful deduction of knowledge, be it scientific or personal, from systematic observations of natural events.

Aristotle's illusion The misimpression that a single object is actually two objects when touched in the following manner: cross two fingers of one hand and have someone touch a marble or similar object to the two fingertips. Note that it is the 'outside' of each finger being touched, the source of the illusion.

arithmetic disorder, developmental A label for a syndrome characterized by a child showing significantly lower performance in arithmetic achievement than one would expect from standardized tests, age, school, IQ, etc.

arithmetic mean ➤ **mean, arithmetic**.

arithmetic series A series which increases or decreases by a constant factor, e.g., 2, 4, 6, 8, 10, 12, . . . is an arithmetic series. Compare with ➤ **geometric series**.

arithmomania Lit., number madness. A compulsive, morbid fascination with counting objects, events, etc.

Army Alpha (and **Beta**) **Tests** Two general tests of intelligence developed for use in screening recruits for the US Army in World War I. These tests were among the first large-scale, group-administered intelligence tests developed by psychologists. The Beta was a *performance test* designed for illiterates and recent emigrés to America whose English was poor; the Alpha was a standard examination which drew heavily on verbal skills.

arousal 1. Generally, a dimension of activity or readiness for activity based on the level of sensory excitability, glandular and hormonal levels and muscular readiness. 2. In physiology, a heightened state

of cortical functioning. Cortical structures are 'aroused' by the stimulation from sensory receptors mediated through lower brain structures such as the reticular formation. Because of the breadth of usage and the generality of meaning, the term is typically used with qualifiers, e.g., cortical arousal (as above), sexual arousal, etc.

arousal theory ➤ theories of *emotion.

array 1. Generally, a display of scores, data, stimuli, etc. 2. More specifically such a display arranged in tabular form. The table may be one-way (usually ranked by magnitude of the scores), two-way (usually arranged into columns and rows by magnitude) or n-way, depending on the number of dimensions represented in the array.

arrest Generally, a stoppage, a cessation of the function, motion, development, etc., of a process. The term is used widely in discussions of physiological, medical, cognitive and emotional processes and its meaning is generally specified by context, e.g. *arrest of emotional development, cardiac arrest*.

arrhythmia Lack of or disruption in normal rhythm; irregularity.

arrow (head) illusion ➤ Müller-Lyer illusion.

arterio- Combining form denoting *artery* or *arterial*.

arteriosclerosis A general label for a variety of pathological conditions involving hardening, thickening and loss in elasticity of blood vessels, especially arteries.

arteriosclerotic dementia ➤ multi-infarct *dementia*.

arthritis Inflammation of a joint.

arthro- Combining form used to denote joint or articulation of structures at a joint.

articular Pertaining to articulation or to the joints.

articulate 1 vb. To join together. 2 vb. To enunciate clearly. 3 adj. Well joined, properly constrained. Articulate speech is well formed, properly pronounced and meaningful; articulate movement is well coordinated and smooth.

articulation 1. Production of speech sounds by complex movements of the vocal organs, the *articulators*. Hence, this meaning refers specifically to the production of consonants and diphthongs, those phonetic elements in speech which require movements of the tongue, jaw, lips, pharynx, etc. Vowels are strictly 'steady state' phonetic elements and typically not considered part of articulation. This fine distinction, however, is not always made nor worried about outside of highly technical writings. **2.** The manner of connection of bones at a joint. **3.** By extension, the joining together of separate elements of a complex system into a coordinate structure. This meaning is used in a variety of applied contexts such as education, organizational psychology, etc. **4.** In ➤ **Gestalt psychology**, the degree of complexity of a structure.

articulation disorder, developmental A general label for the failure of a child to develop appropriate and consistent ➤ **articulation** (1). Most frequently observed with the late-occurring speech sounds, e.g., *r, l, ch, sh, th*. Distinguish from ➤ **dysarthria**. Also called *phonological disorder*.

articulatory store A hypothesized memory system whereby auditory (and perhaps even visual) inputs are stored in a form that reflects their articulatory properties. Contrast with ➤ **acoustic store**, where the hypothesized mechanism is based on sensory systems for receiving sounds.

artifact Generally, any object made or modified by people. var., *artefact*.

artifact, cultural An artifact that has a culturally defined form and function.

artifact, statistical An incorrect or misleading inference due to a bias in collection or analysis of data, or the numbers themselves (taken collectively) which lead to this misleading inference.

artificial intelligence (AI) 1. The interdisciplinary field combining research and theory from cognitive psychology and computer sciences which is focused on the development of artificial systems that display human-like thinking or 'intelligence.' **2.** Any manufactured intelligence, i.e. the goal of the field of study in 1. The work in AI should be, although it often is not, distinguished from work in ➤ **computer simulation**, in which the intelligence is in the programmer of the computer and not the machine itself. Computer-simulation work is concerned with using computers more to test various theories of psychology than to deal with the theoretical aspects of intelligent behavior.

artificialism A ➤ **Piagetian** term used for the tendency to view the world as having been created by people and hence to conclude that naturally occurring phenomena (the stars, the sun, flowers, rain) are the result of human action. Characteristic of the strongly egocentric view of the child in the ➤ **preoperatory stage**, vestiges of artificialism can be found in the myths and folk legends of many (all?) cultures.

artificial language ➤ **language**.

artificial pupil A device which controls the amount of light falling on the eye. The simplest is a pinhole; more elaborate ones have finely calibrated adjustable apertures.

artificial selection The process of selecting particular organisms for special breeding. Compare with ➤ **natural selection**.

artisan's cramp A muscle spasm caused by extended effort of the small muscles of the hand in tasks requiring fine motor coordination; 'writer's cramp.'

asapholalia Poorly articulated speech, mumbling.

ascendance A tendency to assume a leadership role in social interactions and groups. Ascendance is thought by some to lie at one pole of a dimension, the other end being represented by ➤ **submission**. vars. *ascendence, ascendancy*.

ascending-descending series The kinds of

ASCETICISM

series of stimuli used in the ➤ **method of limits**: ➤ **measurement of *threshold** for description.

asceticism A way of living based upon voluntary abstention from sensual, physical pleasures and emphasizing simplicity and self-discipline. The ascetic usually professes to be focusing upon a higher moral/religious value system.

Asch situation A term used for the situation studied extensively by Solomon Asch in his investigations of conformity. The subject is one member of a group of people who are asked to make judgements about various stimuli (e.g., which of two lines is longer). Unknown to the subject, all other members of the group are stooges who deliberately agree that the erroneous answer is the correct one. Such circumstances can have a dramatic effect upon the judgements of people. Also known as *Asch conformity experiment*.

ascribed role ➤ role, ascribed.

-ase Combining form used in the naming of an enzyme by attaching the suffix to the name of the substance it acts on.

asemasia ➤ asemia.

asemia Partial or complete loss of the ability to comprehend the meaning of symbols. Classified by some as a form of ➤ aphasia, although others view it as possibly functional (non-organic) in origin in some cases. vars., *asemasia* and, in some older writings, *asymbolia*.

asexual 1. Literally, without sex or lacking sexuality. 2. Characterizing reproduction without the union of two sex cells. Compare here with ➤ **sexual reproduction**.

'as if' A marvellous example of how specialists can take two perfectly ordinary, high-frequency words and convert them into a technical term with a welter of obscure, dense meanings and usages: 1. A variety of scientific thinking in which one formulates a coherent hypothesis and proceeds with one's explorations or experimentations on the presumption that it is true. The hypothesis so formed is often

called the 'as if' hypothesis. 2. A philosophical point of view based on the notion that many of the most fundamental and useful principles of science are, in fact, hypothetical and as yet unproven. Science, of necessity, functions 'as if' they were valid. 3. Adler, influenced by this philosophical position, extended the domain of the term to the ways in which one's personality develops. The 'as if' became, for Adler, the presumption that one's striving for superiority had actually been achieved. See here ➤ **guiding fiction**. 4. In the study of children's play, the term is commonly used as a label for games of make-believe and fantasy.

asitia An aversion to food.

ASL ➤ American Sign Language.

asocial 1. Without regard to society or social issues. This meaning is used to describe situations, events, behaviors or people which operate independently of (although not in opposition to – ➤ **anti-social**) social values and customs. An asocial person is one who is withdrawn from society. 2. Lacking in sensitivity to social customs. This meaning is closer to that of *antisocial* because the connotation is that such insensitivity can be potentially harmful to a group or society. ➤ **non-social**, **unsocial**.

asonia ➤ tone deafness.

aspartic acid An amino acid suspected of being a neurotransmitter.

Asperger's syndrome (or disorder) A disorder characterized by some of the features of ➤ **autism** such as abnormalities of social interaction and repetitive and stereotyped interests and activities but without the delay or retardation in language and cognitive development that is seen in true autism. Some authorities have doubts about the validity of this syndrome, particularly whether it can be reliably differentiated from mild cases of autism.

asphalgesia Lit, self-pain. A feeling of burning or pain when touching a neutral object; it can be produced occasionally in deeply hypnotized subjects.

56

asphyxia Lit., lack of a pulse. Used, however, for the decrease in oxygen and increase in carbon dioxide produced by any interference with normal respiration.

aspiration 1. Desire, hope, aim; the goal(s) toward which one strives. 2. Breathing in. 3. The act of drawing something in or out by suction.

aspirational reference group ➤ **reference group, aspirational**.

aspiration, level of Quite literally, the level to which one aspires. Operationally defined, a standard set by a person by which success or failure can be personally gauged. Compare and distinguish from ➤ **level of *achievement**.

assault 1. A violent attack on a person. Usually used of physical attacks but the phrases *verbal assault* and *psychological assault* are becoming more and more common. 2. Any invasive medical procedure carried out (illegally) without first obtaining the individual's permission.

assay To examine by test or trial. Hence, the analysis of any complex subject (e.g., a chemical substance, a drug) to determine its components.

A-S scale ➤ **measurement of *authoritarianism**.

assertive behavior facilitation ➤ **assertiveness training**.

assertiveness training A general label for a variety of therapeutic techniques commonly used in the treatment of a variety of disorders which are characterized by a lack of assertiveness, such as ➤ **dependent personality disorder** and ➤ **schizoid personality disorder**, and as a general training program designed to teach persons how to assert themselves in our rather intimidating world. Its most frequent recent advocates have been feminists who argue that women are generally socialized into nonassertive behavior patterns which often prove disadvantageous in interpersonal situations. Also called *assertive behavior facilitation*, although this term is used by some for only one of the various procedures, namely one

based upon the use of assertive models whose behavior the client learns to mimic.

assets–liabilities technique A therapeutic procedure in which the client compiles two lists of his or her behavioral and personality characteristics, one containing traits regarded as being of value (assets) and the other listing traits seen as personal liabilities. The technique is commonly used in behavior therapy as a way of specifying the goals for the client.

assignment therapy Moreno's term for a technique used in group therapy. After a sociometric analysis of the persons involved (➤ **sociometry**), individuals are assigned to particular small groups based on an assessment of which particular collections of persons they can be expected to interact with so as to derive maximum therapeutic advantage.

assimilation The basic meaning is *to take in, absorb* or *incorporate as one's own*. A term which entails such broad connotations has proven hard to resist. In all of the following special usages this general sense is reflected to at least some degree. 1. In physiology, the absorption and conversion of food into protoplasm. 2. In Hering's theory of vision, the anabolism of photochemicals in the retina. 3. In Herbart's theory, when new ideas were incorporated into the existing *apperceptive mass* they were said to have been assimilated. 4. In Piaget's approach to development, the application of a general schema to a particular person, object or event. See, here, the accompanying Piagetian term ➤ **accommodation** (3). 5. In early approaches to the study of memory, it was proposed as a 'law' of memory whereby novel objects or events had to become assimilated into the existing cognitive structure before they could be remembered. 6. In standard psychodynamic approaches, certain pathologies, handicaps or simply unpleasant facts are often said to be assimilated when they are incorporated, in a tolerable way, into one's experiences. The proper antonyms for this meaning are *repression* and *suppression*. 7. In Jung's theory, it is used to characterize the process of altering objects, events or ideas to fit the needs of the individual. **8.** In Thorndike's theory, it was applied to situations in which an animal used a previously learned response in a new situation when there was sufficient commonality between the two. **9.** In phonetics, the process by which two phonemes acquire common characteristics or become identical. **10.** In sociology, the merging of groups or individuals with disparate backgrounds or identifications into one group with common identity. The process here may be one-way, where one is absorbed by the other, or a mutual blending of the two. There are probably other usages in psychology but it seems clear that the term is already suffering from information overload. Some special uses in phrases follow.

assimilation–contrast theory A theory of attitude change based on the assumption that attitudes are modified by changes in the relationship between the originally held position, the opinion articulated by the person attempting to effect the change and the credibility of the source of this new attitude. Depending on these three factors, the person either will form a contrast with the source's opinions and not change (or even perhaps move in the opposite direction) or will assimilate the new attitude.

assimilation, generalizing In Piaget's theory, ➤ **assimilation** (4) based on the child's ability to notice the similarities among objects and to incorporate them into general classes and categories. It follows the development of ➤ **recognitory *assimilation**.

assimilation, law of An obsolete term for the notion that when in a novel situation one will behave in a manner similar to the way one did in similar circumstances encountered previously. In more modern writings, this general idea is expressed more accurately by the terms **analogy** or **generalization**.

assimilation, reciprocal In Piaget's theory, the mutual ➤ **assimilation** (4) of two schemas into each other where both continue but modified by the assimilated components of the other. The interrelated development of visual and motor schemas is assumed by Piagetians to derive from this process.

assimilation, recognitory In Piaget's theory, ➤ **assimilation** (4) based on the child's ability to detect differences between objects and to make discriminative responses to them based on these differences. It follows the primitive ➤ **reproductive *assimilation** and is succeeded in turn by the more sophisticated ➤ **generalizing *assimilation**.

assimilation, reproductive In Piaget's theory, the most basic form of ➤ **assimilation** (4), based on the child repeating the same reaction to a stimulus object or environmental situation whenever it occurs. For example, grasping an object each time it appears allows, according to the theory, the child to assimilate its various features and properties. It is followed by ➤ **recognitory *assimilation**.

assimilative illusion A general label for any illusion in which the pragmatic, functional or emotional context within which the physical stimulus is embedded leads to an illusory misperception. The classic example is the child who, frightened by the dark, misrepresents objects in a room as monsters or threatening beasts. The term derives from the notion that the physical stimulus becomes 'assimilated' into the emotional or cognitive scheme and so is interpreted in an illusory fashion.

assimilative learning ➤ **assimilation** (8).

association 1. Most generally, any learned, functional, connection between two (or more) *elements*. Identifying precisely what these *elements* are (i.e. ideas, acts, images, stimuli and responses, memories, etc.) and specifying the mechanisms underlying their connection (see here ➤ **associative laws**) is a theoretical exercise that has occupied many a philosopher and psychologist for many a year. ➤ **associationism** for discussion of some of these.

2. The bond or the connection itself implied by the above meaning. In the heyday of an associately based behaviorism most theories of learning were couched in terms of *bonds* or *associations* between stimuli (S) and responses (R) or S-R connections. A not insubstantial amount of scholarly activity was aimed at understanding the nature of this link. Practically every conceivable characterization was suggested at one time or another, from simple neural pathways to abstract propositional networks. Interestingly, although this so-called 'S-R' approach has faded, the notion of an association or connection between elements has been revived. See here ➤ **connectionism** (2). **3.** A particular psychological experience evoked by a stimulus or event. For example, you are given the word 'sex' and a sequence of associations emerges. This meaning is entailed by 1 above and usually denoted by qualifiers, e.g., ➤ **controlled *association, free *association. 4.** In statistics, the degree to which changes in one variable are accompanied by changes in another. It is quite common in correlational analyses to speak of the *association* between statistically correlated variables. Note, finally, that the long and tortured history of usage of the term has spawned an enormous number of specialized uses. Most of those that have played or still are playing a role in psychology are listed below with the qualifiers most commonly used.

association areas The areas of the brain where the 'higher mental processes' such as thinking, reasoning, etc., are assumed to occur. In general, those areas of the cortex which do not show clear motor or sensory function are assumed to be association areas. Most frequently cited are the frontal and parietal lobes.

association, backward A connection between one item of a list in a serial learning task and an item or items that preceded it. Backward associations are assumed to be weaker than ➤ **forward *associations.** In either case, however, the more remote the association, the weaker the connection. ➤ **remote *association.**

association by contiguity ➤**associative laws.**

association, constrained A general term for any association procedure in which the stimuli the subject are given or the types of responses allowed are limited. That is, any association other than ➤ **free *association.**

association, controlled A technique used in both clinical and experimental work in which precise instructions are given to put boundaries on the kinds of associations given to stimuli by the client or subject. See, e.g., ➤ **antonym test.**

association cortex ➤ **association areas.**

association, direct An association between two items that is not mediated by other items or mnemonic devices; i.e. it is 'direct.'

association, forward A connection between one item of a list in a serial-learning task and an item or items that followed it. Forward associations are assumed to be stronger than ➤ **backward *associations.**

association, free Any unconstrained association made between ideas, words, thoughts, etc. In a *free-association test* the subject is given a word and asked to reply with the first word that comes to mind. It has been used in such diverse areas as cognitive psychology to explore topics like meaning and syntax and in psychoanalytical investigations and therapeutic procedures, where it mostly serves as a projective device to explore the client's unconscious.

association, immediate Generally, the first, short-latency (➤**latency**) response to a stimulus. An association which is *not* immediate may be either (a) one which is the second, third, etc., association in a chain or (b) one with an uncharacteristically long latency. The former are occasionally termed *mediate associations* (distinguish from ➤ **remote *association**); the latter have no generally accepted term but most psychotherapists consider them to be

ASSOCIATION, INDUCED

important revealers of underlying psychological conflicts and defenses.

association, induced Any idea, image or word which results from a selected word presented to a subject; i.e. the first response to a stimulus on an association test.

associationism A label usually attached to a philosophical/psychological doctrine that asserts that higher-order mental or behavioral processes result from the combination (association) of simpler mental or behavioral elements. Rather than representing an identifiable school of thought, associationism is more of a general principle which has served as the foundation for a variety of specific theories. Its roots can be traced back to the epistemology of Aristotle who, in an essay on memory, proposed the three 'relations' between elements which lead to associations: similarity, contrast and contiguity. Associationism really has two historically important lines, a philosophical and a scientific. The philosophical is best represented by the British Empiricists (Locke, Berkeley, Hume, the Mills, etc.). With their strong antinativist bias they were in need of powerful principles by which complex mental life could be explained by appeal only to experience. Hobbes was the first to suggest that Aristotle's 'relations' could serve as an associationistic model of human cognition. The associationistic approach survived the many variations and points of disagreement between successive Empiricists and reached its highest level of development in Hartley and the Mills, father and son. The scientific approach began with the first experimentation on memory by Ebbinghaus in 1885. The appeal to data to validate associationist doctrine continued through Pavlov's studies on conditioned reflexes and Thorndike's work on 'connectionism' and became, finally, the foundation on which Watson built behaviorism. This orientation differed from the earlier philosophical approach in several ways. First, the primitive elements which became connected were no longer 'ideas' or 'sensations' but became operationally defined stimuli and responses. Second, where the focus previously was on the rationalist analysis of associations already formed – a kind of 'armchair' introspectionism – it shifted to focus on how the associations were formed. Thus, learning became one of the most intensely researched areas in psychology. Third, what were acceptable as legitimate data shifted from mentalistic phenomena, available mainly through introspection, to objectively measurable behavior. While there has been no school which ever called itself 'associationism,' the principle has proven to be one of the most enduring theoretical mechanisms. The basic notions of associationism have re-emerged in recent years in the cognitive sciences under the related term ➤ **connectionism** (2).

association neuron ➤ **interneuron**.

association, paradigmatic/syntagmatic In a free-association test, a *paradigmatic association* is any response that is related to the stimulus word by some semantic link; e.g., replying *table* to *chair*, or *boy* to *girl*, *black* to *white*, etc. A *syntagmatic* association is any in which the response is a word that can syntactically follow in a sentence or a phrase; e.g., replying *runs* to *girl*, or *cloud* to *white*. Children tend to give syntagmatic associations, adult paradigmatic.

association, remote Any ➤ **forward** or ➤ **backward** *association between one item in a serial list and a nonadjacent item. They played an important role in Hull's attempt to explain the ➤ **serial position effect**.

association/sensation ratio The (roughly estimated) ratio of the size of the ➤ **association areas** of the cortex to the sensory areas. Although it has been used by some as a basis for comparing the learning capabilities of different species, conclusions drawn from such a measure should not be taken too seriously.

association test (or **experiment**) A generic label for any procedure, clinical or experimental, based on the presentation of a stimulus (usually, but not necessarily, a word) and having the subject respond with an association (usually, but not necessarily, a verbal one).

association time 1. The response time in an ➤ **association test;** the time it takes for the subject to respond to a stimulus. ➤ **response *latency.** 2. The time it takes for an association to be formed. The time in 1 is relatively easy to measure; that in 2 is not. The problem is that 1 deals strictly with an overt behavior while 2 is an internal, covert mental process. Over the years various techniques have been developed to try to deal with this issue; they range from the early work of Donders (➤ **subtraction method**) to more recent studies with EEGs (electroencephalograms). In many modern writings the term *association time* is less frequently used, having been replaced by any of a number of others such as *retrieval time, reaction time, verification time* and the like depending upon which type of response is under examination.

associative agnosia ➤ agnosia, associative.

associative bond The hypothetical link between the elements in an association.

associative-chain theory An early behaviorist theory of complex behavior which argued that each of the several components in sequential action was linked associatively to the preceding component so that the full act was 'chained off' in a smooth series of elementary acts. The theory is so simplistic that it is almost embarrassing to realize that it was once taken seriously; imagine regarding an uttered sentence as no more than a chain of words or a Bach partita as merely an associately linked series of notes!

associative facilitation An obsolescent term for the facilitation of new associations by previously established ones.

associative illusion A general label for a large class of illusions all of which are produced by interactions between parts of the stimulus such that particular aspects of the display are misperceived. See, e.g., ➤ **Ponzo illusion**.

associative inhibition 1. The inhibition of an established association by a new one. It can occur through either the acquiring of a new response to the old stimulus or learning to associate a new stimulus with the old response. Note that the use of the word *inhibition* here implies that the link between the associated elements has been weakened; the term *associative interference* is frequently used when the writer wishes not to make any presumptions about underlying bonds but rather only to connote that some process is interfering with the retrieval of the old response. 2. A process assumed to be operating when new associations are unusually difficult to establish because of previously learned associations.

associative interference ➤ **associative inhibition** (1).

associative laws A cover term for a number of empirical and theoretical generalizations about the manner in which associations are formed. The most frequently cited and most general is *contiguity*, which states that things which occur together in space and time will become linked with each other. Other associative laws include: *repetition* (or *frequency*), in which it is assumed that elements which occur together often are likely to be associatively linked; *similarity*, whereby stimuli with similar referents are assumed to become associated with each other; *recency*, in which it is assumed that the more recently formed associations are easiest to use or remember; *vividness*, in which unique, compelling associations are stronger than less vivid ones; *contrast*, in which things that differ from one another in compelling ways will tend to be associated with each other; and *succession*, in which serial factors are assumed to be important in ordering associative chains. A careful reading of these should reveal that the dubbing of them as 'laws' was, in essence, wishful thinking. They are rather poorly formed for true laws and, as contemporary psychologists are all too aware, they do not carry much explanatory power. Most of them derive from the early work in ➤

associationism of philosophers and were not founded on hard experimental data. Nevertheless, they do have an often compelling intuitive validity and the sophisticated student of psychology can see how many of these principles have re-emerged in other forms in studies of cognitive psychology, social psychology and dynamic psychology.

associative learning ➤ **learning, associative**.

associative memory ➤ **memory, associative**.

associative shifting One of the basic principles of learning hypothesized by E. L. Thorndike. The fundamental notion was that if a particular response can be maintained while the stimulus environment is gradually shifted (by adding new elements, removing old ones, etc.) the response will eventually be made to an entirely novel stimulus.

associative strength The (assumed) strength of the bond between a stimulus and a response. Used in this fashion, strength is a theoretical variable measured by such procedures as: frequency with which the response is made to the stimulus, resistance of the response to interference, memory for the response, etc. Although the term, theoretically, has broad applications it is used almost exclusively in verbal learning and conditioning studies.

assortative mating ➤ **mating, assortative**.

assumed mean ➤ **mean, assumed**.

assumption The standard dictionary reveals the obvious: an assumption is something taken for granted, a supposition. While this definition is reasonably straightforward, it is important to note that this term is a very general one and that there are various specialized classes of assumptions. To wit: an ➤ **axiom** represents an assumption which is not subjectable to either proof or disproof but rather is universally accepted as given. In logic and mathematics, for example, axioms are accepted as self-evident for the sake of studying the consequences that can be deduced from them. A ➤ **postulate**, on the other hand, is a principle whose apparent truth is not universally accepted as self-evident. Instead, the postulate is adopted within the confines of a particular theory because it seems logically sound to do so, or because the postulate leads to a directly testable conclusion. The postulate, however, is still fundamentally an assumption since it is not a logical deduction within the theory and itself is not directly subjected to proof or disproof.

When the assumption (or, more properly, the proposition) is susceptible to proof or disproof by logical analysis, the proper term is ➤ **theorem**. Theorems, strictly speaking, are not assumptions; they are logical deductions from assumptions (axioms) and serve properly only within the confines of well-formed theories. However, not infrequently, one is confronted with tentative explanations of data or, as yet undemonstrated, potential principles which are 'assumed' to be true. When such an assumption can be stated in such a way as to be empirically evaluated or tested, it is properly called a ➤ **hypothesis**. In short, assumptions are not things to be taken for granted.

astasia Inability to sit upright or to stand owing to severe impairment of motor coordination. Astasia and *abasia* (similar problem seen in walking) often are observed together and an *abasia–astasia syndrome* has been noted that is essentially functional in origin.

astereognosis Partial or complete lack of ability to recognize objects by touch; a form of ➤ **agnosia**.

asthenia Generally, weakness, disability, lack or loss of strength. In physiology and medicine the most common usage is with respect to weakness originating in muscular or cerebellar diseases. In studies of personality and affect, it usually refers to a general sense of debilitation, depression and inhibition.

asthenic feeling An obsolescent term used roughly to denote a sense of depression, despair, grief. ➤ **asthenic type**.

asthenic personality ➤ **dependent personality disorder**.

asthenic type 1. A general label for a person who is chronically exhausted, displaying low energy levels, proneness to fatigue and a general lack of enthusiasm for life. 2. In Kretschmer's old classification system, a lean, slender body type which he believed was associated with a predisposition for schizophrenia.

asthenopia Lit., weakness of the eyes. A condition in which there is tiring of the eyes caused by a fatiguing of the extraocular muscles.

asthma A general term for any of several varieties of bronchial disorders characterized by a spasm of the upper respiratory system with difficult, labored breathing caused by the spasmodic constriction of the bronchial tubes or the congestion of the tubes by the swelling of the mucous membranes. Asthmatic attacks often accompany allergic reactions and occasionally are secondary complications of respiratory infections. However, asthma is usually classified as a psychosomatic disorder because of the tendency for asthmatic reactions to accompany anxiety and psychoneurotic conflicts.

astigmatism An irregularity or defect in the curvature of the lens of the eye which produces distortions in the light falling on the retina. Generally correctable by the use of cylindrical lenses.

astrocytes ➤ **glia**.

astroglia ➤ **glia**.

astrology A pseudoscience, of interest mainly for insight into human gullibility, based on the belief that the stars (some of them!) have an influence on human personality or behavior. The fallaciousness of astrology has been further underlined by modern statistical analysis and demonstrable errors in its purported astronomical basis. Most psychologists are led to the conclusion that the stars have about as much impact on our behavior as we have on theirs. ➤➤ **parapsychology**.

asylum An obsolescent term (from the

Latin for *sanctuary*) for any institution for persons unable to care for themselves.

asymbolia ➤ **asemia**.

asymmetrical distribution ➤ **skewness**.

asymmetry Lacking in ➤ **symmetry**. Used widely of bodies, organs, structures, distributions, logical relations, personal relationships, etc. where there is a lack of correspondence between the two sides. See the discussion under ➤ **symmetry** for various nuances of meaning and usage.

asymptomatic Lit., without symptoms. Generally used when an individual is known through lab tests or other techniques to have some disorder or disease despite the lack of overt physical or behavioral symptoms.

asymptote 1. Mathematically, the limit of the curve of a mathematical function, the line which the curve approaches but never reaches. 2. Behaviorally, the steady state of behavior reached after no further changes in performance are detectable. Strictly speaking this latter usage is not correct since theoretically (i.e. by the former meaning) an asymptote is never actually attained. Nevertheless, psychologists often refer to a subject who has reached maximum levels of performance or learning as being 'at asymptote.'

asynchrony Lack of coordination between events in time. Usage is generally restricted to situations where synchrony is expected or normal. var., *asynchronism*.

asynergia Partial or complete loss of coordination between the muscle groups involved in complex motor acts. Typically, the responses required are made in series rather than as a coordinated 'whole.' The disability is seen in cases of cerebellar disease or injury. var., *asynergy*.

ataque de nervios A ➤ **culture-specific syndrome** found in Latino cultures. Symptoms include uncontrollable shouting and trembling, attacks of crying, a feeling of heat rising in the chest and verbal or physical abuse aimed at others. Precipitating factors are stressful events, typically in the family, such as divorce, death or an accident involving a family member.

ataractic 1 adj. Tranquil, imperturbable. n., *ataraxia*. **2** n. A tranquilizing drug.

atavism 1. Reappearance of an earlier genetic characteristic not manifested in the immediately preceding generations; ➤ **reversion** (2). Atavisms are significant occurrences since they show that genetic potential can survive for remarkably long periods of time without phenotypic displays. **2.** The reappearance of a primitive form of behavior. In this use, the link with genetics entailed by the first meaning is loose and may be missing altogether.

ataxia Partial or complete loss of coordination of voluntary muscular movements. The term is also used somewhat metaphorically to refer to psychic disorders in which the 'loss of coordination' is between emotions and thoughts; ➤ **mental *ataxia**. adjs., *ataxic, atactic*.

ataxia, intrapsychic ➤ **mental *ataxia**.

ataxia, mental An abnormal lack of correspondence between the expression of emotions and thoughts or ideas. The term is generally reserved for cases evincing a lasting discoordination in people whose behaviors frequently are at odds with their emotions, although an acute form can most certainly be induced by highly stressful situations. The best-known example in the experimental literature of what is usually regarded as a clinical syndrome is the pained laughter of many subjects in the obedience-to-authority experiments while they were 'administering' possibly lethal shocks to other persons. See here ➤ **obedience**. Also called *psychic ataxia, intrapsychic ataxia*.

ataxia, optic An *ataxia* characterized by a deficit in the ability to reach for objects under visual guidance.

ataxia, sensory Ataxia caused by dysfunction in afferent pathways; motor coordination is disturbed because of disturbances in conduction of sensory nerves, especially those responsible for proprioception.

ataxia, static Ataxia in which the lack of coordination results in a loss of the ability to maintain a normal standing position.

ataxic aphasia ➤ **aphasia, ataxic**.

ataxic speech A halting speaking pattern in which every syllable is stressed equally and typically with a pause after each. The normal prosodic features of intonation and stress are missing. Also called *scanning speech*.

ataxic writing Severely discoordinated writings.

atelia The maintenance of childish traits and characteristics into adulthood.

atelo- Combining form denoting *incomplete* or *imperfect*. Used typically with respect to developmental factors.

atherosclerosis A form of arteriosclerosis in which there is an accumulation of fatty substances in the blood vessels, obstructing them and impairing circulation.

athetosis A disability characterized by slow, twisting, snake-like movements, particularly in the arms and fingers. A variety of causes are known including encephalitis and *tabes dorsalis*.

athletic type One of Kretschmer's body types (➤ **constitutional theory**) characterized by a well-proportioned, balanced physique.

athymia 1. Lack of feeling or emotional affect. **2.** Absence of the thymus gland or absence of its secretions.

atmosphere effect An obsolescent term for the general-context effect in which the overall circumstances (the 'atmosphere') affect behavior. When the term was first used it referred to the appearance of habits acquired in one context in a similar but inappropriate context; e.g., devout Catholics who inadvertently cross themselves when entering a large imposing building such as a courthouse. The general notions connoted by the term are now carried by ➤ context effects.

atomism 1. The general philosophical position that phenomena are best understood when analyzed into the most elementary components. The term has a mildly derogatory flavor and is used mainly by critics of this position; proponents generally prefer ➤ elementarism. 2. In sociology and social psychology, the approach to the study of groups and societies that argues that all social phenomena must be viewed as the sum of the influences of the individuals that comprise the group. This position is rarely defended these days.

atonia Lack of muscle tone. vars., atony, atonicity.

ATP ➤ adenosine triposphate.

atrium Any cavity or sinus; a chamber.

atrophy A wasting away of tissue caused by disease, old age or injury. Generally refers to muscle tissue; ➤ degeneration (1) is the preferred term for neural tissue.

atropine (sulfate) An alkaloid derived from belladonna (from the deadly nightshade plant). It is a respiratory and circulatory stimulant and counteracts parasympathetic stimulation. Hence, it relaxes nonvoluntary muscles and inhibits secretions by acting as a false transmitter preventing acetylcholine action. Local application in the eye causes pupil dilation and is used commonly in ophthalmological examinations. var., atropin.

attachment 1. Generally, a binding affection, an emotional tie between people. The usual connotation is that this kind of emotional relationship is infused with dependency; the persons rely on each other for emotional satisfaction. 2. In developmental psychology, an emotional bond formed between an infant and one or more adults such that the infant will: (a) approach them especially in periods of distress; (b) show no fear of them, particularly during the stage when strangers evoke anxiety; (c) be highly receptive to being cared for by them; and (d) display anxiety if separated from them. See here ➤

attachment behavior. 3. A tendency on the part of infants to form the kind of bond described in 2. The distinction between meanings 2 and 3 is needed because some authors treat attachment as an innate potential while others view it as a particular pattern of behavior and make no presumptions concerning its genotypic foundations. 4. In anatomy, the connections by which tissues are joined to other bodily parts (usually muscle to bone). 5. The bond between a stimulus and a response.

attachment behavior Bowlby's term for the behavior of an infant with regard to the adult(s) with whom it has formed an ➤ attachment (2). The essential feature of this behavior is that the infant will seek out the adult (usually the mother) and behave so as to maintain maximally close contact. As Bowlby uses the term such behavior is not merely a reaction to separation but a natural response to any distress or uncertainty.

attachment styles Quite literally, the particular styles of ➤ attachment (1 or 2) established between any two individuals. The term originally emerged in the studies of parents and toddlers although it is now used generally, although occasionally authors will refer to 'adult attachment styles' to prevent confusion. The avoidant/insecure style characterizes individuals who tend to avoid interaction and intimacy; the secure refers to those who seek and are comfortable with social interaction and intimacy; and ambivalent/resistant style characterizes those who both seek and reject intimacy and social interaction. Attachments are viewed as consistent patterns of thinking, feeling, and behaving in interpersonal situations. Since the conceptual focus here is on 'consistency' there are those who argue that there is also a disorganized type which is noted by a lack of such consistent patterns of social behavior.

attack 1. Sudden onset of a disease or a symptom. Usually used of major disorders in which the abrupt manifestation is dramatic and serious, such as epilepsy and cardiovascular disease. **2.** Overt, aggressive action. Here the term covers both the physical and verbal varieties.

attack, quiet-biting ➤ predatory attack.

attensity A now obsolete term used by Titchener to refer to the clearness of a sensation which he hypothesized was important in attracting one's attention.

attention 1. A general term referring to the selective aspects of perception which function so that at any instant an organism focuses on certain features of the environment to the (relative) exclusion of other features. Attention may be conscious in that some stimulus elements are actively selected out of the total input, although, by and large, we are not explicitly aware of the factors which cause us to perceive only some small part of the total stimulus array. **2.** The paying of particular notice to the behaviors and demands of another, usually of children or other relatively helpless persons who require that one attend to their needs. **3.** (obs.). Titchener's term for a state of mental clarity in which one aspect of mind is more vivid than others.

attention decrement In *social psychology*, the tendency of people to pay less attention to information that is presented later in a given session. Good propagandists understand this principle implicitly and typically get the important points out early in a message.

attention-deficit disorder (ADD) ➤ attention-deficit hyperactivity disorder.

attention-deficit disorder with hyperactivity (ADDH) ➤ attention-deficit hyperactivity disorder.

attention-deficit hyperactivity disorder (ADHD) A disorder characterized by hyperactivity, attentional deficits, and impulsivity. Although it is first manifested in childhood, it may not be diagnosed until later in life. It is a fairly common disorder and over the years various terms have been used for it and for disorders occasionally thought to be related. Included here are descriptive terms such as *attention-deficit disorder (ADD)*, *hyperkinesis*, *hyperkinetic syndrome*, and *hyperactive child syndrome*, as well as others that imply some organic dysfunction like *minimal brain damage*, *minimal cerebral dysfunction*, and *minor cerebral dysfunction*. Also called *attention-deficit disorder with hyperactivity (ADDH)*.

attention, focal 1. In Titchener's terms, the highest *attention level*. **2.** More commonly, those aspects or objects of a perceptual field which one is devoting attention to.

attention-getting Generally, descriptive of any behavior engaged in for the purpose of securing the attention of others. Used with respect to the various devices children employ, particularly those which would otherwise prove maladaptive (although more than a few adults are pretty good at this little game).

attention level The extent to which one is attending to a stimulus. Historically, the term was used by the structuralists with a rather precise set of levels identified, ranging from the total nonattentiveness of an unconscious person to the vivid clarity of focal attention. Today the term is used without any real specification of levels or steps; rather it connotes a dimension of how much of one's attention is invested in or being attracted by a particular task or stimulus.

attention, margin of The 'edge' of one's attention. The term is used phenomenologically to refer to those components of a stimulus which the individual is only vaguely aware of or only poorly perceives.

attention reflex The change in pupil size when attention is fixed on something. Also called *Piltz's reflex*.

attention span 1. Technically, the number of objects or separate stimulus elements that can be perceived in a single short presentation. See here ➤ apprehension span, subitizing. **2.** The amount of time that a person can continue to attend to one type of input. This latter use is strictly nontechnical.

attenuation Lit., making thin. Thus, attenuating any stimulus means to reduce its strength, intensity, volume or value; an attenuator is any device which functions to attenuate a stimulus.

attenuator model A label for any of several models of selective attention which hypothesize a 'mental attenuator' which reduces the intensity of stimulus inputs not attended to. In the ➤ **cocktail-party phenomenon**, for example, the unattended messages are not completely shut out but rather attenuated so that a familiar or important piece of information, like one's name, 'gets through.' ➤➤ **filter theory**.

attic child A child raised in isolation, often locked away in an attic by parents or guardians. ➤➤ **feral child** for more details.

attitude Psychology regularly gets itself into stormy definitional waters, never more so than when a term like this one is used to denote a concept of fundamental importance in human behavior and when the domain of reference turns out to be much more complex than the original neologists ever imagined. To wit: **1.** Originally the term derived from the Latin *aptitudo* meaning *fitness*. Hence, an attitude rendered one fit to engage in the performance of some task. **2.** In medical parlance, this meaning was (and still is) reflected by using it to refer to bodily position or posture, especially with regard to the positions of the limbs. **3.** In ethology and comparative psychology this meaning was slightly extended to cover the idea of intended action so that a crouching animal may be described as being in an 'attack attitude.' (So far so good, but subtleties are creeping in.) **4.** In traditional personality and social psychology attitudes took on, for the first time, an explanatory role rather than merely a descriptive one. That is, an attitude was viewed as some internal affective orientation that would explain the actions of a person. This meaning is basically an extension of the idea of *inten-*

tion noted in 3, but contemporary usage generally entails several components, namely: *cognitive* (consciously held belief or opinion); *affective* (emotional tone or feeling); *evaluative* (positive or negative); and *conative* (disposition for action). There is considerable dispute as to which of these components should be regarded as more (or less) important. Cognitive theorists usually maintain that the underlying belief is fundamental, behaviorally oriented theorists focus on the conative (indeed, on occasion quite extremely, see 5, below) and most other researchers feel that a combination of the affective and evaluative components are the critical ones. Exactly how the term is used in modern psychological literature will thus depend largely on the theoretical tilt of the writer. **5.** A response tendency. Here the notion is that the concept needs to be rescued from the fuzziness of the usage of 4, and the way to do it is to operationalize it and regard attitudes as things which can only be inferred from observed behaviors.

attitude change This phrase has come to stand as a label for a rather intensely investigated area of social and personality psychology. It covers a number of theories concerning the processes by which individuals can be persuaded to modify their attitudes. The theories reflect a rather overwhelming diversity of attitudes on the part of psychologists about the processes involved; a look at the discussion under ➤ **attitude** (4) gives a hint at this variety.

attitude change, negative and positive Attempts at changing the attitudes of another may work or they may, on occasion, have a reverse effect in which the attitude is changed but in a direction opposite to that intended. The former are called *positive* changes; the latter *negative* changes (or sometimes, ➤ **boomerang effects**).

attitude cluster **1.** A number of attitudes held by a person that are interrelated and distinct from other attitudes. **2.** A set of related attitudes in a population of people that show strong covariance. Technically, high (or low) scores on one attitude within a cluster are accompanied by high (or low) scores on the others. Or, nontechnically, there is agreement across people. Note that 2 does *not* imply 1. For example, attitudes toward fiscal conservatism tend to cluster with attitudes toward sexual expression and victimless crimes in sense 2, but an extreme libertarian will display two distinct attitude clusters on these and related issues in sense 1.

attitude scale Any of a number of devices designed to reveal a person's attitudes. They usually are paper-and-pencil tests in which the subject agrees or disagrees with certain statements that have pre-established scale values. The subject's responses are assumed to reflect the way in which he or she would behave in specific situations – although, admittedly, there has been considerable dispute among specialists as to the degree of correspondence between the assessment of people's attitudes using these scales and the ways in which they actually behave in real-world circumstances. A number of specialized forms of attitude scales exist; see, e.g., ➤ **Likert scale**, **Thurstone-type scales**.

attitudinizing Conscious outward manifestation of particular attitudes for the impact they have upon others in social settings; 'putting on airs.'

attraction 1. A characteristic of an object, activity or person such that it evokes approach responses from other objects or persons. **2.** A tendency to approach an object, activity or person. Meaning 1 places the 'force' in the desired object; Marilyn Monroe held great attraction for many men. Meaning 2 places it in the desirous person; many men felt an attraction toward Marilyn Monroe. It seems pretty clear that any sensible analysis of the psychology of attraction must appreciate that both aspects interact in complex, dynamic ways.

attribute 1. n. A perceived elementary or fundamental quality of a stimulus. The important thing to note here is that the attributes of a stimulus are psychological

not physical. They are relatively invariant and represent whatever remains constant in changing stimulus conditions. For example, the attributes of color are hue, saturation and brightness. **2** n. A defining characteristic of a thing. Concepts may be defined as particular clusters of attributes; see discussion under ➤ **distinctive feature**. **3** n. In Titchener's structuralism, the fundamental characteristics of all sensations which, as he specified them, were *quality*, *intensity*, *duration*, and for some sensations, *extensity* and *clearness*. **4** vb. To describe or impute, particularly to ascribe a particular trait or characteristic to a person. See here ➤ **attribution theory**.

attributional style An individual's style of assigning attributions concerning the good and bad events that occur in life. ➤➤ **attribution theory** and **locus of control**.

attribution error, fundamental A tendency of people observing the action of another to interpret those actions as a sign of or as resulting from an internal disposition or trait. It is regarded as an attribution *error* because making such an interpretation almost always underestimates the impact of the external environment and places too much responsibility for the behavior on the individual's internal traits or tendencies. ➤ **attribution theory**.

attribution of causality The theory, due to F. Heider, that a person's perceptions of the behavior of others are determined largely by what he or she attributes the causes of that person's behavior to. Specifically, the attribution is made either to *internal* personal causes or to the *external* action of the environment, or to some combination of the two. Thus, the argument goes, we evaluate the behavior of others on the basis of perceived motives and intentions. Heider's work forms the conceptual basis of the more general approach known as ➤ **attribution theory**.

attribution of emotion A phrase commonly used to describe the theory of emotion put forward by S. Schachter that argues that the experiencing of emotion is due to both the physiological activation level and to the person's cognitive interpretation of the physiological changes.

attribution theory A general theoretical perspective in social psychology concerned with the issue of social perception. The act of attribution is one in which a person ascribes or imputes a characteristic (or trait, emotion or motive, etc.) to oneself or to another person. Thus, the term represents not so much a formal theory but a general approach to social psychology and personality theory in which behavior is analyzed in the light of this concept. Its roots go back to the ➤ **Gestalt** notion that information acquired through the past experiences of the observer plays an important role in processing new inputs. Modern attribution theory derives from the ➤ **attribution of causality** arguments of Heider and seeks to explain the manner in which people attribute characteristics and traits to people. In capsule form the theory maintains that the following sequence occurs in social situations: a person observes another engaging in some behavior, makes an inference about that individual's intentions based on the perceived actions and then attributes some underlying motivating trait to the person which is consistent with the behavior. There are many variations on this theme, including ➤ **self-perception theory**, in which one's own conceptions of self are handled within this theoretical framework. For more discussion ➤ **person perception**.

attrition From the Latin, meaning *a wearing away*. Hence: **1.** Any loss of material through friction. **2.** A decline in a population over time. The term has an interesting usage pattern which reflects basic lack of concern over the precise cause of the loss. For example, fewer persons graduate from a university than enter it and the loss is usually noted as 'through attrition' with the connotation that somehow the inexorable laws of probabilities are operating. However, the term would not be used should a number of experimental subjects die during an experiment; it would be an impropriety to dismiss the deceased so cavalierly.

atypical Generally and literally, not typical, not conforming to statistical expectations concerning the majority of cases under consideration. The term is common: **1.** In statistical analyses to characterize scores which deviate markedly (usually two or more *standard *deviations*) from the measure of central tendency (usually the *mean*). **2.** In descriptions of special individuals who differ in some fashion from the norm; e.g., disabled persons, gifted children, etc. Note that in this usage there is no evaluative connotation. **3.** In the psychiatric literature as a label for a syndrome or disorder which does not quite fit the standard diagnostic category. For example, a person classified as displaying a dysthymic disorder (disturbed emotional expression) but with periods of up to two or three months of normal affect will be labeled as an *atypical* dysthymic. This usage should be recognized for what it is, a tacit admission of ignorance on the part of those making psychiatric diagnoses accompanied by the fear that the primary diagnostic label may be inappropriate.

atypical autism ➤ **autism, atypical**.

Aubert-Fleischl paradox A perceptual phenomenon whereby a moving stimulus seems to move more slowly when the observer fixates on the stimulus than when he fixates on the background.

Aubert-Förster phenomenon If two objects of different physical sizes are placed at different distances from the observer such that both subtend the same number of degrees of visual are, the physically closer one can be recognized over a greater area of the retina than the physically more distant one.

Aubert phenomenon If a single vertical straight-line stimulus is presented to an observer the line will be perceptually displaced as the observer tilts his head.

audibility limits ➤ **audibility range**.

audibility range The full range of auditory stimuli which can be heard by the average adult subject. Full specification of this range is a complex task since the auditory system is not uniformly sensitive to all frequencies. However, the following rough outlines will suffice: along the frequency (pitch) dimension the range is from about 20 Hz to 20,000 Hz, with the point of maximum sensitivity in the neighborhood of 1,000–4,000 Hz with a diminution in sensitivity for higher and lower pitched tones.

audible Detectable. Used of auditory stimuli that are above the threshold for the average person.

audile ➤ visile.

audi(o)- Combining form meaning *hearing* or *related to hearing*.

audio analgesia Diminished sensitivity to pain produced by loud sounds.

audiogenic Pertaining to any phenomenon produced by or caused by sound.

audiogenic seizure Convulsions produced by long-term exposure to intense, high-pitched sound.

audiogram A graphic representation of a person's absolute auditory threshold. A complete audiogram shows thresholds for each ear separately for a number of different frequencies throughout the normal range of hearing.

audiogyral (or **audiogravic**) **illusion** Misperception of the location of a sound source following disruption in bodily orientation, e.g., by being tilted, being made to think one has been tilted or being rotated rapidly.

audiometer A device for measuring hearing acuity. The standard procedure in audiometry is to evaluate the amount of hearing loss relative to established norms. The loss is generally expressed in decibels, meaning the number of decibels above the norm which were required for the individual being tested to just detect each test frequency.

audiometry The science of testing hearing.

audiometry, averaged electroencephalic A procedure for testing hearing in non-responsive children (very young, autistic, severely retarded, etc.). It is based on the evaluation of changes in the electro-encephalogram made by the perception of sounds and does not require any behavioral response from the subject.

audit Periodic review of a patient or of a pattern of patient care.

audition The broad area of study encompassing the psychological, physiological and psychophysical aspects of sound in organisms; specifically, studies of the mechanisms of hearing. Although many writers adhere to the convention that audition is a *sense* and hearing is a *process* many others do not. Hence, for combined terms not found here, ➤ **hearing** *et seq*.

audition, chromatic A form of ➤ synesthesia in which color sensations are evoked by auditory stimuli. Also called *colored audition* and *colored hearing*.

audito-oculogyric reflex Reflexive turning of the head and eyes in the direction of a sudden or alarming sound.

auditory Relating, in a general way, to the sense of hearing. Several related terms with more limited meanings are: ➤ **acoustic**, which is used for the physical descriptions of sound; ➤ **hearing**, which is more properly used to refer to the full process rather than just the sensory aspects; ➤ **aural**, which is limited to the ear itself; ➤ **otic**, which is limited to the receptor cells; and ➤ **tonal**, which is used to refer to the properties of auditory stimuli.

auditory acuity ➤ acuity, auditory.

auditory agnosia ➤ agnosia, auditory.

auditory aphasia ➤ aphasia, auditory.

auditory attributes (or **dimensions**) ➤ tonal attributes.

auditory canal The passage from the external ear to the eardrum, also known as the *external auditory meatus*.

auditory flicker ➤ flicker, auditory.

auditory image ➤ image, auditory.

auditory localization The perceptual determination of the point in space from which a sound emanates. The primary cues for localization depend on: (a) the fact that the ear closest to the sound source will receive the stimulation a short period of time before the other ear; (b) the head casts a 'shadow' which partially blocks out sound so that the ear closest to the source receives a more intense stimulus and; (c) the two ears receive different phases from the sound wave.

auditory masking See discussion under ➤ masking.

auditory nerve The VIIIth ➤ cranial nerve. It is made up of two principal branches, the *cochlear nerve* which transmits information related to sound and the *vestibular nerve* which transmits information related to bodily balance.

auditory ossicles ➤ ossicles, auditory.

auditory (projection) areas The regions in the temporal lobes of the cortex where the ascending auditory pathways terminate.

auditory space The sense of the physical space surrounding one as perceived through sound. ➤ auditory localization.

auditory span A term occasionally used for the ➤ apprehension span for auditorily presented stimuli.

auditory spectrum ➤ spectrum, auditory.

auditory type Synonym for *audile*; see discussion under ➤ visile.

Aufgabe German for *task*. The term was used primarily by the early Würzburgers (➤ Würzburg school) to capture the notion that each particular task or set of instructions for performing a particular task carries with it a cluster of constraints which invite the use of particular processes. Although today the term is rarely used the concept is important and it is embodied in a variety of other terms including *set, determining tendency, functional fixedness*, etc.

aura A subjective experience that frequently precedes an epileptic seizure or an impending migraine headache. The aura may occur anywhere from a few hours to several seconds prior to onset and usually consists of a variety of sensory-based hallucinations (e.g., a flash of light).

aural Of or pertaining to the ear. ➤ audition, auditory, *et seq*.

aural harmonic A harmonic produced within the auditory mechanism itself.

aural microphonic ➤ cochlear microphonic.

Austrian school A group of early empirical psychologists led by the theologian-philosopher-psychologist Franz Brentano. The emphasis was upon *acts* or processes of mind rather than upon the *contents*, as stressed by those who followed Wundt. Later it evolved into the *Würzburg school* and served as an anticipator of the Functionalist system. ➤➤ act psychology.

authoritarian Pertaining to the method of control by subjugation to authority in which a clear social hierarchy exists and a single individual makes decisions and prescribes procedures.

authoritarian atmosphere K. Lewin's term for the general socio-political climate established when a group is led by a person who uses autocratic, authoritarian techniques. Compare with ➤ democratic atmosphere, laissez-faire atmosphere.

authoritarian character ➤ authoritarian personality

authoritarianism 1. A socio-political system based upon the subjugation of individual rights to the authority of the state and its leader(s). **2.** An attitude or trait characterized by the belief that there should be strict adherence and obedience to authority. Here the term is applicable either to those who are in authority or to those subservient to authority. ➤ authoritarian personality.

authoritarianism, measurement of Various scales were developed during the 1940s and 1950s to assess the hypothesized aspects of the authoritarian personality.

71

They were: (a) the A-S scale for anti-Semitism; (b) the E scale (ethnocentrism); (c) the P-E-C scale (politico-economic conservatism); and (d) the F scale (originally for fascism, later called anti-democratic).

authoritarian personality A term descriptive of one who desires an authoritarian social system, particularly one who seeks obedience, subordination and servile acceptance of authority. The term does not ordinarily refer to the person(s) in authority. Also called *authoritarian character*.

authority **1.** Institutionalized and legal power as manifested within a social system. **2.** The individual who wields such power. Sociologists and social psychologists distinguish various forms of authority; a few main types follow. ➤➤ **power**.

authority, charismatic Authority due primarily to the extraordinary characteristics of an individual. It is uniquely different from other forms of authority in that the power arises outside of legitimate institutions.

authority, legal Authority specifically established by law for the purpose of controlling and regulating social functions. Also called *rational-legal authority*.

authority, nonlegitimate Authority achieved through coercion and force and maintained by systems of reward and punishment.

authority, rational Authority due primarily to the expert knowledge or abilities of an individual. Such authority lies outside factors such as personality or social class and is usually limited to the particular domain within which the expertise is displayed; an auto mechanic will not be an authority on neurosurgery and vice versa.

authority, traditional Authority whose legitimacy and power derive from social and cultural traditions.

autism **1.** The general meaning is reflected by the roots of the word: *aut-* = *self*, and *-ism* = *orientation* or *state*. Hence, the tendency to be absorbed in oneself; a

condition in which one's thoughts, feelings and desires are governed by one's internal apprehensions of the world. Typically usage here connotes pathology. The term implies that the internal state is not consonant with reality and that the individual sees things in terms of fantasies and dreams, wishes and hopes, rather than in terms of a reality shared by and with others. ➤ **infantile *autism. 2.** A tendency to be preoccupied with one's fantasies and daydreams and to derive pleasure from them. This meaning is kept distinct from 1 because the connotations here do not necessarily involve pathology. **3.** The term was originally coined by E. Bleuler for *schizophrenia*. This synonymity is no longer intended, but ➤ **infantile *autism** for lingerings of this idea. adj., *autistic*.

autism, atypical Any case of ➤ **autism** that fails to meet the standard criteria for the disorder in that the symptoms first appear at an unusually late age or the symptomatology is atypical or mild.

autism, infantile A rare but seriously pathological syndrome, appearing in childhood, characterized by a withdrawn state, a lack of social responsiveness or interest in others, serious communicative and linguistic impairments, and a failure to develop normal attachments, all frequently accompanied by a variety of bizarre ways of responding to the environment, usually including a fascination with inanimate objects and an insistence on routine, order, and sameness. Note that the qualifier *infantile* means *lacking or prior to speech* and, hence, the usual criterion for diagnosing this disability is onset prior to 30 months of age. There is considerable dispute among specialists concerning infantile autism. Some argue that the term is really an umbrella category under which a number of similar but probably different disabilities are being inappropriately grouped. These critics cite differential recovery rates, unsystematic evidence of brain damage and occasional development of epileptic seizures later in life, among other factors, all of which call into question the notion of a single 'disease.'

autism, socially shared A term coined by Gardner Murphy to characterize the tendency for groups of individuals collectively to elaborate and perpetuate a particular belief or opinion that has no objective reality. Such 'autistic' (in the sense of withdrawal from reality) thinking presumably functions to fulfill certain needs of the group.

autistic Characterized by or indicative of ➤ **autism**. Used either to characterize a withdrawal from reality into oneself or of a tendency toward internally driven thoughts. The former connotes pathology, the latter eccentricity. The former is more commonly the intended meaning: ➤ **infantile *autism**.

autistic child A child diagnosed as displaying ➤ **infantile *autism**.

autistic fantasy A defense mechanism whereby the individual reacts to conflict and stress by engaging in excessive daydreaming rather than appropriate task-oriented action and thought.

autistic thinking 1. Generally, thinking governed by internal wishes and desires irrespective of external real-world factors. 2. Thinking manifested by (or, better, inferred to be occurring in) an autistic child.

aut(o)- A prefix meaning *self-initiated, self-directed* or *oriented toward the self.* Many combined terms using this prefix are self-explanatory, e.g., autoanalysis is self-analysis, autocompetition is competition with one's previous performances, etc. Terms that are less autoexplanatory follow.

autobiographical memory ➤ **memory, autobiographical**.

autocathartic Descriptive of self-initiated behaviors which have cathartic value for the person (➤ **catharsis**). Often autobiographical writing has such an effect.

autocentric Within the self. Occasionally used of the senses of smell and taste.

autochthonous Lit., from the Greek, *from the land itself.* Hence, it is used to refer to events originating from within an organism (relatively) independently of outside influences. For example, appetites such as hunger or thirst, obsessions, insights, ideas, etc. have all been termed *autochthonous* at one time or another. Some clinicians characterize schizophrenia in this way, since so much of the behavior seems to spring from within the person. Compare with ➤ **allochthonous**.

autochthonous gestalt An organized perception or other experience in which the integrating factors are self-produced rather than identifiable in the stimulus.

autochthonous variable ➤ **variable, autochthonous**.

autoclitic One of the three main categories of verbal behavior suggested by B. F. Skinner in his operant analysis of language. Autoclitics represent a class of utterances intended to suggest verbal behavior that is based upon the speaker's own role and dependent on other verbal behavior. 'I am tempted to add . . .' or 'I agree with . . .' are classic examples.

autoeroticism Lit., self-initiated eroticism. Although masturbation is the classic example of an autoerotic act, the term is also used for a variety of other behaviors and thoughts which have sexual elements, including fantasies, dreams, etc. var., *autoerotism*.

autoerotism ➤ **autoeroticism**.

autogenic Self-originated, self-initiated. ➤ **autogenous**.

autogenic reinforcement The term refers to hypothetical processes whereby a response is strengthened by internal factors independent of the operations of the environment. The usual example is the strengthening of muscular responses by mere repetition of movement without external rewards.

autogenous Usually a synonym for ➤ **autogenic**. However, it also overlaps in meaning with ➤ **endogenous (or endogenic)**, although without carrying the physiological connotations of that term.

autographism ➤ **dermographia**.

autohypnosis Self-induced hypnosis.

autoimmune diseases Generally, any disease that results when the body's own cells are attacked by the ➤ **immune system**. Such diseases often occur following infections, and it is suspected that the immune system somehow becomes sensitized to one of the body's natural proteins and attacks tissue containing it as though it were an invader. Rheumatoid arthritis, lupus, and multiple sclerosis are autoimmune diseases.

autoinstructional device ➤ **programmed instruction, teaching machine**.

autokinesis 1. Voluntary, self-initiated movement. 2. Movement resulting from stimuli that originated within the organism, e.g., movement produced by proprioceptive stimuli. 3. More metaphorically, a shift in cognitive or perceptual set brought about by internal, subjective factors.

autokinetic effect A type of apparent motion in which a small, objectively stationary spot of light in an otherwise dark environment appears to move about. The movement may cover as much as 20° of the visual field (i.e. upwards of 40° measured from point of origin) and is apparently not due to eye movements. Also called the *autokinetic illusion* or *phenomenon*.

automatic 1. Self-operating, capable of functioning without external control. 2. Without reflection or thought, spontaneous, involuntary. 3. By extension, machine-like.

automaticity In cognitive psychology generally, the property of a process that it takes place largely independently of conscious control and of attention. In the classic example, the laborious, deliberative process of first learning how to drive a car gradually becomes replaced by the automatic operations of a well-practiced driver who no longer needs to pay close attention to what he or she is doing. The behavior is said to have become *automatized*.

automatic anxiety ➤ **primary anxiety**.

automatic process ➤ **automaticity**.

automatic speech 1. Speech produced without conscious reflection on what is being said. Easily seen with extremely well-learned material, as with counting, saying the alphabet. 2. Speech which emerges devoid of conscious control. It is observed in some psychoses, in advanced senility and, occasionally, in highly emotional states.

automatic writing 1. Writing produced while attending to content and not to the actual process of writing itself. 2. Writing while one's attention is totally devoted to some other task. In experiments on automatic writing the subject's hand is hidden behind a screen to prevent him or her seeing what is being written. For what it's worth, Gertrude Stein did research on automatic writing while in college (and some of her critics say she never abandoned the technique).

automatism Any act performed automatically, that is, without conscious thought or reflection. The term is primarily used for such undirected behavior as is seen in ➤ **psychomotor *epilepsy**. Occasionally it is used to refer to reflexes and for well-learned or habitual acts, although these latter usages are not recommended.

automatism, sensory Illusions or hallucinations produced by extended focusing on an object.

automatization The development of ➤ **automaticity**.

automatograph Any device for measuring and recording involuntary movements.

automaton A machine that acts like a human being. The term has become particularly important in recent years because of the work in ➤ **computer simulation** and ➤ **artificial intelligence**. A merging of physics, mathematics, computer sciences and psychology has produced a general theory of automata which attempts to translate the behavior of machines into the behavior of humans and vice versa.

automorphic perception The tendency to perceive others as similar to oneself. The term is reserved for instances when obvious differences are overlooked or misperceived.

autonomic 1. Self-controlling or self-regulating. 2. Independent. 3. Spontaneous.

autonomic arousal disorder A ➤ somatoform disorder characterized by persistent or recurrent symptoms (other than pain) that can be attributed to autonomic arousal. The systems or organs typically affected include the cardiovascular (e.g. palpitations, fainting), respiratory (e.g., hyperventilation), gastrointestinal (e.g., vomiting, diarrhea), urogenital (dysuria) and the skin (flushing, blushing).

autonomic balance The normal coordinated functioning between the parasympathetic and sympathetic divisions of the autonomic nervous system.

autonomic nervous system (ANS) A major division of the nervous system with two principal subdivisions, the *sympathetic* and the *parasympathetic*. The system is called 'autonomic' because many of the functions under its control are self-regulating or autonomous. The sympathetic division, anatomically, forms a fairly coherent system (see diagram on page 76). Its neurons originate in the thoracic and lumbar regions of the spinal cord (hence it is also called the *thoracolumbar system*) and synapse with the sympathetic chain of ganglia (also called the *paravertebral ganglionic chain*). Depending upon the specific fibers in question, they either ascend or descend with the chain and exit elsewhere, synapse directly in the chain or pass through it to synapse with other ganglia on their way to their target organ. Taken as a whole, the sympathetic division serves 'arousal' functions, as shown in the figure.

The parasympathetic division has two distinct parts. Some fibers originate in the nuclei of the cranial nerves above the sympathetic division and others in the sacral region of the spinal cord below it. The parasympathetic division is involved in digestion and maintenance of functions that conserve and protect bodily function (see figure) and is dominant during quiet, restful periods. Most (but not all) internal organs are served by both divisions of the ANS. Generally, the actions of the two divisions are *antagonistic*; the sympathetic serving when catabolic processes (those involving energy expenditure) are called on and the parasympathetic when anabolic (those involving energy build-up) are needed. However, pure antagonistic functioning is not the whole picture; the two divisions are interactive and 'cooperative' in many ways – for example, during extreme emotion when involuntary discharge of bladder and bowel may occur, or, in the male, during sex, when erection (parasympathetic) is followed by ejaculation (sympathetic).

autonomous Controlled from within, internally directed, self-regulatory. ant., *heteronomous*.

autonomous complex Jung's term for any complex which evolved unconsciously but, with the passage of time, wended its way into consciousness.

autonomy Independence.

autonomy, functional Gordon Allport's term for the tendency for a motive or motivating force to become independent from the original, primary drive that initiated it.

autonomy, group The characteristic of a group to remain relatively independent from or outside of societal pressures.

autopagnosia An inability to name body parts. Patients with this disorder, which is caused by lesions to the left *parietal lobe*, cannot point to their elbow or knee or other body part when asked to and cannot name body parts when they are pointed to. Also called *autotopagnosia*, it is a form of ➤ agnosia.

autophilia ➤ narcissism.

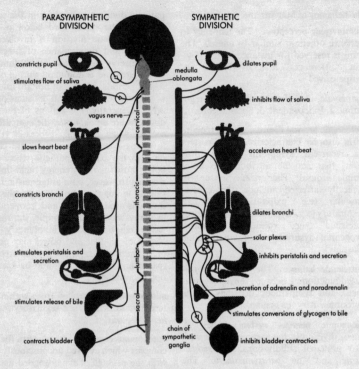

PARASYMPATHETIC
DIVISION

SYMPATHETIC
DIVISION

constricts pupil

stimulates flow of saliva

medulla
oblongata

dilates pupil

inhibits flow of saliva

vagus nerve

cervical

slows heart beat

accelerates heart beat

thoracic

constricts bronchi

dilates bronchi

solar plexus

lumbar

stimulates peristalsis and
secretion

inhibits peristalsis and secretion

stimulates release of bile

secretion of adrenalin and noradrenalin

sacral

stimulates conversions of glycogen to bile

contracts bladder

chain of
sympathetic
ganglia

inhibits bladder contraction

Autonomic nervous system

autoplasty A process by which one's internal psychological system is developed. Autoplastic changes are changes in oneself. Contrast with ➤ **alloplasty**.

autopsychic Descriptive of psychological processes where the primary reference point is in the individual, e.g., delusions are autopsychic. Contrast with ➤ **allopsychic**.

autopsychosis A generic term for a psychotic condition in which the primary symptoms are displayed as disordered ideas concerning the self.

autopsy, psychological A psychological profile developed after the subject's death. The data consist of retrospective analyses of the individual's behavior patterns prior to death collected by reviewing writings

and letters and by interviewing family, friends, co-workers, etc. Such autopsies are usually carried out after suicides and after suspicious cases in which it is not clear whether the death was accidental or self-inflicted.

autoreceptor A receptor molecule on a *neuron* that responds to the *neurotransmitter* that the neuron itself secretes.

autoshaping Automatic *shaping* of an operant response by pairing a stimulus with reinforcement such that the organism is attracted to the *manipulandum*. For example, a pigeon in a Skinner box has a light turned on behind the 'key' (a small plastic disc) every time food is presented. After several dozen such pairings, the pigeon will 'automatically' begin to peck at the key whenever the light comes on even though it has never been specifically reinforced for key pecking.

autosome Any of the paired chromosomes, except for the sex (X and Y) chromosomes.

autosuggestion Lit., self-suggestion. The term comes from a system of self-improvement developed by a Frenchman, Émile Coué (1857–1926), which was very popular in the 1920s and 1930s. The heart of Coué's rather simplistic system was contained in the phrase, 'Every day in every way I am getting better and better,' which he counseled people to repeat twenty to thirty times a day.

autotelic Characteristic of or pertaining to traits and behaviors which are intimately concerned with an individual's purposes and goals, especially those which are self-protective or self-defensive.

autotopagnosia ➤ autopagnosia.

auxiliary 1 adj. Providing support or assistance; helping. 2 adj. Additional, supplementary. 3 adj. Secondary, subsidiary. 4 n. In linguistics, a word with no full meaning of its own but which serves grammatical functions in combination with other words, e.g., conjunctions, prepositions, auxiliary verbs.

auxiliary ego In J. L. Moreno's theory, a person who takes on the role of representing and expressing another person's needs, desires, purposes, etc. Specifically, in a *psychodrama*, one who takes on the role of another person in such a way. For example, the role of the client's father is taken on, but in a manner which reflects the way in which the client sees his or her father.

auxiliary inversion In linguistics, a form of an interrogative in which the order of the verbal auxiliary and the nominal element are inverted, e.g., 'Did she win the race?' Auxiliary inversions yield ➤ yes–no questions.

auxiliary solution Karen Horney's term for a type of ➤ neurotic solution used to

handle, partially or temporarily, conflicts. An auxiliary solution, in her framework, is conceptually similar to a ➤ defense mechanism in that the conflict is not necessarily permanently resolved.

availability 1. In physiology, the extent to which a needed substance is present in a usable form for the tissues under consideration. 2. In studies of memory, the degree to which a particular piece of information can be retrieved from memory. 3. A ➤ cognitive *heuristic in which a decision maker relies upon knowledge that is readily available rather than examine other alternatives or procedures. Although a useful heuristic, it can often lead to erroneous answers to questions or mistaken solutions to problems. For example, when asked whether there are more words in English that begin with the letter 'r' or have 'r' as the third letter, virtually everyone answers 'begin with' despite the fact that there are roughly twice as many words with 'r' in the third position. The error is caused by the fact that words beginning with 'r' are readily available in memory whereas those with 'r' in the third position are not.

average 1. A term which may refer to any one of three measures of ➤ central tendency: the (arithmetic) *mean*, the *median* or the *mode*. In general, when used without further explanation it refers to the mean. 2. Nontechnically: ordinary, typical, representative.

average deviation ➤ deviation, average.

average error ➤ error, average.

average error, method of ➤ measurement of *threshold.

averages, law of 1. The principle that, in the long run, the mean (average) of an extended series of observations may be taken as representing the best estimate of the 'true' value. This generalization is based on the assumption that, with unbiased sampling, the errors that occur will be distributed equally below and above the mean and, hence, cancel each other out. 2. By extension (assuming either a unimodal symmetrical distribution or a very large number of observations), the principle that the mean value will occur more frequently than any other value. **3.** In popular terms, the principle that sooner or later it will all catch up with you.

aversion 1. Originally, a turning away. **2.** Nowadays, a repugnance or dislike for something, an internal negative reaction. This meaning is reflected in a number of combined terms; e.g., ➤ **conditioned *aversion**.

aversion, conditioned A learned ➤ **aversion** (2). A negative reaction toward a stimulus resulting from pairing that stimulus with some other painful or unpleasant stimulus; e.g., ➤ **toxicosis**.

aversion therapy A general term for any of a number of behavior-modification techniques which use unpleasant or painful stimuli in a controlled fashion for the purpose of altering behavior patterns in a therapeutic way. The use of such procedures has been primarily restricted to such disorders as alcoholism and drug abuse (and in a few questionable cases, homosexuality) and, generally speaking, they have not been very successful.

aversive behavior A general term used to describe the study of behavior under conditions of noxious stimulation. Usually the term includes the three major phenomena of *escape learning, avoidance learning* and the effects of *punishment*. Actually, the term is something of an anomaly for there is nothing aversive about the behavior, the interest is in the behavior which occurs under conditions which are aversive.

aversive control In studies of learning, a general term used to characterize any situation where behavior has been brought under control by unpleasant or painful consequences, e.g., *escape learning*.

aversive stimulus Any stimulus which appears to have noxious properties. It is usually identified operationally as any stimulus to which an organism will learn to make some response so as to escape or avoid it, or as any stimulus which when

presented contingent upon a response will produce a lower rate of that response or a cessation of it altogether. This very 'behavioral' definition derives from the simple fact that the term was coined by behaviorists and is used almost exclusively by them.

avoidance–avoidance conflict ➤ **conflict, avoidance–avoidance**.

avoidance gradient The term refers to the increased tendency to avoid a non-desirable goal as the organism gets closer to the goal. This gradient is assumed to be steeper than the *approach gradient*, i.e. negative goals increase in nondesirability with increased proximity more rapidly than positive goals increase in desirability.

avoidance learning (or **conditioning**) A type of instrumental or operant learning in which the subject must learn to make some response to avoid a noxious or aversive stimulus. In the typical avoidance-learning experiment there is a stimulus (e.g., a tone) which signals that the noxious stimulus (e.g., an electric shock) is forthcoming unless the subject makes the appropriate response. If the response is made in time the noxious stimulus does not occur. The assumed reinforcer of such behavior is anxiety reduction. Note that avoidance may be either *active*, when a specific response must be overtly made, or *passive*, when the subject must refrain from making a response which will produce the aversive stimulus.

avoidance response Any 'movement' away from an object or a goal. The notion of 'movement' may encompass anything from overt, physical locomotion away from some object or a metaphorical, covert shift in thoughts, opinions or beliefs.

avoidance rituals E. Goffman's term for the variety of social devices we use to keep social distance between ourselves and others, to maintain a certain formality in social interactions and to preserve individuality. Avoidance rituals and ➤ **pres-**

entational rituals together make up what Goffman called ➤ deference behavior.

avoidant disorder of childhood or adolescence An anxiety disorder in children characterized by persistent and inappropriate shrinking from contact with strangers so severe that it interferes with normal social functioning in peer relationships.

avoidant/insecure attachment ➤ attachment styles.

avoidant-personality disorder A personality disorder characterized by a hypersensitivity to rejection that is so extreme that the individual avoids contacts with others and shies away from forming relationships unless given strong guarantees of uncritical acceptance. There is typically low self-esteem, a tendency to devalue accomplishments and inappropriate distress over personal shortcomings – all accompanied by a desire for affection and acceptance.

avolition Lacking in initiative; the inability to start and persist in goal-directed activity.

awareness 1. An internal, subjective state of being cognizant or conscious of something. 2. Alertness, consciousness. The term has a long history which has found it being used to refer to a wide range of subjective phenomena from simple, primitive detection of very weak stimuli to deep understanding of complex cognitive and affective events. Although it seems clear that the mental processes involved in being 'aware' of the presence of a dim light are fundamentally different from those involved in being 'aware' of the underlying psychodynamic factors which motivate action, the same term is used to cover them all.

awareness, learning without This phrase is often used in discussions of various learning phenomena in which the person is not 'aware' of the behavior or the changes in behavior taking place. There are a number of experimental situations where learning appears to take place without awareness, such as presentation of stimuli under low illumination, concept-formation experiments in which the concept is not easily verbalized, and verbal conditioning studies. It is safe to say that the issue is a highly controversial one and just what each investigator means by 'awareness' is not always clear. For example, a psycholinguist who argues that a person is not aware of the grammatical rules of language means something very different from a psychoanalyst who says that a client is not aware of unconscious attitudes. ➤➤ implicit *learning.

awareness, levels of This phrase has emerged recently because of the recognition that the parent term, ➤ awareness, had accumulated such a wide range of meanings and connotations that confusion was inescapable. Those who use this new term maintain that a variety of levels of awareness exist, ranging from total lack of awareness of events (unconsciousness) to a highly tuned sensitivity to happenings in the environment. A number of more or less synonymous terms are also found, including *states of awareness*, *levels of consciousness*, *states of consciousness*.

awareness, unconscious An oxymoronic term blissfully on its way out of the psychologist's lexicon since it is so clearly a contradiction in terms. Preferred synonyms are ➤ implicit and tacit.

axes Plural of ➤ axis.

axial Pertaining to an ➤ axis, situated in or along an axis.

axial line Any line running along an ➤ axis of the body. Most commonly, the main, *cephalocaudal* axis.

axiom A proposition whose truth is considered self-evident. Axioms are not susceptible to proof or disproof. In logical-theory construction the axioms form the fundamental, primitive elements upon which the whole theory rests. Differentiate from ➤ postulate, in which the truth is not accepted as self-evident and needs to be considered within a chain of reasoning. See the discussion under ➤ assumption. adj., *axiomatic*.

axis 1. A straight line which serves as a reference about which a structure, a figure or its parts may rotate or be conceptualized as rotating. This sense underlies the use of the term: in anatomy, where bodies, organs and their parts may be described with respect to one or more axes; in optics, where lenses may be characterized in terms of lines or passages of light; in chemistry, where arrangements of atoms and molecules are given relative to axes which define planes by which they are defined, etc. **2.** In geometry, one of two (or more, depending on the number of dimensions under consideration) lines which are set to meet each other at a point and which can be used as a reference system to specify the location of any other point. The most commonly used system of axes is the ➤ **Cartesian coordinates. 3.** An underlying dimension, a class of information which may be used to group or to organize data. This meaning is an extension (and a loosening) of that in 2 above and is used in ways similar to ➤ **factor** or ➤ **dimension**.

axis I–V In the **DSM** system of psychiatric classification there are five axes, each designated by a Roman numeral. Axis I notes clinical syndromes, II developmental and personality disorders, III physical disorders and conditions, IV marks the severity of psychosocial stressors, and V is for global assessment of functioning.

axo- Pertaining to ➤ **axis** or to ➤ **axon**.

axoaxonic synapse A synapse of a terminal button of an axon of one neuron upon the axon of another.

axodentrite A neural projection (or *process*) given off by an axon of a neuron.

axodentritic synapse The synapse of a terminal button of the axon of one neuron upon a dendrite of another.

axon A nerve-fiber projection (or *process*) leading from the cell body of a neuron which serves to transmit action potentials from the cell body to other adjacent neurons or to an effector such as a muscle. var. *axone*.

axonal transport The mechanism by which the molecules that participate in the process of synaptic transmission are distributed from the site of synthesis in the cell body to the axon terminal buttons. Compared with ➤ **axoplasmic transport**, it is a rather rapid process, roughly 400 mm per day.

axon hillock The area of a neuron where the axon rises from the soma. It has a lower threshold of excitation than the rest of the axon and an action potential can be readily produced here.

axoospermia Absence of sperm from the semen.

axoplasmic transport The process by which the soluble enzymes within a cell body move to the axonal terminals. Compared with ➤ **axonal transport**, it is very slow, between roughly 1 and 3 mm per day.

axosomatic synapse A synapse of a terminal button of the axon of one neuron upon the cell body (the *soma*) of another.

axotomy Severing of an axon.

azygous Not paired, single.

B

babble Infant vocalizations, presumably produced without any meaning intended. As babbling gradually begins to include sounds typical of the speech environment and to be used for communication, various qualifiers are used, e.g., *directed babbling, controlled babbling*, etc. It is worth noting that even the profoundly deaf infant will babble for the first few months of life in a manner difficult to distinguish from that of normal-hearing infants.

Babinski reflex An upward extension of the toes upon stroking the sole of the foot. A normal reflex in infants but a symptom of certain classes of organic disorders in adults.

Babkin reflex In the newborn, a reflexive opening of the mouth to pressure on the palms.

baby talk A basically silly term with two opposing denotations: **1.** The speech *of* very young children. **2.** The speech of adults and other children *to* very young children. ➤ **motherese**.

background **1.** A person's collective experiences in life as they pertain to some task or job. **2.** The total environmental setting preceding an event. **3.** Any second sensory stimulus, as in 'background music.' **4.** The set of objects and surfaces in the rear of a visual stimulus, the largely undifferentiated portion that contains no figure. ➤ **figure-ground**.

backward Occasionally used to characterize one with mild retardation, e.g., a backward child. n., *backwardness*.

backward association ➤ **association, backward**.

backward conditioning An experimental conditioning procedure in which the conditioned stimulus (CS) follows the onset of the unconditioned stimulus (UCS) rather than preceding it. There is some dispute as to whether conditioning can occur with this arrangement. Contrast with ➤ **delay, simultaneous** and **trace conditioning**.

backward masking ➤ **masking**.

backward reading ➤ **palinlexia**.

bad A term used frequently in clinical psychoanalysis to qualify the unpleasant, feared or malevolent aspects of a psychodynamically important object. Thus, the *bad* mother is the image of the punishing, love-withholding, persecuting mother.

bait shyness A somewhat restrictive term that is used to refer to a particular instance of ➤ **toxicosis**.

balance Any state in which all opposing forces are equalized is said to be 'in balance.' The term is descriptively useful in aesthetics, the study of social interactions, investigations of emotional states, etc. Probably the most common use is in reference to the maintenance of upright posture.

balanced bilingual ➤ **bilingual, balanced**.

balanced scale Any scale (or test or questionnaire) in which items with any potential source of bias are balanced. For example, half of the items may be presented as 'true' and half as 'false,' or, in the case of Likert-type scales, half have the 'positive' or 'most agree' pole on the left side of the page and half have this pole on the right side.

balance theory A general theory of attitudes and attitude change due originally to F. Heider. The main assumption is that a person will seek to resolve or relate attitudes that are 'out of balance' with each other. The term is often used somewhat more broadly as a label for a number of theories that put forward explanations of human behavior in terms of the re-establishment of some form of psychological balance, e.g., theories based on ➤ **cognitive dissonance** or on ➤ **psychological*reactance**.

Balint's syndrome A neurological disorder characterized by three primary symptoms, ➤ **optic *ataxia**, ➤ **ocular *apraxia**, and ➤ **simultanagnosia**, each of which is a disorder of spatial perception. The syndrome is caused by bilateral damage to the parieto-occipital region of the brain.

ballism A motor disorder (i.e. a *dyskinesia*) characterized by violent flailing movements. It is due usually to damage to one of the subthalamic nuclei associated with the ➤ **basal ganglia**. When only one side of the body is affected it is called *hemiballism*.

ballistic Pertaining to or characteristic of the motion of projectiles. The eye movements known as *saccades* are often referred to as ballistic movements because the eye seems to 'throw itself' to its next fixation point. Such movements are easily seen in normal reading of printed materials.

band score In much of the work in tests and measurements a sense of the error variance in a test score is provided by reporting not a raw score but a band score. Thus a person who scored, say, 53% on a particular test would be reported as falling within the band 50%–56%, indicating that a 3% error is not unusual. Band scoring was developed to prevent overinterpretation of scores known to be inexact and variable.

bandwagon effect A social phenomenon wherein people feel pressured to conform with a particular attitude or opinion when it is perceived as being held by a majority of persons in their group or society.

bandwagon technique A propaganda device in which it is claimed that a majority of people hold a position or belief so as to persuade others to adopt that position or belief.

bandwidth In acoustics: **1.** The frequency range of a sound signal. **2.** The frequency range of an instrument or device which

responds to a sound signal.

baragnosis An inability to provide accurate estimates of the weights of lifted objects. Usually a result of lesions of the parietal lobe. Distinguish from ➤ **barognosis**.

Bárány test (or **method**) Bodily rotations of a subject in a special chair (the standard method is one full rotation every two seconds for 20 seconds) so that each of the semicircular canals ends up in a plane at right angles to the direction of rotation. Such rotation produces a characteristic pattern in ➤ **nystagmus**, which can be studied to determine whether the vestibular apparatus is functioning properly.

barbiturate abuse Generally, chronic, pathological use of barbiturates or similarly acting hypnosedatives to the point where the individual cannot stop or reduce the dosage, is intoxicated throughout the day and experiences disturbed and impaired social/occupational functioning as a result.

barbiturate amnestic disorder ➤ **sedative, hypnotic,** or **anxiolytic amnestic disorder.**

barbiturates A very large group of drugs classified as ➤ **hypnosedatives**. Of the over 2,500 barbiturates which have been synthesized, roughly 15 are currently used, in a variety of conditions, including (most commonly) as an aid for sleeping, as an anesthetic and in the symptomatic treatment of epilepsy. Generally, barbiturates depress the activity of all excitable cells, although since the brain is particularly sensitive to them the therapeutic doses in use have negligible effects on other tissues. Barbiturate-induced sleep appears superficially normal but *REM-sleep* (➤ **sleep**) is known to be significantly reduced. Depending on dosage, the effects range from mild sedation, through hypnosis, general anesthesia, coma and ultimately death. As with other drugs which depress central-nervous-system activity, the effects are magnified by alcohol and alcohol–barbiturate poisoning is a significant cause of death both accidental and deliberate.

Barbiturates can be divided into three classes, depending on speed and duration of action. The long-acting include *phenobarbital* and *mephobarbital*. These produce their effects slowly (approximately one hour after ingestion) and last roughly 8–12 hours. The intermediate-acting (15–30-minute onset time; 3–5-hour action) include *pentobarbital*, *secobarbital* and *amobarbital*. The ultra-short acting (1–2 seconds; 15–30 minutes) include *thiopental* and *methohexital*. Those in this last group are used primarily as anesthetics and administration is usually intravenous. With long-term use all the barbiturates produce ➤ **tolerance** as well as both psychological and physiological ➤ **drug *dependence**. These drugs, particularly the long-acting varieties, are sometimes classified as ➤ **antianxiety drugs**. See here ➤ **sedative, hypnotic, or anxiolytic withdrawal**.

barbiturate withdrawal ➤ **sedative, hypnotic, or anxiolytic withdrawal**.

barbiturate withdrawal delirium ➤ **sedative, hypnotic, or anxiolytic withdrawal delirium**.

baresthesia (or **baresthesis**) The sense of pressure or weight. var., *baraesthesia*.

bargaining As a social psychological term it encompasses all of those processes used by two or more persons or groups in their attempts to settle the give-and-take involved in a transaction between them. Buried in this definition are a host of critical variables which affect the bargaining process, such as expected outcomes (e.g., ➤ **mini-max**), gain and loss factors (➤ **payoff matrix**), personality factors (e.g., ➤ **internalization, face-saving**). Bargaining is a problem that has fascinated political scientists, mathematicians and economists for many years but has only fairly recently come under careful scrutiny by psychologists.

bar graph (or **chart** or **diagram**) ➤ **histogram**.

Barnum effect This term honors the master entrepreneur, showman and charlatan, P. T. Barnum, best known for his aphorism, 'There's a sucker born every minute.' It refers to the fact that a cleverly worded 'personal' description based on general, stereotyped statements will be readily accepted as an accurate self-description by most people. This principle is behind the fakery of fortune-tellers, astrologers and mind readers and has often contaminated legitimate studies of personality assessment.

bar(o)- Combining form meaning *weight, pressure*.

barognosis The ability to estimate reliably the weight of lifted objects. Distinguish from ➤ **baragnosis**.

baroreceptor Specialized receptors that respond to changes in barometric pressure. Found primarily in the blood vessels and the heart.

barotaxis An automatic orienting response to a pressure stimulus as displayed, for example, by fish species which swim with (or against) water currents.

barotitis Inflammation of the ear caused by sudden shifts in barometric pressure. It is a not uncommon outcome of an airplane flight, especially if one has an upper respiratory infection which constricts the Eustachian tube and prevents normal adjustment of the ear to pressure shifts.

Barr bodies Spots at the edge of the nucleus of cells from individuals with more than one X chromosome, and hence used to determine chromosomal sex. Barr bodies are found in normal females (XX) but are missing in those with ➤ **Turner's syndrome**. They are also observed in abnormal males, e.g., those with ➤ **Klinefelter's syndrome**.

barrier Any impediment or block preventing an organism from reaching a goal. Although the barrier is often physical it is not improper to refer to barriers which result from an individual's emotional or mental limitations or, more metaphorically, those which are of purely psychological origins.

bar(y)- Combining form meaning *weighty, heavy, dull*.

baryecoia Partial deafness, hardness of hearing.

baryglossia Lit., thick tongue. Hence, slow, thick speech.

barylalia Indistinct 'thick' speech, poor articulation.

baryphonia Difficulty in producing articulate speech. var., *baryphony*.

basal 1. Of primary importance. 2. Pertaining to the base of a thing.

basal age ➤ **age, basal**.

basal forebrain region A brain area just rostral to the *hypothalamus*. It has been implicated in the control of sleep in that destruction of this area produces total insomnia, a condition which causes death in but a few days.

basal ganglia Three large, subcortical nuclei including the *caudate nucleus*, *putamen* and *pallidum* (or *globus pallidus*). These structures and several associated midbrain and subthalamic structures make up the *extrapyramidal system* and are intimately involved in movement. Lesions in the basal ganglia and/or the complex interconnections which they form with the *cortex*, the *subthalamic nucleus*, the *red nucleus*, the *substantia nigra* and the *spinal cord* have been implicated in a variety of motor disorders, including Parkinson's disease, Huntington's disease and Sydenham's chorea.

There are various conventions for labeling parts of the basal ganglia: the caudate nucleus and putamen, being composed of identical cell types, are collectively called the *neostriatum*, with the pallidum being referred to as the *paleostriatum*; the putamen and pallidum, because they together form a lens-shaped structure, are occasionally referred to collectively as the *lenticular nucleus*; the *amygdala* (or amygdaloid complex) is occasionally included as one of the basal ganglia because of its anatomical proximity, although properly it is part of the *limbic system*.

basal metabolism rate (BMR) Measured in calories, it is the minimum energy output needed for minimum bodily functioning. The BMR is calculated by evaluating minimum heat production while the person is at rest some 16 or so hours after eating.

base line 1. The abscissa. 2. ➤ **base rate**. When **2** is the intended meaning, the spelling is usually as one word, *baseline*.

basement effect ➤ **ceiling effect**.

base rate Generally, the normal frequency of occurrence of any response, statistic or other measure per unit of time. Base rates are used as foundations against which to evaluate effects of specific manipulations. For example, in assessing a new reading curriculum one would compare the new reading scores against the base rate prior to its introduction; in operant-conditioning studies, the effects of a novel reinforcer would be evaluated by comparing the new response rate with the base rate responding prior to its introduction. See here ➤ **operant level**.

base-rate fallacy The tendency to ignore the base-rate at which events occur when making decisions. It is surprisingly common; e.g., lotteries survive because people believe they have a much higher chance of winning than the base-rate predicts; more people are afraid to fly than drive despite the much higher base-rate of death on the roads than in the skies.

basi-, baso- Prefixes denoting *base* or *walking*.

basic Pertaining to a base, *fundamental*, *foundational*; occasionally, *primitive*.

basic anxiety Horney's term for a child's feelings of being helpless and isolated. It is assumed to arise from anything which interferes with or disrupts security. This concept is the primary one in her theory of personality development. It is the strategies which the individual develops to deal with basic anxiety which become the fundamental components of personality.

basic conflict Horney's term for the fundamental conflicts that emerge when ➤ **neurotic needs** are discoordinate. In her

84

system, needs are classified into three groups: those involving movement toward people; those involving movement away from people; and those involving movement against people. A basic conflict will emerge if needs from two or three of these groups are activated simultaneously.

basic (level) category ➤ natural *category (2).

basic mistrust ➤ basic trust.

basic need Generally and loosely, any need based on primary, physiological factors; any need vital for survival. See also discussion under ➤ basic needs.

basic needs In Maslow's theory of personality, the primary human needs including those which are physiologically based, like food, water, avoidance of pain, etc. (➤ fundamental needs) and those which are psychologically based, such as security, affection, self-esteem, etc. (➤ intermediate needs). These needs are also termed *deficiency needs*, on the assumption that if the object of need is missing the person will seek to make up for the deficiency. Maslow also assumed that basic needs have a priority hierarchy such that some take precedence over others; when food is missing there is little concern for self-esteem. ➤➤ meta needs, need hierarchy.

basic rest-activity cycle (BRAC) A cycle approximately 90 minutes long in which the body's alertness waxes and wanes. The cycle is controlled by cells in the caudal brain stem. During sleep the BRAC controls the cycles of ➤ REM and ➤ slow wave *sleep. ➤➤ biological clock.

basic skills In education, those skills deemed fundamental for further education and essential for learning other subjects; most commonly included are reading, writing and arithmetic.

basic trust The early development of a sense of fundamental trust in the environment. The concept is fundamental in Erik Erikson's theory of psychosocial development: the first life crisis occurs during the first year and a half, during which the presence of a loving, reliable and responsible caretaker leads to the development of a sense of security and basic trust in the environment whereas unreliable, uncaring and irresponsible caretakers lead to development of anxiety, suspicion and *basic mistrust*. ➤ stages of man.

basilar artery The artery at the base of the brain which connects the blood supply of the vertebral artery and the carotid artery.

basilar membrane A delicate membrane in the cochlea of the inner ear on which the ➤ organ of *Corti is located. It varies in width, stiffness and mass along its length from the base (near the stapes) to the apex. Different portions of the membrane vibrate to different frequencies. The pattern of vibration is central to pitch perception, with the narrow end nearest to the stapes showing maximum displacement to high-pitched tones and the broad, far end showing maximum displacement to low-pitched tones. ➤➤ theories of *hearing.

basket cell A type of interneuron found in the outer layer (the molecular layer) of the cortex of the cerebellum.

basket endings Sensory receptors in the skin, found near the base of the hair follicles. There is some evidence that they respond to touch and pressure stimuli, although such specificity of function is an equivocal issue with the skin senses.

basolateral group The phylogenetically newer part of the ➤ amygdala.

bathy- Combining form meaning *deep*.

bathyanesthesia Loss of deep sensitivity.

bathyesthesia Deep sensitivity. Used for sensitivity in body parts under the skin, in muscles, internal organs, etc.

battered child Any child who has been repeatedly subjected to severe physical beatings and abuses by parents or guardians. ➤ child abuse.

battery (of tests) ➤ test battery.

battle fatigue A term introduced during

BAYES' THEOREM

World War II for what was known earlier as *shell shock* and is now called ➤ **combat fatigue**. ➤➤ **gross *stress reaction**, of which it is an example.

Bayes' theorem The relation among the various conditional probabilities of various events that gives the probability that a particular event (*A*) is a result of one (*X*) of a number of mutually independent events (*B, C, D, . . . , Z*) which might have produced A. The theorem has been used as a model of attitude formation and choice behavior since it provides a mathematical rule for deciding how one's prior opinion or choice(s) should optimally be modified in light of new evidence.

Bayley Scales of Infant Development One of the most commonly used of the ➤ **developmental scales** for assessing the status of infants and young children. The revised version is normed on children from ages 1 to 42 months and uses four scales: *motor quality, attention/arousal, emotional regulation* and *orientation/ engagement*. The test is usually called 'the Bayley' for short.

beat A periodic fluctuation that is heard when two tones of slightly different frequencies are sounded at the same time. The number of these 'beats' heard per second corresponds to the difference in Hz between the frequencies of the two tones. ➤➤ **combination tone, difference tone**.

Beck Depression Inventory (BDI) A self-report inventory for assessing depression. Developed by Aaron T. Beck, the American psychiatrist who is generally regarded as the father of ➤ **cognitive therapy**, it is based on a series of key aspects of behavior and emotion where the individual selects the statement or statements that apply. For example, the person selects one (or more) of four statements concerning decision-making that range from 'I make decisions about as well as I ever could' to 'I can't make decisions at all any more.'

bedlam Originally derived from the Middle English pronunciation of the Hos-

pital of St Mary of Bethlehem ('be*d*lem'):
1. An asylum for the mentally disturbed.
2. Any raucous, noisy place or situation.

bedwetting ➤ **enuresis**.

behavior A generic term covering acts, activities, responses, reactions, movements, processes, operations, etc., in short, any measurable response of an organism. There has been a long (and agonizing) tradition of attempting to put some set of coherent limits on the boundaries of denotation of this term. Doubtless, much of it derives from a well-meant but basically hopeless attempt to define psychology as 'the science of behavior,' a definitional gesture that has resulted in a fascinating kind of futility. The problem has been that as the range of phenomena included within the domain of psychology has increased there has been a need to expand the boundaries of what can be legitimately called 'behavior.'

A quick overview of the history of the discipline reveals that, in general, which activities get included in the class of things called 'behaviors' depends on whether and how they are measurable. For example, strict behaviorists in the tradition of Watson and Skinner tend to include only those responses which are overt and objectively observable. Thus, they would exclude covert mental constructs of consciousness like schemas, ideas, strategies, memories, images, etc. (except as they are manifested in overt behavior). Such an approach, however, leaves out much of what seems essential to an understanding of human behavior and few psychologists today feel comfortable with such a rigid definition of behavior. A more moderate compromise position is that taken by the so-called neo-behaviorists, who permit the inference of internal states, intervening variables, hypothetical constructs, mediational processes and the like. Still behaviorist in their overall approach, such theorists would insist that postulating these covert 'behaviors' is only legitimate when they can be linked with measurables. Still more flexible in their definition of behavior would be those inclined toward a cognitive or mentalistic approach. Here the essence of the 'behavior' is its mental representation rather than the overt measurable behavioral acts. From this perspective the actions and processes of mind are included as aspects worthy of examination. For example, language is studied here with reference to underlying knowledge of rules of grammar and the knowledge itself is the critical feature, not the overt utterances that people may be observed to produce.

Finally, there is the long-standing dispute as to whether or not physiological, neurological processes qualify as 'behavior.' Here the same kind of historical pattern can be discerned. So long as these internal operations were relatively coherent and specifiable (e.g., muscle actions, reflex arcs, glandular secretions) early theorists felt comfortable calling them behaviors. But as the scope of investigation has expanded to include the detailed study of such things as electroencephalography, the relationships between particular neurotransmitters and specific neural pathways, etc., the issues are certainly less clear.

What we have here is a conflict between, on one hand, the deep-felt need to keep psychology objective and precise and, on the other, to extend its domains into cognition and neurophysiology so as to account for what organisms do. The casualty has been, of course, the term *behavior* itself. It is used today in a manner that reflects the theoretical point of view of its user and no longer can be said to have a clear denotative domain. ➤➤ **behaviorism**. var., *behaviour*.

behavioral Pertaining to behavior. Most typically used to characterize or refer to an analysis (theoretical or empirical) carried out the basis of objective behavior. Contrast with ➤ **dynamic**; compare with ➤ **structural**. var., *behavioural*.

behavioral assessment (or **diagnosis**) A general procedure for diagnosing and evaluating psychological disorders by focusing on direct observation and self-reported measures of adaptive (or non-adaptive) functioning. The critical feature which distinguishes this approach from the traditional dynamic or analytical approaches is that interpretive or indirect-assessment techniques are not used.

behavioral clinic ➤ **clinic, behavioral**.

behavioral (or **emotional**) **contagion** ➤ **contagion, behavioral**.

behavioral contract In ➤ **behavior therapy**, a technique in which a contract, typically involving the members of a family, is developed that stipulates responsibilities that the client has and the privileges that he or she is permitted given their fulfillment.

behavioral contrast A phenomenon first reported by G. S. Reynolds. In certain two-choice discrimination situations he found that increases in response rate to one stimulus (S_1) produce decreases in response rate to the other stimulus (S_2) and vice versa. In the typical experiment the introduction of a different schedule of reinforcement for S_1 to either increase or decrease response rate to S_1 produced an opposite (contrasting) change in response rate to S_2. A clear theoretical account of these behavioral-contrast effects is not presently available since classical learning theory should predict the opposite result.

behavioral-directive therapy A general term used of any of a variety of behavior therapies all of which share the assumption that neurotic or maladaptive behaviors can be objectively treated independently of the rest of the client's personality. The term is used by some as synonymous with ➤ **behavior therapy**; other authors will use it as the cover term with behavior therapy considered as but one form of the behavioral-directive therapies.

behavioral dynamics A term used rather loosely to refer to the underlying dynamic structure of motives which, in the psychodynamic approaches, are assumed to be ultimately responsible for observed behaviors of people.

behavioral ecology ➤ **ecology, behavioral**.

behavioral genetics The interdisciplinary science focusing on the study of the relationship between genetics and behavior. This definition uses few words but marks an enormously complex field of endeavor which involves the many techniques of genetic analysis and the scientific analysis of the full range of behavioral manifestations of species.

behavioral homology ➤ **homologous** (2).

behavioral integration ➤ **integration, behavioral**.

behavioral medicine A medical speciality based, in large measure, on the integration of research findings, methods and theory from the social sciences and the more traditional biological, anatomical approaches. The approach has its roots in earlier work on the *psychosomatic* aspects of disease but is a much more vigorously interdisciplinary and open approach to the interactions between mind and body and their impact on disease and health.

behavioral momentum Generally, within Skinnerian behaviorism, resistance to any change in the schedule of reinforcement, including extinction.

behavioral oscillation A term used by Clark Hull to characterize momentary fluctuations in ➤ **reaction potential**. Behavioral oscillation is assumed to be normally distributed. Abbv. $_sO_r$.

behavioral science A general label attachable to any of a number of sciences that study the behavior of organisms including psychology, sociology, social anthropology, ethology, and others. Often used as a synonym for social *science*.

behavioral sink The disorganized and aberrant environment that some theorists feel is an outcome of severe overcrowding. The original studies that led to the coining of the term were carried out with rats and mice which were kept in very crowded cages for extended periods of time. While it seems quite clear that such species are subject to severe disruption of normal behavior under such conditions, current thinking on the problem counsels against extrapolating these findings with rodents

in crowded cages to theorizing about humans in high-density urban environments as some less cautious persons have done. See here ➤ **crowding**.

behavioral teratogens ➤ **teratogen**.

behavior analysis Within the Skinnerian behaviorist tradition, breaking down complex behaviors into their functional parts.

behavior control One of Skinner's favorite phrases. It is used to refer to the general notion that behavior is under the control of the contingencies of reinforcements and stimulation. In the larger perspective of operant theory, behavior control is one of the primary objectives of a scientific psychology.

behavior determinant In Tolman's learning theory, any variable which is causally related to ('determines') behavior.

behavior disorder A very general term used for any aberrant or maladaptive pattern of behavior that is sufficiently severe to warrant the attention of counselors or therapists. The term is preferred over any number of others previously used in this fashion, e.g., *neurosis*. ➤ **disorder** for a discussion of the changing patterns of usage here.

behavior disorders of childhood A general psychiatric label for a number of disturbed behavior patterns found in children and adolescents. Syndromes in this group are less severe than psychoses but considered to be serious enough to warrant therapy. Behaviors commonly cited here are delinquency, overaggressiveness, frequent running away from home, stealing, etc.

behavior episode A term used (rather loosely) for a 'unit' of behavior, a sequence of actions which has some reasonably well-defined beginning and ending.

behaviorism That approach to psychology which argues that the only appropriate subject matter for scientific psychological investigation is observable, measurable behavior. Although flirtations with such a position go back to Hobbes, it was with

John B. Watson in the 1910s (➤ **Watsonian**) that true behaviorism was born. In his polemical reaction to the subjectivism of introspectionism, Watson maintained that a proper scientific approach is one that limits behavior to specific peripheral muscular and glandular responses and regards consciousness and mental states as epiphenomena. This point of view is often dubbed *radical behaviorism* to distinguish it from other, more moderate orientations (e.g., ➤ **neo-behaviorism**). It is represented in contemporary thinking by the perspective of B. F. Skinner (➤ **Skinnerian**)– but with an important difference. Whereas Watson's approach focused on the acts themselves, a perspective that attracted Watson to the work of I. P. Pavlov, whose Russian version of behaviorism was oriented toward physiology and reflexive actions (➤ **Pavlovian**), Skinner's approach is rather pointedly concerned with the *effects* that acts have on the environment. By shifting the focus in this fashion Skinner circumvents (or attempts to circumvent) the problems associated with the determination of exactly what a ➤ **behavior** is (see that term for discussion).

In addition to these points of view, various other positions are sufficiently close to them to have been (occasionally without their defenders' agreement) represented as forms of behaviorism. Included here are Clark L. Hull's neo-behaviorist approach (➤ **Hullian**) and Edward C. Tolman's purposive psychology (➤ **Tolmanian**).

Behaviorism (in any of these guises) was largely an American pastime. Europeans who got involved in the disputes tended to be those with a more philosophical background, such as Gilbert Ryle who, in his attempts to push behaviorism as far as it could go, also helped to reveal its limitations.

Today most psychologists feel uncomfortable with radical behaviorism; there seems to be something unsatisfying about excising the causal role of internal, covert or mental processes in explanations of what it is people do. Yet, in a sense, since all agree that what people *do* is the ulti-

mate test, we still carry the vestiges of behaviorism no matter what general paradigm we may work within. This last point reflects the point of view of those who like to argue that we are all *methodological behaviorists*.

behaviorist One who espouses the theoretical and methodological positions of ➤ **behaviorism**.

behavioristic Pertaining to ➤ **behaviorism**. Generally distinguished from ➤ **behavioral**.

behavior method Generally, the approach to the study of psychological processes that relies strongly on the analysis of overt behavior and rejects mentalistic analyses. The term is typically reserved for those who favor this kind of focus but wish not to be affiliated with the specific position of ➤ **behaviorism**.

behavior modification The process of changing (modifying) a person's behavior. The term is generally used synonymously with ➤ **behavior therapy**.

behavior problem A person, usually a child or adolescent, whose behavior is persistently antisocial. That is, a behavior problem is a person who exhibits ➤ **problem behavior**.

behavior rating Generally, any description or characterization of the overt, observable behavior of a specific subject in a particular situation. The term is restricted to reports which deal only with behavior (who did what, to whom, when, etc.) and not with interpretations of possible underlying motives or personality traits or the like.

behavior sampling ➤ **sampling, behavior**.

behavior setting The general, ecological milieu within which behavior takes place.

behavior therapy That type of psychotherapy that seeks to change abnormal or maladaptive behavior patterns by the use of extinction and inhibitory processes and/or positive and negative reinforcers in classical and operant conditioning situations. The focus is on the behavior itself rather than on some analytical or dynamic analysis of underlying conflicts or other root causes. The argument put forward by the behavior therapists derives from the tenets of behaviorism; in a nutshell, that behavior derives from contingencies of reinforcements and particular responses made in the presence of stimulus situations. Hence, all behavioral disorders are assumed to result from 'unfortunate' contingencies in the life of the individual leading to the acquisition of maladaptive behaviors. There is no need to explore underlying conflicts; effective therapy should aim at modification of the behavior(s) that the client currently manifests. A large array of specific therapeutic procedures and modification techniques exists; e.g., ➤ **assertiveness training, desensitization technique, implosion therapy, reciprocal inhibition, token economy**. ➤➤ **cognitive behavior therapy**.

being-beyond-the-world Within existentialism, the notion that one has responsibility for the possibility of going beyond the (limited) momentary realities of one's existence. Failure to fulfill (or to attempt to fulfill) these potentialities is, in existential analysis, a prime component of feelings of guilt. See and compare with ➤ **being-in-the-world**.

being-in-the-world This term is the generally accepted translation of Heidegger's term *Dasein*. This awkwardly hyphenated phrase is used primarily within the existentialist framework, where it represents the central idea of that philosophy, that one's totality is given by the immediate and inevitable phenomena which comprise the reality of the moment. This phenomenological world is conceptualized as comprising (a) the biological and physical (*Umwelt*), (b) the human and social (*Mitwelt*) and (c) the personal (*Eigenwelt*). ➤➤ **existentialism, existential therapy**.

bel ➤ **decibel**.

belief Generally used in the standard dictionary sense for an emotional acceptance of some proposition, statement or doctrine. ➤➤ **attitude, opinion**.

belief systems ➤ **conceptual systems**.

belief–value matrix Tolman's term for an organism's learned expectations (belief) about the values of objects in the environment and the roles they play with respect to behavior.

belladonna ➤ **atropine**.

belle indifférence, la French for *sublime indifference*. Used of various psychiatric conditions in which the patient seems blithely and inappropriately unconcerned about his or her disabilities. Most commonly seen in ➤ **conversion disorders**.

Bellevue scale ➤ **Wechsler–Bellvue scale**.

Bell–Magendie law The principle, first announced by Bell in 1811 and later (1822) by Magendie, that the ventral roots of the spinal nerves are motor in function and the dorsal roots are sensory. Incidentally, it is Magendie who really deserves credit for this finding. Bell's earlier work was rather poorly done and his conclusions wrong; in fact, he had it backward, claiming that the ventral roots were sensory and the dorsal motor.

bell-shape curve A somewhat substandard term sometimes applied to the normal-frequency distribution because it nicely describes its general shape.

belongingness 1. One of E. L. Thorndike's supplementary principles of learning, it assumes that stimuli are more likely to become associated if they are related to each other in some fashion. In recent work on learning this principle has been 'reactivated' for it is now quite clear that the basic principles of classical and operant conditioning are incomplete without some recognition of the relationship that exists between the items to be associated and the specific properties of the organism undergoing the learning experience. For an example of this principle, see the description of learned taste aversion discussed under ➤ **toxicosis** (2). **2.** In social psychology and sociology, the feeling of inclusion or acceptance by a group.

belongingness, principle of The generalization that an array of stimulus elements will be more likely to be perceived or reacted to as a whole if the elements 'belong' to each other in some recognizable fashion.

Bem Sex Role Inventory A scale developed by S. Bem for measuring the extent to which an individual displays traits or behavioral characteristics traditionally associated with the masculine and/or feminine poles of sex-role identification. The scale is based on 20 items highly associated with the traditional societal view of masculinity (e.g., athletic, dominant, risk-taking) and 20 items similarly associated with femininity (e.g., affectionate, gentle, yielding). The inventory also produces an *androgyny scale*, which reflects the extent to which the testee balances between identifying with the classic masculine and classic feminine traits.

Bender Gestalt Test A test developed in the 1930s by L. Bender. Although there are a number of administrative variations available, the typical procedure is to present the testee with 9 relatively simple standard designs and ask him or her to copy them. The results are interpreted on the basis of the quality of the reproductions, the manner of organization of each copy and the pattern of spatial errors made. Bender originally conceptualized the test as a maturational test for use with children and as a device for exploring regression or retardation and detecting possible brain damage. Today, it is used predominantly for detection of organic cerebral damage. The name of the test derives from the fact that Bender was an advocate of ➤ **Gestalt** psychology and used Gestalt principles in the construction of the test. Also called *Bender Visual Motor Gestalt Test*.

beneffectance The tendency to interpret events in ways that make one's own position or actions seem more favorable, to take credit for things that turned out successfully but to share or even deny responsibility for things that were failures. The term was constructed out of a blending of

beneficial and *effectance* and is used primarily for the process by which an individual egocentrically alters memories of past events so as to increase his or her role in positive events and diminish it in negative ones.

Benham's top A disc, half black, half white with four sets of three curved lines drawn on the white half. When rotated the disc demonstrates a visual anomaly; although itself colorless, colors can be observed. When rotated in one direction the colors appear in spectral order from center to edge, when rotated in the opposite direction the order of colors is reversed.

benign Characteristic of a condition with a good prognosis; one which is nonprogressive and with a hopeful outcome. The term is used for both physical and psychological conditions. Contrast with ➤ **malignant**.

Benzedrine ➤ **amphetamines**.

benzodiazepines A major group of ➤ **antianxiety drugs** including **diazepam** and **lorazepam** that have tranquilizing effects and help to reduce the experience of anxiety. They work by activating the benzodiazepine receptors so that they increase the sensitivity of the ➤ **gamma-amino butyric acid (GABA)** receptors with which they are coupled. Benzodiazepines are most effective against generalized anxiety disorders and have little or no effect on *panic disorder*, *obsessive-compulsive disorders* or *phobic disorders*.

bereavement The emotional reactions felt following the death of a loved one. A full depressive syndrome is considered normal in such a loss and is often accompanied by poor appetite, insomnia and preoccupations with a sense of worthlessness.

berdache 1. Originally, a North American Indian who assumes the manner of dress, life style and sex roles of a member of the opposite sex. **2.** More loosely, a ➤ **transvestite**.

Bernoulli distribution ➤ **binomial** *distribution*.

Bernoulli trial Any trial or situation with two mutually exclusive and exhaustive possible outcomes; e.g., head/tails in a coin flip. A series of Bernoulli trials yields a ➤ **binomial distribution**.

Bernreuter Personality Inventory A personality questionnaire consisting of 125 yes–no items. Factor analysis of the inventory reveals six basic scales, neuroticism, introversion (these two tend to be highly correlated), self-sufficiency, dominance, confidence and sociability.

best fit ➤ **goodness of fit, least squares**.

bestiality 1. Most broadly, any beastly behavior of a person. 2. More specifically, sexual behavior between humans and animals. The latter is the usual meaning. ➤ **zooerasty, zoophilia**.

beta endorphin The most potent of the known ➤ **endorphins**.

beta error ➤ **error, Type I (and Type II)**.

beta motion ➤ **motion, beta**.

beta response In classical eyelid conditioning, a response that occurs shortly after presentation of the conditioned stimulus but anticipatory to the unconditioned stimulus. It is assumed that this is the 'true' conditioned response. Contrast with ➤ **alpha response**.

beta rhythm (or **wave**) A pattern of electrical activity of the brain characteristic of the normal, awake, active person. On the EEG (➤ **electroencephalogram**) it is a wave of somewhat lower amplitude but higher frequency (roughly 17–25 Hz) than the ➤ **alpha rhythm**.

between-group variance ➤ **variance, between-group**.

between-subjects design A research design in which different groups of subjects are run under different conditions. Compare with ➤ **within-subjects design**.

Betz cells Large motor neurons in the precentral gyrus of the frontal lobe of the cerebral cortex and in the motor cortex.

They are involved in mediation of voluntary motor activity.

Bezold-Brücke effect Changes in perceived hue with changes in luminance. Specifically, yellowish reds and yellowish greens are perceived as yellower with increases in illumination and bluish reds and bluish greens appear more blue. Purer reds, yellows, greens and blues do not show this effect.

bi- Prefix denoting *both, two, double, twice*.

bias 1. An inclination toward a position or conclusion; a prejudice. 2. A statistical sampling error; a *biased sample* is one that is not representative of the population about which inferences are to be made. 3. Any systematic factor in an experimental situation that introduces error. 4. As borrowed from *signal detection theory*, any preference for one choice or response over other choices, such as the often observed tendency to select 'heads' over 'tails' in coin flipping. 5. In testing, any aspect of a test which yields differential predictions for groups of persons distinguishable from each other by a factor which, in principle, should be irrelevant to the test. For example, an IQ test which predicted different success rates for blacks and whites with the same measured IQ would be biased in this sense. Needless to say, such a testing bias would render a test useless. 6. A lack of fairness. Often used with qualifiers to specify the type of bias; ➤ e.g., **interviewer bias, response bias, volunteer bias**.

biased sample (or **sampling**) ➤ **biased *sampling**.

bidirectional activational models In the study of ➤ **pattern recognition**, models in which elements are activated and inhibited by both ➤ **bottom-up** and ➤ **top-down processing** operations.

Bidwell's ghost ➤ **Purkinje afterimage**.

bifactor method A procedure in *factor analysis* which extracts a principal factor first and then extracts other factors. The first factor is one which loads on all the subtests and, hence, is taken by some to represent a general factor; the factors extracted later load on isolated clusters and are regarded as of secondary importance.

bilabial A speech sound produced by bringing the two lips together; e.g., [b] in *bat*, [m] in *mat*.

bilateral Having two sides, pertaining to both left and right sides. The general construction of the anatomy and nervous system of most organisms displays *bilateral symmetry*: the left and right sides are more or less mirror images.

bilateral transfer ➤ transfer, bilateral.

bilingual 1 adj. Characteristic of one who is able to speak two languages with approximately equal fluency. **2** n. A bilingual person, in sense 1. ➤ **bilingualism** for discussion of definitional problems.

bilingual, balanced A bilingual who is (approximately) equally fluent in both languages.

bilingual, compound (and **coordinate**) See discussion under ➤ **bilingualism**.

bilingualism The simple definition, fluency in two languages, leaves much unspecified that needs specification. One problem is that what qualifies as 'fluency' is left dangling. Usually the user of the term will specify whether the persons under consideration are bilingual on the basis of some criterion such as reading/writing skills, speaking ability, translating between the languages, etc. A second important issue concerns the conditions under which the two languages were learned. According to a commonly used system of classification, a person who acquires both languages in the same context (e.g., a home where both are spoken interchangeably) is called a *compound bilingual*, one who learns each language in a different setting (e.g., one at home, the other in school) is a *coordinate bilingual*.

bilingual, unbalanced A bilingual who is considerably more fluent in one of the two languages spoken.

bimodal Characteristic of any frequency distribution that has two points or scores that share the property of having the greatest number of cases, that is, a distribution with two ➤ **modes**. Note that the term is used loosely, in that the two modes need not have exactly the same frequency; there needs only to be two points reasonably remote from each other that show a clear concentration of scores.

binary-choice Generally used to characterize decision-making situations in which the subject is confronted with exactly two alternative responses one of which must be made.

binary number system A number system with only two digits, 1 and 0. This system is used extensively in information theory and computer sciences. As the normal decimal system is coded so that each displacement to the left means multiplication by ten, here each displacement means multiplication by two. The following are the decimal-binary equivalents for 1 through 10: $1 = 1$; $2 = 10$; $3 = 011$; $4 = 100$; $5 = 101$; $6 = 110$; $7 = 111$; $8 = 1000$; $9 = 1001$; $10 = 1010$.

binaural 1. Of, or pertaining to, the functioning of both ears simultaneously so that the same input reaches both ears at the same instant. **2.** More generally, pertaining to two ears. Compare with ➤ **dichotic**.

binaural beat ➤ binaural shift.

binaural fusion ➤ fusion, binaural.

binaural ratio The ratio between the physical intensities of sound at the two ears.

binaural shift A term that refers to the phenomenon that when each ear is presented with one of two tones of slightly different frequencies under properly controlled conditions the perceived point in space where the sound is localized seems to shift back and forth. The rate of shift is controlled by the frequency difference. Also called *binaural beat*, which is slightly misleading since ➤ **beat** generally does not involve spatial localization.

binaural time difference The differences

in time of arrival and in intensity of a sound reaching both ears. Such differences are the major cues for sound ➤ **localization**. Also called, simply, *binaural difference* (without the *time*) since the intensity difference is not necessarily entailed by the temporal factors.

binding site That region of the post-synaptic receptor where the *neurotransmitters* attach.

Binet (or Binet–Simon) Scale The first scale of intelligence for schoolchildren, issued by A. Binet and T. Simon in France in 1905 and revised by them in 1908, and again in 1911, adding a set of age norms. The Binet Scale is significant because it was the first of the mental tests to focus on the higher mental functions of cognitive capacity rather than upon the more primitive operations of sensory abilities, reaction times, discrimination, etc. The scale has been revised many times and adapted for many different cultures, the most thorough being that of A. Terman at Stanford University. Still, the origins are honored in name, and casual reference to a 'Binet' is laboratory jargon for the popular *Stanford–Binet Scale* of intelligence.

binge eating ➤ **bulimia nervosa**.

binge-eating disorder An eating disorder marked by binge-eating and related distress similar to that seen in ➤ **bulimia nervosa** but without the self-induced vomiting and purging.

binocular Of or pertaining to the simultaneous functioning of both eyes.

binocular cue Any visual cue for depth perception that requires both eyes, e.g., *retinal disparity*. Compare with ➤ **monocular cue**.

binocular disparity ➤ **disparity, retinal**.

binocular fusion ➤ **binocular rivalry**.

binocular perception ➤ **perception, binocular**.

binocular (or retinal) rivalry A perceptual phenomenon that occurs when the proximal stimuli to the two retinae cannot be resolved into a single percept. The effect may be produced, for example, by presenting a field of blue to one eye and a field of yellow to the other eye. The resulting perception is an irregular alternation from the inputs of the two eyes so that the subject sees first blue then yellow then blue, etc. When the subject can resolve the two different inputs into a single percept (which, of course, is the normal state of affairs) the term *binocular* (or *retinal*) *fusion* is used.

binocular vision ➤ **vision, binocular**.

binomial 1 n. An algebraic expression containing two terms. The binomial expansion is the binomial raised to an arbitrary power, or, e.g., $(p + q)^n$. As the value of n increases the binomial approximates the normal distribution. 2 adj. Characteristic of a thing with two forms.

binomial distribution ➤ **distribution, binomial**.

bio- Combining form meaning *life* or indicating a *relationship to life* or the *living*.

bioacoustics A hybrid field of study borrowing from zoology, biology, physics and psychology which investigates the acoustic communication systems of non-human species.

biochemical antagonism ➤ **antagonism, drug**.

biocybernetics An area of research concerned with the relationships between consciousness and biological functioning. The main interest is in the ways in which people may become aware of and ultimately learn to control biological events which normally are not within the scope of consciousness (e.g., alpha waves, blood pressure, etc.). The 'cybernetics' refers to the frequent use of computers or other devices to provide the feedback to the subject about these biological events. ➤ **biofeedback**. ➤➤ **cybernetics**.

bioenergetics 1. Originally, the study of energy transfer between living systems. 2. A term used for a form of psychotherapy derived from the theories of Wilhelm

Reich. Contemporary advocates of the bioenergetic approach have, by and large, rejected Reich's *orgone* hypothesis but have retained the focus on organismic function and its relationship to emotional stability and well-being. ➤➤ **biofunctional therapy**.

bioethics A field of study concerned with issues of ethics and values as they relate to medicine and related sciences such as biology, physiology, psychology, etc.

biofeedback Information feedback about bodily function. Most biofeedback is mediated through normal sensory channels, e.g., if you close your eyes and hold your arm out away from you, *kinesthetic* feedback informs you of your arm's position and allows you to make adjustments to perform some task. Recent research has shown that biofeedback from an outside source can also be used to enable an organism to modify its functioning. For example, when EEG (➤ **electroencephalogram**) feedback is provided people can maintain some degree of control over their alpha waves. Similar manipulations have been performed with heart rate, blood pressure, blood flow in the extremities, etc. Note that some have taken to using the term as though it meant the direct control of internal, autonomic functions and activities. It should not be used in this fashion. It is merely a descriptive term for the process of providing an organism with information about its biological functions. ➤ **biofeedback therapy**. ➤➤ **biocybernetics**, **feedback**.

biofeedback therapy The use of ➤ **biofeedback** in a fashion that has therapeutic function, as for example, developing a program for a person with hypertension to lower their blood pressure.

biofunctional therapy A cover term for any psychotherapeutic approach that operates on the assumption that bodily functions are primary and that the mental and psychosocial components are secondary. Although pure biofunctional approaches are few (see, e.g., ➤ **bioenergetics, orgone therapy**), many, more eclectic, approaches,

particularly those of the ➤ **human potential movement**, incorporate some aspects.

biogenesis 1. Loosely, the origin and subsequent evolution of the living. **2.** In the phrase, *principle of biogenesis*, the doctrine that living things are begotten from living things which are similar in form and structure; the denial of spontaneous generation.

biogenic 1. Characteristic of or pertaining to processes by which living things give rise through reproduction to other living things. **2.** Characteristic of or pertaining to aspects of behavior which are biological or organic in origin.

biogenic amine hypothesis The general hypothesis that imbalances in the physiology and metabolism of several of the ➤ **biogenic amines** are critical components in the pathogenesis of various psychotic disorders. The amines most suspect are the catecholamines *norepinephrine* and *dopamine* (➤ **catecholamine hypothesis** and ➤ **dopamine hypothesis**) and an indoleamine, ➤ **serotonin**.

biogenic amines Several groups of amines that are of particular interest because of their role in neural functioning. Included are the ➤ **catecholamines**, the ➤ **indoleamines** and ➤ **histamine**.

biological clock A hypothesized biochemical mechanism that is responsible for the control of the behavioral systems which show periodicity. For example, ➤ **biorhythm, circadian rhythm**. Actually, the notion that each organism possesses a single biological clock that monitors the environment and controls all biorhythms is most certainly an oversimplification; it seems clear that there are multiple control systems operating for various functions. Also called *endogenous clock*.

biological memory ➤ **memory, biological**.

biological psychiatry An approach to psychiatry that emphasizes the biological, physical and neurological aspects of behavioral disorders and focuses on pharmacological treatment.

biologic rhythms ➤ **biorhythms**.

biologism The use of biological principles as a basis for describing and explaining human behavior. The term is never used by those who engage in such a theoretically oriented exercise; it is employed disparagingly by the critics of this approach.

biomedical therapy (or **treatment**) An umbrella term used to cover any form of psychotherapy based on biological techniques. Included are the various forms of drug therapies, electroconvulsive shock therapy, and psychosurgery.

biometry (or **biometrics**) The use of mathematical and statistical procedures for the study of organisms.

bionics The study of living systems with emphasis on the construction of artificial systems which will simulate their functions and characteristics.

bionomics Synonym for ➤ **ecology**.

biopsychology ➤ **psychobiology**.

biorhythms A general label covering all forms of periodicity of biological systems. The most intensely studied are the ➤ **circadian rhythms**, although many biological functions show a period other than a daily one, for example, menstrual cycles, bird migrations, protective-coloring changes, etc. Note that in recent years this term has become 'contaminated' by the emergence of a pseudoscience of the same name. Using the so-called 'biorhythm method' its practitioners claim to be able to predict a person's performance on a task on any given day, on the basis of a chart of their biorhythms from their day of birth. An utter lack of supportive evidence for these claims has, predictably, had little impact on public acceptance but it has led scientific researchers to cast about for a new label for their field – ➤ **chronobiology** being the most recent candidate recommended. ➤➤ **biological clock**.

biosocial Characteristic of those features of behavior that are a result of interactions between social and biological factors. The classic example is sexual behavior.

biosphere 1. The portion of the earth that supports life. 2. The environment, particularly when it is characterized and described as an ecosystem, a domain for the support of life. 3. A. Angyal's term for the holistic entity containing the individual and the total environment. In his *organismic* theory the biosphere included the whole person, encompassing the biological, psychological and sociological aspects.

biostatistics 1. ➤ **vital statistics**. 2. The use of statistical procedures and techniques in the study of living organisms.

biotope An ethological term used to describe an area with an overall similar environment. Within any given biotope there may be several habitats or more restricted, specialized environments.

biotransformation Generally, any alteration in a substance within the body.

biotransport ➤ **transport**.

biotype 1. The genetic constitution of an organism and all those who possess it. 2. By extension, a group of organisms with a shared complex of genetic factors.

bipolar 1. Lit., having two poles. The term is used broadly, so the notion of 'pole' here can be taken in several ways. It can be used rather precisely to denote the end point(s) on a well-specified dimension or it can be used somewhat more loosely for two processes or branches of something, or two more-or-less opposed reactions to a person or an event. Hence: 2. In the study of personality, descriptive of traits which are expressible as opposite ends of a single dimension. For example, dominance and submission are considered to be bipolar traits in that they are clear and independent opposites. Note, however, that superficially opposite traits like leadership and followership are generally not called bipolar since good leaders often are good followers, thus the 'negation' of one does not imply the other. 3. In neurophysiology, shortened form of ➤ **bipolar cell** or **bipolar neuron**. 4. An electrode with two poles, one negative and one positive;

such electrodes are commonly used in stimulating and recording from neural tissue.

bipolar affective disorder ➤ **bipolar disorder**.

bipolar cell (or **neuron**) Any neuron with two extensions or processes (axon and dendrite) running in opposite directions from the cell body. Almost always sensory in nature, they are found extensively in the retina where they form connections between the receptors and the ganglion cells. ➤ **unipolar cell, multipolar cell**.

bipolar disorder A major ➤ **mood disorder** in which both manic and depressive episodes occur, i.e. both poles on an affect dimension are manifested. Several subtypes are distinguished and marked as *manic*, *depressed* or *mixed* depending on the currently presenting symptoms; see the following entries for details. Also known as *bipolar affective disorder*, and in some older texts, *manic-depression* and *manic-depressive disorder*. In the most recent texts, owing to the introduction of ➤ **bipolar II disorder**, this condition is often noted as *bipolar I disorder*.

bipolar II disorder A mood disorder where, unlike ➤ **bipolar disorder**, the mood swings are between intense depression and ➤ **hypomania** rather than a full blown ➤ **mania** (2). As with the 'regular' bipolar disorder, the drug of choice is *lithium*.

bipolar disorder, depressed A type of bipolar disorder in which there has been at least one manic episode but the current presenting (or most recent) symptoms are those of a *major *depressive episode*.

bipolar disorder, manic A type of bipolar disorder in which the most recent extreme affective disturbance has been a manic episode: ➤ **mania** (2).

bipolar disorder, mixed A type of bipolar disorder in which the full symptomatic picture of manic and depressed episodes is seen either intermixed or alternating every few days or in which the depressive symptoms predominate although some manic components are observed.

bipolar rating scale ➤ **rating scale, bipolar**.

birth control A very general term used to cover any procedure or practice used to control the number of conceptions and births. The term is not synonymous with *contraception*, but the latter is included as one method of birth control along with, among others, the intrauterine device (IUD) and abortion. Moreover, some authors also use the term to include procedures and techniques for planning and facilitation of conception and birth. ➤ **contraception** for further discussion.

birth cry The reflex crying which accompanies the beginning of natural respiration immediately following birth.

birth defect Generally, any congenital abnormality. The term is used to cover defects which are genetic (e.g., *phenylketonuria*) as well as those that are a result of environmental factors (e.g., defects caused by the mother's ingestion of harmful substances during gestation).

birth injury Any injury to the infant which occurs during birth; ➤ **birth trauma** (2). Distinguish, however, from ➤ **birth trauma** (1).

birthmark A congenital disfiguration; e.g., a *nevus*.

birth order The chronological order of birth of children in a given family. There are small but real correlations between birth order and several other factors such as IQ, eminence, and socioeconomic success, with the first born generally showing a mild advantage.

birth, preterm Birth before the completion of the full, normal gestation period, i.e. prior to the 37th week. ➤ **premature infant** where the definition is more in terms of development than of chronology.

birth rate The number of live births per 1,000 people in the total population. Usually given per year.

birth trauma 1. As argued primarily by Otto Rank, the original and pervasive assault upon the psyche occasioned by being summarily expelled from the comfort of the womb into a hostile, nongratifying world. Rank went on to argue (unconvincingly) that all anxiety neuroses stem from this universal experience. Note, however, that, despite the failure of most theoreticians to be convinced by Rank's thesis, it is still true that many if not most of those with a psychoanalytic orientation assume that the sudden assault of the real world upon the previously protected fetus has lasting effects. The difficulty of such a position is that since everyone is subjected to the same experience it is impossible to establish its true impact on development. To do that we would need subjects who were 'not of women born' to compare the rest of us with. **2.** ➤ **birth injury**.

bisection, method of Bisection simply means cutting into two parts. There are two special references of the bisection *method*: **1.** In neurophysiology the technique of severing one or more of the commissures of the brain to produce a split-brain preparation. **2.** In psychophysics, see the discussion under ➤ **methods of *scaling**.

biserial correlation ➤ **correlation, biserial**.

bisexual 1 n. ➤ **Hermaphrodite** (2) **2** n. An individual whose sexual preferences include members of his or her own sex as well as members of the opposite sex. ➤➤ **heterosexual, homosexual**. **3** adj. Characteristic of such a person. **4.** Occasionally, a synonym for *ambisexual*. This usage is no longer recommended because of the above, much more common, meanings. The state of bisexuality (in senses 2 and 3) is also called *amphigenous inversion*.

bit A contraction of the words '*bi*nary dig*it*.' A bit is a 'piece' of information given as the amount necessary to reduce the alternatives in a choice situation by one half. Hence, if you have four alternatives and are provided with information that eliminates two of them, you have received one bit of information.

bite 1. In operant conditioning a sudden

reduction in response rate followed by a compensatory increase will, when presented in a graph of cumulative responses, make it look like a 'bite' has been taken out of the otherwise smooth curve. Hence, the term has been more or less jokingly adopted to denote this pattern of responses. ➤➤ **knee. 2.** ➤ **byte**.

bite bar A rigid plate which a subject can bite down on firmly so that the head is held steady. Bite bars are commonly used in visual research so that the subject does not move his or her head about needlessly and the experimenter has control over where in the visual field a stimulus is presented.

bitter One of the four primary taste qualities. ➤ **taste** for further discussion.

bivariate Pertaining to conditions where there are exactly two variables.

bivariate association Any statistical relation between two variables; e.g., *product moment correlation*.

black In vision, an achromatic sensation represented as the lower limit in the lightness dimension along the white-gray-black continuum. The percept black, however, is often a relative phenomenon. An object will appear black when it is subjected to low light-levels while surrounded by a relatively brightly illuminated background. The same stimulus may appear to be a neutral or even light gray if this pattern is reversed.

black box A term derived from physics where it was used to stand for a model of the functioning of any complex system based on the hypothesizing of constructs, mechanisms and procedures internal to the system. The basic notion here is that when one cannot know precisely what is inside a system causing it to function in the way it does, one treats it as though it were an impenetrable 'black box' and makes inductive interpretations about its internal properties. The black box then becomes a model of the system and a representation of it that can, in theory, account for how the system functions given the various inputs to it and the observed outputs from it. The use in psychology is obvious: merely let the complex system under examination be an organism. Note that the black box is never empty; it is populated, often richly, with structures, constructs, operations and the like. Some, usually behaviorists who have an aversion for hypothesizing internal mechanisms or for what Skinner called 'spurious physiologizing', have called their approach *black box psychology*. This, of course, is a misuse of the original meaning of the term. See here ➤ **empty organism**.

Black English A label commonly used for the dialect of American English spoken by many Americans of African descent. The term needs to be used with considerable care. While there is an identifiable dialect here with its characteristic patterns of pronunciation, a few syntactic devices not found in other dialects and, of course, a substantial number of specific semantic and idiomatic usage patterns, it is simply not the case that all American Blacks use it. Moreover, there are a number of other regional dialects in the USA, particularly in the South, which have similar dialect features. When used by the experts, the term usually relates to the particular linguistic patterns observed among Black Americans from large urban centers where the divergences between this dialect and the so-called ➤ **Standard English** spoken by the remainder of that particular geographical unit are most evident. Finally, it must be emphasized that there is no evidence whatsoever that suggests that Black English is in any way deficient in communicative or expressive function. There is no disagreement on this point among scholars (despite some unfortunate erroneous statements to the contrary by the uninformed).

blackout 1. Generally, temporary loss of consciousness. 2. The amnesia experienced by some serious alcoholics where they have no memory for a period of time during which they were extremely intoxicated. Such alcoholic blackout periods can be up to several days in duration.

blame avoidance (need) H. Murray's term for, quite literally, the need to avoid blame, a motive for acting in a socially accepted manner so as to avoid censure, disapproval, punishment, etc. Note that Murray, for completeness, also hypothesized a *blame escape need* for a motive which operates when one has not succeeded in avoiding blame and is impelled to flee a situation (physically or psychologically) to escape further censure.

blame escape (need) ➤ **blame avoidance**.

blank trial 1. A trial in an experiment on which some irregular stimulus conditions are introduced. It serves to keep the subject from making automatic responses and to keep attention focused on the task at hand. ➤ e.g., **catch trial**. 2. A trial in an experiment in which reinforcement or information feedback is not forthcoming.

-blast(o)- Combining form meaning *primitive cell, bud, germ*.

blending The synthesis of phonetic elements. The term is used to describe an aspect of the phonic approach to the teaching of reading in which the child is taught letter-sound correspondences and how to synthesize them. Note that blending is more than speeding up the pronunciation of the phonic pattern; the word 'bat' is made up of the phonetic elements buh-ah-tuh but the proper rendering of it is not a rapid pronunciation of buh-ah-tuh (which actually consists of five phonemes and three syllables) but a shingling and synthesizing of the three phonemes / b /, / a /, and / t / to produce the single syllable 'bat.'

blind 1. Lacking in vision, without sight. ➤ **blindness** for discussion of criteria for proper use of this term. 2. Without awareness. See here ➤ **blind analysis**.

blind alley A passage or arm of a maze that is a dead end, also called a *cul-de-sac*.

blind analysis Generally, any analysis carried out without knowledge about conditions or information which might lead to biases in interpretation. For example, in a 'blind' clinical diagnosis the psychologist or psychiatrist would proceed without knowing the results of any other diagnosis that may have been made; a 'blind' analysis of test protocols would be carried out without knowledge of the person from whom they were taken, etc. For extensions of this basic notion see ➤ **double-blind**.

blindness This term is often misused in that it is thought to refer to complete lack of vision. Strictly speaking, there is a continuum of loss of vision and the point at which a person is considered blind is usually a legal problem. The standard generally adopted is of visual acuity of less than 20/200 after correction or the visual field restricted to 20° of arc or less. Moreover, blindness can include a variety of highly specific defects such as loss of vision in one area of the visual field, loss of sensitivity to particular hues, diminished ability to see in low illumination, etc. The following entries describe the more common forms.

blindness, cerebral (or **cortical**) Blindness resulting from a brain lesion.

blindness, functional *Psychogenic* blindness; loss of vision in the absence of any known organic dysfunction. Also called *hysterical* or *psychic blindness*.

blindness, psychogenic Blindness which is psychological or functional in origin.

blindsight L. Weiskrantz's term for 'sight' or better, 'visually guided behavior' that is controlled by stimuli that fall within blind areas (➤ **scotoma**) of the visual system. In such cases the patient displays the capacity to respond to visual stimulation that he or she is not conscious of seeing.

blind spot The small spot on the retina that is insensitive to light. It is at this point that the neural fibers leave the eyeball to form the optic nerve; there are no photo receptors here. The blind spot is located in the horizontal plane about 12–15° of arc toward the nose from the *fovea*.

Also called the *optic disc*.

blink reflex Reflexive closing of the eye lid induced by a bright light, a sudden noise, a puff of air, etc. It has been extensively studied in classical conditioning investigations.

blob A region in the primary visual **cortex** containing **neurons** that are sensitive to specific wavelengths. Part of the ➤ **parvocellular system**, it was given its peculiar name because when stained it appears as a 'blob.'

block 1. Most generally, any obstruction or barrier which prevents a process from occurring. The term is used broadly to cover physical barriers which impede flow through a passage (arterial block), biochemical agents which prevent neural transmission (nerve block or neural block), and psychogenic barriers (emotional blocks). **2.** An abrupt cessation in the flow of some ongoing process. Usage here is generally restricted to processes like speech and thought. ➤ **blocking. 3.** A failure of memory in which the retrieval of information is somehow thwarted. E.g. ➤ **tip-of-the-tongue state. 4.** A group or sequence of trials in an experiment.

block design An experimental design in which subjects are distributed into distinct groups ('blocks') so that each is representative of the population. Each block of subjects is then subjected to particular experimental manipulations. The name for this design comes from agricultural research in which a large area was divided into sub-plots or 'blocks.'

block-design test Any performance (i.e. nonverbal) test using colored blocks or tiles with which the subject is required to match or copy given designs.

block diagram ➤ **histogram**.

blocking 1. Generally obstructing or inhibiting of an ongoing process of thought or language. Most people experience it as a kind of *lacuna*, an absence of processing. **2.** In conditioning, a circumstance where, if an association is first formed between two stimuli (x and y) and then later a compound stimulus ($x + z$) is associated with y, the association between z and y tends not to be learned. That is, it is 'blocked' by the previously established link between x and y.

block sampling ➤ **sampling, block**.

blood–brain barrier A selectively permeable 'barrier' between the circulating blood and the brain which functions by preventing some substances from reaching the brain. The barrier is thought to consist partly of cells making up the walls of the capillaries in the brain. Astrocytes (a type of ➤ **glia**) are hypothesized to function as 'directors' of the growth of capillaries so that they form especially narrow openings which act as the barrier. The blood–brain barrier is selective in that some substances cross it while others do not and it is not uniform throughout the system. See, e.g., the ➤ **area postrema**, where the barrier is more permeable.

blood levels A phrase used to refer to the concentration of a substance in the blood.

blood pressure The pressure exerted by the blood on the artery walls. There are two measures: *systolic*, the maximum pressure produced by the contraction of the left ventricle, and **diastolic**, the minimum pressure when the heart muscle is relaxed.

blue One of the four primary colors. It is experienced when the normal eye is stimulated by a light of approximately 470–75 nm.

blue (color) blindness ➤ **tritanopia**.

blue-yellow (color) blindness ➤ **dichromacy**.

blunted affect A disturbance in ➤ **affect** characterized by sharply reduced intensity of emotional expression.

B-lymphocytes ➤ specific *immune reactions.

BMR ➤ **basal metabolism rate**.

body 1. Generally, in physical or anatomical terms the principal part of a thing, the primary, central portion of an organism, the soma of a cell, a coherent organized collection of tissue, an organ, a small structure within a larger one, etc. 2. In statistics, the main, central component of a distribution; everything but the *tails*. 3. In metaphysics, the material substance of an individual. See here ➤ **mind–body problem**. Many combined terms in psychology expressing these meanings are found; some use *body* (e.g., body type) but many others use either the Latin form *corpus* or the Greek form *soma* as the base.

body-build index Eysenck's measure of body type based on the ratio between one's height and chest circumference. Those within the 'normal' range are called **mesomorphs**, those a standard deviation or more above the mean **leptomorphs**, and those a standard deviation or more below it, **eurymorphs**. See also the discussion under ➤ **constitutional theory**.

body dysmorphic disorder A ➤ **somatoform disorder** characterized by preoccupation with an imagined defect in appearance. The most common complaints involve skin spots, wrinkles, excessive hair (typically facial), and shape of the nose or mouth. Occasionally the term **dysmorphophobia** is used although it is not recommended since the disorder is properly not a phobia.

body image (or **concept**) The subjective image one has of one's own body, specifically with respect to evaluative judgements about how one is perceived by others and how well one is adjusted to these perceptions. Some use the term only for physical appearance, others include judgements concerning body functions, movement, coordination, etc. Disturbed or inappropriate body image is an aspect of many neurotic disorders; see, e.g., ➤ **anorexia nervosa** where it is a hallmark symptom.

body language The complex system whereby information about feelings and emotions is communicated through nonverbal channels involving gestures, body position, facial expressions and other *para-*

linguistic devices. Despite the often misleading and trivial discussions about it that have unfortunately impressed themselves upon the lay public, it is possible to approach this topic in a reasonable and scientifically responsible fashion. E.g., ➤ **kinetics, nonverbal communication**.

body type ➤ somatotype.

bogus pipeline In social psychology, an experimental procedure in which subjects are (mis)informed that their true attitudes can be measured using direct physiological methods. Under these conditions (provided, of course, that they do not figure out the ruse), they tend to respond more honestly than they normally would, especially about socially sensitive attitudes they may hold.

bond 1. n. Generally, a connection or link between things. Hence: **2.** n. The hypothetical link between a stimulus and its associated response, the so-called **associated bond** or **S-R bond**. **3.** An emotional connection between persons. Used here of adults as well as children; see, e.g., ➤ **attachment, pair-bonding**. **4.** A force which binds atoms or molecules together. **5.** The biochemical or biomechanical link between a transmitter substance and its receptor site on a neuron. vb., *to bond* or *to bind*.

bonding Generally, the forming of a relationship. More specifically, that between the mother and her newborn. Some use the term as a synonym for ➤ **attachment** (2); others distinguish it as a separate process that occurs during the first few hours after the birth of the infant.

bone conduction The conduction or transmission of vibrations through the bones of the skull. A bone-conduction test indicates whether sound is mediated without conduction through the ossicles of the middle ear. It enables the audiologist to determine whether a hearing loss is due to defective conduction in the outer or middle ears or to nerve damage in the inner ear.

Boolean algebra Named after its devel-

oper, the English mathematician George Boole, this is basically a system of symbol manipulation that uses algebraic procedures but independently of specific mathematical interpretations. Boolean logic or calculus (as it is also called) has been applied extensively in the computer sciences and in psychology in work on artificial intelligence. These applications are interesting in that Boole conceptualized his original work as representing the operations of basic principles of thought.

boomerang effect A shift in attitude which not only goes against what was intended but actually is in the opposite direction. Most commonly used in attitude-change studies in which a person's attitude is not moved in the intended direction but further away. It is not an uncommon outcome of excessive and insensitive attempts to dissuade persons from prejudices they hold. Also called *negative attitude change*.

bootstrap This term is generally used for operations whereby one uses existing knowledge or information to develop more powerful routines which are then, themselves, used in similar fashion so that the system 'lifts itself by its own bootstraps.' Although no organism or machine can literally bootstrap itself, the term is used metaphorically in cognitive psychology and artificial intelligence to characterize theoretical procedures in which the system (organic or mechanical) 'builds' useful structures for more powerful procedures than were originally programmed (genetically or artificially) into it.

borderline adj. Of or pertaining to cases which are difficult to classify because they lie near to the boundary that separates the categories. Its most frequent use is for equivocal diagnoses of personality disorders and mental retardation, as exemplified by the following entries.

borderline intelligence A term introduced in an attempt to specify the level of intellectual capacity that would differentiate those who were capable of functioning normally and independently in the world from those who would need some form of institutional assistance. The term specifically refers to individuals who are right at the division between these two classes. Occasionally it is used 'quantitatively' by citing IQs in the 70–84 range as defining this category – with the understanding that determination of the capacity to function cannot be made responsibly on the basis of IQ score but requires individual assessment of social, emotional, familial and legal issues. Also called *borderline mental retardation*; see here the discussion under ➤ **mental retardation**.

borderline personality disorder A ➤ **personality disorder** in which the individual chronically lives 'on the borderline' between normal, adaptive functioning and real psychic disability. Usually such a person is identified by any of a number of instabilities with no clear features; e.g., interpersonal relations tend to be unstable, affect shifts dramatically and inappropriately, self-image may be disturbed, displays of anger and temper are common, impulsive acts which are self-damaging like gambling or shoplifting are frequent, boredom can become endemic, etc.

borderline schizophrenia ➤ **schizophrenia, borderline**.

bottom-up processing In cognitive theory, when a process is assumed to be determined primarily by the physical stimulus it is often called by this term. The notion is that the person deals with the information by beginning with the 'raw' stimulus and then 'works their way up' to the more abstract, cognitive operations. Also known as *data-driven processing*. Compare with ➤ **top-down processing**.

boufée delirante A ➤ **culture-specific syndrome** observed in French-speaking areas in West Africa and Haiti. It is characterized by a sudden outburst of agitated and aggressive behavior, marked confusion and occasionally, *hallucinations* and *paranoid ideation*.

boulimia ➤ **bulimia nervosa**.

boundary In addition to the standard dictionary meaning, the term was used by K. Lewin in his topological personality theory. It stood for any hindrance or impediment to the person moving (metaphorically) from region to region in the ➤ **life space**.

bounded rationality ➤ **rationality, bounded**.

bound energy A psychoanalytic term used occasionally for the ego's energy supply. The notion of being 'bounded' derives from the metaphoric role of the ego as being reality-directed and neither wasteful nor frivolous with its energy.

bouton terminal French for ➤ **terminal button**.

bow motion (or **movement**) ➤ **motion, bow**.

bow-wow theory ➤ **theories of *language origins**.

BRAC ➤ **basic rest-activity cycle**.

brachy- Prefix meaning *short*.

brachycephalic Disproportionately short head. ➤ **cephalic index**.

brachymetropia Nearsightedness; ➤ **myopia**.

brady- Prefix meaning *slow*.

bradyacusia Poor hearing.

bradyarthria Abnormally slow and hesitating speech.

bradyesthesia A general term for any reduced perceptual functioning.

bradyglossia An abnormal slowing of speech.

bradykinesia Slowness of motor movements.

bradylalia Slowness of speech.

bradylexia Abnormally slow reading. The term is reserved for cases where the slowness is deemed not to be due simply to overall low intellectual functioning. ➤ **dyslexia**.

braidism An occasional synonym for

103

hypnotism; taken from the name of the English surgeon James Braid.

braille (or **Braille**) A touch-based writing and reading system in which patterns of raised dots are used to represent letters and numerals. Named for its developer, the blind French educator Louis Braille.

brain Simply, that part of the central nervous system encased within the skull. Brain functions are discussed under separate entries dealing with individual parts of the brain.

brain center Any one of a number of areas in the brain in which there are complex interconnections between afferent and efferent fibers. The term has two distinguishable uses. It is used to refer to explicit and identifiable structures such as the hypothalamus and also to refer to hypothetical groups of neurons assumed to control a particular function, such as the speech center.

brain death This phrase refers to the circumstances in which standard electroencephalographic (EEG) data indicate that key components of the brain are no longer functioning. This criterion has been put forward in recent years as the best one for the determination of death, largely because sophisticated life-support systems can keep other organs (heart, lungs, kidneys) functioning and, hence, previously used criteria such as lack of breathing, undetectable pulse, etc., can no longer serve as reliable indicators of death.

brain lesion Any damage to brain tissue produced by injury, disease, surgery, etc. ➤ **lesion**.

brain potential The electrical potential of the brain or the electrical activity of the brain (see here ➤ **electroencephalogram**). Although the term is often used colloquially to mean intellectual potential, it is not used in this sense in the technical literature.

brainstem That part of the brain that is left when both the cerebrum and cerebellum are removed.

brainstorm A sudden insightful idea, usually accompanied by a compelling emotional reaction.

brainstorming A group problem-solving technique in which everyone sits around and lets fly with ideas and possible solutions to the problem at hand.

brainwashing Metaphorically speaking, a systematic attempt to alter a person's ideas, attitudes and beliefs. Actually, the term is used two ways. The dominant use is, as above, with respect to beliefs; the other use is with respect to behavior. This second meaning derives from the work in cognitive dissonance which indicates that changing a person's behavior may produce changes in their beliefs. The term itself, however, derives from a translation of a Chinese colloquialism and first came to be studied after experiences of prisoners of war. Whether such emotional 'laundering' has lasting effects, particularly after the person has returned to his original environment, is open to question.

brain waves Spontaneous electrical discharges of the brain as recorded by an EEC. See discussion under ➤ **electroencephalogram**.

Brawner decision A legal decision regarding the use of an ➤ **insanity defense** in the USA. It states, 'a person is not responsible for criminal conduct if at the time of such conduct as a result of mental disease or defect he lacks substantial capacity either to appreciate the wrongfulness of his conduct or to conform his conduct to the requirements of law.' Compare with ➤ **McNaghten rule**, ➤ **Durham rule** and ➤ **ALI defense**.

Brazelton Scale ➤ **Neonatal Behavioral Assessment Scale**.

breakthrough In psychotherapeutic work, a progressive quantum step in the client's attitudes, reactions, behaviors, feeling of self, etc. The term is generally reserved for such changes when they occur after long periods of no progress.

breast In classical psychoanalytic writings, the term refers to both the anatomical part and to a symbolic representation of it in the mind. In the latter (and psychoanalytically interesting) sense the breast becomes the focus of oral wishes, the source of psychic nutrition, the object which satisfies needs. In short, it becomes the mother but without the personhood of the real mother.

breathing related sleep disorder ➤ **apnea**.

bregma The juncture in the skull where the sagittal and coronal sutures meet.

brief depressive disorder, recurrent A *mood disorder* characterized by recurrent ➤ **major *depressive episodes** that are relatively short-lived (i.e., less than two weeks in duration).

brief psychotherapy A general term used to cover any psychotherapy which is specifically designed to be relatively short in duration. Most such therapeutic programs are quite goal-oriented and the aims are typically well specified; e.g., eliminating a particular phobia.

brief psychotic disorder An acute psychotic disorder with the defining feature that the duration is of no more than two weeks. The diagnosis is made when the individual showed normal adaptive functioning prior to onset and when the episode was precipitated by an identifiable and serious psychologically stressful event. Also called *brief reactive psychosis*.

brief reactive psychosis ➤ **brief psychotic disorder**.

brightness A term with broad usage in a number of contexts: **1.** That dimension of a color that refers to a location along the black–white dimension (contrast here with ➤ **hue** and **saturation**). Sometimes the term *lightness* is used synonymously here. **2.** The perceived intensity of any visual stimulus dependent on the amplitude and wavelength of the light. Note that different subjective brightnesses are produced by different colors having the same physical intensity; e.g., ➤ **Bezold-Brücke effect**, ➤ **Purkinje shift**, ➤ **spectral sensitivity**. **3.** A

relatively high degree of intelligence – a distinctly nontechnical usage. **4.** A subjective quality of tones. ➤ **tonal brightness**. Occasionally called *brilliance*, especially in older writings.

brightness adaptation ➤ **adaptation** (1).

brightness constancy The tendency for a visual stimulus to be perceived as having the same brightness under widely divergent conditions of illumination despite the fact that the different conditions deliver different amounts of physical energy to the eye. ➤ **constancy**.

brightness contrast **1.** The relative brightness of two stimuli. **2.** The effect of modifying the perceived brightness of a stimulus by the prior or simultaneous presentation of another stimulus. ➤ **contrast**.

bril A subjective unit of the perceived brightness of a light. The bril scale is established by equating the subjective value 100 bril with the physical value of 1 millilambert and then plotting brighter and dimmer illuminations relative to this anchor point.

brilliance **1.** ➤ **brightness** and **tonal brightness**. **2.** A nontechnical term for extremely high intelligence or creativity.

Briquet's syndrome A rather loosely defined behavior disorder characterized by vague feelings of unease and poorly articulated, indefinite complaints. ➤ **somatization disorder**.

British empiricism ➤ **empiricism**.

Broca's aphasia ➤ **aphasia, Broca's**.

Broca's area A cortical area involved in the processing of language functions. For virtually all right-handed individuals it is located in the inferior frontal gyrus of the left hemisphere; for the left-handed it is still generally in the left hemisphere although on occasion it is found in the corresponding area on the right. The area was named for the French surgeon Paul Broca who reported in 1861 that many aphasic patients had lesions in this area. Today it is generally acknowledged that this is not 'the' speech center; many different areas of the brain have been implicated in language behavior, of which Broca's area is only one. See, e.g., ➤ **Wernicke's area**.

Brodmann's areas A system for mapping the cortex based on the 'architecture' of the cellular structure. Each of the 44 Brodmann's areas is differentiated from the others on the basis of histologically distinct features. It is worth noting that there is not always correspondence between Brodmann's areas and functional areas established by other mapping techniques such as lesions or electrical stimulation.

broken home A strange term used for a family in which one of the parents is absent owing to death, divorce, desertion, etc. The word *broken* entails the notion of malfunctioning; the coiner of this term was obviously injecting an unwarranted judgement about single-parent homes.

Bruce effect A phenomenon first observed in mice by Hilda Bruce in which the termination of a pregnancy is brought about by substances in the urine of a virile male mouse other than the one which impregnated the female. Having thus eliminated the offspring of the other male, the animal may now impregnate the female himself and thus increase the likelihood of passing his own genes on to future generations.

Brunswik faces A series of schematic faces made up of simple lines for the eyes, nose and mouth. They have been used largely in perceptual and cognitive studies of discrimination and categorization.

Brunswik ratio A way of expressing any perceptual constancy, developed by Egon Brunswik. The easiest example to understand is size constancy: a subject stands at one place viewing a standard stake placed some distance away and is asked to judge which of a series of variable stakes is the same size as the standard. The amount of size constancy is given by the ratio, $P - R/C - R$, where R = relative retinal size (angle of vision subtended on the retina), C =

objective physical size and P = perceived or judged size. Similar ratios are used for other constancies. When the logarithm of the values is used, the formula is called the *Thouless ratio*.

brute force A problem-solving technique where all possible alternatives are attempted or all possible paths to a solution are followed. Brute-force techniques are usually last resorts when ➤ **heuristics** are not known or do not exist.

bruxism Grinding of the teeth, especially during sleep.

buccal Pertaining to the mouth or cheek.

buffer items ➤ **filler (material)**.

buffer (store) A term borrowed from computer science and often used to refer to a limited-capacity memory store in which information is held temporarily while being processed.

bug A problem in a process, an error in a program. The term comes from computer sciences; ➤ **debug**.

buggery Slang for anal intercourse. ➤ **sodomy** (1).

bulb 1. Any expansion of an organ, vessel, neural process, etc. 2. An obsolete term for the ➤ **medulla oblongata**.

-bulia Combining form meaning *will*.

bulimia nervosa An eating disorder characterized by repeated episodes of 'binge' eating followed by misuse of laxatives and self-induced vomiting. In the classic syndrome tremendous amounts of high-calorie foods can be eaten rapidly and with little chewing. Episodes are usually associated with depression and followed by guilt and self-depreciation. Surprisingly, bulimia is frequently found in conjunction with *anorexia nervosa*. var., *boulimia*.

bundle hypothesis A label used derisively by Gestalt psychologists to characterize the early structuralist view that a complex percept is no more than the sum of (a 'bundle' of) its several stimulus elements.

Bunsen–Roscoe law The principle that the absolute threshold for vision is a multiplicative function of the duration and intensity of the stimulus. The law holds reasonably well for short durations up to about 50 msec. An example of ➤ **temporal *summation** in that the effect of a stimulus summates over time.

burned (or **burnt**) A class of olfactory (smell) qualities typified by burned wood. ➤ **Henning's prism**.

burst 1. Generally, any sudden increase in responsiveness. **2.** In operant conditioning, it is used to describe the rapid output of responses after a period of relative quiescence typically found under certain schedules of reinforcement, e.g. *fixed-interval schedules*. **3.** In electrophysiology, it refers to the rapid firing of a stimulated nerve fiber.

buspirone An ➤ **antianxiety drug**.

butaperazine One of the **phenothiazine derivatives** used in the treatment of schizophrenia.

butyrophenones A group of ➤ **anti-**psychotic drugs**, the most commonly prescribed of which is ➤ **haloperidol**. They are similar in action and effect to *chlorpromazine*. ➤➤ **phenothiazines**.

buzz word Colloquial for any word or term which is instantly responded to with a predictable, emotional reaction.

bystander (intervention) effect The phenomenon that the more people present when help is needed the less likely any one of them is to provide assistance. Once thought to be a symbol of the dehumanizing urban environment, the effect is now known to be quite general. Essentially, the more people about the more likely each is to assume that someone else will provide the help – hence, no one helps. ➤➤ **altruism, helping behavior**.

byte A number of binary digits (➤➤ **bit**) taken together as a coordinated unit. The term was introduced in a half-joking manner (many bits make up a *bite* – and this spelling is also found) but it has stuck as a useful term in computer sciences and information theory.

C

C 1. Constant. 2. ➤ **control group**. 3. Centigrade.

c Correction factor.

CA ➤ chronological *age.

CA1, CA2, CA3, and CA4 fields Major subdivisions of the ➤ **hippocampus**. The CA1 and CA3 fields have been most carefully studied, especially with regard to their role in memory. The 'CA' designation comes from *cornu ammonis* (or *Ammon's horn*) which the hippocampus is also called.

cable properties In neurophysiology, the collective properties of axonal transmission of a neural impulse: specifically, those properties that reflect normal modes of action of electrical transmission in any cable whether neural or, e.g., a submarine telegraph cable. Such properties are represented basically as passive conduction of the current in decremental fashion along the length of the axon (or cable).

cachexia Lit., bad condition. Generally, any state of ill health, malnutrition, physical wasting away.

cachinnation Inappropriate, hysterical laughter.

cac(o-) Combining form meaning *bad, diseased, degenerate*.

cacoethes Generally, a bad habit or propensity.

cacogeusia Pathological condition in which ordinarily palatable foods produce a disgusting, putrid taste.

cacosmia An abnormal condition in which normally pleasant or neutral smells are experienced as foul and disgusting.

caffeine An alkaloid found in various common foods including coffee and chocolate. Its stimulating effects are produced by its ability to block the activity of *phos-*phodiesterase*, an enzyme that destroys secondary messengers at cerebral synapses thus increasing activity of many neurons and producing arousal and wakefulness. There is also evidence that caffeine activates *dopaminergic* neurons.

caffeinism Caffeine intoxication. Symptoms are nervousness, anxiety, insomnia and ➤ **psychomotor agitation**. In sensitive persons as little as 250 mg (roughly 2–3 cups of coffee or 3–5 cups of tea) are sufficient to produce these effects.

CAH ➤ congenital adrenal hyperplasia.

CAI ➤ computer-assisted instruction.

calcarine cortex The cortical area surrounding the ➤ **calcarine fissure**.

calcarine fissure The fissure or sulcus on the medial surface of the occipital lobe of the cortex which divides the medial portion of the lobe into superior and inferior portions. The primary visual sensory area is located in the ➤ **calcarine cortex**.

California infant scale(s) Now called, after their designer, the ➤ **Bayley Scales of Infant Development**.

California Psychological Inventory (CPI) A widely used self-report inventory originally derived from the MMPI (➤ **Minnesota Multiphasic Personality Inventory**). It consists of several hundred 'yes–no' questions and yields scores on a number of scales including self-acceptance, self-control, socialization, achievement, dominance and the like.

callosal apraxia ➤ apraxia, callosal.

callosum ➤ corpus callosum.

caloric nystagmus ➤ nystagmus, caloric.

calyx An eggcup-shaped dendritic process in which another cell is embedded.

camera From the Latin, meaning *vault*, a chamber, room, cavity, box, etc. Used in anatomy for internal chambers and in experimental research for specially constructed chambers, e.g., *camera inodorata* or an odor-free enclosure for studying smell.

campimetry The measurement of the visual field.

canal A narrow channel or tube; a passageway. Used more or less synonymously with a number of other terms, e.g., *groove, duct, foramen, tract*, etc.

canal, central A thin canal in the center of the spinal cord filled with cerebrospinal fluid.

canalization **1.** Generally, narrowing, restricting. A thing or process is said to be canalized if its range of manifestation is diminished (often) to the point where only one of the many possible alternatives is observed. **2.** In G. Murphy's theory, a culturally determined narrowing of preferred ways of satisfying drive states. **3.** In neurology, the hypothesized process whereby a neural pathway becomes traversed more easily with increasing use. **4.** In evolutionary genetics, the notion that a particular epigenetic capability or behavior pattern will continue to be manifested in the face of less than optimal environments or, if disturbed or interrupted by extreme conditions, be fairly easily restored when conditions are made appropriate once more.

candela Since an international agreement reached in 1948, the primary standard unit for measurement of the luminous intensity of light. The standard is set by the amount of light radiating from a bar of pure platinum held at the solidification temperature (2,042°K) through a 1.5 mm aperture. This unit is roughly equivalent to the previously used unit, the ➤ **candle**.

candle A unit of luminance measured at the source of light. The intensity of light on a given surface will be presented in terms of foot-candles; that is, the intensity of one candle at 1 ft distance. ➤ **candela**.

cannabis (sativa) *Cannabis* is the name

of a genus of plants. The *sativa* variety is the most common and is cultivated legally for the hemp and illegally for its various psychoactive products which are known by a wide variety of names including *hashish, marihuana* (var., *marijuana*), *charas, bhang, ganja, dagga* and just plain *cannabis* – in addition to an ever increasing number of slang terms. The active ingredients are tetrahydrocannabinols (THC), the primary one being an isomer, delta-9-tetrahydrocannabinol, which has been synthesized and is known to produce central-nervous-system effects. The range of effects of the drug is quite large and is dependent on dosage, the setting in which it is taken, the psychological and physical make-up of the individual and other substances such as alcohol taken at the same time. There is currently considerable debate over the short- and long-range effects of cannabis. There is little evidence of ➤ **drug *tolerance** and no substantial data to support charges of a ➤ **drug *dependence**. The 'social degeneration' occasionally seen with extensive use may be cause as much as effect. ➤ **THC** for more detail.

Cannon-Bard theory ➤ **theories of *emotion**.

cannula A small hollow tube which can be inserted into tissue for the purpose of administering chemical preparations or removal of fluids for analysis. Its most common use is in the study of brain tissue, when the ultrathin tube is inserted into the organism's brain and the action of specific chemical substances can be systemically evaluated.

canon **1.** Any working principle or formula. However, not every formula or heuristic gets to be labeled a canon; the term is generally reserved for important, fundamental principles that seem likely to lead to meaningful truths. E.g., ➤ **Lloyd Morgan's canon**. **2.** A model or standard or a body of such models or standards. See here ➤ **canonical**.

canonical Used generally as derived from ➤ **canon** (2). That is, characterizing or relating to elements or events which are ordered or structured according to some principle or model.

capacity 1. Generally, a synonym of ➤ **ability**. 2. In computer sciences and cognitive science, the amount of information which a given system can handle; e.g., ➤ **channel capacity, storage capacity.** 3. Absorbing or holding power, as in *electrical capacity*. 4. Volume, as in *vital capacity*.

Capgras syndrome The delusion that 'doubles' have replaced persons whom one knows. It is seen only in fairly severe psychoses.

capillary From the Latin, meaning *hairlike*. 1. A minute blood vessel. The capillary system connects the arterial and venous systems. 2. A minute lymph duct through which exchange of nutrients and waste from blood tissue takes place.

carboxyl group A molecule made up of two oxygen atoms and one hydrogen atom bound to a carbon atom (COOH). See here ➤ **amino acid**.

cardiac Pertaining to the heart.

cardinal From the Latin for *important*; *primary, central, fundamental.*

cardio- Prefix meaning pertaining to the heart.

cardiogram A graph of the electrical activity of the heart muscle. A shortened form of ➤ **electrocardiogram**. The device which records the electrical activity is called a *cardiograph*.

cardiovascular Pertaining to the heart and the blood vessels of the circulatory system.

card-sorting task (or **test**) A general term for any task in which the subject is required to sort cards according to some principle or rule. Some are simple sensory/motor tasks in which sorting is carried out according to a specific instruction ('triangles in one pile, circles in the other'), others are more complex, including tasks in which the subject must figure out the rules that determine the correct sorting.

caregiver 1. Generally, anyone involved in any of the phases of healthcare. It may apply to one who identifies illness, helps prevent it, works in treatment or rehabilitation of patients, etc. The term is generally used for community workers, paraprofessionals, orderlies, etc. but may also include trained clinical psychologists or physicians. 2. A parent or other adult who provides childcare, a ➤ **caretaker**.

caretaker A general term for anyone who is intimately involved in the raising of a child. The term is used broadly in child-development studies and may include the natural parents, foster parents, other members of an extended family, a governess, etc.

carnal Pertaining to the flesh. Occasionally used literally, but more often as a euphemism for *sexual*.

carotid artery The artery that serves the rostral (anterior, frontal) portions of the brain.

carpal Pertaining to the wrist.

carpal age ➤ **age, carpal**.

carpentered environment Generally, any physical setting that has been built by humans according to architectural plans that do not follow natural physical forms. Most buildings are built with an eye to square corners, straight lines, even doorways, and hence fulfill this definition. In the study of perception, particularly in cross-cultural and anthropological studies, it is argued that such environments are unnatural and give rise to inappropriate percepts.

carphenazine A ➤ **phenothiazine derivative** used to treat schizophrenia.

Cartesian Pertaining to the theories and discoveries of the great French mathematician and philosopher, René Descartes (1596–1650). The positions represented are a strong form of *dualism* with mind (or soul) being unextended and indivisible and body being extended and divisible; body is mechanical and to be understood through physical and mathematical study, mind through rational means. The *rationalism* which characterized Descartes's point of view led him to articulate a variety of a priori or innate ideas including those of self, of God, of perfection, etc. Descartes's philosophical perspective, ignored by psychologists for the most part during the behaviorist decades, is coming to be regarded as more relevant for the newer approaches of cognitive psychology, cognitive science and the study of language.

Cartesian coordinates A system for locating any point in plane space relative to two axes set at right angles. Developed by René Descartes, it forms the basis for the standard graphing techniques to represent data. The horizontal line is denoted as the x-axis and the vertical as the y-axis. They cross at right angles at the origin or zero point and the position of any arbitrary point is given by its value on each axis.

cary(o)- Variant of ➤ **kary(o)-**.

case 1. Generally, any instance or occurrence of some thing. The 'thing' may be a particular event, a characteristic instance, a disease, etc. 2. An individual who displays the characteristic or a patient who has a disorder or a disease.

case study (or **history**) The detailed account of a single individual. This method is most often used in psychotherapy, where as complete a compilation as possible is made on a single person, including personal history, background, test results, ratings, interviews, etc. In clinical psychology and psychiatry, disciplines which were originally nonexperimental in their approach, case studies often became the basis for generalized theoretical principles.

caseworker A general label for any health-related professional (or paraprofessional) who handles individual cases over an extended period of time. The feature that distinguishes a caseworker from

others in the health and helping professions is this long-term care or supervision of a (usually) small number of cases.

caste 1. A closed hereditary social stratum or class which controls to a considerable degree the marital possibilities, prestige, available occupations, etc. of its members. Some authors restrict the term to the formalized system in India, others use it for any such rigid stratification system. Occasionally qualifiers will be appended to specify the type of caste system, e.g., *color* or *racial caste*, *religious caste*, etc. ➤➤ **social class**. 2. In the social insects, any specialized (functionally and/ or structurally) set of individuals. The honey bee with its three castes (queens, workers, drones) is the classic example.

castrate ➤ **castrating, castration**.

castrating Term used more in the popular literature than in the technical to refer to individuals whose aggressive, dominating style of interacting undermines others and deprives them of opportunities of taking the initiative. It is most frequently used of women with regard to their manner of interaction with males but this restriction is not mandated by the strict meaning of the term. ➤ **castration** (especially 4).

castration 1. From the Latin for *pruning*, the surgical removal of the male gonads, the testes. 2. By extension, the removal of the female gonads, the ovaries. 3. In the classical psychoanalytic literature, the (symbolic) removal of the male external genitalia, especially the penis. See here ➤ **castration anxiety, castration complex**. For meaning 1 *orchiectomy* is an occasional synonym; when non-humans are under consideration, *geld* is often used; for meaning 2 *ovariectomy* is a synonym and, for animals, *spay*. Note that while castration is certainly an effective method of birth control, it should be distinguished from *vasectomy* (in males) and *salpingectomy* (in females), which are surgical procedures for sterilization that do not interfere with normal hormonal processes, as does castration. 4. Metaphorically, the removal of some prized or precious 'possession.' Note that this possession is usually regarded as a pattern of behavior or personality, such as initiative or personal power, and not a physical object. ➤ **castrating**.

castration anxiety A psychoanalytic term for the anxiety resulting from real or imagined threats to one's sexual functions. It is used in sense 3 of the base term and hence refers not to specific threats to one's physical genitals but to symbolic threats. Although the original use of the term applied only to males, whose fear surrounds the loss of masculine erotic function or of the ability to function properly in the male sex role, it can in principle be applied to females; see here ➤ **castration complex**.

castration complex In classical psychoanalytic theory, the fear associated with loss of one's genitals. In the male the complex is supposedly manifested as anxiety surrounding the possibility of loss, in females as the guilt over having already experienced the loss. The original position with regard to males has, of course, been critiqued rather severely but is still generally speaking a part of the standard psychoanalytic theory; the position with regard to females has been so vigorously attacked, especially by female analysts, that it is rarely taken seriously any longer.

castration, hormonal Typically the term ➤ **castration** (meanings 1 and 2) refers to a surgical procedure. When the qualifier is used it is meant to refer to those forms of hormonal treatment that bring about the same biological and behavioral changes but without the surgical intervention.

CAT 1. ➤ **computerized axial tomography**. 2. ➤ **Children's Apperception Test**.

cata- From the Greek, meaning *down*. Also used as a prefix to indicate *from*, *against*, and on occasions *in accordance with* or *repeating* (the latter sense is found in speech and language pathologies). vars., *cath-*, *kata-*.

catabolism 1. Generally, the breaking

down of living things or body structures. 2. The expenditure phase of ➤ **metabolism**. Contrast with ➤ **anabolism**.

catalepsy 1. The rigid maintenance of a body position over extended periods of time. 2. ➤ **flexibilitas cerea** or waxy flexibility. ➤➤ **catatonia** and **catatonic *schizophrenia**.

catalexia A tendency to repeat inappropriate words during reading. ➤ **dyslexia**, of which it is sometimes regarded as a mild form.

catalyst In chemistry the term refers to any substance that affects a chemical reaction but remains itself unaltered. The term now enjoys wide usage and in psychology generally refers to any person or set of stimulus conditions that influences some social or cognitive process. Note that the requirement that the catalytic agent itself remain unchanged by the involvement is often missing in contemporary usage.

catamnesis The medical history of a patient from the point when first seen by a physician or a therapist or from the initial onset of a disability. Compare with ➤ **anamnesis**.

cataphasia ➤ syntactic *aphasia.

cataplexy A sudden loss of muscle tone resulting in the individual collapsing 'like a sack of potatoes.' It may result from a sudden emotional shock or a stroke and is an occasional symptom in narcolepsy where it appears to be due to the person suddenly going into ➤ **REM sleep**, one of the characteristics of which is muscle flaccidity.

catastrophe theory A mathematical theory developed by René Thom which attempts to formalize the nature of abrupt discontinuities in functions. The theory has been seen by many social scientists as potentially useful since many phenomena display these often catastrophic discontinuities, e.g., the dog that suddenly and without warning attacks a person, the precipitate onset of many 'nervous breakdowns' in seemingly undisturbed persons. The theory has been subjected to vigorous criticism both for the possible lack of soundness of the mathematics and the feasibility of useful applications. The jury is still out on it.

catathymic amnesia ➤ episodic *amnesia.

catatonia The term refers literally to muscular rigidity or extreme tonus. It is often observed in cases of ➤ schizophrenia, catatonic type. Note that there are several kinds of catatonic behavior as given in the following entries.

catatonic excitement Excited, apparently purposeless motor activity.

catatonic negativism A fixed, motionless resistance to all attempts to be moved. It may be passive, where the patient simply refuses to move or to be moved, or it may be active, where the patient may do the opposite of what is asked.

catatonic posturing The assumption of an unusual or bizarre posture which the patient may hold for extended periods of time.

catatonic rigidity Maintaining a fixed posture against efforts to be moved.

catatonic schizophrenia ➤ schizophrenia, catatonic (type).

catatonic stupor A reduction in normal, spontaneous movements and activities, often accompanied by a dramatic decrease in reactivity to events in the environment, occasionally to the point of appearing to be in a stupor.

catatonic waxy flexibility A condition where the patient's limbs can be moved or molded into any position, which they will then maintain often for extended periods of time. The term comes from the fact that when the limbs are being moved, they feel as though they were made of wax. Called *flexibilitas cerea* in some older texts.

catch trial A trial in a signal-detection experiment where the signal is not actually present. A positive response on such a trial is termed a ➤ false alarm. ➤ signal detection theory. The original German term here was *Vexierversuch*, meaning *hoax trial*.

catecholamine hypothesis A hypothesis about the possible biochemical basis of schizophrenia. In simple terms the assumption is that excessive build-up of the *catecholamines* (especially *dopamine*, ➤ dopamine hypothesis) in particular synaptic clefts in the brain is responsible for the symptoms of the psychosis. Evidence in support comes from the observation that chronic use of amphetamines produces a 'model' paranoid schizophrenic psychosis and that substances that function to mildly increase the level of the amines (e.g., MAO inhibitors, tricyclic compounds) have anti-depressant effects.

catecholaminergic Of neurons and neural pathways in which the neurotransmitter secreted is one of the ➤ catecholamines.

catecholamines A group of ➤ biogenic amines that includes ➤ epinephrine, ➤ norepinephrine and ➤ dopamine, all of which are known to play significant roles in nervous-system functioning.

categorical 1. Relating to a ➤ category. 2. Absolute, independent of other things. Psychological terminology, especially in studies of perception and cognition, almost always carries meaning 1; more philosophical usages frequently carry 2.

categorical perception The perception of individual stimuli as belonging to a particular category of stimuli rather than as unique, identifiable events. It is most easily observed in the tendency to hear the acoustic variations within a *phoneme* class as all representing the same sound; that is, not to perceive the differences between these variations. Such categorical perception is pronounced when the stimuli are stop consonants (e.g., /b/ versus /p/) but can also be observed in non-speech continua such as plucked versus bowed strings.

categorical scale ➤ nominal *scale.

categorical syllogism ➤ **syllogism**.

category 1. In modern psychological terminology, especially in theories of cognition, this term is used in ways which derive from the extensive concern with its meaning in philosophy. The common notion here is that a category is somehow like a ➤ **concept**, a class or even a system. That is, for example, if there exists the category 'lion' this carries with it the existence of a *concept* 'lion' in the mind, a theoretical *class* of objects which belong in it, an actual *group* of 'lions' and a *system* or set of decision rules about which objects belong in the category and which do not. It should be fairly obvious that a term with connotations like these is going to enjoy (or suffer from) rather extensive and varied usage. Some authors will use it as though it referred to specific, real-world classes which, at least in principle, can be identified and defined perhaps by a list of distinguishing features ('lions' are mammals, felines, predators, have four legs, sleep a lot, etc.), others will use it as though it referred to the mental representation of the class in the mind of the knowing person (i.e. the image or idea of a lion), still others prefer to treat the term in a pragmatic fashion and let patterns of behavior or usage dictate category boundaries ('lion' is a distinct category distinguishable, say, from 'house cat' because the sentence 'My lion spends every evening on my lap purring' is somewhat unlikely to refer to a real-world situations). For more on these issues and usage patterns see related terms such as ➤ **concept**, ➤ **prototype** and ➤ **representation**. 2. In older philosophical writings, a basic mode of thought or being. Aristotle used it for his ten classes which he felt could provide a complete inventory of all things knowable; for Kant it represented the divisions of understanding beginning with quantity, quality, relation and modality. 3. In statistics, any division or grouping of data on specific quantitative criteria.

category, basic (level) ➤ **natural *category** (2).

category estimation ➤ **methods of *scaling**.

category, natural 1. A category which exists by the natural, biological and anatomical structure of the perceiver. For example, colors are natural categories in this sense since all people with a normal, intact visual system respond to the visual spectrum in roughly the same fashion. Even though a person's language may not have separate words for 'red' and 'orange' they will discriminate between them in the same fashion as a speaker of English. 2. A category represented by things that occur naturally in the real world and which share particular features or are reacted to in similar ways. For example, 'furniture,' 'bird,' 'sport' and the like are included here. Note that those who prefer to use the term only in sense 1 will use the term *basic category* or *basic-level category* for sense 2.

catelectrotonus A state of increased excitability of a neuron, nerve or muscle in the region of the cathode (negative pole) when a current is passed through it.

catharsis From the Greek meaning *purification*, *purging*. 1. In psychoanalytic theory this meaning was borrowed to refer to the release of tension and anxiety resulting from the process of bringing repressed ideas, feelings, wishes and memories of the past into consciousness. 2. Lay usage has broadened the meaning a bit and one often sees the term used to refer to any satisfying emotional experience. ➤➤ **abreaction**.

cathexis From the Greek for *retention*, *holding*. In psychoanalytic theory, the investing of libidinal energy in an activity, an object or a person. Thus, one will see references to a goal as being cathected, or of one's ➤ **ego** as an object of a cathection. Freud conceptualized cathexis as a kind of psychic analog of an electric charge and often the terminology used reflects this; the language of cathexis uses expressions like 'charge' and 'current' and these are said to 'flow' and become 'bound' to objects, and even to 'reverse charge' (*anti-cathexis*). vb., *cathect*; var., *cathection*.

cation A positively charged ion. ➤ **anion**.

CAT scan ➤ **computerized axial tomography**.

cauda equina The collection of spinal roots that runs through the lower one-third of the spinal column below the point where the spinal cord itself ends.

caudal 1. Pertaining to the tail or a tail-like structure. **2.** Inferior in position.

caudate nucleus A tail-shaped mass of sub-cortical gray matter. One of the components of the ➤ **basal ganglia**, it is involved in the inhibitory aspects of the voluntary control of movement.

causalgia ➤ **thermalgia**.

causality This term is used for what is essentially a philosophical issue and denotes the abstract quality that links occurrence of some event or state contingent upon the prior occurrence of some other event or state. Because the term is philosophical and refers to an abstract relation it is sometimes distinguished from ➤ **causation**, which is preferred in psychological parlance.

causal texture An old philosophical notion resurrected and streamlined during the 1940s and 1950s by both E. C. Tolman and E. Brunswik. The essential notion is that every event in the environment is linked up with every other event. The degree of dependence may run from the infinitesimal and negligible to absolute causal dependency. The important addition to this hoary idea is that the dependencies are not viewed as certain or deterministic but rather as probabilistic or stochastic. The phrase is used to cover the full spectrum of probabilistically causal interrelationships between events.

causation A basically empirical principle which states that for whatever effects are observed there was a cause that preceded them. The principle of causation (or cause and effect) is asymmetric and unidirectional. In *simple* causation, where there is a single known or knowable cause, it functions as the necessary and sufficient conditions of the effect observed; in *multiple* causation, where there may be several distinguishable causal factors for a particular observed effect, the issues of sufficiency and necessity are weakened. Multiple causation is the modal case in the social sciences.

cautious shift ➤ **choice shift**.

CCC ➤ **consonant trigram**.

ceiling effect The term *ceiling* is used for the maximum score on a test or a limit on the performance on some task. The term *ceiling effect* is taken to refer to: **1.** In testing, the actual limitation on a testee's scores as he or she approaches this theoretical upper bound. The phrase is not used purely synonymously with *ceiling* because chance errors and random fluctuations in performance generally prevent 'perfect' scores. **2.** In studies of behavior, the failure to observe any improvement in performance owing to the fact that the subject is already performing at maximum capacity. Actually, this usage is a bit misleading since the real meaning here is *lack of an effect* (of learning or instruction or whatever) *due to the existence of a ceiling*. The converse is called a *basement effect* or a *floor effect*. **3.** In pharmacology, the maximum dose of a drug that will produce the desired effect.

celeration Event frequency per unit of time; e.g., number of responses per minute per day. The term is mainly used in behavioral analyses.

cell 1. The structural unit of plants and animals. **2.** A compartment in an array or matrix. The former usage, of course, is biological; the latter is restricted to statistical analyses.

cell assembly The central component in the theoretical model of neural circuitry developed by the Canadian psychologist D. O. Hebb to explain certain perceptual phenomena. The cerebral cortex is extraordinarily complexly organized and precious little is known about it. Hebb's notion of the cell assembly was one of the first important attempts to hypothesize about this organization. It is essentially a hypothesized group of neurons that are thought to become functionally interrelated and organized into a complex 'closed circuit' by repeated stimulation.

cell body The integral 'life support' component of a neuron. The cell body (or *soma*) contains the nucleus and other supporting structures. If it is damaged the whole neuron dies.

cellular Pertaining to, derived from or composed of cells.

cenesthesia Lit., common feeling. Hence, the normal collective sense of being alive, of being aware. var., *coenaesthesia*.

cen(o)- Combining form meaning *common, frequent*. var., *coen(o)-*.

cenogamy A rarely practiced form of marriage where two or more men and two or more women unite into a single marital unit. Also called *group marriage*.

cenotrope A similar pattern of behavior exhibited by a group of organisms with common biology and environment. The term was proposed as an ethological replacement for the term ➤ **instinct**, which has suffered a wide variety of abuses from a variety of sources. Unfortunately it hasn't really caught on. var., *coenotrope*.

censor ➤ **censorship**.

censorship **1.** In psychoanalytic theory, the notion that one of the joint functions of the ego and superego is to accept or reject ideas, impulses, wishes, etc. emanating from the unconscious. The term *censor* was first used by Freud in his early writings for the hypothetical agency that distorted dreams and controlled repression. As the theory evolved the censor became the basis for the development of the notion of the superego. For this reason *censor* has typically been used to stand for some hypothetical entity while *censorship* has been used for a set of operations – whether the entity which carries out these functions is actually called the *censor* depends on who is doing the writing and

when. **2.** Any arbitrary regulation of the publishing, communicating or promulgating of information and ideas.

cent A unit of pitch defined as 1/1,200th of an octave.

center **1** n. The mid-point of a body, organ or other structure. **2** n. A collection of nerve cells within the central nervous system that controls or mediates a particular process, activity or function. There are a large number of such structures; those that are germane to psychology are listed under the qualifying term. **3** vb. To focus on a particular aspect of a stimulus, to concentrate on a specific element or feature of something. ➤ **decentration**. var., *centre*.

center clipping ➤ **peak clipping**.

centesis Puncturing of a cavity.

centi- Prefix denoting one-hundredth (1/100th).

centile **1.** Any one of the points on a ranked distribution of scores, each of which contains 1/100th of the scores. Thus a centile rank of 55 means that the score representing the rank is higher than 55% of all the scores in the distribution. Note that this meaning is equivalent to that of *percentile*. **2.** Another, less common, use is to refer not to the points themselves but to the 100 classes that makes up a population. To appreciate the difference note that it makes no sense to refer to a percentile rank of 100 since such a score would have to be higher than all the scores, including itself. But it does make sense to refer to a centile rank of 100 (in meaning 2) since this would refer to the top classification of the distribution of scores.

central **1.** Pertaining or referring to something in the middle, or in the main portion of a body or a structure. **2.** Pertaining to some fundamental or important thing. Sense 1 is generally contrasted with *peripheral* or *distal*; sense 2 with *secondary* or *derivative*. It occurs in a large number of combinatory forms, some of which are semantically obvious; others are given in the following entries.

central canal The narrow tube filled with cerebrospinal fluid that runs the length of the *spinal cord*.

central conflict In K. Horney's theory of personality, the psychic conflict between one's ➤ **real *self** and one's ➤ **idealized *self**.

central deafness ➤ cerebral *deafness*.

central fissure (or **sulcus**) The fissure of the cerebral cortex that separates the motor cortex (the *precentral gyrus*) from the sensory cortex (the *postcentral gyrus*). The pre- and postcentral gyri mark the division between the frontal and parietal lobes of each hemisphere. Also called the *fissure of Rolando*.

central inhibition ➤ inhibition, central.

centralism An old term for the point of view that behavior could only be understood and explained through appeals to brain processes and brain function. Usually contrasted with another old term, ➤ **peripheralism**.

central-limit theorem In nonmathematical terms: as the size of any sample of scores becomes arbitrarily large the sampling distribution of the mean approaches the normal distribution. This theorem gives an intuitive insight into why the normal distribution is so important in statistics, since any sample will eventually approach normality provided enough data are collected. The rate at which the normal distribution is approximated is surprisingly rapid for most of the populations that are investigated in psychology.

central nervous system (CNS) That component of the ➤ **nervous system** composed of the brain, the spinal cord and their associated neural processes.

central nucleus A nucleus in the **amygdala**, it receives sensory information from the primary sensory cortex, the association cortex, and the thalamus. It projects fibers to the hypothalamus, midbrain,

pons, and medulla and is involved in coordinating the various components that make up the expression of emotional responses.

central tegmental tract A noradrenergic system that arises in the medulla and the pons of the brainstem and projects to the hypothalamus. Also called the *ventral noradrenergic bundle*.

central tendency An index of central tendency is a way of describing the typical or 'average' value of any distribution of scores. That is, a measure of central tendency is a ➤ **descriptive *statistic**. The best way to view it is the following: if asked to select just one score from a distribution that best represented the full set of scores you would be wise to select one of the measures of central tendency, namely, the ➤ **mean**, the ➤ **median** or the ➤ **mode**. The ➤ **arithmetic *mean**, for reasons discussed under that term, is the generally preferred measure.

central trait theory Solomon Asch's view that the particular personality characteristics (or *traits*) that an individual displays are of special importance in how we view that person. Asch also argued that the context plays an important role in determining how any particular trait is interpreted.

central vision ➤ vision, central.

centration (or **centering**) ➤ decentration.

centre ➤ center.

centrencephalic Localized in a (relatively) precise area in the brain.

centrifugal swing The tendency for an animal at a choice point in a T-maze to continue in the direction of his previous travel. It was proposed as an explanation for the fact that rats and other animals show strong single-alternation tendencies in maze-learning experiments.

centroid method A factor-analysis technique in which the correlation matrix is represented mathematically on the surface of a sphere. The first axis of rotation is passed through the center of the sphere, the other axes are initially set at right angles to the first (i.e. they are orthogonal to or independent of it) but are then rotated to reveal the various factors.

cephalalgia Lit., pain in the head; a headache.

cephalic Pertaining to the head.

cephalic index An index first used in physical anthropology, it is expressed as the ratio of the length of the head to its breadth × 100. Except in pathological cases the resulting nomenclature (*dolichocephalic* = long head, *mesocephalic* = moderate head, *brachycephalic* = short head) is without any real significance and without correlation with normal or abnormal behavior. Note, if the measurements are taken on the bare skull the index is called *cranial* rather than cephalic.

cephal(o)- Combining form meaning *head*.

cephalocaudad (or **-al**) **development** The hypothesized principle that growth (especially embryological) and behavior development follow a sequence that begins at the head and extends toward the tail end. Generally included in the hypothesis is *proximodistad* (or **-al**) development, which is the tendency for growth and behavior development to proceed from the body toward the extremities.

CER (or **cer**) ➤ **conditioned emotional response**.

cerebellar Pertaining to the ➤ **cerebellum**.

cerebellar peduncles Three myelinated tracts that connect the cerebellum to the brain stem.

cerebellum Lit., the Latin diminutive form of ➤ **cerebrum**, thus: 'little brain.' It is the primary structure in the hindbrain and is involved in muscle coordination and the maintenance of body equilibrium. The cerebellum is particularly important in initiating and controlling very rapid motor sequences of the limbs, movements that

occur so rapidly that they cannot be modulated by sensory feedback. Classic examples in humans are hitting a baseball and returning a serve in tennis. Other species with rapid motor responses, such as birds and monkeys, have well developed cerebellums.

cerebral Pertaining to the ➤ **cerebrum**. Used metaphorically and nontechnically for *intellectual, smart*.

cerebral aqueduct ➤ **aqueduct of Sylvius**.

cerebral blindness ➤ **blindness, cerebral**.

cerebral commissure ➤ **commissure**.

cerebral cortex The surface covering of gray matter that forms the outermost layer of the ➤ **cerebrum**. In evolutionary terms it is the most recent neural development and its approximately 9 to 12 billion cells are responsible for primary sensory functions, motor coordination and control, for mediating most of the integrative, coordinated behaviors and, most important, for the so-called 'higher mental processes' of language, thinking, problem-solving, etc.

cerebral dominance ➤ **dominance, cerebral**.

cerebral hemispheres The two symmetrical (at least superficially – histologically they are known to be distinguishable in a variety of ways) hemispherical halves of the ➤ **cerebrum**.

cerebration 1. Neurological action of the cerebrum. 2. Metaphorically, thinking.

cerebrospinal fluid Lymph-like fluid filling the ventricles of the brain, the central canal of the spinal cord and all other areas in the skull and spinal canal not given over to solid tissues and blood vessels. Its functions are still something of a mystery; the currently favored hypothesis is that it has a role in tissue nutrition and may play a role in sleep.

cerebrotonia One of the three classic components of temperament assumed within ➤ **constitutional theory** (see that entry for details).

cerebrovascular accident ➤ stroke (2).

cerebrum The largest and most prominent structure of the brain. It consists of two hemispheres separated by the longitudinal fissure, below which are the three cerebral commissures connecting the two halves. The inner core is composed of white matter made up of myelinated fibers and the gray basal ganglia; the outer covering (the cerebral cortex) is made up entirely of gray matter. The human cerebrum consists of perhaps 15 billion cells and is the latest brain structure to have evolved. It is involved in processing and interpretation of sensory inputs, control over voluntary motor activity, consciousness, planning and executing of action, thinking, ideating, language, reasoning, judging and the like; in short, all of those functions most closely associated with the so-called 'higher mental functions.'

ceremony A socially or culturally dictated sequence of acts with symbolic significance as defined by the culture's traditions. A ceremony is generally considered a somewhat larger and more elaborate event than a ➤ ritual and, in fact, ceremonies are said by some to be composed of several rituals.

certifiable A forensic (legal) term for someone who, in the opinion of medical or psychological experts, is in need of some form of treatment, guardianship or institutionalization. ➤➤ sectioned.

ceruminous deafness ➤ deafness, ceruminous.

cerveau isolé ➤ *encéphale isolé*.

cervix The neck of any organ or body part, particularly of the womb. adj. *cervical*.

C fibers ➤ free nerve endings.

CFF (or **cff**) ➤ critical flicker frequency.

chained schedule ➤ schedules of *reinforcement.

chaining (or **chained responses**) General terms referring to the linking together of a sequence of behaviors. The initial response in the chain provides a set of cues which becomes associated with and thus elicits the next succeeding response and so forth so that the full sequence is 'chained off.' As an explanatory model of simple rote-learning situations and sequential behavior of lower organisms (e.g., maze learning in rats) it has proven reasonably successful. Attempts to explain complex cognitive behaviors using chaining hypotheses have not been particularly fruitful. Theories based on chaining are usually contrasted with those based on *plans, schemas, scripts*, etc.

challenge In *psychopharmacology*, to administer a therapeutic dose of a drug to observe its effects. For example, the expression 'scopolamine-challenged subjects' refers to subjects given a moderate to high dose of scopolamine.

chance A term that must be used carefully. It has at least two distinct meanings: **1.** To refer to those events occurring within a given system that are caused by factors lying outside of that system. Thus, in any psychological experiment some of the data will be due to manipulations of the independent variables and some will be 'due to chance.' This does not mean that these are random data but merely data for which the causes lie outside of the experiment. Similarly, it may be 'chance' that a tree fell on your car and not somebody else's but it does not eliminate causal factors. **2.** To refer to events that are random in nature and determinable or describable by the use of probability theory. Even in this sense the events are not regarded as wholly causeless but merely as caused by multitudinous independent and interdependent factors that are essentially unknowable, e.g., the sequence of heads and tails in successive coin flips or the exact position of any gas molecule in a large room. Lay language often confuses chance with 'accident' or 'luck.' Such usages are popular but strictly nontechnical.

chance differences In statistical analyses,

any differences due to random factors. Contrast with ➤ **constant *error** and with ➤ **bias**.

chance error ➤ error, chance.

chance-half correlation ➤ correlation, split-half.

chance variation A term generally reserved for genetic variations that have no clearly identifiable antecedents. Darwin made this concept a central assumption in the process of evolution by natural selection.

chancroid A venereal disease characterized by the eruption of a sensitive, inflamed ulcer in the genital area. The infection may spread to the lymph nodes, penis (or vulva) or anus but is localized in these areas. Treatment is usually with antibiotics.

change of life Nontechnical term for the ➤ **menopause**.

change-over delay (COD) A ➤ schedule of *reinforcement used with concurrent operants which allows a response to be reinforced only after a certain amount of time has elapsed since the last change-over from the other response.

channel As borrowed from *information theory*, a complete system for transmitting a signal, from its input phase to its final output phase. The channel generally operates on the basis of some code or language which relates the input and output in systematic ways. The term has become popular in psychology because it is possible to view an organism as a channel so that the receptors are the locus for the input and the responses the locus for the output. Further, any subsystem of an organism such as the visual system or a memory system may be similarly viewed.

channel capacity The maximum amount of information (measured in *bits*) that any channel can carry.

chaos theory A theory imported from the mathematics of nonlinear systems that some have attempted to apply to the behavior of complex systems such as the weather and human beings.

character 1. The original Latin meaning was an inscription or marking which differentiated some one thing from others for identification purposes. Although this meaning is still appropriate, the preferred synonyms here are *trait* or *characteristic*. As the psychological use of the term evolved it came to mean: 2. The sum total or integration of all such markings (traits) to yield a unified whole which reveals the nature (the 'character') of a situation, of an event or of a person. Freudian theory further emphasized this use by the introduction of terms like *anal character*. Today it is much more common to find the term ➤ **personality** (especially 3) used with essentially this meaning.

character analysis 1. Wilhelm Reich's term for his form of psychoanalysis. Unlike the classical Freudian approach, Reich focused less on specific symptoms and more on the total character or personality of the patient. The analysis itself was based on dealing with the client's ➤ **character defenses**. 2. An occasional synonym for ➤ didactic *analysis.

character armor W. Reich's term for an individual's system of defenses.

character defense Generally, any personality trait that functions primarily to fulfill some unconscious defensive purpose.

character disorder Lit. and loosely, a disorder of ➤ **character** (2). It was used originally for individuals who displayed pathological vacillation. Today, it serves as a general label for persons who chronically and habitually engage in maladaptive behaviors, who are inflexible, restrict their own opportunities for growth and usually manage to function in ways that evoke unpleasant reactions from those around them.

characteristic Some individualistic feature, attribute, etc. that serves to identify and 'characterize' something. Generally used synonymously with ➤ **trait** in discussion of personality.

character neurosis K. Horney's term for any long-standing neurotic syndrome manifested first in childhood.

characterology Obsolete term for: **1.** The general study of personality. **2.** The study of personality through physical characteristics; see here ➤ **constitutional theory**. Note, however, that constitutional theory, although lacking in validity and power, was a theory in what was at least a respectable science; characterology was a pseudoscience which focused on irrelevant features such as hair color, complexion, shape of the nose, cranial configuration, etc.

character trait In most usages this term is an unnecessary redundancy; *trait* alone will suffice. However, psychoanalysts occasionally use the full term to refer to behavioral tendencies which are inherited (or at least presumed to be).

charismatic authority ➤ **authority, charismatic**.

Charpentier's bands ➤ **Fechner's colors**.

Charpentier's illusion ➤ **size–weight illusion**.

Charpentier's law A descriptive generalization that holds for visual stimuli at ➤ **threshold** projected on the fovea: $aI = k$; where a is the area of the image, I is the intensity of the stimulus and k is a constant.

cheese effect A potentially serious side effect of ➤ **monoamine oxidase inhibitors**. Foods such as cheese, yogurt, wine, and some nuts and fruits containing pressor amines can cause sympathetic reactions in patients taking these drugs, leading to dangerously high blood pressure levels and heart rates.

chemical antagonism ➤ **drug*antagonism**.

chemical cosh UK slang term for the use of drugs for control purposes in total institutions to pacify or restrain violent or uncooperative detainees, with or without their consent.

chemical sense(s) Those sensory systems responsive to chemical stimuli, namely, ➤ **smell** (or **olfaction**) and ➤ **taste** (or **gustation**).

chemical transmission Generally used to refer to the transmission of information between neurons. The four kinds of chemical involved here, ➤ **neurotransmitters**, ➤ **neuromodulators**, ➤ **hormones**, and ➤ **pheromones**, are used to control the behavior of individual cells, whole organs, or entire organisms. The first three operate within an organism, the last between organisms.

chemo- Combining form meaning *pertaining to chemicals or chemical action*.

chemoreceptor Those sense organs responsive to chemical action. Differentiate from *chemical sense* which refers to the whole modality, while chemoreceptor refers to the actual receptors such as the taste buds.

chemotherapy **1.** Within clinical psychology and psychiatry, any form of psychotherapy that treats behavioral and mental disorders with drugs and chemicals such as tranquilizers, anti-depressants, etc. Some therapists view most, if not all, abnormal reactions as being, in the final analysis, due to biochemical imbalances and will argue that they should be treated likewise. Others take a less definitive position and will use chemotherapy as a way of producing a temporary quiescent state during which more traditional therapy techniques may be employed. **2.** In medicine generally, the term is employed broadly to cover any technique based on chemicals, as for example in the treatment of cancer.

chi (χ) The Greek letter used in many formulas and statistical tests. ➤ **chi-square**.

Chicago school ➤ **functionalism** (2).

chicken game A variation of the ➤ **prisoner's *dilemma** game, in which mutual selection of the competitive response produces the most severe penalty (or lowest reward) for both players.

child A person between either **1.** birth

and maturity, **2.** birth and puberty or, according to some, **3.** infancy and puberty. The last is preferred; ➤ **childhood**.

child abuse Generally, any form of physical or psychological mistreatment of a child by parents or guardians. The most common form involves severe and repeated physical injury (contusions, broken bones), although many will also include as abuse other forms of mistreatment such as starvation, locking the child away in attics or closets, burning with cigarettes or other hot objects, sexual assault (➤ **sexual abuse**) and emotional and psychological degradation. ➤ **child neglect** for a distinction.

child analysis Psychoanalysis of a child.

child development A sub-discipline within the field of ➤ **child psychology**. The key word is *development*; it denotes that the focus is on aspects of physiology, cognition and behavior that show qualitative and quantitative change as the child passes from birth to maturity. Some authors use the term to reflect an emphasis on growth and maturation and a concomitant de-emphasis on learning. This bias is not universally shared and most use it to cover maturation, learning and the critical interactions between them. ➤➤ **developmental psychology**.

child-guidance clinic ➤ **clinic, child-guidance**.

childhood 1 n. Usually, the period between infancy and adolescence. See here ➤ **child**. **2** adj. Pertaining to this period. Used frequently in psychiatry and clinical psychology to characterize the form of a disorder observed in children, e.g., ➤ **childhood *schizophrenia**.

childhood disintegrative disorder A serious disorder of childhood in which there is apparently normal development for at least the first two years of life, followed by significant loss of previously acquired skills in such areas as language, social skills, bowel or bladder control, and sensorimotor coordination. There are problems differentiating this disorder

from ➤ **autism**, although it appears to have a worse prognosis.

childhood, disorders of A commonly found shorthand expression for the full, formal, psychiatric diagnostic category, *disorders first evident in infancy, childhood or adolescence*. The category includes a number of disorders of particular kinds, as follows: (a) disorders found at other points in the life of a person such as *schizophrenia* and *affective disorders*, but which are given special designation as *childhood disorders* in cases where they are first detected prior to adulthood being reached; (b) ➤ **personality disorders**, when they are diagnosed prior to age 18; and (c) a number of other disorders that typically emerge during infancy, childhood and adolescence such as ➤ **mental retardation**, ➤ **conduct disorder**, some ➤ **eating disorders** and the ➤ **developmental disorders** (*pervasive* and *specific*). See each of these for details.

childhood schizophrenia ➤ **schizophrenia, childhood**.

child neglect Because the term ➤ **child abuse** is so frequently associated with severe physical injury inflicted upon the child, the term child *neglect* has come to be used for other less obvious physical forms of maltreatment such as improper attention to health, diet, clothing, education, socialization, etc. The term encompasses maltreatment which results more from omission (as the word *neglect* implies) than from commission.

child psychology Generally taken as the most neutral umbrella term for the interdisciplinary science that studies the child in any of a large number of systematic ways. The actual approach taken by any given child psychologist may differ dramatically from that taken by another. It may be focused either on the normal and adaptive or on the abnormal and pathological; it may be applied or pure in its orientation; it may be concerned with motivation and emotion, with socialization, cognition, learning, or, indeed, any of the processes of psychology generally. The field is actually defined and delimited

CHOLINE

simply by the articulation of age boundaries; any processes observed occurring within the range from infancy to adolescence are 'fair game.' ➤➤ **child development** and **developmental psychology**.

Children's Apperception Test (CAT) A variation on the ➤ **Thematic Apperception Test (TAT)** designed for use with children.

children's culture ➤ **kids' culture**.

chimera 1. In genetics, an individual possessing two (or more) cell types resulting from an *in utero* fusion of two distinct zygotes. 2. Any organism composed of tissues from more than one organism of different species. 3. A mythological creature, a monster made up of the parts of several animals. 4. By extension, a foolish fantasy.

chir(o)- Combining form meaning *hand*.

chi-square (χ^2) A statistical test that allows tests of differences between independent samples using frequency data or between a sample and some set of expected scores. The test is based on differences between observations and expectations: $\chi^2 = \Sigma (O_i - E_i)^2/E_i$; where O_i represents each of *i* observed scores and E_i each of *i* expected scores. There are actually a number of different chi-square tests, although all are based on the same general principle; for example, by using a theoretical model to determine the expected scores the test becomes a test of ➤ **goodness of fit**. ➤➤ **chi-square *distribution**.

chloral hydrate The original sleeping drug. It is one of the non-barbiturate ➤ **sedatives** which, because it has less of a disruptive effect on sleep patterns than the barbiturates (which disrupt ➤ **REM sleep** especially), is frequently prescribed for children. Like most sedatives and hypnotics it interacts with alcohol and the so-called 'Mickey Finn' is a mixture of the two.

chlordiazepoxide A commonly prescribed ➤ **antianxiety drug** of the ➤ **benzodiazepine** class. Trade name, *Librium*.

chlorpromazine The most widely used ➤

antipsychotic drug. ➤ **phenothiazine derivatives**. Trade names, Thorazine, Largactil.

chlorprothixene A ➤ **thioxanthene derivative** used in the treatment of schizophrenia.

choice experiment A general label used for any of a number of basic experimental designs in which the subject is required to select one among two or more responses depending on which one of two or more stimuli was presented. The subject may be working under a *time set*, in which the response must be made as quickly as possible, or under an *accuracy set*, for which speed is relatively unimportant. ➤➤ **reaction time** and the various forms of that term.

choice point 1. Generally, any set of circumstances in which a choice among several alternatives is required. 2. Specifically, the physical point in a maze where the subject may take any one of two or more paths.

choice reaction ➤ **choice experiment**.

choice shift A general term covering the various kinds of changes or shifts in the choices made by a group of persons when compared with the average or typical sentiments about the choices of the separate individuals. In some conditions a *risky shift* is observed when the group decides to choose a more radical, riskier course of action than the individuals would, taken separately, have selected; in others a *cautious shift* is seen when the group takes a more conservative stance than separate individuals favored.

cholecystokinin A hormone found in the intestines and in the brain that has been implicated in the control of eating behavior. High concentrations suppress eating.

choleric Irritable, touchy, easily angered.

choline An amine widely distributed in bodily tissue. It is an essential component in normal fat and carbohydrate metabolism. It is a precursor of ➤ **acetylcholine** (ACh); derived from the breakdown of fats it is taken into neurons where, in the presence of choline acetylase, ACh is produced.

cholinergic Of neurons and neural pathways which, when stimulated, release ➤ **acetylcholine**, those for which acetylcholine is the transmitter substance.

cholinesterase Generally, any enzyme that functions by breaking down choline esters; see, e.g., ➤ **acetylcholinesterase**.

chorda tympani A set of neural fibers that make up part of the VIIth cranial nerve. It carries part of the neural information from the taste receptors and, since it passes through the middle ear where it is accessible to experimentation, it is important in providing information about taste.

chorea Any neurological disorder marked by muscular twitching and jerky, involuntary movements, e.g., Huntington's chorea, Sydenham's chorea.

choreiform movement Nonrepetitive, dance-like movements with a random, irregular quality.

choroid coat (or **membrane**) A delicate pigmented coat of tissue that surrounds the eye (except, naturally, in the front where the cornea admits light). It is just in back of the retina and serves to protect the retina from being stimulated by stray, reflected light.

chrom(a)- Combining form meaning *color*. var., *chrom(o)-*.

chroma 1. In the Munsell color system, the dimension that corresponds with *saturation*, the 'purity' of a color. 2. A quality of any visual stimulus that differentiates it from gray.

chromatic adj. Referring to the hue and saturation dimensions of visual stimuli as opposed to the black–white (or *achromatic*) dimension.

chromatic aberration ➤ **aberration, chromatic**.

chromatic adaptation 1. A decrease in sensitivity to a color stimulus with prolonged exposure. Under conditions of optimal fixation (e.g., the *fixed image* technique) saturation decreases until only a neutral gray is left. 2. Modification in the perceived hue and/or saturation of a light stimulus resulting from prior viewing of a light of different hue and/or saturation.

chromatic audition ➤ **audition, chromatic**.

chromatic color Since *color* is used to cover all aspects of vision including the black–white (or *achromatic*) dimension, this term is used for specific reference to the other two dimensions of hue and saturation of a visual stimulus. A chromatic color is one which cannot be placed in the black–gray–white series.

chromatic contrast ➤ **color contrast**.

chromatic dimming When the brightness of a fixated chromatic stimulus is abruptly lessened the observer experiences dramatic decrease (or 'dimming') in saturation, so much so that occasionally the complementary color appears momentarily.

chromatic induction ➤ **induced color**.

chromaticity The aspect of a color stimulus given by its dominant wavelength (hue) and its purity (saturation) taken together. Also called *chromaticness*.

chromaticness ➤ **chromaticity**.

chromatic valence A relative measure of the hue-producing effectiveness of a chromatic stimulus. When two such stimuli are mixed so that the result is perceived as gray they are, by definition, equal in their chromatic valence.

chromatopsia An abnormal condition in which a chromatic quality is 'added' to stimuli. Achromatic (colorless) objects are seen as having color and everything colored has additional tint to it. It results from taking certain drugs and may occur following exposure to intense visual stimulation. Also called *chromopsia*.

chromesthesia 1. Generally and literally, a form of ➤ **synesthesia** in which non-visual stimuli produce the experience of color sensations. 2. More specifically, the experiencing of color with auditory stimuli. The latter special case is usually intended and, hence, *colored hearing* and *colored audition* are used as synonyms. var., *chromaesthesia*.

chrom(o)- ➤ **chrom(a)-**.

chromopsia ➤ **chromatopsia**.

chromosomal aberrations Variations in either the number of chromosomes or the location of genetic material on chromosomes. ➤ **chromosomal alterations** and **chromosomal anomalies**.

chromosomal alterations Generally, the processes by which rearrangements among chromosomes occur. Three well-documented processes are: *inversion*, in which the bands within a particular chromosome become rearranged; *translocation*, in which two chromosomes fuse; and *reciprocal translocation*, in which there is an exchange of a DNA segment between two chromosomes. All such alterations are assumed to play a role in the evolution of species.

chromosomal anomalies Anomalies or abnormalities involving either loss of one chromosome or the addition of one or more. A number of specific abnormalities are known to occur with some frequency; see, e.g., ➤ **fragile X syndrome** for an instance of a weak chromosome, ➤ **Turner's** (or 45, X) **syndrome** for an instance of a missing sex chromosome and ➤ **Klinefelter's** (or 47, XXY) **syndrome** and ➤ **Down syndrome** (trisomy, 21) for instances of an additional chromosome.

chromosome Microscopic body in the nucleus of a cell which is conspicuous during mitosis. The term literally means *colored body* and chromosomes were so named because they stain deeply with basic dyes. Chromosomes carry the genes, the basic hereditary units. Each species has a constant, normal number of chromosomes. There are 46 in human somatic cells, arranged in 23 pairs; the ovum and sperm contain 23 each, one from each pair. Of this 23, 22 are the *autosomes* and 1 is the sex chromosome (either X or Y). In fertilization the 23 chromosomes from the male

unite with the 23 from the female. The X chromosome is the 'female determining' chromosome, the Y the 'male determining.' Normal female somatic cells are XX, normal male are XY; normal female ova are X, normal male sperm either X or Y. An XX embryo will be female; an XY, male.

chronaxie A value that expresses the sensitivity of a nerve to stimulation. It is measured by first determining the threshold of the nerve, the amount of direct current which if applied indefinitely would just excite it. This value is then doubled and the amount of time this current must be applied before the nerve responds is the chronaxie. var., *chronaxia*.

chronic Generally, long-term, drawn out, extending over a long period of time. Thus, a chronic disease is one in which the symptoms are long-lasting and show a slow progression, a chronic experiment one carried out over an extended period of time. Compare with ➤ **acute** (3 and 4). Various diseases and syndromes are characterized as chronic; they are to be found under the alphabetic listing of the disease or syndrome.

chronic affective disorder ➤ **cyclothymic disorder** and **dysthymic disorder**.

chronic brain disorder (or **syndrome**) One of the standard classifications of behavior disorders. It refers to disorders resulting from large, long-lasting brain damage such as those caused by syphilis, brain tumors, strokes, drugs, etc. The most common by far are those due to changes occurring in old age (senile psychosis) and alcohol (alcoholic psychosis).

chronic (drug) tolerance ➤ **tolerance, chronic**.

chronic pain ➤ **pain, chronic**.

chronic preparation ➤ **preparation, chronic**.

chronic tic disorder ➤ **tic disorders**.

chronic undifferentiated schizophrenia ➤ **chronic *schizophrenia**.

chron(o)- Combining form meaning *time*.

chronobiology A cover term for the study of biological rhythms, biological clocks, circadian rhythms, etc.; in short, any regular pattern of behavior that displays periodicity falls within the scope of this hybrid science. Note that in many texts the term ➤ **biorhythm** is used as a label for this field of study; for reasons explained under that entry the term chronobiology is rapidly becoming the only acceptable name for the science.

chronograph Any device that records and presents graphic records of time intervals.

chronological age ➤ **age, chronological**.

chronometric Lit., of time measurement. It is most often used to characterize the time course of cognitive operations. For example, by continuously increasing the complexity of a task along a known dimension the systematic increase in the time it takes subjects to perform the task will yield a chronometric analysis of the processes involved. For an example of how this technique is used ➤ **subtraction method**.

chronometrics, mental The measurement of the real time for the carrying out of mental processes. ➤ **chronometric**.

chronoscope Any device for measuring time intervals.

chunking A term first suggested by George A. Miller for the organization process whereby distinct 'bits' of information are collected together perceptually and cognitively into larger, coordinated wholes, or 'chunks.'

-cide Word element meaning: **1.** Killer. **2.** Act of killing.

cilia 1. Eyelashes. **2.** Hairlike processes projecting from the surface of various cells (e.g. in the bronchi). sing., *cilium*.

ciliary muscle The smooth muscle that controls accommodation. It is attached to the lens of the eye so that when it contracts the lens is thickened and when it relaxes the lens is flattened, for close-up and distant vision respectively.

cingulate gyrus The cortical part of the limbic system that lies along the lateral walls of the groove that separates the two cerebral hemispheres and just above the *corpus callosum*. It has been shown to be involved in emotional behavior, in hoarding and in the acquisition and retention of avoidance responses.

cingulotomy A form of psychosurgery in which fibers in the cingulate cortex are severed. It is occasionally used in severe cases of bipolar disorder or severe anxiety. ➤ **psychosurgery** for more discussion. var., *cingulectomy*.

cingulum bundle A group of axons that connects the cingulate and prefrontal cortex with the limbic cortex of the temporal lobe. Cutting this bundle has been used as a psychosurgical technique in severe cases of *obsessive-compulsive disorder*.

circadian hour ➤ **circadian time**.

circadian peak (and trough) The points during the 24-hour (i.e., ➤ **circadian**) cycle when body temperature hits its high (peak) and low (trough). Although there are large individual differences, most people's troughs occur at around 4–6 PM in the afternoon and 4 AM in the early morning. Their peaks are usually around 8–10 AM and PM.

circadian rhythm Circadian comes from the Latin *circa* meaning *about* and *dies* meaning *day*. Hence, rhythms with an approximately 24-hour cycle to them are called circadian. Recent work reveals that many biological functions display such a periodicity, including hormone secretions, temperature, blood pressure, etc. Such rhythms seem to be deeply ingrained biologically since they will continue to display their cyclic nature (although some drifting may be observed) even when the normal day/night pattern of light and dark is artificially manipulated. ➤ **biological clock**, **biorhythm**.

circadian rhythm sleep disorder ➤ **sleep–wake schedule disorder**.

circadian time Time as marked by the period of a full circadian cycle in an organism that is allowed to 'free run' (that is, the organism is maintained in a constant environment without the normal day/night or light/dark cycle). In most species the cycle will drift from the 24-hour day to one of roughly 25 hours. Hence, circadian time is based on a 25-hour day and a *circadian hour* is one of roughly 62.5 minutes.

circuit, reverberating ➤ **reverberating circuit** and ➤➤ **cell assembly**.

circular behavior Generally, behavior which stimulates like behavior. Laughter stimulates laughter in another which increases laughing in the first person. The terms *circular response* and *circular reaction* are used as synonyms by many but ➤ **circular reaction** for a special meaning in Piagetian theory.

circular reaction Generally used synonymously with ➤ **circular behavior**. The term has, however, been extended somewhat in its usage in Piagetian theory. Piaget assumed that circular reactions are important operations for making adaptations during the sensorimotor stage. He differentiated *primary* circular reactions from *secondary* and *tertiary*; the primary are centered on the infant's own body, the secondary involve stereotyped manipulations of objects and the tertiary are characterized by repetition with variations from cycle to cycle.

circular reasoning Empty reasoning in which the conclusion rests on an assumption whose validity is dependent on the conclusion. The apocryphal story of the instinct theorist is illustrative: when asked why all the sheep in an open field clustered together he replied, 'Because all sheep have a gregarious instinct.' When pressed as to how he knew they had this instinct he answered, 'It's obvious, just look at them all clustered together in that open field.' The futility of this kind of reasoning is in direct proportion to the amount of energy invested in it.

circum- Combining form meaning *around*.

circumstantiality A psychiatric term for a manner of speaking that is inappropriately indirect and 'circular.' The person tends to talk all around the real topic and delays excessively in dealing with the things under discussion. Compare with ➤ **tangentiality**.

circumstriate cortex ➤ **prestriate cortex**.

circumvallate papilla ➤ **lingual papilla**.

circumventrical system A group of structures around the third ventricle (hence the name) that is suspected of being the area where osmometric and volumetric signals (➤ **thirst**, et seq.) are integrated. Drinking, salt intake, and the secretion of ➤ **vasopressin** are thought to be controlled here.

11-cis retinal ➤ **rhodopsin**.

civilian catastrophe reaction A situational personality disorder brought about by the extreme stress of a major disaster like an earthquake, a plane crash, a flood, etc. See here ➤ **gross *stress reaction**. The symptoms include helplessness, regression, partial amnesia, etc. and are similar to those seen in ➤ **combat fatigue**.

CL (and CLalt) ➤ **comparison level**.

clairaudience The hypothesized extrasensory perception of a distant sound. ➤ **parapsychology** for a general discussion of such purported phenomena.

clairvoyance The hypothesized extrasensory perception of a distant object or event. ➤ **parapsychology** for a general discussion.

clan ➤ **sib** (2).

clang association An association in a verbal task in which two words or other stimulus items become linked because of acoustic similarity.

clarification A technique used in nondirected therapy whereby the therapist provides a summary of what the client says, focusing on and clarifying its meaning.

127

clasp-knife reflex A reaction found in the limbs of decerebrate animals. If pressure is applied to the limb the resistance offered increases owing to the stretch reflex which contracts the muscles. If, however, sufficient pressure is applied the resistance collapses and the muscle becomes extremely relaxed. The name of this reflex action comes from the simile of a spring-loaded knife, the blade of which is hard to pull until it reaches a certain point where it can be moved easily. The reflex acts to protect the extensor muscles from 'overloading.'

class There are several specialized uses here; all carry the basic notion that a class is a grouping, an aggregate or a category of some kind. **1.** In logic, any category of things or events which share common properties or features that can serve as distinctions segregating these things or events from others. **2.** In sociology, a synonym for ➤ **social class. 3.** In education, a group of students taught together as a unit. **4.** In statistics, any of the divisions resulting from a subdividing of a ranked distribution of scores.

class-free test ➤ **culture-free test**.

classical An adjective which, when appended to a theory, method or point of view, carries the implication that it (a) set the standards for the field and formed the basis for later developments and elaborations and/or (b) is a bit antiquated and probably wrong.

classical conditioning 1. An experimental procedure in which a **conditioned stimulus** (CS) which is, at the outset, neutral with respect to the *unconditioned response* (UR) is paired with an *unconditioned stimulus* (US) that reliably elicits the unconditioned response. After a number of such pairings the CS will elicit, by itself, a *conditioned response* (CR) very much like UR. In Pavlov's classic experiments the neutral CS was a bell which was paired with a food US that reliably produced a UR (salivation). After some trials the bell itself was sufficient to produce a flow of saliva, the conditioned response. **2.** The learning that takes place in this type of experimental procedure. Perhaps the best way to think of classical conditioning is that it is a set of circumstances under which responses of an organism established by natural selection come under the control of a new stimulus. ➤➤ **instrumental conditioning, learning, operant conditioning**, and related enteries.

classical psychoanalysis ➤ **classical theory**.

classical theory Since there have been so many variations of psychoanalytic theory developed over the years, this term has come to stand for the 'pure' form of the theory as put forward by Freud and carried on by his disciples without major modification of the basic theoretical framework. Also referred to as *classical psychoanalysis*. See here ➤ **Freudian**.

classification 1. The process of categorizing things or events into mutually exclusive classes. **2.** The result of such a process.

Classification of Mental and Behavioural Disorders (CMBD) The section of the World Health Organization's ➤ **International Classification of Diseases** that deals with the nosology of mental disorders. ➤➤ **Diagnostic and Statistical Manual** for the system approved by the American Psychiatric Association.

classification test 1. Generally, any test in which the individual is requested to sort the stimulus materials into classes. **2.** Specifically, a test designed to facilitate the process of classifying persons for some reason, e.g., for putting them into particular instructional programs.

class inclusion 1. Generally, the notion that if a class A is part of a larger class B then all members of the class A are members of the class B. **2.** In ➤ **Piagetian** theory, the term refers to the child's ability to reason simultaneously about the whole and the parts that make it up.

class interval The range of scores in a ➤ **class** (4) in a frequency distribution.

class limits The upper and lower bounds of a class interval.

clean Laboratory jargon for things which are neat and consistent. Most commonly used of experimental data. Note that through one of those quirks of language the antonym here is not 'dirty' but *noisy*, ➤ **noise** (3).

clearness The original meaning of the term was that proposed by the structuralists: an elementary attribute of phenomenological experience. A clear sensation or a clear image was one which was in the center of attention and stood out vividly from the background. The structuralists with their search for phenomenological consistency characterized both perceptual and cognitive processes in similar ways. The notion of clearness is still used today in both of these areas but the treatments are different. In perception it refers to perceived objects that are definite, distinct and with well-defined boundaries. In cognition it refers to that which is coherent and understandable.

cleft 1. n. A fissure. 2. adj. Split, divided.

cleft palate A congenital fissure or gap in the palate (roof of the mouth). Minor clefts involve only the soft palate although in serious cases it may extend forward through the hard palate, the gum ridge and upper lip.

Clever Hans The most famous of the Elberfeld horses of Germany. Hans seemed to be able to perform rather startling mental tasks such as addition, square roots and multiplication and even spelling words. It was ultimately discovered by the German psychologist Oskar Pfungst in 1907 that the horse was actually performing his apparent mental gymnastics by responding to subtle cues provided by the asker of each question or to his trainer Wilhelm von Osten. Hans' technique was to 'count' up to the answer by stamping his foot the required number of times. He 'knew' when to stop by taking his cue from unconscious and extremely subtle changes in body position and breathing pattern on the part of the humans around him. The term *Clever Hans effect* (or *phenomenon*) has come to stand for any situation in which one unconsciously controls the results of a study or the behavior of others by subtle, implicit communication. ➤➤ **experimenter bias, Rosenthal effect**. Also called commonly by the original German name, *Der kluge Hans*.

client A term preferred by many as a replacement for *patient* in clinical psychology. Originally it was reserved for non-directive therapies such as Carl Rogers's *client-centered* approach but it is now used by many others who wish to move clinical approaches in psychology away from the medically oriented model of aberrant behavior. ➤➤ **analysand** for another, slightly differently motivated, replacement term for *patient*.

client-centered therapy A form of psychotherapy developed by Carl Rogers. The therapist is non-directive and reflective and does not interpret or advise except to encourage or clarify points. The operating assumption is that the client is best able to deal with personal problems and the best course for the therapist is to offer a non-judgemental, accepting atmosphere within which to explore and work them out. Also occasionally known as *non-directive therapy*, although that term may be used to encompass approaches not specifically associated with the Rogerian point of view.

climacteric The ➤ **menopause**.

clinic The original meaning derives from a Greek word denoting *pertaining to a bed*. Obviously, this sense no longer holds; in fact, contemporary usage restricts the term to organizations or places where the patients or clients can walk in. Thus: 1. A place where persons come for individual work-up, diagnosis and/or treatment. In this general sense the term covers both the physical and the psychological. Hence, qualifiers will usually be affixed so that the focus of the clinic is clear; e.g., ➤ **behavioral *clinic, child-guidance *clinic,**

outpatient *clinic, etc. 2. The organization itself, including the building and its staff. 3. A short course or demonstration with either educational or quasi-therapeutic aims. Many have counseled against this usage of the term but their advice has gone unheeded and 'smokers' clinics,' 'speed-reading clinics' and the like abound.

clinical 1 adj. Generally, pertaining to a ➤ clinic, in any of the meanings of that term. 2. Characterizing an approach to personality and psychotherapy that focuses on the individual as a whole rather than seeking for general principles or doing normative studies. 3. Pertaining to medical or other therapeutic practice that relies heavily on intuitive and subjective judgements of the clinician. 4. Characterizing an approach to research which is based on observation (sometimes rather informal, sometimes highly systematic) of a relatively few subjects in natural situations. Often contrasted with the so-called experimental approach, which emphasizes highly controlled studies using large numbers of subjects. ➤ clinical· method, clinical *prediction.

clinical group(ing) Basically, psychiatric nosology, the classification of persons according to symptoms displayed.

clinical method 1. A general cover term for all those methods and procedures of diagnosis, classification and treatment of diseases and other disorders. 2. An approach to the study of psychological phenomena (disordered as well as normal) based on personal, intuitive, subjective analyses. ➤ clinical (3 and 4) and ➤ clinical *prediction. 3. In Piaget's terminology, a method of data collection based on quasinatural interaction with a child in which the experimenter presents some object or task to the child or asks the child particular questions. The child is permitted to respond freely and the experimenter 'takes up' on the responses and moves on to other tasks or asks additional questions. Piaget's term here reflects his recognition that this data-gathering method has much

in common with a psychiatric interview. Distinguish from ➤ clinical trial and ➤ clinical study.

clinical pain ➤ pain, clinical.

clinical prediction ➤ prediction, clinical.

clinical psychology The area of psychology concerned with aberrant, maladaptive or abnormal human behavior. Within the vast umbrella of clinical practices are diagnosis, evaluation, classification, treatment, prevention and research. Although recent years have reflected a trend toward the empirical approach, where the clinician draws on the findings and methodology of the researcher, clinical psychology still largely reflects its historical lineage, which is predominantly medical in orientation. However, to appreciate the enormous range available to the practicing clinician (and even more bewilderingly, to the person seeking psychotherapy) a few of the more recognized and widely practiced therapies should be consulted: ➤ behavior, chemo-, client-centered, cognitive-behavioral, encounter, Gestalt, group, psychoanalysis (various forms), etc.

clinical study ➤ trial (3).

clinical trial ➤ trial (3).

clinical type Any individual case in which the symptoms and behaviors conform to one of the many identifiable syndromes of clinical psychology and psychiatry.

clinic, behavioral Any clinic that specializes in behavior therapy.

clinic, child-guidance A clinic specializing in the psychological problems of children.

clinic, outpatient 1. Generally, a somewhat redundant term for any ➤ clinic (especially 1). 2. Specifically, a clinic specializing in the treatment of individuals who have been released from a hospital or other institution after a period of treatment.

clitoris The highly sensitive structure of erectile tissue that forms part of the female external genitalia. The clitoris develops from the same primordial structures as the penis and, not surprisingly, plays an important role in sexual stimulation and orgasm.

cloaca theory The 'theory' often believed by children that birth takes place through the anus. Not unexpectedly, psychoanalytic theory makes much of this simple but understandable confusion on the part of an unsophisticated child.

clock In operant conditioning, a stimulus some dimension of which varies with time. Thus, expressions like 'FI + clock' mean that the subject is being reinforced on an FI schedule of reinforcement in the presence of some stimulus which is being used to mark time since the last reinforcement. For more detail, ➤ **schedules of *reinforcement**.

clomipramine An ➤ **antidepressant drug** in the category of ➤ **tricyclic compounds**. It is frequently used as an ➤ **antiobsessional drug** since, unlike the other drugs in this category, it is therapeutic in treating obsessive–compulsive disorder.

clone This term comes from the Greek, where it refers to a cutting taken for the purpose of propagation. Hence: **1.** A group of cells which are descended from a single cell. **2.** All of the descendants, taken collectively, produced asexually from a single ancestor.

clonic Pertaining to ➤ **clonus**.

clonic spasm ➤ **spasm**.

clonus Rapid, involuntary contraction and relaxation of a muscle. Contrast with ➤ **tonus**.

closed instinct ➤ **instinct, closed**.

closed question Any question that an individual must answer by selecting one or more of a set number of alternatives. Compare with ➤ **open-ended question**.

closed system A system, actual or theoretical, that is bounded off from other systems and operates or is conceptualized as operating without externally imposed additions or changes.

closure, law of One of the several *Gestalt* laws of organization. It assumes an innate tendency to perceive incomplete objects as complete, to close up or fill in gaps in sensory inputs and to view asymmetric and unbalanced stimuli as symmetric and balanced.

clouding (of consciousness) Perceptually and cognitively confused state.

clozapine An atypical ➤ **antipsychotic drug** that, unlike most others, has minimal *extrapyramidal* effects.

cloze procedure A procedure for studying reading processes. One or more words are deleted from a prose passage and the subject is required to fill in the blanks.

clue A hint, a stimulus that guides behavior. Occasionally used as a loose synonym for ➤ **cue**.

cluster **1.** In factor analysis, a group of variables which have higher correlations with each other than with other variables. **2.** More generally, any group of objects or events which seem, subjectively, to belong together, to form a natural group.

cluster analysis A general label for a variety of mathematical techniques for determining the underlying structure in complex data. Cluster analyses are similar in some respects to factor analyses in that both involve the search for unitary elements (either *factors* or *clusters*) that account for the variability observed in the data.

clustering The tendency to group objects, words, pictures or ideas into clusters which 'belong together' in some subjective way. The effect is seen most clearly in experiments on the free recall of long lists of words in which subjects will recall the list with the similar words grouped together.

cluster suicides Multiple suicides occurring close together in time in a limited geographical area. They most commonly involve adolescents and are suspected of having an element of contagion in that one well-publicized suicide triggers off others among disturbed adolescents. ➤ **Werther syndrome**.

cluttering Rapid, often incoherent speech characterized by eliding words and syllables.

CMBD ➤ **Classification of Mental and Behavioural Disorders**.

CNS (or **cns**) ➤ **central nervous system**.

co- Combining form meaning *along with*, *joint* or *equally*.

coacting group ➤ **group, coacting**.

coarctated Pressed together, narrowed. Used occasionally of behaviors or functions that are inhibited or constricted.

cocaine (hydrochloride) An alkaloid obtained from the coca leaf. It has anesthetic properties when applied locally and stimulating and mood-elevating effects when taken internally by ingestion, injection or inhalation. Both ➤ **drug *dependence** and ➤ **drug *tolerance** develop with continued use. Cocaine acts by blocking the re-uptake of dopamine. Long-term abuse is associated with a toxic psychosis similar to that seen with amphetamines.

coccyx The small bone at the base of the spine in humans and tailless apes. It is formed from four fused rudimentary vertebrae.

cochlea The coiled, snail-shaped (hence its name) structure in the inner ear which contains the receptor organs of hearing. In humans it has 2¾ turns, the base is quite broad and it tapers off as it coils. The cochlea is a bony cavity containing three fluid-filled canals (*scala vestibuli*, *scala tympani*, and *scala media* or cochlear duct) each one running virtually its full length. The three canals are separated from each other by *Reissner's membrane* and by the ➤ **basilar membrane**.

cochlear duct (or **canal**) ➤ **cochlea**.

cochlear microphonic A set of electric potentials that can be recorded in the coch-

lea, considered by many the most likely candidate to be the generator potential for auditory sensation. It is a fluctuating voltage that 'follows' the stimulus even up to frequencies too high for nerve fibers to be firing. It is believed that the traveling wave that stimulates the hair cells at various points (see here ➤ **basilar membrane**) produces the cochlear microphonic.

cochlear nerve ➤ **auditory nerve**.

Cochran Q test A nonparametric statistical test, an extension of the ➤ **McNemar test** for use with more than two samples. It is useful for testing where three (or more) sets of frequencies or proportions differ significantly from each other and can be applied to data which are dichotomous (e.g., 'yes/no' or 'pass/fail').

cocktail-party phenomenon A term coined by C. Cherry to characterize the rather remarkable ability to attend selectively to a single person's speech in the midst of the competing speech of many others. The primary factors responsible for the effect are the context, the ➤ **redundancy** of speech, the physical location of the speaker and the pitch of the speaker's voice.

coconsciousness Term used by M. Prince for the divided, coexisting, consciousnesses seen in cases of multiple personality.

code 1. A set of rules or operations that transforms items, objects or data from one systematic form into another. 2 vb. To perform such a transformation. Thus, for example, the hearer of a sentence will code the sequence of physical, acoustic events into a meaningful form. For precision the term needs to be kept separate from *cipher*, which is a simple system in which one symbol explicitly replaces another. Code (and derived forms of the term) is reserved for the modification of the items so that they are reorganized into different size units or even different numbers of units. To follow up the above example, a person who does not understand French will code a sentence in

French merely in terms of its sounds or phones (indeed, the verb *code* probably shouldn't even be used); a fluent speaker of French will code it in terms of its syntax, semantics, pragmatics, etc. The operation of coding a stimulus input is known as *encoding*, the unscrambling of an already coded input is called *decoding*. Usage here is quite broad. Not only are linguistic messages characterized in this manner but other communicative exchanges as well. For example, a person who facially expresses sadness is said to *encode* sadness; one who perceives sadness in the face is said to *decode* sadness. **3.** A language or dialect form. See here ➤ **code switching, elaborated code, restricted code. 4.** A set of standards or rules for conduct.

codeine An opium alkaloid derived from morphine. It has the usual analgesic and sedative properties of opiates and is commonly used in low doses as an analgesic and a cough suppressant.

co-dependency Quite literally, a mutual dependency such as that between two individuals each of whom is emotionally dependent upon the other. The term has achieved rather wide currency in the non-technical literature. Also written without the hyphen.

code switching The term *code* is used here in sense 3 of that word. Hence, the phrase can have several meanings: **1.** The switching of levels of formality in language; e.g., a politician code switches when moving from the 'smoke-filled room' where a political position is worked out to the political podium where the position is presented to the public. **2.** The switching of dialects; e.g., urban African-Americans who switch dialects depending on the person they are addressing. **3.** The switching of languages, as commonly done by fluent bilinguals.

code test A test in which a message in one form must be converted into a coded form by replacing each symbol with some arbitrarily determined equivalent; e.g., A = 1, B = 2, etc., and the person must 'write' out some message in the numerical form. Occasionally called a *symbol–digit test*. Actually it should be called a *cipher* test since the one-to-one replacement is not a true ➤ **code**.

coding 1. Generally, the process of modifying or transforming a message from its input form into some other form. See the discussion under ➤ **code** (1 and 2). **2.** The transformation of data from one form to another.

coefficient Lit., produced together. Hence: **1.** In chemistry, a figure that indicates the number of molecules of a substance in a reaction. **2.** In mathematics, a constant factor by which other values are to be multiplied. **3.** In statistics, a value that expresses the degree to which some relationship between factors is to be found. This meaning is most commonly found in combined forms, e.g., *correlation coefficient*. Note that many authors prefer the form 'coefficient of ——' over '—— coefficient.' In this volume these terms are listed under the alphabetical heading of the main term.

coefficient of correlation ➤ **correlation coefficient**.

coefficient variation ➤ **coefficient of *dispersion**.

coen(o)- ➤ **cen(o)-**.

cognition A broad (almost unspecifiably so) term which has been traditionally used to refer to such activities as thinking, conceiving, reasoning, etc. Most psychologists have used it to refer to any class of mental 'behaviors' (using that term very loosely) where the underlying characteristics are of an abstract nature and involve symbolizing, insight, expectancy, complex rule use, imagery, belief, intentionality, problem-solving, and so forth. ➤ **cognitive psychology** and **cognitive science**.

cognitive-appraisal theory ➤ **theories of *emotion**.

cognitive-behavior therapy An approach to psychotherapy based originally on ➤ **behavior therapy** and consistent with its basic tenets. The novel aspect involves the extension of the modification and relearning procedures to cognitive processes such as imagery, fantasy, thought, self-image, etc. Proponents of the approach argue, not unpersuasively, that what the client *believes* about the things he or she does and about the reasons for them can be as important as the doing of them. Also known as *cognitive behavioral therapy*.

cognitive contour ➤ subjective *contour.

cognitive derailment A term used loosely in clinical settings to refer to the tendency for thoughts and associations to follow one another in illogical and unpredictable ways. It is often seen in schizophrenic disorders. Also called *cognitive slippage*.

cognitive dissonance An emotional state set up when two simultaneously held attitudes or cognitions are inconsistent or when there is a conflict between belief and overt behavior. The resolution of the conflict is assumed to serve as a basis for attitude change in that belief patterns are generally modified so as to be consistent with behavior.

cognitive dissonance theory Leon Festinger's theory of attitude change based on the notion that we are motivated to adjust our attitudes to remove ➤ **cognitive dissonance**. Also called *dissonance theory*.

cognitive ethology An interdisciplinary field encompassing the work of ethologists, psychologists and zoologists that focuses on the exploration of the mental life of animals, with special attention to their behavior in their natural environments.

cognitive heuristic ➤ heuristic, cognitive.

cognitive impairment disorders An umbrella term covering those disorders whose primary symptoms include impaired cognitive functioning; e.g., ➤ **delirium**, ➤ **dementia** and ➤ **amnesia**.

cognitive map A term coined by E. C. Tolman to describe his theoretical interpretation of the behavior of an animal learning a maze. Tolman argued that the animal was developing a set of spatial relationships – a cognitive 'map' – rather than merely learning a chain of overt responses. Evidence from experiments on *place learning* and *latent learning* was cited as supportive. The notion of a spatial representation that is the mental analog of a real map seems fairly obvious. All one need do is close one's eyes and answer the question, 'How many windows are in my home?', to appreciate the phenomenological reality of an image-like 'map' of the physical layout. Independently of whether rats have them, the notion of a cognitive map is fundamental to human mental processing.

cognitive marker A hypothetical representation of an individual mental process. The term was introduced by R. Ornstein in his theory of the experiencing of the passage of time. According to Ornstein, the phenomenal passing of time is primarily dependent on the amount of cognitive activity going on in a given physical time period and, theoretically, by counting the number of *cognitive markers* or individual mental events one can get an approximate measure of experienced duration.

cognitive operations ➤ operations, cognitive.

cognitive psychology A general approach to psychology emphasizing the internal, mental processes. To the cognitive psychologist behavior is not specifiable simply in terms of its overt properties but requires explanations at the level of mental events, mental representations, beliefs, intentions, etc. Although the cognitive approach is often contrasted sharply with the behaviorist approach it is not necessarily the case that cognitivists are anti-behavioristic. Rather, behaviorism is viewed as seriously incomplete as a general theory, one which fails to provide any coherent characterization of cognitive processes like thinking, language, decision-making, etc. To get a feeling of the general issues and problems within the area ➤ attention, concept formation, information processing, memory (et seq.), psycholinguistics, etc.

cognitive schema ➤ schema.

cognitive science A newly coined name for the cluster of disciplines that studies the human mind. The term refers to an amalgamation; it is an umbrella term which includes a host of once disparate approaches such as cognitive psychology, epistemology, linguistics, computer sciences, artificial intelligence, mathematics and neuropsychology.

cognitive slippage ➤ cognitive derailment.

cognitive style As stated: the characteristic style or manner in which cognitive tasks are approached or handled. Several dimensions have been identified along which individuals' cognitive styles can be shown to differ. See specifically ➤ leveling–sharpening and field dependence–field independence, reflectivity–impulsivity.

cognitive therapy The form of psychotherapy developed by Aaron T. Beck, based on the notion that the way in which an individual structures and interprets his or her experiences determines mood and subsequent behavior. Seeing and thinking negatively are argued to cause negative feelings and behaviors; changing the manner in which an individual conceptualizes things lies at the heart of the therapeutic procedure. The approach and term are Beck's; similar orientations go under the more general heading, ➤ cognitive-behavior therapy.

cognize To know; occasionally, to think.

cohesiveness (or cohesion) The standard dictionary meaning is generally intended in psychology: a tendency to stick together or to be united either physically or logically. The term enjoys wide use in reference to social groups, concepts in education, items in a learning task, elements of a perceptual field, etc.

cohort Originally the term cohort referred to an ancient Roman military unit consisting of from 300 to 600 soldiers. It is more commonly used, however, to refer to: 1. Very generally, any group or band of persons. 2. In demography, a number of persons all possessing a common characteristic; for example, a group of children born in the same year. 3. In ethology, a number of organisms of a given species which function together as a group.

cohort effect An effect or phenomenon whose cause is attributable to the adventitious properties of a ➤ cohort (2). For example, in developing nations a skill like literacy shows strong cohort effects.

coition ➤ coitus.

coitus As the term is typically used it refers to heterosexual, vaginal intercourse culminating with the semen introduced into the female reproductive tract. Thus, coitus interruptus is coitus with the male withdrawing from the vagina prior to ejaculation. ➤ Sexual intercourse is a common synonym but consult that term for some distinctions; coition is generally used synonymously also but is occasionally reserved for the process in general rather than the actual act; copulation is a fairly pure synonym.

coitus interruptus Lit., interruption of coitus. ➤ withdrawal (1).

'coke' Street slang for cocaine.

cold A sensation evoked by any stimulus that is below normal skin temperature (roughly 89°F, 32°C). Note that the sensation of cold is a relative one and depends on the adaptation level of the skin. An object that is at 80°F, which ordinarily feels cool to the touch, can be made to feel warm if the hand is held in 70°F water for a minute or so before touching the stimulus. The equivalent effect occurs with stimuli whose temperature is above normal skin temperature; they can be made to feel cool by adapting the skin to relatively warm water.

cold emotion A phrase used for the agitated physical state experienced with some stimulating drugs (e.g., epinepherine). The bodily conditions mimic those of emotional arousal but there is a lack of true affective experience.

coldness Lack of emotionality; often specifically used of sexual feeling. See the discussion under ➤ **frigidly**.

cold spot A point on the skin where a punctate stimulus that is below adaptation level of the skin will evoke a sensation of cold. It was first thought that such cold spots were due to specific 'cold receptors' in the skin at that point; subsequent microscopic study of the skin has failed to discover any precise relationship between specific nerve fibers and specific sensations.

'cold turkey' Slang for the process of terminating a physiological ➤ **drug *dependence** by abruptly ceasing to take the drug with no support from other drugs. Depending on the severity of the dependence and the form of drug involved, such a process can be a most trying experience. This is particularly true in the case of opiates, amphetamines, alcohol and nicotine.

collateral 1 adj. Accompanying, off to the side. **2** adj. Subsidiary. **3** n. A nonlinearly related kin, a cousin, uncle or aunt. **4** n. A ➤ **collateral fiber**.

collateral fiber A branching fiber from the axon of a neuron. In some neurons, particularly those in the cortex, collateral fibers return to the region of the cell body. Such recurrent collateral fibers act as inhibitors, so that the cell cannot be refired for a time.

collective consciousness ➤ **group mind**.

collective guilt ➤ **group superego**.

collective unconscious Jung's term for that aspect of the unconscious shared by all. This racial unconscious (as it is also called) was assumed by Jung to be inherited, transpersonal and, in his conceptualization, to consist of the residue of the evolution of man. Its components were termed *archetypes*.

colliculus From the Latin for *little hill*, any of four prominent collections of neural tissues of the *corpora quadrigemina* in the brain stem. The two anterior are called the *superior colliculi* and are part of the visual system. In lower vertebrates they represent the sole system; in higher vertebrates they are not as important as the direct retinal-geniculate-cortex system and serve mainly visual reflexes to moving stimuli. The posterior *inferior colliculi* are part of the auditory system and the auditory fibers pass through them on the way to the mediate geniculate nucleus and the auditory cortex.

color The subjective sensation associated with light. Color experience depends on three components of the physical energy: *wavelength*, *purity* and *intensity*. Wavelength corresponds to the psychological attribute of ➤ **hue** (or what the layman would call 'color'), purity to ➤ **saturation** and intensity to ➤ **brightness**. See these terms for details on meaning and usage patterns. Note that the adjective ➤ **chromatic** is used to refer to stimuli that are analyzable into all three of these attributes and ➤ **achromatic** is used for stimuli that only have the brightness attribute. In layman's terms, the former have 'color,' the latter are 'black and white.'

color adaptation ➤ **chromatic adaptation**.

color agnosia The loss of the ability to recognize colors. ➤ **agnosia**.

color antagonism ➤ **complementary *color**.

color attribute Any of the visual qualities of hue, saturation and brightness.

color blindness Any one of a complicated variety of congenital defects in vision that renders a person unable to distinguish two or more colors that normal individuals can distinguish easily. Although there is a form of total color blindness (➤ **achromatopsia** and **monochromacy**), it is quite rare and most colorblind individuals distinguish many wavelengths. The most common variety is *dichromacy*, whereby the colors experienced can be described by using only two hues (i.e. the dichromat can match any given sample using only two wavelengths in mixture, the trichromat with normal color vision needs three). The vast majority of dichromats confuse reds and greens; blue–yellow dichromacy is rare. Color blindness is a sex-linked genetic trait and is far more frequent in males than females with approximately 1 in 15 men showing some defects but only about 1 in 100 women.

color circle A schematic representation of the visible spectrum showing the dimensions of hue and saturation. Hue is given by the position on the circle and saturation by the distance from the center, as in the accompanying figure.

WAVELENGTHS (in nm)

EXTRA-SPECTRAL HUES

color, complementary Any of two colors that can be additively mixed to produce an achromatic gray. Schematically, the hues of complementary colors are found at opposite points on the ➤ **color circle.** ➤ **color mixing** and **theories of *color vision.** Also known as *antagonistic color.*

color constancy The tendency for a color to look the same under wide variation in viewing conditions.

color contrast The fact that the perceived color of any object is somewhat dependent on the color of the surrounding medium. Basically the effect is produced by enhancement of two complementary colors by each other. For example, if blue and yellow fields are juxtaposed a *simultaneous contrast* effect occurs where at the border the colors will seem somewhat bluer and yellower respectively, *Successive contrast* can also be achieved by fixating on one

color for a time followed by presentation of the complementary. Also called *chromatic contrast.*

color deficiency ➤ **color blindness.**

colored audition ➤ **chromatic *audition.**

colored hearing ➤ **chromatic *audition.**

colored noise ➤ **pink *noise.**

color equation A description of the results of a color match in which the subject adjusts the amounts of each of three primary colors needed to match a test color. The equation is usually in the form: $c(C) + r(R) \equiv g(G) + b(B)$, where the lowercase indicates the number of units and the upper-case indicates the color, with C standing for the test color, R for red, G for green and B for blue. Note that '$\equiv$' is typically used here rather than '$=$' because subjective equivalence is given by the equation and not mathematic equality.

color, film A color seen as nonsubstantial, without contour and indefinitely localized. Film colors do not feel like they 'belong' anywhere and are rarely experienced in the real world. The sky on a very clear day comes reasonably close. Compare with ➤ **surface *color.**

colorimeter Any device or instrument for measuring color.

colorimetry The specification and measurement of color. The science of colorimetry is based on the notion that all possible visual stimuli can be specified in terms of but three properly chosen variables. These three are essentially the amount of each of the three primaries which, when mixed, will subjectively match the target stimulus.

color mixing Lit., the mixing of colors. It is important to distinguish between two basic types of mixing: light or 'film color' and paint or 'surface color.' Mixing of lights is an additive process whereby the resulting hue is an interaction of the mixed hues. Mixing of paints is a subtractive process whereby the resulting hue is the

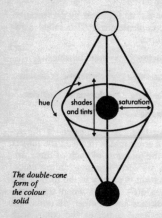

The double-cone form of the colour solid

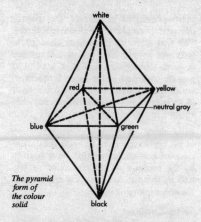

The pyramid form of the colour solid

one not absorbed by the surface. Thus, mixing yellow and blue light produces a gray or white, mixing yellow and blue paint produces a green. In psychology the term is almost always used for the mixing of lights and the mixing is accomplished by presenting two (or more) color stimuli to the same portion of the retina in any of several ways, such as simultaneous projection, rapid succession or alteration.

color pyramid ➤ color solid.

color shades Colors of brightnesses darker than middle or neutral gray. Compare with ➤ color tints.

color solid An extrapolation of the color circle to include the dimension of brightness (or lightness) so that any color may be given as a unique point in the solid depending on its combination of hue, saturation and brightness. Note that the color solid may be presented as either a double cone or double pyramid. The pyramid form is favored by many since the four primaries form the corners. The two forms are shown here.

colors, primary 1. Any three colors (or, more properly, *hues*) no two of which if mixed will produce the third. In this sense there is a very large number of sets of primaries; they are not identified as specific wavelengths but by their relationships to each other and the principles of color

mixing. **2.** As based on introspection, the optimum, purest color experiences – those that appear to an observer as being made up of but a single hue and which cannot be subjectively broken down into other components. Here, four primaries are found: *blue* at approximately 475 nm, *green* at roughly 510 nm, *yellow* at 585 nm and *red*, which is extraspectral and requires a little blue light to get rid of a slight yellowish tinge, at roughly the complement of 495 nm.

Meaning 1 is the one commonly presented in standard general texts in psychology; meaning 2, however, is the one that is accepted in the technical literature on color vision. If 1 is the intended meaning then the proper term for 2 is *unique hues*.

color surface A plane section of the color solid taken at a right angle to the perpendicular. It represents all the hues and saturations at a given brightness level.

color, surface A color seen as belonging to or lying on an object. Surface colors are localized and 'substantial'; part of the real world. Compare with ➤ film *color.

color tints Colors of brightnesses lighter than middle or neutral gray. Compare with ➤ color shades.

color triangle A schematic diagram in the shape of an equilateral triangle (usually) with the apices representing the red, green and blue primaries. The enclosed area represents all the colors possible through mixing these.

color value In the Munsell system of colors, the dimension corresponding approximately with lightness.

color vision, theories of Any of several theoretical models that seek to characterize and explain the basic phenomena of color vision. There are a number of phenomena of color vision that any theory must be able to account for. Briefly they are: (a) the existence of primary colors; (b) the existence of complementary colors and their appearance in contrast effects and afterimages; (c) the laws of color mixing; and (d) the various symptoms of the different kinds of color blindness. The two best-known attempts at a systematic theoretical explanation of these are the Young–Helmholtz theory (also known as the trichromatic theory, or trireceptor theory) and the Hering theory (or opponent process theory).

The Young–Helmholtz theory assumes three types of color receptors. Although each receptor is assumed to respond to all wavelengths, they have different spectral sensitivities, so that one is more sensitive to long wavelengths (reds), one to medium wavelengths (greens) and one to short wavelengths (blues). All other colors are assumed to be perceived by combinations of these so that the perception of yellow, for example, is characterized as being due to the simultaneous stimulation of red and green receptors and their integration in the visual neural pathways and the visual cortex. The theory accounts for the laws of color mixing nicely although it has some difficulty with the other basic phenomena. In particular, the theory cannot easily explain the fact that dichromats who confuse red with green see yellow. It also has difficulty explaining complementary color afterimages.

The Hering theory, now updated by Hurvich and Jameson and known as the opponent process theory, assumes three sets of receptor systems, red–green, blue–yellow and black–white. Each system is assumed to function as an antagonistic pair. As in the Young–Helmholtz theory, each of the receptors (or receptor pairs) is assumed to be sensitive to light of all wavelengths but with maximum sensitivity to wavelengths of particular kinds. The assumption that gives the theory its power is that the stimulating of one of an opponent pair not only produces excitation of that receptor system but also produces an inhibitory effect on the other; red light stimulates the red receptors and simultaneously inhibits the green. The theory accounts for all of the phenomena well including the color-contrast and color-blindness data which are bothersome to the trireceptor theory. At present it is regarded as a better approximation to the true state of color vision. Note, however, that any theory of color vision must eventually deal with the fact that the retina processes visual stimuli differently from the cortical and sub-cortical visual centers. This point is important because the careful examination of the retina has turned up only three types of cone pigments and they correspond rather nicely with the spectral absorption curves derived from the Young–Helmholtz theory. It seems likely that (to force a gross oversimplification) retinal receptors act as per the Young–Helmholtz theory and the signals are then recoded into the opponent process form by higher-level neural systems.

Finally, be it noted that there have been other candidates for a theory of color vision. See here ➤ **Ladd–Franklin theory**, **retinex theory**. The former is not taken seriously for it has many problems; the latter is taken seriously but it is so very different in kind from the others that many researchers are simply not clear how to evaluate and test it.

color, volume Color seen as filling a three-dimensional space. It is perceived as organized and transparent and 'bulky.'

color weakness A term sometimes used in place of ➤ **color blindness**, particularly since most color-deficient individuals are actually color 'weak' and not color 'blind.'

color wheel A simple device for mixing colors by rotating a wheel (usually a disk) the surface of which is covered by colored paper or plastic. By varying the area covered by any color a variety of mixing effects can be obtained. The mixing obtained this way is termed *retinal mixing*.

color zones The retina is not uniformly sensitive to all wavelengths and the differentially sensitive areas are termed color *zones*. For the normal eye all colors can be seen in the *fovea*, which is made up entirely of cones. In the middle zone around the fovea, blues, yellows and the full range of achromatics are perceived, primary red and green are experienced as gray and the other reds and greens have a blue or yellow tinge. In the periphery of the retina (which is made up entirely of rods) there is only achromatic experience.

column 1. In statistics, a vertically arranged series of numbers. 2. In physiology, a nerve which extends longitudinally in the central nervous system.

com- Combining form meaning *with*, *jointly*. var., *con-*, occasionally *col-*.

coma An abnormal state of deep stupor with total absence of consciousness, loss of all voluntary behavior and most reflexes. The term is reserved for cases resulting from injury, disease or other trauma.

comatose In a coma or a coma-like state.

combat fatigue Popularly called *shell shock* or sometimes *battle fatigue*, this was originally classified as a *traumatic neurosis* brought on by extended, dangerous, military action. More recently it has been classified as a ➤ **gross *stress reaction** along with the ➤ **civilian catastrophe reaction**, with which it shares many behavioral and emotional symptoms, and the references to battle and combat have been dropped.

combination tone A subjective tone produced by the simultaneous sounding of two or more tones. Combination tones are formed in the auditory system itself (probably by the mechanical, physical

properties of the cochlea) and are not present in the physical stimulus. If two tones are sounded, for example 1,000 and 1,200 Hz, three types of combination tones will be heard: a *difference tone* of 200 Hz; a *summation tone* of 2,200 Hz; and a series of descending tones produced by a complex relationship between the two original tones.

commensalism A symbiotic relationship between two organisms of different species. ➤ **symbiosis**.

commissive A class of ➤ **speech acts** in which the speaker places himself under obligation to do something or carry through with something; e.g., promises are commissives.

commissural fibers The neural tracts of a ➤ **commissure** that connect corresponding regions on the two sides of the central nervous system.

commissure Generally, any transverse band of neural fibers passing over the midline in the central nervous system and connecting corresponding regions on each side.

commissurectomy Surgical severing of a commissure.

commitment The process whereby an individual is judged to be dangerous either to himself or others or to be incapable of functioning without psychiatric assistance and, hence, is admitted into a psychiatric treatment program. The process may be involuntarily carried out in so far as the individual is concerned, in which case it becomes a forensic (legal) matter, or it may be voluntary when the person judges him- or herself to be in need of the treatment.

common chemical sense A sense of chemical solutions other than those of taste and smell. The receptors are widely distributed, occurring especially in the exposed moist surfaces of the mouth and throat. One of the problems encountered in research on this sense is distinguishing between pain sensitivity and chemical sensitivity. The issue as to whether there is a common chemical sense wholly separate from pain is not yet resolved.

common fate A Gestalt principle that aspects of a perceptual field that function or move in similar manner tend to be perceived together.

common sense 1. In the Aristotelian sense, the capacity to comprehend the qualities of an object by the use of the other senses. **2.** In Thomas Reid's revival of this basic idea the focus was on the ability to apprehend qualities common to all the senses (time, space, numerosity). **3.** Beliefs, opinions, practical understanding of things shared by the 'common man.' **4.** Colloquially, good, reasoned judgement.

common-sense validity ➤ validity, common sense.

common sensibility 1. Originally, tactile sensations. **2.** Occasionally, visceral sensations.

common trait A trait found in all persons in a particular society or culture.

communication 1. Broadly speaking, the transmission of something from one location to another. The 'thing' that is transmitted may be a message, a signal, a meaning, etc. In order to have communication both the transmitter and the receiver must share a common code, so that the meaning or information contained in the message may be interpreted without error. Communication theory, from this very general perspective, has proven useful in psychology in developing models of interpersonal interaction, memory processes, physiological functions, language, etc. ➤➤ channel, code, information theory. **2.** The message or the actual information transmitted. There is a tendency on the part of some writers to use communication as synonymous with ➤ language. This is a mistake and the reasons for keeping these terms distinct are given under that term.

communication disorders An umbrella category for those disorders of speech and language. Included are ➤ expressive lan-

guage disorder, mixed expressive-receptive language disorder, phonological disorder, and stuttering.

communication unit Communications theory usually structures a communication system into an ensemble of elements called a 'unit.' It consists of a transmitter (or sender) which encodes a message, a communication channel through which the message travels and a receiver which receives and decodes the message.

community A settlement of people concentrated in one geographical area. The defining feature of a community is a 'self-consciousness' that each member has that the group is a social unit and that he or she shares group identification with the others.

community psychology An applied branch of psychology in which the practitioner works in a variety of ways with a community. It may include therapy-like interactions with community members but is more often oriented toward improving the quality of life.

companionate love ➤ love, companionate.

comparable forms ➤ forms, comparable.

comparable groups ➤ groups, comparable.

comparative judgement Quite literally, any judgement about a stimulus made relative to (in comparison with) some other stimulus. A common procedure in *scaling* experiments in which a standard stimulus is often used against which all other stimuli are to be judged.

comparative psychology A sub-discipline of psychology concerned with the investigation of the behavior of various species of animals with an eye toward the drawing of comparisons (similarities and distinctions) between them. The approach draws on other areas in psychology such as learning theory and on other disciplines including ethology, physiology, genetics and zoology.

comparison level (CL) In *social psychology*, the average overall level of personal

141

interaction that an individual expects to find in a relationship. People with high CL expect to have rewarding and fulfilling relationships with others. According to the full analysis here, there is also a 'CLalt' or 'comparison level for alternatives' (i.e., other people) which, if higher than the CL, leads a person to be less committed to his or her current relationship.

comparison stimulus ➤ **standard** (especially 2).

compartmentalization 1. Generally, the isolation of various of one's thoughts, feelings and beliefs from each other. My favorite example is a deeply devout Roman Catholic biologist of my acquaintance whose research is on birth control. **2.** K. Horney used the term to describe a sense of disconnectedness that comes from the excessive use of compartmentalization (in the first sense) as a defense mechanism to shield one from the anxiety and tension that such inconsistencies produce.

compatibility 1. Generally, suitability for mixing without producing unfavorable results; characterizing a harmonious coexistence. This meaning is found expressed in psychopharmacology to describe various drug combinations and in social and personality psychology to characterize particular kinds of interpersonal interactions. **2.** In logic, any non-contradictory relation between two statements, principles or propositions.

compensating error ➤ **error, compensating**.

compensation The standard dictionary definition (*making up for, offsetting* or *counterbalancing*) reflects essentially the use that most psychologists make of this term: **1.** Freud elaborated upon it extensively, viewing it as one of the basic defense mechanisms that certain individuals use to make up for particular deficiencies and to cover up the personal shortcomings associated with them so as to prevent them from reaching consciousness. **2.** In Alfred Adler's theory it became the central

concept of his characterization of personality. It was viewed as the primary mechanism by which one could come to deal with feelings of ➤ **inferiority** (see that term for more detail). Compare with ➤ **overcompensation**. **3.** In neurophysiology, the recovery of function following neural damage. The term here is generally restricted to central-nervous-system injury when the neural structures themselves do not regenerate but have their functions subsumed by other tissues.

compensatory movement (or **reflex**) Any movement that functions to restore normal body position or equilibrium.

compensatory trait ➤ **trait, compensatory**.

competence 1. Generally, ability to perform some task or accomplish something. **2.** In forensic psychiatry, ➤ **competent**. **3.** In the study of language and psycholinguistics, the embodiment of the deep, abstract rules of a language. The distinction is made here between competence and ➤ **performance**. A theory of the former would be a theory of linguistic knowledge and grammar, of what an idealized mature speaker-hearer of a language *could* say and understand; a theory of the latter would be a theory of behavior, of what real speaker-hearers actually do say and how utterances of others are understood.

competent In forensic psychiatry, a designation used of a person who has been judged mentally capable to stand trial. The usual criteria for being declared competent are: (a) the person understands the nature of the charges and the legal consequences of adjudged guilt; and (b) the person is able to assist in his or her defense.

competition ➤ **rivalry**.

complement Generally, that which completes something.

complementarity The tendency for people to seek out others that have qualities that they lack or that complement their own.

complementary color ➤ **color, complementary**.

complementary instincts In psychoanalysis, instincts that lie at opposite ends of some dimension. The classic examples are Freud's *eros* and *thanatos*.

complete learning method An experimental procedure in which the subject works with the material until one complete errorless trial is achieved.

completion test Any test in which the individual is given parts of items and must complete them: e.g., a fill-in-the-blanks test.

complex **1.** When the accent is on the second syllable, an adjective treated roughly as the antonym of simple or elementary. **2.** With the accent on the first syllable, a noun referring to a cluster or constellation of emotionally toned ideas or dispositions. Psychoanalytic theory has scattered various complexes liberally throughout its literature (e.g., Oedipus, Electra, inferiority, etc.). Although intended primarily as descriptive devices, they have gradually come to have pathological connotations because of the dominant theme that complexes are often repressed and in conflict with other behaviors. The term, however, should not necessarily convey pathology and it should be used carefully because it will often be misinterpreted.

complex indicator A Jungian term for one or more responses on a word-association test that indicate the existence of a repressed complex. Such response characteristics as stammering, unusually long or short response latencies, highly improbable associates, blushing, etc. are often taken as such indicators.

complex man A label for a general perspective on mankind which presumes that the essential nature of the human being is emotional and motivational complexity and that an effective science of psychology and any worthwhile applications of that science must recognize and be sensitive to the diversity within persons and to individual differences.

complex reaction Synonym for ➤ **choice reaction**.

complex reaction time ➤ **reaction time complex**.

complex tone ➤ **compound *tone**

compliance Generally, yielding to others. Hence, many writers restrict this term to the overt behavior of one person that conforms to the wishes or the behaviors of others. That is, they use it so that there is no notion that the compliant person necessarily believes in what he or she is doing. ➤ **conformity** for more on this point. Compare with ➤ **private acceptance**.

compliant character K. Horney's term for a person who displays neurotic self-effacement, deference and inappropriate yielding. Horney regarded such people as displaying a *neurotic compliance*.

complication **1.** Generally, any secondary factor or set of factors that functions to increase the complexity and intractability of a situation. **2.** In medicine, a second disease or syndrome superimposed on one already present. **3.** In older psychology texts, a combining of sensory experience from two or more senses.

complication experiment An experimental procedure the data from which gave rise to Titchener's ➤ **law of *prior entry** (which see for details).

componential analysis A general term used to refer to any analysis that is based on a determination of distinctive elements or components. In semantics, for example, a componential analysis of a word consists of identifying its primary meaning components. In J. J. Katz's example, 'bachelor' is *human, male, adult, unmarried*.

component instinct ➤ **partial instinct**.

composite A unitary experience or whole made up of elements belonging to several other experiences. The often found compound terms like *composite figure, composite image, composite trait*, etc. are all self-explanatory.

compos mentis Latin for *of sound mind*.

compound bilingual ➤ **bilingualism**.

compound conditioning ➤ **configurational learning**.

compound eye A type of eye found in many insects and crustaceans. Rather than a single focusing unit (lens) and projection surface (retina), it contains many individual optical systems (*ommatidia*) each with its own lens and photosensitive elements. The large compound eye of *limulus* (horseshoe crab) has been the object of considerable study and the source of discoveries about visual systems in general.

compound reaction time ➤ **complex *reaction time**.

compound stimulus Generally, any complex stimulus made of more than one basic element. For example, in animal conditioning, the simultaneous presentation of a tone and a light would function as a *compound stimulus*. ➤ **blocking**.

compound tone ➤ **tone, compound**.

comprehend 1. To understand, with the implication that the understanding is deep and thorough. 2. To combine several ideas or principles under a central theme.

comprehension The act of understanding a thing. The most common uses of the term are in education and psycholinguistics and, perhaps surprisingly, it is used in both contexts with similar connotations. To say that a student *comprehends* a principle entails assumptions about the state of a student's knowledge concerning the material 'containing' (using that word as a loose metaphor) the principle; a similar statement holds for a person who *comprehends* an utterance. Most contemporary cognitive psychologists argue that this comprehension process has two distinct and interlocking components: a *construction* process whereby an interpretation of the material is built up and a *utilization* process whereby the interpretation is matched to other knowledge so that the information can be used to answer questions, deal with new situations, follow instructions, etc. Note that some authors differentiate between *comprehension* and *understanding*, on the grounds that the former is more concrete and deals with specifics while the latter is more abstract and connotes a deeper and more symbolic cognitive act (see here ➤ **understanding**, 1 and 3). This distinction is, however, ignored by most theorists and the two terms are used more or less synonymously.

comprehension test Generally, any test designed to evaluate the understanding of a situation, a principle or some previously presented material. More specifically, a test designed to assess the understanding of material read.

comprehensive solution In K. Horney's theory, a form of a ➤ **neurotic solution** in which one comes to view oneself as being the idealized self.

compromise formation In psychoanalysis, a pattern of reacting to a conflict such that elements of both components of the conflict are expressed. Classical theory regards it as a kind of fusion between the repressed impulse and the repressing agency.

compulsion 1. Behavior motivated by factors that compel a person to act against his or her own wishes. 2. The psychological state in which one feels so compelled. 3. The underlying compelling force itself. Differentiate from ➤ **obsession**, where the focus is more on thoughts and feelings than on behavior and from ➤ **impulse**, where the compelling quality is more sudden and satisfiable. Compulsion usually carries the connotation of repetitiveness and irrationality. Strictly speaking, it may be either endogenous (from within) or exogenous (from without) but the former is usually intended; ➤ **coercion** or *constraint* typically serve for the externally imposed. ➤➤ **impulse control disorder**, **obsessive-compulsive disorder**.

compulsive 1. Characterizing a ➤ **compulsion**. 2. Characterizing a person with a ➤ **compulsive conduct disorder** or displaying a ➤ **compulsive personality disorder**.

compulsive conduct disorder A behavior disorder characterized by a pronounced tendency to engage in repetitive, compulsive acts. ➤ **obsessive compulsive disorder**.

compulsiveness 1. Originally, the tendency to repeat specific motor acts. **2.** More broadly, any tendency for repetitive behavior both affective and cognitive as well as motor. ➤➤ **impulse control disorder, obsessive compulsive disorder**.

compulsive personality disorder A personality disorder characterized by compulsive behaviors, e.g., excessive frugality, obstinacy, cleanliness, etc. Also called *anankastic personality*. ➤➤ **compulsion** and **obsessive compulsive disorder**.

computational metaphor The term refers to the use of computers as models of human functioning and to the extended notion that human cognition is a computational process as opposed to, say, an analog process. ➤➤ **artificial intelligence** and **computer simulation**.

compute In addition to the standard dictionary definitions the term appears in negative form as laboratory jargon (as in the phrase 'does not compute') for a situation that is illogical or an analysis that cannot be carried out because some facts are missing or some data are unavailable.

computer-administered tests A general term for any test that has been adapted so that it can be administered and scored by a computer. Using a television screen, speakers and a keyboard the questions are presented either visually or aurally and the testee types in the answers, which are recorded and analyzed by the computer.

computer-assisted instruction (CAI) Basically, the use of computers to facilitate teaching techniques. Actually, CAI systems are just one (although the most technologically advanced) of the pedagogic developments which have been stimulated in recent years by advances in learning theory and theories of instruction. E.g., ➤ **programmed instruction, teaching machine**.

computerized axial tomography (CAT) A noninvasive technique for examining soft tissue, most commonly the brain. A narrow X-ray beam is passed through the organ repeatedly (for a full brainscan 180 separate scans are made). A computerized system analyzes the pattern of absorption at each point, which yields the data for full visualization of the organ. In a CAT-scan of the brain one can produce a visual representation of important structures including gray matter, the cerebrospinal fluid-filled cavities, blood vessels and any abnormalities like tumors, lesions, etc. Also called, simply, *computerized tomography* or *CT-scan*. ➤➤ **magnetic resonance imaging** and **positron emission tomography**.

computer simulation Quite literally, the use of a computer to simulate something. Generally the 'something' here is human thought or behavior. That is, one attempts to program the computer to behave in a manner that is analogous to thought processes or behavior. In such research the computer itself is relatively unimportant; the critical element is the program – it is literally a theory of the behavior under examination. For example, the General Problem Solver program solves and fails to solve problems in ways that are similar to humans; hence, it 'simulates' human cognition and can be taken as a theory of human problem-solving. Note that the General Problem Solver does not solve just any old problem handed to it; it is not an 'intelligent' beast in that sense. To appreciate this distinction ➤ **artificial intelligence**.

con- Variation of ➤ **com-**.

conation That aspect of the mental processes having to do with volition, striving, willing. The term was used historically to represent a basic mental faculty (along with *affection* and *cognition*) and is rarely used today.

concatenation A general term referring to the stringing or linking together of items into a chain. Thus, a sentence may be spoken of (a bit simplistically) as a concatenation of words.

concaveation Bringing a nonpregnant female animal into contact with young of the species. It can, under the appropriate conditions, produce an approximation to the chain of behaviors associated with parenting, including even lactation in females who have had previous pregnancies.

conceive From the Latin, meaning *to take into oneself*: **1.** To become pregnant. **2.** To form an image, idea or opinion. **3.** To apprehend or understand. By extension of these: **4.** To have or think of a concept.

concentration-camp disorder A well-documented disorder observed in many of those who survived the concentration camps of the Holocaust. Generally regarded as a special form of ➤ **post-traumatic stress disorder**, it is distinguished because of its most significant symptom, ➤ **survivor guilt**.

concept **1.** A complex of objects all of which share some attribute(s) or properties. **2.** The internal, psychological, representation of the shared attributes. Strictly speaking, the term should only be applied to the latter definition since it is the mental representation that *is* the concept and it is the mental representation that is ultimately responsible for behavior with regard to the outside world. There are assuredly things in the world which are chairs but concept of *chair* is 'in the head' and not in the world outside. However, one can get away with meaning 1 on the grounds that in order for the concept to get *into* the head there must be the complex of objects which reflect the properties that are ultimately cognitively represented. In psychological parlance concepts are often ranged along a concreteness–abstractness continuum where something like *chair* is regarded as highly concrete, easily identifiable, easily imaged and (relatively) easily categorized and classified while something like *government* is regarded as highly abstract, not easily identified, poorly imaged and (relatively) resistant to simple categorization. For more on

these problems (which are of legendary difficulty in both philosophy and cognitive psychology) ➤ **category** and related terms.

concept acquisition Generally used to refer to the process whereby one learns ('acquires') a concept not known before. See the discussion under ➤ **concept formation and learning**.

concept discovery A term generally used for the process whereby one discovers which of several previously learned concepts is the proper one for a given situation. In practice, problems arise in actual usage; see the discussion under ➤ **concept formation and learning**.

concept formation and learning These terms are often used synonymously to refer to the process of abstraction of a quality, property or set of features that can be taken to represent a concept. However, there is considerable latitude in actual usage. For example, some authors restrict *formation* to the actual acquisition of the concept and use *learning* for the conditions under which one must learn how to apply a concept that is already known or formed. On this account of things one would study, for example, the *formation* of the concept 'round' in a child while examining how the child *learns* to apply it by responding differently to things which are round and things which are not. If the reader finds this a bit confusing (and the astute reader will, for there are good reasons for arguing that the senses of 'round' here are not differentiable), it should be noted that the literature in cognitive psychology abounds with terms which have been introduced to refer to whatever it is that is going on here: *concept acquisition, concept development, concept discovery, concept identification, concept use, concept attainment, concept construction* and *concept induction* are probably the more frequently used. The reason for this free-flowing use of synonyms and near synonyms is that several interrelated cognitive processes are involved in human conceptual 'behavior.'

To wit: (a) those of the actual induction operations whereby one comes to know symbolically the concept; (b) those of the forming of an underlying mental representation of the concept itself; (c) those which are part of the distinguishing of various concepts from each other; and (d) those of the selection process whereby one discovers which of the concepts is appropriate for use in a particular situation. There is precious little agreement about terminology here and the most useful counsel is careful reading and critical reflection. It is recommended that *concept acquisition* serve for (a), *concept discovery* or *concept identification* serve for (c) and *concept use* for (d). All other terms should wither away from lack of use. There is no simple term for (b), which is really quite all right because no one understands the process anyway.

concept identification Lit., the identification of a concept. Generally used in experiments in which the relevant concept is already known to the subject (e.g., 'roundness,' in an adult) and what needs to be learned is the identity of this concept as the critical one as opposed to some other. See also the discussion under ➤ **concept formation and learning**.

conception 1. Most generally, the mental process of thinking, of conceiving or of imagining. 2. More specifically, the mental process of forming a concept. 3. A mental attitude concerning some thing. 4. The fertilization of an ovum by a sperm. The use of the same term for the creation of both a thought and a life is no etymological accident; it derives from the earliest attempts of the ancients to understand these processes by taking the *epigenetic* point of view for both forms of creation.

conception age ➤ **age, conception**.

conceptual systems O. J. Harvey's term for the kinds of systematically applied processes which he hypothesized underlie the contents of an individual's beliefs. Harvey postulated four such systems, ranging from the first, the primitive concrete and rigid system typical of the authoritarian, progressing through more and more abstract, refined and integrated systems, to the fourth, which is reflected by self-confidence, internal motivation and flexible perspective-taking.

conceptual tempo A general term used to refer to a dimension of cognitive style known more commonly as ➤ **reflectivity–impulsivity**.

concept use ➤ **concept formation and learning**.

concomitant variation *Concomitant* means something that accompanies something else (often, but not always, with the connotation of being subordinate). The full term has two references: **1.** A correlation, a change in one variable that accompanies change in another. **2.** A principle of inductive inference used originally by Mill that states that when two things vary together they are probably either related to each other or to a third common factor. Both usages are neutral on the question of a true causal relation between the factors.

concordance Generally, agreement, harmony. The term is used freely to refer to factors or phenomena that are coordinate, e.g. the degree to which a twin pair share similar traits or diseases.

concordance, coefficient of (W) An estimate of the degree of association among 2 or more sets of rankings. The coefficient, usually abbreviated W, is an index of the divergence of the observed agreement in rankings from the maximum possible agreement. It is also known as *Kendall's coefficient of concordance*.

concrete 1. Specific, precise, represented by some particular exemplar. The opposite of ➤ **abstract** (1). 2. Practical, useful.

concrete intelligence ➤ **intelligence, concrete**.

concrete operations A set of cognitive operations cited by Piaget as characteristic of the thought of a child during the ➤ **concrete operatory stage**. There is a variety of behaviors assumed to reflect these operations and all are characterizable as ways of logically grouping and relating information about the world. As such, they are logical and yet still tied to the physical (concrete) world and to physical (concrete) actions. Distinguish from ➤ **formal operations**.

concrete operatory stage (or **level** or **period**) In Piagetian theory, the stage of cognitive functioning following the *preoperatory stage* and preceding the *formal operatory stage*. It is generally assumed to begin around the age of 6 with the establishment of ➤ **conservation** and to end around age 12 with the beginning of abstract thinking, which marks the formal operatory period.

concrete operatory thought The cognitive operations that exemplify the ➤ **concrete operatory stage**.

concurrent schedules ➤ **schedules of *reinforcement**.

concurrent validity ➤ **validity, concurrent**.

condensation In psychoanalytic theory, a hypothesized process whereby two or more images or elements combine to form a single composite image. The resulting 'condensed' image is assumed to carry the symbolic meaning of the separate images. It is regarded as an essential unconscious process best exemplified in dreams.

conditional probability ➤ **probability, conditional**.

conditional reflex Pavlov's original term for what is more commonly called ➤ **conditioned response**. *Response* came to replace 'reflex' as a more general and neutral term and *conditioned* resulted from an early translator's error. Some researchers are going back to the *-al* form here and many studies of classical conditioning now refer to a *conditional response*.

conditional response ➤ **conditional reflex**.

conditioned 1. Generally, dependent upon something else; conditional. **2.** In studies of conditioning, descriptive of a response that has, through the proper presentation of conditioning procedures, been made dependent upon a once-neutral stimulus. **3.** In studies of conditioning, characterizing the once-neutral stimulus that has, through conditioning, come to elicit a conditional response. **4.** By extension of 2 and 3, descriptive of a laboratory subject reliably displaying a conditioned response.

conditioned aversion ➤ **aversion, conditioned**.

conditioned avoidance (response) Any conditioned response which anticipates and prevents (or 'avoids') the occurrence of a noxious event. The reinforcement for such behavior is assumed to be the reduction of anxiety or fear that follows successful avoidance.

conditioned emotional response (CER) Generally, any emotional reaction which has been acquired through conditioning procedures.

conditioned escape (response) Any conditioned response which terminates (thus allowing 'escape' from) a noxious stimulus.

conditioned flavor (or **food**) **aversion** (or **avoidance**) ➤ **toxicosis**.

conditioned inhibition The suppression of a conditioned response by the simultaneous presentation of another stimulus (usually denoted as CS − to differentiate it from the conditioned stimulus, CS +) which is not associated with the unconditioned stimulus (the US).

conditioned reflex The early Russian physiologists who first studied conditioning preferred to use this term rather than the now more common term *conditioned response* owing to the fact that most of the behaviors which they worked with were reflexive in nature, such as the production of saliva to food placed in the mouth. See the discussion under ➤ **conditional reflex** for other nuances of usage.

conditioned reinforcer ➤ **reinforcer, conditioned**.

conditioned response (CR or Rc) Lit.,

any response which is learned or altered by conditioning. In classical conditioning, the CR is a response that comes to be elicited by a previously neutral stimulus; in operant conditioning, it is a response that has been followed by a reinforcer. Convention has it that the term should be reserved for the classical conditioning situation only, but not all writers follow this.

conditioned stimulus (CS or Sc) Any stimulus that, through conditioning, comes to evoke a conditioned response. The CS is an originally neutral stimulus that develops its eliciting power through pairing with an unconditioned stimulus. This term is used in classical conditioning only; in operant conditioning one generally refers to a *discriminative stimulus* that sets the conditions for the operant response to be made.

conditioned suppression A reduction or suppression in responding in the presence of a previously neutral stimulus. The suppression is produced by pairing the neutral stimulus with a noxious stimulus. For example, if a 1-minute tone is repeatedly followed by a shock, the organism will come to suppress responding during the full minute that the tone is on.

conditioned taste aversion (or avoidance) ➤ toxicosis.

conditioning A generic term for a set of empirical concepts, particularly those that specify the conditions under which associative learning takes place. Often divided into two separate types: *classical conditioning* (or *Type S* or *respondent* or *Pavlovian*) and *operant* (or *Type R* or *instrumental* or *Skinnerian*). The basic difference between the two is that in classical conditioning the outcome of a trial (the unconditioned stimulus or US) always occurs regardless of how the organism responds – Pavlov's dogs received food whether or not they salivated. In operant conditioning the outcome of a trial (the reinforcer) is contingent upon the organism making a specified response – Skinner's pigeons were not given food unless they pecked

the key the requisite number of times under the proper stimulus conditions. The terms classical and operant conditioning, however, will be often used in two ways: (a) to refer to a set of experimental procedures (indeed, this is how they were used above); and (b) to refer to two distinct types of learning that are assumed to occur under the two experimental procedures. The first use is operational, the second is theoretical.

The traditional view used to be that classical conditioning was a kind of primitive, reflex-like process that was elicited from an organism by an appropriate pairing of CS and US while operant conditioning was seen as based on volitional behavior emitted by an organism. However, phenomena like ➤ **autoshaping**, ➤ **blocking** (2), ➤ **sensory preconditioning**, etc., plus the wide acceptance of the ➤ **Rescorla–Wagner theory** show that classical conditioning, this most basic of processes, has previously unsuspected complexities and subtleties. Consequently, in the contemporary literature, the term *conditioning* tends to be used to refer, not to a process, but to an operation, specifically, the arrangement of contingencies among events and the behavioral consequences brought about by such contingencies. Operationally, classical conditioning is subsumed by SS contingencies, as between the CS and the US, and operant conditioning by RS contingencies, as between the organism's response and the environment's stimulus feedback. There are numerous specialized forms of conditioning, some of which are given below; the others may be found under the heading of the modifying term.

conditioning by successive approximations ➤ shaping.

conditioning, excitatory A general term in classical conditioning for situations in which a positive correlation exists between the conditioned stimulus and the unconditioned stimulus, so that increases in responding in the presence of the conditioned stimulus are observed. Compare with **inhibitory *conditioning**.

conditioning, inhibitory A general term in classical conditioning for situations in which there is a negative correlation between the conditioned stimulus and the unconditioned stimulus so that decreases in responding in the presence of the conditioned stimulus are observed. Compare with ➤ **excitatory *conditioning**.

conduct disorder(s) A general psychiatric classification encompassing a variety of behavior patterns in which the individual repetitively and persistently violates the rights, privileges and privacy of others. Various subtypes have been proposed over the years, some based on differing degrees of socialization, on whether or not aggressive tendencies exist, and on whether or not the displays are confined to the family setting or more widely manifested.

conduction 1. The transmission of a neural impulse from one location to another. 2. The mechanical transmission of sound waves through the ear-drum and the ossicles.

conduction aphasia ➤ **aphasia, conduction**.

conduction deafness ➤ **deafness, conduction**.

conductivity 1. Generally, the electric conducting capacity of a substance. 2. Specifically, that of a neuron or nerve.

cones The photoreceptors in the retina that mediate color vision. They are most densely packed in the fovea and thin out toward the periphery. Cones have higher thresholds than ➤ **rods** and function primarily in photopic or daylight vision. Three different cone *opsins* (photopigments) are found each with its own characteristic *spectral sensitivity curve*; the visual system uses the information from these three types of cones to produce color vision.

confabulation Making up details or filling in gaps in memory. This may be a conscious act in which one is adding to elaborating partial memories of events or an unconscious act in which falsification serves as a defense mechanism.

confederate In some experiments in social psychology not all the 'subjects' are real subjects. Frequently the psychologist is interested in the effects of social or peer-group pressure and to insure control over these pressures some of the 'subjects' may be confederates (or 'stooges') of the psychologist who are instructed to act in certain ways to influence the real subjects. See, for example, the discussion under ➤ **conformity**.

confidence 1. Trust; belief in a person's trustworthiness. This is the meaning intended in most social and personality psychology contexts. 2. Assuredness, self-reliance. This meaning is found in a variety of examinations of choice behavior, signal detection, problem-solving and the like where the subjects' confidence that they detected the signal, made the proper choice, found the correct solution, etc. is a factor of considerable importance. In such experiments subjects are frequently required to estimate their degree of confidence on some numbered scale for each response made. 3. In the phrase, 'in confidence,' a secret matter; an agreement that information so passed is not to be divulged. ➤ **privileged communication**.

confidence interval An interval or range of values within which the theoretical probability of an event may be specified. The wider the interval the higher the confidence and vice versa. For example, we may say with almost complete confidence that 'John's IQ is between 50 and 150'; as we narrow the interval our confidence decreases so that we would not be very confident in stating 'John's IQ is between 99 and 101.' The confidence interval is generally given in standard deviation units around the mean.

confidence limits The limits outside of which an event is not expected to occur by chance with more than some specified probability. They mark the *confidence interval* and are usually given in standard units around the mean. Also called *fiducial limits*.

confidentiality Having the characteristic

of being kept secret, an intimacy of knowledge shared by a few who do not divulge it to others. The term is most commonly used with respect to the legal and ethical issues which, in principle, protect this contract of trust particularly as it refers to information passed during psychiatric or psychological therapy. The phrase *confidential communication* is the legal term used to cover such material.

configuration 1. Generally, a particular arrangement of objects, machines, people, stimuli, etc. ➤ **system** (especially 3). 2. In perception the term is used in ways very similar to the term ➤ **Gestalt**. The connotation here is that the essential nature of such an array is the coordinated whole and not the several objects, people, etc. of which it is composed. Occasionally the phrase *configurational tendency* will be used to refer to this tendency to respond to the full, organized arrangement.

configurational learning (or **conditioning**) Learning (or conditioning) where the conditioned stimulus is a compound stimulus (e.g., a light and tone presented together). After extensive training, a conditioned response is only obtained to the full compound stimulus or the 'configuration;' the separate elements (i.e., the light or the tone alone) produce no responding. Compare with ➤ **overshadowing**. Also known as *compound learning* (or *conditioning*).

configurational tendency ➤ **configuration** (2).

confirmation A theoretical construct developed by E. C. Tolman for the fulfillment of an ➤ **expectancy**. In this sense the term provides a theoretical base for the notion of reinforcement since, according to Tolman, confirmation of an expectancy is the basic reinforcer of behaviour.

confirmation bias The tendency to seek and interpret information that confirms existing beliefs. It is seen both in social situations where information that disconfirms one's beliefs is often ignored or misinterpreted as well as in cognitive tasks like problem solving where people test hypotheses that, if true, will confirm already held beliefs rather than entertain hypotheses that would disconfirm these beliefs.

conflict An extremely broad term used to refer to any situation where there are mutually antagonistic events, motives, purposes, behaviors, impulses, etc. The following entries describe the classic conflict situations and the various kinds of conflicts that are theorized to exist.

conflict, actual A presently occurring conflict. In the psychoanalytic approach such conflicts are assumed to derive from *root conflicts*.

conflict, approach–approach A conflict resulting from being drawn toward two equally desirable but mutually incompatible goals. The conflict is generally resolved when one gets closer (physically or metaphorically) to one of the two goals since desirability typically increases with proximity. ➤ **approach gradient**.

conflict, approach–avoidance A conflict resulting from being both drawn and repelled by the same goal. This type of conflict is particularly difficult to resolve in that with distance the goal appears more desirable than fearful whereas with proximity its aversive qualities tend to dominate, causing withdrawal which, of course, leads to an increase in the goal's perceived positive features relative to the negative ones. A classic example is being offered a job with a raise in salary but a substantial increase in work load.

conflict, avoidance–avoidance A conflict resulting from being repelled by two undesirable goals when there are strong pressures to choose one or the other. It is a particularly unpleasant situation which prompts one to select the 'lesser of two evils.' Often when the conflict is intense one will simply 'leave the field' and refuse to choose between the alternatives.

conflict, double approach–avoidance A variation on the simple ➤ **approach–avoidance**

*conflict, in which each of two goals has both positive and negative aspects. A typical example is the conflict felt by a person on a diet faced with a calorie-rich, delicious chocolate cake and a carrot which, for all its nutritional value, still tastes like a carrot.

conformity Generally, the tendency to allow one's opinions, attitudes, actions and even perceptions to be affected by prevailing opinions, attitudes, actions and perceptions. More specifically, it is important to appreciate that there are at least three distinct patterns of use of this term: (a) *behavioral*, when it refers to the tendency to 'go along with the group,' to attempt to act in ways consistent with the majority's; (b) *attitudinal*, when the reference is to a change in attitude or belief, as a result of pressure from others, that may or may not result in behavioral change; and (c) as a *personality trait*, when it implies an underlying characteristic of an individual's personality manifested as being subject to either of the two above tendencies to conform.

confound In experimental work, to fail to separate two variables with the result that their effects cannot be independently ascertained. If, in an experiment on memory and age, all the older subjects are female and all the younger are male, then sex and age are 'confounded' and the memory data cannot be properly interpreted. Contrast with ➤ control – which is what is missing when variables are confounded.

congenital Present at birth. The term is not necessarily synonymous with innate or hereditary. A congenital condition may be due to factors other than heredity, e.g., retardation produced by the mother contracting German measles early in pregnancy.

congenital adrenal hyperplasia (CAH) A syndrome in which the adrenal cortices are prevented from normal production of cortisone and release instead excess adrenal androgens. Females with CAH are born with masculinized external genitalia; males have normal genitalia. CAH can be controlled with regulated doses of cortisone and normal sexual and reproductive functions will develop on schedule. Surgical repair may be needed to feminize the genitalia of girls.

congruence principle The generalization that it is easier to search memory for a match than a mismatch. Most easily seen in experiments where a subject must determine whether or not each of several test stimuli is a searched-for target. Reaction times are far faster for the positive cases (the matches) than for the negative (the mismatches).

congruent attitude change In social psychology, a change in an attitude in the direction of the attitude already held by the individual.

congruent retinal points Two points, one on each retina, that are projections of the same point in the external stimulus configuration. Distinguish from ➤ identical retinal points and contrast with ➤ disparate retinal points.

congruity theory A theory of attitude change that focuses on attitudes about the source and the content of a message. If an individual has positive or negative feelings toward both, the message is congruent and attitudes are not changed. However, if one feels positive toward one but negative toward the other, there is strong motivation to change either one's opinion of the speaker or one's attitude toward the message.

conjoint measurement Measurement wherein that which is being measured is composed of two or more components each of which affects the thing measured. Many psychological variables are conjoint, e.g., preferences, beliefs, utilities, etc. For example, one's preference for a particular auto may be made up of its style, cost, economy, handling, etc. An increase in cost could shift preference dramatically even though the other factors remained constant.

conjugal paranoia ➤ **delusional disorder, jealous type**.

conjugate movement Coordinated movement, as of the two eyes.

conjugate reinforcement ➤ **schedules of *reinforcement**.

conjugation Coupling, joining.

conjunctiva Mucous membranes that line the eyelid and corners of the eyeball.

conjunctival reflex Reflexive closing of the eyelid to stimulation of the cornea or the conjunctiva. Also called *corneal reflex*.

conjunctive concept A concept defined by the mutual presence of two or more aspects. In a concept-identification experiment using various colored shapes as stimuli, a conjunctive concept might be 'red *and* round.' ➤ **disjunctive concept** and **relational concept**.

conjunctive motivation H. S. Sullivan's term for a striving to achieve a permanent, satisfying harmony in the many diversities of life. Compare with ➤ **disjunctive motivation**.

conjunctive schedule ➤ **schedules of *reinforcement**.

connate Appearing at or shortly after birth. ➤ **congenital**.

connection Any link or bond between phenomena. Often used to refer to **1.** the S-R or stimulus-response bond and **2.** the link between neural units in learned behavior.

connectionism 1. E. L. Thorndike's term for his associationistic theory of learning. **2.** In cognitive science, an approach to the study of cognitive processes based on the presumption that a system (like a brain) operates as though it were composed of a network of *nodes*, each of which will have at any point in time a certain level of activation. Each of these nodes is assumed to be interconnected with other nodes at different levels of the system in either an excitatory or an inhibitory manner, so that activating one node will have particular effects on the others. The whole network is assumed to be dynamic in that, so long as inputs are fed to it, it will keep adjusting the levels of activation and the strengths of the various interconnections between the nodes. Connectionist models have proven to be quite powerful and when expressed as computer models (➤ **computer simulation**, ➤ **artificial intelligence**) have provided intriguing insights into human memory, learning, and neurocognitive functioning. Theories based on these principles are also referred to as *associationist models*, *parallel distributed processing* [*PDP*] *models*, or *neural network models*.

connector (neuron) A neuron that lies between and connects two other neurons or a receptor and an effector. Also called an ➤ **interneuron**.

connotative meaning ➤ **meaning, connotative**.

consanguine Having the same forebear. Usually restricted to one, two or at most three generations back, i.e. parents, grandparents, greatgrandparents. A consanguine marriage is one between relatively close relatives.

consanguinity Genetic relatedness.

conscience A reasonably coherent set of internalized moral principles that provides evaluations of right and wrong with regard to acts either performed or contemplated. Historically, theistic views aligned conscience with the voice of God and hence regarded it as innate. The contemporary view is that the prohibitions and obligations of conscience are learned; indeed Freud's characterization of the ➤ **superego** was an attempt to provide an account of its origins, development and manner of functioning. ➤➤ **moral development**.

conscious 1. adj. In its most general sense the term is used to characterize the mental state of an individual who is capable of (a) having sensations and perceptions, (b) reacting to stimuli, (c) having feelings and emotions, (d) having thoughts, ideas, plans and images and (e) being aware of (a) through (d). Note that when the term is applied to nonhuman organisms, the processes under (d) are generally not included, although those under (c) will be for all but the most primitive species. Differentiate the state of *being conscious* from the condition of *having* ➤ **consciousness** (particularly meanings 2 and 3). **2** n. In psychoanalytic theory, the aspect of mind that encompasses all that one is momentarily aware of. This usage generally is marked by the use of the definite article as in 'the conscious' and is differentiated from the ➤ **preconscious** and ➤ **unconscious**.

consciousness **1.** Generally, a state of awareness: a state of being ➤ **conscious** (1). This is the most general usage of the term and is that intended in phrases like 'he lost consciousness.' **2.** A domain of mind that contains the sensations, perceptions and memories of which one is momentarily aware; that is, those aspects of present mental life that one is attending to. ➤ **attention**. **3.** That component of mind available for ➤ **'introspection**. This meaning is found in the older writings of structuralists and other introspectionists. **4.** In psychoanalysis, the ➤ **conscious** (2).

The term has a distinctly checkered history. It has represented sometimes the central focus of psychology (➤ **structuralism**) and at others been banned from the psychologist's lexicon as representing nothing more than the epiphenomenal flotsam of bodily activity (➤ **behaviorism**). The ongoing fascination with it, however, stems from the compelling sense that consciousness is one of the fundamental defining features of our species: that to be human is to possess not only self-awareness but the even more remarkable capacity to scan and review mentally that which we are aware of. As a topic for a scientific psychology it is in clear resurgence, mainly within the areas of cognition, language and neuropsychology. Much of the contemporary focus is on the issue of just which of our cognitive processes such as memory and learning are open for conscious inspection and which are not. See here ➤ **implicit *memory** and ➤ **implicit *learning**.

consensual eye reflex The reaction of both pupils to light when only one eye is exposed to the change in light intensity.

consensual reflex Generally, any reflex observed on the opposite side of the body from the place stimulated.

consensual validation **1.** The use of agreement between two or more persons as providing evidence for the validity of a phenomenon. ➤ **consensual *validity**. **2.** In H. S. Sullivan's theory, the principle that the socially valid meanings of symbols and ideas derive from a coherent consensus among the members of a community. From Sullivan's point of view, normal development is the process of changing from individualistic meanings to socially shared meanings.

consensual validity ➤ **validity, consensual**.

consequent **1.** An event or phenomenon which occurred following some other event such that it 'invites' the inference that it was caused by that event. **2.** In logic, the conclusionary proposition, the so-called 'then' clause. ➤ **antecedent**.

conservation A term introduced by Piaget for the child's (or adult's) understanding that quantitative aspects of a set of materials or other stimulus display are not changed or affected by transformations of the display itself. The key notion here is that one who is a 'conserver' is one who recognizes that the critical quantitative properties are not altered by arbitrary transformation or other modifications of the situation. The amount of fluid in a jar is not changed by pouring it into differently shaped containers, the number of objects in a row is not changed by altering their spatial arrangement, the mass of a quantity of clay is not changed by rolling it into many little balls, etc. Conservation, like other cognitive operations, is assumed by Piagetians to be attained only at certain developmental stages; it is usually taken as the strongest evidence that the child is in the ➤ **concrete operatory stage**. In its 'pure' form conservation is considered to be a singular cognitive operation, the recognition that quantity is preserved no matter what transformations are applied so long as nothing is added and nothing taken away. However, it appears that various applications of this principle by the child require different amounts of experience; typically conservation of number is observed before conservation of length, and weight and volume appear later still. ➤ **horizontal *decalage**.

conservatism In political theory, the point of view that defends the status quo, that maintains that the *conservative* position is to be defended.

conservative 1. adj. In social/political terms descriptive of any point of view or proposal that argues that change is to be resisted, that current modes of functioning should be maintained. 2. n. One who adheres to this point of view.

conservative statistic Any statistic that tends to underestimate. For example, ➤ **Scheffé test**.

consistency Occasional synonym for ➤ **reliability**.

consistency theories A general label for theories of attitude change that assume that people strive for consistency between actions and beliefs. The assumption is that a lack of consistency is psychologically uncomfortable and when a belief is inconsistent with one's behavior the person will be motivated to change something to reestablish consistency. Included are ➤ **balance theory**, ➤ **congruity theory**, and ➤ **cognitive dissonance theory**.

consolidation The hypothesized process that is assumed to take place after acquisition of some behavior. The process assumes long-term neurophysiological changes that allow for the relatively permanent retention of the learned behavior. In its broadest usage it can include any change in the neurophysiological processes relating to that behavior. The exact operations in the nervous system that account for consolidation are not known but are hypothesized to involve any of several possible mechanisms including (a) modifications in the ease with which neurotransmitters affect neighboring neurons, (b) alterations in the amount of particular neurotransmitters in critical neural pathways, or (c) increases in the number of synaptic connections that are made between neurons. Some authors also use the term as a kind of neurological metaphor for the transition from ➤ **short-term *memory** to ➤ **long-term *memory**.

consonant Any speech sound produced by partial or complete closure at some point in the vocal tract accompanied by either audible friction or by a sudden release of air. Consonants include *plosives*, *fricatives*, *nasals*, *laterals* and *glottal stops* (or *catches*). Contrast with ➤ **vowel**.

consonant trigram Any meaningless, unpronounceable combination of three separate consonant letters such as JBK, QKZ. Such CCCs (as they are often abbreviated) are used in studies of memory, perception, verbal learning, etc. where one wishes to keep the meaningfulness dimension to a minimum. Compare with ➤ **nonsense syllable**.

conspecific An ethological term for another organism of the same species as the organism under consideration.

constancy The tendency for perceived objects to give rise to the same (or quite similar) perceptual experiences even though there may be wide variations in the conditions of observation – that is, variations in both the distal stimulus (the objects themselves) and the proximal stimulus (the energy impinging on the receptors) (➤ **distal stimulus**). Essentially all perceptual qualities display constancy to some extent; see, e.g., ➤ **brightness constancy, color constancy, shape constancy**, etc.

constancy hypothesis The hypothesis that strict isomorphism holds between the proximal stimulus and the sensory experience. The hypothesis, in principle, assumes a total lack of any effect of the context within which the observations take place. The hypothesis is really a 'straw man' erected for easy demolition by the Gestaltists (who took the opposing position of ➤ **constructivism**) and attributed to structuralists and behaviorists who never actually defended it in such an extreme form.

constancy of internal environment ➤ **homeostasis**.

constancy of the IQ Lit., the extent to which there is test–retest reliability in IQ. By extension, the question whether IQ tends to remain constant over the years. The test–retest reliability quotients tend to be reasonably high, which some have, erroneously, taken to be evidence for genetically endowed intelligence. How constant IQ is, is critically dependent on the kinds and constancy of environments people are raised in and the kinds and constancy of educational and instructional experiences they have had. ➤ **intelligence** for more on this issue.

constancy of the organism ➤ **homeostasis**.

constant Basically, something that does not vary (as in statistical or mathematical terms) or is not permitted to vary (as in experimental controls).

constant error ➤ **error, constant**.

constant stimuli, method of ➤ **measurement of *threshold**.

constellation 1. Generally, any reasonably well-organized matrix of associations, ideas, images, effects, etc. 2. Specifically, in psychoanalysis, nonrepressed set of coordinated, emotionally charged ideas.

constituent ➤ **immediate constituent**.

constitution Generally, the genotypic endowments of a person, as expressed in the phenotype. Used broadly by some to cover both physical and psychological aspects, used more narrowly by others with the focus on the physical. In the several attempts to construct a ➤ **constitutional theory**, the emphasis was on the physical constitution as the important determinant of the cognitive, social and affective traits that became learned.

constitutional theory A general term used of any of several theories of personality that focused on those aspects of a person that were inherent, particularly those attributes of morphology and physiology that were organic, genetic and relatively stable, and their relationships with psychological and behavioral characteristics. Three theories stand out: (a) Galen's, which was based on four basic types, *sanguine, melancholic, choleric* and *phlegmatic*; (b) Kretschmer's, with three basic types, *pyknic* (stocky), *asthenic* (slender) and *athletic* (muscular) and one mixed type, *dysplastic* (disproportioned); and (c) Sheldon's, which hypothesized three fundamental constitutional types, *ectomorphic* (thin). *mesomorphic* (muscular) and *endomorphic* (fat).

Galen's theory was based on the ancient presumption of bodily humors as controllers of one's psyche, and not surprisingly is the least sophisticated. Kretschmer's was founded on psychiatric observations and sought to relate body type to propensity for particular mental disorders. He argued that the asthenic was prone to schizophrenia, the pyknic to manic-depression and the athletic to sanity. There is little or no evidence to support Kretschmer's claims. Sheldon's theory is the most sophisticated of the three based, as it was, on more modern findings in the structure of embryonic cellular tissue. Moreover, Sheldon sought a general theory of personality and not merely a psychiatric one. He argued that there were three primary components in physique: *endomorphy* (heavy, poorly developed bones and muscles), *mesomorphy* (strong, well-developed bones and muscles), and *ectomorphy* (thin, light bones and muscles) and three primary components in temperament: *viscerotonia* (loving, comfortable, sociable), *somatotonia* (adventurous, vigorous, physical) and *cerebrotonia* (restrained, self-conscious, fearful). Sheldon's attempts to uncover correlations between the three body types and the three classical personality types was a noble effort which reflected a touch of validity, but as a unified theory of personality it was a failure. ➤ **personality** (especially the discussion of *type theories*), **somatotype**.

constitutional types ➤ **constitutional theory**.

constrained association ➤ **association, constrained**.

construct 1. n. The least confusing way to use this term is to treat it as a rough synonym of *concept*, at least in so far as both are basically logical or intellectual creations. Essentially one infers a construct whenever one can establish a relationship between several objects or events. In common use is the notion of a *hypothetical construct*, where the process is not presently observable or objectively measurable but is assumed to exist because it (hypothetically) gives rise to measurable phenomena. The ➤ **ego** is a hypothetical construct in this sense. 2. n. In testing, a quality or a trait; see here ➤ **construct *validity**.

constructional apraxia ➤ **apraxia, constructional**.

construction need H. Murray's hypothesized need to produce, to build things.

constructivism 1. In perception, a general theoretical position that characterizes perception and perceptual experience as being constructed from, in Gregory's words, 'fleeting fragmentary scraps of data signalled by the senses and drawn from the brain's memory banks – themselves constructions from snippets of the past.' The essence of all constructivist theories is that perceptual experience is viewed as more than a direct response to stimulation. It is instead viewed as an elaboration or 'construction' based on hypothesized cognitive and affective operations. Contrast with the theory of ➤ **direct perception**. 2. In social psychology, *social constructivism*

approaches the study of social psychological topics from the same philosophical stance. Social constructivists argue for some extreme but interesting positions, including the notion that there is no such thing as a knowable objective reality. Rather, they maintain, all knowledge is derived from the mental constructions of the members of a social system.

construct validity ➤ **validity, construct**.

consultant Generally, any expert brought in to provide advice and counsel.

consultation In medicine and clinical psychology, diagnosis and treatment plan arrived at through the combined efforts of two or more clinicians.

consultation-liaison psychiatry A psychiatric speciality that is concerned with the overall functioning of a health-care system.

consumer Clearly, one who consumes. The consumer in psychology, particularly social psychology and industrial psychology, is viewed as one who is the recipient and user of services and goods. This goes beyond the simple notion of the consumer as the purchaser of a head of lettuce; a consumer is also one who is a client in psychotherapy, a student in a university, a citizen in a society, and indeed he or she may also be a victim of the functions, operations and decisions of organizations in society. The term, obviously, is used rather broadly.

consummatory response (or *act*) The behaviorist's term for the final response in a behavior chain, the one which terminates in a frequently occurring sequence. Eating, drinking and copulating are all examples.

consummatory stimulus A stimulus that elicits a consummatory response.

contact 1. Generally, any face-to-face interaction between two or more people. 2. Within the contexts of Gestalt therapy and biofunctional therapy, a rich, fulfilled 'relationship.' It may be between a person and his or her bodily processes, between two individuals, between the several aspects of a group interaction, etc. The frequency with which we read, hear or meet people who have 'made contact' with themselves has unfortunately converted a useful phrase into something of a boring cliché.

contact comfort A term used by Harry Harlow to characterize the satisfying feeling that comes from making contact with soft, comfortable objects. The desire for contact comfort is common in many species and is particularly prevalent among the primates. It is known to be an important aspect of early development and for the establishment of normal mother–infant ties.

contact desensitization A variation in the ➤ **desensitization technique** in behavior therapy in which the therapist maintains physical contact with the client to help in lowering anxiety and facilitating the procedures.

contagion, behavioral (or **emotional**) Spread of an activity or a mood through a group. Typified most dramatically by, e.g., group fainting – one child may faint when dissecting in a biology lesson, promptly followed by numbers of others.

contamination The general meaning derives from the Latin for *to render impure*. Hence, any experimental or methodological situation in which one allows previous knowledge, uncontrolled variables, information concerning the expectations of the study, etc. to interfere with the proper collection and interpretation of the data. For example, a clinician searching for a hereditary basis for schizophrenia who knew that someone else in a patient's family already had the disorder would very likely have his or her diagnostic judgement 'contaminated' by this knowledge and tend to interpret any signs of a disorder as schizophrenia.

content 1 adj. With the accent on the second syllable, satisfied with things the way they are. 2 n. With the accent on the first syllable, that which is contained in something else. This meaning is very broad and used to refer to the sensations, images, thoughts, etc. of mind, the particular items or questions on a test, the material expressed in a dream, the elements of a communicated message, etc. Hence, it is usually accompanied by a qualifier, as the following entries show.

content-addressable store A term used in theoretical models of memory, particularly those manifested as computer simulations. The notion is that at least some components of human memory may be characterized as a set of storage registers for holding information, each with an 'address' that gives its 'location' in memory and the 'contents' of the store.

content analysis A general term covering a variety of methods for analyzing a discourse, message or document for varying themes, ideas, emotions, opinions, etc. Most such analyses consist of sophisticated counting schemes in which the frequency of particular words, phrases, affective expressions and the like are determined.

content, latent and manifest These terms derive from depth psychology and are used to distinguish between those aspects of a 'message' that are overt, consciously intended and expressed, and found clearly represented in the material (i.e. they are *manifest*) and those aspects that are presumed to underlie the manifest content but are repressed and hence not consciously or overtly represented (i.e. they are *latent*). The message here may be considered broadly and dreams, narratives, writings, etc. can be the topic of examination, although ➤ **dream content** is the most common and usually what is intended.

content psychology Occasional label for the approach of the early structuralists who were primarily concerned with the use of introspection to examine the contents of consciousness.

content validity ➤ **validity, content**.

content word Any word that has semantic content or meaning. Nouns, verbs, adjectives, adverbs, are all content words. See and compare with ➤ **function word**.

context 1. Generally, those events and processes (physical and mental) that characterize a particular situation and have an impact on an individual's behavior (overt and covert). 2. The specific circumstances within which an action or event takes place. 3. In linguistics, the surrounding words, phrases and sentences that are components of the meaning of any given word, phrase or sentence.

context effects A cover term for those behavioral effects that result from the particular context within which a stimulus is presented or a response is made. No behavior, no thought, no dream – in short, nothing any organism can ever do – can take place in a physical or psychic vacuum. Context effects are necessarily ubiquitous. This is at once a most trivial and most profound statement; ignoring its obvious truth has led more than a few well-meaning theorists to grief. The trick for the scientist is to discern just which context effects are significant and worthy of accounting for and which are negligible.

context specific learning ➤ **learning, context specific**.

context theory A theoretical point of view maintaining that all behavior must be analyzed within the context in which it occurs, that to interpret any act independently of context will ultimately be misleading.

contextualism ➤ **context theory**.

contiguity A state of close proximity or association either in space or in time of two or more events.

contiguity principle 1. Originating with Aristotle, the notion that contiguity between two events is both the necessary and the sufficient condition for a dynamic association between them to be formed. The years have brought many a vigorous criticism of this seemingly straightforward principle. The necessity of contiguity is

challenged by simple memory processes whereby one can recall a previous event and associate it with a contemporary one. The natural rebuttal here is to note that the act of retrieval effectively makes the two contiguous in the mind – but that somewhat robs the principle of explanatory power since all associative operations must be contiguous within the individual and nothing is gained by invoking the principle. See here ➤ **redintegration**. The sufficiency question has been challenged by the principle of reinforcement, which maintains that simple contiguity is not enough for an associative bond to be formed but rather must be accompanied by some reinforcing or rewarding event to 'cement' the link. The standard reply here is to turn the argument back on itself by pointing out that there is no satisfactory theoretical characterization of just what a reinforcer is nor what makes or fails to make any arbitrary event function as one. See here ➤ **reinforcement**. 2. In learning theory, the notion that a response made in the presence of a stimulus will be learned simply by virtue of the spatio-temporal contiguity between the two. See here ➤ **contiguity theory**.

contiguity theory A theory of learning usually associated with E. R. Guthrie. The position he articulated has often been called the ultimate learning theory in terms of parsimony for it had but one principle, that of contiguity. Specifically, the last response to occur in the presence of a stimulus was assumed to be learned. All learning was assumed to be one-trial and all-or-none; the gradual improvement in performance usually observed was argued to be the result of the fact that most behaviors are made up of many complex responses and most stimuli are rather complicated affairs, and so many individual S–R connections were needed for effective behavior. Praised for its elegance and widely tested and debated during the heyday of behaviorism, it has been since abandoned as a viable theory of learning.

continence Self-restraint with respect to:

1. retention of urine, feces and other bodily discharges; **2.** sexual impulses. ·

contingency **1.** In logic the characteristic of a proposition such that it does not have to be true or does not have to hold. **2.** By extension, an event is said to be contingent on another if there exists some demonstrable relationship between them such that the occurrence of one tends to be accompanied by the other. A contingency, stated thus, is a statistical circumstance and may be defined simply as the degree to which the values of one variable are related to the values of another variable. However, there is a strong tendency to use the term with the connotation that the relationship is more than fortuitous, that it is causal and that the occurrence of the second event is dependent (or 'contingent') upon the prior occurrence of the first. Note that 2 does not contradict 1; the second event (or proposition concerning it) need not occur by itself nor hold in isolation but only in conjunction with the first.

contingency coefficient A statistical measure (based on ➤ **chi square**) of the strength of association between two variables.

contingency contract In behavior therapy, a contract drawn up between therapist and client so that it is clear precisely which behaviors the client must produce in order for reinforcements or rewards to be received.

contingency table A two-way table presenting the cross-tabulations of frequencies of occurrences of the categories of events listed in the columns and rows.

contingency theories A term used occasionally for those models of behavior that stress the role of context and circumstances in controlling human action.

continuant In phonetics, a distinctive feature for distinguishing the sounds of a language. Continuants 'continue' over time (e.g., all vowels and consonants like [r, l, th, s, z] etc.), noncontinuants are characterized by a stoppage of the air flow (e.g., [p, t, b] etc.).

continuation ➤ **good continuation** and Gestalt laws of organization.

continuity A characteristic of a system or a process such that it displays continuous, successive gradations. The term is used very generally to refer to physical variables, mental states, social systems, etc. which display uninterrupted changes. ➤ **continuum**.

continuity theory A theory of learning that maintains that associations are formed and gradually strengthened with each reward or reinforced response. Actually it is not so much a distinct theory as a general theoretical principle assumed in a variety of models of the learning process. Contrast with ➤ **all-or-none *learning**.

continuous Characterized by uninterrupted changes, without breaks or steps – or with steps infinitesimally small and thus not detectable. Thus, *continuous scales* are those where the function measured is assumed to be continuous even though the measuring device is broken down into discrete units as with height, weight, etc. Similarly for continuous series, continuous variables and so forth. Contrast with ➤ **discrete**.

continuous reinforcement ➤ **schedules of *reinforcement**.

continuous variable ➤ **continuous**.

continuum **1.** Most generally, any uninterrupted series of changes, any continuous, gradually changing sequence of values. **2.** In mathematics, a variable with a continuous underlying metric such that for any two values there exists a third value between them. **3.** Somewhat less formally, any variable capable of being represented as a continuous series. In psychological work typically such continua are represented by polar labels; e.g., the pleasantness dimension runs from unpleasant to pleasant, with all intermediate points in principle existing.

contour The outline of a figure or object. The term is used metaphorically in that the outline exists only in so far as there is

Several examples of subjective contours

a marked difference in brightness or color between two adjoining places in the visual field. The line of demarcation is strictly psychological.

contour, subjective A contour perceived where there is none in the physical stimulus but only the requisite conditions for its inference by the viewer, as in the accompanying figure. Also known as *anomalous, cognitive* and *illusory contours*.

contra- Combining form meaning *against* or *opposite*.

contraception The term used for any of several methods of birth control which prevent the fertilization of an ovum by a sperm cell; that is, they prevent conception. Strictly speaking, techniques such as intrauterine devices are not true contraceptives since they function by preventing implantation of the already fertilized egg in the uterine wall. This terminological nicety is, however, ignored by many. ➤ **birth control**.

contract, psychological The unwritten set of expectations that exists between the persons in a relationship, the members of a group, the people who work for an organization, etc. The term is used most often in industrial/organizational psychology, where it includes the levels of performance that each member of an organization is expected to reach and each member's own expectations with respect to salary advancement, benefits, perquisites, etc. Moreover, such nebulous components like the quality of life, job satisfaction, personal fulfillment and the like are implicitly a part of the contract.

contracture Relatively permanent contraction of a muscle due to either a spasm (usually temporary) or an abnormal paralytic condition (often permanent).

contradictory 1. n. In logic, either of two propositions such that if one is true the other necessarily is false and vice versa. That is, both cannot be true and both cannot be false. See and compare with ➤ **contrary** 2. adj. Descriptive of an interaction or discourse containing contradictions.

contralateral Pertaining to the opposite side. Contrast with ➤ **ipsilateral**.

contralateral reflex Any reflex occurring on the opposite side of the body from that stimulated.

contrary In logic, either of two propositions such that if one is true then the other cannot also be true although both of them may be false. For example, the proposition, 'all lexicographers are mad' has as a contrary 'no lexicographers are mad' and both are (probably) false. However, the first proposition has a ➤ **contradictory**, 'not all lexicographers are mad,' and here one or the other must be true.

contrast A marked awareness of the differences between two stimulus conditions resulting from bringing them together. The contrast may be *simultaneous*, in that the events or stimuli are presented together in time and space, or it may be *successive*, in that one follows the other in close succession. Simultaneous contrasts are generally more striking. Such effects are observed in a large number of stimulus dimensions. Descriptions of these are listed under the main term, e.g., ➤ **color contrast**.

contrast effect A disproportionate increase in a response with an increase in incentive. That is, if an animal is bar pressing for 1 gram of food reinforcement and is suddenly shifted to 5 grams it will characteristically respond at a higher rate than a comparable animal that has been receiving 5 gram reinforcements all along. There is also a corresponding negative effect. Also known as the *Crespi effect* for the psychologist who did the initial research on it.

contrast, principle of An associationistic principle that observing or thinking about a particular quality tends to produce recall of its opposite.

contrasuggestibility A tendency (seemingly possessed by all children) to take a position counter to or opposite to one which has been suggested.

contrectation 1. Generally, to touch with the hands. **2.** Specifically, sexual fondling and caressing.

control 1. In the abstract, the exercise of the scientific method whereby the various treatments in an experiment are regulated so that the causal factors may be unambiguously identified. The essence of the term is one of exclusion in that the scientist seeks to eliminate the effects of irrelevant variables by 'controlling' them, leaving only the experimental variable(s) free to change. **2.** Manipulation, the ability to modify and change behavior by systematic use of appropriate reinforcements and punishments. This is the sense of the term in the behaviorist tenet that one of the basic goals of psychology is the *control* of behavior.

control experiment A follow-up experiment designed to replicate and solidify the findings of a previous study by specifically evaluating the effects of a variable that was not (or was only partially) controlled in the original.

control group (or **condition**) A group (or condition) in an experiment that is as closely matched as possible to the experimental group (or condition) except that it is not exposed to the independent variable(s) under investigation.

controlled analysis Psychoanalysis in which the analyst is a trainee and is carefully supervised by a qualified analyst.

controlled association ➤ **association, controlled**.

controlled sampling ➤ **sampling, controlled**.

controlled variable ➤ **independent *variable**.

control, statistical When irrelevant factors are beyond direct experimental control it may be necessary to allow for their effects by making mathematical corrections of the actual data. Such corrections are referred to as statistical controls since they do not enter into the analysis until the data are subjected to statistical evaluations.

control variable ➤ **variable, control**.

convenience sampling ➤ **sampling, convenience**.

conventionality 1. Acting according to standard social practices. **2.** A personality characteristic manifested by a tendency to adhere strongly to social conventions. Conventionality is viewed by many as a component of the ➤ **authoritarian personality**.

conventional level of moral development ➤ **moral development**.

convergence 1. Generally, the property of tending toward a particular point. Used of several elements or components of a system that are oriented in a coordinated manner at a specific locale. Hence: **2.** In perception, the turning of the eyes inward to focus on an object that is being viewed binocularly. As a binocular cue for depth perception it is most effective with objects relatively close to the observer. Compare with ➤ **divergence**. **3.** In neurophysiology, the coming together of several neural processes on a single neuron or on a neural pathway or neural center.

convergent thinking ➤ **thinking, convergent**.

convergent validity ➤ **validity, convergent and discriminant**.

conversational maxims H. P. Grice's term for those basic principles of conversations that speakers normally adhere to in order to optimize communication. He identified four such: (a) *quantity*, do not provide too much (nor too little) information; (b) *quality*, do not say that which you know to be false, be genuine; (c) *relation*, be relevant; and (d) *manner*, be orderly, brief and non-obscure. The term ➤ **conversational postulates** is also found but usually relates more to the general issue than to specific principles.

conversational postulates A general label for those social rules for carrying on a conversation which all speakers/hearers are assumed to know and follow and which they assume the person with whom they are talking also knows and is following. ➤ **conversational maxims** for a set of such.

converse In logic, a proposition derived by conversion (reversing the terms) of another proposition.

conversion The standard meaning is the transformation of something from one state to another. Hence: **1.** The dramatic shift from one set of beliefs to another, especially religious beliefs. **2.** The transformation of a psychological maladjustment into physical forms (➤ **conversion disorder**). **3.** The shift of a set of scores from one scale to another. **4.** The interchanging of the terms in a proposition.

conversion disorder A ➤ **somatoform disorder** characterized by the 'conversion' of a psychic conflict into somatic form. The resulting functional disorder may appear superficially to have physical or physiological causes but may frequently follow no known organic system (see, e.g., ➤ **glove anesthesia**). The symptom manifested usually produces some secondary gain for the individual such as avoidance of some noxious activity or garnering of support and concern from others. Also called *conversion reaction*, *conversion hysteria* or *hysterical neurosis*, *conversion type*.

conversion hysteria ➤ **conversion disorder**.

conversion reaction ➤ **conversion disorder**.

convolution A fold of the cerebral cortex, a ➤ **gyrus**. Convolutions are marked as the areas between the sulci or fissures.

convulsant Any agent that produces a convulsion.

convulsion A general, molar, extensive seizure with involuntary muscular contraction and relaxation. Contrast with ➤ **spasm**, which is small and localized, and with ➤ **clonus**, which is a slow and rhythmic contraction.

convulsive disorders A general cover term for a class of pathological conditions in which convulsions are a common symptom. Included are Jacksonian epilepsy, psychomotor epilepsy and other centrencephalic seizures all of which are demonstrably brain disorders with characteristic EEG patterns. Not included are various other conditions which may display seizures as symptoms.

convulsive therapy A generic label for a number of psychotherapeutic procedures based on the artificial inducing of a convulsion. The use of convulsive therapy derived from the observation that epilepsy and schizophrenia rarely co-occur – a classic case of the fallacious inferring of cause and effect from correlation. There seems to be no effect of such therapies on schizophrenic symptoms, although some are of value in certain cases of depression. For details on specific convulsive therapies ➤ **electro-convulsive shock therapy** and **insulin therapy**.

co-occurrence ➤ **covariation**.

Coolidge effect The phenomenon that the males of many species will show high continuous sexual performance for extended periods of time with introductions of new, receptive females. The name for the effect derives from an old and very bad joke about the American president Calvin Coolidge which space limitations prevent telling here.

coordinate 1 vb. To organize or arrange objects, events, concepts, etc. according to a prescribed or harmonious pattern. **2** n. One of the dimensions by which a point is located in space. **3** adj. Equal in rank or value as compared with being *subordinate* or *supraordinate*.

coordinate bilingual ➤ **bilingualism**.

coordinate morality ➤ **archetypal form**.

coordination Generally, harmonious interrelated functioning of the several elements of a system, as in motor coordination or hand-eye coordination.

coping strategies Conscious, rational ways for dealing with the anxieties of life. The term is used for those strategies designed to deal with the source of the anxiety; e.g., a student anxious about an upcoming examination copes by studying especially long hours for it. Compare with ➤ **defensive strategies**, which are directed at the anxiety itself rather than its source.

copro- Combining form meaning *feces, filth, excrement*, etc. A creative person can find no end of uses for this prefix. Existing technical ones are given in the following entries.

coprolagnia ➤ **coprophilia** (2).

coprolalia Excessive use of verbal obscenities.

coprophagia Lit., eating feces.

coprophilia 1. An unusual interest in feces. **2.** A ➤ **paraphilia**, in which sexual arousal and pleasure are obtained from feces. Also called *coprolagnia*.

copulation ➤ **coitus**.

copulin A vaginal pheromone isolated in rhesus monkeys which stimulates the male to copulate. The level of secretion is highest at the time of ovulation, thereby maximizing impregnation.

cord Occasional short-hand for *spinal cord*.

core gender (or **sex**) **identity** A relatively new term introduced into psychoanalytic models of sexual development to refer to the early sense of self as male or female. This identification is assumed to occur in the second year of life, which is several years before the Oedipal stage at which the classic theory had placed this emerging identity.

corium The 'true' skin, the layer lying directly below the epidermis. Hair follicles, sweat glands and smooth muscle fibers all lie in it.

cornea The transparent outer layer of the eye covering the iris and the pupil. The cornea is completely free of blood vessels and it functions as a refractor of light.

corneal reflection technique A procedure whereby one may make a detailed analysis of eye movements by photographing the movements of light reflected off the cornea.

Cornelia de Lange syndrome A congenital syndrome characterized by mental retardation, short stature, skeletal abnormalities, and a variety of facial features including a small, rounded head, bushy confluent eyebrows, and sharply upturned nose. Etiology is unknown, although a hereditary basis is suspected.

Cornell technique Another name for ➤ **Guttman scaling**. Occasionally called *Guttman–Cornell technique*.

cornu ammonis ➤ **hippocampus**.

corollary A proposition that follows naturally from something else, needing no additional proof. Contrast with ➤ **theorem**, which does require proof.

coronal In phonetics, a distinctive feature characterizing sounds produced with the blade of the tongue raised slightly (e.g., *t* in 'top'); in noncoronals the tongue remains in a neutral position (as the *p* in 'pop').

coronal section ➤ **section** (2).

corporal Bodily. Hence, corporal punishment is physical punishment to the body.

corpora quadrigemina Four prominent elevations on the dorsal surface of the midbrain. The anterior pair (also called the *superior colliculi*) mediate visual reflexes, the posterior pair (*inferior colliculi*) contain auditory centers. ➤ **colliculus** for more detail.

corpus A body or a principal part of a body or organ. pl., *corpora*.

corpus callosum The great commissure of the brain, the band of fibers that serves interconnecting functions between the two cerebral hemispheres, located at the floor of the longitudinal fissure. The corpus callosum transfers information from one hemisphere to the other; it is through it that the 'left brain' knows what the 'right brain' has seen, felt, heard, etc. and vice versa. Severing the callosum produces a ➤ **split brain**.

corpuscle 1. Generally, any small round body. 2. An encapsulated sensory nerve ending. See, e.g., ➤ **pacinian corpuscle**.

corpus luteum A progesterone-secreting endocrine structure that develops within a ruptured ovarian follicle. ➤ **menstrual cycle** for more detail.

corpus striatum From the Latin for *striated body*. That portion of the forebrain containing the *caudate nucleus*, *lenticular nucleus* and *internal capsule*.

correction 1. Generally, any specific manipulation that counters the effects of error. Thus: 2. In statistical analysis of data any transformation or manipulation of scores that minimizes errors of observation, chance or other factors. 3. In vision, the use of lenses to correct for refractive errors of the eye. 4. In social/criminological terms, altering an individual's behavior to bring it into conformity with society's norms; prisons are often called (perhaps euphemistically) *correctional institutes*.

correction for chance ➤ **correction for guessing**.

correction for continuity A statistical correction required in the use of some statistical tests when the actual data are from a discrete distribution but the test assumes an underlying continuous distribution.

correction for guessing Adjustment of the scores on a test by subtracting the number of correct answers that presumably could have been produced by pure chance or by simple guessing. Also called *correction for chance*.

corrective 1. n. Generally, any procedure that produces a correction. 2 n. In pharmacology, any drug that modifies the action of another drug. 3 adj. Pertaining to such a drug, or its action.

correlate 1 n. Any of two variables or factors which are systematically related to each other; that is, they 'co-relate.' 2 n. A principle or an argument that is strongly indicated by some other principle or argument. This meaning is a loose way of connoting in nonformal situations what is meant by *corollary*. E.g., 'It is a correlate of computer simulation work that theories will be formally testable.' 3 vb. To place a thing in a situation where it is in a known relation to another thing. 4 vb. To calculate a ➤ **correlation coefficient**.

correlated Descriptive of a relationship between variables such that they show a nonzero correlation coefficient; they reveal some reliable statistical dependency on each other.

correlation 1. In statistics, a relationship between two (or more) variables such that systematic increases in the magnitude of one variable are accompanied by systematic increases or decreases in the magnitude of the other. The existence of such a statistical relationship is traditionally used as a basis for making predictions about the expected magnitude of one variable given the known magnitude of the other. The stronger the relationship (i.e. the

165

further from zero the obtained correlation coefficient) the greater the confidence in the accuracy of prediction. **2.** Somewhat more loosely, any relationship between things such that some concomitant or dependent changes in one (or more) occur with changes in the other(s). Note that in both of these usages one properly withholds the presumption of causality between the variables. Correlations are statements about concomitance; they may suggest but do not necessarily imply that the changes in one variable are producing or causing the changes in the other(s). **3.** In physiology, the overall processes by which the various bodily processes occur in coordinated relation to each other. Distinguish from **neurological *correlation**.

correlational statistics ➤ **statistics, correlational**.

correlation, biserial (r_{bis}) A correlation in which one variable is measured on a graduated or many-valued scale and the other is dichotomous or two-valued. For example, the correlation between the pass-fail rate in a course and scores on an academic aptitude battery consisting of ten separate scales.

correlation, chance-half ➤ **correlation, split-half**.

correlation cluster A group of variables all of which have higher positive correlations with each other than to other groups of variables or single variables. Such a cluster is taken as evidence for the existence of a *factor* in *factor analysis*.

correlation coefficient A number that expresses the degree and direction of relationship between two (or occasionally, more) variables. The correlation coefficient may range from − 1.00 (indicating a perfect ➤ **negative *correlation**) to + 1.00 (indicating a perfect ➤ **positive *correlation**). The higher the value either negative or positive the greater the concomitance between the variables. A value of 0.00 indicates no correlation; changes in one variable are statistically independent of changes in the other. A large number of

statistical procedures exists for determining the correlation coefficient between variables, depending on the nature of the data and the methods of collection. The ➤ **product-moment *correlation** is the most commonly used and when the terms *correlation coefficient* or even simply *correlation* are found without qualifiers they may be taken to be this particular measure. When other forms of correlation are used they are invariably so noted.

correlation, curvilinear Generally, any correlation where the rate (or rates) of change of the variables is nonlinear. ➤ **curvilinear *regression**. Also called *nonlinear correlation* and, on occasion, *skew correlation*.

correlation, direct An occasional synonym for ➤ **positive *correlation**.

correlation, first-order A ➤ **partial *correlation** in which the influences of only one variable are held constant.

correlation, fourfold point ➤ **phi coefficient**.

correlation, indirect (or **inverse**) Occasional synonyms for ➤ **negative *correlation**.

correlation, Kendall rank (and **Kendall partial rank**) ➤ **Kendall tests**.

correlation, linear Any correlation in which unit-sized changes in one variable are associated with unit-sized changes in the other; that is, the *regression line* is a straight line. Most statistical procedures for obtaining a correlation coefficient are based on this assumption of linearity.

correlation matrix ➤ **matrix, correlation**.

correlation, multiple (R) The relationship between one (dependent) variable and two or more (independent) variables. A multiple correlation coefficient yields an estimate of the combined influence of the independent variables on the dependent.

correlation, negative A correlation in which increases in one variable are associated with decreases in the other. Or, if preferred, in which large values in one are associated with small values in the other.

The coefficient will have negative values between 0 and − 1.00. Also called *inverse* or *indirect correlation*.

correlation, neurological A hypothesis that there is a direct correspondence between each distinct mental or behavioral act of an organism and a particular set of unique neurological events.

correlation, nonlinear ➤ curvilinear *correlation.

correlation, part ➤ semipartial *correlation.

correlation, partial The resulting correlation between two variables after the effects of one or more other related variables have been removed.

correlation, Pearson product-moment ➤ product-moment *correlation.

correlation, perfect A correlation in which every change in one variable is matched by an equivalent change in the other; the correlation coefficient here would be either + 1.00 or − 1.00. (Don't hold your breath looking for one of these in the social sciences.)

correlation, phi ➤ phi coefficient.

correlation, point-biserial A correlation in which one variable is measured on a continuous scale and the other is dichotomous or two-valued.

correlation, positive A correlation in which increases in one variable are associated with increases in the other. Or, if preferred, in which large values in one are associated with large values in the other, and small with small. The correlation coefficient will have positive values between 0 and + 1.00. Also called, on occasion, *direct correlation*.

correlation, product-moment (r) The most commonly used method of measuring a correlation between two quantitative variables that are related in a linear fashion. The early work on the mathematics of the procedure was done by Karl Pearson, and it is often called the Pearson product-moment correlation, or simply the Pearson correlation. It is a *parametric* test and, as such, is based on the usual parametric assumptions. The *product-moment*, which is the foundation of the correlation, is the mean (or the sum) of the products of the deviations of each score from the mean of each variable.

correlation, rank-difference ➤ rank-order *correlation.

correlation, rank-order A correlation which is based on the ranks of the scores on the two variables. It is derived from the Pearson product-moment correlation and is the most widely used *nonparametric* correlation. It is often called the *rank-difference correlation* because the critical factor in the calculation of the coefficient is the difference between the ranks on the two variables. Occasionally called *Spearman rank-order correlation*.

correlation ratio A measure of the extent to which a given regression line departs from linearity.

correlation, semipartial A type of ➤ multiple *correlation in which one variable is partialed out but only from one of the several other variables. Also called *part correlation*.

correlation, simple 1. Any correlation based on only two variables, as contrasted with *multiple correlation*. 2. Any linear correlation, as compared with a *curvilinear correlation*.

correlation, skew ➤ curvilinear *correlation.

correlation, Spearman rank-order ➤ rank-order *correlation.

correlation, split-half The correlation between the scores on two halves of a test. ➤ split-half *reliability.

correlation, spurious A correlation that results not from any direct relationship between the variables under assessment but because of their relationships to a third variable (or fourth, or more) that has no connecting relationship between them. For example, there is a significant positive correlation between the number of letters and corresponding letter names that a child knows when entering school and success in reading. However, specific teaching of this information to children during preschool years has proven ineffective in later reading instruction. The correlation was spurious; the critical factor was not knowing letters and their names but being raised in homes where intellectual activity is prized, which almost invariably leads to the alphabet being taught as a matter of course.

correlation table A two-way tabulation of the relationship between the values of two variables. The scores on one variable are given in the row headings, the scores of the other in the column headings, the intersection cells show frequency for the corresponding values on each. Such tables are useful in the preparation and presentation of correlational analyses.

correlation, tetrachoric (r$_t$) A correlation based on two variables each of which is expressed as a dichotomy (two-valued). The tetrachoric, however, is based (mathematically) on the assumption that both variables are continuous and normally distributed but only expressed, for the purposes at hand, as dichotomous.

correspondence bias The tendency to see an individual's behavior as corresponding to an internal disposition or trait. The term is often used interchangeably with ➤ **fundamental *attribution error**.

corresponding retinal points Usually: **1.** A synonym for ➤ **congruent retinal points**. Unfortunately, on occasion: **2.** A synonym for ➤ **identical retinal points**.

cortex This term comes from the Latin meaning *bark* or *rind*. It is used to refer generally to the outer layer of tissue of any organ and specifically, and most commonly, to the ➤ **cerebral cortex**. pl., *cortices*.

cortex, association ➤ **association areas**.

cortex, motor ➤ **motor areas**.

cortex, sensory ➤ **sensory areas**.

cortical Pertaining to a cortex. Usually, although not exclusively, it refers to the ➤ **cerebral cortex**. The following entries give some idea of the ways in which the term is used.

cortical blindness ➤ cerebral *blindness.

cortical center A cortical area or region which serves as a terminal point for incoming sensory nerve fibers or as an origin for motor fibers.

cortical control Control *of* sub-cortical centers *by* cortical ones; not vice versa.

cortical deafness ➤ cerebral *deafness.

cortical dominance See the discussions under ➤ **dominance** (especially 5, 6, 7) and ➤ **cerebral dominance**.

cortical induction Cortical activity in one area resulting from activity in an adjoining area.

cortical inhibition Inhibition or blocking of neural impulses by a cortical center.

corticalization The gradual subsuming of control of behavioral and psychological processes by the cerebral cortex. Corticalization can be seen as an evolutionary process; with ascent up the phylogenetic scale its most prominent manifestation is in the primates. ➤ **encephalization**.

cortical processes Those processes mediated by cortical tissue. The term is frequently used as a synonym for *voluntary* or *conscious* processes. A phrase like 'cortically mediated response' can be read as 'voluntary response.'

cortico- Combining form meaning ➤ **cortical**.

corticobulbar pathway A neural pathway arising in the neocortex (primarily the primary motor area) and synapsing on the nuclei of the Vth, VIIth, and XIIth cranial nerves in the medulla. It is involved in the control of movements of the muscles of the face and tongue.

corticoid ➤ **corticosteroid**.

corticomedial group A group of nuclei

that make up the phylogenetically older part of the *amygdala*. They receive sensory information about the presence of *pheremones* and send it to the *forebrain* and the *hypothalamus*.

corticospinal pathway A complex neural pathway arising in the *cortex* (mainly in the primary motor area) and terminating in the ventral gray matter of the *spinal cord*. The axons that make up the *lateral corticospinal tract* cross over in the medulla and synapse on spinal motor neurons and interneurons that control movements of the arms and hands. Those that make up the *ventral corticospinal tract* cross over near the terminal point in the spine and control movements of the muscles of the trunk.

corticospinal tract ➤ **corticospinal pathway**.

corticosteroid Any of the steroid substances of the cortex of the ➤ **adrenal gland**. Also called *corticoid*.

corticosterone A hormone produced by the cortex of the ➤ **adrenal gland**; it influences metabolism of the carbohydrates and of sodium and potassium.

corticotrophic hormone ➤ **adrenocorticotrophic hormone**.

cortin An extract of the adrenal cortex; it contains several active steroids, e.g., *corticosterone*.

Corti, organ of ➤ **organ of Corti**.

cortisol A hormone of the cortex of the ➤ **adrenal glands** that has physiological effects essentially the same as those of ➤ **cortisone**.

cortisone A hormone isolated from the cortex of the ➤ **adrenal glands**, it plays a critical role in metabolism of fats, carbohydrates, proteins, and in sodium and potassium.

co-twin control An experimental procedure whereby hereditary factors can be controlled. One member of a pair of identical twins is subjected to an experimental treatment while the other is not.

counseling A generic term that is used to cover the several processes of interviewing, testing, guiding, advising, etc. designed to help an individual solve problems, plan for the future, etc. Often the term *counseling psychologist* is used for clinicians who specialize in guidance in marital problems, drug abuse, vocational selection, community work, etc. var., *counselling*.

counseling, marriage ➤ **marital therapy**.

counter- Combining form generally meaning *opposed* but with two different connotations: (a) *against*, as in *countersuggestion* or *counteract*; and (b) *complementary* or *reciprocal*, as in *counterpart*.

counter 1 n. An agent or instrument that counts things; e.g., clocks count seconds. 2 n. In operant conditioning, a stimulus one dimension of which varies with the number of responses that the subject has made. This systematic variation essentially 'counts' responses and, if the organism attends to it, it functions as a source of information about its behavior. 3. An agent or process that functions in an opposing manner, one that counters the actions of another agent or process. vb, *to counter*.

counteraction need H. Murray's term for a need to overcome failure, to strive forward after defeat. Needless to say, not all have it to much of a degree; ➤ e.g., **learned helplessness**.

counterbalancing An experimental procedure for controlling irrelevant factors. A good example is fatigue: If a subject is to perform two types of tasks, *x* and *y*, then the order of running would be counterbalanced so that fatigue factors would be spread equally across both *x* and *y*. To wit: one half of the subjects would perform task *x* first and one half task *y* first. If the experiment were run so that all subjects performed *x* first then it would not be possible to tell whether *y* was more difficult than *x* or merely that the subjects were getting tired.

counter-cathexis ➤ **anticathexis**.

countercompulsion A compulsion adopted to counter the effects of another compulsion.

counter conditioning An experimental procedure where a second, incompatible response is conditioned to an already conditioned stimulus. For example, a rat trained to press a bar in the presence of a light may be counter conditioned to turn a wheel when the light comes on. The general principle here lies behind many of the procedures used in behavior therapy in which the modification in the client's behavior consists of training up new responses to stimuli that are incompatible with the old ones. For example, ➤ **desensitization** basically is conditioning a relaxation response to a stimulus that once evoked anxiety.

counterfactual A contrary-to-fact conditional statement or hypothetical instance which, for any number of reasons, cannot be subjected to empirical evaluation. Some counterfactuals may simply be beyond technology (e.g., 'if the sun's energy were diminished by 10% life on earth could not exist'), others lie outside of ethical considerations (e.g., 'if we do not inoculate, millions will die'), or they may simply be impossible (e.g., historical hypotheticals). Counterfactuals play an important role in the evaluation of theories since they lead one to examine the formal structure of theoretical explanations to see which counterfactuals could be viewed as supportive and which would be viewed as failing to provide support. ➤ **mental *experiment**.

counterfeit role ➤ role, counterfeit

counterformity ➤ anticonformity.

counteridentification In the course of psychoanalysis, on occasion the analyst will identify with the client as a reaction to the client identifying with the analyst; hence, counteridentification.

counterinvestment In psychoanalytic theory, the attachment of an overt feeling that is counter (or opposite) to a supposedly repressed one, such as displaying love where one unconsciously hates (or, for that matter, showing hate where one loves). The difficulty encountered with this notion is how to know what the 'real' emotion is. Projective tests are thought by many to reveal the deep, unconscious motives, but there are problems: ➤ **projective techniques** for a discussion.

counterphobic character A psychoanalytic term for the type of person who regularly engages in and derives pleasure from behaviors and activities that 'normally' would be regarded as dangerous and anxiety-provoking.

countershock phase The second part of the alarm reaction stage in the ➤ **general adaptation syndrome**.

countersuggestion 1. Generally, a suggestion designed to overcome or 'counter' a previously made suggestion. 2. In Piagetian research, a suggestion made to a child that counters or contradicts something the child has previously said or claimed is true. The purpose is to evaluate how robust the child's belief is and to determine how the child will defend his or her belief against the countersuggestion.

countertransference 1. In psychoanalysis, the analyst's displacement of affect (i.e. ➤ **transference**) onto the client. 2. More generally, the analyst's emotional involvement in the therapeutic interaction. In the former sense countertransference is a distorting element in a psychoanalysis and can be disruptive; in the latter sense it is considered benign and, by some, inevitable.

counterwill O. Rank's term for, quite simply, the ability to say 'no.' For Rank this represented the key concept in the development of a healthy personality. Note, this resistance of will covers both external pressures from others and internal impulses.

couples therapy The terms *marital therapy, marriage therapy, marriage counseling* and the like all imply that a couple should be married in order to seek advice and help with their relationship. This term has been introduced to reflect the reality that many persons who are in long-term relationships not graced by state or church are also in need of therapy.

couvade (*coo-vahd*) The experiencing of the rigors of labor and childbirth by the father. The turmoil of the male is quite real and indicative of the effectiveness of psychosomatic phenomena. While it exists as a custom in some societies, it is also found spontaneously occurring in all.

covariance Lit., covariation. Changes in one variable accompanied by changes in another. This coordinated variance is expressed by $\Sigma xy/N$, where x and y are deviations of each score from the means of each variable and N is the number of cases.

covariate Any variable that is controlled for by statistically subtracting out its effects by the use of ➤ **analysis of covariance** or ➤ **multiple regression**.

covariation A relationship between objects or events such that they systematically vary together in ways that entail the conclusion that they are causally linked. The term is used so that it connotes causality as opposed to *co-occurrence*, where the connotation is only that the events occur together. To appreciate the importance of this distinction see ➤ **correlation** (1,2) and ➤ **Rescorla–Wagner theory**.

cover memory ➤ **screen memory**.

covert Covered, disguised, hidden. It is most often used to refer to processes that cannot be directly observed such as imagery, thought, etc.

covert extinction A technique in behavior therapy in which the client imagines that reinforcements are no longer forthcoming for the behavior that is to be extinguished.

covert reinforcement A technique in behavior therapy in which the client imagines reinforcers occurring for the behaviors that are desired. Usually used with anxiety disorders where the client imag-

ines the rewards of successfully coping with the anxiety-producing situation.

covert speech ➤ **subvocalization**.

CPI ➤ **California Personality Inventory**.

CR 1. ➤ **conditional response**. 2. ➤ **critical ratio**.

cranial Pertaining to the ➤ **cranium**.

cranial capacity The volume of the ➤ **cranium**.

cranial division The uppermost part of the parasympathetic division of the ➤ **autonomic nervous system**.

cranial index ➤ **cephalic index**.

cranial nerves The 12 nerves that enter and leave the brain directly rather than through the spinal cord (➤ **spinal nerves**). They are numbered and individually named:

I *Olfactory:* smell; afferent from olfactory receptors.

II *Optic:* efferent controlling vision; afferent from retina.

III *Oculomotor:* efferent to eye muscles; all external muscles except oblique and rectus.

IV *Trocular:* oblique muscles of eye.

V *Trigeminal:* efferent and afferent serving face, nose and tongue.

VI *Abducens:* efferent to rectus muscles of eye.

VII *Facial:* efferent to facial muscles; afferent from taste buds, anterior part of the tongue.

VIII *Auditory-vestibular:* afferent serving hearing and balance. Also called *vestibulocochlear*.

IX *Glossopharyngeal:* efferent to the throat; afferent from taste buds, posterior part of the tongue.

X *Vagus:* afferent and efferent serving heart, lungs, thorax, larynx, pharynx, external ear and abdominal viscera.

XI *Spinal accessory:* afferent and efferent serving neck muscles.

XII *Hypoglossal:* efferent to tongue muscles.

For more detail, see the separate entry for each nerve.

cranial reflex Any reflex mediated directly by one of the cranial nerves. Distinguish from ➤ **spinal reflex**.

cranio- Combining form meaning pertaining to the cranium or, more loosely, the skull.

craniometry Study of the skull, with emphasis on measurement.

craniosacral division Occasional synonym for the parasympathetic division of the ➤ **autonomic nervous system**.

cranioscopy ➤ **phrenology**.

cranium That portion of the skull enclosing the brain.

'crash' Slang term for 'coming down' from an amphetamine- or cocaine-produced 'high.' It only occurs after extended usage and typically involves feelings of anxiety, tremors, heightened irritability and depression.

creationism A point of view derived from theological considerations that argues that life and the existence of species, particularly *Homo sapiens*, are the result of a specific creative act handicrafted by a supreme being. There actually are several creationist points of view, ranging from the pure fundamentalist, which depends on the literal interpretation of the Bible, to the somewhat more 'liberal' perspectives which allow for some Darwinian-type evolutionary processes for lower species but view man as separate from these non-spiritual mechanistic organisms.

creative synthesis A philosophical principle that when several elemental components are organized or coordinated the resulting synthesis has properties and characteristics that are fundamentally different in kind from those of the separate components viewed independently. ➤➤ **emergentism, holism, synthesis**.

creative thinking ➤ **creativity**. Also compare with ➤ **critical *thinking**.

creativity A term used in the technical literature in basically the same way as in the popular, namely to refer to mental processes that lead to solutions, ideas, conceptualization, artistic forms, theories or products that are unique and novel. ➤➤ **divergent *thinking, insight** (3, 4).

credibility Believability. In studies of ➤ **persuasion** the credibility of the source of a statement is an important variable; persons with high credibility, not surprisingly, have more persuasive impact than those with low credibility. adj., *credible*.

credulity A disposition to believe too readily or on too little evidence. Distinguish from ➤ **credibility**.

creole In studies of language, a ➤ **pidgin** that has become the dominant verbal communication system for a people and acquired its own native speakers. This process is called *creolization*.

Crespi effect ➤ **contrast effect**.

cretinism A congenital condition caused by a deficiency in thyroxin and characterized by severe lack of physical growth and mental retardation. Secondary symptoms include rough dry skin, patchy coarse hair, late and erratic dentition, and an enlarged, protruding tongue.

Creutzfeldt-Jakob disease A neurological disorder marked by spastic paralysis of the limbs with tremor and rigidity, and a devastating rapidly progressing dementia not unlike that seen in ➤ **Alzheimer's disease**.

crf Abbreviation for *continuous reinforcement;* ➤ **schedules of *reinforcement**.

crib death ➤ **sudden infant death syndrome**.

cri du chat (*cree-doo-shah*) A chromosomal abnormality resulting in mental retardation, microcephaly, dwarfism and a laryngeal abnormality which gives the infant a cry that sounds like a cat crying (hence the name of the syndrome).

criminal psychopath An individual whose illegal acts stem from uncontrollable psychological problems; e.g., the ➤ **impulse disorders** of kleptomania, pyromania and some of the ➤ **paraphilias** like exhibitionism and rape are included. Also called *criminal sociopath*.

criminal responsibility A legal term relating to the state of mind of a defendant at the time of the crime and the question whether the defendant could distinguish right from wrong and hence be held personally responsible for the criminal actions taken.

criminal type An antiquated term for a type of individual who repeatedly engages in criminal actions and who according to some unreconstructed Lombrosians may possess a constitutional predisposition to do so.

criminology A hybrid science, a blend of law, sociology, psychology and medicine that studies crime, criminals and penology.

crisis 1. From the Greek word for *turning-point*, any inflection point in the course of events. Strictly speaking, a crisis can be either a sudden improvement in things or a sudden deterioration. 2. In medicine, the turning-point in a disease. 3. Any sudden interruption in the normal course of events in the life of an individual or a society that necessitates re-evaluation of modes of action and thought. This general sense of a loss of the normal foundations of day-to-day activity is the dominant connotation of the term and is broadly used. For example, an individual is said to undergo a psychological crisis when abrupt departures from normality occur such as the death of a loved one, the loss of one's job, and the like. 4. In the philosophy and history of science the term is used with similar connotations to refer to circumstances in which the presently accepted principles of a science are directly challenged and found wanting. Note that in all of these usages there is an accompanying sense that a crisis is something that is uncontrollable, that it must be allowed to run its course. pl., *crises*.

crisis intervention A type of psychotherapy focusing on acute, critical situations such as drug overdoses, suicide attempts, profound depressive episodes, etc. Often they are handled over the telephone or through drop-in centers staffed by paraprofessionals.

crisis rites Ceremonies performed at times of crisis. Sociologists and anthropologists usually cite examples – for instance, rain dances in response to droughts – from so-called 'primitive' cultures. So-called 'modern' industrialized democracies also have them, as in voting in the opposition party whenever the economy goes sour. In both cases the rites are ineffectual. ➤ **superstitious behavior**.

crista The organ in the ampulla of each ➤ **semicircular canal** containing the hair cells that respond to movements of the endolymph set up by angular rotation of the head.

criterion 1. Generally, a standard against which a judgement, evaluation or classification can be made. More specifically: 2. A level of performance that is set as a goal by which progress is judged. This meaning is common in studies of learning where some criterion is set and taken as representative·of learning; e.g., in studies of memory one complete errorless run through all items. 3. In signal detection theory, an internal cut-point along the dimension of neural activity below which the response 'no signal' is made and above which the response 'signal' is made. For details ➤ **signal detection theory**. 4. In statistics, the dependent variable. pl., *criteria*; adj., *criterial*.

criterion group A group of selected individuals whose scores on a test may be used to evaluate the test scores of others and to assist in determining the validity of the test. For example, a group of professional musicians might serve as the criterion group for a test of musical aptitude.

criterion score A score in the dependent variable that is predicted on the basis of hypotheses concerning the effects of the independent variable. ➤➤ **coefficient of *validity** for discussion of how criterion scores are used in the determination of the validity of a testing instrument.

173

criterion variable ➤ **variable, criterion**.

critical 1. Pertaining to or characteristic of criticism. This meaning, particularly when used in philosophically oriented work, implies that the approach taken to the work being criticized is *unbiased*, the critic is attempting to review the topic or work without prejudice. 2. Characteristic of skeptical, faultfinding reviews. This meaning, closer perhaps to lay usage, connotes an unfavorable analysis and assessment. 3. Pertaining to ➤ **crisis** in any of the meanings of that term. 4. Characteristic of a judgement or decision that is of great importance, something that is *crucial*.

critical band width In audition, the range of frequencies that interact in special ways within the ear. The term has a variety of extremely technical uses that go beyond the scope of this volume; the interested reader should consult a text on audition or hearing.

critical flicker frequency (cff) The point at which a flickering stimulus is no longer perceived as periodic but shifts to continuous. The cff increases with increases in intensity. Also known as *critical flicker*, *critical fusion frequency*, *flicker fusion point* or *flicker fusion frequency*.

critical period A period of time, biologically determined, during which an organism is optimally ready for acquisition of specific responses. The best-known example is the critical period for *imprinting* in certain species of ducks, which is a 'window' of a few hours following hatching. If imprinting does not occur in the critical period it can never be learned and the duck will not develop normally. ➤➤ **sensitive period**.

critical ratio (CR) The ratio of the difference between two statistics to the standard error of the difference. The CR is a special case of the *t* test.

critical region ➤ **region of rejection**.

critical thinking ➤ **thinking, critical**.

Crocker–Henderson system A system for representing the psychological components of smell using four basic odors, fragrant, acid, burnt and caprylic ('goat'). It was not terribly successful in accounting for psychophysical data; the more complex systems of Henning and Zwaardemaker give better characterizations.

Cronbach's alpha A measure of the internal reliability of the items on a test or questionnaire. It ranges from 0 to 1.0 and reflects the extent to which the items are measuring the same thing. For example, if all respondents who said 'no' to Question 1 also said 'no' to Questions 2 and 3, the alpha for these three would be 1.0.

cross adaptation ➤ **adaptation, cross**.

cross conditioning Incidental conditioning that occurs to an irrelevant stimulus that adventitiously occurred simultaneously with the unconditioned stimulus.

cross-cultural method An experimental method used in social psychology, sociology, anthropology, etc. in which different cultures are evaluated on several different cultural dimensions such as child-rearing practices, literacy, language use, etc. The patterns of scores of the various cultures are then compared. The primary purpose of this type of research is not so much comparison of different cultures, *per se*, as it is comparison of various practices in different cultural settings.

cross-culture test ➤ **culture-free test**.

cross dressing Wearing the clothes of the other gender; ➤ **transvestic fetishism**.

crossed reflex A reflex on the contralateral (opposite) side of the body from that stimulated.

cross-impact matrix method A statistical procedure for making estimates about future trends and events. It is a refinement of ➤ **trend analysis** and projects possible future occurrences probabilistically by extrapolating from known data. The heart of the procedure is the synthesizing of predictions made by a variety of other methods (hence the name). ➤➤ **Delphi method**.

crossing over In genetics, the mutual exchange of genes between two chromosomes. The exchange occurs between corresponding genes on homologous chromosomes during melosis.

cross-modality discrimination Discrimination in which objects presented in one modality (e.g., *vision*) must be identified using another modality (e.g., *touch*).

cross-modality matching ➤ **methods of *scaling**.

cross-parent identification A child's identification with the parent of the opposite sex.

cross-section ➤ section (2).

cross-sectional method An approach to research often used in developmental, clinical and social psychology where large groups of subjects are studied at one point in time (also called the *synchronic method*). Contrast with the ➤ **longitudinal** (or *diachronic*) method where the behavior of individual subjects is followed over an extended period of time.

cross tolerance ➤ **tolerance, cross**.

cross validation A procedure for further evaluating the validity of a test by administering it a second time on a new sample of individuals selected from the same population.

crowd A large but temporary gathering of persons with a common interest or focus. Note that this notion of temporariness is lost when the terms ➤ **crowding** or **overcrowding** are used.

crowding An area of study in social psychology dealing with the impact of numbers of individuals on behavior. While it is clear that the characteristic behaviors that human beings (and other animals) exhibit are affected by the sheer size of the group they are in or the population density of the community within which they live, the manner in which this variable affects behavior is extremely complex. The aberrant behaviors initially re-

ported by researchers (➤ **behavioral sink**) are not always found and, for simplicity's sake, it is reasonable to think of crowding as that situation in which achieved privacy is less than desired privacy. Also called *overcrowding*.

CRT Abbreviation for *cathode ray tube*; the output 'screen' of an oscilloscope.

crucial experiment From the Latin *experimentum crucis* (which is sometimes used), it refers to any experiment the outcome of which will definitely and unambiguously establish the truth or falsity of a proposition or hypothesis. Alas, in science generally and in psychology specifically, the *experimentum crucis* is nearly always an illusion, for a new conundrum always seems to be lurking behind the data.

crude In statistics; **1.** Characterizing data not yet analyzed or transformed; ➤ **raw. 2.** Approximate; a crude statistic is an estimated or approximate statistic.

crude score ➤ **raw *score**.

crutch Generally, any supportive device. It may be used to refer to: (a) a physical device, e.g., to assist in walking; (b) a cognitive *heuristic* like a ➤ **mnemonic** for facilitating learning of and memory for material; or (c) a ➤ **defense mechanism** whereby some affliction, real or imagined, is used to rationalize failure or inadequacy.

cryptesthesia Lit., hidden sensations. A cover term in parapsychology for all forms of extra-sensory perception. See discussion under ➤ **parapsychology**. var. *cryptaesthesia*.

crypt(o)- Word element meaning *hidden, secret, occult*.

cryptogenic epilepsy ➤ **epilepsy, cryptogenic**.

cryptography The study, development and utilization of codes. The term is properly used to refer to artificially developed systems for transmitting messages secretly. Distinguish from ➤ **code**.

cryptomnesia Lit., hidden or unconscious memory. Generally used for ideas and thoughts (often apparently creative and novel) that are really memories of past experiences and events that the individual does not (consciously) recall. Also called *source amnesia* but this term is not recommended for this meaning.

cryptophasia Lit., secret speech. It has been used for the peculiar communication codes occasionally observed in pairs of twins and some pathological cases. The consensus of the psycholinguists who have studied such systems is that they are not true, novel languages as many had first assumed but unsystematic variations on a natural language. Also called *idioglossia*.

cryptorchidism A condition in which one (unilateral) or both (bilateral) testicle(s) are undescended.

CS Abbreviation for ➤ **conditioned stimulus**.

CSF ➤ **cerebrospinal fluid**.

CT scan ➤ **computerized axial tomography**.

cue 1. That aspect of a stimulus pattern that may be used in making a discrimination between that stimulus and any other; an identification mark, a clue. 2. A signal that guides (or 'cues') behavior. It may be either a part of the experimental stimulus, in which case it marks the occasion for an operant response, or part of a response in the form of some feedback from having made it, when it serves as a cue for another response.

cue function The functional role of a stimulus as a guide to or evoker of behavior. ➤ **functional *stimulus**.

cue reversal ➤ **reversal *learning**.

cul-de-sac ➤ **blind alley**.

cult A loosely constructed type of religious organization with an amorphous set of beliefs and rituals. A distinguishing feature of a cult is the adherence to a particular individual who is seen as the guiding

spirit behind these beliefs and rituals. The term is used for both the group of persons in the organization and for the complex of beliefs. See and compare with ➤ **sect**.

cultural Pertaining to culture. The term with its general meaning is used in many combined forms, some of which follow here, some follow the entry for ➤ **culture**. For those not listed there ➤ **social** et seq. or, as a last resort, **group**.

cultural absolute ➤ **absolute, cultural**.

cultural adaptation ➤ **adaptation** (2).

cultural anthropology ➤ **anthropology, cultural**.

cultural artifact ➤ **artifact, cultural**.

cultural assimilation ➤ **assimilation** (10).

cultural blindness The disposition to view the events of the world through the set of values and norms learned in one's own culture; the inability to be aware of or sensitive to the view that others, of different cultures may have, of events and relations between persons. Basically, a synonym of ➤ **ethnocentrism**.

cultural conserve Moreno's term for anything (book, film, work of art, artifact, etc.) that functions to mark and preserve some cultural value.

cultural determinism 1. Generally, the point of view that human behavior is primarily shaped and controlled by cultural and social factors. 2. More specifically, the point of view that culture, transcending as it does the lives of particular persons, must be approached as an object of scientific study independent of the individuals who make it up at any point in time; e.g., the notion that culture is *superorganic*.

cultural drift The gradual shifting of the values and norms of a culture over time. The changes that produce it are typically small and may go quite undetected until they accumulate and the shift in orientation becomes apparent.

cultural integration ➤ **integration, cultural**.

cultural items Those items on a test which clearly reflect specific aspects of a particular culture and which will favor persons with the appropriate learning experiences. ➤ **culture-free test**.

cultural lag Either 1. ➤ **cultural residue** or 2. ➤ **culture lag**. Note that these two have rather different references.

cultural monism The social philosophical perspective that maintains that ethnic, racial and religious minorities should be assimilated into the dominant culture. Advocates of this view maintain that internal strife is less likely with a monistic system than with a cultural ➤ **pluralism** (4).

cultural norms The rules or standards of conduct of a society that specify certain behaviors as appropriate and others as inappropriate. Generally included in a set of cultural norms are rewards and punishments typically meted out for conforming to or violating them.

cultural parallelism ➤ **parallelism, cultural**.

cultural pluralism ➤ **pluralism** (4).

cultural relativism The position that one cannot evaluate, interpret or judge phenomena properly unless they are viewed with reference to the culture in which they originated. The view extends from cultural products such as music, art, literature, industry, etc., to broad concepts like *cultural norms*, *mores* and *ethics*. In general, the operating principle is that the customs of one culture can never be validly judged inferior or superior to those of another.

cultural residue Aspects of a culture that are maintained despite the fact that whatever utilitarian functions they originally had have been lost through technological or attitudinal changes. Typically such *survivals* (as they are often called) are preserved for decorative uses. Sometimes also called *cultural lag[s]*.

cultural transmission The process of learning through which the values, standards; norms, etc. of a culture are passed on to succeeding generations. ➤➤ **acculturation (1)** and **socialization**.

culture 1. The system of information that codes the manner in which the people in an organized group, society or nation interact with their social and physical environment. In this sense the term is really used so that the frame of reference is the sets of rules, regulations, *mores* and methods of interaction within the group. A key connotation is that culture pertains only to non-genetically given transmission; each member must *learn* the systems and the structures. 2. The group or collection of persons who share the patterned systems described in 1.

culture area A geographic region within which common cultural patterns are prevalent. Typically, such an area contains subcultures within it that have their own distinctive elements, although all reflect the shared characteristics.

culture-bound syndrome ➤ **culture-specific syndrome**.

culture complex An integrated, structured pattern of cultural traits and activities that functions as a coordinated unit within a society. Examples run the gamut from the football (soccer) complex in many European and South American countries to the rice-growing complex in many Southeast Asian countries.

culture conflict 1. The conflict occurring in a person or a group when confronted with two or more contradictory cultural standards or practices both of which are partially acceptable and over which there are conflicting loyalties. 2. The actual conflict between groups over such divergent standards and practices. Meaning 1 is that usually intended, the conflict being that *within* the person(s) confronted with the problem.

culture contact Generally, any form of interaction between persons of two distinct cultures that results in mutual modification of the cultures through reciprocal assimilation of traits.

culture-epoch theory The largely discredited theory that holds that (a) all cultures evolve through a series of stages (or

177

'epochs') and that (b) each individual develops in a manner which mirrors this sequence. For more discussion on this general viewpoint ➤ **recapitulation theory**.

culture-fair test ➤ **culture-free test**.

culture-free test A test designed to be, as far as possible, free of any particular cultural bias so that no advantage is derived by individuals of one culture relative to those of another. Such tests generally eliminate or severely underplay language factors and other skills that may be closely tied to a particular culture. A variation is the *class-free test*, which is designed to be fair across socioeconomic classes within a given culture. There is considerable doubt about whether such existing tests are or ever can be made to be truly fair to all persons independent of culture. Also called *culture-fair tests*.

culture island A self-contained community with its own distinct culture existing surrounded by a larger culture. A classic example is the Amish agricultural community in Pennsylvania in the United States.

culture lag Those aspects within a culture that can be observed to be changing less rapidly than other aspects. In most modern industrial societies and in what are euphemistically called 'emerging' societies such lags are common. Compare with ➤ **culture lead**.

culture lead Those aspects of a culture that can be observed to be changing more rapidly than other aspects. In a sense, a lead is an anticipatory aspect of a culture, a shift within a culture that can be interpreted as a preparatory adjustment. Compare with ➤ **culture lag**.

culture pattern 1. Occasional synonym for ➤ **culture complex**. 2. The dominant aspects of a culture.

culture shock The emotional disruption often experienced by persons when they pay an extended visit to or live for some time in a society that is different from their own. The typical manifestations are a sense of bewilderment and a feeling of

strangeness which may last for a considerable length of time depending on the individual and the disparateness of the new culture from the familiar original one.

culture-specific syndrome Any pathological behavioral syndrome specific to a particular culture. See, e.g., Southeast Asian ➤ **koro** and Eskimo ➤ **piblokto**. Note that there are questions as to whether these disorders are really specific to particular cultures. The *ICD-10*, for example, considers them to be local variants of anxiety, depressive, or somatoform disorders. Also called *ethnic psychosis* or *culture-bound syndrome*.

culture trait A very flexible term indeed, used most commonly to denote the simplest significant components of any culture. However, in the hands of different writers, it may serve to stand for any number of things; e.g., a culture-bound material implement such as a cocktail glass, a functionally coordinated set of physically diverse implements such as all the varieties of containers for alcoholic beverages, a social interaction such as a cocktail party, a belief or attitude such as being pro or con cocktail parties, and so forth. Thus this notion of a trait somehow standing for a 'simple' component is very much dependent on the level of analysis undertaken. ➤ **culture complex**.

culturgen A term coined by E. O. Wilson and C. J. Lumsden for the basic individual units that make up culture. The concept emerges as a central one in ➤ **sociobiology**, where the choice between alternative culturgens (e.g., the acceptance or rejection of incest, to use one of the sociobiologists' favorite cases) is seen as a critical element in the evolution of culture.

cumulative 1. Generally, characterizing anything reached by successive additions. 2. In statistics, a method of summing a series of scores in which each successive score is added to the sum of all preceding scores.

cumulative frequency curve A graphic representation of a series of scores summed cumulatively. Generally the scores are arranged in order of increasing magnitude so that the curve reveals the functional relationship. If the underlying distribution is normal, the curve will be an ➤ ogive.

cumulative frequency distribution ➤ distribution, cumulative frequency.

cumulative recorder A device used frequently in operant research which automatically plots responses against time. Paper is fed through the device at a known rate while a pen moves across the paper each time a response is made. Rate of responding can thus be read from the slope of the curve; the steeper the slope the higher the rate. A flat curve indicates no responding.

cumulative scaling method ➤ Guttman scaling.

cuneate nucleus (or **cuneus**) A grouping of neurons located in the lower medulla that relays neural impulses from the upper trunk and arms to the somatic sensory areas of the brain; the first synaptic junction in the pathway. ➤➤ gracile nucleus.

cupula A gelatinous body in the ampulla of the ➤ semicircular canals in which the hair cells of the ➤ crista are embedded.

curare (*kyu-rah-ree*) The common name for d-Tubocurarine. It is a chemical substance found in certain South American plants that causes paralysis in striated muscles. Curare acts by blocking cholinergic transmission at the myoneural junction by competing with acetylcholine at the receptor sites. Its major medical use is by anesthesiologists to induce muscle flaccidity for surgery, but it has also served psychology in a number of experiments that showed that a paralyzed animal can still learn a stimulus–response connection even though the overt response itself cannot be made during the actual training trials.

cure 1. A return to health. 2. Any procedure or treatment that restores health. Compare with ➤ heal.

curiosity The tendency to seek for the novel. Some psychologists regard it as an innate propensity in many species, others are skeptical. Part of the difficulty is in distinguishing between what is entailed by curiosity and what is entailed by simple exploration of one's environment.

curve 1. Any line whose position is given with reference to a set of coordinates. 2. In statistics, a collection of points described by an equation. 3. More generally, a line given to represent a series of values of one or more variables. In this latter sense, for example, one may plot the *curve* of correct responses by trials and generate a *learning curve*. Strictly speaking, a curve may be straight.

curve fitting 1. Any of a number of procedures for obtaining a smooth regular curve that accurately 'fits' or characterizes a given set of data. They may be free-hand approximations (called 'eyeballing' in the trade) or mathematically rigorous procedures ➤ goodness of *fit and ➤ least-squares principle. 2. A slightly derogatory expression used of theoreticians who play loose and fast with the values of the parameters of equations that are taken as theoretical representations of data. The implication is that someone who is 'curve fitting' (usually preceded with a 'merely') is juggling parameters around in an unjustifiable manner so as to make the theoretical curves fit the data.

curve, normal ➤ normal *distribution.

curvilinear Pertaining to a nonrectilinear curve, a line which is not straight.

curvilinear correlation ➤ correlation, curvilinear.

curvilinear regression ➤ regression, curvilinear.

curvilinear relationship Any relationship between two variables that when plotted results in a curved line.

cutaneous Pertaining to or affecting the skin itself or the skin as a sense organ.

cutaneous pain ➤ acute *pain.

cutaneous sense Any sense the receptors

for which lie in the skin, immediately below it, or in the external mucous membranes. Included here are touch, pressure, temperature (warm and cold), pain, and the common chemical senses. Occasionally called *dermal sense*.

CVC (trigram) ➤ **nonsense syllable**.

cybernetics A discipline developed largely through the work of Norbert Wiener and named after the Greek word for *steersman*. It is primarily concerned with control mechanisms and their associated communications systems, particularly those which involve feedback of information to the mechanism about its activities. As it has developed over the years cybernetics has become multidisciplinary, involving engineering, computer sciences, psychology, biology, sociology, etc. In fact the blend with other fields has been so effective that the term itself is falling out of use.

cycle 1. A recurring series of events. 2. A complete vibration of a sound or light wave.

cycle per second (cps) A measure of the frequency of a vibrating stimulus, the term is now 'officially' obsolete and has been replaced by the term ➤ **Hertz (Hz)**.

cyclic adenosine monophosphate In the activation of *receptors*, a second messenger that operates in the production of postsynaptic potentials and in the mediation of the effects of peptide hormones. Also called *cyclic AMP*.

cyclic AMP ➤ **cyclic adenosine monophosphate**.

cyclic disorder ➤ **cyclothymic disorder**.

cyclic GMP ➤ **cyclic guanosine monophosphate**.

cyclic guanosine monophosphate A second messenger with form and function similar to ➤ **cyclic adenosine monophosphate** only with *guanosine* substituted for *adenosine*. Also called *cyclic GMP*.

cyclic nucleotide An umbrella term for those compounds such as ➤ **cyclic adenosine**

monophosphate and **cyclic guanosine monophosphate** that function to mediate the intracellular effects of a variety of neurotransmitters.

cyclopean eye A hypothetical eye in the median plane between the two eyes that can be represented as a theoretical coordinate of the two eyes.

cyclophoria Abnormal rotation of the eyeball due to weakness in the oblique muscles, a form of ➤ **heterophoria**.

cycloplegia A paralysis of the ciliary muscle which controls the pupil of the eye, resulting in a dilated pupil even under high light levels.

cyclothymic disorder A ➤ **mood disorder** characterized by cyclical mood swings or by a fairly consistent elation or depression. Distinguish from ➤ **bipolar disorder**, where the range of the emotions is much more extreme. Cyclothymia is used as a psychiatric label only when there has been an extended disruption in affect (usually two years or more); it is not meant to apply to acute emotional reactions. Also called *cyclic disorder*.

cyesis Pregnancy.

-cyte Suffix denoting **cell**.

cyt(o)- Prefix denoting *cell*.

cytoarchitectonics (or **cytoarchitecture**) Lit., the study of the architecture (the organization and patterns) of the cells within the cerebral cortex.

cytogenetics A branch of the study of heredity specializing in the structure and function of chromosomes and genes.

cytogenic gland Any gland that produces cells; the sex glands, lymph nodes, spleen. See discussion under ➤ **gland**.

cytogenic syndrome A general term used for any condition marked by a variety of physical and behavioral symptoms caused by some abnormality in the size, number, or shape of the chromosomes. ➤ e.g., **Klinefelter's syndrome, Turner's syndrome**.

cytology Science concerned with the

study of the formation, structure and function of cells.

cytoplasm The protoplasm of a cell outside of the nucleus.

cytosine One of the four nucleotide bases

which make up ➤ **deoxyribonucleic acid** and ➤ **ribonucleic acid.**

cytotoxic Destructive of or toxic to cells. Cytotoxic agents are substances that destroy cells or inhibit their multiplication.

D

D **1.** In Hull's theory, *drive*. **2.** In statistics generally, a difference score. **3.** In statistics specifically, a crude measure of dispersion of a distribution of scores given by the difference between the 10th and 90th percentiles.

d **1.** Deviation of a score from a measure of central tendency. Usually the mean is the measure used for the calculation. **2.** A difference score representing the 2 ranks of an individual on 2 separate tests.

d' A measure of the sensitivity of an observer to some stimulus 'event.' The notion of an 'event' here is interpreted broadly. It may be the occurrence of a simple stimulus, the occurrence of some stimulus that differs in some fashion from another stimulus, a part on an assembly line that has a flaw, a shadow on a chest X-ray, etc. The measure *d'* is derived from signal-detection theory as an index of how sensitive an observer is to the stimulus independently of criteria for responding, payoffs for being right or wrong, the probabilities of the stimuli actually being presented and any instructional set that may be given to the subject. It is thus an index for the 'ideal' observer which can, of course, be read for any given subject in a signal-detection experiment. ➤ **signal-detection theory**. Usually pronounced as '*d*-prime.'

DA Abbreviation for ➤ **dopamine**.

dactology Manual sign language.

dactyl From the Greek for *finger* and, by extension, *toe*.

Daltonism Red-green colorblindness. Named for John Dalton, an English chemist who had it and first described it. See discussion of ➤ **dichromacy**.

damping Diminution in the amplitude of a wave.

dance therapy The use of the physical and asthetic aspects of dance as a therapeutic medium. It has been frequently used as a technique for working with disturbed children but wider applications are certainly feasible.

dark adaptation The process of adjustment of the eyes to low intensities of illuminations, the shift from the *photopic* system to the *scotopic* system. Total dark adaptation requires approximately 4 hours, although most of the process is complete in about 30 minutes for the originally brightly illuminated eye. The cones adapt completely first, taking about 7 minutes, the rods continue their adaptation for the full 4 hours. The totally dark-adapted eye is over 1 million times as sensitive as the normally illuminated eye.

dark light Not light at all, rather a phrase used to refer to the fact that the receptors in the eye have a level of spontaneous activity which, under the proper conditions, can be phenomenologically real and detected as a sense of 'light.'

Darwinian fitness ➤ **fitness** (2).

Darwinism The theory of evolution due to Charles Darwin (1809–82). The fundamental tenet of Darwinism is the principle of natural selection, whereby the variations in form displayed by the members of a species have differential survival values. Those variations that are 'adaptive' in the struggle for survival will be the ones most likely to enable those possessing them to live and, if they have reasonably high *Darwinian fitness*, to be passed on to their offspring. This process gradually gives rise to diverse forms leading ultimately, through selective adaptation to specific econiches, to the emergence of new species. Note that the term denotes a gradualist position; other theories which emphasize a saltatory process in which new species are assumed to emerge in a relatively short time period (geologic time) are properly not called Darwinian, nor are other theoretical models such as the Lamarckian hypothesis of *inheritance* of acquired characteristics (although it should be noted that Darwin did accept the possibility of a Lamarckian process). The currently accepted Darwinian-based model is often called *neo-Darwinism*. ➤ **evolution** and **evolutionary theory**.

Dasein Lit. translated from the German the term means *to be* (*sein*) *there* (*da*). However, it is generally rendered in English as ➤ **being-in-the-world**.

Daseinanalyse The original German for what is now generally known as *existential analysis* or *existential psychology*. See the discussion under ➤ **existentialism** and ➤ **existential therapy**.

DAT Abbreviation for *dementia of the Alzheimer's type*. ➤ **Alzheimer's disease**.

data The body of evidence or facts gathered in experiments or studies. *Data* is the plural form of *datum*.

data driven processing In *cognitive psychology*, processing that is determined primarily by the input stimuli, the data. See ➤ **bottom-up processing** for more detail.

data snooping Laboratory jargon for 'scattershot' rummaging through one's data looking for statistically significant effects without an a priori rationale. The 'significant' findings that emerge from such operations are likely to be spurious and due merely to random fluctuations, particularly when the data base is large or the number of factors high. To a certain extent such *fishing expeditions* are carried out by nearly all researchers but the responsible course is to use any adventitious findings as heuristics for future experimentation and not to report them as robust effects based on the original study. Compare and contrast with ➤ **a posteriori tests**.

datum Singular of ➤ **data**.

day blindness ➤ **hemeralopia**.

daydream Mental meandering, fantasies while one is awake. Some distinguish day-

dreams from sleeping dreams by arguing that, among other obvious factors, wishes are not hidden, disguised or repressed in the waking variety. Interestingly, a good deal of research suggests that daydreaming is associated with mental health and stability.

daylight vision ➤ **photopic vision**.

day residue This term is used almost exclusively in the study of dreams to refer to the fragments of recent experiences during waking hours that emerge as dream images.

dB (or **db**) Abbreviation for ➤ **decibel**.

de- Prefix meaning: **1.** *down, away from*; **2.** *apart from, undone*.

deaf-mute A person who can neither hear nor speak. The often-heard slang expression 'deaf and dumb' for such persons is, owing to the dual meaning of *dumb*, inaccurate as well as insulting and should be avoided.

deafness A continuum of hearing losses ranging from partial to total (or *profound*, as it is often called). Like blindness, deafness is often erroneously thought to be an all-or-none affair. Also like blindness, it can be due either to genetic defects, injury, cortical disorder, or to a variety of anatomical/physiological factors. Deafness can be quite specific so that only certain ranges of hearing (e.g., high-pitched tones) are affected. Specialized forms follow.

deafness, cerebral A general term used to cover any form of deafness caused by brain lesions. Several other terms are used in cases where there are good reasons for identifying the locus of the lesion, e.g., *cortical deafness* for lesions in the cortex, *central deafness* for damage to the auditory center in the brain.

deafness, ceruminous The technical term for hearing loss due to build-up of earwax.

deafness, conduction A general term for any form of deafness due to some abnormal condition that interferes with the mechanical conduction system that transmits vibrations from the middle ear to the auditory receptors of the inner ear. It may result from damage to the eardrum, inflammation of the inner ear, otosclerosis (pathological changes in the bones of the middle ear, usually the stapes), ankylosis (rigidity of the bones due to alterations in joints or connecting tissues), etc.

deafness, congenital Lit., deafness existing at the time of birth. Used generally and includes cases due to genetic as well as environmental factors.

deafness, functional **1.** Psychogenic deafness, loss of hearing in the absence of any known organic dysfunction. **2.** Deafness due to a breakdown in the normal functioning of some aspect of the auditory system. These two meanings are at odds with each other; 1 is preferred (➤ **functional disorder**).

deafness, hysterical Obsolete term for ➤ **functional *deafness** (1).

deafness, nerve Deafness resulting from any neurological impairment of the auditory receptors in the cochlea or the auditory nerve. Usually contrasted with ➤ **conduction *deafness**.

death Put simply (but inadequately) the point at which an organism ceases to be alive. Before modern medical support devices such as heart/lung machines, death was determined by the inability of an individual organism to keep *itself* alive. With sophisticated physiological support, the criteria most frequently cited have to do with cerebral functioning (i.e. ➤ **brain death**). The issues here are not simple and not easy; they involve more than the merely biological and touch upon essential questions, ethical, philosophical and theological.

death, brain ➤ **brain death**.

death feigning A response to threatening situations in which an organism goes into a state of *tonic immobility* and appears to be dead. Recovery is rapid and complete

after the threat passes. ➤ **injury feigning**.

death instinct ➤ **Thanatos**.

death wish More a popular term than a technical one, it can be generally taken to refer to an underlying element of the death instinct or *Thanatos*. When used, however, it typically stands for a hypothesized motivational syndrome that is arguably responsible for individuals who consistently put themselves into situations which are life-threatening.

debility Generally, weakness in function, loss of ability. Used commonly of organic and motor functions, occasionally of cognitive.

debriefing Telling the subject in an experiment what it was about and, when necessary, revealing any deception or withholding of information that may have been a necessary element in the study. This latter aspect is sometimes called *dehoaxing*.

debug Laboratory jargon (borrowed from computer sciences) meaning to detect, identify and correct an error in a program, a research project, a logical argument, a complex piece of equipment, etc.

deca- Combining form meaning *multiplied by ten; ten times*.

décalage This term, which translates from the French as, roughly, *discontinuity* or *slippage* (among other meanings), is found primarily in Piagetian approaches to the study of cognitive development. According to a strict Piagetian approach, cognitive development proceeds in a stage-like manner and therefore when a child moves to a higher level of cognitive functioning all the concepts based on the new level ought to appear at roughly the same time. *Décalage* is used collectively for all forms of nonsynchronous appearance of concepts. There are three kinds: (a) *horizontal décalage*, which refers to cases where the various aspects of a single cognitive operation fail to emerge together, as, for example, when a child shows conservation of number but not conservation of mass (see the discussion under ➤ conservation); (b) *vertical décalage*, which refers to transformations in a particular concept (e.g., number, causality) with shifts to new cognitive stages; and (c) *oblique décalage*, which refers to the simultaneous enrichment of existing structures and preparations for later stages. The latter two present no real problem for Piagetian theory; the first does and it is not clear whether horizontal *décalages* reflect differences in task difficulty, differences in the formation of cognitive structures or perhaps erroneous classifications of the behaviors.

decathexis Withdrawal of ➤ **cathexis**.

decay 1. Generally, a wasting away, a gradual deterioration. 2. In the study of memory the term is used as a biological metaphor to characterize the (presumed) gradual degradation and/or disintegration of neural traces. When one refers to a 'decayed' memory trace the implication is that somehow the neural underpinnings of the memory have 'faded' like an unfixed photograph. Presumably, decay can be prevented by the neurological process of ➤ **consolidation**. ➤➤ **forgetting**.

deceleration ➤ **acceleration**.

decentering (or **decentration**) A term used mainly in Piagetian approaches to cognitive development, with two distinguishable but related uses: **1.** The child's transition from an early stage when things are seen as 'centered' on the child's own body and actions (➤ **egocentrism** here) to a more mature stage when the environment is perceived in 'decentered' form and the child's body and actions assume their objective relationships with other objects and events. Several decentration periods are assumed to take place, with respect to action, to representation, and to cognition. **2.** The perceptual or cognitive ability to break frame, to step outside of the sharp demands of a physical stimulus. E.g., *conservation* of volume occurs when the child is able to break away from 'centering' on the height of the liquid in the container and take into account other aspects of the

situation (the width of the container, the fact that no one has added or subtracted any liquid) that provide compensation and balance distortions produced by the more primitive 'centering' process.

decerebrate 1 vb. To remove the cerebrum, typically by transacting the *brainstem*. 2 adj. Of an organism which has been subjected to decerebration or which behaves as though it had been.

decerebrate rigidity A term first used by C. S. Sherrington for the exaggerated muscle tone of limb extensors in cats which had been subjected to a transection of the brain stem between the superior and inferior colliculi of the midbrain.

deci- Combining form meaning *one tenth, divided by ten.*

decibel (dB) A unit of measurement generally used to express sound intensity. It is always given as a ratio between pressures (physical forces) and one must specify the standard used as the reference. The generally accepted system uses 0.0002 dynes/cm^2 for sound measurement; it corresponds roughly to the average human threshold for a 1,000 Hz tone. The intensity of any given tone is thus expressed by

$$dB = 10 \log_{10} I_1/I_2,$$

where I_1 is the intensity under consideration and I_2 is the standard. Since the relationship is logarithmic, increments in decibels are reflected by geometric increases in intensity. At a distance of 5 ft a human whisper is roughly 20 dB, normal conversation 60 dB, a jack-hammer about 100 dB and pain threshold for a broad-spectrum sound (like rock music) about 120 dB. Note, however, that the decibel is not only a measure of sound intensity. A decibel is, literally, 1/10th of a *bel*, a unit used occasionally in electric and light measurement. Since the measure is a ratio of two energies, it is not logically restricted to sound pressure but may be used of other physical continua.

decile One of nine points which divides a distribution of ranked scores into equal intervals. Each interval thus contains 1/10th of the scores.

decision making A generic term used to cover **1.** the process of choosing and **2.** an array of theories and investigations into the question of how organisms make choices between alternatives. The major focus of the work is on human decision making and it is regarded as a subarea within the field of cognitive psychology.

decision theory A label for any theory that seeks to describe and explain decision making. Approaches vary from the highly formal mathematical approaches based on game theory and probability theory to the more informal, intuitive theories which deal with beliefs, attitudes and other subjective factors. The range of problems that fall under this label is quite wide and includes studies of problem solving, choice behavior, utility theory, game theory and the like.

declarative A ➤ speech act in which one tells someone something, i.e. one makes a *declaration*. The function of a declarative is to bring about a new set of circumstances; e.g., 'you're fired.'

declarative knowledge ➤ knowledge, declarative.

declarative memory ➤ memory, declarative.

de Clérambault's syndrome ➤ *psychose passionnelle*.

decode (decoding) ➤ code.

decompensation 1. Lit., failure to compensate. **2.** In psychiatry, a failure of one's defense mechanisms, usually leading to exacerbation of one's condition.

decontextualization Interpretation of a text, a discourse, a dream, etc. based entirely on the literal meaning of the material; i.e. an interpretation that takes no account of the *context* within which the material occurs. Compare with ➤ **rich interpretation**.

decorticate The state of being without a cortex; almost invariably the cerebral

cortex is intended. Certain classes of behavior requiring little or no functioning of the 'higher mental processes' are sometimes referred to as decorticate activities. Occasionally the term is used of species of animals that never evolved a neocortex; e.g., avians.

decrement In general, any decrease in anything can safely be referred to as a decrement. The term is used of behavioral performances, of knowledge, of memory, etc.

decryption Within cryptography, the act or process of converting a coded message back into normal form; *decoding* (➤ **code**).

decussation The crossing over of neural pathways from one side of the nervous system to the other, especially in the midbrain. Owing to the contralateral innervation of many body–brain relations, the locus of decussation is often of interest.

deduction Reasoning that begins with a specific set of assumptions and attempts to draw conclusions or derive theorems from them. In general, it is a logical operation which proceeds from the general to the particular. Deductive inference is, in and of itself, an abstract process which requires no verification other than logical consistency. The proof of the pudding is in the appropriateness and demonstrability of the theorems and conclusions which are deduced. Contrast with ➤ **induction**. Both forms of reasoning have come under close study in psychology, particularly in how they relate to concept formation and problem-solving.

deep 1. Generally, below the surface, as in anatomical descriptions of underlying organs and tissues. **2.** Characteristic of sensations arising in muscles, internal organs, the viscera. **3.** Profound, dealing with the underlying abstract properties of things as opposed to their superficial forms. ➤ **depth of processing**. **4.** In acoustics, pertaining to low-pitched tones. **5.** In vision, pertaining to richly saturated colors. **6.** In psychoanalysis, characteristic of material that the client brings to the analysis that derives from early life experiences or from experiences that have been repressed. ➤ **depth analysis**, **depth psychology**.

deep cerebellar nuclei Quite literally, a set of nuclei located deep within the *cerebellum* that receive and transmit information between themselves and the cerebellar cortex.

deep interpretation ➤ **rich interpretation**.

deep pain ➤ chronic *pain.

deep reflexes Reflexes in underlying tissue. The 'knee jerk' is a good example; it is elicited by a tap on the patellar tendon.

deep sensitivity (or **sensibility**) Sense of pressure, the receptors for which are in deep subcutaneous layers of the skin or in muscles.

deep structure In linguistics, particularly transformational grammar, it is used as part of the distinction between the surface layer of a sentence as given by the actual words and the sentence's underlying structure. To take a classic example, the two sentences 'John is easy to please' and 'John is eager to please' have similar surface structures: proper noun, verb, adjective, infinitive. Yet they have different deep structures as can be shown by attempting to put each of them into equivalent passive forms. The first becomes the acceptable 'It is easy to please John' while the second becomes the anomalous 'It is eager to please John,' indicating that the 'real' subjects of the two sentences in the deep structure were different in the originals. Compare with ➤ **surface structure**.

defect 1. A flaw, an imperfection. 2. A failure to function owing to such. Distinguish from *deficit* and derived terms where the connotation is that there is a *lack* of something rather than a flaw.

defective 1 adj. Imperfect, structurally incomplete, nonfunctional. 2 n. A person so characterized. The most common usage pattern in older writings was to refer to persons who were below average in intelligence. A number of terms were coined, *mental defective, high-grade defective, low-grade defective*, among the least charming. These terms have all but disappeared from the technical literature; their demise from the lay language would not be mourned. ➤ **mental retardation**.

defendance H. Murray's term for the need to defend oneself from criticism, to justify verbally one's actions.

defense 1. Broadly speaking, any action that any organism takes to protect itself. Thus: 2. In medicine, a resistive reaction to a disease or learned pattern of behavior that protects one from possible injury or disease. 3. In clinical psychology and psychiatry, any of a number of reactions that one learns and uses unconsciously to protect one's internal psychic 'structures' (e.g., *ego, self*) from anxiety, conflict, shame, etc. The last meaning here has become the dominant one in psychology and is used in a variety of combined forms each with its own referential nuances. ➤ e.g., **defense mechanism, defense reaction, defensive strategy**, neurotic *defense. var., *defence*.

defense mechanism A term applied to any enduring pattern of protective 'behavior' designed to provide a defense against the awareness of that which is anxiety-producing. The word 'behavior' here needs some clarification. For many writers it denotes some overt pattern of action or some way of thinking or feeling that functions by circumventing or modifying whatever it is that evokes feelings of anxiety or threat. For many others, particularly those with a psychoanalytic bent, the overt behavior is treated as merely a manifestation or symbol of some underlying intrapsychic process – which they take to be the true defense mechanism. These theorists use *defense reaction* for the overt behavior. It should be clear, though, that no matter which nuance is intended everyone seems to agree that the term should be reserved for processes (or behaviors) that are unconsciously motivated, unconsciously acquired, and developed to protect the self or ego from unpleasantness of many kinds. Literally dozens of defense mechanisms have been hypothesized; some of the more commonly cited include *repression*, *regression*, *rationalization* and *projection*.

defense, neurotic Roughly speaking, psychoanalytic theory divides defense mechanisms into those that are *neurotic* and those which are *normal*. As every clinician knows, the difficulty with defense mechanisms is that while they may function as effective protectors of self in some of life's situations, they often prove counterproductive in others. Hence, no matter how one chooses to view them, they can always lead to psychological disorders or, to use the classical term, to a *neurotic breakthrough*. Although various authors differ on classification here, generally all of the defense mechanisms, save successful *repression* and *sublimation*, are regarded as *neurotic* defenses on the grounds that sooner or later they are almost inevitably going to lead one to maladaptive ways of dealing with the world.

defense reaction ➤ **defense mechanism**.

defense reflex Any reflexive, involuntary response to a stimulus; e.g., eye blink to an oncoming object, limb retraction to a hot surface, etc.

defensive attribution ➤ **self-serving bias**.

defensiveness 1. An excessive sensitivity to criticism. Used here with the connotation that the criticism is not merely absorbed in hurt silence but reacted to in a 'defensive' way. In this sense, some use the term as referring to a personality trait or characteristic. 2. A particular manner of behaving which functions to protect one from anxiety, embarrassment or unease, e.g., refusing to answer certain kinds of questions about oneself or one's actions.

defensive strategy A general term for any of a number of strategies that people use to defend themselves from anxiety. It is used in ways similar to the notion of a ➤ **defense mechanism**; i.e. defensive strategies are designed unconsciously to deal directly with the anxiety itself rather than with the source. For example, a student anxious about an upcoming examination spends the evening in a pub, drinks heavily, forgets to set the alarm clock and sleeps through the appointed hour. Compare with ➤ **coping strategies**.

deference behavior E. Goffman's term for a large variety of social behaviors that function to keep social intercourse smooth and civil. The term derives from the fact that such behaviors operate basically by conveying respect for and appreciation of people. ➤ **presentational rituals** and **avoidance rituals** for Goffman's two major classes of deference behaviors.

deference need H. Murray's term for the need to admire and defer to a leader or superior.

deficiency Generally, a lack of something, a condition in which some important element is missing. Distinguish from ➤ **defect**, where the connotation is that there is a failure owing to a flaw or improper arrangement of parts.

deficiency motive Quite literally, the desire to remove deficiencies, the tendency to seek fulfillments based on fairly simple needs. Typically used in contrast with ➤ **abundancy motive**, where one looks toward accretion of things beyond what is required simply to satisfy some basic need.

deficiency needs 1. Generally used to cover any homeostatically based need system such as hunger, thirst, etc. 2. Maslow used the term in his theory of personality in a somewhat broader fashion to characterize his hypothesized level of ➤ **basic needs**. In his sense, not all deficiency needs are based on physiological homeostasis; also included are various social and interpersonal needs.

deficit ➤ **defect**.

definition A marking of the boundary between two classes or groups. Figures that stand out well when viewed are said to have good definition, words whose meanings are well articulated and clearly distinguishable from others are said to be well defined, etc.

definitions Terminological precision is a giant bore when you're in love and positively tedious for a poet. In science, however, it is a high goal and the ambiguity so powerful in good poetry can be the source of monstrous confusion if allowed to slip in undetected. In the attempt to reach for clarity of meaning and use, a large number of definitional devices have been developed. Some of them are rather straightforward, some quite elaborate. The following are the more commonly used procedures for 'marking the boundaries of meaning' of terms in science:

(a) *Nominal:* a definition of a term made by simply supplying a name for a set of observations or events. Often such definitions are but shorthand expressions for cumbersome descriptions; e.g., *IQ* is defined as 100 times the ratio of mental age to chronological age. When new terms are introduced in a science, particularly before the appropriateness or relevance of the term has been evaluated, they are usually introduced by providing a nominal definition.

(b) *Formal:* a definition by specification of the features or characteristics that all members of the class, category or concept under consideration have in common and that can be used to distinguish that class, category or concept from some other. Formal definitions are useful once one understands the properties of the definiendum; e.g. *bachelor* is formally defined as an unmarried, adult, male.

(c) *Real:* a definition that attempts to get at the 'real' nature of the term being defined. It usually carries with it a theoretical connection between several observations or events; e.g., *frustration* as an emotional reaction resulting from being thwarted or prevented from reaching a goal. Here, the validity and relevance are open to test.

(d) *Enumerative:* defining a class by (one hopes) exhaustive listing of all of its members. This is a bit of a cheat and although it works to clarify meaning in cases where the class is small it most assuredly has its limits.

(e) *Operational:* a definition based on the set of operations that produced the thing defined; e.g., *hunger* as a state of affairs resulting from food deprivation. Abstract and hypothetical concepts lend themselves nicely to this type of definition.

(f) *Reduction sentence:* a definition that carries with it a statement about antecedents and consequents; e.g., *anxiety* might be defined as follows: 'If a person is given an anxiety test then he or she is defined to be anxious if and only if his or her score is in the top ten percent.' Note that the definition is in sentence form, that antecedent conditions (the test) and consequences (the score) are specified, and that the sentence may be reduced to logical notation if needed. This kind of definition is useful in dealing with complex, theoretical notions.

The preceding are the more commonly used 'legitimate' varieties. Two other forms are, unfortunately, also rather common although they are distinctly unsatisfactory:

(g) *Tautological:* here one 'defines' a term by using synonyms or variants of the term itself. This dictionary abounds with these but then again so does every other and I won't apologize; after all, a fingernail is a nail on a finger.

(h) *Circular:* a definition where there is a 'circle' (or 'cycle') between two (or more) terms which are used to 'define' each other; e.g., *hormone* as a substance produced by an endocrine *gland* and *endocrine gland* as a producer of hormones. Precious little is gained by 'short cycles' of this kind; oddly though, *long* cycles can prove rather illuminating and as a *reductio ad absurdum* every dictionary is a very long cycle of circular definitions.

The problem of definition is not a simple one and it certainly won't succumb to lexicographical legerdemain. It is, in

189

fact, one of the deepest of philosophical conundrums and has resisted all manner of analysis. Ideally, one needs a metalanguage within which to express one's definitions of terms in the target language. For many areas of science, mathematics and/ or logic serve as the metasystem; for the social sciences we must be content for the nonce with an elaborate 'bootstrapping' operation in which each term in the lexicon is defined by other terms which themselves are defined elsewhere. In this volume I have tried to balance precision with pragmatics; terms are defined 'properly' when possible and usage patterns are laid out where mandated. Analytical philosophers may not approve of this style but my aim here is to improve and refine communication among practitioners and students of psychology and related areas of science; gentle criticisms concerning specific failures to do this should be sent to the publisher or the author.

deflection A defense mechanism that functions by diverting attention or awareness away from the object or situation that arouses anxiety. .

defusion ➤ **fusion** (2).

degenerate 1 n. The standard dictionary definition is usually something like, 'one who deviates markedly from a social norm, particularly in the area of sexuality.' In actual usage the term has a distinctly negative connotation and is, moreover, differentially applied according to gender. For example, a sexually active woman may be so labeled but not a sexually active man – so long as he avoids young boys. adj., *degenerate*. 2 vb. To deteriorate, to decline in function or standards. In this sense the term is applied to mental, moral or biological processes or structures. ➤ **degeneration**.

degeneration 1. In physiology, deterioration of neural tissue caused by injury or lack of critical chemicals. Contrast with ➤ **atrophy**. If individual neurons are examined, two kinds of degeneration can be observed. Severing an axon or destroying the cell body will cause the distal part of the axon to degenerate rapidly; this is called *anterograde* degeneration. If the axon is severed some distance from the cell body, the proximal part of it will also degenerate but more slowly since it still receives nutrients from the cell body; this is called *retrograde* degeneration. 2. Deterioration of moral standards. ➤ **degenerate** (1).

degraded stimulus Any stimulus that has been modified so that it is more difficult to perceive. In formal terms, one says that the *signal-to-noise ratio* has been lowered. A stimulus may be degraded by erasing part of it, embedding it in noise, masking it, putting it out of focus, lowering the volume or intensity level, etc.

degrees of freedom (df) A mathematical concept used to express the fact that in statistical operations there are limits to the values that one is free to choose given particular constraints on the situation. The limit is determined by the number of observations, events or data points one has, minus the number of constraints. The easiest way to understand this is with a simple example: consider a distribution of five scores with mean $\overline{X}$. The last number in the distribution is completely determined by the first four and the value of the mean. That is, one is 'free' up to the fifth number, to choose any four numbers but given them and the mean the last number is fixed in value. In this case $df = 4$ which is the number of observations, 5, minus the one constraint, the mean.

In statistical operations such as *t tests* and analyses of variance, the power of the test depends, in part, on the degrees of freedom. This makes sense intuitively, since as the number of degrees of freedom increases one would expect variability to increase. However, when an experimental effect is real and variability is low then the power of the test is increased. For example, the *t* test with $df = 1$ requires a $t = 6.31$ for significance, while with $df = 10$ only a $t = 1.81$ is required.

dehoaxing ➤ **debriefing**.

dehydroisoandrosterone A natural androgen produced by the adrenal cortices and found in males and females. Compared with *testosterone* it has extremely low biological potency.

deindividuation The loss of one's sense of individuality. The classic example is what often occurs in mobs when the separateness of each person is lost in the surge of the crowd and individual choice is submerged in mob action. Compare with ➤ **anonymity**.

Deiters' cells Supporting cells in the ➤ **organ of Corti**.

deixis A term used to refer to the context-boundedness of language. The deictic aspects of a linguistic message are those elements that refer to time, space and the interpersonal components. Purely deictic segments in English are 'here/there', 'this/that', 'before/after/now', etc. Deixis, of concern to philosophers for some time, has become a topic of interest in developmental psycholinguistics, with the focus on how children acquire these subtle aspects of language.

déjà vu French for *already seen*. A rather compelling illusion of familiarity with a scene that is actually new. It is thought by some to be due to a response to cues in the new situation that are common to old, roughly similar, experiences; others believe it to be due to a kind of momentary neural 'short circuit' so that the impression of the scene arrives at the memory store (metaphorically speaking) before it registers in the sensorium. There is some evidence for the latter view since frequent *déjà vu* experiences are symptomatic of certain kinds of brain damage. There are several *déjà* experiences, e.g., *déjà pensé* or already thought, *déjà entendu* or already heard.

de Lange syndrome ➤ **Cornelia de Lange syndrome**.

delay conditioning An experimental conditioning technique in which the onset of the unconditioned stimulus (US) occurs some time after the onset (although prior to the termination) of the conditioned

stimulus (CS). For most conditioned responses, the optimal delay between CS onset and US onset is approximately 0.4 or 0.5 seconds. Contrast with ➤ **backward conditioning, simultaneous conditioning, trace conditioning**.

delayed instinct ➤ **instinct, delayed**.

delayed matching to sample ➤ **matching to sample**.

delayed reaction (procedure) An experimental procedure in which the subject responds to a stimulus some time after it has been removed from sight. For example, the subject watches while the stimulus object is hidden but is not allowed to search for the object until a delay period expires. It is a difficult task for young children and lower organisms; success is assumed by some to reflect the existence of symbolic capacity.

delayed reinforcement (procedure) Generally, any situation or experimental procedure in which the presentation of the reinforcer is delayed until some time after the response has been made.

delayed response A term used to characterize the major event in the ➤ **delayed reaction procedure**.

delayed sleep-onset insomnia ➤ **insomnia, delayed sleep-onset**.

delinquent Generally, anyone who commits a crime or who violates a legal code. However, the term is almost always used for a juvenile delinquent, where the defining age is set by local legal statute (typically up to around 16 to 18 years).

delirium A disoriented condition with clouded consciousness, often accompanied by hallucinations, illusions, misinterpretations of events and a generally confused quality with reduced capacity to sustain attention to things in the environment. Delirium is frequently of fairly rapid onset (often after head injury or a seizure) but may also develop slowly over time, particularly if metabolic factors are responsible. It is currently classified in psychiatry as an *organic mental syndrome* and several varieties are known, classified usually by cause.

delirium of persecution A term occasionally used for those cases of delirium that have a compelling fearfulness and hallucinations of being threatened as their dominant symptoms. Distinguish from ➤ **delusions of persecution**.

delirium, substance-related A large number of drugs, when abused, can produce a clinical delirium. In some cases it is brought on by large doses (e.g. of amphetamines), in others it follows a period of repeated abuse (e.g., of phencyclidine or PCP), and in others it occurs as a withdrawal syndrome after extended abuse (e.g., *alcohol-withdrawal delirium*).

delirium tremens An acute ➤ **delirium**, with all of its characteristic symptoms, that is associated with excessive alcohol abuse. The definition is pretty straightforward but usage patterns can be rather confusing. Some writers have used the term (and its slang abbreviation, the *d.t.'s*) as though the syndrome were caused by alcohol consumption, which is true but only in a misleading manner. The proper usage is for a delirium whose onset follows, usually by a day or two, the *cessation* of alcohol intake after many years of alcohol abuse. To eliminate this confusion the former syndrome is now called ➤ **alcohol hallucinosis** (which, incidentally, does not have a true delirium, as a symptom) and the latter is known as ➤ **alcohol-withdrawal delirium**.

Delphi method A procedure for predicting future events based on the pooling of judgements made by a number of experts. The procedure is named for the Greek oracle of Delphi.

delta (Δ) A notation (the symbol Δ) used to refer to an increment in some variable or factor. Usually presented in abbreviated form with the thing incremented; e.g., ΔR is an increment in responding, ΔS an increment in the stimulus, ΔI in intensity, etc. Occasionally D will be used instead of Δ, but tradition and the fact that the use of the Greek letter here derives from the notation of the finite calculus make it the symbol of choice.

delta motion (or **movement**) ➤ **motion, delta**.

delta waves Electroencephalographic (EEG) signals of low frequency (1–3 Hz) and high amplitude (approximately 150 microvolts). Delta waves are characteristic of a person in deep sleep.

delusion A belief that is maintained in spite of argument, data and refutation which should (reasonably) be sufficient to destroy it. Care should be taken in the use of the term – one person's delusion may be another's salvation. Also note that the term is not typically used when one's culture or sub-culture subscribes to the belief. Distinguish from ➤ **hallucination** and ➤ **illusion**. With respect to the various forms of psychiatric disorders involving delusions, the official terminology has shifted in recent years. For example, the term 'delusions of grandeur' has given way to 'delusional disorder, grandiose type' and 'delusions of persecution' to 'delusional disorder, persecutory type.' Terms currently recommended by the DSM-IV and the ICD-10 are given below, along with those found in older texts.

delusional disorder An umbrella term for any mental disorder that has as a significant symptom some form of delusion.

delusional disorder, erotomanic type A delusional paranoid disorder that a famous or highly regarded person is in love with oneself.

delusional disorder, grandiose type A delusional disorder which typically takes the form of believing that one has some great but unrecognized talent or insight. Distinguish from ➤ **megalomania**.

delusional disorder, jealous type A delusional disorder where one believes without reasonable cause that his or her mate is unfaithful. In the classic form, the most minute piece of 'evidence,' such as a thread or disarrayed clothing, may be used to justify the belief. Also known as *conjugal paranoia*.

delusional disorder, persecutory type The classic form of ➤ **delusional (paranoid) disorder**. The individual suffers from a cluster of delusions, usually involving a particular theme. They may feel that others are out to 'get' them, that they are being cheated, conspired against, maligned, spied on, and so forth. The oft-used term *paranoid delusion* is no longer recommended when characterizing the symptoms of this disorder, being instead restricted to cases of ➤ **paranoid (type)** ***schizophrenia** where there are delusions of grandiosity and jealousy as well as those of persecution. ➤➤ **paranoia**.

delusional disorder, somatic type A cover term for delusions that involve: (a) the whole body image, as in *anorexia nervosa* where the patient feels 'too fat' despite being emaciated, or (b) parts of the body, as in cases where the patient believes that some part of his or her body is missing (➤ **organic *delusional syndrome**) or imagines that various bodily parts do not function properly or that one emits a foul odor from his or her skin, mouth, rectum, or vagina.

delusional jealousy ➤ **delusional disorder, jealous type**.

delusional (paranoid) disorder An umbrella term for the various forms of paranoid disorders characterized primarily by one or more persistent, nonbizarre delusions with a paranoid flavor. Apart from the delusions and their ramifications, the individual's behavior is not abnormal in any pronounced fashion. The term is used only when there is no evidence of any other mental disorder. ➤➤ **paranoia**.

delusional speech The speech typical of one with a delusion. Seen most commonly in delusions of grandeur, when allusions to personal influence, power, accomplishments, etc. are common, and in delusions of persecution, when the language is rich

with paranoia, suspiciousness, accusations, etc.

delusional syndrome, organic A delusional disorder due to a known organic factor. The term is used broadly to include those disorders brought on by drug abuse (➤ **substance-induced *delusion**) and those that result from epilepsy, brain lesions or other diseases that affect the central nervous system.

delusion, nihilistic A general term for any delusion marked by a sense of nonexistence. It may of the self, parts of the self, or the world. Cases of ➤ **delusional disorder, somatic type** may also be termed nihilistic when they involve the sense of nonexistence of the body or of a body part.

delusion of being controlled A delusion in which the person experiences feelings, impulses, thoughts, and actions as though they were imposed by some external force or some other person.

delusions of grandeur ➤ **delusional disorder, grandiose type**. Also called *grandiose delusion*.

delusions of persecution ➤ **delusional disorder, persecutory type**.

delusions of reference Delusion in which one interprets remarks or references which are neutral or intended for others as having negative significance for oneself. Everyone has a bit of this (➤ **ideas of reference**), but the term itself is reserved for pathological cases.

delusion, substance-related A general label for any of a variety of delusional disorders that result from either extended abuse or single high doses of a drug. A large number of substances are known to produce delusions of various kinds, including alcohol, amphetamines, various hallucinogens, marijuana, cocaine, etc.

delusion, systematized A singular delusion that is marked by multiple elaborations involving other delusions, all of which are traced, in the mind of the individual, back to a single event or theme.

demand 1 n. A requirement, an imperative need. Often used in this sense to refer to either internal or external states that have motivating properties; e.g. nutritional demands or family demands. 2 adj. Characterizing or describing properties of situations that invite or even require particular kinds of behaviors from individuals. E.g. ➤ **demand characteristics**.

demand character A Gestalt term for those characteristics of a stimulus situation that invite particular modes of reaction to it. ➤ **affordance** which is used in similar ways.

demand characteristics 1. Those features of an experimental setting that bias the subject to behave in particular ways, that invite from the subject a particular interpretation of the study and recruit particular kinds of behaviors. When used in this fashion the term refers to confounding features in a study that contaminate the results. ➤ **experimenter bias** for one kind. 2. More generally, the qualities of a particular experimental setting that simply, by their nature, invite certain kinds of behaviors. For example, memory experiments that use nonsense syllables characteristically 'demand' of a subject the use of various mnemonic devices. Here the notion of bias is not connoted; these are features that, by virtue of their properties, are typically going to be associated with one or another behavior pattern. 3. By extension, any social setting that, by its very nature, establishes a set that carries with it behavioral 'demands.'

Note that some authors use the term only to refer to the qualities and properties of the situation (as in the above); others, however, will use it to refer to the feelings, expectations and desires of the individual in such settings. Those who use it for the latter sense typically will use *task demand* or *environmental demand* for the former. ➤➤ **set** (2) which some use as a cover term for all of these effects.

demand feeding ➤ **self-demand (schedule of) feeding**.

dementia Generally, a loss of intellectual capacity to the extent that normal social and occupational functions can no longer be carried out. The term is reserved for multifunctional disorders where memory, reasoning, judgement and other 'higher mental processes' are lost. Typically, alterations in personality and modes of social interaction accompany these cognitive deficits. Some authors use the term only for progressive syndromes with the connotation of irreversibility; others are neutral on prognosis. Usually the writer will be clear on this point. The contemporary approach to the dementias is to treat them as *organic mental syndromes* and use a qualifying term to identify the suspected cause. See following entries.

dementia, alcoholic Dementia observed in the last stages of severe, chronic alcoholism. ➤ **Korsakoff's syndrome**.

dementia, multi-infarct Dementia due to significant cerebrovascular disease that has a distinct 'step-wise' pattern of deterioration. The disorder is not uniformly progressive but goes in steps with a loss in only some intellectual functions early in its course, resulting in a 'patchy' deterioration. The disorder is a result of multiple and often extensive localized cortical lesions and, in addition to the dementia, a variety of neurological signs are symptomatic, e.g., weakness in extremities, exaggeration of deep reflexes, dysphagia, hypertension and other vascular abnormalities. Also called *arteriosclerotic dementia*, *psychosis with cerebral arteriosclerosis* and ➤ **vascular *dementia**; see that term for more detail.

dementia naturalis An obsolete term for extreme mental retardation.

dementia of the Alzheimer's type (DAT) ➤ **Alzheimer's disease**.

dementia paralytica ➤ **paresis**.

dementia praecox Obsolete term for schizophrenia; the literal meaning is *premature dementia*.

dementia, presenile Specifically, a dementia with onset prior to age 65. The criterion here is quite arbitrary but is generally accepted by diagnosticians.

dementia, primary degenerative A form of dementia characterized by gradual and progressive deterioration. It is typically associated with old age (➤ **senile *dementia**) and usually leads to death within 5 to 10 years. The disorder is strongly associated with widespread cerebral atrophy.

dementia pugilistica A chronic dementia caused by multiple concussions. Symptoms include memory loss, speech impairment, unsteady gait, tremors and episodes of confusion and depression. As the name suggests, it is commonly observed among boxers. Known nontechnically as *punch-drunk*.

dementia, senile A general term for any dementia associated with the aged. Senile dementias are of the primary degenerative type and are associated with a variety of causes including *Alzheimer's disease*, *Pick's disease*, certain vitamin deficiencies, cerebrovascular pathologies, etc. Obsolete synonyms are *senile psychosis*, *geriatric psychosis* and *geriopsychosis*.

dementia, vascular A term recently proposed to replace ➤ **multi-infarct *dementia** to reflect the fact that this disorder is due largely to diminished cerebral blood flow.

democratic atmosphere K. Lewin's term for the general socio-political climate established when a group is led by a person with democratic values, where free exchange of ideas and open discussion of issues are encouraged. Contrast with ➤ **authoritarian atmosphere** and ➤ **laissez-faire atmosphere**.

demography The study of the structure of human populations, their distributions, geographic locations, increases and decreases over time, etc. Although demography began with examination of vital statistics, it is now a rich multi-discipline science including such areas of study as fertility, marriage, education, social class, race, distribution of wealth and resources, epidemiology, crime, population migration, etc. and has borrowed heavily from biology, ecology, economics, sociology and psychology.

demonology 1. A legitimate area of study of folklore and cultural myths concerned with demons and spirits. **2.** A pseudo-science which claims to study them as real entities. ➤ **parapsychology**.

demonomania The delusion that one is possessed by a demon or spirit.

demonstration 1. Formally, the presentation of a proof of a theorem. **2.** Less formally, a compelling presentation of an effect which functions to make a point. Many 'experiments' in science are really 'demonstrations' in that they are designed not so much to test a hypothesis as to show that a particular interpretation of a phenomenon is correct. The Gestalt psychologists used this technique masterfully. **3.** A pedagogic technique in which the teaching is by presentation of examples and illustrations.

dendrite The richly branching, tree-like processes attached to the cell body or ➤ **soma** (1) of a *neuron*. Dendrites function as the receiving end of the neuron and are stimulated by *neurotransmitters* which flow across the ➤ **synapse** from the terminal buttons of other (presynaptic) neurons on to the ➤ **dendritic spines**.

dendritic 1. Generally, tree-like, branching. **2.** Specifically, pertaining to dendrites and their structure and function.

dendritic spine A small budlike outgrowth on the surface of a dendrite. Dendritic spines synapse with the terminal buttons of presynaptic neurons.

denervation Removal of the nerve supply to an organ or other tissue. Note that 'removal' here is intended loosely; one may merely sever or otherwise render nonfunctional neural pathways without literally removing the nerves.

denial A defense mechanism that simply disavows or denies thoughts, feelings, wishes or needs that cause anxiety. The term is used purely for unconscious operations that function to 'deny' that which cannot be dealt with consciously.

denotative meaning ➤ meaning, denotative.

density 1. Generally, the degree to which the elements or parts of a display or complex stimulus are grouped together. 2. More specifically, in statistics, the extent to which the various data points lie proximate to the regression line. See here ➤ **regression** (2). 3. In audition, a dimension of experience characterized by the degree to which a tone sounds 'compact' or 'thin.' 4. In demography, the number of persons per unit area, *population density*.

dental A speech sound produced by placing the tongue against the teeth, e.g., $/\theta/$ in *th*in.

dental age ➤ age, dental.

dentate gyrus A part of the ➤ **hippocampal formation** that receives inputs from the ➤ **entorhinal cortex** and projects to an area within the ➤ **hippocampus** itself.

dentate nucleus One of the ➤ **deep cerebellar nuclei**, it plays a role in the control of skilled, rapid movement.

dendrodendritic synapse A *synapse* between the *dendrites* of two *neurons*.

deoxyribonucleic acid (DNA) A large complex molecule made of four nucleotide bases (*adenine, guanine, cytosine* and *thymine*) and a 'backbone' of a sugar molecule (specifically, *2-deoxy-D-ribose*, hence the name). The nucleotide bases are arranged in pairs down the center of the double-helix-shaped molecule and it is the specific arrangement which carries the genetic code determining the functioning of every cell. The code is based on sequences of 3 nucleotide bases each specifying one of 20 amino acids. Since there are 64 possible arrangements there is considerable flexibility in the arrangement and more than enough to code any given protein's sequence of amino acids. Each of the chromosomes in the nuclei of all cells is made up of DNA; it is, thus, the chemical basis

for all heredity and the carrier of all genetic information. ➤➤ **ribonucleic acid (RNA)**.

dependence 1. In statistics, a relationship between variables such that changes in one variable are accompanied by changes in the other. Note that in this sense the term connotes a causal link between the variables. Occasionally an author may wish to use the term while remaining neutral on cause and effect; in such cases the phrase *statistical dependence* is used, with the 'statistical' suggesting that 'true' cause and effect has not been determined. 2. In social psychology, excessive reliance on others for support, opinions, beliefs, ideas, etc. 3. In psychopharmacology, ➤ **drug *dependence**. var., *dependency*.

dependence, drug In recent years the term (and its shorthand form, *dependence*) has come to be favored over the terms *addiction* and *habituation* in scientific writings. Put in simplest terms, an individual is said to have developed dependence on a drug or other substance when there is a strong, compelling desire to continue taking it. Note that this 'desire' may derive from a wish either (a) to experience its effects or (b) to avoid or escape the aversive experiences produced by its absence (see here ➤ **withdrawal symptoms**). Dependence on a drug may in origin be largely psychological (➤ **psychological *dependence**) or physiological (➤ **physiological *dependence**). ➤➤ **substance dependence**.

dependence, physiological Drug dependence produced by alterations in physiological states resulting from repeated administrations of the drug. The characteristic that marks such dependence and differentiates it from ➤ **psychological *dependence** is that severe physiological dysfunctions emerge if the drug is suddenly discontinued or if an antagonist is administered. The opiates and the barbiturates both produce such dependence with prolonged use. Also referred to as *physical dependence*. The term is preferred over the previously used *addiction* and *drug addiction*.

dependence, psychological Drug dependence characterized by a rather pervasive drive to obtain and take the substance. This term is usually defined by exclusion; i.e. it is used for dependences on drugs whose action does *not* produce fundamental biochemical changes such that continued doses of the drug are required for normal functioning. ➤ **Physiological *dependence** covers these other cases. Drugs like marijuana are commonly cited as ones likely to produce psychological dependence with habitual use. The term is preferred over the previously common term, *drug habituation*.

dependency 1. In social and personality psychology, a condition holding between two or more persons in which one relies upon the other(s) for emotional, economic or other support. 2. A characteristic of an individual in such a dependent state; a lack of self-reliance. ➤ **dependence** (2), with which it is often used synonymously.

dependency, morbid K. Horney's term for an extreme, neurotic surrender of self to another such that one person becomes pathologically reliant on another for things social and emotional.

dependency needs A loose cover term for 'vital' needs; those required for normal functioning. Used for both the physical/biological (food, water, warmth, shelter) and the psychological (affection, love, security).

dependent 1 adj. Characterizing ➤ **dependence** or ➤ **dependency** in any of the meanings of those terms. 2 n. A person in a relationship characterized by dependence on others or on a substance; var., *dependant*.

dependent personality disorder A personality disorder characterized by such extreme passivity that the individual allows others to take over responsibility for his or her life. Such individuals are typically lacking in self-confidence, unsure of their abilities and willing to allow decision-making in all matters to be taken over by others. Also called, especially in older writings, *asthenic personality*.

dependent variable ➤ **variable, dependent**.

depersonalization 1. The dominant meaning is that of the existentialists, who used the term to characterize the feeling of loss of self or of personal identity, the sense that one is but a number in a computer memory bank or mere cog in a blundering, dehumanized, social machine. 2. In psychiatric terms, it represents an emotional disorder in which there is a loss of contact with one's own personal reality, a *derealization* accompanied by feelings of strangeness and an unreality of experience. In severe cases, parts of one's body feel alien or altered in size and one may have the experience of perceiving oneself from a distance. To differentiate meaning 1, which does not connote pathology, from meaning 2, which does, the terms *depersonalization disorder* or *depersonalization neurosis* are often used for 2. Compare with ➤ **dissociation**, which is a more general term.

depersonalization disorder (or **neurosis**) ➤ **depersonalization**.

depolarization In neurophysiology, a reduction in the electrical potential of a neuron from its normal resting potential of roughly -70 mV. Very small stimuli produce relatively minor and transient depolarizations; with larger stimuli, those sufficient to depolarize the membrane beyond approximately -60 mV, the neuron 'breaks away' and depolarization becomes complete even to the point of reversing the charge so that the inside of the axon approaches $+40$ mV. This discharge is called the ➤ **action potential**. ➤➤ **all-or-none law** (1).

depressed bipolar disorder ➤ **bipolar disorder, depressed**.

depression 1. Generally, a mood state characterized by a sense of inadequacy, a feeling of despondency, a decrease in activity or reactivity, pessimism, sadness and related symptoms. In this sense depressions are quite normal, relatively short-lived and (damnably) frequent. 2. In psychiatry, any of a number of ➤ **mood disorders** in which the above characteristics are extreme and intense. Depression in this sense may be a symptom of some other psychological disorder, a part or syndrome of related symptoms that appears as secondary to another disorder, or a specific disorder itself. Note that many psychiatrists regard ➤ anhedonia (general lack of interest in the pleasures of life) as a defining characteristic of depression – even to the point of regarding it as sufficient for a diagnosis independent of the individual complaining of being depressed. The following entries describe many of the major variations of depressive disorders. Others are found elsewhere under the modifying term.

depression, agitated A depression in which the individual displays psychomotor agitation as a dominant symptom. The overt symptoms are irritability, excitability and restlessness.

depression, endogenous Depression resulting from 'internal' factors. The term 'internal' is used loosely here to cover both the known physiological causes and psychological disturbances in thought, imagery, etc. The term is used clinically when there is no *apparent* precipitant although many prefer not to use it all on the grounds that it implies that there are *no* precipitating events. Compare with ➤ reactive *depression.

depression, major A ➤ mood disorder marked by a severe and extended ➤ major *depressive episode.

depression, neurotic 'Ordinary' severe depression. A mildly out-of-date term used as a cover for any depression that is not a ➤ psychotic *depression; i.e. one where there is no loss of contact with reality.

depression, psychotic Severe depression in which the individual loses contact with reality and suffers from an array of impairments of normal functioning.

depression, reactive Depression resulting from events occurring in one's life. The use of the term *depression* in this label is a clinical one and connotes that the affective reaction is inappropriate given the events themselves, thus differentiating the mean-

ing of the term from that of *grief*. See also the discussion under ➤ depression. Also called *exogenous depression*. Compare with ➤ endogenous *depression.

depression, retarded Depression characterized by psychomotor retardation as the dominant symptom. The individual tends to be lethargic, laconic and slow to initiate action.

depression, unipolar A ➤ major *depressive episode. The qualifier *unipolar* is used for cases in which the depressive episodes recur without the appearance of the manic phase that is observed in the classic form of ➤ bipolar disorder.

depressive 1 n. One suffering from a ➤ depression (2). 2 adj. Characterizing depression.

depressive anxiety A psychoanalytic term for anxiety provoked by a sense of fear concerning one's own hostile feelings toward others. The usage here derives from the oft-stated interpretation that 'depression is hostility turned inwards.'

depressive disorder A category of ➤ mood disorders marked by either single or recurrent ➤ major *depressive episodes without a history of ➤ mania (2). ➤➤ depression.

depressive disorder, minor A *mood disorder* characterized by periods of depression but lacking the full range of symptoms that mark a ➤ major *depressive episode.

depressive episode, major In psychiatry, a ➤ depression (2) with all of the classic symptoms of ➤ anhedonia, sleep disturbances, lethargy, feelings of worthlessness, despondency, morbid thoughts and, on occasion, suicide attempts. The term is reserved for cases in which there is no known organic dysfunction.

depressive neurosis ➤ dysthymic disorder.

depressive personality disorder A disorder marked by pervasive, low-level depressive thoughts and behaviors. Moods are dominated by gloominess, unhappiness, and pessimism. Such individuals often have low self-esteem and feelings of guilt but, interestingly, often see themselves as merely realistic.

depressive spectrum A syndrome of a diagnosed ➤ **depression** (2) along with a family history of alcoholism and/or one of the ➤ **affective disorders**.

depressor nerve Specifically, a branch of the vagus (Xth cranial) nerve that functions to lower blood pressure. Often, however, one will find any nerve that reduces motor or glandular function referred to as a *depressor*.

d prime ➤ *d'*.

deprivation Strictly speaking the term means loss of some desired object or person and is used to refer either to the act of removing the object or person or to the state of loss itself. There is also a curious technical usage as in phrases like '48-hour food deprivation' and '85% of normal body weight deprivation.' In such cases it refers to an experimental procedure in which the drive or need state of an organism is controlled by specifying (operationally) the level of deprivation.

deprogramming A nontechnical term used to refer to efforts to retrain people who have joined obscure, fanatical cults to live in society again. The assumption is that the cult, using clever techniques of isolation and peer pressure, has 'programmed' these people to their way of life and values (➤ **brainwashing**) and in order to readapt to normal life and values they must be 'deprogrammed.'

depth analysis Psychoanalysis is often called depth analysis since the assumption is that the analysis is probing deeply below the well-defended conscious level of mind to the underlying dynamic factors that presumably motivate the person.

depth of processing In cognitive psychology, a coding dimension that runs from the superficial to the abstract. The further along this dimension a stimulus is processed the greater is the 'depth.' For example, the stimulus 11 may be processed as two straight lines, as a number that

rhymes with another number, as a number between 10 and 12, or as the only 2-digit prime number with both integers the same. Each level here represents a deeper, more abstract analysis than the preceding. According to most contemporary analyses of human memory the greater the depth to which a stimulus is processed the more likely it will be stored in memory for later recall. ➤➤ **short-term *memory** and **long-term *memory**.

depth perception Quite literally, the perception of depth, viewing the world in three dimensions. There are two standard usages here, one to refer to the distance of objects from the viewer and the other to refer to the three-dimensionality of objects themselves.

depth psychology A generic term used to cover any psychological system that assumes that explanations of behavior are to be found at the level of the unconscious. Freudian and Jungian theories are the classic examples and many authors will use the term as a rough synonym for psychoanalysis.

deranged Loosely and largely non-technically, disturbed or disoriented. Used with regard to cognitive, intellectual abilities.

derealization An alteration in the perception of the environment with the sense that somehow one has lost contact with external reality. A common component of ➤ **depersonalization** (2).

dereistic Pertaining to the use of fantasy or imagination, daydreaming. In cases where it is pathological, in that contact with reality is seriously weakened or lost, it serves as a rough synonym for *autistic*.

derivation 1. That which is the result of a formal set of inferences, the outcome of a deductive process. 2. The process itself.

derivative 1. That which is not original, a thing developed, deduced or obtained from something else. 2 adj. Secondary, acquired from something else. 3 adj. In psychoanalysis, characterizing behaviors that emerge from unconscious conflicts disguised or distorted so as not to produce anxiety.

derived Developed out of, transformed from, acquired from, adapted from, etc. The term has a number of combinatorial forms; the following are representative of usage.

derived need A need developed from or learned by close association with a primary need. E.g., ➤ **acquired *drive**.

derived property In Gestalt theory, a property of a stimulus due to the characteristics of the whole situation of which it is a part.

derived scale Any scale that is a result of a transformation from another scale.

derived score Any score that is a result of a transformation from another score, e.g., the *z-score*.

derma 1. Loosely, the skin. 2. Specifically, the layer of skin just below the outermost (epidermal) layer.

dermal sense ➤ **cutaneous sense**.

dermatitis Generally, any inflammation of the skin. Several varieties are known and usually associated with specific causes, but according to many authorities psychosomatic factors lead to a predisposition and/or exacerbation of many forms.

dermatome An area of skin innervated by the fibers of a single dorsal root. For example, there are 12 spinal roots for the thoracic area and there are also 12 dermatomes on the chest and trunk area of the body each corresponding to one of the spinal roots.

dermographia Lit., skin writing; hence, a condition in which tracings made on the skin are followed by marked reddening of the area. Also called *autographia*.

dermooptical perception Lit., seeing with the skin. The term is used in ➤ **parapsychology** for the hypothesized (but undemonstrated) ability to 'see' with one's skin; e.g., to detect the colors of objects by touching them.

Descartes, René ➤ **Cartesian**.

description 1. A full, complete and accurate (to the extent that such is possible) characterization of a situation based on careful observation. In the philosophy of science, description is generally held to be a necessary precursor of ➤ **explanation**. 2. In introspection, reporting psychological processes in a 'pure,' uninterpreted fashion.

descriptive principle The principle that the basic goal of behavioral science is accurate description in terms of relations between observed events such that prediction of and control over behavior may be achieved. The principle represents, at least on the surface, a non-theoretical stance since attempts at developing causal laws and explanations are to be resisted. In its pure form, Skinnerian behaviorism reflects this principle.

descriptive psychiatry A term generally used of any system of psychiatric diagnosis based on the relatively straightforward descriptions of overt, observable symptoms. Usually contrasted with the *dynamic* schools, in which diagnosis is based on underlying, covert psychic factors.

descriptive statistics ➤ **statistics, descriptive**.

descriptive unconscious ➤ **preconscious**.

desensitization Generally, any decrease in reactivity or sensitivity. Used for: (a) reactions to simple stimuli – e.g., a sudden noise will produce a dramatic startle response the first time but after successive presentations within a short time the reaction diminishes and disappears; and (b) more global emotional reactions ➤ **desensitization procedure**.

desensitization procedure A clinical technique used in behavior therapy. The procedure is designed to produce a decrease in anxiety toward some feared object or situation, i.e. to desensitize. It is particularly useful in treating phobias and other behavior problems which are based on anxiety. The basic technique consists of exposing the client to a series of approximations to the anxiety-producing stimulus under relaxed conditions until finally the anxiety reaction is extinguished. For example, a fear of fire engines in a child may be gradually overcome by first exposing the child to pictures of fire engines, then toy models, etc. The technique has come under heavy criticism from psychoanalytically oriented theorists over the issue of ➤ **symptom substitution**. Also called *systematic desensitization*.

desexualization 1. Generally, any procedure that results in the 'removal' of sexual significance from something. 'Removing' here is meant rather loosely and may refer to any of a number of processes; e.g., *sublimation*, concealment, *counter conditioning*, etc. 2. Occasionally, the act of *castration*.

design 1. Any plan or schema for action. The connotation is that there is forethought, that the nature and structure of some plan has been well articulated and reasoned through. ➤ **experimental *design**. 2. A purpose or goal.

design, experimental The overall plan of an experimental investigation. An entire area of experimental psychology is concerned with various ways to design studies to maximize precision and analyzability and to minimize ambiguity and confusion. Topics considered are: selection of experimental subjects, assignment of subjects to conditions, choice of controls, administration of treatments, recording of data, etc. It should be noted that usually experiments are designed with reference to the type of statistics one wishes to use or the kinds of questions one may legitimately ask of one's data. Quite frequently the kinds of statistical analyses one may perform are dependent on the particular experimental design used. ➤➤ **control**.

design, factorial A common type of experimental design in which levels of one treatment are varied over all the levels of another treatment. For example, if one wished to study the effects of different levels of deprivation (say, levels A and B) and different amounts of training (say, levels 1 and 2) on some process like learn-ing in a laboratory rat, then the levels of deprivation would be distributed factorially over the levels of training resulting in four groups of subjects; A1, A2, B1, B2.

destination As borrowed from information theory, the terminus of a message, usually the receiver.

destruction method A method used in physiological research in which the functions of particular areas of the nervous system are studied by surgically destroying them or removing them. The inference is that the resulting behavior is a function of the remaining undestroyed tissue. ➤➤ **ablation, extirpation**.

destrudo A psychoanalytic term (now rare) for the energy of the hypothesized death instinct, *Thanatos*. It was put forward as an analog of *libido*.

desynchronization 1. A term used in physiological psychology with reference to EEG recording. It refers to the disruption of the alpha rhythm as a result of attending to a stimulus. See here ➤ **alpha blocking**. 2. More loosely, of course, it is used for any set of circumstances in which there is a breakdown or disruption in synchrony.

desynchronosis A mismatch between the time one is accustomed to and the time of one's present location; in short, a fancy term for 'jet-lag.'

detached affect A psychoanalytic term for affect which has been removed ('detached') from the painful, anxiety-producing idea or thought with which it was originally associated. In Freud's view, all obsessions resulted from the *reattachment* of such affect to some other, originally neutral, idea or thought.

detachment 1. Generally, a sense of emotional freedom, the lack of feeling of emotional involvement in a problem, with a situation, another person, etc. 2. In K. Horney's theory, a defense mechanism that functions by preventing one from forming emotionally intimate ties with others, resulting (she argued) in a neurotic emotional aloofness with a lack of empathy and sensitivity for others. 'Neurotic' in this context can present a bit of a problem since on occasions a perfectly reasoned and rational choice may be made, depending on the circumstances, to engage in the process of emotional detachment. In such cases the designation 'neurotic' is inappropriate.

detection theory ➤ **signal detection theory**.

detection threshold ➤ **threshold** (especially 1).

deterioration Progressive loss of function. Used in various combinations involving muscular, emotional, intellectual, judgemental, neuronal, etc. functions.

deterioration index A way of estimating the degree of deterioration of mental functioning as measured by the *Wechsler–Bellvue* tests. The index is based on the observation that certain abilities that the test measures decline with age and others do not.

determinant Any causal or antecedent condition or agent. This seemingly straightforward term is used in a most confusing array of combined terms by many authors when they seek to characterize the particular causes of particular patterns of behavior. The terminology here is certainly well-intended but generally rather unsatisfying. To wit: *organismic* determinant is frequently used for causal factors presumed to arise 'within' an organism, *genetic* for those determinants deemed hereditary, *environmental* for those judged to be purely (or at least predominantly) in the external environment, *situational* for momentary determinants of particular acts, *personal* for those argued to derive from personality traits or characteristics, etc. The difficulty, of course, is that one can rarely (if ever) unambiguously determine the locus of the determinants of behavior in this manner; *caveat lector*.

determinant, constitutional Those aspects of a person's general physical and physiological makeup that are regarded (by some theorists) as important factors in one's personality. For more detail here ➤ **constitutional theory**.

determinant, dream In the psychoanalytic approach to dream analysis, those psychic factors that are judged to be significant in giving a dream its essential qualities.

determination 1. From the Latin for *limiting*. Hence, the establishment of limits or boundaries. Often used here with the connotation that the analysis is quantitative, the determinations precise; e.g., the stimulus conditions in a psychophysical experiment are said to receive precise *determination*. 2. By extension, the reaching of a conclusion, the making of a decision. 3. By further extension, a trait of personality characterized by a tendency to push onward toward one's goal despite barriers and hardships.

determination, coefficient of That proportion of the variance of the dependent variable attributable directly to the actions of a specified independent variable. The complement of this statistic, the variance *not* resulting from that independent variable, is called the *coefficient of nondetermination*.

determiner 1. Generally, a cause, an antecedent condition that results in some particular outcome, a ➤ **determinant**. 2. In linguistics, a generic term covering articles (a, an, the), possessives (his, theirs, Mary's etc.), demonstratives (this, that) and a variety of others forms all of which are normally used before attributes in noun phrases.

determining set ➤ **set** (2).

determinism Very loosely, the doctrine that assumes that every event has causes. In classical mechanics it was assumed that were one to know the position and momentum of every particle of matter at one instant in time, then one could, in principle, know their position and momentum at any other point in time future. Such a position is the ultimate in 'hard' (or *nomological*) determinism. This particular view was 'softened' somewhat with the development of quantum mechanics in which the deepest knowable levels of cause and effect appear to be probabilistic in nature, shifting the notion of perfect prediction to probabilistic prediction. In psychology the debate is somewhat less cosmic and considerably less well defined. It generally revolves around the existentialist's and humanist's insistence on a measure of 'free will,' with which a person can remain outside the ever-probing tentacles of the behavioral and cognitive sciences. The debate, however, is probably an empty one. If one wishes to study behavior and the mind scientifically it must be assumed that the things one does have causes and that they are ultimately knowable. The question is really whether there is some 'thing' called *free will* which stands outside scientific analysis of cause and effect or whether it is merely (?) a particular mental/affective state which itself plays a role in the causation of behavior. Most contemporary social scientists, if they think about the issue at all, take a position that can best be described as 'uncomfortable pragmatism.' That is, in their day-to-day work they treat their subjects as probabilistically determined, chalk up what they cannot predict accurately to as yet unknown factors of causation (and perhaps a variation of the uncertainty principle) and prefer to think of themselves as actually operating according to their own free choice independently of a crass determinism that diminishes their sense of their own humanity.

detour problem An experimental setting that requires subjects initially to move away from a goal in order to obtain it eventually. Detour problems require a certain level of cognitive functioning to solve and are difficult for infants and most animals. The problem was first introduced by the Gestalt psychologists under the German term, *Umweg Problem.*

detoxification The process of treatment using rest, fluids and changes in diet to restore proper physiological functioning following disruption by overuse of drugs.

detumescence Subsidence of swelling. Used commonly for the subsiding of the erectile tissue of the genital organs (penis and clitoris) after erection.

deuteranomaly A visual condition in which there is a slight diminution in sensitivity to green wavelengths. A deuteranomalope will require more green light to achieve color matching than one with normal vision.

deuteranopia The more common of the 2 forms of ➤ **dichromacy**; it is characterized by a lowered sensitivity to green light. The term comes from the Greek *deuteros* meaning *second* and the theory is that this form of color blindness is produced by a deficiency in the green-light-absorbing pigment (green being the second primary). Compare with ➤ **protanopia**.

devaluation A defense mechanism in which the individual attributes exaggerated and inappropriate negative qualities to himself/herself or to others.

development 1. The sequence of changes over the full life span of an organism. This is the meaning first introduced into psychology; the area of 'developmental' psychology in the early decades of the century referred to the study of the full life span, from birth to death. Today the tendency is to use the term more restrictively. See, for example, terms like ➤ **developmental disability** and **developmental *aphasia** in which the age range is restricted to birth to adolescence. 2. Maturation. The connotation here is that the process is a biological one and largely dictated by genetic processes. This sense is probably the oldest and etymologically goes back to the Old French *desveloper* meaning to *unwrap* or *unfold*. When used in this sense the term is often contrasted with processes which are the result of learning. See here the discussion under ➤ **child development**. 3. An irreversible sequence of change. In some sense this notion of irreversibility is contained in the above senses of the term but this meaning is marked because of its use in medicine and psychiatry to refer to the *develop-*

mental course of a disease or a disorder wherein stages regularly follow one upon the other. **4.** A progressive change leading to higher levels of differentiation and organization. Here the connotation is one of positive progress, increases in effectiveness of function, maturity, sophistication, richness and complexity. This sense is generally intended in phrases like *human development, social development, intellectual development, emotional development,* etc. Note that the genetic connotations of sense 2 – and also sense 3 – are not found in this meaning; rather the implication is that processes attributable to environmental factors (learning, nutrition, etc.) are responsible.

Clearly, we have a rather loose term on our hands here. And, as is so often the case with terms that reference processes of fundamental importance, it is applied very broadly. In almost any of the above senses the 'thing' that 'develops' may be almost anything: molecular systems, bones and organs, emotions, ideas and cognitive processes, moral systems, personality, relationships, groups, societies and cultures. Not surprisingly, there is a large number of specialized terms based on this one; the more commonly used follow.

developmental Generally, pertaining to ➤ **development**, in any of its senses. Note, however, that there is a tendency to denote a number of clinical syndromes and psychological disorders as *developmental* when (a) they occur only during childhood or (b) the occurrence during childhood is marked and significantly different from occurrence in adolescence or adulthood. Some of these disorders are given below, others will be found under the alphabetical listing of the syndrome or disorder.

developmental age ➤ **age, developmental**.

developmental aphasia ➤ **developmental *aphasia** and **developmental *language disorder**.

developmental arithmetic disorder ➤ **arithmetic disorder, developmental**.

developmental articulation disorder ➤ **articulation disorder, developmental**.

developmental coordination disorder A disorder characterized by marked impairment in motor coordination that is severe enough to interfere with academic achievement or normal living. The term is not used if the lack of coordination is due to a physical disorder or to mental retardation.

developmental disability A general term for any significant handicap appearing in childhood or early adolescence (the criterion often stated is prior to age 18) and which will continue for the life of the individual.

developmental disorder, pervasive A class of childhood disorders characterized by a serious distortion of basic psychological functioning. The notion of distortion here is a general one and may involve social, cognitive, perceptual, attentional, motor or linguistic functioning. E.g., ➤ **infantile *autism**.

developmental disorders, specific A class of disorders that emerge during childhood characterized by disruption or delay in a specific area of perceptual or cognitive functioning that is independent of any other disorder. E.g., ➤ **developmental *arithmetic disorder**, **developmental *language disorder**.

developmental dyslexia ➤ **dyslexia**.

developmental expressive writing disorder ➤ **expressive writing disorder, developmental**.

developmental language disorder ➤ **language disorder, developmental**.

developmental level(s) Levels or classifications of the life span according to fixed ages. The most common set of levels in use is:

birth to 1 year: infancy.
1 year to 6 years: early childhood.
6 years to 10 years: midchildhood.
10 years to 12 years: late childhood (or preadolescence).
12 years to 21 years: adolescence.
21 years to 65 years: maturity.
65 and upwards: old age.

developmental milestones Significant behaviors which are used to mark the progress of development. Walking is a milestone in locomotor development, conservation in cognitive development, production of functional sex cells in sexual development, etc.

developmental norm(s) The average level(s) of performance on some task by a representative group of children at a particular age or developmental level.

developmental psycholinguistics ➤ **psycholinguistics, developmental**.

developmental psychology Strictly speaking, the field of psychology concerned with the lifelong process of change. 'Change' here means any qualitative and/or quantitative modification in structure and function: crawling to walking, babbling to speaking, illogical reasoning to logical, infancy to adolescence to maturity to old age, birth to death. When first articulated as a substantive sub-discipline in psychology by G. S. Hall around the turn of the century, it was quite explicitly this kind of 'cradle-to-grave' field of investigation. However, it should be noted that most of the scientists who call themselves *developmental psychologists* are interested in childhood, indeed so much so that for many the term *developmental psychology* has become equivalent to ➤ **child psychology**. To clarify issues of terminology here various other labels have emerged for more specialized subdisciplines. *Life-span psychology* is used by some for the original meaning and chronologically narrower fields like the *psychology of adolescence* and the *psychology of the aged* (see here ➤ **gerontology**) are recognized.

developmental quotient (DQ) ➤ **developmental *age** divided by chronological age.

developmental reading disorder ➤ **reading disorder, developmental**.

developmental scales A general label for any of a variety of tests and procedures for evaluating the developmental status of infants and preschoolers. Of necessity, all such scales are either performance tests or oral tests and, in general, must be individually administered. E.g., ➤ **Bayley Scales of Infant Development**, **Gesell Development Schedules**.

developmental sequence A general term applicable to the order of appearance of any sequence of behaviors, growth of structures, series of functions, etc. that has a pattern characteristic of a given species.

developmental stage Any period of development during which certain characteristic behaviors appear. This definition is rather 'loose'; see the discussion under ➤ **stage theory** for the rigorous criteria for determining the existence of a developmental stage.

deviance Generally, any pattern of behavior that is markedly different from the accepted standards within a society. The connotation is always that moral or ethical issues are involved and, in use, the term is typically qualified to note the specific form; e.g., sexual deviance.

deviate **1** n. Generally, one who differs markedly from the statistically established central tendency (loosely, the 'average') of a group. Note that, unlike the following, this meaning is evaluatively neutral. On the scale of intelligence, Einstein was a deviate in this sense. **2** n. One who differs markedly from accepted standards of practice in a group, especially standards of morality or ethics. See here ➤ **deviance**. **3** n. One whose sexual behaviors are considered inappropriate by general society; see the discussion under ➤ **sexual *perversion**. vb., *deviate*.

deviation Departure from some norm. The term is used to refer to deviations in behavior, in attitudes and in statistics. In behavior it generally makes reference to disorders or clinical syndromes. In studies of attitudes, the reference is generally to patterns of attitude change. In statistics, it refers to the degree to which a score differs from some measure of *central tendency*, usually the mean.

deviation, average A measure of the variability of a sample of scores from the mean of the sample. It is given as the arithmetic mean of the differences between each score and the mean; i.e., $AD = \Sigma (X_i - \overline{X})/N$, where $\overline{X}$ is the mean, X_i represents the ith score and N is the total number of scores. The average deviation is rarely used; statisticians prefer the ➤ **standard *deviation** as the measure of variability. Also called the *mean deviation*.

deviation score A value giving the degree to which any single score deviates from the mean of all the scores in a sample. Generally denoted as x or d.

deviation, standard A measure of variability of a sample of scores from the mean of the sample. It is given as, $SD = \sqrt{[\Sigma(X_i - \overline{X})^2/N]}$, where $\overline{X}$ is the mean, X_i the ith score and N is the total number of scores. When N is less than about 25 or so, the SD is 'biased' in that it does not give a proper estimate of the true population SD, i.e. the SD of the population from which the sample under consideration was drawn. To correct for this bias with samples under 25, $N - 1$ is used in the denominator. The SD is the preferred measure of dispersion of a set of scores – along with the ➤ **variance**, which is the SD^2. In general, when one is referring to the standard deviation of a sample of scores the notation SD is used; when referring to the standard deviation of a full population or to a theoretical distribution the Greek letter σ is used.

device Any instrument, piece of apparatus or cognitive procedure used for some specific purpose.

devolution 1. Reversal or undoing of evolution. 2. Degeneration, catabolism.

dexter From the Latin, meaning *right* or *favorable*. All derived forms of this term pertain to: 1. The right side of the body in general or the right hand specifically (*dextral*, *dextrality*). 2. Skillfulness, particu-

larly manual (*dexterity*, *dextrousness*). Contrast with ➤ **sinister**.

dexterity test Any sensory/motor test that requires both speed and accuracy of movement.

dextrad Toward the right side (of the body).

df Abbreviation for ➤ **degrees of freedom**.

dhat A ➤ **culture-specific syndrome** found in India. It is marked by anxiety and hypochondriacal concerns with semen, discoloration of urine, and feeling of weakness.

DI ➤ **delta** (Δ).

di- Prefix meaning *two*.

dia- Prefix meaning *within* or *through*.

diacritical marking system (DMS) A writing system developed to assist children in learning to read. The basic intent is the same as with the ➤ **initial teaching alphabet** except that the normal visual patterns of the letters are kept intact and pronunciation cues are supplied by a system of diacritical marks.

diadic Pertaining to two; characterizing things which are paired or arranged in twos. var., *dyadic*.

diad, social A two-person group. Face-to-face encounters between two people are the typical cases although some treat long-range social interactions, such as those occurring over the telephone, as forming social diads. var., *social dyad*.

diagnosis The identification of a disease, disorder, syndrome, condition, etc. In clinical psychology the term has generally been used in the same general sense that it has been in medicine; i.e. classification and categorization are the central concerns. Thus, a person displaying a particular form of aberrant behavior may be diagnosed as having schizophrenia or bipolar disorder or some other specific psychological-psychiatric disorder. Unfortunately, such usage has at times obscured more than it clarified. Such a diagnostic procedure is accurate only to the extent that there, in fact, exist such specific diseases or syndromes. The assumption had always been that these diagnostic categories were as well defined as, say, pneumonia or measles; that is, clinical psychological and psychiatric diagnosis was based on the *medical model*. It is now generally recognized that such an assumption is not always tenable. To deal with the serious problem of inappropriate diagnosis more and more emphasis is placed on behavior, on thought and on affect; in short, on those aspects of what a person does, thinks and feels which are deviant in terms of societal norms or which are counterproductive to living a normal life. The diagnostic emphasis in both psychiatry and clinical psychology has shifted in recent years from identifying and labeling a presumed underlying 'disease' or 'mental illness' to a more objective characterization of symptoms displayed. ➤ **Diagnostic and Statistical Manual**.

diagnosis, differential Diagnosis aimed at distinguishing which of two (or more) similar diseases or disorders an individual has. The term has enjoyed considerable extension beyond the medical/clinical areas and is used for distinguishing between conditions of many kinds in social psychology and the study of personality.

Diagnostic and Statistical Manual (I, II, III, III R, and IV) The full name here is Diagnostic and Statistical Manual of Mental Disorders; it is the official system for classification of psychological and psychiatric disorders prepared by and published by the American Psychiatric Association. The first version, *DSM-I*, was published in 1952 and subsequent revisions (*II*, *III*, *III R*, and *IV*) appeared in 1968, 1980, 1987 and 1994 respectively. Along with the appropriate sections of the ICD (➤ **International Classification of Diseases**) the *DSM* is the major guide for the classification, treatment and prognosis of psychological/psychiatric disorders. It should be clear from the simple fact that five editions have been published in 41 years that psychiatric nosology is hardly

an exact science. Interestingly, during that period the number of identified disorders has grown from about 100 to more than 300 – a fact that should alert all users of the manual to the likelihood that social, cultural, and even political factors play a role in the determination of the categories of psychiatry. Moreover, it should be made very clear that actual usage lags behind the mandated nomenclature; for example, since *DSM-III* there have been no psychiatric conditions that are officially classified as *neuroses* (the more neutral term *disorder* is used), although hardly a textbook exists in personality and/or abnormal psychology which does not use the term. In this Dictionary every effort has been made to include all terms, even the ones no longer receiving the APA's imprimatur, particularly when they are still in wide use. The *DSM-IV* is particularly noteworthy for its extreme specificity. Disorders are quite specifically defined and the emphasis is on behaviors, thoughts, feelings and desires that are counter-productive to the individual displaying them. The shift is away from the identification of specific diseases or 'neuroses.' One important element of the *DSM-IV* is the degree to which its terminology has been coordinated with that of the ICD-10 Classification of Mental and Behavioural Disorders. Up till now these two classification systems had been developed independently and international terminological confusions were all too common. ➤ **diagnosis** for more on this point. Note that the full name here is rarely used; more typically the reference is to the abbreviation, '*DSM-IV*.'

diagnostic interview A common procedure in clinical situations in which the client or patient is interviewed with the purpose of reaching some reasonable determination of the nature of the disorder and its etiology and of planning a method of treatment.

diagnostic test A general cover term for any test or procedure used in an attempt to pinpoint the specific nature and (perhaps) origins of a disability or disorder.

In psychological work the term is used in a somewhat misleading fashion since 'diagnostic' here refers not to the identification of a disease or a syndrome but rather to the determination of the particular source of an individual's difficulties in a certain area. Most tests which are called *diagnostic* evaluate such skills as reading, language, sensory/motor coordination and the like.

diagnostic value Quite literally, the value of a test in making diagnosis; that is, its ➤ **validity**.

diagram 1. Generally, a schematic drawing that presents the essential features of some system. The diagram may represent either the proper physical relations between features in spatial and/or temporal manner or it may present them in a symbolic and/or logical fashion. 2. Common shorthand form of ➤ **scatter diagram**. 3. An arbitrary sign used in a logographic writing system.

dialect A form of a natural language differing from the standard and usually spoken in a particular geographic region. The word 'differing' here is tricky; a dialect is usually regarded as sufficiently distinct in pronunciation patterns, grammar, vocabulary and the use of idioms to be clearly detectable as a separate linguistic form, yet not so different as to be classified as a separate language. However, in practice, political and social issues are often weighed more heavily than linguistic. For example, the Mandarin and Cantonese 'dialects' of Chinese are not mutually intelligible while the Norwegian and Swedish 'languages' to a considerable extent are. Clearly geo-political factors have led to the first two being classified as dialects of one language and the second two as separate languages. Compare with ➤ **accent**.

dialectic 1. Of reasoning involving extensive deductive argument, particularly that aimed at the clarification of the meaning of concepts. The ancient dialectical approach involved the development of contradictions and their solutions as the means of elucidation. 2. Of the philosophy of Georg W. F. Hegel, which was based on the theory that reality develops through the interplay of thesis, antithesis and synthesis. For Hegel every action (thesis) produced a counterreaction (antithesis) and was inevitably followed by an integration of these opposites (synthesis). The *dialectical materialism* of Marx and Engels was greatly influenced by Hegel's principle.

dialectic(al) psychology Loosely, the theoretical stance that argues that conflict and change are the basic principles of life. Dialectics had its origins in Heraclitus and was further developed in philosophical and political forms by Hegel and Marx respectively. As a theory specifically concerned with change, it has found an audience in developmental psychology, where it has become associated with those theories that argue that development is a series or flux of transformations impelled by essential conflicts between the child's cognitive system and reality, or between coexisting cognitive components.

On this position, individuals are seen to transform their environments by action which, in turn, changes them. Thus, people develop through their own labor and action, the resistances they meet, and the conflicts they engender. Major development changes (or 'dialectical leaps') occur when the day-to-day quantitative changes reach a critical number or mass. Piaget's position is often labelled dialectic.

dialysis The process of purifying a liquid by passing it through a membrane.

Diana complex A psychoanalytic term for the (assumed) repressed desire of a woman to be a man.

diaphoresis Profuse sweating.

diary method The study of an individual, usually a child, through a daily record of behavior. Commonly used in the study of longitudinal development of language.

diastole The relaxing phase of the heart cycle.

diathesis An inherited predisposition to a particular disease or other condition. Usually the term will be used with qualifiers specifying the disease or condition.

diathesis–stress hypothesis The generalization that many abnormal behavior patterns are the result of an inherited susceptibility combined with a particularly stressful environment and a lack of learned skills for coping with the stress.

diazepam A commonly prescribed ➤ **antianxiety drug** of the ➤ **benzodiazepine** class. Trade name *Valium*.

dich(o)- Combining form meaning *in two parts*.

dichoptic Stimulation of the two eyes with distinctly different stimuli. The visual equivalent of *dichotic*.

dichotic Stimulation of the two ears with distinctly different stimuli. Contrast with ➤ **binaural** (1) and ➤ **diotic**. The auditory equivalent of *dichoptic*.

dichotomous variable A variable that can take just two values; e.g., male/female.

dichotomy Division or classification into two, not necessarily equal, parts.

dichromacy General term for any of several kinds of color-vision deficiencies. As the name suggests, they have in common the fact that a dichromat can match any given sample hue using only two other wavelengths, as opposed to normal color vision (➤ **trichromacy**) where three are required. Two forms of dichromacy involve weakness in the perception of reds and greens (➤ **protanopia** and ➤ **deuteranopia**); two others involve blues and yellows (➤ **tritanopia** and ➤ **tetartanopia** – although the existence of the latter is not firmly established). Over the years a number of terms have been used synonymously with dichromacy. They include *dichromatism, dichromatiopsia, dichromopsia, dichromia* and *dichromasy*. There are also various adjectival forms for each of the noun forms although, blissfully, only one term

for an individual with the deficit, *dichromat*.

dichromacy, anomalous The term is used by some for either of the rare forms of ➤ **dichromacy** which involve color deficiencies in the blue and yellow regions of the spectrum, i.e. *tritanopia* and *tetartanopia*.

dichromasy ➤ **dichromacy**.

dichromat An individual with any of the various forms of ➤ **dichromacy**.

dichromatism ➤ **dichromacy**.

dichromatopsia ➤ **dichromacy**.

dichromat, uniocular A person who has normal color vision in one eye but is a *dichromat* in the other. Such persons are very rare but are extremely useful subjects in the study of color vision.

dichromia ➤ **dichromacy**.

dichromopsia ➤ **dichromacy**.

Dick-Read method A natural childbirth technique developed in England during the thirties. It is based on giving the mother physiological, anatomical, and hygienic instruction along with training in relaxation and controlled breathing.

didactic Instructional, pertaining to teaching.

didactic analysis ➤ **analysis, didactic**.

didactic therapy ➤ **therapy, didactic**.

diencephalon A major subdivision of the forebrain consisting primarily of the *thalamus* and the *hypothalamus*.

diet The term derives from a Greek word meaning *way of living*. Thus: **1.** Food substances and liquids normally consumed in day-to-day living. However, two other usages are more common these days: **2.** Any specific program of food intake prescribed for a particular reason; e.g., a low-cholesterol diet, a diet for a diabetic, etc. **3.** Any diminished food-intake program for the purpose of losing weight.

dietary neophobia A fear of new foods.

209

It is found in the young of many species who will not eat an unfamiliar food until a parent has consumed it and is not harmed by it. It is also often observed in humans, especially among children, who may exhibit a dislike for new and different foods. Note that the use of *phobia* here is not quite right in that it is not a phobic disorder but a pattern of behavior that has adaptive value. Differentiate from the simple term *neophobia* which, despite being occasionally used synonymously, is properly used only for an irrational fear of new things.

difference limen ➤ threshold.

difference threshold ➤ threshold.

difference tone ➤ combination tone.

differential conditioning Conditioning produced by reinforcing responses made to one of a set of stimuli while withholding responses made to the other(s). ➤ discrimination.

differential diagnosis ➤ diagnosis, differential.

differential extinction Selective extinction of responding by withholding reinforcement for that response while continuing to reinforce other responses.

differential fertility ➤ fertility, differential.

differential growth ➤ growth, differential.

differential inhibition A term coined by Pavlov to describe the gradual elimination of responding to stimuli which are similar to, but discriminably different from, the original, conditioned stimulus.

differential limen ➤ threshold.

differential psychology That approach to the study of psychology that focuses on individual differences in behavior.

differential rate reinforcement In operant conditioning, a term for a class of ➤ schedules of *reinforcement in which the delivery of reinforcement depends on the immediately preceding rate of responding. Included here are *differential reinforcement of high rate* (*drh*), *differen-tial reinforcement of low rate* (*drl*) and *differential reinforcement of paced responses* (*drp*).

differential reinforcement ➤ reinforcement, differential.

differential reinforcement of high rate (drh) ➤ schedules of *reinforcement.

differential reinforcement of low rate (drl) ➤ schedules of *reinforcement.

differential reinforcement of other behavior (dro) ➤ schedules of *reinforcement.

differential reinforcement of paced responses (drp) ➤ schedules of *reinforcement.

differential response Any response made selectively to but one of several stimuli presented. ➤ discrimination.

differential scoring Analyzing the results of a test battery by rescoring the responses along a number of different dimensions so as to extract measures along a number of variables.

differential stimulus ➤ discriminative *stimulus.

differential threshold ➤ threshold.

differential validity ➤ validity, differential.

differentiation 1. In embryology, a process whereby a group of initially similar cells generates a number of different kinds of cells. 2. In mathematics, the process of carrying out a differential. 3. In sociology, the process by which groups, roles, statuses, etc. develop within a society. In psychology proper there are two distinct uses: 4. In conditioning studies, whenever an organism must learn to make two or more different responses to two or more similar stimuli. The particular experimental conditions used dictate whether this set of circumstances is one of *response* differentiation or *stimulus* differentiation. 5. In perception, when a stimulus array changes from perceived homogeneity to perceived heterogeneity so that the various aspects of the array become distinguished. Here one speaks of learning to differentiate between stimulus conditions.

Contrast this meaning with that of ➤ **enrichment**.

diffraction Bending of light or sound waves around the edges of some object in the path of the wave.

diffuse Scattered, spread, not localized. Used of thought or behavior which is undifferentiated, uncoordinated or lacking direction. Used of light that has no clear source.

diffusion 1. Generally, spreading. The connotation is that something found in one locale spreads and scatters through another. Hence: 2. Interpenetration of liquids or gases such that they become mixed. 3. The spreading of the effects of a localized stimulus through neighboring tissues. 4. The scattering of light in the eye produced by characteristics of anatomical structures, principally the spherical aberrations of the lens. 5. In sociology, the spread of culture traits from one society to another or from one distinct group to another within the same society.

diffusion of responsibility ➤ **responsibility, diffusion of**.

digital Pertaining to: 1. The numbers in any given numbering system; e.g., 0–9 in the decimal system, 1–2 in the binary, etc. 2. The fingers and toes.

digit-span test A test of immediate or short-term memory. The subject is given a series of random digits and immediately recalls as many as possible. ➤ **span of *apprehension** and **short-term *memory**.

digraph Any two letters in a word that are pronounced as a single phonetic unit; e.g., the *ch*'s in *church*.

dilatation ➤ **dilation**.

dilation Expansion, enlargement. var. *dilatation*.

dildo(e) An artificial penis.

dilemma A situation in which one is faced with two (or, colloquially, more) mutually exclusive or mutually incompat-

ible alternatives from which to choose when neither can be taken as truly satisfactory. Dilemmas present a fertile domain for the study of choice behavior and the manner in which people balance various positive and negative outcomes in making decisions. See the following entries for a few of the more intensely investigated circumstances.

dilemma, moral A situation in which one is confronted with two choices such that selecting one violates one set of moral precepts and selecting the other violates another. A classic case is that confronting a physician who is asked by a terminally ill patient in great pain to provide a fatal overdose of a drug so that the patient may die with dignity.

dilemma, prisoner's A game based on the classic detective-to-suspect situation. In the typical format each player (prisoner) is told separately that although there is little direct evidence to convict him he has two choices: confess or don't confess. If neither confesses there will be a minor penalty for both, if both confess there will be a relatively severe penalty for both, but if only one confesses they will 'go easy' on him but 'throw the book' at the other. In psychological studies the penalties are usually replaced by small rewards and confessing or not by a choice between two responses, but the principle remains the same. If both subjects make response A both receive a moderate reward, say 5 cents; if both select response B both receive a very small reward (1 cent); but if one chooses A and the other chooses B then the one who chose B receives a high reward (10 cents) and the other a very small one or perhaps none at all. Not surprisingly, the game holds a particular fascination for psychologists because the outcome is always dependent on the choices of both players and on the degree of cooperation they display.

dilemma, social Any situation in which the immediate outcome or payoff for an individual is high if that person 'defects' from social mores but the ultimate outcome for *all* persons is reduced if enough people defect. Examples are ubiquitous and reflect many of the classic and profound ills of any large society. E.g., if you keep your thermostat high your home remains warm but if everyone does then the fuel supply becomes exhausted and all persons will freeze; or, children are one of the few available economic resources to a family in a poorly developed, nonindustrialized society, which encourages each family to have large numbers of offspring, which produces overpopulation, which hinders the development of a sound economy, which would provide each family with other available economic resources, etc.

dimension Originally the term was used only for the three characteristics of physical space: height, width and depth. Now, however, it is used to refer to any well-defined quantitative series. Thus, one speaks of color as having three dimensions (brightness, hue, saturation) or of a pure tone as having three (amplitude, frequency, phase). Moreover, the term has become increasingly common with reference to non-quantitative aspects of complex stimuli, so that references to *semantic dimensions* or *social dimensions* are often seen. Note that in these latter cases the dimensions themselves are frequently difficult to specify. A variety of sophisticated techniques have been developed to extract these dimensions from large data bases; ➤ e.g., **multidimensional analysis, multidimensional scaling**.

diminishing returns Non-technical phrase for negatively accelerated improvement. What is meant is that past a certain point each additional effort results in smaller and smaller amounts of progress; the gain just isn't worth the effort.

dimming In perception, the enhancement of an afterimage by reducing the intensity of the area on which the image is projected.

dimorphism Lit., having two forms or manifestations. Typically used to refer to species of which there are two distinguish-able forms, as in juvenile and adult or male and female.

DIMS *disorders of initiating and maintaining sleep*; ➤ **insomnia**.

DIN color system A color-classification system used widely in Europe. It is based, like the Munsell color system, on the three primary dimensions of hue, brightness and saturation.

ding-dong theory ➤ **theories of *language origin**.

diopter A unit for measuring the power of a lens for bringing parallel rays of light to a focus.

diopteric abberation ➤ **spherical *abberation**.

diotic Stimulation of the two ears with the same stimulus. ➤ **binaural** (1). Contrast with ➤ **dichotic**.

diphenylbutyl piperidines A subgroup of the *butyrophenones* used as ➤ **antipsychotic drugs** primarily in the treatment of schizophrenia. The most common is *pimozide*. They are somewhat less effective in relieving the schizophrenic symptoms than the more frequently used ➤ **phenothiazine** (e.g. *chlorpromazines*), but seem to have fewer side effects.

diphthong (*dif-thong*) Any speech sound produced by gliding from one vowel to another; e.g., the *i* in *ice*.

diplacusis Condition in which a person perceives a different pitch when a tone is presented to one ear from that perceived when the identical tone is presented to the other ear. When both ears are simultaneously stimulated a pitch somewhere between them is heard.

diplegia Paralysis of similar parts on both sides of the body.

dipl(o)- Combining form meaning *double*.

diploid number The normal number of chromosomes in the somatic cells of a particular species. In humans the diploid number is 46. The diploid number is twice the ➤ **haploid number**.

diplopia Vision characterized by double images. The condition results from a failure to fuse properly the images from the two retinas. Contrast with ➤ **polyopia**.

dips(o)- Combining form meaning *thirst*.

dipsomania Uncontrollable craving for alcoholic beverages. Distinguish from *alcoholism*; dipsomania occurs in widely spaced 'attacks' of relatively short duration.

direct 1. Straight, uninterrupted. 2. Unmediated by other processes, not enriched. This latter meaning is most commonly found in the study of perception; ➤ **direct perception**.

direct apprehension ➤ direct perception.

direct association ➤ association, direct.

direct correlation Occasional synonym for ➤ **positive *correlation**.

direct dyslexia ➤ dyslexia, direct.

directed An occasional synonym for *goal-directed*. Used in phrases like *directed movement* for movement aimed coherently at some goal, *directed thinking* for the kind of goal-oriented thinking involved in problem-solving, etc.

directive A *speech act* in which the speaker tries to get the listener to do something for him or her. For example, 'please close the door.' But ➤➤ **indirect directive**.

directive therapy A general label for any psychotherapeutic approach that focuses and directs the client to change. Generally included are *hypnotherapy, rational-emotive therapy, behavioral therapy* (some forms anyway). Also called *active therapy*.

direct perception Referring to a theoretical position about the process of perception put forward by J. J. Gibson. The argument is that perception consists of a cognitively unmediated, inferentially unenriched process whereby the properties of the distal stimulus are directly apprehended. Gibson's position contrasts with

most other theories of perception, which argue that other processes operate to organize, enrich and interpret the percept (➤ **constructivism**). Often the term *direct realism* is used to characterize Gibson's system, on the grounds that the ecologically important aspects of the environment are directly represented in that which is perceived. For more on this point ➤ **ecological validity**.

direct realism ➤ direct perception.

direct reflex 1. Generally, any reflex occurring on the same side of the body as the stimulus. Contrast with ➤ **crossed reflex**. 2. Specifically, the prompt pupil-contraction response to a light shined in the eye.

direct scaling ➤ indirect *scaling.

dirhinia Of both nostrils. Dirhinic stimulation affects receptors in both nostrils simultaneously.

dis- 1. A prefix of Latin origin meaning *apart, away from, lack of, separation from, reversal*. 2. Variant of ➤ **dys-**. Generally, meaning 1 should be sharply distinguished from *dys-*, but the variant spelling of 2 is common, e.g., disorder.

disability Generally, any lack of ability to perform some function. It may be used for congenital impairments or for functions lost through trauma, disease, etc. ➤ **disabled**. In many states there are also governmentally defined criteria. The one used in the US, for example, is: inability to engage in any substantial gainful activity by reason of any medically determinable physical or mental impairment which can be expected to last or has lasted for a continuous period of not less than 12 months.

disabled Characterizing one suffering from a *disability*. Because of the many negative connotations which have developed around the term *handicapped*, many prefer this term to refer to any individual who suffers from a condition that only 'superficially' limits his or her functioning. A look at the entry ➤ **disability**, however, should alert the reader that the word *superficially* needs clarification. The notion entailed by the new usage is that the person may indeed suffer from a most severe (i.e. disabling) condition such as paraplegia but may nevertheless be quite capable of living a rich and fulfilling life provided that certain adjustments are made for the disabling condition such as ramps for wheelchairs, elevators, modified equipment on the job, etc.

disambiguation The act of determining the contextually appropriate meaning(s) of an ambiguous word, phrase, sentence, or other situation.

discharge 1. The firing of a stimulated neuron. 2. The release of pent-up tensions. 3. The flowing away of a bodily secretion or the secretion itself.

discharge of affect Quite literally, the diminishing of experienced affect by displaying and expressing it. The term originated in psychoanalytic theory as part of the 'hydraulic' characterization of psychic energy but is now used more broadly. Distinguish, however, from ➤ **catharsis**.

discipline The several shades of meaning of this term can be captured by the following two primary usages: **1** n. Control of conduct, either of subordinates by a superior or of one's own conduct. Although one usually exercises discipline by the use of punishment it is also possible to exert control by careful manipulations of positive rewards. Strictly speaking it is not correct to use *punishment* and *discipline* as synonyms; one may use punishment to discipline a child but the use of punishment does not necessarily imply that one is really disciplining the child. **2** n. A branch of knowledge or scholarship, e.g. the discipline of linguistics or of biology. Note that the second meaning here derives from the first. Originally the term was used as a rough synonym for education and receiving 'formal discipline' meant that one would develop discipline in particular subjects. vb., *discipline*, for meaning **1**.

discontinuity theory A theory of discrimi-

nation learning that maintains that learning cannot take place until the organism focuses on those aspects of the stimulus that are critical to the required discrimination. Superficially similar to *insight* learning, it belongs to the same general class of theories as ➤ **all-or-one *learning**.

discontinuous Not ➤ **continuous**. Characteristic of variables or measures where not all possible values are 'represented.' Represented is in inverted commas here because a variable or measure may be manifested as a series of discrete values which in fact represent a true underlying continuous scale; e.g., height is usually represented on a discontinuous scale in discrete units like inches or centimeters, and perhaps quarters or tenths thereof, but the underlying scale is continuous and a person passes through all possible heights. Compare with a variable like *number of errors in a learning experiment*, which is truly discontinuous.

discontinuous variable ➤ **discontinuous**.

discourse For want of a better definition, most speech-act theorists call any utterance longer than a sentence a discourse.

discourse analysis In linguistics and related disciplines, the analysis of 'units' larger than the sentence; e.g., in writing, an analysis of paragraphs, in speech, an analysis of turns at talking, etc.

discrete Separate, distinct, individually identifiable, discontinuous.

discriminability Properties of objects or events in the world that permit one to distinguish between them, to discriminate them one from the other.

discriminal dispersion The distribution of responses made in a discrimination experiment.

discriminant analysis A variety of ➤ **regression** (2) analysis that permits one to use continuous independent variables to place individual cases into categories on a dependent variable. For example, one could use variables such as grade point index and number of days absent from school to predict whether or not students would graduate on time.

discriminant validity ➤ **convergent and discriminant *validity**.

discriminated operant An operant whose properties are defined by the stimulus conditions under which it typically occurs and (as is always the case in the study of operant behavior) the effects that it has. Discriminated operant conditioning can thus be thought of as an SRS relationship between the intial Stimuli, the Response emitted, and the Stimulus consequences of the response. ➤➤ **discrimination** (1).

discriminated operant conditioning ➤ **discrimination** (1).

discriminating power The degree to which a test or any individual test item is capable of discriminating between criterial (➤ **criterion**) and noncriterial cases.

discriminating range ➤ **range, discriminating**.

discrimination Two meanings here, one technical and 'neutral,' the other conceptually founded on the technical but alive with the ethical and moral connotations of politics, race, religion, etc. **1.** In technical writing, the ability to perceive differences between two or more stimuli. It also may be looked upon as a class of experimental procedures called, collectively, *discrimination training procedures*. For example, in operant-conditioning experiments, responses in the presence of one stimulus (S^D) are reinforced but responses in the presence of another (S^Δ) are not. In classical conditioning, in the presence of one stimulus the CS (conditioned stimulus) and US (unconditioned stimulus) are paired (i.e. the CS is a 'true' CS – usually denoted as CS^+) but in the presence of another stimulus they are not (i.e. the CS here is not a true CS since it does not signal a US – it is usually denoted as CS^-) In the operant case such training leads to the emitting of responses in the presence of the S^D but not in the presence of the S^Δ. In the classical case it leads to elicitation of the CR in the presence of

the CS^+ but not in the presence of the CS^-. In these examples the term is clearly being used to describe a training procedure whereby an organism learns to respond differentially to different stimuli. Note that the question of **perceptual /learning** (the organism's learning to detect the physical differences between the stimuli themselves) arises only indirectly. In most discrimination-training procedures an a priori assumption is made that the organism does perceive the differences between the stimuli but merely does not react differently toward them because it has never been reinforced for treating them differently. **2.** In perception and psychophysics, the capacity to distinguish between stimuli. For more detail here, ➤ **threshold** (2). **3.** By extension, in social psychology and related areas, the unequal treatment of individuals or groups based on arbitrary characteristics such as race, sex, ethnicity, cultural background, etc. Without going unnecessarily into the politics of this usage of the term it may be noted simply that a careful understanding of the technical meanings can produce considerable insight into the problem. See here ➤ **prejudice**. vb., *discriminate*, used in all senses.

discriminative stimulus (S^D) ➤ **stimulus, discriminative**.

disease Medically, any abnormal bodily condition. By extension, any abnormal psychological condition. The historical roots of the use of the term are traceable to the fact that the first efforts to deal with psychological disturbances came from those trained in medicine. The tradition is quite ancient and goes back to the 15th-century physicians who were required to differentiate between those individuals who were suffering from diseases and those who were suspected of being witches. The legacy of this trend has been to regard psychological disturbances as diseases and to introduce various related phrases such as *mental illness* and *psychological sickness* into the field and to refer to the sufferer as a *patient*. Although no one disputes that biological dysfunctions

215

underlie a number of psychological and psychiatric disorders, under increasing pressure from those who take behavioral and/or cognitive approaches to problems of a clinical nature the medical flavor of the terminology has been diminished in recent years. *Disorder* is generally preferred to *disease*; diagnosis deals more with behavior and patterns of thought than with hypothesized disease-like syndromes; *client* is used by many in place of *patient*; etc. For more on this general point and the changes in terminology entailed, ➤ **diagnosis** and related terms.

disease model   A term used to characterize the medical approach to psychological disturbances. It is usually used by the more behaviorally oriented clinicians with an accompanying sneer and a tone of disdain. See the discussion under ➤ **disease** for the reasons behind this attitude.

disfluency   A general term for any nonfluent speech, e.g., stuttering.

disinhibition   1. As originally used by Pavlov the term refers to the removal of an inhibition by an extraneous stimulus. It is easily seen during the extinction of a classically conditioned response; after a dozen or so trials of extinction of a salivary response the introduction of a sudden novel stimulus will evoke a significant conditioned response. Pavlov was supposed to have discovered the phenomenon serendipitously when an assistant slammed a door during the extinction phase of an experiment. **2.** More generally, the lowering of inhibitions (particularly social ones) that occurs under the influence of some added factor. Alcohol and various other drugs function as disinhibitors in this sense.

disintegration   Generally, loss or serious disruption of organization in some 'system.' The term is used broadly and the system under discussion is usually specified, e.g., behavioral, moral, personality, cognitive, etc.

disjunctive concept   A concept that is defined by the presence of any one of two or more aspects. In a concept-learning experiment using various colored shapes as stimuli, a disjunctive concept might be something like 'red *or* round' so that any red or any round object would be considered correct. Compare with ➤ **conjunctive concept** and ➤ **relational concept**.

disjunctive motivation   Sullivan's term for striving for only the temporary, seeking to achieve only limited or substitute goals. Compare with ➤ **conjunctive motivation**.

disjunctive reaction time   ➤ **reaction time, disjunctive**.

disjunctive syllogism   ➤ **syllogism**.

disorder   Generally, and literally, lack of order, disruption of order once present. In this sense the term has become one of the favored in contemporary psychiatry. In the latest edition of the ➤ **Diagnostic and Statistical Manual** essentially all psychiatric syndromes are listed as various kinds of disorders. It is also gradually taking over the role that the term ➤ **neurosis** previously played in the psychologists' lexicon. The many forms of disorders are listed in this volume under the alphabetical heading of the qualifying term.

disorganized   Characterizing that which has lost or had disrupted its previous structure and functioning. Used commonly in clinical cases where there is disruption in behavior, thought, affect, personality, etc.

disorganized attachment   ➤ **attachment styles**.

disorganized (type) schizophrenia   ➤ **schizophrenia, disorganized (type)**.

disorientation   Inability to orient oneself with regard to spatial, temporal and contextual aspects of the environment. Acute disorientation brought on by alcohol, drugs or dramatic alterations in one's circumstances is not uncommon and not abnormal; long-term progressive disorientation is a symptom of a variety of psychological and/or neurological disorders.

disparate retinal points   Retinal points stimulation of which produces different spatial sensations. The phenomena of ➤ **retinal *disparity** and ➤ **disparation** are due to stimulation of disparate retinal points. Contrast with ➤ **congruent retinal points**.

disparation When an object is either nearer or farther away from the momentary point of fixation of the two eyes there is a difference between the images that fall on each retina, resulting in a blurred, double image. Disparation refers to the difference between the retinal images – not to the double image itself. When this occurs one of the two images is usually suppressed, as can be observed easily if a finger is held in front of the eyes while they are focused on a distant object.

disparity, retinal The slight difference between the two retinal images produced when viewing an object. It is produced by the separation of the two eyes so that each is looking at the object from a different angle, and serves as the basis for stereoscopic vision. In normal viewing it functions as a binocular cue for depth perception. Also called *binocular disparity* and, in some older texts, *visual disparity*.

dispersion 1. Variability, spread. Used primarily in statistics where indices of dispersion are measures which describe the ➤ **variability** of any distribution of scores. In simplest terms, it is a way of describing the tendency for scores to depart from ➤ **central tendency**. The magnitude of a measure of dispersion of a distribution tells something about the relative 'poorness' of the measure of central tendency as a representation of that distribution. Three measures of dispersion are used, ➤ **range**, **average *deviation** and **standard *deviation**, with the last the overwhelming favorite in statistical analyses. ➤➤ **variance**. 2. Spreading out of the population of a group or family. ➤ **inbreeding avoidance**.

dispersion circle The circle of light seen when looking at a single-point source.

dispersion, coefficient of An index of relative variability given by 100 times the measure of dispersion divided by the meas-

ure of central tendency. Usually the ➤ **standard *deviation** and the **mean** serve in these roles. Also known as *coefficient of variability* or *coefficient of variation*.

displaced aggression ➤ **aggression, displaced**.

displaced vision A general term referring to the research on perceptual experiences produced by various modifications of the visual field brought about by wearing special lenses that alter incoming light. The work runs the gamut from dramatic displacements, as with reversing lenses which invert the entire visual world, to more subtle modifications such as 10° displacements, lenses with vertical or horizontal warps, lenses which produce chromatic aberrations, etc.

displacement 1. Generally and literally, the movement of an object from one place to another. An array of extensions of this simple meaning are in common use, to wit: 2. In behavioral terms, the substituting of one response for another, especially when the original response is blocked or thwarted; see here ➤ **displaced *aggression**. 3. The transference of affect or wishes and desires from their original object or person to another object or person. Displacement, in this sense, is regarded as a *defense mechanism*. 4. In vision, ➤ **allelotropia**.

displacement of affect ➤ **affect, displacement of**.

display 1. In ethology, a species-specific behavior pattern that functions to communicate specific information about the state of an animal. Displays are many and varied and function to communicate such states as aggressiveness, submission, receptivity to copulation, etc. They are also used to deceive such as the display of ➤ **death feigning**. 2. In experimental psychology, the presentation of the stimulus.

disposition 1. Generally, an ordered arrangement of elements which stand in a particular relationship to each other such that certain functions may be carried out readily. This is the core meaning and arrives in straight translation from the Latin word for *arrangement*. By extension: **2.** In the study of personality, any hypothesized organization of mental and physical aspects of a person that is expressed as a stable, consistent tendency to exhibit particular patterns of behavior in a broad range of circumstances. In this sense, the literally dozens of special terms used as descriptive labels for tendencies to act like *trait*, *ability*, *habit*, *set*, *instinct*, *drive*, *temperament*, *sentiment*, *motive*, *faculty*, etc., are all interpretable as dispositions. The theoretical problem that has spawned this terminological forest is the need to explain the regularity and consistency of behavior (more or less) independently of variation and alteration in the environment. For a more detailed discussion of this problem, ➤ **personality 3.** A tendency to be susceptible. This meaning is common in psychiatric and clinical psychological writings; e.g., a disposition for schizophrenia. Often it is used in this sense with the connotation that the tendency is inherited; this is not always defensible and often begs an important empirical question.

disruptive behavior disorders An umbrella term for a variety of psychiatric disorders that have disruptive behavior as a significant feature. Included are ➤ **attention-deficit hyperactivity disorder**, ➤ **oppositional defiant disorder**, and the ➤ **conduct disorders**.

dissimilation Occasionally used as the antonym of ➤ **assimilation**, in the general sense of that term.

dissociated vertical deviation A visual condition where the two eyes are discoordinated in a vertical manner. It is associated with various neurological disorders.

dissociation 1. Used generally to characterize the process (or its result) whereby a coordinated set of activities, thoughts, attitudes or emotions becomes separated from the rest of the person's personality and functions independently. Mild forms are seen in ➤ **compartmentalization**, in which one set of life's activities are separated from others, and in the amnesias of hypnosis and some emotional disorders.

More extreme forms are observed in the ➤ **dissociative disorders**. **2.** H. S. Sullivan used the term to characterize the process whereby thoughts or memories that produce anxiety are cut off from consciousness. This *dissociative reaction* (as it is often called) is to be distinguished from schizophrenia on the grounds that each of the dissociated aspects maintains its integrity; one does not observe the general disintegration and loss of contact with reality of the true schizophrenias.

dissociative amnesia ➤ **amnesia, dissociative**.

dissociative disorder A general cover term for those psychological disorders characterized by a breakdown in the usual integrated functions of consciousness, perception of self, and sensory/motor behavior. Generally included here are ➤ **depersonalization disorder**, ➤ **multiple personality** and some forms of ➤ **amnesia** and ➤ **fugue**.

dissociative fugue ➤ **fugue**.

dissociative trance disorder ➤ **trance disorder, dissociative**.

dissonance theory ➤ **cognitive dissonance theory**.

distal Lit., distant, away. Hence: **1.** In anatomy, referring to the farthest point(s) from the center of the body, from the center of an organ or from the point of attachment of an organ or other structure. **2.** In perception, ➤ **distal stimulus**. Compare with ➤ **proximal**.

distal effect The outcome of any response that has some impact on the environment.

distal response Any response with ➤ **distal effects**.

distal stimulus Lit., a stimulus away (distant) from the receptor on which it acts. In the study of perception one differentiates between: (a) stimuli that act directly upon a sensory receptor, e.g., the light waves themselves as they impinge on the retina; and (b) stimuli that are in the external environment, e.g., the chair from which the light waves are reflected. The latter comprise the *distal stimuli*, the former the ➤ **proximal stimuli**.

distance, psychological This term is used broadly and may refer to real, physical distance, as it functions psychologically, or to a mental dimension of separateness or dissimilarity between things. Thus: **1.** In perception, the physical distance between a stimulus source and the receiving organism presented in terms of the psychophysical relations involved. **2.** In social psychology, the degree of apartness between persons usually expressed as a statement about the amount of difficulty experienced when interactions occur. For refinements on meaning here ➤ **social distance**. **3.** In graphic presentations of the outcome of factor analysis or of multidimensional scaling, a measure of the degree of similarity between data points. **4.** In A. Adler's theory, a cover term for any of several psychic devices for coping with situations that could potentially reveal one's weaknesses or shortcomings. Adler identified four such techniques: *functional illness, indecision* or *hesitation, ceasing to try* and the *invention of false barriers*. **5.** The deliberate maintenance of dispassion, a lack of emotional involvement. Here one speaks, for example, of a clinician maintaining psychological distance from his or her clients.

distance receptor Any receptor or receptor system that responds to stimuli arising some distance from the body. The eye, ear and nose are examples. Also called *tele*[o]-*receptor*.

distance vision ➤ **vision, distance**.

distance zones Areas of ➤ **personal space**, specifically zones within which different levels of intimacy are acceptable. There are, of course, many ways to taxonomize such zones; the following four are commonly specified: (a) intimate – out to about 18 inches (approximately 45 cm) from the body; (b) personal – from the boundary of intimate out to about 4 feet (1·2 m); (c) social – from 4 to 12 feet (1·2 to 3·6 m); and (d) public – beyond about 12 feet (3·6 m). ➤➤ **crowding**.

distinctive feature 1. Generally, an attribute ('feature') of some object or event that is critical in distinguishing that object or event from others (i.e. it is 'distinctive'). The term enjoys wide currency in psychology and related disciplines. In most psychological parlance it is used loosely to refer to attributes of persons, places, events or concepts that help to differentiate them from other persons, places, events or concepts; a distinctive feature of a triangle is that it has three sides. **2.** In phonetics, an aspect of a phoneme that distinguishes it from another. Here the features are always presented as binary pairs, i.e. each phoneme either possesses a feature (usually noted as +) or it doesn't (−). For example, *voicing* is a distinctive feature that distinguishes between the phonemes /s/ and /z/ as in *sue* and *zoo* where in *sue* the /s/ is ' − voice' and in *zoo* the /z/ is ' + voice.' **3.** In the study of semantics attempts have been made to discover features which would permit the objective defining of words and concepts. For details on these efforts ➤ **feature model**, **semantic feature**.

distorted room ➤ **Ames room**.

distortion 1. Generally, any twisting or contorting that alters the shape of something so that it no longer faithfully represents the object. Thus intended, the term is used: **2.** In optics and perception for alterations in images produced by the characteristics of lenses. **3.** In studies of memory for modifications in the information stored so that recall data display systematic errors. **4.** In psychoanalysis as a defense mechanism that functions to alter or 'disguise' dream content that would be unacceptable in nondistorted form.

distractibility 1. Quite literally, capable of being distracted (easily). The term is used commonly of children, who are easily 'seduced' by another task or even another thought away from the one at hand. **2.** In a clinical sense it refers to a pathological condition of mental functioning in which the person affected is cognitively so labile that attention is diverted by the most minimal stimulus, internal or external. It is observed in many anxiety disorders, in manic states and in schizophrenia.

distractor 1. Any event or stimulus which diverts attention. In studies of human memory distractors are frequently used in the exploration of *short-term memory*. The typical distractor technique consists of giving the subject a stimulus to commit to memory but then introducing another task that commandeers the subject's attention and interferes with rehearsal and/or coding of the stimulus. **2.** A 'filler' item on a test; an item which is irrelevant to the things actually being tested. Such distractors help keep the test-wise subject from figuring out the focus and purpose of the test.

distractor technique ➤ **distractor**.

distress–relief quotient (or **ratio**) A ratio of the number of verbal indicators of distress to the number of verbal indicators of relief in the statements of a client in psychotherapy. Occasionally used as a 'quick and dirty' method for assessing the amount of progress (or lack thereof).

distributed practice ➤ **practice, distributed**.

distribution Any systematic presentation of scores, data, etc. in such a way that the frequency or probability with which any one score or category of scores occurs is given. Distributions may be theoretical and given by formal mathematical expressions or they may be empirical and simply report the observed data. The following entries describe the distributions most often encountered in psychological research.

distribution, Bernoulli ➤ **binomial** *distribution**.

distribution, binomial The theoretically expected probability distribution when random samples of size N are taken from a (Bernoulli) population containing exactly two categories or classes; e.g., coin tosses, gender. For example, the distribution of the number of heads in some number of coin flips is the binomial distribution. As the sample size becomes large the binomial approximates the normal distribution. Also called a *Bernoulli distribution*.

distribution, chi-square (χ^2) The distribution of the random variable χ^2. If random samples of size 1 are taken from a normal distribution with mean μ and variance σ^2 then, $\chi^2 = (X_i - \mu)^2 / \sigma^2$, where X_i is the sampled score. If the sample size is increased arbitrarily to N then, $\chi^2 = \Sigma N_i = 1 \ (X^i - \mu)^2 / \sigma^2$. As N increases the χ^2 distribution approaches the normal distribution. ➤ **chi-square** for how the distribution is used as the basis for statistical tests.

distribution, cumulative frequency Any listing of scores, observations or data according to ordered classes in which the total number of entries in each class contains all those cases falling in lower classes. The last class thus includes all of the data from the distribution. ➤ **cumulative curve**.

distribution, F The theoretical probability distribution of the random variable, F. If random samples of size N are drawn independently from a normal population each will generate a chi-square distribution with degrees of freedom = N. The ratio of two such chi-squares each divided by its degrees of freedom (df) is called an F ratio and follows the F distribution; i.e. $F = (\chi_1^2 / df_1) / (\chi_2^2 / df_2)$. The F distribution forms the mathematical base for the *analysis of variance* and is of extreme importance in statistical testing and inferential statistics.

distribution-free A term used to refer to a class of statistical operations that makes no assumptions about the theoretical distribution that may underlie the sample data. ➤ **nonparametric statistics**.

distribution, frequency Any distribution based on a listing of the frequency of occurrence of the scores according to classes or categories. Thus, each set of classes is paired with a number that represents its observed frequency. Regardless of the method of presentation (bar graph, frequency polygon, frequency curve, etc.) any such display is called a frequency distribution. Compare with ➤ **probability distribution**.

distribution, grouped frequency Similar to frequency distribution but the scores are classified according to intervals or groups of categories rather than to each possible measurement category. Usually used when either the frequencies are relatively low in individual categories or the number of possible categories is unmanageably large.

distribution, hypergeometric A variation of the binomial and multinomial distributions. Whereas these distributions assume either random sampling *with* replacement or infinitely large populations, the hypergeometric assumes sampling from a finite sample *without* replacement.

distribution, multinomial A generalization of the binomial distribution. It is the theoretically expected probability distribution when the random samples are taken from a population containing more than two categories or classes. Because of the ponderous calculations required whenever the number of classes or categories is large, it is not used very often.

distribution, normal The theoretically expected probability distribution when the samples are drawn from an infinite population in which all events are equally likely to occur. The distribution is continuous for all values from $-\infty$ to $+\infty$; it is symmetrical and unimodal with mean, median and mode at the same value. Some warnings in dealing with the normal distribution: (a) It is specified only by its mathematical rule, it really never exists in nature but is only approximated (this is, of course, true for most of the other distributions as well, but the normal has a tendency to be 'reified' more than, say, the hypergeometric). (b) Although the normal distribution has the familiar bellshaped form, not every bell-shaped curve is a

normal distribution. (c) Finally, the normal distribution is critically important in statistical theory and statistical testing since many statistical tests, in order to be appropriately used, assume that the data approximate normality – that is, it is assumed that the population from which they were drawn was a normal population. ➤➤ **central limit theorem, parametric statistics**.

distribution, Pascal A probability distribution of the number of attempts necessary to obtain a particular number of successes; e.g., the number of flips of a coin it would take to get a total of, say, 10 heads.

distribution, Poisson A special, limited case of the binomial distribution. In particular, it is the theoretically expected distribution when the number of cases sampled is quite large but drawn from a relatively small population that is characterized by one of the two categories being relatively rare.

distribution, probability Similar to frequency distribution except that instead of pairing each class or category with the frequency with which it occurred it is paired with its probability of occurrence. Thus, while the sum of the frequencies in a frequency distribution must be N (or the total number of scores), the sum of the probabilities in a probability distribution must total 1·00.

distribution, ranked Any distribution of scores arranged according to ranks.

distribution, sampling Any distribution that results from taking samples of specified size from a population. See the discussions under ➤ **sample, sampling** and related terms.

distribution, *t* The theoretical distribution of the random variable *t*. If random samples of size N are drawn from a normal population with mean μ, then $t = (\overline{X} - \mu)/(s/\sqrt{N-1})$, where $\overline{X}$ is the sample mean and s is the sample standard deviation. Thus, t is based on the ratio of a statistic to its standard error. The distribution of t approximates the normal with increasing *N*. The various *t*-tests based on the distribution allow one to estimate the level of significance of a statistic of certain size obtained from a sample of given size. As such they are extremely important statistical tools in evaluating the degree to which a sample differs from a theoretical underlying distribution, or the degree to which two samples differ from each other. Also called *Student's distribution*.

distribution, uniform A distribution in which all classes have the same frequency or the same probability. Often called a *rectangular distribution* since the graph of such a distribution is a rectangle.

distributive analysis and synthesis The form of psychotherapy developed by Adolf Meyer. It involves a detailed examination of the client's past life (analysis) with the aim of forming a positive, constructive synthesis. The therapy is a strongly directive one with the therapist giving extensive guidance and direction.

disulfiram A drug used for treatment of alcoholism. It causes acetaldehyde, a breakdown product of alcohol, to accumulate in the blood resulting in a variety of most unpleasant experiences including dizziness, nausea, vomiting, sweating and a throbbing headache. Its use is based on principles of conditioning that predict that the patient will associate the unpleasant experience with the alcohol (the drug has no effect if alcohol is not present) and develop an aversion to it (see here ➤ **toxicosis** for the model conditioning phenomenon). Its success rate in treating alcoholism is not high and one likely reason for the failure is that the alcohol is not the unusual or novel stimulus that the conditioned aversion response requires for effective learning.

disuse, law (or **principle**) **of** One of E. L. Thorndike's original laws of conditioning. It is a generalization that states that a learned association will become weakened by disuse.

disutility Basically, the opposite of *utility*, but with a wrinkle. In economics, game theory, choice behavior, etc. one can speak about the ➤ **utility** (especially 3) of an outcome fairly straightforwardly. However, it is not clear that disutility of a negative outcome will have the same subjective value (quantitatively speaking) as the equivalent positive outcome. That is, it is not clear that the disutility of losing $100 is subjectively as 'bad' as the utility of winning $100 is subjectively 'good.'

diuresis Secretion and passage of unusually large volume of urine.

diuretic Any substance that causes increased secretion and passage of urine.

diurnal (cycle) *Diurnal* means pertaining to day or to the daylight hours; contrast with ➤ **nocturnal**. However, the fuller term, diurnal cycle, is used in a more general way that is essentially synonymous with *daily*. Thus, an expression such as 'changes in blood pressure follow a diurnal cycle' really refers to changes over the full 24-hour period. ➤➤ **circadian** which, properly, is the term for such cycles.

divagation Disorganized, incoherent speech.

divergence 1. Generally, the property of moving away from a central point or of lying in different directions. 2. In perception, the turning outward of the eyes as the point of focus is shifted away from the perceiver. It functions as a binocular cue for depth perception. 3. In neurophysiology, the branching and spreading out of the several processes of an individual neuron or the fibers of a neural pathway. Contrast with ➤ **convergence**.

divergent thinking ➤ **thinking, divergent**.

dizygotic (DZ) Pertaining to two zygotes. ➤ **dizygotic *twins**.

DL Abbreviation meaning *difference* (or *differential*) ➤ **threshold** (the L stands for Latin *limen* = threshold, originally introduced as the equivalent of the German *Schwelle*).

DMS ➤ **diacritical marking system**.

DNA ➤ **deoxyribonucleic acid**.

docile 1. Easily trainable, teachable. **2.** Tractable, manageable.

doctrine ➤ **dogma**.

dogma A transliteration of a Greek word meaning *that which seems good*. It is used for beliefs that are fixed and firmly held, based on authority and accepted independently of facts and other empirical support. The most frequent usage is theological but secular and quasi-scientific dogmas abound. The meaning of the term shades gently and often insidiously with that of *doctrine*. Strictly speaking, doctrine should be used for a teaching or a principle advocated and taught. The conceptual line usually put forward to distinguish between the two is, in principle, *empirical demonstration*. That is, doctrines are usually held to be authoritative statements promulgated with promissory notes that evidence will be forthcoming; dogmas are usually presented as true by fiat and no evidentiary basis for them is sought. Doctrine, which has more or less neutral connotations, is frequently used of extensive theoretical positions that go beyond the available data and invite support on the basis of the still-uncashed promissory note; e.g., Freudian doctrine, behaviorist doctrine, etc. Dogma has, in science, clear negative connotations suggesting that a position is held not merely independently of data but actually in defiance of incompatible facts. In the give and take of doing science, one's opponent's doctrines are dogmas.

dolichocephalic Having a long, narrow head. ➤ **cephalic index**.

dolor Pain; usually physical, occasionally psychic.

dolorology The study of the causes and treatment of pain.

domal sampling ➤ **sampling, domal**.

dominance 1. From the Latin, meaning *ruling*. Hence, in the broadest sense, it refers to a relationship in which any 'thing' is in a position of 'control' over another. 'Thing' here is meant to be taken loosely, as the specialized usages below show, and 'control' may be taken to mean anything from physical control to temporal precedence, relative importance or, simply, preference. **2.** In genetics, the quality through which one *allele* of a pair suppresses the expression of the other and thereby prevails in the *phenotype*. **3.** In ethology, a tendency to exert control over the behavior of other members of a group of conspecifics. See here ➤ **dominance** *hierarchy. **4.** By extension of 3, a personality trait characterized by a tendency to seek and maintain control over other people. See here ➤ **ascendance**. **5.** Preference of use. Generally used in this sense of bilateral anatomical structures in which one side is preferred in normal functioning. ➤ **eye** *dominance, **lateral** *dominance, **handedness**. **6.** Control of one structure or organ by another. This meaning is carried in phrases like *cortical dominance* or *cerebral dominance*. Note that a certain ambiguity exists here; the dominance may be of the brain over other parts of the central nervous system or it may be of one part of the brain over other parts. See here the discussion under ➤ **cerebral dominance**. **7.** ➤ **hemispheric** *dominance. See that term and ➤ **cerebral** *dominance for further discussion on usage. adj., *dominant*.

dominance, cerebral The term refers to the fact that one cerebral hemisphere tends to be dominant in the control of bodily movement and speech. Some loose but defensible generalizations can be made here: In bodily movement the dominant hemisphere is contralateral, that is, for lefthanded individuals the right hemisphere is dominant and vice versa. See here ➤ **handedness** for more detail. In control over speech and language, of those who are righthanded the vast majority are left-hemisphere dominant; of those who are lefthanded a majority, although a considerably smaller one, are also left-hemisphere dominant. Note that the term *cerebral dominance* carries a subtle confusion in that it is easily mistaken to mean dominance of the cerebrum over something else. To avoid this error many authors use other terms such as *hemispheric dominance*, which is literally more accurate anyway; ➤ **laterality**, which covers the full range of effects of brain–body 'sidedness' nicely; or simply ➤ **dominance** (see, especially, meanings 5, 6 and 7).

dominance, cortical See the discussions under ➤ **dominance** (especially 5, 6 and 7) and ➤ **cerebral *dominance**.

dominance, eye The tendency for one eye to be used in focusing on an object. The dominant eye then becomes the one used. In general, when one is scanning a visual field, as in reading, one eye dominates and 'leads' the other from focal point to focal point. Also called the *leading eye*.

dominance, hemispheric See the discussion under ➤ **cerebral *dominance**. In the literature the term cerebral dominance is more often encountered than hemispherical dominance, although the latter is more precise.

dominance hierarchy ➤ **hierarchy, dominance**.

dominance, mixed (cerebral) The contemporary 'received view' on hemispheric functioning is that each cerebral hemisphere plays a dominant role in particular cognitive and sensory/motor functions (➤ **laterality** for explication). The phrase 'mixed dominance' is used for cases where there are reasons to suspect that the 'normal' clear distribution of lateral functioning is not present and one hemisphere does not consistently lead the other in control over particular behaviors. It is suspected by many authorities that mixed dominance is responsible for a variety of dysfunctions, particularly in language and related cognitive functions like reading.

dominance need H. Murray's term for the need to control others.

dominant Generally, displaying the characteristic of ➤ **dominance** in any of the meanings of that term. Note, however, that dominant may have any of four different antonyms depending on the sense of dominance that is intended. To wit:

recessive for sense 2, submissive for 3 and 4, nonpreferred for 5 and nondominant for 6 and 7.

dominant trait ➤ **dominance**.

dominator A retinal ganglion cell that responds over the entire visible spectrum. Such cells do so in a nonuniform fashion and display peak sensitivity at particular wavelengths. Compare with ➤ **modulator**.

Donders' method ➤ **subtraction method**.

Don Juanism ➤ **satyriasis**.

door-in-the-face technique A device for obtaining compliance in which the individual initially requests something very large, so large that it will surely be denied, and then de-escalates to a more modest request, which was the one originally desired. Compare with the ➤ **foot-in-the-door technique**.

dopamine (DA) One of the *catecholamines* that functions as a neurotransmitter. Dopamine appears to function as an inhibitor and has been implicated as important in motor control systems, limbic activity and schizophrenia (➤ **dopamine hypothesis**).

dopamine hypothesis The hypothesis that schizophrenia is associated with 'excessive activity' of the dopaminergic neurons of the limbic system. The 'excessive activity' could, in principle, result from any number of sources, increased production of dopamine and inhibition of re-uptake of it being the most likely.

dopaminergic Characterizing or pertaining to pathways, fibers or neurons in which dopamine is a neurotransmitter.

Doppler shift (or **effect**) A shift in hue or pitch as the source of the stimulation moves relative to the observer. Approaching sources produce increases in frequency (hue shifts toward the blue, pitch toward higher tone); receding sources produce the reverse. The effect is most easily detected with moving sound sources.

dorsal From the Latin, meaning *to the back* or *to the rear*. Used as a directional term in physiology and anatomy. Contrast with ➤ **ventral**.

dorsal column medial lemniscal system One of two main ascending neural systems for somatic sensation (the ➤ **anterolateral system** is the other). The dorsal columns are composed of axons from dorsal-root ganglion cells which ascend ipsilaterally to the medulla, cross over and ascend as the medial lemniscus (see here ➤ **lemniscal system**) to the thalamus. It carries information about touch, vibration and limb position.

dorsal root ➤ **spinal root**.

dorsal tegmental bundle A noradrenergic system the cell bodies of which are in the locus coeruleus of the pons in the brainstem and the fibers of which project to the cerebral cortex, hippocampus, thalamus, cerebellar cortex and medulla.

dorsolateral column A fiber bundle in the *spinal cord* involved in opiate-induced ➤ **analgesia**.

dorsolateral nucleus A thalamic nucleus that projects to the cingulate gyrus. Also called the *lateral dorsal nucleus*.

dorsolateral pathway A neural pathway that runs from the brain stem to the spinal cord and is involved in the control of the muscles used in movement of the forelimbs.

dorsomedial nucleus A thalamic nucleus that receives input from the limbic system and other thalamic nuclei and projects to the prefrontal cortex. Also called the *medial dorsal nucleus*.

dosage 1. The amount of a medicine or other preparation prescribed to be given. 2. The administration of medicine in doses.

dose 1 n. The amount of a medicine or other preparation to be taken at one time. 2 vb. To administer in doses.

double-alternation problem An experimental procedure that requires the subject to make the sequence of responses A–A–B–B.

double approach–avoidance conflict ➤ **conflict, double approach–avoidance**.

double bind A term coined by Gregory Bateson to characterize the situation faced by a person who is receiving contradictory messages from another, powerful person. The classic example, and the one which Bateson once felt may underlie autism and/or schizophrenia, is that of the child who is confronted with a parent who has difficulty with close affectionate relationships but cannot admit to such feelings. The parent communicates withdrawal and coldness when the child approaches, but then reaches out toward the child with simulated love when he or she pulls back from the coldness. The child is thus caught in a 'double bind'; no course of action can possibly prove satisfactory and all assumptions about what he or she is supposed to do will be disconfirmed.

double-blind An experimental procedure in which neither the subject nor the person administering the experimental procedures knows what are considered to be the crucial aspects of the experiment. These procedures are commonly used to guard against the effects of ➤ **experimenter bias**, ➤ **demand characteristics** and ➤ **placebo** effects. Double-blind procedures are used when it is feared that knowledge of what is expected of the subject will influence the subject's performance or when knowledge of what the experiment is about will influence the experimenter's interpretation of what the subject is doing. This kind of control is common in drug studies where neither the subject nor the person administering the preparation knows whether it is a drug or a placebo. The effects of the drug can then be separated from any preconceptions about what the drug is or is not supposed to do.

double-blind crossover A variation on the ➤ **double-blind** technique in which, as an added control, the conditions are crossed in the middle of the experiment. For example, in the course of a study of the effects of a drug those subjects receiving the drug are switched over and administered the placebo and vice versa. In the properly designed study, neither the subjects nor the person administering the drugs know who is in each group, or when (or even whether) the crossover occurred.

double-entry table A table in which the scores are entered by column and row simultaneously; e.g., a *scatter diagram*.

double vibration (dv) An obsolete term for *cycle*. See discussion under ➤ **vibration**.

double vision ➤ **diplopia**.

'downers' Street slang for any drug that has relaxing, anti-anxiety effects. Generally included are the ➤ **hypnotics**, ➤ **minor *tranquilizers** and ➤ **sedatives**.

Down syndrome A congenital condition characterized by a flat skull, stubby fingers, an unusual pattern of skin folds on the palms of the hands and the soles of the feet, epicanthic folds on the eyelids, a fissured tongue and often severe mental deficiency. The disorder is named for the British physician J. Langdon Down, who first described it in 1866. It is the single most common clinical condition with mental retardation as primary symptom and occurs in approximately 1 out of every 700 births. However, the mother's age is a critical factor; in mothers under 30 its incidence is but 1 per 1,000, in mothers over 45 it is as high as 1 per 40. There are actually several variations of the syndrome. By far the most common (over 90% of the cases) are those in which the infant has an extra 21st chromosome or a part of it, making a total of 47 instead of the normal 46. For this reason, the name *trisomy 21* is often used here. This condition is not a truly inherited disorder but rather is due to faulty cell division. In the *mosaicistic* form, which is relatively rare (accounting for less than 2% of the cases), some cells have the extra 21st chromosome but some do not, indicating that the error occurred some time after fertilization. In the *translocation* form the extra 21st chromosome is found attached to another chromosome, usually the 15th. Down syndrome is still occasion-

ally referred to as *mongolism* (which was Down's term for it – he thought that development of the fetus had been arrested at the 'Mongolian' level of civilization and regarded the epicanthic folds as evidence). This term has, fortunately, dropped out of use, although it may still be seen in older texts. Note that in the UK the syndrome is often called *Down's syndrome*.

dowsing The hypothesized location of underground water using two wires, a forked twig, a branch or other 'divining rod.' There is precious little (if any) evidence for this alleged skill; ➤ **parapsychology**.

DQ ➤ **developmental quotient**.

drama therapy ➤ **psychodrama**.

dream A lot of people have wrestled with this one; let's define it simply as 'imagery during sleep.' Dreaming appears to occur in many organisms and is intimately related to rapid-eye-movement (or REM) sleep.

dream analysis A technique originally used in psychoanalysis whereby the contents of dreams are analyzed for underlying or disguised motivations, symbolic meanings or evidence of symbolic representations. In typical dream analysis the individual relates a dream and then free associates about it with the aim of deriving insight into underlying dynamics. Freud, quoting the old proverb, 'pigs dream of acorns and geese dream of maize,' assumed that dreams were expressions of wish-fulfillment. However, according to the standard theory, since most wishes had been repressed, the deep meaning of dreams (➤ **dream content**) had to be interpreted through a veil of censorship, disguise and symbolism. ➤➤ **dream symbolism**.

dream anxiety disorder A ➤ **sleep disorder** marked by repeated waking from sleep with detailed recall of frightening dreams. The dreams are marked by their vividness and often include threats to survival and security. Also known as *nightmare disorder*. Distinguish from ➤ **sleep terror disorder**.

dream content According to psychoanalytic theory the contents of a dream are of two types: (a) *manifest* – that known to the dreamer, the 'surface' of the dream; and (b) *latent* – the deep, hidden aspects that presumably need to be interpreted before their meanings can be made clear. ➤ latent and manifest *content.

dream determinant ➤ determinant, dream.

dream ego Jung's term for a separate component of the ego that he felt was responsible for dreaming.

dream instigator ➤ day residue.

dream interpretation ➤ dream analysis.

dream-series method A technique for studying dreams. The individual keeps a dream diary (recording dreams upon awakening) until some 50 or more have been accumulated. The full set is then examined for patterns, recurring themes, etc.

dream symbolism Within the various psychoanalytic approaches, the disguised expressions in dreams wherein one thing is a 'stand-in' or a symbol for something else. The usual interpretation is that the symbols are necessary for deeply repressed wishes to escape censorship. There are 'standard' interpretations for some commonly occurring dream symbols – towers, pencils, pistons and other entities which share functional, physical or linguistic similarities are almost universally taken as phallic symbols, likewise boxes, doorways and tunnels as vaginal. However, it is misleading to generalize blindly the symbolic elements of dreams. If dream analysis is to be of value it needs to be carried out with a sensitivity to the dreamer's own life and to the manner in which the free-associations to the dream unfold. 'Pop psychology' books on dream symbolism and meaning should be avoided.

dream-work Freud's term for the processes through which the latent content of a dream is transformed into the manifest content.

drh Abbreviation for *differential reinforcement of high rate*. For details, ➤ schedules of *reinforcement.

drive A term with a plethora of uses, some quite precise, others very loose. Probably the clearest usage, and the one from which all other uses derive, is one which treats a drive as a motivational state produced by (a) deprivation of a needed substance such as food, a drug, a hormone, etc. or (b) presence of a noxious stimulus such as a loud noise, excessive cold or heat, a painful stimulus, etc. Note that the term, in this sense, refers to a hypothetical state of the organism and must be inferred either from controlled operations (deliberately depriving the subject of a needed substance) or from observations of the behavior exhibited (e.g., choosing food over sex – or vice versa). Properly, one should differentiate between drive and ➤ need in that need is used to describe states of deprivation and does not necessarily imply a motivational state. The standard view here is to treat need states as producing drive states which motivate behavior. Complications are, to be sure, lurking behind this conceptualization; ➤ incentive for one of them.

drive, acquired (or **secondary**) Any drive whose motivating properties are learned, it is assumed through association with a primary *drive. The classic example is the human drive for money.

drive-arousal stimulus Any stimulus or combination of stimuli which serves to activate a dormant drive state. They may be either internal (think about a juicy, charcoal-broiled steak) or external (the smell of food).

drive, nonregulatory Any ➤ drive (such as sex) that serves functions other than those of maintaining consistent bodily states necessary for survival of an individual organism. Compare with ➤ regulatory *drive.

drive, primary Any drive that arises from an intrinsic physiological characteristic of an organism. There are primary drives that are universal, such as food, water,

227

sex, the avoidance of pain, temperature balance, etc.; there are others that are clearly species-specific such as nest-building, imprinting, etc.

drive reduction   This phrase refers to any event that reduces a drive. The term really only carries meaning within the variety of learning theory championed by Clark Hull, where it relates to the ➤ **drive-reduction hypothesis**.

drive-reduction hypothesis   A general principle that maintains that the goal of all motivated behavior is the reduction or alleviation of a drive state. As used first by E. L. Thorndike and more importantly by Clark L. Hull, it became the theoretical mechanism through which reinforcement operated. That is, any event which served to reduce a drive state was assumed to reinforce (or increase the likelihood of) the response that preceded it. Contrast this usage with ➤ **contiguity theory**. For more on this general issue, ➤ **reinforcement**.

drive, regulatory   Any ➤ **drive** (such as hunger or thirst) that functions so that the organism seeks out substances that serve to maintain consistent bodily states necessary for survival. Compare with ➤ **nonregulatory *drive**.

drive specificity   ➤ **drive stimuli**.

drive stimuli (S_D)   The hypothesized efferent neural impulses resulting from a drive state. In Hull's later theory these were the stimuli the reduction of which was assumed to regulate reinforcement. Note that S_D was also assumed to display *drive specificity*, so that a drive stimulus was associated with the particular set of responses that reduced it.

drl   Abbreviation for *differential reinforcement of low rate*. For details, ➤ **schedules of *reinforcement**.

dro   Abbreviation for *differential reinforcement of other behaviour*. For details, ➤ **schedules of *reinforcement**.

drp   Abbreviation for *differential reinforcement of paced responses*. For details, ➤ **schedules of *reinforcement**.

drug abuse   Improper use of drugs. The usual connotation is that of excessive, irresponsible and self-damaging use of psychoactive and/or addictive drugs. ➤ **substance abuse**.

drug addiction   ➤ **drug *dependence**.

drug antagonism   ➤ **antagonism, drug**.

drug dependence   ➤ **dependence, drug**.

drug-dispositional tolerance   ➤ **tolerance, drug-dispositional**.

drug holiday   A period of time during which a drug is discontinued. Often used as a means of evaluating baseline behavior to determine the therapeutic effects the drug is having and as a procedure to assess side effects.

drug-induced Parkinsonism   ➤ **Parkinsonism, drug-induced**.

drug interaction   The effects of two (or more) drugs taken together, when their combined effects are different from what would be produced by only one of them taken alone. The classic example is that of alcohol and a sedative where the interaction produces central nervous depression far greater than either drug alone would yield. For more details ➤ **drug *antagonism**.

drug tolerance   ➤ **tolerance, drug**.

D sleep   ➤ **sleep, D**.

DSM   Abbreviation for the ➤ **Diagnostic and Statistical Manual**. The DSM, which is the diagnostic guidebook of the American Psychiatric Association, has been revised several times; the current version is *DSM-IV*, which appeared in 1994.

d.t.'s   ➤ **delirium tremens**.

d-tubocurarine   A drug the active ingredient of which is ➤ **curare**.

dual-code hypothesis   The generalization proposed by A. Paivio that human memory is composed of two coding systems, one based on a visual-imagery process and one on a verbal-coding process.

dualism   Any of a number of philosophical positions which admit of two separate states of nature or two sets of fundamental principles in the universe. As originally promulgated by Plato, the distinction was between mind and matter. In contemporary debates the issue is usually divided along lines of mind and body. There can be a strong dualistic position whereby understanding the operation of one sphere has no bearing at all on an understanding of the other, or a softer form of dualism in which some distinctions between, say, mental and physical phenomena are accepted, but without assuming that they are metaphysically different in any fundamental way. The classic forms of dualism are *interactive*, when mind and body are assumed to be separate but interacting, and *parallel*, when mind and body are seen as different manifestations of a complex organism and assumed to 'travel on separate but parallel tracks.' Descartes is usually cited as the strongest proponent of interactive dualism; the early structuralists like Titchener were vigorous defenders of the parallel position, which they often referred to as *psychophysical* dualism. ➤ mind-body problem and ➤ monism.

dual personality ➤ multiple personality.

dual threshold ➤ threshold, dual.

ductless gland ➤ gland.

dull normal An obsolescent category for individuals whose intelligence is below average but not to the point where they are handicapped with regard to typical daily functions. Generally defined as an IQ between 80 and 89. See the discussion under ➤ mental retardation for a contemporary terminology.

dumb Mute, unable to speak.

dummy Synonym of ➤ placebo; used chiefly in Britain.

dummy variable A dichotomous variable that is coded '1' to indicate presence of an attribute and '0' to indicate absence.

Duncan Multiple-Range Test A ➤ post hoc test used after an ➤ analysis of variance has been run. It enables one to test which of the several mean differences are significant.

duplexity (or **duplicity**) **theory** The theory, now universally accepted as correct, which posits that there are two separate receptor mechanisms in the retina: the *cones*, which are color-sensitive and used in high illumination (➤ photopic vision), and the *rods*, which are achromatic and used in low illumination (➤ scotopic vision).

dura mater Lit., *hard mother*. The relatively tough, outermost one of the three meninges covering the spinal cord and brain.

durance H. Murray's term for an identifiable period of time during which a specific activity in one's life is carried out.

duration Generally used with standard dictionary meaning. The early introspectionists, however, spoke of it as a subjective, unanalyzable attribute of a sensation which was regarded as the basis for the experience of the passage of time.

Durham rule A legal principle regarding the use of the ➤ insanity defense. It states that 'an accused is not criminally responsible if his unlawful act was the product of mental disease or mental defect.' It was put forward in 1954 in the USA but is no longer accepted by the courts. ➤ insanity defense.

d.v. Abbreviation for *double vibration*. ➤ vibration for discussion.

dyadic ➤ diadic.

dyad, social ➤ social *diad.

dynamic 1. Generally, characteristic of or relating to things that are in flux or are changeable. 2. More specifically, a label for systems of psychology that emphasize motivation (R. S. Woodworth always referred to his form of functionalism as *dynamic* psychology), those that focus on unconscious processes (Freud and Jung are both considered proponents of a dynamic approach) and those that emphasize complex fields of psychological force

(Lewin's field theory is a good example). Contrast with ➤ **static** and ➤ **structural**. See also the discussion under ➤ **dynamic system**.

dynamic equilibrium Generally, the state of a dynamic system in which, although shifting and changing, the overall pattern of forces or energy is in a stable, organized configuration.

dynamic psychology A general label used for any number of theoretical systems. ➤ **dynamic** (2).

dynamic system A term applicable to any system in which the several elements are all interwoven or interrelated so that changes in one sector of the system have systematic effects on the rest of the system.

dynamic unconscious ➤ **unconscious** (3(a), 3(b)).

dynamism 1. A mechanism of adjustment. Generally used with the connotation that it represents a rather stable manner of behaving, the primary function of which is to fulfill drives and motives and to protect oneself from stress and discomfort. **2.** By extension, H. S. Sullivan used the term to cover a variety of interpersonal relations that function in this manner.

dynamometer Any instrument for measuring strength of muscular response, usually hand-grip.

dyne A unit of force defined as that needed to accelerate 1 gram of matter 1 centimeter per second.

dynorphins ➤ **endogenous opiates**.

dys- A prefix meaning *faulty*, *ill*, *bad*, *difficult*, etc. There are literally scores of technical terms using this prefix and doubtless more coined every day. It is generally used to indicate (a) a particular function that has failed to develop normally (e.g., *dyslexia*) or (b) a function that has been disrupted (e.g., *dysmenorrhea*). Frequently the meaning of the term can be derived from the root word and to save space such terms are not included here;

the less obvious ones follow. Occasional variant, ➤ **dis-**.

dysacousia 1. Inordinate discomfort caused by loud noises. **2.** Difficulty in hearing. The former is the usual meaning.

dysarthria A general term for defective speaking, impaired articulatory ability. Typically used for cases resulting from peripheral motor or muscular defects; compare with ➤ **anarthria**.

dysbasia Difficulty in walking; a form of ➤ **ataxia**.

dysbulia 1. Lit., weakness of will. **2.** Impaired thinking, inability to fix attention on something.

dyscalculia A learning disability in which a child of normal or above normal intelligence experiences inordinate difficulty in learning standard arithmetic. Distinguish from ➤ **acalculia**. ➤➤ **developmental *arithmetic disorder**.

dyschiria Inability to tell which side of one's body has been touched.

dyschromatopsia A general term for any deficiency in color vision. There are several variants here: *dyschromia*, *dyschromopsia*, *dyschromacy*.

dyschronism Generally, disturbed time sense, particularly that caused by flight across 5 to 10 time zones, which maximally disrupts biological rhythms. ➤➤ **desynchronism**.

dysdiadochkinesia Difficulty in performing rapid alternating movements as with the fingers or hands. It is a good example of a neurological ➤ **soft sign**. When the ability is completely absent it is called *adiadochkinesia*.

dyseidetic Characterizing the condition of having poor visual imagery.

dysergasia Lit., inability to work (function) properly. Used in psychology for a disorder characterized by hallucinations, irrational fears, disorientation, dream states and the like brought on by a cerebral nutritional deficit; occasionally caused by a toxic condition like alcohol intoxication.

dysesthesia Generally, inappropriate sensitivity, particularly to touch and pain. The term is used as a cover term for any increased or decreased sensitivity as well as for other more specific syndromes (e.g., *formication*).

dysfunction Broadly, generally and ubiquitously, any disruption in normal functioning.

dysgenic 1. Characterizing abnormal development due to genetic factors. 2. Characterizing those genetic factors leading to abnormal development.

dysgeusia A condition characterized by a disruption of the sense of taste. In serious cases eating the most mundane foods can be an extraordinarily unpleasant experience.

dysgnosia A cover term for any impairment of intellectual functioning.

dysgraphia Inability to write properly or to express oneself through writing. The term is reserved for cases brought about through brain damage.

dyshomophilia A psychosexual disorder in which the sufferer is severely distressed and rendered highly anxious by his or her sexually arousing fantasies about homosexuality. The individual's sexual preferences are not an issue here; the condition can emerge whether the person affected is exclusively homosexual or heterosexual or, indeed, even completely asexual. Compare with and distinguish from ➤ **egodystonic *homosexuality**.

dyskinesia Defects in voluntary movement.

dyslalia Impaired speech due either to psychological (functional) causes or to defects in the peripheral speech organs. When the cause is brain damage ➤ **aphasia** is the proper term.

dyslexia Basically, a failure to learn to read. However, there is a distinct lack of consensus among educators, psychologists and physicians in exactly how to characterize reading failures, particularly in terms of the etiology of the condition, the cognitive and perceptual elements that must underlie it, and precisely how poor one's reading ability should be in order to be classified as a case of dyslexia. Typically, it is regarded as a ➤ **learning disability** and the term is reserved for children who are significantly behind grade level in reading and when there is no evidence of any generally debilitating disorder like mental retardation, major brain injury, severe emotional problems or cultural factors such as coming from a home where the language spoken is not the one used in the larger community. Compare with ➤ **acquired *dyslexia**. Synonymous terms include *developmental reading disorder* and *developmental dyslexia*. Specialized forms of the disorder are listed below. Distinguish from ➤ **alexia**.

dyslexia, acquired A cover term for any ➤ **dyslexia** in an individual who previously read normally.

dyslexia, direct A form of ➤ **acquired *dyslexia** in which the patient can read words aloud but not understand them.

dyslexia, phonological A form of ➤ **acquired *dyslexia** marked by difficulties in learning to sound words out. Phonological dyslexics can learn to read using the ➤ **whole-word method** but have difficulties with new words or names they have not encountered before. Compare with ➤ **surface *dyslexia**.

dyslexia, surface A form of ➤ **acquired *dyslexia** marked by difficulties in recognizing and deriving the meanings from words. Surface dyslexics must sound out the words carefully in order to read them; hence, they have difficulties with irregularly spelled words. Compare with ➤ **phonological *dyslexia**.

dyslexia, word-form A variety of ➤ **acquired *dyslexia** that essentially combines the symptoms of both *surface* and *phono-*

logical dyslexia. Interestingly, such individuals can sometimes still read by laboriously spelling out each word. Also called *spelling dyslexia.*

dyslogia A deficiency in the ability to express ideas verbally.

dysmenorrhea Painful menstruation. *Primary dysmenorrhea* is used of the condition when it appears with the *menarche* (first period), *secondary dysmenorrhea* when it develops later in life usually because of uterine or pelvic pathology.

dysmetria Inability to direct the range and force of voluntary movements. A symptom of some cerebellar lesions.

dysmetropsia Disturbance in the ability to visualize the size and shape of objects.

dysmnesia Generally, any impairment of memory.

dysmorphophobia ➤ **body dysmorphic disorder.**

dysorexia Generally, any disturbance in normal appetite; see, e.g., ➤ **anorexia**.

dysosmia Disruptions in the sense of smell.

dyspareunia A ➤ **sexual pain disorder** marked by recurrent or persistent genital pain before, during, or after sexual intercourse. The term is used for both men and women.

dysphagia An umbrella term for any abnormal eating pattern. Specific forms are ➤ **aphagia, bulimia, hyperphagia, pica**.

dysphasia Disruption of normal speech caused by brain lesion; synonym of ➤ **aphasia**, which is preferred.

dysphemia A speech defect caused by psychological factors.

dysphonetic sequencing disorder A learning disability characterized by phonetic confusions and misperceptions of phonetic sequences. It is generally viewed as a variety of ➤ **dyslexia**.

dysphonia **1.** A general term for any language dysfunction. **2.** A synonym for ➤ **aphasia**. Sense 2 here is not recommended, for etymologically the term does not carry the specific connotation of *aphasia*, namely that language functions once existed and then were lost through neurological damage. See here ➤ **developmental *language disorder**, which is preferred as a synonym for sense 1.

dysphonia, puberum The change in voice in males during puberty.

dysphoria Inappropriate affect, usually used in association with anxiety, restlessness, depression. ant., ➤ **euphoria** (1).

dysphrenia Obsolete term for any mental disorder.

dysplasia Any abnormal development of tissue; any abnormal growth.

dyspnea Difficulty in breathing. var., *dyspnoea.*

dyspraxia Difficulty in moving, painful movement.

dyssocial personality An obsolescent term for a personality disorder characterized by a seriously distorted sense of ethics and morality. Often the 'professional criminal' was so labeled because he might display honored values like loyalty and courage but not in socially desirable ways.

dyssomnia A general label for a group of sleep disorders where the primary disturbance is in the amount, quality, or timing of sleep. Dyssomnias are generally regarded as psychogenic in origin and due primarily to emotional disturbances, high levels of stress, anxiety, etc. Included are ➤ **insomnia**, ➤ **hypersomnia**, and ➤ **sleep-wake schedule disorder**. Compare with ➤ **parasomnia**.

dysspermia Difficult or painful ejaculation.

dysstasia Difficulty in standing upright.

dysthymia Generally, despondency, depression. ➤ **dysthymic disorder**.

dysthymic disorder A *mood disorder* characterized by a general depression, lack of interest in the normal, standard activities of living and a ubiquitous 'down in the dumps' feeling. Dysthymia is not meant to be used for cases of acute depression; the term is only used for these disruptions of normal affect when they last at least a year or two. Distinguish also from ➤ **major *depressive episode**. Also called *depressive neurosis*.

dystocia   Difficult labor.

dystonia   Impaired muscle tone.

dystonic movement   Slow twisting bodily

movement with interspersed periods of muscular tension.

dystrophy   A general term for any condition produced by faulty nutrition or a metabolic dysfunction.

dysuria   Painful or difficult urination.

DZ   Abbreviation for ➤ **dizygotic**.

DZA (or **DZa**)   Abbreviation for a set of dizygotic twins raised apart from each other.

E

E A multifunctional abbreviation used for: **1.** Experimenter. **2.** Experimental group. **3.** Energy. **4.** Error. **5.** Within the theory of learning of C. L. Hull it is found in a veritable 'alphabet soup' of symbols used to refer to various theoretical constructs. A few of the more commonly seen are: $_sE_R$ = excitatory potential; $_sE_R$ = reaction potential (from generalization); $_s\bar{E}_R$ = effective reaction potential. The interested reader is referred to any of the older (1950s) standard texts of learning theory for fuller explanation of these and others; they are rarely used in contemporary work in learning.

ear Most generally, the organ of hearing. Three anatomical divisions make up the full organ. The outer ear consists of the *pinna* (what is, in general parlance, called the 'ear') and the external auditory *meatus* (or canal) up to the *tympanic membrane* (or 'ear drum'). The middle ear contains the *ossicles*, the three bones which transmit vibrations of the tympanic membrane to the *oval window* on the *cochlea*. The middle ear is also connected to the *pharynx* via the *eustachian tube*, which serves to equalize air pressure. The inner ear consists of the cochlea and the *semicircular canals*. Within the cochlea are the receptor cells for audition.

ear drum ➤ tympanic membrane.

eating disorders A general term used to cover a variety of conditions characterized by serious disturbances in eating habits and appetitive behaviors. E.g., ➤ anorexia nervosa, bulimia nervosa, pica and rumination disorder of infancy.

Ebbinghaus curve The classic forgetting curve for nonsense material. It shows a sharp drop in recall immediately after learning, followed by a slow, gradual loss of material. It was discovered by the early German psychologist Hermann Ebbinghaus.

EBS ➤ electrical brain stimulation.

eccentric Lit., off-center. The term used occasionally to characterize persons whose peculiar behavior is accompanied by success.

eccentric projection A term used occasionally to characterize the experiencing of a locus of stimulation as 'out there' in the world rather than at the receptors stimulated. Vision and hearing are the clearest examples; one is conscious of the external scene (the *distal stimulus*) and not the actual events that activate the sense (the *proximal stimulus*).

ECG ➤ electrocardiogram.

echo- Combining form meaning *repetitive*.

echoic The auditory analog of ➤ iconic (see that term for discussion).

echoic behavior Skinner's term for imitations of verbalizations of others.

echoic memory ➤ memory, echoic.

echokinesis ➤ echopraxia.

echolalia The compulsive and apparently senseless repetition of a word or phrase just spoken by another person. Generally symptomatic of a functional disorder, although it is a frequent component of autism in which the sound repeated may be a nonsensical invention of the child and not necessarily one spoken by another. Also called *echophrasia*.

echolocation Lit., the location of objects in space by using the echoes of self-produced sounds. Many species use such information as cues, although in most it is a relatively unimportant process and provides only rough perceptions; a few (bats, dolphins) have evolved it to a rather precise degree.

echopathy A general term for any pathological mimicking of the speech, gestures, actions or mannerisms of others.

echophrasia ➤ **echolalia**.

echopraxia Pathological tendency to repeat the gestures made by others; occasionally seen in schizophrenia of the catatonic type. Also called *echokinesis*.

eclectic Generally, not following any one system but selecting and using whatever is considered best in all systems. In experimental and theoretical work, an eclectic approach tends to be rather loose and informal, no one theoretical position being regarded as universally applicable; if there is any allegiance it is to the attempt to coordinate and reconcile differences between competing theoretical positions in the search for harmony, for synthesis. In clinical psychology and psychiatry an eclectic therapist is one who will use whatever therapeutic procedures seem most applicable to the case. This may mean taking a psychoanalytic bent with one client but a more direct, behavioral approach with another.

In general, eclecticism is regarded as healthy, especially in fields like psychology which are still at too immature a level to expect that any one of its theories or procedures could be universally applicable. Eclecticism is usually put at one pole on a dimension that runs from the eclectic to the formal.

ecmnesia Loss of memory for recent materials while retaining memory for more remote events; ➤ **anterograde *amnesia**.

ecological Pertaining to ➤ **ecology**.

ecological fallacy A logical *fallacy* in which conclusions about individuals are drawn based on data from groups. For example, crime rates tend to be higher in neighborhoods with large numbers of the elderly, but it would be fallacious to conclude that the elderly are more likely to commit crimes.

ecological niche A position or function of an organism (or, more commonly, a species) in a particular environment.

ecological optics Basically, the notion of

➤ **ecological validity** applied to the study of visual perception. J. J. Gibson's theory of ➤ **direct perception** assumes such a process as central to vision.

ecological psychology A term used occasionally to refer to the approach to psychology that elaborates on J. J. Gibson's theory of ➤ **direct perception**.

ecological validity 1. A term originally coined by Egon Brunswik for the degree to which the distal and proximal stimuli co-vary. He conceived of the basic operation of perception as that of learning to estimate the true, physical (distal) stimulus on the basis of the varying proximal stimulus values that actually impinged on the receptor systems. The higher the ecological validity of a proximal cue for a distal stimulus property, the more likely it was to be learned and used. The term is also used with this meaning within the ➤ **direct perception** theory of J. J. Gibson. 2. Loosely, the validity that a principle discovered in a laboratory setting has outside of that setting, in the field, in the real world. 3. Somewhat more specifically, a form of ➤ **criterion-related *validity** based on the degree to which results can be generalized from group to group. Norms established using university students might have low ecological validity when applied to blue collar workers of the same age.

ecology 1. Broadly, the study of the relationship between organisms and their environments. The discipline is concerned with the complex interrelationships of the various plants and animals with each other and with the physical environment in which they live. There are several subdisciplines in the field, dealing with plant ecology, animal ecology and human ecology. 2. In K. Lewin's theory, the study of those psychological factors that contribute to a person's ➤ **life space**. The term also has a variety of specialized uses reflecting either of the two basic meanings that appear in combined forms; some of these follow and others can be found following ➤ **ecological**. Also note that some authors use the term *bionomics* as a general synonym.

ecology, behavioral A term used by some for the extension of the science of ecology into psychology. The focus is on the interaction (or, as the proponents of the approach prefer, the *transaction*) between the environment and the behaviors of the organisms in it. The orientation is strongly holistic and employs naturalistic observation as the primary research tool.

ecology, social The approach to the study of behavior that emphasizes the interactions between individuals and their environment.

ecology, urban A field of study drawing on the researches of various other disciplines such as biology, sociology, psychology and geography. It focuses on the investigation of urban environments as 'natural' ecological systems.

economic In some more technical psychoanalytic writing this term is used as roughly equivalent to or pertaining to energy. Hence, the so-called *economic concepts* are those pertaining to the origin, distribution, transfer and use of psychic energy or libido.

economy, principle of ➤ **principle of *parsimony**.

ecosphere Those portions of the natural environment that are habitable by life forms.

ecosystem A relatively restricted ecological unit.

ecphoria 1. The establishing of a memory trace. **2.** The activation of a previously established memory trace. The term is rare in either sense.

ECS ➤ **electroconvulsive shock**.

ecstatic state ➤ **religious *trance**.

ECT ➤ **electroconvulsive therapy**.

ect(o)- Combining form from the Greek meaning *outside, external*.

ectoderm The outer layer of embryonic

cellular structure that develops into the outer skin, the nervous system, the organs of special sense, the pineal gland and part of the pituitary.

ectogenous Characteristic of that which has its origins outside of the body, *exogenous*.

ectomorphy One of the three primary dimensions of body type (➤ **endomorphy** and ➤ **mesomorphy** being the others) in Sheldon's ➤ **constitutional theory**. An ectomorph is one whose physique is dominated by the embryonic ectodermal component, the outer skin and the nervous system. Hence, ectomorphic persons are thin with large skin surfaces relative to weight.

-ectomy Combining form meaning *removal*, specifically surgical removal.

ectopia Displacement or misposition, particularly of an organ or part thereof.

ectoplasm 1. The outermost layer of cell protoplasm. **2.** In ➤ **parapsychology**, a hypothesized psychic substance said to emanate from the body of a medium in a trance during a séance.

eczema General term for any of several forms of chronic dermatitis. While eczema is typically caused by irritating substances it is generally regarded as having a significant psychosomatic component.

edge Basically, a line in the visual field where there is a detectable difference in some aspect of the stimulus on one side of that line as compared with the other. Note that as the term is used, there is no actual, literal line; the line merely defines the boundary between the two adjacent areas of the visual field.

Edipus complex ➤ **Oedipus complex**.

EDR Abbreviation for *electrodermal response*; ➤ **galvanic skin response**.

educable mentally retarded (EMR) A label for a child who scores below the 'normal' range on a standard IQ test and although formally still classified as mentally retarded (see here ➤ **mental retardation**) can still profit from education and instruction. Contrast with ➤ **trainable mentally retarded** (TMR), which is used for those considered to be sufficiently below normal so as not to be able to profit from a standard education but who can be trained in a minimally demanding skill. Generally the IQ range for the EMR is 50–69; the TMR label is reserved for those scoring between 35 and 49. The EMR child is also classified as one with 'special educational needs' or simply 'special needs.'

education To educe is to draw forth, develop, elicit. Hence, the process of drawing something out, of making a connection, specifically of establishing a connection that reflects the fundamental relations between objects or events.

educational age ➤ **age, educational**.

educational guidance ➤ **guidance**.

educationally subnormal (ESN) ➤ **educable mentally retarded**.

educational psychology A sub-discipline of psychology concerned with theories and problems in education. Generally included within the province of the field are the application of principles of learning to the classroom, curriculum development and reform, testing and evaluation of aptitudes and abilities, socialization processes and their interaction with cognitive functioning, teacher training, etc.

educational quotient (EQ) The ratio of *educational* *age to *chronological* *age times 100.

Edwards Personal Preference Schedule A self-report personality inventory consisting of 225 forced-choice items. The items were selected to correspond to the 15 needs which Henry Murray has theorized are fundamental in human personality. Whether the test really measures what it sets out to is an unresolved issue but the test is interesting because of its attempt to circumvent biased responding due to social desirability – a factor which contaminates many personality tests.

EEG ➤ **electroencephalogram**.

effect 1 n. An event that reliably follows another event, its cause. 2 vb. To bring about a state of affairs, to have an impact on something. 3. In statistics, differences between means that can be attributed to the independent variables in the study. If words at the middle of a list are learned less well than those at the beginning or the end of the list, then there is an *effect* of serial of position on memory. There are ➤ **main effects** (such as this example) and *interaction effects* (➤ **interactions**).

effectance Effectiveness, the capacity to cope with the environment, to be competent. Within Adler's approach, an effectance *motive* is assumed, which functions by making a child feel a strong need to become competent so as to overcome feelings of inadequacy or inferiority.

effect, empirical law of Otherwise known as the 'weak' law of effect, this is a generalization which states that a response followed by a reinforcement is more likely to occur again. It was first postulated by E. L. Thorndike in 1904 and, in its original form, referred to 'satisfying states of affairs' rather than to 'reinforcements.' Thorndike's original formulation also included a ➤ **negative law of *effect**, which was later amended into obscurity. Note that in its simple form the law of effect is inherently circular: a 'satisfying state of affairs' is one which increases responding and any event which increases responding is a 'satisfying state of affairs.' Hence, Thorndike's proposal tends to be viewed as an empirical generalization rather than an explanatory theory. See also the other 'laws' of effect that follow here and also the extended discussion of the theoretical problems attending these concepts under the entry for ➤ **reinforcement**.

effective habit strength In C. L. Hull's theory, the strength of a particular learned response as established by the collective reinforcement processes that have operated on it in the past.

effective reaction potential In C. L. Hull's theory, the ➤ **reaction potential** minus any inhibiting tendencies.

effective stimulus ➤ functional *stimulus.

effective weight ➤ weight (3).

effect, law of 1. Broadly and generally, the principle that events in the world serve to select particular behaviors from the (infinite or at least very large) pool of possible behaviors. Behaviors that lead to 'good' things are repeated, those that lead to 'bad' things are not. It is worth pointing out that from a behaviorist point of view the law of effect is seen as a behavioral parallel of the principle of natural selection – the well-designed behaviors are selected from the pool of responses, their occurrence is made more likely, and the others are allowed to become extinct (➤ extinction). 2. E. L. Thorndike was the first to popularize the term in psychology. Over the years he produced several variations on it; the core meaning is contained in meaning 1 above; the other forms of the 'law' are given under ➤ empirical law of *effect, strong law of *effect and negative law of *effect.

effect, negative law of Originally proposed by Thorndike as the reciprocal of the ➤ empirical law of *effect, the negative law simply postulated that responses that were followed by an 'annoying state of affairs' were less likely to recur. He later 'repealed' the negative law of effect, arguing that it was not a simple converse and that punishment did not 'stamp out' behavior quite the way that reinforcement 'stamped in' behavior. His point, accepted by many, is that punishments did not produce unlearning but suppression of the behaviors that they followed. See here the discussions of related terms, ➤ punishment and suppression.

effector Generally, a muscle or gland at the terminal end of an efferent neural process which produces the observed response.

effect size In statistics, quite literally, the size of an ➤ effect (3). Tests of a null hypothesis may tell you that an effect is significant, but they do not tell you how large the effect is and, of course, if the n is

large very small effect sizes can produce very large significance levels. Measures of effect size such as ➤ omega squared are based on the proportion of variance in the data that can be attributed to the experimental variables and essentially tell you how many standard deviation units the group means are separated by.

effect, spread of To account for the phenomenon of ➤ generalization E. L. Thorndike proposed that the effect of 'satisfiers' or 'annoyers' spread to other stimuli present at the time of the response or to stimuli which are similar in nature to the originally reinforced or punished stimulus.

effect, strong law of An extension of Thorndike's ➤ empirical law of *effect. The strong form states that not only do reinforcements (or, in Thorndike's terms, 'satisfying states of affairs') increase the frequency or probability of the response they follow but their occurrence is a *necessary* condition for a response to be learned. Contrast with the proposal put forth by ➤ contiguity theory.

effeminate Lit., female-like. The most common meaning, however, is descriptive or characteristic of a biological male who displays behavior patterns which, in societal terms, are more closely associated with females. Note that some authors consider effeminacy to encompass physical as well as psychological/behavioral characteristics, although the tendency is to restrict usage to the latter. ➤➤ androgyny. Distinguish from ➤ homosexual; some effeminate men may indeed be homosexual but effeminacy itself is a poor predictor of sexual preference.

efferent From the Latin, meaning *carry away from*. Hence, in neurophysiology it refers to the conduction of nerve impulses from the central nervous system outward toward the periphery (muscles, glands). Efferent neurons and neural pathways carry information to *effectors* and are commonly called *motor* neurons or pathways.

efficacy In Piagetian theory a term used

for a very primitive cognitive experience whereby the young child's emotions and feelings are assumed to be responsible for events in the world.

effort 1. In loose physical terms, the work required to perform some action. However: **2.** In psychology, the subjective sense of the amount of work required to perform some action, usually with the implications that (a) there is some resistance or barrier to be overcome in order to carry out the action and (b) the action carried out is voluntary.

E–F scale A scale from the *Minnesota Multiphasic Personality Inventory* (*MMPI*) made up of 30 items and designed to measure attitudes toward ethnocentricity and authoritarianism (the 'F' is for Fascism).

ego 1. From the Latin for *I*, the 'I' or 'self' conceptualized as the central core around which all psychic activities revolve. This is the foundational meaning and is neutral as regards evaluative connotations and theories of personality. **2.** One of the components in the Freudian tripartite model of the psychic apparatus (along with the ➤ **id** and ➤ **superego**). In the classical theory the ego represents a cluster of cognitive and perceptual processes including memory, problem-solving, reality-testing, inference-making, self-regulated striving and the like that are conscious and in touch with reality, as well as specific defense mechanisms that serve to mediate between the primitive instinctual demands of the id, the internalized social, parental inhibitions and prohibitions of the superego, and the knowledge of reality. In this conceptualization the ego serves like an executive who functions adaptively to maintain psychic balance. **3.** The collected psychological processes that are concerned with ➤ **self**. In semi-technical and even some popular writings this is the meaning usually intended. It connotes a hypothetical entity with which an individual is overly concerned, a kind of psychological touchstone that serves as a basis for one's interests, values, attitudes, desires, etc. This is the meaning captured in terms like *egocentric*, *egoistic* and *egotistic*.

ego-alien ➤ **ego-dystonic**.

ego analysis A psychoanalytic term for a relatively short form of analysis which focuses on the integrative, positive ego functions rather than on the deeply repressed id functions.

ego anxiety In psychoanalytic theory any reaction resulting from threats to the ego; the anxiety caused by conficts between id, ego and/or superego. In the classical theory, the genesis of all *ego defenses* is found here.

ego block A very general term used for anything that is seen, in psychoanalytic terms, as preventing or inhibiting the full development of the ego.

ego, body Freud used this term to capture the notion that at its ultimate core the ego derives from the bodily sensations.

ego boundary A vaguely topological concept that implies that part of the normal ego development consists in establishing a boundary separating self from others. Presumably, anyone who identifies too readily with others at the expense of their own identity is lacking in ego boundary or has a weakly established boundary.

ego cathexis A channeling or focusing of libido on an object within the domain of the reality-oriented ego.

egocentric Pertaining to or characteristic of ➤ **egocentrism**.

egocentricity ➤ **egocentrism**.

egocentric speech Speech which derives from and serves purely internal needs and thoughts. ➤ **egocentrism**.

egocentrism (or egocentricity) As the roots of the term suggest, the perspective in which one is preoccupied with the self and relatively insensitive to others. When used of adults the connotation is of self-absorption and self-centering. When used of children, particularly in the context of

Piagetian theory, it pertains to speech and thought dominated by the child's own internal cognitions.

ego complex A term used by Jung to refer to a group of emotional reactions toward or about oneself. Also called *self-sentiment*.

ego defense The process of harboring the libidinal energies of the id in defense of the ego. In general, all ➤ **defense mechanisms** may be characterized as ego defenses.

ego development The gradual emerging awareness by the child that he or she is a distinct, independent person. The manner in which this takes place is not so easily stated, however. Classical psychoanalysis assumes that the process is one in which the ego progressively acquires functions that enable the individual to master impulses and to learn how to function independently of parents. Erikson's ➤ **stages of man** point of view regards the entire scope of life as understandable only from the perspective of stages of ego development. Piaget, on the other hand, handles the issue by focusing in on cognitive development with considerably less emphasis on dynamic factors. There is precious little consensus here.

ego-dystonic Descriptive of wishes, dreams, impulses, behaviors, etc. that are unacceptable to the ego; or, perhaps more accurately, unacceptable to the person's ideal conception of self. Hence, an egodystonic idea is one that seems to have invaded consciousness, to have come from 'outside' the self. Contrast with ➤ **ego-syntonic**. Also called *ego-alien*. Also spelled *egodystonic*, without the hyphen.

ego-dystonic homosexuality ➤ **homosexuality, ego-dystonic**.

ego-dystonic sexual orientation A condition where the individual's sexual orientation is not in doubt but he or she is unhappy with it and wishes to change it.

ego erotism ➤ **narcissism**.

ego failure A 'breakdown' in ego function, specifically a failure to restrain id impulses so that they conform with the strictures of the superego.

ego function Usually this term refers to the primary role of the ego – to mediate between the id and the superego in ways that are responsive to society and self-protection. However, in the classical psychoanalytic perspective, absolutely anything a person can do is, strictly speaking, an ego function. This usage stems from a simple tautology since in the classical theory all functions are assigned to the ego.

ego ideal The ego's conception of positive ideals; in short, what a person would like to be or prefer to accomplish in terms of that which is positive and good. Generally a distinction is made between the *ego ideal* and the *superego* on the grounds that the former represents prescriptions for life, is modifed through growth and experience, and behavior that violates it produces shame; the latter represents proscriptions, is fixed at a young age, and behavior in conflict with it evokes guilt.

ego instincts Collectively, all impulses for individual self-preservation. In Freud's early writings the ego instincts were distinguished from the id instincts, which were primarily sexual and reproductive. In his later writings this distinction became blurred because of the recasting of instincts into those for life (➤ **Eros**) and death (➤ **Thanatos**).

ego-integrative Tending toward integrating the ego, reaching for a point of coordination and harmony in life.

ego integrity The final of Erikson's ➤ **stages of man**. It juxtaposes ego integrity and despair. Full ego integrity in this conception permits the acceptance of old age and one's ultimate death without despair.

ego involvement 1. A situation of committing oneself wholeheartedly to a task. 2. A situation wherein one determines that a particular goal or task is important to one's ego.

egoism In simplest terms, *self-interest*. Hence: **1.** A label for the point of view that such self-interest is at the base of all behavior (contrast here with ➤ **altruism**). **2.** The tendency to behave strictly or largely according to self-interest. Compare here with ➤ **egotism**.

egoistic Conceited, self-serving, motivated by self-interest. ➤ **egotistic(al)** for discussion of and comparison between these and similar and often confused terms.

egoistic suicide ➤ **suicide, egoistic**.

ego libido Libido invested in the ego. In psychoanalytic writings the term is sometimes used to refer to the psychic energy available for use in carrying out ego functions and sometimes used for self-love. Contrast with ➤ **object libido**.

egomania Pathological preoccupation with one's ego or, better, with one's self. See also discussion under ➤ **-mania**.

ego neurosis A theoretical classification in psychoanalysis that includes neuroses such as paralyses, hysteria, memory loss, etc. that are hypothesized to result from disruption of ego functions.

ego–object polarity The distinction between the self and that which is not-self. It is normally rather sharp, hence the notion of 'polarity.' ➤ **ego boundary**.

egopathy A general term for the tendency to bolster one's own ego by inappropriate hostility and aggression toward others.

ego psychology **1.** Generally, the psychology of the ego. That is, the examination of those developing structures and processes that are regarded as being within the purview of the ego; specifically included here are memory, language, judgement, decision-making and other reality-oriented functions. **2.** A label for those variations of psychoanalytic theory that focus on the ego and its role in personality development.

ego resistance A psychoanalytic term used to characterize resistance on the part of the patient (read, 'the patient's ego') to give up neurotic patterns of behavior, to recognize repressed impulses and to abandon defense mechanisms.

ego strength Psychoanalytic theory characterizes the strength of the ego in terms of its share of available psychic energy. Theoretically, the 'stronger' the ego the greater the resoluteness of character and, according to some, the more likely the individual will be able to withstand the slings and arrows . . . In the final analysis, psychoanalysts use the term in pretty much the same way as it is used in the common nontechnical language.

ego structure A generic term used to characterize the pattern and organization of ego traits, functions, etc. Just what 'structure' the ego 'has' depends entirely upon the theorist under consideration.

ego-syntonic Descriptive of values, feelings, ideas that are consistent with one's ego, that feel 'real' and acceptable to consciousness. An ego-syntonic idea feels 'like it belongs.' Contrast with ➤ **egodystonic**.

ego-syntonic homosexuality ➤ **homosexuality, ego-syntonic**.

ego threat Generally, any danger to the ego's efforts to adapt to the demands of reality. In the psychoanalytic framework, those pressures and instinctual demands of the id that are perceived as incompatible with the constraints of reality and/or the superego's prohibitions.

egotic Pertaining to or characterizing the ego. This term is used by some authors because the other adjectival forms (*egoistic, egotistic, egotistical*) have taken on evaluative connotations that are distinctly negative.

egotism The tendency to regard oneself very highly, specifically to the point of having an annoyingly overblown opinion of self. Compare with ➤ **egoism** (2).

egotistic(al) Conceited, maintaining a high opinion of oneself. Note that this notion of conceit is shared with the term *egoistic* but the connotations of the two are different. Egoistic refers to those who view themselves as at the center of things and who have great concern for their own self-interest; egotistic refers to those who tend to have, in addition, an unrealistic and obnoxious sense of self-importance. One can be very egoistic and have little in the way of egotism and egotistic behavior.

egotization A psychoanalytic term for the process by which some mental process becomes part of the ego or self; i.e. the process by which it comes to be freed from id-based impulses of aggression and sexuality and becomes structured and reality-oriented.

ego trip A nontechnical term used broadly for any pattern of behavior engaged in primarily for the purpose of boosting one's sense of self.

eidetic imagery From the Greek *eidos* meaning *form* (usually taken to mean *form in the mind*), mental imagery that is vivid and persistent. The critical features of those with such imagery (called *eidetikers*) are: (a) that they continue to 'see' a representation of a visual stimulus some time after it has been removed; and (b) that this 'seeing' is a true visual image and not merely memory for the stimulus. A true eidetic image lasts for some time and hence is differentiated from an *icon* (see discussion under ➤ **sensory information store**) and from an ➤ **afterimage**. Eidetic imagery is more common in children (conservative estimates put it at about 5 in 100) than in adults (estimated as occurring in less than 1 in 1,000, with some authorities even putting it as less than 1 in a million).

eidetiker ➤ **eidetic imagery**.

Eigenwelt From the German and literally translated as *self-world*. In existentialism, the relationship between each person and him- or herself. This concept, in isolation, makes precious little sense; its meaning, however, is easily appreciated when juxtaposed against the others used within this theory: *Mitwelt* and *Umwelt*. The former refers to one's relationships with other persons, with one's contemporaries, and the latter to one's relationship with the environment.

eikon ➤ **iconic**.

Einstellung German for *attitude* or *set*. Used to denote a kind of cognitive readiness for a particular stimulus or class of stimuli. A subject in an experiment that had been using only auditory stimulus materials will establish such a set and will be startled by and may not even correctly perceive a visual stimulus if one is suddenly presented. ➤ **set**, especially 2.

ejaculatio praecox ➤ **premature ejaculation**.

ejaculatory incompetence The inability to ejaculate within the vagina during intercourse; in a sense, the reverse of *premature ejaculation*.

EKG ➤ **electrocardiogram**.

ekphorize In psychiatry, to bring back the effect of a particular psychological experience.

elaborated code B. Bernstein's term for the speech mode adopted when one is speaking with persons from different backgrounds from oneself, persons with whom few assumptions can be made concerning shared background or common knowledge. Under such conditions the discourse is relatively slow, words and phrases are carefully selected, the speech is relatively unpredictable and elaborately planned. Compare with ➤ **restricted code**.

elaboration In cognition, any process whereby a particular memory for a stimulus is interpreted, elaborated, associated with other stimuli or in any other way 'fleshed out.' Although it seems fairly clear that such elaborative strategies are used by essentially everyone as aids to memory, there is considerable debate in the field as to whether it is reasonable to regard all of the knowledge in ➤ **long-term *memory** as resulting from the use of elaboration. ➤➤ constructivism for more discussion on a similar point.

elaborative rehearsal Rehearsing of information using ➤ elaboration. ➤➤ rehearsal.

Elberfeld horses A group of superbly trained horses in Germany popular during the early part of the century. The most startling was 'der kluge' Hans (➤ Clever Hans), who could seemingly perform complex mathematical problems, answer factual questions, spell, etc.

elective mutism ➤ selective mutism.

Electra complex ➤ Oedipus complex.

electrical brain stimulation (EBS) The application of a weak electrical current (usually in the form of a series of short pulses) to a specific locale in the brain. The technique is used in a variety of contexts from neurosurgical procedures, in which it helps the surgeon determine the areas of the brain that need to be surgically removed and those that need to be protected, to experimental studies of the relationship between various cerebral structures and the functions they control. Also called by a variety of other names including *electrical stimulation of the brain* (ESB), *intracranial stimulation* (ICS).

electric shock therapy (EST) ➤ electroconvulsive therapy.

electro- Combining form meaning *electric, electrical.*

electrocardiogram (ECG or EKG) A record of the activity of the heart made by recording the spreading electrical potential generated by the heart beat and putting it in graphic form. In addition to its obvious medical applications, ECG has been used as a measure of emotional arousal, of physical exertion, etc., and as such has served the role of dependent variable in studies of classical conditioning, of emotionality and the like.

electroconvulsive shock (ECS) A brief electrical shock applied to the head that produces full-body seizure, convulsions and usually loss of consciousness. ECS is used in two distinct ways: (a) As a research tool to study (in animals) the neurophysiology of memory. Here the usual technique is to pass a current through the brain, producing ➤ retrograde *amnesia (loss of memory for recent past events). There is considerable debate as to whether the technique functions by interfering with the process of ➤ consolidation or whether it disrupts the retrieval of the memory. (b) As a therapeutic procedure for psychiatric disorders; see here ➤ electroconvulsive therapy.

electroconvulsive therapy (ECT) The use of electroconvulsive shock as a therapeutic procedure for psychiatric disorders. The technique consists of applying weak electric current (20–30 milliamps) bilaterally to the temperofrontal region of the skull until a *grand mal* seizure results. The patient is sedated using an ultra-short-acting barbiturate and a muscle relaxant is administered to minimize the intensity of the muscular reactions. ECT produces a period of drowsiness, temporary confusion and disorientation, and a variety of memory deficits, some of which the patient recovers over time, although gaps may remain indefinitely. Recent years have seen a significant drop in the use of this procedure in many large understaffed institutions where it had been used primarily to produce docility in the patient threatened with it. Its only recognized therapeutic use is in the treatment of cases of severe depression that have proven intractable to ➤ antidepressant drugs. Also called *electroshock therapy* (*EST*); distinguish from ➤ electrotherapy.

electroculogram ➤ electro-oculogram.

electrode Generally, any medium for transmitting an electric current to an object or for recording electrical activity from an object. Often one will specify which kind of electrode is in use by appending qualifiers, e.g., *stimulating* or *recording*. Typically the medium is a metallic device and in most psychological and physiological research the object is bodily tissue.

electrodermal response (EDR) ➤ galvanic skin response.

electroencephalogram (EEG) A record of the changes in electrical potential of the brain. Electrodes are generally attached to (or occasionally just under) the scalp and the wavelike potentials are amplified and transferred to paper. Detailed EEG analyses have revealed that the brain undergoes systematic changes in the kinds of potential exhibited during various activities. See, for example, ➤ **alpha wave, delta wave**. Note that the terms *electroencephalogram* and *electroencephalograph* are used virtually interchangeably; the field of study and use of the device is called *electroencephalography*.

electrolyte A substance which when in solution conducts an electrical current and is decomposed by its passage. Salts, bases and acids are all electrolytes.

electromyogram (EMG) A graphic record of the changes in electrical potential in a muscle.

electronarcosis The induction of unconsciousness by passage of an electrical current through brain tissue. ➤ **electroconvulsive shock**.

electronystagmography The recording of ➤ **nystagmus** by detection of the electrical activity of the muscles of the eye.

electro-oculogram (EOG) A device for measuring eye movements by recording the electrical potentials of the muscles that control the eye movements. var., *electroculogram*.

electroretinogram (ERG) A graphic record of the changes in electrical potential of the retina.

electroshock therapy (EST) ➤ **electroconvulsive therapy**.

electrotherapy Therapy using mild, brief electrical stimulation. The term is to be distinguished from *electroshock therapy* and *electroconvulsive therapy*, since the electrical charges used are of a nonconvulsive nature.

element Aside from the standard dictionary meanings this term has several specialized usages in psychology: **1.** The early structuralists used it to represent the basic unit of consciousness, in a manner analogous with its usage in chemistry. That is, the contents of consciousness were assumed to consist of combinations of a finite number of basic mental elements, just as all physical matter consisted of combinations of a finite number of chemical elements. **2.** In G. Kelly's social theory, it referred to an object abstracted out of the rest of the environment by use of a special construct. **3.** In W. K. Estes' mathematical learning theory, a hypothesized unitary component of a stimulus. Estes' treatment of the term is best thought of as equivalent to the notion of a 'point' in geometry: all space is made up of 'points,' all stimuli made up of 'elements.' In this conception, learning becomes the conditioning of stimulus elements to responses. adjs., *elementary* = simple; *elemental* = pertaining to an element, primary, basic. ➤➤ **elementarism** and **reductionism**.

elementarism A cover term for any atomistic philosophical position that maintains that complex phenomena can be understood only by reducing them down to their most primitive (i.e. elementary) parts. The structuralist school in psychology typified this position in that its proponents were searching for the elements of mental content. Similar schools of thought are represented by ➤ **reductionism** and **atomism**. Opposing are ➤ **holism** and ➤ **Gestalt**.

elicit To draw forth, draw out. The term is used to refer to behavior that is not spontaneously produced by an organism but is 'drawn out' by the presentation of the appropriate stimulus. Thus, the term *elicited behavior* becomes synonymous with *reflexive* or *respondent behavior* and is viewed as that behavior characteristically produced by classical conditioning. Compare with ➤ **emit**.

elimination disorders Disorders of childhood in which the child urinates (➤ **enuresis**) or defecates (➤ **encopresis**) in inappropriate places. The term is only used when there is no evidence of organic disorders that might be causing the lack of control.

ellipsis The omission of a word or words from a spoken or written message where the missing words are predictable or determinable from the structure of the sentence or from context. Some psychoanalysts regard the occurrence of ellipses as significant and a form of ➤ **parapraxis**.

elopement In psychiatry, the unauthorized departure of a patient from a psychiatric institution.

emasculation ➤ **castration**.

embedded figure A general class of ambiguous figures in which a particular shape is interwoven with a general pattern, making it difficult to detect. For example, of the following shapes the hexagon (on the left) occurs embedded within the triangle (on the right):

embedded-figures test A paper-and-pencil test that requires that the subject locate a simple figure embedded in a larger, more complex field (see above). It is used primarily as a device to evaluate ➤ **field dependence**.

embolalia Meaningless babbling. var., *embololalia*.

embrace reflex ➤ **Moro's reflex**.

embryo Generally, an organism in the earliest stages of prenatal development. In mammals, the organism during that period before it develops physical similarity to its mature form. In *Homo sapiens*, the organism during the period of about six weeks during which internal and external organs become differentiated. The embryonic period follows the germinal, which itself lasts about two weeks, during which time the fertilized ovum grows into a hollow sphere of approximately 5 mm. After the embryonic stage the term fetus is used.

emergent Descriptive of or characteristic of new or unexpected properties or qualities that 'emerge' as a result of combinations or rearrangements of existing elements. The most prominent examples are *mind* and *consciousness*, emerging from complex neurophysiological and biochemical components. The critical aspect of an emergent property is that one could not predict it from its constituent parts. *Emergentism* is a philosophical position that stresses that objects and phenomena (particularly psychological ones) have emergent properties. Reference is also made to *emergent evolution* as a way of characterizing the appearance of novel phenomena.

emergentism ➤ **emergent**.

emesis Vomiting.

EMG ➤ **electromyogram**.

emission A discharge, a giving out or sending forth. Used broadly to cover bodily discharges, specifically semen during ejaculation, overt responses made by an organism (see here ➤ **emit**), messages output in communication, etc.

emit To produce, to send out. The term is used to refer to behavior that is generated or produced by an organism within the context of an appropriate stimulus. Thus, the phrase *emitted behavior* becomes synonymous with *operant behavior* and is characteristic in free responding situations and in operant conditioning. Contrast with ➤ **elicit**.

emmenia Menstrual flow.

emmeniopathy Any menstrual disorder.

Emmert's law A generalization about the nature of negative afterimages that states that the perceived size of the image varies directly with the distance that it is projected. For example, if one has an afterimage of some object the image will appear smaller if the image is projected on a piece of paper that is fairly close to the subject than the same image projected on to a wall some distance from the viewer. Note that the term 'projected' is used metaphorically here.

emmetropia Normal vision in the sense that when the eye is at rest the light is refracted so that the focus is directly on the retina. Compare with the common refractive disorders of ➤ **astigmatism**, **hyperopia** and **myopia**.

emote To display emotion.

emotion Historically this term has proven utterly refractory to definitional efforts; probably no other term in psychology shares its nondefinability with its frequency of use. Most textbook authors wisely employ it as the title of a chapter and let the material presented substitute for a concise definition. The term itself derives from the Latin *emovere* which translates as *to move, to excite, to stir up* or *to agitate*. Contemporary usage is of two general kinds: **1.** An umbrella term for any of a number of subjectively experienced, affect-laden states, the ontological status of each being established by a label whose meaning is arrived at by simple consensus. This is the primary use of the term in both the technical and the common language. It is what we mean when we say that *love, fear, hate, terror*, etc. are emotions. **2.** A label for a field of scientific investigation that explores the various environmental, physiological and cognitive factors that underlie these subjective experiences.

There is little dispute over 1, other than the sense that it is unfortunate that a term of such importance is used in such loose subjective fashion. The confusing array of usages that confronts the psychologist comes from 2, where the 'definitions' found are really mini-theories about the underpinnings of emotions. Although they differ in the relative contributions assigned to each, nearly all contemporary theories of emotion recognize four classes of factors: (a) *instigating stimuli*: these may be exogenous (events in the world) or endogenous (thoughts, images); (b) *physiological correlates*: included here are general systems (central and autonomic nervous-system activities) as well as more specific patterns of action (e.g., thalamic-hypothalamic interactions); (c) *cognitive appraisal*: the personal significance of an event dictates to a considerable extent the emotions aroused, thus snarling tigers behind clearly strong cage bars do not result in fear, panic or flight; (d) *motivational properties*: emotional arousal is almost always viewed as playing a role in impelling activity. ➤ **motivation**.

In addition to these recognized correlates of emotion, the term generally carries a number of other connotations: First, emotional states are normally regarded as *acute*. They are accompanied by relatively short-lived levels of arousal and desires to act; fear, joy, disgust, pity, love, etc. are regarded as relatively momentary conditions the experiencing of which motivates activity and then subsides. Indeed, in psychiatry many of the *affective disorders* are characterized by an inappropriate chronic experiencing of an emotional state. This sense of the term helps to distinguish it from a term like ➤ **sentiment**. Second, emotions are regarded as intensely experienced states; the point here is to distinguish an emotion from a *feeling*. No one would argue that a fine line exists here; this is merely a terminological heuristic. Third, emotional states are often behaviorally disorganized. This is particularly the case with extreme states of rage, terror, desperate grief and the like, where the individual's behavior may be erratic, chaotic and lacking in organization. Fourth, emotions are, to a certain extent, evolutionarily determined and reflect species-specific survival strategies of considerable genetic antiquity. This point is reflected most clearly in the work in evolutionary biology and ethology as it has affected psychological theory. Fifth, emotional reactions tend to be non-habitual and to result from particular constraints of the environment and how it is appraised. The contrast to be recognized here is with other behaviors that are motivated by underlying biochemical actions like hunger, thirst, and the like, which typically are satisfied by relatively stereotyped, habitual behavior patterns. This issue is related to the fact that emotional states are not cyclical or regular but are dependent on specific situations and how they are evaluated for their personal significance.

For more on the nuances of usage see the following entries as well-related terms: ➤ affect, feeling, mood, sentiment.

emotional 1. Generally, pertaining to any aspect of emotion; characterizing states, processes, expressions etc. that carry the quality of emotion. 2. Characterizing an individual who is experiencing an emotion or one who displays a propensity for emotional reactions.

emotional anesthesia A numbing of one's emotions, a diminished responsiveness to the outside world. Often seen in cases of ➤ post-traumatic stress disorder.

emotional bias Basically a nontechnical term for any personal bias stemming from emotional causes; it is used with the connotation that the individual is not capable of making objective assessments because of this bias.

emotional blocking A general phrase used to refer to an individual's inability to perform complex mental tasks because of a highly intense emotional state.

emotional contagion ➤ contagion, behavioral (or emotional).

emotional deprivation A general term for any situation where an individual is deprived of emotional reactions from others. It is used almost exclusively of children who are raised in situations lacking in love, affection and contact. ➤ anaclitic depression and maturational deprivation syndrome.

emotional disorder Any condition in which emotional reactions are inappropri-

ate for the situations presented. ➤ affective disorder, the preferred term here.

emotional expression Very generally, any anatomical, muscular, physiological, behavioral reaction that accompanies a felt emotion and functions as the manner in which it is displayed. Note, some authors treat the expression of an emotion as distinct (or at least theoretically distinguishable) from the subjectively experienced emotion; others regard the expressive or emotive component as an integral aspect of the whole emotion; and still others (mainly ethologists) consider it to be an evolutionarily selected signal to others about a motive to act in a particular way.

emotional indicator Any of a number of physiological measures which reflect the state of emotional arousal; e.g., ➤ galvanic skin response. ➤ I/E ratio. Also called *emotionality indicator*, for reasons explained under ➤ emotionality.

emotional instability A tendency to be emotionally labile, to display inappropriately abrupt and unpredictably extreme emotionality.

emotionality Because of all the confusion surrounding the connotations of the term ➤ emotion many writers (primarily those with behaviorist leanings) favor this term. Their point is to try to avoid the surplus meanings of *emotion* by operationalizing the term. In this sense *emotionality* is defined in terms of behaviors that are observable and theoretically linked to the (hypothetical) underlying emotion. For example, in animal studies emotionality may be gauged by crouching, trembling, excess urination, defecation, etc. In humans such measures as heart rate, blood chemistry, breathing rate, galvanic skin response, etc. may be used.

Note that this meaning of the term is actually not far removed from the ordinary sense in which it is used; i.e. to refer to the degree with which an individual reacts to emotive situations, with the connotation that such displays are often excessive given the circumstances. In both the behaviorists' technical sense and the layperson's common meaning the underlying notion is that it is the behavioral manifestations that are taken as the critical component in assessment of the emotion experienced.

emotionally unstable personality An obsolete psychiatric label for one who is emotionally labile, especially in the display of inappropriate reactions to minor stresses. ➤ **affective disorder**, the contemporary umbrella term for these disorders.

emotional maturity Loosely, the state in which one's emotional reactivity is considered appropriate and normal for an adult in a given society. The clear connotation in most cultures is one of self-control and the ability to suppress extreme emotional reactions.

emotional release A non-technical term used interchangeably with ➤ **catharsis** and/or ➤ **abreaction**.

emotional stability Used both technically and non-technically to characterize the state of one who is emotionally mature, whose emotional reactions are appropriate for the situation and are consistent from one set of circumstances to another.

emotion, theories of As the extended discussion under ➤ **emotion** suggests, the field of emotion is far from having received a satisfactory theoretical characterization. Nevertheless, a number of legitimate candidates for such a theory have been put forward over the years (as outlined below). They all tend to be complex and (with one exception) to involve both physiological and cognitive components, although the emphasis on each differs considerably from theory to theory.

(a) *James–Lange theory*: C. G. Lange was a Danish physiologist who proposed a theory of emotions so similar to William James's that both are given credit in the name, although the theory is essentially what James proposed in 1890. Letting James speak for himself (always a good

idea): '... my theory is that the bodily changes follow directly the perception of the excitatory fact, and that our feeling of the same changes as they occur *is* the emotion.' Lange's position was similar, albeit he omitted the step on perception and concluded that the vasomotor (bodily) changes were the emotion. The theory has been subjected to rather telling criticism. The strongest objections were raised by Cannon (see below), who questioned the central role of the feedback from the peripheral organs.

(b) *Cannon–Bard theory*. This theory is due primarily to the work of the American physiologist Walter B. Cannon and is often referred to as the *thalamic* theory of emotion. In simplest terms it argues that the integration of emotional expression is controlled by the thalamus sending relevant excitation patterns to the cortex at the same time that the hypothalamus controls the behavior. It was put forward as part of Cannon's critique of the earlier *James–Lange theory* (see above), which had postulated that the sensory feedback controlled the emotional expression. This theory has also been subjected to rather telling criticism in the form of the following more recently developed theories.

(c) *Activation [or arousal] theory*. Not a true theory so much as a generalization about emotions. It is predicated on the assumption that emotions are not unique states but merely lie collectively at the extreme pole of a dimension of neurophysiological arousal or activation opposite the pole represented by coma and deep sleep. This generalization shows up as a component in several other theoretical conceptions of emotions, specifically the *cognitive-appraisal theory*.

(d) *Behavioristic theory*. As one might expect, this point of view deals with all emotions as either unconditioned (i.e. innately given, species-specific) or conditioned (i.e. learned, acquired) responses. Both the physiological and cognitive elements are regarded as unimportant, the focus being on objectively measurable manifestations of what behaviorists like to call 'emotional behavior.' See here the discussion under ➤ **emotionality**.

(e) *Cognitive-appraisal theory*. Here emotions are regarded as subjective states that are the product of an initially evoking stimulus, a set of accompanying physiological changes and a cognitive appraisal or interpretation of the situation as beneficial or harmful, good or bad, for the individual. The key notion here is the cognitive appraisal itself; the argument being that a single physiological arousal state can yield several, even antithetical, emotions depending on how the individual interprets the situation. ➤ **Maclean's theory of emotion, Papez's theory of emotion**.

emotive Characteristic of a situation, event, or other stimulus that elicits emotion.

emotive imagery Quite literally, imagery that evokes emotion. The term is most often used in behavior therapy and cognitive-behavioral therapy for a procedure in which the client images emotion-arousing scenes while relaxed and in a comfortable, protective setting. The technique is based on Wolpe's notion of ➤ **reciprocal inhibition**, in which the positive supportive setting inhibits the anxiety.

empathy 1. A cognitive awareness and understanding of the emotions and feelings of another person. In this sense the term's primary connotation is that of an intellectual or conceptual grasping of the *affect* of another. **2.** A vicarious affective response to the emotional experiences of another person that mirrors or mimics that emotion. In this sense there is the clear implication that an empathic experience is a sharing of the emotion with the other person. **3.** Assuming, in one's mind, the role of another person. This meaning derives from 1, but differs slightly in that there is added the notion that empathy involves taking on the perspective of the other person. This meaning is common in the literature on moral development where some theorists argue that empathy with

another is a prerequisite for the development of a moral code. **4.** In H. S. Sullivan's theory of personality, an unverbalized, covert communication process whereby attitudes, feelings and judgements are passed from person to person without ever being publicly articulated. Sullivan's use of the term is quite broad and encompasses the more restricted connotations of the above meanings. ➤ **sympathy** for more on the terminology of shared affect.

empirical An extremely common term in psychological parlance. It enjoys (or perhaps suffers from) a number of diverse and rather specialized meanings. It is used specifically as: **1.** Relating to facts in general. **2.** Relating to experience in general. **3.** Descriptive of procedures carried out without explicit regard to any theory. **4.** A general synonym for *experimental*. **5.** Descriptive of any procedure based upon factual evaluations. **6.** Pertaining to *empiricism*. Note that all of these usages are based on or relate directly to *data*, to its collection, analysis or evaluation. It is in this general sense that the term is most frequently used. Note that such usage places empirical in opposition (more or less) to ➤ **rational**.

empirical construct Any construct the existence of which is hypothesized or inferred on the basis of empirical evaluation, i.e. on observed facts and data. Although the term *construct* implies an essentially theoretical or hypothetical entity, the adjective *empirical* is awarded when the data are sufficiently consistent and convincing.

empirical equation ➤ **equation, empirical**.

empirical law ➤ **law, empirical**.

empirical law of effect ➤ **effect, empirical law of**.

empirical test The evaluation or assessment of a hypothesis or theory by appeal to data, facts and experimentation.

empirical validity ➤ **validity, empirical**.

empiricism A broad-based philosophical

position grounded on the fundamental assumption that all knowledge comes from experience. Historically, the empiricist tradition stems from the work of a number of British philosophers of the 17th and 18th centuries (Locke, Hume, Berkeley, Hartley). To understand clearly the term one should keep separate empiricism as a *theory* and empiricism as a *method*. As a theory the primary assumption is that knowledge results from experience and learning. In its extreme form (mind as *tabula rasa* or 'blank slate' at birth) it can no longer be seriously defended – the data on developmental stages, on cognitive growth, etc. clearly point to some degree of genetic predisposition for certain kinds of behaviors. The contemporary empiricist position is akin to a mild form of skepticism and is best represented by what it is against: the positions put forward in ➤ **a priorism**, ➤ **nativism** and ➤ **rationalism**. That is, the empiricist relies upon an as yet unworked-out theory of induction for the acquisition of knowledge and rejects any doctrine that argues that the human mind enters the world pre-equipped with ideas or concepts that are independent of personal experience.

As a method, empiricism advocates the collection and evaluation of data. In this sense the focus is on experimentation and an empirical investigation is one guided primarily by induction from observation rather than by deduction from theoretical constructs. Although the theoretical issues are still hotly contested, particularly in contemporary cognitive psychology, it is safe to say that the empirical methods thoroughly dominate contemporary psychological investigation.

empty-chair technique A technique used in Gestalt therapy whereby the client projects the image of a person about whom he or she has unresolved feelings and engages in 'conversation' with the image.

empty organism A phrase, often used derisively by opponents of behaviorism, to characterize that system's unwillingness to make inferences about internal states or to posit hypothetical constructs. See also and distinguish from ➤ **black box**.

EMR ➤ **educable mentally retarded**.

enactive representation A term introduced by J. Bruner in his theory of the development of representative thought. Enactive representations are based on action and movement, are rather primitive compared with ➤ **ikonic** and ➤ **symbolic representations** and are characterized by a failure on the part of the child to distinguish between perception and action. For example, a 'full glass' is represented enactively as 'one which can spill.'

enantiobiosis A relationship between organisms that is mutually antagonistic, the opposite of ➤ **symbiosis**.

enantiodromia Jung's term for the view that eventually all things become transformed into their opposites.

encapsulated nerve endings Structurally the opposite of free nerve endings, these are made up of a free nerve ending which penetrates a capsule of epithelial or muscular tissue and serve as receptors for certain kinds of stimulation. E.g., ➤ **Pacinian corpuscle**.

encapsulation, psychological K. Lewin's term for any behavior that prevents a person from experiencing a painful situation, such as refusing to read newspaper accounts of massacres or covering one's eyes when an accident is imminent.

encéphale isolé A surgical preparation produced by transaction of the brainstem at the caudal end of the medulla just above the spinal cord. An *encéphale isolé* animal is paralyzed but displays normal sleep-wake cycles. When the transection is further up, in the area between the superior and inferior colliculi (the *cerveau isolé* or *mid-collicular* transection), the animal is comatose. A cut made between these, the *midpontine* section, produces wakefulness.

encephalitis Inflammation of the membranes covering the brain or of the brain itself.

encephalization The gradual subsuming of the control of function by the brain. As an evolutionary process it is manifested to a greater and greater degree as one moves up the phylogenetic scale. ➤ **corticalization**.

encephal(o)- Combining form meaning *pertaining to the brain*.

encephalon Relatively rare term for the brain.

encephalopathy General term for any disease or dysfunction of the brain.

encode (encoding) ➤ **code**.

encoding specificity In *cognitive psychology*, the generalization that the initial encoding of learned material will reflect the influence of the context in which the learning took place. For example, learning a word like *jam* in the context *fruit-jam* typically leads to a diminished ability to recognize it when presented later in another context such as *traffic-jam*.

encopresis Fecal incontinence, involuntary expulsion of feces.

encounter group A small group which focuses on intensive interpersonal interactions (or 'encounters'). The group usually has as its goals the removal of psychological barriers and defenses, achieving openness, honesty and the willingness to deal with the difficulties of emotional expression. Group members are encouraged to deal with 'here-and-now' and to eschew intellectualization and personal history. Encounter groups and their use in psychotherapy began with the ➤ **human potential movement**.

encryption Within cryptography, the act or process of converting a message into a coded form; encoding.

enculturation The process by which an individual adapts to a new culture, eventually assimilating its practices, customs and values. ➤ **acculturation** and **socialization**.

end In the social sciences the term usu-

ally carries the connotations of a goal; an end is more than a mere terminus, it is that which is aimed at or desired, the result of purposeful striving.

end brain ➤ **telencephalon**.

end brush The delicate arborization of the ends of an axon.

end button ➤ **terminal button**.

endemic Restricted to a particular geographical area. Used in ➤ **epidemiology**; compare with ➤ **pandemic**.

end foot ➤ **terminal button**.

endo- Combining form meaning *within, inside* or *toward the inside*. var., *ento-*.

endocathection H. Murray's term for an inward cathection (➤ **cathexis**), a preoccupation with one's own feelings and thoughts; the opposite of ➤ **exocathection**.

endocrine Used of glands that secrete hormones internally; that is, their secretions are distributed through the body by the bloodstream, the glands are ductless. Contrast with ➤ **exocrine** and see the discussion under ➤ **gland**.

endocrine gland ➤ **gland**.

endocrinology The study of the body's internal secretions. The term is used broadly and the investigations go beyond the endocrine glands and include internal secretions of any source.

endoderm The inner layer of embryonic cellular structures that develops into the digestive tract and the viscera.

endogamy Limiting marriage to one's social or cultural group such as a caste or clan. Contrast with ➤ **exogamy**.

endogenous (or endogenic) Lit., originating from within. Used to refer to phenomena whose origins are internal or within the body. When the genesis of a phenomenon is clearly physiological the term *somatogenic* is typically used: when it appears to be mental, the term preferred is *psychogenic*. Contrast with ➤ **exogenous**.

endogenous clock ➤ **biological clock**.

endogenous depression ➤ **depression, endogenous**.

endogenous opiates A group of naturally occurring, opiate-like peptides produced by the brain or the pituitary; included are the *endorphins*, *enkephalins* and *dynorphins*. They play important roles in control of emotional behaviors such as those associated with pain, anxiety, fear, and related affective states produced by pain. The binding sites are found in a variety of locations including neurons in the ➤ **periaqueductal gray** and the ➤ **limbic system**.

endolymph The liquid found in the membranous canal of the semicircular canals of the inner ear.

endometrium The mucous membrane that lines the inner surface of the uterus.

endomorphy One of the three primary dimensions of body type (along with *ectomorphy* and *mesomorphy*) in Sheldon's ➤ **constitutional theory**. An endomorph is one whose physique is dominated by the embryonic endodermal component, fatty tissues and the viscera. Hence, endomorphic persons are overweight, have poorly developed muscles and bones, and have low skin surface area relative to weight.

endophasia 1. Internal speech. 2. Making the appropriate lip, tongue and jaw movements of speech but without producing any sound. Meaning 2 entails 1.

endopsychic Characterizing that which is in the mind.

end organ A general term for any sensory receptor.

endorphins ➤ **endogenous opiates**.

end plate Often called a *motor end plate*, the terminus of a neuron that makes functional contact with a muscle cell.

end-plate potential (EPP) The depolarization of the postsynaptic membrane caused by acetylcholine release by the terminus of the end plate. The E P P causes muscle fibers to fire and induces muscle contraction.

end-pleasure See discussion under ➤ **forepleasure**.

end test ➤ **post-test**.

enelicomorphism ➤ **pedomorphism**.

energy One of those terms that have a reasonably precise definition in the physical sciences but lose their clarity when dragged into psychological jargon. The best that can be done here is to point out that the term is usually used as a rough equivalent of *strength* or *vigor* as descriptive of psychological activity.

enervation 1. Diminishing of energy, weakening. 2. The removal of a nerve. Distinguish from ➤ **innervation**.

engineering psychology A branch of ➤ **industrial/organizational psychology** that focuses on the interface between the person and the machine. That is, the study of the behavior of individuals using tools, working with machines, etc. It also includes the design of machines so that they match the behavioral and cognitive capabilities of human operators.

engram A postulated biochemical change resulting from external stimulation. The term engram was coined by the German biologist Richard Semon, who hypothesized it to be the biochemical manifestation of memory, the permanent alteration of neural tissue that represents what has been learned. The decades-old 'search for the engram' as a reified entity has so far been unsuccessful and the term is used as kind of biological metaphor for what must, in principle, exist somewhere in the brain. Note that the term is used with the notion that each engram has a locus but also with the understanding that it may be quite diffuse and widespread.

engulfment R. D. Laing's term for a form of anxiety that is experienced by insecure persons who view relationships with others as threats to their identity.

enkephalins ➤ **endogenous opiates**.

enrichment A term applied to some theories of perceptual learning that assume that perceptual processes go beyond a direct representing of the various aspects of the stimulus field. Gestalt theory, for example, hypothesizes the use of organizational tendencies which structure the input stimulation to give rise to percepts. Contrast with ➤ **differentiation** (5).

enrichment program   A general term used for any educational program designed to enrich the environment of children from socially or culturally deprived circumstances. They typically are developed around special kindergarten classes or other pre-school programs that concentrate on the acquisition of basic verbal skills, although often social and interpersonal skills are part of the curriculum.

entelechy   1. Realization, actuality. In this sense the term is used in specific contrast to potential or that which is on the path to realization. 2. The 'vital force' proposed in the philosophy of ➤ **vitalism**.

enteroceptor   ➤ **interoceptor**.

ento-   ➤ **endo-**.

entoptic   Within the eye. Entoptic phenomena are visual experiences produced by factors within the eye itself; e.g., ➤ **floaters**.

entorhinal cortex   A part of the ➤ **hippocampal formation** that serves as the major input and output communication link between association areas of the neocortex and the ➤ **hippocampus**.

entrainment   A synchrony of movement between two or more persons. Such coordinated responsiveness is observed between adults and children and even in newborn infants reacting to their mother's voice and movements.

entrapment   In social and political psychology, the process whereby individuals and/or groups continue to increase their commitment to a policy that is clearly failing. Those involved become reluctant to relinquish their commitment since to do so is to proclaim that earlier analyses and allocations of resources were in error.

Hence, the commitment is escalated to justify the previous poor judgements. The process is all too familiar.

entropy   Formally, a mathematical measure of the disorganization or 'shuffledness' of a system. The term originally emerged from the study of heat and was first conceptualized as the portion of heat not available for doing work. It was within this context that the second law of thermodynamics stated that the entropy of a system never diminishes, thermal equilibrium (death) is the end state of all isolated systems. Within psychology: 1. In cognitive theory it tends to be associated with *uncertainty*. That is, the greater the uncertainty about the outcome of any situation the greater will be the information contained in it and the greater will be the measure of entropy. In this context see the discussion under ➤ **information**. 2. In psychoanalytic theory, the degree to which psychic energy is no longer available for use, having been invested in a particular object. Note that this distinctly metaphoric usage parallels the original thermodynamic conceptualization. 3. In social psychology, the amount of energy no longer available for producing social change and social progress. Here the metaphoric extension is rather extreme; it is simply unclear what form of 'energy' is referred to. The argument put forward is that increase of this 'social' entropy is responsible for the gradual decline and stagnation of a society or culture.

enuresis   Incontinence, the involuntary passing of urine. Sometimes equated with bed-wetting, particularly when it occurs in young children, although the term applies to a broader class of phenomena.

environment   The term comes from the Old French and translates roughly as *encircle*. Hence, the environment is that which surrounds. Clearly, this general a meaning is going to invite a wide range of uses. Typically the term will have a qualifier appended so that precisely what it is that is being surrounded is made clear. For example, the *cellular* environment consists of the tissue fluids that surround a cell; the *prenatal* (or *uterine*) environment is that enveloping the organism during gestation; an individual's *internal* environment consists of those physiological and psychological events occurring within him, etc. When the term is used without a qualifier it is generally taken to stand for the total physical and social surroundings of an individual organism. Note also that the term carries with it the connotation of influence, i.e. that which is part of a given environment of an organism is that which has some actual or potential role to play in the life of that organism. Hence, a city-council meeting in Cardiff would not be part of the environment of a New Yorker except in the most trivial and uninteresting sense. However, ultraviolet radiation, which one is utterly insensitive to as a stimulus event, would be considered part of each person's environment.

environmental demand ➤ **demand characteristics**.

environmental determinant ➤ **determinant**.

environmentalism A general term for a class of theoretical and philosophical schools that stresses the role of the environment in determining behavior. Contrast with ➤ **nativism** and ➤ **hereditarianism** and ➤➤ **heredity–environment controversy**.

environmentality The proportion of the variance of a particular *trait* in a population that can be traced to environmental factors. This term is preferred by those who feel that the term ➤ **heritability** invites researchers to focus too strongly on genetic factors and neglect the role of the environment on behavior. Environmentality is *1-heritability*.

environmental psychology An interdisciplinary subfield in psychology that draws from the data and theories developed in a variety of areas including social psychology, sociology, ethology, political science, architecture and anthropology and turns them upon, as the name suggests, issues involving the complex interactions between people and their environments.

envy Generally classified as a special form of anxiety, envy is based on, as McDougall put it, 'a grudging contemplation of more fortunate persons.' Usually distinguished from ➤ **jealousy**, where a third party, typically a loved one, is involved.

enzygotic Developed from the same ovum.

enzyme Any of a number of organic catalysts that produce chemical changes in other substances without being changed themselves. Enzymes are complex proteins found particularly in digestive processes that break down complex food substances into simpler compounds.

EOG ➤ **electro-oculogram**.

eonism An occasional synonym of ➤ **transvestism**. The term comes from the Chevalier d'Éon, an 18th-century political adventurer who achieved some notoriety by his preference for women's clothing.

EP ➤ **evoked potential**.

ep- ➤ **epi-**.

ependyma The membrane lining the cerebral ventricles and the central canal of the spinal cord.

epi- Prefix designating *outside*, *above*, *apart from*, *in addition to*. var., *ep-*.

epicritic 1. Generally, pertaining to extreme, highly developed sensitivity, particularly cutaneous sensitivity. 2. In H. Head's system of cutaneous sensibility, one of the two divisions of the afferent neural system which mediated the finely tuned, delicate responses to warm, cold and light pressure stimuli. The other, the ➤ **protopathic**, was assumed to be rather gross and undifferentiated and to be evolutionarily older. The neurological substrata of Head are no longer accepted but the sensitive discriminations he characterized are still called epicritic.

epidemic 1. In medicine, the rapid spread of an infectious disease through a population. 2. By extension, the rapid spread of a social/psychological phenomenon through a population; e.g., an epidemic of suicide occurred when the stock market crashed in 1929.

epidemiology A hybrid science with psychological, sociological, demographic and medical aspects that deals with the study of diseases, their distributions in populations and their environmental impact.

epidermis The outer layer of the skin.

epigenesis The notion that during development the complex morphological properties of an organism develop gradually out of an interaction between the prenatal environment and intracellular processes. Compare with ➤ **preformationism**.

epiglottis The thin valve-like structure of cartilage that covers the *glottis* and prevents food and drink from entering the *larynx*.

epilepsy An umbrella term for a number of disorders characterized by various combinations of the following: periodic motor or sensory seizures (or their *epileptic equivalent*) with or without actual convulsions, clouding of or loss of consciousness, motor, sensory or cognitive malfunctions, and accompanied by an abnormal encephalogram (EEG). A number of classification systems for the epilepsies have been proposed, some based on the etiology of the disorder, some on the cortical locus of the abnormal discharge, others on the EEG pattern manifested, on the clinical form of the seizures themselves, the severity of the seizures or on various combinations of some or all of these factors. The following entries present the most commonly diagnosed forms of epilepsy and give the standard clinical characterizations of each. The root term itself comes from the Greek, meaning *to seize* or *grasp*. Also called *seizure disorder*.

epilepsy, cryptogenic Any epilepsy for which there is no clear-cut cause. Also called *idiopathic epilepsy*.

epilepsy, focal Epilepsy characterized by a relatively localized focus of the cortical dysfunction and manifested by similarly specific sensory-motor seizures. Also called *partial epilepsy*. Compare with ➤ **generalized *epilepsy**.

epilepsy, generalized Epilepsy characterized by diffuse, general seizures with an EEG pattern that reveals pathological activity over the entire surface of the brain. Compare with ➤ **focal *epilepsy**.

epilepsy, idiopathic Epilepsy for which there is no known organic cause. Compare with ➤ **symptomatic *epilepsy**.

epilepsy, Jacksonian motor A form of focal epilepsy characterized by seizures involving involuntary motor movements on the side of the body contralateral to the cortical locus of the disturbance. Usually the movements spread from central muscle groups to others and may involve one whole side of the body. This spreading of the seizure is termed *Jacksonian march*.

epilepsy, Jacksonian sensory A form of focal epilepsy analogous to ➤ **Jacksonian motor *epilepsy**, except that the primary symptoms are specific and localized sensory disturbances.

epilepsy, major Epilepsy characterized by gross convulsive tonic-clonic seizures, loss of consciousness and loss of control over various autonomic functions (e.g., bladder and bowel control). Also called *grand mal epilepsy* and the seizures *grand mal seizures*.

epilepsy, minor A general label for any epilepsy characterized by nonconvulsive seizures (or their epileptic equivalent). Often there is only a momentary lapse of consciousness and/or minor sensory-motor dysfunction. Also called *petit mal epilepsy*.

epilepsy, psychomotor A form of epilepsy characterized by periodic behavior disturbances manifested typically as repetitive and often highly organized movements that are carried out unconsciously and semiautomatically.

epilepsy, symptomatic A general term for any epilepsy for which there is a known organic cause. Compare with ➤ **idiopathic *epilepsy**.

epilepsy, temporal (lobe) Epilepsy where the focus of the cerebral dysfunction is the temporal lobe of the cortex.

epileptic equivalent A general term for any episodic sensory or motor symptom which an epileptic may experience instead of convulsive seizures.

epileptogenic Characterizing factors that cause epilepsy or circumstances that produce seizures in individuals with epilepsy.

epinephrine A hormone of the adrenal medulla whose effects are similar to those brought about by stimulation of the sympathetic division of the autonomic nervous system, e.g., cardiac stimulation, vasoconstriction, arousal. The term itself comes from the Greek and translates as *on the kidney*. It is the preferred synonym of ➤ **adrenalin**; see that entry for reasons why. Note, however, that the adjectival form in general use is still ➤ **adrenergic**; **epinephrinergic** just never took hold even in the technical literature.

epinosic (gain) ➤ **secondary gain**.

epiphenomenalism A term used primarily within a metaphysical context to refer to the doctrine that 'mental life,' 'mind,' 'consciousness,' and other similar constructs are but the manifestations or by-products of a complex neurological system and are without causal influence. O. H. Mowrer put it most succinctly: '. . . epiphenomenalism posits that the physical world is the only true reality and that psychic events are inconsequential excrescences.'

epiphenomenon Any event that occurs in the presence of or incidentally accompanies some other process or event but in fact plays no part in that process or event. For example, a good case can be made for the notion that dreams are epiphenomena that merely accompany biochemical and neurological events during sleep.

epiphysis 1. In the developing infant and child, a boneforming (ossification) center attached to another bone by cartilage. The degree of ossification can be used as a measure of growth. **2.** A shortened form of *epiphysis cerebri*, the ➤ **pineal gland**.

episcotister A device used for studying visual perception. It consists basically of a disc with slots in it. When a light source is placed behind it and the disc rotated, the light will be visible only when it shines through the slots. By varying the width of the slots and the speed of rotation of the disc, precise control over the visual stimulus may be achieved. ➤ **critical flicker frequency** and **Talbot-Plateau law** for examples of its use in early research; it is seldom used today.

episode Any relatively well-defined event or coordinated sequence of events that is perceived as a unit, as a whole. Episodes are generally marked as occurring in particular times and places. See, e.g., ➤ **episodic *memory, psychotic episode**.

episode marker ➤ **marker, episode**.

episode theory ➤ **instance theory**.

episodic amnesia ➤ **amnesia, episodic**.

episodic memory ➤ **memory, episodic**.

epistemology The branch of philosophy that is concerned with the origins, nature, methods and limits of human knowledge.

epistemophilia Love of knowledge, derivation of pleasure from the acquisition of knowledge.

epithelium Any thin layer of tissue that covers the surface or lines the cavity of an organ. Generally performs a secreting or protective function.

eponym A name for a thing, process or function that is adapted from the name of a person.

EPP ➤ **end-plate potential**.

epsilon motion ➤ **motion, epsilon**

EPSP Abbrev. for *excitatory postsynaptic potential*; ➤ **postsynaptic potential**.

EQ ➤ **educational quotient**.

equal and unequal cases method A variation on the *method of constant stimuli*; ➤ **measurement of threshold**.

equal-appearing-intervals method A method of scaling in which the subject is asked to sort stimuli into groups separated by equal steps. The technique is used in psychophysical work, where the stimuli may be lights, weights, tones, etc., and in social psychology, where the stimuli may be statements of opinions, attitudes, preferences, etc. ➤➤ **methods of *scaling, Thurstone-type scales**.

equal-interval scale ➤ **scales**.

equality, judgement of Quite literally, the judgement that two (or more) stimuli are equal. However, the term must be applied loosely since two compared stimuli rarely if ever give the impression of true equality; a judgement of equality is really a judgement of doubt concerning the confidence that the individual has that he has in fact detected a real difference between the stimuli. ➤➤ **signal-detection theory**.

equality, law of A Gestalt principle of perceptual organization stating that, as the several components of a perceptual field become more similar, they will tend to be perceived as a unit.

equal-sense differences method Another term for ➤ **equal-appearing-intervals method**.

equated score(s) Any two sets of scores from different tests or from different parts of the same test (assuming that the same variable is being measured) that have been reduced to a common scale (i.e. 'equated') to facilitate comparisons. *Percentile scores* and *standard *scores* are both examples.

equation, empirical Any mathematical equation that is used to fit observed data. Empirical equations are essentially after-the-fact attempts to characterize quantitatively a set of observations, and the value of such an equation is given by the closeness of the 'fit' between it and the data; theory is not an important issue here. Fechner's psychophysical law is a classic example. Compare with ➤ **rational *equation**.

equation method ➤ **measurement of *threshold**.

equation, rational A logical or mathematical expression based on (rational) assumptions about processes. Such equations differ from *empirical *equations* in that their parameters are derived by deduction from theoretical assumptions and not simply from attempts to fit data. ➤ **stimulus sampling theory** for an example of a theoretical model in psychology that lends itself to such a pattern of logical deduction of formulae.

equi- Word element meaning *equal* or *equally*.

equilibration 1. Generally, achieving a balance between opposing forces. **2.** In Piagetian theory, the process by which a balance between *assimilation* and *accommodation* is maintained and whereby conflicting *schemas* can be integrated into new structures. In a sense it is a cognitive analog of the physiological notion of *homeostasis*, with the added element that as the child centers on new aspects of the environment the process of maintaining equilibrium becomes the mechanism that ultimately produces the transition to a higher cognitive state.

equilibrium Basically the term is used as a synonym of *balance*, with several special usages: **1.** In physiology, the point at which opposing biochemical reactions are stable, *homeostasis*. **2.** In perception, a point at which the body maintains a stable upright posture with respect to its center of gravity. Sometimes called the *equilibrium sense* or *static sense*. **3.** In social psychology, the theoretical tendency for a social system to bring about corrective changes to maintain itself as a functionally integrated unit. Note that this usage carries the notion of a *process*; the others represent it as a point of balance with the process that we know must be there left implicit. **4.** In Piaget's theory, a cognitive state whereby the information available to the child is in equilibrium or balance with the existing cognitive schemas held. Such states may be quite temporary, especially during the early sensorimotor, preoperational and concrete operational stages, or they may be rather stable and permanent as at the formal operational stage.

equipotentiality Lit., of the same potential. There are several specialized usages: **1.** In embryology, a generalization that states that any section of the embryonic tissue can develop into any part of the fully developed organism. In its extreme form this generalization is incorrect, but within limits (i.e. during the germinal phase prior to production of specific enzymes) the phenomenon may be observed. The further down the phylogenetic scale one looks the more valid becomes the generalization. **2.** In neurophysiology, the term refers to the hypothesis that all the neurons that mediate a given sensory modality have a common competing function in addition to their specific functions. That is, each has 'equal potential' for participating in a sensory event within that modality. **3.** By extension, the notion that within certain limits one portion of the cerebral cortex can take on the functions of another part.

equity theory A general label for a class of broad social psychological theories that seek to explain behavior by reference to the concept of equity, i.e. those conditions in which the rewards to individuals in a group are in proportion to their efforts on behalf of the group. The chief argument of its proponents is that such diverse phenomena as *altruism*, *power*, *aggression*, *cooperation* and the like can be subsumed under an analysis of equity/inequity.

equivalence In general, any relationship between two 'things' such that one may be substituted for the other in a particular setting and not alter significantly the situation. The term is often modified so that the particular form of equivalence is specified; e.g., *stimulus* equivalence refers to two or more stimuli that are sufficiently similar that they evoke the same or nearly the same response, *response* equivalence refers to similar responses made to similar stimuli, etc.

equivalence belief A term coined by E. C. Tolman for the hypothesized internal state of an organism such that it responds to a subgoal as it would to the goal. Hence it was used as roughly synonymous with *secondary reinforcement*.

equivalence, coefficient of A correlation coefficient used to evaluate the consistency or reliability of a particular test. Generally carried out by comparing scores on two separate but equivalent forms of the test. ➤ **coefficient of *reliability** and **equivalent forms *reliability**.

equivalence of cues, acquired ➤ **acquired discrimination of cues**.

equivalent forms ➤ **alternate forms *reliability**.

equivalent groups procedure ➤ **matched groups procedure**.

erectile disorder ➤ **male erectile disorder**.

erethism An unusually high sensitivity to sensory stimulation.

ERG ➤ **electroretinogram**.

erg 1. In physics, the work done by a force of 1 dyne acting through a displacement of 1 centimeter in the direction of the force. **2.** In psychology the term is used in a variety of combinations that are metaphoric and relate to energy, force, purpose or dynamic qualities.

-ergic Suffix denoting *work*, *function*, *purpose*. It is used in physiology to characterize a neuron or a neural pathway in terms of the operative neurotransmitter; e.g., *dopaminergic* refers to a neural structure in which dopamine is the substance that 'does the work.'

ergic Purposive. Used by R. B. Cattell to pertain to innate drives or predispositions.

erg(o)- Combining form meaning *work*.

ergodic In probability theory, characteristic of any stochastic process in which every sequence of events is statistically the same and therefore may be taken as representative of the whole.

ergograph Any device for measuring the amount of work accomplished by a muscle or muscle group.

ergonomics The science of the 'fit' between jobs and persons, the study of the relationship between an individual's anatomy, physiology and psychology and the demands of particular forms of work. ➤ **human factors**.

erogenous zones Areas of the body the stimulation of which gives rise to erotic or sexual sensations. Occasionally called *erotogenic zones*.

Eros The Greek god of love. In Freudian theory, Eros refers to the whole complex of life-preservative instincts. Included among them, of course, are the sexual instincts. Compare with Freud's use of ➤ **Thanatos**, the totality of death instincts.

erotic Generally, sexual or libidinal. Used broadly, it may pertain to; **1.** Feelings arising from the genitals specifically. **2.** A more general sense of sexual arousal. **3.** The stimuli that give rise to sexual arousal. **4.** Any motive or need that has sexual components. **5.** Love in any of its manifestations.

erotic apathy ➤ **sexual apathy**.

eroticism 1. Sexual arousal. **2.** A greater than average disposition for the sexual, a tendency to be easily aroused sexually. **3.** Sexual excitement arising from areas other than those specifically sexual, other than the genitals. Usually the area is specified; e.g. *anal eroticism*. var., *erotism*.

erotization A psychoanalytic term for the process by which a body part or bodily function becomes a source of erotic pleasure.

eroto- Combining form meaning pertaining to *sex*, *sexuality*, *love*.

erotogenic zones ➤ **erogenous zones**.

erotomania General term for any exaggerated sexual drive.

ERP ➤ **event-related potential**.

error There are several *general* senses in which this term is used: **1.** A departure from correctness. **2.** A mistaken belief. **3.** The state of holding a mistaken belief. **4.** In statistics, a departure from a true score, a ➤ **deviation 5.** In an experiment, any variation in the dependent variable caused by factors other than variation in the independent variable. **6.** An inappropriate or incorrect response that results in a delay in the learning of the correct response.

There are also scores of *specialized* usages of this inherently appealing term. In the following entries those more often used in psychology are given. Note that qualifiers are often used to locate the source of or characterize the nature of error.

error, absolute The absolute value (i.e. without regard to sign) of the difference between an observed value and the true value of a measure. For example, *over*-estimating someone's height by two inches produces the same absolute error as *under*-estimating by two inches.

error, anticipation An error in a serial-learning task such that the subject responds with an item prior to its correct serial position.

error, average Lit., the average error in a series of observations or judgements.

error, chance Simply, an error that arises from chance factors. Since such errors are in principle random and unbiased they tend to cancel each other out and the sum of chance errors, when a sufficiently large number of cases is considered, approaches zero. Also called *variable error*, *accidental error*, *random error*. Compare with ➤ **constant *error**.

error, compensating Any error that cancels out a previously made error. It may be introduced deliberately to correct for another source of error.

error, constant An error produced by some factor that affects all observations similarly so that the errors are always in one direction and do not cancel each other out. Usually a constant error can be detected and corrected for during statistical analysis. Also called *systematic error*.

error, experimental This term covers a large class of possible errors whose origins lie in the inadequacy of an experimental design or procedure. The history of psychology is well salted with legendary experimental errors due to improper control of some important factor. The most common are failures to control for practice effects, time errors, observer differences, experimenter biases, physiological and species differences and the ubiquitous sampling errors.

error, grouping Any error introduced by the manner in which the data are combined or grouped. In general when data are grouped into classes the statistical operations carried out on those classes are based on the assumption that the combined scores are symmetrically distributed around the midpoint of each class. As a quick look at ➤ **sampling *error** will show, this assumption is often not met and hence some measure of grouping error will emerge during such procedures.

error, instrumental A constant error due to a bias in the apparatus.

error, measurement Any constant error due to a bias in the process of measurement. It may be due to the apparatus, the observer, the subject or the experimenter.

error, perseverative Generally, any tendency for a subject to persevere inappropriately with a particular response. For example, in a serial-learning experiment, remaking a response later in the series than is correct.

error, probable Occasionally used as a measure of the error of estimate or of the sampling error. The probable error is exactly 0.6745 of the ➤ **standard error**.

error, sampling A general term used for any difference between the true value of a statistic within a population and the estimated value of that statistic derived from a sample of that population. Since nearly all work in psychology is based on sam-

ples and not on complete populations, there will almost always be some sampling error. Naturally, one tries to keep this kind of error to a minimum by selecting samples which are representative of the true population and by using as large a sample as is conveniently possible. Note, however, that sampling errors may emerge in two fashions. The first, the one which is inescapable and hence regarded as a legitimate form of error, results from inexorable laws of probability and sampling. The second, the kind which is in principle preventable, results from nonrepresentative sloppy, incomplete or biased sampling. ➤ **sampling** et seq.

error, stimulus To commit the stimulus error, according to E. B. Titchener's brand of structuralism, was to lapse during introspection from the 'psychological' point of view to some other perspective. A stimulus error would result when the subject allowed mediated experience to interfere with the introspection of immediate experience. A butcher who, because of experience with estimating weights, reports that a 2-lb object is 'twice as heavy' as a 1-lb object commits the stimulus error because the response is based on mediated experience with weights rather than on the basis of immediate experience with the weights as they feel at the time of the experiment.

error, subjective A systematic error introduced into observation or interpretation due to an individual's biases or prejudices.

error, time An error in judgement concerning comparisons between two or more events or stimuli based on their temporal order of presentation. By convention, if the first of two objectively equal stimuli is erroneously judged the greater it is termed a *positive* time error; should the second be so judged it is termed a *negative* time error.

error, Type I (and **Type II**) In testing the significance of an experimental result one is, in essence, determining whether to accept or reject the null hypothesis.

Under such conditions there are two types of errors that one is laid open to: (a) the erroneous rejection of a true hypothesis; or (b) the failure to reject a hypothesis that is, in fact, false. The first of these is called a *Type I error* (or, on occasion, an *alpha error*); the second is known as a *Type II error* (or *beta error*). Note that Type I and Type II errors are inextricably linked with each other. If one sets a particularly stringent level of *significance* (or *alpha level*) a Type I error becomes very unlikely but the possibility of a Type II error is raised accordingly; a lenient alpha level lowers the chance of a Type II error but markedly raises the possibility of making a Type I error.

error variance That proportion of the ➤ **variance** that cannot be attributed to controlled factors. Error variance will be inflated by sampling errors, measurement errors, experimental errors, etc.

erythr(o)- From the Greek, a prefix meaning *red*.

erythropia Vision where objects are tinged red. It can result from overexposure to intense light, as in snow blindness. var., *erythropsia*.

ESB ➤ **electrical brain stimulation**.

E scale ➤ **measurement of *authoritarianism**.

escape from reality ➤ **flight from *reality**.

escape learning (or **conditioning**) A form of learning by which the organism acquires an instrumental or operant response that permits it to escape a noxious or painful stimulus. Escape learning is often discussed in conjunction with ➤ **avoidance learning**.

escape mechanism A loose synonym for ➤ **defense mechanism**.

escape training Generally, any experimental procedure in which the subject must learn an escape response.

ESN Abbrev. for *educationally subnormal*; ➤ **educable mentally retarded**.

esotropia A form of ➤ **strabismus** in which one eye turns inward when the other fixates on an object.

ESP ➤ **extra-sensory perception**.

EST 1. Abbreviation for *electroshock therapy*. 2. An acronym for Erhard Seminar Training. A form of psychotherapy based on the 'theories' of Werner Erhard (né Jack Rosenberg, a one-time sales manager). The procedure consists of large group sessions of rather extraordinary intensity. For up to 60 hours several hundred people are gathered in a large hall and subjected to physical privation, guided (some would say forced) meditation and fervent diatribes on the EST way to 'get in touch' with one's inner sense of personal responsibility. Fortunately in recent years EST seems to have diminished in popularity; ➤ **innovative therapies**.

-esthesia, -esthesis, esthesio- Combining forms from the Greek for *sensation* and used for *feeling*, *sensibility*, *sensitivity*, etc. var., *-aesthesia*.

esthesiometer Any device for measuring sensitivity to touch, specifically a compass-like instrument for determining the two-point threshold on the skin.

estimate **1** n. Loosely, a reasonable guess concerning the value of some factor. **2** n. In statistics, somewhat more precisely, a 'best guess' of the value of some variable or statistic based on refined computational procedures which provide both the estimated value as well as a measure of the likelihood that that value falls within ascertainable limits of the true value. An estimate in this sense is an inference about a population based on measurements made on a sample.

estradiol The most biologically potent of the naturally occurring ➤ **estrogens**. It is produced primarily by the ovaries and, in small amounts, by the adrenal cortices.

estriol An estrogenic hormone that is regarded as a metabolic product of ➤ **estradiol** and ➤ **estrone**.

estrogen A generic label for a group of related steroid hormones produced chiefly by the ovaries, but also by the adrenal cortices and, in very small amounts, by the testes. Included are *estradiol, estrone* and their metabolic product, *estriol*. Estrogens are responsible for the morphogenesis of the gonads and the development of most of the female secondary sex characteristics, breast development, maturation of the genitalia, deposition of body fat – but not axillary and pubic hair: growth here is the result of *androstenedione*, an ➤ **androgen**. They are also responsible for the cyclic changes in the uterus that accompany the ➤ **menstrual cycle** – or, in non-primate mammals, the ➤ **estrus cycle**. ➤➤ **progesterone**. var., *oestrogen*.

estrone The less potent biologically of the primary ➤ **estrogens**.

estrus ➤ **estrus cycle**.

estrus cycle The ovarian cycle in female sub-primate mammals. It has four stages: proestrus, estrus, matestrus and diestrus. The second stage, *estrus*, is that associated with ovulation, swelling of the vulva, various uterine processes and receptivity to copulation. The term *estrus* comes from the Greek, meaning *mad* or *frenetic desire*, and is often used for the periodic sexual desire or *heat* displayed by female animals. var., *oestrus*. ➤➤ **menstrual cycle**.

eta A correlation coefficient for curvilinear relationships. Compare with ➤ **product moment *correlation**, which expresses linear relationships between two variables.

eta squared The square of the value of ➤ **eta**. It is an estimate of the proportion of the variance in the data in a curvilinear relationship that can be attributed to the relationship.

ethics A branch of philosophy concerned with that which is deemed acceptable in human behavior, with what is good or bad, right or wrong with human conduct in pursuit of goals and aims. There is a tendency to use the term for theoretical treatises, for examinations of the ideal; when actual human behavior in social and cultural settings is under consideration (particularly with regard to developmental issues and the acquisition of codes of ethics) many authors will use *morality* and related terms. See, for more discussion, ➤ **moral** et seq.

ethinamate A nonbarbiturate sedative used primarily as a sleeping pill. Its effects are similar to *chloral hydrate*.

ethnic group Originally this term was used to refer to groups of people who were biologically related. The usage has been intentionally expanded and an ethnic group is now seen as any group with common cultural traditions and a sense of identity. Thus, ethnic groups may be bound together by a sense of history and tradition (Jews), language (the Dakota Indians), geography (Scandinavians), a sociological definition of race (American Blacks), religion (Moslems), etc. Usually the term is reserved for minority groups, although not always; some social psychologists will call the dominant group in a society an ethnic group. Although ethnic groups will often be racial groups, the terms are no longer used synonymously.

ethnic psychosis ➤ **culture-specific syndrome**.

ethnocentrism 1. The tendency to view one's own ethnic group and its social standards as the basis for evaluative judgements concerning the practices of others – with the implication that one views one's own standards as superior. Hence, ethnocentrism connotes a habitual disposition to look with disfavor on the practices of alien groups. The term is the ethnic analog of egocentrism. 2. In some instances, a synonym for ➤ **sociocentrism**. But see that term.

ethnography A division of anthropology devoted to the comparative study of individual cultures. var., *ethnology*.

ethnomethodology A term originally coined by the sociologist H. Garfinkel to describe the study of the 'resources' available to participants in social interactions and how these resources are utilized by them. The term, which Garfinkel later came to regard as a shibboleth, is generally used to refer to a body of sociological and psychological research on conversational rules, negotiation of property rights and other socially motivated interactions. Such research is generally carried out by naturalistic observation techniques.

ethogram As total a record as is possible of the behavior of an animal in a naturalistic setting. The term carries a theoretical assumption in the notion that within the behavioral repertoire of a species there is only a finite number of fixed, repeatable behavior patterns that can enter into an ethogram. ➤ **ethology** (4).

ethology The term derives originally from the Greek *ethos* meaning *character* or *essential nature* and *-ology* meaning *study of*. Hence, it has been used for: **1.** The study of ethics, especially comparative examination of ethical systems. **2.** The empirical investigation of human character. **3.** The study of cultural customs. All three of these meanings are, however, rarely intended today. The term is, in contemporary psychology, used almost exclusively for: **4.** An interdisciplinary science combining zoology, biology and comparative psychology concerned with precise observation of the behavior of animals in their natural environment and the development of theoretical characterizations of that behavior with regard to the subtle interplay of genetic and environmental factors. The science has its origins in the work of the European naturalists Lorenz, Tinbergen, Thorpe, von Frisch and others. The primary focus of ethological research is the complete, exhaustive analysis of behavior using techniques of ➤ **naturalistic observation**. In this respect it is usually distinguished from ➤ **comparative psychology**, where experimental-manipulative techniques and controlled laboratory techniques are the rule.

etiology The study of the causes of disease. var., *aetiology*.

etymology The study of the historical origins and development of linguistic forms.

eu- Combining form meaning *healthy, well, normal, advantageous.*

Euclidean space ➤ **space** (1).

eufunction A term occasionally used as the antonym of ➤ **dysfunction**. Since *function* is, strictly speaking, a value-neutral term, eufunction is sometimes used to specify positive, healthy functions.

eugenics The study of human heredity patterns with the goal of improving the species through selective breeding. *Positive* eugenics emphasized encouraging individuals with 'desirable' traits to procreate and *negative* eugenics focused on discouraging those with 'undesirable' traits from procreating (often by unethical procedures such as forced sterilization). Unfortunately (or should we say fortunately) agreement about which characteristics it is desirable to perpetuate has not been achieved. Since the founding of the discipline by Francis Galton in the 19th century, eugenicists have been unable to extricate themselves from their own ethnocentrism.

eunuch A prepubertally castrated male. The term is also used to describe the physical characteristics of a eunuch – poor muscle tone, lack of bodily hair, undeveloped genitalia. Occasionally the term is used to refer to a female who has lost the ovaries.

euphoria **1.** A sense of extreme elation generally accompanied by optimism and a deep sense of well-being and heightened activity. In pathological cases it may be totally unrealistic, contain delusions of grandeur and invulnerability and include manic levels of activity. ant., *dysphoria*. **2.** H. S. Sullivan also used it to refer to a feeling of deep satisfaction, well-being and comfort. However, compared with meaning 1, in his sense the emotion is rather constrained and relaxed.

eupsychia A. Maslow's term for the humanistic utopia which would be reached when all persons were psychologically healthy – at least psychologically healthy in the sense characterized by Maslow's particular brand of optimistic humanism.

See, in this regard, ➤ **humanistic psychology** and **need hierarchy**.

eurymorph ➤ **body-build index**.

eustachian tube Small tube of bone and cartilage that connects the middle ear with the pharynx, serving to equalize air pressure on either side of the tympanic membrane.

euthanasia Easy and painless death or the means for producing one. Advocated by many for those suffering from intractable pain that accompanies the terminal stages of many incurable diseases. A distinction worth noting (in respect to matters legal and ethical) is that drawn between *passive* euthanasia, when one simply ceases to supply requisite extraordinary support measures needed to keep an individual alive, and *active* euthanasia, when specific means are taken to terminate life.

euthenics The discipline that seeks to improve the lot of the human being by regulating the environment. The insurmountable ethical problems of ➤ **eugenics** have contributed to the development of this field.

euthymia Tranquility, a pleasant relaxed state.

euthymic mood Normal mood where the range of emotions has neither depressed nor highly elevated states.

evaluation 1. Generally, the determining of the value or worth of something. 2. More specifically, the determination of how successful a program, a curriculum, a series of experiments, a drug, etc. has been in achieving the goals laid out for it at the outset. 3. One of the three hypothesized universal dimensions of *semantic space* in Osgood's theory of word meaning. ➤ **semantic differential**.

evaluation research An area of applied psychology concerned with development of procedures for testing the effectiveness of social, educational, therapeutic or other applied programs. ➤ **evaluation** (2).

event An occurrence, a phenomenon, a slice of reality, indeed anything that happens that has a beginning and an end and can be specified in terms of change. Thus, one speaks of stimuli as events, of responses as events, likewise of reinforcements, of outcomes of trials, and so on. The word is ubiquitous in psychology and everyone uses it in whatever fashion makes them comfortable.

event related potential (ERP) ➤ **evoked potential**.

eviration 1. Castration. 2. Loss of masculine characteristics. 3. A delusion in a man that he has become a woman.

evocative therapy A general term used primarily by behavioral therapists for any form of psychotherapy that focuses on underlying causes of psychological disorders, i.e. the psychoanalytic and psychodynamic. The term was coined by J. D. Frank to emphasize that these approaches functioned by attempting to evoke changes in internal conditions and thereby produce socially acceptable behaviors.

evoke To elicit, call forth. Generally used to refer to responses that are elicited from an organism or from a part of an organism by stimulation.

evoked potential A regular pattern of electrical activity recorded from neural tissue evoked by a controlled stimulus. The term usually applies to potentials from large masses of central-nervous-system tissue, specifically the brain. Also called *event related potential*.

evolution 1. Generally and loosely, orderly development. Here one finds reference to evolution of thought, of theory, of style, and the like. 2. More specifically, the process by which plant and animal forms developed by descent, with modification, from earlier existing forms. See here ➤ **evolutionary theory**.

evolutionary psychology A broad approach to the study of psychology that seeks to understand behaviors in their evolutionary contexts. Although the approach shares with ➤ **sociobiology** a focus on genetic and biological constraints, it places more emphasis on the role of social and cognitive factors which tend to be neglected by sociobiologists.

evolutionary theory Frequently one sees the terms *evolution, evolutionary theory, theory of evolution* and others used as though they were synonyms and all denoting the particular position put forward by Charles Darwin. This pattern of usage tends to be misleading. Evolution is not theory, it is fact; the 'gradualist' position of origin of species by natural selection put forward by Darwin (➤ **Darwinism**) is one attempt to explain that fact. Defenders of creationism frequently mistake disputes over the best characterization of the process of evolution as indications that biologists themselves regard evolution as merely a 'theoretical' notion.

Evolutionary theory has been the stage for many vigorous disputes, ranging from early (indeed, pre-Darwinian) arguments over the role of Lamarckian processes (➤ **inheritance of *acquired characteristics**) to the current debate between the gradualists who, with Darwin, argue that new species developed slowly (relatively speaking) and in an orderly way and the saltationists who defend the position of punctuated equilibrium that argues that new species appear suddenly (relatively speaking) and abruptly, to the seemingly endless argument over whether principles of organic evolution can be applied to the social and cultural milieu (➤ **sociobiology**). These disputes notwithstanding, the impact that evolutionary theory has had upon scientific thought, philosophy and theology is incalculable.

In psychology evolutionary doctrine produced a genuine revolution. It ushered in the study of individual differences with its emphasis on mental testing; it provided the rationale for the field of comparative psychology and made legitimate the inference from animal work to human; it stressed the concepts of adaptation, function and purpose which became dominant in American and European psychology

during the 20th century; it focused attention on the role of genetical material which eventually culminated in the discipline of behavior genetics; and finally, by stressing inheritance, it profoundly influenced the field of developmental psychology. Indeed, there is probably no area of contemporary psychological thinking that has remained immune from its influence.

ex- Prefix indicating *out, out of, away from.*

exafference ➤ **reafference.**

exaptation In evolutionary biology, the process whereby forms or structures that evolved to serve one function are co-opted to serve other functions. The human use of the tongue for speech is a good example.

exceptional child As used in child psychology the term refers to extremely talented and gifted children as well as to those having low intelligence or other learning disabilities. The application of the term to the latter group was well-motivated, to remove from the child the stigma of being classified as 'retarded' or 'minimally functional.' Unfortunately, the effect seems to have been one of altering and contaminating the meaning of the term *exceptional* rather than changing the characterization of the methods of dealing with the children so designated.

exchange theory ➤ **social exchange theory.**

excitable Generally, capable of being aroused or excited. It is widely used as descriptive of: (a) living tissue, specifically neural tissue, that is in a state whereby it will respond to a stimulus; (b) a person who is in a state such that they are easily aroused to emotional reactions; (c) a person who is characteristically easily aroused, etc.

excitant Rare synonym for ➤ **stimulus.**

excitation 1. In physiology, a process whereby some stimulus energy pattern sets up a change or pattern of changes in a receptor. The energy here may be either

265

physical or other neural activity; ➤ **stimulation**. **2.** In the study of learning, a general high level of activity in the whole nervous system; a reasonable synonym here is *drive state*. **3.** In social psychology, an increase in psychological tension; this meaning is intuitively close to conventional usage.

excitatory conditioning ➤ **conditioning, excitatory**.

excitatory irradiation ➤ **irradiation**.

excitatory postsynaptic potential (EPSP) ➤ **postsynaptic potential**.

excitatory potential ($_SE_R$) In Hull's theory, a hypothesized state assumed to reflect an organism's tendency to make a response.

excitatory threshold ➤ **threshold** (3).

excitement–calm (or **excitement–quiescence**) One of the dimensions of Wundt's three-dimensional theory of emotion. The others: pleasantness–unpleasantness and tension–relaxation.

excitotoxin Any agent that overstimulates nerve cells to the point of destroying them.

executive Used primarily in models of cognition, particularly those represented as computer models, it refers to a hypothesized 'master program' that controls and directs small, more limited sub-programs. In some ways the executive program is the modern version of the ➤ **homunculus**.

executive area In neurophysiology, a term used loosely to refer to any cortical area that serves integrative, organizing functions.

executive ego function A term used occasionally in psychoanalytic theory to characterize the management role that the ego plays.

exemplar theory ➤ **instance theory**.

exercise, law (or **principle**) **of** A generalization first formulated by E. L. Thorndike that, 'other things being equal,' repeated performance of any act makes the behavior easier to perform, more fluid and less prone to error. As a generalization it has some merit and certainly seems intuitively obvious. Unfortunately, specifying what 'other things being equal' really means has driven several behaviorially oriented psychologists to grief. See also the ➤ **law of *use** and the ➤ **law of *disuse**, each of which is included within the generalization.

exhaustion **1.** Physiologically, a state in which the metabolic process has been depleted, producing fatigue, weariness and a general lack of responsiveness. **2.** In ethology, the draining of action-specific energy for a particular instinctive act by constant repetition. When used in this sense metabolic depletion is not entailed since the muscles used in the act are not themselves necessarily fatigued. This meaning is also found vaguely represented in the way some psychoanalysts characterize the draining off of libido. **3.** Shortened form of ➤ **exhaustion stage**.

exhaustion delirium An acute delirium occasionally observed under conditions of extreme exhaustion brought about by intense extended physical effort or by other debilitating conditions such as high fever.

exhaustion stage The third stage in the ➤ **general adaptation syndrome**.

exhaustive search ➤ **search, exhaustive**.

exhibitionism **1.** Generally, a strong tendency to make oneself the constant center of attention. **2.** A ➤ **paraphilia** characterized by a compulsion to expose one's genitals under socially inappropriate circumstances.

exhibitionistic need H. Murray's term for the need to be the center of attraction, to entertain others, to amuse, excite and shock others.

existential analysis The generally accepted translation of *Daseinanalyse*. See the discussions under ➤ **existentialism** and ➤ **existential therapy**.

existential anxiety The feeling of fear,

even dread that can accompany a choice involving unknowns.

existentialism An important 20th-century philosophical movement which carved out a domain for itself between rationalistic idealism and totally objective materialism. The emphasis is upon personal decision to be made in a world without reason and without purpose. Existentialism emphasizes subjectivity, free will and individuality and has acted as a philosophical counterbalance to theories that stress the role of society and social groups. It has also spawned a form of psychotherapy (➤ **existential therapy**) that focuses on free will and the necessity for individual choice, action and judgement.

existential psychology This label was once used for the point of view espoused by E. B. Titchener (➤ **structuralism**). However, when found today it almost invariably refers to one or another version of the psychological positions that have emerged from ➤ **existentialism**.

existential therapy A form of psychotherapy based upon the philosophical doctrine of existentialism. In practice the existentialist approach is highly subjective and focuses on the immediate situation (➤ **being-in-the-world** and **Dasein**). It differs from most other therapies in that there is a strict avoidance of intellectual explanation and interpretation; the focus is on the immediate reality shared by client and therapist. Existentialism, by design, resists easy codification and its therapeutic practice runs from the pessimism of the Europeans, especially the followers of Ludwig Binswanger, to the smiling optimism of the American ➤ **human potential movement**.

exo- Prefix designating *out, outside of, external to*.

exocathection H. Murray's term for a cathection (➤ **cathexis**) directed outward, a tendency to be occupied with things external. The opposite of ➤ **endocathection**.

exocrine Used of glands that secrete hormones through a duct. Contrast with ➤ **endocrine** and see the discussion under ➤ **gland**.

exocytosis The process by which a cell secretes its products. The secreted material is held in a container which migrates to and fuses with the cell's outer membrane and then bursts, dumping its contents into the extracellular fluid.

exogamy Marriage outside of one's social or cultural group. Contrast with ➤ **endogamy**.

exogenous (or **exogenic**) Lit., originating from without. Used to refer to phenomena whose origins are external or outside the body. Contrast with ➤ **endogenous**.

exogenous depression ➤ **reactive *depression**.

exogenous opiates Literally, any ➤ **opiate** introduced into the body. Also, ➤ **endogenous opiates**.

exophthalmia Abnormal protrusion of the eyeball.

exopsychic Characterizing mental activity that has effects outside the person.

exosomatic method A term used to characterize the Féré method of evaluating the ➤ **galvanic skin response**.

exotropia Divergent ➤ **strabismus**.

expansive delusion Basically a delusion of grandeur accompanied by feelings of wealth, power, influence, etc.

expansiveness 1. Generally, the term is used with the standard dictionary meaning of outgoingness, friendliness, reactiveness, loquaciousness, etc. However: **2.** In K. Horney's writings, a neurotic condition resulting from the mistaken sense that one has actually achieved ➤ **idealized *self** (2). Here the characteristic behaviors are arrogance, narcissism, vindictiveness, etc.

expectancy 1. Occasional synonym for ➤ **expected value. 2.** An internal state, an attitude or set of an organism that leads it to anticipate (or 'expect') a particular event. Note that in this sense the term is used by both behaviorists and cognitive psychologists; for the former, expectancy must be inferred from objective behavior and is characterized by attentiveness, muscle tension, etc., for the latter it is treated as a mental set with a good deal of conscious cognitive processing involved and is assessed phenomenologically.

expectancy effect ➤ **experimenter expectancy effect**.

expectancy theory One of several names used for E. C. Tolman's purposive psychology. The basic assumption here was that what is learned is a disposition to behave toward stimulus objects as though they were signs for other objects or events whose occurrence is contingent on the appropriate behavior. Thus, in this conceptualization, reinforcement becomes 'confirmation.'

expectancy-value theory Not so much a theory as a way of looking at motivation and behavior. The essential notion here is that any organism (human or otherwise, although the theory is generally used to characterize human motivation) behaves in accordance with the expected outcomes of various courses of action and the values associated with each of those outcomes. ➤ **expectation, expected value**.

expectation 1. The anticipated outcome of a probabilistic situation, the ➤ **expected value**. 2. The ➤ **true *mean**. 3. An emotional state of anticipation.

expected value Most generally, this is the anticipated outcome, in the long run, of a particular strategy. For example, suppose you are offered a game where a head on a coin flip wins you 6 units while a tail loses 5 units. The expected value of this game is + 0.50 units on each toss. The calculation here is simple: multiply the value of each outcome by its probability of occurrence and combine them. Expected values can be calculated for any situation where the probabilities of the several events are known. In statistical analyses, expected values become extremely important because they reveal critical characteristics of distributions. In particular, the mean is the expected value of a distribution. In the theory of decision making, the expected value of a decision is one of the more important determinants of people's behavior. See also in this context ➤ **game**, **subjective probability, utility**.

experience Basically, the term is used in ways commensurate with lay language; that is: 1. Any event through which one has lived. 2. The knowledge gained from such participation in that event. 3. The sum total of knowledge accumulated. However, recent reintroduction of some classic philosophical problems of epistemology into the study of cognition has produced a nuance. Namely, some now use the term with reference to the real world, where experience is characterized in terms of what is 'out there', and others specifically use it only to refer to personal subjective phenomena and the experience is characterized in terms of what is 'in the head.' To appreciate this distinction consider whether or not the 'pink elephants' seen by an alcoholic count as *experiences*.

experiment Modern scientific psychology prides itself (perhaps a bit selfconsciously) on being *experimental*. The intent here is to let it be known that psychological principles are founded on well-controlled and repeatable experiments. In essence, any experiment is an arrangement of conditions or procedures for the purpose of testing some hypothesis. The design of an experiment focuses on: (a) the antecedent conditions themselves, usually referred to as the ➤ **independent *variables** (or *treatments* or *experimental variables*), and (b) the outcome or results of the experiments, usually called the ➤ **dependent *variables**. The critical aspect of any experiment is that there be *control* over the independent variables such that cause-and-effect relationships can be discovered without ambiguity.

There is a tendency to use the adjectival form *experimental* in a broader and looser sense so that it covers casual observations or simple trial procedures that are not always well controlled. This usage is not wrong in any etymological sense, although it should be avoided for it detracts from the rigorous meaning. **➤➤ control** (1), **experimental *design, scientific *method**.

experimental control **➤ control** (1).

experimental design **➤ design, experimental**.

experimental error **➤ error, experimental**.

experimental extinction **➤ extinction**.

experimental group (or **condition**) A group (or condition) in an experiment that is exposed to the independent variable(s) under investigation. Usually the experimental group is matched with a control group (or condition) that receives similar treatment except for the critical independent variable(s).

experimental method **➤ experiment** and **➤ scientific *method**.

experimental neurosis A condition originally described by Pavlov. It was a 'neurosis' that resulted from an attempt to classically condition an impossible discrimination. For example, the positive stimulus may be a circle and the negative one an ellipse. Over several trials the ellipse is gradually formed into a circle so that the discrimination becomes impossible to make. Dogs treated in this manner behaved 'neurotically.' They attempted to avoid entering the laboratory, barked violently during the study, tore and bit at the apparatus, etc. A similar phenomenon may be established by punishing behavior necessary for existence such as shocking a rat every time it tries to eat or drink. The use of the term 'experimental neurosis' has been deplored by some as it adds to the already confused state of the meaning of neurosis, but it has been applauded by others because it provides a possibility for operationalizing the term. The issue, however, has been rendered lexicographically moot (at least in North America) since the DSM (**➤ Diagnostic and Statistical Manual**) no longer uses the term *neurosis*.

experimental psychology A very general term that can be applied to any approach to the study of psychological issues that uses experimental procedures. Once the term was limited to 'laboratory' psychology but now it is used ubiquitously.

experimental variable **➤ independent *variable**.

experiment, controlled In a sense this term is redundant since the assumption is that all experiments are adequately controlled. Nevertheless, one often finds it used to refer to experiments which employ both experimental and control groups.

experimenter bias **➤ experimenter expectancy effect**.

experimenter expectancy effect A bias introduced into an investigation by the experimenter. Such biases can enter most insidiously into many experiments, even those with lower organisms. The common denominator is that when the investigator has certain expectations about the outcome of the experiment these expectations can contaminate the entire scientific process. The experimenter can subtly (unconsciously?) alter his or her behavior in carrying out the experiment in any of a number of ways and so produce biased results. For details on a few of these biases **➤ demand characteristics** and **➤ self-fulfilling prophecy**. Also known by a variety of other names including *expectancy effect*, *experimenter bias*, and, after the researcher who did much of the early work, *Rosenthal effect*.

experiment, mental A kind of speculative non-experiment where the investigator considers the possible results *if* certain manipulations were carried out. Generally, such *thought experiments* (as they are often called) are useful heuristics for exploring the implications of particular theoretical models or for musing about the implications of accumulated facts. Also called *Gedanken experiments*, from the German for *thought*.

experimentum crucis **➤ crucial experiment**.

expiatory punishment **➤ punishment, expiatory**.

explanation An 'account' of a phenomenon or an event or the characterization of some object. Many a scientist's and many a philosopher's lifetime's work has been invested in explication of just what form of 'account' of a thing can be regarded as a true explanation of that thing. Explanations come in various guises; to wit: (a) *causal* – which lays out the necessary and sufficient antecedent conditions for the phenomenon; (b) *historical* (or *ontogenetic*) – where the focus is on articulating the previously occurring events that led to the event whose explanation is sought; (c) *reductive* – where the phenomenon under scrutiny is recast into simpler or more fundamental terms; (d) *constructive* (or *generalized*) – where one is concerned with the elaboration of more general principles or laws that lay out the relationship between the event to be explained and others. Generally, one distinguishes between an explanatory effort and a descriptive one on the grounds that the latter is restricted to reports of observations while the former extends to articulation of relationships between those things observed. In practice, of course, this distinction is not always so easily made. ➤ **causation, definition, description**.

explicit 1. Generally, characterizing that which is direct and clearly specified. 2. By extension, characterizing that which is *overt* and open for observation. 3. By further extension, characterizing that which is consciously known; explicit cognitive processes are those the person is aware of using. Compare here with ➤ **implicit**.

explicit learning ➤ **learning, explicit**.

explicit memory ➤ **memory, explicit**.

exploitive character E. Fromm's term for one who derives satisfaction from exploiting others, who uses others to satisfy his/her own needs without concern for the needs of these others. var., *exploitative*.

exploratory behavior If one places an organism in a novel environment one will generally observe a series of movements and acts the apparent purpose of which is to bring the organism into contact with the various portions or aspects of the surroundings. Such exploratory behavior was something of a problem for early learning theories (particularly Hull's) since there did not appear to be any clear drive state motivating it. Their solution to the conundrum was to hypothesize an *exploratory drive*. Today, with the development of ethological approaches to behavior the tendency is to view such behavior as 'natural' and common to locomoting species (including *H. sap.*) that require information about the nature of novel situations so as to be able to make appropriate responses. The term is also occasionally used for some cognitive processes such as the tendency for people to shift thought patterns from one aspect to another of a novel situation or to consider a variety of possible strategies for action in a particular situation.

exploratory drive ➤ **exploratory behavior**.

exploratory study Any preliminary study designed to provide some feeling for or general understanding of the phenomena to be studied. A good exploratory study will yield cues as to how to proceed with the major investigation. Also called *pilot study*.

explosive disorder ➤ **intermittent explosive disorder**.

exposition need H. Murray's term for the need to explain, demonstrate to and (alas) lecture others.

ex post facto From the Latin, meaning *by subsequent action*. An *ex post facto* experimental design is one in which the groups are matched after the independent variables have already been administered or after the occurrence of the event to be studied. A common example here is the examining of census data collected for other reasons. An *ex post facto* explanation is one in which the findings are explained after the research has been completed. Although *ex post facto* experiments and explanations are less desirable than predictive experiments and explanations, they are often unavoidable.

expression Generally, any outward display. Somewhat more restrictively, an outward display that is taken as implying a particular internal state; see here, e.g., ➤ **emotional expression**.

expressive 1 adj. Characterizing an expression, typically used with regard to facial and/or vocal displays but occasionally extended to cover bodily gestures. **2** n. A class of ➤ **speech acts** which are generally used without any specific function other than to keep social interactions going smoothly. Included here are expressions like 'please,' 'thank you,' 'excuse me,' etc. Unlike most other speech acts, these appear to be learned by children purely by rote.

expressive aphasia ➤ Broca's *aphasia.

expressive dysphasia ➤ developmental *language disorder.

expressive language disorder ➤ developmental *language disorder.

expressive methods A general label for a variety of diagnostic and therapeutic techniques all of which require that the individual freely act out (or 'express') some particular role, part or fantasy. Included here are *psychodrama, play techniques* and *role-playing*. Expressive methods are generally regarded as forms of ➤ **projective techniques**.

expressive writing disorder, developmental A disorder marked by impairment in the development of expressive writing skills. Written texts are marked by spelling and grammatical errors, poor punctuation, and poor organization. The term is not used in cases where the disability is the result of mental retardation, inadequate schooling, or a neurological disorder.

extension 1. The spatial property of an object. **2.** The movement by which the ends of something are pulled apart; hence, any muscle movement that straightens a limb. Contrast here with ➤ **flexion**. **3.** In logic, the domain of a term or concept made up of all those things which fall within it. In less formal terms, extension is roughly equivalent to ➤ **denotative *mean-**

ing. See and compare with ➤ **intension**.

extensor A muscle whose action straightens out a limb. Contrast with ➤ **flexor**. Extensor and flexor muscles generally act to form a pair of ➤ **antagonistic muscles**.

external aim ➤ aim (3).

external auditory meatus The canal from the external ear to the tympanic membrane.

external inhibition ➤ inhibition, external.

externalization A term with a number of usages in a number of disparate areas in psychology. All, however, share the underlying notion that some 'thing' initially internal or 'inside' gets represented, projected or manifested in the external world. Thus: **1.** In learning, the process through which a drive becomes activated through external stimulation; e.g., hunger aroused by the smell of food, sex by erotic literature. **2.** In developmental psychology, the process through which the child gradually comes to differentiate between self and the external world that is not-self. **3.** In social psychology and personality theory, the attribution of cause of behavior to external factors, to chance events or to other fortuitous happenings over which one has (or feels one has) little control. See here ➤ internalization (1) and ➤ locus of control. **4.** By extension, some use the term as approximately synonymous with ➤ projection (especially 1–6). This meaning derives from K. Horney's terms *active* and *passive externalization*, of which the former refers to the process whereby feelings of self are experienced as feelings about others and the latter to the process whereby feelings toward others are experienced as their feelings about oneself.

external rectus One of the muscles controlling the eye.

external validity ➤ criterion-related *validity.

exteroceptor A sensory receptor that is stimulated by changes in the exterior world. Compare with ➤ interoceptor and ➤ proprioceptor.

extinction Outside of evolutionary biology, where it refers to the disappearance of species, this term is used in two ways which are often not kept separate. **1.** An experimental procedure in which the stimulus event that maintains the behavior is removed. In classical conditioning this means presentation of the CS without the US; in operant or instrumental conditioning this amounts to withholding the reinforcer even though the response occurs. **2.** Somewhat more loosely, the actual decrease in the learned response which results from this extinction procedure. Meaning 1 refers to an experimental procedure and, indeed, occasionally the term *experimental extinction* will be used here; in 2 one is referring to the product of the procedure.

extinction burst A sudden burst of rapid and often vigorous responding that frequently occurs when an organism is shifted from reinforced responding to extinction.

extinction, latent In the ordinary extinction procedure using operant or instrumental behavior, the organism makes responses that go unrewarded. If, prior to running standard extinction trials, the organism is placed in the usual setting but without the opportunity to respond, a subsequent sharp decrease in responsiveness will be observed when the extinction procedure is later introduced. This effect of extinction without responding is called latent extinction because of the conceptual parallel with *latent *learning*.

extinction, secondary The weakening of one response when a similar response undergoes experimental extinction.

extinction trial ➤ **trial, extinction**.

extinguish Following the two meanings of the term ➤ **extinction**: **1.** To carry out the procedure of experimental extinction. **2.** To diminish the responsiveness of an organism by running experimental extinction.

extinguished Generally, characterizing a response that has been subjected to extinction procedures. There is also a curious tendency to speak of the organism itself as having been 'extinguished' when the response no longer occurs. This sense of the term is somewhat misleading but fairly common.

extirpation Removal of an organ or bodily structure. Usually used to refer to surgical removal. When only part of the organ or structure is removed the term ➤ **ablation** is generally used.

extra- Prefix meaning: **1.** Outside of, beyond, beside, e.g., *extrasensory*. **2.** By extension, more of a thing; usually hyphenated, e.g., *extra-strong.* var., *extro-*.

extracellular thirst ➤ volumetric *thirst.

extraception H. Murray's term for an outlook on life that is objective, concerned with facts, skeptical. Contrast with ➤ **intraception**.

extradimensional shift ➤ reversal *learning.

extrafusal fibers Muscle fibers that mediate the force extended by contraction.

extrajection An occasional synonym for ➤ **projection** (especially meanings 1–3).

extraocular muscles ➤ eye muscles.

extrapolate To estimate, from a series of known values, the values of a variable that are higher or lower than the known range. The estimation is made on the assumption that the trends already observed in the data will continue. Extrapolations are useful but subject to error because of unpredictable factors that may only reveal their effects at the higher and lower ends of the continuum.

extrapunitive Characterizing the tendency to react to frustration by showing anger toward and investing blame in others. Contrast with ➤ **intropunitive** and compare with ➤ **impunitive**.

extrapyramidal motor system A set of complex, diffuse neural structures both cortical and subcortical including the basal ganglia, cerebellum, parts of the reticular formation and their connections with the motor neurons of the spinal cord and nuclei of the cranial nerves.

extrapyramidal syndrome A neurological disorder with a variety of signs and symptoms including tremors, muscular rigidity, a shuffling gait, restlessness and difficulty in initiating movements. It results from dysfunctions of the extrapyramidal motor system and may occur as a side effect of some psychotropic drugs, especially the phenothiazine derivatives which are used as antipsychotics. ➤➤ **tardive dyskinesia**.

extrasensory perception (ESP) Lit., perception which occurs outside of the use of any known sensory system. It is used as an umbrella term for a number of hypothesized paranormal phenomena including *clairvoyance, precognition* and *telepathy*. ➤ **parapsychology** for a general discussion of these and related terms.

extraspectral hue Any hue that cannot be characterized by a single wavelength. Purple, which requires a mixture of long wavelengths (red) and short wavelengths (blue), is a good example.

extrastriate cortex ➤ **prestriate cortex**.

extraversion Lit., turning outward. Used primarily in personality theory to refer to the tendency to direct one's energies outward, to be concerned with and derive gratification from the physical and social environment. var., *extroversion*. Contrast with ➤ **introversion** and ➤ **extraversion–introversion**.

extraversion–introversion A hypothesized dimension of personality with two theoretical poles, ➤ **extraversion** and ➤ **introversion**. Originally the dimension was entertained as reflecting two unitary personality types which were presumed opposites of each other. Today most theorists doubt that either exists as a singular type and instead regard both as collections of a number of different patterns of behavior. Moreover, it also seems unlikely that the two poles can be validly regarded as opposites since many persons exhibit aspects of both and may increase in their display of behaviors reflective of one pole without necessarily diminishing display of behaviors reflective of the other.

extravert A label used for an individual who displays the behaviors discussed under ➤ **extraversion**. C. Jung also used the term for one of his personality types.

extrinsic 1. Characterizing a property of something that derives its essential nature from relationships with outside factors. Contrast with ➤ **intrinsic**. 2. Characterizing a property of something that lies wholly external to the subject. Contrast here with ➤ **inherent**.

extrinsic eye muscles ➤ **eye muscles**.

extrinsic interest Interest in an object or an activity that derives from its relationship to other, outside factors; e.g., learning to paint because of the prestige or income accruing from the skill. Compare with ➤ **intrinsic interest**.

extrinsic motivation Lit., motivation that originates in factors outside of the individual. Behavior that is motivated by rewards and/or punishments administered by outside forces is extrinsically determined. Usually the question of inner satisfaction or dissatisfaction is considered secondary. Thus, for example, many students strive mightily in school for the extrinsic reward of good grades with little concern for any knowledge or understanding that may be acquired along the way – their behavior is said to be extrinsically motivated. Contrast with ➤ **intrinsic motivation** and see the extended discussion under the base term ➤ **motivation**.

extro- Variation of ➤ **extra-**. Generally (but not always) used in contrast with ➤ **intro-**.

extroversion ➤ **extraversion**.

extrovert ➤ **extravert**.

eye The visual organ. Anatomically the term covers the eyeball (and related structures) and that portion of the optic nerve lying within the eye socket. Moving from the inside of the eye out, there are three coats that make up the eye itself. The innermost is the *retina*, which contains the ➤ **rods** and ➤ **cones**, the specific visual receptors, and a number of other neural structures that mediate the initial processing of visual input; ➤ **retina** for details here. Next is the *uvea*, which is collectively composed of the choroid, the ciliary body and the iris and is primarily nutritional in function. The outermost third layer is made up of the *sclera* and *cornea*. Two cavities are enclosed between these layers: the anterior is the space lying in front of the lens and is filled with a watery *aqueous humor*; the cavity behind the lens is much larger and is filled with the gelatinous *vitreous body*.

'eye-balling' Laboratory slang for taking a quick look at one's data to see if any obvious trends can be perceived prior to (although one hopes not instead of) performing careful statistical analyses.

eyebrow flash A rapid raising of the eyebrows lasting about 1/6 of a second. It is a virtually universal sign of either greeting or flirtation.

eye dominance ➤ **dominance, eye**.

eyelid conditioning A classical conditioning procedure used commonly with humans. The response is the eye blink, usually evoked in response to a puff of air directed at the eye–cheek area.

eye movements Obviously, movements of the eye. There are, however, several kinds of such movements; see, e.g., ➤ **convergence, divergence, fixation, nystagmus, ocular *pursuit, rapid eye movement, saccade.**

eye muscles The term covers two categories of muscles. The *extrinsic* or *extraocular* muscles are a set of six muscles attached to the tough outer coat of the eyeball (the *sclera*) that control the movements of the eyes. The *intrinsic* muscles are those of the iris and ciliary body and are typically not called, collectively, eye muscles but referred to by the structures they control.

eye regression ➤ **regression** (4).

eye span ➤ **reading span**.

eye–voice span The number of words that can be read (out loud) after 'the lights go out.' In other words, it is a measure of how far the eye is ahead of the voice in oral reading. It is often used as a measure of reading skill and as a procedure for investigating reading processes.

eyewitness testimony Basically a legal term for the use of the eyewitness to a crime to provide testimony in court about the identity of the perpetrator. The term, however, is common in ➤ **forensic psychology**, where a large literature exists dealing with the reliability of eyewitnesses and the validity of their testimony.

Eysenck Personality Inventory A self-report personality inventory developed by the German-born British psychologist H. J. Eysenck. The inventory is based on Eysenck's factor theory of personality, which assumes three basic dimensions, *extraversion–introversion, neuroticism* and *psychoticism*.

F

F 1. Fahrenheit. 2. ➤ **F ratio**. 3. **F test**.

F₁, F₂ In genetics, the first and second filial generations. F_1 represents the off-spring of two unlike individuals; F_2 represents the offspring of two individuals of the F_1 generation.

f 1. Frequency. 2. Fluency. 3. Function.

fables test A test in which the individual is required to provide interpretations of fables. Such tests have been used as tests of intelligence and as projective devices (using ambiguous fables).

face saving In social psychology it is used with essentially the same meaning as in common parlance: the protection of one's public image.

face-to-face group ➤ **group, face-to-face**.

face validity ➤ **validity, face**.

facial nerve The VIIth *cranial nerve*. A mixed nerve with efferent fibers to the facial muscles, the platysmal muscle of the neck and the sublingual glands and efferent fibers from the taste buds of the front two-thirds of the tongue.

facial vision Not vision at all, rather the term refers to the ability to detect the presence of an object specifically without vision. Often found in the blind, the cues are provided by air currents. Compare with ➤ **obstacle sense**.

facilitated communication An approach to working with autistic children in which a facilitator holds the child's hand steady while the child 'types' out messages on a keyboard. There are reasons for suspecting that the procedure may be of value with children with neurological disorders that compromise physical functioning; there is no evidence whatsoever that it is of value for autism, despite the lavish claims of its supporters.

facilitation Generally, the act of making

something easier, freeing the act from im-pediments or difficulties. The term is found in many combined forms, some of which follow; others may be found under the listing of the modifying term.

facilitation, neural Lowering the thresh-old for nerve conduction along a neural pathway. It may occur in a number of ways; e.g., by ➤ **summation** of several neural processes, by repeated excitation of the pathways or by inhibiting inhibitory fibers that converge on the synapse.

facilitation, retroactive Strengthening of the association between a stimulus and a response by the formation of new associations.

facilitator A term occasionally used for a therapist who serves as the 'leader' in particular kinds of group therapy settings. The notion is that the leader's role here is not to direct so much as it is to 'facilitate' the group members in their search for their own personal insights.

fact A proposition that has been, in S. J. Gould's words, 'confirmed to so high a degree that it would be perverse to with-hold provisional assent.'

factitious 1. Characteristic of an artifact, made by humans. 2. Not real, not genuine.

factitious disorder An umbrella term for any psychological or psychiatric disorder the symptoms of which are voluntarily produced; factitious disorders are feigned and the disabilities displayed are simu-lated. Usually, however, this classification does not include ➤ **malingering**, in which the illness is claimed for a particular purpose; in a factitious disorder there seems to be no obvious aim other than to play the 'patient role.' These disorders are often classified by patterns of symptoms and referred to accordingly; e.g., *factitious disorder with psychological symptoms* (also called *pseudopsychosis*); *factitious disorder with physical symptoms* (also called *Münchhausen syndrome*). Distinguish from ➤ **somatoform disorder** where the symptoms are not produced 'voluntarily' and are not under the control of the individual.

factitious disorder by proxy A ➤ **factitious disorder** in which one individual produces symptoms in another for the purpose of indirectly assuming the role of a sick individual. It is most commonly seen in a parent artificially creating physical symptoms in a child. When the second individual plays no active role in the creation of the symptoms, they are called *induced factitious symptoms*. Also called *Münchhausen by proxy*.

factitious disorder with physical symptoms The most common factitious disorder, characterized by the plausible presentation of physical symptoms that are apparently under the individual's control. A wide range of symptoms may emerge including back pain, nausea, vomiting, dizziness, rashes, abscesses, fevers of undetermined origin and secondary bleeding stemming from ingestion of anti-coagulants. The patient's medical knowledge and imagination are the only limits. The patient with a true *Münchhausen syndrome* (as it is also called – after Baron Karl von Münchhausen, a notorious teller of tall tales) typically has had multiple hospitalizations and often multiple surgical procedures performed during them.

factitious disorder with psychological symptoms A factitious disorder in which there is the production of various symptoms of psychological disorders seemingly under the voluntary control of the individual. The condition is virtually always superimposed on a severe personality disorder, although the particular symptoms displayed are not explained by that disorder. A typical pattern is for the patient to complain of memory loss, hallucinations, dissociative and conversion symptoms and, often, to be discovered to have been secretly taking various drugs to produce symptoms that would support the diagnosis of a nonorganic mental disorder. Also called *pseudopsychosis*.

fact memory ➤ **memory, fact**.

factor 1. Generally, anything that has some causal influence, some effect on a phenomenon. In this sense a factor is an antecedent condition, a cause. 2. By extension, an independent variable. This usage is common in statistical procedures based on analysis of variance. See here, e.g., ➤ **fixed *factor, random *factor**. 3. In mathematics, any of the numbers which when multiplied together yield a specified product. 4. By extension of 3, one of the products of a factor analysis. Note that the factors in this sense are strictly no more than numbers in a factor matrix that function as given in meaning 3, even though they are typically presented as though they represented some underlying trait (e.g., a *number factor* or a *verbal factor*). ➤ **factor analysis** for clarification of this usage.

factor analysis This term does not really represent a unitary concept, rather it serves as a cover term for a number of statistical procedures all of which function so as to locate a smaller number of dimensions, clusters or ➤ **factors** (4) in a larger set of independent variables or items. The primary distinctive element of a factor analysis is data-reduction. Beginning with an array of correlation coefficients between all of the initial variables in the data base (the number of which may be very large, especially if they are items from a personality inventory or an intelligence test), the factor-analytic techniques extract a small number of basic components that may be viewed as source variables that account for the interrelations observed in the data. Variables that correlate highly with each other become identified as representing a single factor; variables that do not correlate with each other are identified as representing orthogonal (or independent) factors. The ideal factor analysis would identify a small number of factors each of which would be orthogonal to each other; that is, in spatial terms, they would lie at right angles to each other when graphed.

Note that the procedures are all strictly statistical; the factors that emerge from an analysis still have to be subjectively examined to determine whether they represent salient psychological dimensions. For example, on an IQ test the scores on a number of items may be found to correlate highly with each other and emerge as a statistical factor, e.g., examination of these items may reveal that all contain mathematical elements and thus may lead one to hypothesize the existence of a mathematical factor.

There is a tendency, particularly when factor-analytic techniques are applied to personality inventories, to identify the factors that emerge as *traits*. Strictly speaking, the factor is not a trait; the trait is inferred from the factor, it represents an underlying regularity in the data base and the two terms should not be treated as synonymous. The establishment of a valid trait requires additional inferences; ➤ **trait** for discussion of usage and associated problems of meaning.

Factor analysis is an important tool in areas of psychology in which underlying components are suspected but difficult to discern, such as intelligence testing, personality assessment, semantics and the like. The procedures themselves are quite complex and some degree of mathematical sophistication is needed to understand and utilize them. In many of the entries that follow here the conceptual basis of factor-analytical terms is given; for the mathematical foundations and methods of application the reader should consult a text on factor analysis. vb., *factor analyze* (not *factor*, which is to find the multipliers of a product); adj., *factor analytical* (not *factorial*, which derives from ➤ **factor** (1, 2)).

factor analysis, inverse A factor analysis applied to a correlation matrix of 'units' (e.g., individual persons, groups, objects) rather than to the individual items that each 'unit' responded to, which is the more usual technique. Often called the *Q*

technique or *Q factor analysis*. See the discussion under ➤ **R correlation** for details and comparisons with other procedures.

factor axes The set of coordinates that represent the relationships of the various factors to each other and to the full correlation matrix. The particular set that best represents a given data base is determined by a process of *factor *rotation*.

factor coefficient ➤ **factor loading**.

factor configuration In factor analysis, the position of the system of lines or vectors that represents the several tests in the full correlation matrix. In spatial terms, the angles of the vectors to each other specify the correlations between them; right angles reflect orthogonal (or uncorrelated) vectors, acute angles reflect correlations with the degree of acuteness reflecting the degree of correlation. Note that the exact configuration of the factor structure is not unique and one solution may be transformed into another. There are many statistically equivalent ways to represent the underlying dimensions.

factor, first-order A factor that emerges from the matrix of test scores, from the original set of intercorrelations. Compare with a *second-order factor*, which is one that is derived from the intercorrelations among the first-order factors.

factor, fixed Any independent variable in an experiment where the values that the variable may take are set (or 'fixed') by natural circumstances. For example, suppose there exist only 7 different brands of aspirin; an experiment evaluating and comparing them would have the 'brand' variable as a fixed factor. The results that emerge from the study are called *fixed effects* and the data-analysis technique used to evaluate them is termed the *fixed effects model*. Compare with ➤ **random *factor**.

factor, general (g or G) 1. Generally, a factor that is found in all of the tests subjected to a factor analysis. 2. Specifically, a factor hypothesized to be basic to all tests of ability. The notion of a general factor (or *g-factor* or, more simply, *g*) was first put forward in 1904 by the British psychometrician Charles Spearman as representing a single ability that could be taken to represent intelligence. It must be appreciated that *g* has not (and probably cannot) be shown to exist as a separate measurable entity. Spearman identified it on the basis of factor analysis of the various components of an intelligence test. The logical argument was that since the several component skills assessed tended to be positively correlated with each other (i.e. high scores on 'verbal' subtests are accompanied by high scores on 'numerical' subtests, etc.) then they could be all thought of as reflective of a general ability that underlies them. However, it must be recognized that, since *g* is identified in this manner, it is an outcome of a particular form of factor analysis – not all factor analytic procedures will yield such a characterization even when applied to the same data base. This point was made by L. L. Thurstone when he showed that other procedures lead to the uncovering of a number of ➤ **primary *factors** rather than a single core factor. With Thurstone's methods *g*, if it exists at all, is found only as a *second-order factor* and accounts for very little of the data from intelligence tests; with Spearman's methods it accounts for most of the data. Hence, *g* must be viewed not as a 'real' ability but as a hypothetical ability the existence of which is dependent on methodological procedures.

factor, group A factor that emerges from high intercorrelations between two or more tests in the set of tests analyzed but does not correlate with all tests. Most of the factors that have emerged from factor-analyzing intelligence tests (e.g., verbal, arithmetic, analytical) are group factors.

factor, hereditary Simply, a gene. By extension, any transfer of information via the genetic material.

factorial design ➤ **design, factorial**.

factorial invariance The extent to which

the results of a factor analysis remain unaltered when new tests are introduced and the full analysis repeated or when a new set of subjects is run and the full set of data is reanalyzed.

factoring Generally, finding ➤ **factors**. However, factoring is usually reserved for finding ➤ **factors** in sense 3 of that term; for finding *factors* 4 the preferred term is *factor analyzing*.

factor loading A value that expresses the degree to which any given factor accounts for the total variability of the full set of correlations on which the factor analysis has been carried out. That is, the extent to which it correlates with the test itself or the full set of items analyzed. The higher the factor loading the more salient the factor. Also called *factor weight* or *weighting*.

factor matrix In most general terms, a table (matrix) that gives the factor loadings that emerge from a factor analysis. Actually, a variety of specific kinds of factor matrices may be found depending on the kind(s) of transformations one makes on the data. In such cases qualifiers will be used to indicate the kind of matrix under consideration.

factor, primary Any of the factors that emerge in the final stages of factor analysis; i.e. the point at which further mathematical manipulations fail to account for substantially more of the variance and the factors have been located (by rotation) so that the number of factors needed to account for the intercorrelations is minimized. Also called *terminal factor*.

factor, random Any independent variable in an experiment in which the values that the variable may take are very large (or infinite) and the actual values of the factor used in the study are selected at random. Results from a study using such variables are termed *random effects* and the data-analysis technique used to evaluate them is called the *random effects model*. Compare with ➤ **fixed *factor**.

factor reflection ➤ **reflection** (4).

factor resolution R. B. Cattell's term for the finally accepted interpretation of a factor analysis; that is, the particular position of the factor axes after rotation in relation to the test vectors. Thurstone originally used the term ➤ **factor structure** here and many still do.

factor rotation ➤ **rotation** (2).

factor space The region within which a set of factors may be represented. The factor space is defined by the set of inter-correlations in the analysis and is not necessarily two- or three-dimensional and not necessarily Euclidean.

factor, specific A factor that is found in only one test or one unique group of items all of which reflect the same variable. Compare with ➤ **general *factor** and ➤ **group *factor**. Also called *unique factor*.

factor structure ➤ **factor resolution**.

factor theory A general label used of any theory of psychological phenomena that characterizes things in terms of various ➤ **factors**. The term is typically used for theories of personality and of intelligence that have extracted their hypothesized factors from factor-analyzing batteries of tests or personality inventories. However, there is also a tendency to use the phrase for any theory that hypothesizes two (or more) distinguishable processes or components for a psychological process; e.g., the so-called *two-factor theory of learning*, that maintains that both classical and operant conditioning processes are needed to explain complex behavior, or the *two-factor theory of memory* that assumes both episodic and semantic memory systems, etc. The key to distinguishing these two patterns of usage is to note that the base term *factor theory* generally uses ➤ **factor** in sense 4, while terms that begin *n-factor theory* generally use it in sense 1.

factor weight ➤ **factor loading**.

factual knowledge ➤ **declarative *knowledge**.

faculty psychology A faculty was proposed to be a general 'power of the mind,' a cognitive ability such as intellect, will, memory, understanding, etc. Faculty psychology approached the study of the human mind by attempting to account for mental processes in terms of a fixed number of these 'faculties.' The *phrenologists* presented the ultimate in this kind of theorizing. Although regarded as a discredited historical curiosity for decades, it has recently been revived under the name of modularity, where cognitive and perceptual modules (e.g., a language module, a numerical module) are hypothesized. ➤ **modularity hypothesis**.

fading A technique in behaviorally oriented training in which a new stimulus is presented along with an old one to which a response has already been learned. The old stimulus is then gradually diminished in size or intensity or clarity (i.e. faded) and the new one gains control over the response.

failure to thrive A term used occasionally to characterize the poor physical development of infants with ➤ **reactive attachment disorder**.

faith healing Healing accomplished through faith or belief in the power of the healer, the therapist, the therapeutic procedure, or something else. Although one usually sees the term used with reference to religiously based phenomena it has been argued on many occasions that a substantial proportion of the positive outcomes of psychotherapy are accomplished in this fashion.

fallacy An argument involving logically invalid or improper reasoning and, by extension, a conclusion reached by such fallacious reasoning. Note that the meaning of the term depends on the reasoning and not on what is reasoned. Although fallacies usually lead to false conclusions they do not do so by definition; it is quite possible to reach a valid conclusion by faulty means.

fall chronometer A rather clever device from experimental psychology's early days for measuring short time intervals by assessing the distance a weight fell.

fallectomy Surgical severing of the Fallopian tubes, ➤ **salpingectomy**.

false That which is not ➤ **true**, in senses 1 and 2 of that term.

false alarm In signal-detection theory, the statement by a subject that a stimulus was present when in fact no stimulus occurred. Contrast with ➤ **hit**, and ➤ **signal-detection theory**.

false-belief task A task used with young children to assess their understanding of reality and how other people perceive it. Children are asked to predict how some deceptive object will appear to another person. For example, after children are shown a candy box that turns out to hold pencils, they are asked what someone else will expect to see when they open the box. Children around the age of 3 consistently believe the other person will expect to see pencils, older children correctly believe that others will expect candy. ➤ **appearance-reality task**.

false-consensus effect The tendency to overestimate the degree to which one's opinions and beliefs are shared by others. It derives from the ➤ **availability heuristic**, in that people tend to spend more time with others who think and believe as they do.

false memory ➤ **memory, false**.

false negative A case of improper exclusion. Since all tests (e.g., civil service exams, college entrance exams, etc.) are less than perfect, some individuals who score below the cut-off and are thus excluded would actually perform successfully; they are the *false negatives*. Similarly, there will be those who score above the cut-off, are included, but later fail to perform successfully; these are the *false positives*. The concepts underlying this example are quite general and the terms are found widely in medical science, in decision-making, in psychophysical investigations, etc.

false positive ➤ **false negative**.

false transmitter A substance that binds with postsynaptic receptors but does not activate them. Such substances act as antagonists in that by occupying the receptor sites they prevent the normal ➤ **neurotransmitter** from exerting its effects.

false vocal cords ➤ **ventricular folds**.

falsificationism The philosophical point of view associated with the philosopher of science, Sir Karl R. Popper, that holds that scientific theories cannot be proven to be true but only subjected to attempts at refutation. From this point of view, a scientific theory is accepted, not because it is demonstrably a correct codification of a class of phenomena but because it has not yet been shown to be false. This position is usually contrasted with the older position of *verificationism*, in which it is argued that scientific work consists of the attempt to substantiate (verify) the correctness of a theory by logical and empirical means.

familial Lit., pertaining to the ➤ **family**. Generally used with the notion of *common to* members of a family and in this sense it may refer either to factors that are hereditary and genetic or to factors that make up a family's social or cultural heritage.

family 1. In its strictest sense family refers to the fundamental kinship unit. In its minimal or nuclear form the family consists of mother, father and offspring. In broader usage it may refer to the *extended* family, which may include grandparents, cousins, adopted children, etc., all operating as a recognized social unit. Sociologists and anthropologists have literally dozens of other special classifications for various kinds of family units as they are represented in different cultures and societies. 2. By extension, a group of people with close social or personal ties, even though there may be no sanguine connections between them. 3. By further extension, the term is applied to any collection of closely or formally related items or events; in mathematics one refers to a family of curves, in social psychology to a family of traits or attitudes, in linguistics to a language family, etc. **4.** In biology, a level of classification of related genera (or sometimes a single genus) that is grouped into an order.

family constellation The complex set of relationships within a family dictated in large part by the number of persons, their ages and the pattern of functional interactions between them.

family therapy An umbrella term for a number of therapeutic approaches all of which treat a family as a whole rather than singling out specific individuals for independent treatment. The term is neutral theoretically; one can practice family therapy within many different frameworks.

fantasy A term generally used to refer to the mental process of imagining objects, symbols or events not immediately present. However, it is also used to refer to the symbol or image itself. In general, fantasy is assumed to be normal, even indicative of psychological stability and health. It is usually pleasant, often whimsical and frequently creative. The pathological aspects that are often cited are restricted to those cases in which the fantasy becomes delusionary or when it dominates a person's mental life and serves as a retreat from reality rather than an adjunct to it. var., *phantasy*.

fantasy, foster-child ➤ **foster-child fantasy**.

fantasy, rebirth ➤ **rebirth fantasy**.

FAP (or **fap**) Acronym for ➤ **fixed action pattern**.

far point The most remote point distinctly visible under conditions of relaxed accommodation. Contrast with ➤ **near-point**.

farsightedness General term for any visual condition within which objects at a distance are seen relatively clearly but near objects are out of focus. ➤ **presbyopia** and ➤ **hyperopia** for specific forms.

FAS ➤ **fetal alcoholic syndrome**.

fasciculus Generally, a bundle of nerve

or muscle fibers. Usually neural fibers are denoted by the term, to the point where it is an occasional synonym for ➤ **tract**. See, e.g., ➤ **arcuate fasciculus**.

fashioning effect A term used in role theory to describe the fact that the social role adopted by a person influences both that person's behavior and their self-perceptions.

fastigial nucleus A deep cerebellar nucleus, it receives information from the *vermis* and sends its outputs to the *vestibular nucleus* and the motor nuclei in the reticular *formation*.

fasting phase A metabolic phase during which the digestive system is not supplying nutrients. The body's needs during this period are derived from other sources, specifically from glycogen, proteins and adipose tissue.

fast (twitch) muscle ➤ **muscle twitch** (1).

fatalism The philosophical view that all events are subject to fate, a deity, the stars, etc., and that they are predetermined. Free will or any act of volition is assumed to be futile. Differentiate fatalism from ➤ **determinism**; the latter stresses that all events have antecedent causes but does not assume that they were metaphysically *pre*determined.

father complex ➤ **Oedipus complex**.

father figure One who takes the place and hence the role of the real father. It may be used with either of two connotations: **1.** The sense that the person has taken over the full complement of functions of the real father who was replaced; e.g., a stepfather or a foster-father. **2.** The sense that the individual fulfills psychologically important functions, usually that of becoming the male adult with whom one identifies. As the word 'figure' in the term connotes, meaning 2 is the dominant one and indeed may be what is intended even when the father figure is in the role described in **1.** Some authors will use *father surrogate* for 1 to prevent confusion. Also occasionally called *father imago*.

281

father fixation An excessive focusing of emotional attachment to the father. The term implies a rigid focusing, so that there is difficulty in shifting affective attention away from the father to other more socially accepted persons. The equivalent process centred on the female parent is called, not surprisingly, *mother fixation*.

father imago ➤ **father figure**.

father surrogate One who stands in place of the real father. ➤ **father figure** and ➤ **surrogate** for details.

fatigue 1 n. The diminution in ability to do work that results from previously carried out efforts. 2 n. The internal state or condition that results from extended effort and underlies this diminished capacity to perform, a feeling of weariness or tiredness. These meanings are very general; a number of more specific senses are often intended and are usually marked by a qualifier that identifies the source of or the basis for the fatigue. Thus, *sensory fatigue* refers to the reduced responsiveness of a sense organ following prolonged exposure to stimulation (➤ **adaptation** (1)); *neuronal* or *neural fatigue* is a heightened threshold of nerve fibers that occurs as a consequence of previous neural activity (➤ **refractory period** et seq.); *muscle fatigue* refers to the reduced capacity of muscle tissue to contract owing to a buildup of metabolic waste products like lactic acid; *emotional fatigue* is the general debilitated state resulting from excessive conflicts, frustrations, anxieties, etc.; *mental fatigue* refers to a cognitive weariness stemming from either extended mental concentration or boredom; and so forth. Note that these specialized uses are employed to identify the source of the fatigue, some by specifying the external conditions that produced it (e.g., *emotional, mental*) and some by specifying the underlying neurological and/or physiological effects that are responsible for it (e.g., *neural, muscle*). Note, some authors will take a behaviouristic stance here and treat fatigue purely in terms of performance decrements; others will take a sharp physiological line and view it in terms of biological (dys)function; still others will treat it more phenomenologically as an experienced internal state; most, alas, will confound all of these meanings. vb., *to fatigue*. ➤➤ **exhaustion**.

fatty acid Any of three substances (stearic acid, oleic acid, and palmitic acid) that, along with ➤ **glycerol**, make up the adipose (fatty) tissue found beneath the skin and in various locations in the abdomen.

F distribution ➤ **distribution, F**.

fear An emotional state in the presence or anticipation of a dangerous or noxious stimulus. Fear is usually characterized by an internal, subjective experience of extreme agitation, a desire to flee or to attack and by a variety of sympathetic reactions (➤ **autonomic nervous system**). Fear is often differentiated from ➤ **anxiety** on one (or both) of two grounds: (a) fear is treated as involving specific objects or events while anxiety is regarded as a more general emotional state; (b) fear is a reaction to a present danger, anxiety to an anticipated or imagined one. ➤➤ **phobia**, a specific, persistent, irrational fear.

fear-induced aggression ➤ **aggression, fear-induced**.

fear of success ➤ **success, fear of**.

feature An often-used shorthand form of ➤ **distinctive feature**.

feature detector A general term used for any built-in perceptual mechanism hypothesized to detect single distinctive features in complex displays. Usually the feature detected is specified; e.g., *line detector* or *edge detector* in vision, *voice-onset time detector* in speech perception, etc.

feature model A class of models of human memory based on the assumption that information is stored in the form of a set of distinctive (semantic) features that uniquely identify each concept. ➤ **semantic feature** for more detail and compare with ➤ **semantic network model**.

febrile Feverish.

Fechner's colors Subjective color sensations that appear when black and white sectors are rotated moderately rapidly on a color wheel. If the rotation is then slowed somewhat the sensation is of a series of black radii on a white background called *Charpentier's bands*.

Fechner's law A psychophysical generalization that states that the intensity of subjective sensation increases as the logarithm of the stimulus intensity. That is, when physical stimuli increase geometrically the psychological experience increases arithmetically. Formally, $\psi = k$ logS, where ψ = sensation, S = stimulus, k is a constant. Named for its discoverer, the great 19th-century psychophysicist Gustav Theodor Fechner (1801–87), the law is based on early work of E. H. Weber. ➤➤ **Weber's law** and **Weber–Fechner law**.

Fechner's paradox The surprising finding that an object viewed monocularly increases in brightness after being viewed binocularly.

fecundity The capacity to produce offspring, often used with the connotation of being highly fruitful, bountiful. Adj., *fecund*, vb., *fecundate*. Compare with ➤ **fertility**.

feeble-minded ➤ **mental deficiency**.

feedback **1.** Originally in engineering, information that signals an ongoing operation in a system or the state of the system at a point in time. A speedometer provides feedback to the driver about distance traveled per unit time. **2.** In *cybernetics* the meaning was expanded to include such information as it was utilized by the system to make adjustments and modifications in its operations. A thermostat uses feedback about room temperature to turn on or to turn off the heating system. ➤ **servo-mechanism**. Meaning 2 was enthusiastically borrowed in psychology and has been applied to characterize a variety of situations. **3.** In studies of sensorimotor processes, the information provided by kinesthetic report from receptors in muscles and points to guide directed movement. See, e.g., ➤ **Fitt's law**. **4.** In learning, any information about the correctness or appropriateness of a response. The early cognitive theorists adopted this meaning as a replacement for the behaviorists' notion of reinforcement. For example, a light that signalled whether a choice was correct or not in a problem-solving task was *feedback* to a cognitivist – somehow it hardly seemed to qualify as a *reinforcer* in the sense that that term was also applied to food for a rat at the end of a maze. **5.** In social psychology, any reaction from the environment (including other people) that serves as a basis for future action. A smile in return for your smile is termed social feedback. As a generalization, it seems safe to conclude that the term may be used for any information about the functioning of one or more components of a system that leads to modification of functioning. Occasionally the term will be used for the process or the system itself rather than the information that is 'fed back.' To prevent confusion here most authors will use *feedback loop* or *feedback circuit* for the process.

feedback loop ➤ **feedback**.

feeding behavior An umbrella term used to cover all the several behavioral components involved in normal eating. Included are those preparatory behaviors such as foraging for food, actual consumption of the food and the large number of physiological processes involved in the utilization of what has been eaten.

feeding center A term occasionally used for the lateral hypothalamus which, when stimulated, causes the animal to begin to eat. ➤ **hypothalamus** for more detail.

feeding disorder ➤ **eating disorders**.

feeding disorder of infancy or early childhood A general term for any feeding disorder characterized by the infant or child's persistent failure to eat adequately so that he or she either loses weight or fails to gain it at a normal rate. Included are ➤ **rumination disorder of infancy** and ➤ **pica**.

feeding problem A loose term for any difficulty in getting a child to eat properly. It is not used for serious ➤ **eating disorders**.

feeling It is particularly difficult to isolate precise usages for this term since even the most technical are contaminated by popular connotations. **1.** In the most general way, feeling refers to 'experiencing,' 'sensing' or 'having a conscious process.' More specific meanings are: **2.** *Sensory impression*, in which the reference is to feelings such as warmth or pain. **3.** *Affective states*, as in a feeling of well-being, a feeling of depression, a feeling of desire, etc. **4.** One of the dimensions of emotion, particularly where the reference is to the hypothesized elementary emotional continua such as Wundt's three dimensions of feeling. **5.** *Belief*, as in a vague feeling about something not supported by any real evidence.

The difficulty with the term is that its use is nearly always metaphoric and somehow we all seem quite convinced that we know what we mean when we use it. ➤➤ **emotion** et seq., especially ➤ **theories of *emotion** for more on the terminology of this area of psychology.

feeling type One of Jung's hypothesized personality types. ➤ **function types** for details.

female impersonator ➤ **transvestism**.

femaleness The condition of possessing the physiological and anatomical characteristics of a female as they relate to her reproductive capacity. Distinguish from ➤ **femininity**.

female orgasmic disorder ➤ **orgasm disorders**.

female sexual arousal disorder A ➤ **sexual arousal disorder** marked by the woman's persistent or recurrent inability to attain or maintain an adequate lubrication-swelling response of sexual excitement.

feminicula From the Latin, the female form of ➤ **homunculus**.

femininity Lit., the state of an organism reflecting or displaying the appearances, traits and behavior patterns characteristic of the female of the species. Distinguish from ➤ **femaleness**. ➤➤ **masculinity**.

fenestra Latin for *window*. ➤ **oval window** (*fenestra ovalis or vestibuli*) and ➤ **round window** (*fenestra rotunda*).

fenfluramine A serotonin *agonist* that is used to suppress appetite in obese patients.

feral child Feral means wild or existing in a state of nature. A feral child then is one reared in social isolation either by animals or with only indirect contact with humans. The large number of myths about 'wolf children' and the like have great popular and literary appeal, although carefully documented cases are rare. ➤ **Wild Boy of Aveyron** for one excellent case.

Féré phenomenon (or **method**) ➤ **galvanic skin response**.

Ferry-Porter law The generalization that critical flicker frequency increases with the log of the brightness of the stimulus. The relationship is independent of the wavelength of the stimulus. Also known as *Porter's law*.

fertility **1.** Reproductive capability. **2.** Figuratively, mental productivity or creativity, having many novel ideas. adj., *fertile*. Compare with ➤ **fecundity**.

fertility, differential **1.** Generally, differences in the fertility rate in various segments or classes in a society. **2.** More specifically, the difference in the fertility rate of the upper and lower socioeconomic classes of a society. Typically the former is low relative to the latter – a fact which predictably bothers some and not others. **3.** Most specifically, the number of offspring of any one couple compared with others.

fertility rate An index of the fertility of a large population. It is typically taken as the number of offspring born per 1,000 women of childbearing age. Note that various upper and lower limits are used to define this age; the broadest commonly used is 15–49.

fertilization The impregnation of an ovum by a spermatozoon.

fetal Pertaining to the ➤ fetus. var., *foetal*.

fetal alcohol effects A syndrome characterized by some of the features of ➤ fetal alcohol syndrome (FAS) such as hyperactivity, memory disorders, language learning problems, and motoric deficits, but lacking in the severity of the full picture of the typical case of FAS.

fetal alcoholic syndrome (FAS) A cluster of abnormal developmental features of a fetus resulting from alcohol consumption by the mother during pregnancy. The high level of alcohol in the blood combined with a generally reduced level of normal nutrients can produce any (or all) of a number of anatomical and psychological deficits including microcephaly, growth deficiencies, mental retardation, hyperactivity, heart murmurs and skeletal malformations. ➤➤ teratogen.

fetish 1. The object of a *fetishism*. 2. Popularly, a fetishism.

fetishism 1. Generally a fetish is any object of blind devotion or reverence. Fetishism thus connotes a kind of religious activity that emphasizes the worship of inanimate objects believed to have magical or transcendent powers. Often found in connection with ➤ animism. 2. A ➤ paraphilia characterized by obtaining sexual arousal and satisfaction with some object or some part of the body not directly erogenous. Fetishes usually are articles used by others, often but not always of the opposite sex (shoes, gloves, handkerchiefs), or parts of the body (hair, feet).

fetus An organism in the latter stages of prenatal development. In humans, from the third month of pregnancy to birth is called the fetal stage. Prior to that time the developing child is called an ➤ embryo. var., *foetus*.

FFF Abbreviation for *flicker fusion frequency*. ➤ critical flicker frequency.

FI Abbreviation for *fixed interval*. ➤ schedules of *reinforcement.

fiber Any thread-like strand of living material; several fibers running together make up tissues. Fiber is also occasionally used synonymously with *nerve fiber* or *neuron*. var., *fibre*.

fibril Any small, fine filament which runs through the cell body passing out into axons and dendrites, and to peripheral processes.

fibrillation 1. The process of formation of fibrils or other minute fibers. 2. Rapid quivering contraction of muscle fibers.

fiction Generally in psychology and especially in psychoanalytic approaches, any hypothetical entity, internal state or theoretical process that is treated 'as if' it actually existed. See here the discussion under ➤ 'as if.' The term is particularly common in Adler's approach to personality; see here ➤ fictional finalism, guiding *fiction.

fictional finalism Alfred Adler's term introduced to capture his beliefs that (a) one is motivated more by one's expectation for the future than by one's experiences in the past and (b) such projected expectations are often fictional in that they may be unrealizable or unattainable. In Adler's positivistic outlook this fictional finalism may function to motivate great accomplishments. A classic Adlerian neurosis, however, emerges when one cannot step outside of these fictions and confront reality.

fiction, guiding In Adler's approach to personality, a persistent but largely unconscious train of thought or principle by which a person directs, coordinates and categorizes experiences. In the well balanced, these guiding fictions are assumed to approximate reality and to be quite flexible and adaptive. In the neurotic they are assumed to be somewhat divorced from reality and tend to become rigid and nonadaptive. Note that *fiction* is used here as representing abstractions or schemas, they are not necessarily 'fictitious' but tend to function 'as if' they were true. Hence many Adlerians prefer to use the phrase *guiding idea*, which is less ambiguous.

fiducial limits ➤ **confidence limits**.

field 1. Generally, a bounded area. In the most straightforward physical sense areas are defined by boundaries. The notion of an area without bounds is nonsensical; a field of green is defined by the points where it ceases being green. However, in psychological parlance usage tends toward the metaphoric. Generally this presents no problems since the term is rarely used without some qualifier that specifies the boundaries on the field and hence defines it. Examples are *visual field*, for all those points in space that can be seen at a point in time and from a particular location, *attentional field*, for those objects, thoughts, concepts within one's consciousness, etc. 2. In discussions of ➤ **field theory** the term takes on a more dynamic and extended meaning. Here it becomes a generalized kind of psychological space that includes an organism and its environment. The various forms of field theory all emphasize the interactions between an organism and the configuration of the organism's perceptions.

field dependence (and **independence**) Simply, these two phrases represent a continuum along which an individual may be placed to characterize the extent to which his or her perceptions are dependent on (or independent from) cues in the environment (the 'field'). In the first and simplest test used to study this factor a subject had to align a stimulus (such as a rod) so that it was truly vertical when a second stimulus (such as a frame around the rod) was varied with respect to the true vertical. Persons who can set the rod relatively accurately independently of the orientation of the frame are called field independent because they rely on bodily sensation cues rather than on cues in the field. The more the tilt in the field controls the setting of the rod the more field dependent the person is. More elaborate studies were later carried out using chairs and whole rooms that could be tilted. The study of the trait of field dependence began as an investigation of perception but the large individual differences that were found gradually moved the research into the areas of personality, cognitive style and even psychopathology.

field force ➤ **field theory**.

field investigation ➤ **field research**.

field of regard ➤ **regard**.

field research A general term for any research carried out in a natural setting ('in the field'). Included here is almost all the work in ethology using naturalistic observation techniques, a good deal of the work in developmental psychology, and applied areas such as market research and industrial psychology.

field theory Really a broadly based set of theories all of which focus on the total psychological environment and attempt to explain behavior on the basis of the dynamic interactions between the forces in one part of the field and the rest of the field. Field theory developed from Gestalt psychology primarily through the work of Wolfgang Köhler and Kurt Lewin. Köhler drew the parallel between psychological field processes and electromagnetic fields of force. His argument was that any psychological process is dependent upon the interactions in the field and cannot be viewed except from this dynamic point of view. The position is sharply holistic and critical of elementaristic approaches. He extrapolated the general theory into the areas of physiological psychology, particularly the physiological basis of perception, and argued for the existence of electrical brain fields that corresponded to phenomenological experience. ➤ **isomorphism** (2).

Lewin's theorizing focused more on social psychology and personality theory. The field represented the total environment, including the individual and all significant other people, and came to be known as the ➤ **life space**. Behavior was represented as movement through the regions of the life space, some of which are attractive (i.e. those with positive valence) and others unattractive (those with negative valence). Like Köhler's position this perspective is holistic and dynamic.

figural aftereffects Distortions of perception that occur after long exposure to certain stimulus conditions. For example, if a slightly curved line is fixated for several minutes and then replaced by a straight line, the straight line will appear to curve in the opposite direction. The process underlying these effects is quite complex and not well understood. They can occur in any sensory modality that can yield the experience of form, for example, holding a curved block in the hand will produce a figural aftereffect in *haptic* perception; they are not receptor-specific – expose the left eye and the aftereffect is produced in the right eye; and the effects can last for days.

figural cohesion The tendency for all parts of a figure to 'hang together' even though they may be but disjointed lines.

figural synthesis U. Neisser's term for the notion that form perception is based on a process of active construction of meaning from a stimulus.

figurative language ➤ **language, figurative**.

figure Of the multitude of meanings found in standard dictionaries two figure importantly in psychology: **1.** A kind of unitary, cohesive, perceptual experience. Figures in this sense are characterized by contour, structure, coherence and solidity. In this context, ➤ **figure-ground**. **2.** A person who represents the essential attributes of a stereotyped role; e.g., a *father figure*.

figure, ambiguous An umbrella term for any visual stimulus that permits of more than one interpretation. Although a good case can be made that ambiguity is an inherent feature of *all* displays, the term is typically reserved for a class of stimuli that readily lend themselves to two (or

more) interpretations which 'look different' in each version and in which contextual constraints affect what one perceives. The classic example here is Boring's old woman/young woman drawing reproduced above.

Note also that some authors will treat ➤ **reversible figures** and ➤ **embedded figures** as belonging in this category. While this inclusion is defensible in that such figures are indeed ambiguous, other authorities argue that they should be kept separate. The arguments here are: (a) embedded figures are not really available for multiple interpretations but merely difficult to detect owing to the context within which they are embedded; and (b) reversible figures have the property that they shift back and forth spontaneously and are relatively immune to any imposed interpretative bias. There is, however, precious lack of consistency in terminology here.

figure-ground A pair of terms used to describe the perceptual relationship between the object of focus (the figure) and the rest of the perceptual field (the ground). The figure generally has form or structure and appears to be in front of the ground. The ground is seen as relatively homogeneous and as extending behind the figure. The relationship, in many instances, can be reversed by focusing on or attending to the ground rather than the figure.

The best way to conceptualize the notion of a figure–ground relationship is to appreciate that the ➤ **contour** or boundary that 'separates' the figure from the background *physically* belongs to both of them but *perceptually* belongs to the figure. Hence, the figure is given form and shape and the background is left unshaped and lacking in form.

figure, hidden Synonym for *embedded figure*.

figure, impossible Any of a class of figures in which the several components produce conflicting interpretations. In the example given here the right side has cues for a two-pronged object but the left for a three-pronged object. Resolution of the whole figure is thus rendered 'impossible.'

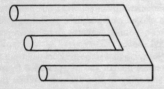

figure, reversible Any of a class of figures that undergo spontaneous reversal of perspective when steadily fixated. The Necker cube given here will shift its orientation when stared at.

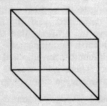

file drawer problem A problem that emerges in attempts to determine whether some effect is real, based on published research. The difficulty emerges when the effect is small (or perhaps nonexistent) and so is only obtained occasionally. Those researchers who find it report it; those who fail to find it tend not to publish their work, leaving it instead in their file drawers. A noneffect can be made to appear real because large numbers of

non-findings are stuck in file drawers while the few anomalous positive findings are published, misleading all concerned. ➤ **Parapsychology** is an area seriously contaminated by this problem.

filial Pertaining to offspring and descendants.

filial generation ➤ F_1, F_2.

filial regression, law of A principle of genetics characterized by a regression toward the mean of traits between the members of filial generations. That is, offspring of two very tall parents will tend to be taller than the average of the whole population but less than the average of their parents' heights. Naturally, the principle is a generalization that holds only when large populations are considered.

filiform papilla ➤ lingual papilla.

filled pause ➤ pause, filled.

filler (material) Material unrelated to the specific experimental manipulations of a study. Such material is often used in studies on language, in questionnaires, on attitude scales, etc. where the filler items help to disguise the true nature of the investigation. Also called *buffer items* or *buffer material*.

film color ➤ color, film.

filter Any device that screens out ('filters') particular stimuli or specific components of a complex stimulus permitting other stimuli or parts thereof to pass through. The term is used broadly; it may be a lens that only transmits certain wavelengths (a light filter), an electronic device that allows only particular sound frequencies to pass (an acoustic filter), a highly restrictive acoustic filter that only passes a narrow band of frequencies (a band pass filter), etc. Note that the term is also used metaphorically for hypothesized perceptual and cognitive processes: ➤ **filter theory**.

filter theory A general term covering any of several models of perception that assume that the basic mechanism in a hypothesized neural filter screens out stimuli that do not 'match' and allows through stimuli that do. For example, the letter 'A' is 'passed' by a filter that is tuned to letters of that shape while another letter such as 'Q' would be screened out by the neural system that detects 'A's'. Filter theories are, in general, too primitive to explain the full complexities of perception and cognition; for example, they fail to provide any real insight into how we could read different handwritings or different typefaces. However, the general notion of filtering or of attenuating incoming stimuli is an important aspect of many more general theories of ➤ **pattern recognition** and ➤ **pattern perception**.

fimbria 1. A complex fiber bundle that runs from the lateral surface of the ➤ **hippocampal formation** to various other regions of the forebrain. The section that runs rostrally from the *hippocampus* forms the *fornix* which, in turn, is divided into the *precommissural fornix*, whose axons run from the *medial septum* to the *hippocampus* and from there to the *lateral septum*, and the *fornix columns*, which convey axons from the *subiculum* to the *anterior thalamic nuclei* and to the *mammillary bodies* of the *hypothalamus*. 2. The long fringelike extremities of the *fallopian tubes*.

final common path C. S. Sherrington's term for the lower motor neurons of the spinal cord and cranial nerve nuclei in their role within any decision-making process involving motor action. His point was, simply, that all processes that are to influence movement, be they monosynaptic spinal reflexes or 'purposive' higher brain functions, must do so by ultimately acting on the motor neurons – hence they were the final common path.

finalism A synonym of ➤ **teleology**.

fine motor movement Simply, fine movements which require subtle muscular coordination in cases where delicate control is needed. Compare with ➤ **gross motor movement**.

finger agnosia ➤ tactile *agnosia.

finger spelling A mode of manual communication in which 26 discrete arrangements of the fingers correspond to the letters of the alphabet and words, names and the like can be spelled out manually. It is an important adjunct to ➤ **sign language**.

first moment The *mean* of a distribution. ➤ **moment** (2).

first-order correlation ➤ **correlation, first-order**.

first-order factor ➤ **factor, first-order**.

first-signal system ➤ **second-signal system**.

Fisher's exact probability test A nonparametric statistical test useful for cases in which the data are from two relatively small samples and fall into two mutually exclusive categories.

Fisher's test A statistical test for determining the significance of a correlation coefficient.

Fisher's Z-transformation ➤ **Z-transformation**.

fishing expedition ➤ **data snooping**.

fission 1. Cell reproduction by division. Each part grows into a normal cell identical to the original. 2. The term is also used analogously in social psychology and the terms *social fission* and *group fission* relate to the splitting of a coherent social group into two separate groups each of which adds members and functions in a manner either similar to or derivative from the original.

fissure Generally, any relatively deep groove or slit on the surface of an organ. However, the term is most commonly used for those furrows on the surface of the brain; e.g., ➤ **central fissure, lateral fissure**. *Fissure* is typically reserved for the deep grooves, ➤ **sulcus** is used for the shallower ones.

fistula A narrow opening or passageway

in an area of tissue produced either artificially by surgery or by abnormal development or incomplete healing. Note that the term is used in two ways: (a) the original meaning above, in which the fistula is an aspect of the tissue of the organism itself, and (b) a derived meaning, in which the fistula is a surgically implanted tube that functions to keep open a passageway in tissue. Strictly speaking, in this latter case the tube is not the fistula, but usage here tends to be loose.

fit **1** n. Medically, a sudden attack or convulsion. ➤ **epilepsy** et seq. **2** n. Statistically, a degree of conformity between observed data and expected data. ➤ **goodness of *fit**. **3** vb. To adjust data to bring them into conformity with some standard. The process is only defensible when there is a set of strongly motivated principles to guide one, otherwise one ends up 'fudging' the data and not fitting them. Distinguish this meaning from that of ➤ **curve fitting**, which does not involve any modification of the data themselves.

fit, goodness of An expression of how well any set of observed data conforms to some expected distribution. There are several tests for evaluating goodness of fit based on the sum of the squared deviations between the observed and the expected values. See, e.g., ➤ **chi square** and **least squares principle**.

fitness **1.** Generally, the extent to which an organism is prepared to succeed in some endeavour. **2.** In evolutionary theory, the degree to which an organism is successful in production of viable offspring. Differentiate this meaning from that of ➤ **adaptation** (3); an individual may have an extremely adaptive phenotype but if it is sterile its fitness will be zero. *Darwinian fitness* is also used for meaning (2). ➤➤ **inclusive fitness**.

fitness, Darwinian ➤ **fitness** (2).

Fitt's law A generalization about sensory-motor processes relating movement time (MT) to the precision of the movement and to the distance of the movement. Specifically, $MT = a + (b \log_2 2D/W)$, where a and b are constants, D is distance moved and W is the width of the target moved toward (the measure of precision). The generalization derives from feedback principles: the longer or the more precise a movement must be the more corrections are needed to perform it and these 'in course' corrections take time.

5-HT ➤ **serotonin**.

fixated response A response that continues to be emitted despite attempts to extinguish or alter it.

fixation **1.** Generally, the process whereby something becomes rigid, set, inflexible; the operation of holding something in a fixed position. This meaning is broadly utilized throughout many areas in psychology: learning, perception, cognition, personality and social psychology, etc. Frequently, the term will have qualifiers appended to designate the specific variety of fixation intended, as the entries that follow reveal. **2.** Within psychoanalytic theory, an extremely common shortened form of ➤ **affective *fixation**.

fixation, abnormal Persistent, compulsive behavior seemingly without rational motivation. Within psychoanalytic theory it is usually assumed to result from ➤ **affective *fixation**.

fixation, affective As derived from classical psychoanalytic theory, the process whereby one becomes excessively attached to (or 'fixated' on) some object or person that was appropriate for an earlier stage of development. The individual is thus said to have become *affectively fixated* at an immature stage. This condition is assumed to produce a variety of neurotic behaviors, such as excessive or irrational attachments to people or objects and an inability to form normal, mature relationships. Sometimes the attachment object itself is called a *fixation* (although this is not recommended) and the point in the developmental sequence at which the individual is arrested is called the *fixation point*. Within the psychoanalytic frame of reference the full term is often (usually) shortened to *fixation*. Within such contexts modifiers are often used; e.g., *father fixation*, *oral fixation*, etc.

fixation, law of In learning theory one speaks of overlearned behavior which is seemingly permanent as being *fixed* or *fixated* behavior. The 'law' here is simply a generalization that states that such fixing of behavior will occur if there is sufficient reinforced practice.

fixation line ➤ visual *fixation.

fixation of affect ➤ affective *fixation.

fixation pause A brief moment when the eyeball is at rest. It is during these fixation pauses that visual discrimination is possible. For example, the visual input for reading takes place during these pauses. ➤➤ **reading span, saccades**.

fixation point 1. ➤ affective *fixation. 2. ➤ fixation pause and visual *fixation.

fixation, visual The orienting of the eyeball so that the projection of the viewed object falls on the fovea and is in focus. The object or location in space is called the *fixation point* and it lies along the *fixation line* which can be 'drawn' from the fovea through the pupil to the object.

fixed action pattern (fap) An ethological term used for certain behavioral sequences that typically occur in a fixed, stereotyped fashion and that have been described in a variety of species. Within classical ethological theory, a fap was assumed to be evoked or released (➤ **releaser**) in a relatively autonomous fashion when the proper species-specific stimulus is encountered. Later research has questioned the stereotypy of the behaviors; it is rarely as compelling as the original theorists thought. Hence this term has been largely replaced by *species-specific* or *species-typical behavior*.

fixed alternative ➤ forced choice (**technique**).

fixed-effects fallacy The results of an experiment run with ➤ **fixed *factors** do not avail themselves of generalizations beyond

those fixed values used. The aptly named fallacy is committed when the experimenter supposes that the experiment was run with ➤ **random *factors** when in fact the variable used was actually a fixed one. The classic example is selecting a sub-set of the large (infinite) set of possible English sentences for a psycholinguistic experiment and treating that set as representing a random factor. On the surface this seems right since the stimuli were taken at random from an infinite population. However, in practice the particular set of sentences selected may (indeed usually will) have rather specific idiosyncratic properties that produce results that do not generalize to the rest of the language. This fallacy can be circumvented most easily by using a different sub-set of materials for each subject run.

fixed effects model ➤ fixed *factor.

fixed factor ➤ factor, fixed.

fixed idea ➤ *idée fixe*.

fixed image ➤ stabilized image.

fixed interval (FI) ➤ schedules of *reinforcement.

fixed ratio (FR) ➤ schedules of *reinforcement.

fixed time (FT) ➤ schedules of *reinforcement.

flaccid Flabby, low in muscle tone.

flaccid paralysis ➤ paralysis.

flagellation The practice of whipping. The term *flagellant* was originally applied to members of a 12th-century sect of religious fanatics who did religious penance by whipping. Flagellation also has strong sexual-arousal properties for some people and the term is commonly used with this connotation. ➤ **masochism, paraphilia, sadism**.

flashback The spontaneous recurrence of the imagery and hallucinations of a drug-like experience without further doses of the drug. Most commonly associated with the hallucinogens (e.g., LSD), such flashbacks may occur for as long as one or two years since the last ingestion of the drug. Since drugs like LSD are metabolized rapidly it seems clear that flashbacks are psychological phenomena and not due in any simple way to the presence of the drug.

flashbulb memory ➤ memory, flashbulb.

flattening of affect The absence of appropriate, outward emotional responses.

flavor A general term used to describe the combined effects of olfactory (smell), gustatory (taste) and touch and temperature sensations of objects in the mouth. var., *flavour*.

flehman A lip curl. It is a common facial expression in mammals usually associated with sniffing and likely functions to convey substances to the ➤ vomeronasal organ.

Flesch index (or **formula**) A formula for evaluating the reading difficulty of a passage of English prose.

flexibilitas cerea Latin for *waxy flexibility*. ➤ catatonic waxy flexibility.

flexion Bending inward, particularly of a limb at a joint. Contrast with ➤ extension (2).

flexor The muscle whose action bends (or flexes) a limb (contrast with ➤ extensor). Flexor and extensor muscles generally act to form a pair of ➤ antagonistic muscles.

flicker Generally, any rapid alternation in a stimulus: typically the stimulus will be a visual one. The point at which the periodic aspect of the stimulus ceases and the flickering stimulus 'fuses' into a continuous one is called the ➤ critical flicker frequency.

flicker, auditory Periodic sound alternation. *Flicker* is really the wrong word here, particularly because of its association with visual stimuli; *flutter* is better and found with increasing frequency. *Jitter* is also used.

flicker fusion point ➤ critical flicker frequency.

flight from reality ➤ reality, flight from.

flight into health A phrase used to characterize the sudden 'recovery' of some emotionally distressed people when they suddenly come face to face with psychotherapy. The usual interpretation is that this 'flight' is a defense mechanism set up to avoid the self-examination required in therapy.

flight into illness A phrase occasionally used to characterize a sudden emergence of psychiatric symptoms. Within psychoanalysis it is viewed as a defense mechanism that is used to mask a deeper conflict the examination of which will be deferred while this new syndrome is made the focus of the analysis.

flight of colors A succession of colored images seen as an afterimage following an intense short-duration stimulus viewed against a dark background.

flight of ideas Continuous, fragmentary stream of ideas, thoughts and images without any coherent pattern or focus, as expressed in speech. Often observed in the manic phase of bipolar disorders.

floaters Tiny substances in the humors of the eye which, although always present, we generally do not notice. Occasionally they are seen as floating specks in the visual field. In some disorders, such as detached vitreous, they can become quite numerous and rather annoying. Also called by the French term, *mouches volantes* (or 'flying flies').

floating affect A psychoanalytic term used to refer to emotional states that are not associated with any specific object or event. The term ➤ free-floating *anxiety is often used in this fashion to refer to generalized feelings of distress which have been 'set free' from the original circumstances that caused them.

flocculonodular lobe A lobe located at the caudal end of the cerebellum that is involved in postural reflexes. It receives inputs from the *vestibular system* and projects its axons to the *vestibular nucleus*.

flooding ➤ implosion therapy.

floor effect ➤ ceiling effect.

flow chart 'Flow' here refers to a sequence of events, hence a flow chart is a graphic or pictorial representation of such a sequence. Originally used in computer programming, the term has been borrowed by psychology along with the general technique as a means of displaying schematically the sequence of events hypothesized to take place in information processing.

flowery A class of olfactory (smell) qualities typified by flowers. ➤ Henning's prism.

fluctuation 1. A generic term characterizing any oscillation or any cyclic change. 2. In biology, a slight variation in form and structure within a species. Contrast here with ➤ mutation. 3. In statistics, a variation in the values of a statistic calculated from successive samples. 4. In perception, a shift in the perceived object when there has been no objective change in the physical stimulus. This last meaning is also expressed by the term *fluctuation of attention*, although such perceptual shifts are not necessarily the result of shifts in attention but may be caused by more basic physiological processes, e.g. adaptation effects.

fluctuation of attention ➤ fluctuation (4).

fluent aphasia ➤ Wernicke's *aphasia.

fluoxetine ➤ antidepressant drug. Trade name Prozac.

fluphenazine An anti-psychotic drug of the phenothiazine group.

flutter ➤ auditory *flicker.

focal 1. Descriptive of the point at which light rays are in focus. 2. By extension, characterizing any integral point that lies at the core of some effect or phenomenon.

focal attention ➤ attention, focal.

focal epilepsy ➤ epilepsy, focal.

focal length As descriptive of a particular lens, it is the distance from the lens to the point at which parallel rays of light are brought into focus.

focal stress The primary vocal stress in a spoken sentence. Such stress plays an important role in the interpretation of an utterance, as can be appreciated by repeating the simple sentence 'What are you doing?' four times with focal stress on a different word each time.

focal therapy A restricted form of psychotherapy where one particular problem is singled out and made the focus of the therapy.

focus 1 n. The point at which the light rays passing through a lens are made to converge. 2 n. The object upon which one's attention or thinking is centred. 3 vb. To adjust an optical system (including the eye) so that the light rays converge at a point. 4 vb. To center one's attention on a particular thing.

focus of attention Quite literally, the 'focus' of 'attention.' The object, event, idea, problem, thought, etc. upon which one is concentrating.

foetal, foetus ➤ fetal and fetus.

foliate papilla ➤ lingual papilla.

folie à deux French for *insanity in pairs*. Descriptive of instances when two closely related people (siblings, husband and wife) display the same mental disorder at the same time. ➤➤ induced psychotic disorder.

folium A convolution or fold on the cerebellum. pl., *folia*.

folklore The complex of songs, legends, stories, etc. that make up the unwritten traditional literature of a culture.

folk mind ➤ group mind.

folk psychology Everyday, commonsense psychology. The kinds of psychological notions, principles, understandings (and misunderstandings) that are held by most lay people.

folkways Social norms or traditional

patterns of behavior in a culture. Folkways are implicit and learned by successive generations through socialization and hence are distinguished from ➤ **mores**, which are the explicitly presented and obligatory standards.

follicle Generally, any small secreting cavity.

follicle, hair A cylindrical invagination in the epidermis with associated sebaceous glands and small muscles through which a hair grows.

follicle-stimulating hormone (FSH) ➤ **menstrual cycle**.

following reaction The species-specific tendency for the young to follow the mother after ➤ **imprinting** has taken place.

fontanel The area in the cranium of an infant that has not yet become ossified. The so-called 'soft spot.' var., *fontanelle*.

food aversion (or **avoidance**) ➤ **toxicosis**.

foot anesthesia ➤ glove *anesthesia.

foot candle A obsolete term for the unit of illuminance defined as the illumination on a surface by a standard candle at a distance of 1 foot. The preferred measure is the ➤ **lux**. ➤➤ **candela** and **candle**.

'foot-in-the-door' technique A device for obtaining compliance in which an individual first makes a small, even trivial, request and once this is granted escalates to larger and more important requests. Compare with ➤ **'door-in-the-face' technique**.

foot lambert An obsolete term for the unit of luminance defined as that produced by a perfectly reflecting and diffusing surface whose brightness is uniformly 1 foot candle. The ➤ **lumen** is now the preferred measure.

foraging In studies of feeding behavior in natural environments the various activities involved in obtaining foodstuffs, e.g., search, identification, procurement, handling, storage, etc.

foramen magnum A foramen is any opening or passageway; the foramen magnum is that opening of the occipital bone of the skull which the spinal cord passes through to become the medulla. Also called the *intervertebral foramen*.

forced-choice (technique) A general label for any procedure in which the subject is required to select one item or answer from a fixed set of two or more alternatives. There are several variations on the technique and they are used in diverse areas such as personality assessment, determination of personal preferences, studies of memory, examinations of decision-making, etc. The basic technique is an extremely important one for it allows one to control for a number of extraneous factors that could easily contaminate the results of an experiment. For example, in the commonly used self-rating personality inventories, social desirability can often disrupt one's findings because in a free-choice setting people tend to put down answers that reflect what society prizes rather than what is appropriate for them. The forced-choice technique demands of the testee the selection of one alternative from a given set even though he or she feels that all (or none) of those provided really fit. By carefully counter-balancing items the social-desirability factor is controlled for. Similarly, in recognition-memory studies individual biases to respond 'yes' or 'no' when in doubt as to an item's status can be eliminated by always giving two or more stimulus items only one of which is correct. Also called, particularly in personality assessment, *fixed-alternative technique*.

force field In physics this term can be given precise meaning, in psychology its use is almost entirely metaphorical and typically refers to any or all of the influences on behavior. It is typically used rather holistically – the force field encompasses all significant factors. Such usage unfortunately tends to be so broad that it robs the term of any real descriptive value.

fore- Prefix meaning *in front of*, *before*.

forebrain During embryonic development the brain evolves three separate portions, the hindbrain, midbrain and forebrain. The latter subdivides into the telencephalon and diencephalon. The telencephalon then develops into the cerebral cortex, the basal ganglia and the limbic system. The diencephalon becomes the thalamus and the hypothalamus.

forecasting efficiency, index of A measure of the extent to which one can use knowledge of one variable to make predictions about another variable given that the correlation between the two is known. Usually symbolized as E, the index is given as $1-\sqrt{(1-r^2)}$, where r is the correlation coefficient.

foreconscious Synonym for ➤ preconscious.

foregrounding A general term for any action taken by a person designed to draw another person's attention to a particular aspect of a stimulus environment. A comment like 'Look at this book' is a good example; it places the book in the person's perceptual/conceptual foreground. Foregrounding is very common in parent-child interactions.

foreign hull In K. Lewin's field theory, all those nonpsychological aspects of the environment that lie outside of but adjacent to the ➤ life space. It is composed of the physical environment and the social and cultural environments that may invade or penetrate the life space.

forensic From the Latin, meaning *of the forum*. Hence: 1. Argumentative, suited for argumentation. 2. Pertaining to the courts of law and judicial procedure. See following entries for specifics.

forensic medicine The application of medical knowledge and medical practice as it pertains to legal issues.

forensic psychiatry A branch of psychiatry dealing with legal questions such as determination of ➤ sanity (see that term for clarification of usage), issues of mental responsibility for acts committed, committability of an individual (to an institution),

etc. Generally distinguished from ➤ **forensic psychology**, although on occasions a forensic psychiatrist may be called to testify on issues that fall within the range of issues discussed under that term.

forensic psychology The field of psychology concerned with the application of psychological knowledge and principles to legal issues. Generally distinguished from ➤ **forensic psychiatry**, it is concerned with an array of problems of a psychological nature including the reliability of evidence, the reliability of eyewitness testimony, the role of human memory, the psychology of decision-making, particularly group decision-making (as in juries), questions of the general credibility of witnesses, etc.

foreperiod Generally, the first part of an experiment; specifically, the term is reserved for experiments on reaction time and refers to the period between the 'ready' signal and the presentation of the stimulus.

fore-pleasure In the classical psychoanalytic approach erotic pleasures are divided into those associated with increasing erotic tension (the *fore*-pleasures) and those associated with release of the tension (*end*-pleasures). Thus, fore-pleasure will be found denoting any activity that functions to increase the desire for end-pleasure.

foreshortening The decrease in apparent length of a line, looked at in an alignment parallel to the line of regard, as compared with its apparent length when seen so that it is at an oblique angle relative to the viewer.

forgetting 1. Broadly, the loss of the ability to recall, recognize or reproduce that which was previously learned. This definition is fairly straightforward and reflects the term's general meaning. However, usage within psychology tends to be tinged with various nuances, nuances that stem from particular theoretical characterizations of the nature of the processes underlying forgetting. In particular: 2. In the traditional approaches to learning forgetting is the weakening of an associative bond. This is presumed to be brought about either by nonreinforcement or by the action of various inhibitory or interfering processes. See here, e.g. ➤ **inhibition**, **proactive *interference**, **retroactive *interference**. **3.** In psychoanalytic theory forgetting is treated as the result of ➤ **repression**. That is, memories are assumed not to be 'lost' but rather rendered nonretrievable by the action of defense mechanisms. **4.** In Gestalt theory, since perception and learning are assumed to be predicated on the organization of coherent wholes, forgetting is viewed as the result of the disruption of or interference with the structured memory. Material is either 'lost' because the coded structure is not retrieved or it is 'modified' by reorganization so thoroughly that it is not any longer recognizable as the original. **5.** The contemporary cognitive approach postulates three types of memory each with a hypothesized forgetting mechanism: (a) the ➤ **sensory-information store** is very short-lived and information is lost through a rapid process of neural decay; (b) *short-term *memory* is a limited-capacity system that retains material through rehearsal and loses it through decay if rehearsal is interfered with. In both of these types material that is forgotten is assumed to be irrevocably 'gone'; (c) *long-term *memory* is a theoretically unlimited memorial system containing all relatively well-coded and organized knowledge. When information is 'lost' from this store the mechanism of interference is generally implicated; forgetting from long-term memory is treated as failure to retrieve. ➤➤ **memory** and related entries.

form Generally this term refers to the outline, shape or overall structure of an object or figure. The critical psychological aspect of any form is that the pattern of the whole figure is usually perceived as more important or significant than the several elements that make it up. The notion of form and form perception is critical in psychology. It was first made into an important issue by the Gestalt psychologists who argued convincingly that form takes precedence over superficial aspects of any display; both o and O are seen as circles, a melody is recognizable whether sung by a baritone or a soprano. ➤ **Gestalt psychology** and related entries.

formal 1. Pertaining to ➤ **form**. **2.** Pertaining to an emphasis on general rules or overall patterns and principles rather than on content.

formal discipline The approach to education that advocates that some subjects ought to be studied, independently of any content that they might have, because they acquaint the student with basic principles (or *forms*) that will ultimately prove of value in other ways and generally serve to 'train the mind.' The enthusiasm for this approach has waxed and waned several times over the years.

formalism A general orientation to the gathering of knowledge that places primary emphasis on organization, consistency and the development of formal principles. Within psychology there have been relatively few theoretical approaches that qualify as formalisms; the most successful have been Hull's *hypothetico-deductive system*, Estes's *mathematical models of learning*, and most recently, the new ➤ **connectionism** (2). The formalist approach is generally balanced against the ➤ **eclectic**; see that term for further discussion.

formal operations A set of cognitive operations cited by Piaget as characteristic of the thought of a child in the ➤ **formal operatory stage**. All involve abstract thinking that is no longer tied to physical objects and events. It is propositional in nature and is concerned with the hypothetical and the possible rather than the real and the perceived. Compare with ➤ **concrete operations**.

formal operatory stage (or **level or period**) In Piagetian theory, the stage of cognitive functioning following the ➤ **concrete operatory stage** assumed to begin around age 12 with the development of abstract thinking. According to Piaget it is regarded as the culmination of 'intellectual' development, although this particular point is vigorously debated by other theorists.

formal operatory thought A term used by Piaget to characterize the 'formal,' logical, cognitive processes manifested by the child in the ➤ **formal operatory stage**.

formal organization ➤ **organization** (2).

formal thought disorder ➤ **thought disorder**.

formal universals ➤ **linguistic * universals**.

formant A spectrographic representation of a speech sound reveals that energy is concentrated in bands at particular frequencies. The concentrations of energy show up as dark areas which are called formants. Each speech sound can be described by the location in the frequency spectrum of four separate formants. The first two (counting up from the lower frequencies) appear to be the critical ones for processing human speech. ➤ **spectrograph**.

formatting ➤ **scaffolding**.

formboard test A class of performance tests in which the task is to fit a set of blocks of varying shapes into slots of varying shapes.

form constancy ➤ **object constancy**.

form–function relation (or **distinction**) In general, this term refers to the role of a thing (its *function*) compared with or distinguished from its physical characteristics (its *form*). The classic distinctions here occur in the study of the psychology of language, where it is often necessary to distinguish between the formal properties of an utterance and its function in a particular setting. For example, the sentence, 'Can you close the door?' is formally a question about one's capabilities but it functions as a request for action.

formication From the Latin *formica* meaning *ant*. A hallucinated sensation that insects or in some cases snakes are crawling on or under the skin. It is a form of ➤ **paresthesia** and a common side effect of long-term abuse of cocaine and of the amphetamines.

forms, comparable A generic term used to refer to two or more comparable or correlated forms of a test. Also called *alternate* or *alternative forms*.

fornication Non-coerced sexual intercourse between persons not married to each other.

fornix ➤ **fimbria (1)**.

fornix columns ➤ **fimbria** (1).

45,X ➤ **Turner's syndrome**, in which there are only 45 chromosomes with only a single (X) sex chromosome present in the genotype.

47,XXX ➤ **triple-X syndrome**.

47,XXY ➤ **Klinefelter's syndrome**, in which there are 47 chromosomes with 3 sex chromosomes present in the genotype.

47,XYY ➤ **XYY syndrome**.

foster-child fantasy The childhood delusion that one's parents are not one's real parents but adoptive or foster parents.

founder effect In genetics, differences between two (or more) populations brought about when one population was founded in a new locale by a small group of individuals who happened to be carrying a subset of genes from the general population. Some unusual patterns of incidence, such as the high rate of schizophrenia among the residents of the area of Sweden above the Arctic Circle, are thought to be *founder effects*.

fourfold-point correlation ➤ **phi coefficient**.

Fourier's law The mathematically demonstrable generalization that any complex periodic pattern, such as sound waves, may be described as a particular sum of a number of sine waves. The sine waves so used are called a *Fourier series* and the description itself, a *Fourier analysis*.

fourth moment The ➤ **kurtosis** of a distribution. ➤➤ **moment** (2).

four-walls technique A technique for obtaining compliance by presenting the individual with a set of questions, the answers to which are designed to produce *cognitive dissonance* should the person fail to comply with the ultimate request. The classic case is the encyclopedia salesperson who begins by asking the customer questions like, 'Do you feel that education is important for your children?' and 'Do you believe that having good reference materials will help your child's education?'

fovea (centralis) A small pit or depression in the retina. When light enters the eye along the visual axis it falls on the portion of the retina called the macula lutea (or yellow spot) in the middle of which is the fovea, a rather small area covering only about 2° of visual angle. The fovea is densely packed with cones (it is rod-free) and is the area of clearest vision. When you focus or look at an object you are turning the eye so that the image of the object is projected on the fovea.

foveal vision ➤ **fovea** and **photopic vision**.

FR Abbreviation for *fixed ratio*. ➤ **schedules of *reinforcement**.

fractional antedating goal response (r_G) A hypothetical reaction assumed to occur in a long response chain. In successive trials it is assumed to move progressively earlier in the chain and provide additional cues which become conditioned to successive responses leading to the goal. Also called *functional anticipatory goal response*.

fractional goal stimulus (s_g) A proprioceptive stimulus which occurs as a result of a *fractional antedating goal response*.

fragile X syndrome A genetic disorder marked by a weak arm on the X chromosome. Affected males have large ears, large testicles, poor speech, and mental retardation; affected females are often subclinical. There is also a suspected link between fragile X syndrome and *autism*.

frame **1.** In ➤ **artificial intelligence**, a set of fixed elements that define ('frame') a situation. For example, the elements in a *room frame* are walls, a ceiling, a floor, doorways, etc. This usage is associated with the work of the American theorist Marvin Minsky. **2.** In social psychology the term is used in similar fashion but much more loosely. Any social situation can be 'defined' in accordance with basic principles that will affect and control the ways in which people involve themselves with and experience that situation. These 'definitions' are frames. Note that the term is used here specifically to refer to the *perceived* and *experienced* organization, the agreed-upon 'frame' within which people function. It is not used to express any necessary statements about objective social reality. The term was first introduced with this meaning by G. Bateson but is primarily associated with the work of the sociologist Erving Goffman.

frame analysis An approach to the study of the experiencing of social situations by analyzing them in terms of ➤ **frames**.

frame of reference The overall context within which a particular event takes place and, hence, is interpreted or judged. ➤ **frame** (2).

framing A ➤ **cognitive *heuristic** in which people tend to reach conclusions based on the 'framework' within which a situation was presented. E.g., people are more likely to recommend the use of a new procedure if it is described as having a '50% success rate' than a '50% failure rate.'

fraternal twins ➤ **dizygotic *twins**.

F ratio In statistics, the ratio of the variances (σ^2) of two samples. The ratio was named in honor of the statistician Ronald A. Fisher and is given by $F = \sigma_1^2 / \sigma_2^2$, where σ_2^2 is always the smaller of the two variances. The size of an F ratio may be used to determine whether there is homogeneity of variance between the two samples from which the two values of σ^2 were estimated.

free association ➤ **association, free**.

freedom A term with two distinct uses in psychology: **1.** The sense that one has personal control over one's choice, decisions, actions, etc. The feeling that external factors play little or no role in one's personal behavior. This meaning is conveyed by sentences that begin 'Freedom to . . .' **2.** The state in which one is (relatively) unburdened by painful situations, noxious stimuli, hunger, pain, disease, etc. This sense is usually intended by sentences that begin 'Freedom from . . .'

To be sure, in the pragmatics of everyday life these two freedoms are intimately interwined, but failure to keep them conceptually distinct leads to philosophical and political muddles. The former is close in conceptualization to the doctrine of ➤ **free will**; the latter relates to issues of ➤ **control** (2). ➤ **social *power** and the behaviorist position on the role of ➤ **reinforcement** and ➤ **punishment**.

free-feeding ➤ **ad lib**.

free-floating anxiety ➤ **free-floating *anxiety** and **floating affect**.

free nerve endings The microscopic, branched endings of afferent neurons that innervate all body tissues unconnected to any specific sensory receptor. They are believed to be the receptors for pain. The thin, slow *C fibers* mediate the slow, diffuse, dull sense of pain; the thicker, myelinated, faster *A-delta fibers* mediate the sharp, localized sense of pain.

free operant A response that may be emitted at any time in a particular situation. In most operant-conditioning experiments the organism is free to respond, and measures of behavior are based on response rate or the number of such free responses made in some unit of time. The key concept here is *emitted*; ➤ **emit** and also the discussion under ➤ **operant conditioning**.

free recall An experimental procedure used in memory research in which the subject is free to recall, in any order, the items given for memorization. Compare with ➤ **serial recall**.

free responding ➤ **free operant**.

free running In the study of ➤ **circadian rhythms**, maintaining an organism in either constant darkness or light so that the normal day/night cycle that constrains the circadian rhythms is no longer present and biological rhythms 'run free.'

free will **1.** A most general term used to refer to a broad class of philosophical positions all of which have in common the assumption that to some degree or another behavior is under control of the volition of an individual. Contrast with ➤ **determinism**. **2.** A hypothesized (and often reified) internal agency that functions independently of externally imposed forces, as in the often-asked question, 'Don't you think people have free will?'

freezing Assuming a position of tonic immobility. The ethological term ➤ **death feigning** is used when the response is a natural one for a member of the species, *freezing* is used by some for the response when it develops as a learned reaction.

frequency **1.** Cycles per second in periodic vibration; e.g., in sound waves, electric current, etc. **2.** The number of occurrences of the several values of some variable.

frequency distribution ➤ **distribution, frequency**.

frequency, law of The generalization that the more often a response is made the more robust and resistant to extinction it becomes. Also known as the *law of repetition*.

frequency method ➤ **measurement of *threshold**.

frequency polygon A way of pictorially presenting a frequency distribution. The frequency of each class interval (➤ **grouped frequency *distribution**) is plotted and a line is drawn which connects these points. ➤➤ **histogram**.

frequency theory ➤ theories of *hearing.

Freudian Of or pertaining to the points of view associated with the brilliant Viennese neurologist Sigmund Freud (1856–1939). Many of the details of specific terms, concepts and principles that emerged from this orientation are dealt with elsewhere in this volume; this eponymous adjective itself is used freely in conjunction with them all. However, there are particular core concepts that characterize the pure term *Freudian*: (a) a focus upon the unconscious, specifically the role of unconscious processes as motivators of behavior; (b) an abiding concern with the cognitive and the symbolic: (c) an affiliation with the basic biological progenitors of human behavior, especially the sexual and the aggressive; (d) a strong presumption that early experiences are the causes of later behaviors; (e) a penchant for deep interpretation, for rummaging down through the layers of the psyche to seek understanding and explanation: (f) the elaboration of the methods of psychoanalytic therapy as a means for producing changes in behavior, thought and feeling.

The many terms that spring to the minds of most educated lay people like *id*, *ego*, *superego*, *cathexis*, *displacement*, *psychosexual stage*, etc. are not really viewed as pure representations of Freudianism any longer. They have become so much a part of the various analytical or depth psychologies that Freudians no longer hold a special claim to them. What truly represents the appellation is: (g) an overarching concern with the most profound conflict of human existence, the agony of recognition of our 'creatureliness' with all of its evolutionarily dictated baseness balanced against our rich cognitive capacity for transcendent thought with its extensions to symbolism, religion and esthetics – and the knowledge derived from this mental capacity that the base creature must eventually die.

Freudian slip ➤ parapraxis.

fricative A speech sound produced by nearly closing the oral cavity so that there is a turbulent air flow, e.g., the *f* in *fat*, the *th* in *that*, both of which are voiceless fricatives, and the *v* in *vat* and the *th* in *this*, both of which are voiced.

frigidity 1. Generally, a lack of sexual desire. 2. More specifically, an inability to enjoy or complete sexual intercourse. 3. Most specifically, an inability to achieve orgasm. The term is used almost exclusively with respect to women; ➤ **impotence** is used for men. The term in any of the above variations lacks clear definitional boundaries: the 'inability' need not be total for the term to be applied but merely too infrequent for a satisfactory sexual life. Some authors will use it strictly with respect to inability to achieve coital orgasm and others to the inability to achieve vaginal orgasm. Both of these 'definitions' are unnecessarily limited; the first is a residue of Victorianism, the second of Freudianism and neither is an accurate reflection of either behavior or biology. Note, when meaning 3 is intended, some authors refer to such women as ➤ **pre-orgasmic**, which avoids the negative connotations of *frigidity*.

fringe of consciousness An occasional synonym for ➤ **margin of *attention**.

frontal Pertaining to the anterior part of a body or organ.

frontal lobe Approximately, that portion of the cerebral cortex that lies in front of the precentral gyrus.

frontal-lobe syndrome ➤ organic *personality syndrome.

frontal lobotomy ➤ lobotomy et seq.

frontal section ➤ section (2).

frottage ➤ frotteurism.

frotteurism A ➤ sexual disorder characterized by intense sexual urges involving touching and rubbing against another, nonconsenting, person. The act itself (*frottage*) is usually carried out in crowded places such as buses or subways. ➤➤ paraphilia.

frozen noise ➤ noise, frozen.

fruity A class of olfactory (smell) qualities typified by fruits. ➤ **Henning's prism**.

frustration Technical usage in psychology is generally limited to two meanings: **1.** The act of blocking, interfering with or disrupting behavior that is directed toward some goal. This is the operational definition; the behavior may be almost anything from overt, physical movement to covert, cognitive process. **2.** The emotional state assumed to result from the act in 1. It is typically assumed that this emotional state has motivational properties that produce behavior designed to bypass or surmount the block.

frustration–aggression hypothesis A 'double-barreled' proposition which assumes that frustration always leads to aggression (whether covert or overt) and that aggressive behavior is always an indication of some prior frustration. Stated this way the hypothesis is circular and an unsatisfying account of behavior. However, the link between frustration and aggression is an intuitively compelling one; what is needed to rescue the hypothesis is independent evaluations of frustration and aggression.

frustrative nonreward (hypothesis) A generalization that assumes that the withholding of a reinforcer is an actively punishing and aversive (i.e. frustrating) event. The hypothesis predicts that behavior following frustrative nonreward will show greater vigor.

F scale ➤ **measurement of *authoritarianism**.

FSH Abbreviation for *follicle-stimulating hormone*. ➤ **menstrual cycle**.

FT Abbreviation for *fixed time*. ➤ **schedules of *reinforcement**.

F test A parametric statistical test that uses the ➤ **F ratio** to determine whether the variances of two samples are significantly different. This simple test forms the basis for the most utilized of all statistical techniques, the *analysis of variance*. The extension was first worked out by Sir Ronald A. Fisher (the *F* honors him), who showed that more than two conditions can be evaluated by setting up an F ratio between a variance estimate based on variability *among* several means and one based on variability among scores *within* each condition.

fugue From the Latin for *flight*, a psychiatric disability the defining feature of which is a sudden and unexpected leaving of home with the person assuming a new identity elsewhere. During the fugue there is no recollection of the earlier life and after recovery amnesia for events during it. Often called *dissociative psychogenic fugue* to distinguish it from other syndromes that have similar symptoms but are caused by known organic dysfunctions.

Fullerton-Cattell law A psychophysical generalization that the error of observation increases with the square root of the stimulus intensity. Proposed as a substitute for ➤ **Weber's law** on the grounds that errors of observation were more psychologically germane than the classic procedures that use introspection to determine a 'real' *just noticeable difference*.

function **1.** In mathematics, a quantity that varies systematically with variation in some other quantity. In the expression, $y = f(x)$, variations in y are given as a function of variations in x. The changes are not necessarily proportional, but are expressed by the nature of f. When used psychologically, x is the ➤ **independent *variable** and y the ➤ **dependent *variable**. Graphic representation can be made of such functional relations by plotting values of x on one axis and values of y on the other. **2.** Often the term is used in something like this mathematical fashion but without the quantification that the above usage reflects. Thus, one will encounter expressions like 'persuasion is a function of the credibility of the source,' where the mathematical meaning is implied with the connotation of one thing being dependent on something else but the quantification of the variables is either missing altogether or represented on a scale of less power (see the discussion under ➤ **scale** and related entries for clarification of usage here). **3.** The proper activity or appropriate behavior of a person, an organ, a structure, a machine or even a socially defined role. Thus one will see references to the function of a teacher, a computer, the liver, a group leader, etc. Compare here with ➤ **structure** (especially 1) and ➤➤ **functionalism** and **structuralism**. **4.** A variation on 3 is also found in which some purpose or goal is specified along with the behavior or activity; e.g., 'a function of the adrenal glands is the production of epinepherine.'

There are other subtle distinctions in the use of the term, but most of them can be subsumed under these general meanings. When variations of meaning are intended they are usually signaled by the use of qualifiers.

functional Pertaining to ➤ **function** (3, 4). When used as a qualifier of some disorder or disability it connotes that the causes are psychological and not the result of known organic or structural factors. ➤ **functional disorder**.

functional analysis **1.** Generally, an analysis of a complex system with an eye to the functions of the various aspects of the system and the manner of integrated operation. Such an analysis usually softpedals the actual form or structure. The 'system' analyzed can be essentially anything; the term is used in this fashion very broadly. **2.** Somewhat more specifically the term is associated with the strong behaviorist point of view of B. F. Skinner. Here the full term is *functional analysis of behavior* and the stress is on examining behavior *per se* while eschewing appeals to internal cognitive or physiological components.

functional antagonism ➤ **drug** *an-tagonism**.

functional autonomy ➤ **autonomy, functional**.

functional disorder An umbrella term for any disorder for which there is no known

organic pathology. In actual practice the term is used for (a) those disorders in which there is *no known* organic pathology (e.g., psychogenic ➤ **fugue**) as well as for (b) those disorders in which there is *known to be no* specific organic pathology that could be directly responsible for the symptoms (e.g., ➤ **glove *anesthesia**).

functional fixedness A conceptual set whereby objects that have been used for one function tend to be viewed as serving only that function even though the situation may call for the use of the object in a different context. For example, a hammer just used for pounding nails may not be perceived as appropriate for use as a pendulum weight. Also called *functional fixity*.

functional fixity ➤ **functional fixedness**.

functional integration ➤ **integration, functional**.

functionalism Within psychology: **1.** A general and broadly presented point of view that stresses the analysis of mind and behavior in terms of their functions or utilities rather than in terms of their contents. **2.** A school of thought formally established at the University of Chicago under J. R. Angell and H. Carr during the 1910s and 1920s.

While the school of thought in 2 reflected many of the characteristics of the approach in 1 it is important to distinguish between them. The formal school (meaning 2), which is often capitalized, represented a particular programmatic approach to the study of consciousness. It had a set of basic tenets put forth by Angell and was designed as a replacement paradigm for the then dominant Structuralist school (➤ **structuralism** (1)). Functionalism in sense 1, which is rarely if ever capitalized, represents a particular perspective that emerged from several influences, namely Darwin's evolutionary theory with its emphasis on adaptation, James's and Peirce's pragmatism with its open-mindedness and liberal attitudes and its focus on the practical utility of action, and Dewey's holism with its bias toward examination of the intact, functioning organism interacting with its environment.

The school of thought of the Chicagoans has expired; the functionalist perspective is still very much alive. It is manifested in modern empiricism and common terms like *purpose, adaptation, function, utility, role*, and many others are its legacy.

3. In philosophy, an approach to the study of mind that views mental states as functional states. Functionalism in this sense is distinguished metaphysically from physicalism in that rather than arguing that two identical mental states are physically identical it argues that they should (can) only be viewed as functionally equivalent. This point of view is represented in work in such fields as artificial intelligence, where a theory of an automaton would be represented in terms of functions rather than of real internal (i.e. physical) structures.

functional knowledge ➤ **procedural *knowledge**.

functional psychology ➤ **functionalism** (1, 2).

functional reasoning A kind of deductive reasoning whereby one's knowledge of the world allows the reaching of a valid conclusion about things not previously known. In the classic example, we probably don't *know* that bananas are not grown in Greenland but by virtue of what we know about geography, climate and growing bananas we can surmise this simple, true fact.

functional relation A relation between two variables such that change in one variable results in change in the other. Philosophically, a functional relation can be characterized as a causal relation.

functional stimulus ➤ **stimulus, functional**.

function engram Jung's hypothesized genetic neurological 'imprint' that serves as the underlying representation of the archetypes and endows symbols with their meanings.

function types Jung's classification of personality types was based on four functions: feeling, thinking, sensing and intuiting. Feeling and thinking were considered *rational*, sensing and intuiting, *irrational*. All persons were assumed to possess all four of these functions, the typing was a reflection of which style dominated in the individual's overall makeup.

function word Any word that has a grammatical (syntactic) role in a sentence as opposed to lexical (semantic) meaning. Prepositions, auxiliary verbs, conjunctions, interjections, articles, etc. are in the class of function words. Also called *functor*. Compare with ➤ **content word**.

functor ➤ **function word**.

fundamental attribution error ➤ **attribution error, fundamental**.

fundamental color(s) Colors (or, strictly speaking, *hues*) that are assumed to correspond with the fundamental color-vision responses of any particular theory of color vision. Thus, in the Young–Helmholtz theory there are three fundamental colors (red, green and blue) which when mixed in proper proportions yield all possible hues with a saturation greater than that possible with any other three wavelengths. ➤ **theories of *color vision**.

fundamental needs The most basic of the ➤ **basic needs** in Maslow's theory of human motivation. They include those generally related to physiological deficits such as hunger, thirst, etc.

fundamental skill Any skill that is a prerequisite for further progress.

fundamental tone The lowest-pitched tone in any compound sound. Practically every sounding or vibrating body vibrates in parts, each part putting out a pure tone dependent on the overall physical structure of the body. The perceived pitch of the resulting compound tone corresponds to the frequency of the *fundamental*. All higher-pitched tones are called *partial tones* or simply *partials*.

fungiform papilla ➤ **lingual papilla**.

funnel technique A technique used in interviewing and in the construction of questionnaires or inventories in which broad, general questions are used in the beginning and gradually the scope is narrowed to specifics.

fusion 1. A generic term used to refer to any process in which the several elements of a complex stimulus are blended or fused together in a whole so that the component parts cannot be perceptually distinguished. The term is very broadly used in this sense and the 'stimulus' may be almost anything from a straightforward physical one in a study on perception to a complex social one in a study of personal interaction. 2. In classical psychoanalytic theory, the balanced coordinated functioning of the life instincts and the death instincts. Fusion is regarded as 'normal,' although different behavioral patterns are assumed to result depending on which instincts dominate. *Defusion* is assumed to lead to various neuroses, especially obsessions.

fusion, binaural The combining of the sounds presented to each ear into a unitary auditory experience.

fusion, binocular The combining of the images presented to each eye into a single visual experience. Also called *retinal fusion*. ➤ **binocular rivalry** for more discussion.

fusion frequency ➤ **critical flicker frequency**.

future shock A term coined by A. Toffler as a way of expressing the view that we in Western society are becoming overloaded in terms of what we can process. The 'shock' produced by the rapid changes in social structures, social values and consumer products is so great that, Toffler argued, many persons simply cannot cope or adapt.

fuzzy set (or **restriction**) The calculus of fuzzy sets is a relatively recent innovation in mathematics dealing with domains and concepts the boundaries of which are not sharply defined. Since much of human cognition seems to operate with such fuzzy concepts (e.g., 'hot,' 'young,' 'approximately equal'), there are many who foresee important applications of this novel calculus to the psychology of thinking, concept formation, judgement, decision-making, etc.

G

G 1. Abbreviation for ➤ **goal**, especially in Hullian theory. **2.** ➤ **g**.

g 1. Abbreviation for ➤ **general *factor**, also denoted as *G*. **2.** In Hull's theory, a fractional part of a goal reaction. See here ➤ **fractional antedating goal response**.

GABA ➤ gamma-amino butyric acid.

GAD ➤ glutamic acid decarboxylase.

gain by illness ➤ **advantage by illness**.

galact(o)- Combining form pertaining to *milk* and occasionally, by extension, to the breast, its milk ducts, lactation, etc.

galactosemia A genetic metabolic disorder characterized by an absence of the enzyme required for conversion of galactose to glucose. If untreated it can lead to irreversible mental retardation. Treatment consists primarily of adjustment of diet to eliminate milk sugar.

Galton bar A device for determining the *just noticeable difference* for visual distance.

Galton whistle A primitive device emitting very high-pitched tones once used extensively to determine upper-pitch thresholds. It is not very accurate.

galvanic Pertaining to direct current.

galvanic skin response (GSR) A measure of the electrical response of the skin as measured by a galvanometer. Two techniques are used, the Féré measure, which records changes in the resistance of the skin to the passage of a weak electric current, and the Tarchanoff measure, which records weak current actually produced by the body. Since the Féré method increases with increasing perspiration it has often been assumed to be an indicator of emotional tension or anxiety. This assumption has proven difficult to substantiate and it is probably best to consider it as merely a measure of physiological arousal; ➤ **lie detector**, **polygraph**. The GSR has alternative names which are generally used synonymously, e.g., *psychogalvanic response* (PGR), *electrodermal response* (EDR), *electrical skin response* (ESR), *Féré phenomenon* and *Tarchanoff phenomenon*.

galvanometer An instrument which measures electric current.

galvanotropism An orienting response to electric current. Also called *galvano-taxis*. ➤ **taxis** and **tropism** for a distinction in terminology.

gambler's fallacy This one is easiest to explain with an example: Suppose you have just flipped a fair, unbiased coin seven times in a row and gotten seven heads. If you think that the chance of getting a tail on the next flip is very high (at least over 0.5) because 'a tail is due' then you have committed the gambler's fallacy – the probability of a tail is still only 0.5. However, you are not alone; in most experiments on choice behavior people's intuitions about the probabilities of independent events do not coincide with a 'rational' implementation of simple probability theory.

gambling The risking of something of value with the possibility of ultimate gain. Not a great deal is known about gambling behavior except what has been derived from studies of risk-taking and game theory and through clinical evaluations of pathological gamblers. It is probably worth pointing out that professional gamblers do not like to call themselves 'gamblers,' on the simple grounds that they do not gamble in the above sense of the term; rather they wager not on the 'possibility' of ultimate gain but on the virtual assuredness of it in the long run.

gambling, pathological An ➤ **impulse control disorder** characterized by chronic inability to resist impulses to gamble. The term is generally not used unless the pattern of behavior disrupts and damages one's personal, familial and vocational life.

game A generic term referring to any pattern of social interaction or organized play with well-defined rules. See some of the following entries for specifics.

gamete A general term for a reproductive cell, either a sperm or an egg cell, in its mature state.

game theory Basically, a branch of mathematics concerned with providing a formal analysis of decision-making, specifically the decision-making process, which takes account of the actions and options for action of another whose own decisions are in conflict with yours (which, after all, is what a game is). In principle, the analyses carried out within this often abstruse realm of mathematics apply to more than simple games, and variations on the basic theory have been directed at studies of interpersonal interactions, economics, labor-management negotiations and international diplomacy. For a not too abstruse example often studied in the laboratory, ➤ **prisoner's dilemma**.

game, zero-sum Any game of which the expected value of playing it is zero for all participants, i.e. a game where in the long run one expects (probabilistically speaking) to lose exactly as much as one wins. Note that games and the associated strategies that players adopt in playing them can usually be evaluated in terms of this notion of expected gain or loss. Naturally, many games and/or playing strategies yield positive expected values (so-called *plus-sum games*) and others result in negative expectations (*minus-sum games*). ➤ **expected value**.

gamma (γ) In psychophysics, the distance of any stimulus from threshold.

gamma afferent ➤ **gamma *motor neuron**.

gamma-amino butyric acid (GABA) An amino acid that functions as an important inhibitory neurotransmitter in many central-nervous-system locations. It is found throughout the gray matter, in the cells of the basal ganglia that project to the substantia nigra, in the Purkinje cells of the cerebellum and in the dorsal horn of the spinal cord. GABA has been implicated in the neurological disorder *Huntington's chorea* and imbalances are thought to play a role in severe anxiety disorders.

gamma motion ➤ **motion, gamma**.

gamma motor neuron ➤ **motor neuron, gamma**.

gam(o)- Combining form used to indicate a marital relationship or a sexual union. This form is typically used as prefix; the suffix forms are *-(o)gamous* and *-(o)gamy*, for adjective and noun forms respectively.

ganglion A collection of cell bodies or nerve cells usually outside the central nervous system. The term is also used on occasion for collections of gray matter in the central nervous system, e.g., the *basal ganglia*. Specific ganglia are found under the alphabetic listing of the modifying term.

ganglion cells Cells in the retina whose axons give rise, at the optic disk, to the optic nerve.

Ganzer's syndrome A ➤ **factitious disorder** (or pseudopsychosis) in which there is voluntary production of (often severe) psychological symptoms. Typically the symptoms are worse when the patient is cognizant of being observed. The displayed symptoms are almost always a reflection of the person's own concept of some disorder and rarely conform to recognized diagnostic categories. The syndrome is often seen in prisons and among army draftees who seek consciously or otherwise to receive special treatment by virtue of their 'disorder.'

Ganzfeld From the German for *complete* or *homogeneous field*, a Ganzfeld is a visual field produced by a set-up in which the entire retina is stimulated by homogeneous light. It has no contours or forms and is totally undifferentiated. In effect, such stimulation is equivalent to no stimulation at all. For example, a colored Ganzfeld becomes an undifferentiated gray after a few minutes and the distance of the field becomes unstable. The easiest way to approximate one outside of the laboratory is to cut a ping-pong ball along the seam and place the halves over your eyes.

Garcia effect ➤ **toxicosis**.

garden-path sentences A rather prosaic name given by psycholinguists to sentences in which the initial few words suggest an interpretation that the later words prove to have been inappropriate. For example, 'The horse raced past the barn fell.'

gargoylism ➤ **Hurler's syndrome**.

GAS ➤ **general adaptation syndrome**.

gaster(o)-, gastro- Combining forms meaning *stomach* or the *stomach region*.

gate-control theory A theory of pain perception that, building on the principle of ➤ **gating**, assumes that pain is only experienced when input from peripheral neurons passes through 'gates' at the points where they enter the spinal cord and lower brainstem. Support for the theory comes from the fact that neurons in the ➤ **periaqueductal gray** in the midbrain have descending axons that terminate on inhibitory neurons in these 'gates' which in turn inhibit transmission of the messages from the peripheral neurons.

gating Essentially, selective damping or inhibiting of sensory input. The 'gate' metaphor is apt: the essence of the effect is that only certain afferent messages get through to be processed consciously. For example, while intently watching a football game one is simply unaware of other aspects of the environment such as itches, cold feet, pickpockets, etc. Also called *sensory gating*.

Gaussian distribution (or **curve**) The normal distribution or curve is often called Gaussian or, simply, Gauss's distribution or curve, in honor of K. F. Gauss (1777–1855), the great German mathematician and astronomer.

gay A sobriquet for homosexual. It has gradually worked its way from the common language into the scientific and is now used regularly in journals and textbooks. Note that some authors only use this term for males; those that do so will typically use *lesbian* for homosexual women. ➤ **homosexuality** et seq. for more detail on usage.

Gedanken experiment ➤ **mental *experiment**.

gemellology The study of twins, particularly the use of twins as the primary data source for evaluating the contributions of heredity and environment on behavior.

gender Strictly speaking, a grammatical term used for classifying nouns. However, because of the many denotative and connotative difficulties with the term ➤ **sex**, it has gradually emerged as the term of choice in discussion of male/female differences, identity, societal roles and the like. The following entries give examples of contemporary usage; ➤➤ **sex**, et seq. for other conceptually related terms.

gender differences ➤ **sex differences**.

gender dysphoria Distress or discomfort with one's gender.

gender identity One's ➤ **identity** (1) as it is experienced with regard to one's individuality as male or female. This sense of self-awareness is generally treated as the internal, private experience of the overt expression of ➤ **gender role**. ➤➤ **sex identity**.

gender identity disorder A class of disorders characterized by a strong and persistent sense of inappropriateness concerning one's gender identification. ➤ **Gender identity disorder in childhood** is manifested by the child's insistence that he or she is the wrong sex, persistent preferences for clothing, games, and pastimes of the other sex, and a tendency for cross-sex roles in fantasy play. In adolescents and adults such disorders are marked by the stated desire to be the other sex, frequent 'passing' as the opposite sex, and the desire to be treated by others as though one were of the opposite sex. Often there is discomfort with one's genitals and one's secondary sex characteristics such as hair and muscles in men and breasts and menstruation in women. ➤ **transsexualism, transvestic fetishism**.

gender identity disorder in childhood Quite literally, a ➤ **gender identity disorder** first noted in childhood. Some classification systems do not view this as a separate disorder. The argument is that while it is true that the characteristic patterns of ideation and behavior gender identity disorder usually appear during childhood, the clinical presentation of psychological distress and depression typically is not manifested until adolescence or adulthood. Some authorities use the term interchangeably with *gender-role disorder in childhood* on the grounds that one's ➤ **identity** (1) is the private experience of the outward expression of ➤ **role**. Both terms are, however, reserved for extreme cases and should not be used in cases of ➤ **gender nonconformity**.

gender nonconformity Quite literally, failure to conform to society's characterization of appropriate sex-role behavior. The term is typically used for children who display preferences for toys and activities generally associated with the opposite sex and who do not show the more common signs of appropriate sex-role identification, i.e. boys who say they just don't 'feel' very masculine or girls, very feminine. Distinguish from ➤ **gender identity disorder in childhood**.

gender role The overt expression of behaviors and attitudes that indicates to others the degree of one's affiliation to maleness or femaleness. It is generally assumed that gender role is the public expression of ➤ **gender identity**. ➤➤ **role** and **sex role**.

gender-role disorder in childhood ➤ **gender identity disorder in childhood**.

gene Any of the functional units of the chromosomes. Genes manifest themselves in heredity by directing the synthesis of proteins. ➤ **deoxyribonucleic acid**.

gene expression The degree to which particular genes or inherited traits are displayed phenotypically. The term is not used for a 'pure' gene process; there are many well-documented phenomena in which environmental effects dictate gene expression.

gene frequency The frequency of occurrence of any particular gene within a population.

gene pair Two genes, one from each parent, that combine to determine a particular inherited trait. The pair is called *homozygous* if both determine the trait in the same way and *heterozygous* if they have different effects. ➤➤ **allele**.

general ability The hypothetical broad-based cognitive ability that some presume to be basic to all the special or *specific abilities* displayed in particular situations. In short, a synonym for ➤ **intelligence**. ➤➤ **general *factor**.

general adaptation syndrome (GAS) The term refers to the physiologist Hans Selye's three-stage characterization of an organism's biological reactions to severe stress. The first stage, the *alarm reaction*, is characterized by two sub-stages, a *shock phase* and a *countershock phase*. During the shock phase body temperature drops, blood pressure is lowered, there is a loss of fluid from the tissues, muscle tone decreases, etc. During the countershock phase there is an increase in adrenocortical hormones and a general biological defensive reaction against the stress begins. The second stage is a *resistance stage*, which continues the recuperative processes begun during countershock. Bodily functions, blood pressure, temperature, etc. gradually return to normal or near normal. However, if the stress is too severe or prolonged the third stage, *exhaustion*, ensues. Here the general pattern of the initial shock phase reappears and ultimately death results.

general aptitude (test) See discussion under ➤ **aptitude test**.

general factor ➤ **factor, general**.

generalization **1.** A process of forming a judgement or making a decision that is applicable to an entire class or category of objects, events or phenomena. There are several features of this meaning that deserve mention. First, generalization in this sense nearly always involves a process of induction; it is derived from a limited number of observations of members of the class and extended (i.e., *generalized*) to the other members. Second, generalization here is the other side of the coin from ➤ **discrimination** (1). That is, when one generalizes a judgement or a response over all members of a category one is, in effect, not discriminating between the individual tokens within that category. ➤ **generalization gradient** for more on this issue. **2.** The process of extending a principle or conceptualization to new objects, events or domains. Note, this process may be similar to 1, in that one discovers that the new object can be classified in a known group and thus included in a previously made generalization, or it may deal with a wholly new set of objects that are still distinguishable from other events but have been shown to lend themselves to explication by some known principle. **3.** In science, any broad principle that can encompass a number of observations. That is, the process of a generalization in sense 2 may yield one in sense 3.

Because these meanings are so 'general,' the term is often qualified by various modifiers that delineate the kind of generalization under consideration. See the following entries for some common examples.

generalization, acoustic A form of ➤ **stimulus *generalization** along an acoustic dimension. One rather compelling example of such generalizations is the startled response that invariably accompanies hearing someone loudly exclaim, 'Oh, sit,' in public. A stimulus other than the original taboo word evokes an emotional reaction because it is acoustically similar to it. Distinguish from ➤ **semantic *generalization**.

generalization gradient In both ➤ **response *generalization** and ➤ **stimulus *generalization** there will be a gradient such that: **1.** in response generalization the more alike the several responses are to the original the more likely they are to occur to the original stimulus; and **2** in stimulus generalization the more similar the several stimuli are to the original the more likely they will be to produce the response. ➤ **gradient**.

generalization, mediated Any ➤ **stimulus *generalization** that is mediated through some other process. The most common form is ➤ **semantic *generalization**, in which the generalization occurs through the semantic content or meaning of a word.

generalization, response The tendency for responses similar to the original reinforced or conditioned response to be made in the conditioning situation. The response is said to be 'generalized' to the situation.

generalization, semantic A form of ➤ **stimulus *generalization** in which the generalization process operates through the semantic properties of the stimuli. For example, a response originally established to the word 'style' may be elicited by the word 'fashion.' Note that although on occasion a writer will blur the distinction, this form of generalization should be kept separate from ➤ **acoustic *generalization**. For example, if the word 'file' elicits the response one, strictly speaking, has a case of *acoustic* generalization even though the word itself does possess semantic content.

Note that while this definition was couched in terms of conditioning, the term is also used by those with a more cognitive bent when they refer to processes of memory and decision-making where it is clear that individuals have categorized or classified words in ways that reflect commonalities amongst their meanings.

generalization, stimulus The tendency for

stimuli similar to the original stimulus in a learning situation to produce the response originally acquired. Generalization gradients are typically found when the stimuli are systematically varied; the more dissimilar the stimulus is relative to the original the less likely the response. A good example here is sound intensity; if the original stimulus is, say, a 70 db tone, as the intensity is varied away from this value the probability of observing the response (or the magnitude of the response or the amount of responding – depending on what response measures are in use) will decrease systematically.

Although there has been a tendency to regard stimulus generalization as a 'fundamental' process, it should be noted that when it occurs it can be viewed as simply the failure of the subject to have established a *discrimination* between the original stimulus and the new one(s). ➤ **discrimination**.

generalization, verbal Simply, ➤ **generalization** with verbal materials; e.g., ➤ **acoustic *generalization**, ➤ **semantic *generalization**.

generalized anxiety disorder A subclass of ➤ **anxiety disorders** characterized by persistent 'free floating' anxiety and a host of unspecific reactions such as trembling, jitteriness, tension, sweating, light headedness, feelings of apprehension, irritability, etc. The term is only used for functional disorders and not for organic disabilities which can produce similar symptoms. Also called, simply, *anxiety reaction*.

generalized inhibitory potential ($_sI_R$) In Hull's learning theory, inhibition conditioned as a result of stimulus generalization.

generalized other A term introduced by the sociologist George Herbert Mead to refer to a person's inculcated notions of some abstract social class or group. An individual develops a generalized other by a process of social interaction through which the attitudes, values, expectations, points of view, etc. of the members of that group gradually become one's own.

Although the initial phases may be quite specific, with particular aspects of the group's values being adopted, over time the full complex of factors becomes interrelated and generalized and it no longer reflects specific attitudes of specific persons. It is through this generalized other that a person comes to interact successfully within the group and reflect its values. Moreover, according to Mead, the generalized other also serves as the basis for abstract thought and problem-solving. ➤ **significant other** and **socialization**.

generalizing assimilation ➤ **assimilation, generalizing**.

general paresis (general paralysis) ➤ **paresis**.

General Problem Solver (GPS) One of the first computer programs to do a respectable job of simulating some limited aspects of human cognitive processes. GPS, developed in 1959 by A. Newell and co-workers, used heuristically guided trial-and-error processes to solve some simple problems and to do so in ways that approximated those used by adults.

general psychology 1. Broadly, that orientation in psychology that seeks general, even universal, principles that apply to all the objects of study. Compare with ➤ **differential psychology**. 2. Even more broadly, the whole of psychology, its theories, findings, principles, etc. as reflected by a standard introductory text.

generation 1. The process of procreation, the forming of a new organism. 2. By extension, any process of creation. Here the meaning extends beyond the organic; see, e.g., ➤ **generative *grammar**. 3. The offspring of an ancestor the same distance removed; e.g., *filial generation* – see here ➤ F_1, F_2. 4. The average period of time between the birth of parents and the birth of their children. This period differs from culture to culture.

generative grammar ➤ **grammar, generative**.

generative semantics ➤ **semantics, generative**.

generator potential Any graded change in electrical potential that occurs in a receptor organ or receptor cell. Generator potentials are related to the initiation of the action potential in the associated afferent neurons; they function much like ➤ **postsynaptic potentials** in that they raise or lower likelihood of a neuron firing. Differentiate from ➤ **receptor potential** and ➤ **action potential**.

generic 1. General, having wide application – at least within the class of objects or events under consideration. **2.** Pertaining to a ➤ **genus**.

generic knowledge ➤ **knowledge, generic**.

generic name The general chemical name for a drug, the nonproprietary name.

genetic 1. Pertaining to the origins and development of any single organism or to an entire species. One speaks of *ontogenetic* when referring to the development of a single organism and *phylogenetic* when referring to the evolutionary process of development of the whole species. **2.** Pertaining to ➤ **genetics**. **3.** Pertaining to ➤ **genes**; ➤ **genic**.

genetic counselling A general term for any health service that tests, advises and counsels prospective parents on any genetic disorder that they may pass to their offspring.

genetic drift Changes in the genetic composition of a population or, more precisely, of the gene pool of that population from generation to generation. The meaning here is not synonymous with ➤ **natural selection** as the changes in the gene pool are not given direction by selection.

genetic epistemology An approach to psychology that focuses on the study of the development of knowledge. The label itself is usually associated with the orientation to development of the Swiss psychologist, Jean Piaget. This point of view stresses: (a) that knowledge develops in the sense of becoming increasingly organized and adaptive to one's surroundings; (b) that this process of development is not based on innately given ideas nor any simple automatic maturation but rather as active construction on the part of the individual, and (c) that this construction of knowledge is initiated and carried through by the need to overcome contradictions produced by functioning in a complex, changing environment. ➤ **Piagetian**.

geneticism One of several terms used for the view that behavior is largely a result of innate characteristics. Note that one could stress either species-specific characteristics shared by all members of the species or the individually inherited traits of single organisms. The distinction is usually marked by appending *phylogenetic* or *ontogenetic* to the base term for these two meanings.

genetic memory ➤ **memory, genetic**.

genetic psychology Generally used as a rough synonym for what is more commonly called ➤ **developmental psychology**. However, note that genetic psychology also includes the branch of ➤ **comparative psychology** and tends to focus on developmental processes that underlie phenomena studied in the mature organism.

genetics A branch of biology that deals with heredity in any of its manifestations.

Genevan school The school of psychology founded by Jean Piaget. For details ➤ **genetic epistemology** and ➤ **Piagetian**.

genic Relating to genes or to that which is caused by genes. A preferred synonym for ➤ **genetic** (in sense 3 of that term).

-genic Combining form used with prefixes to characterize: **1.** The locus or point of origin of something, e.g., *endogenic* = originating from within. **2.** The agent origin of something, e.g., *mutagenic* = mutation-causing.

geniculate bodies Two sets of paired oval tissue masses lying under and to the rear of the thalamus. The ➤ **lateral geniculate bodies** are important synaptic stations for vision and the ➤ **medial geniculate bodies** for audition; see each for details.

genital Pertaining to the genitals, the organs of reproduction.

genital anomaly ➤ **sex anomaly**.

genital character In psychoanalytic theory, the mature synthesis of the previous stages of psychosexual development culminating in the ➤ **genital stage**.

genital eroticism Sensual or sexual pleasure derived from the genitals. var., *genital erotism*.

genitalia ➤ **genitals**.

genitals (or **genitalia**) The reproductive organs.

genital stage (or **level**) In psychoanalytic theory, the culminating level of psychosexual development characterized by the development of relationships with persons of the opposite sex.

genital zones The external genitals and adjacent areas, one of the *erogenous zones*.

genius Loosely used, the term refers to the highest level of intellectual or creative functioning or to a person possessing such capabilities. Although there have been several efforts at giving an explicit definition here (e.g., at one time an IQ of 140 or over was used), such attempts only provide illusory objectivity. Unfortunately (or fortunately) there doesn't appear to be any clear set of attributes that defines genius; all behaviors including the intellectual and creative are subject to a variety of 'noncognitive' factors such as motivation, temperament, emotion and the demand characteristics of the environment, and people who display 'genius' in one setting do not necessarily display it in others. Furthermore, the common language has played such havoc with the term that its usefulness is now suspect even in the most technical context.

genome The full collection of genes of an organism.

genotype **1.** The genetic constitution of an individual organism, the particular set of genes carried. The genotype includes hereditary factors that may be passed on to future generations even though they are not manifested in the individual's ➤ **phenotype**. Usage here, particularly in the study of developmental psychology, typically focuses on the notion of the genotype as a collection of hereditary factors that influences the development of an individual. Rather than referring directly to inherited traits, *per se*, the term relates to inherited influences that help the development of particular traits. Meaning here reflects the complexities of the interaction between heredity and environment and the recognition that a given genotype can be expressed in a variety of phenotypes. **2.** In Lewin's theory of personality, the full compilation of causes responsible for any behavioral phenomenon. This usage is much more inclusive than 1 and is rarely intended any more.

-genous Combining form meaning: **1.** *Producing*. **2.** *Produced by*. Often used as a variation of ➤ **-genic**.

gens ➤ **sib** (2).

genus **1.** In biology, a classification encompassing related ➤ **species** (1). **2.** In Aristotelian logic, a broad category containing subclasses of ➤ **species** (2). pl., *genera*.

-geny Combining form denoting: **1.** *Origin* or *cause*. **2.** *Generation*.

geometric illusion Any of a large class of visual illusions produced by perceptual distortions of straight lines, curves, etc.

geometric mean ➤ **mean, geometric**.

geometric series A series that increases or decreases by a constant proportion or ratio. For example, 2, 4, 8, 16, 32. A geometric series is logarithmic. Contrast with ➤ **arithmetric series**.

geon Any of the simple three-dimensional forms that, according to Biederman's theory, make up the perceptual components of more complex forms. Examples of geons are cubes, cylinders, wedges, slices, etc.

geotropism An orienting response to gravitational forces. Also called ➤ **geotaxis**; ➤ **taxis** and **tropism** for a distinction often ignored.

geriatrics The medical specialty dealing with treatment of the aged.

geriopsychosis ➤ **senile *dementia**.

germ cell A general term for a reproductive cell in any stage of development. Distinguish from ➤ **gamete**, the mature germ cell.

germinal stage (or **period**) The earliest stage of gestation. In humans, it is the period of approximately two weeks from the moment of conception. See discussion under ➤ **embryo**.

gerontology The study of the aged and the aging process. The field is extremely broad and encompasses essentially all aspects of life, physiological, social, psychological, medical, economic, etc., as they are relevant to the understanding of aging.

Gesell Developmental Schedules (or **Scales**) The first of the ➤ **developmental scales** to be constructed and standardized. The schedules were developed by Arnold Gesell and his colleagues to assess four major areas of behavior in the young child: motor, adaptive, language and personal-social. Unlike some later scales (e.g., ➤ **Bayley Scales**), they are weighted toward physical development and are largely based on simple observation of the behavior of the infant and preschooler, and when they are used it is as a supplement to medical, neurological examinations. Two scales are available, an *Infant Schedule* and a *Preschool Schedule*.

gestagen Any of the group of hormones (*progestins*) that function to promote and support pregnancy.

Gestalt (or **gestalt**) A German term which unfortunately has no exact English equivalent. Several terms have been proposed, such as 'form,' 'configuration' or 'shape'; however, 'essence' or 'manner' are also acceptable translations. By and large,

the term itself, rather than any inadequate translation, has moved over into English and is now often spelled without the initial capital.

The primary focus of the term is that it is used to refer to unified wholes, complete structures, totalities, the nature of which is not revealed by simply analyzing the several parts that make it up. An aphorism spawned by this idea is 'the whole (i.e. the Gestalt) is different from the sum of its parts.' This principle forms the core of the Gestalt psychology movement. See the following entries for more details on terminology. pl., *Gestalten* or *Gestalts*.

Gestalt factor Any stimulus situation which tends to produce a perceptual experience of wholeness or unity, a ➤ **Gestalt**. All of the Gestalt laws (or principles) of organization utilize Gestalt factors.

Gestalt laws of organization A cover term for all of those principles of organization that identify the factors that lead to particular forms of perceptual organization. A few of them, with examples, are:

continuation: figure seen as a diamond between uprights and not as a W on top of an M.

closure: figure seen as a square although incomplete.

proximity: figure seen as three groups of two lines each.

similarity: figure seen with two columns of one kind of dot and two of another.

Gestalt psychology A school of psychology founded in Germany in the 1910s. Arguing originally against the structuralists the Gestaltists maintained that psychological phenomena could only be understood if they were viewed as organized, structured wholes (or Gestalten). The structuralist position that phenomena could be introspectively 'broken down' into primitive perceptual elements was directly challenged by the Gestalt point of view that such an analysis left out the notion of the whole, unitary 'essence' of the phenomena (e.g., is an apple *really* a particular combination of primitive elements such as redness, shape, contour, hardness, etc, or does this analysis miss some fundamental 'appleness' that is only apprehensible when the whole is viewed as a whole?).

The early Gestaltists were masters of the elegant counterexample and presented sufficiently convincing arguments and demonstrations to seriously damage the orthodox structuralist view. For example, a particular melody is easily recognized even when its component parts are dramatically altered: it may be sung (in any voice range), played (by any combination of musical instruments), changed in key, embedded in multiple variations, etc., without destroying its recognizable Gestalt. Further, each of the several notes in any particular melody has a different phenomenological sense if played alone or if introduced into a new melody. In all cases, they argued, the whole dominates the perception and it is experienced as different from simply the sum of its several parts.

Learning was regarded by the Gestaltists, not as associations between stimuli and responses (as the behaviorists maintained), but as a restructuring or reorganizing of the whole situation, often involving ➤ insight as a critical feature. The physiology of the brain was viewed in like fashion. Rather than accepting the then conventional view that the cortex was a static, well-differentiated system, they argued for a coordinated physiology in which the cortex was conceptualized as the place in which incoming stimuli interacted in a field of forces. See here ➤ isomorphism (2). In social psychology their work led to ➤ field theory and in education the stress was on productive thinking, creativity.

In general, Gestalt psychology is antithetical to atomistic psychology in all of its varieties (see here ➤ atomism, elementarism) and equal hostility was directed toward the behaviorists and the structuralists. Although as a separate theory Gestalt psychology hardly exists today, many of its discoveries and insights have been incorporated into the contemporary body of knowledge, particularly in the field of perception. The main exponents of the school were Max Wertheimer, Kurt Koffka, Wolfgang Köhler and, by philosophical allegiance, Kurt Lewin.

Gestaltqualität A German term roughly translated as *form quality*. Originally introduced by C. von Ehrenfels, a precursor of the Gestalt movement, it refers to the quality of property of a whole that emerges out of a pattern of stimulation. ➤➤ **Gestalt psychology**, the proponents of which disputed von Ehrenfels' suggestions that a *Gestaltqualität* is merely another perceptual element.

Gestalt therapy A form of psychotherapy associated with the work of Frederick (Fritz) Perls. It is based loosely on the Gestalt concepts of unity and wholeness. Treatment, which is usually conducted in groups, focuses on attempts to broaden a person's awareness of self by using past experiences, memories, emotional states, bodily sensations, etc. In short, everything that could contribute to the person forming a meaningful configuration of awareness is an acceptable part of the therapy process.

gestation 1. The carrying of the embryo in the womb. 2. The period of intrauterine development from conception to birth. 3. By extension, a period of 'incubation' for the development of an idea, a work of art, a scientific theory, etc.

gestational age ➤ conception *age.

gestural language A broad term for any communication system based primarily on gestural operations. ➤ nonverbal communication and sign language.

gesture Any bodily or facial movement used for communication. Gestures may accompany speech or may be used independently, as in sign language.

geusis The process or act of tasting.

g factor ➤ general *factor.

Gibsonian Pertaining to and characterizing the theoretical position of James J. Gibson (1904–80). Gibson's work was focused on that oldest of questions, 'How do we learn about the world?' His answer was simple and yet radical: by direct pickup of information about the invariant properties of the environment. It was 'simple' because it dispensed with the need to take raw sensations into account and because it eliminated the need to hypothesize about internal organizing and inferencing systems that structure and code the sensations. It was 'radical' for these very same reasons. ➤ **affordance, direct perception, ecological optics, ecological validity** for more on Gibson's system.

gifted A generic term used to refer to a person with a special talent. The talent may be a general intellectual one or a quite specific talent such as music or chess playing. The word 'gift' somehow implies that the talent is inherited, a shaky hypothesis at best and one that probably cannot be applied uniformly to all 'gifted' individuals. The term also suffers from the same kind of definitional fogginess surrounding other terms like ➤ **genius**. ➤ **gifted child**.

gifted child 1. A label for any child whose intellectual aptitude and performance dramatically exceeds the norms for her or his age. **2.** More broadly, a child who displays special talents in any area of human behavior that society values. This meaning is based on the notion that giftedness may extend beyond those characteristics and talents assessed through standardized testing instruments. Contrast with ➤ **special child**.

gigantism Abnormal overdevelopment of the skeleton caused by malfunctioning of the anterior pituitary gland before adulthood. ➤ **growth hormone**.

gigantocellular tegmental field A group of cells in the pons. Activity here is hypothesized to be an important component in the control of REM-sleep.

GIGO An acronym for 'garbage in garbage out.' The term is used in computer sciences for the notion that if unreliable data form the input only unreliable outcomes are possible. The acronym has, not surprisingly, achieved wide usage in a variety of psychological contexts.

Gilles de la Tourette's syndrome ➤ **Tourette's syndrome**.

given-new distinction A label for those aspects of communication whereby the speaker assumes that the listener knows something (see here ➤ **presupposition**) and then elaborates upon it by adding new information.

glabrous Smooth, without hair. Usually used of skin.

gland Very generally, any organ or structure that forms a bodily substance or secretes it can be called a gland. There are various subdivisions and classification systems for the glands; to wit: (a) glands of *external secretion* (e.g., sweat glands, kidneys) vs. glands of *internal secretion* (thyroid, pituitary); (b) *endocrine* glands, which are ductless and produce hormones (pituitary, adrenals), vs. *exocrine* glands, which have ducts (salivary); (c) *cytogenic* glands, which produce new cells (lymph nodes, bone marrow, spleen), vs. all others. Moreover, the classifications overlap since some glands (testes, ovaries, liver) produce a hormone as well as a secretion which flows from a duct.

glans The bulbous end of the clitoris and penis.

glaucoma A pathological condition of the eye caused by increasing intraocular pressure resulting in atrophy of the optic nerve, gradually increased visual dysfunction and, ultimately, blindness.

glia Collectively, the 'supportive' cells in the central nervous system. Three primary classes of glia cells have been identified: (a) *astroglia* (or *astrocytes* – so called because of their star-like shape), which play a physical and nutritional supporting role and are involved in 'house-cleaning' of dead cells and the formation of scar tissue following injury – although there is recent evidence that they may exchange information with neurons; (b) *micro-glia* (owing to their small size), which serve as phagocytes (see here ➤ **phagocytosis**); and (c) *oligodendroglia*, which function to produce the *myelin sheath* found on most (but not all) of the axons in the central nervous system. ➤➤ **Schwann cells**. Also called *neuroglia*.

glial Concerning ➤ **glia** and specialized glia cells.

gliosis The replacement of dead neurons with glia cells.

global amnesia ➤ **amnesia, global**.

global aphasia ➤ **aphasia, global**.

globus hystericus A feeling of a lump in the throat. The term is reserved for a psychogenic syndrome often associated with conversion disorder where the illusory lump can actually interfere with swallowing.

globus pallidus One of the subcortical nuclei that make up the ➤ **basal ganglia**. It functions as an excitatory structure of the extrapyramidal motor system. Also called *pallidum* and *paleostriatum*.

glossal Pertaining to the tongue.

glossiness The degree to which a perceived surface reflects light.

glosso- A combining form from the Latin for *tongue*.

glossolalia Artificial, fabricated speech devoid of real, linguistic content. It is observed in persons during religious ecstasy ('speaking in tongues'), under hypnosis and in some psychopathological cases.

glossopharyngeal nerve The IXth ➤ **cranial nerve**. It contains afferent components from the rear third of the tongue and the soft palate which mediate taste and efferent components to muscles in the throat.

glossosynthesis With references to pathological states, the term means to invent nonsense words. Were it not for the (presumed nonpathological) glossosynthetic

predilections of scientists this volume would be about 40% shorter. ➤➤ **neologism**.

glottal 1. Pertaining to the glottis. **2.** A speech sound produced by constriction of the glottis, e.g., the *h* in *hot*.

glottal stop (or **catch**) A speech sound produced by a stopping of the air flow by closing the glottis.

glottis The opening between the vocal folds or cords.

glove anesthesia ➤ **anesthesia, glove**.

glucagon A hormone of the pancreas that functions as part of the process that converts glycogen into glucose.

glucocorticoids A group of hormones of the adrenal cortices, they play an important role in the metabolism of proteins and carbohydrates, particularly when the body is subjected to conditions of stress. Included are ➤ **cortisol** and ➤ **corticosterone**.

glucoprivation Lit., the state when cells are deprived of glucose.

glucoreceptors Cells that are sensitive to glucose. They are found in the lateral hypothalamus and the liver. Also called *glucose receptors*.

glucose A simple sugar that plays a critical role in metabolism. Along with the keto acids glucose constitutes the major source of energy for cerebral tissues.

glucostatic theory A generalization that satiety and hunger are determined by the level or availability of glucose in the blood.

glutamate ➤ **glutamic acid**.

glutamic acid An amino acid that functions as an excitatory neurotransmitter. Also called *glutamate*.

glutamic acid decarboxylase (GAD) An enzyme that converts *glutamic acid* into ➤ **gamma-aminobutyric acid (GABA)**.

glycerine ➤ **glycerol**.

glycerol A soluble carbohydrate that,

along with the ➤ fatty acids, makes up the ➤ triglycerides found in adipose (fatty) tissue. Glycerol is converted into *glucose* by the liver. Also called *glycerine*.

glycine An ➤ amino acid suspected as functioning as an inhibitory neurotransmitter in the spinal cord and lower portions of the brain.

glycogen A polysaccharide (often called 'animal starch'), glycogen is the form in which carbohydrates are stored. It is converted into glucose for use.

glycogenolysis The process of conversion of glycogen into glucose.

-gnosia, -gnosis Combining forms from the Greek for *knowledge* and used widely to denote knowing, cognition, recognition, etc.

goal In psychology the basic meaning is little different from that found in a standard dictionary in that in most usages some end result or object is implied. There are, however, a few subtleties that are worth mentioning: (a) Often the physical location of an object will be called a goal (such as the goal box in a maze) rather than the object itself (food, water, etc.). (b) Occasionally there is a loss of clarity in the distinction between the actual, objective goal and some internal, subjective motivational state. This confusion is most often found in authors who use *purpose* as if it were a synonym for *goal*. While it is probably true that there can be no goal unless there is some motivational state, purpose is still 'internal' and goal, strictly speaking, should be external and operational. (c) In some approaches (e.g., Adler's) goal may be treated as a rather abstract entity such as *superiority* which one strives toward.

goal-directed behavior A neo-behaviorist term intended to serve the same semantic function as the more mentalistic term *purpose*. To wit: goal-directed behavior is a response, or a set of responses, which can only be interpreted in terms of attainment of a known goal. E. C. Tolman once remarked, 'Behavior reeks of purpose.'

He was certainly right, but orthodox behaviorists would have been much more comfortable had he said, 'Behavior reeks of goal-directedness.' So much for poetry.

goal gradient A phrase used to describe the general finding that the closer an organism gets to a goal the more efficient the behavior becomes. That is, speed may increase, error rate goes down, etc. This generalization clearly has limits; when high emotional tone accompanies the approach it often interferes with performance.

goal object Not quite synonymous with ➤ goal, this term is reserved for cases in which there may be a series of subgoals in a complex task and it is used to characterize the final, ultimate goal in the sequence.

goal orientation A general tendency to turn toward or position oneself in the direction of a goal. It applies to cases in which the turning is physical, as well as to more metaphoric orientations of thinking and attention.

goal response Any overt response made to or toward a goal. ➤ goal-directed behavior.

goal stimulus Any proprioceptive stimulus arising from behavior toward a goal.

Goldstein–Scheerer tests A series of tests of concept formation and abstraction used in the diagnosis of brain injuries.

Golgi apparatus A complex of irregular structures of parallel membranes in the cytoplasm of a cell. Basically it is a cell's 'packaging plant.' Secretory cells wrap their products in membrane produced by the Golgi apparatus, the membrane bursts and releases these products after migrating to the outer cell membrane.

Golgi-Mazzoni corpuscles Bulbous encapsulated nerve endings found in the dermis. Once thought to be thermoreceptors, they are currently suspected of mediating pressure sensations.

Golgi neurons (Type I and Type II) Multipolar neurons in the cerebral cortex and the posterior horns of the spinal cord. Type I have long axons, Type II short axons.

Golgi tendon organ Nerve ending located at the juncture of tendon and muscle. It consists of 'stretch' receptors that detect stretch exerted by the muscles (via the tendons) on the bones to which they are attached. Also called *spindle tendon* and *neurotendinal spindle*.

gonad **1.** The embryonic sex gland prior to anatomical differentiation into definitive testis or ovary. **2.** The generic term for the sex glands, testis and ovary.

gonadotrophic hormone A hormone produced by the anterior pituitary gland which stimulates activity in the gonads. For example, ➤ **follicle-stimulating hormone** and **luteinizing hormone**. Also called *gonadotrophin*. Also spelled *gonadotropic*.

gonadotrophin-releasing hormones Hormones that stimulate the gonads which in turn release their hormones. The onset of puberty occurs when cells in the hypothalamus begin secreting these hormones. Also spelled *gonadotropin*.

gon(o)- Combining form meaning *genitals, seed, generation, offspring*.

gonococcus The organism causing gonorrhea.

gonorrhea A venereal disease caused by the gonococcus bacterium. In males the primary symptoms are discharge from the penis, pain and burning sensation during urination. Infected females may be asymptomatic initially but more commonly there is urethral or vaginal discharge, pain during urination and occasionally lower abdominal pain; severe cases can lead to pelvic inflammatory disease, which is quite painful. If untreated the disease may become chronic with a variety of complications including prostate involvement, arthritic conditions and serious inflammation of the membranes lining the heart.

good continuation One of several ➤ **Gestalt laws of organization**. It assumes that there is a tendency to perceive a line as maintaining its established direction. Also called, simply, *continuation*.

Goodenough Draw-a-Person Test It is an intelligence test used with young children (usually under 12) in which the child is asked to draw the best picture of a person he or she can. The test is scored according to the amount of detail present and an assessment of qualitative features. Was once known as the 'Goodenough Draw-a-Man' test, but this sexist bias has been removed.

good Gestalt Any basic, stable configuration. ➤ **Prägnanz**.

goodness of fit ➤ **fit, goodness of**.

good shape, law of One of several ➤ **Gestalt laws of organization**, it assumes that there is a tendency to perceive figures and patterns in the most symmetric, uniform and stable way.

Gottschaldt figures A set of simple figures embedded in more complex ones. They are used as tests for form perception. ➤ **embedded *figure**.

government and binding A class of models of language that are derived from ➤ **transformational grammar**. Government and binding theory quickly gets quite complex but is based on a rather simple assumption, specifically that all grammatical operations are captured by a single transformation 'move X' where 'X' is some abstract aspect of the language such as a noun phrase. The argument is that specifying the parameters for each particular structure 'X' will undercover the universal aspects of all natural languages.

GPS ➤ **General Problem Solver**.

gradation methods A general term for any of the psychophysical methods that use stimuli that change gradually in small discrete steps; e.g., the *method of limits* (➤ **measurement of *threshold**).

graded potential Any slow, gradual electrical potential in a receptor cell or neuron; included are ➤ **generator potential**, ➤ **postsynaptic potential** and ➤ **receptor**

potential. Compare with ➤ **action potential.**

grade equivalent A score on some test that represents level of achievement or performance on that test according to the norms for the population in each grade in school.

grade norm The score (or, more commonly, a range of scores) that is representative of the typical level of achievement in the school population for any given grade. If a single score is used it is almost always the 50th percentile; when a range is used it is usually a fairly narrow one around the 50th percentile.

grade score ➤ **grade equivalent.**

gradient Any standard dictionary will provide several meanings for this term. All of them are variations on the basic connotation: a progressive, continual change in some quantity or variable. In this sense the term is used in both adjective and noun forms in many psychological contexts. For some examples ➤ **approach gradient, avoidance gradient, generalization gradient.**

gradient of effect If, in a sequence of S–R connections, one response is reinforced or punished, those responses preceding and following it show the effects of the procedure. The effect is revealed as a gradient in that responses temporally close to the rewarded or punished response show a larger effect than those more remote. ➤ **spread of *effect.***

gradient of texture One of the monocular cues for depth perception. The fineness of detail or texture that can be seen decreases systematically with increasing distance from the observer.

Graduate Record Examination (GRE) An examination widely used in the USA as a means of selecting among applicants for graduate training. The exam has three general sections and one specialized section. The general tests cover verbal, mathematical and analytic skills; the specialized test is in the student's specific area of concentration.

grain A term descriptive of the record from a ➤ **cumulative recorder.** If the record consists of relatively evenly spaced responses it is said to have a 'smooth' grain; if there are bursts of responding with pauses in between it is said to have a 'rough' grain.

-gram Suffix denoting *written, drawn, sketched.* ➤➤ **-graph.**

grammar The structure of a language, the system of rules that dictates the permissible sequences of language elements that form sentences of that language. It is generally assumed in linguistics and psycholinguistics that a mature speaker-hearer of a language knows, in some implicit fashion, the grammar of the language. That is, she/he knows a set of rules, rules of phonology, morphology, reference, semantics and syntax, that enable the production (or 'generation') of an indefinitely large number of grammatical utterances. It is this knowledge and as yet unanswered questions about how something so complex is acquired that makes grammar an important topic in psychology.

Note that this usage of the term departs from the ways in which the term is used in 'grammar' school. The best way to understand this distinction is to appreciate that the 'grammar' taught in the early grades is *prescriptive,* it consists of rules which dictate usage patterns, while the contemporary grammars of linguistics are *generative,* they specify formal rules for the production of sentences (➤ **generative *grammar*).** For more on usage patterns here see the following entries.

grammar, generative **1.** A field of study in linguistics and psycholinguistics that focuses on the development of a set of formal rules that can provide an explanation of language. **2.** The set of formal rules itself. The point is that rather than treating grammar as simply a set of *prescriptive* rules about acceptability of sentences or a set of *descriptive* rules that can characterize a particular corpus from a language, it is viewed as an abstract set of rules that is, in principle, capable of *gener-*

ating all and only the grammatical sentences of a language. The development of an acceptable generative grammar is one goal of linguistic science. The interest psychologists have in the topic comes from the simple observation that people 'generate' sentences; we continually create novel utterances, we are not merely parroters of previously encountered sentences. Thus, the hope is that a linguistically sound generative grammar will express, in some fashion, the knowledge that normal speaker-hearers of a language possess.

grammar, phrase-structure   A class of ➤ **generative *grammars** that characterizes a language as a set of rules for arranging the elements of a language. The formal base of a phrase-structure grammar is quite simple and is similar to the old 'parsing' systems for analyzing the structure of a sentence; i.e. assigning labels to parts of a sentence and determining the grammatically relevant subparts of phrases. ➤ **rewrite rule** and **tree** (2) for examples of the kinds of operations involved. In general, this class of grammars is regarded as less powerful and less complete than ➤ **transformational *grammars**.

grammar, transformational (generative)   A class of ➤ **generative *grammars** that, as originally put forward by the American linguistic/philosopher A. Noam Chomsky, possess several advantages over the older ➤ **phrase-structure *grammars**. Although the study of transformational generative grammar (or TGG) has become a highly specialized field of its own within linguistics (with all of the accompanying complexity and sophistication of a formal discipline), the essential nature of a transformational grammar may be captured by the accompanying diagram.

That is, a transformational grammar is based on the hypothesization of several components deemed necessary for an adequate characterization of language: the *semantics* component, which contains rules for meaning, feeds into the *deep structure* component where the underlying 'meaning' is represented; the *transforma-*

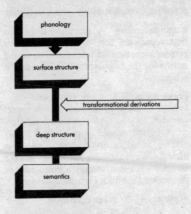

tional derivation aspect is a set of rules for rewriting or mapping deep structures on a *surface* form and the *phonological* component consists of a set of rules for providing the appropriate sound patterns of the language. For more details on these terms ➤ **deep structure, language, phonology, psycholinguistics, semantics, surface structure, transformation** (5). Recently, linguists have begun to downplay transformational grammars in favor of those based on principles of ➤ **government and binding**.

grammar, universal   A hypothesized set of basic grammatical principles assumed to be fundamental to all ➤ **natural languages**. It is argued by some, notably Chomsky, that a universal grammar, formally presented, would also be a theory of the human faculty for language.

grandiose delusions   ➤ **delusional disorder, grandiose type**.

grand mal   ➤ **epilepsy** et seq., especially ➤ **major *epilepsy**.

granular layer   1. Usually, the fourth layer of the cerebral cortex, characterized by many small bipolar cells with short axons. **2.** Occasionally, the fifth and seventh layers of the retina, which have a similar 'granular' structure.

granuloma inquinale   A venereal disease characterized by the appearance of a small, painless lesion on the skin in the genital area followed by a spreading ulceration of surrounding tissue. Treatment is usually with the antibiotic tetracycline.

graph A representation in *n*-dimensional space of the relationship between *n* variables (although in psychology the majority of cases have *n* = 2). The graph is the actual representation of the data, be they statistical, clinical or experimental, in terms of lines, curves or figures that reflect the relationship(s) between the variables.

-graph A combining form from the Greek, meaning *written*, and used to denote: **1.** Something written or drawn. **2.** The instrument or device that writes or records. When used in this latter sense (e.g., *electrocardiograph*) the written output should, for clarity, become *-gram* (e.g., *electrocardiogram*). This convention is not always followed.

graphic analysis Simply, the use of a graph to analyze results. Since a graph can present an enormous amount of information in simple visual form, significant relationships between variables may often be detected and appreciated much more easily than when the data are presented in tabular or numerical forms.

graphic individuality A term that refers to the fact that each of us has an idiosyncratic and unique handwriting or a 'graphic individuality.' ➤ **graphology**.

graphic language Broadly, a means of communicating via written symbols. ➤ **orthography** (the preferred term) for details.

graphic rating scale ➤ **rating scale, graphic**.

grapho- Combining form meaning *writing, drawing*.

graphodyne A device for measuring handwriting pressure.

graphology The investigation and study of handwriting. Forensic graphology has some scientific and legal base: a specialist can detect forgeries or identify certain changes in psychological states by analyzing changes in a person's handwriting. Unfortunately, this limited foundation has spawned a host of charlatans and frauds who make unsubstantiated claims for the value of graphology in assessing personality, diagnosing illness, etc.

graphometry A projective technique in which a blindfolded person makes a drawing and then describes it first while still blindfolded and then again while looking at it.

graphorrhea Uncontrollable urge to write, generally resulting in extended nonsense.

grasp reflex A reflective grasping of an object that stimulates the palm. It is a normal response in infants and is also found in the foot when the sole is stimulated. Also called *grasping reflex*.

Grassmann's laws Those relationships implied by the ➤ **color equation** that have been found to follow the rules of algebra.

gratification The state of satisfaction following the recognition that one has achieved a desired goal.

gray An achromatic visual experience encompassing the brightness dimension from black to white. The grays have neither hue nor saturation. var., *grey*.

gray matter A general term for those parts of the spinal cord and the brain that contain a predominance of cell bodies (which are gray in color) over myelinated nerve fibers (which are whitish).

GRE ➤ **Graduate Record Examination**.

great commissure ➤ **corpus callosum**.

great-man theory A point of view in historical investigations which contends that accomplishments in a field are due primarily to the efforts of 'great men.' This personalistic approach is usually contrasted with the naturalistic approach (often called the *Zeitgeist theory*, from the German meaning *spirit of the times*) which stresses the role of the social, cultural and intellectual climate within which the investigator works and lives. For example, the former would argue that John Watson was responsible for the rise of behaviorism in the early 20th century; the latter that he was merely a historical puppet and that had he not presented this particular theory someone else would have. Doubtless both of these orientations are incorrect in the extreme although, equally without doubt, both have elements of truth in that both the individual and the *Zeitgeist* interact in important ways. As an editorial note, perhaps the first reasonable thing to do would be to change the name of this theory to the great *person* theory. That reflects this writer's *Zeitgeist*.

Greco-Latin square ➤ orthogonal *Latin squares.

green Hue sensation elicited by wavelengths in the vicinity of 515nm.

Greenspoon effect An experimental effect found in some studies on verbal conditioning in which a speaker's use of certain classes of words (e.g., plural nouns) may be made to increase in frequency when reinforced by the listener making appropriately timed gestures of assent like saying 'mm-mmm' or 'uhhuh.' This finding has been taken by some, particularly behaviorists, as evidence that language can be brought under operant control and, by extension, as evidence that language learning takes place through a process of social reinforcement.

gregariousness 1. With respect to animals, the tendency found in many species to live in herds or flocks. 2. With respect to humans, the tendency to want to belong to groups or to derive satisfaction from group activity or group work. Because sense 1 strongly suggests an innate disposition there has been a tendency to assume that sense 2 is also reflective of an instinctive propensity; it is probably wise to resist this extrapolation.

grey ➤ gray.

grief An intense emotional state associated with the loss of someone (or something) with whom (or which) one has had a deep emotional bond. Not used as a synonym for ➤ depression.

grooming In animals, the removal of dirt and parasites from and the smoothing of the fur. Grooming is found in pairs, when two animals groom each other (many species of primates), and singly (rats, cats). Interestingly, grooming frequently appears as a ➤ displacement (2) activity when animals are under stress or placed in a position of conflict.

groove In neurophysiology, a narrow channel or depression. ➤ sulcus.

gross motor movement Generally, any large muscular coordination in which strength is primary. Contrast with ➤ fine motor movement.

gross score ➤ score, gross.

ground 1. The background. See discussion under ➤ figure-ground. 2. The basis for action; a justification for belief.

group 1 n. A collection or assemblage of 'things,' where 'things' may be taken to cover almost any definable category or class of people, animals, events, objects, data, etc. Buried under this notion are a number of important issues; see the discussions under related terms, ➤ category, ➤ class and ➤ concept. 2. A social group; i.e. a group in sense 1 but in which the members are all persons who are classified together on the basis of some social/psychological factor(s). Here the implication is that there is some degree of interrelatedness or interdependence among group members. In many combined terms in sociology and social psychology *group* (as adj.) and *social* are used interchangeably; for such terms not found here see those following ➤ social. 3. vb. To place in classes, to categorize.

group atmosphere ➤ social climate.

group autonomy ➤ autonomy, group.

group behavior Actions of a group that are a result of the subtle interworking of the group as a whole, a kind of emergent property of a group and not simply the summation of the separate behaviors of the individuals in the group. Presumably the activities of the members of a group could not occur were they acting independ-

322

ently. Occasionally the term is used as a rough synonym for 'teamwork,' but this usage is rather superficial.

group climate ➤ social climate.

group, coacting A group of persons engaged in a task at which they work 'side by side' but without interacting.

group cohesion ➤ social cohesion.

group consciousness ➤ social consciousness.

group contagion The rapid spread of an emotional reaction across all of the members of a group.

group decision A decision made by a group. It may be reached by the group acting as a whole, a sort of consensus, or by each member acting individually, in which case the decision usually represents the majority opinion.

group differences Generally, any reliable differences between two or more groups each taken as a whole.

group dynamics 1. Generally, any and all of the collective interactions that take place within a group. 2. The study of groups with an emphasis on dynamic, intragroup processes such as power, power shifts, leadership, group formation, how the group reacts to other groups, cohesiveness, decision-making, etc. Note that some restrict the use of this term to small groups and small-group analyses on the grounds that these dynamic components only emerge when the social unit is small enough for meaningful interactions between members.

grouped frequency distribution ➤ distribution, grouped frequency.

group experiment Generally, any experiment in which a (large) number of subjects is run together in a group.

group, face-to-face A loose term for any small group where the physical proximity of the members to each other is such that 'face-to-face' interactions are possible.

group factor ➤ factor, group.

group, horizontal A group resulting from selection of individuals from a single social class.

group identification ➤ identification.

grouping 1. Generally, the process of classification. Specifically; 2. In statistics, the organizing of data into classes or groups. 3. In education, the classification of students into similar groups, grades, classes, etc.

grouping error ➤ error, grouping.

group integration ➤ integration, group.

group intelligence test A general label for any of a number of paper-and-pencil intelligence tests designed to be administered in groups in a relatively short period of time.

group locomotion Movement and shifting of a group toward some goal or some decision.

group, marginal A group on the edge or 'margin' of a culture, one only partially assimilated into the dominant cultural patterns.

group marriage ➤ cenogamy.

group mind A hypothesized, collective, transcendent spirit or consciousness which was assumed by some to characterize a group or a society. The idea appears in many places, from the theoretical writings of some usually sane philosophers such as Kant to the social theories of William McDougall, who often enthusiastically embraced the outlandish, to some contemporary ethologists who maintain that some social species (e.g., termites, honey bees) function so that some, at least metaphoric, sense of an emergent collective 'mind' can be inferred. This *collective consciousness*, as it was sometimes called, was presumed to exist independently of any single, individual member of the group but to emerge as a synthesized creation when the size of a cohesive group reached some critical mass and organization. Also called *folk mind*.

group norm ➤ norm (2) and for a distinction in usage, ➤ social norm.

group polarization The tendency for the individuals in a group to exaggerate their initial points of view so that the group as a whole takes a more polarized position than the members themselves initially held. Put a group of moderately liberal politicians together and they become more liberal; put together a group of moderately conservative politicians and they become more conservative.

group, primary A group consisting of persons with common values, goals and standards of behavior, and in which there is close personal contact. The adjective 'primary' was originally used to emphasize that these groups (of which the *family* is the prime example) have the earliest impact on the development of an individual's socialization. Compare with ➤ **secondary *group**.

groups, comparable Two groups selected from the same population. The notion of comparability here is not 'strict' but based on principles of unbiased sampling. That is, they are not expected to be identical in all respects but merely reflect the same characteristics of the population from which they were taken.

group, secondary A group consisting of persons who share some values and have some common standards of behavior but only with respect to limited segments of their lives. Professional organizations, fraternities, clubs, etc. are regarded as examples. Compare with ➤ **primary *group**.

group, sensitivity ➤ **sensitivity training**.

group solidarity ➤ **social cohesion**.

group structure Quite literally, the structure of a group. Analysis of group structure typically involves examination of such factors as power and power relationships, sub-groups, their formation and roles with respect to the rest of the group, the various roles that individual members play in the group (i.e. leader, follower, cooperative, competitive, etc.), and so forth. Note that the term is eclectic enough to be employed by sociologists, social psychologists, ethologists, zoologists, clinicians, etc.

group superego ➤ **coordinate morality**.

group test ➤ **test, group**.

group therapy A very general term used to cover any psychotherapeutic process in which groups of individuals meet together with a therapist/leader. The interactions among the members of the group are assumed to be therapeutic and in many cases to be more effective than the traditional client-therapist diad.

groupthink Within group decision making procedures, the tendency for the various members of a group to try to achieve consensus. The need for agreement takes priority over the motivation to try to obtain accurate knowledge to make appropriate decisions. This tendency has been suggested as being one of the prime reasons why politicians operating in closed groups so often make disastrous decisions.

group, vertical A group composed of persons from more than one social class.

growth Generally, gradual progressive increase. The term is widely applied and may refer to: **1.** Increases in size of an individual organism or its parts. **2.** Increases in effectiveness or competence of a function, e.g., growth of cognitive capacity in a child. **3.** Differentiation and refinement of parts and/or functions. This meaning differs from the above in that sheer increases in magnitude as in 1 or performance as in 2 are not entailed; e.g., growth of understanding in a young adult, where the implication is that of becoming more mature. **4.** In mathematics, the increases in a function or a curve.

growth curve A graphic presentation of the growth over time of some measure or variable.

growth, differential A very general term used to refer to those circumstances in which the rate of growth within a complex system is not occurring at the same rate in all parts of the system. The 'system' here is taken very generally and the term is applied in economics, anatomy, mental and intellectual assessment, etc.

growth, horizontal Generally, growth within a given level. The term is usually used with respect to intellectual or sensory/motor skills and refers to the increase in the number of such acts that a person can perform when all are at the same difficulty level. Compare with *vertical *growth*.

growth hormone A pituitary hormone necessary for normal bodily growth prior to adulthood. It also plays a role in regulation of food intake in that it causes the conversion of glycogen to glucose. Also called *somatotrophic hormone*.

growth needs ➤ metaneeds.

growth principle A principle in Carl Rogers' *humanistic psychology* which maintains that emotional and intellectual growth will take place normally in all persons when they are freed from coercion, arbitrary social pressures, punishment or the fear of it, censure and other common components of our daily lives.

growth, vertical Generally, growth between levels. Typically used with regard to intellectual or sensory/motor skills to refer to an increase in the difficulty of acts that can be properly performed. Compare with ➤ horizontal *growth.

GSR ➤ galvanic skin response.

guanine One of the four nucleotide bases that make up ➤ deoxyribonucleic acid and ➤ ribonucleic acid.

guessing bias Any tendency on the part of a subject to display a bias when guessing among possible responses. Such biases are often observed in experiments on learning, decision-making, psychophysics, etc. when the subject does not know the correct response; e.g., a tendency to guess the first alternative presented or to guess the item on the left, etc. Such biases are a source of *constant *error*.

guidance Counseling, leading, directing, advising, assisting, influencing, etc. The term has three broad uses: **1.** *Educational guidance*, where the focus is on providing assistance and advice in school work using instruction, testing and counseling. **2.** *Vocational guidance*, where the task is to assist a person in finding the proper or suitable vocation. A vast battery of tests, intelligence, vocational, interest, aptitude, achievement, etc., is used. **3.** *Child guidance*, which is concerned with the vast array of potential educational, emotional and behavioral problems that children may display. The focus here is generally interdisciplinary and based on coordination between medical, psychological and educational aspects in attempts to assist the child toward the development of a more satisfying life.

guiding fiction ➤ fiction, guiding.

guiding idea ➤ guiding *fiction.

guilt An emotional state produced by the knowledge that one has violated moral standards. Most authorities recognize an emotional state as guilt only when the individual has internalized the moral standards of the society; thus it is distinguished from simple fear of punishment from external sources – guilt is, in a sense, a self-administered punishment. Distinguish from ➤ shame, where knowledge of the transgression by others is part of the concept.

gust A psychophysical unit of taste defined as the subjective sense of sweetness produced by a 1% sucrose solution.

gustation The sense of taste. adj., *gustatory*.

gut A term, in surprisingly common use, for the entire digestive system including the esophagus, stomach, intestines and bowel.

Guttman scaling A method developed by N. Guttman for the measurement of attitudes. Items in a cumulative attitude scale are ranked so that a positive response to any given item is assumed to reflect positive responding to all items of lower rank.

gyn- Combining form from the Greek,

meaning *female*, *woman*. vars., *gyne-*, *gyno-* and a suffix, *-gyny* (for nouns) and *-gynous* (for adjectives).

gynandry ➤ **androgyny**.

gynecomastia The development of breasts on a male. The condition may occur spontaneously, through hormone malfunction, or as a direct result of hormone treatments.

gyrus A convolution or fold on the surface of the cerebral cortex. *Gyri* are bounded by ➤ **fissures** (or *sulci*).

H

H **1.** ➤ **Heritability** or ➤ **heritability ratio. 2.** ➤ **Harmonic *mean. 3.** ➤ **Entropy. 4.** ➤ **Habit strength**. The last of these really represents an array of theoretical terms, all within the behaviorist framework of C. L. Hull. A few of them are: $_sH_R$ = habit strength, $_s\overline{H}_R$ = effective habit strength, $_s'H_R$ = generalized habit strength.

Haab's pupillary reflex A contraction of both pupils when turning toward a bright stimulus in an otherwise dark environment.

habit **1.** Generally, a learned act. Originally the reference was to motor patterns, physical responses; this limitation is no longer recognized and perceptual, cognitive, affective habits are commonly cited. **2.** A pattern of activity that has, through repetition, become automatized, fixed and easily and effortlessly carried out. This meaning, especially in studies of personality, is very close to that of ➤ **trait** (see that entry for some problems in usage that pertain here as well). **3.** An addiction to a drug. The preferred term here is ➤ **drug *dependence. 4.** A pattern of action that is characteristic of a particular species of animal, 'the habits of baboons.' Note that this last meaning differs sharply from the preceding in that it usually connotes an innate, species-specific pattern of behavior while the other usages all clearly entail the notion of the behavior as learned.

habitat The geographical area within which conditions are well suited to the life of a particular species.

habit family hierarchy A concept introduced into psychology by Hull to characterize the fact that there are generally several possible paths to a given goal. As the word *hierarchy* implies, there is preference ordering among the habits, so that if one is blocked the next most preferred will be most likely to occur.

habit formation Obviously, forming a habit: but there have been problems with this term. First, the tendency to use it as a synonym for *learning* should be resisted: such usage implies that all learning is the formation of habits, a theoretical position no one would choose to defend any longer. Second, the very word *formation* invites confusion over whether to apply the term to the actual acquisition of a new habit or to the novel use of a previously acquired habit. For example, rats can certainly run down runways, thus the formation of the habit of straight-alley running relates mainly to the novel use of old behavior. However, in the case of a rat bar-pressing there really is the formation of the new habit. Note that the term is generally restricted to behaviorist approaches to psychology. ➤ **concept formation** and **concept learning** for a related terminological muddle within the cognitive approach.

habit-forming Basically a nontechnical term used loosely to characterize substances that produce either *psychological* or *physiological dependence*. ➤ **drug *dependence** and related terms.

habit hierarchy **1.** In Hull's theory, an ordering of all of the responses that gain in habit strength by virtue of reinforcement of one of them, organized according to amount of gain. **2.** More generally, the organization of simple actions or patterns of behavior (i.e. ➤ **habits** (1, 2)) into more complex, hierarchical systems each 'lower' level of which is subsumed within the higher-order levels. A variety of complex behavioral systems are representable in this fashion, e.g., typing, language. Note, however, that when the behavioristic realm of overt acts is left behind (as in the case of language) the 'habit' is often dropped and the behavior is referred to simply as *hierarchical* or *hierarchically organized*.

habit interference A circumstance that occurs when two or more incompatible responses are acquired to the same stimulus. Either both responses will be inhibited and weakened or one will become dominant.

habit strength As used by Hull it refers to the bond between a stimulus and a response and within this approach is synonymous with *learning*. It is an inferred, hypothetical notion and assumed to be related to four variables: number of reinforcements, amount of reinforcement, stimulus–response interval and the response–reinforcement interval. Symbol: $_sH_R$.

habituation 1. In keeping with the meaning of ➤ **habit** (1, 2), the gradual elimination of superfluous activity in learning. **2.** Somewhat differently, a general kind of adaptation like that of the deep-sea diver who becomes 'habituated' to water pressure. In general, nearly any constant stimulus will produce habituation, e.g., a pure tone sounded for a half-hour may decrease as much as 20 db in perceived loudness. Note that 2 here is similar to ➤ **desensitization**. ➤➤ **adaptation** (1). **3.** In psychopharmacology, ➤ psychological *dependence.

habituation, drug An occasional synonym for ➤ **psychological *dependence**.

haem(o)- ➤ **hem(o)-**.

hair cell A type of cell with hairlike projections (or cilia). They are found in several places, e.g., in the inner ear and in the ampullae at the ends of the semicircular canals, where they function as receptors. The manner of action is similar in both locales; physical force causes a stretching of the membrane to which the hair cells are attached, resulting in a stretching or shearing of the cilia which produces the receptor potential.

halfway house Originally, a facility for persons released from institutions (mental, penal) designed to ease the transition back into the community. Many such facilities function more broadly, however. Rather than being only 'halfway out' houses they may also serve as semi-protective environments for those 'halfway in' persons who can still function productively in the community but need a supportive caring shelter.

hallucination A perceptual experience with all the compelling subjective properties of a real sensory impression but without the normal physical stimulus for that sensory modality. Hallucinations are taken as classic indicators of a psychotic disturbance and are a hallmark of various disorders like schizophrenia. Hence, the term is not usually applied to a variety of other 'false perceptions' that occur normally, like the images that often accompany the transition from waking to sleeping (hypnagogic) or those that occur when first awakening (hypnopompic) or those that occasionally accompany vivid religious experiences. In actual usage the term is generally modified so that the particular modality involved is specified, e.g., *auditory hallucination, tactile hallucination* etc. Distinguish from both ➤ **illusion** and ➤ **delusion**.

hallucinogen Loosely, any of a large group of psychoactive chemical compounds capable of producing hallucinations. ➤ **psychedelic**.

hallucinogen dependence A ➤ **drug *dependence** where the drug is a *hallucinogen*.

hallucinogen intoxication Intoxication brought about by use of a *hallucinogen*. It is typically marked by maladaptive behavioral changes, marked anxiety or depression, impaired judgement, paranoid thoughts, perceptual changes and a host of physiological affects including palpitations, tachycardia, tremors, and the like.

hallucinosis A general term for a condition of extreme susceptibility to hallucinations. It is reserved for conditions in which there is a substance-induced or organic basis for the hallucinations, e.g. ➤ **alcohol hallucinosis**.

halo effect A tendency to allow an overall impression of a person or one particular outstanding trait to influence the total rating of that person. It often emerges as a bias on personal-rating scales.

haloperidol An ➤ **antipsychotic drug** of the butyrophenones group.

halving method A variation of the *method of equal-appearing intervals* whereby a second stimulus is adjusted so that it appears to be half of a given standard (i.e. half as loud, half as bright, etc.). ➤ **methods of *scaling** for more details on this and related procedures.

hammer = *malleus*, ➤ **auditory *ossicles**.

Hampton Court maze The famous English garden maze that was used as a model for many early maze-learning studies with animals.

handedness Generally, a preference for the use of one hand over the other. In actual practice it can be surprisingly difficult to determine unambiguously such a preference. In literate persons the hand used for writing is usually taken as the criterion for determining handedness although even in these relatively clear cases the other hand may occasionally be used preferentially for other tasks, e.g., throwing an object.

handicapped Having an encumbrance or disadvantage that produces a less-than-normal ability to perform. Usually the term refers to the physically impaired but may on occasion be used for the mentally retarded. ➤➤ **disabled**.

haphalgesia Pain sensation when a usually innocuous stimulus touches the skin.

hapl(o)- Combining form meaning *single* or *simple*.

haploid number The normal number of chromosomes in each *gamete* (sex cells, ovum and sperm) of a particular species. The haploid number (which is 23 in *Homo sapiens*) is half of the *diploid number*, the number of chromosomes in each *somatic cell*.

haptic Relating to the cutaneous senses. Haptics, in the broadest sense, is the study of touch.

hard colors A term occasionally applied to the yellows and reds.

'hard' data Laboratory jargon for objective, concrete data. Compare with ➤ **'soft' data**.

'hard' drug Nontechnical term typically used for any drug that produces *physiological *dependence*. Most frequently used for opium-based narcotics.

hardness A perceptual quality. **1.** In tactile perception it characterizes objects which are relatively unyielding to the touch. **2.** In vision, it characterizes color high in saturation and brightness. **3.** In audition, it refers to high intensity and/or high-pitch tones.

hard palate ➤ **palate**.

'hard' psychology A colloquial expression used to refer to those psychological endeavors that are patterned after the natural sciences, e.g., learning, sensory and physiological psychology, psychophysics, etc. The term derives from the notion that the data in these areas tend to be objective and more concrete than in other areas such as clinical psychology or the study of personality; ➤ **'soft' psychology**. Note that this dichotomy into hard and soft is generally not appreciated by 'soft' psychologists, who prefer to call their areas 'complex' and the 'hard' areas 'simple.'

hard-to-get effect In *social psychology*, the phenomenon that people who are selective in their social choices are more desirable than those who are more readily available. The effect is a subtle one because many who act 'hard-to-get' do so in an insensitive manner that simply turns other people off and decreases their social desirability.

hardware In computer terminology, the physical apparatus itself as contrasted with the programs or ➤ **software**.

hard wired Lab slang for genetically pre-programmed. Behaviors that are assumed to be based strongly on genetic factors are spoken of as being 'hard wired.'

harmonic 1 n. An overtone or partial, the frequency of which is a multiple of the fundamental tone. 2 adj. Pertaining to harmony.

harmonic analysis The analysis of a complex wave into its sine and cosine components in accordance with ➤ **Fourier's law**.

harmonic mean ➤ **mean, harmonic**.

harp theory ➤ **theories of *hearing**.

hashish A gummy substance made from the resins of the hemp plant. When smoked or ingested it has psychoactive properties. ➤ **cannabis (sativa)** for further discussion.

hate ➤ **hatred**.

hatred A deep, enduring, intense emotion expressing animosity, anger and hostility toward a person, group or object. Hatred is usually assumed to be characterized by (a) the desire to harm or cause pain to the object of the emotion and (b) feelings of pleasure from the object's misfortunes.

Hawthorne effect Named for the industrial plant where it was first observed, a generalization that states that anything new works: new programs, new methods, curricula, organization, working conditions, etc. – at least for a while. The innovations produce positive results independently of the nature of the modification; in the original study even control conditions designed to lower worker productivity resulted in increases. Presumably the phenomenon results from the enthusiasm that participants feel toward any innovation and from the sense that the changes being introduced show that people are interested in them. The existence of this effect makes a true evaluation of any new program a difficult affair. Note, by implication there will also be an opposite *negative* Hawthorne effect that would be produced in instances where the workers are

unenthusiastic about an innovation, in which case possible legitimate improvements will die aborning.

H cells ➤ **horizontal (H) cells**.

headstart A general label used to cover a number of educational and social programs designed to upgrade the performance of children from impoverished backgrounds.

heal To become healthy again, to make whole, to free from impairment. Note that some will use heal as a synonym for cure, others will distinguish between them. The distinction, when drawn, is based on the argument that heal should be reserved for relatively less severe cases of injury or trauma and cure for more serious diseases and disabilities. Also, some will use heal for providing assistance in the restorative process and cure for more dramatic cases where one intervenes to alter or modify ongoing processes to restore health.

health psychology A field of applied psychology that seeks to use psychological theory and knowledge to promote personal and public health. Specific focuses include problems as diverse as identifying the etiology of illness, understanding the conditions and correlates of well-being, developing techniques for prevention and treatment of illness and improving health care delivery systems.

hearing The perception of sound primarily through the ear. Some authorities prefer to reserve this term for the *process*, using audition for the *sense* of hearing; most others do not and hence, for specialized terms not found below, ➤ **audition** and related entries.

hearing impaired Characterizing a person with a relatively serious hearing loss but who is not to the point of being truly or profoundly deaf. The term is preferred by many over ➤ **deafness** and its various qualified forms.

hearing loss A measure of hearing deficiency usually presented as either: (a) the percentage of normal hearing acuity present for different frequency tones; or (b) the absolute threshold in decibels for different frequency tones. ➤ **audiogram**.

hearing, theories of Although hearing includes a multitude of problems one would almost ensure oneself a Nobel prize upon the presentation of an adequate theory of hearing that could explain satisfactorily no more than the perception of pitch and loudness. There are several candidates, two major ones and several minor. The two most viable are: *place* theory and *periodicity* theory. Place theory (also known variously as *resonance*, *harp* and *piano* theory) originated with the great Helmholtz in the 1860s. It assumes that the perceived pitch of a tone is determined by the place of maximum vibration of the basilar membrane, the portion near the oval window being tuned for high-frequency tones, the far end near the apex of the cochlea for low-frequency tones. Loudness and tonal discriminability are assumed to be determined by the number of neurons activated by the incoming stimulus. Periodicity theory, on the other hand, emphasizes synchronized firing of neurons. It depends heavily on the *volley principle*, which proposes that groups of fibers on the basilar membrane work as squads and fire in synchronized volleys. The volley principle is necessary because the auditory nerve only follows signals with frequencies up to 3,000–4,000 Hz.

The current view seems to favor a kind of amalgamation of these two theories. For stimuli below say 3,000 Hz both place and periodicity combine, for those above, place on the basilar membrane is probably the critical factor. Loudness would seem to be mediated by the overall number of impulses arriving at the brain.

There are other, less well-supported points of view. The classical *frequency* (or *telephone*) theory of Rutherford assumes that the basilar membrane responds as a whole much like a telephone diaphragm. Meyer's *hydraulic* theory stresses the amount of the basilar membrane involved in different tonal patterns. The *sound-pattern* theory of Ewald assumes that different patterns of vibrations are imposed on the basilar membrane by stimuli of different complexities or pitches.

In general, no one theory seems adequate; hearing is very complex. By and large place and periodicity are the leading contenders, the others are (for now anyway) of peripheral importance.

heat 1. Intuitively and subjectively, a sensory experience at the end of the warmth continuum. While it is certainly true that heat is experienced when the skin is exposed to temperatures considerably higher than itself, it is also the case that it is experienced by the separate stimulation of receptors for cold and warm. Grasping a pair of intertwined pipes one containing cold water and one warm will produce a sensation of heat. The assumption is that heat is mediated through a set of neural processes different from those for warm. **2.** A sexually receptive state in a female animal.

hebephrenia ➤ **disorganized (type) *schizophrenia**.

hebetic Relating to youth generally or to occurrences at the time of puberty specifically.

hebetude Emotional dullness, listlessness, a withdrawn lethargy.

hedge Any verbal device that functions to let the listener know that the speaker is not quite so sure as he or she may appear to be, e.g., 'I suspect . . .' or 'I had heard that . . .' are classics. Hedges function to free the speaker from full responsibility for the truth of the utterance.

hedonic Pertaining to or descriptive of the hypothesized affective dimension of pleasure–unpleasure.

hedonic relevance A term used in social psychology to describe the fact that one's personal involvement in another's behavior affects the view one has of the other. If your behavior hurts me personally I am more likely to have a low opinion of you than if your behavior hurts others but does not affect me personally. ➤ **person perception**.

hedonic tone The subjective quality of an experience in terms of the hypothesized pleasure–unpleasure dimension.

hedonism 1. In psychology proper, the theory that behavior is motivated by approach toward pleasure and avoidance of pain. **2.** In ethics, the doctrine that the goal of human conduct ought to be the striving for pleasure and the avoidance of pain. The first usage is descriptive, the second prescriptive.

heliocotrema The small opening at the apex of the cochlea where the scala tympani and scala vestibuli connect.

heliotropism ➤ **phototaxis**.

helping behavior Providing direct assistance to someone in need. The term is used for situations in which the behavior involves no sacrifices, real or potential, on the part of the helper. Distinguish from ➤ **altruism** (or altruistic behavior) where the assistance given involves some risk or personal privation. ➤➤ **bystander effect**.

helping professions Collectively, all those professions whose theories, research and practice focus on the assistance of others, the identification and resolution of their problems and the extension of knowledge of the human condition to further those aims. Included are medicine broadly, psychiatry, clinical psychology and various specialized fields like educational and school psychology, social work, speech and hearing sciences, etc.

helplessness, learned A term coined by M. Seligman to characterize the generalization that helplessness is a learned state produced by exposure to noxious, unpleasant situations in which there is no possibility of escape or avoidance. In the experimental demonstrations that serve as the analog of the effect in humans, repeated inescapable shocking of a dog produces a kind of pathological helplessness so extreme that even when an avenue for escape is provided the animal will not take it. Interestingly, preceding the inescapable shock trials by only a few trials in which

the animal can escape prevents the syndrome from developing.

hem(a)- ➤ **hem(o)-**.

hemat(o)- ➤ **hem(o)-**.

hematocyte 1. A red blood cell. **2.** Any blood cell.

hemeralopia A condition in which vision is normal under dim illumination but poor under normal or high light levels. It is seen in those with achromatism or total color blindness and albinism. Also called *day blindness* and in some older writings, incorrectly, *night blindness*, the proper term for which is ➤ **nyctalopia**. var., *hemeralopsia*.

hemi- Prefix meaning *half* or, when used with respect to organs or organisms that display bilateral symmetry, *on one side*. Most of the combined terms using this prefix are easily understood from their etymological roots (e.g., *hemianalgesia* is lack of sensitivity to pain on one side of the body, *hemiplegia* is paralysis of one side of the body); those that are obscure or used in special ways are given below.

hemianopia Blindness in one half of the visual field. It results from a variety of lesions in the optic pathways and can take a variety of forms. Often used with qualifiers so that the particular form is noted; e.g., *bitemporal* = effecting only the temporal half of the visual field of each eye, *unilateral* = affecting only one eye. vars., *hemiopia*, *hemianopsia*.

hemiballism ➤ **ballism**.

hemilateral Synonym for ➤ **unilateral** (the preferred form).

hemiopia ➤ **hemianopia**.

hemisphere Either half of the cerebrum or cerebellum.

hemispheric specialization ➤ **laterality**.

hem(o)- combining form from the Greek for *blood*. vars., *haem(o)-*, *hem(a)-*, *hemat(o)-*, *haem(a)-*, *haemat(o)-*.

hemocyte ➤ **hematocyte**.

Henning's prism A classification system for smell based on human judgements in which six (theoretically) pure odor qualities (flowery, fruity, spicy, resinous, burnt, putrid) form the corners of a prism with the intermediate qualities lying along the surfaces.

Henning's tetrahedron A classification system for taste in which the four primary tastes (sweet, sour, bitter, salty) are arranged at the corners of a four-sided pyramid with all other tastes arranged at various locations to represent how they are combinations of two or more of the primaries.

hepato-lenticular degeneration ➤ **Wilson's disease**.

Herbartianism An early system of psychological thought developed in the 1820s by J. F. Herbart (1776–1841). It stressed the notion that ideas compete and struggle for recognition. A central concept was *apperceptive mass* (➤ **apperception** (2)), the previously acquired set of ideas to which any new idea must be related. Since these assumptions imply a level of mind of which we are not conscious, Herbart is seen as a precursor of psychoanalytic thought. Herbart's system was also highly mathematical; he was the innovator of mathematical descriptions of the formulation and interaction of ideas. Moreover, he was highly influential with educators and is regarded by many as the initiator of modern educational theory.

herding ➤ **gregariousness**, especially **1.** Also called *herd instinct*.

'here and now' A term popularized by advocates of the ➤ **human potential movement**. It refers, quite literally, to the here and now, the present. It is argued that many maladaptive, neurotic behaviors derive from continuous focusing on past problems, past injustices and that it will be therapeutic to concentrate on what is happening in the 'here and now,' to savor the moment.

hereditarianism A label used for any position stressing the role of heredity in the determination of behavior. Contrast with

➤ **environmentalism**, differentiate subtly from ➤ **nativism** and ➤ **heredity–environment controversy**.

hereditary factor A gene.

hereditary predisposition An inherited predisposition toward a particular trait. However, the term is generally reserved for pathological conditions; one speaks of, for example, a hereditary predisposition toward schizophrenia or epilepsy. Whether or not the pathology develops depends on environmental circumstances.

heredity Most broadly, the biological transmission of genetic characteristics from parent to offspring. The study of heredity is predicated on several fundamental considerations: (a) the biological principles of genetics and genetic transmission; (b) the impact of the environment, the conditions under which an organism is raised and lives; and (c) the complex manner in which these two classes of factors interact with each other. That is, the actual set of physical, behavioral traits manifested (the *phenotype*) is a complex product of the cumulative interactions between the genetic material available at fertilization (the *genotype*) and the various environmental factors that impinge on the developing organism.

Hereditary is the most common adjective form although many others are used more or less interchangeably, e.g., *genetic, biological, inborn, inherited, innate* and *natural*. When used to modify a characteristic or trait they carry the connotation that that characteristic or trait is due, *in some measure*, to genetic factors. However, all these terms must be used with caution since none of them carries any lexical component that denotes the *relative* contribution of the hereditary component to the characteristic under consideration – to describe eye color as 'hereditary' is to suggest one thing, to describe intelligence as 'hereditary' is to suggest quite another. For more on this point ➤ **heredity–environment controversy**. Distinguish all adjectival forms from ➤ **congenital**, which means simply *present at birth*.

heredity–environment controversy Also

referred to as the *nature–nurture debate* or, in philosophical writings, the *nativism–empiricism controversy*. It is a debate of long standing over the relative contributions of experience (nurture, environment, learning) and inheritance (nature, heredity, genetic predisposition) to the make-up of an organism, especially a human organism.

In its earliest incarnation the dispute turned on questions of innate qualities of mind that were assumed to be universal and found in all nonpathological instances. A case in point is vision, where everyone perceives a three-dimensional, Euclidean world: is this because, as the Cartesians argued, we are born with this particular spatial knowledge or, as the empiricists following Locke and Hume maintained, because we learn to see those relationships through experience? (➤ **Molyneux's question**.) This particular form of controversy is recognizable today in the analogous dispute between modern nativists who follow linguist Noam Chomsky in arguing that we are born with the underlying representation of universal grammar that guides language acquisition and the more empiricist-oriented theorists who maintain that there are very general learning principles that can account for how a natural language is acquired without assuming such a rich inherited system.

However, where the nature–nurture dispute has been most explosive is when the issues turn from consideration of those capacities that are *universal*, like vision and language, to the consideration of the roots of the *differences* between individuals, as displayed for example in their scores on intelligence tests. To wit: to what extent does an individual's genetic endowment determine his or her anatomical and behavioral phenotype as it is manifested in ways that are important in terms of society's evaluations? This issue hinges on the notion of ➤ **heritability**, the proportion of the variance in a population of some measurable trait that can be attributed to genetic factors. ➤➤ **environmentalism** and **hereditarianism** and, for a characterization of a recent genetically-based theoretical approach to these issues, ➤ **sociobiology**.

Hering afterimage The first ➤ **positive** *afterimage following a brief, bright, visual stimulus.

Hering grays A series of 50 neutral gray papers graded in subjectively equal steps along the achromatic dimension from extreme white to extreme black.

Hering illusion As shown; the two vertical lines are straight.

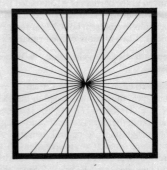

Hering theory of color vision ➤ theories of *color vision.

heritability That proportion of the variance of a particular trait in a population that can be traced to inherited factors. The *heritability ratio* represents this notion as $H = V_G/V_T$, where H is the heritability ratio, V_G is the variance in the population due to genetic (inherited) factors and V_T is the total variance. There are three critical implications of this idea that must be recognized: (a) Even if the value of H approaches 1.0, it does not necessarily mean that there are *large* genetic differences between individuals. While it is true that if the environment were perfectly controlled and identical for all individuals (i.e. the variance due to experience = 0), then any observed differences would be due to genetic factors (since $V_G = V_T$), such a state of affairs would have no bearing on the size of those observed differences. Another way to see this is to appreciate that a century ago blindness would have been scored as low in heritability while today it would be scored as considerably higher. There has not been any change in the occurrence of genetically caused blindness; rather the overall variability (V_T) has been reduced by the development of safety measures and advances in medicine, which are environmental factors, leaving the heritability ratio to increase. Completely removing all environmental causes of blindness might leave an infinitesimal value of V_T and an H of 1.0. (b) The value of H is only interpretable given a population of individuals, it has no implications for individual cases. One cannot argue that so many inches of a person's height are determined by heredity and so many by the environment. That is, H cannot be read as a statement of the amount of a characteristic attributable to genes but only as a statement about the parceling out of the variability to genetic or environmental factors within a given population. (c) No observed group differences on objective measures, no matter how large or small they may be, can be taken as reflective of genetic causes independently of the value of H because H is based on *within*-group variance, not *between*-group variance. For example, one half of a batch of genetically diverse seeds can yield a set of rather tall plants (on the average) and the other half yield a set of rather short ones (on the average) simply by adjusting the richness of the soil. Or, put another way, the fact that one racial or ethnic group scores consistently lower on an IQ test than another group does not mean that the differences between them are genetic in origin even though the value of H for IQ is above 0 as assessed by within-group designs and twin studies. Interestingly, the concept emerged from the work of agricultural breeders who wished to know if it was worth attempts to select for a particular trait. ➤➤ environmentality.

heritability ratio ➤ heritability.

heritage A generic term for transmission from generation to generation. May refer to either biological heredity or to social transmission of customs and traditions.

hermaphrodite 1. In humans, an individual in whom the structures of the reproductive system are so nondifferentiated that an unambiguous assignment of male or female cannot be made. The term derives from Hermaphroditos, the son of Hermes and Aphrodite, who combined with his consort to become a single body possessing both male and female characteristics. Contrast with ➤ androgyny and ➤ pseudohermaphrodite. 2. Characteristic of a species (e.g., many plants) in which both male and female reproductive parts are found in all members.

hermeneutics Interpretative procedures or the science of such. Originally the term was used to refer to interpretation of scripture but it is used today rather more broadly to encompass any interpretative operations.

hermetic Airtight. Occasionally used metaphorically for a pure, uncontaminated process.

heroin An opiate derived from ➤ morphine with analgesic, euphoric and sedative effects. Like all the opiates, repeated dosages lead to development of tolerance and a marked ➤ drug *dependence. The effectiveness of heroin to alter mood, relieve tension, fears and anxieties and produce a gentle drowsy euphoria has made it the most abused of the narcotics.

Hertz (Hz) One cycle per second. The term was introduced to honor the German physicist Heinrich R. Hertz (1857–94) and is now the standard international term replacing *cps* (or *cycles per second*). The term is almost always used in abbreviated form.

hesitation pause ➤ pause, hesitation.

Hess image A third ➤ positive *afterimage appearing after the first two (known as the Hering and Purkinje afterimages respectively). It is exceedingly faint and there is some uncertainty concerning its description.

hetero- Combining form from the Greek, translated variously as *different*, *other*, *unlike*, etc. Contrast with ➤ homo-.

335

heterodox Any belief that is different from what is generally accepted, or the person holding such a belief. The treatment given a heterodox varies widely; in theological realms he or she may be seen as a heretic, in scientific work often as creative and progressive.

heteroerotic Characterizing sexual attraction toward another person. The term is the antonym of ➤ **autoerotic** and is neutral as to hetero- or homosexuality.

heterogeneity Generally, dissimilarity. Used of groups, data, variables, etc. that show marked differences among instances.

heteromorphous Differing from the normal or usual form.

heteronomous Originating or controlled from the outside, externally controlled, the antonym of ➤ **autonomous**.

heteronomous morality stage ➤ **moral realism (stage)**.

heterophemy Saying or writing (although here *heterographia* is the proper term) something other than what one intended.

heterophoria A general term used for any lack of muscular coordination or balance between the two eyes.

heteroscedasticity ➤ **scedasticity**.

heterosexual 1. n. An individual whose sexual preferences are for persons of the opposite sex. 2. adj. Characterizing ➤ **heterosexuality**.

heterosexuality 1. Sexual contact between persons of opposite sexes. 2. An attraction to persons of the opposite sex, the condition in which one's sexual preferences are for the opposite sex. Compare with ➤ **homosexuality**.

heterosis Increased strength, size, vigor and growth rate resulting from cross-breeding of genetically dissimilar members of the same species. Also called *hybrid vigor*.

heterotropia ➤ **strabismus**.

heterozygote A heterozygous organism.

heterozygous Descriptive of any organism possessing two unlike ➤ **alleles** for a particular trait. Contrast with ➤ **homozygous**.

heuristic A method for discovery, a procedure for solving a problem, a technique that operates as a vehicle for creative formulation. Essentially, a heuristic is any sophisticated, directed procedure that functions by reducing the range of possible solutions to a problem or the number of possible answers to a question.

Heuristics operate in the actual 'doing' of science in fundamental ways; they are provisional characterizations that allow for testing, evaluation and refinement of ideas and theories. They emerge, moreover, in a good deal of complex human behavior, particularly in problem-solving, decision-making, concept-learning, memory and the like. Compare with ➤ **algorithm**, which is a procedure that guarantees the finding of a solution, which heuristics do not. adj., *heuristic* or *heuristical*.

heuristic, cognitive A term generally reserved for any of the various ➤ **heuristics** that people use when making decisions, solving problems, and forming beliefs. For some examples, ➤ **anchoring, availability, framing, representativeness**.

hex(a)- Prefix meaning *six*.

Hick-Hyman law A generalization that reflects the fact that reaction time (RT) increases as a function of the amount of information transmitted in making a response. That is, $RT = a + bH$, where a and b are constants and H is the amount of information measured in bits. Thus, as the number of choices available to the subject is increased RT increases; as the number of errors made increases, RT decreases; as the probability of individual choices goes down, RT goes up; and so forth. ➤ **information** and **bit** for details on the patterns of usage of these terms.

hidden figure ➤ **embedded figure**.

hidden observer In Ernest Hilgard's conceptualization of hypnosis, a hypothesized concealed consciousness that is inferred to experience events differently from (although in parallel with) the hypnotized consciousness.

hierarchy Any system of things, events, persons, concepts, etc. in rank order. A very general term, it is found in many cases where the writer wishes to convey the notion of things ranked from 'high' to 'low.' See following entries for some examples.

hierarchy, dominance **1.** A hierarchy of potential responses ranked in terms of the relative likelihood of occurrence under particular stimulus conditions. If behaviors A and B are both conditioned to a given stimulus and A is displayed, it is classified as higher in the dominance hierarchy. In this context, ➤ **habit hierarchy**. **2.** In ethology and comparative psychology, the ranking of members of a group according to relative importance or dominance. The term corresponds to the layman's expression, 'pecking order,' which comes, not surprisingly, from the fact that chickens typically establish such dominance hierarchies within a group.

high Colloquial term for the psychological state produced by psychotropic drugs, especially the hallucinogens and psychedelics.

higher brain centers (or **structures**) Loosely, those cerebral structures that are presumed to be concerned with the so-called *higher mental processes*. Note that words like 'center' and 'structure' are used outrageously loosely – nothing resembling a coherent 'center' for these cognitive processes has been isolated. The best guess is that the cortex of the frontal lobe is a critical area, although many others argue that the brain as a whole operates in this capacity and attempts at localization are futile.

higher mental processes A generic label used to refer collectively to thought, imagery, memory, ideation, language, abstraction, symbolization, judgement, etc.

higher-order conditioning Classical conditioning in which a conditioned stimulus (CS) from an original conditioning series is used as the unconditioned stimulus (US) in a new experimental setting. Also called *secondary* or *second-order conditioning*.

higher response unit Loosely, any complex, integrated response composed of simple responses.

high-grade defective See the discussion under ➤ **defective** (2).

hillock ➤ **axon hillock**.

hindbrain During embryonic development the brain evolves three separate portions, the hindbrain, midbrain and forebrain. The first of these is evolutionarily the oldest; it differentiates into the metencephalon and the myelencephalon. The metencephalon gives rise to the cerebellum and the pons, the myelencephalon to the medulla.

hindsight bias The tendency, after an event has occurred, to think that we knew what was going to happen beforehand.

hippocampal formation A neurologically complex region of the limbic cortex in the temporal lobes which includes the *entorhinal cortex*, the *subicular complex*, the *dentate gyrus*, and the ➤ **hippocampus** itself. It extends from the narrow dorsal part that runs along the corpus callosum to the broad ventral part that forms the floor of the inferior horn of the lateral ventricle. In humans the hippocampal formation plays an important role in the formation of long-term memories; damage to this region or to its inputs and outputs causes ➤ **anterograde *amnesia** for episodic and declarative memories. Note that the term *hippocampus*, although strictly only one part of the formation, is often loosely used for the whole hippocampal region.

hippocampus A part of the ➤ **hippocampal formation**. Cells in the hippocampus itself connect with cortical regions in the brain through the **entorhinal cortex** and subcortical regions through the fimbria/fornix. Also called *Ammon's horn* and *cornu ammonis*.

histamine A *biologic amine* that functions as a *neurotransmitter* in several cerebral pathways. It is also present in nearly all bodily tissue and is released whenever tissues are injured and in allergic reactions. Injection of histamine causes a local red spot, which turns bluish in a minute or two, followed by a spreading redness and a localized swelling which typically itches.

histo- Prefix indicating *relating to tissue*.

histogram A pictorial presentation of a frequency distribution so that the number of cases per class is presented as a vertical bar. Often called a *bar graph* and, occasionally, a *block diagram*.

histology The discipline that studies the microscopic structure of bodily tissue. Basically, it is a branch of biology but histological analyses are an integral part of physiological psychology.

historical method A general term covering any form of therapy, analysis or counseling that deals with the individual by focusing on life history.

histrionic personality disorder A personality disorder usually characterized by immaturity, self-centeredness, attention-getting, manipulativeness and quite often, a vague seductiveness. Such persons are overly dramatic, reactive and intense in their interpersonal relationships and frequently play out classic roles like 'princess' or 'victim.' Also called, especially in older texts, *hysterical personality*.

hit The accurate statement by a subject that an objectively present stimulus was, in fact, present and perceived. Compare with ➤ **false alarm** and see discussion under ➤ **signal-detection theory**.

'HM' The sobriquet of one of neuropsychology's most important early cases. Operated on for intractable epilepsy, he underwent a bilateral midtemporal lobe resection of the amygdala, the anterior two-thirds of the hippocampus, and surrounding cortical tissue. The procedure made the epilepsy manageable but resulted in a severe anterograde amnesia. It was largely through this case that the importance of the midtemporal lobe in explicit memory was first appreciated.

Hobson's choice From the Elizabethan Thomas Hobson, described by the early 18th-century essayist Richard Steele; a choice that is not a choice at all. Hobson, a stable-owner, would only lend out the one horse nearest the stable door no matter how many other of his horses were free. Hence, being presented with Hobson's Choice is to be confronted with a situation in which there are nominally many alternatives from which to choose but the constraints of the situation are such that one's actual choice is forced upon one. The situation presented to the chooser is of considerable interest in social psychological theories of choice behavior. See, for example, ➤ **reactance theory**, **reactive** (2, 3).

hodological space Hodology is a branch of geometry that characterizes geometric relationships in terms of vectors and their paths. K. Lewin's topological theory of personality is based (somewhat informally) on the mathematics of such spaces. ➤ **field theory**, **topology**.

Höffding step In the terminology of Gestalt psychology, the mental step through which the perception of an image makes contact with a memory trace. If you see a 'table' and then think 'chair' the sight of the 'table' does not trigger the associated memory of 'chair' directly. There is an additional step necessary, the step whereby the stimulus 'table' contacts the memory trace of 'table' which then contacts the memory 'chair.' Although the need for the Höffding step has been recognized for nearly a century it has only become regarded as important for theories of pattern perception and pattern recognition in recent years.

holergasia Obsolescent term for any psychiatric disorder that affects the entire emotional, cognitive and behavioral repertoire of an individual.

holism A general label applied to any philosophical approach that focuses on the whole living organism. The basic axiom of a holistic position is that a complex phenomenon cannot be understood by an analysis of the constituent parts alone. Contrast with ➤ **elementarism** and ➤ **atomism**. Gestalt and Freudian theories are classic examples of holistic approaches in psychology.

Hollingshead scales Formulas that allow one to convert the occupation and education level of adults into ordinal scales of socioeconomic status. Each of the scales is appropriate for a particular kind of household; e.g., one scale would be used for a household with a single wage-earner and a different one for a dual-career household. The UK equivalent is called the *Registrar General's scale / categories*. ➤ **occupational hierarchy**.

Holmgren test An early (19th century) test for color blindness using skeins of yarn of various colors that had to be classified into three groups determined by a set of three standard-colored skeins. The test has also been used to evaluate abstracting ability, particularly in patients with brain damage.

hol(o)- Combining form meaning *complete, whole, homogeneous*.

holographic memory ➤ **memory, holographic**.

holophrase A single-word utterance that may function as a whole phrase or even a sentence. ➤ **holophrastic stage**.

holophrastic stage An early stage in the development of language in a child in which single-word utterances dominate. Some theorists argue that such single words (or holophrases) are reduced or telegraphic sentences (e.g., 'milk' represents 'I want milk'), suggesting that memory and motor-control limitations of the young child force the use of these very short 'sentences.' Other theorists argue

that the holophrastic stage is pre-syntactic and that one should not infer that the child in any way 'knows' sentence formation rules, merely that the holophrases are used to indicate primitive concepts like desire, possession, location, etc.

homeo- Combining form denoting *sameness* or *resemblance*.

homeostasis Lit., from the Greek for *same-state*. The American physiologist W. B. Cannon introduced the term for any process that modifies an existing condition or a set of circumstances and thereby initiates other processes that function in a regulatory manner to re-establish the initial condition. A thermostat is a mechanical homeostat. The term is used in physiological psychology to encompass a number of complex biological mechanisms that operate via the autonomic nervous system to regulate such factors as body temperature, bodily fluids and their physical and chemical properties, blood pressure, water balance, metabolism, etc. For example, a drop in body temperature initiates a variety of processes such as shivering, piloerection and an increase in metabolism that produce and conserve heat until a normal temperature is achieved.

home sign Fant's term for the informal, invented manual gestures often seen in communication between deaf children who have been trained through the use of the ➤ **oral method**. ➤➤ **manual method**.

hominid From the name for the primate family, Hominidae, it refers to any of the species so classified – *Homo sapiens* is the only surviving member.

Homo From the Latin for *man*. Usually, but not always, capitalized.

homo- Combining form from the Greek, meaning *same, similar, alike*.

homoerotism **1.** Broadly, any erotic feelings toward members of one's own sex. **2.** Specifically, ➤ **homosexuality**.

homogamy The tendency for people to select mates who are similar to themselves.

It is not clear whether this well-documented tendency is due to a genuine selection of like to like or an artifact of the patterns of social interaction where people typically spend most of their time with those from similar racial, ethnic, and socioeconomic backgrounds.

homogeneity Broadly, similarity, sameness. Applied in various settings to refer to groups, subjects, data, variables, etc. when the items under consideration are not appreciably or meaningfully different from each other.

homogeneity of variance Similarity in ➤ **variance**. Many parametrical statistical tests (e.g., *t* test, *F* test) are based on the assumption that the population variances underlying the samples are the same (in order for the test to provide a valid estimate of any statistical effects). In practice homogeneity of variance means *non-significant heterogeneity*. That is, one does not experience variances to be identical, merely not significantly different from each other so that one may operate on the assumption that the samples actually came from the same underlying population. The ➤ **F ratio** is the most convenient test for this.

homograph Any pair or set of words with identical spellings but different etymologies and hence different meanings. My favorite is the two verbs *cleave* – each is the antonym of the other.

homolateral ➤ **ipsilateral**.

homologous 1. Of biological structures that correspond in type of structure and origin but not necessarily in function. The foreleg of a horse and a bird's wing are homologous structures. Contrast with the biologist's use of ➤ **analog** (2), in which the function is similar but the structure and origin are not, e.g., the wings of bees and birds. 2. By extension, of behaviors that show such a relationship; e.g., territoriality in baboons is often considered to be homologous to territoriality in *Homo sapiens*.

homonym One of two or more words with identical pronunciations and spellings but different etymologies and hence different meanings; e.g., *pool* (the game) and *pool* (the place to swim). See and compare with ➤ **homophone**.

homonymous hemianopia Blindness in the same half of the visual field in both eyes.

homonym symptom A form of speech behavior observed at times in schizophrenics when a polysemous word sends the patient off in what seems like a bizarre narrative. For example, he may begin by telling what he did with his savings and say, '... I took it all to deposit it in the bank ... and there we sat down to fish for a while ...'

homophile 1. A lover of mankind. 2. A homosexual.

homophone One of two or more words with identical pronunciations but, owing to different etymologies, different meanings and written forms. E.g., *bare* and *bear* or *to*, *two* and *too*.

homoscedasticity ➤ **scedasticity**.

homosexual One whose sexual preferences are for members of his or her own sex. ➤ **homosexuality** for further discussion on usage.

homosexuality The term is used rather generally to refer to sexual contact between persons of the same gender. This 'contact' may be fleeting, nonorgasmic and occasional or it may represent an individual's dominant (if not exclusive) mode of sexual expression. In a very real sense then, the term may be found in the psychological literature covering persons ranging from those who have had but one or two half-hearted experiences to those for whom heterosexual contacts have been nonexistent. Comprehensive surveys suggest that perhaps 40% of the population have had at least one homosexual experience leading to orgasm whereas perhaps only 1% of the sexually active population is exclusively homosexual. There has historically been a strong antisocial bias against the homosexual, as evidenced by the inclusion, until the 1980 edition, in the *DSM* (the *Diagnostic and Statistical Manual* of the American Psychiatric Association) of homosexuality in the compendium of mental illnesses. The more recent, enlightened perspective tends to regard it simply as a particular manifestation of sexual preference, without entailing any clinical judgement (for a single exception, ➤ **ego-dystonic *homosexuality**). Note that there is a tendency in the popular literature and even in some technical writings to reserve the word *homosexual* (or *gay*) for a male and to use *lesbian* for a female.

homosexuality, ego-dystonic Homosexuality in which the individual has a persistent concern with changing his or her sexual preference. In the most recent compilation of psychological and psychiatric disorders this is the only form of homosexuality that is classified as a psychiatric disturbance. The critical feature is not the sexual preference *per se*, but the distress and anxiety over it and the persistent desire to be heterosexual. Compare with ➤ **ego-syntonic *homosexuality**.

homosexuality, ego-syntonic Homosexuality in which the individual is comfortable with and accepts his or her behavior as a simple manifestation of natural sexual preference. Compare with ➤ **ego-dystonic *homosexuality**.

homozygote A ➤ **homozygous** organism.

homozygous Descriptive of any organism possessing two like ➤ **alleles** for a particular trait. Contrast with ➤ **heterozygous**.

homunculus Lit., a *miniature man*. **1.** Through the ages the homunculus has served as a half-serious (and occasionally totally serious) physiological and psychological metaphor. At times he has been viewed as inhabiting the reproductive cells and acting as the agent for genetic transmission, as a kind of gremlin in the body regulating morality, or as a little 'green man' in the brain governing decision making. The main problem with the meta-

phor is that it leaves open the question of what kind of beast inhabits the homunculus and governs its acts, *reductio ad infinitum cum absurdum*. **2.** In neurophysiology, a schematic representation of the cortical projections for sensory and motor functions. The body is drawn in proportion to the amount of cortical tissue that subsumes each part. Thus, the motor homunculus has extremely large mouth, lips, tongue, eye and hand and rather diminutive skull, torso, buttock and leg. The sensory version has prominent tongue, lips, face, hand, foot, intra-abdominal region and genitals and small torso, buttock, skull, arm and leg. Not surprisingly, these proportions correspond to sensory discrimination and motor control of these regions. **3.** An obsolete term for a dwarf with normal anatomical proportions.

honestly significant difference test ➤ **Tukey's honestly significant difference test**.

Honi phenomenon Failure of the well-known perceptual distortion effects of the ➤ **Ames room** to occur when a very familiar person such as a parent or spouse is placed in the room.

horizon **1.** In perception, the limit of the range of what can be perceived. **2.** By extension, the limit of knowledge.

horizontal **1.** Pertaining to the horizon. **2.** At right angles to the vertical.

horizontal (H) cells Cells in the retinas of vertebrates with color vision. They have dendrites that hook up with a large number of cones and have been shown to respond in opposite fashion to stimulation of different wavelengths (e.g., red and green). This feature has led to the hypothesis that H cells form part of the neurological mechanism assumed by the *opponent process theory*; for more detail ➤ **theories of *color vision**.

horizontal décalage ➤ **décalage**.

horizontal group ➤ **group, horizontal**.

horizontal growth ➤ **growth, horizontal**.

horizontal mobility Mobility within the same social or occupational class. Also called *horizontal social mobility*.

horizontal sampling ➤ **sampling, horizontal**.

horizontal section ➤ **section** (2).

hormic psychology A school of psychology associated with the work of English-born social psychologist William McDougall. The system is based on a loose collection of basic 'goal-oriented' or 'purposeful' behaviors that were assumed to be motivated by innate propensities or instincts. The term *hormic* derives from the Greek for *animal impulse*.

McDougall, one of the more vigorous critics of Watsonian behaviorism, initially attracted numerous adherents particularly among social psychologists, sociologists and anthropologists, many of whom considered Watson's position simplistic and sterile. The hormic position, however, suffered from major liabilities, the primary being the lack of precision in the definition and use of the concept of instinct. As this, the central pillar of the theory, came under severe attack by the more sophisticated behaviorists the school lost popularity and influence. Today it is mainly of historical interest.

hormone From the Greek, meaning *urging*, *striving*, a general term covering a large number of bodily substances that originate in a gland or an organ, are conveyed to other organic sites and have any of a number of effects on these target cells. Individual hormones are given under separate alphabetic listing. Note that many substances that are listed as hormones by virtue of their production by glands also function as ➤ **neurotransmitters** (e.g., *norepinephrine* and the *endorphins*).

Horner's law The genetic principle that the most common form of color blindness (red–green) is transmitted from male to male through unaffected females.

horopter When both eyes are fixated on a particular point in the visual field there exists a collection of points in the field whose images fall on corresponding retinal points; collectively this locus is called the horopter.

hospice A specialized nursing home for terminally ill patients. Hospices are designed to be caring, peaceful, supportive environments where patients can live out their final days in dignity.

hospital hopper syndrome A quaint but nicely descriptive term occasionally used as a synonym for ➤ **factitious disorder**.

hospitalism ➤ **reactive attachment disorder**.

hostility A long-lasting emotional state characterized by enmity toward others and manifested by a desire to harm or inflict pain upon those at whom it is directed. Often distinguished from ➤ **anger** on the grounds that anger is a more intense and momentary reaction. ➤➤ **animus** (1), **animosity** and **hatred**.

House–Tree–Person Test A projective test in which the subject is requested to draw a house, a tree and a person. The drawings made are interpreted according to a more or less standardized set of criteria involving amount of detail, speed of execution and any comments made by the subject.

5-HT = *5-hydroxtryptamine* ➤ **serotonin**.

hue That dimension of visual sensation corresponding chiefly to the wavelength of the light. The term is roughly synonymous with the common term 'color' and, indeed, hues are specified by names like red, green, yellow, blue, etc. Note that hues are also secondarily related to the amplitude of the light waves since the perceived hue will change somewhat with light intensity. See also entries under ➤ **color** and **spectrum**.

hue, pure A hue whose stimulus is a light source with but a single wave-length. Lasers produce pure hues; they are never seen in the 'real world.'

hues, unique ➤ **primary *colors**, especially 2.

Hullian Pertaining to the theoretical and empirical point of view of the American psychologist Clark Leonard Hull (1884–1952). Although Hull's work spanned several diverse areas including tests and measurements, hypnosis, concept formation, motivation and learning, the term is generally applied only to his work in these last two. Hull developed in the final two decades of his life a rich, elaborate behaviorist theory of learning and motivation. The Hullian approach was wedded to the use of the ➤ **hypothetico-deductive method**, in which one deduces hypotheses from postulates and tests them empirically. Those found wanting are taken as guides to the adjustment of one's postulates so as to deduce new hypotheses, and so forth. Thus, the system was designed to be self-correcting.

The basic principle was that ➤ **habit strength** is increased by reinforcement. A variety of secondary principles articulated the manner in which it could also be modified by drive level, various forms of inhibition and excitation, stimulus and response generalization, etc. The full-blown Hullian system eventually expired of its own hypothetico-deductive excesses. So many variables needed to be introduced as part of the postulate system that by the late 1940s a research paper in the tradition, with all the elaborate notation used as shorthand for the variables, looked like someone had spilled alphabet soup on the page. The power of the Hullian approach that gave it its several decades of influence in experimental psychology derived from several factors: (a) the inclusion of motivational elements in the theory of learning; (b) the strong adherence to a sophisticated positivist philosophy; and (c) the novel manner in which Hull attempted to account for the action of a reinforcer; ➤ **drive reduction hypothesis**.

There are few if any true Hullians left today but many who were profoundly influenced by his thinking.

human engineering 1. An applied discipline allied with industrial and organizational psychology that focuses on the problems of the design of equipment, machinery, work places, working conditions and the like. 2. The art of managing humans as engineers manage machines.

human factors A genetic term used most often as the name of the professional speciality that studies the so-called ➤ **man-machine interface**. The focus is generally on problems of perception, psychophysics, decision-making and other aspects of information processing. The term, however, is also used on occasion to refer to those elements ('factors') that are important within this speciality including the equipment, the physical environment, the tasks and the individuals who do the work. ➤ **industrial / organizational psychology**, which is generally regarded as the broader field within which human factors is a sub-discipline.

humanistic psychology An approach to psychology developed largely by Abraham Maslow, who proposed it as 'a third force' after psychoanalysis and behaviorism. He viewed psychology as too concerned either with that which was neurotic and disturbed (psychoanalysis) or with that which was explainable with mechanistic theory (behaviorism). A humanistic view in Maslow's sense would evolve a science concerned with higher human motives, self-development, knowledge, understanding and esthetics. Other major theorists associated with this general approach are Carl Rogers, Erich Fromm and Rollo May.

human nature An absolutely undefinable term. Usage invariably connotes innateness but precisely what characteristics are presumed to be genetically given depends entirely on the prejudices of the writer. The term's most common use seems to be as an apology for inhuman behavior.

human potential movement A general label covering the vast array of presumably therapeutic techniques such as encounter groups, sensitivity training, assertiveness training, etc. Actually, the number of different theories, techniques and orientations that are part of this essentially eclectic movement is growing daily and in unpredictable ways. Advocates of the movement see it as the cutting edge of a new humanism, critics view it as largely an irresponsible commercial enterprise which preys upon people's vulnerabilities and fears.

There have been enough positive results from the use of some of the techniques for a number of them (particularly sensitivity training) to have actually been introduced into schools and businesses. However, many authorities are highly critical of the movement as a whole because of its tendency to follow the intuitions of practitioners who tend to accept uncritically the claimed virtues of such disparate approaches as Zen Buddhism, psychodrama, art, dance, poetry, mysticism, yoga, meditation, fasting, acupuncture, rolfing, astrology or just plain 'letting it all hang out' independent of any coherent theoretical analysis, controlled experimentation or systematic follow-up on the efficacy of these techniques. In recent years it has blended in with the 'New Age' movement without, alas, gaining anything in reliability, validity or coherence.

humor 1. Any bodily fluid such as the aqueous humor in the eye. Archaic physiological theories assumed that temperament depended on the relative proportions of four cardinal humors in the body. Note that the vestiges of this point of view are still with us in that in common parlance *humor* can be used synonymously with *mood*. **2.** The quality of being pleasant, sympathetic, amusing or funny. var., *humour*.

Humpty-Dumpty rule A rule or principle which has been, perhaps more than any other, the driving force behind the idiosyncratic and often baffling manner of usage of terms in science. It derives, of course, from Lewis Carroll when he had Humpty speak the words closest to his heart: '"When I use a word," Humpty Dumpty said in a rather scornful tone, "it means just what I choose it to mean – neither more nor less."' So it is with the neologistic scientist.

hunger 1. Physiologically, an internal state of an organism that results from particular imbalances in nutrients in the body and whose severity is determined by the degree of these imbalances. ➤ **glucostatic theory**. **2.** An internal state that results from food deprivation and whose severity is measured by the duration of the deprivation. Note that this meaning, which is favored by behaviorists, is essentially an attempt to provide an operational definition for the term. **3.** The phenomenologically experienced state that results from either of the circumstances specified in 1 and 2. This is a distinctly nonbehaviorist meaning. **4.** A drive state resulting from either of the circumstances specified in 1 and 2 that motivates food-seeking behavior. Note that 4 extends 3 by implying that the experienced state is linked ineluctably with motivational components. **5.** By extension, any craving for something that one has been deprived of, a hunger for affection, a sexual hunger, etc. Usage here pulls the term out of its alliance with food but any or all of the specific definitional restrictions exhibited in meanings 1–4 may be found here as well.

hunger, specific A need for specific dietary substances. The term, however, is somewhat misleading in that it connotes, quite literally, that there are specific hungers for specific substances; e.g., that an organism deprived of, say, the vitamin thyamine will have a 'hunger' for it and select out foodstuffs containing it over other foodstuffs lacking it. There is, with the possible exception of salt, precious little evidence for such a phenomenon. What there is evidence for is *learned preference* and *learned avoidance*. That is, an organism will eventually learn to prefer a diet containing thyamine over ones that do not because the ones that do not produce metabolic deficiencies. For more on the model that lies behind this conception, ➤ **toxicosis**.

Huntington's disease An inherited neurological disease characterized by progressive cognitive and muscular deterioration and in the later stages by severe alterations in personality. Patients show deficits in such cognitive areas as attention, retrieval, problem solving, and visuoperceptual functions. Interestingly, the memory dysfunctions are limited largely to recall of material, recognition ability is often unaffected. It is caused by a dominant gene and anyone carrying it will eventually develop the disease. Also called *Huntington's chorea*.

Hurler's syndrome A genetic disorder characterized by severe mental retardation and a variety of physical abnormalities including pronounced spinal curvature and coarse facial features marked by a broad, flat nose, wide set eyes, low set ears and a large protruding tongue.

hwa-byung A ➤ **culture-specific syndrome** in Korea. Attributed to suppression of anger, symptoms include insomnia, fatigue, panic, indigestion and anorexia, generalized aches and pains, and feeling of a mass in the pit of the stomach.

hyalophagia Eating of glass, a form of ➤ **pica**.

H-Y antigen A protein that plays an important role in sexual differentiation. Production of the protein is controlled by a gene on the Y chromosome. When present it stimulates receptors on the surface of the primordial gonads and causes them to develop as testes; when not present they develop as ovaries.

hybrid 1. An offspring resulting from the union of gametes of differing genotypes. Generally used with respect to animals or plants where the parents are of different species or well-marked varieties. 2. By extension, one who is heterogeneous in make-up. Here the meaning extends to social, cultural and linguistic forms. adj., *hybrid*.

hybrid vigor ➤ **heterosis**.

hydraulic theory In general, any theory that models the phenomena under consideration in 'hydraulic' fashion. That is, one based on the assumption that things behave like fluids under pressure, ready to break through any weak spots should

the pressure exceed some critical level. Meyer's theory of hearing is termed hydraulic, as are Freud's personality theory and the Tinbergen–Lorenz ethological theory (although the label, in the last case, is applied derisively, by critics and not proponents of this theory).

hydraulic theory of hearing ➤ **theories of *hearing**.

hydro- Combining form meaning *water* and, by extension, *fluid* or *liquid*.

hydrocephalus Lit., water or fluid in the head. An abnormal accumulation of cerebrospinal fluid within the ➤ **ventricles** (3). The pressure on the brain, if not alleviated, can result in permanent damage to cerebral tissue. adj., *hydrocephalic*.

hydrotherapy A cover term for any use of water in a therapeutic manner.

5-hydroxtryptamine ➤ **serotonin**.

hyp- ➤ **hyp(o)-**.

hypacusia Impaired hearing.

hypalgesia Relative insensitivity to pain. var., *hypalgia*.

hyper- Combining form meaning *above*, *beyond*, *in high degree*, *excessive*. Most of the combinatory forms using this prefix are self-explanatory (e.g., hypercritical); less obvious forms are given below.

hyperactive child Strictly speaking this is a nontechnical term, although it will often be found in the technical literature. It is used loosely for a child who displays any of the various disorders of childhood that have hyperactivity as a feature; for example, ➤ **attention-deficit hyperactivity disorder**.

hyperactive child syndrome ➤ **attention-deficit hyperactivity disorder**.

hyperactivity Vigorous, inappropriate motor activity. ➤ **attention-deficit hyperactivity disorder**.

hyperacusia Excellent hearing.

hyperalgesia Extreme sensitivity to pain. var., *hyperalgia*.

hypercalcemia ➤ **Williams syndrome**.

hypercathexis Investing psychic energy (cathexis) in one process for the (unconscious) purposes of furthering or facilitating another. Generally regarded in psychoanalytic writings as a ➤ **defense mechanism**.

hyperesthesia Extreme sensitivity to touch. On occasion used more generally for any sensory hypersensitivity; under these conditions it will usually be qualified, e.g., *acoustic hyperesthesia*. var., *hyperaesthesia*.

hypergasia Overactivity characteristic of the manic phase of ➤ **bipolar disorder**.

hypergenitalism Excessive early development of the genitals; premature puberty. The condition may be caused by abnormal endocrine secretions of the adrenal cortices or the gonads or by some hypothalamic disorders.

hypergeometric distribution ➤ **distribution, hypergeometric**.

hypergeusia Extreme taste sensitivity.

hyperglycemia Increase in blood sugar.

hyperkinesis Excessive and inappropriate motor activity, extreme restlessness; usually accompanied by poor attention span and impulsivity. ➤ **attention-deficit hyperactivity disorder**. var., *hyperkinesia*.

hyperkinesthesia Extreme sensitivity to kinesthetic sensations.

hyperkinetic syndrome ➤ **attention-deficit hyperactivity disorder**.

hyperlexia 1. Generally, early acquisition of reading. Used specifically of children who learn to read prior to formal reading instruction. 2. A condition characterized by very early and effortless acquisition of oral reading in a child who otherwise shows no special abilities and, in fact, is 'slow' in reaching standard developmental milestones. Used in this sense it refers to what some feel is a form of minimal brain damage.

hypermania Condition exhibiting extreme activity, rapid and erratic behavior and speech.

hypermenorrhea 1. Excessive menstrual flow in amount and/or duration 2. Abnormally frequent menstruation. Each is a form of ➤ **dysmenorrhea**.

hypermetropia ➤ **hyperopia**.

hypermnesia Lit., excessive memory. Hence: 1. A characteristic of some ➤ **savants** in which there is an extraordinary ability to recall names, dates, places, etc. 2. An extremely detailed recollection of a particular past experience. It is observed occasionally in the manic phase of bipolar disorders, during hypnosis and during certain neurosurgical procedures, particularly where the temporal lobe is stimulated. There are questions as to whether these experiences ought to be classified as true memorial phenomena in that the conditions under which they occur make it nearly impossible to determine whether they are real hypermnesic effects or merely elaborations and/or confabulations of events. 3. An increase in the ability to recall material over time. This meaning appears in experimental studies of memory and usually is contrasted with 'typical' forgetting where the tendency is for material once learned to be less likely to be recalled over time. It also is found in some psychoanalytic writings since the techniques of classical psychoanalysis are predicated on a hypermnesic effect in that during analysis the individual is able to retrieve memories of past events that were not recallable prior to the psychic probing of analysis.

hypermotility An occasional synonym for ➤ **hyperkinesis**.

hyperopia A form of farsightedness, the inability to focus clearly on near objects. The shape of the lens of the eye is such that the focal point for light entering the eye is behind the retina rather than directly on it. Contrast with ➤ **myopia**.

hyperorexia Excessive appetite. Contrast with ➤ **anorexia**; differentiate from ➤ **hyperphagia**.

hyperosmia Extreme sensitivity to odors.

hyperphagia Lit., overeating. The term is most often used for a syndrome, experimentally induced by a lesion in the ventro-medial areas of the hypothalamus, in which the normal feeding regime is disturbed, resulting in excessive intake of foodstuffs, increased accumulation of adipose tissue and obesity. ➤ **hypothalamus** and **ventromedial hypothalamic syndrome** for more details here.

hyperphasia ➤ **hyperphrasia**.

hyperphoria Abnormal tendency for one eye to turn upward.

hyperphrasia Pathologically excessive talking. var., *hyperphasia*.

hyperphrenia 1. Excessive mental activity. Not necessarily effective mental activity though; the term is used to characterize the manic phase of *bipolar disorder*. 2. Unusually high intellectual ability. This meaning is rare owing to the former.

hyperplasia Increase in the size of an organ caused by an abnormal increase in the number of cells. Compare with ➤ **hypertrophy**.

hyperpnea Increased breathing either in frequency of respirations or in depth. var., *hyperpnoea*.

hyperpolarization An increase in polarization; in neurophysiology, the increase in the membrane potential of a neuron. See discussion under ➤ **depolarization**.

hyperprosexia An exaggerated fixating on some idea to the exclusion of others; seen in compulsive disorders.

hypersomnia A sleep disorder characterized by excessive sleeping, uncontrollable sleepiness.

hypertension 1. Excessive tension or tonus in a muscle or organ. 2. A condition marked by abnormally high blood pressure.

hyperthymia Excessive emotionality, excitability.

hyperthyroidism Excessive secretion of the thyroid gland, producing accelerated metabolic rate, extreme excitability and apprehension.

hypertonic 1. Of a solution whereby the osmotic pressures between it and cells suspended in it are such that there is fluid transmission from the cell into the surrounding medium. 2. Characteristic of a state of greater than normal (muscular) tension. Contrast with ➤ **hypotonic**.

hypertrophy Enlargement or excessive growth of an organ or organ part. The term is restricted to increases not caused by tumor or excessive proliferation of cells (➤ **hyperplasia**). Opposite of ➤ **atrophy**.

hypertropia Upward ➤ **strabismus**.

hypesthesia Lowered sensitivity. var., *hypaesthesia*.

hyphen psychologist A half-humorous sobriquet applied by the pure behaviorists to theorists who were interested in theorizing about mediational processes, mental constructs, hypothetical entities or any other internal event assumed to intervene between the presentation of a stimulus and the subject's response. The term derives from the desire to theorize about the hyphen in the classic S-R analysis favored by staunch behaviorists.

hypnagogic image(s) Hallucination-like images experienced while first falling asleep. They tend to occur when EEG patterns indicate Stage 1 sleep but in the absence of the rapid eye movements (REM) typically seen during dreaming. Compare with ➤ **hypnopompic image(s)**. var., *hypnogogic*.

hypnoanalysis Psychoanalysis carried out with the patient under hypnosis. Although still used by some analysts it was dissatisfaction with hypnosis that originally led Freud to develop other techniques such as free association and dream analysis. ➤ **hypnotherapy**.

hypnogenic 1. Sleep-producing. 2. Causing or aiding hypnosis.

347

hypnogogic image(s) ➤ **hypnagogic image(s)**.

hypnopaedia Sleep learning. Unfortunately for us all there is absolutely no evidence for this phenomenon.

hypnopompic images(s) Fleeting hallucination-like images that often accompany the first few semi-conscious moments during waking. Compare with ➤ **hypnagogic image(s)**.

hypnosedatives A class of drugs which have both sedative (quieting, tranquilizing) and hypnotic (sleep-producing) effects. Included are drugs like the barbiturates, which in small doses function as sedatives and in larger doses as hypnotics. ➤ **hypnotics** and **sedatives** for more detail.

hypnosis Few terms in the psychological lexicon are so thoroughly wrapped in mysticism and confusion. The problems arise from the tendency that dates back to the discoverer, Franz Anton Mesmer, to regard the process of hypnotism as one which transports the subject into a separate 'state of mind.' Further complications emerged because the phenomenon attracted a coterie of charlatans, faith healers and, more recently, night-club entertainers who make unsubstantiated claims and show a singular reluctance to use proper controls in their work.

The present view is that a hypnotic 'state' does exist. It is somewhat less dramatic than often portrayed but does, in general, display the following characteristics: (a) although it superficially resembles a sleep-like state (which is how it got its name), the EEG pattern does not resemble any of the stages of sleep; (b) normal planning functions are reduced, a hypnotized person tends to wait passively for instructions from the hypnotist; (c) attention becomes highly selective, the individual may hear only one person to the exclusion of others; (d) role-playing is readily accomplished, the hypnotized person frequently becoming quite thoroughly immersed in a suggested role; and (e) post-hypnotic suggestion is often observed, frequently a specific amnesia

where the subject cannot recall things he or she has been told to forget.

It should be noted that all of these effects are of a kind, in that they are also characteristic of a 'normal' person who has voluntarily given up conscious control, a person who evidences extreme suggestibility. Not surprisingly then, there is a school of thought that argues that there is nothing at all special about this 'state' but that it merely represents an extreme pole on the scale of normal suggestibility.

hypnotherapy A general term for any psychotherapy that makes use of hypnosis. Hypnotherapy is generally classified as a *directive* therapy since hypnosis tends to produce a passivity during which the client accepts direction from others. ➤ **hypnoanalysis**.

hypnotic 1. Sleep-producing. **2.** Pertaining to ➤ **hypnosis**. **3.** Pertaining to one of the ➤ **hypnotics**.

hypnotic amnestic disorder ➤ **sedative, hypnotic, or anxiolytic amnestic disorder**.

hypnotic regression ➤ **regression, hypnotic**.

hypnotics A group of drugs that produce sleep by a general (i.e. non-selective) depression of the central nervous system. Some of these drugs are also classified as ➤ **sedatives** or ➤ **hypnosedatives** in that their effects are dose-dependent – sedative in small doses, hypnotic in larger.

hypnotic withdrawal ➤ **sedative, hypnotic, or anxiolytic withdrawal**.

hypnotic withdrawal delirium ➤ **sedative, hypnotic, or anxiolytic withdrawal delirium**.

hypnotism The practice or study of hypnosis.

hypnotize 1. To induce a hypnotic state. **2.** By extension, to influence another by subtle charm and guile.

hyp(o)- Combining form meaning *lesser, diminished, below, under*.

'hypo' Popular slang for a hypodermic syringe or the injection itself.

hypoactive sexual desire disorder A ➤

sexual desire disorder marked by persistent deficient (or absent) sexual fantasies and desire for sexual activity. It is only regarded as a disorder when this lack of libido (to use an older term) causes distress or interpersonal difficulty. Also called *inhibited sexual desire*.

hypochondriac One with ➤ **hypochondriasis**.

hypochondriasis A ➤ **somatoform disorder** characterized by imagined sufferings of physical illness or, more generally, an exaggerated concern with one's physical health. The hypochondriac typically displays a preoccupation with bodily functions such as heart rate, sweating, bowel and bladder functions, and the occasional minor problems like pimples, headaches, a simple cough, etc. All such trivialities are interpreted as signs or symptoms of more serious diseases. 'Doctor shopping' is common; assurances of health are futile. Also called *hypochondria*. adj., *hypochondriacal*.

hypodermic Under the skin.

hypoendocrinism A general term for any abnormal decrease in secretion from an endocrine gland.

hypoergastia Underactivity characteristic of a depressive state.

hypofrontality Reduced blood flow to the frontal and prefrontal regions of the cortex relative to other brain regions. It is seen as a chronic condition in older, mentally deteriorated schizophrenics and in younger ones who are in an acute state brought about by attempts to solve complex problems. Note that when normals are engaged in such cognitive activity these cortical areas typically shown an *increase* in blood supply.

hypogenitalism Underdevelopment of the genitals.

hypogeusia Abnormally diminished taste sensitivity.

hypoglossal nerve The XIIth ➤ **cranial nerve**, an efferent nerve arising in the medulla oblongata and supplying the muscles of the tongue.

hypoglycemia Deficiency of blood sugar.

hypogonadal syndrome A condition in males characterized by a failure of the testes to produce adequate amounts of testosterone.

hypokinesis Abnormally low motor activity.

hypolexia Retarded reading ability. ➤ **dyslexia**, which is the more commonly used term here.

hypologia Abnormally poor speaking ability. The term is generally reserved for cases due to either mental retardation or motor dysfunction; if due to a cerebral disorder ➤ **aphasia** is the proper term.

hypomania Mild ➤ **mania (2)**.

hypomanic disorder An atypical ➤ **bipolar disorder**. The label is used for persons who previously had a depressive episode and now display a mild form of mania.

hypomanic episode A mood disorder marked by a period of ➤ **hypomania**.

hypomenorrhea A form of ➤ **dysmenorrhea** characterized by low volume of menstrual flow but with normally spaced periods.

hypometropia Shortsightedness or nearsightedness. ➤ **myopia**.

hypomnesia A general term for any impaired memory ability.

hypophoria Abnormal tendency for one eye to turn downward.

hypophrenia Mental deficiency, rarely used.

hypophysis ➤ **pituitary gland**.

hypoplasia Defective development of tissue generally producing a structurally diminished organ or organ part. adj., *hypoplastic*.

hypopolarization ➤ **depolarization**.

hyposmia Diminished smell sensitivity.

hyposthenia Subnormal strength, weakness.

349

hypotension 1. Diminished tension or tonus in a muscle or organ. **2.** A condition marked by an abnormally low blood pressure.

hypothalamic hormone Any of a number of hormones released by the neurosecretory cells of the hypothalamus. They are transported to the pituitary where they regulate the synthesis and release of the pituitary hormones.

hypothalamic-hypophyseal portal system A system of blood vessels that joins the capillaries of the hypothalamus with those of the anterior pituitary.

hypothalamic syndromes A general term for any behavioral syndrome that is hypothesized to result from damage to or dysfunction of a part of the hypothalamus. E.g., ➤ **lateral hypothalamic syndrome** and **ventromedial hypothalamic syndrome**.

hypothalamus A relatively small (peanut-sized) but extremely complex structure at the base of the brain (below the thalamus) that is intimately involved in control of the autonomic nervous system and a variety of functions that are crucially related to survival, including temperature regulation, heart rate, blood pressure, feeding behavior, water intake, emotional behavior and sexual behavior.

Anatomically the hypothalamus is divided into three subdivisions: (a) the *periventricular* region, containing many neurosecretory cells that serve as part of the control that the hypothalamus exerts over the pituitary gland; (b) the *medial* region, containing a number of hypothalamic nuclei including the supraoptic, paraventricular, dorsomedial and the important ventromedial (➤ **ventromedial hypothalamic syndrome**); and (c) the *lateral* region, containing a complex system of neural pathways (those of the medial forebrain bundle) and a collection of axons and cell bodies (see here ➤ **lateral hypothalamic syndrome** for discussion of function).

hypothermia Lowering of the body temperature.

hypothesis 1. In scientific work, any statement, proposition or assumption that serves as a tentative explanation of certain facts. A hypothesis is always presented so as to be amenable to empirical test and then either supported or rejected by the evidence. **2.** By extension, a strategy adopted in order to solve some problem. In most complex learning experiments such as those on problem-solving, concept-formation, decision-making and the like subjects typically display consistency from trial to trial, operating as it were on the basis of some hypothesis like, 'if conditions x and y are present I'll make response A, if not then I'll try B.' Strictly speaking, the hypothesis itself is an internal, covert event whose existence must be inferred from the subject's behavior. If the subject is a human being the inference is typically made on the basis of a verbal report from the subject to the effect that he or she *was*, in fact, using such and such a hypothesis – provided that the data from the experiment are in agreement with the verbal statement. If the subject is an animal (or inarticulate human, e.g., an infant) the inference becomes problematical. Much of contemporary learning research with lower species operates on the basis of these quasi-cognitive processes – producing no end of dispute with strict behaviorists. adj., *hypothetical*; vb., *hypothesize*.

hypothesis, null A ➤ **hypothesis** (1) of no difference, no relationship. In the standard hypothesis-testing approach to science one attempts to demonstrate the falsity of the null hypothesis, leaving one with the implication that the alternative, mutually exclusive, hypothesis is the acceptable one.

hypothetical construct As the term suggests, a ➤ **construct** that is hypothetical, i.e. some mechanism whose existence is inferred but for which unambiguous, objective evidence is not (yet?) available. Many critical theoretical entities are hypothetical constructs, black holes being an outstanding example in contemporary science. An interesting example from history is

Harvey's hypothesization of the existence of capillaries from his model of blood circulation. Their hypothetical status was only removed when the microscope verified their existence.

hypothetical syllogism ➤ syllogism.

hypothetico-deductive method A scientific method that focuses on, as the name implies, the deduction of hypotheses. Formally, the process begins with a set of undefined primitive terms or 'givens,' a set of newly defined terms and a set of postulates. It then proceeds, using logical deduction, to theorems and corollaries. Hypothetico-deductive systems are basically 'self-correcting': when new facts are found or new principles discovered that the hypothetical component cannot account for, the superstructure is revised by the modification of the postulate system. Newton's theory of classical mechanics is perhaps the best known and most formalized of such systems. In psychology, Clark L. Hull's herculean efforts to develop a systematic behavior theory (see here ➤ **Hullian**) were structured in terms of a hypothetico-deductive model.

hypothymia Lowered emotionality and depression.

hypothyroidism A deficit in secretions of the thyroid gland resulting in a subnormal metabolic rate. In adults the condition is characterized by weight gain, sluggishness and a tendency to tire easily. In infants, if untreated, it leads to cretinism.

hypotonia-obesity syndrome ➤ Prader–Willi syndrome.

hypotonic **1.** Of a solution whereby the osmotic pressures between it and a cell suspended in it are such that there is fluid transmission from the solution into the cell. **2.** Characteristic of a state of (muscular) relaxation. Contrast with ➤ **hypertonic**.

hypotrophy ➤ atrophy.

hypotropia Downward ➤ strabismus.

hypovolemia A reduction in the volume of extracellular fluid.

hypoxyphilia Deriving of sexual arousal by oxygen deprivation. Typically a noose or ligature is used to cut off oxygen as orgasm nears, although inhaling of volatile nitrates is also used since they diminish blood supply to the brain by peripheral vasodilation. Needless to say this is a rather dangerous ➤ **paraphilia** in which bad timing or equipment failure can lead to death.

hysteria Of all psychiatric disorders hysteria has the longest and most checkered history. Deriving originally from the ancient Greeks it was, until relatively recently, assumed to be solely a dysfunction of women and caused by a 'wandering' uterus (*hysteron* = uterus). Psychoanalytic theory helped in providing a more reasonable etiology, but the link between gender and the disorder was not completely severed: males were rarely so diagnosed. The symptoms that have been cited most often are: hallucinations, somnambulism, functional anesthesia, functional paralysis and dissociation.

The problems with a general classification like this with such an array of symptoms are enormous. The lack of understanding of the disorder may, quite possibly, be due to the fact that there is no single disorder here at all. In all likelihood what we have is a variety of maladaptive behaviors each of which exists more or less independently of the others with the hysterical syndrome existing only in the mind of the diagnostician. In the most recent edition of the ➤ **Diagnostic and Statistical Manual** there is no specific listing for hysteria, rather three, in principle distinguishable, categories of disorders are identified: ➤ **conversion disorder**, ➤ **dissociative disorder** and ➤ **factitious disorder**. Between them they encompass all of the classical symptoms. The oft-hypothesized personality type is now called ➤ **histrionic personality** (the Greek roots still are in evidence) and the acute psychotic form is identified as a ➤ **brief reactive psychosis**. See these terms for details on contemporary usage.

hysterical **1.** Pertaining to or characteriz-

351

ing the symptoms of *hysteria*. **2.** Characterizing or pertaining to functional disorders; e.g., hysterical blindness.

hysterical ataxia ➤ ataxia, hysterical.

hysterical blindness ➤ functional *blindness.

hysterical personality ➤ histrionic personality disorder.

hysteriform Resembling hysteria.

Hz Abbreviation for ➤ Hertz.

I

I Abbrev. for: **1.** *Inhibition*. The symbol has had quite a thorough work-out in ➤ **Hullian** theory. Some of the specialized forms that Hull hypothesized are: I_R = reactive inhibition, sI_R = inhibitory potential, $_sI_R$ = effective inhibitory potential. Other specialized uses of ➤ **inhibition** are found under that term. **2.** *Intensity*.

I That aspect of self which represents the knower of oneself, the component that, in William James's terms, 'is aware of the "me."' See discussion under ➤ **self**, especially 2.

-ia Suffix connoting *abnormal* or *diseased*.

-iasis Suffix meaning *state* or *condition*, used with the connotation of pathology. var., *-osis*.

-iatric Suffix meaning *healing, medical*.

iatric Pertaining to a physician or to medicine.

iatro- Combining form meaning *healing* or *medical*.

iatrogenic disorder A disorder produced by a physician. The term is used generally for any abnormal condition, physical or mental, that was caused by the effects of attempts at treatment. The connotation is that such problems could have been avoided, although such implications are not always fair. Classic examples are functional disorders produced by suggestion or by the anxiety associated with treatment, and drug related disorders (e.g., ➤ **drug-induced *Parkinsonism**).

iatrotropic stimulus The event or symptom that causes a person to seek medical attention. The term covers real symptoms and complaints as well as basically non-medical stimuli, e.g., a premarital examination.

-iatry Suffix meaning *medical* or *physical care*.

Icarus complex H. A. Murray's term for a syndrome characterized by fascination with fire, a history of bedwetting (➤ **urethral complex**), a desire to be immortal, narcissism and lofty but fragile ambition. The complex was named for the figure in Greek mythology who flew with his father on artificial wings and, against fatherly advice, flew too close to the sun. The wax in the wings melted and he plunged to his death.

ICD ➤ **International Classification of Diseases**.

icon ➤ **iconic**.

iconic 1. Characterizing an image, a pictorial representation of something, an idol. **2.** Characterizing a brief visual experience that lasts for a time (perhaps 2 seconds at most) after the termination of a bright stimulus. Often called *iconic memory*, it is considered by many to be one of a class of phenomena within the ➤ **sensory information store**. vars., *ikonic*, *eikonic*. The auditory analog is called *echoic*. n. *icon*.

iconic memory (or store) ➤ **iconic** (2) and **memory, iconic**.

iconic representation ➤ **ikonic representation**.

ICS Abbreviation for *intracranial stimulation*.

ICSH *Interstitial cell-stimulating hormone* ➤ **luteinizing hormone**.

ictal Sudden, abrupt; ictal emotions are transitory, fleeting emotions.

ictus 1. In medicine, a stroke. **2.** In speech, the accentuation of a syllable.

id In the Freudian tripartite model of mind, the primitive, animalistic, instinctual element, the pit of roiling, libidinous energy demanding immediate satisfaction. It is regarded as the deepest component of the psyche, the true unconscious. Entirely self-contained and isolated from the world about it, it is bent on achieving its own aims. The sole governing device here is the pleasure principle, the id being represented as the ultimate hedonist. The task of restraining this single-minded entity is a major part of the ego's function.

All three components of psychoanalytic psyche are, of course, metapsychological constructs. The id is a kind of biological metaphor, a descriptive device. The language of many psychoanalytic writers, however, has led to a kind of personalization, a reification that is unwarranted, unfortunate and misleading. Freud himself was quite clear on this point; the concept of the id should be used only as a descriptive characterization of a system of actions and behaviors. ➤➤ ego, superego.

idea 1. In Plato, the intellectual equivalent to form. An idea in this sense is what is seen, mentally, via one's intellectual vision. In the pure Platonic sense, only ideas are real and they are often capitalized to emphasize this. For example, there is no genuine triangle presented to one's senses; the true, the real triangle is the idea Triangle in the mind. **2.** In Descartes, the notion of this 'true' idea is dropped. Here it became that which is *perceived directly* in the mind. This point of view carries over into the work of Locke and was developed richly by various of the British empiricists. **3.** In contemporary cognitive psychology the term is still used in roughly this fashion. That is, an idea is a mental event, a brain state underlies it, and it is derived in some fashion from experience. In this sense it is treated as being related to the 'real world' with the presumption that the idea itself is the result of some as yet unknown processing of information that yields the phenomenal experience. **4.** In layman's terms, a plan, a scheme, an opinion, an insight, etc.

ideal 1. An abstract representation of the fundamental characteristics of something. **2.** A strived-for goal, one that is

highly desirable. Often used with the connotation that it may not be attainable. This meaning is often carried into theories of personality; e.g., ➤ idealized *self.

idealism 1. A philosophical doctrine that holds that the ultimate reality is mental and that this mental representation forms the basis of all experience and knowledge. From this point of view it is meaningless to speak of the existence of things independent of their perception and experiencing by a conscious observer. Contrast with ➤ realism (2). **2.** An attitude characterized by high personal and societal goals and the general attempt to attain them. Contrast with ➤ realism (3).

idealization 1. In psychoanalytic theory, a defense mechanism in which an object about which one is ambivalent is split into two conceptual representations, one wholly bad and one completely, ideally good. **2.** More generally, the process of dealing with conflict or stress by attributing exaggerated positive qualities to others.

idealized image ➤ image, idealized.

idealized self ➤ self, idealized.

ideal observer A theoretical, perfect observer whose sensory and perceptual systems operate without error and devoid of bias. The notion is used in discussion of sensory and perceptual systems as an abstraction against which to compare a 'real' observer.

ideas of reference A sense that events and incidents occurring about one have a particular meaning that is special to the individual. Distinguish from ➤ delusions of reference.

ideational Pertaining to ideas, to cognitive processes.

ideational agnosia ➤ agnosia, ideational.

ideational apraxia ➤ apraxia, ideational.

ideational fluency A term suggested by Wallach to cover the range of cognitive processes generally subsumed under the label ➤ **divergent *thinking**. It hasn't really 'caught on.'

ideational learning ➤ **learning, ideational**.

idée fixe French for *fixed idea*. A firmly held idea that is maintained without rational reflection and despite the manifest existence of sufficient contrary evidence to persuade a reasonable person of its untenability. Janet used the term to represent an aspect of a neurosis that interfered with the normal flow of information by restricting the individual's attentional capacities.

id-ego 1. Within orthodox psychoanalytic theory, the primitive unit from which the separate id and ego become differentiated. However: **2.** In various other psychoanalytic approaches, a *single* entity whose opposing functions are those of the id and ego, at least as those functions are represented in the classical model. It is difficult to see how one of these two positions could provide greater explanatory power than the other.

identical-elements theory The generalization originally proposed by Thorndike that the degree of transfer of learning that occurs between two tasks is a function of the number of common elements they share.

identical retinal points Any two points, one on each retina, that receive stimulation from the same objective point at infinite distance. Distinguish from ➤ **congruent retinal points**.

identical twins ➤ **monozygotic *twins**.

identification 1. A mental operation whereby one attributes to oneself, either consciously or unconsciously, the characteristics of another person or group. The notion of ➤ **transference** is central here. **2.** A process of establishing a link between oneself and another person or group. Although similar to 1, the connotation of this usage is closer to that of ➤ **affiliation**. **3.** An act of recognizing similarity or identity between events, objects or persons. Here the notions of *labeling* and *classifying* are

roughly synonymous. There are variations on all of these and in many instances a single use has more than one of them; e.g., the common expression, 'identification with the aggressor.'

identity 1. In the study of personality, a person's essential, continuous self, the internal, subjective concept of oneself as an individual. Usage here is often qualified; e.g., *sex-role identity*, *racial* or *group identity*, etc. **2.** In logic, a relation between two or more elements such that either may be substituted for the other in a syllogism without altering its truth value. **3.** Somewhat more loosely, a 'deep' relationship between elements that is assumed to exist despite surface dissimilarities. This meaning is typically qualified to express the level at which the identity is found; e.g., *functional identity*. **4.** Within Piagetian theory, a state of awareness that the relationship described in 3 holds. The classic example here is the case of the child who is aware that a liquid maintains its 'deep' identity even though it undergoes various transformations such as being poured from one container to another of different shape. ➤ **conservation**.

identity crisis An acute loss of the sense of one's identity, a lack of the normal feeling that one has historical continuity, that the person here today is phenomenologically the same as the one here yesterday.

identity formation Quite literally, the forming of one's own ➤ **identity** (1). Most theorists hold to the point of view that mature identity formation emerges when various early, more primitive identifications and influences are rejected.

identity theory In the philosophy of mind, a variation of the more general position of ➤ **physicalism**. The strong form of identity theory (more properly called *type*-identity theory) argues that every mental event or mental state is identical with a particular brain state, an in principle specifiable physiological (i.e. physical) event. Moreover, the theory defends the extension that when two persons share something mental (e.g., both believe that water is wet or both image a dog or both desire to understand psychology) they also have in common in principle specifiable equivalent physical (brain) states. Note that it is this logical extension that earned the label *type* theory, for here *types* of mental events are assumed to correspond to *types* of physical events. Without this extension one has (merely) a *token* identity theory, which is a considerably weaker position, in which only specific, individual (*token*) mental states are assumed to reflect these equivalences.

ideo- Combining form from the Greek, meaning *idea* or *mental image*. Distinguish from *idio-*.

ideogram ➤ logography.

ideokinetic apraxia ➤ apraxia, ideokinetic.

ideomotor act An overt act initiated by an idea.

ideomotor apraxia ➤ apraxia, ideomotor.

idio- Combining form from the Greek *idios*. The general connotation is something *personal*, *private*, *self-produced* and, by extension, *unique* or *distinct*. Distinguish from ➤ ideo-.

idiocy Severe mental deficiency. The term ➤ **idiot** from which it derives is obsolescent (➤ **mental deficiency** and **mental retardation** for discussions of nomenclature) but *idiocy* itself survives in a number of combined forms chiefly of a medical or psychiatric nature identifying syndromes named years ago, e.g. *amaurotic* (*familial*) *idiocy*.

idioglossia ➤ cryptophasia.

idiographic Relating to or dealing with the concrete, the individual, the unique. A psychological system or theory with this orientation is labeled an idiographic approach. The opposite of ➤ **nomothetic**.

idiom Any expression with a special meaning that cannot be determined from the meanings of its component parts.

idiopathic. 1. In medicine, any primary pathological condition. That is, one arising within the affected organ and not as a result of external dysfunctions. **2.** Of any disorder of unknown etiology.

idiopathic epilepsy ➤ epilepsy, idiopathic.

idioretinal light A vague gray perceived in conditions of total darkness with the eyes completely dark adapted. The term is generally used by those who argue that this percept is the result of metabolic processes within the retina; *cortical gray* is the term of choice of those who maintain that cortical action is responsible. The shortened form, *retinal light*, is also found.

idiosyncratic alcohol intoxication ➤ alcohol intoxication, idiosyncratic.

idiot From the Greek *idiotes* which translates roughly as a *person in a totally private state*, *one without knowledge*; by extension, then, an ignorant person. The term is little used today: ➤ **profound *mental retardation** is preferred. ➤ **mental deficiency** for a discussion of this and related terms.

idiotropic Lit., turning inward. *Introspective* is an acceptable synonym, *introverted* is not as it tends to have negative connotations.

idiot savant ➤ savant.

I/E ratio A ratio of the rate of inspiration to the rate of expiration. It is often used as a measure of emotionality with a low number taken as indicative of high arousal.

I.E. scale **1.** A scale of *introversion–extraversion* derived from the ➤ **MMPI**. **2.** A scale that measures the degree to which a person is internally or externally motivated. Usually abbreviated as *I–E scale* to differentiate it from 1. ➤ **locus of control** and ➤ **internal–external scale**.

ikonic ➤ ikonic representation and iconic.

ikonic representation A term introduced by J. Bruner in his theory of the development of representational thought. Ikonic representations are mental representations that are limited to and, almost by definition, correspond to that which is perceptual. That is, they are more sophisticated forms of representation than the ➤ enactive, which are essentially sensory-motor in form, but less so than the ➤ symbolic, which are abstract in form.

il- Prefix used synonymously in some contexts with ➤ in-; e.g., *illicit*.

illegitimate 1. Generally, of things that violate accepted standards, especially sexual standards. 2. Specifically, of children born out of wedlock. Somehow this latter use seems rather unfair – because one's parents chose not to conform to societal mores hardly seems grounds for stigmatizing the offspring.

illicit Generally, not authorized, not permitted. Hence: 1. Not accepted by a culture or not sanctioned by a group. 2. In law, contrary to established legal principle, illegal.

Illinois Test of Psycholinguistic Abilities (ITPA) A test designed to assess psycholinguistic disabilities in children. Constructed along the lines of the theory of communication of Charles Osgood, it has three components, one dealing with communication *channels* (auditory/vocal and visual/motor), one with *processes* (receptive, organizational and expressive) and one with *levels* (representational and automatic). The full battery consists of 10 regular subtests with an additional two optional subtests and is designed for use with children from ages 2 to 10.

illiteracy Generally (and loosely), the inability to read and write where such inability is not the result of either organic dysfunction or mental retardation. Tightening up this loose definition is, however, difficult. Various criteria have been proposed over the years; (a) inability to read at all; (b) inability to read at a particular average school-year level (school years from 2 through 6 have been suggested); (c) inability to read and follow the directions on the typical government form. Depending on which is selected the socio-political 'hot potato' of the national illiteracy rate can be made to mean many different things. ➤➤ reading.

illocutionary act ➤ speech act.

illuminance The light actually falling on a surface. When the source is perpendicular to the surface, illuminance varies with the power of the source and inversely with the square of the distance of the surface from the source. When the source is at an angle with the surface a correction given by *Lambert's cosine law* is made.

illusion Basically, any stimulus situation where that which is perceived cannot be predicted, prima facie, by a simple analysis of the physical stimulus. Often one sees illusions characterized as 'mistaken perceptions,' a designation that is not really correct and misses the point. *Mach bands*, for example, are illusions but they are not 'mistaken perceptions.' Rather, they are perceptions that result from certain retinal and/or cortical processes that cannot be predicted simply from the stimulus itself. If there is a 'mistake' involved it is on the part of psychologists who don't as yet understand the mechanisms that produce the illusions. For a better understanding of the problems here see the separate entries for some of the more common illusions: ➤ Hering, Mach bands, moon, Müller-Lyer, Poggendorff, etc.

Note that the concept of illusion is kept separate from those of ➤ hallucination and ➤ delusion. Illusions are normal, relatively consistent phenomena found across observers and are subject to regular rules. Hallucinations are quite idiosyncratic and despite their compelling sense of reality do not follow interpersonal patterns. Delusions are best thought of as mistaken beliefs. adj., *illusory*.

illusion of control The belief that one has more control over events than one actually does.

illusory conjunction In perception, a phenomenon in which particular features are seen as belonging to the wrong objects. It occurs when stimuli with several features are flashed rapidly, such as a red curved line and a green straight line. The subject will occasionally see a green curved line or a red straight one.

illusory contour ➤ subjective *contour.

illusory correlation A perceived strong association between variables that is either not there or considerably smaller than one believes it is. Some theorists argue that the tendency for people to form such illusory correlations helps to explain the development and persistence of stereotypes and the prejudice that results from them.

im- Prefix connoting *not*.

image The term derives from the Latin for *imitation* and most usages in psychology, both obsolete and contemporary, revolve around this notion. Hence, common synonyms are *likeness, copy, reproduction, duplicate*, etc. Several important variations on this theme are found: **1.** *Optical image* is the most concrete use and refers specifically to the reflection of an object by a mirror, lens or other optical device. **2.** By extension, the *retinal image* is the (approximate) point-by-point picture of an object cast on the retina when light is refracted by the eye's optical system. **3.** Within structuralism, one of the three subclasses of consciousness – the others being *sensations* and *affections*. The thrust of this use was to treat the image as a mental representation of an earlier sensory experience, a copy of it. The copy was considered to be less vivid than the sensory experience but still consciously recognizable as a memory of it. This particular sense of the term has been carried forward into contemporary cognitive psychology where an image is viewed as, putting it somewhat crudely, **4.** a picture in the head. This rather commonsensical notion actually captures fairly well the essence of the term in most contemporary usage but some caveats must be made: (a) The 'picture' is not a literal one – there is no slide-projector/screen arrangement – but rather a kind of 'as if' picture. That is, imagery is a cognitive process that operates 'as if' one had a mental picture that was an analog of a real-world scene. (b) The image is not necessarily treated as a reproduction of an earlier event but rather as a construction, a synthesis. In this sense an image is no longer viewed as a copy; for example, one can image a unicorn driving a motorcycle, which is rather unlikely to be a copy of any previously seen stimulus. (c) This picture in the head seems to be mentally 'adjustable' so that one can image, for example, the unicorn driving its cycle toward you, away from you, around in circles, etc. (d) The picture is not necessarily restricted to visual representation – although this is surely the most common forum for the term to be used in. For example, one can elaborate an auditory image (try forming an image of some well-known tune), a tactile image (image a design of, say, a triangle pressed on your back), etc. Some people claim to even have gustatory and olfactory images. Because of these extensions the term is frequently qualified to indicate the form of image under discussion. Finally, (e) this pattern of usage encroaches on the meaning of an etymologically related term, ➤ imagination.

While these are the dominant uses others are found: **5.** A general attitude toward some institution as in, 'the image of China to westerners.' **6.** The elements of dreams. **7.** As a verb, *to image* means to create an image. Although used as synonym of *to imagine*, the latter can also connote flights of fancy which are generally precluded in the former. That is, despite the subtle overlap between image and imagination, to image something is not, strictly speaking, the same mental act as to imagine something.

image, auditory An image in the auditory system. ➤ image, especially 4(d).

image, fixed ➤ stabilized image.

image, hypnopompic ➤ hypnopompic image.

image, idealized 1. Generally, an inappropriate sense of one's positive aspects. In classical psychoanalysis it is assumed to develop as a defense against the demands of the *ego ideal*. **2.** In K. Horney's theory, a neurotic, unconsciously held image of oneself. Identification with this idealized image results, in her theory, in the development of an *idealized *self*.

imageless thought The reference here is to a theoretical and empirical debate between the Würzburg school (➤ **act psychology**) and orthodox ➤ **structuralism** (1) over whether or not all thought processes were based upon images. Although the issue was never fully resolved, the fact that under the same stimulus conditions the Würzburgers found no evidence for images and the structuralists found traces of sensory images did not augur well for the method of introspection.

imagery In the most inclusive sense the term refers to the whole imaging process. Often it will refer to only the actual images themselves. The whole question of exactly what is being connoted by terms like *image* and *imagery* is most complex; see the discussion under ➤ **image**.

image, visual An image in the visual system. Because so much of imagery seems to involve vision, this term is often taken as equivalent to ➤ **image**. However, see that term, especially 4(d).

imaginal Pertaining to ➤ **image** or to ➤ **imagination**, although usually the former is intended, *imaginary* being the preferred adjectival form for imagination.

imaginary companion An 'invisible' friend, an 'unseen' playmate created by a young child and treated as real. The mythical friend may be very vivid, have a name, stable personality, characteristics and mannerisms of action, and play an important role in the child's life.

imagination The process of recombining memories of past experiences and previously formed images into novel constructions. See here ➤ **image** (4(b)). This term is used in the technical literature very much as it is in the common language. That is, imagination is treated as creative and constructive, it may be primarily wishful or largely reality-bound, it may involve future plans and projections or be mental 'reviews' of the past. Often qualifiers are appended for clarity; e.g., *anticipatory* for the future, *reproductive* for the past, *creative* for the novel, etc.

imagine 1. To engage in the mental process of imagination. 2. An approximate synonym for the verb *to image*, although ➤ **image** (7).

imago 1. In biology, an adult, sexually mature insect or the mature stage of insect life. Used particularly of those forms which undergo a metamorphosis. 2. A term used by Freud to refer to unconscious representations of other persons, typically a parent with whom one identifies closely. Psychoanalytic theory conceptualizes the imago as being formed very early in life and, hence, it is usually an idealized representation and not necessarily reflective of the true person.

imbecile From the Latin *imbecillus* meaning *weak* or *weak-minded*. It is little used today; ➤ **mental deficiency** and **mental retardation**.

imipramine A ➤ **tricyclic compound** used as an ➤ **antidepressant**. It is a noradrenergic and serotonergic antagonist and functions by retarding the re-uptake of norepinephrine and serotonin.

imitation The process of copying the behavior of others. Imitation tends to be used with the sense of intentionality, the one imitating wants to and is trying to model his or her actions on those of another. Distinguish this connotation from that of the related term ➤ **mimicry**. The term also tends to be used so as to imply that the imitative actions are rote and mechanical, a characterization that somehow seems somewhat misleading. A child who imitates his/her mother's way of walking or who adopts his/her peer group's social-interactive manners at play is not 'just imitating.' Such learned behaviors are most complex and mechanical processes are clearly inadequate as explanations or even descriptions. Imitation of this kind involves the notion that the child must know, in some implicit fashion, the underlying rules that govern the social patterns of his/her peer group. ➤ **modelling**, which is the term preferred by many because of the simplistic connotations associated with imitation.

immature 1. Not mature, not fully developed. This meaning is basically descriptive and evaluatively neutral. 2. Displaying less-well-developed traits and characteristics than the norm for one's age. This meaning carries clear negative connotations. The term is found with both meanings in a variety of contexts including the biological and physiological and the emotional, cognitive and social.

immediate 1. Without delay. 2. Without intervening (i.e. ➤ **mediate**) processes.

immediate association ➤ **association, immediate**.

immediate constituent In linguistics a *constituent* is any word or sentential construction that is part of a larger linguistic unit. An *immediate constituent* is any constituent out of which a construction on the next level is directly formed. Lest this sound too obtuse; an example will help. In the sentence, 'The tiger who grew old ate the zoo keeper,' each word is a constituent, as is 'who grew old', but 'old ate' is not (it bridges two phrases); similarly, 'The tiger' and 'who grew old' are immediate constituents since they are part of the higher level unit 'The tiger who grew old.'

immediate experience Early structuralists distinguished between *mediate* and *immediate experience*. Immediate experience was made up of the pure, momentary elements of a perception; mediate experience was an inference or coordinated perception derived from previous learning. If, for example, you look at a table and 'see' a pattern of granularity, roughly trapezoidal in shape, with regular shadows around the edge, etc. you are introspecting on immediate experience; if, however, you 'see' a *table* you are introspecting on mediate experience. Within orthodox ➤ **structuralism** (1), immediate experience was regarded as the proper focus of an experimental psychology, a point of view hotly disputed by, among others, the ➤ **Gestalt psychology** proponents.

immediate memory ➤ **memory, immediate**.

immobility 1. Generally, a state in which there is no visible motion. 2. In ethology, a shortened form of ➤ **tonic immobility**.

immune reactions, nonspecific Immune reactions that are general and do not involve specific antibodies. The ➤ **inflammatory reaction** is a good example.

immune reactions, specific Immune reactions that target specific invader cells. The system learns to recognize the proteins that mark invader organisms and produces specific antibodies (*immunoglobulins*) that attack and kill them. There are actually two systems here, one based on antibodies released into the circulation by the *B-lymphocytes* which develop in bone marrow and the other by the *T-lymphocytes* which develop in the thymus.

immune system A highly complex system that functions to protect the body from infection. It derives its capabilities from white blood cells that develop in bone marrow and the thymus gland.

immunoglobulins A family of five closely related proteins that function as antibodies.

impairment Generally, any loss of or decrement in function. More specifically, such loss or decrement due to injury or disease.

imperative A ➤ **speech act** in which the speaker directly commands or orders the listener to do something.

imperceptible Of a stimulus that is too low in intensity to be perceived; of a stimulus below ➤ **threshold**.

impersonal Characterizing: 1. An objective attitude, a point of view not concerned with personal feelings. 2. A lack of concern with persons.

impersonation Conscious and deliberate assumption of the identity of another.

implantation 1. In placental mammals, the attaching of the embryo to the uterine wall. 2. In physiological psychology, the placement of an electrode in the brain or other tissue of an experimental animal.

implicit 1. Not explicit, hence of something not directly observable. Watson used it in this sense to refer to the subtle muscular and glandular responses that he argued underlay conscious processes such as thinking (which he assumed to be subvocal speech). **2.** Unconscious, covert, tacit, hence of a process that takes place largely outside of the awareness of the individual. The term is used in this sense to characterize cognitive processes that operate independently of consciousness. ➤ **implicit *learning** and ➤ **implicit *memory**.

implicit learning ➤ learning, implicit.

implicit memory ➤ memory, implicit.

implicit personality theory Not a theory in the scientific sense, it is the unconsciously held 'theory' that most laypeople have about the personalities of others. Basically they establish a complex web of assumptions about the traits and behaviors of others and assume that they will act in accordance with those assumptions. Because people hold such views, they are often shocked to discover that some well-loved, gentle neighbor has committed a violent crime – such an act did not fit with their implicit personality profile of that person.

implicit speech ➤ subvocalization.

implosion 1. Generally, a collapsing inward. **2.** Laing extended the term to cover the fear of having one's identity destroyed. It is assumed to result from a sense of emptiness, of vacuousness and the feeling that whatever reality 'fills' this void will annihilate one's fragile sense of identity and reality.

implosion therapy A procedure in which the client is flooded with experiences of a particular kind to such a dramatic degree that he/she either (a) builds up a distinct aversion to them or (b) becomes numbed and no longer responds to them. Outcome (a) is what is hoped for in the use of the technique with habits that one wishes to break, e.g., smoking continuously ciga-

rette after cigarette until the very sight or even thought of a cigarette makes one feel sick. Outcome (b) is the one planned for when the technique is used for phobic disorders where presentation of the phobic stimulus is continued until it no longer evokes the disabling anxiety. Also called *flooding*.

impotence 1. Most generally, lack of potency, weakness, powerlessness. **2.** Specifically, male failure to copulate. ➤ **primary *impotence** and **secondary *impotence**. Currently the term ➤ **male erectile disorder** is recommended as the general label for meaning (2); however, even in the technical literature, the term 'impotence' is still widely used.

impotence, orgasmic ➤ orgasm disorders.

impotence, primary Total coital dysfunction in the sense that there is an inability to achieve or maintain an erection sufficient for coitus on the first and all subsequent attempts. Compare with ➤ **secondary *impotence**.

impotence, psychogenic ➤ impotence (2) in the absence of any organic dysfunction.

impotence, secondary A form of ➤ **psychogenic *impotence**. Unlike ➤ **primary *impotence**, it is difficult to define, because one wishes to differentiate between a male who experiences occasional coital failure and the one for whom it is common enough to pose a problem. The criterion usually accepted is failure to maintain erection sufficient for coitus on 25% (or more) of the attempts. Note, however, that imposing this simple criterion fails to capture important aspects of the syndrome since for many males the impotence is specific to certain individual sex objects or particular situations.

impoverished 1. Of stimuli that have been degraded or occluded so that they are difficult to detect or recognize. ➤ **masking**. **2.** Characterizing any stimulus display or stimulus environment that fails to present all of the variations that it could properly display. For example, the language that an infant hears is argued to be impoverished in that not all of the rules of grammar that the child ultimately comes to be able to use are displayed in it.

impression 1. The presumed neural effects of stimulation. This use is a kind of physiological metaphor for whatever it is that occurs in the brain. **2.** A loosely held belief or judgement; ➤ **impression forma-tion**.

impression formation The coordinating of various bits and pieces of information into a general integrated ➤ **impression** (2). The term is most often used in social psychology with regard to the various 'bits and pieces' of interpersonal perception that give rise to the impression formed of other persons but, strictly speaking, the meaning applies to other psychological domains as well.

impression management Generally and loosely, the full array of devices that people use both consciously and unconsciously in an effort to influence the impression that others have of them.

impression-management theory In *social psychology* the theory that many of our actions are motivated not by a motive to *be* consistent but by a desire to *appear to be* consistent.

imprinting An ethological term used to characterize a kind of ➤ **restricted *learning** that takes place rapidly, within a relatively compressed time span, is exceedingly resistant to extinction or reversal and has a profound and lasting effect on later social behavior with respect to the stimulus objects for the behavior. The classic example is the following response in ducks where a newly hatched duckling will 'imprint' on and follow an object (usually the mother) that it is exposed to during the critical period.

imprinting, negative ➤ **Imprinting** that produces an avoidance of the animal or object rather than an approach or following reaction. ➤ **inbreeding avoidance**.

impulse This term has a variety of uses all of which revolve around the core mean-

ing: **1.** Any act or event 'triggered' by a stimulus and occurring with short latency and with little or no conscious control or direction. Hence, following this general theme: **2.** Any sudden incitement to act; i.e. the internal state that initiates the action in 1 as in 'an impulse to flee.' **3.** In psychoanalytic theory, an instinctual act of the id. **4.** In physiology, a self-propagating excitatory state transmitted along a neural fiber. ➤ **action potential**. **5.** (Rare) An awareness of an ➤ **impulsion**.

impulse-control disorders A class of disorders all marked by failure to resist an impulse or temptation to engage in some act that ultimately proves harmful to oneself. Generally included here are ➤ **pathologi-cal *gambling**, ➤ **kleptomania**, ➤ **pyromania** and ➤ **explosive disorders**. Typically the individual feels a highly increased sense of tension prior to the act and a pleasurable, gratifying feeling afterward. Guilt may or may not be experienced following the act.

impulsion A state of great urgency in which one is highly susceptible to performing an impulsive act. Differentiate from ➤ **compulsion**.

impulsive A general term used of acts carried out without reflection or of the person prone to such acts. ➤ **impulse** and **impulse-control disorders**.

impulsivity ➤ **reflectivity–impulsivity**.

impunitive Characterizing the tendency to react to frustration by assessing the events that led to it without necessarily focusing anger or blame either internally (see here ➤ **intropunitive**) or externally (see here ➤ **extrapunitive**).

in- (**ir-** before words beginning with *r*) Prefix connoting *not* or *lack of*. The usages of terms like *inattention* and *incomprehensible* are straightforward; terms with specialized meanings are given below.

inaccessibility A state of psychological remoteness in which one is unresponsive to ordinary social stimuli. Seen in cases of autism, severe depression and some forms of schizophrenia.

inaccessible memory ➤ **memory, inaccessible**.

inadequacy Most broadly, any inferiority, incompetence or the feeling of such. In usage the term is typically qualified to specify the type of inadequacy; e.g., *sexual*, *intellectual*, etc.

inadequate personality A loose label applied to a person who displays a rather broad range of inadequacies and has a long history of failure.

inadequate stimulus ➤ **stimulus, inadequate**.

inanition 1. General physical weakness due to lack of proper nutrition. 2. Emptiness.

inappropriateness of affect ➤ **appropriateness of *affect**.

inborn Innate, inherited; of characteristics that result from genetic factors.

inbreeding 1. In genetics, the mating or interbreeding (a better term really) of those closely related. Often used in animals to develop a strain with particular hereditary characteristics; most laboratory animals are the result of many generations of careful inbreeding. 2. More metaphorically, a confinement of intellectual or social resources resulting from interactions limited to those individuals with a particular intellectual or social orientation.

inbreeding avoidance The tendency to avoid mating with close relatives. Various mechanisms have been proposed to explain the phenomenon, from cultural systems such as the incest taboo (➤ **incest**) to precultural, genetically determined systems found in many animals such as *dispersion*, where the young leave the home or nest and hence do not have the opportunity to mate with close relatives, and *negative imprinting*, where the young learn to avoid mating with those they have been raised with. ➤➤ **outbreeding**.

incentive Several variations on this term are found – all reflect the underlying notion that an incentive is a *motivator* of

behavior. Indeed, some learning theorists use the hybrid phrase 'incentive motivation' to ensure that this connotation is not missed. Hence: 1. An inducement to respond. In this sense incentives are conditions or objects that are perceived as satisfiers of some need. Water has incentive value for a thirsty organism. 2. A supplemental reward that functions by maintaining behavior prior to reaching the primary goal. Weight watchers' clubs use incentives in this way. 3. A synonym for *value*; the greater the value of an object, the greater is its perceived incentive. Note that here there is a close tie between incentive and the notions of ➤ **drive** and ➤ **need**. That is, the level of the drive state determines the incentive; food has little or no incentive for a satiated organism.

incest Sexual relations between 'close' relatives. 'Close' is defined differently for different cultures although almost all appear to have some form of prohibition against it, the so-called *incest taboo*. Several theories have been proposed to account for this near universality. Some focus on genetic factors, pointing out that the taboo helps to prevent maladaptive, recessive genes from appearing in the population. Others focus on social factors, arguing that the taboo arose because having more than one close, sexual relationship in a family is a fragile and potentially explosive arrangement. However, many nonhuman species have also developed strategies that help accomplish the same end as our incest taboos; ➤ **inbreeding avoidance**. adj., *incestuous*.

incest barrier A psychoanalytic term for the psychosocial prohibitions that operate within a family to free libido from its Oedipal attachment to the opposite-sexed parent and permit the child to become gradually freed from familial ties.

incest taboo ➤ **incest**.

incidence Frequency of occurrence of an event or a condition in relation to the population under examination.

incidental learning ➤ **learning, incidental**.

incidental tests ➤ **post hoc tests**.

incident region ➤ **region, incident**.

inclusive fitness In evolutionary biology, the total measure of the various strategies that an organism may use to ensure genetic success. Inclusive fitness is made up of one's own ➤ **personal fitness** (getting one's own genes into the pool, one's personal reproductive success) plus the ➤ **kin selection** strategy (elevating the reproductive success of a close biological relative).

incommensurable Of two variables having no common measure or standard of comparison.

incompatible The general dictionary meaning – incapable of existing together in harmony – applies in the psychological uses. Thus, one speaks of *incompatible responses* as those which cannot occur at the same time, e.g., anxiety and relaxation; of *incompatible persons* as those whose values or styles conflict so sharply that they cannot associate freely with each other; of *incompatible judgements* as those that cannot both be true, etc.

incompetent 1. Generally, lacking in qualifications, capacities or abilities. **2.** More specifically, a designation for an individual judged to be incapable of making rational judgements and choices and hence not legally responsible. See and compare with ➤ **competent**.

incomplete-pictures test A test in which the subject is shown a series of incomplete pictures of objects, each successive one revealing more of the object. The task is to identify the object as early in the series as possible. It is assumed to measure visual organization and/or set and is occasionally used as a diagnostic tool.

incomplete-sentences test A projective test in which the subject is required to complete sentences like, 'When I am depressed I –' or 'When angry I –.' The responses may be used as a vehicle for leading the subject into discussing a topic that his or her answers suggest is psycho-

logically important or they may be analyzed for the projection of unconscious themes. Distinguish from ➤ **sentence-completion test**.

incontinence Lack of restraint, of ability to hold back. Although the term may be applied broadly (e.g., on occasion one will see it applied to excessive speaking) it usually refers to an inability to hold back bodily functions such as urination, defecation and sexual impulses.

incorporation The roots reveal the general sense of the term: *in-* = *into*, *corpora* = *body*; thus, an act of taking something into the body and, by extension, into the psyche or the self. Hence: **1.** Generally, the ingestion of foodstuffs. **2.** The inculcation of a belief or an attitude. **3.** In psychoanalysis, a primitive defense mechanism operating as fantasy in which a person or part is ingested (figuratively, of course). Distinguish this last meaning from ➤ **internalization** and ➤ **introjection**.

increment Generally, any increase in anything can safely be called an increment.

incremental validity ➤ **validity, incremental**.

incubation 1. A period of brooding required to bring something to a point where it has form and substance. This is the root meaning. **2.** In biology, the period required to bring an egg to hatching. **3.** In cognitive psychology, a period of time during which no conscious effort is made to solve a problem but which terminates with the solution.

incubus A demon supposed to descend upon one during sleep; hence, by extension, a nightmare.

incus One of the three small bones in the middle ear. ➤ **ossicles**.

indecency Obviously, characterizing that which is not decent. Decency, however, is culturally defined and the standards within one society may differ rather dramatically from those in another. Generally, the term is used so that the acceptable degree of exposure of the body is the primary concern.

independence 1. Most generally, a state existing between variables such that there is no significant, relevant correlational or causal relationship between them. In statistical terms this is expressed by stating that changes in one variable are not systematically accompanied by changes in another. 2. In probability theory, a property of two events x and y such that the probability of the occurrence of x is unaffected by the occurrence of y and vice versa. For example, in a random number table each entry is independent of all other entries in just this fashion. 3. In logic, the characteristic of a proposition whose truth is not contingent on the truth of particular other propositions. 4. An autonomous attitude in which one is (relatively) free of the influence of the judgements, opinions or beliefs of others.

independent variable ➤ variable, independent.

indeterminate 1. In mathematics, of values that are not or cannot be determined (i.e. fixed). 2. Occasionally, ➤ underdetermined.

indeterminism A cover term for any doctrine antithetical to ➤ determinism. ➤ free will (1), the most oft-proposed of these.

index 1. Most generally, something used to note, identify, guide or direct; an indication, sign or token. 2. A formula or number, often expressed as a ratio, that notes some relationship between measures or dimensions or one between a measure and a fixed standard. 3. In mathematics, an exponent or an integer in a radical indicating the root. 4. In statistics, a *variable*. Note, however, that the two are not really interchangeable; *index* is used for cases where precision and unambiguous quantification are lacking; e.g., in *stage theories* the various levels of development are taken as indices of some theoretical variable (perhaps cognitive sophistication) but are not properly called variables. 5. By extension of 1 and 4, any measurable

or observable value that can be assessed fairly directly and rigorously and used as an indicator of some other value that cannot be so determined. For example, occupation and income are taken as indices of social status. Note that there is an interesting terminological wrinkle here; in sociology and social psychology some authors will use *indicator* for a single value used in this manner and reserve *index* for a complex set of such indicators. pls., *indices*, *indexes*; adjs., *index*, *indexical*.

index case ➤ proband.

index of variability Lit., any measure of ➤ dispersion. Typically the reference is to the ➤ standard deviation.

indicant Any event used as a token or sign of some other event. Rapid pulse and high GSR (galvanic skin response), for example, are indicants of high arousal. In testing, a score on a psychological test is treated as an indicant of the thing the test is supposed to be measuring. Also called ➤ indicator (1).

indicator 1. ➤ indicant. 2. ➤ index, especially (5).

indices Plural of ➤ index.

indifference Used in essence synonymously with *neutrality*. An *indifferent stimulus* is one that does not elicit a conditioned response; it is neutral with respect to the CR. A *state of indifference* is that when one has no preferences between alternative choices or courses of action. An *indifference point* is the value on some continuum or dimension that represents neutrality.

indigenous Native to a particular geographical area.

indirect 1. Circuitous, not in a straight line, not direct. 2. Mediated, used of things linked by intermediary steps or transformations.

indirect correlation ➤ negative *correlation.

indirect directive A ➤ speech act in which the order or directive is syntactically of another form. For example, 'Do you know what time it is?' is usually taken as a request for the time (and a request not easily denied in most social situations) even though syntactically the utterance has the form of a simple 'yes-no' question. 'It's hot in here' can be an indirect directive to another person to open a window, although here the form of the utterance is that of a simple statement concerning temperature. Unlike ➤ **directives**, this class of speech acts exerts effects in strictly indirect ways and follows fairly complex social and interpersonal rules.

indirect scaling ➤ scaling, indirect.

indirect speech act Any ➤ **speech act** expressed by a construction superficially designed for a function other than the one actually intended. ➤ **indirect directive** for an example of a common form.

indissociation In Piaget's theory, a very early stage of development in which cognitive and perceptual systems are relatively undifferentiated.

individual differences A label used for an approach to psychological phenomena that focuses on characteristics or traits along which individual organisms may be shown to differ. Also called ➤ **differential psychology**.

individualism 1. Personality traits, attitudes or behaviors that reflect personal independence; freedom from the attitudes and opinions of others. Note, this meaning can reflect either a positive connotation, in that one who displays it stands above (or at least outside of) social and peer pressure, or a negative connotation, in that the set of characteristics may describe one who is uncooperative and uncaring. 2. A social philosophy emphasizing the initiative of the individual over governmental social action.

individuality Collectively, those characteristics that distinguish an individual from all others.

individual psychology Historically the term was used roughly synonymously with

what is now called ➤ **differential psychology**. Today it is associated with the personality theory of Alfred Adler; ➤ **Adlerian**.

individual response Any unusual, idiosyncratic response given in a word-association test.

individual symbol ➤ symbol, individual.

individual test ➤ test, individual.

individuation 1. Generally, any process in which the various elements or parts of a complex whole become differentiated from each other, progressively more distinct and 'individual.' The term implies development from the general to the specific. 2. In perception, ➤ **differentiation** (5). 3. In social psychology, the breakdown of social ties and the emergence of individuals lacking in group loyalty. 4. In psychoanalytic theory, the process of becoming an individual who is aware of his or her individuality.

indoleamines A group of ➤ **biogenic amines** including ➤ **serotonin** and ➤ **tryptophan**.

indolones A group of ➤ **antipsychotic drugs** that have biochemical structures that are similar to drugs like ➤ **imipramine** and are used as ➤ **antidepressants**.

induced aggression ➤ aggression, induced.

induced association ➤ association, induced.

induced color A perceived color or color change that is determined by (i.e. induced by) stimulation in other parts of the visual field. ➤ **color contrast**.

induced factitious symptoms ➤ factitious disorder by proxy.

induced goal Any goal whose attainment is induced by outside sources.

induced motion ➤ motion, induced.

induced psychotic disorder A delusional disorder that develops as a result of close contact with an individual who already manifests prominent delusions. The delusions are usually derived from the common experiences of the individuals who, in the typical case, have been together for a long time relatively isolated from others. Also called *shared paranoid disorder* since the delusions are usually of the paranoid variety. ➤ *folie à deux*.

induction 1. A process of reasoning in which general principles are inferred from specific cases. In general, it is a logical operation which proceeds from the individual to the general; what is assumed true of elements from a class is assumed true of the whole class. The experimental method is basically inductive in nature in that conclusions about populations are drawn from observations of individuals and small samples. Contrast here with ➤ **deduction**. 2. A process by which effects are transferred from one 'thing' to another. 'Thing' here is meant most broadly. Emotions are said to be transferred from person to person through *sympathetic induction*, electrical fields through *induction-coils*, neural excitation or inhibition may be induced in one area by the spread of activity from other areas, response rates through the negative effects of *behavioral contrast*, and so forth. 3. A form of parental discipline where the parents use verbal reasoning to induce the child to think about his or her actions and the consequences of them.

induction, sympathetic ➤ **induction** (2).

induction test A general term for any test in which the subject is required to induce a coherent general principle on the basis of a fixed set of exemplars. Such tests are sometimes included as part of more general intelligence-testing batteries.

inductive statistics ➤ **inferential *statistics**.

industrial/organizational psychology A branch of applied psychology covering organizational, military, economic and personnel psychology and including such areas as tests and measurements, the study of organizations and organizational behavior, personnel practices, human engineering, human factors, the effects of work, fatigue, pay and efficiency, consumer sur-

veys, market research, etc. In recent years, as this applied field has grown, there has been a tendency to alter the name by which it is known. Specifically, many contemporary researchers prefer the shortened form *organizational psychology*, on the grounds that the study of organizational behavior is broader than that implied by the qualifier *industrial* since it deals with social structures far removed from industry such as hospitals, prisons, universities, public-service agencies, etc. Often abbreviated *I/O psychology*.

industrial psychiatry ➤ **occupational psychiatry**.

industrial psychology ➤ **industrial/organizational psychology**.

ineffective stimulus ➤ **stimulus, ineffective**.

infancy From the Latin *infantia* which translates as *inability to speak*. This criterion, however, is seldom used and the definition of the stage of infancy depends on who is doing the defining. In law, infancy is often considered to last 18 or 21 years; in developmental psychology, the first year of life is the typically cited period; in layman's terms, it may be up to two or three years.

infant Most generally, an organism within the period of ➤ **infancy**. Although primarily used for members of our species there is a tendency for some to use it for the young of other species during the period of development when they are relatively helpless and dependent on the parents.

infantile Characterizing: 1. ➤ **Infancy**. 2. The behavioral and emotional patterns typical of infancy. Used in this latter sense particularly with regard to such behaviors when they are displayed in an older child or an adult.

infantile amaurotic (familial) idiocy ➤ **Tay–Sachs' disease**.

infantile amnesia ➤ **amnesia, infantile**.

infantile autism ➤ **autism, infantile**.

infantile-birth theories Beliefs of children concerning the actual manner of birth.

Since most parents are loath to deal with these issues in a straightforward and anatomically accurate fashion, children tend to fill in the gaps in what they can discern in rather creative ways. The most common of these 'theories' are emergence through the navel and the anus and some surgical removal techniques. The term is used for child-generated theories, not for cultural myths concerning storks, cabbage patches, mushrooms and the like.

infantile sexuality Within the classical Freudian psychoanalytic theory, the capacity for sexual desire and experience in the infant specifically as manifested by passage through a series of stages beginning with the oral and moving through the anal and early genital.

Since this concept was (is?) so controversial, a comment on terminology is not out of place here: While there are clearly behaviors exhibited by every infant that indicate a focus on the mouth, the anus and the genitals, it is probably the case that the orthodox Freudians were being vaguely anthropomorphic (adultomorphic?) in assigning *sexuality* as the motivator. *Sensuality*, meaning derived from the senses, is probably more accurate and allows us to put the sensuality–sexuality question into a cultural frame where it belongs. Freud, of course, was excoriated by many for being a pan-sexualist, for assigning a sexual base to all sensuality and all pleasure. This issue, as much as any, caused many analysts (such as Jung, Adler and Horney) to abandon the orthodox position.

infantilism 1. A condition of an older child or adult who, for whatever reasons, still displays cognitive and emotional behaviors characteristic of infancy. **2.** Any specific regressive behavior characteristic of infants observed in those more mature.

infant test (or **scale**) Any test or scale for measuring development during infancy. Despite long years of work to develop reliable and valid scales measuring everything from sensory-motor ability to IQ, it is generally acknowledged that such measures do not correlate with measures taken at a later age. The main value of such tests is not as predictors of future success but as diagnostic instruments, for extremely low scores on them are indicative of genuine dysfunctions or disorders. ➤ **Bayley Scales of Infant Development**.

infavoidance need H. Murray's term for the need to avoid failure and, by extension, to avoid attempting tasks that are perceived as likely to lead to failure.

infecundity Sterility in women, barrenness.

inference 1. A logical judgement made on the basis of a sample of evidence, previously made judgements, prior conclusions, etc. rather than on direct observation. **2.** The cognitive process by which such a judgement is made.

inferential statistics ➤ **statistics, inferential**.

inferior 1. Generally, below, lower, worse, in a subsidiary position. **2.** In anatomical descriptions, of a lower part of an organ or a body.

inferior colliculus ➤ **colliculus**.

inferiority complex As originally coined by A. Adler, the term described a collection of repressed fears stemming from organ or bodily inferiority that gave rise to feelings, attitudes and ideas of a more general inferiority. Popular usage has badly mangled the original sense by using the term to refer to any sense of inadequacy or feelings of inferiority; ➤ **inferiority feelings**.

inferiority feelings Loosely, any attitudes toward oneself that are critical and generally negative. Strictly speaking, this is the term that should be used in popular discourse when, for example, someone claims to have an 'inferiority complex.' The problem is that the term *complex* when used in this fashion carries the connotation of some unconscious roots – hence, claimants can know that they have feelings of inferiority but not that they have an ➤ **inferiority complex**.

inferior temporal cortex An area of visual association cortex located on the ventral part of the temporal lobe. It is important in the analysis of information about form and color and plays a critical role in the perception of three-dimensional objects and the ability to differentiate them from their backgrounds.

infertility 1. An inability to produce offspring. **2.** A diminished capacity or a less than normal ability to produce offspring. This meaning is usually indicated by the qualified term *relative infertility*. **3.** The condition of having no offspring. This meaning is rarely the intended one. Note, infertility is typically used for conditions which are temporary or reversible; ➤ **sterility** is preferred for those diagnosed to be permanent or difficult to reverse. ➤➤ **fecundity, fertility**.

infertility, primary Used of females; infertility where there has been no prior pregnancy.

infertility, secondary Used of females, infertility where one or more pregnancies have occurred prior to developing the condition.

inflammatory reaction A complex ➤ **nonspecific *immune reaction** in which the cells damaged by an invading organism secrete substances that cause the area to be inflamed and which attract white blood cells that destroy the invaders.

inflection Lit., a bend or change in the course or direction of something. Hence: **1.** The point in a curve where it changes from concave to convex, or vice versa. **2.** In speech, modulation of the voice by changing pitch. **3.** In linguistics, the suffixing of bound morphemes to a base of a word to express grammatical form and function. In the so-called *synthetic languages* (e.g., Latin) inflection is the primary mode of expression; in *analytic languages* (e.g., English) it is relatively rare. var., *inflexion*.

informal organization ➤ **organization, informal**.

information 1. Within ➤ **information theory** the term is used in a formal manner to quantify an array of items in terms of the number of choices one has in dealing with the items. By definition, the amount of information, measured in *bits* and abbreviated as H, contained in an array of equally likely choices is given by $\log_2 N$ where N is the number of choices. Thus, the answer to the question 'Is it raining?' will provide exactly 1 bit of information since there are only two choices (yes or no) and $\log_2 2 = 1$. (Note, it does not matter whether or not the answer is true.) If one is selecting from 16 equally likely alternatives 4 bits of information will be provided by the choice ($\log_2 16 = 4$). In general, the *less* likely an event is the more information is conveyed by its occurrence.

Intriguingly, this use of information parallels what physicists know as ➤ **entropy** or randomness. When an ensemble is highly structured and not characterized by randomness both entropy and information are low. This meaning of the term is, therefore, concerned not with what is communicated but with what could be communicated; hence, it must be kept conceptually distinct from: **2.** Loosely, any material with content. This sense of the term is close to the standard meaning in nontechnical usage. Information here is basically any knowledge that is received, processed and understood. When ➤ **information processing** models were first introduced in cognitive psychology, the term *information* was used in sense 1. However, the difficulty of specifying just how much information was contained in and hence processed by someone who dealt with a relatively straightforward but complex message (e.g., this sentence) quickly led to a shift to sense 2.

information processing In cognitive psychology, the processing of information. Some clarification is called for here. The term ➤ **information** in the full phrase may, depending on when the writer was writing, reflect either meaning 1 or meaning 2. As discussed under that term, nearly all contemporary usage reflects meaning 2 –

369

any attended input, any idea, image, fact, knowledge, etc. counts as information. Now, *to process* means, basically, to move toward some goal by going through a series of stages or a sequence of acts. Putting these two together yields the notion of organizing, interpreting and responding to (i.e. processing) incoming stimulation (i.e. information). Hence, when one says that information is processed one means that knowledge of some kind is dealt with in some cognitive fashion.

In general, information-processing models of thought and action view cognitive and perceptual operations as taking place in stages or steps, e.g., input, coding, storage, retrieval, decoding, output, and were schematically represented as ➤ **flow charts**. In recent years, however, this approach to cognition has been largely replaced by models based on ➤ **production systems** and connectionist theory. ➤ **connectionism** (2).

information theory More an approach to the study of communications than a 'theory,' it is concerned with the problems of transmission of signals and messages. Strongly interdisciplinary, it draws upon work in engineering, physics, communications, linguistics, psychology, cybernetics, etc. ➤ **information** (1) for details.

information transmission ➤ **information** (1) and ➤ **information theory**.

informed consent Permission to carry out a research or medical procedure where the subject is given information including: (a) the nature of the procedures; (b) potential known risks and benefits; (c) any other alternative procedures that are available; and (d) acknowledgement that such consent is voluntary.

infra- Combining form meaning *low*, *under*, *inferior*, *after*.

infradian rhythms Biological rhythms with cycles of considerable duration, e.g., menstrual cycle.

infrared Pertaining to electromagnetic radiation ('light') the wavelength of which is longer than that to which the normal human eye responds, above roughly 700 nm.

infundibulum 1. Generally, any funnel-shaped passage or structure. **2.** Specifically, the stalk attaching the pituitary body to the forebrain.

ingestive behavior ➤ **feeding behavior**.

in-group A select group in which all members feel a strong sense of identity with the group, a sense of elitism about their group, and tend to act so as to exclude others (the *out-group*). Note that the term connotes strong positive feelings toward the group as an abstraction and not necessarily any such affection toward the individual members of the group who, in fact, may heartily dislike each other. Also occasionally called the *we-group*.

inhalant use disorder A group of disorders brought about by inhaling the aliphatic and aromatic hydrocarbons found in such substances as glue, paint thinners, and gasoline. Also abused are the halogenated hydrocarbons in volatile compounds containing esters, ketones, and glycols. Use produces a psychoactive *inhalant intoxication*; abuse leads to *inhalant dependence* and *inhalant abuse* with serious side effects including neurological, renal and hepatic complications.

inherent From the Latin, meaning *sticking to* or *in*, characterizing a property or attribute of something or someone that is inseparable and permanent. The term is usually contrasted with ➤ **extrinsic** (2). It should be kept distinct from ➤ **inherit** and related terms which have a different etymology that typically denotes genetic origins. vb., *inhere*.

inherit To receive from one's predecessors. In biology, the reference is to the process of genetic transmission; in social, political terms, to a transfer of property and perhaps certain rights and privileges.

inheritance ➤ **heredity**.

inherited trait ➤ **trait, inherited**.

inhibited (female or male) orgasm ➤ orgasm disorders.

inhibited sexual desire ➤ hypoactive sexual desire disorder.

inhibition From the Latin for *restraint*. Hence, very generally: **1.** The restraining, preventing, repressing, decreasing or prohibiting of any process, or the process that brings about such restraining. Somewhat more specifically: **2.** In physiology, the restraining of an ongoing organic process or the prevention of its initiation by neurological or physiological means. There are many specialized forms of inhibition here – see the following entries for details. **3.** In the study of learning, any reduction in or prevention of a response owing to the operation of some other process. Again, specialized terms abound and the more common are given below. **4.** In cognitive psychology, particularly the study of memory, the reduction in performance resulting from the presence of other information that 'gets in the way.' Note that for these two previous usages there is a tendency for some authors to use inhibition as though it were a synonym for *interference*. For meaning 3, the resulting distortion is not serious since the theoretical characterization of such inhibitory process is that other ongoing processes are 'interfering' with the process under consideration (see, e.g., ➤ reciprocal inhibition). For 4, however, such presumed semantic equivalence is, given contemporary theories of memory, misleading and not recommended. ➤ interference (5) for clarification of this point. **5.** In psychoanalysis, the control of instinctual id impulses by the action of the superego. Although some analysts will use the term interchangeably with ➤ suppression (and occasionally even with ➤ repression), such practices are not recommended. In the classical theory inhibition is used as equivalent to *prevention*; the instinctual processes may get repressed or suppressed but only if inhibition should fail. **6.** By extension (and dilution) of 5, any restraining of a momentary impulse or desire.

Not surprisingly, the base term appears in a vast array of specialized contexts and in many agglutinized forms. vb., *inhibit*; adj., *inhibitory*. Combined terms not given below may be found under the alphabetic heading of the modifying term.

inhibition, central This term is used whenever the assumed inhibitory action is taking place within the central nervous system; e.g., *reciprocal inhibition* as exhibited by antagonistic muscles when the neural message to one muscle to contract is accompanied by a relaxation of the other resulting from an inhibition of its motor nerve cells. When action is in the cerebral cortex the term *cortical inhibition* is used.

inhibition, cortical ➤ central *inhibition.

inhibition, external The inhibition of a conditioned response produced when a novel, irrelevant stimulus is presented along with the conditioned stimulus. First discovered by Pavlov, who assumed that it resulted from simultaneous excitations in the central nervous system. Contrast with ➤ internal *inhibition.

inhibition, internal Inhibition that depends on a conditioning process; e.g., that produced by *extinction*, *inhibition of delay*, *conditioned inhibition*, etc. Contrast with ➤ external *inhibition.

inhibition, latent Inhibition established by nonreinforced exposure to a stimulus. The animal learns not to attend to that stimulus so that when it is presented in a reinforcing situation learning is inhibited. Also called the *stimulus preexposure effect*.

inhibition of delay A form of internal inhibition that theoretically produces the characteristic delay of responding during long trace conditioning. The fragile inhibitory nature of the process is demonstrated by the ease with which the response may be *disinhibited* by an extraneous stimulus during the trace or delay period.

inhibition of inhibition The original Pavlovian term for what is now called ➤ disinhibition.

inhibition of (or with) reinforcement The

lessening of a conditioned response when massed, reinforced trials are presented. It is presumably a fatigue factor and responsiveness recovers with rest.

inhibition, proactive ➤ proactive *interference; ➤ interference (especially 4) for why *inhibition* is not the preferred term here.

inhibition, reactive (I_R) Hull's term for the hypothesized inhibitory tendency that builds up as a result of effortful responding.

inhibitory conditioning ➤ conditioning, inhibitory.

inhibitory postsynaptic potential (IPSP) ➤ postsynaptic potential.

inhibitory potential ($_sI_R$) In Hullian theory, the hypothesized state that results from the making of a response and assumed to reflect the organism's tendency to inhibit the making of the response.

inhibitory reflex ➤ reflex inhibition.

initial teaching alphabet (ITA) An alphabetic writing system developed as an aid to teaching reading. The orthography of English in ITA is changed so that every symbol has only one sound value; e.g., 'once' is rendered as 'wuns.' The idea behind such a system has been championed by many, notably G. B. Shaw. However, there are serious problems with ITA and similar synthetic systems; they range from the obvious one of the difficulty of transfer to standard spelling to the not so obvious but nevertheless true fact that English is not really as irregular as most think and that many of its peculiar spelling patterns carry important morphological information (e.g., the *g* in *sign* cues its relationship to *signal*).

initial insomnia ➤ insomnia, initial.

injury Broadly, any damage to bodily tissue.

injury feigning A response to a threatening situation where an animal feigns an injury in order to attract the attention of a predator and lead it away. The classic case here is the ground-nesting female plover, who feigns a broken wing to lure an intruder away from her young. ➤ death feigning.

inkblot test A generic term used for any of the several projective tests that use inkblots. The most widely used is, of course, the *Rorschach Test*.

innate Pertaining to or characterizing that which is natural or native to an organism, that which exists or is potential at birth by virtue of genetic factors. In this vein some more or less acceptable synonyms are *inborn, hereditary, inherited, native, nativistic*. That which is innate is demarcated from that which is acquired, learned or derived from experience. The term is used in two ways: (a) With respect to those properties that are hypothesized to be part of the genetic endowment of each member of a particular species and hence to be observed in the anatomy and behavior of each member. The focus here is universality, those things that are common to all. This sense of the term, long of interest in philosophy (➤ **innate ideas**), is also represented by work in ethology and in some approaches to developmental psychology. (b) To characterize differences between individual members of a species that are not due to environmental factors. Here the focus is on the attribution of genetic cause to observed differences in phenotype among members of a given species. To appreciate these two senses of the term note that walking is innate in the former sense and individual differences in the ability to walk may be innate in the latter sense. Try thinking about an at least partially innate characteristic like body weight in this manner to see this point. See also the extended discussions on usage under ➤ **heritability** and ➤ **heredity–environment controversy**.

innate ideas A hoary philosophical doctrine dating back to the Stoics that holds that certain 'ideas' are innate, existing a priori in all human beings. Descartes was probably the most vigorous defender of the doctrine, suggesting that knowledge of time, causality, perfection and even the

(Euclidean) axioms of geometry were innately given. Locke and other British empiricists attacked the Cartesian position, stressing the role of experience over native endowment. The doctrine has, however, proven rather robust, reappearing in different forms in the writings of Leibniz and Kant and more recently in the theories of the contemporary American linguist and philosopher Noam Chomsky.

innate releasing mechanism In the Lorenz-Tinbergen ethological theory, a postulated mechanism whereby instinctive acts are assumed to be inhibited until the appropriate stimulus (the ➤ **sign stimulus**) occurs. ➤ **action-specific energy**, **fixed action pattern** and **vacuum activity** for details of how this model accounts for various behaviors.

inner-directed A term coined by D. Riesman to characterize a tendency to react according to an internalized set of goals or values. The term is applied to persons exhibiting such internal characteristics as well as to a society that fosters them. Contrast with ➤ **outer-directed**, **tradition-directed**.

inner ear The innermost component of the ear containing the cochlea and the organs of balance. Also called the *labyrinth*.

inner-personal region ➤ **region, inner-personal**.

innervation 1. The neural distribution of and supply to an organ, gland or muscle. This is the usual meaning. On occasion: **2.** The neural excitation of an organ, gland or muscle.

innervation, reciprocal Innervation of a pair of antagonistic muscles through which neural impulses induce flexion in one and extension in the other.

innovative therapies Over the years almost every conceivable form of doing, believing, acting, reacting, hoping, touching, fighting, loving, moving, emoting, provoking, etc., ad nauseam has been turned into some form of psychotherapy – this term acts as an umbrella for them all. A few of these have shown their worth in controlled settings and with proper evaluation and follow-up of cases (e.g., sex therapy), others serve mainly as sources of income for therapists and as something new to try for people who drift psychically about looking for someone somewhere to inject some meaning into their lives. Some of the more exotic forms extant (as of this writing anyway, most are short-lived) are: body therapy, poetry therapy, encouragement therapy, rebirthing therapy, herbal therapy, energy medicine therapy and a whole range of New Age therapies involving crystals, channelling and reincarnation. One hardly knows what to make of these. There are essentially no attempts made to validate the techniques used, no basis for determining success or lack of it and, most damning, no reasonable theoretical basis for assuming that any of them ought to work – short of plain old common sense. After all, poetry is certainly a good thing and reading, writing and understanding poetry would probably have therapeutic value for anyone, but psychology as a pure and applied science is certainly not served well by what has been called this 'southern Californiaizing' of society.

inoculate 1. To introduce a microorganism or other substance into the body usually by means of an injection. **2.** The substance itself. **3.** Metaphorically, to introduce new ideas to someone. Note that the term does not mean to *protect*; this common error derives from the fact that an inoculate of a particular organism can, through the action of antibodies, result in such protection.

inoculation hypothesis In the study of attitudes, the hypothesis that one's belief in some point of view can be strengthened by presenting weak and refutable counter-arguments to it.

input Obviously, something that is put into a system. Broadly, any stimulus may be represented as input in that it is some form of energy that enters some system (an organism). More specifically, the term characterizes a signal fed to an electrical circuit, a message that acts on a receiver, the information entered into a computer, etc. In general one is counseled to ignore the esoterica, all uses are intuitively obvious.

input/output A hybrid term used in various cognitive theories (e.g., *information processing*) to represent the information to a person (input), the behavior of the person (output) and the relationships between them. Cognitive psychologists will talk about input/output relationships in ways analogous to those of behaviorists talking about stimulus–response relationships; the non-trivial difference being that behaviorists prefer to define their stimuli and responses operationally and objectively while cognitivists represent input and output in terms of symbols, codes, structures and the like. Abbreviated *I/O*.

insanity In popular terminology, *not sane*. The term has regrettably been so brutalized by irresponsible writers over the years that its only remaining technical meaning is a forensic one, in its use as a legal designation for the state of an individual judged to be legally irresponsible or incompetent. ➤ **insanity defense**.

insanity defense A legal concept that a person cannot be convicted of a crime if it can be shown that he or she lacked 'criminal responsibility,' that he or she was (legally) insane. Several principles have been accepted by Anglo and American courts on this issue; see, e.g., ➤ **Durham rule**, **irresistible impulse test**, **McNaghten rule**, and **ALI defense (ruling)**.

insect societies ➤ **social insects**.

insecurity A lack of assurance, uncertainty, unprotectedness. Some theorists argue, not without foundation, that essentially all neurotic, destructive behaviors stem from feelings of insecurity and the attendant sense of anxiety. It is difficult to say much else about this term and the manner of its use in psychology. The feelings are ubiquitous in humankind and if

there is one who cannot sense its meaning from personal experience little can be done to explicate further.

insensible Lit., without sensibility. Hence: **1.** Of stimuli that are below threshold or outside the range of the sensory modality under consideration. **2.** Characteristic of an organism in a state of unresponsiveness; e.g., one who is unconscious or in a coma. **3.** Descriptive of individuals who are lacking in feelings or sensitivities. This last usage is generally equivalent to the nontechnical term *insensitivity*.

insight **1.** Most generally, an act of apprehending or sensing intuitively the inner nature of something. There are several more specialized meanings. Two relate to *personal* insight: **2.** In standard parlance, any self-awareness, self-knowledge, or self-understanding. **3.** In psychotherapy, the illumination or comprehension of one's mental condition which had previously escaped awareness. Note that here there are distinctions made between *intellectual* insight, which is a kind of theoretical understanding of one's condition or of the underlying psychodynamics of one's actions but still leaves one alienated from the self, and *emotional* insight, which is regarded as the true, deep understanding. Classical psychoanalysis, for example, regards the intellectual form as a defense mechanism and the emotional form as the critical element of successful therapy.

Two additional meanings relate to situational or environmentally stimulated insights: **4.** A novel, clear, compelling apprehension of the truth of something occurring without overt recourse to memories of past experiences. **5.** Within Gestalt psychology, the process by which problems are solved. In this sense, insight characterizes a sudden reorganization or restructuring of the pattern or significance of events allowing one to grasp relationships relevant to the solution. Here, insight represents a kind of learning and is characterized in an all-or-none fashion. ➤➤ **intuition**.

insomnia A general term for chronic inability to sleep normally, as evidenced by difficulty in falling asleep, frequent waking during the night and/or early morning waking with attendant difficulty in falling back to sleep. In the vast majority of cases insomnia is caused by either anxiety or pain. Over the years a large number of synonyms have been used, including *agrypnia*, *ahypnia*, *ahyposia*, *anhypnia*, *anhypnosis* and other variations of these. The current view is that insomnia is not a single disorder but a complex group of related disorders leading to the suggestion that the term *disorders of initiating and maintaining sleep* (*DIMS*) be used in its place. For additional details ➤ **sleep disorder** and related terms.

insomnia, delayed sleep-onset ➤ **sleep-wake schedule disorder**.

insomnia, initial Difficulty in falling asleep.

insomnia, middle Frequent awakening from sleep accompanied by difficulty falling back to sleep.

insomnia, primary The most common ➤ **sleep disorder** characterized by difficulty falling and/or staying asleep to the point where the individual suffers daytime fatigue and impaired daytime functioning. When the shortened term *insomnia* is used it is typically meant to refer to this disorder.

insomnia, rebound Insomnia occurring following withdrawal from drugs taken to relieve insomnia. It has physicians and researchers concerned, since the rebound insomnia may be worse than the original insomnia the drug was designed to alleviate.

insomnia, terminal Awakening before one's planned or typical time accompanied by difficulty in falling back to sleep.

inspiration 1. Breathing in, inhaling. 2. A sudden apprehension of the essential nature of a thing. This latter use, of course, is derived from the former, owing to the ancient belief that such insights came on the breath of spirits.

inspiration/expiration ratio ➤ **I/E ratio**.

instability ➤ **unstable**.

instance theory An umbrella term for a number of theories in *cognitive psychology* that argue that memory and knowledge systems are built up on the basis of specific instances or episodes. These theorists argue, for example, that if a hairy, four-legged creature should walk into the room, the reason you know it is a dog is because it reminds you of an earlier instance in which a similar looking creature was called a dog. Contrast with ➤ **abstraction theory**. Also called *episode theory* and *exemplar theory*.

instant A 'spot' of time; psychologically, a duration so brief that two or more (perhaps) sequential events are perceived as simultaneous. ➤ **specious present**.

instigation Arousal, stimulation.

instigation therapy A form of behaviorally oriented, directive therapy in which the therapist sets up positive models for the client and actively reinforces progress toward them.

instinct A term with a tortured history indeed. The root is Latin, *instinctus* meaning *instigated* or *impelled*, with the implication that such impulses are natural or innate. There are four general, distinguishable meanings of the term: 1. An unlearned response characteristic of the members of a given species. 2. A tendency or disposition to respond in a particular manner that is characteristic of a particular species. This disposition (2) is the presumed underpinning for the observed behavior (1). 3. A complex, coordinated set of acts found universally or nearly so within a given species that emerges under specific stimulus conditions, specific drive conditions and specific developmental conditions. This meaning is found primarily in ethology; see, e.g., ➤ **innate releasing mechanism**, **fixed action pattern** and related entries. 4. Any of a number of unlearned, inherited tendencies that are hypothesized to function as the motivational forces behind complex human behaviors. This sense, of course, is that expressed by classical psychoanalysis.

In actual use, the manner of application of the term has differed dramatically from theory to theory. The first school of psychology to make instinct a central concept was the ➤ **Freudian**. In his early writings, Freud outlined two classes of instincts, *ego* or self-preserving instincts and *sexual* or reproductive instincts. In his later works he restricted the term to ➤ **Thanatos** (the death instincts) and ➤ **Eros** (the life instincts). However, in both schemes Freud was clear that instincts were fundamentally motivators of behavior but were not presumed to specify particular behavioral manifestations. The emphasis was on that which is *instinctual* rather than on the instincts themselves; that is, meanings 1, 2 and 3 did not apply.

McDougall's ➤ **hormic psychology** used instinct (in senses 1, 2 and 4) as the central theoretical concept. All behavior was treated as purposive or goal-seeking and motivated by underlying species-specific propensities, the instincts. Unlike Freud, McDougall applied the term broadly to all motivational constructs and the resultant proliferation of instincts undermined the scientific basis of the theory.

The use of the term by the ethologists (in sense 3 primarily but incorporating 1 and 2) has stressed the species-specific and biological aspects. Lorenz's definition makes this clear: 'Behavior which is to a large extent determined by nervous mechanisms evolved in the phylogeny of the species.' Note that this use specifically includes behavior, as opposed to the psychoanalytic focus on motivation.

Much of the confusion has resulted from several unresolved (and perhaps unresolvable) issues: (a) *The heredity problem:* The extent to which instincts are biologically pre-programmed or result from environmental factors. See here ➤ **heredity–environment controversy**. (b) *Species specificity:* Are instincts general motivators or can they only be explicated within individual species? The accumulating evidence here tends to favor the ethological approach, which emphasizes intra-species analysis. (c) *Behavioral specifi-*

city: The degree to which specific behaviors are to be incorporated into the concept. While it is clear that some behavioral manifestations are always implied (how else to know the existence of the instinct?), the problem is a serious one. The more specific the presumed behaviors, the greater the chance that the term will take on an unacceptable nebulousness, as it did with McDougall.

Obviously these points are interconnected and, of course, they are not the only ones of import. The point to make is that the general concept is too vital to permit banishment of the term from the psychologist's lexicon, as some have suggested. A less robust concept would long ago have succumbed to its own excesses. Handle with care.

instinct, closed Innate species-specific behavior patterns (i.e. ➤ **instincts** in sense 3) that are rigid and inflexible. They appear if and only if the proper stimulus is provided and are closed to any environmentally guided modification. Much insect behavior falls in this category.

instinct, delayed Any instinct the characteristic behavior of which does not appear until some time after birth or hatching. See here ➤ **critical period**.

instinctive Pertaining to instinct. Note that there is a common misuse of this term in nontechnical writings, as in 'the goalie made a sudden instinctive kick to block the shot.' Here the act is clearly the result of much skilled practice and not in any way truly instinctive; highly practiced automatized acts are not instincts in the technical sense.

instinct, life ➤ Eros, ➤➤ libido.

instinct, open Innate species-specific behavior patterns (i.e. ➤ **instincts** in sense 3) that display flexibility so that the behaviors 'drift' over time and with experience. For example, feedback about the appropriateness of certain materials for nest-building will produce changes in the nest-building behavior of many species of birds. The use of the term *instinct* here is questioned by some, who would prefer to call such modification by experience ➤ **restricted *learning**.

instinctual Pertaining to ➤ **instinct**.

instinctual aggression ➤ **aggression**.

instinctual anxiety A psychoanalytic term for anxiety provoked by fear of one's basic, primal instincts. Used roughly synonymously with ➤ **neurotic *anxiety**.

instinctual fusion ➤ **fusion** (2).

institution 1. In the argot of the sociologist, an organized system of social roles which is a persistent and significant element in a society and which focuses on basic human needs and functions. The term is used broadly and one will find references to economic institutions, institutions of higher learning, marriage as an institution, military institutions, religious orders as institutions, etc. 2. More specifically, and less technically, the term is also used for local clubs, prisons, hospitals, etc. 3. Most specifically, the buildings occupied or used by such organizations. ➤ **organization** (2).

institutionalization 1. The process and development of the stable and formal patterns of behavior that make up an institution. The usage here is quite broad and derives from sociology. 2. The habituation of a person to the patterns within an institution, often to the extent that the person may not be capable of normal functioning outside. 3. The process of having someone placed in an institution.

institutionalize A transitive verb that refers to the process of ➤ **institutionalization** (2, 3) of a person by either (a) indoctrination into a system of social roles or (b) physical placement in an institution like a prison or a mental hospital. Note that in practice, although not necessarily in theory, the former connotation is subtly implied in the latter; individuals placed in institutions (theoretically for rehabilitative or therapeutic reasons) are expected to conform with the 'appropriate' modes of behavior of the place of confinement

and hence to become institutionalized.

institution, total A specialized use of ➤ **institution** denoting places of confinement (total or partial) where life style is sharply restricted, formalized and under the control of special staff. Traditionally, prisons, army camps, convents, mental hospitals, boarding schools, etc. are so classified.

instruction(s) 1. In the singular, directing, teaching, imparting knowledge. 2. In the plural, directions for carrying out some procedures. Used commonly in this sense as a set of directions to a subject in an experiment.

instrument 1. A tool, a device specifically designed for a particular task. 2. Any device or piece of apparatus for measuring some variable or assessing some factor. 3. Any psychological test. The term is used quite broadly to include laboratory hardware as well as any assessment device from sophisticated IQ tests and personality inventories to simple questionnaires and opinion polls.

instrumental Obvious meanings about instruments and tools aside, the psychologist generally uses this term to characterize behaviors that are goal-directed. See, e.g., ➤ **instrumental behavior**, **instrumental conditioning**.

instrumental aggression ➤ **aggression, instrumental**.

instrumental behavior (or **act**) Very generally, any behavior or act that is goal-directed, a means to some end. ➤ **instrumental conditioning**.

instrumental conditioning An experimental procedure in which reinforcement occurs only after the subject has made the proper response. Mazes, straight alleys, puzzle boxes and the like are all examples of experimental apparatuses used to study instrumental conditioning. There are several things of note about this term: (a) The name derives from the fact that the occurrence of the proper response is *instrumental* in producing the reinforcement. Contrast with ➤ **classical conditioning**, in which the US (unconditioned stimulus) appears regardless of whether or not the CR (conditioned response) occurred. (b) Many authors prefer to use the term *operant conditioning* rather than instrumental conditioning. It is, however, not simply a matter of replacing one term with another. Instrumental conditioning traditionally covered discrete-trial situations in which the subject must perform some act within a structured environment. Operant conditioning covers 'free' behavior as well as discrete-trial behavior and includes behavior in which the subject responds in some way which changes (or 'operates' on) the environment. Hence, instrumental conditioning is really a special case of operant conditioning. (c) In general, the term will be used to refer both to the actual learning that takes place and to the experimental procedure itself. ➤ **conditioning** and **operant conditioning**.

instrumentalism A term introduced by John Dewey to characterize his moderate variation on the philosophy of pragmatism. It shares with *operationalism* and other forms of *empiricism* an emphasis on the need to verify concepts through empirical test, but it is somewhat looser in that it does not insist on operational definitions and allows for more conceptual and theoretical analysis.

insula ➤ **island of Reil**.

insulin A hormone secreted by the beta cells of the islets of Langerhans of the pancreas. Insulin is an essential component of proper metabolism; it facilitates entry of glucose and amino acids into cells, provides for proper metabolism of glucose by aiding in its conversion into glycogen and facilitates production of fats in adipose (fatty) tissue. Diminished secretion leads to inadequate metabolism of carbohydrates and fats and the hyperglycemia of diabetes. Secretion of insulin is determined by (a) blood-glucose concentrations, with high levels triggering secretion and low levels inhibiting it, (b) a rise in the level of amino acids and (c) direct efferent nerve impulses from the brain to the pancreas.

insulin shock (or **coma**) Hypoglycemic state produced by excess insulin, resulting in a lowering in blood sugar and a comatose state.

insulin-shock therapy A form of therapy for certain psychological disorders utilizing a large-enough dose of insulin to induce shock and coma. It is a procedure with very real dangers and insufficient evidence for any therapeutic effects; as a result, it is rarely used today.

insult Occasional synonym for *injury*.

integrate 1. Generally, to bring into a harmonious or coordinated whole by rearranging, organizing and occasionally adding or deleting elements or parts. 2. Specifically, to carry out such an operation when the 'elements' are persons who are distinguished by characteristics that play important socio-economic roles in a culture; e.g., race, sex, religion, social class, etc.

integration Very generally, the process of coordinating and unifying disparate elements into a whole; ➤ **integrate**. A variety of special usages is found, typically with qualifiers appended as in the following entries.

integration, behavioral The blending, chaining or combining of several separate behaviors into a coordinated whole.

integration, cultural The blending of cultural traits, which were originally conflicting, to form a modified, integrated system.

integration, functional A general term used to note the functional, operative aspects of any integration.

integration, group ➤ **functional *integration**, in which the system under examination is a group and the several parts are people. ➤ **social *integration**, a near synonym, with the group being a larger segment of a society.

integration, social There are two slightly different uses here: 1. The process of uniting disparate elements or groups into one unified group. **2.** The adoption of existing group standards by an individual so that he or she is accepted into an existing group. In the first, the new group may be totally different after this process; in the second, the group standards remain unchanged.

intellect Originally the term referred specifically to the *rational* thought functions of the human mind; today it is a generic term covering the cognitive processes as a whole.

intellectual **1** adj. Pertaining to the intellect or to intelligence. **2** adj. Pertaining to one with abiding interests in ideas, thinking, creativity. **3** n. A person devoted to matters of the mind. A strange term in many ways, its affective connotations have varied greatly over the years. With skill it can be used as either a high compliment (connotations of intelligence) or a dashing insult (connotations of being narrow, otherworldly, neglectful of emotions, affections, sensations, etc.).

intellectualism A general term for any doctrine that focuses exclusively on intellectual functioning. Used occasionally as a rough synonym of ➤ **idealism** or ➤ **rationalism**, depending on whether one takes the point of view that the intellectual represents the ultimate reality (idealism) or that it represents the basic process by which knowledge is acquired (rationalism).

intellectualization A defense mechanism whereby problems are analyzed in remote, intellectual terms while emotion, affect and feeling are ignored.

intelligence Few concepts in psychology have received more devoted attention and few have resisted clarification so thoroughly. Despite many efforts over the years to develop some independent definition of the term, its connotations have remained intimately intertwined with the techniques developed for its measurement. Binet, the inventor of the individual intelligence test, felt that intelligent behavior

would be manifested in such abilities as reasoning, imagination, insight, judgement and adaptability and so he designed his tests (➤ **Binet tests**) to evaluate just these functions. Other theoreticians have argued that only three fundamental cognitive processes are identifiable (abstraction, learning and dealing with novelty). Still others have argued that all such abilities are only manifestations of a single underlying factor (the so-called ➤ **general *factor**) which is presumed to be at the root of all intellectual functioning. In 1927 the frustrations of dealing with the concept were already being felt. Spearman, the great psychometrician, despaired of the whole notion and called intelligence '. . . a mere vocal sound, a word with so many meanings that finally it had none.'

Such pessimism, however deeply felt, has not dimmed psychology's need for such a concept. Note that before the tests and measurement movement, the term meant 'the ability to profit from experience,' which implies the ability to behave adaptively, to function successfully within particular environments. Hence, any 'intelligence test' that proves to be valid will be one that accurately predicts adaptive and successful functioning within specified environments. Since its inception, the dominant use of the intelligence test has been as a predictor of scholastic success and so, of course, there should be little surprise that the 'adaptive and successful' behaviors have been precisely those of reasoning, judging, learning, dealing with novelty, abstracting, etc. All such intelligence tests will be, by their very existence, socio-culturally determined. They will reflect the ideals and values of the culture of the test designers and 'adaptive and successful' functioning will always mean 'adaptive and successful' functioning within that culture.

There is nothing fundamentally wrong with this. The fact that this set of circumstances invites abuse does not deny a society the right to attempt to discern which of its citizens is most likely to profit from what it has to offer them. Ultimately *intelligence* will be, conceptually, what it has always been, *the ability to profit from experience* and, pragmatically, what it has become, *that which the intelligence tests measure*.

intelligence, abstract ➤ **abstract** and ➤ **intelligence**. Used in a manner similar to ➤ **fluid *intelligence**.

intelligence, adult 1. Psychometrically speaking, the level of intelligence reached when there is a marked decrease in the growth of measured intelligence. Or, more formally put, where the year-to-year average increase in measured mental age becomes small relative to the standard deviation in the scores in the whole population. The age at which this point is reached differs from intelligence test to intelligence test but there is vague agreement that it is somewhere during adolescence (roughly 13–18 years of age). **2.** The average level of intelligence of the adults in a given population. Meanings 1 and 2 are, in many respects, contradictory. On the one hand, if *adult* covers everyone past adolescence then the average *measured* IQ in 2 may very well be lower than in 1 since there is some evidence that IQ scores drop off after middle age. But, on the other hand, if maturity, wisdom, insight, understanding and all those other qualities of the mature adult are to count toward a pragmatic conceptualization of intelligence, then 2 is certainly going to be higher than 1. However, since we haven't the foggiest notion how to evaluate quantitatively things like *wisdom* but think we know how to measure *intelligence*, most authorities have placed themselves in the embarrassing position of defining *adult intelligence* as that possessed by the average *adolescent*.

intelligence, coefficient of Generally, any index of intelligence derived by forming a ratio between the score obtained by an individual on an intelligence test and the norms for that person's age (usually multiplied by some constant); ➤ **intelligence quotient**.

intelligence, concrete Generally, the ability to function effectively with ➤ **concrete**

problems. Used similarly to ➤ **crystalized *intelligence**. See also the general discussion under ➤ **intelligence**.

intelligence, crystalized Intelligence as assessed by those components of an intelligence test that are based on facts and the ability to utilize facts. Used in a manner similar to ➤ **concrete *intelligence**.

intelligence, fluid Intelligence as assessed by those components of an intelligence test that are based on the ability to solve novel problems creatively. Used roughly synonymously with *abstract intelligence* (here, ➤ **abstract** and **intelligence**).

intelligence quotient A measure of intelligence level. Originally defined as 100 times the mental age (MA, determined by a standardized test) divided by the chronological age (CA), it now represents a person's performance relative to peers. Both procedures establish the average as 100. Nearly always abbreviated as IQ.

intelligence test Any test that purports to measure intelligence. Generally such tests consist of a graded series of tasks each of which has been standardized with a large, representative population of individuals. ➤ **intelligence** for a discussion of issues and problems.

intension In logic, the domain of a general term or concept made up of all those terms or concepts that are necessarily true of it. In less formal terms, intension is roughly equivalent to ➤ **connotative *meaning**. Compare with ➤ **extension** (3). Distinguish from ➤ **intention**.

intensity 1. As borrowed from physics, a measure of a quantity of energy. Hence, physical stimuli will be characterized in terms of intensity, e.g., of a light, a tone, an electric current, etc. **2.** The degree of experienced sensation as related to some physical stimulus. Here subjective experience will be so characterized, e.g., intensity of a pain, of an auditory sensation, etc. Sense 1 is quantitative thanks to the successes of the physical sciences; sense 2 is usually qualitative, owing to the complexities of the psychological processes involved, but ➤ scaling and methods of *scaling for attempts to quantify experienced intensity. 3. The vigor or strength of an emitted behavior. This sense is common in behaviorist studies of learning and conditioning. 4. By extension of 3, the degree to which an emotion is experienced, a belief held, an attitude adopted, etc.

In all cases *intensity* refers to or implies the existence of a whole dimension along which the variable can be expressed; hence *intense* is taken to mean, simply, *high intensity* and *intensive* becomes the modifier used to pertain to the full dimension.

intention 1. Generally, any desire, plan, purpose, aim or belief that is oriented toward some goal, some end state. Used by most with the connotation that such striving is *conscious*, although the term occasionally creeps into psychoanalytic writings without the requirement. 2. As represented by the ➤ act psychology school, the essential feature of all conscious processes that they involve outward references to objects. See here ➤ intentionality. Distinguish from ➤ intension.

intentional 1. Deliberate, purposeful, goal-oriented. Generally used to characterize acts undertaken consciously; e.g., ➤ intentional *learning as opposed to ➤ implicit *learning or ➤ intentional *forgetting versus 'ordinary' ➤ forgetting. 2. Pertaining to ➤ intention (2); ➤➤ intentionality.

intentional forgetting 1. ➤ Forgetting due to ➤ repression. Here the notion of *intentional* is compromised somewhat in that it usually carries the connotation of awareness, whereas repression denotes an unconscious process. ➤ intention (1). 2. Directed forgetting, forgetting of material following instructions to do so. This is a touchy issue; it evokes images of the old joke about instructing someone *not* to think about pigmy elephants ... (➤ paradoxical injunction). The argument put forward by some is that such intentional forgetting may result because the person so directed refrains from deep coding or processing of the material and so tends

not to be able to recall it later. See here ➤ depth of processing.

intentionality As borrowed from philosophy, a feature of some (but not all) internal mental or cognitive states in that they are focused outward at objects, events and states of affairs in the real world. The mental state instantiated by saying 'I believe it is raining' would have intentionality. In general, beliefs, intentions, desires, purposes, etc. are *intentional states*. Other mental states characterized by undifferentiated or undirected affect, for example, depression or anxiety, are not so classified.

intentional learning ➤ learning, intentional.

intentional state ➤ intentionality.

inter- Combining term indicating *between*, *among* or *mutual*. Compare with ➤ intra-.

interaction Reciprocal effect or influence. In *social interaction*, the behavior of one acts as a stimulus for the behavior of another, and vice versa. In *statistical interaction* the effects of two (or more) variables are interdependent; e.g., task difficulty and arousal often interact so that increased arousal increases performance on easy tasks but decreases it on difficult tasks.

interactionism ➤ dualism.

interaction variance In statistics, the proportion of the total variance that is not related to the action of single variables but due to the interaction between them.

interactive dualism ➤ dualism.

interaural differences Differences in the sound arriving at the two ears. There are two kinds of interaural differences, *time* and *intensity*. Together they make up the set of cues for localizing a sound source in the environment. ➤➤ binaural time differences.

interbrain ➤ diencephalon.

intercalation 1. Insertion in between the elements of an ordered series. Generally used with the connotation of extraneous, unnecessary. **2.** A speech disorder in which irrelevant, inappropriate sounds or words are inserted.

intercorrelations The correlations of each variable in a set with every other variable in the analysis. A full set of intercorrelations, usually displayed in matrix form, is the basis for a factor analysis.

intercourse **1.** Generally, dealings, interactions or communications between persons and/or groups. **2.** More specifically, an interchange of affect, of emotion. **3.** Most specifically, ➤ **sexual intercourse**.

interest One of those terms that slipped unnoticed into the technical vocabulary of psychology, especially educational psychology. Its meaning is loose at best and at one time or another has been used to imply all of the following: attention, curiosity, motivation, focus, concern, goal-directedness, awareness, worthiness and desire. Most authors merely follow their intuitions in its use; it's hard to go wrong.

interest inventory (or **test**) An instrument designed to evaluate a person's interests in or preferences for a variety of activities. Several such tests have been developed, the ➤ **Kuder Preference Record** and the ➤ **Strong-Campbell Interest Inventory** are two of the more commonly used.

interface **1.** In computer terminology, the circuitry that connects the central processing core of a computer and its peripheral parts. **2.** By extension, the connection between any two functioning units, including organisms. A common phrase in engineering psychology is *man–machine interface*.

interfemale aggression ➤ **aggression, interfemale**.

interference From the Old French, meaning *to strike each other*. Hence: **1.** Very generally, any process in which there is some conflict between operations or acts such that a diminution or decrement in performance results. In layman's terms, things are getting in the way of other things. **2.** In acoustics and optics, the decrease in amplitude of a complex wave form when two or more wave patterns of different phases come together. **3.** In social psychology, a conflict between competing emotions, motives, values, etc. **4.** In learning and conditioning, a conflict among associations formed between stimuli and responses. Commonly used here for circumstances in which there are two mutually incompatible responses and a single stimulus. Often ➤ **inhibition** (especially 3) is an acceptable synonym for this meaning; see, e.g., ➤ **reciprocal inhibition**. **5.** In learning and memory, a conflict between information in memory such that either: (a) new information becomes difficult to learn because of previous experiences – see here ➤ **proactive *interference** – or (b) old information becomes difficult to recall because of current information; see here ➤ **retroactive *interference**. Occasionally one will see ➤ **inhibition** (in sense 4) used as a synonym here. Unlike 4 above, this usage is misleading, particularly in that the theoretical characterization of these memory phenomena is that they are caused by 'things getting in the way of other things' and not by 'things restraining other things' as connoted by the term *inhibition*. **6.** A block or barrier that creates difficulties for another person.

interference, proactive (PI) Interference of material previously learned on material currently being learned. It is 'proactive' in the sense that information acquired in the past has its effects felt 'forward' in time. Proactive interference builds up surprisingly fast, particularly when a person undertakes several highly similar tasks in a short period of time, and performance may drop off precipitously. ➤ **release from *PI**. Compare with ➤ **retroactive *interference**.

interference, retroactive (RI) The interference that the learning of new material has upon the recall of material learned previously. It is 'retroactive' in the sense that current tasks are interfering with the retrieval of memories for learning that took place earlier in time. Compare with ➤ **proactive *interference**.

intergenerational mobility Vertical social mobility from one generation to the next. Typically assessed by comparing occupations of parents and those of their offspring.

interjectional theory ➤ theories of *language origins.

interlocking schedule ➤ schedules of *reinforcement.

intermale aggression ➤ aggression, intermale.

intermarriage 1. Marriage between persons who are blood relations. **2.** Marriage between persons of disparate groups. The groups may be defined by social class, religion, ethnicity or race.

intermediate needs In Maslow's theory, a subclass of ➤ deficiency needs (2). Included here are safety, belongingness, self-esteem, security, etc. ➤ need hierarchy for the relationship between the various classes of needs in the theory.

intermission A symptom-free period in a chronic disorder. Distinguish from ➤ remission.

intermittence tone ➤ interruption tone.

intermittent explosive disorder An ➤ impulse-control disorder characterized by episodes of aggressiveness resulting in serious assaults on people or property. The degree of aggression displayed is dramatically out of proportion to any precipitating event or known external cause. The term is only used when other psychiatric disorders that are associated with loss of control of aggressive impulses have been ruled out. Note that a subcategory of this disorder referred to as an *isolated* form of explosive disorder, where there was but a single such episode, is, for simple logical reasons, no longer officially recognized.

intermittent reinforcement ➤ reinforcement, intermittent.

intermittent schedule ➤ intermittent *reinforcement.

internal aim ➤ aim (3).

internal consistency 1. The degree to which the various parts of a test or other instrument measure the same variables; i.e. the degree to which the test can be said to be 'internally consistent.' **2.** Occasionally, the extent to which an individual's behavior is consistent from situation to situation. The preferred term here is ➤ self-consistency (especially 2, 3).

internal consistency, coefficient of ➤ coefficient of *reliability and split-half *reliability.

internal ear Collectively, the middle and inner parts of the ear.

internal environment A general term used to cover any and all processes and their effects occurring inside the body.

internal–external scale A self-report inventory designed to measure the degree to which a person perceives control of his or her behaviors as arising from internal or from external factors. ➤ locus of control for more detail here. Abbreviated as *I–E scale*.

internal inhibition ➤ inhibition, internal.

internalization 1. The acceptance or adaptation of beliefs, values, attitudes, practices, standards, etc. as one's own. In traditional psychoanalytic theory the superego is assumed to develop through the process of internalization of the standards and values of the parents. Within traditional approaches to social psychology and the study of personality an important issue is the degree to which a person attributes his or her behavior to such internalized motives. See here ➤ locus of control and compare with ➤ externalization. Also, differentiate from ➤ introjection, where the values are 'borrowed' rather than adopted, and from ➤ socialization, where the behavior may conform to societal values without commitment or belief. **2.** Occasionally, although with increasing frequency, the learning of highly abstract rule systems. Thus a child learning to speak is described as having internalized the rules of the grammar of language.

internal rectus One of the muscles controlling the eye.

internal secretion gland ➤ gland.

internal senses The senses of ➤ interoception and ➤ proprioception.

internal validity ➤ validity, internal.

International Classification of Diseases (ICD) A system of classification of diseases developed under the auspices of the World Health Organization. Over the years many revisions of the ICD have been published; as of this writing the most recent system is the tenth, known as *ICD–10*, published in 1992. The ICD has an extensive section on mental and behavioral disorders, which is in wide use in many countries. The other major system in use in clinical psychology and psychiatry is the one laid out in the ➤ **Diagnostic and Statistical Manual** (DSM), which was developed by the American Psychiatric Association. The most recent revision of the DSM (*DSM–IV*) was carried out with a mandate to coordinate terminology with that of the *ICD–10*. The definitions of the various mental and behavioral disorders in this volume reflect the usage patterns of both the DSM and the ICD and hence are appropriate for Europe, Asia, and North America.

International Phonetic Alphabet (IPA) A phonetic alphabet of approximately 95 phones. It is rich and flexible enough for all of the phonemes of the world's languages to be represented.

interneuron A connecting neuron, one that lies between sensory (afferent) and motor (efferent) neurons. Found within the central nervous system. Also called *internuncial neuron* and, in older texts, *association neuron*.

internuncial neuron ➤ interneuron.

interoception The sense of internal functioning, the perception of events within the body. An *interoceptor* is any sense organ or receptor that is activated by stimuli arising within the body. Included are hunger, thirst, nausea, visceral sensations and the like.

interoceptor Any internal sense organ or receptor. Contrast with ➤ **exteroceptor** and ➤ **proprioceptor**. var., *enteroceptor*.

interocular distance The distance between the pupils when the eyes are in normal position for distance viewing, i.e. focused on infinity.

interpersonal 1. Generally, characterizing relations between two or more persons, with the connotation that the interaction is mutual and reciprocal. **2.** Relating to phenomena, properties, effects, etc. that result from such interactions. **3.** Broadly, that which is social.

interpersonal control The term refers to a set of processes whereby a person regulates interactions with others and with the environment. It is considered a dynamic process that changes with conditions to maintain a desired level of interaction.

interpersonal theory A label used to characterize the personality theory of H. S. Sullivan, who theorized that personality dynamics and disorders thereof are due primarily to social forces and interpersonal situations.

interpersonal trust scale A scale developed by J. Rotter that measures a generalized expectation of the believability or trustworthiness of others.

interpolate To estimate, on the basis of two known values of a variable, a value that lies between them. Interpolations are based on the assumption that intermediate points conform to overall trends already observed. They are useful and often necessary but can occasionally lead to errors. Compare with ➤ **extrapolate**.

interpolated reinforcement ➤ **schedules of *reinforcement**.

interposition Partial blocking or obscuring of one object in the visual field by another object. One of the monocular cues for depth perception and one of the more compelling. Also called *occlusion*.

interpretation A process that is usually described as 'explaining a thing in a meaningful way,' or words to that effect. While not wrong, such a definition glosses over an important and complex implication: the very act of interpretation implies the existence of a conceptual schema or model on the part of the interpreter such that what is being observed and interpreted is assumed to conform logically to the facts and explanations inherent in the model.

Hence, there are two broad classes of usage: (a) Scientific interpretation, in which the model is a theoretical one and explanation is a characterization of reality. Thus, whether one interprets a response from a laboratory rat, the action of a neuron, the behavior of a group of people or a dream, the process will involve induction and generalization from some accepted scientific schema. Indeed, all such data *must* be interpreted; facts do not stand in isolation, they are always seen in relationship to other facts and models about these facts. The collection of data and the scientific interpretation of those data are, *ipso facto*, part of the same process. (b) Cognitive interpretation, in which the model is assumed to be the mental scheme within which all the incoming stimuli are identified, classified and reacted to. The interpretative act here is equally essential, since all stimuli are indeed data for the observer and are meaningless (some would say phenomenologically nonexistent) without cognitive interpretation.

interpretative therapy A general term used to characterize any form of psychotherapy in which the therapist interprets the significance and underlying symbolic meaning of the client's statements.

interquartile range The range between the first and third quartiles (i.e. between the 25th and 75th percentiles) of a distribution.

interrater reliability ➤ reliability, inter-rater.

interresponse time (IRT) Simply, the time between responses. It is an important dependent variable in evaluating operant behavior.

interrogative A ➤ speech act in which the speaker requests information from the listener.

interruption tone A tone produced by regular interruptions of a constant tone. If the interruptions are slow, beats are heard; if they are rapid, a tone with pitch corresponding to the rate of interruption is heard. Also called *intermittence tone*.

intersexuality The condition of having both male and female characteristics, particularly the secondary sex characteristics. See the discussion under ➤ hermaphrodite.

interstice A gap or space in a tissue or in the structure of an organ.

interstimulus interval (ISI) In any procedure that uses two stimuli, the time between the offset of the first stimulus and the onset of the second (compare with ➤ stimulus onset asynchrony). It is frequently used as an independent variable in experimental work; for example, in classical conditioning as the interval between the conditioned stimulus (CS) and the unconditioned stimulus (US), in studies of perception and cognition as the time allotted to a subject to process a brief stimulus prior to the presentation of another stimulus. ➤ masking.

interstitial cell-stimulating hormone (ICSH) ➤ luteinizing hormone.

interstitial fluid The fluid that fills the spaces between the cells of the body.

intersubjective Of subjective phenomena that are assumed to be experienced in similar fashion by others than oneself. The term *intersubjective testability* is used to refer to the essential criterion of any science that no event or effect is to be accepted as a legitimate part of the science unless it is of a type that can be described by more than one person. A *dream* is, from this point of view, not an acceptable datum, but the dreamer's *report* of the dream is.

intertrial interval (ITI) The time interval between two trials of an experiment. Often used as an independent variable in experiments on learning and memory.

interval of uncertainty (IU) In psychophysics, the interval between the upper and lower thresholds.

interval reinforcement ➤ **reinforcement, interval**.

interval scale ➤ **scale, interval**.

intervening variable ➤ **variable, intervening**.

intervention (technique) A generic term used for any procedure or technique that is designed to interrupt, interfere with and/or modify an ongoing process. It is used in medicine to characterize particular surgical procedures (e.g., cutting an afferent neural pathway to stop intractable pain), in psychotherapy to disrupt ongoing maladaptive behavior patterns (e.g., removing a child from a home where it was physically abused), in education to reorient a student's approach to learning (e.g., switching the student to a different school), etc.

intervertebral foramen ➤ **foramen magnum**.

interview A directed conversation. In psychology, interviews usually have either information-gathering or therapeutic purposes. Occasionally qualifiers are appended to denote the specific kind of interview under discussion.

interview, depth An interview designed to probe beneath the superficial, to allow for exploration of unknown variables and (the hope is) to provide insight into the nature of the factors discussed.

interviewer bias In an interview, the contaminating effect of the interviewer's opinions, expectations or general lack of objectivity. ➤ **experimenter bias** for an analogous bias in experimental research.

interview, nondirective A loose, less directed interview in which the person being interviewed is given considerable latitude to answer questions and/or to introduce new topics.

intimacy disorder A general term for the inability to become intimate with others, to share emotions, trust others or make a commitment to a stable, lasting relationship.

intimacy, principle of The generalization that the several elements of a Gestalt are intimately related to each other so as to produce, by their mutual interdependence, the perceived 'whole.' Individual elements or parts of a Gestalt may not be removed or replaced without disrupting or changing it; they are not independent from each other nor from the whole percept. ➤ **Gestalt psychology**.

intolerance of ambiguity ➤ **ambiguity, intolerance of**.

intonation A general term covering the modulations of the voice, the stress patterns, and the rise and fall in pitch while speaking. Such modulations play an important grammatical role in the spoken language. For example, a simple sequence of words like 'paint the box brown' can be uttered as many different sentences by varying the intonation pattern (well over a dozen can be generated if you capitalize 'Brown'). ➤➤ **intonation contour, stress** (2).

intonation contour The intonation pattern over a full phrase or sentence. 'Mary slew a tiger' can be either a simple declarative or a question depending on whether the intonation contour is falling or rising.

intoxication 1. Generally, from the Greek for *poison*, the state of having been poisoned by some substance. **2.** Specifically, such a state produced by excessive alcohol intake. In standard psychiatric terminology, mental disorders that result from substance-induced intoxication are classified as ➤ **organic mental disorders** and are typically noted by the responsible substance; e.g., alcohol intoxication, caffeine intoxication, amphetamine intoxication, etc.

intra- A prefix from the Latin meaning *within* or *inside*. Compare with ➤ **inter-** and ➤ **intro-** for a subtle distinction.

intracellular fluid The fluid inside the cells.

intraception H. Murray's terms for an outlook on life that is subjective, internally motivated, imaginative. Contrast with ➤ **extraception**.

intracranial stimulation (ICS) ➤ **electrical brain stimulation**.

intradimensional shift ➤ **reversal *learning**.

intrafusal fibers Muscle fibers that function as stretch receptors. They are arranged in parallel with ➤ **extrafusal fibers** and detect the length of a muscle. Also called *muscle spindles*.

intramural Lit., within the walls; hence, pertaining to events occurring inside the boundaries of an institution.

intransitivity Lit., not capable of passing over or through. Hence, a characteristic of a relation between elements x, y and z such that x is related to y in some fashion and y is related to z in like fashion but without it necessarily being the case that x is so related to z. Liking is such a relation; the fact that a person x likes another y and y likes z does not imply that x necessarily likes z. Intransitivity implies that the scale being used is multidimensional and the relation multicausal. Contrast with ➤ **transitivity**.

intraocular modification An umbrella term covering any change in the visual signal due to the characteristics of the eye; e.g., refraction by the cornea and lens, light scattering, light absorption, etc.

intrapsychic 1. Of anything assumed to arise or take place within the mind. 2. Of interactions between internal, covert factors; e.g., *intrapsychic conflicts* refer to conflicts between beliefs, needs, desires, etc.

intrapsychic ataxia ➤ **mental *ataxia**.

intraverbal In Skinner's behaviorist analysis of language, a class of verbal operants made up of social responses and incidental conversational utterances.

intraversion A common misspelling of ➤ **introversion** produced by the failure to appreciate the distinction between ➤ **intra-** and ➤ **intro-**.

intrinsic From the Latin, meaning *inwardly* or *inward*. Used generally to characterize a property of something that reflects the essential nature of the thing. The connotation is that the property derives none of its character from outside sources. Contrast with ➤ **extrinsic** (1).

intrinsic eye muscles ➤ **eye muscles**.

intrinsic interest Quite literally, interest in an object or an activity that derives from a desire for that object or activity 'for its own sake'; e.g., interest in learning to paint simply for aesthetic pleasure. Contrast with ➤ **extrinsic interest**.

intrinsic motivation A term used to refer to the motivation of any behavior that is dependent on factors that are internal in origin. Intrinsic motivation usually derives from feelings of satisfaction and fulfillment, not from external rewards. Contrast with ➤ **extrinsic motivation** and see the discussion under ➤ **motivation**.

intrinsic validity ➤ **validity, intrinsic**.

intro- Prefix meaning *moving within* or *toward the inside*. Distinguish from ➤ **intra-**, where the notion of movement is absent.

introjection 1. Generally, the process by which aspects of the external world are absorbed into or incorporated within the self, the internal representation then taking over the psychological functions of the external objects. 2. Specifically, in psychoanalysis, that process where the parent figures are the external objects and the *introjects* (as they are called) are the values of the parents; the process here is assumed to lead to the formation of the superego. 3. Reversing the directional flow of 1 and

2, a process of projecting one's own characteristics into inanimate objects; ➤ **animism**.

intromission Placing or inserting one part inside another.

intropunitive Characterizing the tendency to react to frustration by directing anger and blame toward oneself, the internally focused emotions often being experienced as guilt or shame. Contrast with ➤ **extrapunitive** and compare with ➤ **impunitive**.

introspection **1**. Generally, the act of looking inward, the examination of one's mental experiences. **2**. The report of such an inward glance, specifically the mental contents of one's consciousness. ➤ **introspectionism**.

introspectionism Roughly synonymous with ➤ **structuralism** (1), the school of psychology founded on the method of careful and systematic introspection. The basic operation was to present trained observers with controlled stimuli and to have them report back their introspections about covert mental processes while perceiving them. As several critics have noted, introspection is not a true examination of the contents of consciousness, as its proponents claimed, but a retrospective glance back at that which has passed through consciousness.

In a most general way the term *introspection* is still used occasionally in cases where covert mental activity is not easily convertible into directly observable behavior, as in some problem-solving and psycholinguistic experiments, but *introspectionism* as an approach to the study of mind is defunct.

introversion A turning inward. Used in personality theory to refer to the tendency to shrink from social contacts and become preoccupied with one's own thoughts. Although presumably a 'normal' characteristic, there are many who feel that extreme forms of introversion border on the pathological; e.g., *autism*. Curiously, in our culture, such suspicions are rarely voiced of

those exhibiting extreme ➤ **extraversion**.

introversion–extraversion ➤ **extraversion–introversion**.

introvert A label used for an individual who displays the behaviors discussed under ➤ **introversion**. Jung also used it for one of his personality types.

intrusion response (or **error**) In an ordered or serial recall experiment any response that either (a) was not in the original list or (b) occurred in the wrong position in the list.

intuition A mode of understanding or knowing characterized as direct and immediate and occurring without conscious thought or judgement. There are two distinct connotations which often accompany this term: (a) that the process is unmediated and somehow mystical; (b) that it is a response to subtle cues and relationships apprehended implicitly, unconsciously. The former borders on the unscientific and is not recommended, although it is certainly common enough in the nontechnical literature; the latter hints at a number of difficult but fascinating problems in the study of human behavior in the presence of complex situations. See here ➤ **implicit *learning, learning without *awareness**.

intuitive type One of Jung's hypothesized personality types. ➤ **function types**.

in utero Latin for *within the uterus*.

in vacuo Latin for *in a vacuum*. Often used metaphorically to refer to operations or processes carried out without knowledge of related factors.

invalid **1**. Failing to fulfill the canons of logic; used of any statement, proposition, argument or method that does not follow logically from the premises. **2**. By extension, of any test or other evaluative device that fails to measure what it was intended or designed to measure. ➤ **validity** et seq.

invalidate **1**. In logic, to render an argument or conclusion invalid, to prove it false. **2**. By extension, to demonstrate the lack of worth of an experiment and its conclusions either by demonstrating the lack of coherent theoretical analysis of the problem it was designed to explicate or by showing that the procedures used were improper.

invariable hues Hues that do not show the ➤ **Bezold-Brücke effect**, those that do not change with changes in illuminance. Three spectral hues are invariant, 478 nm (a yellow), 503 nm (a green) and 578 nm (a red) and one extraspectral hue that is a mixture of short and long wavelengths (a purple).

invariance Generally, characteristic of that which does not change. The term is most often used with the qualifier *relative*. That is, few things in this world are truly invariant but some display greater invariance, greater consistency from circumstance to circumstance than others. In general, in the study of perception and learning, those aspects of the stimulus world that display the higher invariances, relative to other aspects, are learned most quickly and easily.

invasive 1. Generally, pertaining to any therapy or procedure that 'invades' the body in some direct manner, particularly surgical. 2. Pertaining to tumors or growths that have a tendency to spread. Contrast with ➤ **noninvasive**.

inventory An ordered listing or cataloging of items. The term applies broadly; any check-list, instrument, test or questionnaire that assesses traits, opinions, beliefs, aptitudes, behaviors, etc. may be so labeled; e.g., the *Minnesota Multiphasic Personality Inventory*.

inverse correlation An occasional synonym for ➤ **negative *correlation**.

inverse factor analysis ➤ **factor analysis, inverse**.

inverse nystagmus ➤ **rotational *nystagmus**.

inversion 1. Generally, any process of turning inside out or upside down, or the result of such a process. 2. In statistics, transposing a series of numbers. 3. In mathematics, a momentary reversal of a function or the curve of a function. 4. In genetics, ➤ **chromosomal alterations**. 5. = ➤ **sexual *inversion**. 6. In older psychoanalytic writings, ➤ **homosexuality**.

inversion of affect Sudden switching between two emotions that are at opposite poles on a continuum, usually love and hatred. Typically seen as a sign of a deep ambivalence.

inversion, sexual A more-or-less obsolete term that has been used at various times to mean: 1. Hermaphroditism. 2. Transvestism. 3. Homosexuality, specifically the taking on of the role of the opposite sex in sexual acts. n., *invert*.

inverted factor analysis ➤ **inverse *factor analysis**.

inverted Oedipus (complex) In psychoanalysis, an ➤ **Oedipus complex** in which the parent of one's gender becomes the object of libidinal attachment.

inverted sadism Repressed *sadism*. Note that, as the term is used, it refers to an unconscious state the existence of which is hypothesized on the basis of an extreme withdrawal from any conscious display of aggression, violence, hostility, etc.

inverted-U curve (or **distribution**) Quite literally, any distribution the curve of which is shaped like an inverted letter U, with high frequency for moderate values and low frequency for both very low and very high values. A classic example is performance on a task as a function of arousal level; performance is optimal at moderate levels and drops off with either increases or decreases in arousal.

investment From the Latin, meaning *clothing*. 1. In psychoanalysis, an approximate synonym of *cathexis*; the connotation is of expanding psychic energy, of 'dressing up' an object or figure with one's affect. If one has fear of an authority figure then the fear is said to be *invested in* that figure. 2. In physiology, a covering or sheath.

inviolacy need H. Murray's term for the need to defend oneself, the need to counteract depreciation of self.

in vitro Latin for *in glass*. Hence, to refer to biological or physiological tests or experiments carried out in isolation (e.g., in a test tube) rather than in the whole organism. Contrast with ➤ **in vivo**.

in vivo Latin for *in the living body*. Compare with ➤ **in vitro**.

involuntary 1. Characterizing that which is not volitional, that which occurs because of external compulsions. 2. Characterizing those psychological processes or behaviors that are not under voluntary control. Involuntary behaviors and processes are typically: (a) reflex-like and elicited from an organism by a particular stimulus (see here ➤ **classical conditioning**); or (b) ➤ **fixed-action patterns** which are part of the genetic make-up of a particular species; or (c) extremely well-learned, automatized responses that occur without the sense that one has willed them.

involution From the Latin, meaning *roll into*, used in the sense of a degeneration, a retrograde change, a turning inward. An occasional synonym for *menopause*.

involutional depression An obsolete term once used for depressions that occurred in women following the onset of menopause (➤ **involution**). Such depressions are now treated as a form of a ➤ **major *depressive episode** and not as a special psychiatric category. Similarly obsolete are the terms *involutional psychotic reaction* and *involutional melancholia*.

involutional melancholia ➤ **involutional depression**.

involutional psychotic reaction ➤ **involutional depression**.

I/O Abbreviation for: 1. The field of ➤ **industrial/organizational psychology**. 2. ➤ **input/output**.

ion A charged molecule; *anions* have negative charge, *cations* positive.

ionotropic receptors Receptors that operate by directly opening *ion* channels that allow specific ions to flow in and out of the cell. Compare with ➤ **metabotropic receptors**.

IPA ➤ **International Phonetic Alphabet**.

iprindole A tricyclic compound used as an ➤ **antidepressant drug**.

iproniazide A monoamine oxidase inhibitor used as an ➤ **antidepressant drug**.

ips(a)- Prefix meaning *of one's own*, *of the self*, *the same*. var., *ips(o)-*.

ipsative Reflected or measured against the self. An ipsative personality test, for example, might reveal that an individual is higher in need for achievement than in need for affiliation, but not reveal whether the person is high or low on either need relative to national norms.

ipsilateral Pertaining to the same side. Also called *homolateral*. Contrast with ➤ **contralateral**.

ips(o)- ➤ **ips(a)-**.

IPSP Abbreviation for *inhibitory postsynaptic potential*. ➤ **postsynaptic potential**.

IQ ➤ **intelligence quotient**. Probably the best-known abbreviation in psychology.

ir- ➤ **in-**.

iris The pigmented muscular membrane that projects from the ciliary body of the eye. The aperture in the center is the pupil, which adjusts to control the amount of light entering the eye.

iris reflex ➤ **pupillary reflex**.

iritic reflex ➤ **pupillary reflex**.

irradiation The central notion here is diffusion or radiation of something from a central point of origin and all specialized uses of the term involve this idea of 'spread.' 1. In optics, the spreading of radiant energy from a light source; measured in relation to the radiant flux per unit area. 2. In perception, the phenomenon whereby a bright stimulus appears larger when viewed against a dark background. 3. In physiology, the spread of afferent neural impulses. **4.** In Pavlovian conditioning, two meanings: (a) The elicitation of a conditioned response by stimulation similar but not identical to the original stimulus. This use is essentially synonymous with that of ➤ **stimulus *generalization**. (b) Spread of cortical activity from a central point. Note that this last meaning was introduced by Pavlov to explain that given in 4(a).

irradiation theory An out-of-date term for a theory of learning that makes essentially the same assumptions as ➤ **trial-and-error *learning**, which itself is also out of date as a general theory of learning.

irrational In violation of the rules of logic. Typically used of such cognitive acts as thought, judgement and decision-making that do not follow the canons of logic with the (often implicit) assumption that ➤ **rational** thought or judgements could reasonably be expected under the conditions. Distinguish subtly from ➤ **non-rational**, where reason and logic are seemingly absent but not necessarily violated. A common connotation of irrational is that acts so described are assumed to have been carried out under the pressures of emotional factors that have, somehow, overridden the logical, rational faculties – a connotation which is certainly legitimate in many contexts but which should probably not be applied as widely as it is.

irrational type ➤ **rational type**.

irresistible-impulse test A legal principle set in 1922 in the USA for the establishment of an ➤ **insanity defense**. It states that a person is not to be held responsible for a criminal act if it can be shown that he/she acted through an 'irresistible impulse' which he/she was unable to control because of a mental disorder. It has been rejected by most courts and is rarely used today.

irresponsibility The basis of an ➤ **insanity defense**. In forensic psychiatry and legal parlance, the principle that an individual is not to be adjudged guilty of a crime if it can be determined that the normal conditions under which one could be held to be responsible for his or her actions do, in fact, not pertain. Various legal precedents have been established (and revoked) over the years; see, e.g., ➤ **ALI defense (ruling)**, **Durham rule**, **irresistible-impulse test**, **McNaghten rule**.

irritability **1.** Generally, excitability. All specialized meanings reflect this sense. **2.** Of all living tissue, the property of responding to stimulation. **3.** By extension, the property of an organ, muscle or part thereof such that it responds to particular classes of stimulation. **4.** Of persons, excessive responsiveness, over-sensitivity, impatience.

IRT ➤ **interresponse time**.

ischemia Reduced blood flow to a part of the body. var. *ischaemia*.

Ishihari color plates A series of color plates printed in various hues such that coherent figures (letters, numbers) are visible to the normal eye but not to the color-blind or color-deficient eye. The plates consist of dots that are carefully selected to control saturation and brightness so that only the hue dimension reflects the figures.

ISI ➤ **interstimulus interval**.

island of Reil The insula, a part of the cortex buried totally in the fold of the Sylvian fissure. Largely because of its secluded location little is known about its functional relationships with the rest of the brain. Parts of it have been implicated in motor functions and evidence for projections from gustatory and visceral sensory systems has been offered. It is found only in primates.

-ism A richly polysemous, noun-forming suffix used to denote *usage*, *action*, *practice*, *condition*, *principle*, *characteristic* or *doctrine*. The most common is the last of these and, as some wit put it, if you have enough -ists in agreement you have an - ism.

iso- Combining form meaning *equal* or *the same*.

isochronal 1. Equal in rate, frequency, or time of occurrence. **2.** Equal in ➤ **chronaxie**. var., *isochronous*.

isocoria The normal condition, in which both eyes show equal pupil size even though there may be different amounts of light falling on the two eyes.

isocortex ➤ neocortex.

isolated explosive disorder ➤ **intermittent explosive disorder**.

isolates, breeding ➤ **isolation** (2).

isolation 1. Generally, separateness, apartness. The meaning here is carried into several specialized usages: **2.** In genetics, the condition in which a breeding population is separated from other members of the species. This separation may be brought about by complex social/cultural factors or by simple geographical conditions. Such a group is said to be made up of *breeding isolates*. **3.** In psychoanalysis, a defense mechanism that operates unconsciously and functions by severing the conscious psychological ties between some unacceptable act or impulse and its original memory source. In this sense, the original experience is not forgotten but it is separated from the affect originally associated with it. The classical theory views this mechanism as a common one in obsessional neuroses. Also called *isolation of affect*. **4.** In Jung's terms, a feeling of psychological estrangement from others. Also called *psychic isolation*, Jung argued that it derived from deep secrets, originally from the collective unconscious, which one feels must be kept from others.

isolation amentia An obsolete term for the mental retardation observed in cases of anaclitic depression.

isolation effect ➤ **von Restorff effect**.

isolation of affect ➤ **isolation** (3).

isometric contraction (or **twitch**) Muscle contraction that causes tension but no movement, as when pushing against a wall – there is no actual contraction of the muscle and its length is not altered.

isomorphism 1. In mathematics, a formal point-by-point relationship between two systems. **2.** In Gestalt psychology, the hypothesis that there is such a structural similarity between excitatory fields in the cortex and conscious experience. Note that the correspondence here is not presumed to be between the physical stimulus and the brain but between the perception of the stimulus and the brain.

isophilia Nonsexual attraction and affection toward members of one's own sex. Distinguish from ➤ **homosexuality**.

isophonic contour Lit., equal-sound contour. The line or contour representing the set of coincidences between values of separate dimensions of sound that are perceived as identical. The point made by an isophonic contour is that the dimensions of sound co-vary: loudness, for example, is not merely a function of sound pressure but is dependent on the frequency of the tone. To take one case, a tone of 400 Hz at 61 db is heard as equal in loudness to a tone of 600 Hz at 59 db.

isotonic Lit., equal tension. Hence, an *isotonic contraction* is one in which there is equal tension on the muscle throughout the movement, as occurs in simple lifting of the hand: an *isotonic solution* is one in which the osmotic pressure between it and a cell suspended in it are equal, so that there is no transmission across the cell membrane. Contrast with ➤ **hypertonic** and ➤ **hypotonic**.

-ist Suffix used to denote *agent* or *actor*; an advocate of an ➤ **-ism**.

It 1. Originally a psychosomatic entity, an inner power or psychic force that was assumed to shape both body and mind. **2.** Later, in classical psychoanalysis, the ➤ **id**.

ITA ➤ **initial teaching alphabet**.

itch Itching is, oddly enough, a source of much interest and confusion. It is, as we all know, a rather attention-demanding condition although little is known about the underlying physiology. Presumably, an itch is produced by a fairly low level of irritation of free nerve endings in the skin. The irritation may be chemical, electrical or mechanical, although itching has also been reported in the phantom limbs of amputees indicating that a central component is involved as well. The two main unanswered questions are: (a) What is the relationship between itch and pain? And (b) why does scratching work?

item analysis Generally, the detailed analysis of the individual items of a test or a questionnaire with the purpose of assessing their reliability and validity. Such analyses can focus on content and form or they can be carried out quantitatively in terms of how effectively each item contributes to the overall reliability and validity of the test. In the broadest sense the term covers any analysis including those concerned with factors like item ambiguity, difficulty, time components, etc. In a narrower sense, the term will be used specifically for an assessment of how effectively each individual item contributes to the overall validity of the test. ➤ **validity**.

item difficulty Quite literally, the difficulty of an item on a test. It is defined in terms of the frequency with which the individuals who attempt it answer it correctly.

itemized rating scale ➤ **rating scale, itemized**.

item reliability ➤ **reliability, item**.

item validity The degree to which an individual item on a test assesses what it was designed to assess. ➤ **validity** et seq.

-itis A suffix denoting *inflammation*.

ITPA ➤ **Illinois Test of Psycholinguistic Abilities**.

IU ➤ **interval of uncertainty**.

J

J In Hullian theory, an abbreviation for delay of reinforcement.

jabberwocky Lab slang for artificially constructed verbal materials that are formed using English function words and morphological forms to represent the structure of a sentence frame but using only nonsense for the content words. The term, of course, comes from Lewis Carroll's famous poem in which extensive use of this technique was made ("Twas brillig, and the slithy toves . . .'). Jabberwocky, perhaps not surprisingly, is much easier to read than pure nonsense (i.e. without the function words) but more difficult than ordinary prose.

Jacksonian epilepsy ➤ epilepsy, Jacksonian.

Jacksonian march ➤ Jacksonian motor *epilepsy.

Jacksonian motor epilepsy ➤ epilepsy, Jacksonian motor.

Jacksonian sensory epilepsy ➤ epilepsy, Jacksonian sensory.

Jackson's principle (or **law**) The generalization that the degree of resistance of a mental function to disease or natural deterioration is directly related to the evolutionary antiquity of that function in the species. That is, recently evolved cognitive functions are lost first, those of greater evolutionary age are lost later. Analogous principles have been argued to hold for learned behaviors; the earlier in an individual's life something was learned the more robust that knowledge will be in the face of disease or other insult.

Jacobson's organ ➤ vomeronasal system.

jactation A rare term for an extreme restlessness with uncontrollable jerky movements.

Jamesian Characteristic of or pertaining to the work, theories and overall orientation of the American psychologist/philosopher William James (1842–1910). Although there is no broad, structured theory associated with James's work, the adjectival form is used with regard to the particular point of view that formed the empirical and philosophical underpinnings of his intellectual life. Specifically, these are pragmatism and functionalism, a strong affiliation with evolutionary theory and an openmindedness concerning novel and often unorthodox views. For a glimpse of the Jamesian point of view on a few topics ➤ **stream of consciousness, theories of *emotion, tip-of-the-tongue state**.

James-Lange theory of emotion ➤ theories of *emotion.

jargon 1. Basically, speech that is meaningless to others. Thus, the specialized language of a group or profession will be jargon to one not trained in it and the nonsensical babble of some aphasics will be jargon to all. 2. A type of pre-language vocalization observed in some infants whereby they babble in extended 'phrases' which have an intonation contour like that of real adult sentences. To a casual listener it sounds at first as though the infant is actually talking. Note that use 1 generally implies that there is a meaningful message there somewhere, use 2 does not.

jargonaphasia A form of ➤ aphasia in which the patient's speech is incoherent. Individual words are usually pronounced properly but syntax is garbled and the way the words are used is semantically inappropriate. Regarded by many as a form of ➤ **Wernicke's *aphasia**.

J coefficient A measure of the validity of the several component tests in a vocational test battery. The technique is based on correlations between test scores and job preference (the J is for 'job') with the special feature that each of the specific aspects of a given job is weighted as to its relative importance by both supervisors and workers. The J coefficient is an index of the ➤ synthetic *validity of a test battery.

J curve Generally, any curve of a frequency distribution that when plotted is shaped approximately like the capital letter **J**. That is, distributions have very low frequencies at the low values and rapidly increasing frequencies at successively higher values. There is also a *reverse J curve*, in which the low values reflect high frequencies and vice versa.

jealousy Generally, any emotional state classified as a special form of anxiety and assumed to derive from a lack of sense of security in the affections of one who is loved. The jealousy is directed toward a third party, the rival who is perceived as garnering the affections of the object of love. Distinguish from ➤ envy, where there need be no loved one, merely a desire for things possessed by the rival.

jitter ➤ auditory *flicker.

jnd ➤ just noticeable difference.

job analysis A loose term for the study of the particular aspects of a given job. Those aspects may range from the tasks and duties of the position, to an examination of the desirable qualities of an employee, to the conditions of employment including pay, promotion opportunities, vacations, etc.

Jocasta complex Jocasta was the mother and wife of Oedipus and in keeping with psychoanalytic tradition the term stands for the mother's role in the playing out of the ➤ Oedipus complex.

John Henry effect The tendency occasionally seen in industrial settings where people who know they are in a control group put forth extraordinary efforts in an attempt to outdo those in the experimental group. When it occurs it can negate the purpose of having a control group. The effect is named for the mythical steel worker whose name is a symbol of superhuman effort.

joint event In probability theory, any event that is the simultaneous occurrence of any two (or more) other events. In dealing from a deck of cards, for example, a 'black five' would be a joint event since it consists of all cards which are both black and have five spots.

joint probability The probability of occurrence of a ➤ joint event; it is given as the product of the probabilities of each of the specific events that comprise the joint event.

joking relationship A social relationship that permits the telling of jokes, playing tricks, teasing or displaying a privileged familiarity in a socially approved manner that would be regarded as offensive and insulting if engaged in by persons outside of the relationship. It is basically what permits Jews to tell anti-Semitic jokes to each other and blacks to call each other 'Nigger' without offense.

Jost's law The generalization that (a) within a given time interval material learned recently is more likely to be forgotten than memories of greater antiquity and (b) practice with material facilitates recall of the older memories more than of those more recently acquired. The term is largely obsolete, and both of these principles are now captured by the conceptualization of human memory as comprised of a ➤ short-term *memory and a ➤ long-term *memory. See these terms for clarification.

Joubert syndrome A genetic disorder marked by a failure of normal development of the ➤ vermis. Patients with the disorder often show symptoms of ➤ autism.

judgement 1. Generally, the process of forming an opinion or reaching a conclusion based on the available material; the opinion or conclusion so reached. **2.** The hypothesized mental faculty that func-

JUKE

tions so as to carry out such judgement. This meaning is only found in older writings. **3.** In logic, a statement of the relation between symbols in sentence form. This sense has now been taken over by the term ➤ **proposition**. **4.** A critical evaluation of some thing, event or person. **5.** In psychophysics, the decision concerning presence or absence of the signal or estimations of its intensity relative to other stimuli.

Juke The fictitious name of a large extended family allegedly riddled with all manner of unsavoury characters, social misfits, criminals and degenerates, fully half of whom were supposedly 'feeble minded.' Studies of this family and the equally (in)famous ➤ **Kallikaks** were carried out in the late 19th and early 20th centuries and were taken by many as providing strong evidence for the hereditarian position on intelligence, temperament, socialization, etc. The actual investigations, however, were so badly carried out and the role of the environment so thoroughly neglected in the analyses that they are no longer taken seriously. ➤ **heredity–environment controversy**.

Julesz's stereogram A type of stereogram in which each half-field is made up of an array of computer-produced random dots. The two half-fields are identical except for an inner portion of one which is shifted a bit to one side. The shift produces the retinal disparity required so that when viewed through a stereoscope the inner portion is seen as floating above the background texture or as sunk beneath it.

jumping stand ➤ **Lashley jumping stand**.

juncture In linguistics, a ➤ **suprasegmental** that marks the manner in which speech sounds are joined, specifically the pausing patterns. For example, by changing the pause point a 'light house-keeper' becomes a 'light-house keeper.'

Jungian Pertaining to or representative of the analytical psychology of Carl

Gustav Jung (1875–1961). Although Jung wrote broadly on such diverse topics as word associations, mythology, religion, telepathy, spiritualism and flying saucers, the adjectival form of his name is primarily associated with an approach to psychoanalysis that placed, relative to Freud's, little emphasis on the role of sex and sexual impulses and focused instead on the hypothesized deep, inherited *collective unconscious* with its universal ideas or images, the *archetypes*. Jungian analysis is of the 'deep' variety and concerns itself with rich interpretation of symbols and makes extensive use of dreams.

'junk box' classification A sobriquet applied (critically) to any of a number of diagnostic classifications, especially *aphasia*, *autism* and *schizophrenia*. The implications of the label are that the diagnostic category does not really represent a well-defined syndrome (or disease or condition) but rather is a loosely constructed conceptual 'junk box' into which all manner of individual cases are thrown because of superficial similarities (e.g., all aphasics show some form of language loss) and/or because the diagnostician frankly is unclear about how else to classify them.

just noticeable difference (jnd) The difference between two stimuli that is, under properly controlled experimental conditions, 'just noticeable.' Given the variability of our sensory systems, a stable value cannot be found for the difference. Rather, the jnd is determined to be that difference between two stimuli that is detected as often as it is undetected. Thus, it is viewed as a statistical estimate of the resolving power of a sensory system. For more detail on usage here see the discussion under ➤ **threshold** and ➤ **measurement of *threshold**.

just world bias The belief that we do live in a just world and that life really is fair. People who hold this bias tend to blame the victims of crimes or disasters on the grounds that those who suffer must, for some reason, deserve to suffer.

juxtaposition **1.** Generally, the positioning of two things next to each other. **2.** In Piagetian theory, the cognitive tendency of the young child to tie elements to each other in a kind of primitive 'and then' manner rather than see causal or logical links between them. Contrast this process with that of ➤ **syncretism** (2).

K

K Abbreviation for incentive motivation in Hullian theory.

K' Abbreviation for the physical incentive in Hullian theory.

k The ➤ **coefficient of *alienation**.

kainic acid A ➤ **neurotoxin** that destroys the cell bodies of neurons but leaves the axons undamaged.

kairos Within existential psychology, the critical moment of decision in one's life, a moment of compelling personal experience when the meanings and values attached to living undergo transformation and when decisive personality changes occur. ➤➤ **existentialism** and **existential therapy**.

kakosmia ➤ **cacosmia**.

Kallikak A pseudonym used of two branches of a family tree both of which ostensibly sprang from the loins of one man. The 'good Kallikaks' (who were all, according to H. H. Goddard's report in 1912, fine, moral, upstanding members of the community) supposedly came from his marriage with a middle-class woman; the 'bad Kallikaks' (who, in Goddard's analysis, were nearly all degenerates, feeble-minded, criminals and/or vagrants) descended from his brief affair with a retarded woman. Goddard's eugenicist analysis was so tainted by his own peculiar prejudices concerning the role of heredity in shaping behavior that this once-celebrated case is no longer of any scientific value. ➤➤ **Juke** and the discussion under ➤ **heredity–environment controversy**.

Kanner's syndrome A term occasionally used for ➤ **infantile *autism**.

kary(o)- Combining form meaning *nucleus*.

karyotype A systematic array of the chromosomes of a single cell in graphic form.

kata Variation of ➤ **cata-**.

katasexuality A rare ➤ **paraphilia** in which one's sexual preferences are deceased persons (also called *necrophilia*) or animals (also called *bestiality*).

K complex A sudden, brief, high amplitude waveform in the EEG of a sleeping person. They typically occur at about one minute intervals during stage 2 ➤ **sleep**, but can be triggered by outside noises.

Keller plan A form of personalized instruction developed by the behaviorist Fred Keller. It is based on presenting students with material in relatively small units. When the student feels ready he or she takes a quiz on that unit and, if successful, moves to the next unit. In keeping with the operant-conditioning framework within which Keller worked there are no overt punishments for not passing a unit and only passing grades are awarded. The amount of time needed to complete a course of study is up to the individual student. Teachers are available as resource persons for advice, discussion, clarification, etc.

Kendall tests Any of several nonparametric measures of correlation useful when the data do not satisfy the assumptions of standard correlational analyses. See, e.g., ➤ **coefficient of *concordance, tau coefficient of correlation**.

Kent-Rosanoff List (or **Test**) A free-association test originally developed for assessing imagery and thought patterns in which an individual's associations to a standardized list of words are compared with a set of norms. Although the test itself is not in common use today, the norms continue to be used in studies of verbal learning.

kernel sentence A simple, active, declarative sentence. The term came from early conceptualizations of ➤ **transformational**

*grammar in which such sentences were seen as linguistically (and perhaps psycholinguistically) significant because they are derived from the base with the fewest number of transformations.

ketones Organic acids that are broken down into carbon dioxide and water, releasing energy in the process. They result from the breakdown of fats and, along with glucose, are readily metabolized by the brain and serve as an important energy source. Also known as *keto bodies* and *keto acids*.

ketosteroid A steroid produced by the adrenal cortices and the gonads.

key By extension from locksmithery, any device that contains information necessary to 'unlock' a message, to understand something. Hence: **1.** The set of rules or principles that allows one to encode and decode messages. **2.** The set of correct answers on a test. **3.** The legend on a graph, table or chart that reveals the significance of the notation system in use. **4.** A signal that sets the context within which a particular event is to be regarded; e.g. an art class is keyed to the acceptance of the nudity of a model in a nonsexual manner. **5.** In operant conditioning studies with pigeons, a small disc that the bird must peck in order to receive reinforcement.

Kiddie Mach Test A test designed to assess ➤ **Machiavellianism** in children. ➤➤ **Machiavellian scale**.

kid's culture A half-joking term with a serious and interesting reference. It refers to the notion that children have their own 'culture,' with social rules, games, specialized language devices, rituals, etc. Each person passes through the culture and is appropriately acculturated but only temporarily. An adult peering back to childhood finds it as difficult to apprehend fully the 'culture' as does an anthropologist studying a very different culture from his or her own.

kilo- Combining form meaning *1000*, or *multiplied by 1000*.

kin One's ➤ relatives (4).

kinase Any *enzyme* that causes movement. It is used as a combining form in physiology and physiological psychology.

kine- Combining form indicating *motion, movement*.

kinematics The study of motion.

kineme ➤ kinesics.

kinemorph ➤ kinesics.

kinephantom A movement illusion, particularly of shadows. The most common example is the experience of a rotating spoked object like a fan or wheel looking as if moving backward.

kinesia Motion sickness.

-kinesia Combining form meaning *movement*.

kinesics The study of the movements of the body and their communicative functions. The science, perhaps not surprisingly, shares some interesting parallels with descriptive linguistics. For example, it is possible to identify *kinemes*, which are analogs of *phonemes* in that they are classes of movements which are treated as conceptual categories inasmuch as variations within them are nonmeaningful. Combinations or sequences of kinemes then make up *kinemorphs* which are analogs of *morphemes*.

kinesiology The study of muscles and muscular movement.

kinesthetics The term literally means *feeling of motion*. It is used as an umbrella term to cover the sensations originating in muscles, tendons and joints. Along with ➤ **proprioception** and ➤ **equilibrium** (2), it makes up the sensory system that acquires its information from ➤ **interoceptors**.

kinetic Pertaining to physical motion.

kinetic depth effect A perceptual effect in which a visual pattern will appear to be flat (two-dimensional) when stationary but when moved give rise to an experience of depth (three-dimensional).

kin group A group of persons recognized as being related by blood or marriage.

King's (or Queen's) English The idealized standard form of 'proper' English of Great Britain. In studies of dialectology it is used as the basis for phonetic, semantic and syntactic distinctions in other regional and social class dialects. ➤ **Received Pronunciation, Standard English**.

kinocilia In the inner ear, the tallest of the hairs projecting from the surfaces of the cells of the semicircular canals. Compare with ➤ **stereocilia**.

kin selection In evolutionary biology, selection for activities that, while they may reduce the reproductive effectiveness of a particular organism, function so that the organism's close relatives have an increased likelihood of reproducing. ➤ **personal fitness** and **inclusive fitness**.

kin selection altruism ➤ **altruism**.

kinship A general term used to cover any social relationship based upon family. As the term is used it has components of consanguinal (blood) relationships as well as of those recognized by cultural convention, e.g., marriage and adoption. The roles, rights and obligations that such related individuals have with respect to each other are determined by their culture and not purely by the closeness of the biological relationship.

kinship, ritual A kinship relation based on a societally defined relationship. The most common example is the godfather.

Kleine-Levin syndrome A syndrome characterized by ➤ **hypersomnia** and ➤ **bulimia**. Typically observed in adolescent males.

kleptolagnia Sexual desire and excitement associated with stealing.

kleptomania An ➤ **impulse-control disorder** characterized by recurrent inability to resist impulses to steal. A defining feature of the disorder is that there is no immediate need or use for what is stolen.

Typically there is little or no planning involved but merely a sudden, acute impulse which is acted on.

Klinefelter's syndrome A chromosomal anomaly characterized genotypically by an XXY pattern in the sex chromosomes. Phenotypically such persons are male, but the penis may be unusually small, the testicles abnormally small and often undescended, and there are often marked feminine characteristics such as breast development.

klismaphilia A ➤ **paraphilia** characterized by the deriving of sexual stimulation from having an enema administered.

Kluge Hans, der ➤ Clever Hans.

Klüver-Bucy syndrome A collection of bizarre behaviors including visual *agnosia*, compulsive exploration, hypersexuality and profound changes in emotionality. It is not infrequently observed in cases of tumor removal or brain injuries to the temporal lobe and has been induced experimentally in monkeys by bilateral temporal lobectomy with partial destruction of amygdaloid nuclei and pyriform cortex. The interesting and puzzling aspect of the syndrome is that it involves behaviors that are quite 'cognitive' as well as those that are quite clearly 'emotional.'

knee A specialized term used in operant-conditioning studies to characterize a sudden increase in response rate followed by a compensatory decrease. When such a pattern of responding is presented in a graph of cumulative responding it looks like a 'knee' or bump on an otherwise smooth curve. Compare with ➤ **bite** (1).

knee-jerk reflex A reflex of the lower leg produced by a sharp tap on the patellar tendon just below the knee cap. It was this reflex that Twitmeyer studied in the first experimental investigation of classical conditioning (several years before Pavlov). Because of its long history in the study of the psychology of reflexes, the phrase 'knee-jerk' has taken on vaguely insulting properties and is often used synonymously with unthinking.

knowing how ➤ procedural *knowledge.

knowing self The ➤ I. ➤➤ self (1, 2).

knowing that ➤ declarative *knowledge.

knowledge 1. Collectively, the body of information possessed by a person or, by extension, by a group of persons or a culture. **2.** Those mental components that result from any and all processes, be they innately given or experientially acquired. The term is used in both senses here with the clear implication that knowledge is 'deep' or 'profound' and that it is more than simply a compendium of dispositions to respond or a collection of conditioned responses. To use the term is, prima facie, to deny the applicability of a behaviorist model to human thought. Within the philosophical and cognitive psychological approaches to ➤ epistemology and ➤ cognitive science, various forms of knowledge are typically distinguished; see the following entries for the more commonly cited. Note that *memory* is often used as a virtual synonym of *knowledge*. Combined terms like 'episodic knowledge' and 'declarative knowledge' will be used interchangeably with 'episodic memory' and 'declarative memory.' ➤ memory, et seq., for more detail and for combined terms not found here.

knowledge by acquaintance As distinguished from both ➤ procedural *knowledge and ➤ declarative *knowledge, knowledge of which we are directly aware, knowledge of people, places and things derived from sense data.

knowledge, declarative Knowledge about the world that can be represented as consciously known, factual knowledge. That is, knowledge about which a person can make a declaration; e.g., 'a rose is a kind of flower.' Gilbert Ryle liked to refer to it by the phrase 'knowing that . . .' Also called *factual knowledge*. Compare with ➤ procedural *knowledge.

knowledge, generic General knowledge about things in the world that is held independent of any specific events or episodes. The term is used interchangeably with *semantic knowledge* and ➤ semantic *memory.

knowledge of results Very general term used for any feedback of information to: (a) a subject in an experiment about the correctness of his or her responses; (b) a student in a learning situation about success or failure in mastering material; (c) a client in psychotherapy about progress made, etc.

knowledge, procedural Knowledge about how to do something; knowledge that is operational, practical. Unlike ➤ declarative *knowledge, procedural knowledge lies outside an individual's realm of consciousness. Some classic examples are knowing how to ride a bicycle or tie a knot or, interestingly, speak a language. Procedural knowledge lies behind complex actions and typically is rather resistant to attempts to make it conscious; try explaining to someone how to tie one's shoe-laces – it's much easier to show than to tell. Gilbert Ryle called it 'knowing how . . .' or *practical knowledge*.

known self The ➤ me. ➤➤ self (1, 2).

Kohler-Restorff phenomenon ➤ von Restorff effect.

Kolomogorov-Smirnov test A nonparametric statistical test that may be used to test the significance of the difference between one sample of scores and a population or the difference between two samples. The 'vodka test,' as it is jokingly called, is one of the more powerful nonparametric tests, invariably more sensitive to differences than *chi-square* and approximating that of the *t* test.

kolytic From the Greek for *hinder*, used of processes that are inhibitory.

König bars A set of bars used for measuring visual acuity. The standard for normal vision is a set of bars subtending 3 minutes of visual angle with 1-minute separations between them.

koro A culture-specific disorder found among Southeast Asian males. The primary symptom is a fear that the penis will retract into the abdomen and the belief that this will cause one's death.

Korsakoff's syndrome An ➤ **amnestic syndrome** often found in chronic alcoholics and named for its first systematic describer, the Russian physician S. S. Korsakoff. The most significant symptom is the loss of memory for recent events, although memory for the more remote remains intact. Intriguingly, Korsakoff's patients show much less disturbance of ➤ **implicit *memory** and ➤ **implicit *learning** than they do of learning and memory functions that are based on consciousness and awareness. Autopsies have tended to implicate the medial thalamus and the hippocampus as the brain structures involved. Also spelled Korsakov and Korsakow, and also known as *alcohol amnestic disorder* and *alcoholic dementia*.

Korte's laws A series of generalizations concerning the optimum apparent motion (➤**beta *motion**) in the ➤ **phi phenomenon**. Specifically, they express the relationships that hold between spatial separation of the successively presented stimuli, the intensity of the stimuli, the exposure times, and the interstimulus interval. Specifically: it is more difficult to see apparent motion when spatial separation is very wide, when illumination is very low and when the interstimulus interval is very short, although decrements in one or two variabies can be compensated for by increments in the other(s).

KPR ➤ **Kuder Preference Record**.

Krause end bulb One of the several encapsulated receptors that innervate the skin. It is found typically in mucocutaneous zones, tissue that is transitional between dry, glabrous skin and mucous membranes. Once thought to mediate temperature, they are now suspected of being responsive to mechanical stimulation.

Kretchmer types See discussion under ➤ **constitutional theory**.

K-R formulas ➤ **Kuder-Richardson formulas**.

Kruskal–Shepard scaling A type of multidimensional scaling procedure developed relatively independently by the mathematician W. A. Kruskal and the psychologist R. Shepard. The technique requires that subjects make judgements of the similarity of various stimuli; those judgements are then analyzed to determine the underlying psychological dimensions that were used to make the judgements.

Kruskal–Wallis test A nonparametric analysis of variance. Although it only handles one-way effects (i.e. it cannot test the effects of more than one variable) its sensitivity to difference is quite high, making it a useful test particularly when the assumptions of the *F-test* are not met.

K scale A specialized scale within the *MMPI* that is presumed to detect defensiveness.

K strategy In evolutionary biology, a type of reproductive breeding utilized by many species in which one (or, on occasions, two or three) offspring is born at one time. The K strategy involves considerable investment of energy and resources in the rearing of each offspring and a relatively long interbirth period. This strategy has been adopted by many mammals, most significantly by the great apes and, of course, by *Homo sapiens*. Compare with ➤ **r strategy**. Also called *K selection* or *K selection strategy*.

Kuder Preference Record The prototype of the so-called *interest inventories*. It consists of 168 three-choice items about broad vocational interests from which the individual is to select the one that is most preferred. The test consists of ten scales reflecting areas of vocational interest such as mechanical, scientific, persuasive, artistic, clerical and the like. Note that the test is not normative but ipsative; that is, an individual's score is a measure of his or her particular balance of preferences and does not reflect where he or she is relative to the population at large. The most recent version is known as the *Kuder Occupational Interest Survey*.

Kuder-Richardson formulas Frequently

used measures of ➤ **reliability** of a test. There are several variations for specialized situations although all are based on the correlations between comparable forms of the test. Often abbreviated as *K-R formulas or K-R coefficients of equivalence*.

kurtosis A statistical term used to describe the overall shape of a frequency distribution. The normal curve is *mesokurtic*, a peaked curve is *leptokurtic* and a flat curve is *platykurtic*. Kurtosis is the fourth ➤ **moment** (2) of a distribution.

kymograph A general term used for any device that makes a graphic recording of events. It operates by using a moving pen or marker that responds to pressure applied to it to make a trace on paper wrapped around a revolving drum. Rarely used any more, having been replaced by more sophisticated devices like polygraphs and computer output systems.

kypho- Prefix indicating *humped*.

kyto- A variation of ➤ **cyto-**.

L

L Abbreviation for: **1.** ➤ **lambert**. **2.** ➤ **lumen**. **3.** ➤ **limen**.

L₁,₂, . . . In the study of bi- and multilingualism, L₁ is used to note the first language learned, L₂ the second, etc.

labeling theory An appellation used of contemporary psychiatry by many of its critics who regard most approaches to clinical phenomena as little more than 'labeling' people. Their point, put most simply, is that the traditional diagnostic systems of Western psychiatry are not reflective of any true underlying mental illnesses but rather are merely labels that are attached to behavior patterns deemed 'abnormal' because they are unacceptable to society. Further, they argue, once the label has been attached, professionals, friends, and even the designated individual come to reflect the expectations of the label and behave accordingly, resulting in a classic instance of the ➤ **self-fulfilling prophecy**. This point of view is, to be sure, an extreme one and disputed by most mental-health professionals (although in gentler moments they will admit that it has some merit).

la belle indifférence ➤ *belle indifférence, la*.

labia (sing. **labium** = lip). **1.** Generally, lips. **2.** Specifically the fleshy folds that surround body orifices, especially the vagina.

labial Adjective form of *labium*, *labia*. Used of lips in general, but most commonly with reference to the oral lips. In linguistics it is descriptive of phones produced using one or both lips; e.g., *b* and *p* are *bilabials*.

labia majora The outer fatty folds that surround the vulva.

labia minora The inner, richly vascular folds surrounding the vulva.

labile Changeable, adaptable and, by ex-

tension, not stable. The term is used widely in psychology, most commonly of the changing expression of emotions. Here the connotation is negative, implying a lack of emotional stability.

labile personality ➤ **cyclothymic disorder**.

labiodental A class of speech sounds produced by using the lower lip and the upper teeth; e.g., *f* and *v* in *five*.

labyrinth **1.** From the Greek for *maze*, any structure of intricate pathways. **2.** Because of its complex and intricate membranous and bony construction, the inner ear that contains the sense organs for hearing and balance.

lachrymal Variation of ➤ **lacrimal**.

lacrimal Of or relating to tears. var., *lachrymal*.

lacrimal gland The tear gland. It lies beneath the upper eyelid and secretes tears which moisten the cornea. The tears drain into the nose through the *lacrimal duct*.

lactate **1.** vb. To produce milk. **2.** n. A salt derived from lactic acid.

lactation The production of milk by mammary glands.

lactogenic hormone ➤ **prolactin**.

lacuna A gap, a blank space, a hole. Used most often to refer to gaps in memory or in consciousness.

lacunar amnesia ➤ **episodic *amnesia**.

LAD (or **LAS**) An acronym for *language-acquisition device* (or *system* – bad jokes about masculine and feminine forms abound). It was originally hypothesized by N. Chomsky to be an innately given mechanism that operated upon the linguistic input to elaborate a representative grammar, a kind of 'language organ.' In Chomsky's conceptualization, LAD is preprogrammed with the underlying rules of universal grammar and will, depending on the language to which the child is exposed, select from the full set of rules those that are appropriate for the one spoken. The status of LAD is highly equivocal and most psycholinguists and cognitive psychologists find the idea fascinating but doubtful. However, others will treat it as though its reality was as unchallenged as, say, that of the pituitary gland. Also called LRCS for *language-responsible cognitive structure*.

Ladd-Franklin theory A theory of color vision, not generally accepted today, that assumes a complex photosensitive molecule that responds differentially to red, green, blue and yellow light by releasing substances that stimulate respective nerve endings. The theory is evolutionarily based; dichromatic vision is explained by assuming a less highly developed molecule and achromatic vision by an even more primitive one. ➤ **theories of *color vision**.

lag 1. Generally, any time delay between events. Usually the term is qualified to identify the nature of the lag; e.g., response lag, culture lag. **2.** A brief period after a stimulus has been removed when it may still be perceived. See here ➤ **iconic**.

-lagnia Combining form meaning *lust*.

laissez-faire The idea, first promulgated in 18th-century France, that government should not exert control or influence over the economy. By extension, in social psychology it is used to characterize any leadership system that operates with minimal control. In the true *laissez-faire* system no control is provided by the leader, not even assistance or guidance.

laissez-faire **atmosphere** K. Lewin's term for the general socio-political climate established when the nominal leader of a group maintains a 'hands off' policy and there is little or no guidance or direction imposed. Contrast with ➤ **authoritarian atmosphere** and ➤ **democratic atmosphere**.

-lalia Combining form used in reference to speech, specifically disorders of speech.

lallation 1. An unintelligible, infantile babbling. **2.** The constant use of *l* in place of *r*. Also called *lalling*.

lalo- The prefix form of *-lalia*.

laloplegia Inability to speak owing to paralysis of all those muscles used for speech except the tongue.

lalorrhea ➤ **logorrhea**.

Lamarckianism (or **Lamarckism**) ➤ **inheritance of *acquired characteristics**.

Lamaze method A method of psychological preparation for childbirth. The currently used technique is named for a Frenchman, F. Lamaze. The procedure is a modification of a technique first introduced in the Soviet Union based on Pavlovian conditioning principles. The method focuses on proper anatomical and physiological knowledge, breathing techniques, conditioned relaxation, cognitive control, and a social support system. Also known as the *psychophylatic method*.

lambda (λ) Designation for wavelength of a light.

lambert The luminance of a perfectly diffusing surface either reflecting or emitting light at the rate of 1 lumen per square centimeter. As this is a rather intense level of light, the millilambert (1/1000 of a lambert, mL) is the preferred unit.

Lambert cosine law The illumination of a surface varies as the cosine of the angle of incidence of the light and the surface.

Land effect First demonstrated by Edwin Land (who also developed the Polaroid camera), the effect produces the perception of color from black and white photographs. In the simplest form, two black and white pictures are taken of a scene, one through a red filter and one through a blue-green filter. The two are projected together on a screen, the former through a red filter, the latter through a green one. The resulting scene is seen as composed of a wide variety of colors, including blues that are not normally produced by a mixture of red and green.

Landolt ring(s) A doughnut-shaped figure with an opening in it used for measuring visual acuity. The standard ring has a thickness of 1 minute of visual angle and an opening of 1 minute, other rings have smaller and larger openings.

language All know the meaning of this term – a language is what we speak, the set of arbitrary conventional symbols through which we convey meaning, the culturally determined pattern of vocal gestures we acquire by virtue of being raised in a particular place and time, the medium through which we code our feelings, thoughts, ideas and experiences, the most uniquely human of behaviors and the most ubiquitous behavior of humans. Yet, as the term is used, it may mean all of these, none of them, or even things very different.

The conviction that we know the meaning of this word *language* lasts only so long as we refrain from attempts at specifying what we know. To appreciate the problems of definition and use here consider the following questions: (a) is the system of manual signs used by the profoundly deaf a language? (b) Are the synthetic systems developed for the programming of computers true languages? (c) Are the invented coding systems of socio-political reformers such as Esperanto to be classified as languages? (d) Should the sequences of motor movements, body positions, gestures and facial expressions that convey meaning be regarded as language? (e) Are there valid reasons for labeling the communication systems of other species languages, in particular, bees, dolphins or chimpanzees? (f) At what point in the emerging vocalizations of an infant do we want to conclude that it now has language?

These questions and many more like them cannot easily be answered. They are presented here to illustrate the complexity that the word carries, a complexity that renders any straightforward definition useless. ➤ **linguistics**, **paralinguistics**, **psycholinguistics**, **sign language** and related terms.

language acquisition device (or **system**) ➤ **LAD**.

language centers Those cortical areas known to be involved in the production and/or comprehension of spoken and/or written language. ➤ **Broca's area** and ➤ **Wernicke's area** are the two most often cited. However, the term needs to be used with caution, for these hypothesized centers cannot be thought of as circumscribed areas of the brain that encapsulate all linguistic functions; it is surely the case that vast regions of the cortex are intimately involved in the effective carrying out of language behaviors and there is a large clinical literature to show that neurological insults in many other locales have resulted in language deficits.

language disability An umbrella term for any non-normal language function. The term is nearly always restricted to children; a child displaying it is classified as *language disabled* when the syndrome is general and *specific language disabled* when only fairly precise dysfunctions are identified. There is a tendency to use the term as though it reflected some underlying, subtle, organic dysfunction and the language-disabled child is often assumed to have some form of minimal brain damage. ➤➤ **developmental *language disorder**.

language disorder, developmental A general label used for a number of disorders evidenced by significant impairment in the development of language skills during childhood. The term is restricted to cases in which there is no known neurological or anatomical defect. Often the disorders are divided into the *expressive* types, in which vocal output is disordered but language comprehension is normal, and a *mixed receptive-expressive* type, in which both are impaired. Note, the term *developmental aphasia* has been used for these disorders, but incorrectly; ➤ **aphasia** is reserved for language functions that are *lost*, not for those unacquired. The acceptable synonyms for these varieties of disorder are *expressive* and *receptive dysphasia* respectively: ➤ **dysphasia**. ➤➤ **language disability**, which tends to be used more often in the educational literature than in the clinical.

language, figurative A cover term for those aspects of language used to express ideas by metaphor, simile, allusions and analogies. Figurative language is non-literal and often idiomatic.

language, natural To circumvent some of the problems posed by the term ➤ **language**, the adjective *natural* is often appended when the writer wishes to be clear that only the naturally occurring verbal expression systems of *Homo sapiens* are being referenced. That is, a *natural language* is what the layman generally means when referring to *language*.

language origins, theories of Three general classes of theories were developed during the 19th century. All were highly speculative and dealt only with single words: (a) the *onomatopoetic*, which argued that imitations of sounds of animals and natural events were the beginnings; (b) the *interjectional*, which assumed that emotional exclamations ('ow,' 'ah') were the first words: and (c) the *natural response* theory, which held that automatic vocal reactions to specific environmental stimuli were the initial verbal communications. All three points of view are seriously lacking in explanatory power and are mostly known today by the rather absurd names bestowed by their critics: the 'bow-bow' theory, the 'poohpooh' theory, and the 'ding-dong' or 'splishsplash' theory. There is a great deal of enthusiastic research being done by contemporary anthropologists, psychologists, linguists and biologists on the problem of language origins but no well-developed or widely accepted theory is currently about.

lanugo 1. Fine, downy, infant-like hair. 2. Such fine hair that briefly covers the body of the fetus during the later stage of gestation.

lapse 1. Generally, a slip, a mistake, an error of omission. 2. A brief period during which one is unaware of one's surroundings, especially in mild forms of epilepsy.

lapsus Latin for *slip*. Used in several combined phrases, *lapsus calami* = slip of the pen, *lapsus linguae* = slip of the tongue, *lapsus memoriae* = lapse of memory. Within psychoanalysis all such momentary failures are examples of ➤ **parapraxis** and assumed to be due to unconscious factors.

large numbers, law of In mathematically simplest terms, the larger the sample size the more likely it becomes that the mean of a sample of data will lie arbitrarily close to the true mean of the population from which it was drawn. In essence, given that there are no sampling biases, the larger the data base the more confident one may be that the sample statistics provide accurate estimates of the population parameters.

larynx A cartilaginous structure that sits atop the windpipe. It contains a 'valve' made up of a double set of muscular folds covered with a layer of mucous membrane. The lower set is the true vocal folds (or 'cords') that open and close rapidly during vocalization. During quiet breathing the muscles that control the laryngeal cartilages relax and the folds form a V-shaped opening (called the *glottis*) to allow free passage of air.

Lashley jumping stand A device used for experimenting on small animals (usually laboratory rats). The animal is placed on a stand and must jump toward one of two or more stimuli placed in front of it. The device has been widely used in studies of discrimination and choice behavior.

latah syndrome A rare psychiatric syndrome characterized by symptoms of excitement, *echolalia*, *echopraxia*, *coprolalia* and, sometimes, *fugue* and *hallucinations*. var., *lattah*.

late luteal phase dysphoric disorder A mood disorder in women that begins during the last week of the luteal phase (➤ **menstrual cycle**) and begins to remit within a few days of the onset of menses. The term is only applied in cases where the emotional lability includes persistent anger, marked anxiety and tension, markedly depressed mood and feelings of helplessness severe enough to seriously interfere with work, social activities, or relationships with others. Differentiate from ➤ **premenstrual syndrome** where the mood swings are less dramatic and do not interfere with normal functioning. This term is a highly charged one and many argue that it should not have been included in the *DSM-III-R* on the grounds that it could encourage inappropriate diagnosis and has the potential for stigmatizing women. It has been dropped from the *DSM-IV* although the term *premenstrual dysphoric disorder* (with similar symptoms) is still included as a clinically potential category.

latency Generally, a period of inactivity within a organism. The system is generally an organism and the period of inactivity is marked by some stimulus that initiates it and the occurrence of some response that ends it. The term is broadly used and often qualified as to the particular system and/or the kind of effect referred to; see the entries below for examples. adj., *latent*.

latency period In classical psychoanalytic theory, the period of time from the end of the Oedipal period to the beginning of puberty during which sexual interest is presumed to be sublimated.

latency, response The time between the onset of a stimulus and the occurrence of the overt response to that stimulus. ➤ **association time** (1), **reaction time** and **verification time** for some specialized types of response latencies.

latent Existing in hidden form, dormant but capable of being evoked or developed. It is used adjectivally in a variety of contexts, some of which follow as illustration.

latent content ➤ **latent and manifest *content**.

latent extinction ➤ **extinction, latent**.

latent homosexual Although psychodynamic theories of personality and sexuality go to great lengths to explain this term

it seems clear that a latent homosexual is merely a heterosexual.

latent inhibition ➤ **inhibition, latent**.

latent learning ➤ **learning, latent**.

latent process Very generally, and lit., any process that is *latent*. Often in psychoanalytic theory an infant's ego processes are said to be latent; in cognitive psychology particular intellectual processes that have not yet manifested themselves are referred to as latent; and so forth.

latent schizophrenia ➤ **schizotypal personality disorder**.

latent social identity A social role that, although not 'officially' a factor in functioning in a society, nevertheless has significant impact upon an individual's behavior in a social organization. Gender, race, religion, etc. form part of a person's latent social identity.

latent traits Generally, those genetic traits that do not manifest themselves in the phenotype of an individual but which can be passed on to future generations.

lateral Of or relating to the side, away from the median axis. Used to characterize any number of structures, as the following entries show.

lateral-basomedial group A cluster of nuclei in the *amygdala* that receives visual, auditory and somatosensory information and sends it to the *forebrain* and *hypothalamus*.

lateral corticospinal tract ➤ **corticospinal pathways**.

lateral differences A cover term for any behavioral, cognitive or affective differences between the two hemispheres of the brain and/or the associated peripheral processes. See, e.g., ➤ **laterality** and **handedness**.

lateral dominance Preferential use of one side of the body. ➤➤ **dominance** (5, 6) and **laterality**.

lateral dorsal nucleus ➤ **dorsolateral nucleus**.

lateral fissure The deep groove on the lateral surfaces of the hemispheres of the brain that marks the border between the frontal and parietal lobes (above the fissure) and the temporal lobe (below it). Also called the *Sylvian fissure* or the *fissure of Sylvius*.

lateral geniculate nucleus Two cell nuclei of the thalamus located at the termini of each optic tract from which the visual pathways proceed to the striate area of the occipital cortex. Each lateral geniculate nucleus has a laminar structure such that for the left side the three left layers receive axons from the left side of the left retina and three right layers receive axons from the left side of the right retina. For the right side the reverse is found. Also called *lateral geniculate bodies*.

lateral hypothalamic syndrome A behavioral syndrome observed in animals following lesions in the lateral area of the hypothalamus (LH). It is characterized by aphagia (lack of eating) and adipsia (lack of drinking). If left to their own devices, LH-lesioned animals will die. However, careful nursing and forced feeding will keep them alive and a second stage will be observed during which they 'recover' (more or less – they are still abnormal in other ways) and establish a new, lower but stable, body weight. At first the syndrome was assumed to implicate the LH as a 'feeding' center that operated in reciprocal fashion with the ventromedial hypothalamus (see here ➤ **ventromedial hypothalamic syndrome**). The contemporary viewpoint, however, is that a set of extremely complex neural pathways involving sensory and motor systems – all of which have been shown to play a role in feeding – pass through and around the LH, hence lesions here disrupt the normal pattern of eating and drinking. The LH is thus not a feeding center but part of a network of structures and pathways all of which are part of the complex sensory, motor and affective components of feeding.

lateral hypothalamus (LH) ➤ **hypothalamus** and **lateral hypothalamic syndrome**.

lateral inhibition A set of conditions established when two or more neural cells are interconnected so that excitation of one produces inhibition in the other. Complex lateral inhibitory systems are responsible for the 'sharpening' of perceptions, particularly in the visual system.

laterality Lit., sideness. In general, the term can refer to any preference for one side of the body over the other, such as having a preferred hand or eye. Recently, however, it has come to be used largely to characterize the asymmetry of the hemispheres of the brain with regard to specific cognitive functions. It will often be used to characterize the fact that the brain is organized so that language and speech functions are mediated in the left hemisphere (for most of us, anyway). Although these linguistic capacities are the ones most clearly associated with laterality, there is a growing body of evidence to suggest that a variety of other cognitive, perceptual, and affective components of behavior may also be lateralized: specifically that the left hemisphere is 'analytic' and functions in a sequential, rational fashion and that the right hemisphere is 'synthetic' and functions in a more 'holistic', arational manner. Being precise here is difficult but, to carry this speculation on, some researchers argue that such analytic skills as problem-solving, hypothesis-formation and testing, even perhaps consciousness itself are left-hemispheric whereas other skills like art, music and perhaps even the unconscious are right-hemispheric. All this is great fun, but if we can learn anything from past researches into brain function, it is that these sharp delineations in hemispheric function for specific capacities are painful oversimplifications. ➤➤ **dominance** (5, 6).

lateralization The process by which different functions and processes become associated with one or the other side of the brain. See for more detail ➤ **laterality**.

lateral lemniscus ➤ **lemniscal system**.

LATERAL POSTERIOR NUCLEUS

lateral posterior nucleus A thalamic nucleus that interconnects with the parietal cortex.

lateral preoptic area ➤ **preoptic area**.

lateral thinking A *heuristic* for solving problems in which the individual attempts to look at the problem from many angles rather than search for a direct, head-on solution.

latero- Combining form meaning ➤ **lateral**.

Latin square A balanced two-way classification scheme in which each condition occurs just once in each row and column. For example,

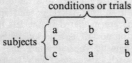

This balancing is often incorporated into experimental designs so that the order of administration of treatments is perfectly balanced across subjects. Two such Latin squares are orthogonal if, when combined, the same pair of symbols occurs only once in the combined square. This composite square is called a *Greco-Latin square*. For example,

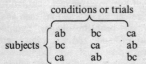

latitude Freedom from narrow restrictions. The term is used in the study of attitudes to refer to the point of view that attitudes, beliefs, opinions and the like should not be viewed as 'points' along a dimension but rather as 'ranges' with some average point representing the core or dominant position taken. That is, each attitude that a person holds exists with some degree of flexibility or latitude.

lattah syndrome ➤ **latah syndrome**.

law **1.** In science, ➤ **scientific *law** and **statistical *law**. **2.** In legal parlance, a

410

governmentally imposed rule of conduct.

law, empirical A principle or generalization relating variables to each other and based on observations or experimental findings. Such laws are basically no more than descriptions of the concordance of events or of facts; ➤ **Weber's law** is a good example of an empirical law.

law, natural **1.** In the natural sciences, a ➤ **scientific *law**. **2.** In social discourse, any established custom or practice adhered to independently of formal legislation. In 1 the sense is of that which occurs in *nature*, in 2 of that which occurs *naturally*.

law of effect ➤ **effect, law of**.

law of exercise ➤ **exercise, law of**.

law, scientific When a generalization or principle has been verified sufficiently often (or has resisted frequent and strong attempts at refutation), when the data base is well defined and when those concerned are satisfied that the relationships specified are, under the appropriate conditions, universal, then one may begin to speak of a scientific law. Psychology, despite the frequent premature announcements, has shown itself to be a discipline particularly resistant to the establishment of such laws. Indeed, it is good counsel to recommend that for the social sciences in general the terms ➤ **generalization** (especially 3) and ➤ **principle** (1,2) are the terms of choice; they tend not to mislead. ➤ **statistical *law**.

law, statistical A ➤ **scientific *law**, when expressed in terms of the probability that the specified relationships will obtain, is a statistical law – given, of course, that the probability is less than 1.0. In some respects such laws are major advances, particularly when they reveal that the underlying lawful processes are themselves probabilistic in nature; in other respects they are admissions of ignorance about the possibility that other poorly understood effects are operating such that precise predictions cannot be made. Most 'laws' in psychology are of this latter kind, an assessment that is generally construed not as criticism of the scientific stature of the field but rather as an acknowledgement of the extraordinary complexity of its subject-matter.

lax In phonetics, a ➤ **distinctive feature** (2) descriptive of speech sounds produced when the vocal tract is in its normal resting position. Opposite of ➤ **tense** (3).

lay Characterizing a nonprofessional; e.g., a layman.

lay analyst One who has received psychoanalytic training and is recognized to practice but who has not taken a degree in medicine.

'lazy eye' ➤ **amblyopia**.

LD Abbreviation for: **1.** ➤ **Learning disability**. **2.** ➤ **Language disability**. Generally used to refer to a child given one of these diagnoses.

leader Anyone who holds a position of dominance, authority or influence in a group. Usually an adjective is affixed to characterize the form of leader or leadership under consideration.

leader, authoritarian A leader with absolute authority, with no requirement to consult with other members of the group in decision-making. Authoritarian leaders are often found in the military, in dictatorships, many organizations, youth gangs, families, etc. In fact, the prevalence of this type of leader has generated considerable interest in social scientists and much concern in social reformers. ➤➤ **authoritarianism**; contrast with ➤ **democratic *leader**.

leader, bureaucratic A leader whose authority stems from the official bureaucratic position held. No other personal or individual characteristics are implied.

leader, democratic A leader whose authority springs from the consensus of the group and who acts in accordance with the beliefs and desires of the members of the group both individually and collectively.

leader, nominal A leader in name only but with no actual leadership role. The implication is that another is actually providing the leadership.

leadership The only really proper use for this term is to characterize the exercise of authority and influence within a social group; that is, to function as a leader is to manifest leadership. It is often used, however, as if it were a personality trait, as if there were a collection of specific skills that reflect leadership capability. Although there is a certain intuitive truth here, this use leads to hopeless confusion because it neglects the role of the situation itself in determining the leadership behavior.

leading eye ➤ eye *dominance.

leading hemisphere Occasionally used for either **1.** the hemisphere of the brain that is primarily responsible for a particular behavior or mode of cognition, or **2.** the dominant (i.e. linguistic) hemisphere. The term was first used by the English neurologist J. H. Jackson in 1868 for meaning 2 on the grounds that language represents the highest mental process and hence the linguistic hemisphere is the one which 'leads' in cognitive functions. ➤ **cerebral dominance**.

learned flavor (or **food**) **aversion** (or **avoidance**) ➤ **toxicosis**.

learned helplessness ➤ **helplessness, learned**.

learned taste aversion (or **avoidance**) ➤ **toxicosis**.

learning 1. The process of acquiring knowledge or the actual possession of such; scholarship. This meaning is very loose and is used in like fashion within various disciplines such as educational psychology and cognitive psychology. The connotations and entailments of this meaning in the technical literature are essentially the same as they are in the nontechnical. However, this looseness is regarded as unsatisfactory within the more behaviorally oriented approaches; hence, here: **2.** In G. Kimble's terms, 'a relatively permanent change in response potentiality which occurs as a result of reinforced practice.' This definition neatly identifies the four major issues that most learning theorists feel are essential to an understanding of the learning process: (a) 'Relatively permanent': the point here is simple, the exclusion of momentary changes in behavior brought about by fatigue, satiation, habituation and the like. (b) 'Response potentiality': this phrase is included in recognition of the learning–performance distinction. It allows the inclusion of the phenomena of ➤ **latent *learning** and ➤ **incidental *learning** in which changes in behavior are not immediately observable, and reflects the truism that learning is really a hypothetical event recognizable solely through measurable changes in performance. (c) 'Reinforced': here is the crux of the issue in so far as most behaviorists are concerned. Presumably, without reinforcement extinction will occur, with it 'relatively permanent changes in response potentiality' will occur. (➤ **reinforcement** for details.) (d) 'Practice': the point here is that for learning to emerge, sooner or later the behavior must be emitted and repeated (reinforced) occurrences will improve learning. This consideration is generally accepted in psychology although some allowances need to be made for the effects of ➤ **imitation, modelling** and **observation *learning**. The practice notion also allows for the exclusion of other behavioral changes of a relatively permanent kind that are generally not considered to be instances of learning, such as native tendencies of particular species (e.g., imprinting) and maturational changes (e.g., flying in birds).

Oddly, the definition and manner of use of the term learning has caused relatively little controversy among theorists and it is used with relatively few encumbrances by developmentalists, educators, cognitive psychologists, behaviorists, etc. The tendency is to use it as a 'chapter heading' word and allow the socially accepted meaning to prevail. The difficulties that do emerge in usage show up when theoretical processes and mechanisms for explaining learning are proposed. Several

of the more hotly disputed are discussed under ➤ **learning theory**.

learning, all-or-none Learning that either takes place completely and successfully 'all at once' (i.e. on a single trial) or not at all (i.e. not that particular trial). All-or-none learning and ➤ **one-trial *learning** are put forward as alternative characterizations to the ➤ **continuity theory** of learning.

learning, associative Learning an association, learning that occurs through the process of linking or binding. What becomes linked or associated is a theoretical question that has received many different answers over the years, from the *ideas* of the early empiricists to the *stimuli* and *responses* of the behaviorists to the *propositions* and *images* of more modern cognitivists. That the term has survived such dramatic shifts in the hypothesized elements is perhaps itself of some significance.

learning, context specific The general principle that, since learning occurs in particular contexts, the material acquired will be best accessed or recalled in that same context. My favorite study here is one that showed that subjects who learned material while under water in scuba diving gear evidenced better recall when tested under water than when sitting by the pool and vice versa for subjects who initially learned while sitting by the pool. For a similar phenomenon ➤ **state-dependent *learning**.

learning curve Any graphic representation of the process of learning or, more precisely, the performance assumed to reflect the learning. Generally the independent variable is plotted on the horizontal axis and the dependent on the vertical. Several decades ago there was a flurry of theoretical activity concerning the shape of *the* learning curve presumed to underlie the process. Although there is something of a consensus that the typical shape is negatively accelerated there is such a large number of variables that can affect the course of learning that no firm generalizations are possible.

learning disability A syndrome found in children of normal or above-average intelligence characterized by specific difficulties in learning to read (*dyslexia*), to write (*dysgraphia*) and to do grade-appropriate mathematics (*dyscalculia*). Since all other cognitive functions are normal it is assumed by most authorities that these disabilities stem from some form of ➤ **minimal brain dysfunction**. Often abbreviated LD with the child so diagnosed referred to as an *LD child*. Note that while the disorder is typically detected and subjected to remediation in childhood, its manifestations are also seen in adults who throughout their lives may have difficulty with particular kinds of verbal and/or quantitative materials.

learning disorder The *DSM-IV* term for various disorders also known as ➤ **academic skills disorders** and/or ➤ **learning disabilities**.

learning, explicit Learning that takes place consciously and results in knowledge that is available to consciousness, learning of which one is aware. When most people use the term 'learning' with reference to the acquisition of complex knowledge in humans, they tend to use it in this sense; that is, the learning is thought of as a *conscious* process. However, ➤ **implicit *learning**.

learning, ideational Loosely, learning based on abstractions, on comprehension. Contrast with ➤ **rote *learning**.

learning, implicit A term coined by A. S. Reber for learning that takes place largely independent of awareness of both the process of acquisition and the content of the knowledge so acquired. Material that has been learned in this fashion can be used to guide behavior, make decisions, and solve problems, although the individual is typically unaware of the complex knowledge held that enables him or her to act in this fashion. The classic examples are the acquisition of language and the process of socialization, where individuals come to speak their natural language and become inculcated with their society's norms and mores but without conscious knowledge of the underlying principles that guide their behavior. Of course, when implicit learning is examined in the laboratory, artificial systems of considerably less complexity are used. ➤➤ **implicit *memory**.

learning, incidental Rather literally, learning that takes place in the absence of intent to learn or instructions to that effect. Distinguish from ➤ **explicit *learning**, where there is clear intention to learn.

learning, latent Learning that has taken place but has not yet manifested itself in changes in performance. The term comes from a series of classic studies carried out some decades ago which showed that if fully satiated animals are allowed to explore a maze they will, when hungry, learn to traverse it for food reinforcement more rapidly than controls which had not had the previous, nonreinforced exposure.

learning, motor A generic term covering, very loosely, any learning in which the basic changes in performance are motoric. Although some movement is ultimately involved in essentially all learning, the term is typically used in contrast with cases in which the critical components are perceptual or cognitive.

learning, observation(al) A term coined by A. Bandura to characterize learning that takes place simply by having the learner observe someone else perform the to-be-acquired response. ➤➤ **modelling**, **social-learning theory**.

learning, one-trial A term used to represent the point of view of E. R. Guthrie, that all learning takes place on a single trial. It only *appears*, he argued, that extended practice improves performance because the behaviors usually under investigation are complex and the gradual improvement reflects a large number of simple components each of which is acquired on a single trial. Contrast with the position expressed by ➤ **continuity theory**. ➤➤ **all-or-none *learning**.

learning, paired-associates Essentially an experimental procedure that is used for investigating a variety of phenomena including memory, concept learning, transfer and interference. The subject is required to learn paired (or associated) relations between a set of stimulus items and a set of response items. The usual procedure is to present the stimulus items one at a time with the subject replying with the associated response items. Often abbreviated *PA learning* or even *PAL*.

learning, perceptual Learning in which the learner comes to perceive the stimuli differently with exposure and practice. Definitionally, not much more can be said but the simplicity of the term is illusory. Specification of exactly what mental changes occur when a perceptual change occurs and explaining the mechanisms underlying such changes are enormous tasks. The major problems surround the issue of *nativism* versus *environmentalism* and the distinction between *enrichment* and *differentiation*.

learning, place Once upon a time there was a very intense theoretical debate over whether an animal learning a maze learned to go to a particular *place* (the goal box) or whether it learned to make a particular set of motor *responses* that led it to the goal box. The issue of contention was that the advocates of place learning were espousing cognitive mechanisms, the response learners peripheral processes. The outcome of the dispute was that both were right – it depends on the experimental setting. Simply, if location of the goal box is clearly marked relative to the general surroundings then place learning will emerge, if it is not then the animal will, of necessity, resort to conditioned motor responses.

learning, probability (PL) Learning the probabilities with which events occur. It is typically studied in simple situations where each of two or three events (e.g., flashing lights on a computer screen) occurs with different probabilities and the subject attempts to predict the event that will occur on each trial. In the typical experiment, subjects' prediction frequen-

cies come to approximate the actual probabilities of occurrence of the several events.

learning, relational A generic term covering cases in which the critical components to be learned are the relations or patterns between stimuli. Roughly synonymous with ➤ **pattern learning** but ➤➤ **pattern recognition** for details.

learning, response See the discussion under ➤ **place *learning**. Note that the term is also used more generally on occasion to refer to *any* situation wherein the subject must learn the response to be made in a particular setting.

learning, restricted An ethological term for a species-specific learning ability whereby the animal possesses the capacity to extract a critical piece of information from the environment that results in precise alterations in the animal's behavior. Restricted learning is close, if not identical, to ➤ **open *instinct**.

learning, reversal This term covers a variety of learning situations during which at some point in discrimination training the original cues for correct responding are modified so that they no longer serve as indicators for the original correct response. For example, a triangle may serve as a cue for a right turn in a maze and a circle for a left. After learning has reached some criterion the cues are reversed so that now right turns to circles are reinforced and left turns to triangles. Originally this procedure was called the *cue-reversal technique* and early work focused on simple motor responses and simple physical cues. However, the technique has been adapted so that it lends itself to the examination of symbolic processes as well. The point is that the reversal need not be so simple as replacing triangles with circles. For example, suppose the original stimuli are circles that vary in brightness and size. On initial training trials all large circles are 'correct' independently of brightness. Now, on reversal trials there may be an *intradimensional* (or *reversal*) shift so that all small circles are now deemed 'correct' or there may be an *extradimensional* (or *nonreversal*) shift so that size becomes irrelevant and all white circles are 'correct' and all dark 'wrong.' Developmental level and phylogenetic differences have both been shown to affect learning, implicating symbolic processes underlying the behavior.

learning, rote Learning (really memorizing) that takes place purely by repetition devoid of meaningfulness of the material or of other operations like organization, inference or the use of mnemonics, etc.

learning, rule This term is commonly used in roughly the same manner as *concept learning*, with the implicit distinction that the *rule* is the formal statement of the structure or pattern that underlies the *concept*. In addition to the problems revolving around just what is learned (➤ **concept formation and learning**), the rule-learning research has yet to deal conclusively with the question of whether rules are learned primarily through implicit means or through apprehension of and conscious knowledge of the rule itself. See here ➤ **implicit *learning**.

learning, selective A very general term applied to those learning situations in which one or a few specific responses are singled out (by an experimenter or by environmental contingencies), reinforced and hence are learned while other similar responses go unreinforced and hence are unlearned.

learning, serial An experimental procedure where the stimulus material consists of a list of items (usually words but pictures or other symbols may be used) that is presented in a fixed order and the subject is required to adhere to that order in attempts at recall. Also called *serial list learning*; ➤➤ **serial recall** (which is used similarly) and compare with ➤ **free recall**.

learning set Most broadly, a kind of attentional focus, a determining tendency that functions so that the subject's perceptual or cognitive system is 'primed' or 'set' for a particular stimulus or pattern of stimuli. The meaning here is close to the old German term *Einstellung*. It has served as a theoretical device for explaining various phenomena such as ➤ **functional fixedness** and ➤ **learning to learn**.

learning, S–R Abbreviation for *stimulus–response learning*. This is one of those relatively rare cases in which the abbreviated form is almost always used. It stands as a kind of cover term for any and all kinds of learning that are assumed to be fundamentally governed by the forming of some link or bond between a particular stimulus and a specific response.

learning, S–S Learning based on the association between two stimuli. The term, which is typically used in this abbreviated fashion, is short for *stimulus–stimulus learning*.

learning, state-dependent The term refers to the general principle that recall of memories of previous events is enhanced if one returns to the original setting of those events. One is much more likely to be able to remember the names of one's first-grade classmates if one returns to the original classroom. The inference, then, is that the learning of the material was 'dependent' upon the original state. For a similar effect ➤ **context specific *learning**.

learning theory Any effort to codify and systematize the operations and hypothesize about the underlying mechanisms of that 'relatively permanent change in response potential' (➤ **learning**) can qualify as a learning theory. Over the years nearly every conceivable form of theory has been seriously proposed from the purely peripheral behaviorism of Watson to the strongly centralist positions of modern cognitive science; from those wholly dependent upon reinforcement such as Thorndike's and Skinner's to those that consider the concept irrelevant like Guthrie's; from those that are founded upon physiological function such as Pavlov's and Köhler's to those that eschew all efforts to physiologize like Skinner's behaviorism. Given all this variation it should be clear that there really is no such thing as a single theory of learning. Theorizing about learning is an exercise in generalization and often can be as polemical as it seeks to be empirical.

learning theory, mathematical A general label for a particular kind of approach to theory construction in the area of learning. The focus is far from unitary; rather, it represents an agreement between theorists to try to use mathematics as the vehicle for maximum precision in the statement of the theory. See, for more detail, ➤ **mathematical model**, **mathematical psychology**, **statistical-learning theory**, **stimulus-sampling theory**.

learning to learn The term refers to the fact that with successive presentations of problems of a similar form the subjects become increasingly successful in learning how to solve them: that is, they learn how to learn. According to some theoretical accounts, learning to learn is predicated upon the formation of an appropriate ➤ **learning set**.

learning trial ➤ **trial, learning**.

learning, trial-and-error Quite literally, learning that is characterized by trial-and-error responding. The course of such learning is typified by the gradual elimination of ineffectual responses and the strengthening of those responses that are satisfactory. Thorndike, in his early theorizing around the turn of the century, argued that this process was central to the acquisition of *all* complex acts, a position now all but totally abandoned. Contrast with ➤ **insight** and **observation(al) *learning**.

learning without awareness ➤ **awareness, learning without**.

least-effort principle The *heuristic* that, given various possibilities for action, an organism will select the one requiring the least expenditure of effort. It has been used to theorize about how rats learn mazes, how children develop articulation skills, how adults act in social settings and how economic systems operate, just to name a few.

least-squares principle The statistical principle that the line of best fit for a body of data is that line which minimizes the sum of the squares of the deviations of the data points about the line. Most ➤ **curve fitting** (1) procedures are based on this principle. ➤➤ **goodness of *fit**.

leaving the field Confronted with insoluble conflict or intensely frustrating circumstances an organism may simply take leave of the field. The escape may be a quite literal physical act or a psychological one such as diverting attention or changing the subject.

Leboyer method A natural childbirth method developed around the assumption that child-bearing can be made less 'violent' for the infant. Delivery takes place in a darkened room, the infant is bathed in warm water and then placed on the mother's abdomen and the severing of the umbilical cord is delayed.

Lee-Boot effect The gradual slowing down of the **estrus cycles** of a group of female mice who are housed together. If they are then exposed to the odor of a male (or to his urine), their cycles begin again. This latter effect, which is called the *Whitten effect*, is caused by a **pheromone** in the male's urine.

left parietal apraxia ➤ **apraxia, left parietal**.

left-right effect The phenomenon that pre-school children have more difficulty learning to make left-right discriminations than those depending on an up-down relationship. Note that the effect is named for the poorer capacity.

legal authority ➤ **authority, legal**.

lek (lekking) The form of mating behavior, commonly seen in birds and some mammals, where the males of the species congregate in specific areas and 'set out their wares' for the females.

lemma In logic, a proposition accepted as true for use in the proof of another proposition. Lemmas are usually distinguished from ➤ **postulates** in that lemmas are, in principle, provable (or supposedly so).

lemniscal system A polysynaptic pathway that ascends through the reticular formation. Made up of the *lateral lemniscus*, which runs rostrally through the medulla and pons carrying fibers of the auditory system; the *medial lemniscus*, which ascends through the medulla and pons carrying somatosensory fibers; and the *trigeminal lemniscus*, which runs parallel to the medial carrying afferent fibers from the trigeminal nerve (the VIIth cranial nerve) to the thalamus.

lens 1. Any transparent refracting medium. **2.** In vertebrate eyes, the transparent, crystalline structure lying just behind the pupil which helps to focus light on the retina. ➤ **accommodation** (2).

lenticular nucleus Collectively the *putamen* and *pallidum* of the ➤ **basal ganglia** (see that entry for details).

-lepsia, -lepsy Combining forms meaning *seizure*.

lept(o)- Combining forms meaning *small, thin, fine* or *weak*.

leptokurtosis ➤ **kurtosis**.

leptomorph ➤ **body-build index**.

lesbian A female homosexual.

Lesch-Nyhan syndrome A genetic metabolic syndrome marked by abnormally high levels of uric acid resulting in severe mental retardation. The main behavioral characteristic of the syndrome is a pattern of severe self-mutilation, including lip biting and finger chewing, often to the point of causing serious deformities. The disorder is associated with a recessive X-linked inheritance and males are primarily affected.

lesion 1. Most generally, any impairment or flaw produced by an injury. **2.** More specifically (and commonly), a circumscribed area of impairment to organic tissue caused by injury, disease or surgical intervention. vb., *to lesion*.

lethologica A temporary inability to recall a proper noun or a name.

letter reversal ➤ **reversal(s)**.

leucotomy ➤ **lobotomy**.

leuk(o)- Combining form meaning *white, colorless*. var., *leuc(o)-*.

leukocyte A white blood cell. var., *leucocyle*.

level 1. Position or rank on some continuum, e.g., intelligence level. **2.** A uniform concentration of a substance in the body, e.g., glucose level. **3.** The magnitude of a quantity measured according to a specified reference value, e.g., decibel level. **4.** A measure of performance, e.g., sixth-grade reading level. Compare with ➤ **phase** and **stage**.

leveling The tendency to smooth over the unusual, irregular or novel aspects of a situation, an event, a story or a drawing such that details are glossed over and what ultimately ends up in memory is a more homogeneous, less incongruous version than what was objectively presented. The reverse tendency is *sharpening*, in which details are (over)emphasized and accentuated. Some have suggested that together these two tendencies represent the poles on a dimension of *cognitive style*; others that essentially everyone displays both tendencies to some extent or other depending on the circumstances and the nature of the material.

level of achievement ➤ **achievement, level of**.

level of aspiration ➤ **aspiration, level of**.

level of confidence 1. ➤ **Significance level**. **2.** ➤ **Confidence** (2). Note, these two meanings are related but different.

level of significance ➤ **significance level**.

levels of consciousness ➤ **levels of *awareness***.

levels of processing ➤ **depth of processing**.

Lewinian Of or pertaining to the general point of view of the Prussian-born psychologist Kurt Lewin (1890–1947). Lewin's work was influenced by the Gestalt movement and by the Freudian psychoanalytic school, both of which emphasized the dynamic and the structured elements of human personality. His general position often goes by the name of ➤ **field theory**, with the concept of the ➤ **life space** holding a central position. Much of Lewin's theorizing about the life space was highly esoteric and was concerned with his attempts to develop a model of personality based on the topology of ➤ **hodological space**. There has been little lasting impact of this specific work; his influence on modern psychology derives largely from his emphasis on groups and group dynamics and his intellectual and personal style, which was democratic, generous and accepting.

lexical-decision task An experimental technique for evaluating the manner in which verbal information is stored in memory. The task simply requests the subject to decide as rapidly as possible whether a string of letters presented briefly is a real word or a non-word. The pattern of response latencies that the subject produces is a sensitive measure of ➤ **lexical *memory**. Also called *word-nonword task*.

lexical memory ➤ **memory, lexical**.

lexicon Most generally an alphabetic listing of the words of a language, a dictionary. By extension, in cognitive theories of human memory, the term is used loosely for the storehouse of words that a person knows – although the restriction that the ordering be alphabetic is always dropped when talking about a mental lexicon. ➤ **lexical *memory**.

lexicostatistics A technique for estimating the historical connection between two languages. By comparing the number of cognates in a standard list of common terms, an evaluation can be made of the duration of separation and evolution from a common parent language.

LH 1. *Luteinizing hormone* (➤ **menstrual**

cycle). **2.** *Lateral hypothalamus* (➤ **hypothalamus**).

libidinal The adjectival form of libido, hence, relating to the sexual energy derived from the id; highly sexual. Distinguish from ➤ **libidinous**.

libidinal (infantile) development In classical psychoanalysis, the series of stages of growth through which each individual passes from infancy to the latency period; namely, the *oral, anal* and *genital*.

libidinal object The object (person or thing) in which libido is invested.

libidinous Excessively sexually active. Distinguish from ➤ **libidinal**, where the connotation of excess is absent.

libido 1. In psychoanalysis, the hypothesized mental energy which, being derived from the id, is most fundamentally sexual. Freud, who introduced the term, modified his usage of it considerably in his later works so that the purely sexual component became less prominent and it took on a meaning closer to *life* energy. This meaning developed along with his reinterpretation of *instinct* to include only Eros and Thanatos, with libido being the energy of Eros. Within the larger scope of psychoanalysis these later modifications never dominated thinking to the extent that the early theory did and libido itself has tended to retain its strongly sexual connotations. Owing, however, to the somewhat conflicting senses of the term it is frequently taken simply to represent: **2.** Any sexual or erotic desire or pleasure, or **3.** Any psychic energy independent of sexuality. Between these two the vast majority of contemporary usages is covered. adj., *libidinal*.

library In cognitive psychology, especially in the study of long term memory, the term serves as a metaphor for the totality of information about the world that a person carries about.

Librium ➤ **chlordiazepoxide**.

lie detector An instrument that measures several physiological processes that may be interpreted as indicators of emotional arousal; e.g., heart rate, blood pressure, breathing rate, galvanic skin response. It is, of course, not a 'lie detector' at all; rather it detects autonomic reactions that are argued to accompany the telling of deliberate falsehoods. Put simply, it detects physiological arousal, not guilt, and therein lies the problem. Such arousal may indeed accompany guilt but it also will accompany many other emotionally arousing circumstances. Law-enforcement officers typically have more faith in the device than do trained scientists. ≫ polygraph.

life 1. The collective total of those properties that differentiate the living from the nonliving. The unsatisfying circularity of this definition will have to suffice for now. It is said with truth that biologists only began making progress when they gave up trying to define this term. 2. The actual state of being alive as manifested by the carrying out of various functions associated with life, e.g., metabolism, growth, reproduction and adaptation to the environment. 3. The time between inception and death. Fixing the two poles here has proved troublesome. The question of whether life (in the sense of an individual, distinct, organism) begins at conception, at birth or at some intermediate point during gestation (e.g., the point where the fetus is capable of survival outside the womb) has troubled judges, theologians, philosophers and scientists with no, as yet, satisfactory resolution. Similar problems arise in defining ➤ death.

life chance(s) The likelihood of any person achieving particular goals, e.g., in education, earning power, marriage, prestige, influence, etc. Strong relationships exist in all stratified societies between such factors as one's sex, race and the socioeconomic status of one's family and one's life chances. ≫ social class.

life cycle 1. The sequence of stages that each member of a particular species goes through from inception to death. 2. By extension, the analogous stages of other social units such as groups, societies, institutions, etc. Note that the term *cycle* here implies that all members or social units undergo these and that they recur from generation to generation.

life goal In Adler's conceptualization, the fundamental aim of achieving the particular form of superiority that will allow one to compensate for one's primary, felt inferiority.

life instinct Synonym for ➤ Eros. ≫ libido.

life lie Adler's term used to cover one's primary defensive rationalization(s) about what one cannot do, what one will surely fail at if attempted, owing to one's personal feelings and weaknesses.

life plan Adler's term for the full complement of defensive reactions and rationalizations that one uses in attempts to achieve superiority and to justify failure. ≫ guiding fiction.

life space The central notion in Kurt Lewin's personality theory. Influenced by the Gestalt perspective, he characterized the world of each individual as a dynamic life space composed of regions representing all the states of affairs, persons, goals, objects, desires, behavioral tendencies, etc. germane to the person. Lewin developed topological models complete with vectors and valences to characterize 'movement,' 'direction' and 'force' within the life space and hoped that mathematical models could be developed to formalize the system. See, for more detail, ➤ field theory and Lewinian.

life span 1. The actual duration of life of an individual organism from inception to death. 2. By extension, the duration of a whole species.

light The stimulus for vision, specifically electromagnetic radiation of wavelengths between approximately 400 and 700 nanometers. Light may be characterized as either individual particles (quanta) or as waves; the latter is most useful for work in psychology, as the definition above reflects.

light adaptation The process of adjustment of the eye to light of relatively high intensity, the shift from the *scotopic* system to the *photopic* system. In the light-adapted eye the pupil is constricted and the cone system is operative, rendering the eye relatively insensitive to lower intensities. Compare with ➤ **dark adaptation**.

light induction ➤ **visual induction**.

lightness That attribute of an object color that permits it to be classified along the series of grays that runs from black to white.

lightning calculator A person who is capable of performing 'in the head' complex feats of mathematical calculation. There are several variations on this general theme. Some such persons can carry out massive multiplication problems like squaring seven digit numbers in a few moments, others are capable of calendar 'look-up' feats such as figuring out the day of the week on which 11 March 2040 will fall, etc. Little is known about the operations or processes used by these people, who frequently (but not always) display little or no other special intellectual talent; ➤ **savant**. ➤➤ **mnemonist**.

light reflex The pupillary response; generally it includes both dilation when light levels drop and constriction when they are raised, although it is occasionally used only for the constriction response.

likelihood 1. Commonly used as a term to describe *subjective probability*; i.e. the estimation by a person of the probability of occurrence of some event. 2. In statistics, the probability that a sample statistic arose from a particular set of parameters in the population from which the sample was drawn.

likelihood ratio In simplest form, the ratio formed between the probability that a signal was present and detected by the subject (a *hit*) and the probability that it was not actually present but was 'detected' by the subject (a *false alarm*). For elaboration of this usage ➤ **signal detection theory**. Naturally, this concept is going to have

considerable generality, for the *signal* can be variously interpreted so as to involve scientific hypotheses, beliefs, stories, expectations about events and the like; hence, the mathematical system underlying likelihood ratios can be applied to more subjective realms of psychology such as choice behavior, decision-making, statistical testing and so forth.

Likert scale A scale developed by Rensis Likert and used primarily in measurement of attitudes. The respondent is given a series of attitude statements and asked to rate them according to his degree of agreement or disagreement. Usually there are five levels, running from 'strongly agree' through 'uncertain' to 'strongly disagree,' although scales with three, seven or even more choices are used and called Likert scales. The importance of the technique is due to the fact that the resulting data are easily amenable to factor analysis which allows the basic underlying dimensions of the tested attitudes to be evaluated.

liking scale A scale developed to measure interpersonal liking. The scale is based on two primary components assumed to reflect liking: a feeling that the liked person is similar to oneself and an overall favorable evaluation of the liked person. Compare these with the components of the ➤ **love scale**.

limb apraxia ➤ **apraxia, limb**.

limbic system A complex set of evolutionarily old structures of the forebrain lying in an arc below the corpus callosum. The specific structures generally classed as limbic are the *hippocampus, anterior thalamus, amygdala, septum,* parts of the *hypothalamus* and their interconnecting fiber bundles. For more details, see the entries for the separate structures.

limen The original Latin term for ➤ **threshold**.

liminal Of or pertaining to ➤ **threshold**. Usually used in combined forms, e.g. *subliminal, supraliminal*.

limit 1. The terminal value of a series. 2.

The end(s) of some continuum, especially a sensory continuum. **3.** The ➤ **asymptote**.

limits, method of ➤ **measurement of** ***threshold**.

limulus The horseshoe crab. Important in psychology because of a very large compound eye that lends itself nicely to experimental study. Much of the work on *lateral inhibition* was performed on *limulus*.

linear **1.** Of or relating to a line. **2.** Specifically, a straight line. **3.** Continuous, as opposed to discrete. n., *linearity*.

linear correlation ➤ **correlation, linear**.

linear-operator model A mathematical theory of learning based on a linear equation that specifies how the probability of a response is hypothesized to increase or decrease as a function of the occurrence of particular events or 'operators' such as reinforcement, punishment, etc.

linear perspective A monocular depth cue based on the geometric fact that as the distance of an object increases the visual angle that it subtends on the eye of the observer decreases. The familiar railroad tracks receding to a single point in the distance are perhaps the most frequently cited example.

linear regression ➤ **regression, linear**.

lingual **1.** Of or pertaining to the tongue. **2.** By extension, pertaining to languages. **3.** In articulatory phonetics, characteristic of sounds made with the tip of the tongue.

lingual papilla A visible protuberance on the surface of the tongue associated with the taste buds. Anatomically, there are four kinds of papillae: *circumvallate*, *folate*, *fungiform* and *filiform*. All but the last contain taste buds.

linguistic **relativity** ➤ **Whorfian** **hypothesis**.

linguistics Broadly, the study of the origins, evolution and structure of language(s). Until fairly recently linguistics and psychology benignly followed their own bents quite independently of each other; but no more. Since the work of Noam Chomsky in the 1960s the two disciplines have become importantly interrelated; in fact, Chomsky has characterized his own discipline of linguistics as a branch of cognitive psychology. ➤➤ **language, psycholinguistics**.

linguistic **universals** ➤ **universals,** **linguistic**.

linkage In genetics, two or more genes are said to be linked if they tend to be passed from generation to generation as a unit. The mechanism of linkage is chromosomal and the closer the genes are to each other on the chromosome the more closely they will be linked. Thus, all the genes on a given chromosome are said to form a *linkage group*. Note, however, that even closely linked genes can become separated as a result of *crossing over*.

liquid In phonetics, the 'flowing' speech sounds *r* and *l*.

lisp An articulatory speech disorder in which sibilant sounds (*s*, *z*, *sh*, *ch*) are mispronounced, usually by substituting a *th* sound.

Lissajou's figures Revolving abstract designs produced either by reflections from vibrating mirrors or on an oscilloscope screen. When watched closely for a time the direction of apparent rotation reverses.

literacy The state of being literate, having the ability to read and write. How to specify precisely what criterial level of these skills determines functional literacy has proven to be something of a problem. ➤ **illiteracy** and ➤➤ **reading**.

lithium (salts) Usually classified as *antipsychotic drugs*, lithium compounds are used primarily in the treatment of ➤ **bipolar disorders**, particularly the manic aspect. Lithium's manner of action in the body is unknown. It does, however, compete with the sodium salts and changes the composition of body fluids. It is also highly toxic and dosage must be carefully controlled. Common side effects include dizziness, slurred speech and ataxia. Note that some authorities classify the lithium salts with the *antidepressant drugs*.

Little Hans The pseudonym of one of Freud's most famous cases, the psychoanalysis of a young boy with a phobia of horses. It was, and still is today, cited by many as a source of supportive evidence for the Freudian theory of psychosexual development in children and how neuroses emerge from deep psychic conflict. It is also cited by many others as a classic case of flagrant overinterpretation – these persons typically are those with a behaviorist orientation who view phobias as the result of conditioning processes.

Lloyd Morgan's canon Articulated in 1894 by the British physiologist/psychologist Conway Lloyd Morgan, it cautioned against the explanatory excesses of the new field of comparative psychology by stating that in interpreting the behavior of an animal it is always preferable to use the psychologically simplest interpretation. Specifically, it is preferable to use the lower or more primitive explanation rather than to assume the action of a higher, more mentalistic process. The canon was very influential in the work of early behaviorists such as Watson and Thorndike. ➤➤ **Occam's razor** and the **principle of *parsimony** with which the canon shares a philosophical basis.

loading ➤ **factor loading**.

loafing ➤ **social loafing**.

lobe Any reasonably well-defined part of an organ.

lobectomy Generally, the surgical removal of a lobe, usually used with a qualifier to denote which one(s).

lobotomy, prefrontal A surgical procedure severing the white-matter tracts between the frontal lobes and the diencephalon, especially those of the thalamic and hypothalamic areas. The original operation was developed by A. E. Moniz in the 1930s and was so heralded as a psychosurgical procedure for severe psychological disorders that he received the Nobel prize for his work. With the accumulation of data from tens of thousands of lobotomies (including one of Moniz's own patients who, ungrateful wretch, shot the good doctor, causing a partial paralysis) the general conclusion is that the procedure does not work. Whatever beneficial results may occasionally be obtained must be balanced against the negative side effects of apathy, insensitivity, impaired judgement and seizures, all of which are irreversible. Recent years have fortunately witnessed its demise. Also called *prefrontal leucotomy*. ➤➤ **psychosurgery**.

lobotomy, transorbital A procedure for performing a ➤ **prefrontal *lobotomy** in which a surgical knife is inserted above the eyeball and moved to cut brain fibers.

localization **1.** Perceptual act of locating the spatial position of a stimulus. The term is used with respect to audition (locating a sound source in the environment), vision (locating a stimulus in the visual field) and tactile sensations (making references to the point of stimulation on the skin). **2.** ➤ **localization of function**.

localization of function A general hypothesized principle concerning brain function that, all things considered, specific functions have relatively precise and relatively circumscribed cortical locations. Contrast with the principle of ➤ **mass action**.

local sign According to the perceptual theory of the 19th-century philosopher Rudolph H. Lotze, every tactual and visual sensation has its particular local sign or 'signature' which is an experiential intensity that is specific for the point stimulated, either on the skin in the case of the tactile or on the retina for the visual. The perception of space was, according to Lotze, produced by the relationships between the local signs as the stimulation shifted across the receptor system.

location error (or **bias**) ➤ **space error** (or **bias**).

loci, method of A mnemonic device in

which the memorizer uses as the basis for learning new material a well-known geographical or architectural structure as a set of locations. For example, the Russian mnemonist S (as he is known in the literature) studied by Luria used to 'place' objects to be recalled in a visual picture of a well-known street. To recall the list of objects he would merely take a 'mental walk' down the street and 'pick up' the objects where he had placed them.

lock-and-key model A model of synaptic transmission based on the assumption that a neurotransmitter affects only those postsynaptic receptor sites that have the correct shape for that particular molecule much as a key fits into a lock.

locomotion Aside from the standard meanings locomotion was used by Lewin in a figurative manner to refer to the movement of a person through his or her ➤ **life space**.

locomotor ataxia ➤ **ataxia**.

locus Generally, a locale, a spot or a place. Used widely as follows: in perception, a point in space; in genetics, the position of a gene on a chromosome; in physiology, a circumscribed area on a organ; etc. pl., *loci*.

locus coeruleus A group of cell bodies located in the dorsal pons. Axons from cells here branch widely and release *norepinephrine* throughout the neocortex, hippocampus, thalamus, the cortex of the cerebellum, medulla, and the rest of the *pons*. Activity in the *locus coeruleus* is closely associated with the sleep–waking cycle.

locus of control A general term in social psychology used to refer to the perceived source of control over one's behavior. It is measured along a dimension running from high *internal* to high *external*, with *internal persons* being those who tend to take responsibility for their own actions and view themselves as having control over their own destinies, and *externals* being those who tend to see control as

residing elsewhere and tend to attribute success or failure to outside forces. Note that *reality* is not being measured here; the question is not whether true control derives from endogenous or exogenous sources but how the individual *perceives* it. ➤ **attribution theory, internal-external scale**.

log 1. logarithm. 2. ➤ **log**(o)-.

logagnosia A condition in which the patient can see and read words but not identify them in terms of their meanings. Some classify it as a form of ➤ **agnosia**, most regard it as a type of ➤ **aphasia**.

logamnesia A condition in which the patient is unable to recognize spoken or written words. ➤ **aphasia**, of which it is a common symptom.

logaphasia An older term for ➤ **motor *aphasia**.

logarithm The exponent to which a number (called the *base*) must be raised to equal a given number. Hence, $\log_{10} 1{,}000 = 3$ since the base (10) must be raised to the 3rd power to yield 1,000. The most common log bases are 2 (➤ **information**), 10 (most of the arithmetic calculations used in psychology) and e (the natural logarithmic system in mathematics in which logarithmic is abbreviated *ln*).

logarithmic curve (or **relationship**) Any curve in which the variables are related to one another according to the equation $y = \log x$.

logarithmic mean ➤ **geometric *mean**.

-logia Suffix meaning relating to *speech* or *speaking*.

logic That normative branch of philosophy that deals with the criteria of validity in thought, the canons of correct predication and the principles of reasoning and demonstration. Logic concerns only the reasoning process, not the end result. Incorrect conclusions can be reached through logical means if the original assumptions are faulty. ➤ **formal *logic, symbolic *logic**.

logic, affective Sequencing of ideas or deductions in which the connecting factors are emotional.

logical 1. Pertaining to **logic**. 2. Characterizing reasoning that is sound, correct.

logical positivism ➤ positivism, logical.

logic, formal Logic based on ➤ **formal** (2) propositions as opposed to logic based on meanings.

logic, symbolic Originally logic referred only to linguistic manifestations of reasoning – see here ➤ **log(o)-**. Symbolic logic was developed using a logical/symbolic language to formalize logical processes and thus remove them from the ambiguities of natural languages.

log law Term used for ➤ **Fechner's law**.

log(o)- Combining form from the Greek *logos* meaning *word* and, by extension, *speech* and even, on occasion, *thought*.

logogen A term introduced by the British psychologist John Morton for his hypothesized memory unit that is assumed to represent a 'node' that interlinks all aspects of a word's representations (i.e. its semantic, auditory, visual and pictorial properties). A logogen is viewed as an integration of all the relevant information with regard to any particular word or concept. The argument is that the actual context within which a word is presented directs the accessing of the relevant components of the total information that the person has in memory.

logography Any writing system based on the use of signs to represent words or morphemes. Mayan, early Egyptian and Chinese are examples. ➤➤ **orthography** and **reading** for details on why such writing systems are of interest to psychologists.

logomania ➤ logorrhea.

logopathy General label for any speech disorder.

logorrhea The roots of the word should be familiar enough. The literal meaning is, of course, an excessive flow or stream of words, usually incoherent. Also called *logomania*, *lalorrhea* and *verbomania*.

logotherapy Viktor Frankl's term for his form of psychotherapy based on focusing the client on a recognition and acceptance of himself or herself in a meaningful way as part of a totality, including the real world within which he/she must function. Often characterized as the third Viennese school (Freudian and Adlerian being the first two), Frankl's approach embodies elements of the dynamic psychologies *existentialism* and *behaviorism*, the latter particularly with regard to the role of learning in the development of neurotic behaviors. Frankl's orientation is also seen as an important component of the ➤ **humanistic psychology** movement.

-logy Combining form meaning *speech* and, by extension, *knowledge* or *science*.

Lombrosian theory A theory of criminality proposed in the late 19th century by Cesare Lombroso. His thesis was that criminality is biological and that 'criminal types' could be identified through physical analysis of head shape. It is without scientific foundation and its main impact was to make life rather unpleasant for some unfortunates with the 'wrong' head shape.

longitudinal 1. Pertaining to length, along the length of something. 2. In anatomy, pertaining to direction or position along the long axis of the body.

longitudinal fissure ➤ sagittal fissure.

longitudinal method Research carried out by following a number of subjects over an extended period of time. Compare with ➤ **cross-sectional method**.

long-term memory (or **store**) ➤ **memory, long-term**.

long-term potentiation A long-term increase in excitatory postsynaptic potentials in the dentate gyrus of the *hippocampal formation* brought about by repeated stimulation. It is hypothesized that the phenomenon is related to the processes of learning and memory, which must, in principle, involve some kind of long-term modification in neural pathways.

looking-glass self A term introduced by C. H. Cooley to characterize a person's perception of himself or herself as a reflection of how he or she appears to others. The self-image is formed as a consequence of the attitudes others have about one.

look-say method ➤ **whole-word method**.

looming A term used to describe the complex of gradient transformations produced as one rapidly approaches some object, or vice versa. Essentially, looming is the cue for an impending collision.

loosening of associations A thought disturbance in which ideas shift in a helter-skelter manner from subject to subject producing an incoherent stream.

lorazepam An antianxiety drug of the ➤ **benzodiazepine** group. ➤ **antianxiety drugs**.

lordosis 1. A severe concavity of the spine and back. 2. A concave arching of the back in response to specific stimulation. It is a common sexual response in many species.

lose-shift strategy ➤ **win-stay lose-shift strategy**.

lost-letter technique A procedure for evaluating ➤ **helping behavior**. A number of addressed, stamped letters are 'planted' in various places such as street corners, hallways, buses, etc. The data consist of the number of letters picked up and mailed by passers-by.

loudness The psychological attribute of an auditory stimulus corresponding to the physical dimension of intensity.

love Psychologists would probably have been wise to have abdicated responsibility for analysis of this term and left it to poets. The confusing litter left behind by lack of wisdom and excess of boldness can, however, be codified by the following classification scheme. First, the two most general uses of the term: 1. An intense feeling of strong liking or affection for some specific thing or person. 2. An enduring sentiment toward a person producing a desire to be with that person and a concern for the happiness and satisfactions of that person. Note that both of these may or may not carry sexual connotations. Certainly 1 is often used in reference to cats, tennis, teachers or academic disciplines, and 2 to refer to parents or children – all without sexual or erotic connotations. However, 1 may apply equally well to paramours and 2 to wives and husbands and lovers. The primary role played by love in either of these senses is that it is an affective state that is assumed to color all interactions with and perceptions of the person or thing loved. It is this component, of course, that makes love so attractive to psychologists.

In psychoanalytic theory, where one might hope to turn for clarification, one finds, in the British analyst C. Rycroft's words, 'as much difficulty defining this protean concept as elsewhere.' It is used variously as: 3. Any affective state defined as basically the opposite of *hatred*; 4. An emotion liable to sublimation or inhibition; and 5. Equivalent to Eros and an instinctive force close either to the life instincts or the sexual instincts – depending on whether one is affiliated with the early or late Freudian point of view here (➤ **libido** for clarification).

Meaning 3 seems to be of little value to psychologists; it merely defers the definitional obligation. Uses 4 and 5 are close to the classic psychoanalytic meaning, particularly in that here all manifestations of love – love of self, of children, of humanity, country or even of abstract ideas – are viewed as manifestations of a basic instinctual force and, hence, subject to the action of defense mechanisms. However, complications do arise, particularly since some theorists append the notion of *object* love, and reinterpret the ideas contained in 4 and 5 as a manifestation of a need to relate to objects – which may include, of course, people.

Using love as a scientific term produces several types of conflicts which we specify here with no attempt at resolution. First, there is the issue of sex and sexual expression: is it an essential component or can love exist totally divorced from it? Second, there is the instinct issue: is love innate or is it an acquired emotional response? Third, there is the problem of the manner or manifestation of the emotions: can the feeling be dissociated from the behavior or does the emotion always contaminate the behavior?

love, companionate Love that is based on a secure and trusting relationship.

love, romantic According to Rubin, that kind of love hypothesized to exist between opposite-sexed peers. ➤ **love scale**.

love scale A scale devised by Z. Rubin to measure ➤ **romantic *love**. The scale is constructed to evaluate three components: affiliative/dependent needs; predispositions to help; and exclusiveness. Differentiate these components from those used in the ➤ **liking scale**. Note that this effort to specify the underlying dimensions of love (at least the 'romantic' kind) is accomplished by dramatically circumscribing the domain discussed under the more general term ➤ **love**.

love withdrawal A form of discipline in which parents control their child's behavior by expressing disapproval. Although the technique consists of disapproving statements to a child like, 'How can you be so stupid,' the implication is that the parent has, by making such a statement, withdrawn their love.

low-balling A two-step device for obtaining compliance in which the individual first secures agreement by requesting something simple and then steps up the request by revealing hidden costs. Compare with ➤ **that's-not-all technique**.

low-grade defective ➤ **defective** (2).

LRCS Abbreviation for *language-responsible cognitive structure*. ➤ **LAD**.

LSD ➤ **lysergic acid diethylamide**.

LTM ➤ **long-term *memory**.

426

LTS Abbreviation for *long-term store*. See discussion under ➤ **long-term *memory**.

lucid interval A period of relatively normal mental functioning between bouts of a psychotic disorder.

lucidity Clarity, especially of mind.

ludic From the Latin *ludere*, meaning *to play*. **1.** Pertaining to behaviors that are seemingly primary in that all display them, yet they have no obvious biological basis. Generally included as ludic activities are exploration, curiosity, intellectual games, humor and the like. **2.** In Piagetian terminology, characterizing that which is make-believe.

lumen In light measurement, the amount of light within a unit solid angle coming from a 1 candlepower source. Abbreviated *L*.

luminance The *luminous flux* emitted, reflected or transmitted by a surface and measured in candles per square meter. Luminance is directly related to the ➤ **illuminance** at the surface times the reflectance of the surface. Thus luminance is equal to RC/d^2, where R is the reflectance of the surface, C is the candlepower of the source and d is the distance of the source from the surface.

luminosity A term with an often confusing array of uses. Once used rather indefinitely for *brightness*, in the contemporary visual sciences it now refers to the property of a stimulus such that the physical characteristics of the energy radiating or reflecting from it are adequate for exciting sufficient numbers of visual receptors for the experiencing of a visual sensation. In older texts this concept was rendered by the term ➤ **visibility**. Some authors will use ➤ **spectral sensitivity** as a synonym for luminosity. This is not wrong, although spectral sensitivity when unqualified is a rather more general term and applicable to any spectrum, not just the visual (e.g. the auditory spectrum).

luminosity coefficient(s) Any of the coefficients expressing the relative luminosity of the visual system to the various wavelengths of the visible spectrum. The coefficients are normalized measures of sensitivity of the system given, relative to the wavelength of peak sensitivity. For the ➤ **scotopic** system the peak is at approximately 510 nm, for the ➤ **photopic** it is at approximately 555 nm. In older texts the term *visibility coefficient* is often used.

luminosity curve(s) Spectral sensitivity curve(s) for the visual system showing the sensitivity of the system to all wavelengths within the visible spectrum. There are a number of such curves depending on a variety of factors such as whether the eye is dark-adapted or not and whether one is evaluating the ➤ **scotopic** or the ➤ **photopic** function.

luminous flux The amount of light radiated or emitted by a source, measured in ➤ **lumens**.

luminous intensity Luminous flux emitted per unit angle about a light source, measured in international *candles* or *candelas*.

lunacy An obsolete term for legal ➤ **insanity**.

lurking variable A third, hidden variable that might explain a correlation between two other variables. For example, there is little doubt that infant distress and ice cream sales would be correlated in a northern urban environment like New York City. The correlation, however, is being driven by a third variable, temperature, which is 'lurking' behind the data.

luteinizing hormone (LH) A hormone that, in the female, regulates progesterone production during the latter stages of the menstrual cycle and, in the male, regulates the production of androgen. Also called *interstitial-cell-stimulating hormone.* ➤➤ **menstrual cycle** for more detail on its manner of action in females.

luteotropic hormone ➤ **prolactin**.

lux A unit of ➤ **illuminance** equal to the amount of light falling on a surface 1 meter from a source of 1 international *candle* or *candela*.

Luys, nucleus of ➤ **subthalamic nucleus**.

lycanthropy The delusion that one is or can change into a wolf.

lymph The alkaline fluid of the lymphatic vessels. Lymph differs from blood in that red corpuscles are absent and the protein content is lower. It is found in tissue spaces all over the body; it is gathered into small vessels and carried centrally, eventually entering the blood stream at junctions with the large veins near the heart.

lymphocytes Specialized white blood cells that manufacture dozens of the natural chemicals involved in the body's immune reactions. The T-lymphocytes are produced in the thymus, the B-lymphocytes in the bone marrow.

lysergic acid diethylamide (LSD) One of the chemical substances derived from lysergic acid, LSD is an exceedingly powerful psychoactive drug capable of producing extreme alterations in consciousness, hallucinations, dramatic distortions in perception and unpredictable mood swings. It was originally classified as a *psychotomimetic* drug because it appeared to produce a state that mimicked a psychosis (in particular, schizophrenia) although this parallel now seems to have little to recommend it. It is difficult to predict what a person's reactions to LSD (or, for that matter, any psychoactive drug) will be. The effects are dependent on a number of factors other than dosage such as the expectations of the user, the setting in which the experience takes place and the individual's general psychological state of mind at the time. There was, for a time, hope that it might have some therapeutic role to play and a few researchers reported some success in treating various disorders from schizophrenia to alcoholism. Follow-up work failed to confirm these early reports and today the drug is regarded as having essentially no clinical value. As a 'recreational' drug it harbors a number of very real psychological dangers.

-lytic Suffix indicating opposition, often used of drugs that oppose a form of action; e.g., a *sympatholytic* drug opposes sympathetic nervous system effects.

M

M Occasional abbreviation for the ➤ **mean**.

m 1. Matter. 2. ➤ **Meaningfulness**.

MA ➤ **mental *age**.

mμ Millimicron (10^{-9} meter).

μ The Greek letter *mu*, a common abbreviation for *micron*.

MacBeth illuminometer A device for measuring the visual effectiveness of light that uses the individual's own eye as the basic measuring instrument. It is rarely used any more since much more efficient and precise photometric instruments now exist; ➤ **photometry**.

Mach bands A phenomenon of brightness contrast produced when a dimly illuminated area merges into a more brightly illuminated one. The perceived change in brightness is considerably sharper than the actual change in light intensity and two bands of dark and light are seen on either side of the gradation. These two bands were named after the 19th-century scientist Ernst Mach.

Machiavellianism Descriptive of a pattern of behaviors including manipulation of others through guile, deviousness, deception and opportunism with the increase of power and control as the central motive. The term 'honors' the name of the 16th-century Italian court adviser Niccolò Machiavelli.

Machiavellian Scale A scale designed by R. Christie to measure Machiavellianism. The subject is asked to agree or disagree with a series of statements, many of which are actually direct quotes from Machiavelli's writings. Also known by the shortened form, *Mach Scale*.

Machover Draw-a-Person Test A popular projective test in which the subject is asked to draw a person and tell a story about the drawing. Both drawing and story are then analyzed. Designed for use with ages 2 and up. Also known as *DAP Test*.

Mach Scale ➤ **Machiavellian Scale**.

MacLean's theory of emotion Taking ➤ **Papez's theory** as a base, MacLean's major modifications were that other areas of the limbic system, particularly the hippocampus and the amygdaloid complex, were involved in emotion as well as the hypothalamus and that the more primitive layers of the cortex played a major role in integrating information. MacLean's theory is part of his more general characterization of the ➤ **triune brain**.

macro- Prefix connoting *large, long* or *thick*. Compare with ➤ **micro-** (1). ➤ **megalo-**, et seq. for terms not found here.

macrobiotic Long-lived, characterizing that which functions to prolong life.

macrocephaly A cover term for any of a number of pathological conditions marked by abnormal enlargement of the head.

macroelectrode A large electrode used for recording the activity of a large number of neurons. Compare with ➤ **microelectrode**.

macromania ➤ **megalomania**.

macropsia Abnormal enlargement of perceived size of visual stimuli.

maculae acusticae Collectively, the *macula sacculi* and *macula utriculi*, the two patches of sensory cells in the utricle and saccule in the vestibular apparatus of the inner ear.

macula fibers Neural fibers which leave the retina from the *macula lutea* and form the central core of the optic nerve.

macula lutea A small yellowish spot in the center of the retina. It contains a pit or depression known as the ➤ **fovea**. Also called the *yellow spot*.

mad (madness) A strictly nontechnical term for ➤ **insanity**, which itself has only a very specialized technical use.

magazine In operant-conditioning procedures, any mechanical device that delivers food, water, etc. to the experimental subject.

magazine training A part of the process of shaping an operant response. The subject is trained to associate the sound and sight of the ➤ **magazine** with reinforcement.

magic Sociologists and social psychologists will classify a practice as magic when: (a) the practitioners believe that supernatural powers are the cause of events; and (b) it is not a part of an organized religion, although this latter criterion tends to be applied rather ethnocentrically.

magical number 7±2 ➤ **seven plus or minus two**.

magical thinking The belief that thinking is equated with doing. Seen in children as a normal stage of development during which the child believes that his thoughts and hopes are the cause of events happening about him. Also observed in adults in a variety of psychiatric disorders. ➤➤ **omnipotence of thought**.

magico-phenomenalist A term in Piaget's theory used to describe the presumed quality of perception of infants prior to the development of ➤ **object permanence**. Basically the idea is that such infants are thought to perceive the world as unorganized, fleeting, sensory impressions.

magnacide The act of assassinating a famous person for no other reason than the fact that they are famous.

magnetic resonance imaging (MRI) A noninvasive procedure that provides a detailed picture of body tissue. An MRI resembles a CAT-scan (➤ **computerized axial tomography**), but uses a strong magnetic field instead of X-rays. Strong magnetic fields cause the nuclei of some molecules in the body to spin. When a radio wave is passed through the body, the nuclei emit energy at various frequencies which are picked up by the MRI scanner; a computer then interprets the pattern of emissions and assembles a picture of the slice of the tissue. MRI-scans have several advantages over CAT-scans and PET-scans (➤ **positron emission tomography**). They present fine detail more clearly; they do not use potentially damaging X-rays; and they can make scans in the sagittal or frontal planes as well as the horizontal.

magnetotropism An orienting response to a magnetic force.

magnitude estimation ➤ **methods of *scaling**.

magnitude production ➤ **methods of *scaling**.

magnocellular system That portion of the pathways of the visual system that is responsible for the perception of form, movement, depth, and small brightness differences. The system is named for the large, rapidly conducting, evolutionarily old cells that make up the magnocellular layers of the lateral geniculate nucleus. Compare with ➤ **parvocellular system**.

Maier's law A cynical 'law' stated by the American psychologist Norman R. F. Maier to the effect that, 'if the data do not fit the theory, the data must be disposed of.' Maier, of course, was chiding his colleagues for excessive affiliation with their own particular theoretical models.

main effect The basic relationship between a single independent variable and a single dependent variable.

mainstreaming The educational practice of removing children with special problems (physical, mental and/or emotional) from special classes and schools and placing them in regular classroom settings.

maintaining stimulus Generally, any stimulus the mere continued presence of which is sufficient to continue to elicit a particular response.

maintenance functions All those physiological processes and behavioral activities that serve to keep an organism in a relatively stable (i.e. *homeostatic*) condition.

maintenance level The physiological steady state of a mature organism after growth has ceased and diet and environmental conditions serve to keep things relatively constant.

maintenance schedule A schedule of feeding, watering, exercising, etc. that keeps an organism at ➤ **maintenance level**.

major affective disorder ➤ **mood disorders**.

major depressive episode ➤ **depressive episode, major**.

major epilepsy ➤ **epilepsy, major**.

major solution K. Horney's term for a form of a ➤ **neurotic solution** in which one engages in vigorous compulsive activity as a way of avoiding anxiety and conflict.

major tranquilizer ➤ **tranquilizer, major**.

mal French for *sickness, disorder, evil*. Used in some combined forms, e.g., *mal de mer* = seasickness, *petit mal* = minor epilepsy, *grand mal* = major epilepsy.

mal- Prefix used to express *faulty, ill, imperfect*. Essentially synonymous with ➤ **dys-**, although the latter is properly reserved for words of Greek origin.

maladaptive Lit., of that which is not adaptive. There are three primary usages here: **1.** In biology, characterizing an organism or aspects thereof that limit the chances of the organism developing the behavioral repertoire needed for survival. **2.** By extension, in evolutionary biology, of such characteristics when displayed by a species. **3.** In psychiatry and clinical psychology, of patterns of behavior likely to produce so much psychic distress that therapy is needed. The last usage here, which is growing in popularity, was introduced to de-emphasize the medical or disease aspects of much of standard psychiatric terminology. The argument put forward by those who favor this term is that many clinical syndromes are fundamentally *maladaptive behavior patterns* and not necessarily signs of *mental illness* or *mental disease*. Not surprisingly, this position is most vigorously espoused by those with a behaviorist orientation. ➤ **adaptive** (2).

maladjustment ➤ **Adjustment** is basically the relationship that any organism establishes with respect to its environment (although see that term for nuances). The connotation is that when this relationship is adaptive the state of adjustment exists, when it is not then there is a condition of maladjustment. Generally, the term is used with respect to social or cultural standards and values although it may legitimately be applied to more basic biological conditions as well. ➤ **adjustment disorder**.

malapropism The inappropriate substitution of one word for another similar in sound. ➤➤ **spoonerism**.

mal de ojo A ➤ **culture-specific syndrome** found in the Mediterranean. The term translates as *evil eye* and is especially found in children. Symptoms include fitful sleep, crying without apparent cause, fever, and various digestive problems.

male erectile disorder A ➤ **sexual arousal disorder** in males marked by a persistent or recurrent inability to maintain an adequate erection. While this term is the one recommended in the *DSM-IV*, the term ➤ **impotence** with its variations is still very much in use for this condition.

maleness The condition of possessing those physiological and anatomical characteristics of a male that relate to his reproductive capacity. Distinguish from ➤ **masculinity**.

male orgasmic disorder ➤ **orgasm disorders**.

malevolent transformation H. S. Sullivan's term for the development of the (neurotic) sense that one is living in the midst of one's enemies, particularly persons with some measure of control over one's life, e.g. doctors, nurses, teachers, parents.

malformation Generally, any deformity. Frequently used with the connotation of it being congenital.

malign 1 adj. Tending to harm, damaging, malignant. 2 vb. To speak about a person in an injurious manner which denigrates or causes harm.

malignant adj. Characteristic of a condition which is growing worse; virulent, harmful, ultimately fatal. Contrast with ➤ **benign**. n., **malignancy**.

malignant narcissism ➤ **narcissism, malignant**.

malingering Deliberate feigning of illness, disability or incompetence. Contrast with ➤ **hypochondria**, in which the condition is not faked but believed. ➤➤ **factitious disorder**.

malleus One of the three small bones of the middle ear. ➤ **auditory *ossicles**.

malpractice Incorrect or negligent treatment especially by a physician, psychologist or other health practitioner. The term has both ethical and legal implications.

Malthusian theory The rather pessimistic theory of Thomas Malthus (1766–1834) which states that in any species the population tends to increase geometrically while the food supply only increases arithmetically. Hence, some check on the population must occur and Malthus cited war, pestilence, famine, disease and plagues as those most likely while counseling for birth control and limitations in family size.

mammal Any member of the Mammalia class of vertebrates. Mammalian characteristics include, in addition to the obvious mammary glands for milk secretion and suckling, hair, a diaphragm for respiration, a lower jaw consisting of a single pair of bones and the ossicles of the middle ear.

mammary glands The compound glands of the female breast that secrete milk.

mammillary bodies Two small rounded projections in the medial area of the hypothalamus that have been implicated in emotional behavior and sexual motivation.

man 1. The genus *Homo* of the primate order of which the species *Homo sapiens* is the only surviving member. 2. By extension, any member of this species. 3. By de-extension, any male member of this species. Raised consciousnesses everywhere concerning the non-equivalence of meanings 1 and 2 and meaning 3 have created no end of linguistic havoc. In this volume I have tried to use gender neutral language as much as possible, hence *man* is only used when it refers to the species as a whole.

management 1. The carrying out of functions of planning, organizing and directing any enterprise. 2. Collectively, those persons in an organization who perform these functions.

managerial psychology A sub-area of industrial/organizational psychology focusing on the role of the manager or supervisor in an organization and the interactive processes between the supervisor and those supervised.

MANCOVA Abbreviation for ➤ **multivariate analysis of covariance**.

mand One of the main categories of verbal behavior suggested by B. F. Skinner in his operant analysis of language. A mand represents a large class of utterances that make demands upon the hearer and are reinforced by fulfillment of the demand. In other words, manding represents verbal behavior primarily under control of its consequences. Classic examples of mands are 'Please pass the salt' and 'Get me my book.' ➤➤ **autoclitic** and **tact**.

mandala A mystic symbol of the cosmos generally of circular form with representations of deities arranged symmetrically around it. Used chiefly in Hinduism and

Buddhism as an aid to meditation, it has become popular in the West for similar functions. In Jungian theory it is the symbolic representation of the striving for unity of the self.

mania 1. Loosely and non-technically, madness; violent, erratic behavior. **2.** A mood disorder characterized by a variety of symptoms including inappropriate elation, extreme motor activity, impulsiveness and excessively rapid thought and speech. It is a component in several ➤ **mood disorders** particularly the manic aspect of ➤ **bipolar disorder**. adj., *maniacal*, *manic*.

-mania A suffix used to indicate an obsessive preoccupation with a particular activity or pattern of thinking or a compulsive need to act in some deviant fashion; e.g., ➤ **kleptomania, megalomania, pyromania**.

maniacal ➤ **mania**.

mania, unipolar ➤ **mania** (2). The qualifier *unipolar* is used for cases in which there are recurrent episodes of mania without the appearance of the depressive phase observed in the classic ➤ **bipolar disorder**.

manic 1 adj. Characteristic of ➤ **mania**. **2** n. One diagnosed as having ➤ **mania** (2).

manic bipolar disorder ➤ **bipolar disorder, manic**.

manic-depressive psychosis (or **illness, reaction** or **syndrome**) ➤ **bipolar disorder**.

manic episode A distinct period during which the predominant mood is ➤ **mania** (2).

manifest anxiety Overt, displayed anxiety; anxiety about which one is conscious. Note, when used in psychoanalytic writings the assumption is that this over-anxiety is a symptom of a deeper, repressed conflict.

Manifest Anxiety Scale (MAS) A scale for measuring manifest or admitted anxiety. Note that this characteristic distinguishes it from other devices for assessing anxiety, which are classified as *projective techniques* since they are designed to deal with repressed or unconscious aspects. The MAS was derived from the *MMPI* and consists of a set of descriptions of anxiety symptoms from which the subject selects those characteristic of him or her.

manifest content ➤ **latent and manifest *content**.

manipulandum Basically, any characteristic of an object that can be manipulated. Most commonly used to refer to the physical object whose movement is associated with reinforcement in an operant-conditioning situation.

manipulative drive A motive to manipulate objects, to handle and explore them. It was hypothesized by neo-behaviorists that organisms, including many lower species, have this drive since they are known to perform other behaviors in which the only reward is the opportunity to manipulate a complex novel object.

mannerism A characteristic quirk or habitual oddity in an individual's behavior or speech.

Mann-Whitney U A nonparametric statistical test based on rank-order data. It compares two samples of scores by evaluating the probabilities of the distribution of rankings. One of the most powerful of the nonparametric tests, it is often used in place of the *t test* when the assumptions of parametric tests are not met. There is also an extension of the test to three samples known as the *Whitney extension*.

MANOVA: Abbreviation for ➤ **multivariate analysis of variance**.

mantra Specifically, a Vedic hymn. More generally, any ritual verbal incantation used devotionally or as an aid in meditation.

manual alphabet ➤ **finger spelling**.

manual language ➤ **sign language**.

manual method A method of teaching communication to the deaf through the use of sign language. For many years a controversy has raged over whether this method is preferable to the so-called *oral* *method*, in which the teaching is through carefully shaped speaking and lip reading. The manual method has the major drawback that it can only be used with others trained in sign language, which eliminates the vast majority of the hearing; the oral method's primary liability is that only a small percentage of those who undergo training reach the fluency needed for easy communication. Most teachers of the deaf today aim for a combination of the two, teaching signing first so that the deaf can communicate with each other and using the oral method later.

MAO inhibitor ➤ **monoamine oxidase inhibitor**.

marasmus Originally the deterioration of tissue in the young caused by poor nutrition. It is, however, often used as roughly synonymous with ➤ **anaclitic depression** and thus incorporates emotional deterioration as an outcome and social and sensory deprivations as causes.

marathon group An aptly named group-therapy technique in which a group of individuals, usually with a fairly singular focus or purpose, meets for an extended period of time ranging anywhere from roughly 6 hours up to 48 hours.

Marbe's law The generalization that in word-association tasks the more frequently a response occurs the more rapidly it tends to occur; latency is inversely related to frequency.

Marfan's syndrome A genetic condition consisting of large, bony fingers, hyperextensible joints and a gaunt, angular face. Often cardiac abnormalities are present, including a weakened aorta.

marginal 1. Generally, on the margin; characteristic of an instance or event of uncertain classification or one on the borderline between two classes or categories. 2. In statistics, of the sums at the margins (or borders) of a table or matrix.

marginal frequency (or **total**) In any data matrix, the sum of any one of the rows or columns; i.e. the frequencies in the margins. For example, in a tabulation of persons by sex and height one set of marginals (as they are often called for short) would give the number of men and the number of women without regard to height; the other set would give the totals of each height without regard to sex.

marginal group ➤ **group, marginal**.

marginal intelligence An occasional synonym for ➤ **borderline intelligence**.

marginal man One who lies between two distinct cultural groups and is faced with the dilemma of which to affiliate with, which cultural values and standards to adopt. Life at the margin is assumed to produce a considerable degree of emotional conflict.

margin of attention ➤ **attention, margin of**.

margin of consciousness ➤ **margin of *attention**.

marijuana (or **marihuana**) A general term for any part of the hemp plant ➤ **cannabis sativa**. See that entry for details.

marital therapy Therapy aimed at the resolution of problems of married couples. Typically both parties are in therapy conjointly although on occasions each may be seen individually. The focus is generally broad, embracing psychodynamic elements, sexual issues, economic factors, etc. The term ➤ **couples therapy** is preferred by many for it encompasses unmarried unions as well. ➤➤ **family therapy**.

marked-unmarked adjectives In adjectives that represent poles along a dimension often one can be 'neutralized' to represent the whole dimension and is considered to be *unmarked* while the other which cannot be so 'neutralized' is called *marked*. For example, in the pair *long-short*, *long* is unmarked and can represent neutrally the concept of time as in the question, 'How long was the movie?' If one, however, asks, 'How short was the movie?' the question is not neutral but presupposes that it was inordinately short.

marker 1. In linguistics, a signal that indicates (i.e. *marks*) a function or a feature. The easiest way to grasp the use here is to note that markers generally designate the presence or absence of distinctive features. Thus, a period is a sentence-boundary marker, voicing marks the phone [b] and distinguishes it from [p], -ed marks the past tense of regular verbs in English, etc. 2. In medicine generally and psychiatry specifically, any sign that can be used diagnostically with respect to a specific disorder. Three kinds are identified, ➤ **episode**, **residual**, and **vulnerability** *marker.

marker, episode A ➤ **marker** (2) or specific symptom that occurs in particular disorders; e.g., fluid in the lungs in pneumonia, auditory hallucinations in schizophrenia. Episode markers allow one to confirm a diagnosis. Compare with ➤ **residual** and **vulnerability** *marker.

marker, residual A ➤ **marker** (2) which is an aftereffect of a disorder and hence 'marks' the patient as having had that disorder even after it has subsided; e.g., certain antibodies following viral infections, subtle sensorimotor deficits following some psychiatric disorders. Compare with ➤ **episode** and **vulnerability** *marker.

marker, vulnerability A ➤ **marker** (2) that exists before, during, and after a particular disorder. Vulnerability markers are, generally speaking, 'risk' factors associated with particular disorders and include such things as particular genes that predispose one to a particular syndrome. Compare with ➤ **episode** and **residual** *marker.

market research The application of statistical and experimental procedures to the study of buying habits, selling techniques, advertising and other attendant economic components of the marketplace. ➤➤ **motivation research**.

marriage Common parlance tends to miss the point that marriage is an institution, a set of social norms. In all cases it sanctions, according to local customs, a union between two (or on occasion more)

persons and, at least theoretically, binds them to a system of obligatory behaviors for the purpose of maintaining a family unit. Although we need not list them here, it should be noted that anthropologists and sociologists distinguish over a score of different kinds of marriage.

marriage counseling ➤ **marital therapy**.

masculine protest An Adlerian term which can take two forms. The uninteresting use is to describe a desire on the part of the female to be male. The interesting one is to characterize the drive for power and superiority which can, of course, be displayed by either sex.

masculinity Lit., the state of an organism reflecting or displaying the appearances, traits and behavior patterns characteristic of the male of the species. As defined, the label does not necessarily implicate gender; it should not be used as a synonym for ➤ **maleness**. ➤➤ **femininity**.

masculinity–femininity scale (MF scale) A scale designed to measure the degree of masculinity and femininity in a person. Note that the scale is gender-free; that is, one's sex does not limit one to scoring on either extreme. This type of scale must always be viewed as tightly culture-bound since what characterizes masculinity or femininity differs dramatically from culture to culture.

masking A general term in the study of perception for any process whereby a detectable or recognizable stimulus (called the *target*) is made difficult or impossible to detect or recognize by the presentation of a second stimulus (the *masker*) in close temporal or spatial proximity to it. Masking may occur in any sensory system; e.g., it may be: auditory, when an above-threshold tone is masked by the introduction of a second tone; visual, when a recognizable form is rendered unrecognizable by introducing an overlapping figure; olfactory, when one odor is covered by another; etc. Masking may also be produced by several temporal arrangements of the target and masker. In *simultaneous masking* the two are presented together; in *backward masking* the masker is presented some (usually very short) time after the target; in *forward masking* the order of presentation is reversed. ➤➤ **metacontrast**, which refers to visual masking when the target and masker are spatially separated.

masking, lateral ➤ **Masking** of a visual stimulus by other stimuli on either side of it. Note that in such cases there will always be mutuality; the target stimulus will mask the masker as well as being masked by it and often the term *mutual lateral masking* is used. ➤➤ **metacontrast**.

masking, remote In audition, the masking of low-frequency tones by high-frequency noise stimuli. It is hypothesized that the effect is produced by distortion processes in the inner ear.

masking, simultaneous ➤ **masking**.

masochism The term derives from the name of the Austrian novelist, Leopold von Sacher-Masoch, and refers most broadly to any tendency to direct that which is destructive, painful or humiliating against oneself. Special uses abound: *sexual masochism* is used when erotic pleasure is associated with the treatment; *moral masochism* is used when such tendencies dominate to such an extent that they seem to represent a character trait, the presumption here being that the person seeks to alleviate guilt by subjecting himself or herself to continuous punishment; *psychic masochism* is used of any kind of hostility or destructive impulse turned upon oneself, a usage which is very general; *mass masochism* refers to whole populations subjecting themselves to pain and hardship.

masochistic personality disorder ➤ **self-defeating personality disorder**.

masochistic sabotage A psychoanalytic term for blatant, overt, self-destructive acts. They are assumed within the theory to result from unconscious motives to punish oneself.

mass In social psychology, any large

number of people both diverse in make-up and without social organization. The interesting aspect of the term is the implication that although the mass is without discernible structure the people involved tend to behave in a relatively uniform fashion. See here ➤ **mass behavior**. Distinguish from ➤ **mob**.

mass-action principle A generalization concerning cortical functioning put forward by the American physiological psychologist Karl S. Lashley. In simplest terms he argued that the cortex operates as a coordinated system, that large 'masses' of tissue were involved in all complex functioning. This position contrasts with the oft-proposed theory that specific local areas of the brain mediate specific behaviors. Lashley's theory rests upon the demonstration that the degree of disruption of a learned behavior is due not simply to the location of brain lesions but to the amount of tissue involved. Note that Lashley was not suggesting that there was no localization of function but that such localization was only part of the story.

massa intermedia Tissue that connects the two lobes of the ➤ **thalamus**.

mass behavior Collective behavior of a ➤ **mass** without any obvious direct or personal communication or mutual influencing of the individuals making up the mass. Fads and fashions, dress styles, political movements, etc. are examples. The assumption is that mass-communication systems are the channels through which the societal influences occur. Also called ➤ **mass contagion**.

mass contagion ➤ **mass behavior**.

massed practice ➤ **practice, massed**.

Massformel German for *measuring formula*. It was Fechner's label for his grand achievement; ➤ **Fechner's law**.

mass movement Spontaneous behavior of a mass of people with some particular focus or goal. Although there may be a common aim the term does not imply that the movement is controlled or organized. In fact, reflecting the meaning of ➤ **mass**, the assumption is that there is no overall plan.

mass reflex Generally, any reflex-like response involving large numbers of muscles and glands; e.g., the *startle response*.

mastery The achieving of some pre-set (and usually high) level of functioning on some task.

mastery test ➤ **test, mastery**.

masturbation The conjectural Latin roots of the term are interesting, particularly in light of so many of the Puritan myths: *manus* meaning *hand* and *stupare* meaning *to defile* or *dishonor*. The accepted meaning of the term is the production of erotic stimulation of the genitals, usually to the point of orgasm, by manual means. Although not explicit, the usual inference is that the stimulation is self-induced.

MAT ➤ **Miller Analogies Test**.

matched-groups procedure An experimental procedure in which control is achieved by matching the groups of subjects on those variables not specifically under investigation. In cases where very fine control is required individual subjects in each group are matched against each other, in the so-called *matched-pairs procedure*. Also called *equivalent-groups procedure*. ➤ **yoked control**, which is a variation on the general procedure.

matched pairs ➤ **matched-groups procedure**.

matched sample ➤ **sample, matched**.

matching law The generalization that an organism will select each of several alternatives with a probability that matches the overall probability that each of the alternatives actually occurs. ➤ **probability matching**, a somewhat more neutral term that merely describes rather than claims 'lawful' status for this phenomenon.

matching test ➤ **matching to sample**.

matching to sample An experimental procedure, simple in basic form but with many complex variations. Most succinctly, the subject is shown a target stimulus and required to choose from a set of alternative stimuli the one that matches the target. The procedure can be extended to study memory processes, by introducing a delay period between the target and the set of choices, or to concept learning, by having the choice set represent abstractions, for example by varying them according to number rather than physical form. Also called *matching test*.

materialism 1. In a sociological sense, a preoccupation with the pursuit of things material to the neglect of the mental or the spiritual. 2. As a philosophical position, the doctrine that the only means through which reality comes to be known is through an understanding of physical matter. Contrast here with ➤ **mentalism** and ➤ **vitalism** and compare with ➤ **mechanism**.

maternal aggression ➤ **aggression, maternal**.

maternal behavior Collectively, all those behaviors related to or associated with being a mother. Often the term is used synonymously with caring for the young. This usage, understandable given much of the behavior of specific species, is misleading when applied universally. In many species, the father displays nurturant behavior and we would do well to use the more neutral word *parental* as the general term with *maternal* and *paternal* reserved for specific cases.

maternal-deprivation syndrome A group of symptoms, including stunted physical growth and retarded emotional development, associated with infants who have been deprived of handling and nurturing. Interestingly, the syndrome emerges with species other than humans and has been documented in several mammals including monkeys and mice. ➤ **maternal behavior** for some terminological issues regarding gender.

maternal drive (or **instinct**) Generally, the tendency of the female of a species to engage in the so-called maternal behaviors of feeding, sheltering and protecting the young. The term can be misleading. The adjective *maternal* suggests falsely that males do not display these behaviors and the nouns *drive* and/or *instinct* imply that they are wholly innate and unitary. The situation is complex and under a variety of conditions females will fail to display the behaviors and under other conditions males will actively engage in them. Moreover, when the various aspects of the criterial behaviors are measured and compared they are found not to correlate. Overall, a term best discarded from the psychologists' lexicon.

maternal impression, influence of The doctrine that the mother's experiences, feelings and thoughts during pregnancy directly affect the fetus. This thesis is of considerable antiquity and is even represented in the Book of Genesis. While it is certainly true that many experiences of the mother have an impact on the fetus (e.g., drugs, diseases, diet, etc.), in the strong form that the doctrine is usually put forward it is utterly false. Listening to Beethoven will not produce musically precocious offspring, nor will a sudden fright produce a birthmark or other deformity.

mathematical learning theory ➤ **learning theory, mathematical**.

mathematical model Any model or theory expressed in formal mathematical terms and hence one making precise quantitative predictions.

mathematical psychology A cover term for any systematic effort to frame psychological ideas, hypotheses and theories in formal mathematical terms. Mathematical psychology does not represent any one idea or interest, although some issues have been found to be more amenable to mathematical analyses than others. In *psychophysics*, *decision-making*, *learning* and *information processing* some progress has been made; other areas such as clinical, personality and social psychology have been virtually untouched.

mathematico-deductive method An occasional synonym for ➤ **hypothetico-deductive method**.

mating, assortative Mating of individuals within a species that are more similar (or more dissimilar) phenotypically than would be expected if only chance mating were to occur. It is termed *positive* when the mating is between phenotypically similar individuals and *negative* when between dissimilar. Compare with ➤ **inbreeding**.

mating behavior A cover term for those patterns of activities associated with mating including pre-, during and postcoital behaviors.

mating, random Mating that occurs essentially at chance, where there are no particular biases that encourage selection of a mate with any particular phenotypic characteristics. Compare with ➤ **assortative** *mating.

matriarchy A social organization using the female (or, more literally, the *mother*) as the base. Sociologists and anthropologists distinguish between various forms of matriarchies depending on which societal aspects are involved. Thus, a *matriarchal family* is a family group organized around the mother as the head and dominant person, a *matriarchal society* would characterize a larger social and/or governmental system in which political and administrative power was invested predominantly in females. Note that in this latter case the original 'mother' meaning is no longer strictly present.

matrilineal descent The passing on of the family name or inheritance through the female line. Also called *uterine descent*.

matrix 1. Any arrangement of data (or numbers or symbols) into a table of rows and columns. 2. A frame or structure that provides form or meaning, a context. Used figuratively, especially for a cognitive or perceptual context that helps to set or determine the meaning of a situation. pl., *matrices*.

matrix, correlation A matrix giving the

coefficient of correlation between each variable in the data set with every other variable.

maturation The core meaning of this is relatively straightforward and parallels that in common language: the developmental process leading toward the state of ➤ **maturity**. The manner in which the term is used by various writers, however, introduces connotative subtleties that reflect the theoretical complexities that underlie it. Nearly all the varieties of usage revolve around one prime issue: the relative contributions of heredity and environment to the maturation process. Consider three 'definitions' found in the literature: **1.** Maturation as a pure biological unfolding. In its simplest form the implication here is that the process is biologically 'pre-wired' and that all behavioral and morphological changes are inevitable. Practically no one holds this position any longer since even the most primitive of maturational processes require some environmental input in order to emerge in normal fashion. **2.** Maturation as a process occurring within inherited boundary conditions. The notion here is that the environmental input is needed for normal developmental changes to occur but that its role is circumscribed by biologically imposed limits. Some who take this position like to think of the environment as acting first as a 'trigger' that initiates the process (this idea is, of course, also captured in the above use) and second as a dictator of the manner in which the biological processes will be manifested. **3.** Maturation as that proportion of the variance in developmental change that is attributable to hereditary factors. The technical term for this meaning is *heritability* and the position is one that reflects the commonly accepted view that heredity and environment interact with each other to control developmental/maturational processes. The various subtleties of usage here are the same as those raised under the more general term, ➤ **heredity–environment controversy**. Note also that in all of these usages the notion of *species specificity* is implicit. All maturational changes must be viewed within the framework of the individual species under consideration.

maturity From the Latin, meaning *ripeness*; the state of adulthood, of completed growth, of full functioning; the end of the process of ➤ **maturation**. The term is widely used, generally with an adjective prefixed to specify the kind of growth achieved; e.g., sexual maturity, intellectual maturity, emotional maturity, etc. Note that while some of these can be reasonably well defined, such as sexual maturity, most cannot. They are generally value judgements made of persons to reflect how successfully they correspond to socially and culturally accepted norms. What is considered emotionally childish in one society may very well be an aspect of emotional maturity in another.

maxim A type of ➤ **heuristic**; a general principle usually regarded as somewhat less compelling than a ➤ **canon**.

maximal 1. Pertaining to or characteristic of a ➤ **maximum** (1, 2). **2.** = ➤ **maximum** (3).

maximal age ➤ **age, maximal**.

maximizing A general term used to characterize any decision-making strategy that is designed to maximize the likelihood of gain. For example, in a probability-learning experiment a subject who always predicted the most likely event would be maximizing.

maximum 1 n. The highest value of a variable, a series or a continuum. **2** n. In a curve, a value that is higher than those immediately preceding and following it. In this sense there can be several maxima in a given function. pls., *maxima, maximums*. **3** adj. Characteristic or descriptive of such values in either of the above senses. In most psychological contexts the maximum value is given by the functional capacity of the organism; e.g., the maximum intensity of a stimulus is the one beyond which further increases in the physical produce no increments in sensation. vb., *maximize*.

439

maximum-likelihood estimator According to the ➤ **principle of *maximum likelihood**, the best estimators of true population values are those whose values, when substituted for the population value, maximize the likelihood of the sample result. To be a good estimator a statistic should be unbiased, consistent, efficient and sufficient.

maximum likelihood, principle of A statistical principle that reflects the very spirit of empirical science and either implicitly or explicitly underlies all statistical inference. To appreciate the sense of the term, note that there are two broad classes of inference that one may want to make: (a) the inference that the obtained values in a sample are truly representative of the population; and (b) the inference that the observed results are in keeping with theoretical expectations (or, better, the inference that one's theoretical predictions accurately reflect the empirical findings). The principle of maximum likelihood states, essentially, that when faced with two or more possible values any one of which may be the true population (or true theoretical) value then the best guess (i.e. the one with the maximum likelihood) is that value which would have made the actual empirical sample have the highest probability.

Maxwell disks Slotted colored disks that can be mounted on a rapidly rotating spindle. By controlling the amount of overlapping of disks of various hues the basic principles of color mixture can be represented.

maze Any experimental apparatus consisting of pathways and culs-de-sac (blind alleys) leading from a start box to an outlet or goal box. Mazes were, along with puzzle boxes, essential pieces of laboratory equipment in the early studies of instrumental behavior. The variety available is rather impressive, from the simplest **T**-*maze* to the complex *Hampton Court maze*. The most common form is the multiple **T**-maze (and its progeny, the **Y**-mazes). There are also water mazes that must be swum through, elevated mazes that consist of narrow ramps, paper and pencil mazes, temporal mazes, straight-alley mazes (which are hardly mazes at all), verbal mazes, etc.

MBD Abbreviation for ➤ **minimal brain dysfunction** or **damage** (the former is preferred).

McCarthy Scales of Children's Abilities A set of developmental scales for assessing the abilities of preschoolers between the ages of $2\frac{1}{2}$ and $8\frac{1}{2}$. There are 18 separate tests combined into six distinct scales: verbal, perceptual, quantitative, memory, motor and general cognitive. The general cognitive scale is based on all but three of the tests and is generally treated as a measure of intellectual development.

McCollough effect (or **afterimage**) A persistent afterimage produced by saturating the eye (or more precisely, the brain) with red and green patterns of different angularity. In the typical experiment a pattern of bright red and black horizontal lines is alternated with a pattern of bright green and black vertical lines every five seconds for several minutes. Following these exposures a pattern of black and white lines at various angles is presented and when the afterimage appears the horizontal white lines are seen as tinged with green and the vertical with red. If the head is tilted 90° the colors change, taking on the appropriate coloration. The effect may last up to four or five days.

McNaghten (or **M'Naghten**) **rule** A legal precedent for the establishment of an ➤ **insanity defense** set in the British House of Lords in 1843. It states that a person is not to be held responsible for a crime if he 'was laboring under such a deficit of reason from disease of the mind as not to know the nature and quality of the act; or if he did know it, that he did not know that what he was doing was wrong.' Compare with ➤ **Durham rule**.

McNemar test A nonparametric test that evaluates whether changes in the variable under consideration are, for a given set of subjects, significant. Since the test is a test of changes, it is particularly useful in experiments in which each subject is used as its own control and scores before and after a particular treatment make up the data.

md, mdn Abbreviations for *median*.

me That aspect of ➤ **self** (see especially, 1, 2) that represents those components of one's total self that derive from the environment, the material possessions, the internalized social values, indeed from the full collection of one's states of consciousness. William James called this 'me' the *empirical* or *known self* and differentiated it from the ➤ **I**, the **knowing self**. George Herbert Mead also used it in a similar fashion but with, predictably, a stronger focus upon the social aspects. Also called the *psychological self*.

mean 1 n. In statistics, any of several measures of central tendency. Properly, the particular measure used will be noted (e.g. *arithmetic mean*, *geometric mean*); when unqualified it invariably refers to the ➤ **arithmetic *mean**. **2** vb. To form an ➤ **intension**. **3** vb. To express a reference, to convey a meaning, to denote or connote something, to imply.

mean, arithmetic The sum of a set of values (or scores) divided by the number of values (or scores). It is the most commonly used and most useful measure of central tendency since, unlike the median and mode, it uses all of the data in the distribution and it serves as the basis for the measures of variability or dispersion. When the shorthand form *mean* is used without the qualifier it can safely be taken as a reference to the arithmetic mean. Symbol: M or $\overline{X}$.

mean, assumed Quite literally, a value assumed as a first guess to be the mean of a set of scores.

mean deviation ➤ **average *deviation**.

mean, geometric A measure of central tendency for a set of n values given by the nth root of the product of the n scores. Less often used than the arithmetic mean, it finds its greatest use in the study of average rates of change. Also called *logarithmic mean*.

mean, harmonic A measure of central tendency of a set of values given by the reciprocal of the arithmetic mean of the reciprocals of the set of values. Of limited use, it is found mostly in averaging rates.

meaning Let us begin with a simple truism: communication consists of three components, a transmitter, a medium and a receiver. Therefore, the *meaning* of a message as communicated or any element thereof (e.g., a word, a phrase, a gesture, etc.) may be defined from any of three perspectives: **1.** That which the speaker or writer intended to convey. As Lewis Carroll put it, speaking through Humpty–Dumpty, 'When I use a word, it means just what I choose it to mean – neither more nor less.' **2.** The representation associated with the physical symbol used, the thing that it designates; 'X marks the spot,' '♀ means female,' 'ψ stands for psychology.' **3.** The apprehended representations of the hearer or reader, the significance of the message as received.

Several cautionary notes are needed here: (a) Specification of senses 1 and 3 is no mean task. There are philosophers and linguists who will tell you that it is the single most difficult task confronting them – and there are others who will tell you it is a hopeless one. No matter what one's view is here, attempts to come to grips with the problem have spawned a large number of specialized forms of meaning; those significant in psychology are given below. (b) Sense 2, taken by itself, is something of an absurdity. The point here is that no symbol 'carries' or 'has' meaning; the meaning is in the minds of the speaker/hearers. The symbol functions as a device for achieving denotative and connotative mutuality. (c) Although meaning (broadly) is often dealt with as though it were codifiable, representable and, at least in principle, explicable, it almost assuredly is a concept that can only be made to make sense when couched in a contextual frame. For example, the standard meaning of *bachelor* is *unmarried male*, but somehow sentences like 'Oscar Wilde was a bachelor' or 'The Pope is a bachelor' or 'My ten-year-old son is a bachelor' miss the mark; they provide contextual frames that do violence to the standard dictionary meaning. Put another way, meaning is in the mind of the beholder. The ludicrous implication of this point is that dictionary-writing is a bad joke, for if words only have meaning (senses 1 and 3, of course) in particular contexts then giving them explicit definitions is an exercise in futility. Recognizing this problem I have attempted to present the terms in this volume as expressing manner of usage; ➤ **definition** for more on this problem. (d) Much of the conveyance of meaning is dependent on the degree of coordination between the intentions of the speaker/writer and the suppositions of the hearer/reader about those intentions. For example, 'She has a lovely voice' can be uttered as a compliment to a singer or a sarcastic remark about a dreadful dramatic performance and if meaning 1 is to be coordinate with meaning 3 then intentions and suppositions must be equivalent.

meaning, affective Basically, if one lists the words that can be used to characterize the sense of another word, that list will capture the affective meaning of the original word. Note that this sense of ➤ **meaning** is quite close to that presented under ➤ **connotative *meaning**. Osgood's ➤ **semantic differential** was designed to measure such meaning.

meaning, associative Loosely, all the things that a person thinks of upon hearing a word represent the associative meaning of that word. Note that these may well include connotative meanings (one thinks of *safety* to the word *home*), denotative meaning (*flare* to *danger*), referential meaning ('*Fido*' to *dog*), or many other links. ➤➤ **meaningfulness**.

meaning, connotative Logicians use *con-*

note as equivalent to *imply*. Taking off here, then, connotative meaning is that which is suggested or implied or signified by a word, symbol, gesture or event. Connotative meanings usually define abstract qualities, common properties or classes of objects, or emotional components. Contrast with ➤ **denotative *meaning**.

meaning, denotative Meaning conveyed by the objects or instances to which a word refers or, by extension, by the generic idea or concept that is represented by that word.

meaningfulness (m) A measure developed in an effort to arrive at an objective characterization of how meaningful a particular word is. It is given as the average number of associations that are produced to that word in one minute. Meaningfulness, not surprisingly, correlates highly with other dimensions such as imageability, familiarity and frequency of the word in the language.

meaning, referential The particular object or event (i.e. the referent) designated by a word. Usually referential meaning is highly context-dependent and quite specific.

mean length of utterance As it says, the mean length, measured in morphemes or words, of the utterances in a sample of speech. It is one of the more frequently used measures of the linguistic sophistication of a child. Although it is a relatively gross measure and does not reflect the child's use of particular syntactic or semantic forms, it gives an excellent first approximation of the stage of linguistic development and allows the researcher to make quantitative comparisons between children. Often used in abbreviated form, *MLU*.

mean, sample The mean of any set of scores. The obtained mean of a sample is the best estimator of the ➤ **true *mean**. Also called *obtained mean*.

means–ends analysis A *heuristic* or rule of thumb incorporated into several models of human problem-solving. In a means–

ends analysis the solver moves towards a final solution by setting up subgoals, each of which is a means toward the final end. The term was first introduced formally in the context of a computer based model of problem solving, the ➤ **General Problem Solver**.

means–ends readiness One of the many 'means–ends' operations in E. C. Tolman's theory of purposive behavior. A means–ends readiness was defined as a state of selective readiness such that an organism will acquire certain expectancies. Although Tolman's theory is no longer influential, this term shows how behaviorists were able to take a subjective unobservable element like *belief* and weave it into an objective behaviorist analysis.

means object (or **situation**) In Tolman's theory, any object (or situation) that brought an organism closer to a goal. He used the term as roughly equivalent to *cue*, with the assumption that it functioned by arousing an expectation concerning the goal.

mean square The average of a set of squared deviations from the mean; i.e. the ➤ **variance**. The root mean square is the square root of the mean square or the ➤ **standard deviation**.

mean, trimmed The mean calculated after the effects of extreme scores (➤ **outliers**) have been accounted for.

mean, true (or **population**) The theoretical value representing the mean of the full compilation of all the possible scores under consideration. The obtained or sample mean is always the best estimate of this, the true mean.

measure 1. vb. To evaluate quantity or magnitude; to make a measurement. 2 n. A value obtained by an act of measurement. 3. A statistic.

measurement There is little difficulty with definition here. The one most generally agreed on comes from S. S. Stevens: 'The assignment of numerals to objects or events according to rules.' The difficulty

with using the term in a scientifically legitimate fashion comes with the problems involved in constructing ➤ **scales of measurement** and understanding the properties that can be ascribed to them.

measurement scales ➤ **scales of measurement** and related terms.

meatus A passageway or an opening.

mechanical ability (or **aptitude**) Quite simply, ability or aptitude for the mechanical. Generally regarded as a relatively low-level intellectual ability and hence often contrasted with ability or aptitude for the abstract, for ideas.

mechanical causality 1. A class of explanations whereby the occurrence of events is represented in terms of physical (mechanical) contacts. 2. In Piagetian theory, a stage in the child's development of an understanding of causality at which he or she can analyze the various components of a causal chain of events; i.e. the child appreciates that when one ball hits another it 'causes' the second one to move.

mechanism 1. A philosophical doctrine that maintains that all events or phenomena, no matter their complexity, can be ultimately understood in a mechanistic framework. The position is strongly deterministic and opposed to a host of other positions including ➤ **dualism**. ➤ **idealism**, and ➤ **vitalism**. Moreover, it implicitly assumes the possibility of ➤ **reductionism** to basic principles of physics and physiology. 2. A theoretical process through which events can be understood and explained. Note that a hypothesized mechanism in this sense can be quite concrete and 'mechanical' (e.g., classical conditioning as understood through the existing mechanism of the reflex arc) or it can be quite abstract (e.g., operant control of autonomic activity as understood through the mechanism of biofeedback). In the approach to science that characterizes most of Western psychological thought, a mechanism of this kind is considered essential for the establishment and acceptance of a phenomenon and the failure to provide one leads invariably to skepticism and often outright rejection of purported findings. For a case study here see the discussion under ➤ **parapsychology**. **3.** A habitual adaptive response. For example, the ➤ **defense mechanisms** of psychoanalytic theories. **4.** A purely mechanical device or machine whose actions are clearly specifiable in terms of physical cause-and-effect systems.

mechanistic organization ➤ **organization, mechanistic**.

mechanistic theory ➤ **mechanism** (1).

medial 1. Pertaining to or situated in the middle. **2.** Toward or near the middle of the body. ➤➤ **median**.

medial dorsal nucleus ➤ **dorsomedial nucleus**.

medial forebrain bundle A pathway in the limbic system leading from the precommissural fornix and the olfactory bulb through the basal forebrain and lateral hypothalamus. It contains axons that interconnect structures in the midbrain and forebrain and has been found to produce highly reinforcing self-stimulation.

medial geniculate nucleus Either of two cell nuclei lying near the rear of the thalamus which are important synaptic waystations in the ascending auditory pathways. Afferent pathways connect the inferior colliculi with the medial geniculate nuclei and these, in turn, project onto the auditory cortex.

medial lemniscus ➤ **lemniscal system**.

medial phoneme Any phoneme pronounced in the middle of the oral cavity; e.g., /r/.

medial plane The sagittal or midline plane that divides the body into right and left halves. Also called *median plane*.

medial preoptic area ➤ **preoptic area**.

medial syllable Any syllable in the middle of a word.

median The middlemost score in a distribution of scores ordered according to the magnitude. As a measure of central tendency it is used less often than ➤ **mean**; its primary value is when dealing with distributions that are dramatically skewed. Although the term is used mostly in statistics, it is also an occasional synonym for ➤ **medial**. abbrev., *md* or *mdn*.

median plane ➤ **medial plane**.

median test A nonparametric statistical test that evaluates the significance of the difference between the medians of two samples. The test is useful when the data consist only of ranked scores and one cannot be sure that they lie on an interval scale.

mediate 1 adj. Descriptive of stimuli, responses, items or events that are in between other stimuli, responses, items or events. **2** adj. Descriptive of behavior or action that is dependent on an intervening process. **3** vb. To arbitrate between two or more disputants. **4** vb. To act as an intervening variable between two or more external processes.

mediate association ➤ **immediate *association**.

mediated generalization ➤ **mediated *generalization** and **semantic *generalization**.

mediate experience ➤ **immediate experience**.

mediation theory A label descriptive of any approach to the study of learning that assumes that some event(s) intervene between the stimulus and the response and that explanations of behavior require explication of these processes. This approach and the term itself are closely tied to the S–R behaviorist orientation. The majority of cognitive psychologists take it for granted that most of what is interesting about psychological processes takes place between the S and the R and don't even bother with a term here.

medical model A general label often used to refer to the approach to psychiatry and clinical psychology based on the assumption that abnormalities and disorders are produced by specific causes and that cure is only possible by removing the root cause. The analogy with the medical approach to somatic diseases is obvious. The term is used relatively neutrally; those who are critical of this particular approach will often call it the ➤ **disease model**, which is always used with clearly negative connotations.

medication-induced movement disorders Movement disorders produced by the taking of medication designed to cure or alleviate some other condition. The most common are the ➤ **neuroleptic-induced** disorders. ➤➤ **iatrogenic disorder**.

mediodorsal nucleus A nucleus in the thalamus that has been implicated in memory. It is one of the areas damaged in ➤ **Korsakoff's syndrome**, in which anterograde amnesia is a striking symptom.

mediola The bony part of the division between the scala media and the scala tympani of the cochlea.

meditation A state of extended reflection or contemplation. Although the term and the characterization of the mental state itself have suffered from considerable abuse – administered mainly by those who make unsubstantiated claims about its therapeutic value – a few aspects of the meditational state have been documented: the E E G pattern generally shows alpha waves, oxygen consumption drops, energy expenditure is lowered and subject reports are consistent in describing the experience as relaxing and salutary.

medium 1. Any intervening substance through which forces act or events are produced. **2.** More generally, the environment. **3.** More specifically, and of doubtful validity, a person through whom paranormal phenomena occur.

medulla 1. Generally, the central or inner core of a structure or an organ. **2.** The ➤ **medulla oblongata**.

medulla oblongata The lowest or hindmost part of the brain, continuous with the spinal cord and containing nuclei which control vital bodily functions such as breathing, circulation, etc.

medullary sheath ➤ **myelin sheath**.

mega-, megalo- Prefixes from the Greek, meaning *bigness, greatness, power*, often with the implication that the characterization is exaggerated. ➤ **macro-** et seq. for combined terms not found here.

megalomania An exaggerated self-evaluation or sense of self-worth. A common component in narcissistic personality disorder. Also called *macromania*.

megalopsia ➤ **macropsia**.

megavitamin therapy ➤ **orthomolecular therapy**.

megrim ➤ **migraine**.

meio- Combining form meaning *decrease in size or in number*.

meiosis The cell-division process in the formation of gametes. The products of meiosis (sperms and ova) are haploid cells containing half the full complement of chromosomes found in diploid cells. Meiosis consists of two successive cell divisions which superficially resemble ➤ **mitosis**, but the chromosomes are duplicated only once, with each daughter cell ending up with the haploid number.

Meissner's corpuscles Specialized nerve endings found in the papillae of hairless skin. It is thought that they are one of the sets of receptors for the sensing of pressure and, on occasion, are referred to as tactile receptors, although the evidence for this role is less than compelling.

mel By definition, the pitch of a 1,000Hz tone; 40 db above threshold is equal to 1,000 mels. Thus, the mel becomes the psychological unit for a scale of pitch.

melancholia From the classic Greek for *black bile*. The archaic theory of temperament was tied to the hypothesized humors or bodily fluids and their balances in the body. Today the term refers to a pronounced depression with feelings of foreboding and a general insensitivity to stimulation.

melatonin An ➤ **indoleamine** produced

principally by the pineal gland. Its secretion during childhood serves to inhibit the development of sexual maturation. It is also suspected of playing a role in sleep. ➤ pineal gland.

member The primary special usage of this term is within the context of Gestalt theory where it is favored over the more common word *part*. The purpose is to communicate the idea that, in accordance with Gestalt principles, a given component of a larger whole is not a separate entity but rather an integrated 'member' of the functioning system or 'whole.' The 'whole' here may be anything from a simple perception to a society, and the member an aspect of a physical stimulus or a person. Other uses of the term are in keeping with the general dictionary meaning.

membership character Extending the Gestalt use of the term ➤ member, the notion is that each member of a group is, to some extent, dependent on the structure of the whole group and each will be affected to a greater or lesser degree by changes in the group. Although the changes, or *characters* as they are called, are presumed to characterize any whole (or Gestalt), the dominant use of the term is within the ➤ Lewinian approach to social psychology. ➤➤ field theory.

membrane Any thin, flexible layer of tissue.

membrane potential The − 70mV electrical charge inside a neuron. The message that is conducted down an axon (➤ action potential) is nothing more than a momentary charge in the membrane potential.

memorial Of or pertaining to memory or to that which is in memory.

memorize To commit to memory. Generally the term carries the implication that the memory process used is rote memory by repeated practice.

memory Since the demise of behaviorism nearly everything about the way in which psychologists characterize memory has changed save the working definition(s) of the generic term. Memory refers to one of the following: 1. The mental function of retaining information about stimuli, events, images, ideas, etc. after the original stimuli are no longer present. 2. The hypothesized 'storage system' in the mind/ brain that holds this information. 3. The information so retained.

Within these definitions there are numerous and varied meanings to be found in the psychological literature. Most of the specialized uses derive from the simple fact that memorial processes are extremely complex and different memory tasks recruit different ones. For example, the rat that 'remembers' to turn left to a bright light and right to a dim one is most assuredly using a different memorial process than the medical student who can recall the twelve cranial nerves, and this latter case is just as profoundly different from that of the person who can recall the meaning of a Socratic dialogue. As a result, *memory* is used almost invariably in psychology with some adjective preceding it to set limits on the kind of memory processes under discussion. The following entries are those in most common use. Note that in nearly every case the type of memory being specified is intimately tied in with the task of the person trying to store away the material and with the type of material being so stored. The exceptions to this pattern are those memorial systems that have theoretical pretensions. The terms *memory* and *knowledge* are often used interchangeably. ➤ knowledge, et seq., for more details and for any combined terms not found here.

memory afterimage An obsolescent term for the kind of memory experience now captured by the term ➤ sensory information store. The older term has been largely abandoned because the word *afterimage* was misleading.

memory, associative This term is used as a label for any memory system that is hypothesized to rest on the notion of an association. Thus the British empiricist assumption of association between ideas, the behaviorist S–R bond, the cognitivist propositionally based associationism and connectionist notions are all classifiable as associative-memory theories.

memory, autobiographical Memory for events that have occurred in one's life. It is a kind of ➤ episodic *memory.

memory, biological Used synonymously with 1. Jung's ➤ racial *memory and 2. ➤ genetic *memory.

memory color Quite literally, the color of an object as it is remembered, which, perhaps not surprisingly, is often rather different from the actual color presented.

memory, declarative Conscious memory, memory that one can communicate or 'declare' to others. Often contrasted with ➤ procedural *memory. ➤➤ explicit *memory.

memory drum A piece of laboratory equipment that presents a series of stimuli to a subject for memory experiments. The stimuli are printed on a rotating drum that stops at controlled intervals so that only one stimulus item is visible at a time. They have been largely replaced by computers.

memory, echoic A residual sensory memory that lasts for a short time (perhaps 2–3 seconds) after a brief auditory stimulus. See the discussion under ➤ iconic (2) and ➤ sensory information store.

memory, episodic A form of memory in which information is stored with 'mental tags' about where, when and how the information was picked up; i.e. the material in memory concerns fairly sharply circumscribed episodes. Compare with ➤ semantic *memory.

memory, explicit Conscious memory, memory for material that one is aware of. Explicit memory for previously presented material is tapped by tasks like *recall* and *recognition* where the individual is consciously aware of the knowledge held and can recall it or recognize it among several alternatives. When most people use the term *memory* they tend to use it in this sense; that is, memory for material is virtu-

ally always thought of as *conscious* memory. However, ➤ implicit *memory to appreciate that not all knowledge held in the mind is available to consciousness.

memory, fact Memory for specific facts, events, or other information carried in a message. Often compared with ➤ source *memory.

memory, false Quite literally, memory for some event that in fact did not happen. False memories are quite common and surprisingly easy to create; e.g., ➤ recovered *memory.

memory, flashbulb Roger Brown's term for the memory that surrounds a particular, significant event in one's life. Such memories are typically very clear and poignant, consisting of where one was, what one was doing, who was there, etc. when the event occurred. In order for such 'sharp' memories to be formed both a high level of surprise and a high level of emotional arousal must be present.

memory, genetic A hypothesized 'memory' for biological events occurring during the eons of evolution of the species. *Memory* here is used in a metaphorical fashion to refer to a genetically coded propensity for particular behaviors and patterns of action which are vestiges of evolutionarily important modifications of the species. The fear of falling and the reflex reactions to a possible plummet have been put forward as an example reflecting an evolutionary adaptive reaction which any successful brachiating primate with a high body-mass-to-surface-area ratio must have. Also called *biological memory*.

memory, holographic A hypothesized memory system suggested by the neuropsychologist Karl Pribram. It is a neurophysiological model of memory based on the assumption that the principles of holography serve as an analog of the neurological processes of memory. Supporters of this point of view cite the *equipotentiality* of neural structures and the consistent failure to identify a neural *engram* as evidence in its favor.

memory, iconic A residual sensory memory that lasts for a short time (perhaps up to 2 seconds) after a brief visual stimulus. ➤ **iconic** (2) and **sensory information store**.

memory, immediate Most often, a synonym of ➤ **short term *memory**. However, some use it as equivalent to *iconic memory*; ➤ **iconic**.

memory, implicit Unconscious memory, memory for material that one is unaware of. Implicit memory for previously presented material can be tapped by a variety of tasks, most commonly ➤ **priming** (4). The existence of implicit memory is compellingly displayed in cases of ➤ **amnesia**, where, despite the patient's inability to explicitly recall previously presented material, performance on tasks like priming is virtually normal. ➤➤ **implicit *learning**.

memory, inaccessible A general term for any memory that, while not 'lost', cannot, for any number of reasons, be retrieved. ➤ **implicit *memory**.

memory, lexical Loosely, memory for the words that one knows; not the meanings but the words themselves with their graphological and phonological features. The meanings of the words are assumed by those who use this term in this fashion to be stored in a ➤ **semantic *memory**.

memory, long-term (LTM) Memory for information that has been well processed and integrated into one's general knowledge store. Once input information has been processed or interpreted in a reasonably deep fashion the underlying abstraction is stored away in this so-called *long-term* system. Thus, LTM is presumed, unlike either ➤ **sensory information store** or ➤ **short-term *memory**, to be without limit either in capacity to store information or in duration of that which is stored. Most of the research on LTM is highly specialized. The search is for the organizational principles and the form(s) of

memorial representation that will explicate memory generally but the work itself tends to focus on specific types of information storage. To appreciate this and get a feeling for the terminological distinctions that are often made, ➤ **semantic *memory, episodic *memory, lexical *memory, associative *memory** and **image**, all of which are presumed to be special cases of the long-term memory processing system. Also called *long-term store (LTS), secondary memory* and *permanent memory*.

memory-operating characteristic (MOC) curve A statistical procedure for analyzing the data from a memory experiment. The technique is the same as that used in analysis of the data from a sensory-detection experiment but instead of plotting detection rates one plots correct recognition responses. For details ➤ **receiver operating characteristic (ROC) curve**.

memory, procedural Memory for procedures or complex activities that have become highly automatized and are acted out without conscious thought about the process, such as driving an auto or riding a bicycle. Compare with ➤ **declarative *memory**.

memory, racial A hypothesized storehouse of memories, feelings, ideas, etc. which, according to Carl Jung, we have inherited from our ancestral past. Racial memory in Jung's theory is a part of the ➤ **collective unconscious**. ➤➤ **genetic *memory**, a term to which it is related but which is used without some of the mystical connotations of Jung's characterizations.

memory, reconstructive Descriptive of the type of memory hypothesized to operate according to principles of reconstruction rather than reproduction. Theories of reconstructive memory assume that abstract principles about the input material are stored away and that the 'memory' is actually reconstructed according to these principles during recall of the material. W. James's theory, outlined in 1890, was the first of this kind and, after a period of many decades during which theories based on ➤ **reproductive *memory** dominated, it is viewed with favor again.

memory, recovered Material that has supposedly been brought back into conscious memory by the use of various techniques such as *hypnosis* and suggestion. This is a very touchy issue, particularly in legal settings, where such 'memories' have been used in evidence in cases of abuse and assault. Alas, there is absolutely no evidence that hypnosis or suggestion can function to recover lost memories; worse, they tend to encourage confabulation and elaboration. Recovered memories are rarely true memories; they tend rather to be constructed at the prompting of the hypnotist or therapist.

memory, redintegrative From the word *reintegrate*, memory of events that is a reestablishment of the original information based on only partial recall of the original material. It is the ability to recall, by piecemeal reconstruction, a past experience by recollecting events, the circumstances surrounding the events, etc. Try, for example, to recall your high-school graduation ceremony or your wedding or your first date or some other such event, to appreciate the processes involved.

memory, reproductive The type of memory hypothesized to operate by the reproduction of the original stimulus input. Reproductive-memory theories imply that images or other forms of mental representations of the original material are stored away and reproduced during recall. Contrast this characterization of memory with that of ➤ **reconstructive *memory**.

memory, semantic Put simply, memory for meanings. Some theorists consider the study of semantic memory to be equivalent to the study of ➤ **long-term *memory** on the grounds that all long-term, relatively permanent memories are those that are coded and stored on the basis of their meaning. However, ➤ **episodic *memory** for another theoretically valid possibility. Compare with *lexical *memory*. Also known as *reference memory*.

memory, short-term (STM) Memory for information that has received minimal processing or interpretation. According to contemporary theories of memory, STM is a relatively limited capacity store capable of holding only about seven or so 'items' (although if the interpretation of the material is rich enough these items can contain a good deal of information; ➤ 7 ± 2). Material is assumed to be held in STM by the operation of rehearsal and should such rehearsal be interrupted the material has a half-life of probably no more than 10 or 15 seconds. Compare with ➤ **long-term *memory** and ➤ **sensory information store**. Also known as *short-term store (STS)*, *primary memory* and *working memory*.

memory, source Memory for the source of a message; e.g., *who* said something rather than *what* was said. Often compared with ➤ **fact *memory**. See also ➤ **source monitoring**.

memory span The number of items immediately reproducible after presentation. True tests of memory span require that the materials used be unrelated sets of symbols, otherwise complex coding systems will artificially inflate the estimate of the span.

memory trace The presumed neurological event(s) responsible for any relatively permanent memory. ➤ **engram**.

memory, unconscious 1. Generally, ➤ **implicit *memory**. 2. Specifically within psychoanalysis, nonretrievable memory for events, feelings, and acts that have been repressed.

memory, working A hypothesized memory system that 'holds' the input while an interpretation of it is worked out. The notion of a working memory is sometimes restricted to theoretical discussions of memory for materials presented in sentence form in which the assumption is that the sentence is held verbatim while its meaning is extracted. Other theorists, however, use the term as equivalent to ➤ **short-term *memory**.

menarche (*menar'kee*) The first menstrual period.

Mendelian Of the genetic principles developed by the Austrian scientist/priest Gregor J. Mendel (1822–84). His three principles were: (a) that separate characteristics are inherited independently of each other via hypothesized elements called genes; (b) that each reproductive cell possesses only one gene from each gene pair; and (c) that some factors are dominant over others.

meninges Collectively, the three membranes (dura, pia and arachnoid) covering the spinal cord and the brain. sing., *meninx*.

menopause That period that marks the permanent cessation of menstrual activity, the period during which menstruation gradually ceases. Also known as the *climacteric* and, popularly, '*change of life*,' both of which can be applied to the analogous period of hormonal change in males, although there is no relatively simple criterion to use with them.

menses ➤ **menstruation**.

mens rea Latin for *intent to harm*. A legal term, used in forensic psychology and psychiatry in cases in which insanity is raised as a defense and questions of intention and motivation are deemed important in adjudging legal guilt.

menstrual cycle The full cycle of changes in the uterus and associated sex organs connected with menstruation and the intermenstrual periods. It begins with growth of ovarian follicles stimulated by the pituitary gland's release of follicle-stimulating hormone (FSH). The follicles produce estrogens which stimulate the hypothalamus which, in turn, causes the pituitary to produce luteinizing hormone (LH). LH causes the follicle to rupture releasing the ovum; the follicle becomes a *corpus luteum* that produces progesterone, which stimulates the uterus to prepare the lining for implantation. If the ovum goes unfertilized, is fertilized too late or if implantation is prevented (as, e.g., by an IUD) the walls of the uterus slough off and menstruation begins.

menstruation The periodic discharge of blood and uterine material in mature women. This term and *menses* are often treated as synonyms, although occasionally the latter is restricted to the actual flow or discharge. ➤ **menstrual cycle** for details.

mental In the most general sense: **1.** Pertaining to ➤ **mind**. Unfortunately, there has been so much bitter dispute as to the very nature of mind that it has never been entirely clear what the adjectival form pertains to. For example, from psychology's earlier days: **2.** Within ➤ **structuralism** (1), pertaining to the *contents* of an introspectible consciousness. **3.** In ➤ **act psychology**, characterizing the *acts* or *processes* of mind. **4.** In ➤ **functionalism** (1, 2), pertaining to the *functional, adaptive aspects* of consciousness.

Now, except within the strict confines of each of these theoretical frameworks, it is difficult to appreciate the distinctions among these last three senses of the term. In fact, so much agonizing hair-splitting went on over these issues that the Watsonian radical behaviorists could argue persuasively that the concept was useless and that unobservable mental events (be they contents, acts or functions) have no role to play in a scientific psychology. The difficulty with the radical behaviorist position, however, was that one simply cannot bully a term out of existence because of confusion over its lexical domain. If anything, the fury of the disputation over what the referent of mental was should have been a cue that there was something of considerable significance here for psychology. Put simply, the term would not die, rather it shifted in its connotations to reflect emerging theory. That is: **5.** Pertaining to mediational processes; those covert events that were interposed between the overt physical stimulus and the observable response of a subject. This meaning was and to some extent still is favored by those with liberal, neo-behaviorist leanings. **6.** Pertaining to those functions that are identified as reflective of intelligence. The sense here is to be distinguished from other internal processes that are regarded as *affective* or *conative*; this meaning, which is rarely intended specifically any more, survives in combined terms like ➤ **mental test** and ➤ **mental retardation**. **7.** Pertaining to that which is causally located in mind. This sense is carried in terms like ➤ **mental illness** and ➤ **mental disease**. Note the distinction here between 6, which superficially suggests the intellectual, and 7, which, while it may include such processes as thought and rationality, also clearly embodies the emotional and motivational. Perhaps a better term for 7 would be *psychogenic*, but it has little currency in these contexts in the literature. **8.** Pertaining (broadly) to all those operations subsumed under the label ➤ **cognitive**. This is, in contemporary psychology, the dominant meaning; a mental process is a cognitive process and the term connotes all that is normally subsumed under the approaches of ➤ **cognitive psychology** and ➤ **cognitive science**.

mental aberration ➤ **aberration, mental**.

mental age ➤ **age, mental**.

mental ataxia ➤ **ataxia, mental**.

mental chemistry A label for a point of view which argues that, in principle, an analogy can be drawn between the fundamental combinatorial principles of chemistry and those of mind. That is, if chemical elements can be combined to produce compounds with emergent properties (➤ **emergentism**) then, so the reasoning goes, separate mental elements can be combined to yield the complex components of mind. The doctrine was first proposed by John Stuart Mill, who viewed the association as the bond that linked ideas together to form synthesized mental compounds. Compare with ➤ **mental mechanics**.

mental chronometrics ➤ **chronometrics, mental**.

mental content ➤ **content** (2).

mental defective This term has been so overworked (as an effective insult) that it no longer has any real scientific meaning. ➤

mental deficiency, which served as a replacement for a time, and ➤ **mental retardation**, which is the now accepted cover term for all forms of less-than-normal intellectual functioning.

mental deficiency As it suggests, a deficiency in mental functioning. There has been a number of attempts at developing a systematic nomenclature to classify and grade various forms of such deficiencies according to intellectual, behavioral and forensic yardsticks. One breakdown, now largely obsolete, used IQ range as follows: borderline deficiency (70–80), moron (50–69), imbecile (20–49), idiot (below 20). In addition to these numerous other terms have put in appearances in the literature: *feeble-minded[ness]* was used for a time for all IQs below 70 (North American usage) and for those in the 50–69 range (British usage); *subnormal* has been loosely used for anyone with IQs under roughly 75 or 80; *amentia* is a sometime synonym for mental deficiency, although etymologically it should really only apply to the extreme low end as *a* means *lack of* or *loss of*. In any event, given the lack of consistency in usage of these several terms, not to mention the distinctly unfavorable connotations that they all have in the common language, most authorities have ceased to use them and the generic label itself is dropping out of the technical literature. The favored cover term now is ➤ **mental retardation**, which should be consulted for currently accepted classifications.

mental deterioration ➤ **deterioration**.

mental development Broadly, all those progressive changes in cognitive development that occur in an individual with the passage of time. Some restrict the term to the period from birth to adulthood, others use it to cover the full life cycle.

mental discipline ➤ **formal discipline**.

mental disease The concept of a mental disease derives from the so-called *medical model* of abnormal behavior, which operates on analogy from diseases of the somatic kind. Hence, any disabling psychological maladjustment or behavioral disorder may be so classified. Once the dominant term, now the synonymous ➤ **mental illness** is more common. See that term and the separate entry on ➤ **disease** for a discussion of problems of usage of these and related terms.

mental disorder A more neutral term than either ➤ **mental disease** or ➤ **mental illness** and preferred by many because it does not convey the assumptions of the *medical model* of clinical phenomena, although it still suffers from the suggestion that the mental sphere is at once an analog of the somatic and yet separate from it. ➤ **disorder** for more on terminological issues here.

mental element ➤ **element** (1).

mentalese Some psycholinguists, in desperation to characterize the hypothesized internal computing language with which the mind represents its contents, came up with this term. With luck it will expire from lack of use.

mental experiment ➤ **experiment, mental**.

mental faculty ➤ **faculty psychology**.

mental function Any cognitive process or act; distinguish from mental ➤ **content** (2). ➤➤ **functionalism** (1, 2).

mental healing An occasional synonym for ➤ **faith healing**.

mental health Although the focus of this term is somewhat more sanguine than its opposite, ➤ **mental illness**, the same medical, logical and empirical problems attend its use. In spite of these issues, the term will probably persist because it is generally used to designate one who is functioning at a high level of behavioral and emotional adjustment and adaptiveness and not for one who is, simply, not mentally ill.

mental hygiene 1. Originally, the art of developing and maintaining mental health. 2. A loose 'catch phrase' for courses generally taught at a very unsophisticated level in many US high schools.

mental illness The generally accepted connotation of this term (and its close synonym, ➤ **mental disease**) is that of a psychological or behavioral abnormality of sufficient severity that psychiatric intervention is warranted – with the implicit assumption that this disability is caused by some psychic 'germ' in a fashion analogous to the manner in which a somatic illness is caused by some biological infestation. There are good reasons for questioning the generality of this assumption; see the discussion under ➤ **disease** and ➤ **diagnosis** for an overview of contemporary terminology.

mental image ➤ **image** (3, 4).

mentalism The doctrine that maintains that an adequate characterization of human behavior is not possible without invoking mental phenomena as explanatory devices. Or, phrased another way, that any reductionistic exercise which seeks to explain cognitive processes (mind) by limiting itself to the physical and the physiological will not succeed in accounting for all phenomena observed.

mentality 1. Loosely, mental or intellectual activity. 2. The quality of mind that is taken as characteristic of a particular individual or class of individuals.

mental level 1. In psychological testing, quite literally, the level of mental functioning. This sense is expressed by a measure of ➤ **mental *age**. 2. In Jungian theory, any of the three divisions or levels of the psyche, *consciousness*, *personal unconsciousness* and *collective unconsciousness*.

mentally handicapped Loosely, descriptive of a person with a slight to moderate degree of ➤ **mental retardation**. See that entry for usage patterns.

mental maturity Loosely, the level of mental functioning of the average adult. ➤ **adult *intelligence** for problems in usage of this or any term that may be introduced to capture this general notion.

mental measurement A generic term used to cover any application of measurement techniques to quantify a mental function.

The term is most often used to refer to various scales that have been developed to assess internal operations and capacities, notably intelligence tests, although it will often be used to cover personality inventories, developmental scales and projective devices and, on occasion, the techniques of psychophysics.

mental mechanics The point of view that an analogy can be drawn between the mode of action of complex, mechanical devices and the workings of the mind. The essence of this perspective, which was championed by James Mill, is that the operations of mind can be viewed as linear and sequential. Compare with ➤ **mental chemistry**.

mental mechanism An occasional (and misleading) synonym for ➤ **defense mechanism**.

mental paper-folding test A test of spatial and configurational skills. Subjects are shown a flat pattern which corresponds to an unfolded cube. They are requested to mentally re-fold the cube and determine whether or not two arrows printed on the faces of the flat pattern would meet when the cube was assembled.

mental process It is difficult to specify the meaning of this term without being tautological. A *process* is an ongoing systematic series of actions or events – if it takes place in the mind, it is a mental process. E.g., ➤ **information processing**.

mental process, higher A largely out-of-date term used to characterize all forms of *thinking*, particularly as contrasted with the more primitive processes of *sensing* and *perceiving*.

mental representation ➤ **representation**.

mental retardation The contemporary term of choice as the umbrella label for all forms of below-average intellectual functioning as assessed by a standard IQ test. The classification system currently in use in the USA specifies four levels: *mild* (approximate IQ range of 50–69), *moderate* (35–49), *severe* (20–34) and *profound* (below 20). Note that this breakdown is predicated on the notion that the term itself should only be applied to persons below −2 standard deviations from the mean. Those within −1 standard deviation (i.e. IQ scores between 86 and 100) are regarded as *normal* or, on occasion for those near the bottom end of this range, as *dull normal*; those within −1 and −2 standard deviations (i.e. 70–85) are regarded as possessing ➤ **borderline intelligence**.

This system is based purely on IQ test scores; no judgements are made about origins or causes, about emotional, motivational, social or familial factors, or about prognosis. In actual practice, of course, such factors are most significant and this is reflected in the manner of application of these various classifications. For example, ➤ **mild mental retardation** is regarded as roughly equivalent to *educable mentally retarded* and *moderate mental retardation* is similarly equivalent to *trainable mentally retarded*.

Note that there is a lingering peculiarity in the core term; what precisely are the connotations of *retardation*? It literally denotes a slowing down and, indeed, there do seem to be at least two aspects of such a retarding of function. First, the developmental rate of cognitive maturation is slowed, so a retarded child reaches the standard milestones at a later age than the normal child. Second, the cognitive processes themselves appear to be slower, so retarded persons typically take longer to carry out cognitive tasks than those of average intelligence. However, the term also connotes more than a simple slowing, it carries the implication of a lowered potential or ceiling: a mentally retarded child is not expected ever to reach normal levels no matter how much time is allowed for development. In other words, mental 'retardation' is really mental 'deficiency' – only that label has been so abused that few use it today (➤ **mental deficiency** for a discussion). One lexical rescue attempt has been the use of *mentally handicapped* as the general term but ➤ **handicapped** has, not surprisingly, its own connotative difficulties.

mental retardation, mild The label generally used for those with IQ scores in the 50–69 range. Such persons can develop reasonably effective social and communicative skills and during their early years (up to roughly 5 or 6 years) are indistinguishable from normals. School subjects up to about the sixth year of schooling are learnable and various skills can be taught. This category constitutes about 80% of the mentally retarded. The term is used roughly equivalently with ➤ **educable mentally retarded**.

mental retardation, moderate The label used generally for those with IQ scores in the 35–49 range. During childhood such persons display poor awareness of social conventions, although communicative skills are reasonably good. Schooling is rarely successful past the second-year level, but with proper assistance and supervision useful unskilled or semiskilled work can be performed. Roughly 12% of the mentally retarded are in this category. These persons are often called ➤ **trainable mentally retarded**.

mental retardation, profound The label used for those with IQ scores below 20. Such persons display minimal sensorimotor functioning as children. As adults some speech and some motor development may take place and they can, on occasion, be taught some limited self-care. Highly structured environments and constant supervision and aid are required. Only about 1% of the mentally retarded are in this category.

mental retardation, severe The label used generally for those with IQ scores in the 20–34 range. During early childhood there is poor motor development, minimal speech and poor or no acquisition of social and communicative skills. Such persons are generally unable to profit from vocational training, although some simple tasks may be carried out with close supervision. About 7% of the mentally retarded are in this category.

mental scale Any assessment device or test for determining an individual's level of mental functioning (i.e. their intelligence).

mental set ➤ **set** (2).

mental-status examination A full clinical work-up of a psychiatric patient including assessment of overall psychiatric condition, diagnosis of existing disorders, prognosis, estimates of suitability for treatment of various kinds, formulation of overall personality, compilation of historical and developmental data, etc.

mental test 1. Generally, any ➤ **test** (1) that is designed to evaluate a particular mental ability or performance. The term, in this encompassing sense, was first used by the American psychologist James McKeen Cattell in 1890 and served as a kind of umbrella term for the mental-testing movement that began soon after. **2.** More specifically, an ➤ **intelligence test**.

mentation Slightly antiquated term for any mental activity.

menticide Lit., the murder of mind; used rarely today although the general sense of the term is captured by the somewhat more colorful term ➤ **brainwashing**.

meprobamate An ➤ **antianxiety drug** with mild tranquilizing and muscle-relaxing effects marketed under the brand names of Miltown and Equanil. It is used mainly to combat insomnia and reduce stress-related anxieties.

mere exposure Zajonc's term for the phenomenon that one's liking or preference for a stimulus is increased by simply being exposed to it.

Merkel's disks Flattened epithelia cells found in glabrous (smooth) skin in the same areas as Meissner's corpuscles. Presumed to function as touch/pressure receptors although the evidence is less than overwhelming.

Merrill-Palmer scale An intelligence scale standardized for children between 2 and 5 years of age.

merycism ➤ **rumination disorder of infancy**.

mescaline A hallucinogenic drug obtained from the peyote cactus. The effects are similar to those of LSD but generally of lesser intensity (depending, of course, on the dosage).

mesencephalon ➤ **midbrain**.

mesial obsolescent synonym for ➤ **medial** and/or ➤ **median**.

mesmerism An old term for ➤ **hypnotism** from its discover, Franz Anton Mesmer.

mes(o)- Combining form meaning: **1.** generally, *middle*, *moderate* or *intermediate*: **2.** in medicine, *secondary*, *partial*.

mesocephalic Lit., moderate head. ➤ **cephalic index**.

mesocortical system A system of dopaminergic neurons with cell bodies in the *ventral tegmentum* and projections to the *prefrontal neocortex*, *limbic cortex*, and *hippocampus*.

mesoderm Middle layer of embryonic cellular structure that develops into the muscles and bones.

mesokurtosis ➤ **kurtosis**.

mesolimbic system A system of dopaminergic neurons with cell bodies in the *ventral tegmentum* and projections to the *nucleus accumbens*, *amygdala*, *lateral septum*, and *hippocampus*.

mesomorphy 1. In Sheldon's ➤ **constitutional theory**, one of the three primary dimensions of body type (along with *ectomorphy* and *endomorphy*). A mesomorph is one whose physique is dominated by the embryonic mesodermal component: muscles, skeleton, circulatory system. Hence, mesodermic persons are strong, well-muscled and have moderate skin-surface-to-weight ratios. **2.** ➤ **body-build index**.

mesopic vision The vision that occurs in the vaguely defined region between *scotopic* (or twilight) and *photopic* (or daylight) vision.

message A communication, the information transmitted in a communication.

There is a good deal of latitude in the usage of this term that derives from the fact that it is used for any (or all) of the three aspects of a communication: (a) the sent message, which reflects the intended meaning of the sender; (b) the transmitted message, which is specified in terms of the medium used; and (c) the received message, which is characterized by the meaning as perceived by the recipient. Clearly, the message in each of these cases may be very different in form, structure and content, depending on a host of psychological and physical variables. ➤ **information theory** and related entries.

messenger RNA ➤ **ribonucleic acid (RNA)**.

meta- A common prefix of Greek origin with a host of connotations including *about*, *beyond*, *among*, *after*, *between*, *behind* or *change in*. The first of these is probably the most common, particularly in philosophically oriented works: the others are used freely in various contexts.

meta-analysis A statistical technique that allows one to combine the findings from a number of studies and determine whether significant trends emerge. It is a particularly powerful procedure because it assists a researcher in dealing with a large number of studies on a topic carried out by different investigators with not-always consistent findings. Meta-analyses look for patterns and trends across studies and provide statistical estimates of the likelihood of significant effects. While such analyses have become common in the social and biomedical sciences, some question the legitimacy of combining data from disparate studies and caution that the results may be misleading. Also spelled *metanalysis*.

metabolism The sum of the processes of ➤ **anabolism** and ➤ **catabolism**; all the energy and material transformations that occur in living cells.

metabotropic receptors Receptors that operate indirectly. When stimulated, they activate an *enzyme* that initiates a series of metabolic processes that opens an ion channel elsewhere in the cell's membrane, allowing ions to pass in and out of the cell. Compare with ➤ **ionotropic receptors**.

metacontrast A variety of ➤ **backward *masking** in which the perception of a visual stimulus (the *target*) is altered by a second visual display (the *masker*). The most commonly used procedures are (a) where the masker consists of two separate stimuli which flank the location of the target and (b) where the masker is an outline which surrounds the location of the target. A variety of factors involving size, location, brightness and timing yield different metacontrast effects. The term ➤ **paracontrast** is generally used to indicate a similar situation but one in which the interest is on ➤ **forward *masking**, i.e. where the flanking or surrounding stimuli are presented first and their impact on the target is evaluated. Not all authors, however, make this distinction.

metaesthetic range That domain of cutaneous responsiveness to stimuli that are not quite intense enough to produce a clear sensation of pain.

metalanguage A language for speaking or writing about an object language. Hence, the language of linguistics as it is used to characterize and describe a natural language is a metalanguage. Similarly, if a treatise on Russian is written in English then English would be a metalanguage in this context.

metalinguistics The study of what people use language for, what they talk about, how they use particular linguistic forms, how language interacts with the rest of culture. ➤➤ **paralinguistics**.

metameric match A perceived match between two color stimuli that actually differ from each other in their spectral characteristics.

metamers Color stimuli that produce ➤ **metameric matches**.

metamorphosis **1.** An abrupt transition in form and structure as occurs in insects

(egg, larva, pupa, adult). **2.** A transformation in personality.

metanalysis ➤ **meta-analysis**.

metaneeds In A. Maslow's theory of personality, the higher human needs, including justice, beauty, order, honor and self-actualization. Metaneeds (or *growth needs* as they are also called) cannot be dealt with, according to the theory, until the prepotent ➤ **basic needs** are fulfilled. ➤ **need hierarchy**.

metaphor A linguistic device whereby an abstract concept is expressed by means of analogy. It is generally concluded that there are no defining features of metaphors, rather that they are, to some extent or another, violations of literalness, and it is from the form of violation that they draw their emotive and cognitive effects. Metaphor and other forms of figurative language (e.g., ➤ **simile**) have long fascinated psychologists because of problems in understanding how they are recognized and understood, what it is that distinguishes a 'good' metaphor from a 'poor' one, what role they play in communication, how such fanciful devices are learned by children, etc.

metaphysics A branch of philosophy that seeks out first principles and, of necessity, must go beyond what can be learned by mechanical or physical analyses. Often, because of its intellectual heritage, it is used as a label for any philosophy that is abstruse. Indeed, William James characterized metaphysics as 'nothing more than an unusually obstinate effort to think clearly.'

metapsychics An occasional synonym for ➤ **parapsychology**.

metapsychoanalysis A general term for an analysis or analytical approach that goes beyond traditional psychoanalysis. Otto Rank's theory, for example, has surely earned this label.

metapsychology **1.** A general label for any theoretical enterprise that attempts to synthesize fact, theory and speculation in a major comprehensive fashion. The *meta-* here means *beyond*, in that such a metapsychological effort is one that goes beyond what has been empirically demonstrated and known and attempts to outline completely general principles of psychology. Such approaches are also called ➤ **nomothetic** psychology. **2.** Within classical Freudian psychoanalysis, such an approach that aims at what Freud regarded as the highest levels of abstraction. Specifically, the analysis of psychic processes in terms of their *dynamic*, *topographical* and *economic* aspects, where *dynamic* included analysis of instinct, *topographical* covered location of a process in the psychic apparatus of id, ego, superego, and *economic* was concerned with the distribution of psychic energy within the system. **3.** Occasionally, a synonym for ➤ **parapsychology**.

metatheory A general term used to cover the theoretical discussions about the construction of scientific theories. For example, the entry ➤ **falsificationism** contains a discussion that is metatheoretical.

metathetic From the Greek, meaning *changed* or *changeable*, it refers to stimulus dimensions within which simple quantitative changes in the physical values produce complex qualitative changes in the psychological sensations. The classic example is the wavelength of light, in which alterations in the continuum produce hue changes. Metathetic continua are a problem for the generality of laws of psychophysical scaling. Contrast with ➤ **prothetic**.

metempsychosis The doctrine of the transmigration of souls, the view that the soul survives bodily death and will, in due course, be reincarnated in another (human or otherwise) body.

metencephalon One of the major subdivisions of the ➤ **hindbrain**, its principal structures include the cerebellum and the pons.

methadone A synthetic narcotic that blocks the effects of other narcotics. It is used occasionally for the treatment of heroin addiction in what are called *metha-*

done maintenance programs. However, methadone itself produces a drug dependence of the morphine type and withdrawal from it is just as traumatic as withdrawal from any of the opioids.

methamphetamine (hydrochloride) A quick-acting and long-lasting ➤ **amphetamine**. Also called *methylamphetamine*.

methaqualone A sedative usually prescribed as a sleeping pill and occasionally combined with an antihistamine, which increases its effects. Its primary effect is to make one drowsy, but frequent side-effects of dizziness, stomach distress and a 'pins and needles' feeling are found. It is marketed under a number of trade names including Quaalude, Melsed, Revonal and Paxidorm. As a street drug it is known as *quaalude* or '*lude*.'

method Very generally, a way of doing things, of working with facts and concepts in a systematic fashion. Now, this is a pretty broad notion and, in practice, the term usually has qualifiers hung on it to specify the form and variety of method under discussion. Several of the more commonly used follow. Note, however, that often the *type* of method receives so much of the focus that the word *method* itself will be dropped; e.g., the *inductive method* is usually referred to simply as *induction*. Hence, for those terms not given here see the qualifying-term entry. See and compare with ➤ **procedure** and ➤ **technique**.

methodological behaviorism ➤ **behaviorism**.

methodology **1.** Broadly, the formulation of systematic and logically coherent methods for the search for knowledge. It is, strictly speaking, not concerned directly with the accumulation of knowledge or understanding but rather with the methods and procedures by which such knowledge and understanding are achieved. Most are prone to use the term as equivalent to *scientific method*, with the implication that the only acceptable methodology is the scientific. The legitimacy of this equivalence depends on just how one characterizes the ➤ **scientific *method** – in the treatment given below, which is representative of the contemporary 'received view,' this synonymity is defensible. **2.** Specifically, the actual procedures used in a particular investigation.

method, scientific The best way to handle this term from the viewpoint of the psychologist is to attack the central issue first: the question as to whether or not psychology is a science. Many persons, both layman and scientists alike, have protested that psychology is not a science, owing to the lack of precision in its procedures and lack of generalizability of its principles. Actually, what makes a given discipline a science has precious little to do with the definitiveness of its findings or the precision of its laws. It rests upon whether the practitioners adhere to the accepted canons of the scientific method. Without unnecessary detail (for the study of the philosophy and methodology of science is a vast and complex field) one can isolate several critical steps that are symptomatic of the scientific approach to any problem.

First, the problem must be defined. This may be no small endeavor; for example, little progress was made in the understanding of human cognition during the several centuries in which the core question was 'What is the nature of mind?' Defining the problem means characterizing it in such a way that it lends itself to careful investigation. Second, the problem must be stated in a manner such that it can be tied in with existing theory and known empirical fact. Without this stage the outcome of a study may be of no value; a science is much more than a compilation of 'raw' facts, it is made up of facts that can be blended with and interpreted in the light of theory and accumulated knowledge. See here ➤ **interpretation**. Third, a testable hypothesis must be formulated. In light of the above, the hypothesis needs to be expressed so that it dovetails with the body of accepted principles and it should be expressed unambiguously so that the outcome of the investigation will be interpretable. There are some fairly

rich arguments concerning this particular issue, ➤ **falsificationism** for one of them. Fourth, the procedures of investigation must be determined. There is enormous latitude here; the possibilities are essentially unlimited so long as one is careful to maintain proper experimental ➤ **control**. Fifth (and sixth), the data are gathered and analyzed and, in accordance with the findings, the hypotheses are either rejected or supported. Seventh, the existing body of scientific knowledge is modified to accommodate the new findings.

Basically, this is a pretty good way to do things, a good way to 'make science.' It has worked well for some time now. It does have some liabilities to be sure. It seems sometimes to be a rather conservative and ponderous procedure and, on occasion, novel findings which appear anomalous in view of the momentary 'state of the science' are cast aside because they do not fit. The classic example here is Mendel's work on genetics, which gathered dust for many years until the field was 'ready' for it. But the exploration of nature, particularly from the point of view of the psychologist, will not suffer unduly from a touch of conservatism. Empiricism is the touchstone of science, experimental control is essential, falsifiable hypotheses necessary, and it all works well – no matter the domain of investigation. For more on related terms ➤ **definition** and **theory**.

methoxyhydroxphenylglycol ➤ MHPG.

methylphenidate A sympathomimetic drug with pharmacologic activity similar to amphetamine but with fewer side-effects. It is routinely prescribed in the treatment of ➤ **attention-deficit hyperactivity disorder** although such treatment remains controversial since not all children so diagnosed respond positively to it. Trade name Ritalin.

Metrazol A circulatory and respiratory stimulant that, in large doses, produces convulsive seizures. Metrazol shock therapy, common in the 1940s and 1950s, is rarely used today. Known as *Cardiazol* in Europe.

metric **1.** Generally, pertaining to measurement. **2.** More specifically, characteristic of measurement in which the elements measured fall on an ➤ **interval** or a ➤ **ratio** *scale. Compare here with ➤ **nonmetric**. **3.** Pertaining to measurement based on the *meter* (38.37 inches) as the unit of length, the *gram* (0.03527 oz) as the unit of weight and the *second* as the unit of time. Occasionally the *liter* (US: 1.057 qt liquid, 0.908 qt dry measure; UK: 1.76 pt liquid, 35 fluid oz) is included as the unit of volume.

-metric, -metrica, -metrika Combining forms meaning *pertaining to measurement*.

metric system ➤ **metric** (3).

-metry Combining form meaning *measurement*.

MF scale ➤ **masculinity–femininity scale**.

MHPG Abbreviation for *methoxyhydroxphenylglycol*. A metabolite of brain *norepinephrine*. MHPG can be measured in urine and levels have been correlated with depression (low levels) and mania (high levels) in patients with a diagnosed ➤ **bipolar disorder**.

micro- **1.** Combining term meaning *very small, minute*. Compare with ➤ **macro-**. **2.** In metric measurement, *one-millionth*.

microcephalic Lit., small-headed. The term is reserved for cases in which the abnormality is so great that retardation results.

microelectrode A very small electrode, specifically one with a tip diameter between 0.5 and 5 microns. Used in neurophysiology for ➤ **single-unit recording**.

microglia ➤ **glia**.

micromillimeter One-millionth of a millimeter; ➤ **nanometer** (preferred).

micron (μ) One-millionth of a meter; used by convention rather than the literal term *micrometer*. pls., *microns, micra*.

microphonia Abnormally weak voice.

microphonic ➤ **cochlear microphonic**.

micropsia Abnormal decrease in the perceived size of visual stimuli. var., *micropia*.

microtome A precision instrument capable of making extremely fine, even sections of tissue for microscopic study.

micturate Urinate.

midbrain During embryonic development the brain evolves three separate portions, the hindbrain, midbrain and forebrain. The midbrain develops into the ➤ **tectum** and ➤ **tegmentum**; see those entries for details.

mid-collicular transection The *cerveau isolé*; ➤ *encéphale isolé*.

middle ear The air-filled space of the ear between the ear-drum and the cochlea containing the ➤ **auditory** *ossicles*.

middle insomnia ➤ **insomnia, middle**.

midline nucleus A thalamic nucleus that relays information from the reticular formation to other thalamic nuclei.

midparent The mean of the measurements of both parents along some dimension – usually weighted for known sex differences – as, for example, in weight or height. It is used as a rough predictor of expectations for the offspring.

midpoint The middlemost point in an interval.

midpontine transection ➤ *encéphale isolé*.

midrange The mean of the highest and lowest scores of a distribution. A 'quick and dirty' estimate of central tendency.

midsagittal plane A plane through the midline dividing the body into symmetrical halves.

midscore The ➤ **median**.

Mignon delusion From the French meaning *darling*, a common childhood fantasy that one's 'real' parents are famous, illustrious persons who will eventually come to the rescue.

459

migraine A syndrome characterized by extremely severe headaches, usually unilateral and often accompanied by nausea, vomiting and visual disturbances. They show a familiar pattern and are often triggered by stress or by particular foodstuffs.

milestone ➤ **developmental milestones**.

milieu The surroundings, the environment, the medium within which events occur. Generally used to refer to the social environment, although the term is extremely flexible.

milieu therapy A general term for any therapeutic setting in which some control is exerted over the socio-environment to accommodate it to the needs of those in therapy. This is (or at least should be) an essential aspect of all inpatient psychiatric institutions.

military psychology A branch of psychology concerned with the application of psychological principles to the special environment that the military life invariably creates. A rather vigorously researched field of applied psychology, it is represented as a special division within the American Psychological Association.

Miller Analogies Test (MAT) A test of the ability to formulate (or, actually, to recognize) analogies. The MAT is used mainly as a screening device for selecting students for graduate schools in the USA and is, after the GRE (Graduate Record Examination), the most widely used of such tests.

milli- Prefix meaning *one-thousandth*.

millilambert One-thousandth of a ➤ **lambert**.

millimicron (mμ) One-thousandth of a micron; ➤ **nanometer** (preferred).

Miltown ➤ **meprobamate**.

mimetic Characterized by mimicry; imitative. Also used as a combining form as in *psychotomimetic*.

mimicry Although some authors use this term as a synonym for the more general term ➤ **imitation**, these days it is more commonly reserved for the evolutionary process whereby one species takes on the phenotypic characteristics of another as a defensive ploy. A classic case is the viceroy butterfly – a juicy mouthful for many birds – whose coloration mimics closely the distinctly toxic monarch.

mind This term and what it connotes is the battered offspring of the union of philosophy and psychology. At some deep level we dearly love and cherish it and see behind its surface great potential but, because of our own inadequacies, we continuously abuse it, harshly and abruptly pummelling it for imagined excesses, and occasionally even lock it away in some dark closet where we cannot hear its insistent whines.

The history of the use of the term reveals two conflicting impulses: the tendency to treat mind as a metaphysical explanatory entity separate and apart from mechanistic systems, and the tendency to view it as a convenient biological metaphor representing the manifestation of the, still not understood, neurophysiological processes of the brain. The following are the more important and common uses of the term and this basic conflict can be seen in all.

1. Mind as the totality of hypothesized mental processes and acts that may serve as explanatory devices for psychological data. In recent years this has become the dominant use of the term. Here, mental components are hypothesized because they have, in the proper theoretical frame, considerable explanatory power. Of interest here is the reluctance, even refusal, of those who adopt this position to speculate about the neurophysiological structures to which it might relate. The focus is typically on the effectiveness of the hypothesized model of mind to explain – not merely describe – the observations of empirical studies. The most frequent users of this meaning are workers in artificial intelligence, modern cognitive psychologists and several schools of philosophy, e.g., ➤ **functionalism** (3). **2.** Mind as the totality of the conscious and unconscious mental experiences of an individual organism (usually, although not always, a human organism). Actually, this use represents an effort to avoid the above-mentioned metaphysical problem but it produces a second-order difficulty of the same kind because of the confusion over how to characterize *consciousness*. Often even those with a behavioristic approach will 'back door' themselves into speculating about mind in this fashion but they will invariably replace *consciousness* with *behaviors* and *acts*. **3.** Mind as a collection of processes. Probably the next most commonly held view, the argument here is that the several processes generally studied under the rubrics of *perception* and *cognition* collectively constitute mind. Here, there is no real effort to define, only to enumerate and to seek to understand those processes enumerated. Strip meaning 1 of theory and you get 3. **4.** Mind as equivalent to brain. This position, which goes back to William James, must in the final analysis be true. Its major liability, of course, is that we know precious little about brain function. As a result, it is more of an article of faith than a true philosophical position. **5.** Mind as an emergent property. The argument here is that of ➤ **emergentism**, that when a biological system reaches a point of sufficient complexity and organizational structure mind (or consciousness) emerges. **6.** Mind as a list of synonyms. For example, *psyche*, *soul*, *self*, etc. Nothing is gained by this use and the definitional problems are compounded. **7.** Mind as intelligence. Really only a colloquial use of the term as in phrases like. 'She has a good mind.' **8.** Mind as a characteristic or trait. Also used nontechnically as in phrases like, 'the mind of an artist,' or 'the Northern European mind.' ➤➤ **mind–body problem**.

mind–body problem One of the classical metaphysical issues concerning the relationship between that which is mental and that which is physical. The issue has its origins in the ancient dualism of Plato and since then many 'solutions' to the problem have been offered; the major ones, classified according to whether they are dualisms, monisms or compromises, follow:

Dualisms: (a) *Interactionism*, wherein mind and body are assumed to be separate entities, obeying separate laws but interacting with and mutually influencing each other. (b) *Psychophysicalism* (or *parallelism*), wherein mind and body are treated as two distinct, independent, but perfectly correlated elements.

Monisms: (a) *Materialism*, which assumes only the physical has reality. (b) *Subjective idealism*, wherein a single basic spiritual or mental realm has reality. (c) *Phenomenalism*, which assumes that neither mind nor body can be substantiated and only ideas and sense impressions exist.

Compromises: (a) *Double aspectism*, wherein it is assumed that the two realities of the physical and the mental come about because each is a particular point of view (or 'aspect') of a single underlying reality. (b) *Epiphenomenalism*, which treats the mental as a noncausal 'shadow' of the physical. ➤➤ **mind**.

mindlessness A term coined by Langer to capture the fact that much of our behavior is carried out 'mindlessly,' that is, without conscious reflection on what we are doing.

mind reading The alleged paranormal ability to know what is going on in the mind of another, a variety of telepathy. Note that when 'mind reading' performances are put on, say by mediums or stage magicians, the phenomenon is quite normal; it consists of the 'reading', not of minds, but of subtle facial and muscular cues and interpreting such factors as tone of voice, manner of speaking, and other pieces of information communicated unconsciously by the one whose 'mind' is being 'read.' ➤ **Clever Hans**.

mineralocorticoids A group of hormones

of the adrenal cortices that effect metabolism of potassium and sodium. E.g., ➤ **aldosterone**.

minimal Pertaining to a ➤ **minimum** and often used interchangeably with that term (in its adjectival form). Many of the related terms such as *minimum audible field* are also found as *minimal* . . .

minimal brain dysfunction (MBD) A general cover term for a variety of behavioral, cognitive and affective abnormalities observed in young children. The term is typically reserved for cases in which the patterns of thought and action are such that one would expect to find some organic abnormality but none is apparent. Generally included as indicative of MBD are ➤ **attention deficit disorder**, ➤ **hyperkinesis**, *impulsivity*, various ➤ **soft signs** and any of a number of learning and language disabilities such as ➤ **dyslexia** and ➤ **dyscalculia**.

The term is often used as though there were an identifiable MBD *syndrome*, a collection of fairly specific disorders that could be taken as hallmarks of some underlying neurological causal mechanisms. Although the issue here is far from settled, the evidence to support a single MBD syndrome is largely unconvincing.

minimal cerebral dysfunction (or **damage**) ➤ **attention-deficit hyperactivity disorder**.

minimal change, method of ➤ **measurement of *threshold**.

minimal cue A ➤ **reduced cue** that still is sufficient to produce the response first associated with the original, full cue.

minimal pair In linguistics, any two words that are pronounced identically except for a single element; e.g. *bill-pill*. The existence of a minimal pair in a language is evidence that the phonetic elements that distinguish the two words are phonemes.

mini-max strategy A general *heuristic* that emerges in economics, problem-solving, decision-making, choice behavior, gambling and even in the design of experiments. The basic principle behind every mini-max strategy is to control the situation so that some effects are minimized (usually one's losses) and others are maximized (usually one's gains).

minimum 1 n. The lowest value of a variable, a series or a continuum. 2 n. In a curve, a value that is lower than those immediately preceding and following it. In this sense there can be several minima in a given function. pls., *minima*, *minimums*. 3 adj. Characteristic or descriptive of such value(s) in either of the above senses; ➤ **minimal**. vb., *to minimize*.

minimum audible field The minimum pressure, measured at a point corresponding to the middle of the head, that will produce a just audible sound. ➤➤ **minimum audible pressure** and **threshold**.

minimum audible pressure The minimum pressure, measured at the eardrum, that will produce a just audible sound. ➤➤ **minimum audible field** and **threshold**.

minimum-distance principle A *heuristic* for sensing the appropriateness of two or more interdependent syntactic forms based on the principle that agreement between them is given by the distance (in number of words) separating them. The perfectly grammatical sentence, 'A number of things is going wrong' feels 'wrong' to most English speakers because it violates this principle; i.e. *things* and *is* are closer together than *number* (the real subject) and *is*. Also called *principle of proximity*.

minimum separable The minimum interspace between two visual contours (i.e. the edges or lines) that can be seen. The typical finding for persons with normal visual acuity is roughly 1 minute of visual angle in the fovea; see here ➤ **acuity grating**. ➤➤ **two-point threshold** for an analogous situation on the skin. Compare this measure of acuity with ➤ **minimum visible**.

minimum visible The narrowest visual stimulus that can be detected. Projected on the fovea of a person with normal visual acuity, the typical finding is roughly

1 second of visual angle. Compare this measure of acuity with ➤ **minimum separable**.

Minnesota Multiphasic Personality Inventory (MMPI) One of, if not the most widely used self-report inventories for the assessment of personality. Published in 1942, the first version consisted of a basic set of 550 items each of which was a descriptive statement about characteristic feelings or behaviors with which the subject indicated either agreement or disagreement. It was originally developed as a clinical diagnostic tool and had eight scales built into it, designed to assess most of the (then) commonly accepted clinical syndromes. Although the MMPI did not prove to be the objective clinical assessment device its developers had hoped for, it turned out to be extremely useful in research into social/personality issues. Indeed, there are currently over 200 separate scales measuring such traits and qualities as *anxiety*, *ego strength*, *masculinity/femininity*, and *internality/externality*, that were developed from the original MMPI item pool.

In response to criticisms concerning many antiquated items, as well as possible biases in the item pool and measurement scales, the inventory was updated in the late 1980's and the scoring system was revised to reflect the results from a large, representative sample of Americans. The revised version contains 567 items, each of which is a statement about oneself which must be answered as *true*, *false*, or *cannot say*. There are now 15 content scales that are related to a variety of psychological problems such as anxiety, depression, anger, social discomfort, family problems, etc., and there is an adolescent version as well as one for adults.

minor depressive disorder ➤ **depressive disorder, minor**.

minor epilepsy ➤ **epilepsy, minor**.

minority group Any identifiable cultural, racial, ethnic or religious group that is subjected to disadvantageous patterns of discrimination and prejudice. As such, the term is not used in its literal meaning; a *minority* group need not be in the numerical minority and being a minority does not necessarily mean classification as a minority *group*. Thus women, though they are neither a minority nor, strictly speaking, a group, are often referred to as a minority group because of discrimination against them by a male-dominated society. At the other extreme are members of certain wealthy, privileged classes who often do form groups and are numerically in the minority but are not classified as such because of the lack of disadvantageous prejudice. These considerations have led some to recommend the term *oppressed group* as a replacement but it hasn't really caught on.

minor tranquilizers ➤ **tranquilizers, minor**.

minus-sum game ➤ **zero-sum *game**.

mirror drawing test A test of sensory-motor skills that requires that the subject trace an object (e.g., a five-pointed star) while viewing the object in a mirror.

mirror self ➤ **looking-glass self**.

mirror writing Writing that, when held up to a mirror, appears in the proper orientation.

mis- ➤ **mis(o)-**.

misandry Hatred of males.

misanthropy Hatred of (literally) males or (more generally) human beings.

mis(o)- **1.** From the Greek, *hated*, *hating*. **2.** From the Latin, *incorrect*, *improper*, *mistakenly*.

misogyny Hatred of females.

miss An inaccurate judgement by a subject that there was no signal present on a trial when one was, in fact, presented. ➤ **signal detection theory** for more details.

missing-parts test A general label for any test where the subject's task is to point out the parts that are absent in a complex pattern or picture. They are often used as items on intelligence tests.

mitosis The cell-division process in which somatic cells divide into daughter cells each with a full complement of chromosomes (the *haploid number*). Compare with ➤ **meiosis**.

Mitwelt ➤ *Eigenwelt*.

mixed In many psychiatric classification systems this term is used to mark disorders that do not display the standard characteristics. In this sense, it is a close synonym of ➤ **atypical** (3).

mixed bipolar disorder ➤ **bipolar disorder, mixed**.

mixed (cerebral) dominance ➤ **dominance, mixed (cerebral)**.

mixed effects model A type of analysis of variance that combines features of the fixed effects model (➤ **fixed *factor**) and the random effects model (➤ **random *factor**).

mixed episode A mood disorder marked by a period of time in which both the symptoms of a ➤ **manic episode** and a ➤ **major *depressive episode** are present.

mixed-motive task Any task or situation where an individual may have more than one conflicting motive operating at the same time. The most frequently studied is the ➤ **prisoner's *dilemma**, in which behaviors that can potentially produce the most favorable outcomes also carry the greatest risk.

mixed receptive-expressive language disorder ➤ **developmental *language disorder**.

mixed schedule ➤ **schedules of *reinforcement**.

mixed transcortical aphasia ➤ **aphasia, mixed transcortical**.

mixoscopia Sexual arousal obtained through watching others engaged in sexual acts. ➤ **voyeurism**.

MLU ➤ **mean length of utterance**.

MMPI ➤ **Minnesota Multiphasic Personality Inventory**.

M'Naghten see under *Mc . . .*

mneme A memory trace.

mnemonic 1. adj. Of or relating to memory. **2.** n. A ➤ **mnemonic device**.

mnemonic device An umbrella term covering any technique for committing material to memory or for improving one's memory. Mnemonics (for short) have a long history, having been developed originally by the ancient Greek and Roman orators who had, by virtue of their profession, enormous memorial burdens placed on them. For examples of some of the more commonly used techniques ➤ **pegword system** and **method of *loci**.

mnemonic trace ➤ **memory trace** and **engram**.

mnemonist One who is expert in the use of various mnemonic devices and capable of feats of memory that seem to most of us to be evidence of extraordinary mental functions. Although most mnemonists (some of whom make a living putting on performances) are quite ordinary mortals who have worked long and hard to develop facility with the mnemonics used, there are the occasional cases of persons whose capabilities appear to be congenital. See here ➤ 'S' for a remarkable instance.

-mnesia A suffix meaning *memory*.

mob As a technical term in social psychology the meaning of mob differs little from that in common parlance: a collection of persons with a specific common purpose and intent. The term is used with the connotation that the emotional level of those in the mob is so high that acts of violence or destruction are likely to occur in the pursuance of the common goal.

mobility Essentially, the reference of this term is the concept of *movement*. It may be literal, physical movement of a stimulus, an object or an organism, or it may be a metaphoric movement through strata which are social, occupational or even cognitive. Because of this wide range of uses the term will usually be accompanied by a qualifier to clarify the reference; e.g., ➤

horizontal mobility, social mobility, vertical mobility.

MOC curve ➤ memory-operating characteristic curve.

modal Relating to the ➤ mode, to the most common score or occurrence.

modality A sensory system, a ➤ sense (1, 2). Usually qualified to specify the sense intended; e.g., the *visual* modality, the *kinesthetic* modality.

mode 1. In statistics, a measure of central tendency of a distribution of scores given by the score of the midpoint of the class interval of scores with the highest frequency. Graphically, it is the peak of a frequency distribution. Although it is the least important of the measures of central tendency (see here ➤ mean and median) it does have descriptive value, particularly in cases where the distribution is *bi-* or *multimodal*. 2. A sense ➤ modality (which is the preferred term). 3. An accepted fashion, a characteristic way of behaving.

model 1 n. A representation that mirrors, duplicates, imitates or in some way illustrates a pattern of relationships observed in data or in nature. The model may be purely mechanical, such as those often constructed to represent the workings of the ear; mathematical, such as those in mathematical psychology; or even a complex blending of these two, as evidenced by research in artificial intelligence. When used in this sense, a model becomes a kind of mini-theory, a characterization of a process and, as such, its value and usefulness derive from the predictions one can make from it and its role in guiding and developing theory and research. 2 n. An ideal, a standard, an example set up as worthy of imitation or copying. In social-learning theory the concept of a model in this sense plays an important role since much of socialization is assumed to take place through the imitation of the behavior of a role model. See here ➤ modeling. 3 vb. To construct a model (in sense 1 above). 4 vb. To serve as the model (sense 2). 5 vb. To imitate, to copy.

modeling (or modelling) 1. The act of constructing a ➤ model (1). 2. A procedure whereby a subject observes a ➤ model (2) perform some behavior and then attempts to imitate that behavior. There are many who feel that it is the fundamental learning process involved in socialization.

moderate mental retardation ➤ mental retardation, moderate.

moderator variable ➤ variable, moderator.

modularity (theory) A cover term for a variety of theories in the cognitive sciences, all of which assume that the mind is composed of relatively independent ➤ modules (1) which are programmed to process particular kinds of information in particular ways. In one ingenious model, Paul Rozin has argued that the evolution of human intelligence can be understood as the gradually acquired capacities for these modules to interact with each other.

modulation transfer function A transfer function is a statement about how a given system passes an input as a function of the frequency of the input; i.e. how it 'transfers' it to an output. When the system is, for example, the lens of the eye and the input is electromagnetic radiation then the transfer function characterizes the manner in which the light waves are modulated by the lens; hence, one has a modulation transfer function that describes the lens.

modulator Any of several types of retinal ganglion cells that have relatively narrow ranges of responsiveness across the visible spectrum. Depending on the species, up to four such modulators have been found with spectral sensitivity peaks in the blue, green, yellow and red ranges. Compare with ➤ dominator.

modulator curve A graph of the spectral sensitivity of individual retinal ganglion cells. ➤ modulator.

module 1. A hypothesized, relatively circumscribed cognitive or perceptual faculty; e.g., a language module, a spatial-perception module. This term, introduced with this meaning by the philosopher

465

Jerry Fodor, is similar to the older term *faculty*; ➤ **faculty psychology** and ➤ **modularity (theory)**. 2. In J. Bruner's theory of cognitive development, an integrated, learned unit of behavior observed in the final phase of the discovery of a solution to a problem (or to a class of related problems) in which the behavior of the problem solver typically becomes well integrated and well organized.

modulus A standard stimulus used as the basis of comparison in studies of scaling of sensory magnitudes.

modus ponens From the Latin for *method of affirming*, a logical inference of the form, *If A then B; A, therefore B*.

modus tollens From the Latin for *method of denying*, a logical inference of the form, *If A then B; not A, therefore not B*.

mogi- Combining form from the Greek, meaning *with exertion* or *with difficulty*. Used freely to connote any difficulty in performance or function; e.g., *mogigraphia* = writer's cramp, *mogilalia* = a speech defect such as stuttering or stammering.

molar The central idea behind the various uses of the term is that it always refers to large units of behavior or to behaviors with holistic functions. Thus, it is used: 1. To characterize learning situations which are large and complex, such as problem-solving or game-playing. 2. Within Gestalt theory, to characterize that which is holistic, in the sense that such a molar phenomenon cannot be analytically broken down into component parts without loss of the intrinsic nature of the whole. 3. In Tolman's theory to describe behavior that is purposive. Contrast with ➤ **molecular**.

molding A technique used in *behavior therapy* where the therapist shapes or molds parts of the client's body, such as folding his or her fingers around a pencil or manipulating his or her mouth to make particular sounds more likely.

molecular 1. Characterizing that which

is small. 2. Pertaining to that which can be analyzed into units or divisions that are small. Hence, reflexive behavior is often called molecular behavior. Contrast with ➤ **molar** (1, 2).

Molyneux's question A query posed in (by most accounts) 1688 by William Molyneux to his friend John Locke. Simply, he asked, would a congenitally blind adult upon suddenly acquiring vision be able to distinguish between a globe and a cube without touching them? Molyneux answered his own question with a vigorous negative and Locke, not surprisingly, agreed. The question, simple though it seems, drove straight at the heart of the extended debate over innate ideas and is today still of deep interest in terms of theories of the extent and form of biological 'preprogramming' of the brain, particularly with respect to questions concerning perception, language and social behavior.

moment Irrespective of seconds and minutes, there are two specialized uses of this term: 1. In the phrase *psychological moment*, it refers to the very short period of time within which successive stimuli will be integrated and perceived as a whole, a kind of discrete quantum of psychological time. For more on this general notion, ➤ **specious present**. 2. In statistics, a moment of a distribution is given by $m_T = \Sigma \chi^i / N$, where m_T is the i-th moment, χ^i is the deviation of each score from the mean raised to the i-th power and N is the number of scores. The first moment of a distribution is the *mean*, the second moment is the *variance*, the third is the distribution's *skewness*, the fourth its *kurtosis*.

monad According to Leibniz's doctrine, monads are indestructible, uncreatable, immutable but quite active entities which constitute the fundamental units of all reality. Through various organizational processes these elemental units can be, he assumed, combined into complex units each of which, by virtue of its coherent structure, is itself a monad.

monaural Pertaining to one ear or to the use of only one ear. Also called *uniaural*.

mongolism ➤ **Down syndrome**.

monism 1. Any of several philosophical positions which argue that there is but one kind of ultimate reality. Several varieties are discussed under ➤ **mind–body problem**; ➤➤ **dualism**. 2. In sociology, ➤ **cultural monism**.

monitor To scan or watch; or one who does so. The monitoring may be of a machine to detect malfunction, of persons to oversee their behavior or of oneself to evaluate personal, internal processes of a cognitive or affective kind. This last sense is similar to that expressed by the more formal term ➤ **introspection**, but without some of its theoretical implications.

mon(o)- Prefix from the Greek, meaning *alone, single, only* or *one*.

monoamine hypothesis The generalization that ➤ **depression** is caused by an insufficiency in the activity of monoaminergic neurons, specifically the serotonergic and the noradrenergic. The hypothesis gains support from the fact that drugs that are monoamine agonists, such as the ➤ **monoamine oxidase inhibitors** and the ➤ **tricyclic compounds**, relieve depression, while those that are monoamine antagonists, such as ➤ **reserpine**, cause it. ➤➤ **biogenic amine hypothesis** for a more general theoretical perspective.

monoamine oxidase (MAO) One of the enzymes responsible for the metabolic breakdown of the ➤ **amines**.

monoamine oxidase inhibitor Any of a class of drugs that operate by inhibiting the action of the enzyme ➤ **monoamine oxidase**, leading to an increase in release of amines such as serotonin and norepinephrine. They are used as ➤ **antidepressant drugs**, although not as often as the ➤ **tricyclic compounds**.

monoblepsia A visual condition in which vision is better when only one eye is used.

monochromacy Complete color blindness. A monochromat can differentiate colors only on the basis of brightness. The term derives from the fact that such an individual can match perceptually all samples using but a single hue. Two forms exist, one in which cones are totally absent (➤ **achromatopsia**) and one in which only a single type of cone is present. In the former (the so-called *rod-monochromat*) all wavelengths are seen as gray, in the latter (called a *cone-monochromat*) they are all presumably seen as one hue. Several synonymous terms have been used over the years, including *monochromatism*, *monochromia* and *monochromasy*.

monochromasy ➤ **monochromacy**.

monochromat One suffering from ➤ **monochromacy**.

monochromatic vision ➤ **monochromacy**.

monochromatism ➤ **monochromacy**.

monochromia ➤ **monochromacy**.

monocular Pertaining or relating to one eye or to the use of only one eye. Also called ➤ **uniocular**.

monocular cue Any visual cue for depth or distance perception that requires only one eye to be processed. Compare with ➤ **binocular cue**.

monocular suppression ➤ **suppression, monocular**.

monogamy A mating (or, in humans, a marriage) system in which each party has but a single mate. Contrast with ➤ **polygamy**. The usual connotation of the term is that the pair maintain mutual sexual fidelity.

monogony Asexual reproduction.

monomania Once used as equivalent to *paranoia*, monomania now refers, almost colloquially, to any inflexible, irrational fixation.

monomyoplegia Paralysis in a single muscle.

monophasic Lit., having but one phase. The most specialized use of the term is to characterize a biological rhythm that has only one full phase per day, such as the typical human sleep/waking cycle.

monoplegia Paralysis of a single limb or a single muscle group.

monoptic   With one eye, *monocular*.

monorchid   A male with only one testicle.

monorhinic   Pertaining to smelling with only one nostril.

monosynaptic reflex arc   The simplest possible reflex arc, consisting of only two neurons, one afferent and one efferent with a single synapse between them. Such 'neural circuits' are rare in higher organisms where even the simplest reflexive systems are polysynaptic.

monotic   With or to one ear. Contrast with ➤ **diotic** and ➤ **dichotic**.

monotonic   Characterizing a relationship between two variables in which for each value on one there is a unique value on the other. Such a monotonic relationship will, when graphed, produce either a continuously rising or a continuously falling function with no level spots and no inflection points.

monovular twins   ➤ **monozygotic *twins**.

monozygotic (MZ)   Lit., one zygote; ➤ **monozygotic *twins**.

Monte Carlo procedure   Generally, any procedure that generates 'pseudo-data' according to a specific set of probabilistic rules. These methods are used frequently to test mathematical models, since the pseudo-data exemplify what the real data should look like if the mathematical model were correct. Often data from individual 'pseudo-subjects' are produced in this fashion and called 'stat-rats' or 'stat-subjects.' Monte Carlo methods are widely used in other sciences, economics and physics in particular, to produce estimated solutions to mathematically intractable problems.

mood   **1.** Any relatively short-lived, low-intensity emotional state. Used freely. **2.** A relatively pervasive and sustained emotional state. Although this meaning clearly conflicts with the original usage, this is the sense found in the latest edition of the ➤ **DSM** and is reflected in the umbrella diagnostic category ➤ **mood disorders**.

mood-congruent psychotic features   *Delusions* or *hallucinations* whose content is consistent with displayed mood. For example, manic states accompanied by delusions of great wealth, inflated power, and grandiosity. *Mood incongruent features* are also often seen, e.g., manic states accompanied by delusions of persecution without grandiose content.

mood disorders   A category of disorders characterized by disturbances of mood or emotional tone to the point where excessive and inappropriate depression or elation occurs. Included are the ➤ **bipolar disorders**, ➤ **cyclothymic disorder**, ➤ **dysthymic disorder**, ➤ **mania** (2), and ➤ **depression**. Also known as *affective disorders*.

mood disorder with seasonal pattern   ➤ **seasonal affective disorder**.

mood-incongruent psychotic features   ➤ **mood-congruent psychotic features**.

mood-stabilizing drugs   An umbrella term for several classes of drugs that are used in the treatment of major mood disorders. All function to stabilize the patient's affect. Included are the *tricyclic compounds* and the *monoamine oxidase inhibitors*, both of which are used for depression, and *lithium* which is used for *bipolar *disorders*.

moon illusion   The illusion that the moon appears larger when on the horizon than when viewed overhead, despite the fact that the retinal image is the same size in both cases.

moral   All of the subtle nuances in the meaning of this term focus on the central notion of pertaining to considerations of right and wrong conduct, of that which is right and that which is wrong within a particular ➤ **moral code**. See the following entries for usage patterns.

moral anxiety   ➤ **anxiety, moral**.

moral code   A code or set of sanctions and rules for classifying that which is regarded as right and proper within a particular group or society. The implication is that the code is applicable to all who regard themselves as members of that group of society.

moral development The development of morality, the process whereby individuals, particularly children, come to adopt and internalize the standards of right and wrong of their society. As such, the term acts as a cover term for a substantial sub-area within the study of developmental psychology. Classic issues within the field concern how children come to perceive what their society's moral code is, how they learn to resist temptations to transgress, how they react should transgressions occur, how they respond to the knowledge or observance of others who have violated the code, etc.

Usage of the term is often bound up with theory. The most influential and frequently referred to is the interactionist stage theory of Lawrence Kohlberg, which is an extension and elaboration of the early work of Piaget on the problem. Kohlberg's analysis distinguishes three primary levels of moral thinking, each with two stages, yielding six (at least theoretically) distinguishable stages. Level I is classified as *premoral*, in that behavior is evaluated only on the basis of personal outcomes without any concept of right or wrong. Stage 1 here is characterized by avoidance of punishment, Stage 2 by hedonistic motives and mutual favoritism. Level II is considered to be the *conventional* level, in that behavior here is dominated by external sanctions. Stage 3 within it is dominated by a desire for approval from others, Stage 4 is characterized by adherence to strong, legitimate authority. It is assumed that guilt emerges during Level II as an anticipation of possible punishment. Level III is regarded as the highest level, in which moral judgement is based on personal principle. Stage 5 is characterized by concern for the values of the community, a just moral order and self-respect, Stage 6 by a reflection upon personal conscience and deep personal principle.

Balanced against this point of view are

two other major schools of thought, within which terms like *moral* and *moral development* will reflect different connotations. Within psychoanalysis the development of morality is assumed to have a stage-like course but here the primary mechanism is assumed to be *identification* with the values of the parents and *internalization* of those values into the superego. The stages here are not stages of moral development *per se* as they are in Kohlberg's theory; rather they are linked to the more general progression through the stages of psychosexual development.

The other major theory is the social-learning theory of Albert Bandura, which emphasizes learning principles, in particular observational learning and modeling. Unlike the other approaches to moral development, Bandura's theory makes no pretenses to being a stage theory and hence no specific sequence of moral judgements or behaviors is predicted. Development of morality is assumed to take place through the dispensing of rewards and punishments by adults and peers who serve as models for acceptable behavior.

The fact that three such disparate theories could all coexist and all be considered viable says something important about the enormous complexity of the problem of moral development, the difficulty of collecting definitive data that will differentiate between each position and the lack of precision with which each is posed, rendering empirical comparisons among them exceedingly difficult.

moral dilemma ➤ dilemma, moral.

moral independence (stage) In Piaget's characterization of moral development, the later stage during which the child's determination of what is right and proper is modified to fit the particular circumstances. Compare with ➤ **moral realism (stage)**. Also called *autonomous morality stage*.

morality 1. A doctrine or set of principles for action, a *moral code*. **2.** A quality of an act such that, according to a particular moral code, it is deemed to be right

469

and proper or not. Morality, while it derives from a social codification of right and wrong, may be treated as either internal and hence part of an individual's personal code or external and imposed by society. Although certain truths seem self-evident, it is probably not the case that a universal code of morality either exists or can be established (*pace* Kant); as with ➤ **ethics**, a relativistic stance is recommended.

moral obligation An expectation that some particular act is required of one owing to a given set of socially accepted moral standards.

moral realism (stage) In Piaget's characterization of moral development, the early stage during which the child accepts as right and proper those rules given by authority. Compare with ➤ **moral independence (stage)**. Also called *heteronomous morality stage*.

morals Principles, or the behaviors which are the manifestations of the principles, judged with respect to rightness and wrongness. If ➤ **morality** is an abstraction that underlies action, then morals are the concretizations. The relationship with ➤ **ethics** is strong; in fact it is so closely related that many treat the terms as synonymous.

morbidity rate The number of cases of a disease or other disorder per unit of population (usually per 100,000) in a given period of time (usually 1 year). Compare with ➤ **mortality rate** (1).

Morenogram A sociometric method developed by Jacob Moreno; ➤ **sociogram** for details.

mores (*more-rays*) Social norms and customs that provide the moral standards of behavior of a group or a society. Mores are important codes of behavior and conformity is regarded as essential for proper functioning of the society; nonconformity is severely sanctioned. The term is typically restricted to social customs that have not been formally enacted into law. sing., *mos* (rare).

Morgan's canon ➤ Lloyd Morgan's canon.

moron From the Greek, meaning *dull*. It is little used today, ➤ **mild *mental retardation** being preferred. ➤➤ **mental deficiency** for further discussion of terminology.

Moro reflex An immature startle reflex observed in very young infants characterized by a drawing of the arms across the chest in an embrace-like manner. Also called *embrace reflex*.

morpheme The minimal linguistic unit that carries meaning. It may be either *free* in that it can stand alone (e.g., *book, eat*) or *bound* in that it cannot be used without being affixed to another morpheme (e.g., *un-, -ed*).

morphine Named for the minor Greek deity Morpheus, the god of dreams and the son of the god of sleep, a powerful narcotic derived from the opium poppy. It is the principal alkaloid of opium; its primary action is as a depressant producing euphoria, drowsiness and relief of pain. Its use as an analgesic is limited by the development of increasing tolerance for the drug and the ease with which drug dependency develops.

morphogenesis From its roots, the meaning is evident: *morph-* = *form* or *structure, genesis* = *origin* and *development*.

morphological Generally, the study of the form or structure of something. Used very broadly.

morphological index A single figure derived from the relative proportions of ectomorphic, endomorphic and mesomorphic characteristics that make up a person's physique. ➤ **somatotype**.

morphology 1. In biology, analysis of form and structure of organisms. 2. In linguistics, analysis of language at the level of the ➤ **morpheme**.

morphophonemics In linguistics, the study of the interrelationship between ➤ **phonemes** and ➤ **morphemes**; it is generally conceded that a full characterization of any natural language is going to have to have a morphophonemic component, since the two levels are intimately interdependent.

mortality rate 1. Specifically, the death rate, usually given as number of deaths per unit of population (typically 100,000) in a specific time period (usually 1 year) and often expressed as an age-specific rate. Compare with ➤ **morbidity rate. 2.** Metaphorically, the failure rate in colleges, medical schools, training programs, etc.

mortido The energy of ➤ **Thanatos**, on analogy with libido as the energy of Eros.

mos ➤ **mores**.

mosaic 1. Generally, a structure or design composed of many diverse pieces. **2.** In genetics, a chromosomal anomaly in which some cells have the normal complement of chromosomes and others do not.

mosaicistic Down syndrome A rare form of ➤ **Down syndrome**.

Moses test A nonparametric test that assesses the difference between two sets of scores by comparing the number of extreme scores from one sample with the number from the other.

mother complex ➤ **Oedipus complex**.

motherese E. Newport's unfortunate term for the speech of adults to young children ('parentese,' 'adultese'?). Such speech is different from adult-to-adult speech in important ways. Utterances are shorter, less complex syntactically, contain very few fragmentary or ungrammatical sentences and have sharply restricted lexical selections. Incidentally, further confounding the term is the fact that older children also use it when speaking to the very young. Motherese should not be confused with the singsong 'baby talk' often used when speaking to infants, pets or other cute creatures.

mother figure The female analog of ➤ **father figure**.

mother fixation ➤ **father fixation**.

mother surrogate One who stands in

place of the real mother. ➤ **surrogate**.

motile 1. adj. Of biological entities, capable of movement. **2.** n. In the study of imagery, a person whose images of movement are particularly vivid.

motion The displacement of a mass. Compare with ➤ **movement**, which, strictly speaking, is used when the mass that is displaced is an organism or a part thereof – a lexicographic nicety that is generally ignored in psychology, in which the two terms are often used interchangeably. For ease of reference all combined forms and varieties have been included here under *motion*, although the terms will often be found in the literature under *movement* as well.

motion aftereffects A class of apparent motion effects. All are produced by first fixating for a time on a steadily moving stimulus and then shifting one's gaze to a stationary stimulus, which will appear to move in the opposite direction. Watching a spiral spin inward will result in a stationary object that 'moves' outward; staring at a waterfall for a time will make the trees on the bank appear to 'swim' upward.

motion, alpha Apparent motion of change in size produced by presenting successively larger or smaller copies of a figure. The perception is of an expanding or shrinking single figure.

motion, apparent A cover term for a large number of perceptual phenomena in which one 'sees' motion when the objects are, in fact, stationary. For some examples ➤ **motion aftereffects, autokinetic effect** and **phi phenomenon**. Also called *phenomenal motion*.

motion, beta The optimal apparent motion in the ➤ **phi phenomenon**. Specifically, perceived motion of an object from one place to another produced by successive static presentations of the object spatially separated from each other.

motion, bow A form of ➤ **beta *motion** produced when an obstructing stimulus is introduced between the two stimulus objects causing the apparent motion to 'bow' around the obstruction.

motion, delta A form of apparent motion in which the seen position of an object shifts with changes in illumination.

motion, epsilon Apparent motion produced when a white line on a black background is abruptly changed into a black line on a white background.

motion, gamma Apparent motion of expansion and contraction of a figure when the luminance is increased and decreased.

motion, induced The perception of motion of a stationary stimulus object produced by real motion of another stimulus object. If, for example, in an otherwise dark room, a moving square perimeter of light is presented with a stationary dot of light inside the square, the square will be seen as stationary and the dot as moving.

motion parallax A general term used to cover a class of cues for the perception of relative motion all of which are reflective of the fact that as the observer moves there are systematic movements in the visual field. ➤ **motion perspective**.

motion perspective J. J. Gibson's term for the flow of visual information surrounding a moving observer. The term is used with the focus on the critical point that as one moves about in the environment objects at different distances move with different speeds according to their distance and position relative to the observer. The resulting complex of movements (➤ **motion parallax**) makes up the overall perspective that provides the cues for the veridical perception of real motion in a complex, three-dimensional world.

motion, pure ➤ **phi phenomenon**.

motion, real Strictly speaking, motion that is perceived when either one (or both) of two conditions occur: (a) the image of a stimulus on the retina remains fixed as the eye tracks the stimulus; or (b) the eye remains stationary and the image travels across the retina. Note, however, that

such motion is not perceived during a *saccade*. The cues for the perception of real motion are extremely complex and only partly understood; see here ➤ **motion perspective**.

motion sickness The feeling of nausea produced by certain patterns of motion. Oddly, exactly what produces this common and often disabling effect is not known. It seems fairly clear that it involves the semicircular canals but just which patterns of movement are effective and which are not is still an open question. Head movement, vision and anxiety also contribute and, to complicate the issue, there are very large individual differences in susceptibility and adaptability.

motion, stroboscopic Any of a class of apparent motion effects produced by presenting a series of stationary stimuli separated by brief intervals. Motion pictures are the best known example; there is no 'real' motion on the screen, merely a sequence of still frames presented in succession. The discovery of the ➤ **phi phenomenon** was the major impetus to the study of the more general stroboscopic motion effects.

motivate 1. To impel to action, to induce a state of ➤ **motivation**. 2. To function as a goal, an incentive.

motivated error An error that is (theoretically) caused by some underlying need or desire. In classical psychoanalysis, all errors and mistakes are presumed to be caused by such unconscious motives. ➤ **unconscious *motivation** and **parapraxis**.

motivation The most typical use of this extremely important but definitionally elusive term is to regard it as an intervening process or an internal state of an organism that impels or drives it to action. In this sense motivation is an energizer of behavior. There are, however, several variations on this theme. Some theorists view the motivational state as one of general arousal without any specific goal or directionality but rather as what is known as a *generalized energizer* or a *generalized drive*. The behavior that actually occurs, they will argue, is the one that was dominant in that particular situation. Most other theorists, on the other hand, argue that motivational states are specific to particular drives and needs and must always be analyzed in terms of specific goals and directionality. Indeed, in the study of human psychosocial motivation this aspect is generally taken as axiomatic. Hence, motivation here is often characterized by the notion that a particular behavior or behavioral tendency is observed *because of* a specific motivational state.

Note, however, that motivation is not a concept that can be used as a singular explanation of behavior. Motivational states result from the multiple interactions of a large number of other variables, among them being the *need* or *drive* level, the *incentive* value of the goal, the organism's *expectations*, the availability of the appropriate responses (i.e. the learned behaviors), the possible presence of conflicting or contradictory motives and, of course, unconscious factors.

Most contemporary research on motivation falls into three broad orientations: (a) The *physiological*, which aims at an analysis of neurological and biochemical underpinnings. Most work here is limited to the so-called *primary drives*, such as hunger, thirst, temperature maintenance, pain avoidance, sex, etc. that have clear organic bases. E.g., ➤ **drive**, **homeostasis**, **limbic system**; (b) The *behavioral*, which is concerned largely with elaborations and refinements of drive theory and learning theory. Note that these two orientations are very strongly complementary. E.g., ➤ **drive** (and related entries), ➤ **incentive**, ➤ **need**; (c) The *psychosocial*, which is oriented toward explanations of complex, learned, human behaviors. Except for a sharing of many similar basic concepts, this latter focus is quite separate from the other two. See here ➤ **need for achievement**, **need for affiliation**, **need hierarchy**, **unconscious *motivation**.

Finally, note that the topic of motivation is intimately intertwined with that of ➤ **emotion**. Emotional states tend to have motivational properties and the energizing elements of a motivational disposition often have a strong emotional tone to them. Moreover, the physiological structures identified in one context tend to be implicated in the other.

motivational hierarchy ➤ **need hierarchy**.

motivation research An effort on the part of advertisers and their clients to manipulate the buying patterns of consumers by exploitation of the real and/or imagined motivations of the public. The 'research' part relates to systematic and controlled efforts to determine just how to package, label and advertise a product to maximize sales. It is a rather sad commentary on our society and its values that it is here, in the 'marketplace,' that scientific psychological procedures and techniques have most effectively wended their way from the laboratory to the 'real world.' ➤ **market research**.

motivation, unconscious By definition, motivation that is not in the conscious awareness of the person. Many agree that herein lies the single most important contribution of one Sigmund Freud: not all motivated behavior can be seen as the result of the rational, the conscious or the willful. Much of behavior is motivated by unconscious factors working through a network of defense mechanisms, symbolic disguises and psychosexual cloaks.

motive 1. A state of arousal that impels an organism to action. 2. A rationalization, justification or excuse that a person gives as the reason for his or her behavior. Note that this second, largely non-technical, meaning carries the same essential theoretical component as the first, more technical, one – it provides a characterization of the cause of the behavior. 3. Occasionally, a general global attitude, as in a phrase like 'his actions reflected altruistic motives.' ➤ **motivation** for more details on usage.

moto- Combining form of *motor*.

motoneuron ➤ **motor neuron**.

motor Very generally, pertaining to or

characterizing that which involves muscles, muscular movements and, by extension, glandular secretions. In short, anything that gives rise to or results in stimulation of effector organs. Almost invariably used in combined form as the following entries show. Contrast with ➤ sensory.

motor aphasia ➤ aphasia, motor.

motor apraxia ➤ apraxia, motor.

motor area (s) Most generally, those regions of the central nervous system that have direct descending connections to motor neurons. The area most often cited is the *primary motor area* of the precentral gyrus, which is, in many aspects, a mirror of the sensory area; upon both is found the body representation known as the ➤ homunculus (2). The innervation here is contralateral, with the exception of the facial area where there is bilateral control of lower face and jaw muscles. A second *supplementary motor area* exists on the medial wall of the cortex, below the primary area. Although much smaller, this area seems to have independent output function in that in experimental animals stimulation here produces movement even if the entire primary motor cortex has been destroyed and its accompanying efferent system has degenerated. In the dominant hemisphere in humans this area has been implicated in the planning of the movements and motivation for speech. Lesions here produce ➤ transcortical motor *aphasia. Note that although motor responses can be elicited by stimulation of some *sensory areas* and many of the *association areas*, these are not technically considered motor areas because of the lack of direct connections with spinal and cranial motor neurons.

motor cortex ➤ motor area(s).

motor end plate The terminus of a motor neuron on muscle fiber. ➤ myoneural junction.

motor equivalence A term used to characterize the fact that many motor responses may be functionally equivalent in that

they bring about the same result though they may be very different topologically; a bar press may occur because a rat uses its teeth, its paws or its head, but all will qualify as bar presses that display motor equivalence.

motor homunculus ➤ homunculus (2).

motoric region ➤ perceptual-motor *region.

motor learning ➤ learning, motor.

motor nerve A bundle of peripheral nerve fibers connecting the central nervous system with an effector.

motor neuron Any single nerve cell that activates an effector.

motor neuron, alpha A motor neuron with cell body in either the ventral horn of the spinal cord or one of the motor nuclei of the cranial nerves. Stimulation produces contraction of extrafusal muscle fibers.

motor neuron, gamma A motor neuron with cell body in either the gray matter of the spinal cord or the motor nuclei of the cranial nerves. They synapse on intrafusal muscle fibers.

motor projection area(s) The motor areas, because they are the parts of the cerebral cortex where the nerve pathways to the striate muscles originate, are often referred to as motor *projection* areas. ➤ motor area(s) for details.

motor reaction type ➤ reaction type (2).

motor response A somewhat redundant phrase used primarily to refer to: **1.** An action of an organism that is emitted without significant covert components, a reflex-like response. **2.** That portion of a complex series of actions that is motoric; e.g., in a decision-making task a complex sequence of perceptual and cognitive processes may be manifested by the making of a simple *motor response* such as pressing one of two buttons.

motor sense A more or less nontechnical term for ➤ kinesthesia.

motor theory of consciousness The

strongly peripheralist theory, originally proposed by the arch-behaviorist John B. Watson, to the effect that consciousness was no more than an epiphenomenon, muscular and glandular action representing the true realities. What one may actually experience is argued to be a mere correlate of action and what one senses or perceives is presumed to be dependent on how one reacts to it. The theory has precious few adherents these days.

motor theory of speech perception A theory of speech perception due largely to A. M. Liberman. The main point is that speech is assumed to be perceived by an implicit, covert system that 'maps' the acoustic properties of the input against a set of deep motor representations of idealized articulation. The theory was developed to account for the phenomenon of ➤ **categorical perception**, which indicated that speech was not processed in the same manner as other acoustic inputs. Note that the 'motor' aspect of the theory is at a deep representational level and, hence, the theory should not be confused with the peripheralist ➤ **motor theory of consciousness**; in Liberman's conceptualization, one does not actually have to *make* a motor response in order to perceive speech properly.

motor unit The basic unit of action of the neuromuscular system; it includes a single efferent neural fiber from a single motor neuron along with the muscle fiber it innervates.

mouches volantes ➤ **floaters**.

movement 1. Any ➤ **motion**. 2. Any change in the position of an organism or of one or more of its parts. All specialized compound forms involving use 1 are to be found under ➤ **motion** et seq., those involving use 2 under ➤ **motor** et seq.

movement afterimage ➤ **motion aftereffects**.

movement disorders A class of psychiatric disorders including ➤ **tic disorders** and ➤ **Tourette's syndrome**.

movement disturbances A cover term for a large array of abnormal patterns of bodily movement. Included are ➤ **choreiform movement**, ➤ **dystonic movement**, *dyskinesia* (➤ **tardive dyskinesia**), *spasms*, etc.

movement, illusion of Any illusion that a part of one's body or the whole body is moving when it is not.

MRI ➤ magnetic resonance imaging.

mRNA Abbreviation for *messenger RNA* ➤ **ribonucleic acid**.

msec Abbreviation for millisecond, 1/1000th of a second.

mucous membrane A general term for any moist epithelium and the connective underlying tissues found in vertebrates.

Müllerian ducts The structures in the embryo that develop into the female internal sex organs.

Müllerian system In the developing embryo, the precursors of the internal female sex organs.

Müller-Lyer illusion One of the best known of the visual illusions, in which the perceived length of a line depends upon the shape and position of other lines that enclose it. The simplest form, the so-called 'arrowhead' illusion, is shown here; lines *a* and *b* are exactly the same length.

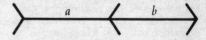

Müller-Urban method In psychophysics, the procedure that sets the threshold as the median value of the ogive fit to the data obtained from a constant-stimulus method. ➤ **measurement of *threshold**.

multi- Latin prefix meaning *many*. Properly it should only be used with terms of Latin origin. ➤ **poly-**, which is used with those of Greek origin.

multidimensional Of variables and factors that are represented as lying along more than one dimension.

multidimensional analysis A variation on ➤ **factor analysis** procedures. Rather than searching for basic factors in a complex array of interdependent variables, this type of analysis allows one to identify a small set of dimensions which account for the variability observed in a larger number of scales. ➤ **Kruskal-Shepard scaling** and **multidimensional scaling**.

multidimensional scaling A statistical procedure for making a multidimensional analysis. All such techniques operate by searching for a small set of dimensions that will provide the best fit for a large number of data points. E.g., ➤ **Kruskal-Shepard scaling**.

multi-infarct dementia ➤ **dementia, multi-infarct**.

multimodal Of a distribution with more than one ➤ **mode**. Compare with ➤ **bimodal**, which refers to distributions with exactly two modes.

multimodal theory of intelligence The position that maintains that intelligence is composed of many separate abilities. It is in strong contrast with the theory that holds that all intellectual abilities derive from a single ➤ **general factor** (2). ➤➤ **intelligence** for more on this topic.

multinomial distribution ➤ **distribution, multinomial**.

multiparous Pertaining to a female who has borne more than one offspring. Usually the term connotes more than one pregnancy, but it is also used for cases of multiple births from a single pregnancy.

multiphasic Lit., having many phases. Used (a) to describe testing devices that were designed to measure a variety of facets of personality at the same time, e.g., ➤ **Minnesota Multiphasic Personality Inventory**, and (b) for biological rhythms with more than one phase per day. Compare with ➤ **monophasic**.

multiple-aptitude test ➤ **aptitude test**.

multiple causation ➤ **causation**.

multiple-choice experiment Any experiment where the subject must make a single choice from among several alternatives. Such experiments are most commonly found in the study of perception and cognition.

multiple correlation ➤ **correlation, multiple**.

multiple personality A relatively rare disorder in which the usual integrity of one's personality becomes so fractionated that two (or more) relatively independent subpersonalities emerge. The condition of multiple personality is an abnormality of degree, not of kind. Most normal persons show pronounced changes in style, behavior and reactivity as they move between different social situations and different social roles. The pathological condition is marked by circumstances in which these varied manifestations of self become so bifurcated that the sense of underlying integrity is lost. There is a suggestion that the disorder is associated with a history of severe abuse during childhood where fantasy became the only escape from painful reality. Lay people often confuse multiple personality with schizophrenia, probably because of the persistent and erroneous use of the colloquialism 'split personality' for schizophrenia (the 'split' in schizophrenia is between affect and thought and not between 'personalities').

multiple regression (equation) A statistical technique that is an extension of simple ➤ **regression** and allows one to make predictions about performance on one variable or measure (called the ➤ **criterion *variable**) based on performance on two or more other variables (called the ➤ **predictor *variables**). If the regression equation is in standard score form then the relative weights or contributions of each of the predictor variables may be assessed. The basic term *multiple regression* is often used with the understanding that the regressions are linear. ➤➤ **multiple *correlation**.

multiple-reinforcement schedule ➤ **schedules of *reinforcement**.

multipolar cell (or **neuron**) A neuron with more than two neural processes rising from the soma. One of these is the axon, the others are 'trunks' of dendritic 'trees' which undergo multiple branchings. Of the three varieties of neurons (the others are unipolar and bipolar) in the central nervous system, the multipolar are the most common.

multistage theories A generic label applicable to any number of theories that hypothesize the existence of various stages of *processing* or of *development*. The most common of the former kind are *information processing* theories, theories of ➤ **semantic** ***memory** and theories of *decision making*; of the latter kind Piaget's theory of *cognitive development* and Kohlberg's theory of *moral development* are exemplary. In this latter category, however, the simpler form ➤ **stage theory** tends to be the term of choice.

multisynaptic reflex arc ➤ **polysynaptic reflex arc**.

multivariate Pertaining to any procedure, experimental or statistical, in which the effects of more than one variable are assessed simultaneously. ➤ **multivariate analysis**.

multivariate analysis A generic term used to cover any of several statistical techniques for examining multiple variables at the same time. Included are ➤ **factor analysis**, ➤ **multiple linear regression**, ➤ **multivariate analysis of variance**, and ➤ **multivariate analysis of covariance**.

multivariate analysis of covariance (**MANCOVA**) An extension of ➤ **analysis of covariance** to situations where multiple dependent variables are under analysis.

multivariate analysis of variance (**MANOVA**) An extension of ➤ **analysis of variance** that permits one to test the significance of more than one dependent variable simultaneously. Unlike a regular analysis of variance which merely provides significance levels for each dependent variable, a MANOVA also yields an estimate of the proportion of variance in the sample data that can be traced to the effects of each of the several dependent variables.

Münchhausen syndrome ➤ **factitious disorder with physical symptoms**. Also occasionally spelled Münchausen.

Münchhausen syndrome by proxy ➤ **factitious disorder by proxy**.

Munsell color system The most widely used of the color specification systems. In it several hundreds of color samples are analyzed according to their *hue, saturation* and *brightness*. The samples in the Munsell Atlas that are used as the basis of comparison for a stimulus were selected to represent psychologically equal steps along the three dimensions and a notational system was developed that reflects these steps.

Murphy's 'laws' A number of semi-humorous 'laws' which, alas, are true entirely too often. Although long lists of variations on the legendary Murphy and his laws exist the three original ones are: **1.** Anything that can possibly go wrong will go wrong. **2.** Anything that goes wrong will do so at the worst possible time. **3.** Anything you plan will cost more and take longer. Anyone with the slightest familiarity with probability theory or even a touch of fatalism about the outcome of the most carefully planned research will appreciate the a priori truth of these 'laws.'

muscarinic receptor A type of acetylcholine receptor that is stimulated by muscarine and blocked by atropine. They are found throughout the central nervous system. ➤➤ **nicotinic receptor**.

muscle Any tissue made up of variously modified elongated cells operating together as a contractile unit. Muscles are made up of muscle cells for contraction, connective tissue for binding and vascular tissue for nourishment. Muscles are generally differentiated according to structure of the cells and to function. E.g., ➤ **cardiac** ***muscle, smooth** ***muscle, striate** ***muscle**.

muscle-action potential The sequence of electrical and chemical events that occurs when a muscle cell is stimulated by a motor neuron across the myoneural junction. The polarization reversal that occurs has the same general characteristics as that in a nerve cell when it propagates an impulse. ➤ **action potential**.

muscle, cardiac Specialized muscle tissue found only in the heart. The cells are intermediate in both structure and function between the smooth and striate muscles and have the automaticity typical of most smooth muscle as well as the rapid contraction rate of striate muscles.

muscle sensation That aspect of kinesthesis that provides an awareness of muscle movement and muscle position.

muscle, smooth Specialized muscle tissue found in the viscera, the blood vessels, the sphincters, the iris and the piloerectors. Structurally they are the simplest of muscles, functionally they are relatively slow contractors. Innervated by the autonomic nervous system, they are sometimes called 'involuntary' muscles, although we can learn voluntary control over some as in toilet training.

muscle spindles ➤ **intrafusal fibers**.

muscle, striate (or **striped**) Muscles that move the body about by pulling on the bony 'levers' of the skeleton – hence, they are also referred to as *skeletal muscles*. The individual fibers are larger than those in smooth muscle and they have a much faster contraction rate. Often called *somatic muscles*, they are for the most part under voluntary control.

muscle tone (or **tonus**) The resting, partial-contraction state of healthy muscle.

muscle twitch 1. A complex sequence of contraction and relaxation of a muscle from a single momentary stimulus. Muscles are often distinguished on the basis of the speed with which the twitch takes place, i.e. *fast-twitch muscles* have short reaction times and *slow-twitch muscles* long reaction times. **2.** A rather derogatory, although admittedly humorous, so-

briquet which critics of behaviorism have used to label the basic response unit that lies at the core of that approach; indeed some call the behaviorist approach 'muscle-twitch psychology.' To be fair, modern variations of behaviorism really don't deserve this label.

mutagen Any substance or agent that causes genetic mutations.

mutation A saltatory change in genetic material brought about by factors other than normal Mendelian recombinations. Mutations become part of the genetic material (i.e. they are *genotypic*), although their impact may not be observed in an individual organism's *phenotype*. The majority of mutations involve individual genes, although gross alterations of chromosomes, involving many genes, also occur. A mutation may also take place in a cell body (called *somatic mutation*) which is transmitted by mitosis from that cell. From the perspective of the adaptive value of a mutation for an individual organism, the outcome is strictly random; their role in evolution comes about through the process of natural selection. Generally speaking, large (macro) mutations are deleterious to the organism and, hence, do not get passed on; small (micro) mutations, according to the standard viewpoint, are said to be the very 'stuff' of evolution.

mute adj. Descriptive of one who lacks speech. The condition of *mutism* may be due to failure to develop the necessary organs for speech, to congenital or early deafness or to severe emotional factors. n., *mute*.

mutual exclusivity assumption An observed constraint on the learning of the meanings of new words in which the learner assumes that a second novel word for an object refers not to the object itself but to some part of it. If, on a trip to the zoo, mother says, 'Look at the ring-tailed lemur,' the child, who already knows the word 'lemur,' assumes that 'ring-tailed' refers to the creature's most distinctive feature. Compare with ➤ **whole object assumption**.

mutualism An occasional synonym for a true symbiotic relationship; ➤ **symbiosis**.

mutual lateral masking ➤ **lateral *masking**.

mutually exclusive (events) Events that cannot occur simultaneously; the occurrence of one prevents the possibility of the occurrence of the other(s). A rat may turn either right or left in a T -maze; one choice eliminates the other so far as that trial is concerned and hence they are mutually exclusive. The concept is extremely important in probability theory and statistics.

myasthenia Muscular disability or weakness.

mydriasis Abnormal dilation of the pupil of the eye. Contrast with ➤ **myosis**.

myelencephalon One of the major subdivisions of the ➤ **hindbrain**. Its principal structure is the medulla oblongata.

myelin A white fatty substance that forms a sheath along many nerve axons in vertebrates. The myelin coating usually begins just below the cell body and covers the entire axon except for the very fine terminal end brushes that synapse on other cells. The sheath is interrupted every 2 mm or so by the nodes of Ranvier. Myelinated fibers propagate neural impulses at roughly 20 times the speed of nonmyelinated fibers. In general, small-diameter fibers do not have myelin sheaths, a fact which is apparent by the distinction between *white matter* and *gray matter* in the central nervous system; the former is composed of myelinated fibers, the latter of nonmyelinated ones.

my(o)- Combining form meaning *muscle, muscular*.

myoclonic movement Any sudden arhythmic contraction of a single muscle or a small group of muscles. Although these movements characterize some motor disorders, they are also commonly observed in almost everyone. The most frequent occurrence is the so-called *myoclonic jerk*, which often accompanies the first stages of sleep and which can awaken the sleeper.

myogram Any graphic representation of muscular activity: e.g., *electromyogram*.

myograph Any instrument for measuring muscular strength.

myoneural junction ➤ **neuromuscular junction**.

myopia Nearsightedness, the inability to focus clearly on distant objects. The shape of the lens is such that in normal accommodation the focal point for light entering the eye is in front of the retina rather than directly on it. Contrast with ➤ **hyperopia**. adj., *myopic*; n., *myope* (person).

myosis Abnormal contraction of the pupil of the eye. Contrast with ➤ **mydriasis**.

myotactic reflex ➤ **stretch reflex**.

myotonia Excessive muscle rigidity.

mysticism 1. A doctrine that knowledge of ultimate reality (theological or otherwise) comes about in non-ordinary ways, i.e. through means other than sensory inputs and cognitive processes. 2. The practice of making vague speculations without reasonable foundation. Use 1 is not at all derogatory and the value of establishing such a philosophical position is usually related to the current (non-mystical) knowledge and/or lack thereof concerning emotional states, intuition, cognitive processes and other psychological issues. The mystical experiences (or revelations) that have been reported by respected persons reflect an intriguing unanimity, one component of which is great difficulty in providing verbal descriptions of them except in negative and/or metaphorical terms. Use 2, however, is generally a slur applied to those who either eschew the scientific method or apply it badly.

mysticotranscendent therapy An umbrella term used to cover a number of approaches of a therapeutic/religious sort which advocate the achievement of understanding of life and self through mystical and/or transcendental experience. Although most contemporary forms lie outside of any well-developed theory of personality or self, the roots of these approaches can be found in the writings of many with an analytic bent, particularly Jung, Fromm and Laing. Frankly, it is not clear that the term *therapy* is really appropriate here; what is generally advocated is a new orientation toward the vagaries of life and a new perspective that transcends the mundane reality – this may or may not prove therapeutic. Indeed, many of the practitioners recommend that one should first be freed of all neurotic tendencies through conventional therapies before one can truly profit from the experience.

myth **1.** From the Greek, meaning *tale* or *speech*; a story that is of unknown or unverifiable origin but is part of the traditions of a culture or a group. Usually a myth carries some explanatory component that ostensibly relates historic events, particularly those of importance to the culture. In Jungian theory, myths became one of the units for analysis of the collective unconscious. **2.** A false, unsupportable, but nevertheless widely held, belief.

myxedema A condition of severe depression of nervous-system activity with symptoms of lethargy, low basal-metabolism rate and general weakness. It occurs in adults with thyroxin deficits. var., *myxoedema*.

MZ Abbreviation for ➤ **monozygotic**.

MZA (or MZa) Shorthand notation for a pair of ➤ **monozygotic** *twins* reared apart from each other.

MZT (or MZt) Shorthand notation for a pair of *monozygotic* *twins* reared together in the same home.

N

N A common abbreviation for *number*, as in the number of scores in a distribution, a population, a sample, an experimental condition, the number of reinforcements, a number factor, etc.

n Abbreviation for: **1.** The number of scores or cases in a subclass or subcategory of a larger population. **2.** Need, as in *nAch* (*need for achievement*).

nAch ➤ need for achievement.

naevus ➤ nevus.

naïve Lacking sophistication or experience; used to describe a subject in an experiment who is unaware of the nature and purpose of the experiment, n., *naïveté* (or *naïvety*), *naïveness*.

nalorphine A narcotic antagonist that blocks the primary pharmacological effects of opium-based drugs. When administered alone, however, its effects are of the morphine type.

naloxone An opioid antagonist that reverses the pharmacological action of ➤ endogenous and ➤ exogenous opiates by competing with them for receptor sites in the brain. Used in experimental work as well as in clinical settings to treat opiate overdoses. Unlike other narcotic antagonists, when administered alone it does not have the morphine-type pharmacological effects.

Nancy school A 19th-century group of psychiatrists who, under the leadership of Hippolyte M. Bernheim, maintained that the state of consciousness induced by hypnosis was an extension of a normal state of high suggestibility rather than an abnormal state akin to hysteria, as many others argued. ➤ Salpêtrière school.

nano- Prefix meaning *one-billionth*.

nanometer (nm) One-billionth of 1 meter. It is the preferred measure for the wavelength of light; 1 nm is equal to 1 millimicron.

narcism Variant of ➤ narcissism.

narcissism The term comes from the Greek myth of a young man's unfortunate emotional investment in his own reflection. In its most general sense it stands for an exaggerated self-love. However, the term may have any of a variety of meanings depending on the particular orientation of the author. For the specific meanings in psychoanalytic theory ➤ primary *narcissism, ➤ secondary *narcissism and ➤ narcissistic neurosis; for the contemporary usage in standard psychiatry ➤ narcissistic personality disorder. Note, in some writings narcissism is called *ego erotism*.

narcissism, malignant A form of ➤ narcissistic personality disorder characterized by suspiciousness to the point of paranoia, feelings of grandiosity, and sadistic cruelty accompanied by a complete lack of remorse.

narcissism, primary In classical psychoanalysis, the early stage of development when libido is overly invested in the self or the ego, or, more simply, in the body. Note that the stage is considered normal in the very young; should it persist into adulthood it is usually classified as a neurosis and is generally characterized by a love of self that precedes, if not precludes, love of others.

narcissism, secondary In classical psychoanalysis, the love of self that results from a withdrawing of libido from objects and persons and the investing of it in oneself.

narcissistic injury A psychological wounding of one's essential self. Such a blow to one's core identity typically lowers one's self-esteem and produces feelings of humiliation, shame, and rage.

narcissistic libido ➤ ego libido.

narcissistic neurosis A neurosis characterized by such excessive self-love that normal love for others is impossible. In the classical theory of psychoanalysis, such a neurosis can prevent the individual from forming a transference. For a nonpsychoanalytic characterization ➤ **narcissistic personality disorder**.

narcissistic object choice As the term suggests, the object that is chosen for narcissistic reasons. The choice is either the self or one very much like oneself.

narcissistic personality disorder A personality disorder characterized by an exaggerated sense of self-importance, a tendency to overvalue one's actual accomplishments, an exhibitionistic need for attention and admiration, a preoccupation with fantasies of success, wealth, power, esteem or ideal love, and inappropriate emotional reactions to the criticisms of others. This symptom-based definition is preferred over that found under the older term ➤ **narcissistic neurosis**.

narcissistic wound A rather clumsy phrase which simply means any blow to or attack upon one's self-esteem.

narc(o)- A prefix meaning *sleep*, *numbness* or *stupor*.

narcoanalysis A form of psychoanalysis carried out under the influence of drugs which produce a sleep-like stupor, most commonly one of the barbiturates. The procedure is rarely if ever used today.

narcolepsy An ➤ **organic *sleep disorder** characterized by recurrent, uncontrollable, brief episodes of sleep. No more descriptive phrase exists than that in Taber's *Cyclopedic Medical Dictionary* (Philadelphia, 1977): 'Here sleep reasserts itself excessively and under conditions not to the best interests of the patient.' Although some narcoleptics appear normal except for these transient episodes, many others display related symptoms, including excessive daytime sleepiness, cataplexy and disturbed nighttime sleep.

narcomania Obsolescent term for: **1.** Extreme desire for narcotic drugs. **2.** A psychotic state resulting from long-term abuse of narcotics.

narcosis A state of markedly reduced responsiveness, both in behavior and in normal physiological functioning, induced by narcotic drugs.

narcotherapy A general term for any therapy that makes use of narcotic drugs. ➤ **narcoanalysis**, which is sometimes used as an approximate synonym but carries a more restricted set of connotations.

narcotic **1.** In psychopharmacology, any drug that has both *sedative* (sleep-inducing) and *analgesic* (pain-relieving) properties. Hence, the classification is restricted essentially to the opiates and opiate-like drugs. **2.** In some (ill-advised) legal systems, a drug classification that includes the true narcotics (1, above) as well as marijuana and cocaine. The problem here is that these other drugs are pharmacologically unrelated to the narcotics and have different patterns of drug dependence associated with them. Hence the term 'narcotic' is rarely if ever used in the technical literature any more. Rather the particular class of drugs under consideration (usually the ➤ **opiates**) is specified.

narcotic analgesic ➤ **narcotic** (2).

narcotic blocking agent Any drug that functions as a narcotic *antagonist*. Included are naloxone, methadone and other agents that are structurally similar to the opiates and presumably function by competing with them for the receptor sites in the central nervous system.

nares The nostrils; sing., *naris*.

narratophilia A ➤ **paraphilia** characterized by deriving erotic stimulation from listening to or reading erotic works to the extent that such narratives are necessary for maintaining sexual arousal and to achieve orgasm. The term is not used for simple enjoyment of erotica or for the use of such literature as an adjunct to sexual activity.

nasal **1.** In phonetics, a ➤ **distinctive fea-**

ture (2) for distinguishing the sounds of a language. A phonetic element is called nasal when the velum is lowered and the sound is permitted to resonate in the nasal cavity (e.g., *m* and *n*); it is marked as non-nasal when the nasal cavity is blocked off (e.g., most of the other phonemes in English). 2. Generally, pertaining to the nose.

nascent Incipient, beginning, just born.

naso- Combining form meaning *nasal*, *pertaining to the nose*.

nasopharynx Collectively, the nasal passages, the mouth, and the upper part of the throat.

native Innate, inherited.

nativism 1. Historically, the doctrine that the capacity to perceive time and space is inborn. This point of view, in its strongest form, argued for the ability for normal perception independent of experience, a position no longer defensible. ➤ Molyneux's question. 2. More contemporarily, and more loosely, any orientation to psychology or philosophy that stresses the genetic, inherited influences on behavior and thought over the acquired, experiential influences. Modern variations on nativism have focused on 'issues' such as language (➤ LAD) and social behavior (➤ sociobiology). Compare with *empiricism* and see the extended discussion under ➤ heredity–environment controversy.

natural category ➤ category, natural.

natural childbirth A general term covering a number of methods of childbirth in which the focus is on the psychological and social aspects and the meaning of birth rather than on the mechanical, medical and physiological.

natural experiment A naturally occurring situation that has many of the trappings of a formal, laboratory experiment in that one can identify factors that function as independent variables although they are not controlled in the usual sense. For example, one could study the role of schooling in vocabulary development in children by comparing the number of new words learned during the summer with the months just preceding and following.

naturalistic approach ➤ *Zeitgeist*.

naturalistic observation The collection of data by careful observation of events in their natural setting. The oldest of the various scientific methods, it is used widely in ethology, ethnomethodology, developmental psychology and other areas.

natural killer cells White blood cells that attack and destroy cells that have been infected by viruses. They are part of the body's immune system.

natural language ➤ language, natural.

natural-response theory ➤ theories of *language origins*.

natural selection First proposed by Charles Darwin and Alfred Russel Wallace in 1858, natural selection is now recognized as the primary mechanism of evolution. The principle of natural selection asserts that of the range of inheritable variations of traits in a population, those that contribute to an organism's survival will be those most likely to be passed on to the next generation. Hence, the contributions to succeeding generations are not random but are 'selected' by the natural process of the viability of the trait. ➤ Darwinism, evolution, evolutionary theory.

natural sign ➤ sign (1).

nature Three, more or less distinct, general meanings of this term can be isolated: 1. Those traits or characteristics of an organism that are assumed to be innate or inherited. The issues raised by this connotation are reflected in what is often called the nature–nurture or ➤ heredity–environment controversy. 2. The complex of events, forces and phenomena that make up the totality of the universe as we know it. Combined with the preceding meaning, this usage produces a most annoying confrontation of meanings since by 'nature–nurture' (nature in sense 1) we could literally mean 'nature–nature' (nature in sense 2). 3. The intrinsic qualities, attributes or characteristic modes of behavior of a person. This sense is strictly nontechnical and is found mainly in off-hand remarks like, 'What do you expect, that's just his nature.'

nature–nurture controversy ➤ **heredity–environment controversy**.

nature, second 1. A nontechnical phrase used to imply that a piece of behavior is habitual and occurs almost reflexively and without conscious thought. 2. Occasionally, in psychoanalytic writings, the *super-ego*.

NE ➤ **norepinephrine**.

near point 1. The point closest to the eye that an object can be clearly seen. Since this point reflects the ability of the lens to focus the image it is often called the *near point of accommodation*. 2. The point closest to the two eyes where an object can be seen with proper binocular fusion. Often called the *near point of convergence*.

nearsightedness ➤ **myopia**.

near vision ➤ **vision, near**.

Necker cube ➤ **reversible *figure**.

necro- Combining form meaning *dead*.

necromania Pathological fascination with death and the dead. Similar in meaning to ➤ **necrophilia** but without the erotic component.

necrophilia A fascination with the dead, specifically an obsessive erotic attraction toward corpses.

necropsy An examination following death to determine its cause, an autopsy.

necrosis Localized tissue death with accompanying degeneration while still in contact with living tissue; e.g., as occurs at the site of a wound.

need 1. Some thing or some state of affairs which, if present, would improve the well-being of an organism. A need, in this sense, may be something basic and biological (food) or it may involve social and personal factors and derive from complex forms of learning (achievement, prestige).

2. An internal state of an organism that is in need of the thing or state of affairs. Note that 1 refers to that which is needed while 2 refers to the hypothetical state of the organism in the deprivation condition.

These two definitions, straightforward though they may be, mask some important subtleties of usage that are reflected in the technical literature. For example, there is a tendency among some to treat *need* as equivalent to ➤ **drive**. This use extends the meanings above in theoretically interesting but occasionally troublesome ways. The equation with drive endows the need state with motivational properties that are not explicitly present in 1, although they are implicit in 2. To appreciate the problem here one must realize that there are needs for which there are no drives, such as the need for oxygen, for the distress felt when you hold your breath is not a drive for oxygen but a drive to reduce carbon dioxide levels.

Within the behaviorist tradition attempts have been made to handle the concept of need with a strictly operationalist analysis. That is, a given need is characterized in terms of procedures. An organism's 'need' for food, for example, is specified by any of several devices such as a statement of its body weight relative to what it would be under normal (ad lib) feeding conditions or a specification of the number of hours since it has eaten. While this lexicographic device helps to clarify some issues, it doesn't aid in understanding the complex interrelationships between biological needs, social needs and the problem of ➤ **motivation**.

There are other variations of usage but they are neither as common nor as compelling as these. For example, need will, on occasion, be used as a synonym for such terms as *motive, incentive, wish, desire, craving*, etc. The plethora of quasi-synonyms is symptomatic of concepts whose underlying characteristics are essential for a theoretically sound psychology but whose connotations are so diverse that conceptual boundary conditions have not been arrived at. In general, most authors will use qualifying phrases to delineate their particular sense of the term, as the following entries show.

need cathexis A more 'mechanical' use of ➤ **cathexis** than that commonly found in psychoanalytic theory. It conveys the same general connotation but physiological needs are assumed in place of *libido*. The need here is assumed to become attached to or invested in some object or person as a means to its gratification or fulfilment.

need–drive–incentive model A model motivation that assumes that basic, physiological needs are produced by states of deprivation, that such needs produce drives that are the true instigators of action and that the action is directed toward the incentive components of the goal state.

need for achievement As characterized by D. C. McClelland and J. W. Atkinson, the desire to compete with a standard of excellence. It is treated as a socially characterized need with two critical components: a set of internalized standards that represent personal achievement or fulfillment, and a theoretical energizing or motivating condition that impels the person toward attempts to meet these standards. Need for achievement is generally measured by the use of a projective test, using, specifically, several pictures similar to those from Murray's Thematic Apperception Test. Usually used in abbreviated form, *nAch.* ➤➤ **achievement** et seq.

need for affiliation H. Murray's term for the need to be with other people, to socialize, form friendships, cooperate, etc.

need for cognition A personality variable that reflects the extent to which an individual enjoys effortful cognitive activities. People who are high in need for cognition crave information, like to analyze complex situations, and enjoy solving problems, particularly difficult ones.

need for intimacy The need for close, warm, and intimate relationships.

need hierarchy According to A. Maslow's theory, all human motives can be viewed as components of a hierarchical need system. Although the hierarchy can be broken up in various ways (see, e.g., ➤ **basic needs, intermediate needs, metaneeds** and **deficiency needs**), the following are the seven main divisions in Maslow's system: 1. Physiological needs: food, water, etc. 2. Safety needs: freedom from threat, security, etc. 3. Belongingness and love needs: affiliation, acceptance, etc. 4. Esteem needs: achievement, prestige, status, etc. 5. Cognitive needs: knowledge, understanding, curiosity, etc. 6. Esthetic needs: order, beauty, structure, art, etc. 7. Need for self-actualization: self-fulfillment, realization of potential.

Maslow conceptualized the hierarchy as invariant (although this claim is disputed by many theorists) and argued that the lower the need the more prepotent it will become if unfulfilled – a starving person is unlikely to be much concerned about self-esteem. It is this assumption, of course, that gives Maslow's conceptualization its hierarchical properties; without it all you have is a list.

need-integrate H. Murray's term used to characterize the dynamic integration of behaviors, including pathways, movements, goals and goal objects of a person. They can (at least theoretically) be subjected to analyses that reveal the particular patterns of needs of the individual.

need-press ➤ **press**.

need, primary Any unlearned need, one determined by innate factors, a *basic need*.

need reduction The result of any event or behavior that diminishes a need. ➤➤ **drive reduction**.

need state ➤ **need** (2).

need, tissue The primary physiological need(s) of tissue for substances necessary for life such as oxygen, food, water, etc.

neencephalon Lit., new brain, the most recently evolved structures of the brain, the cortex and coordinated structures. All the rest is the *paleencephalon* (var. *palae-oencephalon*) or *old brain*.

negation 1. In logic, the denial of a proposition. **2.** Generally, any act of denial, dispute. **3.** ➤ **negativism** (1).

negative acceleration ➤ **acceleration**.

negative adaptation ➤ **adaptation** (1) where there is a gradual diminution in sensitivity.

negative afterimage ➤ **afterimage, negative**.

negative attitude change ➤ **attitude change, negative and positive**.

negative feedback Descriptive of any feedback loop that diminishes or terminates a process. See discussion under ➤ **feedback**.

negative law of effect ➤ **effect, negative law of**.

negative priming ➤ **priming, negative**.

negative recency In experiments on guessing and predicting events (e.g., ➤ **probability learning**), the tendency to predict an event that has not occurred recently. In a simple case like flipping a coin, the less recently a head has occurred the more likely people are to guess 'heads' on the next flip. Contrast with ➤ **positive recency** and see the discussion under ➤ **gambler's fallacy**.

negative reference group ➤ **reference group, negative**.

negative reinforcement ➤ **reinforcement, negative**.

negative sensation An archaic term for a stimulus whose intensity is below threshold.

negative symptoms Symptoms of psychoses characterized by a lack of behavior or affect that is normally present; e.g., flat affect, thought blocking, and social withdrawal. Compare with ➤ **positive symptoms**.

negative transfer ➤ **transfer, negative**.

negative transference ➤ **transference**.

negative valence ➤ **valence**.

negativism 1. A general attitude characterized by resistance to suggestions of others (*passive* negativism) and a tendency to act in ways opposite to directions or commands (*active* negativism). The hallmark of such behavior, particularly when displayed by young children, is the lack of any possible objective reason for the negative stance. **2.** A general term for any philosophy based on negative principles, e.g., skepticism, agnosticism.

neglect A neurological disorder in which the patient is simply not cognizant of (i.e., 'neglects') particular categories of information. For example, the patient may be unaware of the left half of the space about him or her (as, for example, when the lesion causing the disorder is in the right hemisphere) and not consciously see, hear, or feel stimuli that originate there.

neighboring region ➤ **region, neighboring**.

ne(o)- Prefix used to denote that which is new or recent. Also often used to indicate a theoretical position or a point of view that is derivative of an earlier position.

neoanalyst ➤ **neo-Freudian**.

neoassociationism A general term applicable to a number of variations on the classical associationist theory. Neoassociationism tends to be cognitive in character; behavior is viewed as resulting from links between abstract, mental entities such as propositions, images, ideas and the like rather than links between stimuli and responses as in a strict behaviorism. Oddly, these modern theories are hardly *neo-*. They are actually quite close in spirit to the associationist ideas of the early British empiricists. For more on usage patterns here ➤ **associationism**.

neobehaviorism A very general label used as descriptive of any theory or approach that, like classical behaviorism, focuses on the behaviors of organisms as the source of one's data but also allows for the use of unobservable and covert processes as explanatory devices.

neocerebellum The evolutionarily newest part of the cerebellum; it is composed of the lateral cortex and the dentate nucleus. Once thought to be concerned solely with rapid skilled movements, there is increasing evidence that its structures may play an important role in cognitive functions such as language and memory.

neocortex The evolutionarily most recent and most complex of neural tissue. The frontal, parietal, temporal and occipital lobes of the brain consist of neocortex.

neo-Freudian A term descriptive of any psychoanalytic approach, theory or individual analyst that departs from or modifies significantly the orthodox ➤ **Freudian** position. Those analysts who emphasized social, cultural and interpersonal factors while still maintaining a basically dynamic point of view, such as Sullivan, Horney or Fromm, are so labeled. Those who made a clean break from Freud and established their own schools of thought, like Jung and Adler, are not so classified.

neologism 1. A new word or phrase or a new meaning attached to an existing word or phrase. 2. The act of coining such; *neology*.

neology The coining of new words or terms or the use of existing words or terms in novel ways. Often considered a creative act of an innovative person, it is also regarded as a symptom characteristic of certain pathological conditions such as schizophrenia and some forms of aphasia.

neonatal abstinence syndrome A pattern of behaviors observed in the infants of mothers who are heroin 'addicts' (see here ➤ **drug dependence**). The syndrome is characterized by irritability, excessive loud crying, tremors and a voracious appetite unaccompanied by usual weight gain. There is evidence to suggest that the syndrome is associated with decreased attention span and hyperactivity in later childhood.

Neonatal Behavioral Assessment Scale A test of behavioral development constructed by T. B. Brazelton and often simply referred to as 'the Brazelton.' It consists of assessing an infant's reactions to a variety of stimuli such as a light in the eyes, a rattle, a moving ball, etc. It is simple, easily administered, but surprisingly effective at providing an initial assessment of the child. A variety of abnormalities are easily detected using it.

neonate Lit., a newborn child. Occasionally, however, it is used metaphorically to characterize anything novel or new, e.g., a neonatal idea.

neopallium All of the tissues of the cerebral cortex except the olfactory area.

neophasia The speech often observed in some forms of schizophrenia. Although there are some who argue that it has grammatical and semantic structure, the evidence presented to date to support this view is less than compelling.

neophilia 1. Generally, a desire for the new or novel. 2. Specifically, a tendency to try new foods.

neopsychoanalysis ➤ **neo-Freudian**.

neostriatum Collectively, the caudate nucleus and putamen of the ➤ **basal ganglia**.

neoteny The retention of immature characteristics in adulthood.

nerve 1 n. A bundle of independently conducting neural fibers along with accompanying connective tissue. Specific nerves are listed in this volume under the qualifying term. 2 adj. Of or pertaining to such a bundle of neural fibers. There are several adjectival forms freely used with this latter meaning, e.g., *nerve*, *nervous*, *neural* and *neuronal*. The standard conventions for usage are as follows:

(a) *Nerve*. Specific reference to anatomical structures, e.g., *nerve tissue*, *nerve cell*, *nerve fiber*.

(b) *Nervous*. General reference to pathological conditions, particularly those characterized by instability and excitability. However, also firmly fixed in the physiologist's lexicon as a synonym of *nerve* (above sense), e.g., *central nervous system*.

NERVE BLOCK

(c) *Neural.* Originally used to refer to
functions and operations of nerve fibers;
now often used as a 'blanket' adjective for
anything involving nerves and nerve cells
– structural or functional.

(d) *Neuronal.* Relating to individual
nerve cells, ➤ **neurons**.

While these conventions are followed
to a considerable extent, they are hardly
adhered to slavishly; all in all these various forms are used with great latitude in
the technical literature. If a particular combined form is not found in this volume
under one qualifier see the other three.

nerve block Temporary inhibition of
neural transmission by either chemical or
mechanical means.

nerve cell 1. Usually, a ➤ **neuron. 2.**
Occasionally, the ➤ **cell body** of a neuron.

nerve center 1. Generally, any point in
the nervous system that has the function
of integrating and coordinating neural information. **2.** Specifically, a locus of
neural tissue where *afferent* information
makes the transition to *efferent*
information.

nerve deafness ➤ **deafness, nerve**.

nerve ending Generally, the terminus of
a neuron in a peripheral structure. Usually
the term is used in combination with qualifiers that specify structure (e.g., *free nerve
ending*) or function (e.g., *efferent nerve
ending*). Note, the term is not used of
neurons that terminate on other neurons;
➤ **synapse**.

nerve fiber 1. An elongated process of a ➤
neuron (usually the axon) that carries
neural impulses. This is the preferred
reference. **2.** Occasionally, a ➤ **nerve** or a
bundle of such nerve fibers. var., *nerve
fibre*.

nerve impulse ➤ **impulse** (4).

nerve-muscle preparation A procedure
used in the study of neural-muscular function. A muscle with its efferent nerve still
attached is removed and mounted so that
stimulation of the nerve produces muscle
contraction.

nerve pathway The path or route
through the nervous system of a particular
neural impulse.

nerve process ➤ **neural process**.

nerve tissue Loosely, any and all the neurons, the cells that comprise the nervous
system.

nerve trunk The main stem of a peripheral nerve.

nervios ➤ *ataque de nervios*.

nervous 1. Originally, pertaining to ➤
nerve. See that entry, especially 2, for
various points on usage of the several
near-synonyms, *nerve*, *neural* and *neuronal*. **2.** Loosely and largely nontechnically,
descriptive of persons of elevated emotionality, hyperexcitability, tenseness. **3.** By
extension of these two meanings, referring
to a broad class of disorders whose
origins may be either neural or emotional.
The looseness of usage apparent in the
above has led to a gradual abandonment
of this term in the technical literature.
Although it still survives in popular parlance (e.g., *nervous breakdown* for a serious
acute emotional disorder and *nervous
energy* for an elevated level of drive and
activity), the technical meanings once associated with it are now for the most part
captured by one or another synonym –
with the obvious exceptions of phrases
like *central nervous system* and *peripheral
nervous system*, where usage appears
entrenched.

nervous breakdown A non-technical term
for a severe emotional disorder. ➤ **nervous**.

nervous habit Non-technical term for an
oft-repeated set of movements (e.g., nail-
biting, finger-tapping, facial and bodily
mannerisms) that occur when one is under
tension.

nervous impulse ➤ **neural impulse**.

nervous system Collectively, the full
system of structures and organs composed
of neural tissue. Depending on the focus,
various schemes exist for dividing up the
nervous system. The most common anatomical division is into the *central nervous*

system (brain and spinal cord) and the *peripheral nervous system* (the rest). Other taxonomies focus on function, the division into the *somatic nervous system* and *autonomic nervous system*, with the former subserving voluntary, conscious sensory and motor functions and the latter the visceral, automatic, nonvolitional.

nervous tissue *neural tissue*.

network models **1.** A class of models of ➤ **semantic *memory** based on the assumption that the representations in memory are stored in a complex network of interrelations and associations. The links between concepts are represented by operations so that a concept like *apple* would be linked to the concept *round* by a link labelled *is*. Compare with ➤ **set-theoretic model**. **2.** A class of models of learning and memory based on the principles of modern ➤ **connectionism** (2). Note that many of the models here are designed to mimic various aspects of the central nervous system and hence are often referred to as *neural network models*.

neural Pertaining to nerves and neurons. ➤ **nerve** (2) for comments on the use of this term and its several approximate synonyms.

neural arc Generally, any network or path of afferent, interneural and efferent neurons that forms a functional unit from a receptor through the central nervous system interconnections to an effector.

neural conduction The transmission of neural excitation along a nerve fiber (➤ **action potential**) or between two neurons (➤ **synaptic transmission**).

neural crest A band of cells arranged longitudinally along the ➤ **neural tube** of a vertebrate embryo that gives rise to the cells that form the cranial, spinal and autonomic ganglia.

neural discharge The firing of an individual neuron, the propagation of a neural impulse down its length and onto either an effector or another neuron. ➤ **action potential**.

neural facilitation ➤ **facilitation, neural**.

neural fold One of two longitudinal elevations of the embryonic ➤ **neural plate**, which, in vertebrates, unite to form the *neural tube*.

neuralgia Any sharp, relatively severe pain felt along the pathway of a nerve.

neural groove The groove along the *neural plate* in the vertebrate embryo that eventually forms the *neural tube*.

neural impulse ➤ **impulse** (4).

neural induction ➤ **induction** (2).

neural integration The processes by which both excitatory and inhibitory ➤ **postsynaptic potentials** interact to control the firing of neurons.

neural network models ➤ **network models** (2) and ➤ **connectionism** (2).

neural plate The thickened layer of ectodermal cells in the vertebrate embryo from which the central nervous system develops.

neural process **1.** Anatomically, any filament of a neuron, i.e. an axon, dendrite, terminal branch or collateral fiber. **2.** Loosely, any functional change in nerve tissue.

neural quantal hypothesis ➤ **quantal hypothesis**.

neural reverberation ➤ **reverberating circuit**.

neural tube The tube formed by the fusing of the ➤ **neural folds** in the vertebrate embryo from which the central nervous system develops.

neural-tube defects A general term for those congenital defects involving a failure of the ➤ **neural tube** to close properly during the early stages of gestation. Failures to close at the top result in *anencephaly* (no or at best a rudimentary brain), which is always fatal; failures to close along the spine result in *spina bifida*, which can have either a reasonably hopeful or a very poor prognosis depending on location and other characteristics of the opening.

neurasthenia As a psychiatric diagnostic category *neurasthenia* has had a long and confusing history as it has fallen in and out of favor. When in favor it is regarded as a ➤ **somatoform disorder** characterized by mental and physical fatigue and weakness after performing ordinary chores that normally would not require unusual effort and a failure to recover with normal periods of rest or relaxation. The exhaustion is often accompanied by headaches, dizziness, sleep disturbances, irritability, and intestinal distress.

neuraxis The spinal cord and brain represented as a line of reference along the vertical axis of the body. In anatomy, directions within the nervous system are given relative to the neuraxis.

neurilemma The thin membraneous covering of the ➤ **myelin sheath** of the axons of peripheral neurons. Neurilemma is made up of ➤ **Schwann cells**. var., *neurolemma*.

neurin A protein found coating the membrane of presynaptic vesicles.

neuritis Inflammation of a nerve, usually associated with a degenerative process.

neur(o)- A combining form meaning *relating to a nerve, neuron, nerve tissue*, etc.

neuroanatomy The study of the structures and functions of the nervous system.

neurobiotaxis The phenomenon of the growth of dendrites and the shifts in orientation of nerve cell bodies during development toward the area where their primary impulses are initiated.

neuroblast An embryonic cell from the ➤ **neural tube** that gives rise to a neuron.

neurocognition An area within *cognitive psychology* which explores the relationships between neuroanatomical structures in the brain and particular cognitive functions.

neurocyte A nerve cell, ➤ **neuron**.

neuroeffector junction A junction between an efferent neuron and an effector such as a smooth muscle or a gland.

neurogenesis 1. Growth and development *of* nerve tissue. 2. Growth and development of structures originating *from* nerve tissue.

neuroglia ➤ **glia**.

neurogram Synonym of *engram*.

neurohumor ➤ **neurotransmitter**.

neurohormone Any of several substances that are chemically equivalent to ➤ **neurotransmitters** but classified as ➤ **hormones** because they are secreted into the blood rather than onto other neurons.

neurohypophysis ➤ **pituitary gland**.

neuroleptic induced A cover term for those *medication-induced movement disorders* that result as a side effect of one of the ➤ **neuroleptics**. Included are neuroleptically induced *Parkinsonism, dystonia, akathisia*, and *tardive dyskinesia*. ➤➤ **antipsychotic drugs**.

neuroleptics An occasional synonym for the ➤ **antipsychotic drugs**. The term tends to be used only for those dopamine agonist drugs that have their effect through the pathways of the ➤ **extrapyramidal system**. These include, of this writing, virtually all antipsychotic agents used in the USA, although there are some available elsewhere (e.g., clozapine) that have few extrapyramidal effects.

neurolinguistic programming A technique developed to influence and modify an individual's behaviors and beliefs. It is based on assumed (but largely undocumented) sets of relations between linguistic forms, eye and body position and movement, and memory. Used primarily as a form of therapy, its proponents also promote its use in advertising, management, and education. There is virtually no reliable evidence for its effectiveness.

neurolinguistics A hybrid discipline made up of contributions from psycholinguistics and neurology. The primary focus is on the neurological brain functions and processes that underlie language. It is often included as one of the several disciplines in ➤ **cognitive science**. Distinguish from ➤ **neurolinguistic program-ming**.

neurological correlation ➤ **correlation, neurological**.

neurological soft signs ➤ **soft signs**.

neuromodulators Chemical substances that function as ➤ **neurotransmitters** but, rather than being restricted to the synaptic cleft, are dispersed widely, modulating the action of many neurons in a particular area.

neuromuscular junction A junction between a somatic motor neuron and a skeletal muscle fiber. Also called ➤ **myoneural junction**.

neuron A nerve cell, the basic structural and functional unit of the nervous system. Although found in a wide variety of shapes and sizes and subserving a vast array of functions, all neurons consist of a cell body or soma that contains the nucleus and its neural processes, an axon and one or more dendrites. var., *neurone*.

neuronal Of or pertaining to a ➤ **neuron**. ➤ **nerve** (2).

neuropathic Variously used in the past as characterizing either organic or functional nervous disabilities. Today the term is generally restricted to the organic, with either *psychogenic* or *neurotic* being the terms used for functional disorders – however, ➤ **neurosis** for comments on the usage of that and related terms.

neuropeptide Y A *peptide* that plays a role in feeding. Fasting causes its secretion into the lateral *hypothalamus*; eating diminishes its secretion. If introduced artificially it stimulates ravenous eating. It has also been implicated in control over *circadian rhythms*.

neuropsychiatry A branch of medicine that deals with the relationship between neural processes and psychiatric disorders.

neuropsychology A sub-discipline within physiological psychology that focuses on the interrelationships between neurological processes and behavior.

neurosecretory cell A neuron that secretes hormones or similar substances into the extracellular fluid.

neurosis 1 (obs.). A disease of the nerves. 2. A personality or mental disturbance *not* due to any known neurological or organic dysfunction, i.e. a *psychoneurosis*. This meaning, dominant since Freud, has been used: (a) *descriptively*, to denote an identifiable symptom or group of related symptoms that, while distressing and painful, is relatively benign in that reality testing is intact and by and large social norms are adhered to, and (b) *etiologically*, to indicate a causal role played by unconscious conflicts that evoke anxiety and lead to the use of defense mechanisms that ultimately produce the observed symptoms.

Within this conceptual framework a number of specific neuroses were identified and labeled, beginning with Freud's original four subtypes of *anxiety, phobic, obsessive compulsive* and *hysterical* and expanding to include *depressive, depersonalized, character, narcissistic, organ*, etc. The vagueness of these various syndromes, the failure to find features that could reliably characterize each and serve to distinguish it from others, and the inherent ambiguity produced by the use of the core term for both a description and an etiological process have all conspired to rob the term of any coherent (or even consensual) meaning.

Recent years have seen two terminological adjustments: (a) The use of the phrase *neurotic disorder* as a generic cover term for any enduring mental disorder that is distressing, recognized by the individual as unacceptable and alien, but where contact with reality is maintained and there is no demonstrable organic disorder. *Neurotic disorder*, thus, fulfills the *descriptive* role of neurosis but is neutral with regard to etiological factors. This lexical device is the one adopted in the ➤ **International Classification of Diseases**.

(b) The elimination of the term as denoting a psychiatrically identifiable diagnosis, accompanied by a reassignment of the various, previously recognized neuroses to other diagnostic classifications. This is the resolution of the terminological problem taken in the ➤ **Diagnostic and Statistical Manual** of the American Psychiatric Association, in which various specialized terms are introduced for each previously recognized neurotic disorder.

A final note: the term *neurosis* itself is surely not about to expire any time soon. It is deeply entrenched in both the technical literature and the common language. The principle of 'resting semantic inertia' suggests that it will continue to be used technically (especially by those with psychoanalytic training) to mark what many believe to be an etiological process and popularly to refer to, in Ernst Becker's lovely phrase, 'a miscarriage of clumsy lies about reality.' Specialized forms can be found under the alphabetical listing of the defining term. ➤➤ **neurotic**, et seq.

neurotendinal spindle ➤ **Golgi tendon organ**.

neurotic 1 adj. Pertaining to or characterizing specific behaviors that are actually displayed by a person diagnosed as having a neurosis. 2 adj. Characterizing, loosely, those types of behaviors typical of or resembling those of a neurosis. 3 n. A person displaying such behavior. See the discussion under ➤ **neurosis** for comments on contemporary usage.

neurotic anxiety ➤ **anxiety, neurotic**.

neurotic breakthrough ➤ **neurotic *defense**.

neurotic character 1. Specifically, in Adler's theory, the collection of qualities and traits that one uses as a defense against feelings of inferiority and which dispose one to develop overt manifestations of neurosis. 2. More generally, an individual with a personality that predisposes him or her to neurosis. 3. Loosely, a label for one diagnosed as having a neurosis.

neurotic claim K. Horney's term for an inappropriate sense of one's superiority such that one feels that others should rightfully fulfill all one's wants and needs.

neurotic compliance ➤ **compliant character**.

neurotic defense ➤ **defense, neurotic**.

neurotic depression ➤ **depression, neurotic**.

neurotic disorder ➤ **neurosis**.

neurotic fiction In Adler's theory, a ➤ **guiding *fiction** that is so inappropriate and divorced from reality that it can never be achieved, leaving the person hopelessly in pursuit of selfish, unattainable goals.

neurotic inventory Any questionnaire for examining tendencies toward neuroticism. Typically, statements from and about actual clinical cases are given to the subject, who is asked to indicate whether or not he or she agrees with them.

neuroticism 1. A state of being neurotic, of having been diagnosed as neurotic. 2. The underlying abstract core that is the etiological basis for a neurosis. See the discussion under ➤ **neurosis** for caveats concerning usage here, especially 2.

neurotic needs K. Horney's term for irrational solutions to the problems of ➤ **basic anxiety**. According to her theory, people develop a variety of strategies for dealing with this anxiety, many of which eventually become well-learned characteristics of one's personality. They can lead, however, to neuroses because the needs that underlie these strategies are not always rational or appropriate. In the full theory, Horney described ten such needs including a need for power, a need for prestige, a need for affection, a need to exploit others, etc.

neurotic pride ➤ **pride, neurotic**.

neurotic process In Horney's theory, the core inner conflict between one's idealized self and one's real self.

neurotic solution In Karen Horney's theory, any resolution of a conflict that is based on excluding the conflict from awareness. This may be accomplished by a variety of devices such as distortion, neutralization, minimalization or avoidance, but all are presumed to function by relieving the tension and anxiety produced by the conflict. ➤ **auxiliary solution**, **comprehensive solution** and **major solution**, the three types of these neurotic solutions noted by Horney.

neurotic trend K. Horney's term for a pattern of behavioral tendencies focused primarily on security and the need to decrease basic anxiety. She hypothesized that such a basic trend was almost always acquired in childhood.

neurot(o)- Combining form meaning *neurotic*.

neurotoxin Literally *nerve poison*. Any substance that destroys the cell bodies of neurons.

neurotransmitter Any of the many substances that function as the vehicles of communication across the synaptic gap between the terminal buttons of one neuron and the membrane of the receiving cell on the other side. The effect of a neurotransmitter is to produce a brief alteration in the post-synaptic membrane of the receiving cell, either depolarization or hypopolarization (see here the discussion under ➤ **postsynaptic potential**). There are many different neurotransmitters whose actions and locations in the nervous system have been identified; e.g., ➤ **acetylcholine, dopamine, serotonin**. Note that some substances that are listed as neurotransmitters by virtue of their production within neurons are chemically identical to substances that also function as ➤ **hormones** (e.g., *norepinephrine* and the *endorphins*). ➤ **neurohormones**. Also called *neurohumor, transmitter substance*.

neurovegetative system Occasional term for the ➤ **autonomic nervous system**, specifically the parasympathetic division.

neutral Indifferent; characterizing values that are not categorized as reflecting properties of specific classes; lying at or arbitrarily close to the zero point on some dimension.

neutral color Any achromatic color, one

along the black–white continuum.

neutral gray A gray that lies at the midpoint of the continuum of brightness, one that is intermediate between black and white.

neutralization In psychoanalysis, the process by which the sexual and aggressive impulses of infancy are softened ('neutralized') and lose their primitive, infantile quality.

neutral stimulus ➤ **stimulus, neutral**.

nevus A congenital discoloration of an area of the skin. var., *naevus*.

newborn In humans, by convention, an infant under the age of one month. The term is, however, used loosely and the upper age limit will depend on the species under consideration and the author's preferences.

New Look A label attached to an approach to the study of perception that is today not so new (having been most influential in the 1940s and 1950s). It emphasized the roles of emotion and motivation in perception and produced much interesting work on problems like *perceptual vigilance* and *perceptual defense*.

Newman–Keuls test One of the ➤ **post hoc tests**.

nialamide An ➤ **antidepressant drug** of the monoamine oxidase inhibitor class.

nicotine A stimulant found in tobacco. It stimulates ➤ **acetylcholine** receptors and increases the activity level of ➤ **dopaminergic** neurons. It is also highly addictive; statistically speaking, nicotine dependency is as difficult to break as dependency on opiates.

nicotine withdrawal A syndrome that results from abrupt cessation of nicotine-containing substances. It is marked by a craving for nicotine, irritability, feelings of frustration, anxiety, restlessness, and increased appetite with occasional weight gain. The symptoms begin within a few hours of cessation and may continue for days, weeks, or, in some cases, months.

Nicotine withdrawal is regarded by many as an ➤ **organic mental disorder** and the term *nicotine-induced organic mental disorder* is used synonymously. Also called, in some older texts, *tobacco withdrawal*.

nicotinic receptor A type of acetylcholine receptor that is stimulated by nicotine and blocked by curare. They are found on skeletal muscles and to some extent in the *central nervous system*. ➤➤ **muscarinic receptor**.

nictitating membrane A tough, inner eyelid found in many birds, fish, and mammals that, when the eye is threatened, moves laterally from the nasal to the temporal side. It is used in studies of the neural basis of conditioning.

night blindness ➤ **nyctalopia**.

nightmare Generally, any frightening or anxiety-producing dream. The typical nightmare occurs, like other dreams, during *REM* sleep and is contrasted with ➤ **sleep terror disorder**, which occurs during *NREM sleep*.

nightmare disorder ➤ **dream anxiety disorder**.

night vision ➤ **scotopic vision**.

nigro-striatal bundle An axon bundle originating in the substantia nigra of the pons and terminating in the caudate nucleus and putamen.

nihilistic delusion ➤ **delusion, nihilistic**.

nirvana 1. Roughly, the Buddhist notion of liberation from the cycle of death and rebirth. Although there are variations on this theme in the several Buddhist positions, all share the notion that the state is primarily defined negatively as freedom from worldly concerns, particularly concerns of self, self-interest and desire. Such freedom, in principle, allows for the achievement of true wisdom and final liberation. Within some psychoanalytic approaches total loss of individuality, the so-called *nirvana principle*, is argued to represent the manifestation of Freud's death instinct or Thanatos. 2. In some

recent ➤ **innovative therapies**, a state of bliss and ecstasy supposedly achieved through meditation and work. Somehow this usage cheapens the philosophically deep and historically important concept expressed in 1.

Nissl bodies Granular bodies found in the cytoplasm of the cell bodies of neurons and glia. Because they are readily stained by various dyes, the Nissl substances make it possible to examine nuclear tissue in the nervous system separately from the fiber bundles which, made up of axons that do not contain Nissl bodies, are not affected by these dyes.

nit A measure of luminance of a surface equal to ➤ **lux** times I *k*. Nit (symbol: nt) is a relatively new term in photometry introduced to replace the *meter-candle* or *foot-candle*. Multiplying it by 0.292 gives *foot-lamberts*.

nitrazepam A ➤ **benzodiazepine** used principally as a sleeping drug.

nm Abbreviation for ➤ **nanometer**.

nociceptive Pertaining to *pain* or to harmful although not necessarily painful stimuli. Protective reflexes are sometimes referred to as *nociceptive*.

noctambulation Lit., walking at night; sleepwalking; ➤ **somnambulism** (preferred).

nocturnal emission Ejaculation in males during sleep; usually during a dream.

nocturnal myoclonus A condition characterized by sharp muscular twitches that occur during sleep. It is regarded as an ➤ **organic *sleep disorder**, although in mild cases the individual with the disorder is oblivious to it; it only bothers their bedmates.

nodal points Two points in an optical system located along the axis of a lens such that a ray of light sent through one will produce a parallel emergent ray through the other.

node 1. In anatomy, a knob, a swelling, a protuberance; any small rounded organ or structure. 2. By extension, and metaphorically, a point in a network upon which a number of operations impinge. ➤ **network models** for an example of this usage. **3.** The zero amplitude point in a wave.

nodes of Ranvier ➤ **Ranvier, nodes of.**

noesis **1.** In philosophy, a mental event grasped by pure intellect. **2.** In psychology, the general functioning of the intellect; cognition. adj., *noetic*.

noise **1.** Any stimulus that is aperiodic, unstructured and patternless. Although the usual reference here is to auditory stimuli (e.g., ➤ **white noise**), references to *visual noise* are not uncommon. **2.** An unwanted, interfering stimulus. The denotations of meaning 2 may be very different from those of meaning 1. For example, a Beethoven symphony could never qualify for 1 but it could very well be noise in sense 2 if it were to interfere with some other ongoing task. On the other hand, real, auditory noise in sense 1 may not be considered noise in sense 2 if, for example, it is used as a background sound that masks other stimuli and assists one's ability to concentrate on some other task. **3.** As derived from information theory, any contaminant that clutters up the communication of a message or increases the variability or the error rate in some ongoing process. This general sense has been extended beyond the formal confines of information theory and one often sees references to 'noisy data' or 'noisy procedures'; phrases which imply that various uncontrolled factors have contaminated some process or operation.

noise, frozen A segment of ➤ **white noise** that has been recorded and is repeated over and over. This procedure reduces the variability inherent in standard white noise and ensures that each presentation is equivalent to every other.

noise, pink In acoustics, any ➤ **noise** (1) in which the distribution of frequencies is not uniform. Often called *colored noise*; compare with ➤ **white noise.**

noise, white An auditory stimulus that

has all frequencies represented in random fluctuation and sounds like an ongoing 'shhh.' Note that the term derives from the analogy with white light, where all wavelengths are present. White noise is the most frequently used ➤ **noise** (1) in experimental work where a controlled background sound is needed; see here ➤ **signal-to-noise ratio.** Compare with ➤ **pink *noise.**

nomadism A tendency to change residences or, by extension, occupations frequently. Used only for pathological cases.

nominal **1.** As derived from Latin, pertaining to names or naming; classifying, designating. The connotation here is that of distinguishing one thing from another by their names or designations and not by any factual or empirical properties they may have. **2.** By extension, characterizing that which is of limited or only superficial importance.

nominal aphasia ➤ **anomic aphasia.**

nominal definition ➤ **definitions.**

nominalism **1.** A philosophical point of view that maintains that abstract ideas or concepts have no objective reality and are therefore not legitimate foci for scientific investigation. Nominalists argue that reality consists solely of objective particulars and that notions like *mind, society, personality* and so forth are without scientific value. It represents an extreme form of ➤ **empiricism.** Compare with ➤ **positivism** and ➤ **operationalism**; contrast with ➤ **realism** (1). **2.** A tendency to accept the naming of something as providing evidence for its reality. Those who espouse 1 eschew 2.

nominal scale ➤ **scale, nominal.**

nominal weight ➤ **weight** (2).

nominating technique A sociometric technique for the exploration of the structure of a group in which each member nominates the person who best satisfies some criterion; e.g., best liked, easiest to work with, etc.

nomological Pertaining to general laws of nature; ➤ **nomothetic**.

nomothetic From the Greek, meaning relating to or dealing with the *abstract*, the *universal* or the *general*. Any scientific or philosophical system so oriented is called a nomothetic approach. Contrast with ➤ **idiographic**. Also called *nomological*.

non- A prefix meaning *not, without*. Generally, the connotation is negative in the sense of the absence of the thing referenced rather than of the opposite or reverse of it. Some specialized terms are given below; the meaning of most others is obvious from the root word.

nonadditive Quite literally, pertaining to objects, variables, scores, etc. that cannot be added together without somehow disrupting the nature of the things so summed. There are at least three important cases of nonadditivity and the reasons for each having this property are different in each case. (a) When variables or objects are measured on a ➤ **nominal *scale** they cannot be added, because of the lack of quantification in nominal scales; e.g., it makes no sense to add the numbers on football players' uniforms. (b) When objects are reflective of underlying structures that are unrelated they are nonadditive; e.g., one cannot add a person's IQ and their weight, the resulting number has no meaning. (c) When a structured configuration, a ➤ **Gestalt**, is under consideration the elements that comprise it are nonadditive in the sense that each is so intimately related to the whole that they cannot be legitimately distinguished as separate summable entities. Note that case (c) designates the antithesis of (b); in (c) the elements are too closely related to be separately summed, in (b) they are too disparate to be sensibly summed.

nonalcoholic Korsakoff psychosis ➤ **Amnestic syndrome** in which alcoholism is not the cause. The term is not recommended since ➤ **Korsakoff's syndrome** is specifically associated with long-term alcohol abuse.

nonbarbiturate sedatives ➤ **sedatives**.

496

non compos mentis Latin for *not of sound mind*.

nonconscious Not conscious. Used to refer to (a) that which is inanimate and therefore lacking consciousness and (b) those components of mental functioning in sentient beings that are not part of awareness. In this latter sense the term is properly synonymous with ➤ **implicit** and ➤ **covert**. It is also used as a synonym of ➤ **unconscious** in sense 2a and 2b, but should be distinguished from *unconscious* in senses 3a and 3b.

noncontingent reinforcement ➤ **reinforcement, noncontingent**.

nondeclarative memory Occasional synonym for ➤ **procedural memory**.

nondecremental conduction A phrase used to characterize the conduction of a neural impulse down an axon which occurs in an all-or-none fashion.

nondetermination, coefficient of ➤ **coefficient of *determination**.

nondirective therapy A cover term for any therapy in which specific counseling, advice or direction on the part of the therapist is kept to a bare minimum. ➤ **client-centered therapy** for more discussion. Compare with ➤ **directive therapy**.

nondisjunction In genetics, the failure of a pair of chromosomes to separate during meiosis.

nondominant Not dominant; but see the discussion under ➤ **dominant** for specifics on usage.

nonexperimental method An umbrella term for any research method that does not involve the systematic manipulation of independent variables. Naturalistic observation and correlational methods are the most common examples.

nonfluent aphasia ➤ **Broca's *aphasia**.

nonintermittent reinforcement schedule Either *continuous reinforcement* or *extinction*. ➤ **schedules of *reinforcement** for details.

noninvasive 1. Characterizing devices or

procedures that do not 'invade' the body in any direct manner. **2.** Pertaining to tumors or other growths that are local and do not spread.

nonlegitimate authority ➤ **authority, nonlegitimate**.

nonlinear Characterizing any function that cannot be represented by a straight line. Also called *curvilinear*.

nonlinear correlation ➤ **curvilinear *correlation**.

nonlinear regression ➤ **curvilinear *regression**.

nonliterate Basically an anthropological term for any culture whose spoken language does not have a written form. Note, incidentally, that the majority of the world's known languages do not have written forms. Distinguish from ➤ **illiterate**.

nonmatching to sample A variation on the ➤ **matching to sample** procedure where the subject must select the alternative that fails to match the target.

nonmetric 1. Generally, referring to that which is not measured (but not necessarily not measurable) in a quantitative manner. **2.** More specifically, characterizing measurement where the elements measured fall on an ➤ **ordinal *scale**. ➤ **methods of *scaling**.

nonmetric scaling ➤ **methods of *scaling** (especially 3).

nonnutritive sucking procedures Any of several procedures for assessing an infant's attentional and perceptual processes using a pacifier nipple as the basic apparatus. The infant's rate of sucking is recorded as various stimuli are presented and inferences about perceptual and cognitive processes are drawn from the observed changes in sucking rate.

nonoperatory thought An occasional synonym for ➤ **preoperatory thought**.

nonparametric statistics A class of statistical procedures for determining relations between variables which can be used without making assumptions about particular parameters of distributions. Note that although these nonparametric statistical tests are often called *distribution-free* they are not *assumption-free*, for each particular procedure is dependent on certain criteria. Compare with ➤ **parametric statistics** and ➤ **parameter**.

nonpreferred Not preferred; ➤ **dominant** for specifics on usage.

nonprobability sampling ➤ **sampling, nonprobability**.

nonrational This term is used quite literally to refer to thinking, believing, decision-making, etc. where the notions of reason and logic are simply not applicable. However, it should be distinguished from ➤ **irrational**, which implies that logic and reason are violated and not merely irrelevant. Also called *arational*.

nonregulatory drive ➤ **drive, nonregulatory**.

non-REM sleep ➤ **NREM sleep**.

nonreversal shift ➤ **reversal *learning**.

nonsense syllable Any pronounceable but nonsensical combination of consonant-vowel-consonant with the restriction that the two consonants be different; e.g., DAX, TUZ. Invented by H. von Ebbinghaus in the 1880s to study memory (relatively) unencumbered by meaningfulness, they have enjoyed over a century of use in experimental psychology. Also called *CVC trigram*.

non sequitur Latin for *it does not follow*. The term is generally reserved for a conclusion that does not even remotely give an appearance of being a valid argument and not for one drawn invalidly simply because of fallacious reasoning.

nonsocial 1. Descriptive of one who remains outside of, or is relatively indifferent to, social groups or gatherings. **2.** Pertaining to phenomena that are not social, that do not pertain to groups of individuals or to the effects of such groups. Note that ➤ **asocial** (1) is an acceptable synonym; ➤ **antisocial** is not.

nonsomniac A normal individual who needs little sleep, in some cases as few as one or two hours a night. Differentiate from one who suffers from ➤ **insomnia**, which is a ➤ **sleep disorder**.

nonspecific 1. Lit., not specific; general. This meaning is straightforward. 2. Characterizing effects or phenomena that cannot be attributed to identifiable causes or factors. This meaning really functions as a gentle euphemism for ignorance; it is used in circumstances where one simply does not know the origins of some disorder, the causes of some disease, or the basis for the effects that a drug may have on a given individual, etc.

nonspecific immune reactions ➤ **immune reactions, nonspecific**.

nonverbal This term is almost always used in combined form to express those characteristics of a task, a process or a situation that exclude the specifically linguistic. See the following entries for examples.

nonverbal communication A general term covering any and all aspects of communication that are expressed without the use of the overt, spoken, language. Gestures, body positions, facial expressions, contextual factors, presuppositions and the like all fall within the realm of the components of a communication system which transmits information without the use of that which is specifically linguistic. ➤➤ **kinesiology, paralinguistics, proxemics**.

nonverbal intelligence Intelligence that is manifested through performance on tasks that require minimal use of verbal materials. Note that the existence of *verbal* and *nonverbal* intelligence tests does not necessarily imply that there are two different kinds of intelligence. The nonverbal (or *performance*) tests were devised to evaluate intelligence in persons who may, for any number of reasons, have problems with verbal materials, e.g. those tested in their second language, those who speak various dialects, the very young, the mentally retarded, those with sensory deficits, etc. See here ➤ **performance test(s)**.

nonverbal tests ➤ **performance test(s)**.

nonvoluntary ➤ **involuntary**.

noology Frankel's term for the study of that which is uniquely human. In Frankel's hierarchy, psychology is encompassed by noology (although most of the rest of us would reverse this inclusionary clause). It's worth noting, just to understand Frankel's perspective, that he had *theology* encompassing *noology*.

noradrenalin ➤ **norepinephrine**.

noradrenergic Characterizing neurons and neural fibers and pathways which, when stimulated, release ➤ **norepinephrine**. Note that although the preferred term for the neurotransmitter itself is *norepinephrine*, this adjectival form, *noradrenergic*, remains in use. See the discussions under ➤ **adrenalin** and **adrenergic** for the reasons for this pattern of usage.

norepinephrine (NE) A ➤ **catecholeamine** that functions as a neurotransmitter. In the central nervous system NE-containing cells are found in the locus coeruleus in the brain stem; in the peripheral nervous system NE is the transmitter in the postganglionic neurons of the sympathetic nervous system.

norm 1. Statistically, a number, value or level (or a range of such numbers, values or levels) that is representative of a group and may be used as a basis for comparison of individual cases. In this sense any of the measures of central tendency (or a range of values around the measure, usually 1 or 2 standard deviations) may be taken as a norm. 2. Somewhat less formally, any pattern of behavior or performance that is 'typical' or 'representative' of a group or a society. See here ➤ **social norm**. 3. An occasional synonym for ➤ **standard**. This usage is not recommended since it deprives *norm* of the quantitative component explicit in 1 and implicit in 2.

normal 1. Generally, as derived from ➤ **norm** (1, 2), conforming to that which is characteristic and representative of a group; not deviating markedly from the average or the typical. 2. In statistics, characterizing a distribution of scores that does not deviate markedly from the 'bell-shaped' Gaussian curve. ➤ **normal *distribution** for details. **3.** In biology and medicine, regular, natural; not subjected to special consideration or treatment; occurring naturally and not as a result of disease or experimentation. **4.** Free from disease, mental disorder, mental retardation or other psychological dysfunction. That is, *not abnormal*.

Meanings 1 and 2 carry statistical, quantitative connotations and so long as this component of the term is intended there are few problems with usage. Meaning 3 also provides sufficiently clear boundaries to defuse confusion. Meaning 4 is, putting it bluntly, a lexicographer's nightmare. The difficulties in usage stem from the original, well-intentioned attempt to have the term reflect the statistical underpinnings of 1 and 2; that *normal behavior*, for example, should be that behavior that reflects the typical patterns that are observed in society. Unfortunately, many who use the term allow their theories of behavior or their own beliefs about the 'quality of life' to determine the boundary that separates normal and abnormal. That is, normal becomes, for them, that which is right and proper, a standard for behavior and action which may have precious little relationship to the norms that are statistically observed. For more on this definitional problem ➤ **abnormal**.

One interesting attempt to deal with this problem that has been suggested is the specification of the *norm group*. For example, cannibalism may once have been deemed 'normal' among certain peoples in New Guinea but not in, say, Canada. However, this device does not always work; divorce is still regarded as vaguely abnormal in the United States despite the fact that the divorces outnumber the marriages in many states. To appreciate the semantic nuances here, compare the sense of the phrases 'divorce is now the norm in America' and 'divorce is now normal in America.' The statistical sense is carried in the former by *norm* but an evaluative element emerges in the latter and even

one who recognizes the truth of the former feels a little uncomfortable accepting the latter. If there is a resolution to this that may work, it lies in the desire of many psychologists to characterize that which is normal in a manner that blends the group-norm idea with the consideration of the individual; i.e. to ask the question: 'Is the behavior functional and adaptive for that person in that social system?' If so, then it will be considered *normal* and if not, it will be regarded as *abnormal*. This particular use has much to recommend it, particularly because it helps to remove the subjective opinions of the theoretician and the diagnostician and allows the individual under consideration some rights in making the designation. (See here, for a classic case, the discussion under ➤ **homosexuality**.) Its obvious weakness is that it drastically reduces the strength of the generalizations that one can make concerning what is normal.

normal curve ➤ **normal *distribution**.

normal distribution ➤ **distribution, normal**.

normality The state or condition of being adjudged ➤ **normal** in sense 4 of that term.

normalize 1. To transform a set of scores such that the resulting distribution approximates the *normal *distribution*. **2.** To adjust a set of scores such that the highest score is set equal to 100 and the lowest equal to 0 and, thus, they may be read as percentiles. **3.** To adjust something so as to bring it into accordance with an accepted ➤ **norm** (2).

normative Pertaining to norms or standards. A set of *normative data* is that collected for the purpose of establishing norms and getting a sense of the underlying distribution. ➤ **norm** (especially 1 and 2). Distinguish subtly from the sense of the term as carried in the phrase ➤ **normative science**.

normative-reeducative strategy A strategy for social change based on the principle that new attitudes, values and behaviors can only be successfully introduced to a society or group when one takes account of the traditional cultural factors of that society or group and makes allowances for them. Compare with ➤ **power-coercive strategy**.

normative research methods A class of non-experimental research methods based on the collection of observational data from normal subjects of various ages and developmental levels. The purpose is to establish a set of norms that reflect typical behavior.

normative science Any discipline that seeks to develop correct patterns of behavior and conduct. Given the standard characterizations of science (➤ **scientific *method**), this term is something of a misnomer in that normative 'science' tends to be prescriptive rather than descriptive or explanatory. Ethics and esthetics are often regarded as normative sciences. ➤➤ **normative**.

normative survey ➤ **survey, normative**.

norm group The group that one uses to establish a standard against which to measure performance or evaluate behavior. ➤ **normal** (4) for an example of how this term is used.

normless suicide ➤ **anomic *suicide**.

norm of reaction In behavioral genetics, the full range of phenotypic outcomes that can be expressed by a given *genotype*. This notion imposes no practical limits on phenotypic variability and anticipates that, when extreme variations in the environment occur, a larger phenotypic range may be expressed than is generally assumed. ➤ **reaction range**.

nortriptyline An ➤ **antidepressant drug** of the tricyclic group.

nose The organ of ➤ **olfaction**, including the entrance that warms, moistens and filters the air. ➤➤ **olfactory epithelium, smell** and related terms.

nose distance The distance between the noses of two persons in a social interaction. As silly as it sounds, it is actually an important variable in various kinds of personal interactions that occur and in the comfort or discomfort felt by the participants. ➤ **distance zone**, ➤ **personal space**.

nos(o)e- Combining form from the Greek, meaning *disease*.

nosology The systematic description and classification of diseases.

nosomania Obsolescent term for the delusion that one is diseased or has a disease.

notochord The embryonic precursor of the spinal cord and brain.

'not otherwise specified' The phrase used in the ➤ **DSM** for disorders with symptoms that do not match the category in precise ways. For example, *amnestic disorder not otherwise specified* would be used to classify a clear case of *amnesia* that failed to meet any of the specified criteria for identified forms of the disorder. The ➤ **ICD** uses the simpler term *unspecified*.

noxious Painful, injurious. The common use is in the phrase *noxious stimulus*, which is used to characterize (operationally) any stimulus which will function as ➤ **punishment** if presented to an organism or as a ➤ **negative *reinforcer** if removed.

NREM sleep Those stages of sleep not characterized by rapid eye movements (REM). Also called *non-REM sleep*; ➤ **sleep** for more details.

nuclear complex (or conflict) Within a number of psychoanalytic or psychodynamic theories, a fundamental conflict occurring during infancy or early childhood that is assumed to be a root cause of a number of psychoneurotic disorders that may only emerge later in life. For Freud, the Oedipus complex fulfilled this hypothesized role, for Horney it was a child's feeling of helplessness, for Adler it was feelings of inferiority, etc. A nuclear complex is not the same thing as a ➤ **universal complex**, although it is true that all nuclear complexes are assumed (within each theory) to be universal. Also called *nuclear problem* or, on occasion, *root conflict*.

nuclear family ➤ family (1).

nuclear problem ➤ nuclear complex.

nucleic acids A group of complex acids found in the cells of all living things. They are intimately involved in the self-duplication mechanisms that are fundamental to life and form the core of the processes by which hereditary characteristics are transmitted. Those nucleic acids containing ribose are known as ➤ ribonucleic acids (RNA); those containing deoxyribose are the ➤ deoxyribonucleic acids (DNA).

nucleo- Combining form meaning *pertaining to a nucleus*.

nucleolus A spherical organelle contained in the nucleus of a cell that produces ribosomes. pl., *nucleoli*.

nucleus From the Latin, meaning *kernel*. **1.** The central portion of an atom. **2.** A spherical structure within the cytoplasm of most cells (not, e.g., in viruses). It contains the chromosomes, one or more nucleoli and functions as an integral part of the living cell; if removed the cytoplasm dies. **3.** A histologically identifiable mass of neural cell bodies in the brain or spinal cord. Specific nuclei are listed in this volume under the modifying term. **4.** Any physical core or central point about which elements or factors are gathered, e.g., 'governmental nucleus,' 'social-power nucleus.' **5.** In factor analysis or multi-dimensional analysis, a cluster of correlations around which many factors or dimensions lie.

nucleus accumbens (septi) A dopaminergic area in the basal forebrain near the septum. It is suspected of being intimately involved in ➤ reinforcement, in that natural reinforcers such as eating, drinking, and engaging in sexual behavior all cause the release of *dopamine* in this area.

nucleus basalis An acetylcholinergic nucleus in the basal forebrain whose neurons innervate most of the cerebral cortex. It undergoes degeneration in *Alzheimer's disease*.

nucleus of the solitary tract A nucleus in the medulla that receives taste information from the tongue and the visceral organs. It appears to play a role in sleep.

nucleus raphe magnus One of the nuclei of the *raphe*. It receives neural projections from the periaqueductal gray and is involved in producing *analgesia*.

null hypothesis ➤ hypothesis, null.

nulliparous Pertaining to a female who has never borne offspring.

null result Any experimental outcome that was not significant. Generally, null results tend not to be reported in the scientific literature – which is occasionally unfortunate since the knowledge that such and such an effect does not obtain is often of considerable importance.

number completion test A test in which the subject is given a series of numbers arranged according to some rule and asked to complete it; e.g., 1, 2, 3, 5, 8, 13, –.

number factor A factor found in many analyses of performance on intelligence tests and other tests of cognitive ability that emerges as a cluster of skills all of which are seemingly representative of a facility with numerical and quantitative operations.

numerical value ➤ absolute *value.

nurturance **1.** The act of supplying support, food, shelter, protection, etc. to the young, weak or helpless. **2.** The tendency to do so.

nurture The collective impact of all environmental factors that affect growth and behavior. Contrast with ➤ nature (1 but see also 2).

nyctalopia Abnormally poor vision under low illumination conditions. The condition may be due either to a deficiency in vitamin A or to a congenital retinal defect. The former is temporary and correctable; the latter is a permanent condition. Also known popularly as 'night blindness.' Watch for authors who

501

incorrectly use this term when ➤ **hemera-lopia** is meant.

nyctophilia A preference for darkness or night. Also called ➤ **scotophilia** (2).

nymphomania An exaggerated sexual desire in females. The term is used almost unconscionably loosely and often attached to sexually active women whose erotic desires and behaviors happen to exceed one's own particular preferences about what is right and proper. As a true clinical syndrome, it is rare and is generally regarded as a manifestation of some deep psychological disorder and accompanied by other symptoms.

nystagmus A set of movements of the eyes made up of small-amplitude, rapid tremors and a large, slower, return sweep. They are normal and, in fact, are critical for proper vision. Their presence and/or absence under various conditions is used in diagnosing a variety of visual and neurological disorders. Compare with ➤ **saccades** and ➤ **stabilized image** for a discussion of the result of neutralizing their function.

nystagmus, caloric Nystagmus produced by introducing either cold or warm water into the canal of the external ear. Warm water produces nystagmus in the direction of the ear stimulated, cold water in the opposite direction.

nystagmus, galvanic Nystagmus produced by a mild electric current passed through the auditory labyrinth.

nystagmus, optokinetic Nystagmus produced when following a moving target with the eyes. The eyes will track the target briefly then sweep back to the original position and so forth. This appropriately named 'optokinetic' response will persist for a time after the visual stimulus has been removed.

nystagmus, physiological In the sequence of eye movements described under ➤ **nystagmus**, the fine, rapid tremors which average roughly 30 Hz with travel no greater than about 20 seconds of arc.

nystagmus, rotational Nystagmus caused by rapid rotating of the body. The slow, large amplitude phase is in the direction of rotation; when the bodily rotation is stopped, a *secondary* or *post-rotational nystagmus* in the opposite direction occurs. ➤ **Bárány test**.

O

O Abbreviation for: **1.** ➤ **Observer** (2), as the subject in studies on perception is often called. **2.** ➤ **Organism**. ➤ **Subject** (1) is an acceptable synonym in both cases. **3.** ➤ **Oscillation**.

$_SO_R$ ➤ **behavioral oscillation**.

ob- Combining form meaning *against, in the way of; toward.*

obedience Simply, acting so as to conform with rules or orders. In most contemporary work in psychology the term is used as roughly synonymous with ➤ **compliance**, i.e. with the connotation that one need not believe in what one in fact does but merely that one feels compelled to obey.

obesity Most definitions of this term are phrased in language that characterizes an individual as being, to some degree or another, overweight. Properly, this is not correct. Obesity is characterized by excess body fat, not excess body weight. While the two are typically correlated, exceptions exist. An athlete, for example, can be 'overweight' when compared with established norms because of extensive muscle development but would not be properly classified as obese. However, since the procedures for determining obesity from a nutritionalist's point of view have become quite complex and involve a variety of factors, some general rule of thumb is still needed. Thus, for practical purposes, an individual is regarded being obese if body weight is in excess of 30% above normal, with normal generally given by standard tables of ranges of optimal weights for age, sex and body type. Obesity can be caused by a large number of factors ranging from the purely physiological to the psychological. Several of the most frequently differentiated types are given in the following entries.

obesity, dietary Obesity which results from simple overeating, particularly when there is an excess of high fat and high carbohydrate foods in one's diet.

obesity, endogenous Obesity, the primary cause of which is some organic abnormality, e.g., an endocrine imbalance, faulty metabolism.

obesity, exogenous Obesity, the cause of which is external, i.e. it results from excessive food intake and not from some specific organic dysfunction.

obesity, genetic Obesity that is dependent (in part) upon genetic factors. The contemporary point of view is that it results from an overabundance of fat cells which are inherited.

obesity, hypothalamic Obesity resulting from dysfunction of the ➤ **hypothalamus**, specifically a lesion in the ventromedial area.

obesity, morbid Obesity where the individual's weight is in excess of 50% of what is regarded as normal for age, sex and body type.

obesity, ovarian Obesity hypothesized by some to result from imbalances in the sex hormones. This form of obesity is identified with females, who in later life tend more toward obesity than males.

object **1** n. Most broadly, *anything.* **2** n. Within the study of perception and cognition, an aspect of the environment of which one is aware. This sense is expressed in phrases like *stimulus object*, for a physical entity that one detects, senses or recognizes, *object of regard*, for that which one attends to or looks at, *object of thought*, for that which one contemplates or thinks about, and so forth. **3** n. A goal or an end state; here the term is really a shortened form of an *objective.* **4** n. In psychoanalytic theory, a person, a part of a person, or a symbol representative of either, toward which behaviors, thoughts and desires are oriented. In the classical model, an object is required for one to obtain satisfaction of instincts.

Note that these meanings run quite a gamut from the physical to the perceptual, the conceptual and the symbolic as well as from the inanimate to the personal. Not surprisingly, it tends to be a term used in combined form so that the object or the subject of the object is specified; see the following entries for examples.

object-assembly test A general term for any test in which the subject is required to put together objects which have been disassembled.

object assimilation Modification or alteration of the perceived form or function of an object over time. Jung used the phrase to describe such changes, which he theorized were due to a person's needs. Gestalt psychologists and some contemporary memory theorists use it to refer to modifications in the memorial representation of the object over time, with the stipulation that these modifications bring the memory of the object more in line with that which is typical of the category. ➤➤ **assimilation**.

object blindness ➤ **agnosia**.

object cathexis In psychoanalysis, investment of energy in an ➤ **object** (4). ➤ **object choice**.

object choice In psychoanalytic theory, an ➤ **object** (4) as the focus of love, affection or, more generally, of libido. When there is identification with an object similar to oneself, it is called *narcissistic object choice*; when it is based upon differences from the individual, it is called *anaclitic object choice*.

object color The color of an object – which is not quite as tautological as it sounds at first, for an object's color must be either a ➤ **surface *color** or a ➤ **volume *color** and hence differentiated from a ➤ **film *color**. See those terms for details.

object concept In Piagetian theory, a

mature object concept is achieved when the child sees an object as a real, physical entity which exists and moves in the same space as the child. ➤ **object permanence** for more on usage.

object constancy **1.** A very general term for the tendency for objects to maintain perceptually their characteristics under wide variations of viewing. Total object constancy is produced by several more elemental constancies, namely those of *color, brightness, size* and *form*. ➤ **constancy**. **2.** In psychoanalysis, the maintenance of a psychic connection with a specific ➤ **object** (4). The term is used here with the implication that an object constancy once established functions so that possible replacements for the object tend to be rejected.

objectivation The use of the defense mechanism of ➤ **projection** (1) – with a 'twist.' It refers to the case in which one projects one's own feelings upon another who actually has those feelings.

objective **1** adj. The basic meaning here derives from the notion of an object as a thing which is real, demonstrable or physical (➤ **object**, 1, 2 and 3) and hence whose status or function is publicly verifiable, externally observable and not dependent on internal, mental or ➤ **subjective** experience. This general sense of the term is reflected in the following, more specific, usages. **2** adj. Characterizing a thing whose nature is determinable through the use of physical measurement. Weight, wavelength and frequency of a sound wave are 'objective' characteristics of things which correspond to the 'subjective' dimensions of heaviness, hue and pitch. **3** adj. Free of bias, uncontaminated by the emotional aspects of personal assessment. ➤ **clinical *prediction** for a classic example of the contrast between objective and subjective. **4** adj. External to the body or mind. **5** adj. Sensed or experienced as externally localized. **6** adj. Pertaining to an ➤ **object**, in any of the several meanings of that term. **7** n. A goal; ➤ **object** (3).

objective anxiety Real anxiety in the

sense that there is a clear, objective cause. Note that the meaning here is, in a way, somewhat contradictory to the usual connotations of ➤ **anxiety**.

objective examination (or **test**) Any test in which the correct answers are objectively given and no subjective judgements enter into the scoring.

objective psychology A label covering any approach to scientific psychology in which the only data considered 'legitimate' are those based upon measurement in physical, objective terms. Specifically excluded are data based on introspection or interpretation. ➤ **Behaviorism** is as close to being an objective psychology as one could probably put up with.

objective scoring ➤ **objective examination**. Contrast with ➤ **subjective scoring**.

objective set ➤ **set, objective**.

objective test ➤ **objective examination**.

objective vertigo ➤ **vertigo**.

objectivism In ethics the point of view that there exist particular moral truths independent of whether or not, in a given society, they are believed in or practiced. To take the classic example, one could argue that the stricture 'No one should inflict pain merely to derive pleasure from the suffering of another' is true everywhere, even in a society of sadists, just as $5 + 5 = 10$ is true everywhere even in a society where no one can count. Contrast with ➤ **subjectivism**.

objectivity 1. The quality of dealing with objects as external to the mind. 2. An approach to events characterized by freedom from interpretative bias or prejudice. Sense 2 is assumed to be derived from 1 in that the nonsubjective quality results from approaching phenomena as having an external (*objective*) reality uncontaminated by internal interpretation. E.g., ➤ **objective psychology**.

object libido ➤ **libidinal object**.

object loss In psychoanalytic theory, the loss of an ➤ **object** (4) who was perceived as

benevolent and loved. The term is used for either the loss of the love or the loss of the object.

object of instinct In psychoanalysis, the ➤ **object** (4) that is the focus of an instinct.

object, part In psychoanalytic theory, some particular aspect of an ➤ **object** (4) that plays a role in fulfilling needs, e.g., a breast or a penis.

object permanence A critical aspect of a child's development of what Piaget calls the ➤ **object concept** is the notion of its permanence. Specifically, the reference here is to the awareness that a physical object is permanent, that it continues to exist even when the child no longer interacts with it.

object relations The emotional bonds between oneself and another. Typically expressed in the sense of one's capacity to love and care for another as balanced against interest in and love for the self.

object representation A term used in psychoanalysis to emphasize the internal mental representational aspects of an ➤ **object** (4). The point is that a psychic process, say *object cathexis*, is assumed to take place with respect to one's mental representation of the object and not the real person.

object size Lit., the actual physical size of a thing as opposed to its perceived size. When ➤ **size constancy** holds, the two measures of size are equivalent.

object, transitional An object used by a child as a comforter. Usually there is considerable emotional attachment invested in the object, which is typically a piece of cloth or a doll. The term derives from psychoanalytic theory, where the object is viewed as a psychological bridge allowing the child to make the transition from primitive narcissism to a more mature emotional attachment to others. It is used, however, by many without the psychoanalytic interpretation.

oblique Characterizing a line or a plane that intersects another line or plane at an angle other than 90°. In graphic representations of factor analysis, two axes (representing factors) that are correlated appear as oblique.

oblique décalage ➤ **décalage**.

oblique rotation ➤ **rotation** (2).

oblique solution In factor analysis, a solution whereby the axes that represent the underlying factors are situated so that they are not at right angles to each other. In such a solution, the factors themselves are correlated. Compare with ➤ **orthogonal solution**. Also called *oblique-axes solution*.

obliviscence An old term for the loss of information from memory. It is currently being resuscitated as the convenient antonym of ➤ **reminiscence**. One reason for its revival is that the notion of ➤ **hypermnesia** may conveniently be defined as reminiscence minus obliviscence.

oblongata ➤ **medulla oblongata**.

obscenity From the Latin, meaning *of evil omen* and, by extension, *disgusting, offensive*. Modern usage restricts the meaning to those acts, words or pictures that are regarded as indecent and offensive about sexual and excretory matters. The difficulty with the term emerges from the words 'are regarded' in the previous sentence. Typically, appeals are made to 'accepted standards in society' or to 'prevailing social morality' or other ill-defined criteria. In the final analysis, obscenity is much like beauty and exists primarily in the eye of the beholder.

observation 1. Most generally, any form of examination of events, behaviors, phenomena, etc. 2. By extension, any individual datum, score, value, etc. that represents an event, behavior or phenomenon. Note that on occasion observation may be used in contrast with *experiment*. This distinction marks the fact that many regard scientific work based on the so-called ➤ **observational methods** as non-experimental. In this sense, the distinction is justified, although on the other side of the coin lies the argument that such a differentiation is really unnecessary since an experiment is merely one way of making an observation. Where the terms need to be kept conceptually separate is when one wishes to distinguish between research that is controlled by the manipulation of independent variables and research that is carried out by the use of ➤ **naturalistic observation**. 3. A casual or informal commentary upon or interpretation of that which has been observed.

observation(al) learning ➤ **learning, observation(al)**.

observational methods Generally, any of the procedures and techniques that are used in nonexperimental research to assist in making accurate observations of events. Included is the use of various devices such as audio and video recorders, cameras, stopwatches, check lists, etc.

observation trial Any trial in an experiment in which the subject is not required to make any response but merely to observe the stimulus presented. ➤ **observation(al) *learning**.

observer 1. One who makes an ➤ **observation**. 2. One who is engaged in ➤ **introspection**. Note that in sense 1 the observer is the scientist carrying out a study and collecting data, while in 2 the observer is the subject in an experiment who reports on experiences (➤ **introspection**) or attends to stimuli presented (➤ **observation(al) *learning**). Symbol: *O*: but only used for 2.

observer drift The tendency for the observers in a study to become inconsistent in the manner in which they make and record their observations. More likely to occur in long-term studies, it is a bias that reduces reliability.

obsession Any idea that haunts, hovers and constantly invades one's consciousness. Obsessions are seemingly beyond one's 'will' and awareness of their inappropriateness is of little or no avail. Compare with ➤ **compulsion** and ➤➤ **obsessive-compulsive disorder**.

obsessional neurosis Originally, a neurosis characterized by obsessional thoughts, ideas, etc. Because such obsessions tend to occur along with compulsive behavior, the more inclusive term *obsessive-compulsive neurosis* was introduced. Today, owing to difficulties with the term ➤ **neurosis** itself, the preferred label is ➤ **obsessive-compulsive disorder**.

obsessive-compulsive disorder (OCD) A sub-class of ➤ **anxiety disorders** with two essential characteristics: recurrent and persistent thoughts, ideas and feelings; and repetitive, ritualized behaviors. Attempts to resist a compulsion produce mounting tension and anxiety, which are relieved immediately by giving in to it. The term is not properly used for behaviors like excessive drinking, gambling, eating, etc. on the grounds that the 'compulsive gambler,' for example, actually derives considerable pleasure from gambling (it's the losing that hurts); one burdened with a true obsessive-compulsive disorder derives no pleasure from it other than the release of tension. Recent evidence indicates that the disorder is associated with damage to or dysfunctions of the *basal ganglia*, *cingulate gyrus*, and the *prefrontal cortex*. The disorder does not respond well to standard therapies but often does to ➤ **antiobsessional drugs**.

obstacle sense The ability of many blind persons to avoid obstacles in their path. The sense involved is hearing and the ability is due to ➤ **echolocation**. Compare with ➤ **facial vision**.

obstruction method An experimental procedure in which the subject (usually a rat) is separated from a goal by some obstruction, usually an electrically charged grid floor. Typically, the motivational state of the animal and the aversiveness of the electric shock are manipulated and the strengths of various drives can be compared.

obtained mean ➤ **sample *mean**.

obtained score ➤ **raw *score**.

Occam's razor The principle, *entia non sunt multiplicanda praeter necessitatem* (entities are not to be multiplied beyond necessity). William of Occam (or Ockham) was a 14th-century Franciscan philosopher and theologian who argued that reality exists only in individual things and events. Often called the *principle of ontological economy*, Occam's razor is similar to the more modern ➤ **Lloyd Morgan's canon** and to the more general principle of ➤ **parsimony**.

occipital Pertaining to the back part of the head, skull or brain.

occipital lobe The posterior lobe of the cerebral hemispheres.

occlusion An obstruction, a block, closure. Used in physiology and medicine for a blockage or closure of a passageway. In the study of perception it is an occasional synonym for ➤ **interposition**.

occult From the Latin for *covered* or *concealed*, involving the supernatural. The study of the occult involves magic, spiritualism, and other branches of the paranormal, particularly as such 'powers' may be used to control natural events. Modern science is partly occult in its origins, yet oddly most contemporary occultists are vigorously anti-science. ➤➤ **parapsychology**.

occupation **1.** Specifically, any activity or set of activities carried out for purposes of earning a living. That is, an occupation is a ➤ **role** that has both economic and social elements to it. **2.** More generally, any activity that one carries out; whatever keeps one occupied.

occupational analysis ➤ **job analysis**.

occupational family A cluster of occupations or professions all of which share similar training and requisite abilities. Distinguish from ➤ **occupational group**.

occupational group A group organized and defined by the common occupation of its members. Professional societies, labor unions and the like are examples. Distinguish from ➤ **occupational family**.

occupational hierarchy Any ranking or ordering of occupations according to some set of criteria. The most commonly used are: (a) the more or less objective criteria such as intellectual and/or skill requirements, the amount of education and/or training needed for success in each occupation; and (b) the social-esteem criteria such as the prestige and social status associated with each occupation. Although such hierarchies are invariably tinged by social/political biases, they are generally useful in the study of such issues as social mobility, social power and the study of social-class differences. ➤ **Hollingshead scales**.

occupational interest inventory ➤ **interest inventory**.

occupational psychiatry A subfield of psychiatry concerned with diagnostic and preventive issues within the workplace. The focus is on problems such as returning psychiatric patients to work, emotional stability in the work environment, absenteeism, accidents and accident proneness, problems of retirement, etc. Also called *industrial psychiatry*. Distinguish from ➤ **occupational therapy**.

occupational therapy Simply, therapy based on giving the individual something purposeful to do. It may be either physical therapy, in which the tasks are designed to exercise and develop certain muscles and sensory-motor coordination, or psychologically oriented therapy, in which the work is designed to improve one's general sense of self. Distinguish from ➤ **occupational psychiatry**.

OCD ➤ **obsessive-compulsive disorder**.

octa- Combining form meaning *eight*. var., *octo-*.

octo- ➤ **octa-**.

ocular Pertaining to the eye. ➤ **Ophthalmic** is an acceptable (and preferred) synonym; ➤ **optic** is not.

ocular apraxia ➤ **apraxia, ocular**.

ocular dominance An obsolescent term for ➤ **eye *dominance**.

ocular pursuit ➤ **pursuit movement**.

ocular torsional movement ➤ **torsion** (2).

oculist Obsolete term for *ophthalmologist*.

oculo- Combining form meaning *the eye* or *pertaining to the eye*.

oculogyral illusion The apparent movement of a stationary spot of light when the observer is rotated about rapidly. The illusion of movement is a result of reflexive eye movements caused by the rotation; see here ➤ **rotational *nystagmus**.

oculomotor A cover term used to characterize any of the several kinds of eye movements. Included are the movements of the eyeball as controlled by the extrinsic muscles, the movements of accommodation and the movements of the muscle controlling the iris.

oculomotor nerve The IIIrd ➤ **cranial nerve**. It originates in the oculomotor nucleus of the superior colliculus and the third ventricle in the midbrain and consists primarily of efferent fibers to all the ocular muscles except the exterior rectus and superior oblique. Although this motor function is primary, it also contains some proprioceptive (afferent) fibers.

oculomotor nucleus ➤ **oculomotor nerve**.

odd–even technique ➤ **split-half *reliability**.

odds In probability calculations, the ratio of success to failure. For example, the odds of drawing a spade at random from a deck of cards is 13 to 39 or 1 *to* 3. Note that calculating the odds is not the same as calculating the ➤ **probability** (1). For the example given, the probability of drawing a spade is .25 or 1 *in* 4.

odiferous Having an odor.

odor Either **1.** the sensory experience of smelling a gaseous substance, or **2.** the substance itself. ➤ **olfaction, olfactory, smell**, etc.

odorimetry ➤ **olfactometry**.

odor prism ➤ **Henning's prism**.

Oedipus complex A group or collection (i.e. a *complex*) of unconscious wishes, feelings and ideas focusing on the desire to 'possess' the opposite-sexed parent and 'eliminate' the same-sexed parent. In the traditional Freudian view, the complex is seen as emerging during the Oedipal stage, which corresponds roughly to the ages 3 to 5, and is characterized as a universal component of development irrespective of culture. The complex is assumed to become partly resolved, within this classical view, through the child making an appropriate identification with the same-sexed parent, with full resolution theoretically achieved when the opposite-sexed parent is 'rediscovered' in a mature, adult sexual ➤ **object** (4). Freud viewed the Oedipus complex as the ➤ **nuclear complex** of all psychoneuroses and, in his view, a variety of neurotic fixations, sexual aberrations and debilitating guilt feelings were theoretically traceable to an 'unresolved' Oedipus complex.

Interestingly, the theoretical genesis of the complex – which derives its name from the mythical figure Oedipus, the hero of two of Sophocles' tragedies who unknowingly killed his father and married his mother – was Freud's own self-analysis, carried out after his father's death. At first, *Oedipus* referred only to the male complex, *Electra* being used for the female. Today, however, both are subsumed under *Oedipus* largely for convenience, although it should be noted that Electra's sins were different from Oedipus'. Rather than directly murdering her mother, she urged her brother to do it.

Contemporary psychoanalytic theory places somewhat less importance on the complex than did Freud and his immediate followers. Rather, there is more emphasis on the earlier relationship between the child and the mother and the Oedipal behaviors are now viewed as derivative of previous experiences and conflicts. Var., *Edipus*.

oestrus ➤ **estrus cycle**.

'off' cells Ganglion cells in the retina that respond to the termination of stimulation. ➤➤ **'on' cells**.

ogive Specifically, an elongated, ʃ-shaped curve which results from the transformation of a normal curve into cumulative proportions or frequencies. More generally, although not completely accurately, the term is sometimes used for any graph of a cumulative-frequency distribution with this approximate shape.

Ohm's (acoustic) law Due to the German physicist G. S. Ohm, a principle that says that a complex tone is analyzed *by the hearer* into its frequency components. Although this analysis, which Ohm likened to a Fourier analysis, is not normally part of our awareness, with training a hearer can learn to perceive individual harmonics in a complex sound. Note that Ohm's law is a theoretical statement about the perceiver and thus must be differentiated from a ➤ **Fourier analysis**, which is a theoretical statement about the physical stimulus. The word *acoustic* in the law, which was put in to distinguish it from Ohm's electrical law ($I = E/R$, where I = current in amperes, E = volts and R = resistance), was an unfortunate choice, for it confuses the issue. As has often been pointed out, it would have been better to have called it Ohm's *auditory* law.

-oid Suffix denoting *resemblance, similarity*.

oleic acid ➤ **fatty acid**.

olfactie Zwaardemaker's unit for measuring odor intensity. It is established as the number of centimeters exposed on a Zwaardemaker olfactometer when the threshold for that odor is reached.

olfaction 1. The sense of smell. 2. The act of smelling. The receptors for olfaction are found in the olfactory epithelium in the upper part of the nose; the stimuli for olfactory experience are chemical substances in gaseous forms that can dissolve in the mucus that coats the olfactory epithelium.

olfactometry Measurement of the capacity of a gaseous substance to produce an olfactory experience. Also called *odorimetry*.

olfactory Pertaining to the sense of smell or act of smelling.

olfactory brain ➤ **rhinencephalon**.

olfactory bulbs Two enlargements at the terminus of the olfactory nerve (Ist cranial). They lie at the base of the brain just above the nasal cavity.

olfactory epithelium Two patches of mucous membrane located at the top of the nasal passageways that contain the receptors for the sense of smell.

olfactory nerve The Ist ➤ **cranial nerve**. An afferent nerve carrying odor information from the receptors in the olfactory epithelium via the mitral cells, whose axons make up the olfactory bulbs and olfactory tracts, along to the cerebrum.

olig(o)- Combining term meaning *little* or *few*.

oligodendroglia ➤ **glia**.

oligoencephaly Lit., somewhat like Pooh-bear, 'of little brain.' Specifically, mental deficiency caused by abnormal brain development.

oligologia Lit., of few words. Specifically, characteristic of one with a small vocabulary. Obviously, an affliction uncommon among psychologists.

oligophrenia Generally, any mental deficiency.

olivary body (or **nucleus**) ➤ **inferior *olivary nucleus**.

olivary nucleus, inferior A rounded, olive-shaped mass of cells in the ventral part of the medulla oblongata that forms part of the reticular system. Also called *olivary body*.

olivary nucleus, superior A small nucleus of cells in the tegmental region of the pons.

-ology Suffix denoting *study of, knowledge of* or *science of*.

omega squared A measure of the strength of association between variables. It provides the proportion of the variance in the dependent variable that is associated with the variability in the dependent variable. It is somewhat more conservative than other measures of effect size such as r^2.

omission training An occasional synonym of *differential reinforcement of other behavior*; ➤ **schedules of *reinforcement**.

ommatidium Each of the separate elements of the compound eye of insects and crustaceans. The ommatidia of *Limulus* (the horseshoe crab) have served physiological psychologists well as a model system in which the operations of ➤ **lateral inhibition** have been studied.

omnibus test **1.** In *statistics*, any overall test of statistical significance among three or more groups such as the ➤ **F test**. When omnibus tests yield significance, planned comparisons (➤ **post hoc tests**) are run to specify the differences that exist among the groups. **2.** In **psychometrics**, any test that has several generalized subtests distributed throughout it designed to evaluate a number of related psychological factors. Most intelligence tests are omnibus tests.

omnipotence of thought In psychoanalytic theory, the belief that one's wishes, hopes or thoughts can affect external reality. Some theorists assume that it is a normal stage of childhood (➤ **magical thinking**), others regard it as a sign of alienation from and even denial of reality. Freud thought that it was a fundamental aspect of the development of animism, magic and religion.

onanism From the practice of the biblical character Onan, *coitus interruptus*. However, the term is often used to refer to sexual self-stimulation, masturbation.

'on' cells Ganglion cells in the retina that respond to the onset of stimulation. ➤ **'off' cells**.

onco- Combining form meaning *mass, tumor, swelling*.

oneiric Pertaining to dreams or dreaming.

oneiromancy The supposed prediction of the future by the interpretation of dreams. The term is only used in examinations of the paranormal, where it is assumed to be one aspect of precognition; it is not used for dream interpretation in psychoanalysis or other depth psychologies.

oneirophrenia A dreamlike state with some characteristics of simple schizophrenia but without the dissociation typical of that disorder.

one-tailed test ➤ two-tailed test.

one-trial learning ➤ learning, one-trial.

one-way screen (or **mirror**) Any device, commonly a mirror, that permits one to observe events on the other side without being seen.

'on–off cells' Ganglion cells in the retina that respond to both the onset and termination of stimulation. ➤➤ 'off' cells and 'on' cells.

onomatomania A disorder in which particular words acquire unnatural, deep significance and are obsessively thought about or repeated.

onomatopoeia The formation of a word by imitation of the thing named; e.g., *cuckoo* as the name of the bird that makes that call. All of the onomatopoetic ➤ theories of *language origins assume that such mimicking lies at the core of the genesis of human language.

onset 1. In medicine, the point at which a disorder first manifests itself. 2. In experimental psychology, the instant in time when a stimulus is presented. Actually, onset is determined by the point in time when the event is noticed, even though it may have been physically present prior to that time; e.g., the onset of a gradually increasing stimulus is when it is above threshold and the observer first notices it.

onto- Combining form meaning: 1 generally, *existence*; 2 specifically, *a living being*.

ontoanalytic model A label occasionally used for the existential approach; ➤ existentialism et seq. for details.

ontogeny (ontogenesis) From the roots of the word, the origin and, by extension, the development of an individual organism. By convention, *ontogeny* is used for the abstract and the general; *ontogenesis* for the particular. Compare with ➤ phylogeny and ➤ phylogenesis, which are used for the origin and development of species. ➤ development and developmental, which are generally preferred in discussions of child psychology.

ontology Generally, an aspect of metaphysical inquiry concerned with the question of existence apart from specific objects and events. Existence here can be taken broadly to cover cases such as the *ontological argument* concerning the existence of God, discussions about the conceptual reality of categories, e.g., numbers, trees, languages, etc. (➤ category and ➤ concept), or assumptions concerning the underlying conceptual systems of theories of mind.

onychophagia Excessive nail-biting.

oo- Combining form meaning *egg*.

opaque 1. Impenetrable by visible light, not transparent. 2. By extension, not open to conscious awareness.

open classroom 1. A class (room) made up of children of different ages and achievement levels. 2. A class (room) that the children and teachers can move freely in and out of.

open class (words) ➤ pivot grammar.

open-ended question Any question that an individual can answer freely as compared with a ➤ closed question that has to be answered by selecting one of several specific alternatives. Open-ended questions are often used in political polling, opinion sampling and clinical interviews since they permit a wide range of responses and are not limited by the set of preselected possible answers. They also have a liability in that it is difficult to score and analyze the responses so obtained.

open instinct ➤ **instinct, open**.

open study (or **trial**) A preliminary experimental study of a drug or a therapeutic technique in which the experimenter and the subjects know the purpose of the study, what factors are being examined, who is an experimental subject and who a control, etc. Generally used as a pilot study prior to running a fully controlled experiment. Compare with ➤ **double-blind**.

open system Any system that has flexibility and can be adjusted and modified. **1.** In biology, an open system is one which is characterized as not amenable to the standard thermodynamic laws about the conservation of energy, entropy, etc., but is 'open' to new inputs, growth and change. **2.** In the study of communication, a system is called 'open' if any arbitrary message can be expressed. In this sense, only human languages are truly open. ➤ **language** and **natural *language**.

operandum A term preferred by Skinnerians to ➤ **manipulandum**.

operant **1** n. Any behavior that is emitted by an organism and can be characterized in terms of its effects upon the environment. Note that the critical feature in this definition is the notion of the changes or effects that the response has on the environment; hence an operant is actually a *class* of responses all of which share the same effect. For example, a rat in a Skinner box may press the bar with any paw or even with its nose and all will be considered as instances of the same operant – a bar press. To be sure, this issue can be more finely represented so as to include various means for distinguishing between the finer overt aspects of such an operant. ➤ **topography** (2) for a discussion of these. Operants, unlike ➤ **respondents** (which are elicited by specific stimuli), occur without specific antecedent stimulus conditions. When an operant has been brought under the control of a discriminative stimulus, ➤ **operant conditioning** has occurred. **2** adj. Pertaining to or characterizing a response that displays these properties. Compare with ➤ **instrumental**.

operant aggression ➤ **instrumental *aggression**.

operant conditioning A type of ➤ **conditioning** in which an ➤ **operant** response is brought under stimulus control. The operation through which such conditioning occurs is the presentation of reinforcement contingent upon the organism's emitting the response. This 'operational' aspect is the critical one in distinguishing the operant conditioning procedure from the ➤ **classical conditioning** procedure, where the 'reinforcement' (the *US*) occurs whether or not the organism makes the response. Perhaps the easiest way to view operant conditioning is to regard it as a set of circumstances under which new responses that are within the organism's volitional repertoire come to be 'strengthened' by contingent reinforcement.

Often *operant conditioning* is used synonymously with *instrumental conditioning*, although there are subtle distinctions between these terms that need to be appreciated. ➤ **instrumental conditioning** for a discussion of these. Finally, note that the phrase operant conditioning itself is used for both the actual procedures as described above as well as for the kind of learning that occurs under such conditions. ➤➤ **Skinnerian**.

operant level **1.** The rate at which an ➤ **operant** is emitted prior to reinforcement. **2.** The response rate after experimental extinction has taken place.

operant reserve The number of operant responses emitted by an organism after the termination of reinforcement. It is used as a measure of resistance to extinction. Occasionally treated as a synonym of ➤ **reflex reserve** but see that entry for a distinction.

operant response ➤ **operant** (1).

operating characteristic **1.** Generally, a formal statement concerning the likelihood of observing specific effects under specified conditions. This notion appears in various, more circumscribed usages in psychology; to wit: **2.** In statistics, the likelihood of failing to reject the null hypothesis, given each statistically defined set of conditions for a particular test of significance. **3.** In the study of perception, ➤ **receiver operating characteristic (ROC) curve. 4.** In the study of memory, ➤ **memory operating characteristic (MOC) curve**.

operation Generally, a performing, a carrying out – or the act so performed or carried out. An operation may be *empirical* if it manipulates aspects of physical reality, *logical* or *mathematical* if it alters the relationships between symbols of a formal system like symbolic logic, or *cognitive* or *mental* if it modifies mental states, ideas, thoughts, images, etc. Note that these usages run the gamut from the objective and physical to the subjective and mental and various derived terms may reflect one or more of these connotative aspects. For example, ➤ **operationalism** stresses the overt, physical and objective whereas the many combined terms in Piagetian theory (e.g., ➤ **operatory thought**) deal with processes which are covert and subjective.

operational Generally, pertaining to an ➤ **operation**. However, that term has such a wide range of usages that many writers will use this adjectival form only when referring to the overt, objective components of action or to the formal aspects of symbolic systems. The variant *operatory* is then reserved for discussions of the subjective and/or cognitive operations, specifically within the confines of the Piagetian approach. These conventions, needless to say, are not followed by all.

operational definition ➤ **definitions**.

operationalism A point of view vigorously expounded (although not originated, as some suppose) by the physicist P. Bridgman. Essentially, it argues that the concepts of science be operationalized – that they be defined by, and their meaning limited to, the concrete operations used in their measurement. Operationalism was embraced in psychology by radical behaviorists and their theoretical and empirical terminology was derived largely through the use of *operational definitions*.

Thus, for example, the strength of a 'hunger drive' was defined as a specified number of hours of food deprivation, 'classical conditioning' was regarded as a given set of experimental procedures, etc. Even abstract concepts were operationalized: 'intelligence' became that which an intelligence test measured – leading to the implication that it would be defined differently according to the test in use.

Operationalism, however, was soon discovered to have many problems. While praising its objectivity one needs to recognize its limitations. In the final analysis, many of the critical terms and concepts of psychology carry a 'thingness' or a 'deep' meaning that is simply not captured by even the most thorough operational characterization; the meaning and causal role of 'hunger,' for example, is just not represented by the kinds of operational definition given above. Also called *operationism*.

operational research ➤ **operations research**.

operationism A variant of ➤ **operationalism**.

operations, cognitive 1. Generally, and loosely, the procedures of thought. **2.** Specifically within the Piagetian approach, the principles involved in ➤ **operatory thought** as evidenced by ➤ **concrete operations** and ➤ **formal operations**.

operations research A general term covering any approach to an analysis of a complex system to determine its overall mode of operation and maximize its effectiveness. The 'system' here may be an individual organism, a group of persons, an organization, a machine or any combination of these. Also called *operational research*.

operator 1. In mathematics and statistics, any symbol that denotes the operation to be performed on other symbols or numbers. **2.** Any individual or part or aspect thereof that carries out some action or process.

operatory Pertaining to an ➤ **operation**. This adjectival form is found primarily in the Piagetian approach to cognitive development; ➤ **operational** for discussion of usage patterns.

operatory stages In Piagetian theory, those stages of cognitive development characterized by ➤ **operatory thought**.

operatory thought Piaget's general label for the cognitive principles involved in ➤ **concrete operations** and ➤ **formal operations**. Note that Piagetians restrict the use of the term operatory to these two cognitive stages in which the child displays behavior that reveals thinking that is governed by a logical system. See and compare with ➤ **preoperatory thought**. Also called, on occasion, *operational thought*; see here the discussion under ➤ **operational** for a note on usage.

ophthalmic Pertaining to the eye. In this, and in all other terms using the *ophthal-*prefix, the *ph* is pronounced *f*. This is probably the most consistently mispronounced group of words in all of science and medicine. Compare with ➤ **ocular**; distinguish from ➤ **optic**.

ophthalmology A medical speciality concerned with treatment of the eye. Ophthalmologists hold the MD degree and their practice includes surgical and pharmaceutical treatment. Compare with ➤ **optometry**.

ophthalmometer A device for measuring corneal curvature.

ophthalmoscope An instrument that allows one to see the inside of the eye. Most important, it permits one to make a careful inspection of the retina without any surgical intervention.

-opia (-opy) Suffixes meaning *visual defect*.

opiate receptors Specific, post-synaptic receptors in various parts of the brain (anterior amygdala, central gray regions, hypothalamus) that take up drugs of the opiate group. The opiate receptors function ideally (and naturally) for the ➤ **endor-**phins but will also take up the other ➤ **opiates**, the natural as well as the synthetic.

opiates A class of drugs including: (a) the naturally occurring opiates, all of which are derived from the opium poppy; morphine is the drug of reference here, codeine the other commonly found alkaloid of opium; (b) the semi-synthetic opiates including heroin and various other preparations such as dihydromorphinone; (c) the synthetic opiates including methadone, meperidine and phenazocine, all of which are wholly synthetic compounds with a morphine-like pharmacological profile; (d) the narcotic antagonists which when used in conjunction with an opiate block its effects but when used alone have opiate-like properties (note, however, that *naloxone* is an important exception to this pattern, being an opiate antagonist but having no analgesic or narcotic properties by itself); and (e) the ➤ **endogenous opiates** that occur naturally and are found in various parts of the brain.

As a class the opiates all have both analgesic and narcotic effects; they also produce (often rapidly) both ➤ **drug *tolerance** and ➤ **drug *dependence**. var., *opioids*.

opinion Generally, a tentatively held and expressible point of view. The term is used with the connotations of an opinion as being intellectually held and based on at least some facts or data. These aspects help differentiate opinion from ➤ **belief**, where an emotional component is entailed, and from ➤ **attitude** (especially 4), which has a much broader range of semantic implication. To appreciate these distinctions note that we have opinion polls but not belief polls or attitude polls; beliefs and attitudes require more elaborate and intensive devices in order to be properly assessed.

opinion poll Any survey of opinions, most generally through the use of a simple questionnaire.

opinion, private One's internally held opinion on some issue. Depending on various factors, particularly the current ➤

public *opinion (1) on the issue, a person's private opinion may or may not differ significantly from his or her openly stated opinion – a fact that confounds much work in opinion polling.

opinion, public **1.** The general point of view expressed by a group or society, i.e. by the public. The term is used so that it reflects the modal position; there is no implication that the opinion is held universally. **2.** An individual's overtly stated opinion on some issue; compare here with ➤ **private *opinion**.

opioids ➤ **opiates**.

opium The substance obtained from the unripe pod of the opium poppy (*Papaver somniferum*). Pharmacologically, it has both narcotic and analgesic properties. adj., *opiate* or *opioid*. ➤ **opiates** for more details.

opo- Combining form meaning *derived from juice*.

opponent process Generally, a complex interacting mechanism in which the functioning of one aspect of the system simultaneously inhibits the functioning of the other and vice versa. An opponent-process system operates (roughly) like a balance beam: elevation of one arm depresses the other. This general notion has been incorporated into various theoretical models of psychological processes; e.g., ➤ **opponent-process theory of motivation** and ➤ **theories of *color vision**.

opponent-process theory of color vision ➤ **theories of *color vision**.

opponent-process theory of motivation A theory of motivation, due largely to Richard L. Solomon, which assumes that the functioning of an intact organism is predicated on the maintenance of a moderate position of 'motivational normality.' Any swing toward either pole on a motivational dimension produces an opponent process that operates to bring the system back into balance; terror and fear will produce a tendency toward joy and ecstasy and vice versa. An axiom of the theory is that excitation of one pole produces a simultaneous inhibition of the other; hence, if the conditions that produced the original state are removed there will be an 'overshift' to the opposite side of the balance point owing to the action of disinhibition.

opposites test A test in which the subject is required to respond to a stimulus word with its opposite.

oppositional defiant disorder A developmental disorder marked by defiant, hostile, and negativistic behavior, but without the serious antisocial characteristics observed in the ➤ **conduct disorders**. Such children are argumentative, lose their temper easily, and are resentful, angry, and easily annoyed. Typically these patterns of behavior are only displayed with adults the child knows (like parents), and hence may not be seen during clinical interviews.

oppressed group ➤ **minority group**.

opsin A protein that occurs in several forms, one of which is one of the metabolic products that occurs in the breakdown of ➤ **rhodopsin**; a form more properly called *rod opsin*.

optic Originally used to refer to the branch of physics known as *optics*. However, it is also freely used to refer to the eye and to vision and occurs in various combined forms that denote neurological structures, e.g., *optic nerve*, *optic tract*. var., *optical*.

optic agnosia ➤ **visual *agnosia**.

optical axis The line of vision as given by a straight line through the centers of curvature of the lens and the cornea.

optical defect Generally, any impairment of vision that is *optical* in the sense that the light rays are distorted by the eye's optical system (lens and cornea) prior to reaching the retina. E.g., ➤ **astigmatism**, **hyperopia**, **myopia**.

optical illusion Any ➤ **illusion** involving vision.

optical image ➤ **image** (1).

optical projection 1. The projection of an image by some optical method, e.g., a slide projector, a movie projector, etc. 2. The set of points in space that correspond with the image on the retina. That is, a mapping (or 'projection') of space such that objects are in those locations which would produce a particular retinal stimulus given the particular refraction patterns of the lens and the cornea of the eye.

optic ataxia ➤ **ataxia, optic**.

optic aphasia ➤ **aphasia, optic**.

optic chiasm The point at the base of the brain where the fibers from the two optic nerves join and diverge. Fibers from the nasal (or inside) areas of each retina cross over at the chiasm; fibers from the temporal (or outside) portions of each retina remain on their original side. Thus the functional distribution of fibers is such that should there be damage to, say, the left *optic nerve* (prior to the chiasm), it would produce blindness in the left eye; damage to the left *optic tract* (after the chiasm) would produce lack of visual functioning in the left half of each retina, which would yield blindness in the right half of the visual field. var., *optic chiasma*.

optic disc The area of the retina where all the nerve fibers collect and leave as a bundle (the ➤ **optic nerve**). This area is also known as the ➤ **blind spot**, in that since there are very few receptors it is insensitive to light stimulation. Also called the *optic papilla*; var., *optic disk*.

optician One who is skilled in grinding lenses and fitting glasses. Distinguish from ➤ **ophthalmologist** and ➤ **optometrist**.

optic nerve The IInd ➤ **cranial nerve**. Composed of two branches, each branch carries visual information from the ganglion cell layer of the retina of each eye to the ➤ **optic chiasm**, where the decussation (crossing over) of axons that carry information from the nasal halves of each retina produces two nerve tracts each carrying a representation of half of the visual field to the ➤ **lateral geniculate nuclei**. The portion from the optic chiasm to the lateral geniculate bodies is called the *optic tract*.

optic papilla ➤ **optic disc**.

optics A branch of physics concerned with the study of light and its relationship to vision.

optic tract That part of the visual pathway from the ➤ **optic chiasm** to the ➤ **lateral geniculate nuclei**.

optimality theory In evolutionary theory the generalization that the traits that evolve will be those that are optimal in the sense that their benefits exceed their costs by a greater amount than all other alternatives. The theory has been applied primarily to analysis of behaviors like food-gathering and mating, where there are reasonably precise quantitative measures (e.g., calories gained or lost or number of fertilizations per opportunity).

optimum That value of the range of values available that produces the maximum gain for the purpose under consideration. adj., *optimum, optimal*; vb., *optimize*.

optional-stopping fallacy The unplanned stopping of an experiment at a point other than after the full set of trials that properly should have been run. It occurs in two forms: (a) stopping the experiment when it looks like one's hypothesis is being supported; and (b) continuing to collect data past the point originally planned because it appears that one's hypothesis has not (yet) been supported. Either procedure leads to the drawing of fallacious conclusions.

opto- Prefix denoting *vision* or, on occasion, the *eye*.

optogram The image on the retina of an external object: it results from the bleaching of the photopigments in the receptor cells.

optokinetic Pertaining to eye movements.

optokinetic nystagmus ➤ **nystagmus, optokinetic**.

optometrist One trained in ➤ **optometry**. Distinguish from ➤ **ophthalmologist** and ➤ **optician**.

optometry 1. The actual measurement of the refractive power of the visual apparatus. 2. A label for the profession of correcting vision by exercises and the fitting of corrective lenses. Distinguish from ➤ **ophthalmology**.

opy- ➤ **opia**.

oral Pertaining to either 1. the mouth, or 2. its primary product, speech. Most psychological terms embodying the former meaning are psychoanalytic and/or anatomical; most using the latter are concerned with language and speech and psycholinguistics. It is used mainly in conjunction with another word or phrase, as revealed in the following entries. Distinguish from ➤ **aural**.

oral-aggressive In psychoanalytic theory, a pattern of aggressive behaviors in the adult which results, at least theoretically, from sublimation of the late oral stage. Behaviors assumed representative are ambition, envy, a pronounced tendency to exploit others and aggressiveness in personal interactions.

oral cavity The cavity extending from the pharynx to the lips.

oral character In psychoanalytic theory: 1. A personality characteristic displayed by persons with fixations at the ➤ **oral stage** of development. 2. A personality type characterized by excessive derivation of satisfaction from oral eroticism. In the classic theory such personalities are assumed to be manifested through a tendency to be either (a) optimistic, dependent, generous and elated, or (b) pessimistic, depressed and aggressive. The former cluster of traits is assumed to result from abundant and pleasurable early oral experience, the latter from restrictive and harsh early oral experience.

oral dependence In psychoanalysis, the desire to return to the earliest stages of oral development. This desire is presumed to be representative of the seeking of the sense of security and safety that this stage was characterized by. In theory, the specific focus is the comfort of being held to the mother's breast and of suckling.

oral drive Broadly, any drive focused on oral satisfaction, most specifically those drives associated with suckling and chewing.

oral dynamism Loosely, the interplay of psychic factors associated with oral characteristics.

oral eroticism Any tendency to obtain pleasure from oral activity. In psychoanalytic theory, oral eroticism normally characterizes the ➤ **oral stage** of development. When adults display excessive orality it is taken, within the theoretical framework, as evidence of regression to, or fixation at, this stage. Such behaviors as excessive smoking, talking, chewing, etc. are considered to be symptomatic. var., *oral erotism*.

oral-incorporative 1. Generally, in the young child, characterizing the tendency to put nearly everything into the mouth. 2. In psychoanalytic theory the term has the same behavioral reference, but it carries the connotation that this tendency is reflective of the desire on the part of the child to 'incorporate' the mother, particularly through the nipple, into itself. Some analysts argue for a distinct *oral-incorporative stage* of development, others maintain that it should merely be viewed as an aspect of the ➤ **oral stage**. The classical theory hypothesizes that possessiveness, greed, miserliness and the like are behaviors rooted in this tendency.

orality Pertaining to: 1. Specifically, ➤ **oral eroticism**. 2. More generally, any oral component emerging in a psychoneurosis or other disorder.

oral libido stage ➤ **oral stage**.

oral method A method of teaching language to the deaf through lip-reading and the shaping of speech. ➤ **manual method** for a comparison and further discussion.

oral neurosis A term used by some

psychoanalysts for various speech impediments such as stammering or stuttering, on the assumption that they result from disorders of the oral libido. There isn't much evidence on this point and, frankly, it is far from clear as to what would constitute evidence anyway. ➤ **speech disorders**.

oral-passive ➤ **receptive character**.

oral personality ➤ **oral character**.

oral primacy In psychoanalytic theory, the concentration of libido upon the mouth, evidenced by using the tongue and lips to explore things and by deriving pleasure from sucking, biting and chewing. In infancy it is regarded as normal, in adults abnormal.

oral reading Moving the lips while reading 'silently.' Everyone does it to some extent, particularly when first exposed to difficult material, as it helps in coding and understanding. If it persists when reading comic books, it is usually considered a problem if for no other reason than it limits reading speed.

oral regression A tendency to return to the ➤ **oral stage**.

oral sadism In psychoanalysis, the desire to inflict pain through oral means. Generally, biting is considered the prime behavior, although some analysts include verbal attack as symptomatic.

oral stage The first and most primitive of the psychosexual stages of development hypothesized by classical psychoanalytic theory. During this stage the mouth is the focus of the libido and satisfaction is obtained through sucking, biting, chewing, etc. In some analytical frameworks the stage is subdivided into an *early* component characterized by passivity and a *late* component characterized by activity, particularly aggressive activity. Also called *oral libido stage*.

oral test Loosely, any test in which the materials are presented and responded to orally.

oral triad A rather specialized psychoanalytic term used for three, theoretically coordinated, desires to be suckled by, sleep with and be devoured by the breast.

ora terminalis The very edge of the retina.

Orbison figures The figure on the left is actually a perfect square, the one on the right a circle.

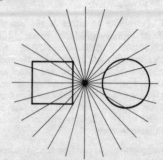

orbital Pertaining to any orbit but most frequently used in reference to the bony cavity in which the eye is set.

orchiectomy Surgical removal of a testicle. ➤ **castration**. var., *orchectomy*.

orchi(o)- Combining form meaning *testicle*.

order Most of the meanings of this word in psychology derive from standard dictionary definitions. A few, however, rate explication: **1.** Any arrangement of facts, data, events, etc. in time (*temporal order*) or space (*spatial order*) or both (*spatiotemporal order*). **2.** Any position in an ordered series of events. **3.** A category in the phylogenetic classification system just above *family* and below *class*. The first two uses, here, have a verb form so that the phrase *to order* means to arrange facts, events, data etc. in a particular fashion. See the following entries for some special forms. Note, *ordering* is a common synonym for 1 and 2.

order, cyclic An ordering of items that displays a regular cycle, e.g., 112233112233 . . .

order effects Effects that are attributed to the order in which treatments are presented in an experiment. Order effects can confound an experiment and typically ➤ **counterbalancing** procedures are employed as a control.

order, linear An order in which all items are presented as though they were on a line, e.g., 1st, 2nd, 3rd, 4th. Note that only order is implied here, not magnitude of the interval. Thus, the 3rd score is not necessarily that much larger than the 2nd than the 2nd is larger than the 1st., ➤ **ordinal *scale**.

order of magnitude 1. An ordering of data or events from the lowest to the highest. This use of the term is essentially synonymous with ➤ **linear *order**. **2.** A tenfold increase.

order statistics Statistical tests which can be carried out on data that only reflect ➤ **ordinal *scale** properties. All order statistics are ➤ **nonparametric statistics**, although the reverse is not true.

ordinal (position) A somewhat redundant phrase (in that *ordinal* is a close synonym of *positional*) used to refer to ranked location in an ordered array, i.e. 1st, 2nd, etc.

ordinal scale ➤ **scale, ordinal**.

ordinate The vertical coordinate of a point in a plane Cartesian coordinate system. Commonly, although strictly speaking not correctly, the y-axis is called by this name. In standard notation, values of the *dependent *variable* plotted on the ordinate. ➤➤ **axis**; **Cartesian coordinates**.

orectic Pertaining to the appetitive and affective aspects of behavior. In psychoanalytic writings, the orectic is often contrasted with the cognitive. var., *orexic*; n., *orexis*.

organ Generally, any structural part of an organism that has a specific function (or functions) to perform. Note that the adjectival form ➤ **organic** has several addi-

tional meanings other than, simply, pertaining to an organ.

organelle A specialized part of a cell that performs a specific function.

organ eroticism In psychoanalytic theory, the experiencing of eroticism associated with a particular organ. Also called *organ libido*; var., *organ erotism*.

organic 1. Pertaining to an organ. **2.** Essential or vital. **3.** Pertaining to the intrinsic organization of a thing, to its existence as a synthesis of elemental parts. **4.** Pertaining to that which is somatic as opposed to that which is mental. In this last sense, organic is contrasted with ➤ **functional**. **5.** Occasionally, pertaining to an organism; ➤ **organismic** is preferred here.

organic affective syndrome ➤ **affective syndrome, organic**.

organic anxiety Anxiety resulting from known organic dysfunction. The term may refer to normal apprehension resulting from the awareness of the very real consequences of a serious disease or to a neurotic overanxious reaction to a disability. ➤ **anginaphobia** for an example of the latter.

organic anxiety syndrome An ➤ **organic mental syndrome** characterized by prominent, recurrent panic attacks or generalized anxiety caused by some specific organic factor such as an endocrine disorder or the abuse of psychoactive substances.

organic brain syndrome ➤ **organic mental syndrome**.

organic delusional syndrome ➤ **delusional syndrome, organic**.

organic disorder Loosely, any disorder that is caused by a known organic condition. Contrast with ➤ **functional disorder** and, for more details, ➤ **organic mental syndrome** and ➤ **organic mental disorder**.

organic hallucinosis ➤ **hallucinosis**.

organicism A sociological theory, first expressed by Herbert Spencer, that treats society as an analog to an organic, biological system. This 'organic' model draws the parallel between units and elements of society and the biological organ. Sometimes called *social organism model*.

organic mental disorder An umbrella term in contemporary psychiatry for a large number of disorders all of which are associated with some organic (brain) dysfunction, either transitory or permanent, and in which the etiology of the disorder is either known or can be presumed on the basis of other facts and data. It is this factor regarding etiology that distinguishes usage of this term from ➤ **organic mental syndrome**. Note, however, that the diagnosis of an organic mental disorder is predicated on an initial diagnosis of an organic mental syndrome; hence a general diagnosis such as *dementia* is regarded as an organic mental syndrome, while specific forms (e.g., *primary degenerative dementia*) are classified as organic mental disorders. Recognize, also, that in contemporary clinical psychology and psychiatry most researchers and practitioners operate on the presumption, taken as an article of faith rather than on any definitive evidence, that ultimately all serious disorders (or psychoses) will be shown to be organic in origin. The existence, therefore, of distinct classes of organic disorders does not necessarily imply that nonorganic (i.e. functional) disorders are independent of brain processes. Rather, the nonorganic diagnoses tend to be used when either of two criteria pertain: (a) social/behavioral factors provide a cogent characterization of the disorder (e.g., *adjustment disorder*), or (b) the presence of a specific organic factor, although suspected, has not been established (e.g., the *schizophrenias*).

organic mental syndrome A cover term for a number of disorders including ➤ **amnestic syndrome**, ➤ **delirium**, ➤ **dementia**, ➤ **organic *delusional syndrome**, ➤ **organic mood syndrome**, and ➤ **organic *personality syndrome**. Each of these disorders is characterized by particular symptoms, but, unlike the ➤ **organic mental disorders**, no reference is made to the etiology of the disorder. Also called *organic brain syndrome*.

organic mood syndrome An ➤ **organic mental syndrome** characterized by a prominent and persistent depressed, elevated or expansive mood resembling the kinds of moods seen in a ➤ **manic episode** or ➤ **major *depressive episode**. The term is only used when there are toxic or metabolic factors in the etiology.

organic organization ➤ **organization, organic**.

organic personality syndrome ➤ **personality syndrome, organic**.

organic psychosis Loosely, any severe mental disorder due to either known or strongly suspected brain pathologies. For more on contemporary terminology, ➤ **organic mental disorder** and ➤ **organic mental syndrome**.

organic repression ➤ **repression, organic**.

organic sensations A term now largely abandoned for the more appropriate ➤ **visceral sensations**.

organic variable In post-Watsonian behaviorism, any internal process or state that was assumed to play a role in determining the response observed. In the initial behaviorist conceptualization, all behaviors were viewed simply as S–R processes; that is, the stimulus (S) was regarded as the sole causal agent of the response (R) once conditioning was complete. More sober minds soon recognized that there was a need for 'organic' variables within the behaving organism upon which the stimuli impinged and which played a role in the production of the observed behavior, i.e. S–O–R processes. Although the term itself is rare today, the argument that covert, internal factors play an integral part in the causal chain leading to the overt behaviors one observes is essentially universally accepted. abbrev., *O variable*. ➤➤ **organismic variable** (a descriptively more accurate term) and ➤➤ **intervening *variable**.

organ inferiority As proposed by Adler,

the notion that deficiencies in organ function (real or imagined) can produce a sense of inferiority.

organism Loosely, any living thing be it plant or animal, bacterium or virus. This sort of definition is only moderately satisfying for it is little more than a list of those entities generally regarded as being organisms. Ideally, we should have a clear definition of what is meant by *living*, and thus dispense with our list – and also eliminate arguments over just what things deserved to be listed; not all would put viruses on it. The difficulty, however, is that the attempts to deal with defining ➤ **life** are themselves lists; e.g., a living thing is that which carries out some (or all) of the basic physiological functions of ingestion, excretion, reproduction, locomotion, etc. As there is currently no agreed-upon criterial set of features for determination of that which is living, there is no rigorous definition of that which qualifies as an organism. Generally speaking, the term is used in psychology to refer to an animal, particularly one used in an experiment or other scientific study. It served as a useful term for many behaviorists who, while working primarily with rats, pigeons and the like, preferred to phrase their results and conclusions so as to connote that their findings generalized to all living things. It is certainly no surprise that one of the seminal works in this tradition was B. F. Skinner's 1938 work, *Behavior of Organisms*.

organismic In simplest terms, pertaining to an organism. However, this straightforward use is rare. More often, the term is used to refer to any of several theoretical approaches that emphasize the need to view a behaving organism as a biological entity, one which must be approached as the coordinated functioning of a multitude of interrelated processes. Organismic approaches are uniformly *monistic*, rejecting mind–body dualism, and tend to focus on larger, more molar analyses to the relative neglect of reductionistic analyses. They may derive from a surprisingly wide range of stances; J. R. Kantor's is clearly behavioristic, K. Lewin's historically derivative of the Gestalt school and K. Goldstein's represented a biological/functionalist point of view, yet all are called organismic psychologies.

organismic determinant ➤ **determinant**.

organismic psychology ➤ **organismic**.

organismic variable Lit., a variable inside an organism; a process or operation that occurs internally but is hypothesized to play a causal role in determining overt responding. ➤➤ **organic variable**.

organization 1. A characteristic of any complex system that reflects the degree to which its several, structurally distinguishable parts are functionally coordinated and interrelated. 2. The process that operates so as to bring about such a coordinated system. 3. The system itself as it displays such properties.

This term, particularly in sense 3, represents a very powerful concept in the social (and, for that matter, the physical) sciences. In all cases the central connotation is one of *structure*; diverse parts or elements are coordinated to form an integrated, coherent and systematic whole. This notion of an organization is represented in such areas as: (a) ➤ **Gestalt psychology**, where it refers to the processes whereby a perceptual ➤ **Gestalt** is formed (➤➤ **Gestalt laws of organization**); (b) cognitive theory, where it serves as a vehicle for expressing the notion that thought is more than a simple linear arrangement of primitive processes (➤ **cognitive *organization**); (c) social psychology, where it refers to a ➤ **group** (2) as a structured collection of individuals; see here ➤ **social *organization**; and (d) ➤ **industrial/organizational psychology**, where the reference is to a complex social system made up of individuals, their facilities and the products yielded. In this last sense, which is admittedly very general, a small corner store qualifies as an (albeit relatively simple) organization as does a multinational corporation, a political party or a university. Because of the great latitude of reference here, several criteria are usually

521

applied so as to limit the meaning. To wit: there must be coordination of effort of the personnel, they must have some set of common goals or purposes, there has to be some division of labor within the larger structure and also some degree of integrated functioning, including a hierarchy of authority. vb., *organize*; adj., *organized, organization*. See the following entries for a number of other specialized usages of the basic term.

organizational dynamics A term used to refer collectively to the various patterns of shifting (i.e. dynamic) elements within an ➤ **organization** (3(d)). It is used commonly within a framework put forward by J. P. Kotter, in which seven conceptual elements are viewed in interrelated fashion: organizational processes; external environment; employees; formal structure; the internal social system; technology; and coalitions within the organization.

organizational psychology ➤ **industrial/ organizational psychology**.

organization, cognitive An extension of the connotations of the Gestalt ➤ **principle of *organization** from the study of perception (where it was first introduced) to the subject-matter of cognitive psychology in general. The essential notion remains the same, that it is the coherent, structured whole that dominates what one perceives or knows; however, the force of the qualifier *cognitive* is to drive the meaning of the term organization beyond the perceptual issues and to apply it to the cognitive domain in all manifestations. To wit: the meaning of a sentence is determined by the whole and not by a summation of the meanings of its several words; the meaning of a position in a chess game is given by the entire configuration and not by the individual pieces in isolation; the knowledge that a researcher or practitioner of psychology has of the field is derived from the coordination of many diverse facts, principles and experiences and is not simply a compendium of, say, the terms used in the discipline.

organization, formal A term occasionally

used of an ➤ **organization** (in senses 3(c) and 3(d)) to differentiate it from an ➤ **informal *organization**.

organization, informal A term used to cover the set of integrated and coordinated activities that the individuals in a group have with each other. The adjective *informal* is used to differentiate these patterns of behavior, which are often spontaneous and function without well-articulated rules or blueprints for interaction, from the more *formal* patterns entailed by the simple term ➤ **organization** (especially in senses 3(c) and 3(d)).

organization, mechanistic An ➤ **organization** (3(d)) characterized by a rigid overall structure with clearly defined roles for its members and a clearly specified hierarchy of authority. Mechanistic organizations are relatively easy to establish, but have the disadvantage that they do not respond well to change. Compare with ➤ **organic *organization**.

organization, organic An ➤ **organization** (3(d)) characterized by a loose overall structure without a clear hierarchy of authority and underdefined tasks and responsibilities for its members. In such organizations the individuals involved set up the structure in a kind of 'organic' fashion. Organic organizations are difficult to establish, but once set up have the advantage of responding well to change. Compare with ➤ **mechanistic *organization**.

organization, principle of As proposed by the Gestalt psychologists, the principle that the separate elements of a ➤ **Gestalt** are not all equally important in determining what is perceived. Rather, it is the integration or organized whole that is deemed critical. According to W. Köhler, who championed this view, this structuring of the stimulus information is assumed to occur without consciousness. For an extension of this basic idea, ➤ **cognitive *organization**.

organization, social 1. The (relatively) stable set of behavioral patterns of individuals and groups within a society, particularly as they are representative of the ➤ **social norms**, ➤ **rules** (3) and ➤ **roles** of the society. **2.** Loosely, a formally established social group; ➤ **organization** (especially 3(c) and 3(d)).

organized play   ➤ **play, organized**.

organ libido   ➤ **organ eroticism**.

organ neurosis A term from classical psychoanalysis which has been largely replaced by ➤ **psychosomatic disorder**.

organ of Corti The complex structure in the cochlea of the inner ear including the basilar membrane, the hair cells which are attached to it and the tectorial membrane to which they in turn attach. Vibrations produce deflections of the basilar membrane relative to the more rigid tectorial membrane, which stretches the cilia of the hair cells resulting in the receptor potential. The structure is named after the Italian anatomist Alfonso Corti.

orgasm A complex sequence of processes occurring at the climax of sexual activity involving involuntary movements of the genital organs, voluntary movements of related muscle groups and neurophysiological responses keyed by spinal action that result in strong pleasurable sexual feelings culminating in an abrupt sense of relief of tension and, in the male, the ejaculation of semen. adj., *orgasmic, orgastic*.

orgasm disorders A category of ➤ **sexual disorders** marked by persistent or recurrent delay in, or absence of, orgasm following a normal phase of sexual excitement. The term is only used when there is no evidence of another condition that can interfere with sexual functioning, such as depression or drug use. It should not be applied unless there is evidence that the condition causes marked distress or interpersonal difficulty. There are many individuals with little or no orgasmic function who are quite content in that state, and applying the term to them is inappropriate. The term is gender neutral. A variety of other terms has been used over the years for these disorders, including *female*

(or *male*) *orgasmic disorder*, *inhibited* (*female* or *male*) *orgasm*, *orgasmic* (or *orgastic*) *dysfunction* (for females), and *orgasmic impotence* (for males).

orgasmic dysfunction   ➤ **orgasm disorders**.

orgasmic impotence   ➤ **orgasm disorders**.

orgastic dysfunction/impotence   ➤ **orgasm disorders**.

orgone theory A theory due to Wilhelm Reich, a creative and innovative thinker who, in his search for truth, pushed his basically psychoanalytic system into what became, alas, utterly ludicrous and totally dismissible forms. Essentially, it is a theory of being, based on the hypothesization of a specific form of energy (orgone energy) which was assumed to fill all space and account for all life. Such a concept invites all manner of metaphysical problems; not the least is the problem of identifying the orgone, for in order to demonstrate the existence of something one must be able to ascertain where it is not, so as to know where it is. Put simply, if something is uniformly everywhere it might as well be nowhere. Recognition of this problem led Reich to build his 'orgone accumulator,' a device which ultimately led to serious legal problems with the US Food and Drug Administration. ➤➤ **orgonomy**.

orgone therapy   ➤ **orgonomy**.

orgonomy The term generally used for the personality theory and accompanying therapeutic practices developed by Wilhelm Reich. The central theoretical concept is the hypothesized universal energy form, orgone (➤ **orgone theory**), and the therapy (*orgone therapy*) is based on a rather elaborate program of massage, manipulations, probing, prodding and directing the client toward the ultimate orgastic release that Reich conceived of as the prime evidence of therapeutic breakthrough. ➤➤ **biofunctional therapy**.

orientation In Middle English *orient* acquired the meaning, *the East* or *the sunrise*. Hence, the noun: **1.** Turning or focusing. Used in this sense in ethology specifically with regard to adjustment of the body or parts of the body with respect to specific stimulation. See here ➤ **taxis** and ➤ **tropism**. **2.** The specific position of a body or part thereof. Here one sees references, e.g., to the orientation of a cell or of a limb. **3.** Knowledge, awareness of one's location and position. Used in this sense either literally concerning physical space and time or, by extension, with regard to one's figurative place in terms of the social, interpersonal, and conceptual framework. **4.** A cognitive ➤ **set** (2), a conceptual point of view that yields a characteristic disposition to react to events. **5.** A particular 'world view,' a very general perspective on life, science, philosophy, etc. Meaning 5 is distinguished from 4 only in degree of generality. **6.** A program of instruction designed to assist one to orient oneself in any of the above senses. This meaning is, however, typically expressed in a more restrictive fashion and applied to achieving an orientation of types 3, 4 or 5 with a view to some occupation or some task. Indeed, many jobs and occupations have an *orientation program* associated with them for newcomers. vb., *orient*; adjs., *oriented* (the preferred form), *orientated*.

orienting reflex ➤ **orienting response**.

orienting response **1.** Most generally, any turning of the body with reference to the position of a specific stimulus. In this sense, the term is essentially synonymous with ➤ **tropism**. **2.** In Pavlovian terms, any attentional response made to a stimulus, e.g., head turning, ear raising. **3.** Any response of an organism that functions to bring it into a position whereby it is optimally exposed to stimulation. This meaning is an extension of 2 which connotes a rather reflex-like quality (and indeed, *orienting reflex* is often used for meaning 2) and applies the concept to a more 'directed' kind of behavior.

ortho- Combining form from the Greek, literally meaning *straight* and, by extension, *correct, normal, proper*.

orthogenesis Lit., straight from the begin-

ning; hence, a label used for any of several doctrines predicated on the notion of development as set at the beginning such that it will proceed in a particular fashion controlled by internal forces unless catastrophically disrupted by outside forces. It has been proposed at various times as a theory of evolution, as a model of ontogeny and as a theory of social and cultural development. adj., *orthogenic*.

orthogenital Relating to patterns of sexual behavior that are regarded as 'normal' or 'proper.' While it seems fairly clear that heterosexual coitus is orthogenital it is far from obvious which sexual practices lie outside the domain of the term. ➤ **paraphilia**.

orthognathy An anatomical situation in which the jaw does not project far beyond the cranium; i.e. the jaw and the cranium lie approximately along the same vertical plane. The term is used in evolutionary biology as descriptive of particular species and in anthropometry as a measure of an individual's facial-profile angle. Contrast with ➤ **prognathy**.

orthogonal At right angles. By extension, characteristic of any set of variables in an experiment that are independent of each other. This meaning derives from the concept that underlies the compound term; ➤ **orthogonal solution**.

orthogonal rotation ➤ **rotation** (2).

orthogonal solution In factor analysis, a solution in which the axes that represent the underlying factors are situated so that they are at right angles to each other. In such a solution, the factors are uncorrelated. Compare with ➤ **oblique solution**.

orthogonal trait In a factor-analysis matrix, any trait that is independent of, and hence shows a zero correlation with, all others.

orthography A generic term used to cover any writing system. For details on various types ➤ **alphabet, logography, semasiography, syllabary**.

orthomolecular psychiatry An approach

to psychiatric therapy that focuses on the attainment of appropriate balances and concentrations of normal bodily substances. This approach has as its basic assumption the notion that abnormal behaviors are the result of biochemical imbalances or, as it is commonly phrased, 'for every twisted mind there must be twisted molecule.'

orthomolecular therapy A general label for any of a number of therapeutic procedures based on the administration of large doses of various substances. ➤ **Orthomolecular psychiatry** is often specified as providing the foundation in principle for this approach to therapy, although many practitioners go far beyond the scope of the scientific basis of that discipline – as, for example, in the use of massive doses of vitamins (popularly called *megavitamin therapy*) for all manner of disorders.

orthopsychiatry A discipline dealing primarily with the prevention and early treatment of mental and emotional disorders. Although the term *psychiatry* is in the name of the field, in practice the discipline extends beyond psychiatric medicine and involves clinical psychology, pediatrics, social work, education, etc.

os 1. Mouth or opening. pl., *ora*. **2.** Bone. pl., *ossa*.

oscillation By and large, the standard dictionary definition of 'a fluctuation between states' will do quite well; all uses in psychology carry this basic notion of a swinging back and forth. Note, however, that often, particularly in usages that derive from physics, the implication is that the oscillation is regular, like a sine wave. This sense is not always carried over into psychological usage where the notion frequently is that the oscillation is irregular and variable; e.g., ➤ **behavioral oscillation**. abbrev., *O*.

oscillometer Any device for measuring oscillations.

oscilloscope An electronic device for recording and displaying in a visual form the wave form of changing electrical cur-

rent, voltage or any other quantity that can be represented as electrical change. The most common form is based on a cathode-ray tube, similar in principle to a television picture tube. Their most common research uses are in psychophysics for inspecting and calibrating the stimuli and in physiological psychology for recording and visualizing neural impulses.

-osis ➤ **-iasis**.

osm(o)- Combining form: **1.** From the Greek *osme*, pertaining to *smell* or *odor*. **2.** From the Greek *osmos*, characterizing an *impulse*, a *thrusting forth*. **3.** By extension of 2, pertaining to ➤ **osmosis**.

osmometric thirst ➤ **thirst, osmometric**.

osmoreceptor The inferred receptors that respond to changes in osmotic pressure in cells and, hence, serve as the mediators of ➤ **osmometric *thirst**. The available evidence suggests that they are located in the nucleus circularis of the hypothalamus and function by regulating the secretion of antidiuretic hormone.

osmosis The diffusion of a solvent through a semi-permeable membrane on either side of which are solutions of different concentrations. The solvent passes through from the side of the lower concentration to the side of the higher and tends to equalize the concentrations.

osphresiolagnia Erotic experience produced by an odor.

osphresis ➤ **olfaction**, the sense of smell.

ossicle Any small bone.

ossicles, auditory The set of three small bones (the *malleus* or 'hammer,' the *incus* or 'anvil' and the *stapes* or 'stirrup') in the middle ear which transmit the vibrations of the ear-drum to the cochlea.

ossify Lit., to become bone-like; figuratively, to harden, to become inflexible.

O technique ➤ **R correlation**.

Othello syndrome A serious, morbid

jealousy accompanied by delusions that one's spouse is unfaithful.

other behavior A term used primarily in the operant-conditioning literature to refer to any behavior other than that which is specifically being reinforced or punished.

other-directed ➤ **outer-directed**.

other, the **1.** Most generally, everyone and everything but oneself. In essence this meaning encompasses the entire matrix of events, stimuli, persons, etc. that make up the psychological environment. **2.** More specifically, another person not oneself. **3.** Most specifically, G. H. Mead's term, used in the plural to refer collectively to the ➤ **significant others** in one's life.

otic Pertaining to the ear or, more specifically, to the receptor cells in the inner ear.

otitis Inflammation of the ear; usually marked as *externa, media* or *interna* depending on the location of the inflammation.

ot(o)- Combining form·meaning *the ear*.

otogenic tone A tone produced by the mechanisms within the ear and not objec-tively present in the environment. E.g., ➤ **combination tone**.

otolaryngology A medical specialization dealing with the ear (otology), nose (rhinology) and the throat (laryngology).

otoliths Tiny calcium crystals suspended in the endolymph of the labyrinth of the inner ear. Movements of the head set the endolymph in motion and the otoliths stimulate the receptor cells, thus providing feedback information that assists in the maintenance of body balance.

otology The science concerned with the ear, its anatomy, physiology and pathology.

otosclerosis A condition characterized by chronic, progressive of loss of hearing caused by a buildup of bone around the oval window with attendant immobility of the stapes.

outbreeding The tendency to mate with individuals who are not closely related genetically; the opposite of ➤ **inbreeding**. The limits on outbreeding are usually established at the species boundary in that matings further removed typically do not produce viable and fertile offspring. ➤➤ **inbreeding avoidance**.

outcome Very generally: **1.** Any change in the environment that occurs as a result of an organism's behavior. **2.** Any change in an organism as a result of events in the environment.

outer-directed Within the sociological framework of D. Riesman, a tendency to conform to societal values and to be overly sensitized to the expectations and preferences of others. According to Riesman, modern urban societies foster such outer-directedness. The term is used both for the person who displays these characteristics and for the society itself. Also known as *other-directed*. ➤➤ **inner-directed** and **tradition-directed**.

out-group Quite simply, a group comprised of any and all persons not in one's ➤ **in-group**. Also occasionally called *they-group*.

out-group homogeneity bias The tendency of members of one group to assume that there is greater similarity among the members of out-groups than there actually is.

outlet Loosely, any activity that serves to relieve a state of tension, reduce a drive, satisfy a need, etc.

outlier Any subject or data point that has an extreme value on some variable. Outliers may represent anomalous data points (e.g., a subject who didn't sleep the night before an experiment, a trial during which the subject sneezed) and can distort one's interpretation of the data. Statistical procedures exist that correct for the effects of outliers.

outpatient Any nonhospitalized patient who regularly visits a hospital or clinic for treatment.

outpatient clinic ➤ **clinic, outpatient**.

output 1. Generally and literally, that which is 'put out,' any response from an organism or any product of a system. 2. In information theory, the signal emitted.

ova Plural of ➤ **ovum**.

oval window The membrane in the wall of the cochlea to which the stapes is attached. It is through the vibration of this membrane that sound waves are carried to the inner ear.

ovarian Pertaining to the ➤ **ovary**.

ovarian follicle ➤ **menstrual cycle**.

ovariectomy Surgical removal of the ovaries. var., *ovariotomy*.

ovary One of a pair of the primary reproductive organs in the female. The ovaries are glandular organs connected via the Fallopian tubes to the uterus. Ovaries produce the ova (pl. of ovum) and the estrogens.

over- A common prefix meaning *excessive, more than what is required*. In psychoanalytic writing, it often carries the implication of a pathological condition of sheer excess.

overachiever One whose actual performance on a task or in a situation (e.g., school) is higher than one would have predicted. The word *predicted* is often used rather loosely here; strictly speaking there should be valid test scores from which to make the predictions, otherwise labels like *overachiever* and *underachiever* (its opposite) lack real meaning.

There is a curious aspect of these labels: *over*achiever has a vaguely insulting connotation whereas *under*achiever carries a kind of subtle praise. It is as if we hold higher what we believe people are capable of doing than what they actually do. Or, then again, maybe it is that we think that our tests of intelligence and aptitude are better than they actually are.

overanxious disorder An anxiety disorder of childhood characterized by excessive and inappropriate anxiety and fearfulness that is not focused on or associated with a specific situation or object and not due to a particular psychosocial stressor. Children with the disorder display an inordinate concern about future events, are overly concerned about their own performance (scholastic, social, athletic) and often have a variety of psychosomatic complaints.

overcompensation A term used with somewhat less precision than the root word, ➤ **compensation**. The basic idea is that the *over*compensatory behavior is that which is more than is really required to make up for or offset some liability. Part of the confusion with the term comes from the fact that some writers use it with a distinctly positive connotation (implying that through extraordinary effort a person has achieved great heights in spite of, or perhaps because of, initial deficiencies) while others use it to connote a kind of negative overreaction (implying that the individual is somehow engaging in pathological and harmful excesses).

overcrowding ➤ **crowding**.

overdetermined Generally, having many causes. The term is often used in psychoanalysis where a dream, an act, an emotion, etc. will be considered to be overdetermined if it can be seen that it has resulted from the expression of more than one drive, conflict or other unconscious determiner. It was axiomatic in Freud's thinking that all human behavior was motivationally overdetermined and that, in analysis, one always had to search beyond the first unconscious causes.

overeating ➤ **hyperphagia**.

overexclusion A perceptual/cognitive deficit characterized by a tendency to exclude, rather rigidly, alternative responses or choices. The term tends to be used for genuine deficits and not for simple ➤ **undergeneralization**.

overexpectation In animal conditioning, a learning situation where two conditioned stimuli are conditioned separately and then the combined stimulus is conditioned. Later testing with either of the original two stimuli separately shows lower responding than was found during initial training. The term is used to suggest the notion that, after the combined training phase, the animal's 'expectations' are raised and the subsequent presentation of either original stimulus alone is something of a 'let down.'

overextension ➤ overgeneralization.

overflow activity ➤ vacuum activity.

overgeneralization The extension of the use of a word to cover circumstances, events or objects beyond those that the word is normally used for. Such *overextensions* (as they are also called) are common in young children, for example, calling a horse a 'doggie.' Compare with ➤ **undergeneralization**.

overinclusion A perceptual/cognitive deficit characterized by a failure to screen out the irrelevant, the inefficient and the inappropriate. The term is generally used only for genuine deficits and not for cases of simple ➤ overgeneralization.

overjustification The phenomenon in which an individual who has been carrying out some task for the simple intrinsic pleasure of it become less likely to again perform the task for no reward after a period in which they received extrinsic rewards.

overlapping factor In a factor analysis, any factor that is common to (i.e. overlaps with) more than one test.

overlearning Overlearning is said to occur when a response has been over-learned. This painfully tautological definition is not very satisfying; the problem is that one can only classify a response as *overlearned* when one has some established criterion against which to measure it, hence overlearning is always relative. In the typical experimental study of overlearning some defining condition for learning is set, say 10 correct responses in a row. Some subjects are then run to some overlearning point, say 20 consecutive correct responses, and the impact of this additional training is assessed. Thus, the con-

cept itself is necessarily arbitrary and is always definitionally contingent upon some previously set notion of what is to be considered learning.

overload Laboratory jargon used primarily in the information-processing approach to cognitive psychology for the condition of having too much information to deal with at a point in time or too much material to commit to memory in the time available.

overpopulation ➤ crowding.

overprotection A term commonly used to characterize parental behavior that is indulgent, pampering, solicitous, encapsulating, sheltering, and fostering of dependencies to an excessive degree. The problem with this usage is in that word *excessive*. Usually, clinicians will consider the parents to have been overprotective when the child fails to develop normal independence. Hence, the term functions in an entirely *post hoc* fashion.

overreaction Very generally, any response that is greater than one would have expected given the circumstances. The implication is that there is an emotional element and, indeed, the adjective *emotional* is often prefixed in psychological writings.

overshadowing In animal conditioning, a learning situation in which a compound conditioned stimulus is used but where one element of the stimulus (e.g., a rather loud tone) dominates the other (e.g., a dim light). After training, the dominant stimulus 'overshadows' the other and only it will produced responding when presented alone. Compare with ➤ **configurational learning**.

overshooting In a ➤ **probability learning** experiment, predicting the most likely of two (or more) events with a higher probability than actually occurs. Compare with ➤ **maximizing** and ➤ **probability matching**.

overt That which is open, available, detectable by whoever observes it. Overt behavior is usually what the strict behaviorist argues should be the subject-matter of psychology. Note that the use of the term has expanded in recent decades as technology has made that which was covert open for observation. ➤ **covert**.

overtone Any partial tone produced by a vibrating body other than the ➤ **fundamental tone**.

ovum The female sex cell, the egg. pl., *ova*.

own-control design An experimental design in which each subject serves as his or her own control. It consists of repeatedly alternating procedures with the same individual and assessing the effect(s) that each has. It is used routinely in intensive case studies in psychiatry, particularly in the use of drug-treatment programs.

oxazepam A ➤ **benzodiazepine compound** used as an antidepressant.

oxytocin A hormone secreted by the posterior lobe of the pituitary gland which acts on the blood pressure, strengthens uterine contractions and controls the milk-ejecting function of the mammary glands.

P

P 1. ➤ probability ratio. 2. The symbol for *stability of personality* in Eysenck's theory. 3. ➤ substance P.

p 1. The *probability* of a specifiable event or outcome. Here the common use is as a statement of ➤ **statistical significance**. 2. The *proportion* of events in a population exhibiting a particular characteristic and distinguishable from a mutually exclusive proportion of events, *q*, such that $p + q = 1$. 3. A *percentile*. 4. A percentage.

PA Abbreviation for *paired-associate* or *paired-association*. ➤ **paired-associates** *learning.

pacemaker 1. Generally, any physiological structure or system that displays periodicity and has some regulatory output that helps to control another structure system. The ➤ **suprachiasmatic nucleus** is often called a pacemaker. 2. More specifically, a region in the heart that functions as an integral part of the system that is rhythmically active and controls the rate of cardiac contraction.

pacing 1. Controlling the speed (i.e. 'pace') of an act. Used generally to refer to experimental procedures in which the sequence and timing of trials or behaviors are carefully controlled. 2. Structuring a learning program or educational curriculum so that materials are introduced gradually over time so as to correspond with the developmental level of the learner.

Pacinian corpuscle Large, specialized nerve endings located in the deep, subcutaneous fatty tissue. The largest of the nerve endings found in the skin, they occur abundantly in the feet and hands, in joints, ligaments, in the genitals and elsewhere. It is likely that these receptors transmit pressure information in response to rapid changes.

paedia- ➤ pedia-, ped(o).

paed(o)- ➤ pedia-, ped(o)-.

PAG ➤ periaqueductal gray.

pain This term comes from the Latin word for *penalty* or *fine* and has an exceedingly wide range of uses, not all of which reflect the original meaning. Here we shall skip the metaphoric, figurative and poetic; in psychology there are three distinguishable primary senses of the term – each with a variety of more specialized forms. To wit: 1. Loosely, the opposite of ➤ **pleasure**, that is, ➤ **unpleasure**. 2. Physical or psychic distress. While now rather common, this admittedly vague meaning emerged within psychoanalysis where it was often referred to as 'unpleasure' or 'displeasure' and is assumed to result from an excess of affect caused by tension and/or conflict. It should be noted that Freud used two separate words to differentiate these two forms of pain. One, *Schmerz*, was translated unambiguously into English as *pain*, the physical kind; the other, *Umlust*, is harder to fit in English and although *displeasure* or *aversion* are more or less acceptable, most translators avoided the issue of nuance and simply used *pain* for it as well – causing no end of confusion. 3. The experience that results from certain kinds of physical stimulation. In this context various kinds of pain are distinguished; see many of the following entries.

pain, acute Generally, any relatively short-duration pain with known organic cause. Acute pain is contrasted with ➤ **chronic *pain**, both in manner of cause and in the underlying neural pathways which mediate them. By and large, acute pain is externally caused, experienced immediately, and felt as a sharp, sudden sensation which diminishes fairly quickly. Also called *cutaneous pain*, *sharp pain*, and *surface pain*. ➤➤ **pain pathways**.

pain, chronic Deep, long-lasting, intractable pain. As contrasted with ➤ **acute *pain**, it is caused by internal factors and is experienced as deep, dull and diffuse; it tends to increase in intensity over time. Also known as *deep pain*. ➤➤ **pain pathways**.

pain, clinical Pain resulting from disease, injury, surgery, etc.

pain disorder An umbrella term for a class of ➤ **somatoform disorders** marked by the existence of pain as part of an individual's overall clinical picture when that pain causes marked distress or significant impairment in social or occupational functioning. The disorder may be subclassified as *psychological type* if psychological factors are judged to be the significant causes, *secondary type* if nonpsychological medical conditions account for the condition, or *combined type* if both factors contribute. Also called *psychogenic pain disorder* and *somatoform pain disorder*.

pain endurance Loosely, the ability of a person to endure pain. Many theorists treat it as a personality characteristic and there is evidence that the ability to tolerate pain (➤ **pain tolerance**), assessed objectively, predicts how well a person will be able to endure chronic pain resulting from natural causes.

pain pathways The afferent neural pathways leading from the receptors to the central nervous system that transmit the sensation of pain. The pathways for ➤ **acute *pain** are made up of rapidly conducting fibers that travel to the ventrobasal complex of the thalamus and from there to the somatosensory cortex; those for ➤ **chronic *pain** are made up of slow conducting fibers that travel to the midline nuclei of the thalamus and from there to various areas, including the limbic system and the frontal lobes of the cerebral cortex.

pain, pricking A form of ➤ **acute *pain** experienced when a sharp momentary stimulus is applied to the skin.

pain principle The striving for death or for nirvana. In Freud's early psychoanalytic formulations this notion is only hinted at; later it was made explicit in the form of Thanatos, the death instinct, which was conceived of as operating along with Eros, the life instinct. There are some terminological confusions to be found in the writings of psychoanalysts with regard to the pain principle. On one hand it is used as above but on the other it also finds expression in the compound phrase ➤ **pleasure – pain principle**, for which there are rather different connotations.

pain, referred The sensation of bodily pain in a location other than the place stimulated. It is particularly common in the abdominal area and often makes medical diagnosis difficult.

pain threshold The minimal intensity of a stimulus that is perceived as painful. While this threshold appears to be biologically determined, an individual's ➤ **pain tolerance** has a large psychological component.

pain tolerance The upper threshold for endurance of painful stimulation. Experimentally, it is assessed by the point at which a subject (paid volunteers!) will terminate the stimulation.

pair-bond In ethology, a lasting male–female union. The term is only used for nonhuman species.

paired-associates learning ➤ **learning, paired-associates**

paired-comparisons method A very general procedure for measuring (scaling) objects or stimuli and assessing the dimensions that underlie them. In the standard, complete method of paired comparisons, every object in a set is presented for judgement in a pair-wise fashion with every other object in the set. The method is extremely powerful and general and, in principle, can be used with any collection of objects or stimuli that can be compared with each other in some psychologically real manner. For example, in a simple psychophysical problem, such as the experience of loudness, a number of tones of varying intensities are presented in pairs and the subject is asked to judge which of

PAL

the pair is louder. In more complex areas such as emotion or esthetics, subjects might be asked to compare paintings according to beauty, odors according to pleasantness, faces according to similarity, etc. The power in the procedure results from the application of multidimensional and factor-analytic techniques to the data to reveal the underlying dimensions along which the judgements were made. ➤ scaling et seq.

PAL ➤ paired-associates *learning.

palaeoencephalon ➤ neencephalon.

palaeopsychology ➤ paleopsychology.

palatable Agreeable to the palate, pleasant-tasting. Interestingly, however, the palate is essentially devoid of taste receptors. Nevertheless, the term continues to be used, in even the most formal presentations, for the acceptability of foodstuff.

palate The roof of the mouth; it is divided into the anterior hard palate and the posterior soft palate.

PA learning ➤ paired-associates *learning.

paleencephalon ➤ neencephalon.

paleo- Combining form meaning ancient, old, prehistoric. var., palaeo-.

paleopsychology A rather esoteric area of psychology in which processes suspected of having been carried over from earlier evolutionary eras are studied. Some of the research into the origins and evolution of language (➤ theories of *language origins) falls into this area, as does much of Carl Jung's speculations about the ➤ collective unconscious. var., palaeopsychology.

paleostriatum = ➤ globus pallidus.

palilalia Repeating one's own words and phrases. It is a symptom in some ➤ tic disorders. ➤ echolalia.

palin- Combining form meaning backward or repetitive.

palindrome Any word, phrase or sentence that reads the same forward and backward. For obvious reasons, the author is rather partial to them.

palingraphia An obscure term for the more common ➤ mirror writing.

palinlexia Reading backward. There are two forms, one in which a sentence is read with the word order reversed, the other where each word is read with letter order reversed. ➤ dyslexia.

palinphrasia Pathologically frequent repetition of particular words or phrases during speech.

pallesthesia The sensation of vibration. Also called palmesthesia. var., pallaesthesia.

palliative Anything that eases pain.

pallidum ➤ globus pallidus.

pallium Obsolescent term for the cerebral cortex.

palmaesthesia ➤ pallesthesia.

palmar Pertaining to the palm of the hand or the sole of the foot. Also called, especially in older writings, volar.

palmar conductance (or resistance) Lit., the electrical conductivity or resistance of the skin of the palm. ➤ galvanic skin response.

palmar response The grasping reflex of a newborn when pressure is applied to the palm. It normally disappears at around the fourth or fifth month of life.

palmesthesia ➤ pallesthesia.

palmistry The practice of personality and character assessment based on the interpretation of the lines, wrinkles and other features of the palm. In Ambrose Bierce's terms, the practice often works, for the wrinkles in the palm of the subject invariably spell out 'dupe.' ➤ pseudoscience, of which palmistry is an example.

palmitic acid ➤ fatty acid.

palpitation(s) Rapid heartbeat. It often

532

accompanies a ➤ **panic attack** and can itself be quite frightening.

palsy Generally, paralysis. Typically used in combined form to specify the nature, location or type of disability.

pan- Combining form meaning *all* or *every* (*where*). var., *panto-*.

pandemic In epidemiology, occurring over a wide geographical area; by extension, universal.

Pandemonium An early and influential computer model of pattern perception developed in the 1950s by O. Selfridge. In its simplest form it was based on a number of perceiving elements (called *demons*) that were tuned to detect specific features (e.g., a straight line, a half-circle). Each low-level demon that was activated 'shouted out' and the higher level demons decided what stimulus was presented by sifting through the pandemonium.

panic attack A discrete period of intense fear or discomfort accompanied by various symptoms which may include shortness of breath, dizziness, palpitations, trembling, sweating, nausea, and often a fear that one is going crazy. The attacks are initially unexpected and typically last no longer than 15 minutes. ➤ **panic disorders**.

panic disorders A class of ➤ **anxiety disorders** characterized by recurrent ➤ **panic attacks**. The term is not used in cases where a known organic factor is responsible. Panic disorder is typically classified as with or without ➤ **agoraphobia**.

panpsychism A philosophical position that holds that the ultimate, meaningful (or perhaps *only*) reality is psychic or mental; that all that exists is 'mindlike.' In the final analysis it represents a rather naive effort to resolve the ➤ **mind–body problem** and when drawn to its (logical?) extreme emerges as ➤ **animism** in disguise.

pansexualism A sobriquet thrust often upon the classical Freudian point of view

by its critics, who argue that the strong emphasis on sexual determinants that that view embodies is unwarranted.

pantheism The doctrine that God and the cosmic totality are coterminous. It served as a convenient perspective for rescuing ➤ **subjective idealism** from ➤ **solipsism**.

panto- ➤ **pan-**.

panum phenomenon A visual effect obtained using a stereoscope such that one is first presented with two parallel lines to one eye and a single line, at the same distance and similarly parallel, to the other eye. Adjusting the single line so that it fuses stereoscopically with either of two lines from the other eye will cause the fused line to appear to be closer to the viewer than the other line.

paper-and-pencil test A general label for any test (achievement, aptitude, intelligence, etc.) that uses only pencil and paper as testing instruments.

paper-folding test ➤ **mental paper-folding test**.

Papez's circuit A complex neural circuit consisting of the mamillary bodies, the anterior thalamus, the cingulate cortex, the hippocampus and the various fibers interconnecting them.

Papez's theory of emotion One of the first theoretical attempts to delineate the specific cortical mechanisms underlying emotion. It was developed by J. W. Papez in the 1930s and proposed three interlocking systems (sensory, hypothalamic, thalamic) all of which were hypothesized to be combined in the cortex, where the 'psychological products' of emotion emerged. The theory has not stood up to careful anatomical study but it was influential in implicating the hypothalamus and by focusing attention on the integrative role of the cortex. ➤➤ **MacLean's theory of emotion**, which built on several of Papez's ideas, and the general discussion under ➤ **theories of *emotion**.

papilla Any small nipple-like protuberance. E.g., ➤ **lingual papilla**.

-para- Combining term with two origins. When from its Greek roots it means: **1.** *Next to* or *along side of.* **2.** By extension, *beyond.* **3.** By further extension, *unusual, irregular,* even *abnormal.* When from its Latin roots: **4.** *To bear, to bring forth.* It is used in this sense to characterize a woman with respect to her viable offspring; e.g., *nullipara* for one who has had none, *multipara* for one who has had two or more. A shorthand expression is also used here, *para-0*, *para-1*, *para-n*, for a woman who has had none, one, or *n* offspring.

parabiosis 1. Lit., living alongside; hence, the joining together of two individuals either congenitally, as in Siamese twins, or artificially, as in a ➤ **parabiotic preparation**. **2.** An obsolete term for a temporary suppression of the conductivity of a nerve.

parabiotic preparation An experimental preparation that is, roughly, an artificially created pair of Siamese twins in which the skins of two genetically similar animals are surgically joined. The animals share, to a limited degree, circulating blood which allows for a number of ingenious experiments to be carried out on such problems as the role of hormones and other humoral factors on behavior.

parabrachial nucleus A nucleus in the ➤ **pons** that relays information about taste to the gustatory area of the ➤ **thalamus**.

paracentral vision ➤ **vision, paracentral**.

parachlorophenylalanine A substance that prevents the synthesis of ➤ **serotonin** by blocking the action of ➤ **trytophan**.

parachromatopsia A general term for color deficiency, ➤ **color blindness**.

paracontrast ➤ **metacontrast**.

paracusia 1. Selective deafness to low-pitched tones. **2.** A label for what was once thought to be the paradox that a paracusic (in the previous sense) could actually hear better when there was background noise. The effect turns out to be due simply to the fact that those who are speaking to the paracusic tend to raise their voices to compensate for the noise – which the paracusic cannot hear anyway.

paradigm 1. Any series of linguistic forms all of which reflect a common underlying element, e.g., give, gives, gave, giving, given, etc. This general notion is also found in other levels of linguistic analysis including phonemic, morphemic and syntactic. **2.** An orientation to or plan for research using a particular focus. Thus one reads, for example, of an attack on a problem using the *psychoanalytic paradigm*. **3.** A particular experimental procedure, e.g., the *classical conditioning paradigm*. **4.** In T. S. Kuhn's influential analysis of the history of science, the collective set of attitudes, values, procedures, techniques, etc. that form the generally accepted perspective of a particular discipline at a point in time. Note that all of these uses from the linguistic to the historical/philosophical reflect the original Greek word *paradeigma*, meaning *pattern*.

paradigmatic association ➤ **association, paradigmatic**.

paradox A situation wherein, on the basis of a number of premises generally taken to be true, contradictory conclusions are reached without violating logical deductive reasoning. Note that the contradiction here can arise not only from logical deductions, but also from an experimental outcome that 'contradicts' (using that term loosely) the predictions of a generally agreed-upon theoretical analysis. From an empirical standpoint many scientific paradoxes are but momentary states of affairs that are best viewed as symptoms of a lack of understanding; i.e. usually the premises from which one is working should not have been so uncritically accepted as true. For a nice example of a still not completely resolved paradox in cognitive psychology ➤ **word-superiority effect**.

From a logical point of view there is a

large and important class of paradoxes that are significant for philosophy, mathematics and psychology – the *self-referencing paradoxes*. The most famous (and oldest) is the liar paradox in which Epimenides (who is from Crete) remarks, 'All Cretans are liars.' Attempt to determine whether Epimenides is speaking the truth or not to see the paradox.

paradoxical cold A sensation of coldness when an actually rather warm object of about 113°F (45°C) or above stimulates a ➤ **cold spot** on the skin.

paradoxical injunction A command not to do something that, by virtue of the command, cannot be carried out. The classic example: I command you *not* to think about gorillas.

paradoxical intention A psychotherapeutic technique used within Viktor E. Frankl's ➤ **logotherapy** wherein the individual is encouraged (with appropriate humor – a point that Frankl strongly emphasizes and which some others, to their peril, fail to appreciate) to do exactly what he or she is afraid of doing or to imagine that his or her worst neurotic fears have actually transpired. The technique is used primarily with obsessions; e.g., the case of a man who was terrified to leave his house because of an obsession with having a heart seizure who was told, 'Go on out, have a heart attack, have two, it's still early in the day; might as well use the day well, have a stroke too.' Clearly, this is a procedure to be used judiciously; it is not recommended for one not trained in Frankl's approach.

paradoxical sleep A term occasionally used for what is now more commonly referred to as ➤ **REM sleep**. The phrase paradoxical sleep was introduced because the EEG pattern during REM sleep looks like that of a normally awake person. Also known as *D sleep*.

paradoxical warmth A sensation of warmth experienced when an object of roughly 84° to 88°F. (29°–31°C.), which normally feels cool, stimulates the skin.

paraesthesia ➤ **paresthesia**.

parafovea The area of the retina immediately surrounding the fovea.

parageusia A general term for any gustory (taste) illusion.

paragraphia Habitual inappropriate insertion of words into writing.

parahippocampal cortex (or **gyrus**) Part of the limbic system adjaceent to the ➤ **hippocampal formation**. It and the *perirhinal cortex* relay information between the hippocampus and the rest of the brain.

parakinesis ➤ **psychokinesis** (1).

paralalia Habitual inappropriate substitution of sounds during speech.

paraldehyde A quick-acting, nonbarbiturate sedative with anticonvulsive effects. It is normally administered by injection as it is rather foul-tasting, leaves a distinctly unpleasant odor on the patient's breath and irritates the stomach.

paralexia A form of ➤ **dyslexia** in which words and/or letters are misread. Often the misreading involves transposition of letters, syllables and even whole words.

paralinguistics The study of those aspects of communication that are not 'purely' linguistic, i.e. not morphophonemic, syntactic or semantic. Specifically, the meanings conveyed by tone of voice, pacing, pausing, emphasis, hems and haws, snorting, etc. qualify as paralinguistic. Note that some will use the term so as to include social mannerisms, gestures, facial expressions and the like. A paralinguistic analysis of an utterance or a discourse is one which is concerned primarily with *how* something is said rather than with the actual words used. ➤ **kinesics, metalinguistics, nonverbal communication**.

parallax A term borrowed from geometry to refer to the patterns of shifts in apparent motion of objects in the visual field as the observer moves laterally. For more on usage here ➤ **motion parallax** and ➤ **motion perspective**.

parallel distributed processing (PDP) models A class of theoretical models in *cognitive psychology* that are based on the assumption that systems operate by having a number of internal nodes or units that function in parallel with each other. For more detail ➤ **connectionism** (2).

parallel forms ➤ **alternate forms** *reliability.

parallelism, cultural A term borrowed from anthropology and used to describe the situation in which a set of similar, if not identical, cultural patterns and conventions are found in widely separated and presumably totally independent cultures. Cultural parallelisms are cited as evidence for the theory that all cultures progress through a similar developmental sequence.

parallelism, psychoneural A variation on ➤ **psychophysical *parallelism** in which it is assumed that for every event in the mental domain there is a corresponding unique event in the neural domain.

parallelism, psychophysical The philosophical doctrine often associated with the empirically oriented psychology of the late 19th and early 20th century. It was an attempt to resolve the mind–body problem by assuming that the two domains were merely separate 'tracks' and that for every mental or psychic event there was a corresponding physical event and vice versa. ➤ **mind–body problem** and **dualism**.

parallel play ➤ **play, parallel**.

parallel processing ➤ **processing, parallel**.

parallel search ➤ **search, parallel**.

paralysis Any partial or complete loss of some function. Unless specifically noted, the reference is nearly always to the voluntary musculature. Although there are many special subclassifications of paralyses which we needn't list here, physicians typically group paralyses into the *spastic* and the *flaccid* types. In the former, where there is damage to the upper motor neurons, there is loss of control over musculature with tremors or spasms; in the latter,

where the lesions are in the lower motor neurons, there is loss of voluntary control and no movement. ➤ **-plegia** for additional details. Occasionally the term will be used figuratively for sensory function and even for the sense of a crippling or loss of effectiveness of cognitive processes.

paralysis agitans ➤ **Parkinson's disease**.

paralytic dementia ➤ **paresis**.

parameter 1. Mathematically, in the simplest of terms, an *unspecified constant*. Specifically, it is the value of this constant in a function that will satisfy the conditions of the function. 2. In statistics, the value that enters into the mathematical function for a probability distribution. This sense, which is an application of the above, is most clearly realized as a summary measure of a *population* of scores; e.g., the population mean (μ) is a parameter and so is the population standard deviation (σ). Note here, that the term parameter is not used of *samples*; the mean and standard deviation of a sample of scores are called *statistics*. For more detail on usage here ➤ **parametric statistics**. 3. In various quantitative approaches to psychology the term is found with essentially these same meanings. For example, a PDP model of learning (➤ **connectionism** (2)) will have a learning parameter that must be specified in order to determine the rate at which the system will set up its representations. 4. In experimental work, any variable that is set for a particular study to one or more values but can be changed to other values for other parametric variations on the original study. For example, one may study one motivational level in one experiment and double or triple that level in a later parametric extension. 5. In psychotherapy, an aspect of a therapeutic program that can be systematically altered, e.g., number of therapy sessions, their length, etc.

parametric 1. From the Greek words *para* (meaning *near*) and *metron* (meaning *measure*), pertaining to a ➤ **parameter**. 2. From the Greek words *para* (*near*) and *metra* (*uterus*), pertaining to the tissue area surrounding the uterus.

parametric statistics A general label covering those statistical procedures that require that the sample data under analysis be drawn from a population with a known form, most generally the normal distribution. Moreover, parametric techniques also require; (a) that the samples under analysis are taken independently; (b) that when more than one population is being sampled they have the same variance or a known ratio of variances; and (c) that the data be in a form such that all arithmetic operations (addition, multiplication) can be carried out on them. As a rule, parametric procedures are to be preferred over ➤ **nonparametric statistics** (provided that the conditions hold) because they have greater statistical power and are more likely to detect statistically significant effects.

paramimia A form of ➤ **apraxia** in which the kinesic system (gestures) is at variance with other behavioral indicators of emotionality. In simple terms, the body and face do not accurately reflect the underlying affect felt.

paramnesia The Greek roots of the word are *para*, meaning *irregular* and *mnesia*, *memory*: hence a distorted or false memory for things. E.g., ➤ *déjà vu* and ➤ **confabulation**.

paramnesia, reduplicative A paramnesia where the patient believes that two or more places (such as hospitals) with virtually identical features exist. It is typically associated with frontal lobe damage.

paranoia In the standard psychiatric nosology, a functional disorder characterized by symptoms of delusions of jealousy, and delusions of either grandeur and/or persecution, which cannot be explained by other disorders such as *schizophrenia*, *organic mental disorder* or *organic mental syndrome*. In the classic form, the delusions develop insidiously and become knit together into a rational and coherent set of beliefs that is internally consistent and, once the initial set of assumptions is accepted, compelling and vigorously defensible. In paranoia,

intellectual functioning is unimpaired and the paranoid is quite capable of coherent behavior within the delusional system. adj., *paranoid* or *paranoiac*; n., *paranoid* or *paranoiac*. In the standard nomenclature, paranoia is considered a ➤ **delusional disorder** and specialized terms can be found under that heading.

paranoiac (and **paranoid**) Originally *paranoiac* was used to refer to a person suffering from a diagnosed paranoia and *paranoid* to one manifesting some of the suspiciousness and delusional tendencies typical of the disorder. This distinction, which was useful, is pretty well lost today and both terms are often used interchangeably.

paranoid anxiety A psychoanalytic term for anxiety produced by fear of attack from hostile others. Also called *persecutory anxiety*.

paranoid character ➤ **paranoid personality disorder**.

paranoid delusions One of the key symptoms of ➤ **paranoid type *schizophrenia**.

paranoid disorders ➤ **delusional (paranoid) disorder**, the currently approved term and, for more detail, ➤ **paranoia**.

paranoid ideation The typical pattern of thinking displayed in cases of paranoia; it is characterized by suspiciousness and beliefs that one is being followed, plotted against, persecuted, etc.

paranoid personality disorder A ➤ **personality disorder** characterized by excessive suspiciousness, hostility and sensitivity to accusations or even hints of accusation. Distinguish from ➤ **delusional (paranoid) disorder** in that there is no fully developed persecutory system. Called in some old writings *paranoid character*.

paranoid schizophrenia ➤ **schizophrenia, paranoid type**.

paranoid state An acute form of ➤ **delusional (paranoid) disorder** brought about by an abrupt shift in occupation or in living conditions. Seen in immigrants, refugees, prisoners of war, young people leaving home for the first time, etc. The condition is almost always temporary.

paranoid states A term used in earlier editions of the International Classification of Diseases. The currently preferred term is ➤ **delusional (paranoid) disorder**.

paranoid trend An older psychiatric term for the pattern of suspiciousness, jealousy and feelings of persecution and/or grandeur often displayed by one with a ➤ **paranoid personality disorder**.

paranormal Lit., outside of the normal. Generally used for the 'phenomena' studied under ➤ **parapsychology**, and related areas such as the occult, astrology, magic, etc.

paranosic (gain) ➤ **primary gain**.

paraphasia A general term used as a cover for any habitual inappropriate use of words in speech.

paraphemia The habitual use of the wrong word or the wrong phonetic unit in speech.

paraphilia An umbrella term for any mode of sexual expression in which arousal is dependent upon what are generally considered to be socially unacceptable stimulating conditions. Typically a paraphiliac is not one who simply enjoys an exotic passing fancy with something 'offbeat' but is rather obsessively concerned with and responsive to the particular erotic stimuli of his or her sexual mode. Human sexual expression is extraordinarily varied and a large number of paraphilias has been identified and studied. For those interested in such matters ➤ **coprophilia** (2), **exhibitionism** (2), **fetishism** (2), **frotteurism**, **klismaphilia**, **masochism**, **necrophilia**, **pedophilia**, **pictophilia**, **sadism**, **scophophilia**, **transvestic fetishism**, **troilism**, **urophilia**, **voyeurism** and **zoophilia**.

paraphobia Any mild form of a phobia.

paraphonia Generally, any weakness or other abnormal change in voice quality.

paraphrase **1** n. The relation that holds between two sentences when they both have the same underlying meaning but differ in their surface forms, e.g., the active and passive forms of a simple sentence, 'Max ate the eggs' and 'The eggs were eaten by Max.' **2** n. By extension, shared meanings of larger units of language, paragraphs, essays, stories etc. The strict relationship between underlying structures that can be shown to hold for cases like **1** is not implied in this sense of the term; *meaning* is used more loosely here. **3** vb. To produce either form of paraphrase.

paraphrasic error A speech error marked by substitutions of incorrect words or sounds, usually by transposing syllables, words, or even whole phrases. They are common in the speech of patients with ➤ **Wernicke's *aphasia**.

paraphrenia ➤ **schizophrenia, paranoid type**.

paraplegia Paralysis of the lower limbs.

parapraxis Any minor slip-up or error; most typically observed in speech, writing, small accidents, memory lapses, etc. According to Freud, these were no mere innocent gestures but the result of the operations of unconscious wishes or conflicts that could often be used to reveal the functioning of the unconscious in the normal healthy individual. Commonly referred to as *Freudian slip*. pl., *parapraxes*.

paraprofessional Generally, an individual who has received sufficient training in a specialized field to assist and work under the direction of one who has had full professional training.

parapsychology A more or less (with the emphasis on the *less*) accepted branch of psychology concerned with paranormal phenomena; that is, those that are presumed to be unexplainable using known laws and principles. Generally included are extrasensory perception (ESP), telepathy, precognition, telekinesis, clairvoyance, and the like. Although there is a great deal of interest in parapsychology and many actively pursue the scientific basis of the various claims that have been made, the majority of psychologists are deeply skeptical and for good reason.

First, the results of the individual experiments that have reported positive findings have proven notoriously difficult to replicate. Reproducibility is essential in all sciences; it is a touchstone of the scientific method and demand for independent verification is found everywhere. This aspect of science is, moreover, absolutely essential in any branch that makes frontal assault on accepted laws and principles. Second, the reported phenomena often entail conclusions that violate known laws of science. For example, the further away a light source is the weaker the light, the greater the distance between two bodies the weaker the mutual gravitational pull. Yet, *psi* abilities (as they are often called) have been argued to operate equally well at distances of 1,000 miles or 10 feet. Most scientists are loath to abandon general principles like the inverse square law (which accounts for both light and gravity in the above examples), particularly when the phenomena that 'mandate' their rejection resist replication so thoroughly. It is more reasonable to distrust the data from the nonrepeatable experiment than to jettison laws that function in all other domains. Third, no mechanism has ever been proposed that could explain these purported paranormal phenomena in any way that is coherent in view of the rest of scientific knowledge. Precognition, for example, invites the hypothesization of time travel by the mind or, phrased differently, hypothesization of time travel by some force that moves from the future to have an impact upon someone's mind here in the present. Such a mechanism entails reversal of cause and effect (tomorrow affects today) not to mention conflicting with the basic principles of relativity theory and the laws of thermodynamics. Fourth, and this reason is perhaps unfortunate, many charlatans and fakes argue strongly for paranormal phenomena and many of the purported effects have been shown to be the result of outright fraud. If psi effects are real (and skepticism – reasonable skepticism – does not outlaw

them nor uniformly reject them) their vigorous espousal by obvious frauds makes objective analysis extremely difficult.

Finally, many of the skeptics wonder why those persons who claim to have these extraordinary capabilities don't simply hie themselves off to the nearest gambling casino or race track and put them to good work. If nothing else, they could use the profits to fund further research in parapsychology.

parasagittal Of a plane parallel to the ➤ **sagittal** (2) plane of an organ or body.

parasexuality Lit., anomalous sexuality or, by extension, perverted sexuality. Unfortunately, since the notion of just what is anomalous and/or perverted in sexual behavior changes with the passage of time and with the societally regulated attitudes of the persons making the classification, it is simply not clear which behaviors are truly parasexual and which are merely uncommon among clinicians. ➤ **paraphilia**.

parasomnia A general label for a group of sleep disorders characterized by abnormal episodes that occur during sleep. Included are ➤ **somnambulism**, ➤ **dream anxiety disorder**, and ➤ **sleep terror disorder**. When these disorders occur in childhood they are usually due to developmental factors; in adults they are primarily psychogenic. Compare with ➤ **dyssomnia**.

parasympathetic nervous system ➤ **autonomic nervous system**.

parataxic distortion H. S. Sullivan's term for a distortion of reality brought about by inferring a causal relationship between events that are actually independent. Contrast with ➤ **syntaxis**.

parataxis **1.** From the Greek, meaning *placing side by side*; in linguistics, characterizing phrases or sentences placed together without a conjunction as in Caesar's famous remark, 'I came, I saw, I conquered.' **2.** By extension, within H. S. Sullivan's theory, a mode of thinking lacking in integration or a personality in which skills, attitudes, personal relationships, etc. are largely separated from each other.

➤ **parataxic distortion**. 3. By further extension, a general abnormality in emotionality wherein the various components of emotion (ideas, thoughts, feelings, attitudes) are poorly integrated.

parathyroid glands Several small endocrine glands located in the back and lower edge of the thyroid gland. They secrete a hormone *parathormone* which is essential for calcium–phosphorus metabolism.

paratypic Lit., diverting from a type. Hence, by extension, characterizing influences that are environmental; not inherited.

paraventricular nucleus A nucleus of cells within the hypothalamus. The cell bodies of the nucleus produce antidiuretic hormone and oxytocin and transport them through their axons to the posterior pituitary gland.

paraverbal ➤ **paralinguistics**.

paravertebral ganglionic chain ➤ **autonomic nervous system**.

paraxial On either side of the axis of the body or of an organ.

parental behavior Behavior characteristic of a parent, behavior that is specifically focused on the care, protection, feeding, nurturing, etc. of offspring. It is used as either (a) a term for those behaviors that are 'gender-free,' i.e. those that are normally carried out by either the male or female parent, or (b) an umbrella term encompassing all behaviors of both parents. ➤ **maternal behavior** and **paternal behavior** for some additional comments on usage.

parental investment The time, energy, and risk to one's survival that a parent must invest in order to produce, feed, and rear each offspring. Or, phrased another way, the future reproductive capacity lost by the parent for each offspring produced and nurtured.

parent image 1. The image or memory one has of one's parents. Needless to say, this image does not necessarily correspond to the reality. 2. A parent ➤ **surrogate** (2).

paresis 1. Generally, incomplete, partial paralysis of organic origin. 2. Specifically, an ➤ **organic mental disorder** characterized by progressive mental deterioration and paralysis. It is the result of central nervous system damage caused by tertiary syphilis. Also called *dementia paralytica*, *general paresis*, *general paralysis of the insane*.

paresthesia Abnormal skin sensations such as tickling, itching, burning. E.g., ➤ **formication**. var., *paraesthesia*.

parietal bones The parts of the cranium, in the middle of each side, lying between the occipital and the frontal bones.

parietal lobes The areas of the cerebral hemispheres lying below the parietal bones i.e. in between the frontal and occipital lobes and above the temporal lobe. They contain the somatosensory cortex and are involved in spatial perception and both memory for and planning of motor sequences.

Parkinsonism, drug-induced A syndrome with many of the classic symptoms of ➤ **Parkinson's disease** produced as a side effect of long-term use of ➤ **antipsychotic drugs**. It is treatable with antiparkinsonian agents. Also called *pseudoparkinsonism*.

Parkinson's disease A neurological disorder named for James Parkinson, the English physician who first described it. The primary symptoms are a rapid coarse tremor, masklike facial expressions, loss of sensory-motor coordination, loss of the ability to initiate action and a general tendency toward exhaustion. There are also subtle cognitive deficits involving learning and memory that may be difficult to identify in individual cases. The disease is caused by dopamine deficiency in the basal ganglia. Also called *parkinsonism* (or *Parkinsonism*), in older texts *paralysis agitans* or sometimes simply *palsy*.

parophresia ➤ **parosmia**.

parorexia Craving for strange, unusual foods. Used only for truly pathological cases.

parosmia Generally, any disorder in the sense of smell. Also called *parophresia*.

parotid glands The large salivary glands in the cheeks just below and in front of the external ears. It was the parotid glands of the dog which, under the orchestration of Ivan P. Pavlov, produced some of psychology's most important early data.

parous Pertaining to females who have borne at least one viable offspring.

paroxysm 1. Specifically, a spasmodic fit or convulsion. 2. More generally, any sudden increase in the severity of a disease or of an emotional disorder. 3. Figuratively, any sudden rage or anger.

parsimony, principle of A general *heuristic* which states that if two scientific propositions or two theories are equally tenable the simpler one is to be preferred. The principle is eminently reasonable, applying it is another matter. In practice it turns out that two equally tenable propositions or theories are about as rare as hen's teeth. Moreover, how tenable a theory is typically is judged by its effectiveness in handling known phenomena and not by additional insights that it may yield; the more complex of the competing theories may indeed turn out to have greater predictive validity. In psychology and other social sciences, the issue is further confounded because, unlike some branches of the physical sciences and unlike pure mathematics (where the principle has its strongest role to play), determining the complexity of theoretical propositions is often impossible. Finally there is the everpresent problem that this rational principle must be applied by the human scientist, a creature not known for its rationality. Nevertheless, the principle has merit and keeps reappearing in various guises; ➤ **Lloyd Morgan's canon, Occam's razor**.

part correlation ➤ **semipartial *correlation**.

parthenogenesis From the Greek, meaning *virgin origin*, the production of a viable offspring from a female egg without male fertilization.

partial 1 adj. Pertaining to that which is less than the whole of some object, system or organization. 2 n. A ➤ **partial tone**.

partial aim In psychoanalytic theory, any means for deriving sexual gratification to the development of the genital stage.

partial correlation ➤ **correlation, partial**.

partial hospitalization A treatment program for patients who only require hospital care part of the time, usually overnight or on weekends.

partial instinct In classical psychoanalytic theory, instincts are assumed to develop from the specific manifestations of a number of component instincts. These more molecular elements are the *partial* (or *component* or, simply, *part*) instincts. For example, the sex instinct is assumed to derive from the partial libidinal contributions of the oral, anal and genital.

partialism A ➤ **paraphilia** marked by the individual's sexual interest being exclusively focused on a single part of the body.

partialization O. Rank's term for the process now captured by the term ➤ **differentiation**, in sense 5 of that term.

partial regression (equation) ➤ **multiple regression (equation)**.

partial reinforcement A somewhat ambiguous synonym for ➤ **intermittent *reinforcement**. ➤ **schedules of *reinforcement**.

partial-reinforcement effect The generalization that behavior maintained with partial or intermittent reinforcement has greater resistance to extinction compared with behavior maintained with continuous reinforcement. Despite the preference for the term *intermittent reinforcement* over *partial reinforcement*, the generalization goes by the latter.

partial relations Relations between variables discovered by subdividing a larger sample into subsets (or 'parts').

partial-report method An experimental procedure in which the subject is required to report only part of a stimulus display rather than the whole display.

partial tone Any of the separate tones produced by a vibrating body. The lowest and loudest is the *fundamental tone*, the rest form the *harmonic* or *overtone series*. Also called, simply, *partial*.

participant ➤ **subject** (1).

participant observer In the study of groups, communities and societies an observer who is simultaneously a full participant in the group. Often this role is taken by a psychologist, anthropologist or sociologist in order to examine group processes *in situ*.

participation 1. Taking an active, sharing part in a game, a group, an experiment, etc. 2. By extension, the dynamic characteristic of a complex activity that results from the 'participation' of a number of interacting components. This sense is often expressed in Piaget's writings, particularly as it pertains to the young child's manner of thinking about external and internal realities.

participative management In industrial/organizational psychology, a form of management of an organization in which the employees are involved in managerial decision-making on issues that directly concern them.

particular complex In psychoanalysis, any individual or idiosyncratic complex as contrasted with those complexes assumed to be universal. ➤ **nuclear complex**, **universal complex**.

particularism In sociology and social psychology, an approach to social theory in which standards of conduct are developed with a recognition of the role of individual circumstances and possible mitigating contexts. Compare with the more absolutist approach of ➤ **universalism**.

partile Any of the set of points that divides an ordered distribution of scores into a series of equal-sized divisions. The most commonly found are *percentiles* or *centiles*, although logically any subdivision

is possible, e.g., *quartiles, quintiles, deciles*, etc. Note that sometimes these terms are used to designate the points themselves, as above, and sometimes to designate divisions between any two points. See the discussion under ➤ **centile** for clarification of this often confusing usage.

part instinct ➤ **partial instinct**.

partition measure Any measure or statistic that partitions off one part of a distribution of scores from other part(s). Most commonly used are ➤ **partiles**.

part learning method ➤ **whole learning method**.

part object ➤ **object, part**.

parturition The act of giving birth.

parvocellular system A neural pathway in the visual system that is composed of small, slowly conducting cells. It is responsible for the perception of color, fine detail, and high contrast. The system, which is found only in primates, is named for the evolutionarily newer **parvo cells**, that make up the parvocellular layers of the lateral geniculate nucleus. Compare with ➤ **magnocellular system**.

Pascal distribution ➤ **distribution, Pascal**.

passing stranger (effect) The often observed phenomenon that a person will divulge the most private information about him or herself to a perfect stranger – information that even the person's spouse or therapist may not be privy to. Sometimes it is called the 'stranger on a train' effect, because trains are a likely place for such encounters. The explanation seems simple enough: the stranger will probably never be seen again and so the cathartic release of unburdening oneself can take place without fear that the information will ever be used against one.

passive 1. Not active, at rest. 2. Characterizing a particular attitude or stance whereby one permits outside influences to control a situation. 3. Characterizing a submissive posture whereby one allows oneself to be controlled by outside influences or persons, particularly in matters sexual. ➤ **active and passive** for Freud's use of the term and its opposite.

passive-aggressive Descriptive of patterns of behavior in which aggressiveness is displayed but in a passive rather than in an active manner. It is commonly seen in persons in a relatively low power position in which overt aggressiveness would surely lead to reprisals.

passive-aggressive personality disorder A ➤ **personality disorder** marked by a pattern of passive resistance to requests for appropriate social and/or occupational performance. The individual typically procrastinates, becomes sulky and irritable when asked to do things he or she does not wish to do, works slowly (in a seemingly deliberate manner) on jobs and avoids obligations or responsibilities.

passive analysis ➤ **passive *therapy**.

passive avoidance ➤ **avoidance**.

passive-dependent personality ➤ **dependent personality disorder**.

passive learning ➤ **incidental *learning**.

passive therapy ➤ **therapy, passive**.

passive vocabulary ➤ **vocabulary, passive**.

pastoral counseling Psychological counseling carried out by members of the clergy who have been trained to work with members of their congregation who seek help with emotional problems.

past-pointing 1. The inability to place accurately one's finger on some specified part of the body. It is a sign of various neurological disorders. 2. The tendency to point past a specific spot following rapid rotation of the whole body. It is, unlike 1, normal and a sign that one's vestibular system is functioning properly.

patella The kneecap.

patellar reflex The ➤ **knee-jerk reflex**.

paternal behavior Collectively, all those behaviors relating to or associated with being a father. The caveats concerning

usage outlined under ➤ **maternal behavior** apply here as well. ➤ **parental behavior**.

paternalism 1. Specifically, a leadership pattern in which the males in a position of authority use their power to provide protection and control in return for loyalty and obedience. 2. More loosely, any relationship in which adults are treated like children and denied the right to personal control.

path 1. Simply, a line connecting two points. More specifically: 2. In neurophysiology, a route formed by neurons (cell bodies and axonal and dendritic processes) along which nerve conduction takes place. 3. In simple learning experiments, a route through a maze. 4. In K. Lewin's field theory, a topological metaphor for a route over which a person moves psychologically. 5. In sociometry, a component in a theoretical model which displays the hypothesized causal relationships between variables. In all these uses, the synonym *pathway* may be used, particularly in 2.

path analysis A type of multivariate analysis that enables a researcher to discern the causal relations that exist between several variables. The relations are represented by graphs called *path diagrams* that show the various 'paths' that these causal influences travel.

pathergasia A. Meyer's term for the syndrome in which a personality or behavior disorder is associated with an anatomical or structural abnormality.

pathetic fallacy ➤ **anthropomorphism**.

pathetism A rare synonym for ➤ **hypnotism**.

pathic Pertaining to disease, disease-like.

-pathic Suffix used to indicate: 1. An experience or feeling that one has been affected in a particular way: e.g. *telepathic*. 2. A diseased condition; e.g., *cardiopathic*. 3. A general disorder; e.g., *sociopathic*. 4. A form of therapy or treatment; e.g., *osteopathic*.

path(o)- Word element borrowed from

the Greek *pathos* and carrying essentially the original meaning of *suffering, disease* or, more generally, *feeling*.

pathobiography The use of largely historical data to perform a psychoanalytic, biographical analysis on a person.

pathogenesis As the roots of the word suggest, the origin and development of disease.

pathognomic 1. Generally, capable of recognizing emotions and feelings. 2. More specifically, capable of recognizing and diagnosing disease.

pathognomonic Relating to a symptom or group of symptoms that are diagnostic 'trademarks' of a particular disease or disorder.

pathological gambling ➤ **gambling, pathological**.

pathological intoxication ➤ **alcohol intoxication, idiosyncratic**.

pathology 1. An abnormal condition or biological state in which proper functioning is prevented. The specific medical usage connotes an *organic* dysfunction or disease and not a *functional* one. However, in clinical psychology and psychiatry, the usage has been extended so that disorders for which there are no known biological components are included, hence the term, *psychopathology*. 2. A general label for the scientific study of such conditions. 3. A suffix used to specify a particular scientific or medical field, e.g., *neuropathology*. Note, however, that the simple term *pathologist* is still reserved for a medical specialist who deals with organic tissue abnormalities. Other specialists are always referred to by appending a qualifying prefix. adj. (for 1), *pathological*.

pathomimicry The feigning of a pathological state, mimicking the symptoms of some disease. The term is a general one and is used to include conscious, deliberate ➤ **malingering** as well as more subtle, unconsciously motivated ➤ **hypochondriasis**. ➤➤ **factitious disorder**.

pathoneurosis A neurotic condition marked by an excessive concern with a diseased or malfunctioning organ or with an organ that was previously diseased or malfunctioning.

pathway Synonym for ➤ **path**, especially meaning 2.

-pathy 1. Suffix denoting *disease, suffering* or *feeling*. 2. Combining form used to denote names of systems or methods of treatment, e.g., *osteopathy*.

patient In medicine: 1 n. One who is receiving treatment for a diagnosed illness or injury. 2 n. One who is receiving medical care. Meaning 2 is more general and covers persons with no demonstrable illness who are undergoing tests for possible disease. In psychology: 3 n. An individual in psychotherapy.

Meanings 1 and 2 are straightforward, meaning 3 is not. Within psychology the use of the term for a person in therapy derives from the influential ➤ **medical model** of psychological and psychiatric disorders which assumes that a ➤ **mental disorder** is a ➤ **mental disease** analogous to an organic, somatic disease. While there are good reasons for regarding many mental and behavioral disorders as diseases and for viewing those suffering from them as patients in the medical sense (e.g., a seriously deteriorated schizophrenic who requires hospitalization and is receiving antipsychotic drugs under the care of a psychiatrist), it is far from clear that the term should be applied to an individual who consults a psychiatrist or a clinical psychologist for weekly sessions to work through feelings of insecurity (➤ **client**) or to persons who are undergoing psychoanalysis (➤ **analysand**).

patrilineal descent The passing on of the family name or inheritance through the male line.

pattern 1. A model or sample. 2. A configuration or grouping of parts or elements with a coherent structure. In the former sense, one will see references to 'patterned behavior' or 'patterning' with the connotation that the behavior is modeled after or copied from another. ➤ **model, modeling, observational learning**. In the latter sense, the connotation is that the separate parts of an array, although distinguishable, form a coherent, integrated whole which is emphasized and which is the pattern. See here ➤ **configuration, Gestalt, pattern perception** and **pattern recognition**. In both of these senses one will also find verb forms, so that *to pattern* will mean either to copy or model or to integrate or organize the elements of a stimulus array into a conceptual structure.

pattern analysis A statistical technique whereby one attempts to discover the set of test items that 'belong together.' That is, they enable the tester to make more successful prediction of some criterion. Note that in a pattern analysis, unlike an analysis based on ➤ **multiple correlation**, the implication is that the discovered pattern of scores is interactive and representative of an underlying ability.

pattern discrimination The process whereby a ➤ **pattern** (2) is discriminated or detected in a complex stimulus array; e.g., discriminating a melody rather than just a sequence of notes. The term is used roughly interchangeably with ➤ **pattern recognition** on the grounds that discrimination entails recognition of the pattern and recognition of a pattern entails discrimination of that which is recognized as being distinct from other things. ➤➤ **pattern perception**, which is used as a cover term here, thus obviating these lexical difficulties.

patterning 1. Behaving so as to copy or model a ➤ **pattern** (1); see here ➤ **modeling** (preferred). **2.** The act of imposing a coherent structure or a ➤ **pattern** (2). **3.** The acquisition of a response to a ➤ **pattern** (2) rather than to any of its sub-elements. **4.** A program of physical therapy used in treating children with brain damage. The child is guided through the 'normal' sequence of sensory-motor development, beginning with crawling and creeping, on the assumption that cortical tissue that is undamaged will subsume the lost

functions. The assumption, it should be noted, is distinctly presumptive; there is precious little evidence that the procedure works.

pattern learning A term often used synonymously with ➤ **relational learning**. But see the discussions under ➤ **pattern perception** and ➤ **pattern recognition** for further development and special meanings.

pattern perception Loosely and generally (and, alas, tautologically), the perception of a ➤ **pattern** (2). Actually, most of what is really interesting about ➤ **perception** involves the perception of patterns. In fact, it is trivially true that *all* perception involves patterning in that even in the case of the simplest possible visual stimulus display, a single point of white light, there is a pattern in that the perceiver distinguishes the spot from the background (see here ➤ **figure–ground**). Thus, the term **pattern perception** has come to be used in the technical literature as an umbrella term and may refer to any or all of the issues involved in the *detection, discrimination* and *recognition* of patterns.

pattern recognition The separate words define the phrase rather nicely; pattern recognition is the act of recognizing that a particular array of stimulus elements or sequence of stimulus events is representative of a particular ➤ **pattern** (2). The simple definition of the term, however, covers some very tricky theoretical issues which can be illuminated by posing a few simple questions: How does one recognize that a particular collection of facial movements is a smile and not a frown? That a particular configuration of wood, cloth and stuffing is a chair rather than a sofa? That a particular four-legged, hairy beast is a dog and not a wolf? And so on. These questions have proven rather resistant to simple answers; see here the entries on ➤ **category** (et seq.) and ➤ **concept** (et seq.) to see how various terminologies have been introduced in an attempt to deal with them. Note also that many authors will use *pattern recognition* interchangeably with ➤ **pattern discrimination**; see this term for discussion on why this synonymity is attractive. ➤➤ **pattern perception**, which serves as an umbrella term.

pause 1. Generally, any short interruption in an ongoing process. More specifically: **2.** In operant analyses of behavior, a momentary cessation of operant responding. **3.** In normal speech, a break in the speech stream. Here, several kinds of pauses are distinguished; ➤ **filled *pause**, **hesitation *pause**, and **silent *pause**. **4.** In the study of eye movements, a ➤ **fixation pause**.

pause, filled In speech, a pause in the ongoing flow of words which is filled with other 'verbal gestures' such as 'ah,' 'um,' 'well,' etc. Since silence is often a cue for turn-taking during conversation, filled pauses act like 'floor holders' and keep the speaker from being interrupted.

pause, hesitation A short hesitation in the flow of speech. Although some use this term synonymously with ➤ **silent *pause**, it seems better to reserve it for those short spots of silence which serve linguistic function; e.g., appreciate how different the meaning is in the following sentence depending on whether the speaker puts a hesitation before or after the word *not*: 'He was not surprisingly killed by the blast.' Distinguish from ➤ **juncture**, which is phonemic.

pause, silent A pause in the flow of speech, a short period of silence. Most silent pauses (as well as most ➤ **filled *pauses**) have a 'computational' or 'lexical selection' function. That is, they are pauses during which the speaker plans the next phrase or sentence or searches memory for a particular word. Some use the term as a synonym for ➤ **hesitation *pause**, a practice not recommended (see that term for reasons). Also called *unfilled pause*.

Pavlovian Of or pertaining to the empirical and theoretical work of the great Russian physiologist Ivan Petrovich Pavlov (1849–1936). Although Pavlov's researches took him from the study of the heart through a series of investigations of the physiology of digestion (for which he

was awarded the Nobel Prize in 1904) to an extensive program of experimentation on conditioned responses, in psychology it is in this last area of research that he is best known and it is this work that is denoted by the adjectival form of his name. For details on specifics of the Pavlovian approach ➤ **classical conditioning**, **conditioned response**, **conditioned stimulus**, **conditioning**, **Pavlovianism**.

Pavlovian conditioning A term often used for ➤ **classical conditioning**.

Pavlovianism A variation on the physicalist ➤ **identity theory** associated closely with the work of I. P. Pavlov. The doctrine maintains that psychological states and processes are identical with physiological states and processes in the brain and, by extension, that investigations of the physiology and neurology of the brain (through, for example, the study of conditioning) are the only approaches likely to prove scientifically fruitful. It is this last proposition that kept Pavlov from ever referring to himself as a psychologist, preferring instead to regard his work as quintessentially physiological. ➤➤ **Pavlovian**.

pavor (*diurnus* and *nocturnus*) ➤ **sleep terror disorder**.

payoff The outcome of a trial expressed in terms of costs and/or benefits associated with taking a particular course of action. The term is used primarily in studies of choice behavior, decision-making, problem-solving, signal detection, games and the like where it is preferred to the behaviorist's term ➤ **reinforcement**.

payoff matrix A matrix or table that gives the various costs and benefits associated with each of the possible outcomes in a signal-detection experiment, a game, a decision-making experiment, etc. For example, ➤ **prisoner's *dilemma**.

PCP ➤ **phencyclidine thiophene**.

PDP models ➤ **parallel distributed processing (PDP) models**.

peak-clipping The elimination or 'clipping' off of the high-amplitude portions (the 'peaks') of a speech wave. Peak-clipping produces strange sounding speech but surprisingly little reduction in its intelligibility, particularly when compared with *center-clipping*, although, to be sure, the size of the 'clip' is an important factor.

peak experience A term coined by Abraham Maslow to characterize a profound moment in a person's life, an instance when they feel in harmony with all things, clear, spontaneous, independent and alert and often with relatively little awareness of time and space. Maslow was interested in the occurrence of such moments of reverie, particularly their relationship to the attainment of ➤ **self-actualization**.

Pearson chi-square (χ^2) **tests** There are several statistical tests included here, all of them variations of the basic ➤ **chi-square** statistic. They are used as tests of ➤ **goodness-of-fit** between a large sample and a population and as tests of association between two samples.

Pearson product-moment correlation ➤ **product-moment *correlation**.

pecking order The term derives from studies of chickens in which the order of dominance and its attendant privileges and priorities is expressible in terms of which chicken pecks which chicken. The phrase is used quite generally as a metaphor to characterize any graded ordering of privilege quite independently of fowl. Actually, since the phrase has become so common in everyday language, psychologists now prefer the phrase ➤ **dominance hierarchy**.

P-E-C scale ➤ **measurement of *authoritarianism**.

pedagogy Broadly, the science and art of teaching. The latter aspect being the ascendant one stamps the lie upon the former.

pederasty Specifically, anal intercourse with a young boy. Occasionally, although not correctly, it is used to mean any anal intercourse between two males. ➤ **sodomy**.

pederosis ➤ **pedophilia**.

ped(i)- Combining form meaning *foot*.

pedia-, ped(o)- Combining forms meaning *infant* or *child*. vars., *paedia-, paed(o)-*.

pediatrics Medical specialization concerned with the diseases of childhood.

pedication A catch-all term for a host of unusual sexual practices including pederasty, bestiality and sodomy.

pedigree A schematic representation of the structure of a family showing marriages, offspring, etc.; in short, a richly detailed 'family tree.' In genetics research, a complex system of notation has been adopted so that specific aspects of gene-linked conditions are represented in a pedigree.

pedologia Lit., infantile speech.

pedomorphism Investing adults with child-like characteristics; interpreting adult behaviour using concepts more appropriate to interpreting that of children; *infantilization*. The reverse tendency is called *enelicomorphism*. Distinguish from ➤ **pedomorphosis**.

pedomorphosis The retention of juvenile characteristics into adulthood; used typically when making cross-species comparisons. Distinguish from ➤ **pedomorphism**.

pedophilia Lit., attraction for children. However, as the term is used, that attraction is always sexual in its connotations and the meaning of the term is restricted to the sexual feelings of an adult for a child. Pedophilia is classified as a ➤ **paraphilia** only when it results in actual sexual activity and the child is pre-pubic.

peduncle Any of several stalk-like bundles of nerve fibers in the brain.

peeping Tom A term that has wended its way from the common tongue to the technical. Simply, a *voyeur*; ➤ **voyeurism**.

peer From the Latin for *equal*, characterizing individuals who may be regarded as equal with respect to some function (e.g., skill, educational level) or some situation (e.g., socioeconomic status). Generally, the term is not used in the technical literature for persons who happen to be, say, of the same age or from the same neighborhood. The term ➤ **peer group** is preferred by many.

peer group Any group the several members of which have roughly equal status within the confines and functions of the group. The term is most often used to describe children's or adolescents' groups, although it is applied to groups of adults in which the notion of equal status holds. Note, however, that legal issues may often intrude here on usage. That is, a peer group may also be defined as those of equal rank or of equal standing before the law. This latter meaning may or may not encompass the former – and vice versa.

peer rating A rating by one's peers in the sense of members of one's ➤➤ **peer group**. ➤➤ **peer review**.

peer review Quite literally, a review by one's peers or by the members of one's peer group. Hence: **1.** In social psychology, a process whereby one's behavior is analyzed and evaluated by other members of one's social group. **2.** In the actual functioning of science, a set of procedures whereby one's colleagues in a scientific field evaluate one's contribution in that field. In this sense, peer review is used to determine the publishability of scientific papers, to evaluate research proposals, to assess the fundability of grant applications, etc.

pegboard test Any of several performance tests of manual dexterity in which pegs must be placed in holes as rapidly as possible.

peg-word system A mnemonic technique in which the memorizer uses the components of a previously learned system as 'pegs' upon which to 'hang' new material. Perhaps the most common is the 'one-bun, two-shoe, three-tree,' etc. rhyme which, once learned, can be used to memorize a long list of new words by associating the first word with a bun, the second with a shoe, and so forth.

pellet A small, round bit of laboratory chow of standardized size, weight and nutritional content used as a reinforcement in animal experiments. The term has come to be used as a general euphemism for reinforcement of any kind, and offhanded jokes (especially by behaviorists) about what people will do for their pellets are not uncommon.

penalty As a simple extension of its standard meaning, the term is used in some experimental work to refer to the outcome of a trial on which the subject makes an error. The term is used in this sense as roughly equivalent to ➤ **punishment**, although that term has additional meaning.

penetrance In genetics, the frequency of expression of a particular trait in a population of organisms all of whom possess the genetic configuration for that trait.

penile Pertaining to the penis. Compare with ➤ **phallic**.

penis The male copulatory (and, in mammals, urinary) organ. Distinguish from ➤ **phallus**.

penis captivus A set of circumstances in which the penis is held within the vagina and cannot be withdrawn. It does exist as a momentary normal component in the copulatory behavior of some species but it is clinically unknown in humans.

penis envy The hypothesized envy of the penis. The primary usage is with regard to women who, according to the classical Freudian view, are universally afflicted with a repressed wish to possess a penis. This position, stemming as it does from Freud's characterization of women as incomplete men, has been vigorously criticized and is rarely taken completely seriously any more. The secondary usage is with respect to young boys, who often display envy of the adult male.

pentatonic Of a musical scale based on five tones.

pentobarbital A short-to-immediate-acting ➤ **barbiturate**.

peotomy Surgical removal of the penis. Distinguish from ➤ **castration**.

pepsin An enzyme secreted by the stomach that breaks peptide bonds and thus initiates the process of breaking the proteins in food into their constituent amino acids.

peptic Pertaining to the stomach and to digestion.

peptide A chain of amino acids held together by peptide bonds. The molecules, made up of several amino acids, are called *polypeptides*, and when the chains become links of over 50, *proteins*. Many peptides produced in the body function as ➤ **neurotransmitters, neuromodulators,** and **hormones**.

peptide bond A bond between the amino group of one amino acid and the carboxyl of another.

perceive Simply, to be aware of the source of that which impinges on the sensory receptors. Usage, however, is far from simple; ➤ **perception** for discussion.

perceived self ➤ **self, perceived**.

percentile Any of the 99 numbered points that divide an ordered set of scores into 100 parts, each of which contains 1/100th of the total. This straightforward meaning unfortunately often gets lost in confusion; ➤ **centile** and **partile** for discussion.

percentile score A score given as a percentile and representing the percentage of scores in a sample that fall below it. That is, a score at the 50th percentile indicates that 50% of the scores fall below it. Note that the highest possible percentile score is 99; one of 100 makes no sense since a score cannot be greater than itself.

percept That which is perceived. Note that percept should not be confused with either the physical object (the ➤ **distal** stimulus) or the energy that impinges on a receptor (the ➤ **proximal stimulus**). In the final analysis, the percept is phenomenological or experiential; it is the outcome of the process of ➤ **perception**.

perception 1. Collectively, those processes that give coherence and unity to sensory input. This is the most general sense of the term and covers the entire sequence of events from the presentation of a physical stimulus to the phenomenological experiencing of it. Included here are physical, physiological, neurological, sensory, cognitive and affective components. Because this manner of use of the term is so broad, it should be seen as encompassing many of the more specialized and restrictive senses that follow. **2.** The awareness of an organic process. This meaning is designed to focus on perception as a conscious event; the actual experiencing of a chain of (organic) processes initiated by some external or internal stimulus. **3.** A synthesis or fusion of the elements of sensation. This usage is found in the approach of ➤ **structuralism** (1). **4.** An intervening variable, a hypothetical internal event that results directly from stimulation of sensory receptors and is affected by drive level and habit. This meaning, of course, is that expressed within ➤ **behaviorism**. **5.** An awareness of the truth of something. This sense is largely nontechnical and connotes a kind of implicit, intuitive insight. **6.** A label for the field of psychology that studies any or all of the processes entailed in the above meanings.

Not surprisingly, the full range of connotations of the term envelops nearly every aspect of psychology and existing theories of perception are far-reaching indeed. In essence, the study of perception always begins with recognition of the fact that what is perceived is not uniquely determined by physical stimulation but, rather, is an organized complex, dependent upon a host of other factors. While there is no doubt that the incoming stimulus is an essential feature of what is ultimately perceived, the old structuralist argument that perceptions are built up entirely out of sensations is accepted by virtually no one today. The following is a quick review of the factors that determine what is perceived; terms of importance are treated in more detail elsewhere in this volume.

(a) *Attention.* In order to perceive an event it must be focused upon or noticed. Moreover, attention itself is selective, so that attending to one stimulus tends to inhibit or suppress the processing of others. See here ➤ **attention, cocktail-party phenomenon, information processing**.

(b) *Constancy.* The perceptual world tends to remain the same despite rather drastic alterations in sensory input. A book seen from an angle is still perceived as rectangular although the retinal image is distinctly trapezoidal. See here ➤ **constancy, unconscious inference**.

(c) *Motivation.* What is perceived is affected by one's motivational state; hungry people see food objects in ambiguous stimuli that sated people do not. See here ➤ **New Look, perceptual defense, perceptual vigilance**.

(d) *Organization.* Perception is not a simple juxtaposition of sensory elements, it is fundamentally organized into coherent wholes. ➤ **Gestalt** and related entries.

(e) *Set.* The cognitive and/or emotional stance that is taken toward a stimulus array strongly affects what will be perceived. See here ➤ **attitude, set** (2).

(f) *Learning.* There are two issues here. One concerns the question of how much of perception is innate and how much acquired from experience; ➤ **heredity–environment controversy** and **nativism**. The other concerns the question of how learning can function to modify perception; ➤ **perceptual *learning**.

(g) *Distortion and hallucination.* Strong emotional feelings can distort perceptions rather dramatically and hallucinations can be produced by a variety of causes including drugs, lack of sleep, sensory deprivation, emotional stress, psychosis, etc. These 'misperceptions' are an intriguing problem because the essential perception seems to come from 'inside the head'

rather than from the environment. ➤ **hallucination**.

(h) *Illusion.* There are many circumstances in which what is perceived cannot be easily predicted from an analysis of the physical-stimulus array. ➤ **illusion**.

There are, of course, other elements involved in both the study of perception and the impact of perceptual research on other areas of psychology. Many of these are dealt with in the entries below. Others are found under the alphabetical listing of the modifying term.

perception, binocular Normal perception with both eyes such that the two retinal images fuse into a single percept. ➤ **binocular** and **depth perception**.

perception, span of ➤ **apprehension span** and **span of *attention**.

perception, subliminal A curious phrase since *subliminal* means below the threshold for perception. The term actually refers, not to *perception* in the usual sense of that term, but to the effect of a below-threshold stimulus upon an individual's behavior. There has been considerable scientific debate over the reliability and/or validity of the effects of subliminal stimuli and extensive discussion of the ethical issues raised by even the possibility that such effects might be real and thus be used by unscrupulous advertisers or politicians. If there are reliable effects here (➤ **perceptual defense, perceptual vigilance, subception**), they are small and there is no evidence that they can be used to modify attitudes or emotions. Indeed, the best overview of the research on subliminal advertising (the application feared by many) was given by the American psychologist J. V. McConnell: 'All things considered, secret attempts to manipulate people's minds have yielded results as subliminal as the stimuli used.'

perception time A largely obsolete term for the time it takes the brain to carry out a particular perceptual process. The procedure used to measure perception time was the ➤ **subtraction method**, whereby one subtracts the time required for various parts of a reaction. Interestingly, the principle involved has found new life in recent work in cognitive psychology, although the term itself has resisted attempts to revive it.

perceptive Only loosely related to the meaning of ➤ **perception**, perceptive is most commonly used as descriptive of persons who are sensitive in picking up important cues in social situations.

perceptual Pertaining to ➤ **perception**. Almost always used in combined form, as the following entries exemplify.

perceptual anchoring A phrase generally used to refer to any situation in which what is perceived is dependent, not so much on the physical properties of the stimulus, but on one's frame of reference.

perceptual cycle A term used by U. Neisser to characterize his argument that a critical aspect of perception consists of a set of cognitive anticipations about to-be-perceived information. The full perceptual cycle consists of three components: (a) a set of cognitive schemata which direct perceptual processes; (b) a set of perceptual-exploration responses which sample information; and (c) the actual stimuli of the physical environment. The information thus picked up modifies the existing cognitive schemata, which affect the exploration processes and so on around the cycle. The term is Neisser's but the general notion of feedback and adjustment is common to many theories of perception.

perceptual defense Operationally, perceptual defense is said to occur whenever recognition threshold for a stimulus is raised. Evidence for such an effect was put forward by workers in the so-called ➤ **New Look** approach in which tachistoscopically presented words with unpleasant connotation and taboo words had higher thresholds than neutral words. Such effects were hailed as significant demonstrations of the role of emotional and motivational factors in perception – not to mention as support for psychoana-

lytic theory, where considerable stress is placed on unconscious defenses. Enthusiasm was tempered somewhat when it was recognized that these early experiments did not clearly distinguish between *unconscious* perceptual defense and *conscious* response inhibition; to wit, is it perceptual defense that prevents a subject from seeing a taboo word, or response inhibition that prevents the subject from reporting that that 'dirty word' was, in fact, *really* presented by the experimenter? Some more recent studies run with proper controls seem to suggest that perceptual defense (and its opposite, ➤ **perceptual vigilance**) may be real phenomena, although their effects are very small. Contrast with ➤ **subception**.

perceptual field A very general term used to refer collectively to all of those aspects of the physical stimulus that an individual is conscious of. Because of the factors discussed under ➤ **perception**, the elements of the perceptual field rarely, if ever, correspond with those in the environment in any simple one-to-one fashion.

perceptual induction An occasional synonym for ➤ **empathy**.

perceptual learning ➤ **learning, perceptual**.

perceptual-motor region ➤ **region, perceptual-motor**.

perceptual organization ➤ **organization** and ➤ **principle of *organization**.

perceptual schema ➤ **schema** (1).

perceptual sensitization A phenomenon said to occur when the recognition threshold for a stimulus is lowered, i.e. the subject is more 'sensitive' than is usual. The term is preferred by many over ➤ **perceptual vigilance**, although this latter term is still more common in the literature – despite the connotative difficulties it has.

perceptual set ➤ *Einstellung* and **set** (2).

perceptual structure Loosely, the overall cognitive-perceptual organization of a complex stimulus. See here ➤ **Gestalt** and related entries.

perceptual transformation A general term for any modification in the percept produced by (a) additions to, deletions from or alterations in the physical stimulus, or (b) novel interpretations of the stimulus, changes in set or attitude, or sudden insights concerning the material.

perceptual vigilance A synonym for ➤ **perceptual sensitization** which, although clearly preferred on semantic grounds, is not as common in the literature. The word *vigilance* is a little tricky here because it carries the connotation that the subject is actively, even consciously, looking for a particular stimulus event and most of the theories of the phenomenon (and its opposite, ➤ **perceptual defense**) assume that unconscious processes are responsible. Nevertheless, the word *vigilance* is kind of 'catchy' and continues to be the term of choice for most psychologists.

perch An antiquated term for a ➤ **fixation pause** in reading.

percipient 1. Generally, one who perceives, a perceiver. 2. In parapsychology, one who supposedly receives a telepathic message.

perfect correlation ➤ **correlation, perfect**.

perfect pitch ➤ **absolute pitch**.

perforant path A neural pathway connecting the ➤ **entorhinal cortex** with the ➤ **dentate gyrus** of the ➤ **hippocampal formation**.

performance In its broadest sense performance can be equated with behavior; that is, any activity or set of responses that has some effect upon the environment. However, there are nuances of usage found in specific contexts. To wit: (a) Performance is sometimes equated with *achievement* in the sense that some measure of the adequacy of the behavior is involved. The point here is that performance is often viewed as behavior in some particular situation requiring particular responses, as in a test. Distinguish this usage from ➤ **performance test**, where one is specifically alluding to tests in which the role of language is minimized, or tests which involve only motor coordination. (b) Performance is often used in a general way to include only that which is overt. In this sense, one finds distinctions between *performance* and ➤ **competence** (3) or between *performance* and ➤ **learning**. In these cases *performance* refers to the overt, observable behavior while *competence* or *learning* refers to the covert, hypothesized states or processes inside the organism. For a trivial example to make the point, consider that a fully satiated rat which has just received several dozen reinforcements for bar pressing still 'knows' how and when to press even though the performance level may be at zero owing to changes in motivation.

performance test Any test designed to rely on nonverbal performance. There is a variety of such tests using form boards, mazes, picture completions, puzzles, etc. The correlations between scores on these tests and on standard verbal tests designed to evaluate the same processes are moderately positive although, given our cultural orientations, it is not surprising that the verbal tests have the higher predictive validity.

performative A ➤ **speech act** in which, by its very utterance, the speaker performs something. Examples: judge to prisoner, 'I sentence you to five years in prison,' or delegate at a political convention, 'I nominate Joe Blow for president.' Verbs typically used performatively include, *appoint*, *order*, *urge*, *promise*, *guarantee*, *state*, *request*, *thank*, etc. ➤➤ **commissive** and **declarative**, which are other speech acts that can have performative properties.

peri- Combining form meaning *around, about, outside* or *beyond*.

periaqueductal gray (PAG) An area in the midbrain surrounding the cerebral aqueduct. It contains opiate-sensitive cells that play an important role in inhibiting pain through descending axons that synapse onto neurons in the lower brainstem and spinal cord that mediate *analgesia*. It also plays a role in control over aggressive behavior and the female sexual response.

perimacular vision ➤ **vision, perimacular**.

perimeter In vision, a device for mapping the sensitivity of the retinal field.

perinatal During the period just preceding, during or just following childbirth.

period 1. The time for a complete oscillation of a cyclic (periodic) event. 2. The days of the menstrual flow. 3. The menstrual discharge itself.

periodicity theory of hearing ➤ **theories of *hearing**.

periodic reinforcement Descriptive label for any reinforcement presented on a regular time schedule. ➤ **schedules of *reinforcement**.

period prevalence In epidemiology, the total number of cases of a disease that occurred within a specified time period. Compare with ➤ *point prevalence*.

peripheral A multipurpose adjective used in a variety of circumstances when one wishes to distinguish between things, events or processes that are external, on the outside (i.e. on the periphery), from those which are internal or central. Thus, it is used to pertain to: 1. The surface or outer part of an organ or body. 2. The sensory (afferent) and motor (efferent) neurons connecting the surface of the body with the central nervous system, i.e. the *peripheral nervous system*. 3. Those psychological processes assumed to be intimately connected with that which is muscular, glandular, visceral, skeletal or sensory. That is, processes not considered to be intrinsic to the higher brain centers. This use, as many have noted, is highly arbitrary. Theorists who argue for ➤ **peripheralism** include many processes here that others would classify as central; e.g., Watson even made *thinking* a peripheral process. 4. That which is of marginal or doubtful relevance or importance.

peripheralism A theoretical perspective that focuses on peripheral processes as explanatory devices. The strongest proponent of this point of view was the origina-

tor of radical behaviorism, John B. Watson, who took the arguments about as far as they could go – to the point of characterizing thinking as merely subvocal laryngeal movements and all emotions as mechanical glandular responses. From this orientation, conscious experience was regarded as epiphenomenal and without a causal role in determining behavior. Although the ➤ **Watsonian** position was, at the time, an understandable reaction against the extreme centrist views of *structuralism* and *psychoanalysis*, the peripheralist perspective has little to recommend it today.

peripheral nervous system ➤ **nervous system**.

peripheral vision ➤ **vision, peripheral**.

periphery of the retina The outermost area of the retina, that farthest from the fovea. It is not sharply defined, but generally regarded as the area where the cones are effectively absent. Peripheral vision is relatively poor, low in acuity and strictly achromatic.

perirhinal cortex ➤ **parahippocampal cortex**.

periventricular hypothalamus ➤ **hypothalamus**.

Perky effect A confusion between imagery and perception. In the basic procedure, the subject is asked to image an object, say an apple, on an initially blank screen. A very dim picture of an apple is then projected on the screen and the subject is often incapable of detecting that the real picture of the apple is other than the imaged apple.

permanent memory ➤ **long-term *memory**.

permeable Capable of being permeated. In physiological work, descriptive of a membrane that is capable of passing certain substances through it. Somewhat more metaphorically, characterizing any boundary that can be penetrated.

permissiveness An attitude or characteristic of persons such that they tend to be liberal, granting considerable behavioral freedom and latitude to others over whom they have authority. Contrast with ➤ **authoritarianism**.

pernicious trend Pernicious means *ruinous, harmful*, even *fatal*. Hence, this term is used as descriptive of any serious, regressive trend away from normal development. It is also used by researchers to describe a pattern in the data that consistently supports someone else's theory.

persecutory anxiety ➤ **paranoid anxiery**.

perseverance ➤ **persistence**.

perseveration Several uses are common here; all contain the notion of a tendency to persist, to persevere. **1.** The tendency to continue with a particular pattern of behavior. Often used with the connotation that such perseveration continues to the point where it is no longer appropriate. Compare with ➤ **stereotypy**. **2.** The tendency to repeat, to a pathological degree, a word or phrase. **3.** The tendency for a particular memory or idea or piece of behavior to recur without any (detectable) stimulus for it. The term invariably carries negative connotations. Compare here with ➤ **persistence**.

perseveration deficit ➤ **deficit, perseveration**.

perseveration set A ➤ **set** (2) that one carries over from one situation to another. The usual connotation here is that such sets are often inappropriate and reflect an inability to shift strategies appropriately.

perseverative error Any error made repeatedly.

perseverative functional autonomy Allport's term for an extreme form of ➤ **functional *autonomy** displayed as inappropriate repetitions and ritualized acts. Compare with ➤ **propriate functional autonomy**.

perseverative trace ➤ **trace, perseverative**.

persistence Similar in meaning to ➤ **perseveration** in that it reflects a behavioral tendency to persevere or persist, but with two important differences. First, the negative connotations of perseveration are generally not present; persistence suggests an admirable striving against opposition. Second, persistence typically refers to *behavior*, while perseveration is generally suggestive of a tendency. In this sense persistence will be used to refer to processes which continue in time after the stimulus that initiated them is no longer present. syn., *perseverance*.

persistence of vision ➤ **iconic** (2).

person Psychology, in one guise or another, concerns itself with entities that behave, act, think, emote and do so within the context of some social and physical environment. When such an entity is a member of the species *Homo sapiens* the term *person* is appropriately used as label.

persona From the Latin, meaning *person*. In classical Roman theater, it was a mask which the actor wore expressing the role played. By extension of this notion, Jung used the term in his early formulations to refer to the role a person takes on by virtue of the pressures of society. It is meant to refer to the role that society expects one to play in life and not necessarily the one played at a deep psychological level. The persona is public, the face presented to others. Compare with ➤ **anima** (2).

personal **1.** Relating to some thing, event or characteristic having the quality of a person. **2.** Relating to some thing, event or characteristic which is intrinsic to a particular person. Sense 1 is general, the reference is personhood; 2 is specific, the reference is a single individual.

personal construct The central concept in George Kelly's theory of personality. It is a cover term for each of the ways in which a person attempts to perceive, understand, predict and control the world; each of an individual's personal constructs functions like a hypothesis, a possible way of constructing the physical and social environment. They may be altered if conflicting information is perceived, or become fixed and incorporated as basic aspects of one's personality. ➤ **Rep Test**.

personal determinant ➤ **determinant**.

personal disjunction The disparity between what one would ideally like to get from a situation (or from life in general) and what one actually expects to get. Note that the discrepancy is not between desires and reality, it is between what is wanted and a judgement of how likely it is that these wants will be fulfilled.

personal disposition G. W. Allport's term for ➤ **personality trait**.

personal document Any self-produced document that provides information about an individual; diaries, personal essays, autobiographical sketches, letters, recordings, etc. are included. The 'personal' aspect is what makes them of interest. Because they are intrinsically motivated rather than responses to questionnaires or interviews, they presumably provide insights into those aspects of social and personal life that the person regards as most salient.

personal equation The term was coined by the 19th-century astronomer F. W. Bessel to refer to a procedure for correcting for differences in reaction time between two observers of stellar transit. Bessel proposed the 'equation' as a mathematical method to correct for the individual differences of astronomers so as to prevent such factors from contaminating astronomical research. By extension, it became a phrase used to mean any adjustment for difference in simple reaction times between any two subjects.

personal fitness In evolutionary biology, an individual organism's reproductive success. Also called *Darwinian fitness* and, simply, ➤ **fitness** (2).

personal identity 1. The phenomenological sense that one has of one's own intrinsic self independent of all others and transcending the biological and psychological emendations and amputations produced by a world in flux. See here ➤ **self**. 2. The fact that each person is a separate individual. Meaning 1 is the existentially more interesting one; it reflects the essential quality of selfness and if lost the continued existence of 2 hardly seems to make much difference.

personalism 1. Generally, an approach to psychological science that maintains that the individual personality is the central construct against which all else must be considered. 2. More specifically, descriptive of the general principle that one perceives and interprets the actions of another partly by reference to the extent to which such actions were directed personally at the perceiver. Thus, one will read of the personalisms of another's behaviors, meaning the degree to which they are seen as directed at the perceiver. 3. A synonym for ➤ **personalistic psychology**.

personalistic approach See the discussion under ➤ **great-man theory**.

personalistic psychology The orientation that argues that psychological principles only have meaning when they are mapped into or shown to be reflections of personal life and personal experience.

personality One of the classic 'chapter heading' words in psychology. That is, a term so resistant to definition and so broad in usage that no coherent simple statement about it can be made – hence the wise author uses it as the title of a chapter and then writes freely about it without incurring any of the definitional responsibilities incurred were it introduced in the text. Rather than repeat here the folly of several score unwise authors (G. W. Allport, back in 1927, was able to cull nearly 50 different definitions from the literature and heaven only knows how many one could find today), we shall not characterize the term definitionally but rather according to its role in personality theory. This approach seems best, since each author's meaning of the term tends to be colored by his or her theoretical biases and by the empirical tools used in evaluation and test of the theory. The easiest procedure is to present a few of the most influential general orientations and outline how each characterizes the term:

1. *Type theories*. The oldest of these is that of Hippocrates, who hypothesized four basic temperaments, choleric, sanguine, melancholic and phlegmatic. The assumption here, as in all subsequent type theories, was that each individual is a representation of a particular balance of these basic elements. The most complete typological theory was that of W. H. Sheldon, who elegantly (but unconvincingly) argued that body types are intimately related to personality development. ➤ **constitutional theory** for a discussion. Carl Jung's approach, although belonging properly under the psychoanalytic theories (see below), is sometimes pigeonholed as a type theory because of his emphasis upon classifying individuals according to types, e.g., *introvert* v. *extravert*.

2. *Trait theories*. All theories of this kind operate from the assumption that one's personality is a compendium of *traits* or characteristic ways of behaving, thinking, feeling, reacting, etc. The early trait theories were actually little more than lists of adjectives and personality was defined by enumeration. More recent approaches have used techniques of factor analysis in an attempt to isolate underlying dimensions of personality. Probably the most influential theory here is that of R. B. Cattell, which is based on a set of ➤ **source *traits** that are assumed to exist in relative amounts in each individual and are the 'real structural influences underlying personality.' According to Cattell, the goal of personality theory is to have the individual trait matrix formulated so that behavioral predictions can be made.

Note that the *type* and *trait* approaches complement each other and, indeed, one could argue that they are two sides of the same coin. Type theories are primarily concerned with that which is common among individuals, trait theories focus on that which differentiates them. However, they certainly entail very different connotations of the base term *personality*.

3. *Psychodynamic and psychoanalytic theories*. A multitude of approaches is clustered here including the classic theories of Freud and Jung, the social psychological theories of Adler, Fromm, Sullivan and Horney, and the more recent approaches of Laing and Perls, among others. The distinctions between them are legion but all contain an important common core idea: personality for all is characterized by the notion of *integration*. Strong emphasis is generally placed upon developmental factors, with the implicit assumption that the adult personality evolves gradually over time, depending on the manner in which the integration of factors develops. Moreover, motivational concepts are of considerable importance, so that no account of personality is considered to be theoretically useful without an evaluation of the underlying motivational syndromes. syn., ➤ **character** (2).

4. *Behaviorism*. The focus here has been on the extension of learning theory to the study of personality. Although there are no influential, purely behavioristic theories of personality, the orientation has stimulated other theorists to look closely at an integral problem: how much of the behavioral consistency that most people display is due to underlying personality *types* or *traits* or *dynamics* and how much is due to consistencies in the environment and in the contingencies of reinforcement? Not surprisingly, the points of view below, all of which were influenced to some degree by behaviorism, look beyond the person for answers here and, to some degree or another, actually question the usefulness of the term *personality*.

5. *Humanism*. This orientation emerged as a reaction to what was perceived as the dominance of psychoanalysis and behaviorism in psychology. Thinkers such as Maslow, Rogers, May, and Frankl focused upon ➤ **phenomenology**, where subjective mental experiences are paramount, on ➤ **holism**, where the reductionism of behaviorism is rejected, and on the importance of the drive toward ➤ **self-actualization** (2). Humanism's main problems concern the difficulty of testing scientifically many of its theoretical notions. Nevertheless, it has remained an important approach to the study of personality

and has given rise to the ➤ **human-potential movement**.

6. *Social learning theories*. Much of the theorizing from this point of view derives from the problem of balancing the impact of the environment with that of naturally given properties. However, the notion of personality is treated here as those aspects of behavior that are acquired in a social context. The leading theorist here is Albert Bandura, whose position is based on the assumption that although learning is critical, factors other than simple stimulus–response associations and reinforcement contingencies are needed to explain the development of complex social behaviors (such as *roles*) that essentially make up one's personality. In particular, cognitive factors such as memory, retention processes and self-regulatory processes are important and much research has focused on modeling and observational learning as mechanisms that can give a theoretically satisfying description of the regularities of behavior in social contexts.

7. *Situationism*. This perspective, championed by Walter Mischel, is derivative of behaviorism and social learning theory. It argues that whatever consistency of behavior is observable is largely determined by the characteristics of the *situation* rather than by any internal personality types or traits. Indeed, the very notion of a personality trait, from this point of view, is nothing more than a mental construction of an observer who is trying to make some sense of the behavior of others and exists only in the mind of the beholder. The regularity of behavior is attributed to similarities in the situations one tends to find oneself in rather than to internal regularities.

8. *Interactionism*. This position is a kind of eclectic one. It admits of certain truths in all of the above, more single-minded, theories and maintains that personality emerges from interactions between particular qualities and predispositions and the manner in which the environment influences the ways in which these qualities and behavioral tendencies are displayed. It is far from clear that personality can be said to exist as a distinct 'thing' from this perspective. Rather it becomes a kind of cover term for the complex patterns of interaction.

It is interesting to note that the above theoretical approaches can be seen as representing two distinguishable generalizations concerning the very term *personality*. For 1–3 it represents a legitimate theoretical construct, a hypothetical, internal 'entity' with a causal role in behavior and, from a theoretical point of view, with genuine explanatory power. For 4–8 it is seen as a secondary factor inferred on the basis of consistency of behavior – while other operations and processes play the critical causal roles in dictating behavior – and, hence, as a notion that has relatively little explanatory power.

The foregoing does not, of course, exhaust the theoretical approaches that have had their turn in the scientific spotlight (e.g, ➤ **existentialism, field theory**) but it should suffice to give a feeling for the diversity of forms of meaning that the term *personality* can express. The term is also found in a wide variety of combined forms, the more commonly used of which follow.

personality disintegration Since many personality theorists regard *integration* as one of the key aspects of a normal, well-adapted, functioning ➤ **personality**, this term will be used to designate the circumstances in which the various components (behavioral, emotional, motivational) lose their integrated, structured quality. However, since various theorists propose various ways of conceptualizing the components of personality there will be similarly various ways of conceptualizing just what personality disintegration is.

personality disorder This term has served for a considerable length of time as an umbrella term for any of a number of psychological disorders. The primary difficulty in determining just what belongs under the umbrella and just how it is being used derives from the fact that several 'official' definitions have been 'traded in' for newer models over the past several decades. To wit: **1.** Originally, any mental disorder manifested by maladjustments in motivation and maladaptive patterns of relating to one's social environment. This sense of the term was used so broadly that it encompassed minor neuroses as well as full-blown psychotic disturbances. It also had a tendency to be applied rather arbitrarily to styles of social interaction that were outside of one's particular perspective concerning what was right and proper. Because of this looseness of usage, this meaning was abandoned – and it is surely of interest that the term itself survived this (and a further) adjustment in denotation rather than simply succumbing of its excesses. **2.** A class of behavioral disorders, *excluding* the neuroses and psychoses, manifested as pathological developments in one's overall personality and marked by relatively little anxiety or distress. Within this general use of the term three subclasses of disorders were identified: (a) The *general personality disorders*, including ➤ **compulsive,** ➤ **cyclothymic,** ➤ **paranoid** and ➤ **schizoid personalities**. (b) The *sociopathic disorders*, which were characterized by a general lack of appropriate affect, little or no guilt following transgressions and an inability to form lasting emotional bonds with others. Included here were ➤ **antisocial,** ➤ **dyssocial,** ➤ **psychopathic** and ➤ **sociopathic personalities**. (c) The *sexual deviants*, whose primary mode of sexual gratification was generally regarded as socially undesirable. This sense of the term was the dominant one until the third edition of the US *Diagnostic and Statistical Manual* in 1980, which revised the use of the term considerably. Many of the subcategories of personality disorder given in the following are carry-overs from those in 2; however, the label *personality* which was attached to each disorder has been altered so that *personality disorder* is now the preferred term; e.g., *schizoid personality* is now *schizoid personality disorder*. **3.** A mental disorder the essential features of which are deeply ingrained, enduring, maladaptive patterns of relating to, thinking about and perceiving the environment

that are extreme to the point where they cause impairment in social and behavioral functioning. Personality disorders are generally recognizable in childhood or adolescence and continue through most of adult life. Note, however, if diagnosed before age 18, the proper diagnostic category is ➤ **disorder of *childhood**. Included in this category are ➤ **paranoid, schizoid, schizotypal, histrionic, narcissistic, antisocial, borderline, avoidant, dependent** and **compulsive personality disorders**. See any or all of the specific disorders listed above for details.

personality dynamics A general term used for the study of the complex, interactive, dynamic aspects of motivation, emotion and behavior. ➤ **dynamic**.

personality integration Generally the coordination, organization or unification of the disparate traits, behavioral dispositions, motives, emotions, etc. that make up one's personality. ➤➤ **personality disintegration** and the core term ➤ **personality**.

personality inventory A personality-assessment device based on a large number of items to which the subject responds by indicating those that apply to or are descriptive of him or herself. Three types of inventories are common: in one the individual responds to a statement with 'yes,' 'no' 'questionable'; in another the individual chooses between pairs of statements the one that best applies; and the third uses the ➤ **Likert scale**. E.g., ➤ **Minnesota Multiphasic Personality Inventory**.

personality organization ➤ **personality integration**.

personality problem A basically non-technical term used as a catch-all label for any minor, persistent or recurring behavioral, motivational or emotional pattern that makes a person unhappy.

personality, segmentalized A term borrowed from sociology and used for one who has developed, as a response to societal pressures, a diverse and inconsistent set of social roles and ways of behaving. It is argued by some that complex urban societies are more likely to produce this type of personality than small, more coherent, rural societies. Distinguish from ➤ **multiple personality**.

personality sphere R. B. Cattell's term for the entire range of measurable human personality. As the beginning point in his investigations he took over 4,500 trait adjectives from a dictionary, reduced the list to 200 by grouping synonyms and factor-analyzed these to get 35 ➤ **surface *traits** and 16 ➤ **source *traits** which he argued give full coverage to the entire personality sphere.

personality, split A strictly nontechnical term used in popular parlance more or less appropriately for ➤ **multiple personality** and more or less inappropriately for ➤ **schizophrenia**.

personality syndrome The original meaning of *syndrome* carried with it the notion of a characteristic pattern of symptoms of a disease. This meaning has been extended to the notion of personality such that syndrome here refers to a set of maladaptive behavioral characteristics that have been shown to be common to many persons. When the unqualified term is used, the 'disease' aspect has been largely dropped, on the grounds that the causal factors are largely social and cultural rather than biological. However, when physiological factors are clearly implicated, the term ➤ **organic *personality syndrome** is used.

personality syndrome, organic Any marked alteration in personality where a specific biological factor has been identified. Typical symptoms include socially unacceptable action, extreme emotional liability, loss of impulse control and lack of recognition of the consequences of one's actions. E.g., ➤ **Pick's disease**. Occasionally the term *frontal-lobe syndrome* is used for these disorders.

personality test Very loosely, any device or instrument for assessing or evaluating personality. Typically, *direct tests* (e.g., the ➤ **Minnesota Multiphasic Personality**

Inventory) are distinguished from the *indirect* or *projective tests* (e.g., the ➤ **Rorschach**).

personality theory ➤ **personality**.

personality trait Loosely a ➤ **trait** of personality. That is: **1.** Some hypothesized underlying disposition or characteristic of a person that, in principle, can be used as an explanation of the regularities and consistencies of behavior. See, here, the discussion under ➤ **personality** (especially 2). **2.** A simple description of an individual's characteristic modes of behaving, perceiving, thinking, etc. Sense 2 is used descriptively without explanatory intent; sense 1 is grounded in a particular approach to personality theory.

personality type Generally, any label used for classifying an individual's personality. There are many different typologies, each with its own categorization system. All, however, are predicated on the assumption that coherent patterns of behavior or consistent styles of action exist which are sufficiently well defined so that individuals may be classified as falling into one or more types. This assumption, although certainly questionable, does have heuristic value and personality typing is endemic in social and personality research and theory. ➤ **personality** (especially 1).

personalized instruction A general term for any educational program designed with sufficient flexibility to be adapted to individual students of differing capabilities. E.g., ➤ **Keller plan**.

personal space The area immediately surrounding an individual. It may be a large area or a small one depending on a host of momentary factors (whom you are with, your mood, the nature of the interaction, etc.) and more permanent factors (cultural traditions, physical size, etc.).

personal unconscious Jung's term for an individual person's unconscious as distinguished from the transpersonal, ➤ **collective unconscious**. Jung conceived of the personal unconscious as consisting of repressed, suppressed, forgotten or even ignored experiences and treated it very much like Freud's ➤ **preconscious** in that material in it could and often did enter consciousness.

personification 1. Generally, the inputing of human or personal qualities to some 'abstraction.' The abstraction may be a social group or a social structure, an image or representation of some real person, or even that which is not human. ➤ **anthropomorphism** and **animism. 2.** More specifically, a type of defense mechanism in which the individual attributes qualities or the blame for things to others as a result of personal frustrations. See here ➤ **projection**, of which personification is generally regarded as a form.

personnel 1 n. Specifically, the employees in an organization. **2** n. More generally, the human aspect in business and industry. **3** adj. Pertaining to the personnel in either sense.

personnel psychology A general label for that aspect of industrial/organizational psychology concerned with (a) the selecting, supervising and evaluating of personnel, and (b) a variety of job-related factors such as morale, personal satisfaction, management-worker relations, counseling and so forth.

personology 1. The label Henry Murray applied to his herculean efforts to develop a comprehensive theory of personality. His viewpoint was strongly organic and holistic. He insisted that no isolated piece of behavior could ever be understood without taking into account the fully functioning person. **2.** Loosely, the study of personality. 1 is clearly the preferred usage.

person perception A general label for an area in social psychology concerned with the issue of how we perceive other persons. Although the basic principles of perception certainly apply, there is a variety of additional variables and factors which make other persons rather special objects of perception. To appreciate the kinds of issues involved here, ➤ **attribution theory, impression formation, prejudice**.

perspective 1. A mental view, a cognitive orientation, a way of seeing a situation or a scene. **2.** The arrangement of the parts of a whole scene as viewed from some conceptual, physical or temporal vantage point. The implication in this meaning is that this vantage point provides the proper point of view, the perception being more veridical than from some other. **3.** The arrangement of objects on a flat surface such that the viewer receives the impression of a three-dimensional scene.

perspective taking 1. In the Piagetian approach, the capacity of a child to view the environment from the position other than the one the child is in. In the classical experiment to study the effect, a puppet is placed in a room away from the child who is asked what the puppet can see. **2.** In *social psychology*, the capacity to appreciate the point of view of another person with whom one is interacting. In this sense, it is an essential feature of smooth social relationships.

persuasion A process of inducing a person to adopt a particular set of values, beliefs or attitudes. Studies of this process have been far-reaching and implicated a number of factors both rational and nonrational. E.g., ➤ **cognitive dissonance, credibility, persuasive communication**.

persuasive communication Quite literally, a communication that persuades. Identifying the set of factors that make up such a message is an important goal in social psychology. Both external aspects (the message itself, the arguments presented, the credibility of the source, the medium used, etc.) and internal aspects (the person's original beliefs, credulity, etc.) are involved.

persuasive therapy An approach to psychotherapy based on the use of direct suggestion, the giving of specific advice and direct counseling.

pervasive developmental disorder ➤ **developmental disorder, pervasive**.

perversion As derived from the Latin *perversio* (= facing the wrong way), a perversion is any turning away from the right course, any distortion from the proper path to the proper end. With this general connotation, the term can be and is used to refer to thought processes, emotions, judgements or actions which are, in some sense, warped or distorted. However, the overwhelmingly common reference is to behaviors that are sexual – so much so that many use the term as if its sole semantic domain were sexual. In an effort to disabuse readers of this unnecessary restriction of the use of the term, the sexual aspect is given under the separate entry, ➤ sexual *perversion.

perversion, sexual Any form of sexual behavior that is a distortion of the 'proper goal' of sex (➤ perversion). Ascertaining precisely what constitutes the 'proper goal' and hence what shall characterize perverted sexual behavior has proven something of a problem. If one takes the point of view that procreation is the only proper goal, then anything other than heterosexual intercourse under the biologically appropriate circumstances is a sexual perversion; if one assumes that sexual pleasure is a legitimate and proper goal then it becomes difficult to exclude anything. Many psychiatric nomenclatures, deriving as they do from the early decades of this century, will list *homosexuality*, *voyeurism*, *exhibitionism*, *fetishism*, *sadism*, *masochism*, *bestiality*, *pederasty* and *sodomy* as sexual perversions. More modern (enlightened?) nosologies restrict the domain of the term to those sexual acts that violate the personal rights and desires of others, and hence include *exhibitionism*, *rape* and *child molesting*. Modes of sexual expression such as *sadism* or *sodomy* are only regarded as perversions when they are imposed on an unwilling partner or a juvenile. ➤➤ paraphilia.

Peter principle The notion that a person gets promoted up through the ranks of an organization until he or she reaches his or her level of incompetence.

petit mal ➤ minor *epilepsy.

petrification R. D. Laing's term for a defensive reaction, used by the insecure

when under severe psychological threat, in which the individual depersonalizes either himself or herself ('turns oneself to stone') or the outside other who is the source of the threat.

peyote 1. Specifically, the peyote cactus (*Lophophora williamsii*) from which the psychoactive drug ➤ mescaline is derived. **2.** Loosely, mescaline itself.

PGO waves Bursts of activity originating in the pons (P), moving to the geniculate nucleus (G) and the occipital cortex (O), characteristic of ➤ REM sleep. While they have only been recorded in animals, they are assumed to occur in humans.

PGR Abbreviation for *psychogalvanic response*. ➤ galvanic skin response.

phacoscope An instrument for observing the changes in the images reflected from the lens of the eye (➤ Purkinje-Sanson images) during accommodation.

-phagia, -phagy Combining form from the Greek, meaning *eating*.

phagocytosis Lit., cell-eating. Used of the complex process in which particular cells in the body engulf and digest neurons that have died.

phallic Pertaining to: **1.** ➤ Phallus **2.** ➤ Penis. Sense 1 is preferred, particularly when symbolic reference is made; ➤ penile is best used for meaning 2.

phallic character An adult who compulsively displays behaviors which, according to psychoanalytic theory, are referable to the phallic stage of development. The dominant trait here is regarding sexual behavior as a display of power and potency. Contrast with ➤ genital character.

phallic love In boys, love of the penis; by extension, in girls of the clitoris.

phallic phase ➤ phallic stage.

phallic primacy In psychoanalysis, the focusing of erotic interest upon the penis or the clitoris during the early ➤ genital stage.

phallic stage (or **level** or **phase**) In psychoanalytic theory, the stage of psychosexual development marked by great interest in (Freud called it a preoccupation with) one's penis or, by extension, in girls one's clitoris. Theoretically, this stage follows the ➤ **anal stage** and is succeeded by the ➤ **Oedipal stage**.

phallic symbol Anything that can be interpreted from a psychoanalytic perspective as symbolically representing a phallus. Most writers limit this class of objects to things pointed or upright, but this often underestimates the ingenuity of the interpreter.

phallic woman In psychoanalytic theory, the notion of a female with phallic traits. Theoretically, this is how the pre-Oedipal child views its mother. The idea of a phallic woman is also commonly found in folklore and myth and, according to some interpretations, is manifested in the (unconscious) conception of women in masochistic, submissive men.

phallocentric A sobriquet for the classical theory of psychoanalysis. The term was first applied by Ernest Jones as a critical comment upon the theory for placing so much emphasis on the penis and phallic symbolism, in particular the tendency to view the psychological development of the female as a reaction to the discovery that she did not have a penis.

phallus While *penis* is used as an anatomical term, the connotations of *phallus* are primarily symbolic. The reference then is the image or representation of the penis as a symbol of power. Jung is generally credited with the comment that nicely sums up the distinction, 'The penis is only a phallic symbol.'

phantasy ➤ **fantasy**.

phantom 1. Generally, an image or semblance of something perceived but not physically present in the stimulus environment. E.g., ➤ **phantom limb. 2.** In psychoanalysis, an unconscious representation of a person.

phantom limb A subjective experience of sensations arising from a limb that has been amputated. Although the amputation of the limb removes the peripheral extremity itself, it does not destroy the neural representation of the limb, particularly in the cortex. Hence, many amputees have feelings and sensations that are experienced as though they came from this nonexistent, phantom limb.

pharmacodynamic tolerance ➤ **tolerance, pharmacodynamic**.

pharmacologic antagonism ➤ **drug *antagonism**.

pharmacology The science of the study of drugs. For its relevance to psychology, ➤ **psychopharmacology**.

pharmacopeia 1. Specifically, an authoritative treatise on drugs, their preparation, chemical make-up, properties and recommended dosages and manner of administration. **2.** More loosely, the full compendium of available drugs.

pharyngo- The combining form for ➤ **pharynx**.

pharynx The part of the oral cavity, including the surrounding muscles and membranes, connecting the mouth and nose with the larynx and esophagus.

phase 1. An aspect of appearance or state of some thing or event which recurs as the thing or event passes cyclically through various modes or conditions. The key word in the use of this term is *recur*. Thus one sees references to the phase of a sound wave, the phases of the moon, the manic phase of manic-depression, etc. **2.** a temporary *stage* in a person's life in which characteristic behaviors are observed. Strictly speaking, this usage is not proper, because the notion of recurrence is missing – unless one assumes that the recurrence is not within a single organism but rather across many (all?) organisms of that species. It is frequently used in this latter sense in developmental and/or psychoanalytic works (e.g., *phallic phase*) and is particularly common in nontechnical writings with regard to periods during which children exhibit behaviors that their parents hope will soon cease. If a combined term with the word *phase* is not found below, look under ➤ stage, which is preferred when the recurrence notion is not fulfilled.

phase difference A difference in the phase relations of any two sound waves. When the phase difference is zero and the peaks and troughs of the two occur simultaneously, they are said to be *in phase*. If the peak of one occurs simultaneously with the trough of the other, they are said to be *in opposite phase*. Phase differences are measured in phase angles with 180° representing opposite phase. Phase differences are perceived as beats, slight increases and decreases in intensity, and can be used as cues for the localization of a sound source.

phase locking In neurophysiology, the tendency of a cell to fire in a manner coordinated with particular portions of a cyclically repetitive stimulus. Many auditory fibers display this property, which was, interestingly, predicted by the *volley theory* of hearing long before it had been empirically identified. ➤ **theories of *hearing**.

-phasia Suffix meaning *speech disorder*, used with the implication that the disorder is due to a cortical lesion. E.g., ➤ **aphasia**.

-phemia Combining form meaning *speech disorder*, used with the implication that the disorder is due to psychological i.e. non-organic factors.

phenazocine A synthetic ➤ **opiate**.

phencyclidine A hallucinogen chemically known as phenylcyclohexyl-piperidine hydrochloride (PCP), with effects that are dose-related and range from a mild euphoria at low doses to tenseness, palpitations, disorientation and hypertension to convulsions and possible death at higher. Recovery from an overdose is not infrequently followed by an acute delirium, which may last for several days. PCP is a frequently abused drug with the street name of 'angel dust.'

phenobarbital One of the more frequently prescribed long-acting ➤ **barbiturates**.

phenocopy A phenotypic syndrome that, owing to environmental factors, mimics a genetic syndrome.

phenomenal field Rather inclusively, absolutely anything that is in the total momentary experience of a person, including the experience of the self. The emphasis is on *experience* independent of the physical stimuli; thus, those things imaged, emoted and thought are part of the phenomenal field even if not present physically but those things present physically but not noticed or attended to are not. Also called *phenomenological field*.

phenomenalism 1. The philosophical point of view that knowledge and understanding are limited to 'appearances,' to the ways in which objects and events are perceived, that true reality outside of that which is phenomenological is unknowable. **2.** A synonym for **phenomenology** – which is a somewhat different philosophy from 1. **3.** A Piagetian term used to refer to the sense that if any two events occur in temporal contiguity then one of them must have caused the other; see here ➤ **phenomenistic thought**.

phenomenalistic introspection ➤ **introspection** that is a free-flowing report of experience given in everyday language. As used by those with a phenomenological approach, it differs quite dramatically from the structured, systematic introspections of the *structuralists* and the *act psychologists*.

phenomenal motion ➤ **apparent *motion**.

phenomenal pattern That which is experienced or perceived in contrast with the objective, physical stimulus. For example, in cases like ➤ **ambiguous *figures**, the objective stimulus remains constant but the phenomenal pattern changes.

phenomenal regression The term refers to the fact that neither the principles of perspective and geometry nor the principles of object constancy accurately predict what is perceived. The perceived size of a distant (and necessarily familiar) object tends to be slightly larger than geometric, line-of-sight estimates predict and somewhat smaller than if it were regarded as an object of constant size. The *regression* in the term is because, with practice, the perceived size tends to shift toward the predictions of the geometric principles.

phenomenal self ➤ **self, phenomenal**.

phenomenistic causality ➤ **phenomenistic thought**.

phenomenistic thought A term used by Piaget to characterize the reasoning of the young child whose cognitive structures are predominantly organized around the physical appearances of the things in its environment. Phenomenistic thought gives rise to *phenomenistic causality*, in which simple physical co-occurrence is endowed with causal status; e.g., the child who remarks, 'Trains go fast 'cause they're big.'

phenomenocentrism The tendency to accept one's own personal, immediate experience as revealing the true aspects of mind. It is a fallacy akin to ➤ **ethnocentrism** (1) and ➤ **anthropomorphism**. The phenomenocentric perspective suffers from the general failure to recognize that immediate personal experiences, no matter how poignant and convincing they may seem, are still the products of social presuppositions and personal histories and cannot be taken as valid indicators of general mental processes.

phenomenology In simplest terms, a philosophical doctrine that advocates that the scientific study of immediate experience be the basis of psychology. As developed by Edmund Husserl, the focus is on events, occurrences, happenings, etc. as one experiences them, with a minimum of regard for the external, physical reality and for the so-called 'scientific biases' of the natural sciences. Note that there is no attempt here to deny the objective reality of events; rather, the basic issue for a phenomenological analysis is to avoid focusing upon the physical events themselves and instead to deal with how they are perceived and experienced. Real mean-

ing for a phenomenologist is to be derived by examining the individual's relationship with and reactions to these real-world events. Compare with ➤ **phenomenalism** (1).

phenomenon 1. As taken from the Greek, *an appearance, that which appears*; hence, any perceptible change, any occurrence that is open to observation. This meaning, which is very general, embodies two aspects each of which is represented in the following more restricted senses: 2. A physical occurrence, a fact, a proven event. Note also that the term is often used in this sense without consideration of the causes of the happening. 3. An internal experience of which one is aware, the data of personal experience. This meaning is reflected in the perspective of ➤ **phenomenology**. 4. In Kantian terms, appearance or knowledge of events or objects interpreted through categories; phenomena here serve as the basis for inferring reality.

phenothiazines A major group of ➤ **antipsychotic drugs** used in the alleviation of severe psychological disorders, notably schizophrenia. Chlorpromazine and thioridazine are the most frequently prescribed. All drugs of this group have important effects on the autonomic nervous system, including epinepherine and norepinepherine blocking at sympathetic receptors and acetycholine blocking at postganglionic parasympathetic receptors. They depress sensory input to the reticular formation and raise the general threshold for such stimuli in the brain stem. As a result, all have a sedative effect, although it differs from that of the *barbiturates* in that there is little *ataxia*, and the patient can be aroused easily. They also alleviate the nausea and vomiting caused by other drugs and/or conditions (not, however, motion sickness). Side effects include disruption of temperature-regulation processes in the hypothalamus, some disruption of the endocrine system and a variety of motor disorders including tremors from muscle weakness and, with long term administration, ➤ **tardive dyskinesia**.

phenotype The actual, physical, observable; the manifested structure, function or behavior of an organism. For more detail ➤ **genotype**.

phenylketonuria (PKU) A genetic disorder of amino-acid metabolism in which the enzyme *phenylalanine hydroxylase*, necessary for the oxidizing of phenylalanine, is missing. In most industrialized societies, babies are screened for the disorder a few days after birth and, if diagnosed, a diet low in phenylalanine is instituted and untoward effects are prevented. If left untreated the resulting buildup of phenylpyruvic acid causes severe and permanent mental retardation (called *phenylpyruvic oligophrenia*).

phenylpyruvic oligophrenia ➤ **phenylketonuria**.

pheromone A chemical substance used as a means of communication between members of a species. Pheromones serve a variety of functions in different species, signalling sexual receptivity, alarm, marking territory, etc. E.g. ➤ **Lee-Boot effect**, **Bruce effect**.

phi (φ) coefficient An index of the relationship between any two sets of scores, provided that both sets of scores can be represented on ordered, binary dimensions, e.g., male–female; married–single. Also called the *fourfold-point correlation*.

-philia Combining form meaning *love of*, *friend of*, *affinity for*.

phil(o)- Combining form meaning *loving*, *friendly*.

philology Lit., the love of words. Generally used as the name of a branch of linguistics concerned with the study of the origins and evolution of the meanings of words. Occasionally, in some older writings, a synonym for *linguistics* itself.

philosophical psychotherapy An approach to therapy predicated on the assumption that one's beliefs, attitudes and general *Weltanschauung* (overall outlook on life) have a profound impact on one's behavior, feelings and ways of dealing with reality. The basic goal is to alter the client's philosophical attitude or posture. Phenomenological approaches like Rogers's client-centered therapy and Frankl's logotherapy have philosophical-psychotherapy components but the prototype of the approach is *existential therapy*.

philosophy In that most hackneyed of phrases, 'the search for the truth.' There are various ways to conduct this search that properly belong within this discipline and various domains of nature into which it has, over the millennia, led. The most convenient division is to break philosophy into two broad sub-disciplines, ➤ **epistemology** and ➤ **metaphysics**. The former encompasses efforts to understand the origins, nature and the limits of thought and human knowledge, the latter includes similar exercises into the ultimate reality of existence. Other prominent branches are *esthetics, ethics* and *logic*.

phi motion ➤ **phi phenomenon**.

phi phenomenon 1. Specifically, a form of ➤ **apparent *motion** produced when two stationary lights are flashed successively. If the interval between the two is optimal (in the neighborhood of 150 msec), then one perceives movement of the light from the first location to the second. 2. More generally, Max Wertheimer used the phrase to refer to the 'pure' irreducible experiencing of motion independent of other factors such as color, brightness, size, spatial location, etc. The phi phenomenon in the first sense here was considered by Wertheimer to be a good example of the second sense and hence is sometimes called the *pure phi phenomenon*.

-phob- Combining form meaning *fear, dread* or *aversion*. The *-phobe* form is used to characterize the person displaying the fear, the *-phobia* form is used for the condition itself, and the *-phobic* form serves adjectival functions.

phobia A term from the Greek for *fear* or *dread*; in keeping with this etymology, specific phobias are properly given Greek root qualifiers, e.g., *pyrophobia* = fear of fire, *nyctophobia* = fear of the night, etc. In standard psychiatric work, a reaction requires several factors before it is properly classified as a phobia. Specifically, the fear must be persistent and intense, there must be a compelling need to flee or avoid the phobic object or situation and the fear must be irrational and not based on sound judgement. Both the technical and the common terms for specific phobias can be found in Appendix B.

phobia, simple Any persistent fear of a specific stimulus object or situation. Specifically excluded from this category are ➤ **social *phobia** and a fear of having a ➤ **panic attack** (➤➤ **panic disorder**). The most common simple phobias involve animals, blood, closed spaces, and heights; see Appendix B for a full list. Also called *specific phobia*.

phobia, social An ➤ **anxiety disorder** marked by a persistent fear of particular social situations in which the individual is subjected to possible scrutiny by others and fears that he or she will act in some way that will humiliate or embarrass. The actual fear itself may be quite circumscribed, such as being unable to speak in public, choking on food while eating in the presence of others, having one's hand tremble when attempting to write in front of others, etc. Social phobias often coexist with ➤ **panic disorder** and any of various ➤ **simple *phobias**.

phobic anxiety The fear experienced by one with a phobia when presented with the phobic object or circumstances.

phobic character A psychoanalytic term for an individual who tends to deal with difficult or anxiety-provoking situations by the simple expedient of avoiding them, usually by restricting his or her activities in life and seeking a protective environment.

phobic disorder Earlier nomenclatures used this term as a synonym for ➤ **phobia**. It

is rarely found in contemporary writing.

phobic neurosis A ➤ **neurosis** manifested as a ➤ phobia. The term is not used in contemporary nosologies.

phocomelia A birth defect characterized by incomplete development of the limbs.

phon A measure of the subjective loudness of a tone. The phon scale is based on comparisons with a 1,000 Hz standard.

phonation Generally, the production of speech sounds; more specifically, the production of speech sounds by the vibration of the vocal cords.

phone Any discrete speech sound the characteristics of which can be specified independently of that sound's role in any specific language. Compare here with ➤ **phoneme**, which is language-specific. Phonetic elements are traditionally denoted by placement within square brackets, [ ]. ➤➤ **International Phonetic Alphabet**.

phoneme The minimal unit of speech in a given language that 'makes a difference' to the fluent speaker of that language. This 'minimal unit' is not really a discrete speech sound, but rather a *class* of sounds, and is represented in speech through one of its *allophones*. To use every linguist's favorite example, in English the classes of sounds denoted as /r/ and /l/ are two distinct phonemes while in Korean they are treated as allophonic variations of a single phoneme. Phonemic notation is traditionally given, as in the above example, in slashes / /. There is a temptation to regard the letters used in alphabetic writing as representing phonemes. This should be resisted, for it completely misrepresents the role of the phoneme in language. Ultimately, phonemes are cognitive/perceptual abstractions and as such are independent of writing systems. To appreciate this point ➤ **orthography** and related entries. Compare with ➤ **phone**.

phonemic Pertaining to: 1. ➤ **phoneme**. 2. ➤ **phonemics**.

phonemic restoration effect The generalization that a dramatically altered acoustic element in speech is extremely difficult to detect: e.g., replacing a /t/ with a 'click' sound still sounds like proper speech. The listener fills in or 'restores' the missing or distorted components by the use of other cues in the message. The effect is not found in isolated speech sounds.

phonemics The study of the speech sounds of a specific language. That is, the examination is focused on the *phonemic* patterns of a language, not the *phonetic*. For example, the English words *pan, span* and *nap* contain three different 'p' sounds, but a phonemic analysis treats them all similarly because they are allophonic variations of a single ➤ **phoneme**, /p/. Compare with ➤ **phonetics**, where the differences between the three are taken into consideration in the analysis.

phonetic Pertaining to:1. ➤ **phone**. 2. ➤ **phonetics**.

phonetic alphabet ➤ **International Phonetic Alphabet**.

phonetic method Any method of speech training that focuses on the relationship between movements of the articulators (tongue, lips, etc.) and speech sounds. Distinguish from ➤ **phonic(s) method**.

phonetics The study of speech sounds, including classification, transmission, production and perception of phonetic elements. Generally considered to consist of two sub-disciplines: *articulatory phonetics*, which analyzes the methods of production of speech sounds; and *acoustic phonetics*, which analyzes their physical properties. The former is grounded in biology, the latter in physics. Compare with ➤ **phonemics**, noting particularly that *phonetics* is language-free and *phonemics* language-dependent.

-phonia Combining form used to denote a vocal disorder.

phonic Of sounds, specifically speech sounds.

phonic(s) method A method of reading

instruction in which the focus is on the relationship between letters and letter groups and the sounds of the language they represent. Compare with ➤ **whole-word method**. Distinguish from ➤ **phonetics method**.

phonism A form of ➤ **synesthesia** in which sounds are experienced when stimuli from other, non-auditory modalities are presented.

phon(o)- Combining form meaning *sound, voice* or *vocal*.

phonography Any writing system based on the sounds of the spoken language. E.g., ➤ **alphabet, syllabary**.

phonological disorder ➤ **developmental *articulation disorder**.

phonological dyslexia ➤ **dyslexia, phonological**.

phonopathy A general term for any vocal disorder.

phonoscope Any device that converts sound energy into a visible form. ➤ **spectrograph** for the most commonly used variety.

phon scale ➤ **phon**.

phoria Generally, the orientation of the two eyeballs while focusing on an object. Specifically, any abnormality in which there is a lack of coordination between the two eyes.

phorometry Measurement of the balance of the muscles that turn the eyeballs.

phosphenes Luminous images produced by mechanical stimulation of the eye or the visual cortex. They can easily be produced by gently pressing on the side of the eye with the lid closed or by a blow on the head. They also occur normally, but less dramatically, during *accommodation* and *convergence*.

phosphodiesterase ➤ **caffeine**.

phot A unit of illuminance. Specifically, that falling on a surface 1 centimeter from a point source of light of 1 candle.

photerythrous Descriptive of persons

who have a heightened sensitivity to long-wavelength light.

photic Pertaining to light.

photic driving The use of a stroboscopic (i.e. rapidly flashing) light to accentuate or 'drive' brain-wave patterns, particularly the alpha waves.

photism 1. The hallucination of a bright light. 2. The experience of colors when stimuli from other, non-visual modalities are presented, a form of ➤ **synesthesia**.

phot(o)- Combining form meaning: **1.** *Relating to light*. **2.** *Of photography*.

photochromatic interval The range of luminous stimulus intensities sufficient to stimulate the *rods*, and thus produce a sensation of light, but insufficient for the *cones*, so that no hue is perceived.

photographic memory A non-technical term for a perfect memory. As used in the common language it has no reference, for, as a look at ➤ **memory** et seq. will show, such a perfectly recording memory is not to be found in creatures of organic origin. The closest thing to it is the phenomenon of ➤ **eidetic imagery**.

photokinesis In lower organisms, a movement or general activity to light.

photoma A hallucinated flash of light.

photometer ➤ **photometry**.

photometric brightness ➤ **luminance**.

photometric measurement ➤ **photometry**.

photometry A general term covering the devices, procedures, and theory of the measurement of the visual effectiveness of light. The essential problem in photometry is that the eye is not uniformly sensitive to all wavelengths; as a result all modern *photometers* have a set of built-in standards that are based on an internationally agreed-upon characterization of the normal human visual system.

photon An obsolete term for what is now called a ➤ **troland**. The usage of the term photon in physics forced this change in terminology.

photophobia An abnormal sensitivity to light. Note, not fear of light, as the root *phobia* seems to imply. Photophobia occurs in albinos, who lack pigmentation, and in a variety of other conditions.

photopic vision Normal daylight vision; vision under sufficiently high illumination conditions that the cones of the retina are functioning. Photopic vision has the following general properties: (a) hues are perceived; (b) the visual threshold is, relative to *scotopic vision*, high; (c) the *luminosity curve* shows maximum sensitivity to a wavelength of approximately 555 nm, with a rapidly decreasing sensitivity to longer and shorter wavelengths; and (d) because the fovea is entirely made up of cones, visual acuity is high. Compare with ➤ **scotopic vision**.

photopigment Any of several light-sensitive chemicals found in the receptor cells (rods and cones) of the retina. Photopigments absorb light and undergo chemical changes that represent the first stage in the transduction of light energy to visual experience. ➤ **rhodopsin**, the photopigment of the rods.

photoreceptor Any of the receptor cells of the retina that are stimulated by light energy and give rise to the experience of vision. ➤ **rods** and **cones** for details.

phototaxis An orienting response with regard to light. *Positive* phototaxis is movement toward the source, *negative* away from it. The term is properly reserved for such movements in animals; *phototropism* is used for plants. *Heliotaxis* and *heliotropism* are occasionally found as synonyms. ➤ **taxis**.

phototherapy The use of light in therapy. The most common use is in the treatment of ➤ **seasonal affective disorder**.

phototropism ➤ **phototaxis**.

phrase 1. In linguistics, a group of words and morphemes arranged according to grammatical rules and functioning as a 'unit' within a sentence. 2. In speech, a group of words and sounds spoken with an intonation contour that reflects the underlying meaningful structure of the 'unit.' Note that the phrase in 2 is not necessarily a phrase in sense 1.

phrase-marker ➤ **tree** (2).

phrase-structure grammar ➤ **grammar**, **phrase-structure**.

-phrasia Combining form used to denote speech disorders.

-phren-, -phrenia, phreno- Combining forms referring generally to *mind, mental, mentality*.

phrenasthenia Lit. mental weakness.

phrenology Originally conceptualized by the anatomist Franz Josef Gall as the science that studied the relationship between mental faculties or functions and specific brain areas. The practice of phrenology was based upon three assumptions: (a) that there was a clear relationship between specific brain areas and particular mental functions; (b) that the more developed a function was, the larger that area of the brain was, and (c) that the shape of the skull conformed to the shape of the brain. On the assumption that all three held, Gall developed the practice of 'reading' mental capacity, emotions and even personality from the bumps on the head. Alas, all three turned out to be wrong and today phrenology is a pseudoscience and its practitioners most definitely frauds.

phylaxis 1. Specifically, the body's active defense against infection. 2. More generally, protection, defense.

phyl(o)- Combining form meaning *race* or *tribe* based upon kinship; by extension, any biologically defined group.

phylogenesis ➤ **phylogeny**.

phylogenetic ➤ **phylogeny** and **genetics**.

phylogenetic memory A memory or idea that is presumed universal in all individuals, reflecting an early phyletic stage. Phrased this way it is a rather empty concept; if one recasts the idea into the framework of *species-specific* behavioral tendencies, it is not quite so bizarre.

phylogenetic principle ➤ **recapitulation theory**.

phylogeny (or **phylogenesis**) The origin and, by extension, the evolution of a species or other form of animal or plant; its evolutionary history. Contrast with ➤ **ontogeny**, which refers to the origin and development of an individual organism.

phylum A primary division in the classification of animals and plants.

physical 1. Pertaining to properties of matter, energy, etc.; in short, to the physical sciences. 2. By extension, pertaining to material elements of nature other than those peculiar to living matter, external to an organism, e.g., a *physical stimulus*. 3. Pertaining to the body, to *physique*; *somatic*. 4. By extension, vigorous, active. The mutually contradictory nature of 1 and 2 versus 3 and 4 actually causes less trouble than one might suppose; context typically determines the sense intended. Antonym for 1 and 2 is *biological*; for 3 and 4 it is *mental*.

physical dependence ➤ **physiological *dependence**.

physicalism A philosophical point of view that all scientific propositions can be expressed in the terminology of the physical sciences. The variety most influential in psychology is ➤ **identity theory**. ➤ **operationalism** and **positivism**, with which it is closely aligned.

physical stimulus A stimulus specified in terms of its properties of energy and energy changes. See the discussion under ➤ **stimulus** for details.

physical teratogen ➤ **teratogen**.

physio- Combining form from the Greek, meaning *pertaining to nature*. Given the breadth with which the term ➤ **nature** is used, this suffix can be taken to relate to that which is biological or to that which is material. In psychology, the reference is virtually always the former, so much so that 'physio' is used as lab jargon for *physiological psychology*.

physiodynamic therapy A cover term for

a number of psychotherapeutic procedures including ➤ **electroconvulsive therapy**, ➤ **insulin-shock therapy**, ➤ **narcotherapy** and ➤ **psychosurgery**.

physiogenetic Characterizing that which originates in the body or in a part thereof.

physiognomic 1. Pertaining to physiognomy. **2.** Characterizing an empathic reaction in which emotional qualities are interjected into perceptual/cognitive judgements; e.g., a brand-new car looks 'alert.'

physiognomic perception The perception of emotions and feelings. Gestalt psychologists maintained that it was as primary an aspect of perceptual experience as 'ordinary' qualities. For example, in music a melody is not heard as a sequence of notes but as an organized whole with emotive content.

physiognomy 1. The physical appearance of the face. **2.** Specifically, the use of the face and facial expressions to judge mental abilities, character, emotional attitudes, etc. Sense 1 represents a simple exercise in description; sense 2 is sheer quackery – e.g., ➤ **Lombrosian**.

physiological age ➤ **age, physiological**.

physiological antagonism ➤ **drug *antagonism**.

physiological dependence ➤ **dependence, physiological**.

physiological limit The theoretical asymptote or upper limit of performance as presumably dictated by biological factors.

physiological motive A generic term for any motive based on body needs or tissue needs, e.g., food, water, avoidance of noxious stimulation, etc. See here ➤ **drive** and ➤ **primary *drive**.

physiological nystagmus ➤ **nystagmus, physiological**.

physiological psychology A branch of psychology that is oriented toward description and explanation of psychological phenomena based on physiological and neurological processes. It shares much of its subject-matter and many of its techniques with biology and physiology and typically reflects either a *correlational* orientation, in which the search is for the physiological correlates of behavior, or a *reductionistic* orientation, in which the final explanation for action and thought is sought in physiological principles. A number of synonyms and near synonyms is used for this field including *biological psychology*, *biopsychology*, *psychobiology* and *psychophysiology*.

physiological zero The temperature to which a response neither of warm nor of cold is experienced. All other things being equal, this point of thermal indifference corresponds to the temperature of the skin, or roughly 32° C (90° F). The zero 'point' is not a true point but a small range of temperatures within which no thermal sensation is reported. Note also that the level of adaptation of the skin and the area of the body where stimulation occurs will also affect the measured zero point.

physiology Broadly, the discipline within biology that studies the functions of cells, tissues and organs or living organisms.

physique The structure and anatomical organization of the body; usually, but not exclusively, the human body.

physostigmine An acetylcholine *agonist* that functions by inactivating *acetylcholinesterase*.

PI ➤ **proactive interference**.

Piagetian Of the theories and perspectives of Jean Piaget (1896–1980) and his colleagues, who established the so-called *Genevan school* of developmental psychology. Piaget's work focused on the attempt to understand the development of cognitive functioning in the child and is typically expressed in terms of his *stage theory*, in which the child is seen as passing through a series of cognitive periods, each displaying its characteristic modes of thought. See here ➤ **concrete operations**, **formal operations**, **preoperatory thought**, **sensorimotor intelligence**.

Piaget's original training was in zoology, and his interest in children derived from his concerns with epistemology, the origins, nature and limits of knowledge. His approach is often called ➤ **genetic epistemology**, for it reflects his deep conviction that the development of intelligence can be seen as naturalistic and biological, the result of a dynamic interaction between the child and the environment. The Piagetian orientation, however, is not nativistic in the usual sense of ➤ **nativism**; he did not conceptualize the child as emerging preequipped with *innate ideas*. Rather, he maintained, phylogenetic evolutionary pressures have resulted in a neonate with very general regulatory mechanisms and modes of processing the environmental inputs. It is the interplay of these (e.g., ➤ **accommodation** (3), **assimilation** (4), **equilibration** (2)) that yields the modes of thought representative of the several stages.

pia mater The innermost of the three meninges covering the brain and spinal cord. The term literally means *tender mother*; the membrane is thin, highly vascular and closely envelops the underlying tissue.

piano theory of hearing ➤ **theories of *hearing**.

piblokto A *culture-specific syndrome* found among Eskimos. The primary symptom is an acute attack of screaming and crying and running uncontrollably through the snow. var., *pibloktoq*.

pica From the name of a genus of birds which includes the voracious magpie, a persistent eating of non-nutritive substances, e.g., chalk, clay, bits of trash, etc. It often accompanies mental retardation and in such cases is classified as a ➤ **feeding disorder of infancy or early childhood**. Also called *allotriophagy*. ➤➤ **eating disorders**.

Pick's disease A presenile degenerative brain disease affecting the cerebral cortex and particularly the frontal lobes. Symptoms include severe intellectual deterioration, stereotyped behavior, emotional lability and a loss of social judgement. It is suspected of having a hereditary basis.

pico- Combining form meaning *1 trillionth*.

pictogram A picture or symbol used to represent an object or a concept.

pictophilia A ➤ **paraphilia** characterized by the deriving of erotic stimulation from viewing sexually oriented pictures or films to the extent that such viewing is necessary to maintain sexual arousal and to achieve orgasm. The term is reserved for those whose sexual behaviors are dependent on such pictures and is not used for the normal arousal experienced by most people when viewing erotic material.

picture-arrangement test A test consisting of a series of cartoon-like pictures presented in a haphazard order. The subject's task is to arrange them as quickly as possible so that a coherent story is represented. Such tests are a common feature of intelligence tests.

picture-completion test A test in which incomplete pictures are presented to the subject (e.g., a picture of a person with a missing foot, a cow with only one horn, etc.) who must identify the omitted detail.

picture-interpretation test A generic term for any test or part thereof where the subject is given a picture and asked to interpret it.

pidgin A verbal communication system that develops when two different language communities make occasional contact with each other. Pidgins emerge when the contact is not general enough to motivate the learning of each other's language, hence a 'simplified' blend (the pidgin) is devised. Note that pidgins are not usually classified as natural languages (see here ➤ **language**) until or unless they become creolized (➤ **creole**).

piecemeal activity, law of Thorndike's term for the generalization that a part of a learning situation may become prepotent and evoke responding even though other aspects of the situation are altered or removed.

pie chart A way of presenting proportional data in the form of a circle (the *pie*) with each category represented by a *slice*, the size of which reflects the proportion of the whole for that category.

Pierre Robin syndrome A congenital syndrome marked by a small head; a small receding chin and an abnormal tongue. In cases where there is brain damage there may be mental retardation, although in most cases intelligence is normal. There is often poor respiration and feeding problems and children with the disorder may fail to thrive.

pigment 1. Generally, any substance, usually in the form of nonsoluble particles, that differentially absorbs light of particular wavelengths and thereby gives color or hue to a surface. That is, a red pigment is perceived as red because it contains particles that absorb more light of medium and short wavelength relative to light of long wavelength, which it reflects back to the viewer. 2. In physiology, any such substance in tissues that gives them color.

pigment layer The first layer of the retina containing the pigmented cells.

pill-rolling Obsessive behavior such that the person affected continuously rolls little balls ('pills') of fabric or paper around.

pilo- Combining form meaning *hair*.

piloerection The state when one's hairs stand on end.

pilomotor response Pimpling of the skin with accompanying piloerection; commonly known as 'goose-bumps.'

pilot study Common synonym for ➤ **exploratory study**.

Piltz's reflex ➤ **attention reflex**.

pimozide An ➤ **antipsychotic drug** used in the treatment of ➤ **Tourette's syndrome**.

pineal body (or **gland**) A tiny structure located sufficiently close to the geographical center of the brain for Galen to have believed that it regulated the very flow of thoughts and for Descartes to have hypothesized that it functioned as the locus of interaction between the body and the rational soul. Its actual functions are not completely known but are cur-

rently believed to be somewhat less cosmic. It does play an important role in the hormonal changes that occur during adolescence. The gland secretes during childhood a hormone, ➤ **melatonin**, that inhibits sexual maturation. When secretion diminishes during adolescence sexual development begins.

There is also evidence that the gland plays a role in sleep regulation in humans, and in various other species it has been implicated in exerting control over the full diurnal cycle. In some species, such as lizards, it contains light-sensitive neurons. Also called the *epiphysis cerebri*.

pink noise ➤ **noise, pink**.

pinna The fleshy outer part of the external ear. It serves some sound-gathering functions.

Piper's law A generalization which states that for moderate-sized, uniform areas of the retina outside of the fovea, the absolute threshold is inversely proportional to the square root of the area stimulated. Compare with ➤ **Ricco's law**.

PI, release from A technique for measuring the buildup of ➤ **proactive *interference** (PI) in a learning task. It consists of giving the subject successive tasks with similar materials (which builds up PI) and then abruptly switching the type of materials. The performance on the new material relative to the original performance on the first trial with the old material gives a measure of the amount of PI 'released.'

pitch 1. The dimension of psychological experience that corresponds (roughly and complexly) with the frequency of an auditory stimulus. The typical range of the normal (and young) human ear is from approximately 20 to 20,000 Hz, with low-frequency tones sounding 'low' in pitch and high-frequency tones sounding 'high.' 2. In linguistics, a ➤ **suprasegmental** phonetic element which marks the fundamental frequency of a component of speech. The role of pitch is most easily appreciated by comparing the uttering of a simple sentence like 'That's a book' first with a 'flat' pitch contour, which yields a simple declarative, and second with a rising pitch at the end, which produces a question.

pituitary gland The 'master gland' of the endocrine system, so called because of its role in regulating actions of the other endocrine glands. It is attached to the base of the brain by the infundibular stalk and divided into two lobes. The anterior lobe (*adenohypophysis*), which is connected with the *hypothalamus* via the hypothalamic-hypophyseal portal system, produces: *somatotrophic hormone* (STH), which regulates growth; *adrenocorticotrophic hormone* (ACTH), which controls the activity of the adrenal cortex; *thyrotrophic hormone* (TTH), which regulates activity of the thyroid gland; the *gonadotrophic hormones*, including, among others, *follicle-stimulating hormone* (FSH), which stimulates development of ovarian follicles in females and spermatogenesis in males; *luteinizing hormone* (LH) or *interstitial cell-stimulating hormone* (ICSH), which, in conjunction with FSH, stimulates secretion of estrogens, ovulation and the development of corpus luteum; and *lactogenic hormone*, which controls milk production in a mature mammary gland. The posterior lobe (*neurohypophysis*) secretes the *antidiuretic hormone*, which controls water metabolism, *vasopressin*, which induces contraction of the smooth muscles of blood vessels, and *oxytocin*, which strengthens uterine contractions and the milk-ejecting functions of the mammary glands. Also known as the ➤ **hypophysis**.

pivot class (words) ➤ **pivot grammar**.

pivot grammar A grammar proposed as a description of the early two-word stage of language development. It is based on the division of the child's vocabulary into two classes of words, *pivot* (P) and *open* (O). The former class includes a small number of high-frequency words that function by attaching other words to them to form utterances; all the other words are members of the open class. Utterances are hypothesized to be of three types: P + O ('allgone milk'), O + P ('Daddy home') and O + O ('Daddy read'). Pivot grammars were vigorously criticized on many grounds, primarily that they are overly simplistic, and are rarely taken seriously any more as valid generalizations of early child language.

PK Abbreviation for ➤ **psychokinesis** (1).

PKU ➤ **phenylketonuria**.

placebo A preparation with no medicinal value and no pharmacological effects. In studies on the effects of a drug or other substance, a placebo control condition is invariably used (➤ **double blind**) to separate the true pharmacological effects from the psychological effects of the subject (or the experimenter) believing that a real drug is being administered.

placebo, active A ➤ **placebo** that mimics the side-effects of the drug under investigation but lacks its specific, assumed therapeutic effects. Employed in cases where the side-effects of the experimental drug could be used as clues by the subjects to enable them to identify whether they are in the experimental or the control group.

placebo effect Any observed effect on behavior that is 'caused' by a ➤ **placebo**. Although the term was first introduced in the context of pharmacological research, it has been widely used and may be found in situations having nothing to do with the study of drugs. For more on the central issues here ➤ **double blind** and **experimenter bias**.

place cells Neurons in the hippocampus that respond to the specific location that an organism is in.

place learning ➤ **learning, place**.

placement Generally, the process of determining the appropriate position for a person. The term is used in educational settings, where it refers to placing a student in an appropriate class for instruction; in foster care, where it is used for the settlement of a child with foster parents; and in industrial and organizational settings, where it refers to finding the optimum position for a worker.

placenta In mammals, an organ consisting of embryonic and maternal tissue to which the fetus is attached via the umbilical cord. The placenta is the 'life support system' for the fetus; oxygen, food substances and antibodies enter through it, metabolic waste products leave through it. In general, there is no admixture of maternal and fetal blood. The placenta also serves as an endocrine organ producing various hormones so that the uterus remains properly adapted during pregnancy.

place theory of hearing ➤ **theories of *hearing**.

plain-folks technique A form of propaganda in which, in order to gain the support of others, a person attempts to persuade them that he or she is not of high station or possessing of great power but is, rather, 'just plain folk' and 'one of them.'

plan 1. An outline or design for an experiment usually including the nature and number of subjects to be used, the experimental and control groups that will be run, the procedures to be implemented, and the data analyses to be carried out. **2.** An articulated, verbalized statement about how some action or procedure is to be carried out. **3.** A covert, mental, hierarchical operation that is assumed to exist 'inside the head' of the organism and to guide behavior. Note that when the organism here is either nonhuman or nonverbal this type of plan is not necessarily considered to operate in the same way as is assumed in sense 2. However, when the subject is verbal there is a tendency to take meanings 2 and 3 as equivalent, with the assumption that 2 is merely the conscious expression of 3. To put it mildly, this equivalence is debatable.

plane A two-dimensional surface representing a slice, real or imaginary, through a body or organ. Planes are used as points (actually 'planes') of reference for indicating various anatomical aspects of the organ or body under discussion. A plane is the result of a ➤ **section** (2); see that entry for details on various kinds.

planned comparison ➤ **a priori** (or **planned**) **tests**.

planned parenthood The voluntary regulation of the size of a family by planning the spacing and number of children. The term is inclusive of any number of procedures that operate to prevent unplanned births. Also called *voluntary parenthood*.

planned tests ➤ **a priori** (or **planned**) **tests**.

planning, social A general term applied to any large-scale, organized effort to deal with current and projected problems of a society and to proposed solutions and goals.

planning, urban Social planning for an urban area.

planophrasia Erratic flight of ideas.

plantar reflex Toe flexion to a stroking of the sole of the foot.

plantigrade Characterizing a mode of walking in which the whole sole is placed on the ground. It occurs in infants around 6–10 months of age.

planum temporale A part of ➤ **Wernicke's area**. Abnormalities here have been implicated in developmental ➤ **dyslexia**.

plasticity Flexibility, modifiability, malleability, adaptability, teachability, etc. The term is used widely; e.g., (a) in neurophysiology, the ability of brain tissue to subsume functions normally carried out by other tissue (see here ➤ **equipotentiality** (3)): (b) in education, a creative, flexible cognitive style; (c) in social psychology, nonrigid adherence to roles; (d) in the study of imagery, the ability to shift and modify images, etc.

plastic tonus ➤ **catatonic waxy flexibility**.

plateau 1. A period of time during the learning of a response when no improvement is detected. **2.** A period of time during an operant-conditioning experiment when no responses are made. In both cases the term derives from the fact that a plot of the data reveals a flat portion in the curve – the plateau.

Platonic Relating or pertaining to the philosophical doctrines of Plato (*c.* 427–347 B.C.E.). Most typically this adjectival form is used in combination with other terms, as in the following entries; var., *platonic*.

Platonic idea Plato argued for a strong form of ► **dualism** in which mind and body were made up of different 'stuff' and obeyed different laws. The mental was, for him, the supreme, and the general form – the idea – represented the true basis for reality. Platonic ideas were to be achieved through a kind of dialectic induction, making the apprehension of the idea a truly rationalist endeavor.

Platonic ideal The nonphysical manifestation of a thing apprehendable only through rational thought. ►► **Platonic idea**.

Platonic love Friendship, affection, comradeship, love (the intensity of the emotion being a matter of debate) that is without sexual feelings. For Plato, this kind of love transcended the physical and reached the contemplation of the spiritual ideal. The modern usage of the term, however, has debased it somewhat and it tends to be used to refer simply to a nonerotic heterosexual relationship.

platonize To make a thing ► **Platonic**. Specifically: **1.** To render a relationship nonerotic. **2.** To idealize. **3.** To think rationally about a thing without carrying out any action. **4.** In psychoanalysis, to use the defense mechanism of *platonization*. This mechanism is assumed to function in one of two ways. One is to use the process in 1 above, and here platonization is treated as very similar to ► **sublimation**; the other is to use those in 2 and 3, where the mechanism is essentially identical with ► **omnipotence of thought**.

platoon-volley theory of hearing Another name for the *volley theory*; ► **theories of *hearing**.

platy- Combining form meaning *broad, flat*.

platycephalic Lit., flat-headed.

platykurtosis ► **kurtosis**.

play An *abridged* dictionary we consulted gave 55 distinguishable meanings for this term. At the core of all is the notion that somehow play involves diver-

sion or recreation, an activity not necessarily to be taken seriously. For psychologists, the study of play is almost entirely within the realm of childhood, and while diversion and recreation seem to be strong elements, it would be a mistake to conclude that such things are not taken seriously by the participants. Although many kinds of play have been studied and authors frequently create specialized terms for them, Piaget's three classes serve well as a general framework within which to view the current research: (a) games of mastery (building, copying, designing); (b) games with rules (marbles, war games, hide-and-seek, etc.); and (c) games of make-believe and fantasy. See following entries for other special forms.

play, organized Play that is planned in advance and carried out under rules agreed upon by the participants.

play, parallel Play that is not coordinated with the activities of a 'playmate.' It is often observed in early childhood where, according to Piaget, it results from a failure of the young child to accommodate to his or her playmates, a failure to decenter. Note, however, that although this side-by-side play is uncoordinated, presence of the other increases interest and activity. See here ► **social *facilitation**. This quality is carried through to adulthood in games like golf.

play therapy The use of play situations in a therapeutic setting. There is a variety of sophisticated procedures involved in such therapy but they can all be grouped into two main classes: (a) diagnosis, in which the child's behavior in a play situation reveals patterns that are indicative of his or her particular emotional and social-interactive difficulties; and (b) treatment, in which the play environment provides a forum within which pent-up emotions and feelings can be expressed freely. The first use is, in many respects, a real-life *projective* test, the second is derived from the theoretical concept of *catharsis*.

pleasant 1. Characterizing an emotional experience which has positive, agreeable, qualities. See here ➤ **pleasure**. **2.** Characterizing any environmental situation or stimulus conditions to which an organism will learn to make responses to bring them about and not learn to make responses that result in their termination. This, of course, is the behaviorist's usage. ➤➤ **unpleasant**.

pleasure An emotional experience that many regard as fundamentally undefinable. Some treat it as though it were a pole on a continuum, its opposite number being either ➤ **unpleasure** or ➤ **pain**. Those with a behaviorist bent eschew the subjectivity entailed by either of these devices and typically regard it as an internal state manifested by an organism's engaging in certain behaviors and avoiding other behaviors. Neither of these approaches is very satisfying. The use of a pleasure–unpleasure or a pleasure–pain continuum leaves more problems than it solves, as a look at the entry under ➤ **pain** will clearly show; the behaviorist characterization somehow seems to miss the internal affective state that most people associate with the term. What is interesting about these lexicographic conundrums is that pleasure, by virtue of its undefinability, may simply be a fundamental emotional experience characterizable as a desire to have the stimulation that produced it repeated. If this is still unsatisfying, see the extended discussion of ➤ **reinforcement**, a term used rather differently but one which entails the same kind of definitional problems.

pleasure center(s) A term coined by James Olds for areas in the brain which when stimulated with mild electric current produce what seems to be pleasure. Olds's work was with lower organisms and, in a flagrant display of anthropomorphism, he took the fact that the animal would make large numbers of responses in order to receive the stimulation as evidence of the experience of pleasure. The specific areas implicated lie along a predominantly dopaminergic pathway from the brainstem through the lateral hypothalamus and other parts of the limbic system to the frontal lobes. ➤ **pleasure**.

pleasure–pain principle One often sees this term in its shortened form, *pleasure principle*. The reference here is to a hypothetical early and primitive id function that seeks to satisfy any need either by direct means or through hallucination and fantasy – with the implication that at this point in an infant's development there is a failure to differentiate the fantasy from the reality. However, this focus upon the 'pleasure' aspect is slightly misleading since, as the classical theory of psychoanalysis developed, the operations involved here were viewed not simply as strivings for pleasure but as coordinated strivings for gratification *and* withdrawals from or avoidances of the unbalanced tension and excessive affect of pain and/or unpleasure.

According to the standard Freudian model, the primitive, pleasure-seeking, pain-avoiding operations gradually become modified by the ➤ **reality principle** as ego functions are developed and the child comes to replace the fantasized wishfulfillment with more appropriate and reality-oriented adaptive behavior. Note also that the *pain* of the principle is different in meaning from the *pain* in the ➤ **pain principle** where a striving **for** pain is hypothesized, not an avoidance of it. Note that the term *pleasure–unpleasure principle* is also used. ➤ **pain** for reasons why *pain* and *unpleasure* are often interchanged within psychoanalysis.

pleasure principle ➤ **pleasure–pain principle**.

pleasure–unpleasure principle ➤ **pleasure–pain principle**.

-plectic ➤ **-plegia**.

-plegia A suffix from the Greek, meaning *stroke*. It is used to connote paralysis or loss of function due to a stroke or other neural damage; e.g., *hemiplegia* is a paralysis on one side of the body, *diplegia* involves both sides, *paraplegia* is a paralysis of both lower limbs, *monoplegia* of only one limb or a single muscle group, *facialplegia* involves the facial muscles, etc. adj., *-plectic*.

pleio-, pleo-, plio- Combining forms meaning *more*.

pleiotropic Of a gene that influences more than one phenotypic trait. The majority of genes appear to function in such a manner. n., *pleiotropy, pleiotropism*.

plethysmograph A device for measuring volume, usually that of blood supply, in a part of the body.

plexus Any network of nerves or of blood or lymphatic vessels.

plosive A speech sound that is produced by a momentary stoppage of the flow of air followed by a sudden release of the articulators and a rush of air. Plosives may be *voiced* (e.g., *d, b, g*) or *voiceless* (e.g., *t, p, k*).

plot 1 vb. To present data in graphic form. 2 n. The result of such an operation. There is a tendency to reserve the term for scatter diagrams, although most use it for any form of graphic display.

pluralism 1. A philosophical point of view that ultimate reality consists of more than one form of basic substance or principle. Strictly speaking, ➤ **dualism** is a pluralism, although the terms are usually kept distinct; ➤ **vitalism**, when appended to a dualistic approach, is an example. 2. The tendency to search for multiple causes. This sense is very general and characterizes any number of theoretical approaches that assume that psychological phenomena result from a multiplicity of causal factors. 3. The tendency for social groups to break up into smaller units. This usage is strictly descriptive. 4. A social-philosophical perspective that maintains that the diverse cultural characteristics of minority groups are important aspects of a whole society and that they should be encouraged by the more powerful majority. This usage is clearly prescriptive. The term *cultural pluralism* is often used to help distinguish this meaning from the above.

pluralistic ignorance A term introduced by Floyd Allport to characterize the feeling that one's beliefs or attitudes are not shared by others when they actually are –

but the 'others' aren't talking. Allport suggested that sudden observed changes in societal mores may come about when all the silent ones begin to express their previously covert beliefs.

plurel A term used primarily in sociology and social psychology to refer to a category or class containing any number of persons greater than one.

plus-sum game ➤ zero-sum *game.

PMAs Abbreviation for ➤ **primary mental abilities**.

PMS ➤ premenstrual syndrome.

pneumat(o)- Combining form meaning pertaining to *air, respiration*.

pneum(o)- Combining form meaning *lung*.

pneumogastric nerve Obsolete term for the ➤ vagus nerve.

pneumograph An instrument for recording breathing.

Poetzl effect The later appearance in dreams and waking imagery of parts of tachistoscopically presented pictures which were not reported as being perceived when actually presented. var., *Pötzl*.

Poggendorff illusion As depicted:

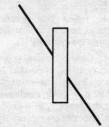

point-biserial correlation ➤ correlation, point-biserial.

point-for-point correspondence ➤ isomorphism.

point of regard ➤ regard.

point of subjective equality (pse) The point along a stimulus continuum at which two stimuli are perceived as nondistinguishable from each other. Actually, the *point* here is a statistically derived one and represents one of the following: (a) the value of the comparison stimulus that is most frequently judged as nondiscriminable from the standard; (b) the point at which either of two stimulus values is equally likely to be judged as being greater or lesser than the other; or (c) the value half-way between the upper and lower thresholds for the stimulus continuum.

point prevalence In epidemiology, the number of cases of a disease at a specific point in time. Compare with ➤ **period prevalence**.

point source A source of light sufficiently small in area such that for photometric purposes (➤ **photometry**) it may be regarded as a single point.

point-to-point correspondence ➤ **isomorphism**.

Poisson distribution ➤ **distribution, Poisson**.

polar continuum Any continuum whose poles are opposites. Various hypothesized psychological continua are represented as reflecting this characteristic of polarity. Some are straightforward, such as psychophysical dimensions like light–heavy, loud–soft; others are less obvious, such as many of the personality traits that are assumed to reflect this property like introversion–extraversion, dominance–submissiveness. ➤➤ **polarity** (1).

polarity 1. Generally, the property of having two poles or opposites. Magnets have polarity as do various continua or series; see here ➤ **polar continuum**. **2.** In neurology, the property of a neuron such that ions of opposite charges are separated by the semipermeable membrane of the cell. See here ➤ **action potential, depolarization**. **3.** The expression of opposite extremes of emotions, behaviors or traits, e.g., the polarized 'love–hate' relationship many children have with their parents. **4.** In a group setting, the focusing of attention on a single individual. ➤➤ **bipolar** et seq.

polarization 1. The treatment of light such that all vibrations are confined to a single plane. **2.** Concentration of electrical potential at one pole. **3.** The equilibrium of electrically charged ions on either side of a cell membrane. See here ➤ **depolarization**. **4.** Adjusting behaviors and opinions so that they are oriented or conform to one end of a bipolar continuum. **5.** The state of a group such that its activities have become focused on a central figure.

polar opposites Any two aspects of things (i.e. behaviors, objects, events, feelings, etc.) that represent the extreme poles on a continuum. That is, the pair *hot–cold* would be considered polar opposites but the pair *warm–cool* would not.

poll The original meaning is the *crown of the head* and contemporary uses in the social sciences still reflect this sense in that a poll is a 'head count' of opinions or attitudes. Note that modern polling no longer literally counts all the heads but rather uses sophisticated sampling techniques to provide estimates of populations of individuals from relatively small samples of persons. ➤ **sampling** et seq.

Pollyanna mechanism A defense mechanism in which one believes that all is well despite all evidence that it is not. The name comes from a character in an Eleanor Porter novel who was hopelessly and blindly optimistic.

poly- Combining form from the Greek, meaning *many*. Generally used in combination with words of Greek origin; words of Latin origin properly use ➤ **multi-**.

polyandry A mating (or, in humans, a marriage) system in which a single female may mate with (or marry) two or more males. Rare in humans, it tends to occur in species (like the seahorse) where the highest ➤ **parental investment** is made by the male. Compare with ➤ **polygyny**.

polyandry, fraternal A form of polyandry in which the woman's husbands must all be brothers.

polychromatic Having many colors.

polydactyl Possessing more than the usual complement of fingers.

polydipsia A general term for excessive drinking.

polydipsia, psychogenic A relatively rare psychological disorder characterized by the drinking of extreme amounts of water. It can, on occasions, prove fatal since sodium levels in the blood can be so severely reduced that coma and convulsions ensue.

polygamy A mating (or, in humans, a marriage) system involving the pairing of more than two individuals. For specialized forms, ➤ **polyandry** and ➤ **polygyny**.

polygamy, serial A marriage system in which a person may have more than one legal spouse but only seriatim, that is, only one at a time. This most common of marriage systems is often called *serial monogamy*, although this term is not preferred in the technical literature because the *mono*-prefix clearly denotes *one*.

polygenic Characterized by many genes. The term is used most often to refer to traits or structures that are determined by many genes.

polyglot One who speaks many languages. Contrast with ➤ **polylogia**.

polygnandry A mating system in which each male may mate with two or more females and each female with two or more males. It is seen in species that live in troupes, such as chimpanzees. The term *promiscuity* used to be used for this situation, which, while accurate, had a bit of an edge on it. *Polygnandry* is clearly the euphemism of choice.

polygraph Lit., multiple graph. Hence, any apparatus that reports or graphs data from more than one system at a time. The most common is the multi-channel recorder that simultaneously collects data (typically presented on moving graph paper) on a variety of events such as breathing, heart rate, perspiration, galvanic skin response, etc. Although used in a wide variety of laboratory situations, the polygraph has been so identified in the public eye with the lie detector that the phrase 'polygraph test' is often used synonymously with 'lie-detector test.' This equivalence is unfortunate and surely misleading. ➤ **lie detector**.

polygyny A mating (or, in humans, a marriage) system in which a single male may mate with (or marry) two or more females. It tends to occur in species (like many mammals) where the highest ➤ **parental investment** is made by the female. Compare with ➤ **polyandry**.

polygyny, sororal A form of polygyny in which the man's several wives must all be sisters.

polylogia Continuous, incoherent speech.

polymorphous Appearing in many forms or varieties.

polymorphous perverse A term often used to characterize the sexual nature of the young child as it is depicted within the classical theory of psychoanalysis. According to this model, the infant is viewed as deriving sexual pleasure in a variety of erotic forms, oral, anal, etc., which would be regarded (at least were in Freud's time) as ➤ **sexual *perversions** in an adult.

polyneuritic psychosis An occasional synonym for ➤ **Korsakoff's syndrome**.

polyonomy In linguistics, a situation in which a language has a large number of specific terms for the various aspects of a thing. For example, the Eskimo languages have separate words for fresh snow, hard-packed snow, walk-on-able snow, light-windblown snow, etc. all of which require extensive use of adjectives in English. The existence of polyonomy in a particular perceptual or conceptual area reflects a particular cultural/linguistic view of the world and helps to perpetuate it within the culture. Polyonomy has also been a focus of various theories concerning the interrelationship between language, perception and thought; see here ➤ **Whorfian hypothesis**. Contrast with ➤ **polysemy**.

polyopia Lit., more than one image. The term is reserved for conditions in which, because of irregularities in the refraction of light by the lens and/or the cornea, more than one image is formed on the retina. Contrast with ➤ **diplopia**. var., *polyopsia*.

polypeptide ➤ **peptide**.

polyphagia Excessive eating. E.g., ➤ **bulimia**.

polyphony 1. In linguistics, descriptive of single graphemes that are used to represent many different sounds; e.g., the English letter *s* as in *s*in, *s*ure, trea*s*ure, and lo*s*e. 2. In music, descriptive of having two or more melodies simultaneously.

polyphrasia A synonym for ➤ **logorrhea**.

polysemy Lit., many meanings. Used generally of single words with many distinguishable meanings; e.g., *rose* as a flower, the past tense of *rise*, a color, etc. Note that in comparative linguistics, it is also used to refer to two or more words in different languages which have the same original root.

polysubstance dependence ➤ **substance-related disorder** characterized by the use of three or more drugs, no one of which predominates. The term is not used when nicotine or caffeine are among the drugs.

polysynaptic reflex arc Any reflex arc in which the basic neural pathway has two or more synapses. The simplest will consist of an *afferent* neuron, an *association* *neuron* and an *efferent* neuron. Also called *multisynaptic reflex arc*.

pons 1. Generally, tissue that connects two or more parts. 2. Specifically shortened form of ➤ **pons varolii**.

pons varolii Rounded prominence on the ventral side of the brain stem connected with the cerebellum and containing fibers that link the medulla oblongata and the cerebellum with the higher regions of the brain. Several of the cranial nerves have their origins at its borders. Also known simply as *pons*.

pontine nucleus The gray matter in the pons varollii.

pontocerebellar-angle syndrome A syndrome produced by a tumor that exerts pressure on the auditory-vestibular (VIIIth cranial) nerve. Because the nerve carries fibers that serve both audition and balance, the syndrome displays both movement disorders (ataxia with staggering gait, vertigo, hemiplegia) and hearing disturbances (tinnitus, progressive hearing loss). Occasionally the facial (VIIth cranial) nerve is involved as well as producing a facial anesthesia and loss of the corneal reflex.

Ponzo illusion As depicted; also known, not surprisingly, as the *railway illusion*. Both horizontal bars are the same length.

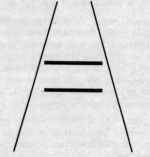

pooh-pooh theory ➤ **theories of *language** origins**.

pooling A term used in various contexts to express the notion of combining things, usually data. Thus: 1. Combining scores from several variables to produce a single measure; e.g., overall academic achievement as measured by pooling scores from all types of tests, grades on exams, papers, etc. 2. Combining data from more than one group of subjects; e.g., all 3rd- and 4th-grade children grouped together and compared with 5th and 6th graders as a separately pooled group. In both types of pooling, *weighting* procedures are usually required to prevent distortions.

population 1. All of the organisms of a specific kind (usually, but not necessarily, people) within a defined geographic area at a particular point in time. 2. In statistics, the total number of cases about which a specific statement can be made. Note that in this sense of the term, the population may be: (a) finite, existing and knowable (e.g., all the students enrolled in a particular school); (b) finite, existing but effectively unknowable (e.g., the population of the UK on the day of publication of this volume); or (c) infinite (e.g., all possible coin flips). Distinguish from ➤ **sample**, which is some observed or selected subset of a population. ➤➤ **sampling population**.

pornography Lit., from the original Greek, *writing about prostitutes*. Contemporary usage has expanded the domain of the term considerably and it is typically defined today as any form of written or pictorial representation that either is obscene or has as its sole function sexually to arouse the beholder. There are serious problems with both criteria here. Equating pornography with that which is obscene merely shifts the definitional burden; ➤ **obscenity** for a discussion of semantic problems. Characterizing it by reference to that which is sexually arousing makes the definition dependent upon the sexual preferences of the beholder. There seems to be no simple solution here and the actual connotations of the term are invariably colored by the writer's subjective point of view.

Porter's law ➤ **Ferry-Porter law**.

position The core meaning here is *place* or *location*, and all specialized usages of the term reflect this. Specific meanings are: **1.** In perception, a location of an object with reference to the point of view of an observer. **2.** In sociology and social psychology, a place in a social class or a system of social relationships. Note that this meaning is similar to ➤ **status** in that a social *position* entails social *roles*. **3.** In ethology, a point in a ➤ **dominance hierarchy**. **4.** In Lewin's field theory, a region in a ➤ **life space** where an event, fact, thing, etc. takes place. **5.** In general, a point of view or attitude that one assumes.

position factor Generally, any effect of temporal or physical location of a stimulus on a response. E.g., ➤ **position preference**.

position habit A learned ➤ **position preference**.

position preference Any preference, learned or otherwise, that an organism has for one temporal or spatial location over others. For example, a tendency to select the stimulus on the right over the one on the left in a two-choice discrimination experiment; a tendency to select the first of the alternatives in a multiple-choice exam or questionnaire, etc. Generally, such position factors need to be carefully controlled for by randomizing position of the stimuli on test items.

positive acceleration ➤ **acceleration**.

positive adaptation ➤ **adaptation** (1) where there is a gradual increase in sensitivity.

positive afterimage ➤ **afterimage, positive**.

positive attitude change ➤ **attitude change, negative and positive**.

positive correlation ➤ **correlation, positive**.

positive feedback Descriptive of any ➤ **feedback** loop which accelerates or increases a process.

positive recency In experiments on guessing and predicting, the tendency to predict the event that has occurred most recently. Contrast with ➤ **negative recency**.

positive reinforcement ➤ **reinforcement, positive**.

positive symptoms Symptoms of psychoses marked by the presence of bizarre behaviors and thoughts such as hallucinations and delusions. Compare with ➤ **negative symptoms**.

positive transfer ➤ **transfer, positive**.

positive transference ➤ **transference**.

positive valence ➤ **valence**.

positivism A philosophical point of view generally cited as having been formulated by Auguste Comte, although he was clearly influenced by Francis Bacon and by the British Empiricists. The *positive* aspect is used in the sense of that which is given, that which is accepted as it is found. Comte's point here was to argue against the attempts of metaphysics and theology to inquire about first causes and/or ultimate ends; that is, to argue that it is not possible to go beyond the objective world given to observation. Hence, for the positivists, all knowledge is contained within the boundaries of science and only those questions answerable from the application of the scientific method can be approached. The general perspective has emerged in a number of versions including ➤ **operationalism**. In psychology, the positivist approach is most closely associated with ➤ **behaviorism**, with its focus on objective observation as the basis for the formulation of laws. Positivism is sublimely 'hard-headed' and often praised for its common-sense approach. It is also, interestingly, occasionally defended on pragmatic grounds even by those who are unconvinced that all questions of knowledge can be ultimately reduced to scientific terms uncontaminated by metaphysics, mentalism and/or theology. It is also, however, not defended in strong form by very many contemporary scientists on the grounds that it places too many sharp limitations on what can legitimately be included in a scientific program.

positivism, logical A variant of ➤ **positivism** that had at its core the argument that any nontautological proposition that cannot, in principle, be verified by empirical, observational means is utterly devoid of meaning. The focus was to relegate all nonempirical aspects of philosophy and science such as metaphysics, theology, esthetics and ethics to the status of expressions of emotion and belief. The doctrine was ultimately hoist by its own petard for, among other difficulties, it was simply not clear that its own central principle of verifiability could be verified in the dictated manner.

positron emission tomography (PET) A procedure that provides an analysis of the amount of metabolic activity taking place in various parts of the brain. To do a PET-scan the patient is injected with a radioactive glucose-like substance that is absorbed into cells, particularly those that are metabolically active. The individual's

brain is scanned in a manner similar to a CAT scan. A beam of X-rays is passed through the head and the activities of the radioactive molecules are detected by the computer, which compiles a picture of the brain revealing the differential metabolic activity of various structures. ➤ **computerized axial tomography** and **magnetic resonance imaging**.

possessive instinct The drive for power and control over others, which is considered by some psychoanalysts to be an instinct. The sucking and swallowing behaviour of the infant is assumed to be an early manifestation of it.

possessiveness Strictly speaking, this term can be used for any tendency to attempt to gain and hold ownership over things. The psychologically interesting aspect, however, is when these 'things' are people. In fact, some authors use the term so that its sole connotative domain is the tendency to maintain power and control over others, to treat them as though they were one's owned possessions. It is most commonly observed in parents' attitudes toward their children and husbands and wives toward each other.

post- A combining form meaning *after*, *later*, *behind*.

postcentral gyrus The ➤ **gyrus** or ridge just posterior to the ➤ **central fissure** containing the primary somatosensory cortex.

postconcussional disorder An organic mental syndrome occurring following a head injury. A wide array of behavioral symptoms may be manifested so that it can resemble any number of other disorders. Typically present are giddiness, headaches, insomnia, a subjective sense of impaired cognitive functioning, wide mood fluctuations and low tolerance for mental or physical stress.

postconventional level of moral development ➤ **moral development**.

post-encephalic amnesia ➤ **amnesia, post-encephalic**.

posterior In time, *following*; in space,

behind. Contrast with ➤ **anterior**. In human anatomical terminology, *posterior* is frequently found as a synonym for *dorsal*, *anterior* as a synonym for *ventral*.

posterior root ➤ **spinal root**.

postganglionic neurons Efferent neurons of the autonomic nervous system that synapse directly onto their target organs.

posthallucinogen perception disorder An ➤ **organic mental disorder** characterized by ➤ **flashbacks** where one reexperiences the perceptual disruptions of a hallucinogen following cessation of the drug. The term is only used when the symptoms cause psychological distress.

post hoc Latin for *after this*. The term is generally used to refer to hypotheses or explanations developed on the basis of contiguity or correlation. Such hypotheses are not necessarily valid, because they assume causality without proper verification. Note that the phrase is actually a shortened form of *post hoc, ergo propter hoc* or, literally, *after this, therefore because of it*. A *post hoc* fallacy is the unwarranted presumption of causality of *x* on *y* simply because one has observed that *x* preceded *y*.

post hoc tests Any of several statistical procedures for determining which specific comparisons in a multifactor experiment are significant. These comparisons are run after (*post*) a general procedure such as an analysis of variance or a regression analysis has shown overall significance. Two of the more frequently used *post hoc* tests are the ➤ **Tukey honestly significant difference** and the ➤ **Scheffé**; others are the *Duncan* and the *Newman-Keuls*. Also known as *incidental tests*. ➤➤ **a posteriori tests**.

posthypnotic amnesia Generally, the inability to recall afterward some event that occurred while one was hypnotized. It is a form of posthypnotic suggestion in which the subject is specifically told that he or she will, upon waking, not be able to remember a particular fact or event.

posthypnotic suggestion A general term

for any suggestion given to a hypnotized subject that he or she will behave in a particular way after they have been wakened. ➤ **hypnosis**.

postnatal After birth; compare with ➤ **prenatal**.

postpartum Latin for *after childbirth*.

postpartum depression Loosely, any acute depression occurring within three months following childbirth. If psychotic symptoms are present, such as delusions, hallucinations, marked illogical thought, loosening of associations, the term *postpartum psychosis* may be used. Note, the three-month criterion is not universally adhered to and a variety of time periods may be cited as diagnostically relevant.

postpsychotic depression of schizophrenia ➤ **postschizophrenic depression**.

postremity (principle) The principle that the most probable response an organism will make in a particular situation is the last one it made in that situation. The principle played an important role in E. R. Guthrie's ➤ **contiguity theory** of learning.

postrotational nystagmus ➤ **nystagmus, postrotational**.

postschizophrenic depression A major depressive episode that occasionally occurs during the residual phase of ➤ **schizophrenia** or ➤ **schizophreniform disorder**. Also known as *postpsychotic depression of schizophrenia*.

postsynaptic Of a cell that is on the 'receiving side' of a synapse, the cell upon which the terminal buttons synapse.

postsynaptic potential (PSP) Generally, any change in the membrane potential of a postsynaptic neuron. PSPs are produced by transmitter substances released by the presynaptic terminal buttons. The *excitatory postsynaptic potentials* (EPSPs) are *de*polarizations which lower the threshold of the neuron and increase its likelihood of firing, the inhibitory postsynaptic potentials (IPSPs) are *hyper*polarizations which have the opposite effect.

post-test A general term for any test given at the end of an experiment, a training program, a course of instruction or the like. By comparing the score on the post-test with that on the ➤ **pretest** (2), one gets a measure of the effectiveness of the procedure. Also called *endtest*.

post-traumatic amnesia ➤ **amnesia, post-traumatic**.

post-traumatic stress disorder (PTSD) An ➤ **anxiety disorder** that emerges following a psychologically distressing, traumatic event such as a natural disaster, accident, war, rape, or the like. The syndrome includes reexperiencing the trauma in dreams, recurrent thoughts and images, a kind of psychological numbness with an accompanying lessening of feeling of involvement with the world about, hypervigilance, and an exaggerated **startle response**. As a psychiatric diagnosis, the term is not applied until the symptoms have continued for at least a month; prior to that it is called an *acute stress disorder*.

postulate An ➤ **assumption** that is accepted as true for the purpose of further reasoning. Postulates are similar to ➤ **axioms** in so far as neither is directly susceptible to proof or disproof but, unlike axioms, postulates are not universally self-evident. Their apparent truth is limited to the confines of a particular theory. Postulates also differ from ➤ **theorems** in that they are not logical deductions and from ➤ **hypotheses** in that they are not open to direct empirical evaluation.

postulational method A synonym for ➤ **hypothetico-deductive method**.

postural Pertaining to posture. Used specifically for position of the body and, more metaphorically, for mental attitudes or beliefs.

postural reflexes Collectively, the variety of reflex-like responses responsible for maintenance of body posture.

postural set A body position that is preparatory for a particular response.

postural tremors Fine, rapid tremors most commonly of the fingers and hands and occasionally of the head, mouth or tongue that emerge when the affected body part is held in a fixed posture; e.g., hands outstretched, mouth held open. A side effect of ➤ **lithium**, they are regarded as a ➤ **medication-induced movement disorder**.

posture 1. The overall position of the body. 2. A mental attitude or belief.

pot Slang for *marijuana*. ➤ **cannabis sativa** for details.

potency 1. Most generally, power. Some authors use it to refer to actual manifested power although, properly, the central connotation is that of *latent* power. ➤ **potential**, which shares the same etymology. 2. Effectiveness, particularly that of a drug. 3. Sexual capability, specifically the relative ability of the male to 'perform' sexually. Potency in this sense is independent of fertility; a sterile man may have great sexual potency. ➤ **impotence** for more on usage. 4. One of the three hypothesized universal dimensions of *semantic space* in Osgood's theory of word meaning. ➤ **semantic differential**.

potential 1 adj. Characterized by ➤ **potency**. 2. adj. Relating to the condition of ➤ **potentiality**. Note, however, that potential is often used as a shortened form of potentiality, i.e. as a noun denoting this condition rather than an adjective relating to it. 3 n. In electricity, voltage or electrical pressure. With respect to the electrical changes associated with neural impulses, ➤ **action potential** and ➤ **evoked potential**.

potentiality A present set of circumstances that suggests a latent ability; characteristics that are used to infer that some property or talent not currently manifested will develop or be learned (the faint hope that many parents cling to when they look at their children). ➤ **potential** (2).

poverty A relatively low standard of living in terms of goods and materials. *Relative* here is characterized in terms of the general standard of living in the society, its distribution of wealth, one's social status and one's personal expectations. The term is also used more metaphorically to characterize a relative lack of mental functioning, e.g., a poverty of ideas.

power The basic meanings are rather concrete: **1.** In mathematics, either the product of a number multiplied by itself or the exponent indicating the number of times the self-multiplication operation is to be carried out. **2.** In optics, the magnification of a lens. **3.** In physics, a measure of the rate of doing work. **4.** Muscular strength. **5.** = ➤ **social *power**. **6.** = ➤ **statistical *power of a test**.

power assertion A form of discipline where parents control the behavior of their children by using or threatening to use punishments and rewards.

power-coercive strategy A label used to cover any of a variety of strategies based on the use of political, economic or social power to bring about social change. Usually, only techniques utilizing some degree of coercive pressure are included here, e.g., strikes, boycotts, sit-ins, etc. Compare with ➤ **normative-reeducative strategy**.

power elite C. Wright Mills's term for the 'intricate set of overlapping cliques'· within the government, the military and the business world the members of which make the basic decisions about national events.

power field(s) In Lewin's field theory, those regions in the life space over which the individual has control. They may be objects, events or other persons.

power figure An individual as an identifiable representative of authority and power. The authority and power may be real or imagined; the primary role of the power figure is that of being someone with whom one can identify.

power function **1.** In statistics, an index of the power of a statistical test to reject, at a specified risk level, a false null hypothesis; see here ➤ **statistical *power of a test**. **2.** In psychophysics, an equation that expresses a particular theoretical relationship between the magnitude of a physical stimulus and the intensity of the sensory experience it evokes. ➤ **power law**.

power law A generalization, due primarily to the work of S. S. Stevens, that states that the psychophysical relationship between a physical stimulus, S, and the psychological experience of that stimulus. ψ, is given by the equation, $\psi = kS^n$, where n is the exponent or the power to which S must be raised that is characteristic of that particular continuum, and k is a constant. Stevens amassed a great deal of evidence to support his contention that when dealing with ➤ **metathetic** continua, the power law represents the 'true' psychophysical law. Note that ➤ **prophetic** continua do not follow this generalization and that other laws have been proposed and defended, e.g., *Fechner's* ➤ **log law**. ➤ **methods of *scaling, psychophysics** and **scales**.

power law (of performance) A generalization about learning that states that the speed of performance of a sensorimotor task increases as the power of the number of times the task is carried out. In layperson's terms, practice makes perfect (or at least makes you faster!).

powerlessness A psychological state in which one feels deprived of power, control or influence over events. The state may relate to feelings vis-à-vis social and political events or to feelings with respect to one's own personal psychological needs.

power of a test, statistical A measure of the probability that any given statistical test will detect a significant relationship when one actually exists in the data. Or, in the more usual phrasing, the probability that the test will reject, at a given level of risk, the ➤ **null hypothesis** of no relationship when, in fact, that hypothesis is false. The power of any statistical test increases as the sample size increases. ➤➤ **statistical significance**.

power, social Social psychologists and sociologists typically view power as the degree of control that a person or a group has over other persons or groups. Power is thus viewed in terms of relationships;

maximum power is the ability to exert total control over others while remaining simultaneously immune from attempts of the powerless to do likewise. Such power may be manifested in any of a number of ways. Formal ➤ authority carries with it formal, legal power, but surreptitious manipulations can often render it impotent. Physical force and coercion are obvious vehicles for exerting control but subtle and more genteel persuasions based upon deceit and deception are probably more common. Moreover, it must be recognized that an important aspect of social power is the degree to which one can compel another to act against his or her will. Thus, one means of wresting power from another is simply to withdraw one's emotional investment. This particular device is commonly observed in marital relationships and in the functioning of small social groups.

The more behavioristically inclined have a rather simple and not inelegant way of expressing the components of social power: 'Power is the degree to which one may dispense rewards and punishments to others while remaining unaffected by such attempts at dispensation by these others.' Bertrand Russell remarked that the social sciences ought to follow through on their oft-stated desire to emulate the natural sciences and, as physics has done, make power the fundamental concept. Since there are few areas of psychology with more obvious relevance to the 'real world' there are many who believe he was right.

power spectrum In acoustics, a graph of the mean square amplitude of a sound wave.

power test Any test that measures ability by determining the degree of difficulty of material that can be mastered with no time pressures on the test taker. Compare with ➤ speed test.

practice An abridged dictionary I checked provided 21 separate definitions for this term and, without much stretching, one could find almost all of them represented in the psychological literature.

However, the following four account for most of the term's use in psychology: **1.** The repetition of an act or a series of acts. **2.** The repetition of an act or a series of acts for the purpose of improving functioning. These two senses are kept separate because of theoretical debates over the relationships between ➤ **learning** and ➤ **performance** and the impact of repetitions of behaviors upon either or both. **3.** Any habitually performed, ritualized behavior. **4.** Any behavior that is customary or traditional, particularly within a particular culture.

practice, distributed In the study of learning, circumstances in which the practice trials are separated by rest periods or by periods of 'other' activity. Compare with ➤ **massed *practice**, in which there are no such pauses. Also called *spaced practice*.

practice effect Basically, the effect of practice. The term is used to refer to a factor that needs to be carefully controlled in experimental work to take into account effects of experience that are not relevant to the situation under study. For example, re-using the same IQ test with a person may invalidate it as a device for measuring his or her intelligence because of the practice effect produced by taking the test the first time.

practice, massed In the study of learning, an arrangement in which the subjects complete many trials with very short or no intertrial intervals. Learning under such conditions is generally slower than that with ➤ **distributed *practice**.

practice material Material given to a subject to familiarize him or her with the general experimental procedure prior to collecting the real data.

practice period **1.** A period during which the subject works with ➤ **practice material**. **2.** A period during an experiment or test in which the subject is permitted to practice.

practice theory of play The generalization that play, particularly that observed in lower organisms, is adaptive, in that it provides the opportunity to practice behaviors that will be of value as the organism matures. In the past, this hypothesis was also applied to children's play, although it accounts for only little of the observed data here. ➤ **play**.

practice trials One or more trials in which the subject is given practice materials to work with prior to actually running an experiment or administering a test.

Prader-Willi syndrome A congenital syndrome typically but not always marked by mental retardation ranging from mild to severe. Physical characteristics include short stature, generalized obesity, underdeveloped genitalia, and occasionally abnormal metabolism. Bizarre eating patterns are common. Also known as *hypotonia-obesity syndrome*.

prae- Variation of ➤ **pre-**.

Praegnanz Variation of ➤ **Prägnanz**.

pragmatic Concerned with the outcome rather than with the process; preferring that which is practical to that which is theoretical; favoring the concrete over the abstract.

pragmatics 1. As originally developed, the study of the relationship between the signs used (words, expressions, etc.) and the uses of them. 2. More recently, due largely to the work of Austin and Searle in the 1950s and 1960s, a rather general endeavor encompassing philosophical, linguistic, sociological and psychological aspects of the use and effects of verbal signs and forms. Pragmatics differs from most other areas of linguistic endeavor in its emphasis on the function of various language forms rather than on the forms alone. Pragmatics is often equated with ➤ **speech-act theory**, although it should be noted that the latter is more properly only one theory of pragmatics.

pragmatism A philosophical doctrine in which values, meanings and truths of propositions are taken as equivalent to the practical, empirical consequences derivable from them. Several of psychology's foremost early theorists were exponents of pragmatism, including John Dewey and William James.

Prägnanz A Gestalt principle of organization that holds that perceived or experienced forms tend toward a more coherent structure, i.e. better defined, more symmetrical, more stable, simpler and more meaningful. The term itself derives from the German word for *pregnant* and this is, indeed, the core of the connotation. It is occasionally referred to as the *law of pregnance* or the *law of precision*.

prandial Relating to a meal; e.g., prandial drinking is drinking associated with eating.

-praxia A word element meaning *doing* or *practice*.

pre- A combining form meaning *before, in front of*. var., *prae-*.

preadolescence By convention, the two years before puberty.

preattentive processing Unconscious processing of information that takes place prior to awareness of what has been heard or seen.

precategorical acoustic store (PAS) An unnecessarily long synonym for ➤ **echoic** **memory*. The point of the term, as its users argue, is that it specifies that the material in the PAS has not been processed or categorized.

precedence effect In perception, a phenomenon where the first of two or more stimuli to be noticed attracts one's attention so that the other(s) are not perceived as accurately. ➤ **law of *prior entry** for a similar phenomenon.

precenter To provide a fixation point in the visual field prior to presentation of a stimulus. By having the subject focus on this point, the area of the retina upon which the stimulus will fall is controlled.

precentral gyrus The ➤ **gyrus** or ridge just in front of the ➤ **central fissure** containing the neural tissue that controls the skeletal muscles.

precision, law of ➤ **Prägnanz**.

precision of process (h) In statistics, the reciprocal of the variance: i.e. $h = 1/\sigma^2$. Just as σ^2 reflects the uncertainty associated with observations drawn from a population, h reflects certainty.

precocity Generally, premature, rapid development. Although the term is most often used with respect to particularly early appearance of some intellectual or artistic ability, it can be applied to any early-maturing function. var., *precociousness*; adj., *precocious*.

precoding Determining the coding system to be used prior to the collection of the data.

precognition The hypothesized paranormal ability to have knowledge of future events. The term is not used for well-reasoned inferences and predictions made on the basis of current knowledge. ➤ **parapsychology**.

precommissural fornix ➤ **fimbria**.

preconcept Piaget's term for the primitive concepts used by a preoperatory stage child. Such concepts tend to be concrete and action-oriented; see here ➤ **transductive reasoning**.

preconscious A psychoanalytic term that refers to knowledge, emotions, images, etc. which are not momentarily in consciousness but which are easily accessible. Sometimes called the *descriptive unconscious* or the *foreconscious*; distinguish from ➤ **unconscious** and compare with ➤ **subconscious**.

preconventional level of moral development ➤ **moral development**.

precursor Generally, any thing that precedes another thing, with the implication that the first-occurring plays an essential role in the determination of the nature of the subsequent. The term is used most often with regard to various biochemical substances that play a role in the synthesis of other substances; e.g., *L-dopa* is a precursor of *dopamine*. Occasionally, a preliminary training program and/or learning experience may be called a precursor of the acquisition of other, more complex, skills.

precursor load strategy A psychopharmacological treatment method for various psychiatric disorders in which the patient is given doses of the precursor for a needed substance. The strategy is used in cases in which the required substance does not cross the blood-brain barrier but the precursor will, e.g., the oral administration of L-dopa in Parkinson's disease.

predation A cover term for all those behaviors associated with an animal's hunting, attacking and seizing other organisms for food. *Predator* is used for the animal that carries out these behaviors; *prey* for the victim. adj., *predatory*.

predatory aggression ➤ **aggression, predatory**.

predatory attack The kind of physical attack typically seen when an individual of a predatory species attacks one of its normal prey. The pattern of behavior has been artificially elicited in experiments with cats by stimulation of the brain; under such conditions it is called, descriptively, a *quiet biting attack*.

predelay reinforcement (procedure) A variation on the ➤ **delayed reaction (procedure)** in which the subject is reinforced in a particular place and then prevented from returning for various lengths of time before being permitted to attempt to go to the proper location.

predestination ➤ **predeterminism**.

predeterminism A philosophical point of view that maintains that the full script for the universe has already been written and that all that happens is merely the acting out of the grand design; all that transpires is predestined. A curious thing about this doctrine, which its adherents never quite seem to understand, is that it makes absolutely no difference whether it is true or false. Distinguish from ➤ **determinism**.

predicate (or **predicative**) **thinking** Reasoning whereby two objects are assumed to be similar or even identical because they share the same predicate; that is, they possess the same attribute with respect to a subject. Many psychoanalysts argue that the *id* 'thinks' predicatively, and Piagetians consider it a central aspect of preoperatory thought in the young child. Note, however, that the primitiveness implied by these usages is not the whole issue; predicate thought is also an element in cognitively sophisticated symbolism and symbolic thought where generalizations concerning concepts are made on the basis of shared features.

predication In logic (originally) and linguistics (more recently), a formal linking between a subject and a predicate. In simple terms, making a statement or proposition which attributes characteristics to a subject; e.g., 'Richard is a dirty rat' predicates of a person, Richard, a particular characteristic, dirty-ratness. Predication always involves the notion of linking or asserting.

prediction Simply, a statement about what will be observed before it actually occurs. In all scientific endeavors, prediction is a sophisticated operation involving detailed knowledge of the phenomena under consideration, including relevant facts and basic principles. Accurate prediction is usually regarded as the most stringent test of a scientific theory. In psychology, essentially all predictions are couched in forms probabilistic – although it should be recognized that this may be considered true in all sciences, the difference being that the probabilities are closer to 1.0 in some than in others.

prediction, clinical A term usually used in opposition to *statistical* or *empirical prediction*. The issue involves the question of whether predictions about an individual's behavior are more accurately made on the basis of an essentially subjective understanding that results from close individualistic scrutiny (i.e. *clinical*) or from statistical judgements made by evaluating the person with respect to objective scales and population norms (i.e. *statistical* or *empirical*). Note that both procedures may use 'hard' and 'soft' data; the

critical distinction is in how these data are combined subjectively and intuitively or objectively and mechanically.

prediction, differential Basically, any *either/or* prediction.

prediction, empirical ➤ clinical *prediction.

prediction, statistical ➤ clinical *prediction.

predictive efficiency A measure of the success of a test, a rule, a principle, a theory, etc. in making accurate predictions. Usually, in cases of relatively simple and well-defined situations, such as predicting who will succeed in an academic setting, the measure is given as a proportion of correct to total predictions.

predictive index ➤ index of *forecasting efficiency.

predictive validity ➤ validity, predictive.

predictor variable ➤ variable, predictor.

predisposing cause Any factor which although not *the* precipitating cause of an event, plays an important role in the manifestation of that event. The term is most frequently found with regard to diseases, hereditary syndromes and clinical disorders.

predisposition 1. Specifically, any genetic factor or set of factors that increases the likelihood of its possessor displaying a particular trait or characteristic. 2. More generally, a ➤ disposition.

preemie A ➤ premature infant.

preference Basically, a liking of one thing more than another thing. In practice, many psychologists prefer to operationalize the term and preference will often be used with reference to a turning toward or the actual selection of one alternative over another; that is, *choice* is taken as the indicator of preference.

preference test 1. Generally, any experimental situation where the subject must select the preferred of two or more alternatives. 2. Specifically, any of several tests of personal preference; e.g. *Kuder Preference Record*.

preformationism In its earliest form, the doctrine that all traits and structures were present in the germ plasma. The usual assumption here was that a ➤ **homunculus** (1), a miniature form of the organism, was present at the time of conception. The more modern variation holds that the characteristics and traits of an individual are present at conception in the form of a genetic code and that development is an unfolding of these 'preformed' patterns. Compare with ➤ **epigenesis**. Also called *preformism*.

prefrontal Pertaining to the anterior part of the frontal lobes of the brain.

prefrontal lobotomy ➤ **lobotomy, prefrontal**.

preganglionic neurons Efferent neurons of the autonomic nervous system that synapse on ➤ **postganglionic neurons**.

pregenital stage (or **level** or **phase**) In psychoanalytic theory, a stage of psychosexual development preceding the genital stage. The infant during this period is presumed to derive libidinal satisfaction from the oral and anal zones. Thus, the term is used so that it encompasses both the oral and anal stages.

pregnance, law of ➤ **Prägnanz**.

pregnant 1. Pertaining to the state of pregnancy. 2. Pertaining to a figure or a Gestalt having the characteristic of ➤ **Prägnanz**.

prehensile Capable of grasping.

prehension 1. The physical act of grasping. 2. Occasionally, the mental act of understanding. The connotation in both cases is that of a rather primitive kind of act.

prejudice 1. The literal meaning is with reference to an act of 'prejudging', a forming of an attitude prior to having sufficient information, a preconception. In this 'pure' sense, a prejudice can be either negative or positive in evaluative terms; it can

be about any particular thing, event, person, idea, etc.; and it can even be seen as an aspect of coherent scientific work when a hypothesis formulated on little evidence can legitimately be called a prejudice. 2. A negative attitude toward a particular group of persons based on negative traits assumed to be uniformly displayed by all members of that group. 3. A failure to react toward a person as an individual with individual qualities but rather to treat him or her as possessing the presumed stereotypes of his or her socially or racially defined group. Meanings 2 and 3 are connotatively very different from meaning 1; they are also the more commonly intended ones.

Prejudice (senses 2 and 3) is often thought of popularly as being characteristic of the members of the majority group in a society with respect to that society's minority groups. In fact, it tends to be an endemic attitude in many (all?) areas of social life. Prejudice should be differentiated from the notion of a *preconception*, largely because of the connotative element, the evaluative aspect. Contrast also with ➤ **discrimination**, which tends to be reserved for behaviors while prejudice is more clearly reserved for attitudes – which may or may not have behavioral accompaniments.

preliterate Used synonymously with ➤ **nonliterate**; distinguish from ➤ **illiterate**.

prelogical thinking A very general term for any mode of thought that does not follow the principles of logic. The prefix *pre-* implies that logical thought is somehow within the range of the individual's cognitive potential but simply hasn't made its appearance yet. Hence, it is typically used of young children.

Premack principle The generalization put forward by David Premack that if any two behaviors differ in their momentary probability of occurrence, the opportunity to engage in the more probable will serve to reinforce the less probable. The principle presents ➤ **reinforcement** as relative, not absolute. For example, food will reinforce running for a hungry rat but running may be made to reinforce eating if the rat is fully satiated but has been physically confined for a time and deprived of the opportunity for exercise.

premature ejaculation Undesired ejaculation during sexual intercourse which occurs too soon to satisfy the coital partner. Note that this functional definition has absolutely nothing to do with real time.

premature infant A viable fetus born 'prematurely.' 'Prematurely' here has been dealt with in a variety of ways over the years. Originally, the number of days since conception was used, with 250 days set as criterial for prematurity. Difficulties in obtaining accurate and objective data on conception led to a shift to birth weight as the critical factor with the generally accepted criterion being 2.5 kg (approximately 5.5 lb). When date of conception can be reasonably well identified, the concept of *weight appropriateness* relative to gestational age is used so that terms such as *small for date*, *preterm*, or in extreme cases, *very low birth weight* (usually restricted to infants below 1000 g) will be used.

premenstrual dysphoric disorder ➤ **late luteal phase dysphoric disorder**.

premenstrual syndrome (PMS) Minor mood lability in women associated with the late luteal period. The irritability and mood swings typically disappear within a few days of the onset of menses. Distinguish from ➤ **late luteal phase dysphoric disorder**.

premise In any argument, one of the propositions upon which another proposition (the conclusion) is based. ➤ **syllogism**.

premorbid Prior to the onset of a disorder. The term *premorbid functioning*, for example, is used to refer to the physical or psychological level of function before the disruptive effects of a condition or disorder.

premorbid personality A loose term used for an individual whose characteristic modes of behavior and thought are taken

as signs of a predisposition for a psychosis, notably schizophrenia.

prenatal Prior to birth.

prenatal influences Very generally, anything that has an effect upon the developing fetus. The term is used neutrally and should be distinguished from the doctrine of the ➤ **influence of *maternal impression**.

prenubile Pertaining to the period from birth to the onset of puberty.

pre-Oedipal stage (or **level** or **phase**). In psychoanalytic theory, the stage(s) of psychosexual development prior to the ➤ **Oedipal stage**. During this period the child is conceptualized as rather single-mindedly devoted to the mother.

preoperational thought ➤ **preoperatory thought**.

preoperatory stage (or **level** or **period**) In Piagetian theory, the stage of cognitive development following the ➤ **sensory-motor stage**. It is first detectable with the establishment of ➤ **object permanence** and ends with the emergence of ➤ **concrete operations**. During this stage, the child is characterized largely by dependence upon perceptual features of the world and thinking is intuitive in nature rather than logical, although the child is capable of some early forms of symbolic representational thought. Also called the *preoperational stage*.

preoperatory thought A term used by Piaget to refer to the kinds of cognitive capabilities manifested by a child during the ➤ **preoperatory stage**.

preoptic area An area just rostral to the *hypothalamus*, it is usually divided into the *lateral* and *medial* preoptic areas. The medial preoptic area is the forebrain region that is most responsible for male sexual behavior; lesions eliminate the copulatory response, stimulation produces it.

preorgasmic ➤ **frigidity** (3) and ➤ **orgasm disorders**.

preparation **1.** Most generally, the act of preparing, of getting ready to perform some behavior **2.** In problem-solving, the preliminary stage, during which the solver attempts to gather the relevant information needed for attempted solutions. **3.** In physiological psychology, an organism prepared for examination or experimentation.

preparation, acute A ➤ **preparation** (3) studied for a short period of time, specifically while the temporary (i.e. *acute*) effects of some drug or surgical procedure are being manifested by the experimental subject.

preparation, chronic A ➤ **preparation** (3) studied over an extended period of time. A common example in physiological work is the permanent implantation of an electrode in an animal's brain.

preparatory interval In experiments, particularly those in which *reaction time* is the major dependent variable, a short period of time between a 'ready' signal and the presentation of the stimulus for responding.

preparatory response A term used by some learning theorists to refer to all the responses in a sequence of behaviors (except the very last response) which lead the organism to a single reinforcement. Since, strictly speaking, reinforcement only follows the very last of a chain of responses, it was the only one that was directly reinforced. Hence, the previous responses in the sequence were dubbed 'preparatory.'

preparatory set ➤ **set, preparatory**.

preperception A rarely used term which refers to the host of vague processes taking place just prior to perceiving a stimulus. It is most clearly experienced with ambiguous figures.

prepotent reflex (or **response**) Any reflex or response that take precedence over any other potential reflex or response that an organism might make.

prepotent stimulus Any stimulus that takes precedence over all the others in the environment at a given point in time, the

stimulus with the greatest attention-getting capacity.

preprogramming Technical jargon for the extent to which the behavior of a species or individual organism is genetically programmed. Typically used with respect to the degree to which the neural patterns of the brain are assumed to have been genetically 'prewired' for particular behaviors. See here ➤ **heredity–environment controversy**.

prepsychotic Loosely, pertaining to behaviors or emotional or cognitive states that a clinician considers to be indicative of an incipient psychosis.

prepuberal stage A synonym for the period of ➤ **preadolescence**. Also spelled *prepubertal*.

presby- A combining form meaning *old, aged*.

presbyacusis Loss of sensitivity to sound stimuli with increasing age. The term is used specifically to refer to the common partial or complete deafness in the aged, although essentially everyone past childhood is somewhat presbyacutic, especially for high-pitched stimuli (above roughly 15,000 Hz).

presbyophrenia A type of senility characterized by chronic memory deficits but with relatively normal level of mental alertness and awareness.

presbyopia A visual defect produced by a hardening of the lens. The rigidity of the lens, which is common in old age, causes a loss of accommodation such that the ability to focus on close objects is lost. Bifocals correct for the condition.

preschool **1.** The period of life prior to reaching school age. **2.** Any kindergarten and/or nursery school.

presenile dementia ➤ **dementia, presenile**.

presenile onset ➤ **presenile *dementia** and ➤ **senile**.

presenium The period of life before the age of 65.

presentation **1.** Generally, any manner in

which material is put before a person for learning or understanding. **2.** In experimental work, the act of placing a stimulus before a subject. **3.** The stimulus itself. **4.** In psychoanalysis, the manner in which an instinctual drive is expressed. **5.** In ethology, the sequence of behaviors engaged in by a female animal indicative of receptivity of coitus. **6.** In social interactions, the manner in which a person expresses him or herself; e.g., ➤ **presentational rituals**.

presentational rituals E. Goffman's term for the many things we do to promote social interactions in a polite manner. He cites four classes of rituals: salutations, invitations, compliments and minor services. Presentation rituals and ➤ **avoidance rituals** together make up what he calls *deference behavior*.

presenting symptom 1. The symptom that causes a person to seek medical or psychological therapy. **2.** The symptom that a patient 'presents' as the initial one during the first intake work-up by a physician or a therapist. They may not be the same symptom.

presolution variability A term used for the general observation that prior to the discovery of a solution to a complex problem there is typically considerable variability in behavior as many different strategies are employed in an attempt to find the correct route to take.

press In Henry Murray's theory of personality, those aspects of the environment that are effective determinants of behavior. Press are (note that Murray used the term in the plural) external and represent features of objects that have straightforward implications for the individual in his efforts to fulfill needs which are conceptualized as internal. In actual behavior, a *press-need pattern* emerges which collectively represents the various actions taken to satisfy the needs produced by press. For example, the press of poverty may produce a need for financial security and the person may, according to circumstances, cheat, work hard, train for a lucrative profession, etc.

press-need pattern ➤ **press**.

pressure The basic dictionary definition of exertion of force against something is generally adequate in psychology. There are a few specific uses, as follows: **1.** The sensation experienced when physical force is applied to an area of the body; see here, ➤ **pressure sensation**. **2.** The emotional experience of feeling compelled to respond to someone's wishes or to some external forces. **3.** The use of coercion to persuade another to act in a particular manner. ➤ **social pressure**.

pressured speech Extremely rapid, frenzied speech. Seen in cases of mania.

pressure gradient The gradient of deflection of the skin away from the point where the pressure is applied. This gradient is the critical stimulus for ➤ **pressure sensation** as can be shown by placing one's finger in a jar of mercury. Although there is considerable physical pressure everywhere, the only sense of pressure is where there is a gradient, at the surface.

pressure sensation The perceptual experience when sufficient tissue distortion to establish a detectable ➤ **pressure gradient** takes place. The phrase 'tissue distortion' is used here to emphasize that, although in the normal course of affairs pressure is typically experienced when a stimulus deforms the skin inward, outward deflections are similarly perceived as pressure, as are tensions in muscles, joints, tendons and internal organs. Occasionally one will see reference to qualitatively different pressure sensations, e.g., light or heavy, surface or deep, sharp or diffuse, etc. These references should not necessarily be taken as reflective of neurologically distinct pressure systems or distinct receptors but rather as phenomenologically different experiences of different patterns of physical stimulation. Although there are many unresolved issues, there is evidence to implicate the *Pacinian corpuscles*, the *Meissner corpuscles* and the *free nerve endings* as pressure receptors.

pressure-sensitive spot Any small spot on

593

the skin with lower threshold for the sensation of pressure than the surrounding area. There is a close correspondence between these spots and individual hairs, with most of them found to the 'windward' side of hairs.

prestige Loosely, an attribute of being held in high regard by one's associates. Prestigious persons are generally influential in a group or society although, since prestige may be limited to a specific area or field of endeavor, their influence may be tempered by limited credibility.

prestige suggestion The process of persuading others by associating prestigious persons with the point of view one is attempting to put forward. ➤ **persuasion** and related entries.

prestriate cortex Visual association cortex that surrounds the primary visual cortex (➤ **striate cortex**). It receives fibers from both the primary visual cortex and the superior colliculi (➤ **colliculus**). Also called *circumstriate cortex* and *extrastriate cortex*.

presupposition 1. Generally, a supposition made in advance, an assumption, a postulate. 2. In studies of language, an assumption that a speaker makes about the listener's knowledge in order that an utterance will make sense. For example, in uttering a simple sentence like 'Pat is sick too,' the speaker presupposes that he and the listener share knowledge of a person named Pat and another unnamed person of their acquaintance whom they both know is sick.

presynaptic Of a neuron that synapses on another; the cell on the other side of the synapse from the ➤ **postsynaptic** neuron.

pretest 1. A practice test, some number of trials or some period of time during which the subject in an experiment becomes familiar with the materials being used. 2. A preliminary test or series of trials given prior to the actual experimental manipulations. Scores on the pretest form a baseline against which to measure the effects of the manipulations. 3. A final

run with a questionnaire or survey prior to full-scale implementation, a kind of last-minute 'shakedown' to detect any existing problems in design, wording of questions, etc.

prevalence The total number of cases of a disease or a disorder in a specified population at a point in time.

preverbal A general term used to refer to the time prior to the acquisition of language.

prewiring ➤ **pre-programming**.

priapism A chronically erect penis. The term is properly used for an abnormal condition in which the persistent erection occurs without sexual arousal. It should not be used as a synonym for ➤ **satyriasis**.

pricking pain ➤ **pain, pricking**.

pride The state of satisfaction with oneself for efforts made and gains accomplished.

pride, neurotic K. Horney's term for the neurotic condition in which the sense of one's worth far exceeds what the data actually warrant.

primacy Generally, the property of being first in any respect. In psychoanalytic writings, the meaning is often not a simple temporal or logical one but may connote *prepotence*. That is, a tendency which has *primacy* is one which is strong and can withstand regressive tendencies or other infantile id pressures. adj., *primary*.

primacy effect 1. In cognitive psychology, the common finding that in a free recall situation, the materials that were presented first in a series are better recalled than those that were presented in the middle. ➤➤ **recency effect** and **serial position effect**. Also called the *law of primacy* or the *principle of primacy*. 2. In social psychology, the finding that information about an individual presented early on has a greater impact on impression formation than information presented later.

primacy, law or principle of ➤ **primacy effect**.

prima facie Latin for *at first appearance, at first view*. In scientific work, it refers to the circumstances in which a fact or an observation is put forward which is suggestive of a particular interpretation but requires further analysis or research before conclusions can be legitimately drawn. In *forensic* matters, it refers to evidence deemed indicative that an event has occurred and, unless rebutted, probably legally acceptable. Note that we find scientists here somewhat more conservative in their stance than lawyers and judges.

primal First in a temporal sequence, first in time. Often used as equivalent to *primitive* or *primordial*, particularly in psychoanalytic works.

primal anxiety In psychoanalytic theory, the anxiety experienced immediately after birth when the infant is expelled from the protective womb and thrust into the frenetic stimulation of the outside world. Note that some psychoanalytic theorists have continued to maintain that this primal experience (the so-called *birth trauma*) is the source of all anxiety; Freud himself revised his thinking on this issue considerably in his later writings. ➤ **primary anxiety** and **signal anxiety**.

primal father ➤ **primal horde**.

primal horde Freud's term for the primordial community hypothesized originally by Darwin in which social structure was organized around a dominant male (the *primal father*), a number of females whom he reserved for himself and the subordinate males whom he kept in subjugation. It should be appreciated that Freud's notions were based upon psychoanalytic theory, not archeological or anthropological data, and that Darwin's original hypothesis was based upon the observation of nonhuman primates.

primal repression ➤ **repression** (1).

primal scene A recollected or confabulated scene from childhood of some early sexual experience, most commonly one's parents copulating.

primal trauma A term used very generally in psychoanalytic approaches to refer to some painful childhood experience. The experience of birth, an especially severe punishment, the death of a parent, witnessing parental coitus, the knowledge that your parents do not love you, etc. have been so labeled by various theorists.

primary First, in the broadest possible sense. The basic idea here is that a thing is primary with respect to other things if these things can be ordered in some logical, coherent fashion, e.g., according to time, spatial location, order of development, order of magnitude, relative importance, etc. Note that distinctions between this term and its various partial synonyms are occasionally made. To wit: *prime* = first in importance, *primal* = first in a temporal sequence, *primitive* = first in a series of things of increasing complexity, *primordial* = first in an evolutionary or geological time sequence. Compare with ➤ **secondary**. n., *primacy*.

primary abilities ➤ **primary mental abilities**.

primary amentia A mental deficiency assumed to be due to genetic factors.

primary anxiety In psychoanalysis, the emotional experience that accompanies the dissolution of the ego. In Freud's later theorizing about anxiety, he regarded this form as the basic, fundamental (i.e. *primary*) anxiety and distinguished it from ➤ **signal anxiety**, which was conceptualized as having a protective, altering function. Distinguish from ➤ **primal anxiety**.

primary circular reaction ➤ **circular reaction**.

primary color ➤ **colors, primary**.

primary degenerative dementia ➤ **dementia, primary degenerative**.

primary drive ➤ **drive, primary**.

primary factor ➤ **factor, primary**.

primary feeblemindedness Obsolete synonym of ➤ **primary amentia**.

primary gain 1. In psychoanalytic theory, the basic relief from anxiety that results from the initial development of a neurosis. 2. More generally, an initial gain achieved through the development of any disorder. Also called *paranosic gain*. Compare with ➤ **secondary gain** and ➤➤ **advantage by illness**.

primary group ➤ **group, primary**.

primary hue ➤ **unique *hues**.

primary identification In psychoanalytic theory: 1. The total devotional identification the infant feels with the mother before an awareness of the existence of others develops. 2. More generally, identification with the same-sexed parent.

primary insomnia ➤ **insomnia, primary**.

primary integration Freud's term for the initial recognition by the child that it is an integrated whole, separate and distinct from the rest of the environment. Piaget used the term ➤ **subject–object differentiation** in a similar manner.

primary memory ➤ **short-term *memory**.

primary mental abilities The basic, fundamental mental abilities that have been hypothesized as being the components of intelligence. The term derives from and tends to be associated closely with the factor-analytic studies of L. L. Thurstone, which yielded seven of these (verbal, word fluency, numerical, space, memory, perceptual and reasoning). Often abbreviated *PMAs*.

primary motivation Motivation that derives from basic, biological needs and which is assumed to be common to all members of a particular species. See the discussion under ➤ **motivation**.

primary motor cortex The ➤ **precentral gyrus**.

primary narcissism ➤ **narcissism, primary**.

primary need ➤ **need, primary**.

primary object In psychoanalytic theory, the initial or first ➤ **object** (4) to which the infant relates, usually the mother or the breast.

primary object-love The infant's emotional experience associated with the ➤ **primary object**.

primary process In psychoanalytic theory, mental functioning operative in the *id*., Primary processes are conceptualized as unconscious, irrational, ignorant of time and space and governed by the pleasure–pain principle. Compare with ➤ **secondary process**.

primary quality ➤ **primary and secondary *quality**.

primary reinforcement ➤ **primary *reinforcer**.

primary repression ➤ **repression** (1).

primary sensory cortex A general term for those areas of the cerebral cortex that contain the primary inputs from one of the sensory systems. Typically modifiers are used to reflect the sensory modality under consideration; e.g., primary visual cortex, primary auditory cortex.

primary sex characteristics ➤ **sex characteristics, primary**.

primary zone In psychoanalysis, the zone that provides maximum libidinal satisfaction at each particular stage of psychosexual development.

primate Any member of the Primates, the highest order of mammals. There are three sub-orders, Lemuroidea, Tarsioidea and Anthropoidea; the last counts our own species among its members.

prime 1 adj. Primary, in the sense of first in importance or quality. 2 n. A mark (') used to designate a symbol. 3 n. The fundamental tone, the first partial. 4 n. A prime number. 5. Any event that functions so that the phenomenon of ➤ **priming**, in any of its various senses, occurs. 6. vb. To make ready, to prepare.

priming 1. Generally, the process of presenting an event or episode (the ➤ **prime** (5)) that prepares a system for functioning. 2. In animal learning, the presentation of a specific experience that makes the animal more sensitive and/or responsive to a wider ranger of stimuli. **3.** In cognitive psychology, the triggering of specific memories by a specific cue; e.g., *river* will prime one meaning of *bank* while *money* will prime another. Interestingly, this priming can take place outside of consciousness; one can fail to recall or even recognize words that were previously presented yet respond with those words when 'primed' by something like the first three letters. ➤ implicit *memory.

priming, negative The reverse of regular ➤ priming (3). Here, one typically finds slower and less accurate responding to an aspect of the stimulus display that the subject had previously been told to ignore.

primipara A female who has borne offspring but once.

primitive 1. Loosely, undeveloped. **2.** Characterizing or referencing the (theoretical) earliest stages of the development of man. **3.** Pertaining to a ➤ nonliterate people or culture. The first two usages are fairly unambiguous (➤ primary); the third is not and fortunately is gradually dropping out of use. The issue here is that there is no reason to suppose nor is there any evidence to support the view that 'primitive' people in sense 3 are 'primitive' in senses 1 or 2.

primitivization A loose synonym for ➤ regression (1).

primordial ➤ primary.

primordial image ➤ unconscious ideation.

principal First, leading, of greatest importance. Distinguish from ➤ principle.

principal-component method A technique in factor analysis whereby a major axis representing a factor is first determined and a second axis that accounts for as much of the remaining variance as possible is located at right angles to it.

principle 1 n. A general, basic maxim; a fundamental truth. **2** n. A generally accepted rule of procedure, particularly a scientific procedure. There are some fine distinctions between *principles, canons, rules* and *laws* which are drawn, the most common being that *law* should be reserved for cases in which the uniformity and validity are beyond doubt, while the other terms serve for more problematical cases. In actual usage, the connotations of these terms overlap so much that distinctions often become academic. However, ➤ scientific law. **3.** The active ingredient of a substance. Distinguish from ➤ principal.

principle of proximity ➤ minimum distance principle.

prior entry, law of A generalization, first formulated by E. B. Titchener, that of two simultaneously presented stimuli the one upon which one's attention is focused will be perceived as having occurred first. ➤ precedence effect for a similar phenomenon.

prism In optics, a wedge-shaped lens that bends and disperses light in accordance with its wavelength. Note that although the term is specifically optical, any wedge-shaped object may be, on occasion, called a prism; e.g., ➤ Henning's prism.

prism diopter In optics, the unit of measurement of the strength of a prism given as 100 times the tangent of the angle through which the light is bent.

prisoner's dilemma ➤ dilemma, prisoner's.

prison psychosis ➤ Ganser syndrome.

private 1 adj. Generally, of an individual, with respect to a person, not shared, personal. **2** adj. Belonging to a single individual, e.g., private property. **3.** Internal, subjective.

private acceptance The covert accepting of the opinions or beliefs of others, conforming to the attitudes of others. The term is used so that there is no entailment of behavior; i.e. one who privately accepts the beliefs of others is not necessarily expected to act upon them. ➤ conformity for more on this point. Compare with ➤ compliance.

private opinion ➤ opinion, private.

privation A lacking of satisfaction or the

means to achieve satisfaction of one's needs. Compare with ➤ **deprivation**, which is the loss or removal of such means.

privilege Any advantage accruing to some members of a group or society and not to others. In the context of social psychology, the term is restricted to advantages guaranteed by virtue of social status. In psychiatry and clinical psychology, it denotes the legal rights of patients to the confidentiality of what is divulged during therapy: ➤ **privileged communication**.

privileged communication Generally any document, statement or other form of communication that is not open for public inspection. Within the confines of psychotherapeutic proceedings, material that emerges in the course of treatment is generally regarded as such – although the laws pertaining to what can and cannot be divulged in court differ from locale to locale.

pro- A combining form meaning: **1.** *In front of, before.* **2.** *In account of.* **3.** *In favor of.*

proactive Generally, descriptive of any event, stimulus or process that has an effect upon events, stimuli or processes that occur subsequently. E.g., ➤ **proactive *interference**. Compare with ➤ **retroactive**.

proactive inhibition ➤ **proactive *interference**.

proactive interference ➤ **interference, proactive**.

probabilism The philosophical perspective that maintains that events may be empirically and rationally predicted but only with some probability, $p < 1.0$. Actually, there are two varieties of this position. One argues that the probabilistic aspect is a result of the complexity of the phenomena under examination and of our current level of ignorance, which force us to be content with probabilistic estimates. The other maintains that the underlying reality is probabilistic in nature. ➤ **determinism** for other issues and terms.

probabilistic functionalism A theory of

598

perception and, by extension, a general theory of behavior, due primarily to Egon Brunswik. The theory stresses that perception is a process of discovering which aspects of the stimulus provide the most useful or functional cues, i.e. those that produce the greatest probability of successfully reacting to the environment. ➤ **ecological validity**.

probability **1.** In the simplest, nontechnical sense, the likelihood of an event. Specification of the number that corresponds, more formally, with that likelihood is determined by the ratio of the number of ways that that event can occur to the total number of possible events under consideration. Thus, the probability of any event A is a statement of the expectation of the proportional frequency of As observed in the long run. **2.** Somewhat more loosely, the state of being probable, of being likely to occur. **3.** Shorthand for ➤ **probability theory**.

probability, conditional The likelihood of an event A dependent upon the occurrence of some other event B, denoted as $p(A/B)$. Note that, in a very real sense, all probabilities are conditional probabilities in that the estimating of the likelihood of any event entails certain preconditions; the term, however, is used only for those circumstances where there is a probabilistic quality to the conditional event.

probability curve **1.** Very generally, any graph of the probabilities of particular outcomes. ➤ **probability distribution**. **2.** Specifically, the normal probability curve. ➤ **normal distribution**.

probability density When dealing with a continuous random variable the probability of occurrence of any exact value of the variable is zero. Hence, in such situations, reference is made to a small range or interval of values of the variable and probability is given by the *probability density* of the variable in the interval under consideration.

probability distribution ➤ **distribution, probability**.

probability function Simply, a formal expression that gives the pairing of each event in a particular situation and the probability of its occurrence. On occasion, the term is used synonymously with the normal probability curve; see here ➤ **normal distribution**.

probability, joint The probability of a joint event, i.e. the likelihood that two (or more) events occur simultaneously.

probability learning ➤ **learning, probability**.

probability mass function A graph (or its functional rule) of a discrete random variable with the values it may assume on the x-axis and the probability units on the y-axis.

probability matching In a ➤ **probability *learning** experiment, the condition when the subject predicts the several events with the same probabilities that they are actually occurring. Compare with ➤ **maximizing** and **overshooting**, and ➤➤ **matching law**, a somewhat more ambitious-sounding term used in roughly the same fashion.

probability of response The frequency of occurrence of a particular response (or, more precisely, of the various instances of a *class* of responses) relative to the theoretical maximum frequency of occurrence of that (class of) response(s) under specified conditions. Strictly speaking, the term should be restricted to circumstances in which one knows the number of possible responses, in which the likelihood of each has been empirically determined and in which a mathematically meaningful probability may be calculated, e.g., in a two-alternative, forced-choice recognition experiment. One should, properly, resist the temptation to embellish one's research with bogus quantification by using the term otherwise. Workers in operant conditioning are often guilty of this misuse of the term when they refer to the 'probability of a bar press' when what is really meant is the frequency of bar presses relative to some base rate; frequency alone does not a probability make.

probability ratio The ratio of the number of occurrences of an event of a specific class to the total number of occurrences of events in a specified set.

probability sampling ➤ **sampling, probability**.

probability space For any given, finite set of events, the specification of the probability of occurrence of each.

probability, subjective A belief about the likelihood of occurrence of some event or about its relative frequency of occurrence. Such beliefs are often not consciously held and people may have considerable difficulty in expressing specific values that reflect them. Nevertheless, their behavior often reflects strongly held subjective-probability estimates. E.g., ➤ **probability *learning**.

probability theory The discipline within mathematics that deals with probability. The mathematical foundation of probability theory forms the basis for all the statistical techniques of psychology. Probability theory had its origins in gambling where, on the basis of a relatively small number of trials (roulette-wheel spins, dice throws, poker hands), some decisions needed to be made about the likelihood of particular events occurring in the long run, given the basic assumption of the uniformity of nature and the mutual cancellation of complementary errors. The logic of modern statistical theory is entirely consonant with this notion; given a relatively small number of observations in an experimental setting, one needs to make decisions about the likelihood of such observations in the long run.

probable error ➤ **error, probable**.

proband The individual who first comes to the attention of investigators and, because of his or her mental or physical disorder, leads to a detailed study of the genetic-transmission pattern within the family to determine if there is a pattern of disorders that might be genotypic in nature. Also called the *propositus* or the *index case*.

probe **1** vb. To penetrate with intent to explore. **2** n. An instrument or a stimulus used in such a manner. For example, in the so-called *probe technique* for the study of memory, a subject is given a list of stimulus items to memorize followed by a final stimulus (the probe); that is, a list like 7, 1, 6, 9, 5, 4, 8, 3, 5 might be followed by the stimulus '9' as the probe and the subject would be asked to recall the number that immediately preceded or followed the '9' in the list.

problem Basically, a situation in which some of the attendant components are known and additional components must be ascertained or determined. Problems are of interest to psychologists when the unknown characteristics which lead to solution are neither obvious nor easily ascertained. ➤ **problem-solving**.

problem behavior Loosely, behavior which may lead to psychological problems. Generally included are behaviors that are incomprehensible to others, and those that are antisocial, destructive, disruptive or broadly maladaptive. Distinguish from ➤ **behavior problem**.

problem box ➤ **puzzle box**.

problem check-list A self-report personality inventory which contains a list of typical problem situations (e.g., those having to do with money, sex, interpersonal relationships, achievement in school or on the job, etc.). The subject checks off those that are germane.

problem child Loosely, a child whose behavior is such that his or her parents, teachers, friends, etc. cannot deal effectively with him or her. Although this definition seems to put the 'burden' on these other persons and not on the child, it really is the only accurate characterization of the situation.

problem-solving **1.** The processes involved in the solution of a problem. **2.** The area of cognitive psychology that is concerned with these processes. For some examples of classic problems ➤ **anagrams**, **puzzle box, water-jug problem**. For some

classic issues which emerge in the study of problem-solving, ➤ **functional fixedness**, **insight** and **trial-and-error *learning**.

procedural knowledge ➤ **knowledge, procedural**.

procedural memory ➤ **memory, procedural**.

procedure Generally, any technique for controlling the relevant factors for the purpose of examining some phenomenon. The term is similar in use to ➤ **method** but with the connotation that a procedure is a more concrete manipulation of specific conditions whereas a method generally suggests a broader orientation. For example, the phrase *experimental procedure* refers to the specific techniques used in a specific experiment while *experimental method* refers to a general class of techniques used in doing experimental work.

proceeding Henry Murray's term for a complex 'unit' of behavior. Proceedings involve interactions either between persons or between persons and objects; they have beginnings and endings; and they are regarded as psychological 'wholes' in the sense of being coordinated but elementary pieces of any behavior sequence. In Murray's theory (➤ **personology**) they are the basic data of analysis although, admittedly, in practice it is often difficult to determine where one proceeding begins and another leaves off, for they are commonly overlapping. ➤ **serial**.

process A term with a rather rich variety of meanings in psychology. Note, however, that in spite of the seeming diversity in usage, all derive from the Latin *processus* meaning *a going forward*, and the underlying connotation is always that of a series of steps or a progression toward some aim or some goal. Hence: **1.** Very generally, any change or modification in a thing in which directionality or focus can be discerned. The usual sense here is that the form or structure of an organism or object is relatively static or stable and that any systematic modification in it over time represents some underlying, meaningful process that leads to a different form or structure. *Process* here is regarded as *active*, the *structure* itself as *passive*. This general meaning is applicable in almost any domain of the social sciences and, as many have argued, psychology is basically a study of processes. **2.** The manner in which some change is brought about. The usual reference here is to some set of operations that produces a particular result, e.g., the *learning process*, the *extinction process*. **3.** In cognitive psychology, any operation that is a component of the organizing, coding and interpreting of information. The so-called *cognitive processes* include memory, thinking, interpreting, problem-solving, creativity and the like. See here ➤ **information processing** and related terms. The above three uses all have the verb *to process*, meaning to engage in or carry out any of these operations. **4.** In physiology, the underlying (causal?) operations of behavior. The implication here is the indisputable fact that some physiological or biological *process* underlies all observed behavior. **5.** In anatomy, any slender extension or projection from an organ or cell; axons and dendrites are processes. **6.** In Titchener's structuralism, a conscious content without reference to its meaning, value, or context.

processing error Any error introduced during the processing (i.e. analyzing, organizing, reporting, etc.) of the data from an experiment.

processing, parallel Information processing in which more than one sequence of processing operations is carried out simultaneously or 'in parallel.' The processing may involve extremely low level, nonsymbolic components such as those used in the ➤ **parallel distributed processing models** and ➤ **network models** (2), or it may be based on higher level elements such as those used in retrieval of information about words where meaning, spelling, pronunciation, and role in syntax are all accessed at virtually the same time. Compare with ➤ **sequential *processing**.

processing, sequential Information processing in which complex stimulus inputs are processed by the manipulation of pieces of information in series or 'sequentially.' Most consciously controlled information processing is sequential in nature. For a simple example, try attending to two conversations at the same time – the only way it can be done is to shift attention back and forth rapidly so that the multiple processing is not really carried out at the same time but rather in a sequence of shifts of attention. Also called *serial processing*. Compare with ➤ **parallel *processing**.

process schizophrenia ➤ **schizophrenia, process**.

prodigy From the Latin *prodigium*, meaning a *prophetic sign*. As such, its original meaning was as a reference to something extraordinary, something so unusual that it seemed to be an omen of things to come. Contemporary usage has narrowed the reference to a person with some extraordinary talent or power, specifically when it emerges at an early age.

prodromal Pertaining to the earliest stages of an illness, the period between the very first symptom and the full appearance of the disorder. n., *prodrome*, = a premonitory symptom.

production In psycholinguistics, actual verbal output; e.g., a child's language *production* capabilities are often compared with its *comprehension* of language, with the suggestion that the latter typically precedes the former.

production method A general label for any of several kinds of experimental procedures in which the subject is required to produce a response relative to a particular stimulus. The most common use is in psychophysical scaling where the subject adjusts a stimulus to correspond to some value, e.g., producing a light half as bright as a standard light. See here ➤ **methods of *scaling**.

production systems A class of theoretical models of human cognitive functioning that are based on sets of rules for dealing with the situation at hand (the *productions*) and sets of rules for applying them. They have proven especially useful in representing problem solving; e.g., a simple production system can play perfect tic-tac-toe using simple rules like 'if your opponent already has two X's in a row insert an O to block.' More complex models have successfully simulated human problem solving in a variety of contexts.

productiveness 1. ➤ **productivity**, in the sense of the industrial psychologist. 2. A characteristic of a person's behavior that serves to increase the development and well-being of himself and of the groups of which he is a part. This latter meaning is quite general and encompasses creativity and originality as well as simple output.

productivity 1. In industrial psychology, a measure of the effective output of some system. The system here may be an individual worker, a unit in a business or factory, the entire organization, etc. 2. In academe the term carries the additional connotation of originality or creativity.

product-moment correlation ➤ **correlation, product-moment**.

product scale ➤ **scale, product**.

profession A term generally used of any occupation that requires a high degree of skill and extensive specialized training for the purpose of performing a specialized societal role. Professions tend to have their own codes of ethics and conduct within their practice and, owing to the high degree of specialization and the monopoly of knowledge and skills, they tend to be highly resistant to control or 'interference' in their affairs by outside groups.

professional manager In industrial and organizational psychology, one who is specifically trained for a managerial position, as distinguished from an owner/manager.

profile 1. A drawn or sketched outline of a thing. 2. A graphic display of a set of scores, usually in the form of a *histogram* or *bar graph*. 3. A ➤ **profile analysis**.

profile analysis A profile of a person in the sense of a sketch or general presentation of the personality traits and characterisitcs displayed, relative to a set of norms for the population as a whole. The analysis may take the form of a literal ➤ **profile** (2), in which the data are presented in graphic form (educational profiles of students often use this method), or it may be a more general metaphoric profile in the sense of a general overview of the individual's characteristics or traits presented in summary form.

profile chart ➤ **profile, profile analysis**.

profile-matching system In industrial and organizational psychology, a system of selecting personnel in which the profiles of each job candidate, including all of the variables deemed important for the position, are compared with the profiles of successful workers and personnel decisions are made on the basis of the closeness of the match.

profound mental retardation ➤ **mental retardation, profound**.

progeria A serious disability characterized by stunted growth (especially dwarfism) and a premature disruption of mental capacity that is similar to senility.

progesterone A hormone produced by the corpus luteum following ovulation and, during pregnancy, by the placenta. ➤ **menstrual cycle**.

progestin 1. A synthetic hormone with progesterone-like effects. 2. In older writings, ➤ **progesterone**.

prognathy An anatomical arrangement in which the jaw projects out in front of the cranium. ➤ **orthognathy** for more detail.

prognosis 1. Specifically, the predicted (in the sense of the best-educated guess) eventual outcome of a disease or other disorder. **2.** More generally, a prediction of the course and outcome of any process, be it educational, industrial, methodological, programmatic, etc.

prognostic test A general label for any test designed to provide data for making predictions about the eventual outcome and likelihood of success of some program of education or training for an individual person.

program 1. An extended plan of research. The term is used in this sense for the research of anything from a single individual to a whole institution and even to the abstract notion of the research program of an entire field or discipline. **2.** A set of instructions to a computer for the purpose of having it perform some specified operations. **3.** In genetics, the set of instructions coded in the DNA molecules. var., *programme* (not for 2).

programmed instruction (or learning) A generic term covering the use of any machine or other device as a technological aid to learning. The commonest of such aids are the ➤ **programmed text** and the computer; see here ➤ **computer-assisted instruction**.

programmed text Any text that presents the material to be learned in a series of small, graded steps in accordance with the operant principles of ➤ **shaping**. It is one of the devices commonly used in programmed instruction.

programming In computer terminology, the operation of preparing the set of instructions for the computer to carry out a specific function or solve some problem.

progression 1. In mathematics, a series in which each term is related to the preceding by some specifiable constant relation. For example, 1, 4, 7, 10, 13, ... is an *arithmetic* progression derived by adding a constant; 1, 2, 4, 8, 16, 32, ... is a *geometric* progression derived by multiplying by a constant. **2.** Any advance or movement forward. Used here to refer to

simple locomotion (walking, running) as well as to more abstract forms such as the *progression of knowledge* or *ideas*.

progressive 1 adj. Moving forward, advancing. **2** adj. Pertaining to progress. **3.** In medicine, characterizing the progression of a disease or disorder. Note that 1 and 2 both carry generally sanguine connotations while 3 carries a distinctly negative sense.

progressive education A general orientation toward educational theory and practice that derives primarily from the theories of John Dewey. The core of Dewey's thinking in philosophy, psychology and education stressed flexibility, function, holism and pragmatism and, not surprisingly, the educational program he espoused revolves around these principles. Most progressive education programs (e.g., A. S. Neill's Summerhill) reflect a focus on the individual students and their intrinsic interests and needs, their skills and desires. It reflects a generally experimental attitude, a corresponding vigorous denial of the values of dogmatism and a pragmatic ethic in which education is tied to functioning in the real world.

Progressive Matrices Test A performance test consisting of 60 designs (the matrices) each missing a part. The subject must select the omitted aspect from a set of alternatives. The matrices run from very simple designs to extremely abstract logical relations.

progressive-relaxation therapy ➤ **relaxation therapy**.

progressive teleological-regression hypothesis A theory of schizophrenia maintaining that the disorder results from a process of active concretization, i.e. a purposeful returning to lower levels of psychodynamic and behavioral adaptation which, while it may prove momentarily effective in reducing anxiety, tends ultimately toward repetitive behaviors and results in a failure to maintain integration. The term is Silvano Arieti's and was chosen because the disorder itself is viewed as *progressive*, the direction is *regressive* and the regression itself appears to function as though it had a purpose, i.e. it is *teleological.*

projection Standard dictionary definitions here all carry the basic idea of a jutting out or protruding; technical uses also reflect this notion but with the understanding that, in many uses, the projecting may be abstract and/or symbolic. To wit: **1.** In classical psychoanalysis, the process by which one's own traits, emotions, dispositions, etc. are ascribed to another. Typically used here with the implication that there is an accompanying denial that one has these feelings or tendencies, that the projection functions as a defense mechanism to protect the individual from anxiety and that some underlying conflict has been repressed. **2.** In other psychodynamic theories, the process of ascribing unwittingly one's beliefs, values or other subjective processes to others. This usage, which is typical of the Kleinian approach, has a different connotation. Here, the process is viewed as a normal aspect of psychological development and not necessarily reflective of neurotic tendencies. **3.** The perceiving of events and environmental stimuli (particularly ambiguous ones) in terms of one's own expectations, needs, desires, etc. This meaning is completely neutral with regard to the issue of the pathological aspect of projection. Rather, it is accepted as axiomatic of the operation of the process itself and, hence, forms the theoretical basis for the use of ➤ **projective techniques**. **4.** The attribution of one's own faults and short-comings to another. This sense of the term is the one generally assumed in everyday speech and is not technically correct, because of the limitation to faults and shortcomings, which is but one component of the technical meanings. In anatomy and physiology: **5.** Any anatomical or neurological protuberance. **6.** The efferent connection between the neurons in one specific cortical region and those in another. **7.** The spreading out of the sensory fibers through the cerebral cortex after emerging from the spinal cord. The spatially separate areas in the cortex where the neural representations

are mapped are called *projection areas.* In factor analysis: **8.** The mapping or plotting of the factor loadings onto some surface, usually a sphere.

projection areas ➤ **projection** (6, 7).

projective device ➤ **projective technique**.

projective identification Similar to ➤ **projection** (1, 2, 3), but with a twist: the individual does not fully disavow what is projected. Instead, the person remains aware of his or her own feelings or impulses, but misattributes them and regards them as being justifiable reactions to the behavior of the other persons involved.

projective play A general label for any of several projective techniques utilizing a play situation with children. With all such techniques, the assumption is that the child's repressed feelings, conflicts, attitudes, etc. will emerge in an unstructured situation. The most commonly used techniques revolve around dolls, houses and interpersonal interactions. ➤ **play therapy**.

projective technique A cover term for any test, device or set of procedures designed to provide information about or insight into an individual's personality by allowing him or her the opportunity to respond in an unrestricted manner to unstructured or ambiguous objects or situations. As the name suggests, all of these procedures are based upon the general sense of ➤ **projection** – as captured by meanings 1, 2 and/or 3. Very roughly, one can identify three types of techniques here: (a) Those based on the assumption that there are deeply repressed, unconscious factors underlying personality which can be revealed through projection onto highly ambiguous stimuli. The prototype here, of course, is the ➤ **Rorschach Test**. (b) Those based on the assumption that underlying patterns of needs are revealed by interpretations of stories or pictures. Murray's ➤ **Thematic Apperception Test** (TAT) is the best known of these. Note that, as Murray characterized the TAT, it was not designed to probe the deep unconscious like the Rorschach but rather to provide a forum whereby needs, desires, beliefs and attitudes that are part of the individual's psychosocial make-up can be revealed. These need patterns may even be consciously known by the person, but without the ambiguity of the projective device they may never be articulated. (c) Those procedures based on the assumption that some ego defense, either momentary or firmly established, is blocking awareness and a projective procedure is needed to circumvent it. Projective-play techniques, picture-completion tests and the like are examples.

Note that there is vigorous debate over the use of projective techniques in any and all of their forms. The points of contention range from the scientific issues of whether they have the reliability and validity required of psychological assessment devices, to the pragmatic issue of whether they are worth the time and expense when other, more objective, procedures exist, to the political/ethical question of whether they violate basic civil liberties and the right to privacy. (The last issue, of course, is only germane if the first two should be decided in the affirmative.) Also called *projective device*.

projective test   A label for any of a variety of devices used in personality assessment and clinical psychology in which an individual is presented with a standardized, unstructured set of stimuli and requested to respond to them in as unrestricted a manner as possible. Note, some authors use the term only to refer to a ➤ **projective technique** that has been standardized (e.g., the Rorschach *Test*. the Thematic Apperception *Test*); others have abandoned it entirely on the grounds that they are not really *tests* since they do not provide *scores* and there is doubt about what they *measure*. For the latter, the generic terms *projective technique* and *projective device* are used.

prolactin   A hormone secreted by the anterior pituitary responsible for the onset and maintenance of lactation in mammals after birth of the young. Also called *lactogenic* or *luteotropic hormone*.

proliferation   The root meaning is biological and relates to growth by cell division. However, its connotations have been extended to cover any rapid growth, e.g., of people, ideas, theories and, obviously, technical terms.

prolonged withdrawal syndrome   ➤ **withdrawal syndrome, prolonged**.

promiscuous   **1.** Characterized by a rather jumbled, haphazard heterogeneity. **2.** Lacking discrimination or selectivity, casual. From these original meanings we have ended up with the now dominant: **3.** Unselective and haphazard sexuality.

promise   A ➤ **speech act** in which the speaker is understood to commit himself to something. Promises are ➤ **commissives** and are generally more cognitively complex and learned later by children than some other speech acts like ➤ **directives**.

prompt   A hint, suggestion or assist; the act of presenting such. Often used in experiments on memory, particularly as a measure of the degree of learning of verbal materials. For example, the fewer the prompts necessary during recall the better the learning of the material can be assumed to have been.

prompting method   ➤ **anticipation method** (2).

pronation   **1.** Lying face downward. **2.** Turning one's arm so that the palm faces down. Opposite of ➤ **supination**.

pronomenalization   A linguistic procedure whereby condensation of a message is achieved by substituting a simple expression (like a pronoun) for a more complex and longer one (like a full noun phrase).

pronoun   A nominal form that can take the place of a noun. Once the reference of the pronoun is clear (➤ **pronomenalization**), pronouns share the same privileges of occurrence in linguistic messages as nouns. How the young child learns this is a much-researched problem.

proof 1. Within a formal system, a proof of a conclusion *C* is a sequence of well-formed propositions *P* such that each follows from the initial set of axioms and preceding *Ps* according to proper rules of inference and culminates in a *P* = *C*. 2. Somewhat more loosely, any conclusionary proposition derived validly from true premises. 3. Even more loosely, any demonstration that provides logical or evidentiary support for a belief.

Properly, proof needs to be treated in several distinct fashions. Specifically, meanings 1 and 2 need to be distinguished from 3. Within axiomatic systems, proof amounts to a formal demonstration that a proposition follows inferentially and deductively. That is, one can, in Euclidean geometry, *prove* propositions concerning points, lines and spaces; within a system like general relativity theory, one can *prove* propositions concerning the bending of light in the neighborhood of large masses and, within mathematical learning theory, one can *prove* that the probability of a correct response increases according to a specific function with the number of reinforced trials. But *proof* here is no more than a statement that, *within the system*, the syntax of the sentence that forms the conclusion is proper and follows from premises. That is, they are proofs in senses 1 and 2.

Sense 3 has different and problematical connotations; it extends the domain of the term into the realm of data and theory. It invites one to take, for example, Euclid's geometry as *proved* if it describes the three-dimensional world of our senses, relativity theory as *proved* if light bends while passing a star, or mathematical learning theory as *proved* if the learning data from experiments conform to the theoretical function. That is, all appear as evidentiary support for a belief about nature. Clearly, this kind of proof is a rather different kind of thing from that in 1 and 2 – so much so, that in the technical literature meaning 3 is typically not found. Proof is properly dealt with here from the point of view of the failure of attempts at disproof; see here ➤ **falsificationism**.

proof-reader's illusion There is some confusion here because the term is used in two slightly different ways, neither of which is really representative of an illusion: 1. The failure to notice that written material does not make sense because one is doing 'low level' proof-reading, i.e. looking for typographical errors, misspellings, etc. 2. The failure to notice a 'low level' error in written material because one is concentrating on 'higher level' processing, i.e. comprehension, understanding, etc. The latter is the more common meaning.

propaedeutic Pertaining to or having the characteristic of being preliminary. Psychology, in its contemporary form, has been referred to as a *propaedeutic science*.

propaedeutic task 1. Specifically, a task or teaching aid used in the instruction of the retarded or the handicapped. Such tasks involve instruction in things that are preliminary to and necessary for future instruction. 2. More generally, any task that is designed to impart preliminary knowledge; e.g., memorizing the alphabet is a propaedeutic task for learning to read English.

propaganda Most broadly, a generic term covering any attempt to manipulate opinion. In practice, social psychologists find it useful to impose some conditions on the use of the term. Specifically, a message will be regarded as propaganda only if it (a) represents a conscious, systematic and organized effort, (b) conceals the true nature of the debate by presenting only one side of the issues and (c) is characterized by an attempt to disguise the fact that it is, indeed, propaganda. vb., *propagandize*.

propagation 1. Generally, reproduction. 2. The transmission of a neural impulse down the axon of a neuron. ➤ **action potential**. 3. The dissemination or spreading of information, particularly through a group or society. Distinguish this last sense from ➤ **propaganda**.

propensity A very general term for any strong, persistent tendency for action. It is used broadly and terms like ➤ **drive** and

➤ **disposition** (2, 3) are rough synonyms. Note that some will use the term with the clear implication that a propensity is innate; others are neutral on this issue.

prophylactic **1** n. Any measure or device that produces ➤ **prophylaxis**. **2** adj. Characterizing such a device or measure.

prophylaxis Generally, the use of any preventive measure. Specifically, the use of measures designed to prevent disease.

proportion **1.** A ratio of magnitudes, either of one part to another or of a single part to the whole. Note that in the latter case the proportion can be expressed as a percentage. **2.** In esthetics, a pleasant balance between the parts of something.

proposition **1.** Generally and inclusively, whatever can be stated, asserted, contended, supposed, presupposed, derived, negated or implied. That is, whatever can be expressed in the standard form of an indicative sentence. Various types of propositions are distinguished: **2.** A *formal* proposition is a statement that relates objects, events and properties (or their symbolic representations) to each other in well-defined ways. Such propositions are ultimately neither true nor false; their truth value consists in their conforming to the principles of logic. The formal proposition 'apples are red' is deductively true or false depending upon preceding propositions regarding apples, color, perceptual principles, etc. **3.** An *empirical* proposition is a statement of a similar kind but the elements consist of observable objects, events or operations (or their symbolic representations) and can be tested empirically for its truth. The empirical proposition 'apples are red' is demonstrably true or false based upon observations of apples and determination of their color. **4.** A *linguistic* proposition is a formal statement that represents a component of the underlying meaning of a sentence. Here, the sentence 'apples are red' would be represented as (apple, all, red). The notion of truth here is irrelevant; the concern is with whether or not the proposition provides an accurate characterization of the underlying meaning of the sentence being analyzed.

propositional attitudes Those particular stances that people take toward propositions; i.e., they may *believe* that a proposition is true, *wish* that it be true, *doubt* that it is true, etc.

propositional content In linguistics, the full set of ➤ **propositions** (4) expressed by a sentence or paragraph or extended discourse.

propositus ➤ **proband**.

propriate functional autonomy Gordon Allport's term for a level of ➤ **functional *autonomy** which included personal interests, values, life style, etc. Such behaviors are assumed to be learned and largely internally motivated. Compare with ➤ **perseverative functional autonomy**.

propriate strivings ➤ **proprium**.

proprio- Combining form meaning *one's own*.

proprioception A general term used to cover all those sensory systems that are involved in providing information about position, location, orientation and movement of the body (and its parts). The two primary groups of *proprioceptors* are those in the vestibular system of the inner ear and the kinesthetic and cutaneous systems (collectively, the somatosenses).

proprioceptor Any of the sensory receptors that mediate ➤ **proprioception**.

proprium A term coined by Gordon Allport to cover the full range of acquired functions that comprise the various elements of selfhood. Seven aspects of the proprium were hypothesized, from the sense of bodily self that appears in childhood to the sense of self as a reasoning, cognitive person capable of handling distant goals that emerges during adolescence. Other components dealt with self-image, self-identity, self-esteem, characteristic patterns of thought, cognitive style, etc. The proprium was, for Allport, an encompassing concept equivalent to *selfhood*. The term itself was chosen in an

PROSENCEPHALON

attempt to clarify some of the issues which had become muddled through the repeated re-using of terms like *self* and *ego*. ➤ **self** (especially senses 1, 2 and 5) to appreciate what these conceptual problems are.

prosencephalon The embryonic ➤ **forebrain**.

proso- Combining form meaning *forward, anterior*.

prosocial A general descriptive label for those social behaviors that are cooperative in nature. Usually included are friendship, empathy, altruism, helping behavior, etc. ant., **antisocial, asocial**.

prosodic features Features of language such as stress, pitch, pitch changes, intonation, juncture, pausing, etc. Prosodic features are generally treated as distinct from the ➤ **suprasegmentals** in that they are not typically phonemic. That is, they serve to mark function or intention rather than to distinguish meaning. Examples of prosodic features would be rising intonation contour, which generally cues a question; strong sharp stress, which can convey anger or an order; high pitch, which may signal insecurity or anxiety, etc. Note that some of these prosodic features may also be regarded as phonemic in some situations.

prosody 1. All those aspects of language related to the use of ➤ **prosodic features**. **2.** All those aspects of language related to the use of the prosodic features and the ➤ **suprasegmentals**. Sense 1 is preferred.

prosopagnosia A neurological disorder characterized by an inability to recognize faces. In serious cases it may include a failure to recognize one's own face.

prospect theory A perspective on decision making based on the assumption that people typically show ➤ **risk aversion**; hence, when making decisions they view whatever losses may be involved as more painful than equivalent gains are desirable.

prostaglandin A hormone first discovered in the prostate (hence the name). It sensitizes free nerve endings to histamine thereby playing a role in pain perception. Aspirin's analgesic effects come from its ability to interfere with the production of prostaglandins.

prosthesis Any artificial device used in addition to or in place of a dysfunctional or missing body part.

prostration 1. Lit., being spread out, prone. Technically, the term is used here to characterize extreme exhaustion, due to disease or shock, to the point where many normal bodily reflexes cannot be elicited. **2.** Somewhat more loosely, any extreme physical or mental exhaustion. **3.** Metaphorically, the act of throwing oneself down in a gesture of humility or abasement.

protanomaly A visual condition in which there is a minor diminution in sensitivity to long-wavelength light. ➤➤ **protanopia**.

protanopia A form of ➤ **dichromacy** characterized by a lowered sensitivity to long-wavelength light. The Greek prefix *proto-*, meaning *first*, is used for this condition because this form of color-deficient vision is assumed to be due to a deficiency in the red-light-absorbing pigment in the retina and red is considered to be the first primary color. Compare with ➤ **deuteranopia**.

protensity An archaic term used by Tichener to refer to the direct experience of the duration of sensation.

prothetic The basic meaning of the word connotes the addition of a thing without a change in the qualitative aspects of that to which it was added. It is used to characterize stimulus dimensions that do not change qualitatively with changes in physical intensity. For example, *weight* is prothetic because systematic increases in mass produce systematic increases in perceived heaviness; likewise for the loudness of sounds, brightness of lights, etc. Compare with ➤ **metathetic** continua such as the wavelength of light or the concentration of some odors. By and large, prothetic continua produce *power functions* when scaled, metathetic continua do not.

608

proto- A common prefix from the Greek, meaning *first, original, primary, primitive.*

protocol The original record of an experiment or other investigation made during or immediately after the event.

protopathic 1. Generally, primitive and undifferentiating. Used most commonly with respect to cutaneous sensitivity. 2. See discussion under ➤ **epicritic** (2).

prototaxis H. S. Sullivan's term for a mental state in which events are experientially undifferentiated. He felt that it was normally characteristic of infants and only occurred in adults in extreme cases of psychosis. adj., *prototaxic.*

prototype 1. The original, primitive type or form of a thing. 2. The most 'typical' instance of a class or category of things. Note that a prototype, particularly in sense 2, is regarded as an abstraction based on shared features or functions of the members of the class or category. It is not treated as necessarily represented by any one instance. For example, a robin is regarded by most people as a more 'typical' bird than, say, a chicken or a penguin; in fact a robin is often regarded as more bird-like than any other instance. This, however, does not mean that the robin is the prototype of the category *bird*; only that it is closer to the abstract, prototypical bird. This notion of a prototype plays an important role in many theories of memory and thinking; e.g., ➤ **category, concept, natural *category.**

pro-verb In linguistics, a verbal form which, once the reference is clear, can be used in place of a full verb phrase; e.g., *do so.*

provisional try An antiquated term for *trial-and-error behavior* (which itself is a bit out of date, ➤ **trial-and-error *learning**).

proxemics The study of space and its use in different social and cultural situations. Major areas of interest include ➤ **crowding,** ➤ **territoriality** and the study of ➤ **personal space.**

proximal From the Latin, meaning *near to, close.* Hence: 1. In anatomy, referring to points near to the center of the body, to the center of an organ or to the point of attachment of an organ or other structure. 2. Touching or contiguous. Compare with ➤ **distal.**

proximal response Any direct internal response, e.g., one that is muscular or glandular.

proximal stimulus The physical energy that actually impinges upon a receptor. The dog that just walked into the room is the ➤ **distal stimulus,** the pattern of light reflected off the dog that stimulates your retina is the proximal stimulus.

proximate explanation In evolutionary biology an explanation of a species' behavior in terms of the mechanisms and immediate circumstances that bring on that behavior. E.g., explaining the mating behavior of a male elephant seal by focusing on shifts in temperature that stimulate increased production of testosterone which in turn stimulates particular brain centers, etc. The focus is on environmental stimuli and physiological mechanisms. Compare with ➤ **ultimate explanation.**

proximity, law of One of the Gestalt laws (or principles) of organization. A generalization that states that, other things being equal, objects or events in the perceptual field which are proximate to each other either spatially or temporally will be perceived as belonging together in a unit.

proximodistad (or proximodistal) development ➤ **cephalocaudad development.**

proxy variable ➤ **variable, proxy.**

pseudesthesia Generally, any sensory illusion. Usually used of illusions of location of stimulation, e.g., the ➤ **phantom limb.**

pseud(o)- A prefix denoting *false, fake, counterfeit.* The connotation is that the 'pseudo' event or object is a copy of the real one.

pseudoangina The functional chest pain that resembles a heart attack.

pseudochromesthesia An unnecessarily long synonym for ➤ **chromesthesia.**

pseudoconditioning An increase in the frequency of occurrence of a response to a stimulus which has not been systematically paired with an unconditioned stimulus. Pseudoconditioning can be observed most clearly just after a series of true conditioning trials have been run, when the subject will produce the 'conditioned' response to some neutral stimulus. It is presumably due to *sensitization* of the subject.

pseudocyesis False pregnancy. This can be a most compelling functional syndrome that may include abdominal swelling and cessation of the menses.

pseudodementia A temporary drop in performance of intellectual functioning brought about by emotional conditions. It is observed in cases of depression and is usually temporary.

pseudohermaphrodite An individual whose external genitalia are of one sex and the internal organs of the other. The individual is not a true ➤ **hermaphrodite** since there is no ambiguity in the external genitalia and, hence, no question about gender assignment at birth.

pseudoinsomnia Not a true ➤ **insomnia**, but a condition where the individual dreams that they are lying in bed awake. Although they actually have had a normal night's sleep, they wake up thinking that they spent a sleepless night.

pseudo-isochromatic charts Color charts made up of random patterns of dots of various hues and saturations. The hues are so arranged that they form recognizable shapes (numbers, letters, etc.) in the array. Careful selection of the hues and careful controlling of saturation and brightness provide a sensitive test for color deficiencies, since the shapes can only be seen by using the hue information. E.g., ➤ **Ishihari color plates**.

pseudolalia Nonsensical babbling.

pseudomemory Lit., any false memory; ➤ **paramnesia**.

pseudomnesia A term occasionally used

for a pseudomemory that is severe or pathological.

pseudoneurotic schizophrenia ➤ **schizotypal personality disorder**.

pseudoparkinsonism ➤ **drug-induced *Parkinsonism**.

pseudophone A device which transposes the spatial location of sounds so that those that normally would enter the right ear enter the left and vice versa. It was developed to study the process of sound localization.

pseudopsychology Lit., fake or false psychology. The term has two common uses. **1.** To characterize those unscientific endeavors that are clearly fraudulent and whose practitioners are obvious quacks, e.g., graphology, palmistry, phrenology. **2.** To characterize one's scientific foes who insist on adhering to theoretical points of view that one knows are clearly unscientific. Here everything from psychoanalysis to behaviorism to parapsychology has been called a pseudopsychology at one time or another. ➤ **pseudoscience**.

pseudopsychosis ➤ **factitious disorder with psychological symptoms**.

pseudoretardation A syndrome often seen in intrinsically normal but culturally or socially deprived children who, because of a lack of stimulation, socialization or parenting, or through some emotional disturbance, show up initially as retarded on standard intelligence tests.

pseudoscience Generally, the improper use of the scientific method, a fake or false science. Most pseudoscience has the superficial trappings of real science but is contaminated by such factors as poor control over experimental conditions, improper analysis of data, illogical deductive reasoning and, occasionally, outright fraud.

pseudoscope An optical device that transposes the images to the two eyes such that light that would fall on the right retina falls on the left and vice versa. Distinguish from ➤ **reversing lenses**.

psi (ψ) The Greek letter. When the letter itself is used it serves as an abbreviation for *psychology*; when spelled out in English it refers to the parapsychologist's *psi processes*.

psilocybin A hallucinogen extracted from a Mexican mushroom. It has actions similar to LSD and shows ➤ **cross *tolerance** with it.

psi-missing In parapsychology, a situation in which a paranormal 'process' seems to be working in a negative fashion; e.g., rather than being able to predict the turn of a card with greater than chance probability, the subject makes many more errors than chance guessing would predict. ➤ **parapsychology** for a discussion of the general issue of such presumed phenomena.

psi process A general term used of any individual paranormal ability, e.g., telepathy. ➤ **parapsychology** for a discussion. Also called, simply, *psi*.

PSP ➤ **postsynaptic potential**.

psychalgia A cover term for disorders the dominant symptoms of which are pains of a mental origin, most commonly headaches or backaches, not due to any other psychiatric disorder and with no detectable organic dysfunctions.

psychasthenia Pierre Janet's term for a disorder characterized by anxiety, obsessions and fixed ideas.

psyche **1.** The oldest and most general use of this term is by the early Greeks, who envisioned the psyche as the soul or the very essence of life. **2.** More conventionally, the connotation is limited to *mind*. Although both of these senses reflect a kind of ➤ **dualism**, 2 is considerably less problematical and is the favored meaning. It is also the sense carried in the original meaning of *psychology*. **3.** The ➤ **self**. adjs., ➤ **psychic** (1 or 3), *psychical*.

psychedelic An invented term constructed by combining the Greek words *psyche* meaning *mind* and *delos* meaning *manifest* or *visible*; hence, *mind-manifest-*ing. It is used to distinguish the group of hallucinogenic drugs that have specific and reliable changes in mood, perception and judgement as their dominant effects from others that have hallucinogenic side-effects independent of their primary use. Thus, psychedelic is used for drugs that are self-administered for the primary purpose of producing these experiences, e.g., *LSD*, *mescaline*, *psilocybin*, *marijuana*.

psychiatric social work A specialization within social work in which the social worker is trained for collaborative work with psychiatrists and clinical psychologists.

psychiatrist A person trained in medicine who specializes in the prevention, diagnosis and treatment of mental disorders. The actual practice of the psychiatrist and the clinical psychologist overlap considerably; the primary difference being that the psychiatrist, by virtue of the medical license, is legally authorized to prescribe drugs while the clinical psychologist is not. ➤ **psychiatry**.

psychiatry A specialization within medicine encompassing prevention, diagnosis, treatment and research of mental disorders. Psychiatry, although parallel in many respects to ➤ **clinical psychology**, is historically and presently a branch of medicine and psychiatrists hold the MD degree whereas clinical psychologists hold a PhD or other professional degree. The historical issue here is more important than many realize, for psychiatry has traditionally taken the point of view that emotional and behavioral disorders are medical problems and that a person with a serious behavioral or emotional disability is mentally ill; see here ➤ **medical model** and ➤ **mental illness** for more on terminology. As such, the psychiatrist is trained specifically in abnormalities and their prevention and cure, and little training is received in theories of normal behavior, experimental design, collection and analysis of data, etc. The practice of psychiatry is extremely broad and includes aspects that are indeed strictly medical, such as drug treatment, electroconvulsive-shock therapy, legal issues of institutionalization and hospitalization and organic disabilities with psychological manifestations. However, it also includes many aspects that have little to do with the domain of medicine in a strict sense, including behavior modification therapy, psychoanalysis, etc. Indeed, in these endeavors the practicing psychiatrist is little different from the practicing clinical psychologist.

psychic 1 adj. Generally and loosely, pertaining to mind and that which is mental, and/or to person and the dimensions of personality – in short, a synonym of *psychological*. 2. More narrowly, pertaining to various aspects of ➤ **parapsychology**, usually spiritualism. In this sense the noun form refers to one who claims to have supernatural powers. 3. Pertaining to psychogenic or functional disorders. Although this meaning is fairly well rooted in usage (e.g., *psychic blindness*), it is, given meanings 1 and 2 above, misleading to many and ➤ **psychogenic** is generally preferred. var., *psychical*, particularly for 2.

psychical ➤ psychic (especially 2).

psychic(al) research Research in ➤ **parapsychology**.

psychic anaphylaxis ➤ psychological *anaphylaxis.

psychic ataxia ➤ mental *ataxia.

psychic blindness 1. = ➤ functional *blindness. 2. = ➤ agnosia.

psychic determinism A form of ➤ **determinism** reflecting the point of view that all psychological processes are causally determined by antecedent factors. The term is used primarily by psychoanalytical theorists with respect to unconscious motives and causes.

psychic impotence 1. ➤ Impotence which is psychogenic. 2. A temporary inability to carry out normal psychological processes.

psychic isolation ➤ isolation (4).

psychic numbing A diminished responsiveness to the outside world, a numbing of one's emotions. Often seen in cases of ➤ **post-traumatic stress disorder**.

psychic reflex ➤ psychic secretion.

psychic secretion I. P. Pavlov's original term for those first few drops of saliva elicited by a once-neutral stimulus. More generally, any conditioned salivary response. The more general term *psychic reflex* is also used here.

psychic trauma A general term used for any painful psychological experience. Typically used with the implication that the impact of the experience is long-lasting and that it interferes with normal functioning.

psychic vaginismus ➤ vaginismus.

psychism ➤ parapsychology.

psycho- Combining form meaning pertaining to *mind, psyche* or *psychology*.

psycho Nontechnical slang for an individual suffering from a psychosis.

psychoacoustics A discipline within psychology concerned with sound, its perception and the physiological foundations of hearing. A hybrid field with contributions from physics, biology and applied areas in audiology and the speech sciences, it is now a fundamental part of many other areas including the study of language, speech, music, etc.

psychoactive substance (or **drug**) Generic terms for any substance or drug that affects consciousness, mood and awareness. At one time or another all of the antipsychotics, antidepressants, antianxiety drugs, stimulants, sedatives, psychedelics and hallucinogens have been so classified. Actually, this kind of categorizing doesn't help very much because essentially any drug could be placed in this group; aspirin, when it relieves a headache, can change one's consciousness and awareness. Nevertheless, the term has achieved a certain currency, but its use is properly restricted to substances that produce a marked psychological effect. ➤ **psychotropic**, an approximate synonym.

psychoactive substance use disorders A category of disorders marked by various cognitive and behavioral changes associated with the regular use of psychoactive substances that affect the nervous system. ➤ **substance-related disorders**, the preferred term.

psychoactive substance abuse ➤ **substance abuse**.

psychoactive substance dependence ➤ **substance dependence**.

psychoactive substance-induced organic mental disorders ➤ **substance-induced disorders**.

psychoanalysis 1. A theory of human behavior. 2. A doctrine associated with this theory. 3. A set of techniques for exploring the underlying motivations of human behavior. 4. A method of treatment of various mental disorders. Meaning 1 typically is used for the comprehensive theory due to Sigmund Freud (➤ **Freudian**), although it may be found referring to any of a variety of related dynamic theories that are derivative of it even when quite distinct from the orthodoxy of classical Freudianism, e.g., Adler's individual psychology, Jung's analytical psychology. Note, some prefer the term *neopsychoanalysis* for these to prevent muddying the definitional waters. Sense 2 refers to a cultural and social movement that has had an impact upon a variety of endeavors anthropological, political, esthetic, literary and philosophical. It is a very loose doctrine that may or may not reflect Freudian purity; its application is detectable largely by the extensive use of interpretation, hypothesization of unconscious motives and a search for deep causes. Meaning 3 covers the basic methods Freud developed over a period of several decades and which have been elaborated and extended by many others. The core components here are *free association, rich interpretation* and *transference*. In a nutshell, the subject free-associates; the ana-

lyst interprets the associations produced, the obstacles that bar others and the subject's feelings toward the analyst. Sense 4 is the extension of 3 in a systematic fashion to treat the psychoneuroses.

psychoanalyst 1. One who practices ➤ **psychoanalysis** (4). Here, the term is reserved for persons who have had psychoanalytic training at a recognized institute. They may have had any of a number of different forms of training prior to the psychoanalytical, e.g., an MD degree with a psychiatric residency, a doctorate or other advanced degree in psychology or even a master's degree in social work or counseling. The term *lay analyst* is often used for practitioners who have not taken a medical degree. 2. One who is given to interpretations of events in accordance with psychoanalytic theory. This usage reflects those who use ➤ **psychoanalysis** in senses 2 and 3 of that term.

psychoasthenia Mental deficiency, mental retardation.

psychoasthenics The study of mental retardation.

psychobiology 1. Originally, a school of thought in psychiatry based on the theoretical orientation of Adolf Meyer which stressed the mechanisms of integration of the biological, the psychological and the social experiences. 2. Contemporarily, a general term for the study of psychological process from a biological point of view. The approach is a broad one and work in *behavior genetics, endocrinology* and *physiological psychology* can all be found classified as psychobiological. syn. *biopsychology* (for 2).

psychoceramics As conceptualized by the once and future Professor Josiah Carberry of Brown University, a highly specialized sub-discipline dealing with the crackpot in all his manifestations. The much-traveled Professor Carberry is said, like Freud, to have developed his theories largely from intensive self-examination.

psychodiagnosis Specifically, procedures

for diagnosing psychological abnormalities, mental disturbances, etc. Somewhat more generally, the term is used for any psychological or personality assessment procedure. ➤ **diagnosis** for more details on usage.

psychodiagnostics 1. Any of the more or less valid techniques of assessing personality by interpreting behavior patterns, particularly nonverbal ones, e.g., facial expressions, body posture, gait, etc. 2. Occasionally, the use of the Rorschach Test.

psychodrama A psychotherapeutic technique developed by J. L. Moreno in which the individual acts out certain roles or incidents in the presence of a therapist and, often, other persons who are part of a therapy group. The procedures are based on the assumption that the role-taking allows the person to express troublesome emotions and face deep conflicts in the relatively protected environment of the therapeutic stage. Common variations are *group psychodrama*, in which all the actors are in the therapy group, and *family groups*, in which difficult domestic scenes are enacted.

psychodynamic 1. A label used freely for (a) all those psychological systems and theories that emphasize processes of change and development, and/or (b) those systems and theories that make motivation and drive central concepts. In short, psychological theories that deal with that which is ➤ **dynamic** will all be included. 2. Occasionally, a synonym for *psychoanalytic*.

psychoendocrinology The study of the interactive role of the endocrine glands with various neurological processes, and their combined effects on thought, emotion and behavior.

psychogalvanic response (PGR) ➤ **galvanic skin response**.

psychogalvanometer A device for measuring the ➤ **galvanic skin response**.

psychogenesis 1. The origin and, by extension, development of the psyche. In this sense the term is used very generally for essentially any aspect of psychological functioning. 2. The origin and development of a specific psychological event within a particular organism. adj., *psychogenetic, psychogenic* (for 2).

psychogenetics 1. The study of the genetic basis of psychological processes. See here ➤ **behavioral genetics**. 2. In some older texts, the study of ➤ **psychogenesis** (1).

psychogenic 1. Psychological in origin. Used here primarily as a qualifier for disorders that are assumed to be functional in origin, i.e. those in which there is no known organic dysfunction. 2. Occasionally, pertaining to ➤ **psychogenesis**; properly only in sense 2 of that term.

psychogenic amnesia ➤ **dissociative *amnesia**.

psychogenic disorder Any disorder for which there are no apparent organic bases; see here ➤ **functional disorder**.

psychogenic fugue ➤ **fugue**.

psychogenic motives (or **needs**) H. Murray's term for needs that are nonphysiological. ➤➤ **motivation and need**.

psychogenic pain disorder ➤ **pain disorder**.

psychogram 1. Generally, a profile of an individual on a variety of standard tests. 2. Specifically, H. Murray's term for a representation of an individual's pattern of needs and *press*.

psychography ➤ **psychohistory**.

psychohistory A general term used for any literary work that attempts to understand historical events by providing a detailed psychological analysis of the characters involved. Psychohistorical analyses differ slightly from the so-called ➤ **pathobiography** in that the latter term is almost invariably used for psychoanalytic works while the former are eclectic. Also called *psychography*.

psychoimmunology ➤ **psychoneuroimmunology**.

psychokinesis 1. A hypothesized parapsychological phenomenon whereby an individual supposedly influences a physical event without direct intervention. Also called *parakinesis* and abbreviated *PK*. **2.** Occasionally, in psychiatric writings, manic behavior.

psycholagny Sexual excitement brought about by the use of one's imagination, usually by forming mental images.

psycholepsy A sudden loss of mental alertness, a feeling of hopelessness, helplessness, depression.

psycholinguistics A field that was created and named during an interdisciplinary conference held in the USA in 1953. Despite protestations from one of the prominent participants, Roger Brown, that the name sounded more like a description of a deranged polyglot than a scientific field, both it and its evergrowing subject-matter have become a permanent part of psychology. Most broadly, the focus is upon the study of any and all behaviors that are linguistic. Subfields include the acquisition of language, bilingualism, pragmatics, speech-act theory, studies of grammar, the psychology of reading, the relationship between language and thought, etc. Because of the ubiquity of verbal behavior in humans, many psycholinguistic issues emerge in other areas as well, e.g., cognitive psychology, memory, information processing, speech and hearing sciences, sociolinguistics, neuropsychology, clinical psychology, etc. Compare with ➤ **verbal learning**.

psycholinguistics, developmental A division of ➤ **psycholinguistics** that focuses on the study of the acquisition of natural language by the child.

psychological **1.** Pertaining to psychology in any and/or all of its manifestations. **2.** Characterizing an event, process, phenomenon or theory so as to emphasize its role in psychology as opposed to any other connotations which it may have: e.g., psychological test, psychological warfare, etc. **3.** Pertaining to that which is mental in origin, ➤ **psychogenic** (1).

psychological anaphylaxis ➤ **anaphylaxis, psychological**.

psychological autopsy ➤ **autopsy, psychological**.

psychological contract ➤ **contract, psychological**.

psychological dependence ➤ **dependence, psychological**.

psychological distance ➤ **distance, psychological**.

psychological environment Taken loosely, this term refers to all aspects of the environment that are psychologically relevant to an individual at any point in time. Exactly what constitutes this environment, however, is viewed very differently by different writers. For behaviorists it is characterized essentially in physical, objective terms; for Gestalt theorists it includes imaged, imagined and memorial aspects; for psychoanalytic thinkers it includes unconscious elements, motives, etc.

psychological factors affecting physical condition An unnecessarily long phrase put forward as a cover term for those mental factors that play a significant role in ➤ **psychosomatic disorders**.

psychological freedom ➤ **freedom**.

psychological me ➤ **me**.

psychological moment ➤ **moment** (1).

psychological present ➤ **specious present**.

psychological reactance ➤ **reactance, psychological**.

psychological refractory period ➤ **refractory period, psychological**.

psychological scale ➤ **scale, psychological**.

psychological space ➤ **life space**.

psychological teratogen ➤ **teratogen**.

psychological test A cover term for all tests of a psychological nature. ➤ **test** and related entries for discussion and definitions of various kinds of tests.

psychological time ➤ **time, psychological**.

psychological type ➤ **type** (especially 3).

psychological warfare Originally, the use

of psychological manipulations in the waging of wars. Most attempts are essentially morale 'boosters' for one's allies and 'depressors' for the enemy. More recently, the use of the term has been extended beyond the military domain and it will be found used for similar morale-manipulating techniques used in marriages, business, sports, etc.

psychological weaning ➤ **weaning, psychological**.

psychologism The most common meaning is to refer to the point of view that psychology is *the* fundamental science and to treat the events of the world from that perspective. What the term means depends, of course, on who is using it. Many non-psychologists use it as a form of reproach, psychologists typically don't.

psychologist Determining just to whom this term applies is no simple matter. The difficulties stem from the fact that some who claim it do so because they *practice* psychology, others because they *apply* it, others because they *teach* it, and still others because they *research* it. When a formal definition is provided, it is usually done so as to satisfy some particular practical and/or legal issue. For example, many governmental bodies that regulate licensing of psychologists require that the individual have completed an advanced degree (a master's minimally, often a doctorate) at a recognized institution, undertaken one or more years of a supervised internship or practicum and passed a written examination. Criteria of this kind are most often used when defining a psychologist as one who is recognized to undertake any of a number of professional duties, e.g., clinical psychologist, consulting psychologist, forensic psychologist, school psychologist, etc. However, when assessing whether one who teaches and/or does research in psychology 'deserves' this four-syllable mantle, things become less clear. For example, the standard characterization of a psychologist that is usually offered is that he or she is one who (a) holds at least a master's degree or preferably a doctorate and (b) studies psychological processes. The degree requirement presents problems. What degree counts? Whatever are we to call Erik Erikson, the great analyst and humanitarian who never received a university degree, or Herbert Simon, Nobel laureate in economics who is one of the leading theorists in the field of cognitive psychology, or Jean Piaget, who remade developmental psychology despite being trained in biology, or William James, perhaps the greatest of them all, whose first course in psychology was the one he taught?

The other requirement, that a psychologist study psychological processes, is equally futile, for each new development in psychology implicates processes once thought to lie in other domains. This volume contains hundreds if not thousands of terms derived from sociology, anthropology, biology, physiology, medicine, philosophy, computer sciences, linguistics, mathematics, chemistry and physics; the scientists who studied these processes often did not presume to be studying psychology but they were. How shall we call them?

The bottom lexicographical line here is that the term gets 'awarded' by two different kinds of collective agencies. One is a legally constituted body; it determines who shall be called a psychologist according to governmentally regulated standards which have been designed to protect the public, to ensure that the 'psychologist' who offers his or her services does, in fact, possess the training and skills that one should legitimately expect them to have. The other is a loosely federated community of scholars and it operates much less formally. It functions according to implicit criteria concerning an individual's accomplishments. Here, one who has taught, written, lectured and/or researched about those phenomena that fall within the confines of psychology will end up not only being called a psychologist but, in the long run, defining what it is those who are called psychologists (by the former set of criteria) actually do. He or she may and usually will have a doctorate degree and it probably will be in psychology, but these are not defining features of the label. Many who claim the label through these latter criteria would not qualify for it via the former. For more on these definitional issues, ➤ **psychotherapist** and, of course, ➤ **psychology**; for distinctions with those persons with medical training, ➤ **psychiatrist** and ➤ **psychiatry**.

psychologist's fallacy An oddly named phenomenon which is, simply, the tendency to project one's point of view or one's interpretation onto another – when committed by a psychologist. For example, a clinical psychologist who makes a fallacious inference about a client in therapy, an introspectionist who reads unwarranted interpretations into the observer's reports, etc.

psychology Psychology simply cannot be defined; indeed, it cannot even be easily characterized. Even if one were to do so today, tomorrow would render the effort inadequate. Psychology is what scientists and philosophers of various persuasions have created to try to fulfill the need to understand the minds and behaviors of various organisms from the most primitive to the most complex. Hence, it really isn't a thing at all, it is about a thing, or about many things. It has few boundaries and aside from the canons of science and the ethical standards of a free society it should not have any imposed upon it either by its practitioners or its critics. It is an attempt to understand what has so far pretty much escaped understanding, and any effort to circumscribe it or box it in is to imply that something is known about the edges of our knowledge, and that must be wrong.

As a distinct discipline it finds its roots a mere century or so back in the faculties of medicine and philosophy. From medicine it took the orientation that explication of that which is done, thought and felt ultimately must be couched in biology and physiology, from philosophy it took a class of deep problems concerning mind, will and knowledge. Since then, it has been variously defined as 'the science of

mind,' 'the science of mental life,' 'the science of behavior,' etc. All such definitions, of course, reflect the prejudices of the definer more than the actual nature of the field. In the course of writing this volume, a rather strange metaphor has emerged that somehow seems to capture the essential quality of our discipline. It is like an amoeba, relatively unstructured but very much identifiable as a distinct entity with a peculiar mode of action in which it sends out a projection of itself toward some new technique, some novel problem area, some theoretical model, or even some other distinct field of science, incorporating it and slowly pulling itself clumsily into another shape. Not very flattering perhaps, but accurate. For more on the lexicographical problems here ➤ **psychologist**.

psycholytic Lit., mind-loosening. Used occasionally of the hallucinogenic or psychedelic drugs.

psycholytic therapy A radical form of psychotherapy which is based, in part, on the administration of psychedelic drugs. There has been a good deal of controversy over its therapeutic value compared with more traditional approaches, and it is rarely used today.

psychometric Lit., pertaining to the measurement of that which is psychological. Hence: **1.** Pertaining to mental testing in any of its facets, including assessment of personality, evaluation of intelligence, determining aptitudes, etc. **2.** Pertaining to ➤ **psychophysics**. **3.** Pertaining to issues of the application of principles of mathematics and statistics to the data of psychology.

psychometric function Generally, a mathematical expression relating the values of a physical variable to the psychological experiencing of each value. E.g., ➤ **power law**.

psychometrician Broadly, a specialist in the study of that which is ➤ **psychometric**. Usually, however, the reference is to an individual who is an expert in sense 1 of that term, a specialist in the theory and/or practice of administering, scoring and interpreting the results of mental tests. It is also used in the other two senses of *psychometric*, but somewhat less frequently.

psychometrics Collectively, the branches of psychology concerned with measurement. ➤ **psychometric** for details.

psychometrist A relatively rare synonym for ➤ **psychometrician**.

psychometrizing A paranormal process in which information about a person or event is supposedly obtained by touching or holding an object belonging to or related to the person or the event. ➤ **parapsychology**.

psychometry 1. The fields that embody ➤ **psychometric** research; generally used in sense 1 of that term, rarely if ever for the other meanings. 2. ➤ **psychometrizing**. The use of the same label for two fields, one reasonable and the other not, is unfortunate.

psychomimetic Generally, of that which mimics or resembles a natural psychological process. ➤ **psychotomimetic**, which has a more specific reference.

psychomotor Loosely, pertaining to mental events which have motor effect or vice versa. ➤ **sensorimotor**.

psychomotor agitation Excessive motor activity that is marked by nonproductivity and repetitiveness and associated with feelings of inner tension. Typical behaviors are an inability to remain seated, constant pacing, hand-wringing, tugging and fussing with one's clothes and rapid, complaining speech.

psychomotor epilepsy ➤ **epilepsy, psychomotor**.

psychomotor retardation A general slowing down of motor action, movements and speech. Seen as a common symptom of various disorders, notably depression.

psychoneural parallelism ➤ **parallelism, psychoneural**.

psychoneuroimmunology An interdisciplinary science that studies the interrelationships between the psychological, behavioral, neuroendocrinal processes and immunology. Also called *psychoimmunology*.

psychoneurosis 1. A term used more or less interchangeably with ➤ **neurosis**. It is preferred by many writers because etymologically it emphasizes the functional, nonorganic aspects. The original, but now largely obsolete, meaning of *neurosis* made reference to disorders of the nervous system and its actions and the *psycho-* prefix was first appended to distinguish clearly between the *neurotic* and *neural*. **2.** A diagnostic category comprising a group of disorders characterized by anxiety including *conversion reaction*, the *phobias* and *obsessive-compulsive reaction*. Note, however, that this category is gradually being dropped from the diagnostic classification system of mental disorders – at least in the USA, where the *Diagnostic and Statistical Manual* no longer lists it. ➤ **neurosis** for more on contemporary terminology here.

psychoneurotic inventory ➤ **neurotic inventory**.

psychonomic 1. Relating to or concerned with that which is lawful in psychology. A psychonomic enterprise is one which searches for general principles and underlying lawful relationships. Although there are variations in use, generally it characterizes an approach to psychology patterned after the natural sciences. **2** (obs.). Pertaining to environmental effects on psychological development.

psychooncology The psychological study of the conditions of having cancer.

psychopath A term with two uses, both of which are falling out of favor. **1.** A general label for a person with any severe mental disorder. This usage is now absent from technical writings but still occurs in popular literature. **2.** An individual diagnosed as having a ➤ **psychopathic personality**. Note, however, that that term has been largely superseded first by ➤ **sociopathic personality disorder** and more recently by ➤ **antisocial personality disorder**.

psychopathic ➤ **psychopathy**.

psychopathic personality A personality disorder characterized by amorality, a lack of affect and a diminished sense of anxiety and/or guilt associated with commission of transgressions. The term, once popular, was replaced for a time by ➤ **sociopathic personality** in order to emphasize the social aspects of the disorder. However, since it is clear that the disorder involves much more than a diminished sense of guilt and is typically accompanied by a variety of related behaviors, all of which have an antisocial quality to them, the current term of choice is ➤ **antisocial personality disorder**.

psychopathology The scientific study of mental disorders. Strictly speaking, the term refers to a scientific domain that includes the research work of, among others, psychologists, psychiatrists, neurologists, endocrinologists and pharmacologists, and is distinguished from the actual *practice* of clinical psychologists and psychiatrists in the treatment of those with mental disorders. adj., *psychopathological*. Distinguish from ➤ **psychopathic**.

psychopathy 1. Any abnormal mental condition of which the etiology is unknown and a diagnosis has not been (or cannot be) made. In this sense, the term is an open admission of ignorance. Alternatively: **2.** A forensic psychiatric term for the condition described under ➤ **psychopathic personality**. Note that this meaning, which has had a long history of use (and abuse) in medico-legal proceedings, is now rare. The problems with diagnosis alluded to under *psychopathic personality* as well as the confusion caused by using the same term for meaning 1 above have contributed to its gradual demise. See here the related terms ➤ **sociopathy** and ➤ **sociopathic personality** for more details and ➤➤ **antisocial personality disorder**, which is the contemporary term of choice for 2.

psychopedics Clinical child psychology.

psychopharmacology The study of drugs, specifically with a focus on their psychological effects. It is a hybrid field deriving its foundations from biology, physiology, biochemistry, medicine and psychology.

psychophysical 1. Pertaining to ➤ **psychophysics**. **2.** Pertaining to the oft-hypothesized division between that which is mental and that which is physical. E.g., ➤ **dualism, psychophysical *parallelism**.

psychophysical function Generally, any mathematical function relating sensory experience with physical stimuli. The ➤ **power law** is a good example.

psychophysical measurement Generally, the process of determining some scale of measurement that relates the values of a physical variable with the psychological experiences associated with those values. See, for details here, ➤ **measurement of *threshold, methods of *scaling, scales of measurement** and related entries.

psychophysical methods Broadly, any and/or all of those methods developed in the study of *psychophysics*. See, for details, ➤ **measurement of *threshold, methods of *scaling, scales of measurement**.

psychophysical parallelism ➤ **parallelism, psychophysical**.

psychophysical scale ➤ **psychological *scale**.

psychophysics An area of psychology concerned primarily with the quantitative relationships between physical stimuli and the psychological experience of them. The study of psychophysics began formally with the work of Gustav T. Fechner in the 1860s, although, in his mind, it was the larger science of determining the formal relationship between mind (psyche) and body (physics). As it developed, two broad classes of problems emerged, the determination of ➤ **thresholds** (1, 2) and the establishment of ➤ **psychophysical *scales**. See these and related entries for details on method and theory.

psychophysiological Pertaining generally to the relationship between physiological processes and psychological experience.

psychophysiologic disorder ➤ **psychosomatic disorder**.

psychophysiology ➤ **physiological psychology**.

psychoprophylactic method ➤ **Lamaze method**.

psychose passionnelle The relatively rare delusion that another person, usually one of high social status or a celebrity, is deeply in love with one. Also called *pure erotomania* and *de Clérambault's syndrome*.

psychosexual **1.** Broadly, relating to all aspects of sexuality, the mental as well as the physical and physiological. **2.** Relating to the mental components of sexuality, particularly in a context where they are considered more important than the somatic components. **3.** Within psychoanalytic theory, pertaining to the notion that psychological processes originate in that which is sexual. For example, *development* in classical Freudian theory is often characterized as ➤ **psychosexual development**. In this phrase all three meanings of the term are incorporated.

psychosexual development Within the classical psychoanalytic model, a series of stages of development characterized by the interaction between biological drives and the environment. According to the standard model, balanced, reality-oriented development takes place when there is a proper resolution of this interaction; unbalanced development with attendant conflicts and fixations results in psychological disturbances which may lie latent or be manifested as personality or behavioral disorders. The stages assumed by the theory are the familiar, ➤ **oral**, ➤ **anal**, ➤ **phallic**, ➤ **latency** and ➤ **genital**; see each for details.

psychosexual disorder ➤ **sexual disorders**.

psychosexual dysfunction ➤ **sexual dysfunctions**.

psychosis **1.** Originally, but now rarely, the total mental condition of a person at a specific moment. **2.** A ➤ **psychotic disorder**. pl. *psychoses*.

psychosis with cerebral arteriosclerosis ➤ **multi-infarct *dementia**.

psychosocial Generally, a grab-bag term used freely to cover any situation where both psychological and social factors are assumed to play a role.

psychosocial deprivation During childhood, the condition of getting less than appropriate psychological and social interaction, contact, experience, etc. The term is generally used to characterize an aberrant home environment in which there is inadequate parenting. It is suspected of being one of the primary causes of mild mental retardation, since in many cases enriching the environment causes tested IQ to rise sharply to normal levels.

psychosocial development A term that may be used loosely and literally for an individual's psychological/social development but that is more commonly associated with Erik Erikson's characterization of personality growth and development, which stresses the interaction between the person and the physical and social environment. ➤ **stages of man** for more details on the hypothesized process.

psychosomatic Generally, pertaining to that which is presumed to have both *psychic* (mental) and *somatic* (bodily) components. The usual implication here is that these two aspects interact, each having impact upon the other. ➤ **psychosomatic disorder** and **psychosomatic medicine**.

psychosomatic disorder A general label used for any disorder with *somatic* (bodily) manifestations that are assumed to have at least a partial cognitive and emotional etiology, i.e. they are to some degree *psychological*. There are several approaches taken to these disorders: the one taken dictates the connotations that the term will have. From one widely held perspective, three subcategories of disorders can be distinguished: (a) those related to the individual's overall personality (e.g., highly anxious people show a higher incidence of respiratory disorders); (b) those intimately connected to one's life style (e.g., persons in high-pressure stressful occupations show a higher rate of hypertension and gastric dysfunctions); and (c) those manifested primarily by heightened reaction to substances and conditions (e.g., allergies which, while stimulated by foreign substances, are differentially experienced depending on psychological factors).

However, there is another general point of view that is predicated on the assumption that the manifestation of *all* somatic disorders is psychological to some degree. This orientation suggests a rather different nosology. Here, the disorders are named and classified according to the organ system involved, e.g., gastrointestinal, respiratory, cutaneous, etc. ➤➤ **somatoform disorder**.

psychosomatic medicine The branch of medicine concerned with the relationship between psychological states (conceptualized broadly) and somatic disturbances. While much of the focus is on ➤ **psychosomatic disorders**, the basic operating hypothesis is that there are subtle but critical interactions between somatic and organic dysfunctions and psychological/emotional factors in *all* cases. Distinguish from ➤ **somatopsychology**. ➤➤ **somatoform disorder**.

psychosurgery A general label for any surgical procedure performed on brain tissue for the purpose of alleviating psychological disorders. Procedures range from major surgical interventions (➤ **prefrontal *lobotomy**) to minor techniques that are carried out under local anesthetic (➤ **transorbital *lobotomy**). Other techniques involve severing pathways that mediate limbic-system activity (➤ **amygdalotomy**) and the dramatic procedure of severing the fibers of the *corpus callosum* (➤ **split-brain technique**).

There has been extensive and vigorous debate over the practice of psychosurgery. Typically, even its strongest proponents approach it with extreme caution, prefer-

ring it only when all other procedures have proved ineffectual. Fortunately the increasing sophistication of the psychiatric pharmacopeia has dramatically reduced the number of cases referred for such 'heroic' procedures.

psychotechnician One trained specifically and only to administer certain kinds of psychological and educational tests.

psychotechnology A sometime synonym for *appled psychology*. Used rather loosely, its meaning depends upon the theoretical orientation of the author.

psychotherapeutic 1. Pertaining to ➤ **psychotherapy**. **2.** Pertaining to that which has curative value in psychological disorders. These two meanings are not necessarily equivalent.

psychotherapist Generally, one who practices psychotherapy. Note, in fact, that in some locales the term has taken on a legal definition and may be formally distinguished from that of ➤ **psychologist**. That is, some governmental bodies and professional licensing boards recognize a person with some special training to function as a licensed psychotherapist (e.g., one trained in social work or school or counseling psychology), while reserving the title *psychologist* for those with doctoral degrees and recognized internships.

psychotherapy In the most inclusive sense, the use of absolutely any technique or procedure that has palliative or curative effects upon any mental, emotional or behavioral disorder. In this general sense the term is neutral with regard to the theory that may underlie it, the actual procedures and techniques entailed or the form and duration of the treatment. There may, however, be legal and professional issues involved in the actual practice of what is called psychotherapy, and in the technical literature the term is properly used only when it is carried out by someone with recognized training and using accepted techniques. For more on this issue ➤ **psychiatrist, psychoanalyst, psychologist** and ➤ **psychotherapist**. The term is often used in shortened form, *therapy*, particularly when modifiers are appended to identify the form of therapy or the theoretical orientation of the therapist using it. Specific forms are included in this volume under the modifier.

psychotic 1 adj. Pertaining to a ➤ **psychotic disorder**. Often used in combined form here to mark a disorder when the symptoms are characteristic of or strongly resemble a psychosis; e.g., *psychotic *depression*. 2 n. One who has been diagnosed as having a psychotic disorder.

psychotic depression ➤ **depression, psychotic**.

psychotic disorders A general cover term for a number of severe mental disorders of organic or emotional origin. In contemporary psychiatric nosology, the defining feature of these disorders is gross impairment in ➤ **reality testing** (2). That is, the person makes incorrect inferences concerning external reality, makes improper evaluations of the accuracy of his or her thoughts and perceptions and continues to make these errors in the face of contrary evidence. Classic symptoms include delusions, hallucinations, severe regressive behaviors, dramatically inappropriate mood and markedly incoherent speech. The standard clinical literature lists as psychoses: ➤ **bipolar disorder**, ➤ **brief reactive psychosis**, the ➤ **schizophrenias**, various ➤ **organic mental disorders**, and some of the ➤ **mood disorders**.

psychotic episode ➤ **brief reactive psychosis**.

psychotic surrender A term used occasionally to characterize a reaction in individuals who are seen as reaching a point where they 'throw in the towel,' a giving up on their battle to face reality and surrendering to a psychotic withdrawal.

psychotogenic Generally, characterizing events, circumstances or substances that produce psychotic states.

psychotomimetic Lit., mimicking a psychosis. First used of those psychotropic drugs whose actions were assumed to mimic psychotic disorders, specifically hallucinogens like LSD. This assumption has been found wanting and the term is now used loosely to characterize drugs that produce a state similar to or symptomatic of a psychotic disorder.

psychotropic Lit., mind-altering or mood-altering. Most often used to characterize drugs that affect psychological functioning, such as those used in drug therapy like the antianxiety, antidepressant and antipsychotic drugs as well as the hallucinogens such as LSD, mescaline, etc. Like its near synonym. ➤ **psychoactive**, the term tends to be used loosely.

psychro- Combining form meaning *cold*.

P technique ➤ **R correlation**.

ptosis Dropping, drooping. Used of organs or parts, e.g., the drooping of the eyelid from paralysis.

PTSD ➤ **post-traumatic stress disorder**.

puberal Pertaining to ➤ **puberty**. var., *pubertal*.

pubertas praecox ➤ precocious *puberty.

puberty The period of life during which the sex organs become reproductively functional. Onset in the female is fairly clearly marked by the menarche; in the male it is less obvious, but the growth and pigmentation of underarm hair is often taken as criterial. The end of puberty is difficult to specify and many authors simply select an arbitrary cut-off point based on age (e.g., 14 in the female and 15 in the male are often used), although it should be recognized that there is considerable variation in age of onset and rate of development and so such a procedure is of questionable value.

puberty, precocious Lit., early puberty. The term is reserved for the abnormal condition in which, owing to pituitary malfunction, the normal maturational sequence is speeded up and the onset of puberty, including the maturation of the sex organs and the emergence of the secondary sex characteristics, occurs at an abnormally early age. Also called *pubertas praecox*.

puberty rites Generally, any cultural ritual concerning the passage into adult status. Note that although the term is most often used in anthropological discourses on tribal lore and tradition in preliterate societies, many modern social, ethnic and religious groups have similar practices. Compare with ➤ **pubic rites**.

puberum dysphonia ➤ **dysphonia, puberum**.

pubes **1** n. sing. The hair or the entire hairy region of the lower abdomen and genital area. **2** n. pl. The pubic bones that form part of the pelvis.

pubescence The process of first reaching puberty.

pubescent Of one in the early period of puberty.

pubic Pertaining to the external genitals and the immediate genital area; pertaining to the pubes.

pubic rites Any ritual or ceremony involving the genitals. They may or may not be associated with ➤ **puberty rites**; e.g., circumcision is usually performed soon after birth.

public **1** adj. Open, unrestricted, available. **2** adj. Pertaining to the people or, by extension, the government of the people. **3** n. A large aggregate of persons. Note that this last use is generally broken down so that it may refer to: (a) the full complement of persons in a state or country, which is the meaning usually conveyed by the simple use of the definite article as in 'the public.' or (b) a number of persons who share a common set of interests, which is the meaning usually conveyed by the use of delimiting adjectives as in the 'golfing public' or the 'buying public.' Note that this particular use of the term is similar to that of the term *group* but without the connotation of *organization*. ➤ **group** for discussion.

public opinion ➤ **opinion, public**.

pudenda The external genitals. sing., *pudendum*.

puerile Childlike. Usually used as descriptive of the behavior of an adult that is inappropriately childish.

puerperal Pertaining to childbirth or to the weeks immediately following. Often used in phrases that relate to disorders accompanying childbirth, e.g., *postpartum depression* is also called *puerperal depression*.

puerperium The period following childbirth, often specified as 42 days.

Pulfrich phenomenon A visual phenomenon in which a regularly swinging pendulum will be perceived to follow an elliptical path when viewed monocularly through a medium-density filter.

pulmonary Pertaining to the lungs.

pulse **1.** Generally, any regular rhythmic throbbing. **2.** Specifically, the beating produced by the rise and fall of pressure in the arteries resulting from heart-muscle action.

pulvinar An area of the thalamus that projects fibers to the visual association areas in the parietal and temporal lobes.

punch drunk ➤ **dementia pugilistica**.

punctate Marked with or by points. A punctate stimulus is one applied to a point on the skin.

punctuated equilibrium A model of evolution which argues that new species evolve in rather rapid (geologically speaking) fashion rather than in the gradual manner depicted by the standard Darwinian model. The term connotes that evolution can be seen as periods of relative stability occasionally punctuated by the saltatory emergence of new species. Compare with ➤ **Darwinism**.

punisher Any event that operates opposite in sign to a ➤ **reinforcer**. That is, a *positive punisher* reduces the probability of responses that produced it and a *negative punisher* reduces the probability of responses that terminated it. ➤➤ **negative *reinforcer, positive *reinforcer**.

punishment **1.** The administration of

623

some aversive stimulus contingent upon a particular behavior. **2.** The aversive stimulus itself. Behind these formal definitions of the term lies a variety of issues, and the exact connotations of the term depend on the manner of its use. To wit: (a) the aversive stimulus itself may be short, simple and well-defined, as in most laboratory studies where electric shock is used, but it may also be an extended, complex event as when society incarcerates a legal offender; (b) the punishing event may be the presentation of some aversive stimulus (an electric shock, a spanking) or it may consist of the withdrawal of some desired or pleasant thing (a fine, a parent's withdrawal of love); (c) the punishment may be either for the performance of some response (a rat pressing the wrong bar, a felony) or for the nonperformance of a response (failure to press the bar, not studying for an exam). Moreover, some authors use the term so that the threat of punishment is considered to be a punishment. This extension is defended by the argument that the anxiety associated with the possibility of the infliction of the aversive stimulus is, in itself, punishing. Compare with and distinguish from ➤ **negative *reinforcement**.

punishment by reciprocity Punishment that takes account of the nature and severity of the transgression and is logically related to it, punishment that 'fits the crime' and makes clear to the transgressor the implications of the offense. Older children tend to favor such as compared with ➤ **expiatory *punishment**.

punishment, expiatory Punishment that is painful in proportion to the seriousness of the transgression but not necessarily dependent on the nature of the offense committed. Younger children tend to favor such as compared with **punishment by reciprocity**.

punitive Pertaining to punishment especially with the connotation of the use of punishment or the threat of it to control the behavior of others. Compare with ➤ **impunitive**, **intropunitive** and **extrapunitive**.

pupil 1. The adjustable opening in the iris of the eye through which light passes. **2.** Any child in the elementary grades. **3.** Any student being tutored.

pupillary reflex A change in the size of the pupil of the eye. Contraction of the iris muscle causes constriction of the pupil, relaxation produces a dilated pupil. The reflex is produced by a variety of stimuli, including changes in light level, changes in point of focus and emotional aspects of the visual stimulus – although these latter changes in pupil size are probably conditioned responses and not true reflexes. Also called *iris reflex* and *iritic reflex*.

pure 1. Unadulterated, free from extraneous factors, homogeneous; e.g., a *pure tone* consists of only a single frequency, a *pure hue* of only one wavelength. **2.** Uncontaminated, morally sound, virtuous. **3.** Not applied. Here the term is used for research aimed at the accumulation of knowledge, understanding and explanation independently of possible applications. This is not to suggest that applications may not be made, only that such potential is not a motivation in the actual research itself.

pure alexia ➤ alexia, pure.

pure erotomania ➤ *psychose passionnelle*.

pure hue ➤ hue, pure.

pure phi phenomenon ➤ phi phenomenon.

pure-stimulus act ➤ act, pure-stimulus.

pure tone ➤ tone, pure.

pure word deafness ➤ auditory *aphasia.

Purkinje (Purkyně) afterimage The second ➤ **positive *afterimage**, which occurs following a bright stimulus; it is in the hue complementary to the original.

Purkinje (Purkyně) cells Large neurons in the cerebellum. They are the major efferent projections from the cortex of the cerebellum to its deep nuclei. The cells have extensive dendritic processes that project to the molecular layer of the cortex.

Purkinje (Purkyně) effect (or phenomenon or shift) The phenomenon that when the illumination of a multihue display is reduced those hues toward the long-wavelength end of the spectrum (reds, oranges) lose their perceived brightness more rapidly than those toward the short-wavelength end (greens, blues). This shift is due to the fact that the rods, which have greater overall sensitivity than the cones, are also maximally sensitive to short wavelengths.

Purkinje (Purkyně) figures (or network) The perception of the network of interwoven blood vessels of the retina. Under the proper conditions (low room illumination, a small relatively bright light held just under the eye, stare at a blank wall) it can be seen.

Purkinje (Purkyně)–Sanson images Three distinct images of an object that a person is viewing that can be observed by looking at that person's eye under the proper conditions. One is from the surface of the cornea, one from the front of the lens and the third from the back of the lens.

purple A hue (or, better, a series of related hues) that results from mixtures of blue and red light. The purples are often referred to as *extraspectral* because there are no single wavelengths in the visible spectrum that produce them; hence they are defined by specifying the wavelength of their complements, e.g., the greens and yellow-greens in the neighborhood of 550 nm.

purpose 1. The internally represented mental goal or aim which is set by an individual and which guides and directs his or her behavior. **2.** A hypothetical determiner of behavior inferred from an organism's behavior that reveals directedness, persistence and focused orientation toward some goal. Meaning 2 was introduced by E. C. Tolman to permit behaviorists to theorize about purpose in sense 1 but not admit to it. ➤ **purposive psychology**.

purposive psychology An orientation of psychological science that stresses the role of purpose in the determination of behavior. The term was introduced by the neobehaviorist Edward Chace Tolman to characterize his theoretical position that behavior could not be properly understood from the pure behaviorist perspective, which stressed only the mechanical chaining of reflexive, physiological processes. Note, however, that several other theoretical positions, while not necessarily labeled as *purposive*, make similar assumptions about behavior, e.g., the hormic psychology of McDougall and virtually all of the depth or analytic approaches.

pursuitmeter Any device for measuring a subject's ability to follow (pursue) an erratically moving target. The most commonly used are the *pursuit rotor*, in which the target follows a rough and erratically varying circular path, and the *pursuit pendulum*, in which the target traces a varying pendular path.

pursuit movement Eye movement made while tracking a moving object. The eye moves relatively smoothly and in a manner so that the image remains on the fovea. Compare with ➤ **saccadic movement**.

pursuit, ocular ➤ **pursuit movement**.

pursuit pendulum ➤ **pursuitmeter**.

pursuit reaction Generally, any set of movements that serves to keep an organism oriented with respect to a moving stimulus.

pursuit rotor ➤ **pursuitmeter**.

push-down stack 1. In computer terminology, a temporally ordered list. It refers to a limited-capacity storage system in which each new incoming stimulus occupies the topmost position in the stack, 'pushing down' the previously stored stimuli. When the capacity of the stack is reached, each new stimulus 'pushes out' the oldest of the stored ones. **2.** In cognitive psychology, a metaphor for the mode of operation of human ➤ **short-term *memory**, which displays many of these properties.

putamen One of the large subcortical nuclei that comprise the ➤ **basal ganglia**.

putrid An olfactory quality typified by rotting organic matter. ➤ **Henning's prism**.

puzzle box Generally, any experimental apparatus consisting of a locked box and an unlocking device which must be manipulated in the proper manner by the subject to either (a) obtain a reward locked in the box, or (b) get out of the box in which it is locked. The unlocking device may be either a simple lever, bar or string or a complex mechanism, depending upon the cognitive sophistication of the subject in the experiment. E.g., ➤ **Thorndike puzzle box**.

Pygmalion effect 1. From the play by G. B. Shaw, the oft-observed effect in which people come to behave in ways that correspond to others' expectations concerning them. ➤ **self-fulfilling prophecy. 2.** From the name of a king in a Greek myth (from which Shaw borrowed the name), a pathological condition in which one falls in love with one's own creation. syn. (for 2), *pygmalionism*.

pyknic Referring to a compact, thick body type. ➤ **constitutional theory** for more detail. var., *pyknik*.

pyramidal cells Multipolar cells with triangular-shaped bodies and extensive dendritic processes found in the cerebral cortex and the hippocampus.

pyramidal (motor) system ➤ **pyramidal tract**.

pyramidal tract A neural system consisting of a long monosynaptic pathway running from the cortex to the motor neurons of the cranial-nerve nuclei and ventral horn of the spinal cord. Most of the fibers in the system decussate at the medulla, the others further down the pathway. It contains axons of the lateral and ventral *corticospinal tracts* (➤ **corticospinal pathway**). Also called *pyramidal motor system*.

pyramids Compact elevated bundles of nerve fibers in the medulla.

pyromania An ➤ **impulse-control disorder** characterized by a recurrent failure to resist impulses to set fires and a deep fascination with watching them burn. A defining feature of the disorder is that the fire-setting is undertaken without obvious motivations such as money, revenge or political ideology.

pyrosis Heartburn.

Q

Q Abbreviation for: **1.** ➤ **Quartile deviation. 2.** When subscripted, a ➤ **quartile**; Q_1, Q_2, Q_3, designate the first, second and third quartiles. **3.** *Question*, as in *Q* and *A* (answer). **4.** *Questionnaire*, used generally here.

q The proportion of events in a population failing to exhibit a particular characteristic and thereby distinguishable from a mutually exclusive proportion of events, *p*, such that $p + q = 1$.

Q data Any data obtained from a questionnaire.

Q method A general term for the use of questionnaires in research.

Q sort A technique used in personality assessment based upon a series of statements and trait names which the subject sorts into categories from 'most characteristic of me' to 'least characteristic of me.'

Q technique ➤ **R correlation**.

Q test ➤ **Cochran Q test**.

quadrant 1. One of the four cells in a 2 × 2 table. **2.** One of the four equal-sized areas of a plane created by subdividing it with intersecting perpendicular lines.

quadrigemina ➤ **corpora quadrigemina**.

quadriplegia Paralysis of all four limbs.

quale The singular of **qualia**.

qualia The simple, uninterpreted elements of experience. What role such basic, raw aspects of experience play in mental life (given that they can be shown to exist) has been long debated by philosophers and psychologists. From the point of view of ➤ **structuralism** (1), qualia form the primary data of psychology; from the ➤ **Gestalt psychology** perspective, their existence is doubted if not denied. sing. *quale*.

quality 1. Originally, in early forms of structuralism, a basic attribute of a sensa-

tion, an aspect of a thing that enabled it to be distinguished from other things. Qualities were expressed by names and labels, adjectives and modifiers, e.g., pink, F#, hard, etc. The point of this usage was to divorce the concept of quality from that of ➤ **quantity**, the latter to be reserved for reference to differences in amount, degree or intensity of sensations and the former for differences in kinds of sensations. The distinction is not as easy to make as once thought. **2.** A more or less quantitative assessment of the value or worth of a thing. Note, this meaning differs sharply from 1, having a distinctly quantitative connotation.

quality, primary and secondary A distinction first drawn by Democritus and revived several times by the likes of Galileo, Descartes, Newton and, most significantly, Locke to the effect that the qualities that things possess may be separated into the primary and the secondary. The former encompasses those qualities that objects actually have (solidity, extension, shape, motion, number), while the latter covers those qualities that are only reactions to these (sounds, colors, tastes, etc.). The distinction is surely inviting and historically clearly robust, but it has turned out to be epistemologically problematic and is rarely made any more.

quanta Plural of ➤ **quantum**.

quantal Pertaining to that which: **1.** Changes in small discrete steps. **2.** Occurs in small elemental units.

quantal hypothesis The hypothesis that continuous increments in a physical variable produce discrete (quantal) increases in sensation. The hypothesis has been extended to the neurological level where it is called, not unexpectedly, the *neural quantal hypothesis*.

quantity An aspect or property of a

thing that renders it countable or measurable in numerical terms. See and contrast with ➤ **quality** (1).

quantum **1.** In physics, the elemental unit of radiant energy. **2.** More generally, any discrete amount of anything. pl., *quanta*.

quartile **1.** One of the three points that divide an ordered distribution into four parts each containing one quarter of the scores. **2.** One of the four parts of the distribution so divided. See the discussion under ➤ **partile** and ➤ **centile** for problems of usage encountered because of the inconsistency of meanings here.

quartile deviation One-half of the difference between the third and first ➤ **quartiles** (1). Occasionally used as a 'quick and dirty' estimate of the variability of a distribution, particularly when the median is used as the measure of central tendency. Also known as the *semi-interquartile range*, it is, in a normal distribution, equal to the *probable error*.

quasi- A combining form used freely as an affix, an adjective or an adverb. The usual connotation is that the thing so qualified is but a resemblance of or only superficially similar to some other thing.

quasi-experimental research An umbrella term for any research carried out without full control over the independent variables. Much naturalistic social psychological research comes within this category, such as analysis of people's reactions to natural disasters when the subjects are those who just happen to fall victim to the disaster and are not selected by any controlled sampling procedure.

quasi group A sociological term often used to refer to an aggregate of persons

with the, as yet unrealized, potential for forming into a true ➤ **group**.

quasi need A term occasionally used for any nonbiological need.

Queen's English ➤ **King's English**.

questionary A rarely used synonym for ➤ **questionnaire**.

questionnaire Broadly, any set of questions dealing with any topic or group of related topics designed to be answered by a respondent.

quick and dirty Laboratory slang for any simple technique for making a rough estimate. For example, 'eye-balling' a regression line, using the quartile deviation as a measure of variability, etc. Such procedures are called 'quick' because they are, and 'dirty' because they typically have a high error rate.

quickening The first fetal movements *in utero*. Typically felt between the 18th and 20th weeks, although earlier movements are not uncommon.

quiet biting attack ➤ **predatory attack**.

quota control A way of establishing control over the sample of subjects selected for an investigation by using ➤ **quota *sampling**. See that entry for details.

quota sampling ➤ **sampling, quota**.

quotidian Daily, occurring daily.

quotidian variability Day-to-day variability.

quotient The result of the operation of dividing one number by another. Quotients are commonly used to express data in psychology, e.g., IQ = ➤ **intelligence quotient**. Their mathematical status as such is often misunderstood.

R

R A (sometimes confusingly) polyfunctional abbreviation. To wit: **1.** *Response*, as in the common shorthand *S–R* for *stimulus–response*. **2.** *Stimulus*, from the German word *Reiz*. The confusion once produced by these two conflicting uses is lessened these days as this latter use is now rare. **3.** ➤ **Multiple *correlation** coefficient. **4.** A general *reasoning* factor hypothesized by some to be a primary mental ability.

R$_C$ An infrequent abbreviation for *conditioned response*; *CR* is more common.

R$_G$ In Hull's theory, any goal-attaining response, e.g., eating, drinking.

R$_{1.23...n}$ ➤ **multiple *correlation** coefficient.

R$_P$ The probability of a response. This abbreviation is little used, *p* being the more common notation for probability, with the response under consideration usually being clear from context.

R$_u$ An infrequent abbreviation for *unconditioned response*; *UR* and *UCR* are encountered more often.

r **1.** The ➤ **product-moment *correlation** coefficient: ➤ **r$_{xy}$**. **2.** In Hull's theory, the efferent reaction leading to an overt response. Also called a ➤ **pure-stimulus *act**.

r$_{bis}$ The ➤ **biserial *correlation** coefficient.

r$_G$ In Hull's theory, a ➤ **fractional antedating goal response**.

r$_{12.34}$ ➤ **partial *correlation** coefficient. It denotes the correlation between the variables to the left of the point (here, 1 and 2) after the influences of those to the right (here, 3 and 4) have been removed.

r^2 The square of the value of a ➤ **product-moment *correlation** coefficient. It provides an estimate of the proportion of the variance in the data that can be attributed

to the relationship. Occasionally written *r-squared*.

r$_t$ The ➤ **tetrachoric *correlation** coefficient. Also denoted as r_{tet}.

r$_{tet}$ ➤ **r$_t$**.

r$_{xy}$ The ➤ **product-moment *correlation** with the variables (*x* and *y*) that enter into its computation denoted.

race A term born in anthropological innocence and meant simply to designate the major subdivisions of *Homo sapiens*. A race was defined as any relatively large division of persons that could be distinguished from others on the basis of inherited physical characteristics such as skin pigmentation, blood groups, hair texture and the like. In actual practice, it is nearly impossible to classify or distinguish individual persons by such physical characteristics, for no specific set of them truly constitutes criterial features. If the concept has any residual meaning in this respect, it is only when the relative frequency of occurrence of physical traits in a population is assessed. For example, there are many 'blacks' with lighter skins than many 'whites,' so skin color cannot serve as a definitive criterion for any arbitrarily selected individual. However, among the population of persons who identify themselves as 'black' there will be a higher relative frequency of dark-skinned individuals than among the population of those who identify themselves as 'white.' Since the key criterion here is *identify themselves as*, it is clear that the working definition of race is one that is dependent upon a social-cultural-political identification and not one that can be unambiguously determined by genetic classification. ➤ **race differences**.

race differences Those characteristics that are supposedly distinctive of the members of one race and serve to distinguish them from those of other races. When large populations of persons are under consideration, a variety of physical traits can be identified and, with the proper caveats (➤ **race**), the use of the term in this domain is not disputed. The difficulties with it emerge when non-obvious characteristics such as intelligence and aptitudes for particular professions are examined with respect to possible differential distributions in different races. These difficulties come in two forms. First is the problem of the determination of the existence of racial differences on such psychological dimensions. Here the research is badly muddled because of the difficulties of measurement associated with factors like ➤ **intelligence** (which see for discussion). Second is the problem of assignment of cause for any differences that may eventually emerge. Strictly speaking, the use of the term *race differences* does not necessarily entail the presumption of genetic differences since sociocultural differences associated with racial identification in a society may yield differences that emerge on standard tests. However, as the term *race* itself carries unambiguous genetic connotations, many authors use race differences with this implication as well.

It is an unhappy commentary that this phrase rates such an extensive entry in a contemporary lexicon of psychology. The focus on the assessment of differences to the neglect of that which is universal distorts issues of paramount social, political and individual importance.

race prejudice Any ➤ **prejudice** based on race. ➤ **racism** (especially 2).

racialism ➤ racism.

racial memory ➤ memory, racial.

racial unconscious ➤ collective unconscious.

racism 1. A ➤ **prejudice** based on race and characterized by attitudes and beliefs about the inferior nature of persons of other races. This sense is close in many ways to ➤ **ethnocentrism** (1). **2.** A social/political doctrine that argues for differen-

tial social, economic, educational and legal treatment of persons based on their race. Sense 1 does not entail adherence to the doctrine of 2 nor to its program of discriminatory practices; 2, however, assumes the attitudes of racial superiority of 1. See the discussions of ➤ **race** and ➤ **race differences** for more on the connotations of usage. var., *racialism*.

radial arm maze a maze consisting of a central hub out from which a number of arms (usually six or seven) radiate.

radiance ➤ **Radiant energy** as measured by the rate of emission and the area of the source.

radiant energy Electromagnetic energy usually conceptualized as propagated in wave form. Although the full spectrum of radiant energy runs from the very long wavelengths (e.g., radio waves with peak-to-peak wavelengths of up to 3×10^{15} nm) to the very short wavelengths (e.g., cosmic rays, 3×10^{-9} nm), the area from roughly 400–750 nm is visible and generally called light.

radiation 1. Generally, the spread of energy from some source through space or matter. Specifically: **2.** Neural radiation, usually expressed as the spread of neural excitation. **3.** The radiation of pain from a source. **4.** = ➤ **radiant energy**.

radical The core meaning here is *pertaining to a root*. Thus: **1.** In mathematics, a sign ($\sqrt{}$) signifying the operation of factoring the quantity under it into its roots. **2.** In social/political terms, descriptive of any point of view or proposal that argues for basic, fundamental change. **3.** A person who advocates such change. ➤ **radicalism**.

radicalism 1. Generally, any sociopolitical point of view that advocates extreme, rapid and fundamental change. Radicalism is, strictly speaking, a nonconformist point of view with dramatic societal change as its aim and, thus, is not necessarily associated with either the left or the right poles of the political spectrum. However: **2.** An extreme ideological perspective of the left.

rage A term usually taken to refer to the extreme end of the domain of emotionality denoted by ➤ **anger**, i.e. anger that has gotten out of control. It is usually identified by the same patterns of visceral and muscular responses as anger, but the pattern is more extreme, more intense, and an attack response is considered more likely.

railway illusion ➤ **Ponzo illusion**.

ramus 1. Any branch of a nerve or vein. 2. Any of the several branches of each of the spinal nerves.

random Most dictionaries attempt to define this term by listing synonyms or near-synonyms. The typical list includes words or phrases like *haphazard, by chance, occurring without voluntary control, aimless, purposeless*, etc. While it is true that random is used in ways that correspond to these (e.g., one frequently sees references to *random activity, random thinking*, etc.), such clustering of synonyms tends to miss the essential point that randomness is a mathematical or statistical concept; the term means simply that there is *no detectible systematicity* in the sequence of events observed. Strictly speaking, random refers not to a thing but to the *lack* of a thing, the lack of pattern or structure or regularity. For more discussion, see another often misunderstood term, ➤ **chance**.

random activity The usual reference of this term is behavior that is aimless or purposeless. Note, however, that it is not used to imply that the activity so labeled is intrinsically without aim nor that it is acausal; rather it is used to label behavior in which the observer cannot discern any clear aim, purpose or eliciting stimulus. ➤ **random**.

random effects model ➤ **random *factor**.

random error ➤ **chance *error**.

random factor ➤ **factor, random**.

random group ➤ **random *sample**.

randomization test One of the more powerful nonparametric statistical tests. It is based on the determination of the exact probabilities of an observed set of differences in scores between two matched samples and the assessment of just how likely such a difference would be under the null hypothesis of no difference in the underlying distributions.

randomize 1. To select or choose objects, events, experimental subjects, etc. such that there are no detectable biases or systematic patterns. That is, to make one's selections so that each event has an equal and independent chance of being sampled. 2. To arrange a sequence or collection of events such that there is no detectable pattern or systematicity. ➤ **random, random *sample**.

random mating ➤ **mating, random**.

random movement ➤ **random activity**.

random noise = ➤ white *noise; ➤➤ noise (1).

random number The concept of a single random number makes no sense except in terms of the manner in which it was selected or chosen, i.e. a number that has been selected at random from a ➤ **random-number table**.

random-number table A large collection of digits tabulated such that there is no statistically detectable pattern or systematicity in the table. In all practical cases, where the table consists of but several thousand digits, true randomness is only approximated. Nevertheless, these tables are important research tools in experimental and survey procedures where there is a need to prevent any systematic bias in the order of presentation of stimuli or conditions or in the order of selection of subjects. The need for tables approximating randomness led in the past to the publication of a book consisting of 1 million random digits – surely the most boring book ever published. Today, sophisticated computer programs exist for generating sequences of random numbers.

random observation Any observation or

series of observations made without any systematic pattern and without preconception about what is to be observed. Random observation is an important control procedure, particularly in naturalistic studies where periodic observations may produce biased data. Note that a random-observation schedule is not necessarily unplanned; rather it may be carefully planned but with the aid of and according to a random-number table.

random ratio (RR) An occasional synonym for *variable ratio*. ➤ **schedules of** *reinforcement.

random sample ➤ **sample, random**.

random variable Any variable, the values of which are determined randomly. *Random* here refers to the manner in which the values are chosen, not to the variable itself. For more detail, ➤ **random**.

random variation Those differences in the values of a variable that are due to chance. For example, you take two random samples of people. In your first sample you find 40 brown-eyed people and 10 blue-eyed; in the second, 42 with brown eyes but only 8 with blue. The differences here are due to random variation. In the long run random variations will cancel each other out. Also called *random error*.

range The standard dictionary meaning is basic to all uses in psychology; i.e. the extent to or the limits between which variation can occur. Thus: **1.** The interval or 'distance' between the highest and lowest scores in a distribution. **2.** In statistics, a crude measure of the variability or dispersion of a set of scores. It is obtained by subtracting the lowest score from the highest. **3.** In sociology and ethology, the physical area over which a particular group lives or a particular species is found. Compare here with ➤ **habitat**. **4.** In psychophysics, the domain or interval over which a particular sensory system functions, e.g., the *audibility range*.

range, audibility ➤ **audibility range**.

range, discriminating The range of scores on a test that have reliable predictive values. For example, the scores above roughly the 90th percentile on the Graduate Record Examination lie outside of this range since there are no reliable predictive differences found between those students who score within this interval.

rank **1** n. In statistics, the position in an ordered series of scores. The rank of a score on some measure tells only where that score is relative to all others (i.e. 1st, 2nd, 3rd, ..., *n*th); it reveals nothing about the distance between the scores. Scores that are ranked form an ➤ **ordinal** *scale and hence only nonparametric statistics may be used in analyzing them. **2** vb. To order or arrange scores, events, individuals, etc. in a ranked order.

rank-difference correlation ➤ **correlation, rank-order**.

ranked distribution ➤ **distribution, ranked**.

rank order Any ordering of scores according to their ➤ **ranks**.

rank-order correlation ➤ **correlation, rank-order**.

Ranschburg effect The generalization that under tachistoscopic viewing conditions more individual stimuli can be recognized if all are different than if some are identical.

Ranvier, nodes of Small gaps in the myelin sheath of nerve fibers.

raphe **1.** In anatomy generally, a crease or seam marking the joining of two halves. **2.** Specifically, a complex of nuclei in the core of the brainstem that plays a part in the brain's complex sleep mechanism. var., *rhaphe*.

rapid cycling A term used to note cases of ➤ **bipolar disorder** where the shifts between states is unusually rapid.

rapid eye movements (REM) The rapid, jerky, eye movements characteristic of one particular stage of sleep. For details here, ➤ **REM-sleep, sleep** and related terms.

rapport **1.** Generally, a comfortable, relaxed, unconstrained, mutually accepting interaction between persons, especially when the persons are a tester and a subject in psychological testing, a client and a therapist in therapy, and the like. **2.** In *hypnosis*, the affective contract between hypnotist and subject so that the latter will 'accept' the suggestions of the former. **3.** In *parapsychology*, the presumed relationship between a medium and his or her spiritual contact.

RAS (or **ras**) ➤ **reticular activating system**.

rate **1** n. A ratio of the number of occurrences or observations of some event within a specific period of time divided by either (a) the total number of possible occurrences of that event, or (b) a standardized number of units. For example, annual birth rate can be given as the number of births per year relative to either (a) the total number of women of childbearing age, or (b) a standardized number of such women, e.g., 100, 1,000, 1 million, etc. **2** n. The number of occurrences of some event within a specified time period; e.g., *response rate* is a common dependent variable in operant-conditioning experiments and is usually given as the raw number of responses per minute or some other time unit. **3** n. Shorthand for ➤ **rate of change**. **4** vb. To assign a number or score reflecting ordinal position or ➤ **rank** on some variable. **5** vb. To assign a ➤ **rating**.

ratee A person being rated.

rate law In neurophysiology, the generalization that the strength of a stimulus is represented by the rate at which the axon of a neuron fires. ➤➤ **all-or-none law** (1).

rate of change An expression that reflects the ➤ **rate** (1 or 2) at which change is observed to occur. It is expressed as a ratio of the amount of change observed in a given time period to the value prior to the change.

rater One who carries out a ➤ **rating**.

rater reliability ➤ **interrater *reliability**.

rate score In time tests, a score based on

the number of problems or tasks completed per unit time.

rating **1.** An estimate or evaluation of an object, event or person (including oneself, the so-called *self-rating*). Ratings are used commonly in social and personality research to measure qualities and characteristics that are subjective and for which no objective measurement techniques exist. ➤ **rating scale** et seq. **2.** An occasional synonym of ➤ **rank** (1). This semantic equivalence derives from the fact that rating procedures often utilize ➤ **ordinal *scales**.

rating, behavior The use of rating techniques in a fairly restricted manner such that only overt, objectively observable behaviors enter into the assessment. The term is used to refer to either an assessing of the degree to which specific behaviors are observed to occur or a simple recording of the presence or absence of particular behaviors.

rating scale Generally, any device used to assist a rater in making ratings. Social scientists have developed a rather impressive array of such devices; the more commonly used are listed below.

rating scale, bipolar Any rating scale where the dimensions along which the ratings are made are specified by the two opposing poles, with the scale itself laid out between them. A typical scale of this kind may consist of a list of dimensions like 'good–bad,' 'pleasant–unpleasant,' 'cooperative–uncooperative,' etc.; the respondent marks the point between or at one of the two poles which is appropriate for what or whomever is being rated.

rating scale, check-list A rating scale based upon a list of traits or characteristics in which the rater checks those that apply to the person being rated. Such scales are often used in self-reporting procedures.

rating scale, graphic Any rating scale that utilizes a graphic or pictorial format. The most commonly used is for an attitude statement, which is presented with a line marked from positive at one end, through neutral in the middle, to negative at the other end. The ratee marks a spot on the line at the point that represents his or her attitude with respect to the statement.

rating scale, itemized A rating scale based on a series of ordered categories (e.g., most negative to most positive, most desirable to least desirable, most characteristic to least characteristic, etc.). The rater selects the one category that is most applicable to the item or person under consideration.

ratio A quotient, a relationship between any two magnitudes expressed as the product of division.

ratio estimation ➤ methods of *scaling.

rational 1. Relating to or suggestive of the use of reason, the process of reasoning or the property of being reasonable. 2. Pertaining to that which is correct or, at least, justifiable by reason; e.g., a rational decision. 3. Descriptive of an organism capable of high mental functioning; man is often called (seriously as well as in jest) the *rational animal*. 4. Connoting sanity or lucidity. 5. Primarily cognitive in nature as opposed to emotional.

rational authority ➤ authority, rational.

rationale The reason or the grounds offered for an opinion, attitude, decision, etc. The usual implication is that a rationale is reasonable (➤ **rational**) and that it is consciously reached and expressible.

rational-economic man A general model of behavior predicated on the assumption that the basic, fundamental principle underlying human nature is the rational (*sic!*) striving for self-interest, particularly economic and material gain.

rational-emotive therapy A form of psychotherapy developed by Albert Ellis which focuses on the rational, problem-solving aspects of emotional and behavioral disorders. Ellis's approach is highly directive (see here ➤ **directive therapy**), consisting in large measure of telling the client what he or she must do in order to

be happy and then 'encouraging' him or her, often through confrontation and encounter, to act and think accordingly. Although related in some ways to the behavior therapies, the rational-emotive approach is distinguishable from them in being strongly cognitive and emotive.

rational equation ➤ equation, rational.

rationalism Any of several philosophical perspectives all of which share the assumption that truth is to be ascertained through the use of reason, of rational thought. Older forms of rationalism (e.g., Platonic, medieval theological) maintained that *only* through reason could ultimate truth be discovered. More modern perspectives (e.g., Chomskyan linguistics) are not quite so totally antiempirical; rational deductions are generally treated as susceptible to empirical demonstration and test.

rationality A state characterized by reasonableness, a willingness to accept that which is well reasoned.

rationality, bounded 1. A particular characteristic of human decision-making under conditions of extreme complexity. 2. A theory of cognitive processes as they are displayed under such conditions. In either usage, the reference is to the notion that in the face of complexity one cannot behave in a totally rational manner, simply because one's information-processing capacities are too limited to encompass all the knowledge required for such ideal decision-making. The theory of bounded rationality describes individuals as decision-makers who circumscribe the situation by limiting (or 'bounding') the amount of information to be dealt with – often in creative and imaginative ways – and then behaving in a rational fashion with this limited knowledge base. The theory is most closely associated with the work of the American economist-philosopher-psychologist, Herbert Simon.

rationalization 1. In general terms, the process through which things that were confusing and obscure and irrational (or, better perhaps, *non*rational) are made clear, concise and rational. **2.** In psychoanalytic theory, the term carries this general sense but with the additional connotation that it serves to conceal the true motivations for one's actions, thoughts or feelings. In this sense, it is usually classified as a ➤ **defense mechanism. 3.** The outcome of the rationalization process in either of the above senses.

rational learning A general term used for any learning which is based on logical, conscious reasoning.

rational-legal authority ➤ **legal *authority**.

rational problem-solving The reaching of a solution to a problem through the use of logical, systematic reasoning. Most cognitive psychologists agree that this excludes procedures based on blind trial and error or on faulty logic even when they lead, fortuitously, to acceptable solutions. There is, however, considerable disagreement as to whether solutions achieved through nonconscious processes such as ➤ **insight,** ➤ **implicit *learning,** ➤ **incubation** and the like should be classified as rational.

rational psychology A covering term for any approach to psychology in which the overall theoretical structure for interpretation and understanding of psychological phenomena is grounded in a theological and/or philosophical framework. Note that the term really has a rather narrow reference in that defense of the position derives from the philosophical foundations of ➤ **rationalism**. Rational psychology is, thus, usually contrasted sharply with empirical or scientific approaches to psychology.

rational types In Jung's classification of personality types, individuals whose dominant mode of functioning is based on feeling and thinking. These types were contrasted with the so-called *irrational types*, who tend to utilize sensing and intuiting. Note that by *irrational*, Jung really meant *nonrational*. ➤➤ **function types**.

rational uniformity Social uniformity based on the (rational?) assumption that it is usually easier and ultimately to one's advantage to conform to social norms. The term is used to characterize behavior based, not on one's true personal desires or values, but rather on the belief that one can profit by going along with others.

ratio production ➤ **methods of *scaling**.

ratio reinforcement ➤ **reinforcement, ratio**.

ratio scale ➤ **scale, ratio**.

'rat man' In the psychoanalytic literature, the sobriquet for the man described by Freud in his classic analysis of an obsessive neurotic.

rauwolfia alkaloids A group of drugs derived from an Indian climbing shrub that includes ➤ **reserpine** (see for more detail).

raw data Data which have not been coded, transformed or analyzed. ➤ **raw *score**.

Rayleigh equation A quantitative relationship between the proportions of red and green needed to match a given yellow. Typically, the subject is given a spectral green and a spectral red and required to mix them until they match the hue of a spectral yellow target. The resulting equation is a sensitive test for *anomalous *trichromacy*.

R correlation In the personality theory of Raymond B. Cattell, in which traits are identified through correlational analysis, four techniques are identified: O, P, Q and R correlations. When no letter precedes, it is understood that the R technique is referred to. In a standard Cattell analysis, the data will consist of (a) persons, (b) their performance on specific tasks and (c) particular task conditions. The R technique looks for correlations between tasks; the Q technique correlates persons; the P technique correlates each person with the tasks and conditions; the O technique analyzes the intercorrelations between tasks and conditions. The R and Q techniques yield single correlations, the P and O techniques produce correlation matrices. The traits and factors that make up Cattell's complex theory of personality derive from analyses of these kinds.

reactance, psychological An unpleasant drive state brought about by a threat to one's perceived freedom.

reactance theory A point of view which maintains that, under the appropriate circumstances, people will react against attempts to restrict or control their choices and decisions. The theory makes two important predictions: (a) because the attractiveness or desirability of an object or activity is assumed to be related to the opportunity to choose it or engage in it, the more the individual perceives that others are attempting to limit his or her opportunities the more attractive the object or activity becomes; and (b) when an individual perceives that strong pressure is being exerted to force a particular decision or attitude, the person will tend to become contrary and resist the pressure by selecting an opposing perspective. ➤ **reactive** (3).

reaction 1. Basically, a 're-action,' response, act, movement, etc. that an organism makes when stimulated. 2. By extension, a group or social response against social change. The connotation here is that this kind of reaction is politically or culturally conservative in the extreme, or *reactionary*. 3. In psychiatry, a cluster of behaviors or a syndrome characteristic of a particular disorder. Often the longer phrase, *reaction pattern*, is used; ➤ **reaction formation**.

reaction chain ➤ **chaining**.

reaction, false 1. Any response to an inappropriate stimulus. 2. A ➤ **false alarm**.

reaction formation The process through which unacceptable feelings or impulses are controlled by the establishing of behavior patterns which are directly opposed to them. According to classical psychoanalytical theory, reaction formation operates by repressing the original impulse, which is assumed to continue to exist unconsciously in its original form and is, thus, likely to emerge under some circum-

stances. The concept has played an important role in theoretical analyses of various clinical cases, e.g., those where a pattern of antisocial behavior precipitously emerges in a person with a past history of kindliness and solicitude.

reaction pattern ➤ **reaction** (3).

reaction potential In Hull's learning theory, the likelihood of occurrence of a particular response.

reaction process A general term used to refer to the full sequence of acts involved in ➤ **reaction time** experiments.

reaction range In behavioral genetics, the limits on the expression of a *phenotype* that are imposed by the *genotype*. Compare with ➤ **norm of reaction**.

reaction-specific energy ➤ **action-specific energy**.

reaction time (RT) Generally, the minimum time between the presentation of a stimulus and the subject's response to it. The RT is one of experimental psychology's oldest dependent variables and several specialized types have been studied. They are described in the following entries. Note that the term is used for the actual time that it takes a subject to respond as well as the experimental procedure that uses RTs as the basic data. When unqualified, the term refers to ➤ **simple *reaction time**.

reaction time, associative In word association experiments, the time between the presentation of the stimulus word and the subject's verbal response.

reaction time, choice An extension of ➤ **simple *reaction time** in which the subject is confronted with two (or more) stimuli and two (or more) corresponding responses.

reaction time, complex (or **compound**) Any reaction time where two (or more) stimuli and/or two (or more) responses are employed, i.e. all possible variations other than the ➤ **simple *reaction time**.

reaction time, discrimination A variation

of ➤ **choice** ***reaction time** in which there are two distinctive stimuli and the subject is instructed to respond to but one of them and refrain from making a response to the other.

reaction time, disjunctive An umbrella term covering ➤ **choice, complex,** and **discrimination *reaction time** procedures.

reaction time, simple The minimum lag between a single simple stimulus (e.g., a light, a tone) and the subject's making of a single simple response (e.g., pressing a button, releasing a switch).

reactivation of memory A term often used with respect to memories which have been 'triggered' by some external cue or event. For example, ➤ **priming**.

reactive 1. Very generally, a synonym for ➤ **responsive**. However, there are two additional meanings of the term that are occasionally intended: **2.** Pertaining to or characterizing an action that is a reaction. That is, of an action that is not internally motivated but rather occurs as a response to a particular stimulus or to particular actions of another. This is the sense intended in most of the compound terms containing this word as given in the following entries. **3.** Contrary. This usage amplifies the preceding by appending the notion that the reaction is an attempt to rescue one's personal freedom from attempts by others to restrict choice or direct behavior. ➤ **reactance theory**.

reactive attachment disorder A disorder of childhood or infancy characterized by the failure of the child to develop normal social relatedness prior to the age of five. The disturbance is marked either by persistent failure of the child to initiate or respond appropriately to social interactions or (in older children) by indiscriminate sociability particularly with strangers and other socially inappropriate individuals. The disorder is presumed due to grossly pathological early care marked by a lack of normal physical and social stimulation, since it has been observed even when there is good nutrition and sanita-

tion. Note, the term is not used if there is evidence of mental retardation or any other pervasive developmental disorder. Also called *hospitalism*; ➤➤ **anaclitic depression** and **failure-to-thrive**.

reactive depression ➤ **depression, reactive**.

reactive inhibition ➤ **inhibition, reactive**.

reactive psychosis A general term for a psychosis that stems from strong environmental pressures and stresses. ➤ **brief reactive psychosis**.

reactive reinforcement In psychoanalysis, a hypothesized process whereby conscious attempts at emotion and affect bolster ('reinforce') the opposite emotion at an unconscious level. Conscious aggression theoretically stimulates unconscious non-aggression and vice versa.

reactive schizophrenia ➤ **schizophrenia, reactive**.

reactive type A general term applied to individuals whose primary mode of behaving is by reacting to others.

readability 1. Loosely, a measure of the understandability of written text as given by an analysis of a variety of factors, including syntactic complexity, vocabulary, thematic expression, continuity of themes and the like. **2.** A measure of how readable a text is based on the average grade level of readers who can read and understand it.

These two usages are insidiously contradictory and lead to anomalous constructions like 'One would be advised to lower the readability of the school's text books.' What such a statement means in sense 2 is that the texts used for, say the 5th-graders, are written at too high a level for the average 5th-grade student. However, in sense 1 it connotes that the understandability of the text should be lowered; that it should be made harder to read. Since both meanings are used widely, caution is advised.

readiness 1. A position of preparedness in which an organism is set to act or to respond. **2.** A state of a person such that they are in a position to profit from some experience. Depending on the type of experience, this state may be conceptualized as relatively simple and biologically determined (e.g., sexual readiness) or developmentally and cognitively complex (e.g., reading readiness).

readiness, law of In Thorndike's early theory of learning, the hypothesized principle that satisfaction was derived from the functioning of behavioral 'conduction units' (a notion that was never clearly specified) which were ready to function. This 'law' and its corresponding *law of unreadiness* (functioning is unpleasant if the unit is not ready) are now only of historical importance.

readiness test A general label for any test that assesses ➤ **readiness** (2). Such tests are a common feature of educational programs.

reading 1. In simplest terms, the process by which information is extracted from written or printed text. This process, in fact, is extremely complex and only partly understood, although two critical aspects of it deserve mention here. First, the process of reading is dependent on the written format, the ➤ **orthography**. To read an alphabetic system of writing like English requires that one decode the phonetic relationships that exist between the marks on the page (letters) and the sounds of the spoken language, whereas to read a logographic system like Chinese requires one to match the marks on the page (the ideograms) with the word or concept in the language that each represents. Thus, alphabetic systems carry an intervening stage of decoding of the phonetic component, a stage not involved in the use of logographic systems. The term *reading*, therefore, entails different cognitive and perceptual processes depending on orthographic form. Second, reading consists of both a phonetic/acoustic process and a semantic/syntactic process. Consider the hypothetical example of an illiterate Greek farmer and his English professor friend whose schooling has taught him how to

pronounce all the Greek letters and letter combinations although he cannot speak a word of modern Greek. The professor pronounces what for him are the nonsense sounds from a Greek newspaper for his illiterate friend, who comprehends their meaning perfectly. Neither of the two can be said to be *reading*, yet between them they represent the skills that a reader must have. The purpose of raising these points here is to clarify to the reader that many simplistic definitions of reading which characterize the process in terms of pronouncing words are misleading and blur the deeper, more important aspects of this complex process. It is likely that many of the problems involved in the teaching of reading derive from our failure as yet to understand fully these various processes.
  2. By extension of the word *text* in the simple definition given above, the term is also applied to the extraction of information from Braille symbols, from musical notation, from patterns of lip movements, of gestures, etc. 3. In parapsychology, the interpretations of a fortune-teller, phrenologist, palmist, etc.

reading age 1. The typical age at which a normal child is generally expected to begin to learn to read. This meaning is outmoded and simplistic; see the discussion under ➤ **reading readiness**. 2. A score on a standardized reading test given in terms of *age equivalent* scores.

reading disability (or **disorder**) ➤ **developmental *reading disorder**.

reading-disabled child ➤ **developmental *reading disorder**.

reading disorder, developmental An ➤ **academic skills disorder** characterized by a marked failure in learning to read. It is usually (but not always) reserved for a child who falls significantly (i.e. two or more grades) below the norms for his or her age and educational level (provided that the child does not show any significant mental retardation and no obvious neurological pathology). ➤➤ **dyslexia**.

reading readiness A term used to characterize the degree to which a child is prepared to profit from instruction in reading. Exactly what competences and skills define this 'readiness' are far from clear, but a variety of factors, perceptual, cognitive, emotional and motivational, have been implicated. The notion that chronological age is, in any sense, the indicator is misleading.

reading span Roughly, the amount of written text that can be perceived within a single ➤ **fixation pause**. Although various values such as seven to ten letter-spaces are often cited as typical, several facts about this span must be noted: (a) the size of the span corresponds to foveal vision and the number of letter-spaces within this region will depend on the size of the type used in the printing of the material and the distance at which the text is held from the eyes; (b) some information outside the foveal area can be used by a fluent reader during the course of normal reading, e.g., spaces between words, capital letters, etc.; (c) the fovea is circular and most measurements of reading span are made only linearly using a single line of text at a time. In normal reading, information from adjacent lines is also often picked up and used. Occasionally called *eye span* or *visual span*.

reafference A cover term for those sensory events that are produced by voluntary movements of a sense organ, e.g., those resulting from the movement of an image across the retina that accompany voluntary movements of the eye. They are contrasted with *exafference*, or those sensory events produced by changes in the stimulus itself, e.g., those resulting from movement of an image across the retina that accompany real displacements of the physical object.

real **1.** Existing, actual, nonimaginary. **2.** Empirical, as opposed to theoretical. **3.** Physical, as opposed to mental; objective, as opposed to subjective.

real anxiety = ➤ **objective anxiety**.

real definition ➤ **definitions**, especially (c).

realism **1.** A philosophical point of view which argues that abstract concepts have a coherent real existence and are thus subject to empirical study. Contrast with ➤ **nominalism** (1). **2.** A philosophical point of view which maintains that the physical world has a reality separate from perception and mind. Contrast with ➤ **idealism** (1). **3.** An attitude generally characterized as the recognition that there are limits to the impact that one can have upon the world. Distinguish from ➤ **conservatism**, which resists change, and from ➤ **idealism** (2), which ignores issues of pragmatics. **4.** A term used by Piaget in some of his earlier writings to characterize a young child's belief that its perceptual perspective is shared by others; e.g., if the child can see a photograph held up by an adult the child assumes that the adult can also see it. See here ➤ **egocentrism**, which is used more or less equivalently.

reality **1.** Most restrictively, those aspects of the physical universe that are directly or indirectly measurable. In this sense, reality is objective and limited to what can be publicly and reliably measured. **2.** By extension, the term may be used to include constructs that are inferable or interpretable from logical induction or theoretical analysis, but not measurable in the above sense; e.g., gravity, natural selection, personality, etc. would all be regarded as parts of reality by 2, although they may be problematical by 1. **3.** By yet another extension, the term is used by many to include all that which forms an integral part of what an individual believes to be 'real.' Thus, free will, ghosts, God, etc., form a compelling part of reality for some but not for all. See, for an extension of this last meaning, ➤ **social *reality**.

reality adaptation In psychoanalytic theory, the process through which the infant gradually brings its perceptions, desires, needs, etc. into line with the external reality. It is often characterized as a trading-in of the pleasure–pain principle for the reality principle.

reality, contact with Perceiving and assessing the environment in ways coordinate with one's social and cultural schemes and values. Note that in this phrase the word *reality* is used in the sense of ➤ **social *reality** and not necessarily in any of the other meanings that it has; see here ➤ **reality**.

reality, flight from Generally, the use of fantasy and imaginary satisfactions to avoid dealing with a harsh reality. It may be manifested in any number of ways including excessive daydreaming, inappropriate rationalization, a resorting to drugs or alcohol and, in extreme cases, ➤ **fugue**. Also called *retreat from reality*.

reality monitoring A term coined by M. K. Johnson for the cognitive functions involved in paying attention to, coding, and processing the events in one's life.

reality principle 1. In psychoanalytic theory, the recognition of the real environment by the child, the growing awareness of its demands and the need to accommodate to them. Normal development is seen here as the acquisition and strengthening of this reality principle to function as a brake on or modifier of the more primitive, unreal, pleasure principle. **2.** In speech-act theory, the assumption that the speaker is talking about real things and events.

reality, social ➤ **Reality** (3) that is dependent upon or, indeed, defined by the consensus of a group. The term is applicable to anything from very small groups to a whole society. Thus, the social reality shared by a small band of fanatics who are awaiting the end of the world on a mountain-top is as 'real' as the nearly universal belief in the value of education.

reality-testing 1. Very generally, any process by which an organism systematically assesses the limits upon its behavior which the external environment imposes. This meaning is inclusive of the following more specialized uses of the term. **2.** A set of perceptual, cognitive and sensorimotor acts that enables one to determine one's relationship with the external physical and social environments. This meaning is typically expressed with the connotation that one is determining just how far one can go in having an impact on the environment, in attempting to modify or alter events and processes. In childhood, this is viewed as an intimate aspect of cognitive growth and socialization. A breakdown of reality-testing in this sense in adulthood is taken as symptomatic of a ➤ **psychotic disorder**. **3.** In psychoanalytic theory, a set of ego functions that enable the child to distinguish between subjective impression and external reality and to adjust the primitive subjective components to the constraints of the objective environment. ➤ **Delusions** and ➤ **hallucinations** are viewed here as failures of reality-testing.

real motion ➤ **motion, real**.

reason 1 n. A rough synonym for logical thought. Originally, reason was viewed as an integral mental *faculty* which functioned in a purely *rational* manner. This meaning is rarely intended in contemporary writings. **2** n. A justification offered as an explanation (or apology) for one's actions, usually expressed in terms of one's motivations. **3** n. An objective cause for some event. **4** n. A logical, sound mind. **5** vb. To think rationally and logically.

reasoning 1. In general, thinking, with the implication that the process is logical and coherent. **2.** More specifically, problem-solving, where well-formed hypotheses are tested systematically and solutions are logically deduced. Note that the term is used so that it is the cognitive processes that are of concern, not whether the correct outcome is achieved. Perfectly logical reasoning can easily lead to the wrong solution if one's initial assumptions are at fault.

reassurance A label for the myriad of devices that psychotherapists use to 'reassure' their clients that the therapy really is worth all the trouble and that a favorable outcome is in the offing.

reattachment ➤ detached affect.

rebelliousness, neurotic One of Karen Horney's forms of what she called ➤ **neurotic *resignation**. It is characterized by a continuous, active reaction on the part of the person. Horney hypothesized it as being directed either against outside persons and societal influences or toward one's own internalized regulations.

Reber's law This law, never before publicly articulated, was the outcome of work on this dictionary. It states, quite simply, that the closer anything is examined, the more complex it is seen to be.

rebirth fantasy In psychoanalysis, a fantasy of being born. Often expressed in symbolic form, e.g., a dream of emerging from water.

rebound (effect) 1. Generally, any phenomenon characterized by a distinct increase in some behavior following a period during which it was depressed or inhibited, e.g., a physical rebound following an illness. **2.** In the phrase *rebound effect*, however, the meaning usually is restricted to an increase in some physiological function following a period of inhibition or deprivation, e.g., an increase in REM sleep following one or more nights of REM deprivation.

rebound insomnia ➤ insomnia, rebound.

rebus A writing format based on the notion that two words that are homophones (sound alike) can be expressed using the same sign. Thus, we can cryptically render Shakespeare into a rebus orthography:

The rebus principle has been used as a teaching device in some reading curricula because it is a fairly painless way to introduce the child to the notion that, in alphabets and syllabaries, the marks on the page represent sounds and not meanings.

recall 1. The process of retrieving information from memory. Lest this definition appear disarmingly simple, the complexities lurking behind it can be appreciated by seeing ➤ **memory** et seq. **2.** An experimental procedure for investigating memorial processes whereby the subject must reproduce material previously learned. Compare with ➤ **recognition**.

recall test ➤ test, recall.

recapitulation theory As embodied in the rather catchy phrase, 'Ontogeny recapitulates phylogeny,' the doctrine that the development of an individual organism is a microcosmic replaying of the evolution of its species. The theory has had two, not unrelated, manifestations, one which focuses on biological and physiological factors (particularly the embryological) and one that focuses on the development of cognitive and perceptual skills. Taken literally, the generalization does not have much value, but the concept is still of interest as a heuristic for investigating various problems in evolutionary biology and developmental psychology. For an anthropological variation on this theme, ➤ **culture-epoch theory**.

Received Pronunciation (RP) The phonetician's technical term for the idealized standard pronunciation pattern of British English. The term derives from the sense of 'received' as 'accepted at court.' Hence, the phrase ➤ **King's English** is also used for this speech pattern. ➤➤ **Standard English**.

receiver In information theory, that which picks up the physical signal and converts it into a usable form. The term is used broadly and may refer to an electronic device, an organism's sensory-receptor system with its accompanying neural circuitry, or the organism itself, depending on context.

receiver-operating characteristic (ROC) curve A way of representing the data from a signal-detection experiment. The ROC curve plots the number of *hits* (trials in which the subject responds 'yes' and there was a signal) and *false alarms* (subject responds 'yes' but there was no signal) depending on the number of *catch trials* (trials where there was, in fact, no signal present). The result is a sensitive measure of the subject's true sensory sensitivity. ➤ **signal-detection theory** for more detail.

receiving hospital A hospital to which patients come for diagnosis, evaluation and preliminary treatment. Those deemed to require long-term care or hospitalization are referred elsewhere.

recency effect The common finding that in a free-recall experiment the items that were presented toward the end of a list (i.e. most recently) are more likely to be recalled than those in the middle. ➤ **primacy effect** and **serial position effect**. Also known as the *law* (or *principle*) *of recency*.

receptive aphasia ➤ **Wernicke's *aphasia**.

receptive character Fromm's term for an individual who is excessively passive and requires a great deal of support and guidance from those about. Also called *oral passive*.

receptive dysphasia ➤ **developmental *language disorder**.

receptive-expressive aphasia ➤ **global *aphasia**.

receptive field 1. With respect to any single cell in any part of the visual system, that area in the retina which, upon presentation of a visual stimulus, will produce a reliable change (either excitatory or inhibitory) in that cell's pattern of firing. 2. By extension, an analogous region on the body surface.

receptive language disorder ➤ **developmental *language disorder**.

receptivity 1. Openness, acceptance, passivity. Note that, depending on the context, the term may have positive connotations, in that one who displays receptivity may be seen as non-dogmatic, flexible and reasonable, or it may have negative connotations, in that the characterization is of one who is weak, passive and dependent

(see here ➤ **receptive character**). 2. A state in a female animal of a willingness to copulate.

receptor In most general terms, a specialized neural cell or part thereof that transduces physical stimuli into receptor potentials. That is, a cell that is responsive to a particular form of stimulation and which reliably undergoes a particular pattern of change. Such a definition is wide enough for all of the following to be properly regarded as receptors: (a) peripheral cells in the various sensory systems that respond to specific forms of physical energy, e.g., rods and cones in the retina, hair cells in the organ of Corti of the inner ear, pressure-sensitive cells in the skin, taste buds in the tongue, etc.; (b) proprioceptors that respond to internal stimulation, e.g., the hair cells in the semicircular canals of the inner ear, the stretch receptors in the viscera, the kinesthetic receptors in the joints and tendons, etc.; and (c) the postsynaptic neurons that respond to the release of neurotransmitter substances within the nervous system; see here ➤ **receptor site**.

Several systems for classifying receptors have been used over the years. Some are keyed to location of the receptors in the body, e.g., exteroceptors, interoceptors and proprioceptors; some are based on the specific modality served, e.g., visual receptors, auditory receptors, etc.; some are dependent on identification of the form of the physical stimuli to which the receptors are sensitive, e.g., chemical receptors such as those serving taste and smell, mechanical receptors for pressure and audition, photic receptors in vision, temperature receptors for warm and cold, etc.; and others are keyed to the neurotransmitter substances that mediate the neural pathway that serves the particular receptor system, e.g., cholinergic receptors, dopaminergic receptors, etc. Note that this last classification system is predicated on central-nervous-system considerations rather than on the specific sensory systems that initiate the neural changes. Generally, the context within which the particular receptors are discussed makes clear the classification system in use.

receptor potential A graded potential change in receptor cells that lack axons and, hence, do not produce action potentials. Receptor potentials are transmitted (chemically or electrically) to neurons with axons. They function by raising or lowering the likelihood of firing of these axonal neurons. ➤ **action potential** and *generator potential*.

receptor site A specific area of the membrane of a cell that is sensitive to a particular neurotransmitter or hormone. The presence of that substance will initiate a characteristic sequence of changes in the cell.

recess 1. A period of rest between periods of work or activity. 2. In anatomy, a small depression or cavity in an organ or structure.

recessive 1. Generally, not dominant, holding back, receding, not expressed. 2. In genetics, of one allele of a gene pair which is suppressed by the other and therefore is not expressed in the phenotype. 3. In genetics, characterizing a trait that only emerges in the phenotype when both parents contribute the recessive gene, a trait that remains latent if suppressed by the dominant gene. See here ➤ **dominance** (especially 2); ant., *dominant*, but see that entry for specifics on usage.

recessive trait ➤ **recessive** (3).

recidivism From the Latin for *relapse*, a return to delinquency or crime. Most restrict the term to forensic matters: a recidivist is typically defined as one who has had a second (or further) conviction or incarceration. Some, however, extend the meaning to cover the recurrence of a mental disorder, although this is not generally recommended.

recidivism rate The proportion of persons in a sample who are incarcerated or institutionalized again within some specified period of time after discharge. It is often used as a measure of the effectiveness of treatment programs.

reciprocal 1 n. In mathematics, a number the product of which when multiplied by another number is unity; the reciprocal of any number n is $1/n$. 2 adj. Descriptive of any relationship in which the elements operate in coordinated opposition to each other, e.g., ➤ **reciprocal inhibition**.

reciprocal altruism ➤ **altruism**.

reciprocal assimilation ➤ **assimilation, reciprocal**.

reciprocal inhibition 1. The inhibition of the action of one neural pathway by the activity of another, e.g., ➤ **reciprocal *innervation**. 2. The inability to recall a word, name or image owing to the activation of another word, name or image. This meaning is dropping out of use; see the discussion under ➤ **interference** (4, 5) for reasons. 3. The inhibition of one response by the occurrence of another mutually incompatible response. This meaning is the one expressed in ➤ **reciprocal-inhibition therapy**.

reciprocal-inhibition therapy A form of behavior therapy based on the notion of ➤ **reciprocal inhibition** (3). Developed by Joseph Wolpe, it uses the technique of conditioning a new response that is incompatible with the response that is to be eliminated. For example, anxiety and relaxation are incompatible responses and a phobic disorder can be removed by conditioning a relaxation response to the stimulus that previously evoked an anxiety response. For more detail here, **desensitization procedure**.

reciprocal innervation ➤ **innervation, reciprocal**.

reciprocal roles ➤ **roles, reciprocal**.

reciprocal translocation ➤ **chromosomal alterations**.

reciprocity There are several specialized uses of this term, all of which carry the underlying meaning of mutual exchange, the notion of equal give and take. To wit: 1. In sensory psychology, the generalization that the duration and intensity of a stimulus interact to produce sensation, the so-called ➤ **Bunsen-Roscoe law**. **2.** In Piaget's theory of *cognitive* development, the cognitive process of recognizing that one can neutralize or control a factor for the purpose of studying a second factor and then later reintroducing the first. Such thinking does not emerge until the ➤ **formal operatory stage**. **3.** In Piaget's theory of *moral* development, the attitude that one should return a favor in kind ('You scratch my back, I'll scratch yours'). ➤➤ **punishment by reciprocity**. **4.** In Heider's ➤ **balance theory**, the principle that social attraction is mutual; if I know you like me, it increases the likelihood that I will like you.

recognition **1.** The awareness that an object or event is one that has been previously seen, experienced or learned. **2.** An experimental procedure for the study of memory; ➤ **recognition procedure**. **3.** Acknowledgement, taken generally, i.e. of achievement, of the validity of a statement, of a kindness, etc.

recognition memory Memory assessed by use of the ➤ **recognition procedure**.

recognition procedure (or **method**) An experimental procedure used in the study of memory in which the subject is required to respond to a series of test stimuli by stating whether or not they were among those stimuli presented in a learning session held earlier. Actually, there are many variations on this basic theme. The subject may be required to respond 'yes' or 'no' to each individual stimulus, to select previously seen stimuli from a large array, to sort new and old items, etc. Compare with ➤ **recall**.

recognition span An occasional, but slightly misleading, synonym for ➤ **reading span**.

recognition test Any test which relies on differentiating old, previously seen material from new material. Most multiple-choice exams are of this type.

recognition vocabulary ➤ **passive *vocabulary**.

recognitory assimilation ➤ **assimilation, recognitory**.

recollection A general term for 'remembrance of things past.' It is little used now in technical writings.

reconditioning Conditioning again. Thus we get two confusing usages: **1.** To 'recondition' a weakened response by reintroducing the unconditioned stimulus. **2.** To 'recondition' a new response to an old stimulus and thereby 'de-condition' the old response. Most authors intend the former, reserving ➤ **counterconditioning** for the latter.

reconstruction **1.** Generally, the act of restoring the original order or structure of a thing. **2.** In psychoanalysis, a procedure whereby extensive biographical and autobiographical data on an individual are interpreted (i.e. 'reconstructed') to provide understanding of contemporary behavior. **3.** In the study of memory, a procedure whereby the subject is required to restore a disrupted stimulus sequence to its original form or order. ➤ **reconstructive *memory** for further discussion.

reconstruction method ➤ **reconstruction** (3).

reconstructive memory ➤ **memory, reconstructive**.

recovered memory ➤ **memory, recovered**.

recovery **1.** Generally, the return to or re-establishment of the normal, original state of a person, an organ, a response, a neuron, etc. **2.** The act of retrieving information from memory.

recovery time The time required for a neuron to recover its normal state of excitability following firing. See here ➤ **refractory period**.

recruitment The neural process by which successive or prolonged stimulation increases the number of nerve cells excited. Also called *recruiting response*.

rectilinear Forming, characteristic of or characterized by a straight line. Used synonymously with ➤ **linear**.

rectilinear distribution ➤ **uniform * distribution**.

rectilinear regression = ➤ **linear * regression**.

recurrent brief depressive disorder ➤ **brief depressive disorder, recurrent**.

recurrent collateral ➤ **recurrent inhibition**.

recurrent inhibition A neurological phenomenon in which a cell, upon firing, produces a self-inhibiting action. Some motor neurons, for example, have a *recurrent collateral* process which, via an inhibiting neuron (a *Renshaw cell*), synapses back on itself and produces an inhibitory postsynaptic potential that prevents the motor neuron from firing for a time.

red The hue experienced when the normal eye is exposed to wavelengths in the range 650–730 nm. Actually, the reds in this range are perceived as having a slight tinge of yellow or blue in them and to produce a 'pure' red a small quantity of short-wavelength light must be added.

red-green (color) blindness The most frequently occurring form of partial color blindness, in which reds and greens are not differentiated. ➤ **dichromacy**.

redintegration 1. Generally, the re-establishing of a whole by the bringing together of its several parts, a 're-integration.' 2. More specifically, the capability of one aspect of a complex stimulus to evoke a response originally associated with the whole stimulus. 3. The recalling of many (or all) of the details of a complex memory upon presentation of one detail; ➤ **redintegrative *memory**. Also called *reintegration*.

redintegrative memory ➤ **memory, redintegrative**.

red nucleus A group of nerve cells in the tegmentum that forms part of the extrapyramidal motor system. It is an important link in the transmission of information along the corticorubrospinal system that runs from the cortex through the red nucleus to the spinal cord.

red-sighted 1. Heightened sensitivity to long-wavelength light, to the reds. 2. A tendency to see objects tinged with red.

reduced cue Any diminished or partial *cue*. Generally, after extensive learning or conditioning, a reduced cue can evoke the response originally associated with the full cue.

reduced score Any score or datum from which a constant has been subtracted.

reductio ad absurdum The reducing of a proposition to an absurdity. Generally used of arguments which disprove a proposition by showing that it leads to an absurd conclusion. Note that in logic it also refers to an indirect method of proving a proposition by showing that the denial of that proposition leads to a demonstrably false conclusion.

reduction division The type of cell division that occurs in ➤ **meiosis**.

reductionism Stated broadly, a philosophical point of view which maintains that complex phenomena are best understood by a componential analysis which breaks down the phenomena into their fundamental, elementary aspects. The core of the reductionist's position is that greater *insight* into nature will be derived by recasting the analyses carried out at one level into a deeper, more basic level. As such, the issue of reductionism in science is really an issue of degree, of pragmatic considerations and of that mysterious quality, elegance. The degree of reductionistic endeavor espoused by a theorist typically has little to do with the stated, 'pure' arguments of reductionism like final demonstrations of adequacy or underlying causal explanations of reality; rather it turns on pragmatic issues, and the debates that ensue are invariably over questions of the richness and depth of understanding provided by ceasing the effort at one point or another. This latter point is a subtle one and some examples may help.

No one doubts for a moment that neurological and biochemical factors ultimately underlie all behavior, but many question whether significant insights into psychological phenomena could ever emerge by characterizing them in such terms. The history of psychology abounds with such debates. The early structuralists attempted to reduce perception to elementary sensations, the Gestalt theorists countered by arguing that to do so *loses* explanatory power, for the perceived whole is not equivalent to the sum of its parts; contemporary behaviorists seek to reduce all complex acts to stimulus–response terms, cognitive theorists maintain that images, thoughts, plans, ideas, etc. exist as entities with causal roles to play in behavior whose reality is distorted by a re-casting into an S–R format; some personality theorists argue that personality is composed of distinguishable traits or that types of individuals can be identified, proponents of organismic and humanistic approaches insist that such an analysis does violence to the integrity of the whole person. In each of these cases, the debate is typically not over whether the more molecular components *exist*, it is over whether or not greater insight into the underlying nature of the phenomena under consideration can be achieved by reaching down to them. To borrow an analogy, we know that all of mathematics can be ultimately reduced down to the notions of set and set-inclusion, but this fact is of no pragmatic value to one who is attempting to establish an algorithm to solve a set of simultaneous equations. Insight into simultaneous equations is unlikely to emerge from considerations of set theory. In psychology too much has been made of ultimate reduction, especially with regard to the underlying physiological representations, without an appreciation of the fact that most of the issues surround points which are essentially ones of pragmatic reduction.

reduction screen In its simplest form, a large piece of cardboard that blocks the visual field except for that which can be seen through one (or two) tiny, clean-edged pin holes punched in it. The device is used in experiments where contextual cues provided by the background need to be excluded from the visual field.

reduction sentence ➤ **definitions**, especially (f).

reductive interpretation Jung's term for an analytic interpretation in which a particular piece of behavior is evaluated as an indicator of the existence of some unconscious process.

redundancy In information theory, the degree to which a message is constrained. One usually speaks of the amount of redundancy in terms of the predictability of the letters or words based upon what has gone before. For example, in the message, 'Today is Emily's birthday, she is ten years —,' the last word is essentially perfectly predictable and hence is utterly redundant. However, if the message is, 'My phone number is 386 847–,' then there is no way to know the last digit other than guessing and hence there is zero redundancy in the message. ➤➤ **entropy, information theory** and related entries.

reduplicative paramnesia ➤ **paramnesia, reduplicative**.

re-education 1. A true 're-'education in the sense that a lost skill or capability is re-acquired or relearned. **2.** A learning of a new set of adaptive habits to replace maladaptive ones. The former sense is generally found in discussions of persons recovering from disabling injuries or mental disorders, the latter sense in discussions of criminals, delinquents and, under some governmental systems, wrong-thinkers.

re-enactment Loosely, any re-experiencing of the feelings, actions, images or thoughts of an early event in one's life. The usual connotation is that the important feature of a re-enactment is the emotional, that the process has value in the alleviation of anxiety. ➤ **abreaction**.

reference axes In factor analysis, the axes of two orthogonal (independent) factors which are used as the frame of reference for the location of other factors.

reference group Any group with which a

person feels some identification or emotional affiliation and which is used to guide and define his or her beliefs, values and goals. The term is used even though the individual may not belong, nor even wish to belong, to the group; indeed, his or her perceptions of the group's values may be wildly distorted. Also called *positive reference group* to distinguish it from ➤ negative *reference group.

reference group, aspirational Any reference group which an individual aspires to membership in. The implication is that such a group has a more compelling impact on one's beliefs and values than a simple ➤ reference group in that the aspirational component demands a greater conformity to the ideals of the group.

reference group, negative A reference group which an individual uses as a countervalent balance point in guiding and defining his or her values. The negative reference group's values serve as a motivator for oppositional opinions and beliefs.

reference memory ➤ semantic *memory.

reference vector In factor analysis, the set of axes that define the basic coordinate space into which the various relations between factors given in the correlation matrix can be placed. In normal Euclidean space the ➤ Cartesian coordinates represent the reference vector.

referent The entity in the real world that is indicated or picked out by word, phrase or expression. Strictly speaking only concrete objects or events can be considered as referents, although some authors will stretch the term to cover abstractions which can be operationalized.

referral 1. The act of sending a patient or client to another physician, therapist or clinic for treatment. 2. The person so sent.

referred pain ➤ pain, referred.

referred sensation Generally, any sensory experience that is subjectively localized at a point other than the one actually stimulated; *e.g.*, ➤ referred *pain.

reflected color The color reflected off an object, its ➤ surface *color.

reflection 1. The core meaning is that of a rebounding, a casting back or returning of a thing, and it is used freely in the technical literature with this general meaning. There are also three more specialized uses: 2. A synonym for ➤ introspection. 3. A thinking about a thing, particularly with the notion of meditation upon a previous experience or event and its significance. 4. In factor analysis, changing of the signs of one (or more) columns or rows in a correlation matrix.

reflection of feeling A technique used in nondirective therapy in which the therapist rephrases what the client has said with an emphasis on the emotional aspects.

reflection spectrum ➤ spectrum, reflection.

reflectivity–impulsivity A hypothesized dimension of ➤ cognitive style based on the observation that in the solving of problems some people tend to be rather 'impulsive' and react quickly on the basis of the first thing that comes to mind while others are more 'reflective,' more systematic and tend to think the problem through before acting.

reflex 1. Generally, any relatively simple, 'mechanical' response. Reflexes are usually regarded as species-specific, innate behaviors which are largely outside of volition and choice and show little variability from instance to instance. This is the preferred meaning in the technical literature. 2. An unlearned stimulus–response relationship. This sense merely extends the above by including within the definition the stimulus conditions for evoking the reflex. 3. More metaphorically, any unthinking, impulsive act. This sense extends the above considerably and, although common, is not recommended.

Many authors will interchange *reflex* and *response* despite the fact that the term *response* carries none of the species-specific, innate connotations of *reflex* (at least in its preferred meaning). Hence, many compound terms have ended up in the literature under either or both general headings; e.g., the so-called *startle response* is often called the *startle reflex*. Terms not found below can be found either following ➤ **response** or under the alphabetical listing of the modifying term.

reflex arc The hypothesized neural unit representing the functioning of a reflex. This abstract arc is schematically represented by a sensory (afferent) neuron stimulated by physical energy and a motor (efferent) neuron to which the impulse is transmitted via an intermediary neuron. Also called *reflex circuit*.

reflex association V. M. Bekhterev's term for ➤ **conditioned response**; ➤ **reflexology**.

reflex circuit ➤ **reflex arc**.

reflex, conditioned (or **conditional**) ➤ **conditioned response**.

reflex facilitation The increase in the magnitude of a reflex by presentation of another stimulus that would not, by itself, produce the reflex. The classic example is increase in the knee-jerk reflex by grasping and squeezing an object.

reflex inhibition The inhibition of one reflex by a mutually incompatible one. See here ➤ **reciprocal inhibition**.

reflex latency The time between the presentation of the eliciting stimulus and the appearance of a reflex.

reflexology A mechanistic, behavioristic point of view that argues that all psychological processes may be represented as reflexes and combinations of reflexes. The label generally associated with the Russian physiological approach, beginning with I. M. Sechenov and developed further by I. P. Pavlov and V. M. Bekhterev, the latter being credited with coining the term.

reflex reserve A term originally used by B. F. Skinner to refer to the hypothetical reservoir of responsiveness remaining after reinforcement had terminated; operationally it was given as the number of responses made by an organism during experimental extinction. Although occasionally used as a synonym of ➤ **operant reserve**, it should really be restricted to cases of classical conditioning.

reflex sensitization An approximate synonym for ➤ **pseudoconditioning**.

reflex time ➤ **reflex latency**.

refraction 1. Generally, the bending or changing of direction of a wave of light, sound or heat as it changes speed when passing obliquely from one medium into another. 2. In vision, the ability of the eye to focus light to form an image on the retina. The ability in 2 is, of course, dependent on the principle of 1, where the cornea and lens are the refractive media.

refraction, error of An umbrella term covering a variety of conditions in which the refractive characteristics of the eye are such that the image that falls on the retina is out of focus.

refraction, index of A measure of refraction, a value that expresses the degree to which a ray of light is bent when passing from one medium to another.

refractoriness 1. An occasional synonym for ➤ **satiation** (2). 2. The state of a neuron during the various *refractory periods*.

refractory Stubborn, unmanageable, unresponsive. Clearly, a term with these meanings is going to have considerable currency in a field like psychology. It is used for people (especially children) who are unmanageable, for abnormal conditions that resist attempts at therapy, for diseases that are difficult or impossible to cure, for neurons that do not respond to stimulation, etc.

refractory period, absolute A very brief period of time during which neural tissue is totally unresponsive. It corresponds to the period of actual passage of the neural impulse along the axon, and, depending on the properties of the cell, ranges from 0.5 to 2 milliseconds.

refractory period, psychological A short

period of time during the processing of and responding to one stimulus when the processing of and responding to a second stimulus is slowed.

refractory period, relative A brief period of time following the ➤ **absolute *refractory period** during which the excitation threshold of neural tissue is raised and a stronger than normal stimulus is required to initiate an action potential. This period lasts for a few milliseconds before the threshold returns to normal.

regard That which can be seen or that which is being looked at; e.g., *point of regard* is the fixation point, *field of regard* is the visual field with the head held stationary, etc.

regeneration From the Latin, meaning *a making over, producing anew*. Thus: **1.** Generally, an emotional or intellectual renewal. **2.** In biology and physiology, the restoration of a neuron, organ or other bodily part.

region **1.** An area, a physical space. **2.** In K. Lewin's topological *field theory*, a psychological area in one's life space defined by present and contemplated acts, facts, feelings and thoughts and enclosed by boundaries. Lewin specified a variety of such regions, the more important of which are given below.

region, incident A ➤ **region** (2) that can be reached from another region without any other intermediary region being traversed.

region, inner-personal The ➤ **region** (2) in Lewin's theory that represents the inner psychological components of the individual. It is represented as differentiated into smaller regions and is surrounded entirely by the ➤ **perceptual-motor *region**.

region, neighboring Any of two ➤ **regions** (2) with a common boundary.

region of rejection In statistics, an interval of values sufficiently extreme for any result falling within it to be so unlikely under the assumptions of the null hypothesis that one can feel secure in rejecting the null hypothesis in favor of the alterna-

tive hypothesis. A result within this preset region (or regions if a ➤ **two-tailed *test** is being used) is considered to have ➤ **statistical significance**. Also called the *critical region*.

region, perceptual-motor A ➤ **region** (2) conceptualized as completely surrounding the ➤ **inner-personal *region** so that the only path of communication between the environment and the inner-personal region is through this area.

region(s), private Those ➤ **regions** (2) that are most personal and which, in a particular culture or under particular social constraints, are of relatively little public interest.

Registrar General's scale/categories ➤ **Hollingshead scales**.

regnancy H. A. Murray's term for the 'totality of brain processes occurring during a single moment.' Most other writers, when they borrow this term, focus upon the psychological aspect that a regnancy represents a single, brief, organized unit of experience; however, it should be recognized that for Murray a *regnant process* was a brain process.

regnant process ➤ **regnancy**.

regression A richly polysemous term in psychology. The core meaning of the term which underlies the various specialized uses is that of reverting, a going backward, a retreating; the opposite of *progression*. Thus: **1.** A reverting to an earlier, more primitive or more childlike pattern of behavior. When the term is used in this sense, the individual so characterized may or may not have ever actually engaged in the exhibited primitive behavior; a 12-year-old child may show regression by thumb sucking even though he or she never did so as an infant. Contrast here with ➤ **retrogression** (2). Moreover, the connotation of *relapse* is always present; regression is not used for primitive behaviors that were never lost. Contrast here with ➤ **fixation**. It should be appreciated that this meaning of the term has different evaluative connotations in different areas of usage: (a) in psychoanalytic theories, it has a negative implication, i.e. the notion that stress or anxiety is causing the individual to flee from reality into a more infantile state, but (b) in cognitive/developmental theories, it refers to a temporary falling back upon an earlier form of thinking in order to begin to learn how to deal with new complexity, and is viewed as a way-station in an ultimately progressive development of cognitive processing. **2.** In statistics, a relationship between the selected values on one variable (x) and the observed values on a second paired variable (y). When the ➤ **regression equation** for a set of data is worked out, the most probable value of y can be predicted for any value of x. The term in this sense is actually a shortened form of ➤ **regression toward the mean. 3.** In genetics, the ➤ **law of *filial regression. 4.** In reading, any eye movement back over material already read. The frequency of such regressions is related to the difficulty of the material and the reading skills of the individual. **5.** In conditioning studies, the reappearance of a previously acquired response. Such regression to a response lower on the ➤ **habit hierarchy** is most frequently observed during punishment of the dominant response. Many behaviorists take the effect here as a laboratory analog of regression in sense 1. adj., *regressive*, *regressed*; vb., *regress*.

regression analysis 1. Generally, any statistical use of ➤ **regression** (2) to analyze one's data. **2.** Somewhat more restrictively, the use of qualitative ratings on one variable to make quantitative predictions on another variable.

regression coefficient In a linear ➤ **regression equation**, the constant that represents the rate of change of one variable (y) as a function of variations in the other variable (x). When the *regression line* is plotted graphically, the coefficient represents the slope of the line and is thus a measure of its steepness.

regression curve The smooth curve fitted to a set of paired entry data from a correlation table. If the regression is linear, the curve will be a straight line, if it is quadratic there will be a single inflection point, etc.

regression, curvilinear Any nonlinear regression wherein the regression equation for changes in one variable (y) as a function of changes in another (x) is a quadratic, cubic or higher-order equation. It should be appreciated that although it is always possible mathematically to have a regression equation that will fit every 'squiggle' in the curve, most of these perturbations are due to sampling or measurement error and nothing is gained by such a 'perfect' fit. Whether a curvilinear regression is appropriate for a set of data is not always easy to determine, although there exist statistical tests for determining whether each higher order of equation increases significantly the goodness of fit for a given set of data.

regression equation The equation representing the relationship between the values of one variable (x) and the observed values of another (y). The equation is, thus, a formula which permits the prediction of the most probable values of y for any known x. Linear regression equations are of the form, $y = ax + b$, quadratic of the form, $y = ax^2 + bx + c$, etc.

regression, hypnotic Regression produced by the use of hypnosis. The phenomenon has been vigorously debated, some arguing that a true ➤ **regression** (1) actually takes place, others that the hypnotized subject merely acts out (i.e. mimics) the immature state suggested.

regression, linear Any regression that is represented by a linear ➤ **regression equation**. Linear regressions are always represented by straight lines; compare with ➤ **curvilinear *regression**.

regression neurosis A generic term for a neurosis which has ➤ regression (1) as its dominant symptom.

regression of y on x A phrase used to characterize the typical ➤ **regression equation** where values of x are used as the basis for making predictions about the most likely values of *y*.

regression time The amount of time spent in making regressive eye movements during reading. ➤ **regression** (4).

regression toward the mean A generalization, stated simply, that given any standard score on one variable, *x*, the optimal linear prediction of the standard score on another paired variable, *y*, will be closer to the mean of all the *y*-scores than *x* was to the mean of all the *x*-scores. The phenomenon is a result of the statistical assumptions built into the use of ➤ **regression** (2) as a means of making predictions and should not necessarily be viewed as a feature of nature.

regression weight A synonym for ➤ **regression coefficient**.

regret Generally, the feeling that, in retrospect, one might have behaved differently in the past or that things might have turned out better had events gone differently. ➤➤ **anticipatory *regret**.

regret, anticipatory A feeling that often accompanies a decision-maker when the various alternatives are considered. It is essentially a vague sense of worry about the possible negative elements that might result if a given choice is actually made, a kind of 'I will regret this action tomorrow' feeling.

regulatory behavior 1. In biology, any behavior that serves to maintain balance or equilibrium. Used here in the sense of the maintenance of ➤ **homeostasis**. 2. By extension to psychological systems, daily rituals and habits that help maintain emotional stability.

regulatory drive ➤ **drive, regulatory**.

rehabilitate 1. To restore to good form or proper functioning condition. 2. To restore to a previous condition or status. Note that the former meaning is not necessarily equivalent to the latter; in psychological writings the usual connotation is meaning 1. n., *rehabilitation*.

rehearsal 1. Practice of an act in anticipation of a time when its performance will be required. 2. Repetitive review of material previously learned with an eye toward a later need to recall it. In some contexts the process is viewed as a rather 'shallow' cognitive process dealing primarily with the surface, physical form of the material and not necessarily with its underlying meaning. In this sense, it is hypothesized by some as the procedure for keeping information in ➤ **short-term *memory**.

reification From its Latin roots the term literally means 'thing-a-fying.' It is the making real and concrete that which is abstract and/or hypothetical: or, better, the acting as if one believed that the abstract or hypothetical were real. From a purely rationalistic perspective it is a cognitive/emotional act of children and other unsophisticated folk; in reality, it is one of the more seductive ways in which social scientists distort and misrepresent the status of many of their hypothetical entities and constructs. When this occurs it is called the *reification fallacy*.

reification fallacy ➤ **reification**.

reinforce 1. To shore up, to strengthen, to solidify a thing. 2. To present a ➤ **reinforcement** or (more properly) a ➤ **reinforcer**. See both of these terms for details.

reinforcement There is considerable diversity in usage of this term. Most of the definitional variations, however, stem from theoretical issues in learning theory about what reinforcement is and how it functions. At the core of them all is a relatively simple meaning: 1. The operation of strengthening, supporting or solidifying something, or the event that so strengthens or supports it. Since the term is most commonly found in the literature on learning, the 'something' strengthened is generally considered to be a learned response of the bond between that response and a stimulus. 2. In classical conditioning, the unconditioned stimulus (US) when it is presented either simultaneously, overlapping with or shortly following the conditioned stimulus (CS). The US in these circumstances clearly functions as a reinforcer of the CS–US 'bond' in sense 1, since if it is omitted extinction of the CR occurs.

These first two meanings are relatively uncontroversial; 1 is a harmless tautology ('reinforcement reinforces') and 2 is a description of an empirically demonstrable state of affairs. The difficulties with the term emerge when definitions are offered which contain theoretical assumptions about the mechanisms involved, particularly when operant or instrumental behaviors are under consideration. To wit: 3. Any set of circumstances that an organism finds pleasurable or satisfying. While it is likely true that pleasurable or satisfying events will 'reinforce' behavior, this definitional effort only serves to pass along the problem. Since pleasure and satisfaction are no more definitionally tractable terms than reinforcement, nothing is gained here. Compare this usage, however, with that of ➤ reward, which some authors will treat as a synonym for reinforcement in this sense. 4. Any event or act which serves to reduce a drive. This is, of course, not a definition so much as a theoretical statement about the mechanism of reinforcement; see here ➤ drive-reduction hypothesis. As such, it has been largely abandoned because of a failure to find evidence for the operation of drive reduction in all those cases where reinforcement effects (in sense 1 above) are observed. 5. A termination or modification of a particular stimulating condition. This definition derives from ➤ contiguity theory which maintains that the last act performed in a situation is the one learned. Actually, as the defenders of this point of view were quick to note, it is no definition at all but rather an attempt to do away with the term *reinforcement* altogether. 6. Any behavior with higher momentary probability of occurrence than some other behavior. This meaning is expressed by the so-called ➤ Premack principle (which see for details) which emphasizes the relativity of reinforcement. 7. Knowledge of results, feedback about the correctness or

appropriateness of one's behavior. This sense is the one intended in essentially all areas of psychology where human beings are the primary experimental subjects.

This array of partially overlapping and, on occasion, contradictory definitions pleases no one, least of all psychologists, who find themselves often trapped lexicographically into the use of the term. In a very real sense, part of the difficulty results from attempts to treat the concept as if it represented a single fundamental principle that operated in all circumstances. Somehow, this seems rather wrongheaded; it seems rather unlikely that the same principles pertain when a hungry rat is fed after a bar press as when the Nobel prize is awarded for a brilliant scientific discovery – yet both 'reinforce' the behavior, in that the rat returns to press the bar and the scientist to the laboratory to work on other problems. Moreover, physical pain functions as reinforcement for the masochist, punishment may reinforce confession in one who experiences a deep sense of guilt, altruism is reinforcing for the noble and abdication of responsibility will serve for the authoritarian personality. The range and diversity of things which can function as reinforcement (in sense 1) is essentially without bound and the failure to discern any unitary underlying mechanisms has led to: 8. Any event, stimulus, act, response or information which, when made contingent upon the response that preceded it, will serve to increase the relative frequency or likelihood of occurrence of that response. This is the so-called 'neutral' definition, because it begs no theory and makes no presumptions about the underlying action or role of reinforcement. It is also inherently circular: the existence of reinforcement is predicated upon the observation of increased responding and increased responding is, perforce, evidence of the existence of there having been some reinforcement. Many have railed against this definition and with good reason. This kind of semantic boot-strapping is a feeble definitional basis for one of psychology's most used constructs. Nevertheless, it is the dominant meaning, it reflects fairly accurately the way in which the term is most often used and thus, for now, it will have to suffice.

Note, in all of the senses outlined the term itself may be found referring to (a) the procedure of presenting or removing the reinforcing event, (b) the theoretical process that is presumed to be involved in its action, or (c) the actual event or act itself. It is recommended that *reinforcement* only be used for the first two and the term *reinforcer* serve for the last.

Finally, there are uses of the term that do not touch upon the various disputes of meanings 1 to 8: **9.** In studies of reflexes, the operation whereby one reflex strengthens or increases the operation of another reflex: e.g., the magnitude of an eye-blink response will be reinforced by heightened muscle tone. **10.** In dream analysis, the process whereby the theme of a dream is amplified and supported by a secondary dream within the primary one.

reinforcement, periodic Any ➤ schedule of *reinforcement based on varying time intervals.

reinforcement, contingent Quite literally, reinforcement that is contingent upon some response. In the vast majority of uses of the unqualified term ➤ reinforcement, this is the intended meaning. Compare with ➤ noncontingent *reinforcement.

reinforcement, continuous A ➤ schedule of *reinforcement in which every response is reinforced. abbrev., *crf* or *CRF*.

reinforcement, differential 1. The reinforcement of only one response to a particular stimulus. All other responses made to that stimulus either are not reinforced or are punished. **2.** The reinforcement of a response to only one of several stimuli. Responses made in the presence of the other stimuli either are not reinforce or are punished. **3.** A label for a class of ➤ schedules of *reinforcement all of which are dependent upon responses being emitted at specified rates, e.g., *differential reinforcement of low rate*.

reinforcement gradient (effect) A generalization that the 'closer' a given previously unreinforced response is to a reinforced response, the more it is strengthened. Note that 'closeness' here may depend on spatial, temporal and/or structural conditions.

reinforcement, intermittent An umbrella term for all those ➤ schedules of *reinforcement in which some of the responses made go unreinforced. That is, all those schedules of reinforcement other than ➤ continuous *reinforcement and ➤ extinction. Also called *partial reinforcement*.

reinforcement, interval Any ➤ schedule of *reinforcement based on time intervals.

reinforcement, negative 1. Any procedure or method of training that uses a negative reinforcer. **2.** Any event, stimulus or behaviour which, when its removal is made contingent upon a response, will increase the frequency or likelihood of that response. See here ➤ negative *reinforcer, which is the preferred term for this meaning. Contrast with ➤ punishment, which is the presentation of an aversive stimulus, and with ➤ extinction, where reinforcement (of any kind) is no longer presented.

reinforcement, noncontingent Reinforcement which occurs independently of any behavior. For a sense of the role that such reinforcement can play in the development and maintenance of behavior, ➤ superstitious behavior.

reinforcement, positive 1. A procedure or method of training which uses positive reinforcers. **2.** Any event, stimulus or behavior which, when made contingent upon a response, serves to increase the frequency or likelihood of occurrence of that response. See here ➤ positive *reinforcer, which is the preferred term for this meaning.

reinforcement, ratio Any ➤ schedule of *reinforcement in which reinforcements are delivered on the basis of some number of responses; consult that entry.

reinforcement, schedules of Quite literally, any of the schedules under which reinforcements are presented to a subject dependent upon some spatial, temporal or sequential aspect of the response. In what follows, it is assumed that *operant* behavior is under consideration; although some of the schedules have been used in classical conditioning (e.g., *continuous reinforcement*) the use of the term schedule of reinforcement is rare in those contexts.

The fascination that many psychologists, particularly *Skinnerian* behaviorists, have with schedules of reinforcement derives from the simple fact that the reinforcement of behavior in day-to-day living is typically irregular and nonuniform. Gamblers do not collect after every bet, not every seed planted grows and many a political speech ends without persuasion of a voter. Yet, gamblers continue to lay wagers, farmers to plant crops and politicians (alas) to give speeches. Hence, there has been considerable effort invested in the examination of the effect that the schedule with which reinforcements appear has upon the development and maintenance of behavior. The following list includes the most thoroughly studied schedules of reinforcement. The classification system used here is more or less standard, although others may be found in the technical literature: first the 'simple' schedules, where there is a single type of contingency between responding and reinforcement, are presented; next the 'compound' schedules, where two or more simple schedules are in force, are described; finally the 'special' schedules, which do not fit neatly into either of the preceding classes, are outlined.

It will be clear, in practice, to anyone who plods through the following outline that the range of possibility is nearly without bound. The reader may also get the feeling that much of the research is little more than an exercise in esoterica. Even Skinnerians are occasionally beset with such intimations. Recovery from such self-doubt usually takes the form of listing the various applications in educational, industrial, organizational and therapeutic settings that have been made (which, admittedly, are many).

I. *Simple schedules*. All of the following are schedules in which there is but one, constant contingency between the response and the occurrence of the reinforcer. **1.** *Continuous reinforcement* (*crf* or *CRF*). Quite simply, every response is reinforced. **2.** *Extinction* (*ext* or *EXT*). No responses are reinforced. **3.** *Fixed ratio* (*FR*). A class of schedules in which the ratio between responses and reinforcements is fixed; i.e. reinforcement is contingent on a fixed number of responses being made since the preceding reinforcement. Thus, *FR 10* means that every 10th response is reinforced. Note, according to this usage, CRF is actually a fixed ratio schedule, specifically, FR 1. **4.** *Variable ratio* (*VR*). A class of schedules where the ratio between responses and reinforcements varies in some random or semi-random fashion but with a specific mean value. Thus, *VR 10* means that on the average every 10th response is reinforced. **5.** *Random ratio* [*RR*]. A variation on the VR schedules in which a ratio specifies the probability that any given response will be reinforced. In an RR 10, for example, there is a .10 probability that any given response will be reinforced, independent of the number of responses made since the previous reinforcement. **6.** *Fixed interval* (*FI*). Time-contingent schedules in which the last response made after a given interval of time since the preceding reinforcement has passed is reinforced. Usually the notation is given in minutes: *FI 3* means fixed interval 3 minutes. **7.** *Variable interval* (*VI*). Time-contingent schedules in which reinforcements are 'set up' on a random or semi-random sequence of intervals with a specific mean value. Thus, *VI 3* means that on the average the interval between potential reinforcements is 3 minutes. Note that VI schedules tend to produce very regular response rates while FI schedules tend to produce bursts of responses followed by periods of few or no responses. **8.** *Fixed time* (*FT*). A class of schedules where, like FI schedules, reinforcements are delivered at fixed time intervals but, unlike FI schedules, independently of any responses made or not made by the subject. **9.** *Variable time* (*VT*). Like FT schedules but here the time between reinforcements varies. **10.** *Differential reinforcement of low rate* [*drl* or *DRL*]. A class of schedules based on a specified rate of response which must not be exceeded for reinforcement to occur. Thus, in *DRL 10* (seconds), 10 seconds must pass between responses or no reinforcement is delivered; a response made too soon 'resets' the clock and another 10 seconds without a response must pass **11.** *Differential reinforcement of high rate* (*drh* or *DRH*). In contrast to DRL, here the rate must exceed some set value for reinforcement to occur. *DRH* 1 (second) means that the interresponse time must be less than 1 second. **12.** *Differential reinforcement of paced responses* (*drp* or *DRP*). A class of schedules that combines aspects of both DRL and DRH in that the rate of responding must fall within certain limits in order for reinforcement to occur. **13.** *Differential reinforcement of other behavior* (*dro* or *DRO*). A schedule which reinforces the failure of a specific response to occur. Thus, *DRO 30* (seconds) means that reinforcement will occur after 30 seconds provided that the response under consideration has not occurred in that interval; in effect, all 'other' behaviors emitted during that interval are being reinforced.

II. *Compound schedules.* The following are schedules where two or more simple schedules are combined into compound form. They may be either 'sequential,' in which case one component of the schedule must be satisfied before the other(s) is in effect, or they may be 'simultaneous,' in which case two or more schedules are in effect concurrently. **1.** *Tandem* (*tand*). A sequential schedule in which reinforcement depends upon the successive completion of two or more simple schedules. Thus, in *tand FI 2 FR 5*, the FI 2 component must be satisfied before responses count toward the FR 5. The full sequence is carried out without discriminative cues to the subject about which component is

in effect at any point in time. **2.** *Chained* (*chain*). A sequential schedule similar to *tand* except that a discriminative stimulus is associated with each component. **3.** *Mixed* (*mix*). A sequential schedule in which two or more simple schedules are presented either alternating or at random. As with *tandem* schedules, no discriminative cues are used. **4.** *Multiple* (*mult*). The same as a *mixed schedule* with the addition of discriminative stimuli to mark off each of the components. **5.** *Alternative* (*alt*). A simultaneous schedule where satisfying any one of the components produces reinforcement. After reinforcement, the schedule 're-sets.' Thus, in *alt FI 5 FR 50* reinforcement occurs after either the 50th response if it is made in under 5 minutes or after the 1st response at the end of the 5-minute period since the last reinforcement has elapsed. **6.** *Conjunctive* (*conj*). Similar to *alternative* except that here all components must be satisfied before reinforcement is delivered. **7.** *Concurrent* (*conc*). A general label used to cover all situations in which two or more schedules that are set up independently of each other operate simultaneously.

III. *Special schedules.* These schedules have time or rate components that do not easily fit into the above categories. **1.** *Interlocking* (*interlock*). A class of schedules where reinforcement is delivered upon completion of a given number of responses but where this number is changed as a function of the time since the last reinforcement. For example, a linear reduction in number of responses might be programmed so that the longer the subject waits the fewer the number of responses required for reinforcement. **2.** *Adjusting* (*adj*). A class of schedules wherein the requirements for reinforcement are adjusted systematically as a function of the subject's performance. For example, an FR may be increased or decreased depending upon whether the latency of the first response after a reinforcement is greater or less than some predetermined value. **3.** *Conjugate* (*conjug*). A schedule in which the intensity level of some reinforcing stimulus increases or decreases with the rate of responding; e.g., the brightness of a TV screen changes systematically with response rate. **4.** *Interpolated* (*inter*). A schedule in which a small block of reinforcements on one schedule is introduced, without discriminative stimuli, into a different ongoing schedule.

There are others but enough is enough. ➤ **clock, counter, cumulative recorder, operant conditioning, reinforcement, shaping, Skinnerian, time-out** and related terms.

reinforcement, social Broadly, any social event which serves to increase the likelihood or frequency of some behavior which preceded its presentation.

reinforcement theory A general term used for any of a number of theories of behavior that assume that the fundamental explanatory concept for understanding the acquisition, maintenance and extinction of behavior is ➤ **reinforcement**. The theories of B. F. Skinner (➤ **Skinnerian**) and Clark L. Hull (➤ **Hullian**) are classic examples of this genre.

reinforcer Any event or behavior which functions as a ➤ **reinforcement**, which has reinforcing properties. Note that although *reinforcement* and *reinforcer* are often used interchangeably (including in this volume), the former is best reserved for the operation or the process, the latter for the event or stimulus.

reinforcer, conditioned A reinforcer whose properties are not intrinsic to it but are due to association with another reinforcer, a learned (i.e. *conditioned*) reinforcer. Money is, of course, the classic example. ➤ **higher-order conditioning**, and compare with ➤ **primary *reinforcer**. Also called *secondary reinforcer*.

reinforcer, negative Any event or behavior whose reinforcing properties are associated with its removal and, conversely, whose presentation functions as ➤ **punishment**. Note that whether a particular aversive stimulus (e.g., an electric shock) is referred to as a *negative reinforcer* or as a *punisher* depends on the relationship between its presentation and/or removal contingent upon some operant response.

Terminating an existing electric shock after a rat presses a bar is a *negative reinforcer* for it will increase bar-pressing behavior; presenting a shock contingent upon a bar press punishes the response and decreases bar-pressing. Compare with ➤ **negative *reinforcement**, which is a synonym only in sense 2 of that term.

reinforcer, positive Any event, stimulus or behavior whose reinforcing properties are associated with its presentation and, conversely, whose removal will produce extinction. It is further proposed by some that removal of a positive reinforcer has punishing properties (➤ **punishment** for a discussion). Compare with ➤ **positive *reinforcement**, which is a synonym only in sense 2 of that term.

reinforcer, primary Basically, any event or behavior whose reinforcing properties are a naturally occurring result of the intrinsic characteristics of the species under consideration. In classical conditioning, the unconditioned stimulus (US) is such a natural event, as its presence under the proper conditions (➤ **classical conditioning** for these) reinforces the conditioned response (CR). In operant conditioning, the situation is somewhat more complex. While it seems clear that some events are manifestly primary reinforcers by virtue of the physiology of a species (e.g., food, water, moderate temperatures, sex, etc.), in many cases no simple way of making the determination exists. Compare with ➤ **conditioned *reinforcer**.

reinforcing stimulus ➤ **stimulus, reinforcing**.

reintegration ➤ **redintegration**.

Reissner's membrane The delicate membrane in the cochlea that separates the cochlear canal from the scala vestibuli.

Reiz German for *stimulus*. In some older works where the term was borrowed straight from the German it was abbreviated *R*, which caused no end of confusion since English-speaking psychologists were using this abbreviation for *response*.

rejection The core meaning is a failure or refusal to assimilate or to accept. Thus, a body can reject an organ transplant or a food substance, a parent can reject a child, an adult a lover, a committee an idea, a society a cultural value, etc. In all cases there is an implied system or structure that refuses or fails to incorporate a thing.

rejection, parental A parent's rejection of the child. There is no simple term for the reverse.

relapse Generally, the falling back into a previous state or into an earlier behavior pattern. It is used rather freely in moral, mental, physical and medical cases.

relation 1. Generally, a relationship between two or more events, objects or persons. The precise nature of the connection may vary considerably from author to author. Usually one of the following is intended: 2. A connection between two variables such that variation in one is accompanied by variation in the other; see here ➤ **correlation**. 3. A connection between propositions such that the truth or falseness of one implicates the truth or falseness of the other. 4. A connection between events such that one serves as an antecedent condition for the other. Note that one can, in a sense, order these last three meanings along a dimension that reflects the strength of relation, with 4 suggesting a strong, causal connection that is only hinted at in 3 and logically absent in 2. 5. A kin or ➤ **relative** (4).

relational learning ➤ **learning, relational**.

relational problems A loose term for difficulties in a relationship that are sufficiently serious to become the focus of clinical attention.

relationship 1. = ➤relation. 2. = ➤kinship.

relationship, primary In interpersonal relations, a basic, long-lasting relationship founded upon strong emotional ties and a sense of commitment to the other person. Unlike ➤ **secondary *relationships**, they tend to be rather diffuse, covering a variety of roles, behaviors and situations; they are generally not bounded by strict rules of interaction and the persons involved generally know each other extremely well. Primary relationships are such that one member cannot simply replace the other with a new person.

relationship, secondary In interpersonal relations, a relatively short-lived relationship between persons characterized by limited interaction, rather clear rules for relating and fairly well-defined social roles. Unlike a ➤ **primary *relationship**, they rarely have much in the way of emotional involvement and the members in the relationship can rather easily be replaced.

relative 1 adj. Loosely, characterizing a condition where an event or datum is regarded as having a ➤ **relation** to another event or datum. 2 adj. Not ➤ **absolute** (1); dependent upon other data, events or considerations for its meaning. The value, effectiveness or even the very nature of a relative event or datum is derived by taking into consideration its relationship with other events or data. 3 adj. Partial, incomplete. Here, for example, a response may be referred to as relative when it is but a part of the full response that might potentially be made. 4 n. A person with a particular ➤ **kinship** relation to another person.

relative deprivation/gratification The generalization that the rewards one receives are not valued absolutely but as relative to one's expectations. Being promoted to the post of general manager in a company may be viewed as relatively gratifying to a person whose expectation was an assistant manager's post but as relatively depriving for one who anticipated a vice-presidency. Note that a social/cultural element is generally implied in the use of the term in that one's expectations are often established relative to what other persons, particularly one's peers, value and achieve.

relative infertility ➤ **infertility** (2).

relative refractory period ➤ **refractory period, relative**.

relative risk The ratio of the ➤ **incidence** of a particular disorder or condition to the number of individuals exposed to the predisposing conditions. Relative risk is an important factor in recommending particular treatments that have known side effects or carrying out studies that have some potentially harmful consequences; they allow one to estimate whether the gains are worth the risk.

relativism ➤ **relativity**.

relativity (or **relativism**) A general principle that maintains that all experimental and physical events have meaning only with respect to their relationships to other events. From a relativistic perspective, events have no intrinsic meaning independent of other events or of a general framework within which they may be viewed. The principle, in some form or another, is found in nearly every branch of science.

relaxation 1. Most generally, the state of low tension in which emotional level is diminished, especially the level of emotions such as anxiety, fear, anger and the like. 2. The process used to bring about this state; see here ➤ **relaxation therapy**. 3. More specifically, the return of a contracted muscle to its normal resting state.

relaxation therapy Generally, any psychotherapy that emphasizes techniques for teaching the client how to relax, to control tensions. The procedure used is based upon E. Jacobson's *progressive relaxation techniques* in which the individual learns how to relax muscle groups one at a time, the assumption being that muscular relaxation is effective in bringing about emotional relaxation. Jacobson's techniques are often used in various forms of behavior therapy; ➤ **desensitization procedure**.

relearning 1. Simply, learning again material that had been forgotten or responses that had undergone extinction. 2. A procedure for studying memory or retention in which the effort required to learn the material a second time is compared with the effort needed on the initial learning experience.

releaser In ethology, any ➤ **sign stimulus** that serves communicative function and initiates social behaviors. In older texts, this notion is captured by the term *object of instinct*.

release therapy Generally, any therapeutic procedure based on the assumption that there is therapeutic value in the releasing of deep, pent-up, emotional conflicts. The client is invited, indeed encouraged, to express openly and actively anger, hostility, aggression, etc. Such techniques are often used in *play therapy*, *psychodrama*, *Gestalt therapy* and others. ➤➤ **catharsis**.

relevant other An occasional synonym for ➤ **significant other**.

reliability 1. Very generally, dependability. 2. In personality assessment, a characteristic trustworthiness; a reliable person is a responsible person, one who can be counted upon. 3. In psychological testing (and in measurement generally), a generic term used to cover all aspects relating to the dependability of a measurement device or test. The essential notion here is *consistency*, the extent to which the measurement device or test yields the same approximate results when utilized repeatedly under similar conditions. Compare here with ➤ **validity**. The degree to which a procedure is reliable can be assessed through a number of procedures; the more commonly used are listed below.

reliability, alternate forms A method of determining the reliability of a test by developing two (or more) parallel sets of items of similar types and difficulty and correlating the scores obtained from one form with those from the other(s). Also called *equivalent* or *parallel forms reliability*.

reliability, coefficient of A correlation coefficient expressing the degree of relationship between two sets of scores in which these sets of scores are the results from two testing sessions with the same instrument. The coefficient is then used as a quantitative expression of the ➤ **reliability** (3) of the testing instrument or measurement procedure. There are several different coefficients of reliability depending on the particular scores that are being compared. For example, the *coefficient of stability* is obtained in the *test-retest* method (➤ **test-retest *reliability**), a *coefficient of equivalence* provides an estimate of reliability when *alternate* or *parallel* forms of a test are used (see here ➤ **alternate forms *reliability**), a *coefficient of internal consistency* is obtained from intratest manipulations like the *split-half* procedure (see here ➤ **split-half *reliability**).

reliability, index of A statistic that provides an estimate of the correlation between the actual scores obtained from a test and the theoretical true scores. The index is given as the value of $\sqrt{r}$ where r is the calculated ➤ **coefficient of *reliability**.

reliability, interrater The degree to which two or more independent observers agree in their assessment of behavior. Whenever one is dealing with data that are dependent on highly subjective interpretations of situations, for example where shifts in facial expression of people in a conversation are being studied, high interrater reliability must be shown before the data can be accepted as valid. Also called *rater reliability*.

reliability, item The reliability of a test determined by the degree to which the items on a test measure the same construct. Also called *scale reliability*.

reliability, sampling Any evaluation of the degree of consistency of two samples of scores taken from the same population. ➤ **sampling** and related entries.

reliability, scale ➤ **item *reliability**.

reliability, split-half A general label for several methods of determining the reliability of a test by evaluating the test's overall internal consistency. The methods are logically similar to the equivalent forms procedure (➤ **alternate forms *reliability**); the single test is split into two forms and a ➤ **coefficient of *reliability** between the

two is obtained. The two halves of the test may be produced in any way provided the result is two comparable forms. Some common procedures are to put the odd-numbered items on one form and the even on the other, to alternate blocks of items from form to form or to assign items to forms on a random basis.

reliability, test-retest A method for determining the reliability of a test by administering it two (or more) times to the same persons and obtaining a ➤ **coefficient of *reliability** between the scores, on each testing. Usually a reasonably long period of time is allowed between the test and the retest, for obvious reasons.

religion Basically, a system of beliefs with either an institutionalized or a traditionally defined pattern of ceremony. Religion is regarded by many as a cultural universal which emerges invariably as an outcome of the need to understand the human condition. Most, although not all, religions share certain characteristics, notably the concept of a (or several) supreme being(s), the promise of a pathway to an ideal existence and an afterlife.

religion, comparative An interdisciplinary field that encompasses the work of sociologists, anthropologists, philosophers, social psychologists and theologians. The primary foci are: (a) those universal needs of human existence which (presumably) stimulate the development of religions: and (b) comparisons between the various theological and cultural factors which have given rise to the diversity of forms in which contemporary and past religions appear.

religion, psychology of A subdiscipline within psychology concerned with the origins of religions, their role in human existence, the nature of religious attitudes, of religious experiences, etc.

religiosity Involvement, interest or participation in religion. Although the term is used by some authors to denote a high degree of religious involvement, it properly refers to a continuum of degree of participation in religious ritual and practice, and one may also correctly characterize a person as displaying low or moderate religiosity.

religious instinct An assumed ➤ **instinct** (see that term for a discussion of the caveats involved in its use in a context like this) in *Homo sapiens* for religious beliefs. The virtual universality of religion in known human cultures has led some to conclude that it must be part of our native endowment, that it is 'instinctive.' Others, to be sure, have differing viewpoints.

religious trance ➤ **trance, religious**.

REM ➤ **rapid eye movements**.

remedial Of a training or educational program designed to correct deficiencies and to elevate the student or trainee to an acceptable (i.e. *median*) level. n., *remediation*.

remember To recall, recollect, retrieve, reinstate or reproduce an earlier experience, event, stimulus, etc. ➤ **memory** and related entries.

remembrance The act or product of remembering; ➤ **reminiscence** for more detail.

reminiscence 1. The general meaning is similar to that of ➤ **remembrance** except that it is often regarded as the unconscious recall of information while a remembrance is considered to be the result of a conscious effort to retrieve information. **2.** A rambling, sequential recalling of information about some earlier experience. In this sense, the connotation is that the process is a rather leisurely and enjoyable one. **3.** Simply, a synonym for ➤ **recall** (1). The unconscious aspect is absent in 2 and 3. ➤ **obliviscence**, the loss of information from memory.

remission A cessation of the symptoms of a disorder or disease. The connotation of ➤ **cure** is entirely absent from this term; the disorder or disease is still assumed to be present even though there are no apparent symptoms. The term is often used with the (guarded) connotation that the symptoms

are not expected to reappear; distinguish, on these grounds, from ➤ **intermission**.

REM latency The period of time between the onset of sleep and the first period of *REM sleep*. There are suggestions that unusually short REM latency is a symptom of depression.

remote Distant, removed, far away. The term is used in a variety of contexts, as given in the following entries.

remote association ➤ **association, remote**.

remote conditioning A relatively rare synonym for ➤ **trace conditioning**.

remote dependency Any statistical relationship between non-adjacent events. For example, in a pattern-learning experiment the stimulus that appears on trial n may be made to depend upon the stimulus that appeared on some remote, earlier trial $n - y$, where $y > 1$.

remote masking ➤ **masking, remote**.

remote perception Perception of a stimulus object through some intermediary device not normally used for the gathering of such stimulus information, e.g., the perception of the shape of an object probed with a stick or cane while blindfolded.

REM sleep A stage of sleep named for the rapid eye movements which are among its most salient characteristics. For more detail, ➤ **sleep**.

REM storm Extremely vigorous episodes of rapid eye movements (REM) during sleep. During such bursts the eye movements have very large amplitude and are often accompanied by facial movements, brow raising and eye opening. They are relatively common in neonates up to about 5 weeks of age and less frequent thereafter.

renal Pertaining to the kidney.

renifleur A *paraphilia* in which erotic stimulation is derived from odors, specifically from the smell of the urine of others.

renin A hormone of the kidney. Release of renin is produced by sympathetic stimulation or by reduction in blood flow in the kidneys. When released, it causes angiotensinogen in the blood to convert to angiotensin which, in turn, produces thirst as well as stimulating the adrenal cortex, resulting ultimately in sodium retention.

Renshaw cell A small neuron with a short axon that functions as an inhibitor of motor neurons. ➤ **recurrent inhibition**.

renunciation A tricky term with three related but different usages: **1.** In common parlance, a surrendering of self, will, title, inheritance, etc. **2.** In the psychology of religion, the surrendering of one's personal will or desires to what one perceives to be the will of one's God. **3.** In psychoanalysis, the *refusal* of the ego to surrender to either the primitive demands of the id or the unrealistic restrictions of the superego.

reorganization theory The theory that the primary process involved in learning is the altering or modifying of existing mental structures. This generalization appears most frequently in research in cognitive and perceptual processes and, like its base word, ➤ **organization**, its meaning derives from the assumptions of ➤ **Gestalt theory**. As such, it stands in strong opposition to associationistic theory, which assumes that learning is essentially the appending of new responses without structural reorganization; ➤ **associationism**. The term is used in a variety of contexts and it is not infrequently found in studies of personality and social psychology where the link with Gestalt theory is not always apparent.

repair mechanism In interpersonal communication, any statement or utterance designed to correct a misunderstanding. Repair mechanisms are of particular interest in early language development, during which a parent must frequently 'repair' a miscommunication caused by using a linguistic form beyond the child's competence or by a lack of attention on the part of the child.

reparation In psychoanalysis, the reduc-

tion of guilt by the doing of good works. In Melanie Klein's approach, reparation was considered a nonneurotic defense mechanism used to resolve ambivalent feelings toward objects and persons.

repertoire The full compendium of behaviors of an organism or a species. Some authors restrict the term to those behaviors which a given organism can currently perform, others use it more generally to include potential behaviors that a member of that species may perform. The latter meaning is more often the intended one.

repetition **1.** The practicing or repeating of some act. When this operation functions merely to *hold* information in memory, the term is essentially synonymous with ➤ **rehearsal**: when it functions to *improve* performance, the meaning is synonymous with ➤ **practice**. **2.** Any replica or reproduction. **3.** A single trial in an experiment. The repetitive aspect is missing in this meaning.

repetition blindness ➤ **repetition effects**.

repetition compulsion **1.** Generally, a common form of compulsion in which there is an irrational and rather irresistible desire to repeat some behavior. **2.** In psychoanalytic theory, the impulse to re-enact emotional experiences from early life independent of any advantage that may be derived from so doing.

repetition effects Quite simply, the effects on perception and memory of repeating a stimulus. One may observe *repetition priming* (➤ **priming**), where an earlier presented stimulus increases the likelihood it will be perceived or recalled on a subsequent test, or *repetition blindness*, where, perhaps surprisingly, the second of two rapid presentations of a visual stimulus is often not noticed.

repetition, law of ➤ **law of *frequency**.

replacement sampling ➤ **sampling with replacement**.

replicate To reproduce, to duplicate. Specifically, to duplicate as precisely as possible an experiment in an effort to see if the same results are obtained, to run a ➤ **replication** (1).

replication A term commonly used in discussions of experimental methodology but with two different (although semantically related) meanings: **1.** A second experiment that reproduces or replicates an earlier study. **2.** Each of the subdivisions of an experiment which contains all of the basic parametric variations of interest. Note that some use the term in sense 2 to refer to the operation of subdividing the experiment; in these cases, the term *replica* will be used to denote each part.

replication therapy A technique used in some behavioral-therapy approaches in which an attempt is made to reproduce real-life situations or to encourage reactions in the client which are similar to those made in real-life situations.

represent **1.** To stand for, in the sense of a symbol or substitute. See here ➤ **representation, representative**. **2.** To present again; often spelled re-present to distinguish from 1.

representation A thing that stands for, takes the place of, symbolizes, or represents another thing. In studies of perception and cognition one often sees reference to the *mental representation* of a stimulus event which, depending upon theoretical orientation, may be characterized as a direct mapping of the stimulus (➤ **direct realism**), an elaboration of the stimulus (➤ **constructivism**), a mental code of it (➤ **idea, image**) or an abstract characterization of it (➤ **proposition**). In psychoanalytic theory, dreams, memories, fantasies and the like are also called representations of unconscious factors and repressed impulses.

representative Having the characteristic of being able to take the place of a thing or to be substituted for it without disrupting the overall structure or introducing systematic bias. E.g., ➤ **representative *sampling, representative score**.

representative measure ➤ **representative score**.

representativeness A ➤ **cognitive *heuristic** in which decisions are made based on how representative a given individual case appears to be independent of other information about its actual likelihood. For example, when people read about a man who is conservative, enjoys mathematical games, tends to wear white, short-sleeve shirts, and has little interest in politics they are more likely to believe he is an engineer than a lawyer – and will continue to believe this even if told that he was selected randomly from a group composed of 70 lawyers but only 30 engineers. Representativeness is one of the reasons why people commit the ➤ **base-rate fallacy**.

representative sample ➤ **sample, representative**.

representative score A single score or number which, within recognized limits of confidence, can be taken as representative of a large number of scores. The term is most frequently used of the *mean* as a measure of central tendency that best characterizes ('represents') all the scores from which it is calculated. Also called *representative measure* and *representative value*.

representative value ➤ **representative score**.

repress **1.** Outside of psychoanalytic theories the term is used in ways similar to the common sense, i.e. to hold or put down, to suppress, keep from occurring. **2.** Within psychanalysis, to engage the operations of the defense mechanism of ➤ **repression**; see meaning 1 of that term for details.

repressed Loosely, characterizing any mental element that has been relegated to or maintained in the unconscious. Thus we have repressed wishes, repressed complexes, repressed desires, etc.; ➤ **repression** (especially 1) for a discussion of usage.

repression The basic meaning here derives from the root verb, *to repress*, which in various contexts means to put down, to suppress, control, censor, exclude, etc. Hence: **1.** In all depth psychologies from the classical Freudian model onward, a hypothesized mental process or operation that functions to protect the individual from ideas, impulses and memories which would produce anxiety, apprehension or guilt were they to become conscious. Repression is considered to be operative at an unconscious level; that is, not only does the mechanism keep certain mental contents from reaching awareness, but its very operations lie outside of conscious awareness. In classical psychoanalytic theory, it is regarded as an ego function and several processes are included under it: (a) *primal repression*, in which primitive, forbidden id impulses are blocked and prevented from ever reaching consciousness; (b) *primary repression*, in which anxiety-producing mental content is forcefully removed from consciousness and prevented from re-emerging; and (c) *secondary repression*, in which elements that might serve to remind the person of that which has been previously repressed are themselves repressed. An important corollary of this analysis is that that which is repressed is not deactivated but continues to have a lively existence at the unconscious level, making itself felt through projections in disguised symbolic form in dreams, parapraxes and psychoneuroses. Within these analytic psychologies, the term has a fairly clear referential domain and should be contrasted with other seemingly synonymous terms such as ➤ **suppression** and ➤ **inhibition. 2.** In sociology and social psychology, the limitations of a group's or an individual's freedom of expression and action by a dominant group or individual.

repression, organic A vaguely misleading term for the inability to recall past events owing to organic dysfunction, brain damage, etc. The word *repression* is misused here since the term is properly restricted to those conditions with an organic basis, whereas ➤ **repression** is used very differently. ➤ **amnesia**, which is preferred, especially ➤ **anterograde *amnesia.**

repression–sensitization scale A personality-assessment scale designed to evaluate an individual's defensive reactions against threatening stimuli. *Repressors*, as compared with *sensitizers*, have difficulty with threatening stimuli, often tending not to notice them. They also show poorer memory for threatening materials they have learned, have lower overall awareness of anxiety and a more positive self-image.

reproduction 1. Generally, the process of re-producing a thing, or the product of such a process. **2.** The process that produces a new organism from one (asexual reproduction) or two (sexual reproduction) parents.

reproduction method (or **procedure**) **1.** In the study of memory, any procedure in which the subject is required to reproduce as completely and accurately as possible all of the stimulus materials originally learned. **2.** In psychophysics, a synonym for the *method of adjustment*; see here ➤ **method of *scaling** and ➤ **measurement of *threshold** for details.

reproduction theory A theory of mental imagery or ideation that maintains that an image is a copy or point-by-point reproduction of the original stimulus. The last word on this discredited theory was provided by William James in 1890, who dubbed such a faithful mental image or ideal 'as mythological an entity as the Jack of Spades.'

reproductive assimilation ➤ **assimilation, reproductive.**

reproductive facilitation An increase in the ability to reproduce previously learned material caused by the interpolation of some other unrelated activity or material between the learning and the time of recall. This facilitation effect seems to result from a release of proactive interference; ➤ **release from *PI.**

reproductive function A biological term for those activities of organisms that result in new organisms. Note that both sexual and asexual reproduction are included.

reproductive interference A decrease in the ability to reproduce previously learned material resulting from the interpolation of some other activity or material between the learning and the time of recall. The effect seems to result from ➤ **retroactive *interference**.

reproductive isolation ➤ **isolation** (2).

reproductive memory ➤ **memory, reproductive**

reproductive ritual Any cultural ritual that centers on sex, sexuality, sex roles or other factors relevant to reproduction. Generally included are puberty rites, male or female initiation rites, elaborate taboos, as for example those surrounding menstruation, birth practices such as couvade, and the like.

Rep Test A personality-assessment test designed by George Kelly to facilitate the process of coming to know how an individual views his or her world. The full name of the instrument is *Role Construct Repertory Test* and it is used for diagnosing or assessing one's *personal-role constructs* which, in Kelly's theory, are essential components of personality. ➤ **personal construct** for more detail.

Rescorla–Wagner theory A generalization about conditioning due to R. Rescorla and A. Wagner that maintains that organisms do not merely respond to the *co-occurrence* of the conditioned stimulus (CS) and the unconditioned stimulus (US) but rather are sensitive to the actual *covariations* that exist between them. The point is that conditioning only occurs when a particular CS is a good predictor of the US. The theory provides an answer to the question, 'Why didn't Pavlov's dogs salivate to Pavlov since he was the one who administered the food?' The reason is because Pavlov was also there when the food was *not* delivered. Thus, unlike the bell, he was not a reliable predictor of the arrival of food; he merely co-occurred with it.

research Theodorson and Theodorson in their *Modern Dictionary of Sociology* (New York, 1969) provide one of the best comments on this term we've seen: 'Any

honest attempt to study a problem systematically or to add to [our] knowledge of a problem may be regarded as research.' No more really needs to be said; if more is wanted ➤ **scientific *method**, which is how most research is carried out in psychology as well as the other sciences.

reserpine An alkaloid of the Indian shrub *Rauwolfia serpentina*, this was the first ➤ **antipsychotic** drug to be used widely. In low doses it has a marked calming and sedative effect, in large doses it may cause seizures and, on occasion, severe depression. These side-effects make it no longer a legitimate choice as an antipsychotic, the ➤ **phenothiazine derivatives** being favored. It is, however, still used in small doses for hypertension because of its marked effects in reducing blood pressure and heart rate.

reserve 1. A reluctance to participate in social interactions. 2. That which is kept back, that which remains; ➤ **operant reserve** and ➤ **reflex reserve**.

residual 1. Generally, characterizing that which is left over or remains behind after some operation or event has occurred. 2. Pertaining to the perceptual function remaining following an accident, injury or operation, e.g., *residual vision*. 3. In factor analysis, characterizing that portion of the variance that remains after that accounted for by all of the factors has been extracted. n., *residual*.

residual phase That phase of an illness or disorder that occurs after the initial symptoms that mark the full disorder.

residual marker ➤ **marker, residual**.

residual schizophrenia ➤ **schizophrenia, residual**.

resignation Generally, an attitude of acquiescence, a giving up of the 'good fight' and accepting, with vague negative feelings, one's fate. However, note that Karen Horney differentiated between ➤ **dynamic *resignation** and **neurotic *resignation**.

resignation, dynamic Horney's term for a conscious, planned resignation in a situation where the person feels that it is mom-entarily unfavorable to further efforts on his or her part. It characterizes a situation in which the individual does not admit defeat and is alert for changes in the situation that may turn things in his or her favor. Compare with ➤ **neurotic *resignation**.

resignation, neurotic Horney's term for a psychoneurotic withdrawal from a conflict. She hypothesized three different forms which it could take, ➤ **persistent *resignation**, ➤ **shallow living** and ➤ **neurotic *rebelliousness**; see each of these for details and distinguish this class of reactions from ➤ **dynamic *resignation**.

resignation, persistent A form of ➤ **neurotic *resignation** manifested by inertia, ennui, passivity and a generalized lack of initiative in dealing with the ordinary conflicts and decisions of daily living.

resinous An olfactory quality typified by pine pitch; ➤ **Henning's smell prism**.

resistance 1. Generally, any action of a body that opposes, withstands, strives against or 'resists' a force. **2.** In electronics the opposition of any circuit or body to the passage of an electric current. **3.** In biology, the ability of a body to resist infection or stress. **4.** A personality trait typified by a reluctance to follow orders, respond to group pressures, etc. **5.** In psychoanalysis, opposition to making what is unconscious conscious. Note that some psychoanalysts also use the term somewhat more pragmatically to refer to the opposition against accepting the interpretations made by the analyst. In either case, the resistance is generally regarded as caused by unconscious factors. It is also regarded as universal in psychoanalysis.

resistance, conscious Deliberate, conscious refusal to divulge information by a client in a therapeutic situation. Distinguish from ➤ **resistance** (5), but appreciate that some theorists argue that unconscious resistance is the motivator of this conscious form.

resistance stage The second stage in the ➤ **general adaptation syndrome**.

resistance to extinction The extent to which a learned response continues to be made after experimental extinction procedures have begun. It is used as a measure of the strength of conditioning, particularly in comparing the effectiveness of various ➤ **schedules of *reinforcement** in maintaining operant behavior.

resistance to temptation Quite literally, the ability to resist temptation, specifically the temptation to engage in forbidden or taboo behaviors. Within psychoanalysis it is commonly interpreted as a measure of superego functioning.

resolution Generally, the solution of a problem by the coordination of all relevant elements and/or the taking of a novel but workable perspective. This meaning is applied broadly in the study of problem-solving, in decision-making and in psychotherapy, where 'resolution of a conflict' is often taken as the key to establishment of normal, nonneurotic functioning.

resolving power 1. Generally, in optics the ability of a lens to produce separate images of distinct but spatially proximate objects. **2.** Specifically, a similar ability of the eye. **3.** Metaphorically, the cognitive capability to make subtle discrimination between situations.

resonance 1. Sympathetic vibration in a body produced in response to an external vibration. **2.** Metaphorically, a property of a situation where two or more people are in agreement about the emotional aspects of a situation. This latter meaning, although basically nontechnical, has worked its way into the literature, particularly in the writings of humanistic psychologists.

resonance theory (of hearing) ➤ **theories of *hearing**.

resonance-volley theory (of hearing) ➤ **theories of *hearing**.

resonator Any device that uses the principle of ➤ **resonance** (1) to amplify a tone.

respiration rate Breathing rate. Commonly used as a measure of emotionality and arousal by comparing relative amounts of time spent on inspiration and expiration; see here ➤ **I/E ratio**.

respondent **1** n. Any behavior that is elicited from an organism by a specific stimulus, a classically conditioned response. **2** adj. Characterizing such a behavior. See and compare these two meanings with ➤ **operant**. **3** n. Loosely, any organism that responds to a stimulus – although this meaning is virtually always restricted to a person responding to items on a questionnaire.

respondent conditioning Skinner's term for ➤ **classical conditioning**.

response (R) There are real problems with defining this term. The difficulties are caused by its ubiquity and by the fact that in most contexts it is used with qualifiers. As a 'pure' term, one can identify several denotative domains, as follows: **1.** Any reaction of an organism to, or in the presence of, a stimulus. This usage is utterly general and utterly inclusive. **2.** Any muscular or glandular reaction or process made to, or in the presence of, a stimulus. This meaning was favored by early behaviorists. **3.** Any answer to any question. This sense is mostly found in research work using questionnaires and survey techniques. **4.** A unitary process that serves as a theoretical category representing all behaviors that share sufficient similarity to be regarded as functionally equivalent for the topic or issue under consideration. This meaning, although rarely specified, underlies all of the above. It is a necessary aspect of any definition of the term, since individual 'responses' differ from instance to instance. No two bar-presses are identical, all gaits are different, repeated utterances of even simple sentences may vary in their own ways as much as interpretations of a Beethoven sonata, and so on. This issue is made explicit in the Skinnerian definition of the term: **5.** A class of behaviors all of which have the same effect. Note, however, that in this context one further distinguishes operant re-

sponses (*operants*) and reflexive responses (*respondents*).

Note, finally, that there exists a large number of partial synonyms, e.g., *reaction*, *behavior*, *act*, *movement*, *process*, etc. Just how synonymous each is depends on the context and the biases of the writer. Generally, one can get away with almost any interchanging of these terms.

response amplitude The magnitude of a response measured along some set dimension, e.g., number of drops of saliva, size of a galvanic skin response. Note that the term is almost invariably restricted to discussions of classically conditioned responses. ➤ **response magnitude**.

response attitude ➤ **response * set**.

response bias Generally, any preference for making one particular response over any of the other alternatives available where that preference is exhibited independent of the relevant stimulus conditions. Response biases often pose difficult problems in research. For example, in experiments on ➤ **absolute *threshold**, subjects who are rather liberal with their 'yes, I detected it' responses will produce rather different data than those with a more conservative bias, even though presumably their sensitivity to the stimuli is about the same. ➤ **catch trial** and ➤ **signal-detection theory**. Difficulties stemming from response biases also emerge in social and personality inventories and questionnaires; ➤ **forced-choice technique**.

response class A term occasionally used to clarify the meaning of ➤ **response** when the author is using that term in senses 4 or 5.

response differentiation ➤ **differentiation** (especially 4, 5).

response generalization ➤ **generalization**, **response**.

response hierarchy Essentially a synonym for ➤ **habit hierarchy**, although *response hierarchy* probably has greater currency since *habit hierarchy* is tinged with specific connotations from its use in Hullian theory.

response latency ➤ **latency, response**.

response learning ➤ **learning, response**.

response magnitude A general term for those characteristics of a response that presumably reflect response strength. Usually included are factors such as intensity, duration, frequency, speed, latency, etc. It should be appreciated that these measures can be very misleading; a given response could be exceedingly gentle, slow, quiet and rare but still have extremely high ➤ **resistance to extinction**, a factor which ultimately is a better measure of the 'strength' of a response.

response-operating characteristic ➤ **receiver-operating characteristic curve**.

response probability ➤ **probability of response**.

response rate The number of responses per unit time. It is a commonly used measure of learning in operant conditioning experiments.

response set ➤ **set, response**.

response-shock interval ➤ **temporal avoidance conditioning**.

response strength 1. Quite literally, the 'strength' of a response as reflected by its magnitude; ➤ **response magnitude** for a discussion of usage. 2. More abstractly (but more correctly), the degree to which a response continues to be made after extinction procedures have been instituted; ➤ **resistance to extinction** for a discussion.

response time The time required for a response to be made. ➤➤ **reaction time**, **response *latency**.

response variable Basically, the ➤ **dependent *variable** in an experiment.

responsibility, diffusion of Quite literally, the diffusion of one's sense of responsibility to act in a particular situation owing to the presence of many other persons all of whom may be viewed as potentially

responsible for acting. ➤➤ **bystander-intervention effect**.

responsive Characterizing: **1.** Any organism or part thereof that makes a response to a particular stimulus. **2.** Any organism that gives evidence of being prepared to respond or capable of responding. **3.** A person who provides pertinent and appropriate responses to questions or requests.

rest 1. A state of not responding (relatively speaking). **2.** A state of relaxation; typically used here with the connotation of a recuperative or rehabilitative function.

rest-activity cycle ➤ **basic rest-activity cycle**.

resting potential The electrical potential of a neuron at rest. See and compare with ➤ **action potential**.

Restorff effect ➤ **von Restorff effect**.

restricted code B. Bernstein's term for the speech mode adopted when one is speaking with peers with whom one shares close identification, similar views and common backgrounds and knowledge. Under such conditions, especially when the topic under discussion is in the 'here and now,' the discourse is rapid, relatively simply planned, relatively predictable and often contains 'in-jokes' and shorthand expressions. Compare with ➤ **elaborated code**.

restricted learning ➤ **learning, restricted**.

restructure 1. Quite literally, to modify or adjust an existing structure. Generally used here with respect to the internal (mental) structure of an image, a memory, a situation, etc. **2.** In ➤ **field theory**, to alter in fundamental ways the relationships between the various aspects of a field.

retardation 1. Generally, a slowing of any process. **2.** More specifically, a slowing of mental, intellectual or scholastic progress. ➤ **mental retardation** for details on usage.

retarded depression ➤ **depression, retarded**.

retention 1. Generally, the process of holding onto or retaining a thing. Most commonly used with respect to issues surrounding the retention of information, where the basic presumption is that some 'mental content' persists from the time of initial exposure to the material or initial learning of a response until some later request for recall or re-performance. ➤ **memory** et seq. and ➤ **forgetting** for more details. **2.** In physiology, the retaining either voluntarily or involuntarily of feces or urine.

retention curve A label applied to any of a number of possible graphic representations that present the course of retention of material over time.

reticular From the Latin, meaning *net, network*.

reticular activating system (RAS) That component of the ➤ **reticular formation** that was once assumed to function as an activating center that when stimulated 'aroused' the rest of the brain. Although the ➤ **locus coeruleus** in the reticular formation does play a role in some aspects of sleep (particularly REM sleep), there is no compelling reason to think of it or any other structure in the brain stem as functioning as the brain's 'activating' system.

reticular formation A complex system of over 90 nuclei and a diffuse network of neurons with complex and extensive axonal and dendritic processes. It occupies the central core of the brain stem from the medulla to the upper part of the midbrain, receiving input from various ascending pathways and projecting fibers to the cord, the thalamus and ultimately to the cerebral cortex. It plays a role in attention, movement, sleep and arousal, and various reflexes.

reticular membrane A membrane formed by the plates at the termini of supporting cells in the organ of Corti in the cochlea of the inner ear.

reticular nucleus A thalamic nucleus that relays information from the cortex to the reticular formation.

reticulospinal tract One of the ➤ **ventromedial pathways**, it runs from the ➤ **reticular formation** to the gray matter of the spinal cord and controls the muscles responsible for postural movement.

reticulothalamic tract (or system) An offshoot of the ➤ **spinothalamic tract** that carries afferent information about temperature and pain.

retina The innermost of the membranes of the inner surface of the posterior portion of the eye. Although extremely complex neuronally, with up to ten layers or zones identifiable, the usual description divides it into three major layers, from front to back: the *ganglion-cell layer*, the *bipolar-cell layer* and the *photoreceptor layer*. This last layer contains the approximately 115 million ➤ **rods** and 6 million ➤ **cones** which serve as the primary visual receptors. The cones, which are responsible for color vision and perception of fine details, are packed into the rod-free ➤ **fovea** and thin out toward the periphery of the retina (see here ➤ **photopic vision**). The rods, which handle low-illumination vision, begin just outside the fovea and increase in relative proportion toward the periphery (➤ **scotopic vision**). pl., *retinas* or *retinae*.

retinal 1 n. A small molecule derived from vitamin A which, along with *opsin*, makes up the basic chemical constituents of photopigments. ➤ **rhodopsin** for more detail. Also called *retinene*; distinguish from ➤ **retinol**. **2** adj. Pertaining to the retina.

retinal densitometry A technique for measuring the amount of light absorbed by the rods of the retina. The basic principle involves the reflecting of light back off the dark choroid sheath behind the retina. The light passes through the retina twice and whatever is absorbed by the retinal pigments will be absent in the final measurement.

retinal disparity ➤ **disparity, retinal**.

retinal field The pattern or array of retinal receptors stimulated by a stimulus field.

retinal fusion ➤ **binocular rivalry**.

retinal image ➤ **image** (2).

retinal light ➤ **idioretinal light**.

retinal rivalry ➤ **binocular rivalry**.

retinal zones ➤ **color zones**.

retinene ➤ **retinal** (1).

retinex (theory) Edwin Land's theoretical model of color vision. He hypothesized three separate visual systems (retinexes), one responsive primarily to long-wavelength light, one to moderate, and the third to short-wavelength light. Each is represented as an analog to a black-and-white picture taken through a particular filter, with each one producing maximum activity in response to red, green and blue light for the long-, moderate-, and short-wavelength retinexes respectively.

retinol Vitamin A; it is an essential precursor for the synthesis of ➤ **retinal** (1).

retinotopic representation The topological representation of the retina on the visual cortex. It is not a linear representation, since the fovea, which is physically a small spot on the retina, provides roughly 25% of the cortical representation, but it does maintain the spatial code. That is, stimulating two neighboring regions on the retina produces excitation of two adjacent areas on the cortex. Also called *retinotopy*, *visuotopic representation* or *visuotopy*.

retinotopy ➤ **retinotopic representation**.

retreat from reality ➤ **flight from *reality***.

retrieval This term, absent from older lexicons of psychology, has become one of the more common – even voguish – words for the process of recalling information from memory. ➤ **recall** and **memory** (et seq.) for discussion.

retro- Combining form meaning *behind* or *backward in time or in space*.

retroactive Generally descriptive of any event, stimulus or process that has an effect on the effects of previously occuring events, stimuli or processes. Compare with ➤ **proactive**.

retroactive association In serial-learning experiments, an association between an item on a list and any preceding item.

retroactive facilitation ➤ **facilitation, retroactive**.

retroactive inhibition ➤ **retroactive *interference**.

retrograde 1. Generally, moving backward, retreating, retiring. 2. With respect to the orderings of events, reversed or inverted. 3. In biology, showing degeneration or deterioration.

retrograde amnesia ➤ **amnesia, retrograde**.

retrograde degeneration ➤ **degeneration** (1).

retrogression 1. A synonym for ➤ **regression** (1). Used in this sense by some authors who wish to avoid the psychoanalytic connotations that often accompany *regression*. 2. A reverting to an earlier form of behavior that was actually engaged in by the individual. Lewin stressed this meaning and many others use it as well; it should, unlike meaning 1, be contrasted with **regression**.

retrospection Lit., inspecting and reporting on that which has passed. There was an interesting debate among the early structuralists, some of whom argued that *retrospection* needed to be contrasted with *introspection* (observing and reporting on present experience), others maintained that the processes were equivalent. Auguste Comte put this latter position forward succinctly: 'In order to observe (introspect) your intellect must pause from activity and yet it is this activity you want to observe. If you cannot effect the pause you cannot observe, if you do effect it, there is nothing (present) to observe.'

retrospective falsification Unconscious modification and distortion of previous experiences so as to make them conform with present needs. ➤ **confabulation**, which may or may not have the connotation of *unconscious*.

Rett's syndrome (or **disorder**) A developmental disorder characterized by normal development for the first six months followed by a gradual loss of purposive hand movements with accompanying stereotypic hand-washing movements, a failure of normal head and trunk growth, ataxia, and marked delay and impairment of language development.

re-uptake The reabsorption of a substance. Used commonly of transmitter substances that are 'taken up' again by the terminal buttons from which they had been liberated.

reverberating circuit In Donald O. Hebb's theory, a ➤ **cell assembly** that, functioning as a whole unit, continues to respond after the original stimulus that initiated its response has been terminated. Also called *reverberatory circuit*.

reverie A rather unstructured, relatively purposeless mental state characterized by aimless mental meanderings and fantasies. As the term is typically used, the connotation is that the state is a distinctly pleasant experience.

reversal In psychoanalysis, the turning about of an instinct, e.g., sadism changes to masochism. Anna Freud argued that reaction formation as a defense mechanism occurs because of the capacity for reversal.

reversal error ➤ reversals.

reversal formation An occasional synonym for ➤ **reaction formation**.

reversal learning ➤ learning, reversal.

reversals (or **reversal errors**) Errors made in reading and writing characterized by the reversal of symbols. Such errors are most often single-letter reversals (e.g., *b* and *d*) or reversals of letter order (e.g., *was* for *saw*), although occasionally word-order errors will also be called reversals. Note that the technical term, *strephosym-*

bolia, which literally means the *twisting of symbols*, is dropping out of usage here and, for once in science, an easily understood term is replacing an awkward one.

reversal shift ➤ reversal *learning.

reversibility The property of a series of operations such that reversing their order restores the original state. In Piaget's theory, apprehension of this principle is an element in the establishment of *conservation*.

reversible figure ➤ figure, reversible.

reversible perspective ➤ alternating perspective.

reversing lenses (or **prisms**) Lenses which, when worn, reverse the visual field. They have been used in research on perceptual learning and re-learning. See, for more here, ➤ **displaced vision**.

reversion 1. Generally, the act of reversing. 2. In genetics, the reappearance of a recessive genetic trait which had not been present in the phenotypes for one or more generations. 3. Loosely, ➤ regression (1).

revival 1. Generally, bringing back to life. 2. In the study of memory, the process of recall in the sense that a dormant memory has been triggered or 'revived'.

reward Loosely, any event or thing that is pleasurable or satisfying that is obtained when some requisite task has been carried out. The similarity between this notion and that of the term ➤ **reinforcement**, especially sense 3, has led some authors to treat them as synonyms. For the meaning of compound terms using *reward* in this fashion, see the equivalent term following *reinforcement*: e.g., *primary reward* = ➤ **primary *reinforcement**. However, most prefer to distinguish them in a manner best expressed by the following example. 'For the children in the study, a reward of 1 penny served as the reinforcement for each correct response.' It is possible to split many a hair over the subtle semantic overlaps between reward and reinforcement; see the extended discussion under ➤ **reinforcement** for a few of them.

reward expectancy In Tolman's learning theory, the internal process that occurs when an organism recognizes that it is in a circumstance that has been previously associated with a reward.

rewrite rule In linguistics, a rule that specifies how one linguistic form is to be altered to produce a grammatical phrase or sentence. E.g., NP → Art + N is a rewrite rule that specifies that a noun phrase (NP) can be written out as an article (Art) plus a noun (N), with the arrow indicating 'rewrite as.'

RGB system A system for specifying colors; see, for details, ➤ **color equation**.

Rh Abbreviation for *rhesus*, a species of monkey. ➤ **Rh blood group**.

-rhage Combining form meaning *discharge, bleeding*.

rhaphe ➤ **raphe**.

Rh blood group A blood group found in roughly 80% of all humans: the name is derived from the rhesus monkey, where it was first discovered. Its presence is noted as Rh+ (or Rh positive), its absence as Rh− (or Rh negative). If the factor is introduced in those who are Rh− it causes the production of antibodies (anti-Rh agglutinin) and subsequent transfusions of Rh+ blood will cause serious reactions. During pregnancy, an Rh− woman may become sensitized if the fetus is Rh+ and subsequent pregnancies with Rh+ fetuses are potentially dangerous because the Rh antibodies in maternal blood may cross the placenta and destroy fetal blood cells.

-rhea Suffix meaning *flow*.

rheo- Combining form denoting *flowing, fluidity* or *current*.

rheobase In neurophysiology, the threshold of excitability of neural tissue; it is given as the minimum direct current which if applied indefinitely would be sufficient to produce excitation. ➤➤ **chronaxte**.

rheotropism An orienting response to the flow of water.

Rh factor ➤ **Rh blood group**.

Rhine deck ➤ **Zener cards**.

rhinencephalon Lit., the smell (or olfactory) brain. It includes the olfactory bulb, olfactory tract, pyriform area, parts of the pyriform cortex and parts of the amygdaloid complex.

rhinal fissure A small fissure that marks the boundary between the ➤ **hippocampal formation** and the neocortex.

rhino- Combining form meaning *nose, nasal*.

rho (*p*) The symbol for a correlation coefficient resulting from an analysis of rank-order data on two variables.

rhodopsin The photopigment of the rods. It consists of rod ➤ **opsin** and ➤ **retinal** and its breakdown in the presence of light is the first part of the long chain of events in the transduction of light energy to visual experience. Retinal has two forms, a bent form (called *11-cis retinal*) and a straight form (*all-trans retinal*); only the 11-cis form can attach to rod opsin. The 11-cis form is, moreover, very unstable and exists only in the dark. Hence, when rhodopsin is exposed to light, the 11-cis form straightens out to become the all-trans form and rhodopsin breaks down into its constituents, which causes the photoreceptor to hyperpolarize.

rhombencephalon The ➤ **hindbrain**.

rhythm Regular recurrence of a pattern of events, particularly with a uniform system of beats, accents or grouped sequences. Rhythm and rhythmic structures are important as mnemonic aids; e.g., the common 7-digit telephone number is usually coded rhythmically as '''(pause)'''' or '''(long pause)'' (short pause)''.

RI Abbreviation for ➤ **retroactive *interference** (or *retroactive inhibition*).

ribonucleic acid (RNA) A large, complex molecule made up of a sequence of four nucleotide bases (*adenine, guanine, cytosine* and *uracil*) attached to a sugar-phosphate 'backbone' (specifically, *ribose*, hence the name). *Messenger RNA (m RNA)* is copied from one strand of ➤ **deoxyribonucleic acid (DNA)** and delivers genetic information from part of a chromosome to a ribosome where *transfer RNA [tRNA]* coordinates the assembling of the proper amino acids into enzymes for cell specialization.

ribosome A small structure found in all cells that function as site for protein synthesis.

Ribot's law The generalization that the progressive memory loss seen in various forms of neurological disease follows evolutionary lines such that those processes dependent on phylogenetically older structures are spared impairment. ➤ **Jackson's principle**, which is more general.

Ricco's law A generalization that states that for very small areas of the retina (i.e. less than 10′ of arc) the absolute threshold is inversely proportional to the area stimulated. Compare with ➤ **Piper's law**. Ricco's law also holds reasonably well for thermal thresholds on the skin.

rich interpretation Extended and expanded interpretation of a text, a discourse, a dream, etc. that brings to bear all that is known about the culture, the persons involved and existing theoretical models about the processes under examination. The term is found in psycholinguistic studies of a person's understanding of textual material, in discourse analysis involving interpretations that go beyond the information literally contained in the material, in dream analysis where the latent content of a dream is deeply interpreted, and the like. Also called *deep interpretation*. Compare with ➤ **decontextualization**.

rickets A bone-development disease in children caused by deficiencies in vitamin D.

right and wrong cases, method of ➤ measurement of *threshold.

right-associates learning An obsolete term for ➤ **paired-associates** *learning.

righting reflex Quite as it says, a reflexive reaction of an organism to being tipped off balance or turned over by which the organism attempts to regain normal posture.

rigid Inflexible, unyielding, nonpliant, etc. Used in a wide variety of contexts to characterize thinking that is invariant, muscles that are tense, attitudes that are inflexible and unmodifiable, etc. Note that the usual connotation is a distinctly negative one.

rigidity 1. In physiology, a state of strong muscular contraction. **2.** In personality theory, a trait characterized by cognitive, perceptual and/or social inflexibility. Distinguish from ➤ **perseveration**.

risk An action that jeopardizes something of value. Risk and the role it plays in psychological phenomena have been studied extensively; e.g., ➤ **choice shift, game** (et seq.), **utility** and **value** (1, 3).

risk aversion The general tendency to be afraid of taking risks even when they also carry substantial potential gain. To take a classic case, when offered a choice between (a) a sure gain of $3000 and (b) an 80% chance of a gain of $4000 and a 20% chance of nothing almost everyone chooses (a). However, if asked to choose between (a) a sure loss of $3000 and (b) an 80% chance of losing $4000 and a 20% chance of losing nothing, most people choose (b). That is, most people are risk aversive and choose so as to avoid taking risks when looking for some gain; they will submit to risky propositions but only when attempting to avoid a sure loss.

risk-taking A hypothesized personality dimension reflecting the degree to which an individual willingly undertakes actions that involve a significant degree of risk.

risky-shift ➤ **choice shift**.

Ritalin ➤ **methylphenidate**.

rite 1. A culturally directed format for a ceremony. **2.** Occasionally, a ➤ **ritual** (2), but see that term and ➤ **ceremony** for distinctions in usage.

ritual **1.** Generally, any sequence of actions or behaviors that is highly stylized, relatively rigid and stereotyped. **2.** A culturally or socially standardized set of actions dictated by tradition (usually religious, magical or nationalistic), rather precisely defined and revealing little or no variation from occurrence to occurrence. Occasionally this meaning is treated as a partial synonym for ➤ **rite** or ➤ **ceremony**, although ceremony is often taken as a more general term, several rituals comprising a ceremony. **3.** An oft-repeated pattern of behavior which tends to occur at appropriate times, e.g., the morning ritual of washing, grooming, dressing, etc. **4.** A fairly elaborate, stereotyped set of behaviors that perhaps had functional origins but they are no longer apparent. The term *routine* is also used for 3 and 4. **5.** Irrational, repetitive behaviors often observed in the ➤ **obsessive-compulsive disorder**.

It should be appreciated that some authors use the term with the connotation that all rituals, no matter how mundane their manifestation, have some symbolic role to play either in a culture or in the psychological make-up of an individual.

rivalry A state of interaction between two or more entities (which may be persons, groups, institutions, biological structures, etc.) such that they are in a competitive pursuit of the same goals or things. The term is used generally and the participants in the interaction may be either in direct contact with each other or they may pursue the goals separately. *Competition* is a common synonym for the case where there is direct contact but is generally not used when it is indirect.

rivalry, sibling A popular term for the often aggressive, contentious interactions between siblings. The term has little technical value since it is used so inclusively that almost any competitive interaction is so labeled no matter what the initiating cause or underlying dynamics may be.

RL An old abbreviation for *absolute* ➤ **threshold** (1); it comes from the German,

Reizlimen meaning stimulus threshold.

RMS ➤ **root-mean square**.

RNA ➤ **ribonucleic acid.**

robust **1.** Generally, strong, sturdy, resistant. **2.** In statistics, characterizing a statistical test that remains useful even when some of its basic assumptions are violated.

ROC curve ➤ **receiver-operating characteristic curve**.

rod and frame test A test used primarily in measuring ➤ **field dependence**. The subject is presented with a rectangular frame and a rod within the frame. The orientation of the frame is changed from trial to trial and the subject attempts to set the position of the rod to the true vertical. The amount of error and its relationship to the orientation of the frame yield a measure of the subject's field dependence.

rods The achromatic photoreceptors in the retina. Rods have lower thresholds than ➤ **cones** and function under conditions of low illumination; see here ➤ **scotopic vision**. There are no rods in the fovea, where maximum acuity is found. Scotopic vision is both colorblind and lacking in fine detail. Rods contain a single photopigment, ➤ **rhodopsin** (which see for more detail).

rod vision ➤ **Scotopic vision**; vision under low-illumination conditions, specifically below the threshold for the ➤ **cones**.

Rogerian Of or pertaining to the theories and clinical practices of Carl Rogers. For details, ➤ **client-centered therapy, humanistic psychology**.

Rolandic fissure ➤ **central fissure**.

role A word derived from the early French theatre, where a *role* was the roll of paper upon which an actor's part was written. In social psychology, it refers generally to any pattern of behavior involving certain rights, obligations and duties which an individual is expected, trained and, indeed, encouraged to perform in a given social situation. In fact, one may go so far as to say that a person's role is precisely what is expected of him or her by others and ultimately, after the particular role has been thoroughly learned and internalized, by the person him or herself. Roles may assume rather wide manifestations. They may be momentary, e.g., the winner of a game; they may be indefinable in time, e.g., child, parent, spouse; or they may be essentially permanent, e.g., male, female, Black. The term is also used in a variety of specialized ways, as the following entries show. ➤ **status** and **stereotype**, which are used in ways that may overlap subtly.

role, achieved Quite literally, any role that has been achieved or earned, e.g, corporation president. Contrast with ➤ ascribed *role.

role, ascribed A role ascribed to one, a role handed to one at birth (e.g., male, upper class) or at some point later in life (e.g., adult).

role conflict A situation in which a person is expected to perform in two or more roles that conflict in fundamental ways with each other. The classic example here is the situation confronted by a military chaplain.

Role Construct Repertory Test ➤ **Rep Test**.

role, counterfeit Any role assumed falsely, usually to protect oneself from the social stigma of the truth, e.g., the divorced person who plays the role of widow or widower.

role diffusion Erik Erikson's term for a developmental stage, characteristic of adolescence, in which there is a lack of harmony between the various identifications made with others (the role models).

role discontinuity A term used descriptively of situations in which a sudden and often dramatic shift in one's primary role is necessitated. The recent retiree is a good example.

role distancing The process of playing out a role without really meaning it, with-out actually accepting the role but rather doing it with some other motive in mind. The 'distancing' component is meant to convey the sense that the internalization process, which is normally regarded as central to the adoption of a ➤ **role**, is missing.

role-enactment theory A theory of hypnosis which argues that the hypnotized person basically is acting out a role. The point of interest here is that the subject is not assumed to be in an 'altered state' but merely so deeply involved in the enactment of the suggested role that his or her actions take place without conscious intent.

role model ➤ **model** (2).

role-playing 1. The acting out or performing of a particular role. As a procedure, it has rather wide currency in psychotherapy, in education and even in industrial settings. 2. The acting out in an appropriate fashion of the role one perceives as properly characteristic of oneself. Note that 1 and 2 conflict in meaning. Those who use the term for sense 2 generally use the phrase 'playing at a role' for sense 1.

role rehearsal The preliminary playing out of an adult role by a child. The phenomenon is extremely common and is generally taken as an important component of socialization whereby the child identifies with an adult and mimics that person's role behavior. It is also seen in various infrahuman species, particularly primates.

role reversal A reversing of the social roles of two persons involved in a ➤ reciprocal *roles relationship; e.g., the teacher becomes the pupil and vice versa, the dominant member of a pair becomes the submissive and the submissive the dominant.

role set Within the study of organizational behavior, a term preferred by many over the more general term, ➤ **group**. The point here is that *role set* emphasizes the notion that a functioning group of individuals within an organization is given primarily by the *role* relationships that exist between a *set* of individuals. The term was first used by the sociologist R. K. Merton in his analysis of social status and social structure.

roles, reciprocal Roles that are defined by the relationship between persons, particularly those where the relationship produces an inseparable intertwining of the roles. Husband–wife, teacher–pupil, mother–daughter, etc. are examples.

romantic love ➤ **love, romantic**.

Romberg's sign The inability to maintain body balance when standing with eyes shut and feet close together. It is a sign of neurological damage.

Romeo and Juliet effect The increase in the attractiveness between two people resulting from an attempt on the part of their parents or others to keep them apart.

root 1 n. In mathematics, any number which, when multiplied by itself a given number of times, yields a given quantity; e.g., 2 is the second (or square) root of 4, the third (or cube) root of 8, the fourth root of 16, etc. 2 n. In linguistics, a morpheme that serves as the basis of an inflectional paradigm: e.g., 'talk' is the root for 'talks,' 'talked,' 'talking,' 'talker,' etc. 3 n. The embedded base of a growth such as a hair, a nail, a tooth. 4 n. A collection of nerve fibers entering or leaving the central nervous system. 5 adj. Primary or basic; e.g., the root cause, the root idea, etc.

root conflict (or **problem**) In the depth psychologies, the underlying conflict that is assumed to be primarily responsible for an observed psychological disorder. Compare with ➤ **nuclear conflict**, which tends to be used in broader fashion.

rooting reflex A sequence of head-turning and mouthing movements elicited in an infant by a gentle stroking of the cheek.

root-mean square (**RMS**) $\sqrt{(\Sigma X^2/N)}$, where X represents each of the scores in the calculation and N is the number of scores. In the special case where $X =$ deviation of a score from the mean of the distribution, RMS = ➤ **standard *deviation**.

Rorschach ranking test A simplified variation on the ➤ **Rorschach test** in which the subject is given each of the ten inkblots along with a list of nine possible responses and asked to rank them as to their values as adequate descriptions of each inkblot.

Rorschach test The grandfather of all ➤ **projective tests**, designed and developed by the Swiss psychiatrist Hermann Rorschach. The administration of the test consists of a structured interview using a series of ten standardized, bilaterally symmetrical inkblots. Five of the blots are achromatic, two have some color and the other three are in various colors. Each blot is presented to the subject, who is requested to state freely what he or she sees either in the blot as a whole or in any part of it. Extremely complex scoring and interpretation systems have been developed and lengthy training is required to become proficient in its use. According to the classical interpretation, responses to color are supposedly reflective of emotional responsiveness of the subject to the environment; form and location responses are taken as indices of overall orientation to life; movement responses are assumed to reflect tendencies toward introversion; originality theoretically reflects intelligence but bizarre originality is seen as indicative of neurotic tendencies, etc.

There is a certain fascination with this test that affects all, professional and layman alike. In some ways, particularly among lay people, it is seen as a symbol of psychology itself. It reflects that strange belief which many have that psychologists and psychiatrists can somehow tell you something about yourself that you would never be able to ascertain on your own, as if they possessed some mysterious ability to read through the veils of defenses and posturings which are opaque to all but these shamans and their testing procedures. Among the professionals its magnetic qualities are equally strong. The literature on the Rorschach is simply enormous and literally dozens of other ➤

675

projective devices have been developed based on similar theoretical principles. Yet, in the midst of all of this activity, devotion and fascination, there is essentially no evidence whatsoever that the test has even a shred of validity. Its supporters display an almost religious fervor in its defense and their claims often read like theological discourses and not scientific analyses; its attackers are merciless and maintain that it is totally worthless and may even be harmful because it can lead the clinician astray.

When debates of this intensity and polarity occur between honorable people there are likely to be elements of truth on both sides. The following is a personal view. It seems not unreasonable to assume that the test can be of value in a clinical setting, but perhaps not necessarily because of any intrinsic property of the Rorschach itself nor of the manner of its administration. Rather, it is likely the case that the test provides an opportunity for an extended, unbounded interaction between client and therapist with the inkblots acting as the vehicle for the interaction. Given such an intensive, open setting, particularly where the client believes the test has a valid psychological role to play in the ongoing dialogue, the perceptive clinician can gain insight into the personality characteristics of the client. Thus, the usefulness of the Rorschach will depend upon the sensitivity, empathy and insightfulness of the tester totally independently of the Rorschach itself. An intense dialogue about the wallpaper or the rug would do as well provided that both parties believe.

Rosanoff list (or **test**) ➤ **Kent-Rosanoff list.**

Rosenthal effect A term derived from the extensive research of Robert Rosenthal on the manner in which one's beliefs, biases and expectations can have an impact on the phenomena under investigation. For special instances of the effect ➤ **demand characteristics, experimenter, expectancy effect, self-fulfilling prophecy.**

rostral Lit., toward or pertaining to the beak. Hence, toward the head or the front end of a body.

rotary-pursuit procedure ➤ **pursuit meter.**

rotation 1. Generally, any movement about some central point. **2.** In ➤ **factor analysis**, the operation of moving the axes so as to find the orientation that maximizes the loading. Such rotations may be *oblique*, when the angles between the ➤ **factor axes** are acute, indicating that they are correlated with each other and that a *second-order factor* exists, or they may be *orthogonal*, when the axes meet at right angles, indicating that the factors do not correlate with each other.

rote learning ➤ **learning, rote.**

rote memory ➤ **rote *learning.**

round window A small, round, membrane-covered opening in the ➤ **cochlea** of the inner ear which vibrates back and forth, functioning to alleviate the pressures set up by the vibrations of the ➤ **oval window.**

routine The kinds of ➤ **rituals** discussed under meanings 3 and 4 of that term are often referred to as *routines*, on the grounds that whatever symbolic elements the behaviors once had are now lost. The connotation is that somehow a routine is a more mundane, stereotyped behavior pattern than a ritual. ➤➤ **ceremony.**

RP ➤ **Received Pronunciation.**

RR Abbreviation for *random ratio*. ➤ **schedules of *reinforcement.**

R–R conditioning Conditioning of a series of responses in which each response is the precondition for the next response.

-rrhagia, -rrhea Combining forms used to denote *discharge, eruption, bursting forth*, with the connotation that it is an abnormal or unusual condition.

R–R laws Conditioning principles based on underlying response relationships. Although not all authors are consistent in their notation, many reserve the upper case for overt responses and use *r–r* for discussions of covert or mental responses. Compare with ➤ **S–R laws**.

R–S interval ➤ **temporal avoidance conditioning**.

r strategy In evolutionary biology, a type of reproductive breeding utilized by many species in which many offspring are born at a time. The r strategy involves the expenditure of little or no energy or effort in the rearing of the offspring and is usually accompanied by relatively short periods between one birthing and the next. Most insects utilize this strategy, as do other species such as sea turtles, many fish, etc. Also called *r selection* or *r selection strategy*. Compare with ➤ **K strategy**.

RT 1. ➤ **reaction time**. 2. ➤ **response time**. Usually 1 is intended.

R technique ➤ **R correlation**.

rubella A relatively mild disease with one serious complication. In a pregnant woman during the first two or three months of pregnancy, it can produce a number of fetal anomalies including mental retardation, cataracts, heart disease and deafness. The dangers are greatest during the first month and lessen thereafter. Also commonly called *German measles*.

Rubin's figure The common ambiguous figure which is seen as either a vase or as two faces in profile. It is named for E. Rubin, who studied such reversible figures extensively.

rubrospinal tract The efferent nerve tract running from the red nucleus to the spinal cord.

rudiment 1. A basic element, a first principle. 2. A beginning, a first emerging appearance of a thing. 3. In biology, an organ or part of an organ that is incompletely developed, arrested in development, or one that no longer serves any identifiable function, a vestige.

Ruffini corpuscle Encapsulated, branching nerve ending in subcutaneous tissue;

suspected of mediating the sense of warmth. Also called *Ruffini cylinder*.

Ruffini end organ Branching nerve ending found in subcutaneous tissue and suspected of functioning as a mediator of constant skin indentation and thus playing a role in the sense of pressure. Also called *Ruffini papillary ending*, *Ruffini plume* or *Ruffini ending*.

rule A formal expression that codifies and specifies a particular set of relations. In this sense, the term is used in ways surprisingly close to the term ➤ **concept**. Indeed, many *concept learning* experiments are also referred to as *rule learning* experiments. The point of commonality here is the notion that as a concept is defined by some rule, to learn the concept is to display knowledge, albeit implicit, of the rule. ➤ **concept** et seq.

rule learning ➤ **learning, rule**.

rule of inference ➤ **transformation** (3).

rule of thumb ➤ **heuristic**.

rumination disorder of infancy A serious eating disorder characterized by repeated regurgitation of food. In the typical syndrome, partially digested food is regurgitated by the infant and either ejected or chewed and reswallowed. There is no nausea, retching or obvious gastrointestinal malfunction. Also called *merycism*.

rumor An unverified and typically inaccurate report, story or characterization which travels through a community usually by word of mouth. Rumors tend to occur during periods of societal stress and usually are concerned with persons or events in whom or about which there is considerable interest but little concrete, verifiable information. With propagation, rumors tend to undergo both *leveling* (becoming shorter and simpler) and *sharpening* (emphasizing particular details and neglecting others).

rumor-intensity formula A formula proposed by G. Allport and L. Postman that captures the generalization that the intensity of rumors tends to be a function of the importance of the subject and its ambiguity, i.e. $R = ia$, where R is the intensity of the rumor, i = importance and a = ambiguity. Note that a multiplicative relationship is assumed; if either i or a is zero, there is no rumor.

run **1.** vb. To carry out an experiment or a single trial in an experiment. **2** n. The experiment or trial itself. **3** n. A sequence of identical symbols; e.g., AAAA is a run of As of length four.

runs test A nonparametric statistical test that determines whether a single data sample is significantly different from random by analyzing the pattern of ➤ **runs** (3) that is observed. ➤➤ **Wald-Wolfowitz runs test**, which is used to evaluate differences between two samples.

runway Any straight alley maze or a longish straightaway in a maze.

rut **1.** In lower animals, a seasonal period of sexual excitement. ➤ **estrus, heat** (2). **2.** In animals, copulation.

S

S Abbreviation for **1.** *Stimulus*; see here ➤ S^+, S^-, S^Δ, S^D, S–R. **2.** *Subject*. **3.** In some older writings, *sensation*. This last use is generally restricted to instances in which *R* is used for stimulus; ➤ *Reiz*. **4.** In psychophysics, the ➤ standard (2).

'S' The pseudonym of a *mnemonist* studied extensively by Alexander Luria. A man of average intelligence, S's seemingly inexhaustible memory capacity was aided by his use of a variety of mnemonic devices and coding schemes, a remarkable ability to form associations between things and a most unusual and bizarrely developed *synesthesia*.

S^C A relatively rare abbreviation for the ➤ conditioned stimulus; CS is preferred.

S^D ➤ drive stimulus.

S^D Abbreviation for ➤ discriminative *stimulus. In operant-conditioning studies, S^D denotes the stimulus in the presence of which responses are reinforced and S^Δ the stimulus in the presence of which responses go unreinforced. Compare with S^+ and S^-.

S^Δ See discussion under S^D.

S^G Abbreviation for ➤ goal stimulus.

S^+, S^- In discrimination-learning experiments, the positive stimulus (responses to which are reinforced) is generally denoted as S^+ and the negative stimulus (responses to which go unreinforced) by S^-. In this sense, $S^+ = S^D$ and $S^- = S^\Delta$. Note, however, that in some circumstances S^- is used to denote a stimulus in the presence of which responses are punished. In these cases, S^- has a distinct negative component that S^Δ does not.

S_u An occasional abbreviation for ➤ unconditioned stimulus; US and UCS are more common.

s **1.** Sensation. **2.** The standard deviation in a data sample. **3.** Any variable stimulus. This use is generally restricted to the area of psychophysics.

$s\bar{x}$ In Hullian theory, a ➤ fractional goal stimulus.

s^2 ➤ variance.

$s_{\bar{x}}$ ➤ standard error of mean.

SAC ➤ stimulus as coded.

saccade A quick eye movement, a jump from one fixation point to another. Saccadic movements are seen most clearly during reading and the scanning of visual displays. The eye was once thought to be functionally blind during a saccade; it is now known that some vision does occur although fine details are not picked up. vb., *saccade*.

saccadic movement An eye movement made while scanning a scene or fixed display. ➤ saccade for more detail.

saccule The smaller of the two vestibular sacs in the inner ear. Like the ➤ utricle, it is approximately round in shape and has a layer of receptors on its 'floor' that respond to changes in orientation of the head.

sacral Pertaining to the area around and including the ➤ sacrum.

sacral division A division of the ➤ autonomic nervous system (see that entry for details).

sacred Characteristic of those aspects of a society or culture which are treated with great respect. They may be physical objects (a cross, an ark), or they may be spiritual, supernatural or even emergent ideas derived from the shared values of a society (patriotism). In the social sciences the term encompasses more than the religious or the divine; in fact, it can be taken to refer to anything which is not to be taken frivolously.

sacrifice To terminate the life of an experimental animal for the purpose of carrying out a post-mortem examination. The term is a euphemism for any number of other words and serves obvious palliative functions.

sacrum The triangular bone at the lower end of the spine that connects with the hipbones to form the dorsal part of the pelvis. adj., *sacral*.

SAD ➤ **seasonal affective disorder**.

sadism 1. The association of sexual pleasure with the inflicting of pain upon another. Note that *pain* here may take many forms other than the purely physical. As the term is used, causing psychic pain, humiliation, debasement, exploitation, etc. may all be regarded as sadistic acts. The term covers the actual derivation of sexual satisfaction as well as cases in which the sadistic behavior serves as an arousal function as a prelude to further sexual action. When it is necessary for sexual gratification, it is classified as a ➤ **paraphilia**. The term derives from the rather singular sexual orientation of the notorious essayist, novelist and revolutionary, Donatien Alphonse François, the Marquis de Sade. 2. Somewhat more generally, the derivation of pleasure from the inflicting of pain and suffering on others. As with 1, *pain* may take forms other than the purely physical. In this usage, the sexual connotation may or may not be present. adj., *sadistic*; n., *sadist*. ➤ **masochism**.

sado-masochistic 1. A hybrid term reflecting the oft-noted tendency for sadistic and masochistic manifestations to occur together in the same person. 2. Characterizing a relationship between persons in which one enacts the role of sadist and the other the role of masochist. ➤ **sadism** and **masochism**.

safety device Horney's term for any of the techniques one uses for defending and protecting oneself from the difficulties of life. The usual usage is with respect to neurosis and the devices used by neurotics.

safety motive 1. Generally, any desire for

or tendency to strive for safety and security. 2. A tendency to avoid failure or the threat of failure by withdrawing from a situation or by lowering one's level of aspiration or one's goals. Note that the first usage is a simple description of a state of affairs; the second is a hypothesized explanatory mechanism.

sagittal 1. From the Latin for *arrow*, pertaining to the arrow-shaped suture joining the two parietal bones of the skull. 2. Pertaining to the plane passing through the long axis of the head which schematically divides the body into symmetrical right and left halves, or to any other plane parallel to this one.

sagittal axis The line of reference from the center of the retina through the centers of the lens and pupil to the visual field.

sagittal fissure The fissure that separates the two cerebral hemispheres. Also called the *longitudinal fissure*.

sagittal section ➤ **section** (2).

salience Distinctiveness, prominence, obviousness. The term is widely used in perception and cognition to refer to any aspect of a stimulus that, for any of many reasons, stands out from the rest. Salience may be the result of emotional, motivational or cognitive factors and is not necessarily associated with physical factors such as intensity, clarity, size, etc. adj., *salient*.

Salpêtrière school The psychiatric institute at the Salpêtrière Hospital in Paris was long a significant institution. Its fame began with the administration of the facilities by Philippe Pinel in 1793 and continued through the guidance of Jean Martin Charcot and Pierre Janet. The specific school of thought noted by the term, however, is that associated with the point of view of Charcot, who developed the so-called clinicoanatomical approach to mental disorders, whereby neurological diseases were associated with and classified according to the anatomic and pathological conditions, outlined a general theory of psychopathology based on neurological principles and proposed a theory of hypnosis based on the assumption that it was a pathological state rooted in a neurological disorder and associated with hysteria. This last theoretical position was vigorously criticized by those of the ➤ **Nancy school**.

salpingectomy The surgical procedure of cutting, tying off or removing the Fallopian tubes. It is the simplest of the various surgical contraceptive procedures in women. ➤➤ **vasectomy**, the analogous procedure in men.

saltatory Characterized by leaps, discontinuous, quantal. n., *saltation*.

saltatory conduction The conduction of action potentials in myelinated neurons where the potential jumps from one ➤ **node of *Ranvier** to the next.

salty One of the four basic qualities of ➤ **taste**.

sample 1 n. A part of a ➤ **population** selected (usually according to some procedure and with some purpose in mind) such that it is considered to be representative of the population as a whole. 2 vb. To take such a selected part of the population. The term is frequently qualified to specify the kind of sample or the sampling procedure under discussion; the more frequently used ones are given below. When unqualified, a ➤ **random *sample** is generally meant. Note that *sample* and *sampling* are often used interchangeably, especially in compound forms. If a term is not found immediately below, see those following ➤ **sampling**.

sample, adequate A sample of sufficient size that the intended level of accuracy can be achieved. Note that the term pertains only to size and has no connotations concerning representativeness.

sample bias Any factor that decreases the likelihood of a ➤ **representative *sample** being drawn.

sample distribution The distribution of scores on some variable that is found in a

particular ➤ **sample**. Distinguish from ➤ **sampling *distribution**.

sample, matched Any sample selected so that it reflects the same characteristics as another sample. ➤ **matched-groups procedure** for an example.

sample, nonrepresentative Any sample the characteristics of which do not reflect those of the population from which it was drawn.

sample, random A sample which has been drawn such that each member or object in the population has an equal (and independent) probability of being selected. ➤ **random *sampling**.

sample, representative Any sample which is an accurate reflection of the population from which it was drawn; an *unbiased sample*. All systematic sampling procedures are designed to yield representative samples.

sample space The totality of events which are potential candidates for any sample; in other words, the *population*.

sample, time Any sample based on the taking of observations at specified times or during specific time periods. Ideally the times are selected in an unbiased fashion and the sample data are the behaviors exhibited during them. ➤ **behavior *sampling**.

sampling The operation of drawing a sample from a population. If unqualified, it is safe to assume that ➤ **random *sampling** procedures are being used. Note, in many cases, particularly in the many compound terms, *sample* and *sampling* are used interchangeably – for terms not found below see those following ➤ **sample**.

sampling, accidental Sampling the events or elements of which are drawn essentially 'by accident' and without regard for representativeness. Such samples are invariably *biased*. The typical 'person on the street' polls that radio and television stations are so fond of taking are of this kind.

sampling, area Generally, any sampling

method based on selection of subjects from geographical regions.

sampling, behavior A recording of the behavior exhibited by a subject during specific time periods. These specific periods are chosen so that the behavior observed during them (the sample) can be taken as representative of the overall patterns of behavior the subject displays.

sampling, biased Any sampling procedure in which some events or elements have a greater or lesser chance of being selected than they should, given their frequency in the population. Biased samples are nonrepresentative and hence inferences from them will contain systematic errors.

sampling, block A sampling procedure in which the elements to be sampled are broken into groups (or blocks) and separate samples are taken from each. E.g. ➤ **area *sampling, stratified *sampling**.

sampling, controlled A generic term covering any sampling procedure where some measure of control is exerted over the manner in which the sample is selected. E.g., ➤ **matched *sample, stratified *sampling**.

sampling, convenience Sampling based, not on representativeness, but on convenience. Despite statements that the subjects in such and such a study were selected 'at random,' most experimental psychology with human subjects is based on these samples being drawn, not from the population at large, but from a convenient subset of it – usually students taking Introductory Psychology.

sampling distribution ➤ **distribution, sampling**.

sampling, domal A specialized form of ➤ **area *sampling** in which specific restrictions are placed on who is sampled. For example, only every fifth house (*domal* = domestic, or household) may be chosen and only the head of the household is used in each sample.

sampling error ➤ **error, sampling**.

sampling fraction The percentage of the full population that is in a given sample.

sampling, horizontal Sampling of subjects from within a single socioeconomic or social class. Contrast with ➤ **vertical *sampling**.

sampling, nonprobability Sampling in which the probability of each event or element being drawn is not known, e.g., ➤ **accidental *sampling, quota *sampling**. Compare with ➤ **probability *sampling**.

sampling population Strictly speaking, the population from which a sample is actually drawn is, by definition, the sampling population. However, it may not, in actual practice, correspond with the real, theoretical population. For a simple, omnipresent exemplary case, consider that almost all psychological experiments that investigate the cognitive processes of normal human beings are performed on samples of college undergraduates. The theoretical inferences made are based on the presumption that this sampling population is representative of the true population or *universe* (i.e. all cognitively normal human beings) – there are, obviously, many reasons for questioning this extension. Hence, although many authors will use *population* and *sampling population* as synonyms, there are subtle but potentially important reasons for keeping their denotative domains separate. ➤ **population**, especially 2, for more details on usage.

sampling, probability Sampling in which the events or elements are drawn according to some known probability structure. Note that ➤ **random *sampling** is a special case of probability sampling where the probability structure is one which specifies that all elements are equally likely to be chosen. Compare with ➤ **nonprobability *sampling**.

sampling, quota A variety of ➤ **stratified *sampling** in which a specific number of cases (the quota) is selected from each stratum.

sampling, random The classic procedure for drawing a sample in which each event or element in the population is independent of every other and each is equally likely to be included in the sample. ➤ **random** for more on usage.

sampling reliability ➤ **reliability, sampling**.

sampling, representative Sampling which yields a truly ➤ **representative** *sample*.

sampling, snowball Sampling in which each person in the sample is asked to provide the names of several other persons, who are then added to the sample, etc.

sampling, stratified Sampling in which the population as a whole is separated into distinct parts (or 'strata') and each is drawn from separately. Contemporary political polling uses this type of sampling, which helps to ensure that the full population is properly represented.

sampling, systematic Sampling based on a systematic rule such as 'every 10th case' or 'every other element.' Many experiments which report random sampling actually use this procedure, in particular studies in which the first subject who shows up goes into one group, the second into the second group, the third into the first group, etc.

sampling theory A branch of mathematical statistics concerned with the principles and applied techniques for drawing representative and adequate samples from populations such that valid inferences can be made. ➤ **probability theory**, which lies at the core of sampling theory and, indeed, all statistical procedures.

sampling validity ➤ **validity, sampling**.

sampling variability The variability of successive samples drawn from a population evaluated relative to what a truly random sample would reflect.

sampling, vertical Sampling of subjects from two or more social socioeconomic classes. Compare with ➤ **horizontal** *sampling*.

sampling without replacement Sampling in which each selected element is not replaced in the sample set and is thus not available for future sampling. Compare with ➤ **sampling with replacement**.

sampling with replacement Sampling in which each element selected is placed back in the sample set so that it is available for future sampling. Compare with ➤ **sampling without replacement**.

samsara From the Sanskrit for *transmigration*, the doctrine of the continuous cycle of death and rebirth. ➤➤ **metempsychosis**.

sane (and **sanity**) Terms which, despite their high frequency of usage in both the technical and popular literatures, really have no clear, agreed-upon definitions outside of the legal domain. Presumably, a sane person is one who is ➤ **normal** (see that entry for a discussion of usage) and capable of adequate, adaptive functioning on a day-to-day basis. For the legal issues involved here, ➤ **insanity**.

sangue dormido A ➤ **culture-specific syndrome** found among Portuguese Cape Verde Islanders. It is marked by pain, numbness, paralysis, and, in extreme cases, convulsions and blindness.

sanguine Lit., bloody. It is used typically to label a person of rather optimistic temperament with an air of hopefulness and warmth. The origins of the term go back to the ancient classification of personality types based upon the presumed bodily humors.

Sanson images ➤ **Purkinje–Sanson images**.

Sapir–Whorf hypothesis ➤ **Whorfian hypothesis**. Edward Sapir, as Whorf's teacher and collaborator, often has his name attached to this theory.

Sapphism From the Greek lyric poet Sappho of the island of Lesbos, female ➤ **homosexuality**.

saralasin ➤ **subfornical organ**.

SAT ➤ **Scholastic Aptitude Test**.

satellite cell A cell that functions to

683

support neurons in the peripheral nervous system; e.g., ➤ **Schwann cell**.

satiation 1. ➤ **satiety**. 2. A state of dramatically reduced sensitivity to new stimulation resulting from fatigue from immediately preceding multiple stimulations. syn.; *refractoriness*.

satiety A state of an organism in which desire or motivation for a thing no longer exists because the need has been satisfied.

satiety center A term used occasionally for the ventromedial area of the ➤ **hypothalamus**.

satiety mechanisms Any mechanism that operates to alert the body that some need has been satisfied. The interesting feature of such mechanisms is that they operate in anticipation of the tissue needs being fulfilled. For example, your thirst is quenched after drinking a glass or two of water even though the water has not yet had a chance to replace that which is missing in your cells.

satisfaction An emotional state produced by achieving some goal. Interestingly, early behaviorists (e.g., Thorndike) used this term freely, despite its inescapable mentalistic qualities. ➤ **satisfier** for Thorndike's attempts to circumvent this difficulty.

satisfice To accept a choice or judgement as one that is good enough, one that satisfies. According to Herb Simon, who coined the term, the tendency *to satisfice* shows up in many cognitive tasks such as playing games, solving problems, and making financial decisions where people typically do not or cannot search for the optimal solutions.

satisfier As originally used by the early behaviorist Edward Lee Thorndike, any stimulus possessing pleasant or desirable properties. Defined operationally, a satisfier is a stimulus which an organism will approach or learn some behavior in order to obtain. Hence, a satisfier is a goal that results in the state of ➤ **satisfaction** – although Thorndike himself would doubt-

less not have approved of this last sentence. For more on the general class of theoretical problems buried beneath this term, ➤ **reinforcer** and **reinforcement**.

saturation 1. In the study of color, the dimension that reflects purity or richness. A highly saturated color is vivid and rich, a poorly saturated one is faded or washed out. 2. In factor analysis, the extent to which any particular factor is correlated with a test.

satyriasis An exaggerated sexual desire in males. The term derives from the Greek deity who displayed a fondness for erotic revelry. Compare with ➤ **nymphomania** and ➤ **erotomania**. Also called *Don Juanism*.

savant From the French meaning *knowledgeable*. The term is used for persons who display special, indeed extraordinary, mental capabilities, such as individuals who have had no formal music training but are able to play on the piano any piece heard but once, or those who display a computer-like capacity to perform arithmetic calculations or are able to calculate the day of the week on which any given date in the future will fall. Such persons were once called *idiot savants* because they often have rather limited overall social and/or mental capabilities; fortunately, that term is falling out of use.

savings, method of A procedure for studying memory developed by Ebbinghaus in the 1880s. The subject is required to relearn old material and a comparison is made between the number of trials (or time) needed to relearn and the number of trials (or time) required for the original learning. Comparison between the two yields a *savings score*.

S-B ➤ **Stanford-Binet Scale**.

Sc Relatively rare abbreviation for ➤ **conditioned stimulus**; CS is preferred.

scaffolding An interactive behavioral process whereby structure is provided by one person in the form of behaviors that another person can respond to. As the second person becomes more and more adept at making appropriate contributions, the first individual loosens or modifies the structure, thereby increasing the demands on the second until basically both have learned the full system. Often seen in developmental settings, particularly when a parent is teaching a child a new game. Also called *formatting*.

scalability To make a long story short, the property of being representable in an ordered series of some kind. To make this short story long, ➤ **scale of measurement** and **methods of *scaling**.

scala media ➤ **cochlea**.

scalar analysis An analysis that yields information about where on a known scale a particular item or variable falls.

scala tympani ➤ **cochlea**.

scala vestibuli ➤ **cochlea**.

scale 1. Generally and inclusively, any procedure or device that is used for the purpose of arranging objects or events in some progressive series. This meaning, which is the dominant one, entails the notion that in each and every case there exists some rule for assigning numbers or values to the objects or events to be scaled. The rule(s) applicable in individual cases are what reflect the meaning that the scale values can have. **2.** Any progressive numerical arrangement which can be used to assign magnitudes to events or objects. The primary difference between 1 and 2 here is between the abstract and the concrete. For example, a thermometer is a scale in meaning 2 – it reflects the temperature scale in sense 1. **3.** A testing instrument which has items or tasks arranged along some dimension. The dimension may be any of several such as *difficulty*, as is typical in *intelligence scales*, or *preferences*, as in *attitude scales*. Note that these concrete scaling devices may yield various kinds of measurement scales. vb., *to scale*, meaning to assign numbers to events according to some rule.

scale, absolute A ➤ **ratio *scale**. The term *absolute* is occasionally used here because the establishment of the true zero point permits the conversion of an interval scale into a ratio scale, and *true zero* is also called *absolute zero*.

scale, additive = ➤ **interval *scale**. The term is derived from the fact that the most powerful arithmetic operation one can carry out with such scales is addition.

scale, difficulty A general term for any scale or test with the items marked for order of difficulty.

scale, interval A scale that reflects precise statements about the differences between observed magnitudes; i.e., the *interval* of measurement is specified. The classic examples here are the temperature-measurement scales (Fahrenheit, Celsius), where the interval between, e.g., 40° and 30° is the same as that between 20° and 10°. However, while the intervals are specified, the numbers used in measurement are arbitrary; i.e. the zero point on such a scale is not a true zero as it is on a ➤ **ratio *scale**. Since interval scales are the simplest true quantitative scales, most psychological measurement procedures aspire to at least this level. Interestingly, most of the scales given as examples under ➤ **ordinal *scale** are often treated as though they were, in fact, interval scales. Aside from sheer pragmatics (i.e. only very limited mathematical and statistical operations can be carried out with ordinal data), there are a few quasi-legitimate procedures for making interval scales from ordinal scales, the most common being the assumption of normality in the underlying distribution and the interval units of the scale then being adjusted to match the observations. This procedure, in fact, is what is done with IQ data from intelligence scales.

The statistical operations of addition and subtraction can be carried out with interval scales and means and standard deviations can be calculated. The major limitation is that proportions cannot be specified; e.g., to use temperature measurement again, 80° is most assuredly not twice as warm as 40°. See and compare with ➤ **nominal *scale**, **ordinal *scale**, and **ratio *scale**. Also called *additive scale*.

scale, nominal The most primitive of the possible scales of measurement, this is essentially a system of notation for identifying, classifying and naming observations. In fact, some authorities maintain that the term *scale* is misapplied here since quantification and magnitude are not relevant. The numbers on athletes' uniforms, the taxonomy of biologists, psychiatric nosologies, are examples. Nominal scales since they are strictly qualitative are not particularly interesting as scales; the only formal operation that can be performed on data so scaled is the determination of equivalence and the only statistic permissible is the mode. Also called *categorical scale*. See and compare with ➤ **interval *scale**, **ordinal *scale**, and **ratio *scale**.

scale of measurement A cover term for any of the ➤ **scales** in sense 1 of that term that can be used for measuring some quantity. It is worth noting that a number of mathematical assumptions are always made, either implicitly or explicitly, when actually measuring something along some scale – and not all things are or can be measured in the same manner. For details on the various scales of measurement that are in common use in psychology see the four most important: ➤ **nominal**, **ordinal**, **interval**, and **ratio *scale** as well as some of the other less-used: ➤ **ordered metric** and **product *scale**.

scale, ordered metric A scale of measurement that lies in power and degree of generality between ➤ **ordinal** and **interval *scales**. The basic assumption is that an ordered metric scale results when measurement techniques permit the ordering of the magnitudes of intervals between measured objects.

scale, ordinal A scale with 'order' properties in the specific sense that it is a ranking of observations along some dimension. The assignment of a larger number to one ordinally scaled observation than to another means that there is 'more of' the thing being measured in the first case than in the second. Examples are the hardness scale for minerals, the order of finish in a race, the pleasantness rankings of odors or tastes, etc. Such scales are limited, in that true magnitude cannot be expressed, only relative magnitude. For example, we know that a mineral marked as 7 is harder than one marked 6 and a 6 is harder than one marked 5, but we cannot know whether a 7 is that much harder than a 6 than a 6 is harder than a 5. Because of this intrinsic limiting factor, statistics such as the mean and standard deviation ought not to be used with data on ordinal scales. However, since many scales that psychologists use to measure subjective and covert properties that are of prime importance in the field are ordinal (e.g., attitudes, personal attractiveness, locus of control, anxiety, intelligence, aptitudes, etc.), pragmatic considerations occasionally condone a certain amount of irregular statisticizing. Formally, only medians, percentiles and rank-order statistics are permissible with ordinal data but see the discussion under ➤ **interval *scale** for one of the standard tricks that allows researchers to calculate means and standard deviations. See also and compare with ➤ **nominal *scale** and **ratio *scale**.

scale, psychological Essentially any scale that specifies some kind of system or device for measuring a psychological variable. Note that some authors differentiate between *psychophysical scales*, in which there is a known physical variable to which the psychological one is related (e.g., frequency of a tone and pitch), and *psychological scales*, which have no counterpart in the physical domain (e.g., intelligence).

scale, ratio A scale of measurement on which ratios of magnitudes of those observations being scaled can be expressed. Most of the measurement scales in the physical sciences have this property, e.g., weight, where it is the case that an object weighing 10 grams is twice as heavy as one weighing 5 grams. The fundamental property of a ratio scale is the existence of a true zero point, the one property that ➤ interval *scales lack. They are the most powerful of scales and all mathematical and statistical operations are permissible on observations measured on ratio scales. They are actually relatively rare in psychological measurement, although psychophysical methods exist for establishing ratio scales for some basic sensory systems (e.g., the *sone* scale for loudness; see here ➤ methods of *scaling). It is worth noting that the measurement of observations has often moved upward from scale to scale as new techniques and theories have been developed. For example, temperature measurement was on an *ordinal scale* when only subjective sensations of 'warmer' or 'cooler' were available; it became an *interval scale* with the invention of the thermometer, and a *ratio scale* upon the extrapolation of the absolute zero point based upon the thermodynamics of ratios of gases. Also called *absolute scale*. See and compare with ➤ nominal *scale, ordinal *scale and interval *scale.

scale reliability ➤ item *reliability.

scaling Scale construction and utilization, most commonly the former. Typically in the social sciences, the construction of a scale consists of the evaluation of subjective psychological experience and the development of a numerical system for its measurement. To take as examples some seemingly trivial but actually rather fundamental and important questions answerable by principles of scaling: Does a 20-lb weight *feel* twice as heavy as a 10-lb weight? Does doubling the power output of a radio make it *sound* twice as loud? Does 10 minutes *seem* twice as long as 5 minutes? In each case the answer can only be obtained by constructing a scale along a psychological dimension (heaviness, loudness, time) which is mathematically related to some known physical dimension. For further discussion of related terminology, ➤ methods of *scaling, multidimensional scaling, scale, scale of measurement.

scaling, indirect A cover term for those methods of scaling based on indirect evaluations of experience such as *bisection* or the *method of adjustment*. They are to be contrasted with the more direct scaling methods such as *magnitude estimation*. See the discussion under ➤ methods of *scaling for descriptions of these and other procedures.

scaling, methods of Simply, procedures for ➤ scaling. Although a century of research on the construction of psychological scales has produced dozens of variations, the most common procedures can be summarized under three general classes: 1. *Interval scaling*. Here subjects are requested to judge stimuli on the basis of intervals or differences. In *bisection*, the subject must adjust a stimulus so that it lies half-way between two other stimuli; in *categorical estimation*, he must categorize different stimuli into a small number of categories; in the *method of equal-appearing intervals*, stimuli are to be sorted into groups so that the intervals between them are subjectively equal. 2. *Ratio scaling*. Here the subject estimates the subjective experience by assigning numbers either directly or indirectly to stimuli so that they reflect their judged experiential magnitude. In *magnitude estimation*, each stimulus is assigned a number that reflects its proportionate intensity relative to some standard; e.g., if the standard is called '10' then a stimulus subjectively twice as great is assigned '20,' one half as great is assigned '5,' etc. In the *method of production*, the subject is asked to produce a stimulus that corresponds to some proportional value of a standard, e.g., twice as bright, one-third as loud, etc.; this procedure is also called the *method of adjustment*. In *cross modality matching*, the magnitudes are arrived at indirectly; e.g., the loudness of a tone is adjusted so that it sounds as loud as a given weight feels heavy. 3. *Non-metric scaling*. These are procedures for dealing with psychological variables that are *non-metric*, i.e. those that cannot be simply dealt with in interval scale form. Scaling of preferences, tastes, value judgments and the like fall under this heading. The typical technique here consists of providing the subject with pairs of stimuli and asking him or her to judge them in terms of desirability or preference; e.g., would the subject rather have a cheese sandwich or a ham sandwich. Several mathematically sophisticated procedures exist whereby these ordered judgements can be made to yield true interval scales. ➤ **multidimensional scaling**.

scallop A term used in operant-conditioning studies as reflective of the shape of the graph of cumulative responses typically produced by an organism run for some time on a fixed-interval schedule of reinforcement. The 'scallop' pattern is produced by the fact that relatively few responses occur immediately after a reinforcement, with the number increasing dramatically toward the end of the interval.

scalogram analysis = ➤ **Guttman scaling**.

scan **1** vb. To produce a picture of a slice through the soft tissue of the body, most commonly the brain. **2** n. The picture itself. **3** n. The procedure that produces the picture. The three most frequently used procedures are ➤ **computerized axial tomography** (CAT-scan), ➤ **magnetic resonance imaging** (MRI-scan) and ➤ **positron emission tomography** (PET-scan).

Scanlon Plan A group incentive plan used in many industries and other organizations. It is based on notions of learning theory and social needs of workers. In it workers are encouraged to offer suggestions for improving working conditions and procedures and if such are successfully implemented the savings are returned to the workers as percentage increases in pay.

scanning speech ➤ **ataxic speech**.

scapegoat *Scape* is an archaic form of *escape*, the goat is the animal upon whom, in the ancient Hebraic practice, the accumulated sins of the people were placed on Atonement Day. The goat thus symbolically burdened was then driven into the wild. Hence, scapegoating is the act of blaming a convenient (but innocent,

as was the goat) person or group for one's own frustrations, grievances, guilts, etc. This phenomenon is found as a defense mechanism in individuals as well as a deliberate form of propaganda in governments.

scatological **1.** As derived from the Greek word for *dung*, referring to excrement or to an abiding interest in excrement. **2.** More loosely, characteristic of obscene language independent of fecal references.

scatter **1.** n. The degree to which a set of scores (or the data points representing them, ➤ **scatter diagram**) is clustered about some central score, typically the *mean*. In this sense, it is a synonym for ➤ **variability** or ➤ **dispersion**. **2.** n. The degree to which there is high variability in scoring, particularly intrasubject variability on a particular test. Persons who obtain high scores on some parts of a test but low on others or students who achieve high grades in some subjects but low in others are said to show high scatter. vb., *scatter*, used in either sense.

scatter diagram (or **plot**) A diagram, plot or table of two-valued data points such that all the *x*-scores are plotted with their respective *y*-scores. When presented in graphic fashion and fitted with a regression line, a pictorial sense of the amount of ➤ **scatter** (1) in the data can be obtained.

scedasticity The relative variability displayed in rows and columns of a scatter diagram. *Homoscedasticity* is the condition in which the measures of variability (usually the *standard deviation* or *variance*) lie within the range expected of chance variability; *heteroscedasticity* is the condition in which they are greater than would be expected by chance.

schedule **1.** A plan or organization used particularly with respect to a series of operations that are repeated. **2.** An outline or a form, especially one set up for a questionnaire or for conducting an interview.

schedule of reinforcement ➤ **reinforcement, schedules of**.

scheduling theory A general theory concerned with the mathematically complex problems of scheduling a large number of individual operations or processes that must be carried out to perform some complex task. Originally developed by computer operations theorists, it has been applied by industrial and organizational psychologists in handling problems in industry and by cognitive scientists as a basic model of how the brain allocates priorities and schedules various cognitive processes in the performance of complex tasks.

Scheffé test A common ➤ *post hoc* test used to test specific comparisons after an analysis of variance or other statistical test has shown overall significance. It is a conservative test that tends to err on the side of underestimating the significance of differences between means, and it deals well with the problem of unequal numbers of cases in particular cells.

schema 1. A plan, an outline, a structure, a framework, a program, etc. In all or any of these meanings the assumption is that the schemata (or schemas) are cognitive, mental plans that are abstract and that they serve as guides for action, as structures for interpreting information, as organized frameworks for solving problems, etc. Thus, we find references to a linguistic schema for comprehending a sentence, a cultural schema for interpreting a myth, a prehensile schema for a child learning how to grasp an object, a means–end schema for solving logical problems, etc. A schema is more than a ➤ **set** (2) because it is more elaborate and less restricted to a particular situation; it is more ideational or implicit than a ➤ **strategy** (1) and conceptually richer than a ➤ **hypothesis** (2). 2. A general framework or structure within which data or events can be recorded, particularly one that emphasizes the overall relationships between major effects and down-plays fine details. 3. By extension, a model or organized outline touching on the main or primary elements of a system. Compare with ➤ **scheme**.

schematic 1. Usually, diagrammatic; presented in skeletal form. 2. Less often, pertaining to a ➤ **schema** or a ➤ **scheme**.

schematize To present in schematic form.

scheme An organized plan. Some use this term interchangeably with ➤ **schema**; others reserve scheme for the more concrete kinds of cognitive structures that are formed consciously. This distinction is particularly true of Piaget's use of the terms.

schizo- A combining form meaning *splitting, separating, cleavage.*

schizoaffective disorder A psychosis marked by either a major depressive episode or a manic episode occurring concurrent with classic symptoms of ➤ **schizophrenia** such as delusions, hallucinations, lack of volition, disturbed speech patterns, etc.

schizoid A term with a tortured pattern of usage: **1.** Pertaining to or descriptive of ➤ **schizophrenia** or of an individual so diagnosed. Here the reference is clearly to a ➤ **psychosis**. **2.** Resembling some of the behavioral and cognitive characteristics of schizophrenia but displayed in a manner that is merely eccentric and not the least psychotic. See here ➤ **schizothymia**. **3.** Shorthand form of ➤ **schizoid disorder of childhood or adolescence**. **4.** Shorthand form of ➤ **schizoid personality disorder**. Usages 3 and 4 are, in contemporary writings, the ones usually intended. Meanings 1 and 2 have been dropped by most authorities because of the confusions involved in using the same term for a psychotic disorder and a simple pattern of eccentric but normal behavior.

schizoid disorder of childhood or adolescence A childhood disorder marked by a lack of ability to form friendships with peers, a lack of interest in doing so and a decided lack of pleasure derived from such interactions when encouraged or arranged by others. Such children are withdrawn, aloof and seclusive and typically react negatively to demands from others for social interaction. They display, however, none of the signs of a psychosis such as loss of reality testing. If the disorder continues into adulthood it is termed ➤ **schizoid personality disorder**.

schizoid personality disorder A personality disorder characterized by an emotional coldness, secretiveness, solitude, withdrawal and a general inability to form intimate attachments to others. It is not regarded as a form of schizophrenia and is diagnostically differentiated from a ➤ **schizotypal personality disorder**; see that entry for details.

schizophrasia A term occasionally used for disconnected speech such as that observed in some forms of schizophrenia.

schizophrenia A general label for a number of psychotic disorders with various cognitive, emotional and behavioral manifestations. The term originated with Eugen Bleuler, who offered it in 1911 as a replacement for ➤ **dementia praecox**. It literally means *splitting in the mind* and was chosen by Bleuler because the disorder seemed to reflect a cleavage or dissociation between the functions of feeling or emotion on one hand and those of thinking or cognition on the other. That is, the 'split' here is horizontal and not vertical; the latter dissociation yields ➤ **multiple personality**, a decidedly different psychiatric syndrome.

Although there are various distinguishable schizophrenias which display differing etiologies and have distinguishable prognoses, certain features are taken as hallmarks of all: (a) deterioration from previous levels of social, cognitive and vocational functioning; (b) onset before midlife (roughly 45–50 years of age); (c) a duration of at least six months; and most tellingly, (d) a pattern of psychotic features including thought disturbances, bizarre delusions, hallucinations (usually auditory), disturbed sense of self and a loss of reality testing.

The borderline that distinguishes schizophrenia from other disorders is fuzzy and differential diagnosis is problematical. See for details here ➤ **borderline *schizo-**phrenia, ➤ **schizoaffective disorder**, ➤ **schizoid personality disorder**, ➤ **schizophreniform disorder**, ➤ **schizotypal personality disorder**. Note also that, although many authorities are convinced that a relatively straightforward (although still largely unknown) neurochemical cause exists for the disorder, it is not given as a diagnostic label when there is evidence of an ➤ **organic mental disorder**. There is strong evidence that schizophrenia shows familial patterns of incidence, suggesting that there is a genetic predisposition for individuals to display the disorder.

A number of terms have been and are used as equivalent to schizophrenia; they include *schizophrenic disorder*, *schizophrenic reaction* and *schizophrenic psychosis*. The various forms of schizophrenia that have been labeled at one time or another are given in the following entries. Those that are part of the contemporary psychiatric nosology (that is, they are recognized by either the ➤ **DSM–IV** or the ➤ **ICD–10**) are marked with an *.

schizophrenia, borderline A vague classification used of persons who display some of the features of schizophrenia but do not fit the full profile of the psychosis. The preferred diagnostic label for such cases is ➤ **schizotypal personality disorder**.

schizophrenia, catatonic (type)* A type of schizophrenia characterized by a tendency to remain in a stupor-like state during which the patient may hold a particular posture, sitting or lying in the same position for extended periods of time, sometimes for weeks or even months. Mutism, waxy flexibility and mindless stereotypy are also common. Frequently the catatonic state gives way to short periods of frenetic activity during which the patient is capable of considerable damage to others as well as to him- or herself. Note that there is a school of thought that views this syndrome, not as a schizophrenia, but as an ➤ **affective disorder**. Also called *schizophrenic disorder*, *catatonic type*.

schizophrenia, childhood Simply, schizophrenia occurring in childhood. Many experts question whether this is in fact a category of disorder separate from any of several others occurring during childhood. E.g., ➤ **infantile *autism**.

schizophrenia, chronic A diagnostic label used for any schizophrenia the symptoms of which have continued for an extended time and proven relatively refractory to therapeutic intervention.

schizophrenia, deficit (type)* A subtype of schizophrenia recently suggested for cases where the clinical picture is dominated by enduring, disabling *negative symptoms* in the absence of disorganized behavior, speech, or affect.

schizophrenia, disorganized (type)* A type of schizophrenia which is, in a sense, the prototype of the disorder. The primary symptoms are the erratic speech, strange, often childish mannerisms and general bizarreness of behavior that are regarded as hallmarks of the psychotic. A variety of other symptoms are often although not always noted including hearing voices, elaborate fantasies including the belief that one is someone else, withdrawal from day-to-day realities, delusions of grandeur and/or persecution, strange bodily feelings including the delusion that vital organs are missing, etc. This is the single most common diagnostic category in Western mental institutions. Also called *hebephrenia*, *hebephrenic schizophrenia* and *schizophrenic disorder*, *disorganized type*.

schizophrenia, hebephrenic ➤ **disorganized (type) *schizophrenia**.

schizophrenia in remission A diagnostic label used for cases in which the patient has had a history of schizophrenia but currently is symptom-free. The term is used whether or not the individual is taking medication for the disorder. Just how long the person should remain free of symptoms before the diagnostic label is dropped is a matter of dispute among authorities.

schizophrenia, paranoid (type)* A type of schizophrenia characterized primarily by delusions of persecution or grandiosity or hallucinations with persecutory or grandiose content. Delusional jealousy is often part of the disorder and any of a number of associated symptoms may be found, including unfocused anxiety, anger, argumentativeness, doubts about gender identity, stilted formal quality, aloofness. Unlike many other forms of schizophrenia, the patient is usually of relatively normal appearance and clean in habits and if the delusions are not acted on impairment in functioning may be minimal. Also called *paraphrenic schizophrenia* and *paraphrenia*. Distinguish from ➤ **paranoia**, ➤ **paranoid personality** and ➤ **delusional (paranoid) disorder**.

schizophrenia, positive paranoid (type)* A new label suggested for the subtype of schizophrenia known as *paranoid (type) schizophrenia*. The term emphasizes the positive aspects of the disorder; ➤ **paranoid (type) *schizophrenia** to appreciate this point.

schizophrenia, process A term used loosely for chronic schizophrenias attributed more to organic causes than to environmental. They are marked by gradual onset and generally poor prognosis and distinguished from the so-called ➤ **reactive *schizophrenia**.

schizophrenia, reactive A term used loosely for schizophrenia marked by abrupt onset and relatively short duration. As the term *reactive* suggests, it is generally attributed to predisposing factors and/or precipitating environmental events. The prognosis is regarded as favourable. Contrast with ➤ **process *schizophrenia**.

schizophrenia, residual (type)* A psychiatric category for cases in which the individual has a history of at least one episode of schizophrenia, currently displays no prominent psychotic symptoms, but still manifests evidence of maladaptive behavior such as unusually low or inappropriate affect, erratic or illogical thinking, strange associations, social withdrawal, etc.

schizophrenia, simple A form of schizophrenia characterized by an extreme lack of what are considered normal emotional reactions to the real world. Emotions of joy, sadness, anger, resentment and the like are missing; ambition and initiative likewise; apathy, indifference and resignation dominate. With social and economic impoverishment, vagrancy often results.

schizophrenia, undifferentiated (type)* A diagnostic category for clinical cases considered to be schizophrenic because they display some of the classic symptoms of the disorder such as delusions, hallucinations, incoherence and disorganized behaviors but who fail to display any one cluster of these symptoms clearly enough to meet the criteria for any of the other types.

schizophrenic episode, acute A relatively brief (a few weeks or months) episode of schizophrenic symptoms, typically, clouding of consciousness, emotional turmoil and disorganized thought. Also called ➤ **reactive *schizophrenia**, but see that term for further discussion of usage.

schizophrenic thought disorder ➤ schizophrenia.

schizophreniform disorder A psychotic disorder characterized by all the classic features of schizophrenia but in which the duration is more than two weeks but less than six months.

schizophrenogenic Generally, pertaining to any factor hypothesized to be causally related to the development of schizophrenia. Two broad classes of factors have been identified, *genetic* and *environmental*, leading to three broad theoretical models of the etiology of the disorder: (a) the *specific gene theory*, which assumes that the disorder is caused by one (or more) faulty genes that produce metabolic disturbances; (b) the *environment theory*, which views schizophrenia as a reaction to a stressful environment rife with anxiety-producing conditions (see here ➤ **schizophrenic parent**); and (c) the *constitutional-predisposition theory*, which combines these two, arguing that a variety of disparate dispositions are inherited but that the emergence of a diagnosable schizophrenic disorder is dependent upon the degree of these dispositions and the extent to which they are encouraged by particular kinds of environmental conditions. This last point of view has the largest number of adherents among specialists.

schizophrenogenic parent A term used for a parent who is cold, rejecting, distant, aloof, but dominating. Theoretically, such a parent puts the child in a hopeless double-bind in that dependency is being simultaneously fostered and rejected. Whether such a parenting style actually can cause a child who is not genetically predisposed to become schizophrenic is a highly debatable question.

schizothymia The tendency to display erratic patterns of thought and behavior. A schizothymic is regarded as a quite normal individual, merely eccentric. ➤➤ **schizoid** (2).

schizotypal personality disorder A personality disorder characterized by markedly eccentric and erratic thought, speech and behavior and a tendency to withdraw from other people. The disorder is characterized as similar to but less severe than ➤ **schizophrenia**, although it is occasionally called *borderline schizophrenia*. This diagnostic category is used in the DSM as roughly equivalent to the ICD's ➤ **simple *schizophrenia**. Distinguish from ➤ **schizoid personality disorder**, where the eccentricities of thought, speech and behavior are not present.

Schmerz ➤ pain (3).

Scholastic Aptitude Test (SAT) In the USA, the most widely used of the college-admission tests. It consists of two aptitude tests, one in verbal and one in mathematical aptitude, and a series of achievement tests in particular subjects.

school Outside of the obvious, a loosely organized group of scholars or researchers whose approach to a field of study is rather doctrinaire and structured around a particular theoretical point of view. Frequently the school is tied in with the theory of one person, e.g., the Freudian school; often, however, the orientation prevails without eponym, e.g., the Gestalt school.

school phobia 1. Irrational fear of school or the school situation. 2. = ➤ **school refusal**. The synonymity of 2 is not recommended, as is explained under that entry.

school psychology A sub-discipline within the discipline of educational psychology. Typically the school psychologist is concerned with counseling and advising primary and secondary schoolchildren, assisting in curriculum development and in testing for and assessing potential emotional and/or learning disabilities.

school refusal Refusal on the part of a child to attend school or, by extension, go away to camp, stay at a friend's house, etc. It is generally taken as one of the hallmark features of ➤ **separation-anxiety disorder**. Note that some authors use the term as a synonym for ➤ **school phobia**. This equivalence is not recommended; strictly speaking, a refusal to go to school may be caused by a school phobia but most school refusals are due to separation anxiety. In a true school phobia the child will show the phobic reaction even if the parents are present.

schwa (ə) In phonetics, a common midcentral neutral vowel. It plays an important role in the sound patterns of English in that it appears as a reduced, unstressed vowel in syllables that are stressed or accented; e.g., in most American dialects, the phrase 'the lovely attitude' is pronounced so that the italicized *e*, *o* and *i* are all schwas.

Schwann cells The cells that provide the ➤ **neurilemma** that covers the myelin sheath of axons in the peripheral nervous system. They differ from the oligodendroglia (➤ **glia**) found in the central nervous system in that they aid in regeneration of damaged axons by guiding the route of regrowth. Regeneration does not occur in the central nervous system.

Schwann sheath = ➤ **neurilemma**.

science 1. A body of knowledge, particularly that which has resulted from the systematic application of the ➤ **scientific *method**. 2. A branch of study or a discipline focused on the derivation of basic principles and general laws. 3. A system of methods and procedures for the investigation of natural phenomena based upon scientific principles.

scientific attitude (or **approach**) Simply, that orientation toward the study of phenomena that presumes that basic understanding is best achieved through the systematic application of the ➤ **scientific *method**.

scientific law ➤ **law, scientific**.

scientific method ➤ **method, scientific**.

scientific psychology Basically, the pursuit of psychological knowledge using the ➤ **scientific *method**. Given the breadth of procedures and interpretative laterality involved here, the term includes essentially all of psychology.

scientism A term typically used in a critical vein toward those who, in the eyes of the critic, place too much emphasis on science to provide solutions to problems and understanding of phenomena.

sciosophy Any body of beliefs about the natural or supernatural systematized by tradition or imagination independently of scientific thinking or scientific methods.

sclera The thick, fibrous, white, opaque outer covering of the eyeball. Also called the *sclerotic coat* or *layer*.

sclerosis Generally, a pathological hardening of tissue.

sclerotic coat (or **layer**) ➤ **sclera**.

scoliosis An abnormal lateral curvature of the spine, usually consisting of two curves in opposite directions.

scope The domain within which some action takes place.

-scope Combining form meaning *device* or *instrument for viewing*.

-scopia, -scopy Combining forms meaning *examination*, *viewing*, *scrutiny*.

scopic Measured or evaluated by direct (visual) observation as opposed to by the use of instruments.

scopolamine (hydrobromide) An alkaloid obtained from plants of the nightshade family. It is used as a sedative and, in combination with either phenobarbital or morphine, to produce 'twilight' sleep. Despite the fantasies of spy novelists, it is not a truth serum.

scopophilia The deriving of sexual pleasure from visual sources, e.g., watching others make love, nudity, pornographic pictures or films. If an individual requires such activity for sexual arousal, it is classified as a ➤ **paraphilia**; see here ➤ **voyeurism**. vars., *scotophilia*, *scoptophilia* (neither is recommended).

-scopy ➤ **-scopia**.

score A number or other quantitative value used to represent: **1.** An individual response, where the term *response* is meant to encompass any measurable act of a subject. **2.** A summed or totalled value based on a number of individual *scores* (in sense 1, above). This meaning is usually found in testing when a final score is composed of several subtest scores. The term typically occurs in combined form with qualifiers which specify the kind of score under consideration; the more common are given below.

score, gross Any score presented in the original units of measurement.

score, raw The originally observed and recorded value. A score that has not been subjected to any transformation or statisti-

cal analysis. Compare with ➤ **derived score**. Also called *obtained score*, *observed score*, *crude score*.

score, standard **1.** Generally, any derived score that is based on the ➤ **standard *deviation**. **2.** More specifically, and more commonly, a ➤ **z-score**.

score, transformed Any score that is derived from a transformation in which the original score is mapped onto and expressed in a different scale. E.g., ➤ **arc sine transformation**. Occasionally called *transmuted score*.

score, true The value of a population statistic. All observed scores from samples are assumed to be made up of this 'true' score plus or minus some ➤ **error**. In theory, since sampling errors are assumed to be random, they cancel each other out and with increasingly large data bases the observed values will approach the true values. In actual practice, the mean of the observed scores, within its standard error, is taken as an unbiased estimate of the true score. Also called *true value*.

scoring Generally, procedures for assigning values, for making measurements. Usually one distinguishes between *objective scoring* and *subjective scoring*; the former is used for situations in which some unambiguous rule or code essentially guarantees that any competent observer will arrive at the same conclusion concerning the scores, the latter for situations in which complex and sophisticated evaluations are made based on often non-specifiable and subjective procedures. Multiple-choice examinations are scored by the former, essay examinations by the latter.

scoterythrous A loss of color sensitivity to the long-wavelength lights; ➤ **protanopia**.

scoto- Combining form meaning *dark*, *darkness*.

scotoma A totally or partially blind area of the retina. The term is generally reserved for pathologies, although some authors refer to the normal *blind spot* as *physiological scotoma*. pl., *scotomata*; adj., *scotomatous*.

scotomization A defense mechanism in which the person develops 'blind spots' (metaphorically speaking) to certain kinds of emotional or anxiety-producing situations or conflicts.

scotophilia 1. = ➤ **scopophilia**. 2. Preference for darkness or nighttime; also called *nyctophilia*.

scotopic adaptation ➤ **dark adaptation**.

scotopic vision Twilight vision, vision under conditions of low illumination such that visual experience is that provided by the rods of the retina. Scotopic vision has the following general properties: (a) hues are not seen, vision is in terms of black and white; (b) the brightness threshold, compared with that of ➤ **photopic vision**, is low; (c) the luminosity curve shows maximum sensitivity to a wavelength of approximately 510 nm with rapidly decreasing sensitivity to longer and shorter wavelengths; (d) because the rods exist only outside of the fovea, visual acuity is poor.

scratch reflex A reflexive scratching response elicited from an animal by a sharp stimulus such as a pinch on the back or the flank.

screen 1 n. Any device for blanking out part of the visual field. 2 n. A device upon which a stimulus is displayed. 3 n. In psychoanalytic theory, any event or object that serves a defensive function and prevents a person from realizing the underlying meaning of an event, a symbol, a dream, etc. 4 vb. To select a small sub-set of events or things from a larger population. These events or things may be stimuli, in which case an observer is said to *screen* (or to *filter*) *out* some while attending to the others, or they may be persons applying for a position, in which case certain candidates are said to be *screened out* of the selection process. Note that, in these usages, the rejected items or persons are referred to as having been *screened out*, the others are said to *pass the screening* or to *pass through the screen*.

screen memory A psychoanalytic term for the memory for events dating from early childhood, fleeting, elusive memories that have managed to filter through the ego's defensive efforts at repression. The usual interpretation is that such memories function as 'covers' for other emotionally dangerous information which they, in fact, help to repress. Hence, a common synonym is *cover memory*.

script 1. In sociology and social psychology, a scenario, a characterization of the events that occur in a particular social setting. 2. In the cognitive sciences, an individual's knowledge of these events in terms of appropriate behavior to be carried out, knowledge of who does what, when, to whom and why. Usually scripts are qualified to specify the setting of circumstances; e.g., a restaurant script, a picnic script. 3. Cursive handwriting.

S-curve ➤ **S-shaped curve**.

SD ➤ **standard *deviation**.

SDT ➤ **signal-detection theory**.

SE ➤ **standard error**.

seance 1. A sitting, as a session of a learned group or a class for the purpose of discussion or deliberation. 2. A sitting for the purpose of communicating with spirits. The second meaning has, unfortunately, become the dominant one.

search In cognitive psychology: 1 vb. To scan through one's memory for some specific fact or other piece of information. 2 n. the process of making such a scan. The following entries give the various kinds of memory searches that have been hypothesized; note that most of them derive their names from recent work in ➤ **information processing** and ➤ **artificial intelligence** and hence have a kind of computer-like character to them.

search, exhaustive A memory search in which all possible alternatives are considered. Compare with ➤ **self-terminating *search**.

search, parallel Any memory-search

695

process in which more than one type of scanning goes on simultaneously. ➤ **parallel *processing**.

search, self-terminating A memory-search process where one considers alternatives until the 'target' has been found. Compare with ➤ **exhaustive *search**. Note that most theories of memory that hypothesize a self-terminating search routine assume that it has a time component; i.e. if the searched-for target is not found within some period of time, the search terminates and the individual is said to have forgotten the material. ➤ **forgetting** for more on usage here.

search, serial A memory search in which pieces of information are examined one at a time in a series. ➤ **sequential *processing**.

Seashore tests A series of tests of auditory and musical ability developed by Carl E. Seashore.

seasonal affective disorder (SAD) The most common form of ➤ **seasonal mood disorder**; it is characterized by depression, lethargy, and sleep disturbances. It typically occurs during the winter months and can often be treated by regular exposure to bright lights. Also called *mood disorder with seasonal pattern*.

seasonal mood disorder An umbrella term for any ➤ **mood disorder** that shows a regular temporal pattern such as recurring every summer or over every winter. ➤ **seasonal affective disorder**.

seasickness ➤ **motion sickness**.

seclusion need Murray's term for the need for privacy, aloneness, inconspicuousness.

secondary 1. Second, particularly in importance, rank or significance. The fundamental idea is that a thing is considered secondary with respect to other things when they can be ordered in some way, in time, in space, in magnitude, etc. **2.** Dependent on something else; based on or derived from a primary thing. The term enjoys wide currency in combined phrases; see the following. Contrast with ➤ **primary**.

secondary advantage ➤ **secondary gain**.

secondary circular reaction ➤ **circular reaction**.

secondary (or second-order) conditioning ➤ **higher-order conditioning**.

secondary drive A learned or ➤ **acquired *drive**.

secondary elaboration A psychoanalytic term for the tendency to fill gaps, make inferences and reorganize one's memory of dreams upon awakening.

secondary extinction ➤ **extinction, secondary**.

secondary gain 1. Generally, any continuing gain derived from being ill. **2.** More specifically, the advantages derived from a neurosis, e.g., the avoidance of conflict and lessening of anxiety. Compare with ➤ **primary gain**. ➤ **advantage by illness**. Also called *epinosic gain*.

secondary group ➤ **group, secondary**.

secondary identification Identification with someone other than the usual parental figure.

secondary integration Freud's term for the integration of the psychic elements of the pregenital stage into a coherent psychosexual identity.

secondary memory ➤ **long-term *memory**.

secondary narcissism ➤ **narcissism, secondary**.

secondary personality In cases of multiple personality, the aspect that separates off from the main personality.

secondary process In psychoanalytic theory, mental functioning which is conscious, rational and logical. Secondary processes are conceptualized as intimately linked with the ego and the reality principle. Compare with ➤ **primary process**.

secondary quality ➤ **primary and secondary *quality**.

secondary reinforcer ➤ **conditioned *reinforcer**.

secondary relationship ➤ relationship, secondary.

secondary repression ➤ repression (1).

secondary reward A secondary or ➤ conditioned *reinforcer.

secondary sex characteristics ➤ sex characteristics, secondary.

second messenger Generally, any chemical within a cell that initiates a series of steps involved in synaptic transmission. They are called *second messengers* with the understanding that the ➤ neurotransmitters are the *first*.

second moment The ➤ variance of a distribution. ⇒ moment (2).

second-order conditioning ➤ higher-order conditioning.

second-order factor ➤ first-order *factor.

second-signal system In the ➤ Pavlovian approach, stimuli or signals are separated into two domains, those that are due to direct physical events (the *first-signal system*) and those that are generated internally, inside the organism (the *second-signal system*). Pavlov viewed speech and language as the primary vehicles for the functioning of the second-signal system, but more recent Russian theorizing has extended the domain to include all forms of ideational, mental, imaginal and mediational activity.

sect A group that espouses a particular set of religious beliefs and practices. A sect is generally viewed as a separate, exclusive entity, with abstract ideals, existing within another, larger religious organization. Compare with ➤ cult.

section 1. Generally, a subdivision or the act of creating a subdivision. 2. More specifically, a slice of tissue or the cutting or slicing of tissue. They are various types of sections that are commonly made in physiological work: (a) *Transverse sections* are cuts straight across the longitudinal axis at right angles to it. Note that other terms are used to specify particular kinds of transverse sections: *cross section* is used generally, *frontal section* when the cut is made toward the front of the organ and *coronal section* when it is made toward the rear. (b) *Horizontal sections* are cuts made parallel to the ground. (c) *Sagittal sections* are made perpendicular to the ground.

sectioned The process of determining that an individual is certifiable as suffering from a severe mental disorder and may be committed to a mental institution. The term is common in Great Britain where it derives from the holding of the individual under the appropriate *section* of the Mental Health Act. ⇒ certifiable and commitment.

secular 1. Observed but once in a century or an age. Generally descriptive of processes that evolve slowly, e.g., cultural change. 2. Worldly, temporal, as opposed to religious or spiritual.

secure attachment ➤ attachment styles.

security A sense of confidence, safety, freedom from fear or anxiety, particularly with respect to fulfilling one's present (and future) needs.

security operations 1. H. S. Sullivan's cover term for all those efforts engaged in by individuals to maintain or increase security and avoid anxiety. 2. In Fromm-Reichmann's approach, security operations are essentially synonymous with *defense mechanisms.*

sedative, hypnotic, or anxiolytic amnestic disorder An ➤ amnestic disorder brought about by prolonged, excessive use of any sedative, hypnotic, or anxiolytic drug.

sedative, hypnotic, or anxiolytic withdrawal An organic mental disorder resulting from the cessation of prolonged, moderate or heavy use of a sedative, hypnotic, or anxiolytic drug. The symptoms of nausea, weakness, anxiety, irritability, and the like are similar to those of ➤ alcohol withdrawal. This disorder is often called 'uncomplicated' to distinguish it from cases where *delirium* is one of the symptoms.

sedative, hypnotic, or anxiolytic withdrawal

697

delirium Similar to ➤ **sedative, hypnotic, or anxiolytic withdrawal**, but with delirium, vivid hallucinations, and marked autonomic hyperactivity including tachycardia and sweating. The disorder is typically not seen unless the drug has been used heavily for five or more years prior to the withdrawal.

sedatives A class of drugs all of which produce drowsiness and are prescribed most frequently in cases of insomnia. Sedatives are usually classified into the ➤ **barbiturates** (of which there are several; see that entry for details) and the *non-barbiturates*; the latter group includes ➤ **chloral hydrate**, ➤ **ethinamate**, ➤ **glutethimide**, ➤ **methaqualone** and ➤ **paraldehyde**. All of these drugs function similarly to depress, nonselectively, central-nervous-system functioning. Depending on the size of the dose, they produce mild sedation, 'hynotic' sleep (see here ➤ **hypnotics**), anesthesia, coma and death from respiratory failure. All are subject to buildup of tolerance, so that increasing doses are needed to maintain the same effect, and all produce drug dependence. They also diminish sensorimotor skills and interact strongly with many other drugs, significantly alcohol. Other drugs are occasionally included in the category of sedatives, in particular ➤ **antihistamines**, which have drowsiness as a side-effect, several ➤ **anticholinergic drugs** (e.g., *scopolamine*) and some ➤ **antianxiety drugs**.

segmentation 1. Generally, the process of dividing up a whole into its component parts or segments. **2.** In linguistics, the dividing of the surface structure of a sentence into its constituents and phonetic elements.

segregation 1. In Gestalt theory, the perceptual process whereby the coherent, organized figure is seen as phenomenologically distinct from the rest of the field (the ground); see here ➤ **figure-ground. 2.** By extension from perception to cognition, the compartmentalization of thought processes. **3.** An ecological process whereby particular demographic units – usually

cities – become subdivided into distinct, functional/cultural districts; e.g., industrial, residential, upper-income, slum, high-rise, ethnic, etc. **4.** A subdividing of the residential areas of a city and their accompanying services including schools, shopping facilities, transportation, churches, theaters, etc. such that their availability to persons is controlled and determined by racial, ethnic or religious characteristics. In this context ➤ **racism** and **prejudice** and compare with ➤ **discrimination**. Note that 4 is, in a sense, included in the more general, neutral meaning of 3, although 4 has become the dominant sociopolitical meaning. **5.** In genetics, the process of reduction division (➤ **meiosis**) in sexual reproduction such that only a single gene from each gene pair is in the gamete.

seizure 1. Generally, any sudden attack of a disorder or malady. **2.** More specifically, a convulsion.

seizure disorders A term often used synonymously with ➤ **epilepsy**. The various forms of seizure disorders can be found under that heading.

selected group Generally, any group or sample which results from the application of some rule such that the members are specially selected from a larger population. Note that a selected group may be chosen so as to be either (a) deliberately nonrepresentative of the population, e.g., a group composed of Nobel prize winners or a group of psychologists who have authored lexicons, or (b) deliberately more representative of the population than a similarly sized random sample could reasonably be expected to be, e.g., a stratified sample, as is often used in modern polling techniques. ➤ **sample** et seq.

selection 1. Broadly, choice. The term is used freely with respect to any operation whereby some individual, group, subject, item, etc. is chosen to be included in a sample, an experiment, a group, etc. **2.** In evolutionary biology, the process whereby individual organisms, possessing particular genetic characteristics which make survival and reproductive success in their environmental niches more likely, cause a progressive sequence of changes in the genes for that species. Strictly speaking, it is the *genes* themselves that are selected for by this process, although it is the success of their associated phenotypes that is the causal process. ➤➤ **natural selection**. **3**. In operant behavior analysis, the process whereby particular behaviors become part of an organism's repertoire of responses by virtue of the particular consequences of those behaviors. It is used analogously with meaning 2, only instead of features of species being selected for, behaviors of individual organisms are. ➤➤ **shaping**.

selection index A formula for assessing the power of a particular test or item on a test in discriminating individuals from each other.

selection, social An obsolete term used originally as a sociological analog of natural selection. It was the basic principle hypothesized to operate in the so-called social Darwinian model of social change. ➤ **social Darwinism** for discussion.

selective adaptation ➤ **adaptation, selective**.

selective attention The process involved in situations in which one is confronted with multiple stimulus inputs and must select but one aspect of them and attend to it. In a sense, the term is redundant since the simple term ➤ **attention** carries the sense of selectivity; nevertheless, the compound form is often used.

selective breeding Controlled mating for the purpose of producing offspring with particular characteristics.

selective inattention **1**. A lack of conscious attending to some aspect of a stimulus. **2**. A synonym for ➤ **perceptual defense**.

selective learning ➤ **learning, selective**.

selective mutism Quite literally, selecting not to speak. Classified as a childhood disorder, it is characterized by a failure to speak in specific social situations where speech is expected, such as school. The condition typically lasts only a few months. Also called *elective mutism*.

self One of the more dominant aspects of human experience is the compelling sense of one's unique existence, what philosophers have traditionally called the issue of personal identity or of the *self*. Accordingly, this term finds itself rather well represented in psychological theory, particularly in the areas of social and developmental psychology, the study of personality and the field of psychopathology. The diversity of uses, not surprisingly, is extremely broad and rather unsystematic and the meaning intended is often confounded by the fact that the term may be used in ways which interact subtly with grammatical forms. To appreciate this problem, see the separate entry for the combining form, ➤ **self-**.

The following are what appear to be the six primary intentions of the users of the term *self*: **1**. Self as inner agent or force with controlling and directing functions over motives, fears, needs, etc. Here the self is a hypothetical entity, an assumed aspect of the psyche with a particular role to play. This meaning is found in Adler's notion of the ➤ **creative *self**, in Sullivan's ➤ **self-system** and in Jung's early writings. **2**. Self as inner witness to events. Here, self is viewed as a component of the psyche which serves an introspective function. This self presumably can scan and introspect upon the self expressed in meaning 1. William James pointed out in 1890 that these two meanings might best be spoken of as the *me* and the *I*, the *me* being the self known, the self as object as in 1, and the *I* being the knowing self, the self as subject as in 2. **3**. Self as the totality of personal experience and expression, self as living being. Here the term is used inclusively and relatively neutrally and other terms like *ego, person, individual, organism*, etc. are acceptable synonyms. **4**. Self as synthesis, self as an organized personalized whole. The meaning here is similar to 3 but with the additional connotation that one is concentrating upon the integrated aspect. Those who use

SELF-

the term in this fashion often present it as a logical construct which is inferred indirectly by an individual's experience of personal continuity despite changes over time. Thus generally, the term ➤ **personality** is an acceptable synonym for this meaning (but consult that entry for a discussion of the difficulties in usage). **5.** Self as consciousness, awareness, personal conception; self as identity. Gordon Allport's term ➤ **proprium** is an appropriate synonym here. **6.** Self as abstract goal or end point on some personalistic dimension. This meaning is embodied specifically in the later writings of Jung, in which self became conceptualized as the ultimate archetype lying between consciousness and the unconscious, the achievement of self thus being the final human expression of spiritualistic development. Maslow also expressed this meaning but only tangentially in the combined term ➤ **self-actualization**. Note that meanings 1–5 are regarded, in one form or another, as existing aspects of one's personhood; meaning 6 is not, it is rather a potential of one's personhood.

self- A reflexive prefix used in a rather impressive array of psychological terms, as the following entries show. There are several forms of it which are not always immediately apparent and the manner of use of each carries some subtle connotations concerning the presumed meaning of the root word ➤ **self**. For example, in phrases like *self-control*, the subject is treated as essentially identical with the object – the self controls the self; in phrases like *self-actualization*, the subject has an indirect-object-type relation – the self becomes actualized; in phrases like self-consistency, there is an adverbial relation with the subject – the self acts consistently; in phrases like *self-evident*, the whole combined form is treated as an adjective modifying some other proposition.

self, abandoned A term used by William James to refer to an attempted identity, a model characterization of oneself that one has given up. Often used in the plural

under the assumption that most people have several of these littering their lives.

self-abasement 1. An act of self-depreciation; used with the connotation that the critical self-evaluation is inappropriately excessive. **2.** Submission of will or of independent action to another.

self-abuse A perfectly ludicrous term for *masturbation* which has its origins in puritanical attitudes toward sex and sexuality. As several critics have pointed out, it is a uniformly inappropriate term misrepresenting both of the base words, *self* and *abuse*.

self-acceptance Quite literally, an acceptance of oneself. The term is used with the specific connotation that this acceptance is based on a relatively objective appraisal of one's unique talents, capabilities and general worth, a realistic recognition of their limits and a rich feeling of satisfaction with both these talents and their boundaries.

self, actual Horney's term for the momentary psychic totality. The term is really a shorthand expression used for referring to everything psychological about a person at a moment in time, including unconscious elements. ➤ **idealized *self** (2) and **real *self**.

self-actualization 1. A term originally introduced by the organismic theorist, Kurt Goldstein, for the motive to realize all of one's potentialities. In his view, it was the master motive – indeed, the only real motive a person has, all others being merely manifestations of it. **2.** In Abraham Maslow's theory of personality, the final level of psychological development that can be achieved when all basic and meta needs are fulfilled and the 'actualization' of the full personal potential takes place. Meanings 1 and 2 are similar. For Goldstein it was a motive and for Maslow it was a level of development; for both, however, roughly the same kinds of qualities were expressed: independence, autonomy, a tendency to form few but deep friendships, a 'philosophical' sense of humor, a tendency to resist outside pressures and a general transcendence of the environment rather than a simple 'coping' with it.

self-alienation ➤ **alienation**.

self-appraisal ➤ **self-esteem**.

self-awareness Generally, the condition of being aware of or conscious of oneself – in the sense of a relatively objective but open and accepting appraisal of one's true personal nature. Compare with ➤ **self-consciousness** (1).

self-concept One's concept of oneself in as complete and thorough a description as is possible for one to give. Contrast with ➤ **self-esteem**, where the emphasis is on the evaluative judgements.

self-consciousness 1. Generally, ➤ **self-awareness**, but with a 'twist,' the additional realization that it is possible that others are similarly aware of oneself. 2. Specifically, a sense of embarrassment or unease that derives from the sense expressed in 1 when the individual suspects that the awareness that others have contains critical evaluative aspects that are incompatible with one's own personal self-assessment or reveals one to be inadequate.

self-consistency 1. Generally, the characteristic of any system when its several parts all display or reflect a pattern of broad-based compatibility between all of its elements. When the system under consideration is a questionnaire or a test, the term ➤ **internal consistency** is used. 2. By extension, a pattern of behavior of a person that reflects this characteristic. The term tends to be used here with the additional assumption that the displayed consistency is determined by internal factors of a psychological nature rather than by external, environmental factors.

self-control Quite literally, control of self. The term is generally reserved for the ability to control impulsiveness by inhibiting immediate short-range desires; its dominant connotation is that of repressing or inhibiting.

self-correlation In testing, the correlation between the scores from two administrations of a test (see here ➤ **test-retest *reliability**) or between two forms of a test (see here ➤ **equivalent forms *reliability**).

self, creative In Adler's personality theory, the prime mover of behavior, the inner striving for superiority which acts to give meaning to life.

self-criticism Basically, criticism of oneself by oneself with the connotation that such a critical evaluation is an objective and realistic appraisal of one's strengths and weaknesses, talents and shortcomings, etc. Such an analysis of self is part of a healthy self-acceptance. Note that some authors will distinguish between *externally* imposed self-criticism, which focuses on failure to live up to societal standards, and *internally* imposed self-criticism, which focuses upon personal standards.

self-deception The deceiving of onself in the sense of the inability to have accurate insights into one's limitations; a self-deceiver cannot display ➤ **self-acceptance**.

self-defeating personality disorder A ➤ **personality disorder** characterized by a pervasive pattern of self-defeating behavior, including avoiding or undermining pleasurable experiences, being drawn into situations with a high likelihood of failure, seeking out relationships that are likely to be unrewarding, and preventing others from providing help. Also called *masochistic personality disorder*. This disorder was hotly debated in psychiatric circles over the past several years because of possible gender bias and, interestingly, is not included in the *DSM-IV*.

self-demand (schedule of) feeding Feeding upon request. Used in animal experimentation synonymously with ➤ **ad lib** (feeding) and in child-rearing to refer to a flexible-feeding arrangement whereby the infant is fed whenever it shows signs of hunger. Also called *demand feeding*.

self-denial The practice of deliberately

forgoing pleasures and satisfactions. Typically practiced by those who value asceticism, who argue that they forsake the superficial and trivial pleasures for greater psychological gain.

self-desensitization In behavior therapy, the use of the ➤ **desensitization technique** by an individual in everyday situations as a way of dealing with anxiety.

self-determination Roughly, internally controlling one's behavior, acting on the basis of personal beliefs and values rather than on the basis of social norms or group pressures. Some theorists, particularly those with an existentialist orientation, maintain that it is an integral component of the optimal functioning of a person while others, notably Skinnerian behaviorists, regard it as an illusion. ➤➤ **self-direction**.

self-development 1. Generally, growth of self, movement toward emotional and cognitive maturity. 2. In Maslow's model, progress toward ➤ **self-actualization** (2).

self-direction A rough synonym of ➤ **self-determination** but used more 'neutrally.' That is, this term does not invite the theoretical disputes that underlie the connotations of its approximate synonym.

self-discipline 1. Usually, controlling one's behavior, particularly controlling immediate impulsiveness. Here it is essentially a synonym of ➤ **self-control**. 2. Occasionally, self-punishment.

self-dynamisms In H. S. Sullivan's theory of personality, an umbrella term used for all of the basic motivational aspects of the self, i.e. the biological as well as the social and the learned as well as the unlearned. ➤ **self-system**.

self-effacement 1. Generally, modesty or humility. 2. Specifically, in Karen Horney's theory, a neurotic pattern in which one comes to idealize and identify with the originally least admirable characteristics of one's personality.

self-efficacy Bandura's term for an individual's sense of their abilities, of their capacity to deal with the particular sets of conditions that life puts before them.

self-embedded sentence Any sentence with a relative clause between the subject and the verb of the main clause, e.g. 'the man who wore the purple snow boots has already left.' Single embedded sentences such as this one are relatively easy to comprehend; double, triple, and more highly embedded ones seriously strain one's intepretative and memorial capabilities.

self, empirical One of William James's alternative terms for the ➤ **me**; ➤ **self** (1, 2).

self-esteem The degree to which one values oneself. Note that although the word *esteem* carries the connotation of high worth or value, the combined form, self-esteem, refers to the full dimension and the degree of self-esteem (high or low) is usually specified. Contrast with ➤ **self-appraisal**, where the evaluative component is absent. Also called *self-appraisal*.

self-evaluation ➤ **self-rating**.

self-evident Characterizing any proposition, statement, principle, etc. the truth of which is evident on the face of it and requires no independent demonstration. It should be recognized that as the term is used there is an oft-hidden connotation that the evidentiary aspect is to be appreciated only by one who really understands the situation; therefore, vigorous debates over the self-evident status of particular propositions are more common than the definition would lead one to expect.

self-expression 1. The acting out of one's inner feelings, beliefs, attitudes, etc. In many contemporary psychotherapeutic orientations, such a display is assumed to have therapeutic value. 2. Any behavior carried out for the sheer pleasure and satisfaction that it provides for the individual. It should be appreciated that this meaning is what lies behind the presumption of the therapeutic value in sense 1.

self-fulfilling prophecy A term used to refer to the fact that frequently things turn out just as one expected (or prophesied) that they would – not necessarily because of one's prescience but because one behaved in a manner that optimized these very outcomes. A teacher who predicts that a student will ultimately fail tends to treat that student in ways that increase the likelihood of failure, thus fulfilling the original prophecy. See also the related concepts: ➤ **demand characteristics**, ➤ **experimenter bias**.

self-handicapping Engaging in behaviors that sabotage one's own ability to function in particular situations, thereby providing a convenient subsequent excuse for failure.

self-help Essentially, helping oneself. The term is often used in the *human potential movement*, with respect to psychotherapeutic issues, to encourage one to grow, mature and assume responsibility for oneself without unnecessary dependence upon others, particularly establishment specialists.

self, idealized 1. Generally, a perfected and lofty characterization of self in the sense of what one would like to become. When used this way, the term refers to a kind of personalistic goal of a well-adjusted individual. 2. In Karen Horney's theory, a neurotic self-image in which one comes to believe that one has indeed achieved this glorified state.

self-identification The process whereby one develops affection and admiration for another person who possesses qualities and traits which resemble those of oneself. That is, one sees (identifies) oneself in another; as the term is used, there is no suggestion of confusion in personal identity, however.

self-image The imaged (or, better perhaps, imagined) self; the self one supposes oneself to be. Many models of neurosis, particularly that of Karen Horney, are built on the commonly observed circumstances in which a person's real self is rather dramatically incongruent with their self-image. ➤➤ **perceived *self, self-perception theory**.

self-inventory Any self-evaluation device (most commonly in the form of a questionnaire) in which the subject checks off those personality traits or characteristics which he feels are characteristic of himself. ➤➤ **self-report inventory**.

selfish gene The term refers metaphorically to a hypothesized characteristic of a species genotype. In simplest terms, the behavior of any organism is hypothesized to maximize the survival of its genes, which are then passed on to future generations. Hence, the genes are 'selfish'; they appear to function so that the organism whose behavior they are an important determiner of will survive and breed and thereby ensure their survival. This hypothesis lies at the core of the viewpoint of ➤ **sociobiology**.

self·love A general term used for any form of extreme love of oneself; e.g., ➤ **narcissism** and ➤ **egoism**.

self-monitoring The process by which we become aware of our self-presentation and adjust it to match the demands of particular social situations.

self-observation 1. Simply, observation of one's behavior, observation of oneself. 2. More specifically, a synonym for ➤ **introspection**.

self, perceived 1. The ➤ **self** which one is aware of. 2. The self as represented in ➤ **self-perception theory**.

self-perception theory A theoretical point of view which argues that people's attitudes, beliefs and self-characterizations are, to a considerable degree, determined by observation of their own behaviors. The underlying principle is simple: just as we tend to judge the feelings of others by what we see them do, so we infer our own attitudes by self-observation. The theory's importance stems from its basically neo-behaviorist slant, which sets up, in principle at least, the conditions for attitude change. That is, if attitudes are determined by behavior rather than the other way around, then modification of behavior will produce concomitant modification of attitude. ➤➤ **attribution theory**, to which it is related.

self, phenomenal **1.** The self as known through direct, unmediated experience. Generally the phenomenal self is presumed to derive from the environment (or, more precisely, from the interaction between the individual and the environment) and its ultimate expression is through one's direct, conscious, noninferential perception. See here ➤ **phenomenology**. **2.** The ➤ **perceived *self** (1).

self-presentation Quite literally, the process of presenting oneself in relationship to socially and culturally accepted modes of action and behavior. The connotation is that the process is based on the use of specific strategies designed to shape what others will think of one.

self-preservation An umbrella term for any behaviors which function to increase the survival chances of an organism. The term covers a wide range of processes, from the rather primitive aggressive behaviors and flight responses to sophisticated operations like the defense mechanisms for handling anxiety.

self psychology A generic label for any approach to psychology that makes the self the central concept against which all other events and processes are interpreted.

self-rating Any evaluation of oneself. The term is generally used with respect to personality-assessment devices in which the individual supplies information about him- or herself. Also called *self-evaluation*.

self, real In Karen Horney's system, a hypothesized font of psychic energy which can be utilized to orient a person toward a normal, nonneurotic life. Compare with ➤ **actual *self** and ➤ **idealized *self**.

self-realization More or less nontechnically, the fulfillment of one's potential.

self-reference effect The generalization that we have better memory for material that was relevant to ourselves than material that was not.

self-regard **1.** Observing oneself. **2.** High self-esteem. **3.** Concern for one's personal interests.

self-report inventory Any broad-based personality-assessment device in which the subject is asked to check off from a list of characteristics and traits the ones that are self-descriptive and to indicate which of a variety of behaviors in imaginary situations and hypothetical choices are characteristic of him- or herself.

self-selected groups design A research method in which the subjects 'select themselves' by virtue of having particular characteristics or demographic properties.

self-sentiment **1.** ➤ **ego complex**. **2.** W. McDougall's term for a sentiment in which the self is the object.

self-serving bias Quite simply, any bias in interpreting events in the world that operates in a self-serving manner. My (and most professors') favorite example: most students regard exams they did well on as valid indicators of their ability but exams they did poorly on as poor indicators. Also called *defensive attribution*.

self, social A general term used in several ways, all of which reflect some aspect of the 'interface' between society and self: **1.** Those aspects of self that are largely determined by societal values and social influences. **2.** The (usually delimited) aspects of one's self or personality which are readily perceived by other persons in social interactions. **3.** Those components of personality that an individual regards as important in social interactions. **4.** The general characterization of one's self that an individual perceives as being perceived by others. ➤➤ **person perception, self-perception theory**.

self-stimulation Lit., stimulation of oneself. Used in various situations, e.g., of children who, when left in relatively uniform environments, will babble, wave their hands, etc. in an effort to provide their own varied stimulation, and of animals in electrical brain-stimulation studies who can deliver stimulation to their own brains by making an operant response.

self-system Harry Stack Sullivan's term for the ➤ **self-dynamism** that is composed of a set of tendencies that function to protect one from anxiety and to provide security so that one can behave effectively. As Sullivan viewed it, this self-system, like the defence mechanisms of the more orthodox psychoanalytic theorists, can have serious drawbacks in that in protecting the individual from anxiety it may also prevent growth and productive change.

self-terminating search ➤ **search, self-terminating**.

semantic component 1. ➤ **semantic feature**. 2. In some linguistic theories, that aspect of a grammar that contains the formal rules and procedures for representing meaning. In this sense, the semantic component is distinguished from the ➤ **syntactic component**.

semantic conditioning The conditioning of meaning. Used to refer to either (a) the simple association of a word with its referent, or (b) the more complex association of some other response to a particular meaning. When a child learns to associate a spoken word like 'sheep' with a real sheep, then (a) has presumably occurred; if a person shows a response originally associated with 'sheep' to a semantically similar word like 'lamb,' then (b) has occurred. Note that the occurrence of (b) is, in effect, a demonstration that the conditioning in (a) was really *semantic*.

semantic confusion Any confusion over which stimulus was presented, based upon semantic factors. Remembering *wolf* when the actual stimulus was *fox* is an example. Compare with ➤ **acoustic confusion**.

semantic differential A technique due to Charles Osgood and his co-workers for evaluating the connotative meanings of individual words. A subject rates the meaning of each word along a number of polar dimensions such as hot–cold, weak–

strong, tense–relaxed, rough–smooth, etc. Factor analyses of the data generally reveal three primary factors underlying connotative meaning: *activity*, *potency* and *evaluative*.

semantic feature Broadly, any defining characteristic of the meaning of a word which serves to distinguish its meaning from that of other words; e.g., 'widow' is distinguished from 'widower' by the semantic feature, *female*.

semantic generalization ➤ **generalization, semantic**.

semantic memory ➤ **memory, semantic**.

semantic network (model) A class of theoretical models of the structure of human ➤ **long-term *memory**. Such models assume that information is stored in the form of words, concepts or propositions as independent units which are interconnected by links or relations. For example, *cat* is assumed to be represented by links such as 'has fur,' 'is domestic,' 'is a mammal,' etc. The network formed by the central node and all of its associated links represents the memorial representation of the concept 'cat.'

semantics The study of meaning in any and all of its manifestations.

semantic satiation A curious phenomenon best explained by example: repeat any word (e.g., giraffe) over and over several times (10 or 15 will do). The curious sense of loss of meaning of the word that you experience is called semantic satiation. Nobody has yet presented a compelling explanation or how or why it happens.

semantics, generative An approach to the study of language that focuses on the development of a grammar that generates underlying meanings of sentences and transforms the meaning into actual sentences.

semantic space A term used metaphorically to refer to the mental representation of word meaning in theories of ➤ **semantic *memory** that hypothesize a kind of spatial model of the memorial form. E.g., ➤ **semantic network (model)**.

semantic therapy A technique used in a number of therapies in which the focus is on getting the client to reinterpret distorted connotations of emotionally tinged words.

semasiography The most primitive of orthographies (writing systems) and the first to have been invented. It consists essentially of the representing of a concept or a meaning by some sign. Semasiographies preceded *logographies*.

semeiology 1. ➤ **semiotics**. 2. The study of the signs (i.e. symptoms) of disease.

semeiotics ➤ **semiotics**.

semen 1. The cloudy, viscous fluid in which the male sperm are suspended. 2. The sperm themselves. Typically the former is intended. adj., *seminal* (used much more generally, e.g., seminal idea).

semicircular canals The three semicircular tubes that are part of the labyrinth of the inner ear. Each consists of a membraneous canal filled with endolymph. They lie roughly at right angles to each other and approximate the three planes of the head. Movement of the head causes movement of the endolymph, which produces a shearing of the hair cells of the crista (the organ containing the receptors) in the ampulla (the enlargements at one end of each canal).

semi-interquartile range ➤ **quartile deviation**.

seminal vesicles The two sacs at the base of the bladder in males that store semen.

semiology ➤ **semiotics**.

semiotics According to one of its leading researchers, Thomas Sebeok, it is the study of 'patterned communications in all modalities,' and hence its subject-matter ranges from evolutionarily primitive animal communication to sophisticated linguistic systems. Two forms are usually specified: (a) *anthroposemiotic systems*, which are largely linguistic and specific to

Homo sapiens, and (b) *zoosemiotic systems*, which are nonverbal and paralinguistic and are characteristic of all species. vars., *semeiotics, semeiology, semiology*.

semipartial correlation ➤ **correlation, semipartial**.

semi-tone A half-tone; ➤ **tone** (2).

semi-vowel A speech sound having some basic vowel-like qualities in that the air passage is relatively unobstructed but with more friction, e.g., /w/ in *wit*. Unlike vowels, semi-vowels cannot form syllables without support from other speech elements.

senescence 1. Old age. 2. The process of becoming old. 3. The years during which one becomes old. At one time it was used as a rough synonym for *senility*; this meaning is no longer found; ➤ **senility** and **senile**.

senile Aged; used particularly with respect to those patterns of thought and behavior characteristic of old age. Note that, although this definition is basically evaluatively neutral, the term has taken on negative connotations and tends to be used almost exclusively to refer to those patterns of thought and behavior that show the deterioration often but not universally observed in the aged. In an effort to overcome these connotations some have taken to using the term with a strict criterion of age 65. Thus *senile onset* is reserved for conditions that first appear after age 65 and *presenile onset* before age 65. Compare with the more neutral term, ➤ **senescence**.

senile dementia ➤ **dementia, senile**.

senile onset ➤ **senile**.

senile psychosis ➤ **dementia, senile**.

senility 1. = ➤ **Senescence**, in the neutral sense of that term. 2. The state or period of life of being ➤ **senile**.

senium The period of life after the age of 65.

sensate focus 1. Generally, developing

and maintaining the focusing of attention upon particular sensory inputs. **2.** Specifically, such a focusing on sensual experiences. **3.** By extension, a technique of sex therapy designed to overcome the fears and anxieties that accompany many forms of orgasmic dysfunction by gradually building up a recognition of and ability to focus on pleasurable sensual experience.

sensation 1. Any unelaborated, elementary experience of feeling or awareness of conditions within or outside of the body produced by the stimulation of some receptor or receptor system, a *sense datum*. This definition has represented a kind of operating principle for a variety of theories of sensory experience and tends to be what is presented in most introductory textbooks, where *sensations* are usually distinguished from *perceptions*, the latter being characterized as resulting from interpretation and elaboration of sensations. It should, however, be appreciated that many psychologists dispute the very notion that one can have any experiential sense at all without elaborating, interpreting, labeling or recognizing what the experience is. **2.** In Titchener's structuralism, one of the three basic elements of consciousness (along with *feelings* and *images*). **3.** The process of sensing. **4.** A label for the field of psychology that studies these basic processes of sensory experience. The focus is primarily on the examination of physiological and psychophysical principles.

sensation level The sensed or experienced level of intensity of a stimulus, e.g., how loud a particular sound is heard as, how bright a light is seen to be, etc. They are measured by using the individual's own absolute threshold as the reference level.

sensation-seeking A dimension along which individuals may be rated according to the degree to which they search out and enjoy partaking in activities with high levels of sensation.

sensation threshold ➤ absolute *threshold.

sensation type One of Jung's hypo-

thesized personality types; ➤ **function types** for details.

sense 1. n. A subjective category of sensory impressions grouped together on the basis of shared experiential features; a sense modality, e.g., the sense of hearing, of smell, of vision, etc. **2.** n. A similar classification but with the defining feature being a common receptor system rather than common experience. This usage often appears in qualified phrases like 'sense organ for hearing.' These two meanings are not as synonymous as they may initially appear. One may have a sense 1 without a true receptor organ for that sense 2, as in the phenomenon of the ➤ **phantom limb**; one may have two or more senses 1 with but one sense 2, as in ➤ **synesthesia**; or one may have a single sense 1 with several anatomically different receptor organs for that sense 2, as is the case with pressure on the skin and muscles. **3.** n. A classification of subjective experiences not clearly linked in a simple way with any particular sense (as in meanings 1 and 2) but coordinated in some complex fashion with a dimension of the physical world; e.g., sense of time, sense of space, etc. **4** n. A form of awareness of some abstract quality or concept; e.g., a sense of humor, a sense of fair play, a sense of justice. **5** n. A summary of the general meaning of a thing, the gist of some event, episode, story, etc. **6** n. A well-considered or intelligent judgement, as in 'she showed good sense.'

In addition to these noun forms there are several verb forms: **7.** To experience by virtue of a categorical judgement made with reference to a sensory modality. **8.** To experience by virtue of the direct stimulation of a receptor system. Note that 7 is the verbal form of 1, and 8 of 2. **9.** To have an emotional or cognitive experience that reflects one's judgement about an event or episode; e.g., 'I sense unhappiness behind his smile.'

There are also many combined phrases based on these meanings and in many instances derived forms are used in place of the core-term sense. Although there is something less than universality in usage, generally speaking ➤ **sensory** is preferred when referring to those which are based on meanings 1, 2, 7 and 8, i.e. those dealing with sensation and the sensory processes; while ➤ **sensitive** (1,2) and ➤ **sensitivity** are preferred when referring to those based on meanings 3, 4, 5, 6 and 9, i.e. those dealing with the emotional, judgemental and intellectual functions. ➤ **Sensible** is, unfortunately, used rather haphazardly for both domains but is becoming increasingly rare in these contexts in the technical literature. For combined forms not found following one of these, see the others.

sense datum ➤ sensation (1).

sense illusion An obsolete term for a perceptual illusion. The word *sense* was once used to emphasize the point that such illusions were thought to be due to basic sensory processes and not higher cognitive functions.

sense impression Generally, any piece of sensory data. The term was a favorite among some early behaviorists who wanted to theorize about perception and perceptual processes without admitting it.

sense limen ➤ absolute *threshold.

sense modality ➤ modality.

sense organ Loosely, any specialized neurological structure that responds to particular classes of stimulation. syn., ➤ receptor (preferred).

sense perception A somewhat confusing term originally used to refer to the processes by which one derived perceptual experiences from sensory inputs. The inextricable relations now known to exist between sensation and perception have rendered the term relatively useless.

sense quality ➤ quality (1).

sense, special A cover term used for those senses whose receptors are in the head: vision, audition, smell and taste. It should be appreciated that, although the typical reference includes only the above-

mentioned four modalities, the sense of balance, or vestibular sense, ought also to be included here since its receptor system, the semicircular canals, is in the head.

sensibility The capacity for being ➤ **sensible** in any of the meanings of that term – although meanings 4 and 5 are the usually intended ones.

sensible Reflecting the several meanings of ➤ **sense: 1.** Pertaining to that which is an effective stimulus for a sensory receptor, an above-threshold stimulus. **2.** Pertaining to any stimulus object or event that is apprehended through the senses. **3.** Pertaining to an individual who shows the capacity for responding to stimulation. **4.** Having meaning. **5.** Displaying good judgement. **6.** ➤ **sensitive** (1 or 2). Meanings 4 and 5 are the more common in contemporary writings.

sensing The process whereby one becomes cognizant of a stimulus which has impinged upon one's sensory organs. ➤ **sensation** and **perception** for discussions of the complexities involved in these processes.

sensitive 1. adj. Generally, pertaining to sensitivity. **2.** adj. Characteristic of one who is emotionally labile, easily moved by events. **3.** n. One who presumably possesses certain paranormal abilities in communication and perception. See here ➤ **parapsychology**.

sensitive period 1. ➤ critical period. **2.** A loosely defined period of time during which an organism is sensitive to particular forms of stimulus inputs and physiologically and psychologically ready for the acquisition of a particular response or a particular type of knowledge. Sense 2 here is much less sharply specified than 1; e.g., one speaks of a sensitive period for acquiring language (ranging from a few months of age up to roughly puberty). ➤ **critical period** for a comparison example.

sensitive zone Any bodily area with a particularly high sensitivity to certain classes of stimulation; e.g., the erogenous zones.

sensitivity **1.** Generally, susceptibility to stimulation. **2.** More specifically, responsiveness to weak stimuli, having a low threshold. **3.** Cognizance of the feelings of another, particularly an awareness based on relatively minor cues. **4.** A personal vulnerability whereby one is easily hurt or offended.

sensitivity training A generic term for a variety of quasi-therapeutic group procedures developed originally in the 1940s by Kurt Lewin and Ronald Lippitt. They served as forums for the members of a group or organization to develop greater awareness of group dynamics and their own roles within the group. Lately, the techniques have merged with many others used within the so-called *human potential movement*, and much of the original scientific focus and the influence of the late K. Lewin has been unfortunately obscured in faddism. Also known as *T-group* ('T' for *training*).

sensitization The process of becoming highly sensitive, usually with the implication that one is not uniformly sensitive to all stimuli but only to specific events or situations. ➤ **desensitization** for the opposite process.

sensor That which senses, hence: **1.** An individual receptor, e.g., a free nerve ending, a retinal rod or cone, etc. **2.** A receptor organ, e.g., the eye, the ear, etc. The former is the more common denotation. ➤ **receptor**.

sensorimotor **1.** Generally, pertaining to those processes which are theorized as being essentially made up of afferent (sensory) and efferent (motor) mechanisms. Although it is trivially true that virtually all behaviors, from the most primitive reflexive acts to the most complex cognitive processes, are in some sense sensorimotor, the term is typically reserved for those acts which are predominantly so; e.g., an infant reaching for a toy is so characterized, but the movement of a chess piece in a game is not. **2.** More specifically, the neural circuit from a receptor to the central nervous system and back to a muscle. Often the variation *sensory-*

motor is used synonymously, although its original meaning was restricted to 2.

sensorimotor intelligence A general term used to refer to the types of cognitive capabilities exhibited by children during the ➤ **sensorimotor stage**. According to Piaget, such thinking is characterized by the differentiation and elaboration of the basis action schemas such as grasping, sucking, looking, etc.

sensorimotor rhythm A moderately rapid (12–14 Hz) brain wave which can be recorded from the scalp over the sensorimotor areas of the cortex.

sensorimotor stage (or **level** or **period**) In Piagetian theory, the stage of cognitive functioning beginning at birth and continuing until the development or establishment of ➤ **object permanance** and the beginnings of symbolic thought.

sensorium Loosely, those areas of the brain that handle conscious registering and processing of incoming sensory information.

sensory Pertaining very generally to the senses, the sense organs, the sense receptors, the afferent neural pathways, sense data, sensation, etc. Contrast with ➤ **motor**. ➤➤ **sense** (1,2) and **sensation** (1).

sensory acuity ➤ **acuity, sensory**.

sensory adaptation ➤ **adaptation** (1).

sensory aphasia ➤ Wernicke's *aphasia.

sensory area(s) Most generally, those areas of the central nervous system that are the termini of ascending sensory neurons. Specific areas are typically specified by the sensory modality they serve, e.g., visual area, somatosensory areas, etc. Also called *sensory projection areas*.

sensory ataxia ➤ **ataxia, sensory**.

sensory automatism ➤ **automatism, sensory**.

sensory conditioning ➤ **sensory preconditioning**.

sensory cortex ➤ **sensory areas(s)**.

sensory deprivation Descriptive of a

709

situation either natural or experimentally arranged in which there is a marked reduction in incoming sensory information. Relatively short periods of time in sensory deprivation are mildly pleasant and relaxing; long periods are extremely aversive and produce time-sense distortions, bizarre thoughts and images, hallucinations, etc.

sensory discrimination Essentially, differential responding to different stimuli. If the subject is a nonverbal organism, sensory discrimination between two stimuli is said to have occurred if the subject reliably makes one response to one and another response to the other; with human subjects a verbal response that a difference is detected is sufficient. ➤➤ **discrimination** (1).

sensory drive A drive for some specific sensation.

sensory field 1. = ➤ **perceptual field**. 2. = ➤ **receptive field**.

sensory gating ➤ **gating**.

sensory homunculus ➤ **homunculus** (2).

sensory information store (SIS) A memory system of extremely short duration. Immediately after the removal of a stimulus a sensory representation of the stimulus seems 'suspended' in the mind for a brief time – on the order of one of two seconds. The capacity of SIS is limited by the information that can be apprehended in one short exposure to the stimulus; the form of the memory is essentially a direct match of the stimulus. Material is assumed to be lost from SIS by a process of decay which is completed in a very short time unless the material is passed into the ➤ **short-term memory** system. For a specific example, ➤ **iconic** (2). Also called *sensory memory* and *sensory register*.

sensory memory ➤ **sensory information store**.

sensory modality ➤ **modality**.

sensory-motor ➤ **sensorimotor**.

sensory-motor intelligence ➤ **sensorimotor intelligence**.

sensory-motor stage ➤ **sensorimotor stage**.

sensory nerve An afferent nerve, one that conveys sensory information to the central nervous system.

sensory neuron Any individual afferent neuron.

sensory organization Generally, the process of coordination and organization of the sensory imput. ➤ **organization** et seq. for more details.

sensory preconditioning An experimental procedure where two neutral, nongeneralizable stimuli are repeatedly presented together followed by the conditioning of one of them to a particular response. Sensory preconditioning is said to have occurred if the other, nonconditioned stimulus evokes the conditioned response on a test trial. Also called *sensory conditioning*, but *preconditioning* is more accurate.

sensory process Loosely and inclusively, any process conceptualized either physiologically or psychologically which relates to sensation, sense data, sensing, etc.

sensory projection areas ➤ **sensory area**(s).

sensory psychophysiology That aspect of the field of ➤ **physiological psychology** that is concerned with sensory systems and their manner of functioning.

sensory quality ➤ **quality** (1).

sensory-reaction type ➤ **reaction type** (2).

sensory register ➤ **sensory information store**.

sensory-seeking motives Generally, those motives to increase stimulation and heighten arousal and tension; e.g., desires to engage in sporting events, parties, rides in amusement parks, etc. ➤➤ **sensation-seeking**.

sensory stimulus A distinctly redundant term used by some authors for stimuli that are above threshold; that is, stimuli that evoke a sensation.

sensory transduction ➤ **transduction** (2).

sensual Generally, pertaining to gratification of the senses. Usage, in practice, is restricted to the carnal and erotic. syn., *sensuous*.

sentence A self-contained, grammatical, linguistic unit consisting of one or more words syntactically and semantically related to each other such that some assertion, question, command, etc. is expressed. In the written format, sentences are usually marked by appropriate punctuation; in the spoken format, sentences are rather less clearly marked, although there is generally a phonetically distinguishable pattern of stress, pitch and pausing. The sentence has become the primary unit of analysis of modern linguistics and, by extension, an important component in the study of psycholinguistics.

sentence-completion test (or **method**) A procedure in which a subject is given partial sentences (the 'stems') and required to complete them. It is used as a technique for assessing linguistic knowledge as well as a projective device. Note that in the latter case it is usually capitalized.

sentience **1.** The state of being capable of sensing. **2.** A fairly primitive, undifferentiated state of consciousness, 'pure' sensation without interpretation. Compare with *sentient*.

sentience need H. Murray's term for the need for sensual pleasures.

sentient Following from the general meaning of ➤ **sentience**: **1.** Capable of responding to stimuli. **2.** Capable of a minimal consciousness of awareness of stimulation. But, by further extension: **3.** Capable of awareness of or conscious recognition of the perception of detail; in short, intelligent. This last meaning, which goes much further than the earlier senses of the term, is now the dominant.

sentiment Although etymologically this term is derived from ➤ **sense**, it tends to be used much more broadly. To wit: **1.** A complex disposition based upon one's feelings toward some person, situation, idea, etc. A sentiment is more general and more complex that an *attitude* or a *judgement* and behavior is typically implied. That is, a given sentiment is more than just a complex affective state, it implies action; e.g., a person with a strong nationalistic sentiment is likely to defend their country vigorously. **2.** R. B. Cattell's term for a learned, dynamic trait structure which focuses and mediates attention and reaction to classes of objects in characteristic ways.

sentimentality Emotionality which is shallow, maudlin, romantic and, in some respects, suspect in its veracity. Distinguish from ➤ **sentiment**.

separation anxiety **1.** In psychoanalysis, the hypothesized anxiety on the part of the infant or child concerning possible loss of the mother object. **2.** By extension, anxiety over the possible loss of any other person or object upon whom one has become dependent. ➤ **separation-anxiety disorder**.

separation-anxiety disorder An anxiety disorder of childhood in which the dominant feature is excessive and inappropriate anxiety on separation from the primary attachment figure (usually one or both parents) or from the home environment. Common manifestations are unrealistic worries about harmful things happening to the attachment figure while away, persistent fears of being lost, kidnapped or even killed if separated, social withdrawal, ➤ **school refusal**.

separation-individuation Margaret Mahler's term for the child's awareness of its discrete identity, separateness and individuality apart from the mother. In her theory, this process follows the *symbiotic stage*, when the mutually reinforcing relationship between mother and child is dominant.

septum **1.** A dividing wall or membrane separating two cavities of an organ or other structure; e.g., the nasal septum separates the nostrils. pl., *septa*. **2.** A portion of the limbic system lying between the walls of the anterior portions of the lateral ventricles.

sequela Any abnormal condition resulting from a disease which continues chronically after the disease has been cured. pl., *sequelae*.

sequence 1. A consecutive ordering of events, numbers, etc. in some seriated fashion usually in time or space, or with respect to some dimension like size, magnitude, etc. **2.** In mathematics, a quantitative series in which each element is derived from the preceding by the application of a particular operation. adj., *sequential*.

sequence preference A response bias based upon a sequential pattern; e.g., rats in mazes often show a single-alternation sequence preference, turning left-right-left-right, etc.

sequential analysis Statistical analysis of data performed at a particular point in an extended study to determine whether enough data have been collected to evaluate properly the hypothesis under consideration, or whether to collect more. Such analyses are frequently used in large-scale *clinical trials*.

sequential marriage ➤ serial *polygamy.

sequential (statistical) test Generally, any statistical test based on the sequence of responses made by the subjects in an experiment. Many of these can be rather complex mathematically: ➤ **runs test** for a simple example.

serendipity The finding of one thing while engaged in a search for something else. The term was first used with respect to scientific discovery by the physiologist Walter Cannon. It entered the language via Horace Walpole, who coined it in 1754, basing it on *The Three Princes of Serendip*, a tale by a 16th-century Venetian writer named Michele Tramezzino. The princes traveled the earth searching fruitlessly for certain things but always managing through careful observation and subtle logical reasoning to make other unanticipated but exciting discoveries. Serendipitous findings of import are, thus, not just a matter of random good fortune; it takes a shrewd and insightful person to understand the significance of some event 'stumbled across.' Probably every person who ever owned a dog has seen it salivate to a non-food stimulus like a can opener, but it took the genius of a Pavlov to recognize the magnitude of that *psychic secretion*, as he first called it when it accidentally occurred in his laboratory during the course of another experiment.

serial H. Murray's term for a 'long functional unit of behavior.' Serials are organized but intermittent successions of ➤ **proceedings** and are exemplified by friendships, marriages, careers, etc.

serial-anticipation method An experimental procedure in which each stimulus in a list is a cue for a response to follow. The subject's task is to make the proper response before being prompted with it.

serial association Generally, any association between one item on a list and the next succeeding item. ➤ **serial *learning**.

serial behavior Generally, behavior that consists of a series of responses or acts where the order in which they are carried out is a critical feature. ➤ **chaining** for behaviorist and cognitivist perspectives on such behavior.

serial exploration, method of ➤ **measurement of *threshold**.

serial learning ➤ learning, serial.

serial monogamy ➤ serial *polygamy.

serial polygamy ➤ polygamy, serial.

serial-position curve A graphic display of the probability of a correct recall of an item plotted against the serial position of the item during presentation. The classic curve is bow-shaped with high probabilities for the first few and last few items. ➤ **serial-position effect** for more detail.

serial-position effect The generalization that in a free-recall experiment the likelihood of an individual item from a list being recalled is a function of the location of that item in the serial presentation of the list during learning. Items which were toward the beginning of the list (the 'primary' items) and those toward the end (the most 'recent' items in time at point of recall) are more likely to be correctly recalled than those in the middle. The full serial-position effect is, thus, composed of two more local effects, the ➤ **primary effect** and the ➤ **recency effect**; see each for details.

serial recall An experimental procedure used in memory research in which the stimulus materials are presented to the subject in a fixed order and must be recalled in that particular order. Compare with ➤ **free recall**.

serial search ➤ **search, serial**.

seriation In a series, in a consecutive order.

series An arrangement of items in succession such that by using some principle (temporal, spatial or logical) the items can be represented by the number series.

serotonergic Characterizing or pertaining to pathways, fibers, or neurons in which ➤ **serotonin** is the *neurotransmitter*.

serotonin A ➤ **neurotransmitter** found in neural pathways of peripheral ganglia and in the central nervous system. Also known as *5-hydroxytryptamine* or *5-HT*, it is an inhibitory transmitter whose actions have been implicated in various processes including sleep, pain and the psychobiology of various affective disorders, specifically depression and bipolar disorder.

servomechanism Any device used to control a system which functions by sensing the difference between the actual state of the system and the desired state and acting so as to minimize this difference. The simplest example is a thermostat.

SES ➤ **socioeconomic status**.

set **1** n. A classification, aggregate or series of things sharing some defining property or properties such that they can

be regarded collectively. This general meaning encompasses a variety of uses from the purely mathematical characterization embodied in set theory, through the more common-sense denotations such as the *set* of respondents to a questionnaire, the *set* of stimulus items in an experiment, the country-club *set* in upper-class society, etc. Note that sets may be infinite in size (the set of integers), finite (the set of correct answers on a multiple-choice test), empty (the set of immortal persons) or poorly defined (the set of all young persons, see here ➤ **fuzzy set**). **2** n. Any condition, disposition or tendency on the part of an organism to respond in a particular manner. Note that the term 'respond' here may encompass a number of acts. Thus, one may have an attentional or ➤ **perceptual set** for particular kinds of stimuli (see here ➤ *Einstellung*), a task-oriented set for a problem (see here ➤ *Aufgabe*), a functional set which directs the manner of use of objects (see here ➤ **functional fixedness**), a muscular set in which a particular motor act is optimized (➤ **preparatory *set**), etc. To distinguish among these various uses, many authors will use qualifiers, as in some of the following entries. It should also be recognized that the term is generally used with the connotation that the set under consideration is a temporary (although potentially recurring) one and, as such, its meaning is contrasted with terms like ➤ **habit** and ➤ **trait**, which refer to enduring dispositions or conditions, and distinguished from ➤ **schema** (1), which is used for more general orientations to situations. The longer term *determining set* is often used synonymously for 2, particularly for sets that exert some measure of control over how the organism is to respond. adj., *set*; vb. (for 2), *set*.

set, hypnotic A term used roughly equivalently with ➤ **posthypnotic suggestion**; ➤➤ **hypnosis**.

set, motor **1.** A preparatory readiness to perform a particular motor response. **2.** The actual pattern of muscle tone accompanying such a state of readiness.

set, objective A readiness in which one is prepared to perceive a stimulus as a physical event in the external world, a set that is as free of interpretative, subjective bias as possible. ➤ set (2).

set point The desired value in a servomechanism such that when departures from it are detected, compensatory activities ensue to reduce them. Various biological systems operate using a set point in roughly this fashion; e.g., ➤ **thermoregulation**.

set, preparatory Any stance or posture which prepares an organism for a particular response. Usually used with respect to motor responses, ➤ **motor *set**.

set, response A readiness to respond to a stimulus. For example, in the simple reaction-time experiment, the subject is in a set that calls for the making of a response as rapidly as possible as soon as the stimulus is sensed. Occasionally called *response attitude*. Contrast with ➤ **stimulus *set**.

set, stimulus A readiness to sense a stimulus. Generally the term is used in situations in which there are two or more possible stimuli and the subject is set to react to them differentially. For example, in the choice reaction-time experiment, the subject is in a set in which one of two responses must be made depending upon which of two stimuli occurs. Occasionally called *stimulus attitude*. Contrast with ➤ **response *set**.

set-theoretical model Generally, any model which treats the units or entities under consideration as elements arranged in sets and formally represents the relations between the elements in terms of set theory. Such models have been applied to the study of semantic features, word meaning and human long-term memory.

seven plus or minus two (7 ± 2) George A. Miller's 'magical number.' The term denotes the approximate number of discrete pieces of information that can be held in short-term memory at one time.

Note that this limit is based on the conceptualization of these pieces of information as 'chunks' or coded aggregates and not merely as a summing up of the total amount of information in each. Thus, for example, one can hold approximately seven discrete, unrelated phonetic elements in memory at one time or one can hold approximately seven discrete, unrelated nonsense syllables in memory at one time – despite the fact that these seven nonsense syllables may contain well over 20 separate phonetic elements.

severe mental retardation ➤ **mental retardation, severe**.

sex 1 adj. Pertaining to those biological distinctions which differentiate female from male. This form of the term is used broadly and can encompass the functional, reproductive aspects as well as the specific organs, hormones and structures that anatomically differentiate female from male. When used in combined forms and phrases, however, the usual reference is to properties and characteristics that are functional and biological and not to those that involve either the amorous or the erotic – the form ➤ **sexual** is properly reserved for these cases. For example, one has *sex hormones* but not *sexual hormones* and one engages in *sexual intercourse* but not in *sex intercourse*. In those instances where both forms are found, their meanings are (or should be) appropriately distinguished. Thus, *sex dominance* refers to a broad pattern of dominance of one sex over the other while *sexual dominance* refers to the dominance of one individual over another during sexual activity. Similarly, *sex roles* refers to encompassing patterns of behavior and affect of persons relating to their maleness or femaleness, one component of which would be their *sexual roles*. Note also that the term *gender* has become increasingly common as a synonym for sex in this adjectival sense. Although the original meaning of gender restricted its use to grammar, its connotative neutrality has made it the euphemism of choice for many contemporary writers. For combined terms not

found below, see those following ➤ **gender**.
2 n. Either of the two forms biologically present in most (but not all) species, distinguished as male (the sperm-cell producer) and female (the egg-cell producer). **3** n. By extension of 2, the totality of characteristics that may be used as distinctive features for identification of male or female. **4** n. The process, considered broadly, of reproduction. **5** n. Those organic and/or physiological pleasures and satisfactions associated with sexual activities.

sex- Combining form meaning: **1.** *Sex*. **2.** *Six*.

sex anomaly Any individual case where the sex organs differ dramatically from the normal, e.g., *hermaphrodite*. Also called *genital anomaly*. Distinguish from ➤ **sexual anomaly**.

sex assignment The sex or gender assigned at birth. In cases of genital anomalies the assignment may be problematic.

sex change ➤ **sex reversal**.

sex characteristics Very generally, those characteristics or traits that are strongly associated with one sex relative to the other. The term is used uniformly for biological and behavioral features. Also called *sex characters*.

sex characteristics, primary Those genetically determined sex traits that are differentially associated more strongly with one sex than with the other and are intimately, biologically bound up with the functions of reproduction, e.g., the genitals, the organs of reproduction. Also called *primary sex characters*.

sex characteristics, secondary Those genetically determined sex traits that are differentially associated more strongly with one sex than with the other but are not functionally necessary for normal reproduction, e.g., body hair, fundamental pitch of the voice, patterns of musculature, etc. Also called *secondary sex characters*.

sex chromosomes ➤ **chromosomes**.

sex differences Those differences that are statistically distributed in the population such that when large numbers of individuals are considered they can be used as distinguishing features between males and females. There are three potential referential domains here: (a) ➤ **primary *sex characteristics**; (b) ➤ **secondary *sex characteristics**; and (c) *mental, emotional* and *social behavior patterns*. The divergences between the sexes diminish as one moves from (a) to (c). No one disputes the differences in primary sex characteristics, but the term is rarely, if ever, used in this sense. The differences observed in secondary sex characteristics are now known to be not quite so large nor so unequivocal as some had thought, but generally they are not disputed as existing but and, like those in (a), are to a considerable extent genetically determined. The difficulties with the term emerge only in the case of (c) and it is here that we find the domain of reference in virtually every case that the term *sex difference* is used.

The problems that arise in applying the term to the factors included in (c) are due in large measure to the varying tendencies on the part of various authors to extrapolate from the known genetic determinants in domains (a) and (b) – this despite the fact that the term itself is neutral with respect to genetic factors and their entailment is a theoretical step and not a definitional one. The underlying causal factors for those sex differences that can be observed in category (c) have yet to be unequivocally determined. Many authors, in an effort to avoid the need to distinguish between the domains of (a) and (b) on one hand and (c) on the other, use the term *gender differences* for (c), thereby defusing, at least partially, the genetic-determination issue that is so problematical here.

sex distribution The distribution of males and females in a population. ➤ **sex ratio**.

sex education 1. Broadly, education in all aspects of sex and sexuality including physiological, reproductive, performative, emotional and interpersonal. **2.** More narrowly, education in only the physiological and reproductive aspects of sex.

sex identity One's learned identity as it pertains to one's sex. ➤ **gender identity** for more detail.

sex-influenced character or **gene** A genetic characteristic that is dominant in one sex and recessive in the other.

sexism A prejudice based on sex. In practice, as the term is used, its meaning goes beyond this simple definition in two ways. First, a prejudice is generally treated as an attitude or belief, while the term sexism (like the related term *racism*) generally connotes differential action and behavior toward persons which discriminates between them on the basis of their sex. Second, the term is nearly always used with respect to discrimination against females, a unitary focus that derives from the objective data of society but which unfortunately delimits the meaning of the term.

sex-limited character or **gene** A genetic characteristic that is expressed in only one sex.

sex-linked character or **gene** A genetic characteristic that is controlled by genes located on the sex chromosomes.

sex object 1. A ➤ **sexual object** toward which or upon whom sexual activities are focused. **2.** Popularly, a person responded to in such a fashion that sex and sexuality are the primary aspects of the interaction. Typically, it is a man who so treats a woman, but this limitation is social and not definitional. Note that being a sex object in sense 2 does not necessarily entail sense 1; you may treat someone as a sex object (2) but not have any of the specific sexual intentions that are connoted in meaning 1.

sex offender In legal parlance, one who has violated local statutes concerning sexual behavior. Since laws differ from community to community and country to country, it is not possible to provide a precise definition of the term, although rapists and child molesters are almost universally so classified.

sexology The scientific study of sex and sexuality.

sex ratio The proportion of males or females in a population. Usually presented as the number of males (or females) per 100 persons.

sex reassignment A cover term for the legal, personal, behavioral and surgical actions involved in the reassignment of sex identity.

sex reversal A surgical procedure, with accompanying hormonal treatments, for changing one's sex.

sex rivalry In classical psychoanalytic theory, the hypothesized competition between a child and the same-sexed parent for the affections and attentions of the other parent.

sex role The full complement of behaviors and attitudes of one's role in life as it is associated with one's sex. ➤ **gender role** and **role** for further discussion.

sex-role inversion ➤ **transsexualism**.

sex-role steroype The typical beliefs concerning the particular patterns of behavior that are expected of persons according to their sex.

sex therapy A general term used to cover any therapeutic enterprise aimed at the relief of sexual dysfunctions or disturbances. Included are therapies aimed at altering one's attitudes toward sex and sexual behavior so as, for example, to relieve irrational fears or guilt feelings which inhibit performance and enjoyment, therapies specifically concerned with identifiable dysfunctions such as impotency, premature ejaculation or orgasmic dysfunctions, 'family' therapies which focus on communication and interactive difficulties that a couple may be experiencing, and so forth.

sexual 1. Characterizing reproduction by the union of two sex cells, one provided by a female and one by a male of the same species. Contrast with ➤ **asexual** (2). **2.** Relating to, in a very general way, the behavioral and affective component of ➤ **sexuality**. Compare with ➤ **sex** (1).

sexual abuse Sexual mistreatment of another person. As the term is used it virtually always refers to the abuse of children by an adult. ➤➤ **sexual harassment**.

sexual aim The goal of the release of sexual tensions by orgasm. ➤ **Aim** is used here synonymously with ➤ **goal** rather than with ➤ **object** or ➤ **target** – see these several terms for the distinctions implied. See also and compare with ➤ **sexual object**.

sexual anesthesia ➤ **frigidity**.

sexual anomaly Generally, any sexual practice that is 'anormal,' i.e. outside of the generally accepted practices of a society. Many authors use this term specifically to denote any of a variety of sexual behaviors that are statistically anomalous when they wish to be clear that no connotation of pathology or perversion is intended; e.g., they will call homosexuality or fetishism sexual anomalies. For more on this point ➤ **sexual *perversion**. The term should not be used as a synonym of ➤ **sex anomaly**, which is reserved for the biological and anatomical.

sexual anorexia ➤ **anorexia, sexual**.

sexual apathy A general term for any unusually low interest in sex and sexuality. Also called *erotic apathy*.

sexual arousal disorders Those ➤ **sexual dysfunctions** characterized by a lack of the appropriate physiological responses that accompany sexual excitement. Included are ➤ **female sexual arousal disorder** and ➤ **male erectile disorder**. Like the ➤ **sexual desire disorders**, the term is only used when the condition causes marked distress or interpersonal difficulties.

sexual aversion disorder A ➤ **sexual desire disorder** marked by persistent or recurrent aversion to and avoidance of genital sexual contact with a sexual partner.

sexual desire disorders Those ➤ **sexual dysfunctions** marked by absent or diminished interest in sex and sexual activity. Included are ➤ **hypoactive sexual disorder** and ➤ **sexual aversion disorder**. Sexual desire is a personal thing and the label is used only when the condition causes marked distress or compromises interpersonal interactions. Many people have low libido and are quite content to be that way. Also called *inhibited sexual desire*.

sexual dimorphism Dimorphism means *two forms*; hence, relating to the circumstances in which a species has two distinct forms differentiated on the basis of sex characteristics.

sexual disorders An umbrella psychiatric category covering all disorders of sexual behavior and function. Included are the ➤ **paraphilias** and the ➤ **sexual dysfunctions**. See those entries for details and for disorders classified under each. Occasionally called *psychosexual disorders*.

sexual drive ➤ **libido**.

sexual dysfunctions A subclass of ➤ **sexual disorders** marked by inhibition of arousal or of the psychophysiological aspects of the sexual response cycle. The term is only used when there is no evidence of an organic disorder that might cause the symptoms. Included are the ➤ **sexual arousal disorders** and the ➤ **sexual desire disorders**. Occasionally called *psychosexual dysfunctions*.

sexual harassment *Harass* comes from the Old French meaning *to set a dog on* and generally means to persistently disturb, pester, plague, or torment. The term applies to cases where such badgering has a sexual component to it, particularly when there is a power imbalance between the parties. Overwhelmingly, such cases involve men harassing women. The term is not used for cases with children; ➤ **sexual abuse**.

sexual identity One's identity with respect to sexual preferences. The term is usually restricted to labeling oneself as hetero-, homo- or bisexual. Note that the

717

term is used so that it does not necessarily encompass sexual behaviors; there are, for example, many persons who express a strong personal homosexual identity but who not infrequently engage in heterosexual activity and vice versa. See here ➤ **sexual preference**.

sexual instinct 1. In psychoanalysis this expression originally stood as a cover term for the impetus assumed to underlie any pleasure-seeking. This remarkably inclusive meaning derived from Freud's early characterization of sexuality as the foundational motive for all pleasure. More recent usage puts boundaries on the term in that a hint of sexuality needs to be present for it to be applied. 2. In ethology, the underlying drive to engage in patterns of behavior oriented around courtship and sexual union.

sexual intercourse Essentially a synonym for ➤ **coitus**. The term does, in fact, have a wider meaning in that it is also used for other forms of genital interaction, although typically these additional meanings are signaled by qualifiers, e.g., anal intercourse, homosexual intercourse, etc.

sexual inversion ➤ **inversion, sexual**.

sexual involution ➤ **involution**.

sexuality 1. Generally, all those aspects of one's constitution and one's behavior that are related to sex. Some authors use this meaning with a clear restriction to sex, others use it so that one's dispositions toward love and deep affection are included, even if not associated with the sex organs *per se*. Typically, the former is intended. 2. The state of having sex and sexual functions; the quality of being sexual. Note that this usage is occasionally amplified by the notion of excessiveness; that is, sexuality to some authors is not just the quality of being sexual but the quality of being too sexual. This evaluative component of the term is less common than it once was.

sexual latency ➤ **latency period**.

sexually dimorphic nucleus An area in

the *medial* ➤ **preoptic area** that is considerably larger in males than females.

sexual maturation Biological maturation of the organs of reproduction to a functional level. ➤ **maturation**.

sexual object The individual or thing toward which sexual actions are directed. Distinguish from ➤ **sexual aim** and ➤➤ **sex object**.

sexual pain disorders A class of ➤ **sexual dysfunctions** marked by physical pain during sexual intercourse. Included are ➤ **dyspareunia** and ➤ **vaginismus**.

sexual perversion ➤ **perversion, sexual**.

sexual preference The preferred sex of one's sexual partner(s). The term is relatively new and was introduced in response to the rapidly accumulating data that indicate that relatively few persons are purely heterosexual or homosexual, the more common pattern being to have had some experiences or feelings of both kinds but with a marked preference for one or the other.

sexual reproduction The activities and processes of organisms which result in the production of new organisms through the union of sex cells. Compare with ➤ **asexual** (2), in which new organisms are produced by grafts, spores or the fission of a single cell.

sexual selection The process by which the differences between males and females of a species in secondary sex characteristics derive from preferential selection of individuals displaying these characteristics by individuals of the opposite sex.

sexual trauma 1. Generally, any trauma of a sexual nature. 2. More specifically, a disturbing or anxiety-producing childhood event related to sex that has lasting effect on sexual adjustment.

s factor ➤ **specific *factor**.

shadow 1. n. In Jung's approach, one of the archetypes; a complex of undeveloped feelings, ideas, desires and the like – the 'animal' instincts passed along through evolution to *Homo sapiens* from lower, more primitive forms that represent the negative side of personality; the 'alter ego.' **2 vb.** To follow, see here ➤ **shadowing**.

shadowing Following a spoken message by repeating as rapidly and accurately as possible what is said. It is used extensively as a control procedure in experiments on attention, since shadowing a message commandeers one's attentional focus so thoroughly that little or no attention can be directed toward any other stimulus that may be present.

shallow living One of Karen Horney's three forms of ➤ **neurotic *resignation**, manifested by a hectic life style in which the individual compulsively engages in so many activities that only the surfaces of things are dealt with and deep conflicts can be avoided.

shaman A practicer of magic, particularly one who attempts to use magic and spiritualism to heal. In popular jargon, a medicine man or witch doctor.

shame An emotional state produced by the awareness that one has acted dishonorably or ridiculously. The term is usually reserved for situations in which one's actions are publicly known or exposed to real or potential ridicule. Distinguish from ➤ **guilt**.

sham feeding (procedure) A surgical procedure in which an esophageal fistula (tube) is implanted so that whatever is swallowed exits without reaching the stomach.

shamming Faking, feigning. Used as a protective device in some species; e.g., ➤ **death feigning**.

sham rage A pattern of behavior mimicking a rage reaction, produced by artificial means. Two procedures have been studied. In one the entire cortex of an experimental animal is removed; in the other, areas of the hypothalamus are stimulated in an intact animal. In the first procedure, the rage reaction occurs to almost any stimulus and is totally indirected (the deco-

rticate animal is blind); in the second, the animal displays the characteristics of a normal rage response except that it terminates abruptly with cessation of the hypothalamic stimulation.

sham surgery Surgery in which all procedures are carried out save the one under specific experimental study. It is used as a control procedure in animal experiments involving surgery to protect against the possibility that any effects observed could be caused by the trauma of the surgery. For example, in animal studies of intestinal-bypass surgery, the control subjects will receive exactly the same surgical procedures as the experimental subjects except that the severed intestine will be resutured rather than bypassed.

shape The physical form of something. The shape of a stimulus is perceived and, hence, 'defined' by its contours or boundaries, the locus of points where there are sharp gradations in texture, shading, color, brightness, etc.

shape constancy The tendency to perceive the shape of a rigid object as remaining fixed despite alterations in the viewing conditions. A swinging door looked at head-on is still perceived as rectangular despite the fact that as it is opened and closed its retinal projection changes from rectangular to trapezoidal.

shaping The gradual building up of an operant behavior by reinforcing successive approximations. Shaping functions by the selective use of reinforcement to convert existing simple behaviors into more complex patterns of responding. Also called *approximation conditioning* and *conditioning by successive approximations*.

shared paranoid disorder ➤ **induced psychotic disorder**.

shenkui A ➤ **culture-specific syndrome** reported in Chinese men. It is marked by anxiety and panic with accompanying somatic complaints such as dizziness, backache, sexual dysfunctions, and insomnia that have no physical basis. Prevailing folk wisdom attributes it to excess loss of semen through frequent intercourse or masturbation.

shock **1.** A clinical syndrome that accompanies disruption of the oxygen supply to tissues, particularly brain tissues. Shock, to some extent, accompanies every injury although it is generally detectable only when there has been a major trauma such as serious injury, surgery, an overdose of certain drugs, extremely strong emotional experience, etc. **2.** The result of passing an electric current through the body. Severe shock (2) can produce shock (1). ➤ **shock therapy**.

shock phase The first part of the *alarm reaction* stage in the ➤ **general adaptation syndrome**.

shock–shock interval ➤ **temporal avoidance conditioning**.

shock therapy A general term covering the use of shock-inducing procedures for the treatment of emotional disorders. The most commonly used is ➤ **electroconvulsive shock**; other procedures such as *insulin shock* which were once popular are now little used. ➤ **electroconvulsive therapy** for a discussion.

shoe anesthesia ➤ **glove *anesthesia**.

short-circuit appeal A propaganda technique designed to arouse by appeals to emotional rather than cognitive or rational considerations.

short-term memory (or **store**) ➤ **memory, short-term**.

shotgunning Lab slang for a broad-based hit-or-miss approach to a problem. Rather like letting loose a shotgun blast in the hope that some pellets are on target.

shoulds Karen Horney's term for the elaborate set of internalized demands upon one's behavior. Although all persons are certainly replete with these internal pressures. Horney reserved the term for those excessive and irrational pressures and internal standards that contribute to neurotic obsessive and compulsive behaviors.

shrink Popular US slang for a psychiatrist or clinical psychologist.

shut-in personality A semi-technical term for an extremely withdrawn person.

shuttle box An experimental apparatus consisting of a box divided into two halves. Typically the subject must move from one side to the other to receive reward, escape or avoid an aversive stimulus, etc.

shwa ➤ **schwa**.

sib **1.** Short for ➤ **sibling** (1). **2.** In anthropology, a kin group composed of all of the lineal descendants of a single person. Usually a sib may be either matrilineal or patrilineal, although some authors who use the term *clan* for matrilineal cases will use *gens* for the patrilineal and *sib* as generic.

sibilant In phonetics, any speech sound produced by the turbulent passing of air between two articulators. e.g., *s*ure, *ch*urch, *j*eer.

sibling **1** n. Generally, one of two or more offspring in a family, a brother, a sister. Some restrict the term to cases in which the parents of both siblings are the same, using *half-sibling* when there is only one common biological parent. **2** adj. In biogenetics, characterizing two species which are genetically very closely related.

sibling rivalry ➤ **rivalry, sibling**.

sibship All the brothers and sisters in a given family.

Sidman avoidance ➤ **temporal avoidance conditioning**.

SIDS ➤ **sudden infant death syndrome**.

sight ➤ **vision**.

sighting line ➤ **visual axis**.

sight method ➤ **whole-word method**.

sight vocabulary ➤ **vocabulary, sight**.

sigma:
Σ A symbol denoting *summation*; e.g., ΣX means 'add up all the X values.' The symbol is read as 'sum of' and not 'sigma,'

which is reserved for the lowercase form, σ.

σ A symbol denoting ➤ **standard *deviation**. In some older texts it may be seen used as an abbreviation for *millisecond*.

σ_M = ➤ **standard error of the mean**.

$\sigma_{(M)}$ = ➤ **standard error of measurement**.

sigma score   ➤ **z-score**.

sign   **1** n. Most generally and inclusively, an indicator, a hint, a clue. When the sign is a characteristic element of some thing or event, it is often referred to as a *natural sign* or a ➤ **signal**; e.g., fire is a (natural) sign that something is burning. When the sign has an arbitrary social or cultural component it is generally referred to as a *conventional sign* or ➤ **symbol**; e.g., fire, in some cultures, is a (conventional) sign for life. **2** n. By extension, an event or an action that serves as a signifier of something with meaning or manifestations beyond its own self. For example, to an archeologist a pottery shard is a sign of human habitation, to a clinician tightly clenched fists are a sign of tension or anxiety in a client. This use, in discussion of pathologies, is similar to, although not identical with, ➤ **symptom**. Compare, for example, the meanings in 'A fever is a sign of infection' and 'A fever is a symptom of infection.' **3** n. An event which, by virtue of temporal and spatial contiguity with some other event, becomes capable of substituting for that event in eliciting a response. In Pavlov's original classic conditioning experiments, for example, the bell became a *sign* for salivation after being paired with food. Note that although the bell–food relationship here is arbitrary and learned, the term *symbol* is generally not used because the arbitrariness is not within the experimental subject's domain. **4** n. A physical gesture, especially a characteristic sequence or pattern of hand movements, used to stand for a word or a concept as in ➤ **sign language**. **5** n. A mathematical expression which stands for a particular operation or set of operations, e.g., a + sign. Note, however, that *sign* and *symbol* are often interchanged here; a + sign is referred to as an example of a mathematical symbol, although the latter term is typically reserved for the generic. **6** n. In linguistics, a word considered as a *symbol* of a thing. Here, the sign is the concrete element that represents the abstract or symbolic. **7** n. One of 12 divisions of the zodiac. vb., *to sign*, to indicate a thing or to communicate about a thing by the use of signs (in any of the senses above). Compare here with the verb *to signify*, which is used for either (a) to show or indicate a thing by signs, or (b) to have meaning.

signal   **1** n. Most generally, a ➤ **sign**, especially in meaning 1 of that term, that serves to communicate something. **2** n. More specifically, an agreed-upon event or object that functions as an occasion for some action. **3** n. A stimulus, particularly as in ➤ **signal-detection theory**. **4** n. In neurological work, any event that is transmitted along neural pathways. **5** n. Any transmitted event, e.g., a radio signal. See here ➤ **information theory**. **6** vb. To indicate or denote a thing. adj., *signal*.

signal anxiety   In Freud's later writings about anxiety, he hypothesized a mechanism that served an alerting, protective role. This so-called *signal anxiety* was seen as a response to threats to the equilibrium of the ego and served as a warning device to prevent the devastating experience of ➤ **primary anxiety** which accompanied ego dissolution.

signal-detection theory (SDT)   A mathematical theory of the detection of physical signals. The theory is based on the assumption that sensitivity to a signal is not merely a result of its intensity but is also dependent upon the amount of noise present, the motivation of the subject and the criterion which the subject sets for responding. The essential nature of the theory is captured in the figure (see overleaf). One assumption is that the amount of neural stimulation is normally distributed and that the subject's decision to respond 'yes' (i.e. 'I detected a signal')

721

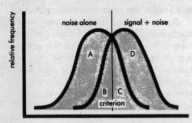

Key
A: Correct "no" responses
B: Misses; incorrect "no" responses
C: False alarms; incorrect "yes" responses
D: Hits; correct "yes" responses

is given by whether the *total* stimulation contributed either by noise alone or by noise plus signal exceeds the set-response criterion. The criterion is easily adjusted by changing the ➤ **payoff matrix** so that the costs and benefits associated with *hits* and *false alarms* are modified. The proportion of *hits* to *misses* in any given situation yields a measure of the subject's sensitivity (➤ **d′**) independent of the criterion set or other possible bias. Also called simply, *detection theory* because the principles apply to any situation, e.g., detecting a flaw in parts coming off a production line, detecting an abnormal feature in a patient's X-ray, etc.

signalling system A term often applied to the communication systems of non-human species. It is preferred in these contexts to ➤ **language**. ➤➤ **semiotics**.

signal-to-noise ratio Quite literally, the ratio between the energy in the signal to which one is attending and that in the background noise. abbrev., s/n.

signature ➤ **local sign**.

sign Gestalt (expectation) E. C. Tolman's term for a cognitive process involving a stimulus environment, a particular response and the anticipation that this particular response in this situation will lead to the fulfillment of the organism's expectations. ➤➤ **expectancy** and **means–ends readiness**.

significance Importance, meaning, the quality of having importance or meaning. E.g., ➤ **statistical significance**.

significance level An arbitrary value used as a criterion for determining whether a given data set departs sufficiently from what would be expected were only chance factors operating that it can be classified as statistically significant. The usual level adopted in the social sciences is 5% or, as it is usually denoted, $p < 0.05$, where p is the probability of the observed results or more extreme results occurring by chance alone. Occasionally called the *alpha level*. ➤➤ **statistical significance**.

significant difference ➤ **statistical significance**.

significant other As originally introduced by H. S. Sullivan, any person who is important and influential in affecting an individual's development of social norms, values and personal self-image. Usually a significant other is someone who has power over one and provides a point of reflection for accepting and rejecting values, norms and behaviors. ➤➤ **socialization** and **generalized other**.

signify ➤ **sign**.

sign language A language based on gestural communication. Typically the term refers to the rich, elaborate and fully grammatical manual system used by the deaf. Note that *finger spelling*, although it is an integral part of such communication since it is necessary for signing names, novel words and specialized terms which have no manual sign, is generally regarded as a separate component of communication by sign and not as part of the sign language itself.

sign learning E. C. Tolman's term for learning that consists primarily of acquiring an appreciation for the relations between signs, their references and the outcomes of behavior emitted with respect to them.

sign stimulus In ethology, a species-specific stimulus that is effective in triggering a ➤ **fixed-action pattern**. Occasionally called a ➤ **releaser**, although properly a releaser is but a particular kind of sign stimulus. ➤➤ **innate releasing mechanism**.

sign test A nonparametric statistical test useful for situations in which the data consist solely of whether the observed scores exceed (+) or fail to exceed (−) some theoretical values or some other scores. The test compares the observed proportions of plus and minus signs against what would be expected by chance.

sign tracking An occasional synonym for ➤ **autoshaping**.

silent pause ➤ **pause, silent**.

silent speech ➤ **subvocalization**.

similarity A dimension of sameness, resemblance. Generally used with respect to the notion of shared features or shared principles; the more features or principles two things have in common the greater their similarity.

similarity, law of **1.** The generalization that thoughts, images, words, etc. are more likely to elicit other similar thoughts, images, words, etc. than those that are dissimilar. **2.** In Gestalt psychology, one of the laws (or principles) of organization that, other things being equal, parts of a stimulus field that are physically similar to each other tend to be perceived as belonging together as a unit.

simple causation ➤ **causation**.

simple correlation ➤ **correlation, simple**.

simple phobia ➤ **phobia, simple**.

simple schizophrenia ➤ **schizophrenia, simple**.

simple structure In factor analysis, the stage in which the factor rotation has yielded an arrangement where the factors are located such that the sum of the number of factors required to describe each test is a minimum.

simple tone ➤ **pure *tone**.

simulate **1.** Generally, to mimic, to assume the appearance of, to copy. **2.** In psychiatry and clinical psychology, to malinger, to engage in a conscious attempt to pretend to be suffering from a mental disorder.

simulator Generally, an apparatus designed for training that mimics real-life situations. Airline pilots' training programs, for example, make extensive use of them.

simultanagnosia An ➤ **apperceptive *agnosia** in which the patient can recognize individual elements of a complex picture one at a time but cannot appreciate the overall sense of the scene.

simultaneous conditioning An experimental conditioning procedure in which there is simultaneous presentation and termination of the conditioned stimulus and the unconditioned stimulus. Compare with ➤ **delay conditioning** and ➤ **trace conditioning**.

simultaneous contrast ➤ **contrast**.

sine wave A wave form characterized by regular oscillations with a set period and amplitude such that the displacement amplitude at each point is proportional to the sine of the phase angle of the displacement. A pure tone is propagated as a sine wave.

single-blind An experimental technique in which the subjects are ignorant of the experimental conditions but the researcher running the experiment knows them. The procedure helps to reduce expectation effects but does not control for possible experimenter-bias effects as well as the ➤ **double-blind**.

single-cell recording ➤ **single-unit recording**.

single-channel model The generalization that for the most part one can attend fully to only one sequentially structured stimulus input at a time.

singleton **1.** An only child, one without siblings. **2.** Any mammal born alone, with no litter mates.

single-unit recording In neurophysiology,

recording the electrical activity of a single neuron with the use of microelectrodes (tip diameter less than 10 microns). Also called *single-cell recording*.

single-variable principle The empirical principle that when but one factor is permitted to vary while all others are held constant, any observed systematic effects must be due to the single variable manipulated. ➤ **control**.

sinister From the Latin, meaning *left* or *unfavorable*. The original use was with reference to omens which appeared on the left side, which were always thought to be portents of evil. The derived forms used in science today deal only with the notion of sideness, the evaluative meaning having been discarded. Thus, *sinistrad* is toward the left, *sinistral* refers to the left side of the body or to left-handedness, etc. Contrast with ➤ **dexter**, which still retains the old meaning of favorable in both the technical and popular language, as well as the notion of right-sided.

sinistrality Any marked preference for the left side of the body. ➤ **sinister**.

sinus From the Latin for *hollow* or *curve*, any cavity with a relatively narrow opening.

sinusoid(al) Pertaining to: **1.** a sine wave; **2.** a sinus.

-sis A suffix from the Greek, meaning *state* or *condition*. Depending on the vowel that precedes, it may take any of several forms: *-asis, -esis, -iasis* or *-osis*.

situation 1. Simply, a place, locale or position. This meaning, restricted largely to circumscribed physical domains, is actually rather uncommon in technical writing. **2.** A complex whole representing the multiple stimulus patterns, events, objects, persons and affective tone existing at some point in time. In this sense the term is close in meaning to 'state of affairs' or 'set of circumstances.' In essentially all combined forms with the term, this is the meaning intended. adj. *situational*.

situational analysis The study or analysis of events and phenomena in the natural surroundings as opposed to the laboratory setting. This term has been largely replaced by ➤ **naturalistic observation**, particularly when the subject of the analysis is subhuman.

situational approach An approach to group management and group leadership which stresses that there is no single individual or particular set of skills that makes for optimal leadership in all situations. Rather, that different situations and circumstances require different skills and have different types of people who are best qualified to take managerial and leadership roles.

situational determinant ➤ **determinant**.

situational neurosis A neurotic syndrome produced by a particular environmental situation, usually one which caused a great deal of stress, anxiety or other trauma. E.g., ➤ **gross *stress reaction**.

situational psychosis ➤ **brief reactive psychosis**.

situational stress reaction A minor cognitive and personality disorientation to the stress of encountering difficult, new life experiences like a new job, moving to a new city or country. The duration of the disorder is typically brief as the individual adjusts to the novel circumstances.

situational test A contrived and necessarily disguised test in which the person being evaluated is put in a situation which simulates a particular slice of real life, to determine whether the appropriate response is made. For example, testing an applicant for a proof-reader's job by handing him or her an application form with several typographical errors in it.

situation, defining the The process of examining, evaluating and assessing a particular situation prior to making decisions about how to behave in an appropriate fashion.

16 PF ➤ **Sixteen Personality Factor Questionnaire**.

Sixteen Personality Factor Questionnaire A personality assessment inventory developed by Raymond Cattell based on the 16 personality factors or ➤ **source *traits** that emerged from his factor analyses of a wide range of ➤ **surface *traits**. The test itself consists of self-report statements concerning personality traits, e.g., 'sober v. happy-go-lucky.' Also called the *16 PF*.

sixth sense Colloquially and erroneously, the paranormal sense. The problems with this term surround the question of its existence (see the discussion under ➤ **parapsychology**) and the number used, which implies that there are but five normal senses (hearing, vision, taste, smell and touch), which grossly misrepresents the true situation since kinesthesis, equilibrium, the sensing of warmth (and coldness), at least two varieties of pain, etc. are omitted by this count.

size constancy The tendency to perceive the veridical size of familiar objects despite the fact that the size of the retinal image undergoes dramatic variation owing to changing conditions of viewing, most significantly the changing distance of the object from the perceiver.

size–weight illusion The tendency to estimate the weight of large objects as lighter than small ones with identical physical mass. Also called *Charpentier illusion*.

Skaggs-Robinson hypothesis The generalization that little or no similarity between stimuli causes both little or no interference and little or no facilitation in processing them.

skeletal From the Greek for *dried up*, pertaining to the skeleton, to the body framework composed of 206 separate bones.

skeletal age ➤ carpal *age.

skeletal muscle ➤ striate *muscle.

skew correlation ➤ curvilinear *correlation.

skewness The degree to which the curve of a frequency distribution departs from per-

fect symmetry. Skewness is described as *positive* (or *to the right*) or *negative* (or *to the left*) depending upon whether the tail of the distribution extends toward those values relative to the mode. Skewness is the third ➤ **moment** (2) of a distribution.

skill The capacity for carrying out complex, well-organized, patterns of behavior smoothly and adaptively so as to achieve some end or goal. Although the term was originally used largely with respect to motor activity, it is now common to see references to verbal and social skills. Note, however, that in these latter cases there is a tendency to use the term with the connotation that the skill is part of a pattern of behaviors aimed at influencing and manipulating other persons.

skin The external covering of the body. Consisting of epidermis, dermis and subcutaneous tissues, it is an extremely complex and vital organ involved in the mediation of the senses of temperature, pressure and pain and playing important roles in protection and temperature regulation.

skin conductance response (SCR) ➤ **galvanic skin response**.

Skinner box An experimental apparatus named for its inventor, B. F. Skinner. Although there is an almost limitless number of variations, the basic design is simplicity itself: a small enclosed chamber with two essential components, a manipulandum (button, bar, key, lever, etc.), which the experimental subject can operate, and a device which delivers reinforcements (food hopper, water tube, etc.). Other common components are projectors and speakers for presenting visual and auditory stimuli, an electrifiable grid floor for studying aversive conditioning, additional manipulanda for investigations of choice behavior, etc. The apparatus has become the prototypical device for the controlled laboratory study of ➤ **operant behavior**.

Skinnerian Pertaining to or characteristic of the general theoretical point of view of the great American advocate of ➤

behaviorism, Burrhus Frederic Skinner. The Skinnerian position embodies a strong ➤ **positivism** with its attendant ➤ **operationalism**, a denial of the usefulness of hypothesizing unobservable mental acts, an eschewing of formal theory (although Skinner himself was seemingly irresistibly drawn to informal theorizing) and a denial of the explanatory value of concepts such as freedom, will, dignity, etc. Like most comprehensive orientations, the Skinnerian has its own set of procedures (➤➤ **operant conditioning, schedules of *reinforcement, Skinner box**), its own technical journal (*Journal of the Experimental Analysis of Behavior*) and its own often arcane terminology (for some of the more unusual, ➤ **autoclitic, knee, mand, perch, scallop, time-out**).

Skinnerian conditioning ➤ **Operant conditioning** is occasionally so referred to in honor of B. F. Skinner.

skin potential The electrical potential of the skin, which is measured as the ➤ **galvanic skin response**.

skin senses Those senses for which the receptors are in the ➤ **skin**.

sleep Basically, a particular loss of consciousness characterized by a variety of behavioral and neurophysiological effects. In modern psychology sleep and the various stages of sleep are typically defined and characterized by particular physiological events, in particular brain-wave patterns as recorded by an electroencephalograph, metabolic processes, muscle tone, heart and respiration rates and the important presence or absence of rapid eye movements (REMs). The typical division is into *REM sleep* and *NREM* (or *non-REM*) *sleep*. REM sleep is characterized by its primary defining feature, the rapid eye movements, and several less detectable but important factors including a lack of delta waves (slow, large-amplitude brain waves), flaccid musculature, fluctuating heart beat, erratic respiration, genital changes and, significantly, dreaming (in approximately 80–85% of cases studied, subjects awakened from a REM period

reported dreaming). NREM sleep is usually divided into four separate stages based on the proportion of delta waves observed: Stage 1 shows essentially 0% of the total brain activity as delta (but with no REM), Stage 2 has up to 20% delta, Stage 3 between 20 and 50% delta, Stage 4 over 50%. Not surprisingly, Stages 3 and 4 are often referred to collectively as *slow-wave sleep* (SWS). These stages also show a progressively deeper and deeper sleep and all are characterized by a lack of REM, a regular heart beat, rhythmic respiration, low levels of metabolic activity and moderate-to-high muscle tone. Although dreaming is strongly associated with REM sleep, there is roughly a 15% chance that dreams will be reported by persons woken from NREM sleep, although these dreams lack the clear imagery, emotional tone and structure of REM sleep dreams. However, a variety of atypical sleep phenomena such as ➤ **somnambulism** and ➤ **sleep terror disorder** tend to occur during Stage 4. ➤➤ **dream, dream analysis, hypnagogic imagery**. Note that many authors prefer the notations ➤ **D *sleep** and ➤ **S *sleep** for REM and NREM sleep; see those entries for reasons.

sleep apnea ➤ **apnea**.

sleep attack An overwhelming urge to sleep. Much more compelling than mere sleepiness, it occurs in ➤ **sleep disorders** such as ➤ **narcolepsy**.

sleep center A term once applied to an area of the hypothalamus thought to control sleep. It is now known that there is no such identifiable neural center; brainstem and forebrain structures have both been implicated in control over the complex sleep–waking cycle.

sleep, D A common synonym for *REM sleep*. The notation *D* is favored by some because REM sleep shows a *d*esynchronized EEG pattern and because it is usually accompanied by *d*reaming. ➤ **sleep** for more detail. Compare with ➤ **S *sleep**.

sleep disorder An umbrella term for any

significant departure from the normal sleep–waking cycle. Contemporary terminology distinguishes between the ➤ **organic** ***sleep disorders** that are caused by neurological or physiological factors and the ➤ **nonorganic *sleep disorders** that are regarded as primarily psychogenic. This latter category is subdivided into the ➤ **dyssomnias**, which include disorders in the amount, quality or timing of sleep, and the ➤ **parasomnias**, which include disorders marked by abnormal events occurring during sleep. See each of these terms for more detail.

sleep disorder, nonorganic Any sleep disorder in which emotional factors are deemed to be the primary cause. See ➤ **dyssomnia** and ➤ **parasomnia** for details.

sleep disorder, organic Any sleep disorder in which organic, nonpsychogenic factors are deemed to be the primary cause. Included are ➤ **narcolepsy**, ➤ **apnea**, and ➤ **nocturnal myoclonus**.

sleep, disorders of initiating and maintaining (DIMS) ➤ **insomnia**.

sleep epilepsy ➤ **narcolepsy**.

sleeper effect 1. Originally, Carl Hovland's term for the fact that attitude changes produced by a message often do not become evident until a period of time has passed. 2. More specifically, the generalization that a message from a low credibility source that originally had no effect on people's attitudes will show an effect after some time has passed. People remember the message but forget the source. ➤ **source *memory**. 3. In developmental psychology, an early event or circumstance that does not produce an effect until some time has passed.

sleeping sickness The common name for the infectious disease *Encephalitis lethargica* characterized by increasing drowsiness, lethargy and apathy.

sleep learning ➤ **hypnopaedia**.

sleep paralysis The temporary inability to move when muscle flaccidity and accompanying paralysis of REM sleep intrudes on an awake period. Such episodes usually occur immediately before or after sleep and can be mildly frightening.

sleep, pathological A general term for any abnormal pattern of sleep. ➤ **sleep disorder**, et seq.

sleep, S A common term for *NREM sleep*. The notation *S* is used to denote the fact that the EEG of a person in NREM sleep is characterized by *s*low waves, is *s*ynchronized and shows *s*leep *s*pindles. ➤ **sleep** for more details. Compare with ➤ **D *sleep**.

sleep, slow-wave A term occasionally used for the sleep in Stages 3 and 4, in which the EEG displays the large-amplitude, slow, delta waves. ➤ **sleep** for more detail. abbrev., *SWS*.

sleep spindles Short (about 1 second) bursts of rapid (12–14 Hz), low-voltage brain-wave activity. They are observed in Stages 2, 3 and 4 of ➤ **sleep**; see that entry for details.

sleep terror disorder A sleep disorder marked by repeated episodes of waking in what appears to be a state of intense anxiety with dilated pupils, sweating, rapid breathing, and a rapid pulse. After the agitation subsides, the individual usually reports a vague sense of terror with fragmentary dream-like images. Typically there is no memory in the morning. The disorder generally begins in childhood and, unlike ➤ **dream anxiety disorder**, occurs during Stages 3 and 4 of sleep and not during REM sleep. Also called *pavor nocturnus* or, when occurring during daytime naps, *pavor diurnus*.

sleep, twilight The delirium-like state produced by an injection of scopolamine, morphine and phenobarbital.

sleep–wake schedule disorder A type of ➤ **sleep disorder** marked by a mismatch between the person's natural (*circadian rhythm*) sleep–wake cycle and that which is expected by their environment (e.g., their job). The most common form is ➤ **delayed sleep-onset insomnia** where the person tosses and turns often for hours before falling asleep. Also called *circadian rhythm sleep disorder*.

sleepwalking ➤ **somnambulism**.

slip of the tongue ➤ **parapraxis**.

slope With respect to curves, the tangent of the angle made by a straight line drawn from a point on the curve by the *x*-axis. ➤ **acceleration**.

slow Basically a nontechnical term used to characterize: **1.** A child whose development is retarded relative to the norm. **2.** Any person with below-normal intellectual functioning. See also terms beginning with ➤ **brady-**.

slow learner 1. A mildly retarded child. **2.** A child with normal intellectual potential who, for any number of reasons, takes longer to learn material than is typical for that age. ➤ **mental retardation** to appreciate the distinction between these two meanings.

slow (twitch) muscle ➤ **muscle twitch** (1).

slow-wave sleep ➤ **sleep, slow-wave**.

small group By arbitrary convention, a group of individuals numbering approximately ten or fewer. Most small-group research involves the study of such small numbers of persons in face-to-face contact in either laboratory settings or natural environments.

small-sample theory The mathematical/statistical theory and accompanying techniques that permit the derivation of inferences from relatively small samples to larger populations.

smell 1 n. The sense modality of *olfaction*, that sense for which the stimuli are particular classes of chemicals in gaseous form. See here ➤ **olfaction, olfactory** and related entries. **2** n. A sensation produced by stimulation of the olfactory receptors and nerves. **3** vb. To process information in the olfactory modality, to perceive via the stimulation of the olfactory receptors and nerves. **4** vb. To emit an odor (despite the famous anecdote concerning Dr Johnson).

smoothed curve A curve whose erratic changes in slope have been evened out so that the general trend can be more easily seen. The fitting of a smooth line by a *least-squares* procedure is a commonly employed method.

smooth muscle ➤ **muscle, smooth**.

s/n ➤ **signal-to-noise ratio**.

Snellen chart A chart used as a rough test for measuring visual acuity. Letters are printed in various sizes on the chart, which is placed at a fixed distance from the viewer. The letters are based on a scale of 5×3 minutes of visual angle, with the size of the letters adjusted for the viewing distance.

snowball sampling ➤ **sampling, snowball**.

snow blindness An impairment to vision, typically temporary, caused by exposure to extremely high-intensity light such as that reflected off of a snow field under a bright sun. Complete blindness is rare, more commonly acuity is dramatically reduced and objects have a reddish tinge for a time.

SOA ➤ **stimulus onset asynchrony**.

sociability The tendency to have and make personal relationships; friendliness.

sociability index (or **rating**) A rating that expresses one's sociability. A ➤ **sociogram**, for example, yields, among other measures, an assessment of the sociability of the various members of a group.

social A splendidly broad adjective which can safely be used for any situation involving two or more conspecifics (members of a species). Note that this is really the appropriate definition. Although the vast majority of uses of the term involve the species *Homo sapiens*, it is also used freely by comparative psychologists, ethologists and sociobiologists. As the many following entries suggest, it is rarely used as a free-standing term but generally qualified to narrow and specify its intended meaning. For combined terms and phrases not found here, see those using ➤

cultural or ➤ group as the base term.

social accommodation ➤ accommodation (4).

social action Any organized, concerted effort on the part of a group of persons to change or reform some (usually political or institutional) aspect of society.

social adaptation ➤ adaptation (2).

social adjustment ➤ adjustment (1).

social-adjustment theory A theoretical approach to the study of attitudes and attitude changes as social-adjustment operations. It draws upon basic principles of experimental psychology, especially psychophysics, to assess the processes involved in the establishment and modification of evaluative judgements. There are two general models, ➤ assimilation-contrast theory and ➤ adaptation-level theory; see each for details.

social anchoring A term used to describe personal decision-making and attitude formation which is dependent primarily upon an external group's decisions or attitudes. The person is said to 'anchor' decisions on those of some reference group. The effect is presumed by some theorists to be sufficiently strong to account for the bandwagon phenomenon in politics, where the candidate perceived to be ahead suddenly attracts the support of the undecided voters, who take their cue from the majority.

social anxiety Feelings of unease and discomfort in social settings typically accompanied by shyness and social awkwardness. Distinguish from ➤ social *phobia.

social atmosphere ➤ social climate.

social attitude A term used in several contexts to refer to any attitude which can be characterized as social in origin or in manner of manifestation. Thus: 1. The attitude which underlies a person's tendency to behave in a particular fashion toward other persons. 2. A particular pattern of beliefs common to a group of persons or a society. 3. Any personal belief which is acquired as a result of socialization processes.

social behavior 1. Loosely, any behavior of an individual which has social components. That is, behavior that is influenced by the presence, attitudes or actions of others; behavior that influences the presence, attitudes or actions of others; or behavior learned primarily as a result of social factors. 2. More specifically, ➤ group behavior or that behavior which takes place in and is primarily determined by a group.

social being A more or less nontechnical term for any organism or species whose intrinsic nature and behaviors are dependent on the presence of and interactions with others.

social-breakdown syndrome The generalization that some of the symptoms of various mental disorders are the result of conditions and facilities of treatment and not primary components of the psychiatric disorder itself. Generally included as contributing factors here are labeling (➤ labeling theory), learning the role of 'sick person' (➤ advantage by illness), atrophy of social skills and identification with the sick.

social casework ➤ social work.

social category A collection of persons who are classified together by virtue of societal criteria but do not form a group or an organization, e.g., adolescents, secondary-school teachers, unemployed persons. Compare with ➤ social class.

social change Generally, any alteration in the social organization or structure of a society. In practice, the term is typically reserved for major, significant changes in a society as a whole and is not applied to minor perturbations or to changes in subgroups within the society.

social class A social category in a stratified society which is usually defined by its members having roughly equivalent ➤ socioeconomic status relative to other strata of that society. There is some debate as to the generality of this criterion of socioeconomic status. Some authorities stress that less obvious factors such as life style, prestige, attitudes, identifications, etc. are better descriptive measures and many use the notion of ➤ **life chance(s)** as the primary defining feature. Others, notably those with a Marxist orientation, stress that the means of production in a society dictate social class sufficiently strongly to outweigh other factors. Usage, thus, follows theory.

social climate A more or less nontechnical term for the general tenor or inclination of any society, or segment thereof, that has effects on the attitudes and actions of its individual members. Also called *group climate* or *social* (or *group*) *atmosphere*.

social climbing A nontechnical term for which we provide here a technical definition: behaving so as to attempt to move from *social class n* to social class *n + j*, where *n* and *j* are integers and the various social classes may be represented on at least an ➤ **ordinal *scale**.

social code A general term for any set of rules, mores or regulations, formal or informal, which exerts control over the conduct of persons in a group or society.

social cognition A subfield that is essentially a blending of social and cognitive psychology which focuses on how individuals perceive, recall, think about, and interpret information about the actions of themselves and others.

social cohesion The tendency for any group or society to maintain itself, to hold together its several components. The degree of cohesion of a group is usually reflected by its resiliency to disruption by outside forces.

social comparison The use of others as a basis for comparison in evaluating one's own judgements, abilities, attitudes, etc.

social consciousness 1. Generally, the awareness that one has of one's social nature and of one's role in a group or society. **2.** Somewhat more specifically, the recognition that one's needs, feelings, attitudes and beliefs are not utterly unique but are shared by others, particularly those with similar social backgrounds. **3.** A synonym for *group consciousness, collective consciousness* or ➤ **group mind**.

social constructivism ➤ **constructivism** (2).

social contagion The rapid spread of attitudes, ideas or moods through a group or a society, as, for example, through *rumour*.

social control The control that a society exerts upon the individuals within it. The form that this control takes is primarily through the socialization process and the resulting internalization of the norms and values of the society. The term is generally not used to refer to the use of personal or group power to effect exploitative or selfish control over others although, to be sure, by the very nature of society such forms of social control do exist. Most social theorists find it useful to distinguish between *negative* social control, which functions through disapproval, ridicule, punishment, the threat of punishment, etc., and *positive* social control, which operates through rewards, approval, tangible benefits, etc.

social Darwinism The theory that social and cultural development could be explained by analogy with the Darwinian theory of biological evolution. The basic principle here, first articulated by the British philosopher Herbert Spencer, is that society functions primarily through competition and conflict and that the fittest survive and prosper, the weak and poorly adapted are eliminated. The theory is indefensibly simplistic but has, unfortunately, been used by some as a defense of a rather ugly form of *laissez-faire* economics which ignores the importance of social class and related factors in affecting one's chances of success.

social desirability 1. Those characteristics generally approved of socially and which, if possessed, make one a socially attractive person. **2.** A bias or set to respond to self-evaluative questions in a socially approved manner so as to appear more socially desirable either to oneself or to others.

social determinism ➤ **cultural determinism**.

social differentiation Collectively, the processes through which a society becomes divided into various statuses, classes, groups, strata, roles, etc.

social dilemma ➤ **dilemma, social**.

social distance Generally, the degree of separation between groups or individuals in a society. Social distance is a complex concept and reflects patterns of personal and social interaction, the degree of intimacy and the mutual sympathy for values and ideals between persons in a society. It has been characterized in various ways, ranging from the extent to which a given stratum of a society is accessible to other persons from another stratum, to the internal sense of disparateness an individual feels with respect to a particular segment of society, to the degree to which a person will willingly associate with another from a distinct social group. Note also that the terms *horizontal* and *vertical* are often used for social distance between persons of the same and different socio-economic classes respectively.

social distance scale A sociometric instrument for measuring ➤ **social distance**. The subject indicates the degree of intimate interaction he or she would willingly have with other persons from other social, racial, ethnic or national groups. The scale is based on a series of graded categories from 'exclude from my country' to 'admit to my family through marriage.' Also known as the *Bogardus Social Distance Scale*.

social drive Loosely, any drive for social interaction, a drive with interpersonal aims rather than physical or material aims. Distinguish from ➤ **socialized drive**.

social dyad ➤ **diad, social**.

social dynamics **1.** Loosely, the processes that underlie social change. **2.** Any approach to social psychology or sociology that is primarily concerned with the study of social change. Compare with ➤ **group dynamics**.

social ecology ➤ **ecology, social**.

social equilibrium ➤ **equilibrium** (3).

social-exchange theory A model of social structure based on the principle that most social behavior is predicated on the individual's expectation that one's actions with respect to others will result in some kind of commensurate return.

social facilitation A general phenomenon revealing that activity is increased (facilitated) by the presence of ➤ **conspecifics**. Examples abound. Fully satiated chickens will eat if placed among chickens who are eating hungrily, athletes perform better if an audience watches, children play more enthusiastically if a playmate is near by, even if only engaged in parallel play, and even cockroaches will learn a maze faster if watched by other roaches. Note that this facilitation effect occurs with relatively well learned or automatic behaviors; the presence of others can inhibit or interfere with behaviors that are not well learned or that are highly complex.

social factor Broadly, any variable that has an impact on behavior in a social setting.

social fission The splitting apart of a group or other social unit. ➤ **fission**.

social heritage The compendium of folkways, mores, traditions, institutions, laws, customs, etc. passed on within a social system from generation to generation. Thus, the term captures the same essential meaning as the term ➤ **culture**.

social identity theory The hypothesis that people seek out others like themselves (➤ **ingroup**) because it enhances self-esteem.

social immobility ➤ **social mobility**.

social indicators Generally, those aspects of group or social behavior that can be used as cues to general societal trends.

social influence A cover term for all those processes through which a person, group or class influences the opinions, attitudes, behaviors and values of other persons, groups or classes.

social inhibition The restraining of behavior by social factors. The obviousness of this effect can be appreciated simply by considering where and when one takes off one's clothes.

social insects Any of several species of insects whose mode of existence is fundamentally social, particularly those the hive or nest of which is hierarchically structured so that duties and behaviors are delegated to particular groups or classes.

social instinct Gregariousness, the tendency to seek out and form social contacts. The term is ill-advised; the word ➤ **instinct** is loaded with species-specific, genetic connotations that are far from the whole picture here.

social institution ➤ **institution** (1, 2).

social integration ➤ **integration, social**.

social interaction ➤ **interaction**.

social interference ➤ **social facilitation**.

social isolate A person who forms relatively few interpersonal ties with others. The causes may be either internal or external.

sociality ➤ **sociability**.

socialization 1. Generally, the process whereby an individual acquires the knowledge, values, facility with language, social skills and social sensitivity that enables him or her to become integrated into and behave adaptively within a society. Strictly speaking, this definition applies uniformly to persons of all ages and, in a very real sense, socialization is a lifelong experience. However, the dominant usage of the term is with respect to the processes by which the child becomes inculcated with society's values and with his or her own social roles. 2. The process of the taking over by the state of the services, industry and other institutions of a society

for the (ostensible) benefit of all members. 3. In industrial/organizational psychology, the process whereby a new recruit of an organization learns to adapt to that organization's norms and roles; in the layman's terms, 'learning the ropes.' 4. The respective outcomes of any of the above processes.

socialize 1. To bring about ➤ **socialization** in either sense 1 or 2 of that term. 2. To interact freely with other persons. 3. To encourage such interactions in others.

socialized drive Any primary drive which has had its mode of manifestation shaped by social learning so that its satisfaction is achieved through socially accepted behaviors. Distinguish from ➤ **social drive**.

social lag ➤ **culture lag**.

social learning theory An approach to the study of social behavior and personality due primarily to the work of Albert Bandura and Robert Walters. The theory is based upon the role of observation and the mimicking or imitating of behaviors observed in others, usually referred to as models. For more details on specifics of the theory, ➤ **model, modelling** and **observational *learning**.

social loafing The tendency for individuals to reduce the effort that they make toward some task when working together with others. The effect has been found in a wide variety of circumstances; people put less effort into pushing a car or to solving cognitively complex problems when the tasks are carried out in a group.

social man A perspective on mankind that assumes that the basic principle underlying human nature is a complex set of social and interpersonal needs.

social meaning The meaning of a situation, event or other social phenomenon as given by the shared understandings and interpretations of those present. Social meaning is derived from shared attitudes and beliefs of the persons in a group or a larger society.

social mind 1. ➤ **group mind**. 2. The

dominant opinion within a group or society.

social mobility 1. A dimension that characterizes the degree to which individuals in a particular society can move along the social scale. Rigid, fixed, social systems are characterized by social immobility such that a person's hereditary role largely determines his or her life chances; open, more democratic systems are typically characterized by somewhat greater social mobility. 2. The movement from class to class of individuals in a society. Although the term can, strictly speaking, cover both upward and downward movements, it is generally applied only to upward ones.

social motive Generally, any learned motive. Social motives are typically not essential for life, are learned through social interaction and are satisfied by social outcomes. Originally these 'secondary' motives were contrasted with the 'primary,' physiologically based motives, but it is, in practice, often difficult to separate them; for example, sexual motivation is inextricably tied to both aspects.

social need Generally, any ➤ **need** with a social basis, e.g., ➤ **need for affiliation**.

social norm Any pattern of behavior that occurs so often within a particular society that it comes to be accepted as reflective of that society and taken as sanctioned by the members of that society. Sometimes called *group norm*, although that term is probably best reserved for smaller social units.

social object An ➤ **object** that is a person or a group of persons.

social order 1. The totality of the institutions and structures that make up a society; usually preceded by the word *the*. 2. A relatively stable condition in a society in which things are harmonious and major conflicts are rare.

social organization ➤ **organization, social**.

social pathology ➤ **social problem**.

social perception Broadly, any aspect of ➤ perception that has a social element. The term is generally used with respect to an individual's awareness of the behaviors of others which are revealing of their motives or attitudes. See here ➤ **person perception**; compare with ➤ **self-perception theory**.

social phobia ➤ **phobia, social**.

social power ➤ **power, social**.

social pressure The collective coercive influences of others, particularly when they are acting as a coordinated group. Usually used only when such patterns of pressure lie outside of the formalized value systems of society. ➤ **pressure** (2, 3).

social problem An umbrella term for any situation which, from the point of view of a significant number of persons in a community, is deemed to constitute a problem of sufficient severity to require reform. Typically included here are drug abuse, juvenile delinquency, poverty, gangs, unemployment and the like.

social psychiatry Loosely, any approach to psychiatry or clinical psychology that focuses on social factors in the etiology and treatment of mental disorders.

social psychology That branch of psychology that concentrates on any and all aspects of human behavior that involve persons and their relationships to other persons, groups, social institutions and to society as a whole. Gordon Allport captured this general sense in his now classic definition of social psychology as the discipline that 'attempts to understand and explain how the thought, feeling or behavior of individuals are influenced by the actual, imagined or implied presence of others.' Social psychology exchanges freely ideas, models and methods with other social sciences, particularly sociology. In fact, this exchange is so rich and ubiquitous that it is often difficult to distinguish the two fields. Some authorities maintain that the sociologist begins with the domain of society and works toward the individual while the social psychologist reverses the order. However, since in practice both disciplines invest most of their resources in the ambiguous middle ground, the distinction is blurred.

social pyramid A term used for the vertical model of the social classes in a society which, if schematically represented with the size of each stratum reflecting the number of persons in it, has a pyramidal shape with the numerous lower classes at the base and the less numerous elite classes at the apex.

social reality ➤ reality, social.

social recognition A general term used to cover a number of processes that relate to the ability of an individual to recognize particular social attributes and characteristics of other individuals or groups. Included here are processes like recognition of species identity, group membership, sexual receptivity, social status, reproductive status, genetic relatedness, etc. The term is used for humans as well as other species.

social reinforcement ➤ reinforcement, social.

social role ➤ role.

social sanction Social approval of action or choice.

social scale The various social classes ordered according to some set of criteria. Any number of social scales may be formed; the most common are those based on ➤ socioeconomic status or ➤ social class.

social selection 1. A term first used by those espousing ➤ social Darwinism for a hypothetical process by which certain individuals, groups or classes survived and prospered while others did not. The presumption was that social systems could be viewed as analogs of biological systems, with social selection operating as did ➤ natural selection. This meaning is obsolete. 2. More loosely, the role of social factors in determining differential survival of individuals. From this point of view, ➤ sexual selection may be regarded as an example of social selection in many species in that interactions between individuals in attracting and maintaining a mate are important components in reproductive success.

social self ➤ self, social.

social sensitivity ➤ sensitivity (3). The *social* is often appended to distinguish this meaning of sensitivity from the others that it has.

social space A region with both geographical and social boundaries which represents the social, interactive domain for an individual. One's social space may shift over time as new relationships are formed and old ones dissolve, as group membership changes and as one's social perceptions are modified. Compare with ➤ personal space.

social status ➤ status, social.

social stratification The alignment of a society into social classes.

social structure The relatively stable, organized pattern of interrelated roles, statuses, norms and institutions characterizing a group or a society at a point in time.

social studies Generally, those aspects of a school curriculum which touch upon social issues, social problems, etc.

social support Generally and loosely, all those forms of support provided by other individuals and groups that help an individual cope with life.

social tension ➤ tension (4).

social time ➤ time, social.

social transmission ➤ cultural transmission.

social value ➤ value (2).

social welfare (programs) Any of the programs of formal agencies, private and public, which are designed to assist the disadvantaged in a society.

social work A professional field which bridges community psychology, clinical psychology and sociology. Social work is concerned broadly with the application of social-science principles to social problems. Although the field is difficult to circumscribe, particularly because new problems, theories and procedures tend to extend its domain, it is typically divided into three broad areas: (a) social casework with a focus on individual and family therapy; (b) group work with emphasis on work with gangs, youth, churches, etc.; and (c) community relations, with an orientation toward local organizations, neighborhood groups, institutions, etc.

societal Pertaining to society or to that which is social in nature.

society 1. Inclusively, all of humankind taken as a whole. This meaning is rare these days. 2. A collection of persons with: (a) a recognized set of norms, values, roles and institutions which forms the basis of a common culture; (b) a relatively well-circumscribed geographical region which they populate; (c) a sense of unity; and (d) a feeling of belongingness or relatedness to those cultural norms and customs. 3. Any organized, relatively long-lasting group of organisms of a species. This last definition, in a sense, encompasses 2, but it is deliberately vague so as to include species other than *Homo sapiens*. That is, one might wish to state that bees have a society in sense 3 but surely not in sense 2.

socio- A combining form meaning *social* or *societal*.

sociobiology A science that focuses on the study of the biological basis of social behavior. The dominant paradigm in the field is the application of the principles and theoretical framework of evolutionary biology in an attempt to explain those structural and behavioral aspects of organisms as they pertain to social behavior. ➤ **evolutionary biology**.

sociocenter The person who lies at the center of a ➤ **sociogram**, the one to whom most of the arrows point.

sociocentrism 1. The perspective of a person that their social group represents the ideal standards of behavior, opinions etc. against which the worth of other groups is judged. Like ➤ **egocentrism** and ➤ **ethnocentrism**, it implies a lack of sensitiv-

ity to the values and practices of others. 2. = ➤ **ethnocentrism**, which usually connotes a larger scope, but some authors will use the terms synonymously.

sociodrama ➤ **psychodrama**, but with an emphasis on role-taking in groups.

socioeconomic status (SES) Quite literally, a rating of the status of an individual's position in a stratified society based on a variety of social (e.g., family background, social class, education of parents, education of self, values, occupation, etc.) and economic (income of family, of self) indices.

sociofugal Characterizing environments arranged to minimize intimacy among the users. Public places like waiting rooms in hospitals and train stations where the furniture is set in rows are good examples. Compare with ➤ **sociopetal**.

sociogenic 1. In sociology, pertaining to the origins of society. 2. More generally, characterizing the social origins of various behaviors; e.g., juvenile delinquency is usually regarded as a sociogenic problem. var., *sociogenetic*.

sociogram In ➤ **sociometry** a diagrammatic representation of the structure of interactions between the members of a group. The typical procedure is to represent the interactions by arrows connecting individuals, with each arrow marked for attraction or antagonism.

sociolinguistics A field of study predicated on the principle that language normally functions in a social context and focused on the investigation of the broad range of interaction between language behavior and social behavior. Generally included are the study of linguistic variations, particularly those which are related to social class, ethnic groups and geographic regions, the interaction between linguistic variation and child-rearing patterns, the role of gesture and other paralinguistic devices in communication, the study of nonverbal communication, and the like. ➤ **psycholinguistics** and related entries.

sociology The discipline that focuses on the study of human behavior from the perspective of the social dimension. Sociology concentrates relatively less upon the individual as a separate entity than does social psychology, tending to view behavior as it occurs in social interactions, in groups, etc. ➤ **social psychology**.

sociometrics Loosely, any attempt to measure, quantify or formalize interpersonal relationships. The most developed is J. Moreno's ➤ **sociometry**.

sociometric test A social rating test in which each member of a group is asked to select which other members of the group she or he likes or dislikes, would or would not be willing to work with, spend time with, etc. In the original format, the rattings were usually based on the liking and disliking dimension; however, many variations on the procedures are now used, often for rather specific purposes such as the selection of committees, work groups, social organizations, etc., and so questions of liking are often deemed less important than other factors such as work-oriented compatibility. The results of a sociometric analysis are typically displayed diagrammatically as a ➤ **sociogram**.

sociometry 1. Lit., the measuring of things social. **2.** Specifically, the techniques and theory due largely to the work of Jacob L. Moreno that form the basis of the most oft-used procedures for measuring of things social. Moreno's techniques consist primarily of laying out the network of interrelationships that exist between the various members of a group. The procedure for establishing the set of relationships is the ➤ **sociometric test** and the resulting schematic diagram that is constructed from the test is called a ➤ **sociogram**.

sociopath One with a ➤ **sociopathic personality**.

sociopathic personality A personality disorder characterized by disturbed, maladaptive, social relationships, particularly those that reflect clear antisocial behav-

iors. The term itself was introduced some time ago as a replacement for ➤ **psychopathic personality** because it more clearly noted the *social* aspects of the disorder and because the base term ➤ **psychopathy** had suffered so much lexical abuse in other contexts. However, terminology keeps changing and the current term of choice is ➤ **antisocial personality disorder**.

sociopathy The condition described under ➤ **sociopathic personality**.

sociopetal Characterizing environments arranged to increase intimacy among the users. In most homes, for example, the furniture is arranged so that people face each other. Compare with ➤ **sociofugal**.

sociotechnical model An approach to the study of social systems that is predicated on the notion that all productive social organizations (or parts thereof) are dynamic products of their *technology* and their particular *social systems*. Technology is characterized broadly here and includes the physical layout, any apparatus or other technical devices that may be in use, the specific requirements of those persons involved in the organization, etc.; the social system is viewed as the dynamic interrelationships between those persons involved in the organization. The approach emerged from the work of the London-based Tavistock Institute in the 1950s and 1960s.

sociotherapy An umbrella term for any form of therapy in which the emphasis is on the socioenvironmental and interpersonal aspects rather than on the intra-psychic. Various forms of group therapy, psychodrama and the like are included.

sodomy 1. Originally, as characterized in Genesis, anal intercourse. **2.** More generally, bestiality or zooerasty. **3.** In some legal instances, any 'unnatural' sex act; a ➤ **paraphilia**. ➤ **sexual *perversion** for a discussion of the problems involved in definitions such as this.

'soft' data Laboratory jargon for subjective data, e.g., subjective impressions, ratings, clinical case studies, interviews, projective test analyses, etc. Compare with ➤ **'hard' data**.

'soft' drug A nontechnical term for any drug that either has no clear ➤ **physiological *dependence** associated with it (e.g., marijuana) or is legal (e.g., caffeine, nicotine).

softening of the brain Obsolescent term for the deterioration of brain tissue of advanced syphilis; ➤ **paresis** (2).

softness A perceptual quality which is used to characterize a variety of perceptual experiences. In tactile perception, it is a characteristic of objects that yield readily to the touch; in vision, of objects whose colors are low in saturation and brightness; in audition, of tones that are low in intensity and/or pitch.

soft palate ➤ **palate**.

'soft' psychology Laboratory jargon for those areas in psychology that focus on the social-science as opposed to the natural-science aspects; e.g., personality, abnormal psychology, developmental psychology, social psychology, etc. ➤ **'hard' psychology** for more discussion on terminology here.

soft sign Any of a number of minor abnormalities that emerge in childhood and are used as diagnostic indicators of minimal brain damage; e.g., *dysdiadochkinesis*, difficulty in carrying out alternating movements (like tapping) with one's fingers or hands. Soft signs are subtle and difficult to detect reliably; they tend to run their developmental course with no clear locus of origin and are not regarded as indicators of any specific neurological disease. The 'soft' in the term comes from the difficulties of interpretation and the uncertain association with structural brain damage. Also called *soft neurological sign*.

soft spot ➤ **fontanel**.

software In computer terminology, the program. Contrast with ➤ **hardware**.

'soldier's sickness' An old euphemism coined after the First World War to refer to the morphine dependence that many soldiers had developed from the rather free use of the drug to ease the pain of wounds received.

solidarity ➤ **Social cohesion**, but used with the connotation of a collective, cooperative effort toward group goals.

solipsism The philosophical position that holds that the only thing of which one can be certain is one's own personal experience and, by extension, that one's experiences represent all of reality – the outside world existing only as an object of one's consciousness. An extreme variation of ➤ **idealism** (2) rarely held these days.

solution In order of specificity: **1.** The value(s) that fit the conditions of an equation. **2.** The answer to a question or problem. **3.** The resolution of a set of difficulties or conflicts. Meaning 1 derives from logic and mathematics; 2 is the usual sense in the study of thinking, problem-solving, concept formation, etc.; 3 is the intended meaning in the study of personality, social psychology and clinical psychology and psychiatry.

solution learning A neobehaviorist term for ➤ **trial-and-error *learning**.

soma **1.** The cell body of a neuron. **2.** The body, taken as a whole and represented as distinct from mind. **3.** All of the cells in the body except the germ cells, *somatoplasm*. adj., *somatic*.

soma- Combining form meaning *body*, *bodily*.

somaesthesia ➤ **somesthesia**.

somasthenia Chronic bodily weakness; syn., *somatasthenia*.

somatasthenia ➤ **somasthenia**.

somatesthesia ➤ **somesthesia**.

somatic **1.** Pertaining to the body. Hence, contrasted with either (or both, depending on the author's intentions) the *environment* or the *mind*. **2.** Pertaining to all the cells except the germ cells. **3.** Pertaining to all of the body except the nervous system. This meaning, confusing as it is given 1 and 2, is still found; e.g., *somatic disorder* (1).

somatic delusion ➤ delusion, somatic.

somatic disorder 1. Generally, any non-neurological disorder; i.e. a disorder of the body. 2. More specifically, an ➤ organic disorder. Generally, meaning 2 is intended.

somatic nervous system ➤ nervous system.

somatic therapy A cover term in psychiatry for those forms of therapy that are founded on the biological rather than the psychological, e.g., electroconvulsive therapy, the use of various forms of psychopharmacological agents, etc.

somatization disorder A ➤ somatoform disorder characterized by a history of recurrent and multiple physical symptoms for which there are no apparent physical causes. The disorder virtually always begins in the teens or twenties and has a chronic but fluctuating course involving a wide variety of complaints about organic dysfunctions. Common complaints are vague pains, allergies, gastrointestinal problems, psychosexual symptoms, palpitations and conversion symptoms.

somato- Combining form meaning *somatic*.

somatoform disorders A class of mental disorders in which there are clear and present physical symptoms that are suggestive of a somatic disorder but where there is no detectible organic damage or neurophysiological dysfunction that can explain the symptoms and there is a strong presumption that they are linked to psychological factors. ➤ autonomic arousal disorder, ➤ body dysmorphic disorder, ➤ conversion disorder, ➤ hypochondriasis, ➤ neurasthenia, ➤ somatization disorder, and the ➤ pain disorders. Cases with volitional symptoms (e.g., ➤ factitious disorder) are specifically excluded.

somatoform disorder, undifferentiated Quite like it says, a ➤ somatoform disorder without a clearly differentiated

set of symptoms. The term is used for cases with physical complaints such as fatigue, loss of appetite, and intestinal and urinary complaints associated with psychological factors of stress and conflict.

somatogenic need Any biological or tissue need, a ➤ primary *need.

somatopsychic An occasional synonym for ➤ psychosomatic.

somatopsychology The study of the psychological factors that typically accompany severe physical disabilities (e.g., blindness, facial disfiguration) and serious diseases (e.g., cancer, heart attacks). Distinguish from ➤ psychosomatic medicine.

somatopsychosis 1. Any psychosis the primary symptoms of which involve delusions concerning one's own body. 2. Any psychosis the mental disorder of which is a symptom of a bodily disease. Both uses are rather loose.

somatosenses Collectively, those sensory systems that mediate the various 'touch' receptors, e.g., pressure, tickle, warm, cold, vibration, limb position, limb movement, pain. Generally classified into the *cutaneous*, the *kinesthetic* and the *visceral* senses.

somatotonia One of the three classic components of temperament assumed by ➤ constitutional theory. The somatotonic is characterized by highly developed physical abilities.

somatotopy The orderly mapping of the somatic sensory system on the cerebral cortex. The somatotopic representation of the body surface on the post-central gyrus yields the sensory homunculus; ➤ homunculus (2) for more detail.

somatotrophic hormone ➤ growth hormone.

somatotype Lit., body type. The term is virtually always found in the context of ➤ constitutional theory relating physique to temperament.

some- Combining form meaning *body* or *bodily*.

somesthesia The sense associated with body contact; the skin senses, kinesthesis and internal sensitivity taken collectively. vars., *somaesthesia, somatesthesia*.

somnambulism Sleepwalking. Interestingly, sleepwalking tends to occur during the deepest stages of NREM sleep and not during REM sleep when most dreaming occurs. ➤ **sleep** for details. If recurrent and disruptive it is classified as a ➤ **sleep disorder**.

somniferous Sleep-inducing; ➤ **soporific**.

sonant A voiced speech sound.

sone The basic unit of a ratio scale of loudness. It is defined as the experienced loudness of a 1,000-Hz tone at 40 db above absolute threshold.

sophistry The deliberate use of nonvalid argument with the intention of deceiving others. Most 'good' sophistry embeds the fallacy in convoluted syllogistic form, giving it the surface illusion of rigorousness and/or profundity.

soporific Sleep-inducing. Used with respect to either drugs such as the barbiturates and narcotics or to boring, dull experiences. syn., *somniferous*.

S–O–R A modification of the classic S–R characterization of behavior. Whereas ➤ **S–R theory** focused primarily on the stimulus (S) and the resultant (R), the modification explicitly put the organism (O) into the equation.

sororate The custom whereby an unmarried sister of a deceased woman marries the widower.

sorting test A general label for any test or task in which the subject is required to sort stimulus items according to some given principle.

Soto's syndrome A congenital disorder marked by rapid early growth leading to heavy features, a long, large head, large, protruding jaw, wide-set eyes and large, broad hands. Mild to moderate degrees of mental retardation are typical. Also called *Soto's cerebral gigantism*.

soul Outside of the realm of theology: **1.** An obsolete term for *psyche* or *mind*. ➤ **dualism**. **2.** Popularly, the affective, emotional domain of one's personality as contrasted with the analytical, intellectual aspects.

soul-image Jung's term for the remote, unconscious domain of mind which he hypothesized to be composed of the ➤ **anima** and ➤ **animus**.

sound **1.** In physics, a pattern of energy represented as condensation and rarefaction of molecules in an elastic medium. **2.** In psychology, that sensory experience resulting from the physical energy in 1 stimulating the auditory and neurological mechanisms of an organism – with the proviso that the frequency and intensity characteristics of these mechanisms are appropriate; a sound (sense 1) of 40,000 Hz will be a sound (sense 2) for a bat but not for a human. Note that appreciating the distinction here will permit one to answer that hoary philosophical puzzle, 'If a tree falls in the forest and there is no one about to hear it, does it make a sound?' For related terms see the following entries and also ➤ **acoustic**, ➤ **auditory**, and combined terms with these as a base.

sound intensity **1.** In physics, the power of a sound wave, typically expressed in dynes/cm^2. **2.** In psychological terms, an occasional synonym for ➤ **loudness**.

sound-level meter A device for measuring the sound level at various frequencies. Such meters do not give 'raw' sound levels but contain weighting networks which adjust the power at each frequency in accordance with the known properties of the spectral sensitivity of the average human ear.

sound-pattern theory (of hearing) ➤ **theories of *hearing**.

sound perimetry A procedure for determining the boundaries of the auditory space for an individual subject.

sound-pressure level (SPL) The physical

intensity of a sound stimulus as specified against an objective standard. The standard typically used is 0.0002 dynes/cm² which corresponds approximately to the absolute threshold of the normal human ear for a 1,000-Hz tone.

sound, sensation level of The pressure level of a sound given in decibels above threshold.

sound shadow A region in a field in which the sound is reduced owing to an object which blocks, obscures, absorbs or reflects the physical energy. The sound shadow produced by one's head serves as a cue in the location of sounds of relatively high frequencies.

sound spectrograph The full, proper name for what is more generally referred to as a ➤ **spectrograph**.

sour One of the four primary taste qualities. ➤ **taste** for more detail.

source 1. Generally, the original location for some process or event. 2. In communication theory, the entity (typically an organism but occasionally a machine) that emits a signal. 3. In psychophysics, the device that puts out a stimulus. 4. In psychoanalysis, the underlying condition that initiates an instinct. 5. In social psychology, the locus of a socially important message, e.g., a rumor, a news story.

source amnesia ➤ **amnesia, source**.

source memory ➤ **memory, source**.

source monitoring The cognitive capacity to track and store (➤ **source *memory**) information about where and when particular events occurred or particular pieces of information were acquired. Disruption in source monitoring can have serious consequences, such as when one fails to differentiate fact from fantasy or cannot recall whether some medical advice came from one's doctor or from the local tabloid.

source, primary An original source of information. In the social sciences, any original document or first-hand report such as

a diary, paper, tape recording, etc. that provides data for analysis.

source, secondary Any source of information based on a ➤ **primary *source**. Secondary sources include reviews, interpretations and/or revisions and summaries of primary sources.

source trait ➤ **trait, source**.

'sour-grapes' mechanism From Aesop and his famous fox, a term used to characterize a defense mechanism whereby one devalues goals which one cannot obtain.

space 1. Fundamentally, space is an abstraction, a geometric characterization of a system of location of m objects in n dimensions. In the classic model of physical space, m is finite and $n = 3$. This so-called *Euclidean space* is such a compelling aspect of human experience that it has often been presented as a nativistically given form and *space* is often taken as denotatively equivalent to Euclidean space. However, such a limitation is inappropriate; any mathematical representation of m objects in n dimensions will satisfy the definition and although it may not be as natural, one can conceptualize and formalize a two-dimensional plane space, a spherical space, a saddle-shaped space, etc. 2. In social psychology and environmental psychology, the experiential space in which one lives and functions. This sense of space is often contrasted with the raw physical space in the classical Euclidean sense; e.g., ➤ **personal space**. 3. In factor analysis, the conceptual space containing all the factors that emerged from the data analysis. This meaning is usually expressed by the phrase *factor space* to keep it distinct from other senses. ➤ **factor analysis** et seq. for details here. 4. In multidimensional scaling, an abstract representation of an n-dimensional space that characterizes the hypothetical psychological character of the stimuli being scaled. For details here, ➤ **multidimensional scaling** and ➤ **methods of *scaling** (3). Note that in senses 3 and 4 the number of dimensions may, and typically does, exceed three and the formal representation need not be, and typically is not, Euclidean. See, for a common example, ➤ **semantic space**. **5.** In K. Lewin's field theory, the representation of an individual as represented in terms of a topologically complex ➤ **life space**; see that entry for details. **6.** The area around something. **7.** The distance between two things. adj., *spatial*.

spaced practice ➤ **practice, distributed**.

space error (or **bias**) Generally, any systematic bias in choice behavior, discrimination learning, maze learning, etc. toward some spatial location or direction. Also called *location error* (or *bias*).

space factor A hypothesized underlying factor which presumably is what accounts for the several ➤ **spatial abilities**.

space life ➤ **life space**.

space orientation ➤ **spatial orientation**.

space perception Quite straightforwardly, the perception of ➤ **space**. Typically meanings 1 and 2 of that term are intended here: 1 as the physical space surrounding an individual and 2 as the experienced sense of space within which one behaves. The term is, thus, used rather freely to cover depth perception, spatial relations, real movement, apparent movement, personal space, etc.

space psychology The application of psychological principles and methods to the study of space-related issues. Much of the work involves extensions of the techniques of personnel selection and the study of human factors in the highly specialized circumstances surrounding space flight and living in outer space.

span of apprehension ➤ **apprehension, span of**.

span of attention ➤ **attention span**.

span of consciousness An obsolete term for the number of objects that can be apprehended simultaneously. For the contemporary point of view on this topic, ➤ **seven, plus or minus two**, ➤ **short-term *memory**, ➤ **subitizing**.

spasm Generally, any sudden, convulsive, muscular movement. Spasms may be *clonic* (alternating contraction-relaxation of the muscle) or *tonic* (continuous contraction); they may involve skeletal (striated) muscle or visceral (smooth) muscle.

spasmophemia Any speech disorder caused by spasms. Occasionally used as a synonym for *stuttering*.

spastic **1.** Pertaining to or resembling a spasm. **2.** Characteristic of a disability caused by spasms. **3.** A person suffering from any disorder with spasms as a primary symptom, e.g., cerebral palsy.

spasticity ➤ **spastic paralysis**.

spastic paralysis Any condition displaying extreme muscular tension and muscular rigidity with a partial paralysis. Typically lesions in the upper motor neurons are responsible. When muscular tension and rigidity are not accompanied by a paralysis, the more general term *spasticity* is used.

spastic speech The erratic, jerky speech seen in persons with spastic conditions of the muscles involved in speech production.

spatial Pertaining to *space*. For combined terms not found below here, see those following ➤ **space**.

spatial abilities Those perceptual/cognitive abilities that enable one to deal effectively with spatial relations, visual-spatial tasks, orientation of objects in space, etc. Frequently *visual* and *nonvisual* spatial abilities are distinguished.

spatial discrimination A somewhat confusing term for the ability to detect two disparate points of stimulation on the skin. See here ➤ **two-point threshold**.

spatial orientation **1.** The ability to orient oneself in space relative to objects and events. See here ➤ **field dependence**. **2.** Awareness of self-location.

spatial summation ➤ **summation, spatial**.

spatial threshold ➤ **two-point threshold**.

spay To sterilize a female animal by ovariectomy.

speaking in tongues ➤ **glossolalia**.

Spearman-Brown formula **1.** A technique for predicting the reliability of a full test made up of two separate subtests when the reliability of each of the sub-tests is known. **2.** A technique for estimating the gain in reliability of a measure with an increase in the number of observations. Meaning 1 is also occasionally called the *Spearman Brown prophecy formula*.

Spearman rank correlation ➤ **correlation, rank order**.

special-aptitude test ➤ **aptitude test**.

special case **1.** Generally, any instance in a category that somehow stands out from the others. **2.** Any exemplar of a category isolated for special treatment or analysis for some particular reason.

special child A child with problems, emotional, social, physical or mental. This term has been adopted by many as the euphemism of choice for handicapped, retarded or autistic children. Occasionally confusion is created, for some authors will also use the term for children who are well above the average or show special talents but others will use ➤ **gifted child** for such cases. ➤➤ **exceptional child**, the other common euphemism which suffers from similar problems.

special class (or **school**) ➤ **special education**.

special education **1.** The area within the field of educational psychology that is concerned with the ➤ **special child**. Some aspects are highly theoretical and focus on issues of cognitive and perceptual competence of such children, other components are more applied and focus on the problems of their education. **2.** Loosely, any educational program, class or school for the education of special children.

special factor(s) ➤ **general factor**.

special senses ➤ **senses, special**.

speciation The process of the development of a new species.

species **1.** In biology, a classification immediately below ➤ **genus** (1). It is the smallest category commonly used and is generally identified on the grounds of commonality or mutual resemblance of organisms. When possible, the criterion of the ability. to breed among themselves is used; i.e. a species is a category of organisms that forms a reproductively isolated group whose genes are freely admixed but not with those of other species. This criterion, however, cannot always be applied, as with bacteria and various plants. pl., *species*. **2.** In Aristotelian logic, a category or class differing from other categories within a larger class or ➤ **genus** (2) by specified characteristics. When the terms *species* and *genus* are used in this fashion they carry no biological implications, although it is clear that the biological meaning derived from the Aristotelian.

species-specific adj. Of the behavior of virtually all the members of a given species under roughly equivalent circumstances. The term is used to characterize those behaviors of a given species that are specific to that species; it approximates to the original usage of the more common term ➤ **instinct**. However, as is outlined under that entry, many contemporary authorities prefer *species-specific* and its synonym *species-typical* and have dropped *instinct* from their technical lexicons. Although the term, like *instinct*, tends to carry the connotation of innateness, such an inference is not logically implied.

species-typical ➤ **species-specific**.

specific **1.** Pertaining to a ➤ **species**. **2.** Distinctive, outstanding, highly detectable. **3.** By extension, in factor analysis, uncorrelated with other things or factors.

specific ability In theory, any ability that is specific to a particular kind of task; in practice, any ability that is identified by factor-analytic techniques as one that shows little or no correlation with other abilities. Compare with ➤ **general ability**.

specific developmental disorder ➤ **developmental disorder, specific**.

specific developmental dyslexia ➤ **dyslexia**.

specific energies doctrine ➤ **specific nerve energies, doctrine of**.

specific phobia ➤ **simple *phobia**.

specific hunger ➤ **hunger, specific**.

specificity 1. Preciseness, uniqueness. The term is used here with the connotation that the thing so characterized is relevant to but a single phenomenon or event. For example, stimuli are said to display specificity when they are only associated with a single response, adaptive structures show specificity when their functions have not generalized beyond specific boundaries, etc. 2. In sociology, a narrow pattern of expected behavior in a particular situation; specificity is displayed here when only a small aspect of one's full social role emerges in a given social context. 3. In factor analysis, the proportion of the variance not correlated with the main factors.

specific language disability ➤ **language disability**.

specific nerve energies, doctrine of The generalization originally put forward by Johannes Müller that the various qualities of experience derive, not from differences in the physical and environmental stimuli that impinge upon us, but from the specific neural structures that each excites.

specious present The psychological sense of the present, of 'nowness.' This notion of a true *present* in the measurement of time has about the same status as the notion of a *point* on a line or in space does in geometry: it exists as a locus relative to other loci. It is the point that divides past from future, what happened from what is still to happen. Yet, introspectively, this is not very satisfying nor does it feel intuitively correct; this 'timeless moment,' as it has been called, seems to have temporal duration, brief perhaps but most palpable.

spectral Pertaining to or related to a ➤ **spectrum**.

spectral-absorption curve A curve of the relative absorption of each wavelength of light for the particular substance under examination.

spectral color The color or (more accurately) the *hue* of any visual stimulus whose dominant wavelength is within the visible spectrum.

spectral-emission curve In optics, a curve showing the relative number of quanta emitted by a light source as a function of wavelength.

spectral hue ➤ **spectral color**.

spectral-sensitivity curve A curve that displays the sensitivity of a receptor system across the full range of a particular spectrum. Such a curve for the human auditory system, for example, would show a peak sensitivity around 4,000 Hz, with diminishing sensitivity for higher- and lower-pitched tones.

spectro- Combining form meaning *appearance*, *image*.

spectrograph A device that provides a visual representation of sound. The resultant *spectrogram* is a display that presents all three acoustic dimensions of sound: *time* is represented on one axis of a two-dimensional display, *frequency* is given on the other and *intensity* of the sound at each frequency and point in time is represented by the darkness of the display (see here ➤ **formant**). Spectrographic analyses are primarily used in the study of speech production and perception. Their use in courts of law has created a lively controversy with proponents arguing that *voiceprints* (as they are often called) can be used to identify individuals and critics maintaining that the procedures lack reliability. So far the critics' case appears the stronger and few courts permit their use.

spectrophotometer In vision, a device for determining the ➤ **absorption *spectrum** of a translucent substance. Typically, the device is used for evaluation of the light quanta absorbed by photopigments at various wavelengths. A known number of quanta of monochromatic light at each wavelength is passed into a container filled with the pigment, the number of quanta that emerge is evaluated and the difference between these reflects the proportion absorbed. ➤➤ **photometry**.

spectrum Generally, a range of components of some energy source (e.g., a light wave, a sound wave) separated and arranged along some dimension (e.g., wavelength, frequency). Note that there is a strong tendency to use this term as though it pertained only to the physical dimension of radiant energy and the visual modality. This restriction is not accurate; properly the term should be used with qualifiers to specify the particular spectrum under consideration, e.g., ➤ **absorption *spectrum**, **auditory *spectrum**, ➤ **visual *spectrum**, etc. pl., *spectra* (the preferred form) or *spectrums*.

spectrum, absorption In optics, the proportion of incident light absorbed by a body as a function of wavelength; ➤ **spectral-absorption curve**.

spectrum, auditory The sound frequencies that are within the normal human range of hearing, i.e. those ranging from approximately 20 Hz to roughly 20,000 Hz.

spectrum, reflection In optics, the proportion of incident light reflected back off of a body as a function of wavelength.

spectrum, visual (or **visible**) The wavelengths of light to which the normal human eye is sensitive, i.e. those ranging from approximately 380 nm to roughly 740 nm.

speculative psychology An approach to psychology that begins with empirical studies and known facts about behavior and proceeds in an attempt to elaborate a speculative conceptualization of the nature of the human mind or the human condition. As an accepted discipline in psychology it has few self-proclaimed practitioners; as an unacknowledged practice

it lurks, often unrecognized, behind nearly every theoretical advance in the field – despite the publicly articulated allegiances to pure formalisms, positivisms, hypothetico-deductivisms, logical behaviorisms and the like.

speech act An occurrence of an utterance in a language such that the person who uttered it can be viewed as intending, with his or her words, to communicate something, to make something happen or to get someone to do something. Common speech acts are *commissives*, *declaratives*, *directives*, *expressives* and *representatives*; see each for details. The study of speech acts is usually regarded as part of the larger field of ➤ **pragmatics**. syn., *illocutionary act*.

speech block A momentary inability to speak, a form of *stuttering*.

speech center ➤ **Broca's area**.

speech disorder A cover term for a number of abnormalities in speaking. There is precious little agreement on exactly which language disabilities belong in this category and how they should be classified. Some authorities differentiate between *functional* or *psychogenic disorders* (e.g., most cases of ➤ **stuttering**) and those with an organic basis (e.g., the ➤ **aphasias**); some will distinguish between those that affect linguistic functioning (e.g., ➤ **dysarthria**) and those that affect voice quality without disturbing communicative performance (e.g., the ➤ **voice disorders**); and some will keep the language-reception abnormalities (e.g., ➤ **alexia**) in a separate diagnostic category whereas others include them, arguing that pure receptive disabilities showing no deficit in language production are rare.

speech disorder, acquired Any speech disorder that appears as a result of some event occurring after birth, e.g., the ➤ **aphasias**.

speech disorder, congenital Any speech disorder due to an abnormal condition present at birth, e.g., those associated with cerebral palsy or with a cleft palate.

speech impediment Loosely, anything that disrupts, inhibits or prevents normal fluent speech.

speech-retarded child A child who learns to speak at a later age than the norm. Note that the 'retardation' in this case is a literal slowing and it carries no connotations concerning eventual levels of performance; the typical child here ultimately shows fully normal language ability but achieves it relatively late.

speech synthesizer Any machine that can produce intelligible, speech-like sounds. The output of such a device is called *synthetic speech* and recent advances in computer technology and acoustics have seen the development of sophisticated synthesizers whose speech quality is sufficiently 'human' that they are used to generate stimuli for many experiments on language and hearing as well as being widely used in business and industry.

speech therapy Loosely, any therapy aimed at correcting a speech disorder.

speed/accuracy tradeoff The generalization that when speed is of the essence accuracy will decrease and vice versa, hence there is a tradeoff in functioning between them.

speed reading Since the average fluent reader reads somewhere between 100 and 140 words per minute (depending on the nature of the material), speed reading is defined simply as reading at rates significantly in excess of these norms. An issue of interest here (particularly in view of the popular and expensive programs that claim to teach this skill) is whether such rapid rates can be achieved without sacrificing comprehension. The problem is a complex one but the evidence available indicates that they cannot.

speed test A general term for any test that measures ability by determining the number of problems that can be dealt with successfully within a fixed time period. Compare with ➤ **power test**.

spelling dyslexia ➤ **dyslexia, word-form**.

sperm 1. Semen, the male ejaculant containing spermatozoa. 2. Spermatozoa, the mature male sex cells.

spermatozoa The plural of ➤ **spermatozoon**.

spermatozoon A mature, male sex cell.

spheresthesia Occasional synonym of ➤ **globus hystericus**.

spherical aberration ➤ **aberration, spherical**.

sphincter Any circular muscle which constricts during muscular contraction, thereby closing an orifice.

sphincter control Control over the sphincter muscles of the urinary and anal passages.

sphincter morality A psychoanalytic term for a pattern of attitudes and behaviour hypothesized to result from early, abrupt, toilet training.

sphygmo- A combining form meaning *pulse*.

sphygmograph A device for measuring and recording the shape and force of the pulse.

sphygmomanometer A device for measuring arterial blood pressure.

sphygmometer = ➤ **sphygmograph**.

spicy A class of olfactory qualities typified by spices. ➤ **Henning's prism**.

spike In the recording of the electrical activity of a neuron, the conspicuous tracing that is indicative of the rapid reversal of membrane potential of the ➤ **action potential**. Or, put more simply, the sharp peak in the record that indicates that the neuron has fired.

spinal Pertaining to or characteristic of the backbone (the spine) or the spinal cord.

spinal accessory nerve The XIth ➤ **cranial nerve**. A motor nerve to the trapezius and sternomastoid muscles of the neck and the pharynx. The 'accessory' portion joins the vagus (Xth cranial) nerve supplying motor and cardioinhibitory fibers.

spinal animal An experimental preparation in which the neural pathways between the spinal cord and the brain have been severed. In such an animal, whatever control still exists over the muscles and sensory receptors of the periphery is that which is mediated by the spinal cord.

spinal canal The canal, containing cerebrospinal fluids, that runs through the vertebral column.

spinal column The vertebral column, more commonly referred to as the *backbone*. It encloses the spinal cord and consists of 33 vertebrae: 7 cervical, 12 thoracic, 5 lumbar, 5 sacral (fused to form a single bone) and 4 in the coccyx (also fused to form one bone).

spinal cord The long column of neural tissue running through the spinal canal from the 2nd lumbar vertebra up to the medulla.

spinal fluid ➤ cerebrospinal fluid.

spinal ganglia Enlargements on the dorsal root of each spinal nerve made up principally of the cell bodies of somatic and visceral afferent neurons.

spinal nerves Nerves arising from the spinal cord. In *Homo sapiens* there are 31 pairs of them: 8 cervical, 12 thoracic, 5 lumbar, 5 sacral and 1 coccygeal. Each is attached to the cord by two ➤ spinal roots, one dorsal (or posterior) and one ventral (or anterior).

spinal reflex Any reflex mediated entirely at the spinal level. A spinal reflex can be elicited even in a ➤ spinal animal, where the controlling influence of the brain has been removed.

spinal root Collections of neural fibers through which the ➤ spinal nerves are attached to the spinal cord. Spinal roots occur in pairs; the *dorsal root* of each pair carries afferent fibers, the *ventral root* efferent fibers. Each pair fuses to form one of the spinal nerves.

spindle tendon ➤ Golgi tendon organ.

spinoreticulothalamic tract ➤ spinothalamic tract.

spinothalamic tract (or **system**) A complex ascending neural pathway that runs through the spinal cord to the thalamus. Actually the term is slightly misleading for in reality only a small proportion of the fibers ascend directly to the thalamus, most of them synapse at lower levels in the brain stem, specifically in the reticular formation. ➤ **reticulothalamic system**. These pathways are major carriers of pain fibers from the periphery. Also called ➤ **spinoreticulothalamic tract**.

spiral aftereffect ➤ motion aftereffects.

spiral ganglion A spiral-shaped collection of myelinated bipolar neurons located in the bony hub of the cochlea. The axonal processes of these cells run toward the organ of Corti and innervate the hair cells.

spiral test Generally, any psychometric instrument in which the several kinds of items (e.g., quantitative, verbal, general knowledge) are presented in a repeating series where each new cycle 'spirals' upward in difficulty.

spirometer A device for measuring breathing.

SPL ➤ sound-pressure level.

splanchic Pertaining to the viscera.

split-brain technique The severing of the ➤ corpus callosum (and, on occasion, the ➤ optic chiasm) thus eliminating the exchange of information between the cerebral hemispheres. The procedure is used in humans only in cases of severe and intractable epilepsy. Those who have undergone the operation serve as natural laboratories for the study of ➤ laterality.

split-half correlation ➤ correlation, split-half.

split-half reliability ➤ reliability, split-half.

split-litter method A control procedure in which litter mates are divided into experimental and control groups. It serves as a partial control over genetic factors and has advantages over random assignment of either individual animals or whole litters to different groups.

split-off consciousness William James's term for those aspects of consciousness which are relatively well organized and structured but exist more or less independently of the rest of consciousness. The term is rarely used today.

split personality ➤ **multiple personality**.

splitting A defense mechanism in which one deals with conflict and stress by compartmentalizing (or 'splitting') the positive and negative aspects of oneself or others. Use of this mechanism is marked by a tendency to view oneself and others in alternating polar opposites, switching back and forth between highly positive and highly negative images.

spongioblast A cell that develops from the embryonic neural tube and is a forerunner of ependymal cells and astrocytes. See here ➤ **glia**.

spontaneity test Moreno's term for that aspect of a ➤ **psychodrama** in which the individual is in a very lifelike situation and must spontaneously act out feelings with respect to the others present.

spontaneity therapy A general label occasionally applied to J. L. Moreno's ➤ **psychodrama** procedures which emphasize role-playing, emotional expression, empathy, etc.

spontaneous 1. Natural, unconstrained. **2.** Not premeditated. **3.** From within, endogenous, personal.

spontaneous discharge Generally, any neural impulse not directly initiated by a known external stimulus. Also called *spontaneous firing*.

spontaneous recovery The reappearance of an extinguished conditioned response following a rest period.

spontaneous regression Age regression under hypnosis.

spontaneous remission The lessening or abatement of the symptoms of a disease or disorder independent of any therapeutic intervention. ➤ **remission**.

spoonerism The exchanging of the initial phonetic elements of two (or more) words in a single phrase or sentence. The term 'honors' the Rev. W. A. Spooner of Oxford, who had a rather extraordinary penchant for such confusions. Of the countless incidents attributed to the good reverend, our favorites are his attempted reference to Victoria Regina as 'our queer old dean,' and his tongue-lashing of an inattentive student, 'you have tasted the whole worm.' Independent of the humorous aspects, spoonerisms are evidence of the psychological reality of the phoneme and clearly show that whole phrases and sentences are planned in advance of their being uttered.

spreading activation 1. In cognitive psychology, a generalization that the activation of a memory tends to spread to conceptually associated memories, making them likely to be themselves activated. **2.** In neurophysiology, a hypothesized set of neural processes that, in principle, underlies the kinds of effects given in 1.

spreading depression The phenomenon that a stimulus applied directly to the surface of the cortex produces a depression of electrical activity that spreads from the locus of stimulation and inhibits cortical responses to other stimuli.

spread of effect ➤ **effect, spread of**.

spurious 1. Not genuine, not authentic. **2.** Having superficial resemblance to something but with deeper, more important differences.

spurious correlation ➤ **correlation, spurious**.

spurt Generally, any sudden increase in performance, growth, learning, etc.

SQ 3R method A reading/study method based on the presumption that information from a text can best be learned by *S*urveying the material first, *Q*uestioning the basic issues, *R*eading thoroughly, *Re*-citing the basic points and then *R*eviewing the material once more.

squint ➤ strabismus.

S–R ➤ stimulus–response.

S–R learning ➤ learning, S–R.

S–R psychology ➤ stimulus–response psychology.

S–R theory ➤ stimulus–response theory.

SS ➤ standard *score.

S-shaped curve ➤ ogive.

S–S interval ➤ temporal avoidance conditioning.

S–S learning ➤ learning, S–S.

S sleep ➤ sleep, S.

SST ➤ stimulus-sampling theory.

stabilimeter A device for measuring stability. It measures bodily sway while the subject, who is usually blindfolded, attempts to stand perfectly still.

stability 1. In physics, the relative lack of motion of a body compared with the motion of the surroundings. 2. In genetics, the relative invariances in genetically determined factors over generations. 3. In personality theory, a trait characterized by a lack of excessive emotional change. Here the qualifier *emotional* is often used. 4. In statistics, the reliability and consistency of a statistic. See here ➤ statistical stability.

stability, coefficient of ➤ coefficient of * reliability and test-retest *reliability.

stabilized image An image (or, more properly, a proximal stimulus) that has been stabilized or fixed so that it falls on the same spot on the retina regardless of the movements of the eye (see here ➤ nystagmus and ➤ saccade for characterizations of these). There are several techniques for accomplishing this. One common one is to provide the subject with a contact lens with a small mirror attached; the stimulus is reflected off the mirror onto a screen via a series of other mirrors which control orientation. The resulting image is stabilized, because no matter how the eye moves the image also moves and the area of the retina onto which the stimulus is projected is fixed. Under these conditions, the perception fades rapidly, presumably from fatigue of the retinal receptors. Also called *stabilized retinal image, fixed image* and *stopped image.*

stabilized retinal image ➤ stabilized image.

stable 1. Characterizing an individual whose behavior is relatively reliable and consistent. ant., *unstable* (1, 2). 2. Characterizing a statistical result which is significant. ➤ statistical stability.

stage An identifiable period in an extended, ongoing process; specifically, one that appears to have its own internal coherence and so stands out from other, similarly identifiable periods. Compare with ➤ level, which is reserved for a particular point in the process or on a continuum, and with ➤ phase, which connotes cyclicity.

stages of man In Erik Erikson's characterization of personality, the life of man (generically speaking) is viewed as a sequence of eight stages during which an individual either displays or fails to display a characteristic set of behavioral and emotional qualities. Each stage is conceptualized as an either/or configuration, reflecting Erikson's notion that at each point in one's life one may or may not be strong enough to accept the potential hazards of the next stage. The stages are: (1) trust v. mistrust, (2) autonomy v. shame and doubt, (3) initiative v. guilt, (4) industry v. inferiority, (5) identity v. role diffusion, (6) intimacy v. isolation, (7) generativity v. stagnation, (8) ego integrity v. despair. The first four correspond roughly to the Freudian stages up to adolescence, stage 5 encompasses late adolescence and early adulthood, stage 6 is the so-called 'prime of life' period, 7 corresponds to middle age and the last to old age.

stages of sleep ➤ sleep.

stage theory A label applicable to any

theory of development that characterizes growth, be it physical, sensorimotor, cognitive, moral, etc., as a progression through a sequence of stages. Stage theories tend to be either *maturational* or *interactionist*, i.e. basically biologically determined or resulting from interactions between the biological and the experiential. Standard criteria of scientific adequacy dictate that a stage theory have at least four critical properties. First, it must predict qualitative differences in behavior over time and experience. Second, it must assume invariance of the sequence of stages – the rate of sequencing may be accelerated or retarded but the order must remain the same from individual to individual. Third, it must assume structural cohesiveness of a stage; that is, the behaviors within a stage must share a common conceptual base. Fourth, there must be hierarchical integration of structures from stage to stage so that a later stage incorporates and expands upon the structures from an earlier stage. Exemplary theories here are Gesell's for sensorimotor development, Piaget's for cognitive development, Kohlberg's for the development of morality and, somewhat more loosely, Freud's theory of psychosexual development and Erikson's stages of man.

stain To apply a pigment to tissue for histological examination.

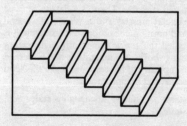

staircase illusion As depicted above. Stare at the figure: the perspective will reverse so that it will be seen from above or from below.

staircase method ➤ up-and-down method.

staircase phenomenon ➤ treppe.

stammering ➤ stuttering.

stance reflex A general term for the variety of postural adjustments, taken collectively, that an organism makes to maintain proper orientation and normal stance.

standard 1. Generally, a basis for comparison for making evaluative judgements or measurements. **2.** In physics, a fixed unit for standardizing international scientific measurement, e.g., standard meter, standard candle. **3.** In scaling, an arbitrary stimulus that serves as the basis for making estimates of psychological magnitudes; ➤ **methods of *scaling. 4.** In the social sciences generally, any socially agreed-upon and expected behavior within a society. Distinguish from ➤ **norm**.

standard deviation ➤ deviation, standard.

standard difference The difference between two means divided by the standard error of that difference. Also called the *standard ratio*.

Standard English In the USA, the idealized form of spoken American English. References to Standard English are found primarily as a basis for comparison with other dialects, e.g., ➤ **Black English**. Perhaps the only time, however, that one hears true Standard English spoken is by trained elocutionists and some radio and TV commentators. ➤➤ **King's English** and **Received Pronunciation** for similar terms used in Britain.

standard error The standard deviation of a theoretical sampling distribution. It provides an estimate of the variability which can be expected in the actual samples drawn from the underlying theoretical population and is, thus, a population ➤ **parameter**. ➤➤ **standard error of the mean**, which is the estimate of standard error most frequently used to assess the representativeness of a sample. abbrev., *SE*.

standard error of estimate An estimate of the degree of error likely to occur when one uses a regression equation to predict (or estimate) the values of one variable from the values of another correlated variable. It is derived from a formula based on the standard deviation of the dependent (or predicted) variable, the correlation coefficient between the two variables and the size of the sample. The chances are about 0.67 that any actual value will lie within one standard error of its predicted value.

standard error of measurement An estimate of the degree to which a particular set of measurements obtained in a given situation (e.g., a test or one of several parallel forms of a test) might be expected to deviate from the true values. Denoted as $\sigma_{(M)}$.

standard error of the mean The standard deviation of the theoretical sampling distribution of the mean. In practice it is used as an estimate of the degree to which the obtained mean of the sample may be expected to deviate from the true population mean. Denoted as σ_M.

standardization The processes and procedures of establishing a set of norms for a test.

standardization group A selected group of persons that is presumed to represent the population under consideration and is used for the standardization of a test. For example, a test designed to evaluate typing skill would be standardized on a group of professional typists.

standardize 1. Generally, to adjust something so that it is brought into some standard frame of reference; e.g., ➤ **standard *score**. 2. To establish a set of norms of standards. 3. In testing, to establish, for a particular test, the set of procedures for its administration, the scoring techniques to be used and the methods of evaluation and interpretation of obtained scores.

standardized test ➤ test, standardized.

standard measure ➤ standard *score.

standard observer In the study of sensory processes and perception, the hypothetical observer whose sensory receptor systems function ideally.

standard ratio ➤ standard difference.

standard score ➤ score, standard.

standard stimulus ➤ standard (3).

Stanford-Binet Scale (or **Test**) The first test of intelligence known by this name was the one prepared by A. Terman and his associates at Stanford University in 1916. It was designed to be a revision of the Binet–Simon Scale of 1911 (see here ➤ **Binet Scale**) for American culture and language, but it introduced so many changes that it was essentially a new test. Several revisions have appeared over the years (most recently in 1986) which incorporate a large number of modifications, including extensive norms and the scales for measuring adult IQ.

stanine From 'standard nine,' a statistical unit representing exactly 1/9th of the full range of scores in a distribution.

stapedial muscle A muscle in the ear attached to the *stapes*. It contracts as a response to loud noises, pulling the stapes away from the oval window and thereby dampening the vibration passed on to the receptive cells in the inner ear.

stapes One of the three small bones in the middle ear. ➤ **auditory *ossicles**.

startle reflex ➤ startle response.

startle response (or **reaction**) A complex, involuntary reaction to a sudden, unanticipated stimulus. There is a flexion of most skeletal muscles and a variety of visceral and hormonal reactions. Occasionally it is called the *startle reflex*, although, except in newborns, the magnitude and patterned complexity of the response make this term somewhat inappropriate.

stasis A stable, unchanging state. adj., *static*.

state 1. A condition of a system in which the essential qualities are relatively stable. Note that it is the *qualities* of features that are unchanging; the features themselves may, in actuality, be dynamic. Thus, references to a *hyperactive state* or a *state of flux* are not uncommon. 2. A form of organized society with legitimate sovereignty over a geographical area, political authority and a national government.

state-dependent learning ➤ **learning, state-dependent**.

static Stable, unchanging. Contrast with ➤ **dynamic**.

static ataxia ➤ **ataxia, static**.

static equilibrium A stable, unchanging condition.

static reflex (or **response**) Any posture-adjusting or orienting response. The *stance reflex* maintains proper posture under normal conditions, the *righting reflex* regains normal posture; both are examples of a static reflex.

static sense ➤ **equilibrium** (2).

statistic 1. Generally, any value derived from mathematical or statistical manipulations. 2. More specifically, a value summarizing a characteristic of a sample and theoretically reflecting the population from which the sample was drawn; e.g., the sample mean is an estimate of the true population mean; the sample mean is a statistic, the population mean is a ➤ **parameter** (2).

statistical 1. Pertaining to or characteristic of a ➤ **statistic**. 2. A shorthand form, meaning of ➤ **statistical significance**; e.g., the common phrase, 'There was no statistical effect' means 'The statistical analysis led to a value of p greater than the established criterion for concluding statistical significance.'

statistical artifact ➤ **artifact, statistical**.

statistical association Any statistical relationship between two or more variables such that change in one is accompanied by change(s) in the other(s). Such associations are captured by correlational analyses; ➤ **correlation** et seq.

statistical attenuation A term used to refer to the fact that all correlations based on sample data are theoretically reduced (attenuated) to some extent through errors of measurement. There are procedures for estimating the size of the attenuation and thus for estimating the maximum true correlations that theoretically could exist in the population under consideration.

statistical control ➤ **control, statistical**.

statistical dependence ➤ **dependence** (1).

statistical error A general term for any inaccuracy in sampling or in the recording of analysis of the data that makes valid conclusions impossible to draw.

statistical inference The process of drawing generalizations about a population on the basis of sample data. ➤ **inferential *statistics**.

statistical interaction ➤ **interaction**.

statistical law ➤ **law, statistical**.

statistical-learning theory A term introduced in the early 1950s by W.K. Estes to cover a variety of attempts to formulate and quantify basic principles of learning theory. E.g., ➤ **stimulus-sampling theory**.

statistical power ➤ **power of a test, statistical**.

statistical psychology An obsolescent form for the use of statistics and statistical principles to derive general laws and principles in psychology. The broader term ➤ **mathematical psychology** now encompasses it. Note, the term does not refer to the use of statistics to evaluate empirical data for the purpose of testing hypotheses.

statistical significance The degree to which an obtained result was sufficiently unlikely to have occurred under the assumption that only chance factors were operating, and therefore the degree to which it may be attributed to systematic manipulations. The degree itself is typically specified and denoted as a probability; e.g., $p < 0.05$ means that the results obtained (or more extreme results) could only have occurred by chance in fewer than 5 cases in 100. The smaller the p-value, the more significant the results; that is, the less likely that they occurred by chance. ➤ **significance level**.

statistical stability An occasional synonym for ➤ **statistical significance**. The connotation of the term is that any statistically significant result is 'stable,' in the sense that if the experiment were repeated one could confidently expect similar results.

statistical test Any procedure whereby sample data are evaluated statistically to determine an estimate of the probable truth of a hypothesis about a population.

statistics 1. Very generally, the branch of mathematics, pure and applied, which deals with collecting, classifying and analyzing data. 2. Sets of procedures developed to describe and analyze particular types of data and enable a researcher to draw various kinds of conclusions on the basis of those data. This sense is the one commonly found with qualifiers that identify the specific class of statistics under consideration; e.g., *descriptive statistics*, *inferential statistics*. The most often used in psychology are given below. 3. Loosely, in popular usage, numbers used to represent facts or data.

statistics, correlational A general label for all those statistical procedures which are based on ➤ **correlations**. Note that most consider these procedures to be part of ➤ **descriptive *statistics**.

statistics, descriptive A general label for the use of statistical procedures to describe, organize and summarize samples of data. Basically, a descriptive statistic is a number that represents some aspects of a sample of data. The most common are measures of ➤ **central tendency**, measures of ➤ **dispersion** (or ➤ **variability**) and measures of ➤ **correlation** – although some authorities treat the last category separately.

statistics, inferential The use of statistical procedures for the making of inferences. Basically, they utilize the mathematics of probability theory to infer or induce generalizations about populations from sample data. ➤ **statistical inference**, ➤ **parametric**

statistics and compare with ➤ **descriptive *statistics**. Also known as *inference statistics* and *inductive statistics*.

statistic, sufficient A statistic that makes use of all of the available data in a sample in providing an estimate of a population parameter.

statoacoustic nerve Another name for the VIIIth ➤ **cranial nerve**; more commonly called the ➤ **auditory nerve**.

statokinetic response Any of the many postural responses or reflexes that maintain stable posture while the body is in motion.

stat rat (or subject) Short for *statistical rat (or statistical subject)*, a sort of laboratory slang for a theoretical experimental subject whose hypothetical behavior is generated by a computer or other device. In the most common situation, the computer is programmed to behave (metaphorically speaking) like a theoretical rat (or other subject).

statue of Condillac The subject of a thought experiment of the 18th-century philosopher Étienne Bonnot de Condillac. His fantasized statue was marble and in human form. Condillac imagined it to be endowed, one by one, with the several normal human senses, first smell, then taste, followed by hearing, vision and finally touch. He argued that each of the components of human consciousness, thought, memory, feelings, etc. could be thus seen as fundamentally sensationalistic in nature.

status 1. Generally, a state of affairs, a condition. 2. A reasonably well-defined standing in the social order of a group or a society. Status, here, may be characterized in one of two ways: (a) in terms of rights, privileges, prestige, power, etc. relative to others in the social hierarchy; and/or (b) in terms of roles, the patterns of socially accepted and expected behaviors. The former tends to emphasize position or location in a social structure and is often called *social status*, the latter tends to emphasize the obligatory behaviors of persons in particular positions. ➤ **role, social class. 3.** In medicine, a pathological or abnormal condition. Here the term comes straight from the Latin and is usually italicized.

status, achieved Any status that is acquired by effort, competition, knowledge, special skills, etc. Examples are the occupational statuses of physicians, professors, artists, etc. Compare with ➤ **ascribed *status**.

status, ascribed Any status based on inherited factors and not on individual ability, skills, etc. Compare with ➤ **achieved *status**.

status epilepticus A rapid succession of convulsive epileptic seizures without the patient gaining consciousness in the intervals. *Status epilepticus* is a neurological emergency which, if left untreated, may be fatal.

status group 1. A group of persons classified together on the basis of social status, shared patterns of behavior and privileges, and a sense of awareness of their group membership, e.g., a caste. **2.** Any number of persons classified together because of a sharing of social status and life style, but not necessarily forming a group, e.g., factory workers.

status grouping A grouping of persons according to equivalent statuses.

status need A need to achieve a high social position.

status sequence A succession of statuses that occur in a set pattern. The classic example is the sequence, medical student–intern–practicing physician.

status, social ➤ **status** (2).

status symbol More of a popular term than a technical one, used to refer to any visible mark, activity or affectation of behavior that conveys one's membership in a particular status group or one's status aspirations. The term is typically restricted to symbols of high-status groups and aspirations.

status validity ➤ **concurrent *validity**.

steady state A general term for any unchanging condition. ➤ **homeostasis**.

stearic acid ➤ **fatty acid**.

stellate cell Generally, any cell with a starlike shape; specifically, those found in the cerebral cortex, particularly the fourth layer, and in the molecular layer of the cerebellum.

stem-completion task A task commonly used in *cognitive psychology* where the subject is given a word stem (e.g., MOT . . .) and asked to complete it with the first word that comes to mind. Also called *word completion task* and *word stem-completion task*.

stenin A protein found coating the membrane of synaptic vesicles.

step function Any function with discrete, quantal increments or decrements.

step interval An occasional synonym for ➤ **class interval**.

stepwise phenomenon In Gestalt theory, the sense that a sequence of discrete steps along a continuum is an organized, smooth progression. For example, a sequence of lights of increasing brightness is seen as a stepwise progression. However, a sequence of lights of increasing wavelength is not so perceived; it is seen, rather, as a discontinuous progression moving through various hues. The stepwise phenomenon occurs with ➤ **prothetic** continua but not with ➤ **metathetic**.

stereo A combinatory form taken from the Greek meaning *solid*. By extension, it is also used for *heavy, deep* and *three-dimensional*.

stereochemical theory (of smell) A theory of olfaction based on the physical shapes and electrical charges of odorous molecules. Seven primary odors are assumed (camphorous, musky, floral, minty, ethereal, pungent and putrid) and all others are represented as occurring through combinations of these.

stereocilia In the inner ear, the shorter hairs projecting from the surface of the cells of the semicircular canals. ➤ **kinocilia**.

stereognosis Perception of or, more literally, knowledge of objects derived through touch.

stereogram A pair of two-dimensional pictures arranged such that when viewed through a ➤ **stereoscope** they fuse into a single, three-dimensional picture.

stereopsis 1. Loosely, stereoscopic vision; vision through a stereoscope. **2.** Specifically, the displacement of two objects in the third dimension; ➤ **retinal *disparity**. See that entry for details here. **3.** The extent to which objects may be discriminated in three dimensions. ➤ **stereoscopic *acuity**.

stereoscope Any device for viewing two-dimensional pictures (stereograms) so that the perception of depth is produced. There are several such devices using different principles, but all function so that the perception of depth arises from having one eye view a scene from a slightly different perspective than the other eye. ➤ **retinal *disparity**.

stereoscopic acuity ➤ **acuity, stereoscopic**.

stereoscopic vision ➤ **vision, stereoscopic**.

stereotaxis A method for precisely locating areas in the brain. It is used in both experimental research on lower organisms and in certain neurosurgical procedures on human patients. A stereotaxic instrument permits the positioning of an instrument (e.g., an electrode for recording electrical activity of neural tissue) when guided by features of the skull and a detailed, three-dimensional atlas of the species' brain.

stereotropism Generally, any orienting response to a solid object.

stereotype This term derives from its use in printing, where it refers to a solid printing mould or plate which, once cast, is difficult to change. In keeping with this etymology, the term has typically been used in the social sciences to stand for: **1**

n. A set of relatively fixed, simplistic over-generalizations about a group or class of people. Here, the negative, unfavorable, characteristics are emphasized, although some authorities will regard positive but biased and inaccurate beliefs as components of a. stereotype. Given the ubiquity of this meaning it is of interest that empirical studies of people's attitudes toward social groups and classes other than their own have not supported the theory invited by this definition, particularly with regard to the notions of rigidity and inaccuracy. Hence: **2** n. Within a culture, a set of widely shared generalizations about the psychological characteristics of a group or class of people. This rather more neutral definition is preferred, as it (a) allows for stereotypes to change, as we know they do, (b) permits the inclusion of positive and accurate characteristics and (c) emphasizes that stereotypes must be widely shared sets of beliefs – somehow when held by only a few the term hardly seems justified. **3** vb. To form or utilize such sets of beliefs, to classify or categorize an individual on the basis of them. ➤ **prejudice**.

stereotyped behavior Rigid, inflexible behavior that tends to be made despite changes in the context and outcomes which normally should produce modifications in how one acts. ➤➤ **stereotyped movement** and **stereotypy**.

stereotyped movement A persistent postural, gestural or verbal response that is without apparent meaning and tends to recur inappropriately. Such repetitive behaviors are symptoms in a number of mental disorders.

stereotypic movement disorder A ➤ **movement disorder** characterized by nonfunctional repetitive behaviors such as rocking back and forth, hitting, biting or scratching parts of one's body, repetitive vocalizations, etc. It is associated, especially in its more pronounced forms, with severe or profound mental retardation and often accompanies *autism*. Also called *stereotypy/habit disorder*.

stereotypy Generally, any condition characterized by a high degree of stereotyped behavior and movement. Note, however, some authors restrict usage to psychopathological or neuropathological conditions; others will apply it to the normal recurrent mannerisms of those who are free of disorder. The connotations of the term clearly depend upon how the author uses it.

stereotypy/habit disorder ➤ **stereotypic movement disorder**.

sterile 1. Not fertile, having the condition of ➤ **sterility**. 2. Free from microorganisms, free from contamination. 3. Impoverished or barren in thought and ideation; unimaginative, uncreative.

sterility A condition of inability to serve as one of the partners in sexual reproduction; in the female the inability to become pregnant, in the male the inability to impregnate. Sterility can result from a truly remarkable variety of causes, physiological, anatomical and psychological. See and compare with ➤ **infertility**.

sterilization 1. The process of destroying the ability of an individual to reproduce, the act of rendering one ➤ **sterile** (1). It can be accomplished through the surgical removal of the testes or ovaries (see here ➤ **castration**), by irradiation which inactivates the germ-producing tissue or by tying off or removing portions of the reproductive ducts (➤ **vasectomy** in the male, ➤ **salpingectomy** in the female). 2. The process of destroying all microorganisms on a substance or object; the act of rendering a thing ➤ **sterile** (2).

Sternberg task A simple procedure developed by Saul Sternberg to study human memory. The subject is given a small set of items (four or five will do) to memorize. Then a single item is presented and the subject must say, as rapidly as possible, whether that item is a novel one or one from the original set.

steroids Hormones made up of small, fat-soluble molecules that are readily absorbed into cells where they attach themselves to receptors in the nucleus. Steroids

such as the sex hormones secreted by the testes and ovaries and those secreted by the adrenal cortex have *anabolic* properties and, as such, are often abused by individuals seeking additional muscle mass. It should be noted that steroid abuse has a number of unhappy side effects including sexual impotence.

Steven's power law ➤ **power law**.

sthenia From the Greek, meaning *strength*. ant., ➤ **asthenia**.

sthenometer Any device for measuring muscular strength.

stigma Greek for *mark* or *brand*. Hence: 1. Any mark or spot on the skin. Typically, this meaning is restricted to cases in which the blemish itself is benign but thought to be symptomatic of a degenerative condition. 2. In genetics, a criterial feature of a genetic disorder. 3. Figuratively, a mark or blemish on one's reputation. pl., *stigmata* or *stigmas*; vb., *stigmatize*.

Stiles-Crawford effect A term used for either of two closely related effects. 1. The generalization that the light entering the eye through the center of the pupil appears brighter than light entering near the edge. The effect is related to the distribution of cones in the retina; clustered as they are near the center in the fovea, they are less likely to be affected by light at an angle than by light arriving head on. The effect does not occur in the dark-adapted eye and hence is not due to rod action. 2. The generalization that when monochromatic light enters the eye, oblique rays entering off-center result in the experiencing of slightly different hues than those entering through the center. The effects holds even when the stimuli have been equated for brightness. With short and long wavelengths there is a slight positive shift (e.g., oblique long wavelengths look 'too red') while in the middle wavelength region it is negative (e.g., an oblique 540-nm stimulus looks 'too yellow').

Stilling test A test for color deficiencies consisting of numbers arranged in complex dot patterns on complexly arranged dot-pattern backgrounds. The saturation and brightness of the dots are carefully controlled, leaving only hue as a feature for detecting each number. The color-weak eye will see only the random dots.

stimulant drug with arousing, altering, stimulating properties. Included in this large category are the powerful ➤ **amphetamines**, ➤ **methylphenidate**, ➤ **cocaine** and many common, less potent substances such as ➤ **caffeine** and ➤ **nicotine**. All produce, in varying degrees, alertness, talkativeness, enhanced physical performance for gross sensorimotor acts, increased confidence and a diminution of appetite. To some extent all have an associated ➤ **drug *dependence**. The primary medical uses are in ➤ **obesity**, ➤ **narcolepsy** and childhood ➤ **hypokinesis**.

stimulation 1. Broadly, any event that arouses an organism, or the actual arousal itself. **2.** More specifically, a particular event that, when applied to a sensory receptor or receptor cell, causes it to become active. Note that in 1 the term can be used for either the event or the arousal; in 2 it only refers to the event, the term ➤ **excitation** (1) serving to cover the resulting state of arousal. vb., *stimulate*.

stimulus (S) Attempting to provide a precise definition for this term has led many psychologists to grief. Since it is the primary term in the theoretical orientation that has, historically, been regarded as one of the most objective yet produced by psychology (➤ **stimulus–response theory**), one would anticipate that there would be a relatively unambiguous definition for it or, barring that, at least an agreed-upon manner of usage. Alas, neither is to be found. However, among the diverse meanings and patterns of usage outlined below it is possible to perceive several commonalities, and it helps to specify them at the outset: (a) a stimulus must be characterized, or must in principle be characterizable, in physical terms – a ghost cannot serve as a stimulus; (b) a stimulus must fall within the range of receptivity of the

organism under consideration – a 40,000 Hz tone may be a stimulus for a bat but not for a human; (c) a stimulus either must evoke a response from a receptor or must provoke or 'stimulate' some action or behavior from an organism; and (d) a stimulus must be external to either the organism itself or to some internal but circumscribable part of an organism. With these points in mind, the following are the six most common meanings of the term, from the most general to the most specific: **1.** Any thing (i.e. any event, any occurrence, any change in a thing, any percept, or concept, internal or external) that has some impact or effect on an organism such that its behavior is modified in some detectable way. Although the following definitions all attempt to delimit the referential meaning of the term in some degree or fashion, in the final analysis this utterly inclusive definition represents the connotative meaning that the term almost invariably has. Note, however, like the term ➤ **response**, it often is used with qualifiers which are introduced in an attempt to specify the limits of applicability. **2.** Any event or change in an event that alerts or arouses an organism. This meaning is preferred by some because it carries with it the original sense of the term ➤ **stimulation** (2). **3.** Any change that is sufficient to excite a receptor or receptor system. This meaning is most commonly found in studies of sensory processes and occasionally in the study of perception. **4.** A signal for action. Here, the definitional focus is on the role of a stimulus as a sign or initiator of behavior. **5.** Some mental or internal event that provokes or prods an organism on, an *incentive*. This meaning is rare in technical writing but common in popular texts. **6.** The environmental circumstances regularly present at the time of occurrence of a particular response. This definition is favored by Skinnerian behaviorists because the focus is on the objective, physical environment; e.g., ➤ **discriminative *stimulus**, **eliciting *stimulus**, **reinforcing *stimulus**, all of which reflect this meaning.

Finally, note that in any or all of these

there is a theoretically important question that is glossed over. Specifically, what is the relationship between the physical characterizations of the stimulus in objective form and the internal representation of that stimulus to the organism? There is no simple answer to this question but there are specialized terms whose meanings reflect attempts to deal with it. E.g., ➤ **adequate *stimulus, functional *stimulus, inadequate *stimulus, stimulus as coded**.

stimulus, adequate Any stimulus that will produce a response in a receptor or receptor system. As the term is used, such a stimulus will necessarily have two properties: (a) it will be above the threshold for that sensory system; and (b) it will be an appropriate energy form for that sense. Compare with ➤ **inadequate *stimulus**.

stimulus as coded A phrase used for the simple fact that, in reality, the stimulus in any given set of circumstances can rarely be represented by a straightforward physical description of its objective properties but rather must be viewed as functioning according to how the subject interprets or codes it. abbrev., *SAC*. ➤➤ **functional *stimulus** for more on this general point and several examples.

stimulus attitude ➤ **stimulus *set**.

stimulus-bound 1. Generally, characteristic of situations in which what is perceived is determined virtually entirely by the physical properties of the stimulus. As the discussion under the entry ➤ **perception** points out, this is usually not the case. 2. In personality research, characteristic of persons who tend to be rather rigid and inflexible and who tend to react on the basis of external stimuli rather than on reflection or interpretation of the situation.

stimulus continuum Generally, the underlying dimension that represents a continuous variable that any individual stimulus is a part of. For example, any given achromatic light represents a particular point along the black-white stimulus continuum.

stimulus control A phrase that refers to the extent to which behavior can be said to be under the control of environmental stimulus conditions. Those with a cognitive orientation tend to downplay stimulus control, arguing that it is the underlying mental processes which are more important in determining behavior; those with a behaviorist point of view see stimulus control as a central component in the explanation of an organism's behavior, even to the point of using the phrase 'bringing behavior under stimulus control' as a (somewhat awkward) synonym for *learning*.

stimulus differentiation ➤ **differentiation** (especially 4 and 5).

stimulus, discriminative In operant-conditioning studies of discrimination learning, any stimulus in the presence of which responses are reinforced and in the absence of which they are not. Abbrev., S^D.

stimulus element ➤ **element** (3).

stimulus equivalence ➤ **equivalence**.

stimulus error ➤ **error, stimulus**.

stimulus field A very general term used for the totality of stimuli impinging upon an organism at any point in time. Typically, the term is reserved for external stimuli; if mental or covert aspects are included the qualifier *internal* is usually appended.

stimulus, functional The stimulus or the aspect of the stimulus which is, in reality, functioning to exert some control over responses. For example, if several bright, colored, moving objects are used as stimuli for a pigeon and a cat in a discrimination-learning experiment, the movements are likely to be the functional components of the stimulus for the cat while the hue and brightness of the stimuli will serve as the primary functional components for the pigeon. Similarly, an English-speaking subject given the nonsense syllable MIF in a memory experiment may code it as an acronym for 'my intimate friend,' which then becomes the functional stimulus. ➤➤ **stimulus as coded**, which speaks to the same general issue. Also called, on occasion, *effective stimulus*.

stimulus generalization ➤ **generalization, stimulus**.

stimulus, inadequate A confusing and, fortunately, obsolescent term for any stimulus whose energy form is not normally effective for a particular sensory modality. For example, slight pressure on the side of the eyeball will produce a visual sensation, and in some older texts will be called an inadequate visual stimulus. A better term here is *anomalous stimulus*. ➤➤ **adequate *stimulus**. Compare with ➤ **ineffective *stimulus**.

stimulus, ineffective Quite literally, a stimulus that is ineffective in producing a response or in exciting a receptor. The lack of functional effectiveness may derive from any of several reasons; e.g., the stimulus may be below threshold, it may be outside the range of receptivity of the organism's sensory system, or the organism's attentional focus could be directed elsewhere. Compare with ➤ **inadequate *stimulus**.

stimulus, neutral 1. In operant conditioning, any (all, in fact) environmental events that have no effect upon behavior at a given point in time. 2. In classical conditioning, any stimulus that does not naturally elicit the conditioned response and, as a result, can serve as a conditioned stimulus.

stimulus object A loose term used to cover any object that functions as a stimulus for some behavior. The word *object* here may be taken to stand for things, persons or even abstractions depending on the context.

stimulus onset asynchrony (SOA) The time between the onsets of two stimuli. The term is often used in studies of ➤ **masking** where the SOA is the time between the onset of the target and the onset of the masker. Compare with ➤ **interstimulus interval**.

stimulus pattern Generally, any complex stimulus that functions as a whole in which the separate elements form a structured array. In some reductionistic sense, all but the most primitive unidimensional stimuli are stimulus patterns, but the term is typically applied only to situations where it is the pattern itself which is the functional coded stimulus. The classical example is a musical melody. ➤ **functional *stimulus, pattern, stimulus as coded** et seq.

stimulus population In ➤ **stimulus-sampling theory**, the full complement of independent elements that make up the stimulus present on a given trial in an experiment.

stimulus preexposure effect ➤ **latent *inhibition**.

stimulus, reinforcing Within the ➤ **Skinnerian** approach, any environmental event that is present immediately following a response and functions so as to maintain that response. ➤ **reinforcement**, especially (8).

stimulus–response Of or representing the bond between a stimulus and its associated response. The term is used as a shorthand expression for a particular approach to psychology, specifically that predicated upon conditioning principles and affiliated with the general position of ➤ **associationism**, and it serves as an all-purpose adjective for phenomena, hypothetical mechanisms and general theories that are based on this bond. E.g., ➤ **stimulus–response psychology, stimulus–response theory**. Often referred to by the abbreviation, *S–R*.

stimulus–response learning ➤ **S–R *learning**.

stimulus–response psychology Loosely, that approach to psychology that views the stimulus–response bond as the foundation of behavior and conceptualizes the goal of a scientific psychology as the discovery of the functional relationships between stimuli and responses. Note that while essentially all approaches to psychology that may be classified as stimulus–response are, in fact, behavioristic, it is not necessarily the case that they must be. It is, perhaps, only a historical accident that the behaviourists commandeered the terms and forbade the reference to mental stimuli and cognitive responses. Hence, stimulus–response psychology (often abbreviated as *S–R psychology*) is contrasted with ➤ **cognitive psychology**, **dynamic psychology**, **Gestalt psychology** and **psychoanalysis**.

stimulus–response theory Loosely, any of the associationistic learning theories that have as their theoretical foundation the forming of a bond between a stimulus and a response. Often referred to by the shorthand, *S–R theory*. ➤ **S–R *learning**.

stimulus-sampling theory A mathematically formal theory of learning due largely to the work of William K. Estes. Each stimulus is assumed to be made up of elements. On each trial of a learning experiment the subject samples some proportion of these elements and makes a response. When that response is reinforced, those elements become conditioned to it. Hence, the probability of that response on any given trial can be specified by the proportion of all stimulus elements conditioned to that response. By introducing additional responses, by assuming that the subject can only sample certain elements from the full population, by assuming that some stimuli come in patterns of elements and so forth, the theory can provide rather precise predictions about behavior in a variety of rather complex learning experiments.

stimulus set ➤ **set, stimulus**.

stimulus situation The full complement of environmental stimuli in the presence of which an organism behaves. The term connotes holistic and contextual effects as opposed to the atomistic, objective analysis preferred by the behaviorists.

stimulus–stimulus learning ➤ S–S *learning.

stimulus trace Hull's term for the sensory aftereffects of a stimulus which are represented in the nervous system after the

physical stimulus has been terminated. ➤ **iconic** for a slightly different perspective on the same issue.

stimulus value A loose term for any quantitative aspect of a stimulus.

stimulus variable Any of the ➤ **independent variables** in an experiment that can be characterized as a change in a physical stimulus. For example, children of varying ages might be asked to read words of varying length. Both age and word length would be independent variables but only word length would be a stimulus variable.

stimulus word Loosely, any word used as a stimulus. Most often, a word presented to a subject in a word-association study or a reaction-time study or a word used as the stimulus in paired-associates learning.

stirrup = ➤ **stapes**. ➤ **auditory *ossicles**.

stochastic From the Greek, meaning *skillful in guessing*, characteristic of any process or any sequence of events that can be described by using probability theory. Used roughly synonymously with *non-deterministic* and *probabilistic*.

Stockholm syndrome An emotional bond between hostages and their captors which is frequently observed when the hostages are held for long periods of time under emotionally straining circumstances. The name derives from the instance when it was first publicly noted, when a group of hostages was held by robbers in a Stockholm bank for five days.

stocking anesthesia ➤ **glove *anesthesia**.

stooge A person who poses as a subject in an experiment but who is actually a confederate of the experimenter.

stop consonant A speech sound produced with a momentary complete closure of the mouth at some point; the /p/ in *pan*, /t/ in *tan*.

stopped image ➤ **stabilized image**.

storage = *memory*. The term is very common in cognitive psychology. ➤ **memory** et seq. for details on contemporary terminology.

storage capacity As borrowed from computer sciences, the upper limit on the amount of information that can be stored in memory. Typically used with regard to limited-memory systems such as ➤ **short-term *memory**.

store 1 n. = ➤ **memory**. **2** vb. To commit to memory.

strabismus From the Greek, meaning *squint*, a lack of coordinated fixation between the two eyes due to muscular disorders. The condition may be *unilateral*, when the same eye always deviates, *alternating*, when either may deviate while the other fixates, *convergent*, when the deviant eye turns inward, *divergent*, when it turns outward, or *vertical*, when it turns downward.

straight-line processing Loosely, linear, sequential thinking.

straight-line sensory system A phrase used occasionally to refer to the primary afferent neural pathways from the peripheral sensory receptors to the brain.

strain 1 n. Generally, the state of a system when severe demands are placed upon it. This general meaning comes from the Old French for *bind* or *draw tight* and appears in a variety of contexts, typically with the connotation that the system is deformed in some way by the stress. Thus, references to muscular strain, the straining of a joint or tendon, psychological strain, eye strain, etc. are common. **2** n. The line of reproductively isolated members of a particular species. Common laboratory rats and wild rats represent two strains of a single species. This meaning derives from the Old English for *acquire*. **3** vb. To pass through a filter. **4** vb. To injure by the placing of excessive demands or severe stress. **5** vb. To engage in excessive efforts to accomplish something.

strange situation An experimental procedure developed by Ainsworth in which a young child is placed in a series of increasingly stressful 'strange' situations and emotional reactions are observed. The situations range from the least stressful where the child is playing with a parent through the moderately stressful where a stranger enters the room during play to the most stressful where the parent leaves the child alone in the room. The procedure is most commonly used with one- and two-year-olds.

strategy 1. As derived from the Greek for *generalship*, a plan of conduct or action, a consciously arrived-at set of operations for solving some problem or achieving some goal. **2.** Occasionally, particularly in psychoanalytic writings, an unconscious program of operation. References to the 'id's strategies for circumventing the ego' reflect this meaning. **3.** In ethology and sociobiology, a species' collective pattern of adaptive behaviour, e.g., *survival strategy*, *reproductive strategy*. Note the rather different ways in which the question of consciousness is handled here. In meaning 1 the clear connotation is that a strategy is conscious, in 2 it is generally taken as an unconscious process, in 3 the question is irrelevant.

stratification In sociology and social psychology, the arrangement of the social classes in a society into a horizontal, layered arrangement such that the roles, statuses and life chances of those in each layer are relatively differentiated from those in other layers.

stratified sampling ➤ **sampling, stratified**.

Stratton's experiment The term honors G. M. Stratton, who in 1896 published the original experiments with special prisms which invert the perceived visual field by rotating it through 180° of arc. ➤ **displaced vision** for more here.

streaming ➤ **tracking** (2).

stream of action The behavioristic, functionalistic analog of James's ➤ **stream of consciousness**.

stream of consciousness 1. As introduced by William James, a term used to emphasize the notion that consciousness was not a static thing made up of discrete elements, as conceptualized by the defenders of ➤ **structuralism** (1), but rather was a confluent, continuous, multifarious succession of images, ideas, feelings, memories and thoughts. **2.** A phrase used to characterize speech and/or writing which has an unedited quality, so that, 'whatever worm makes it to the top, pops out.' It is not used for the speech or writing of those with diagnosed mental disorders but rather for those whose minds are 'normal' but whose verbal style is eccentric.

strephosymbolia From the Greek, meaning *twisting of symbols*: **1.** Left–right reversal of the location of symbols, e.g., reading *sag* as *gas*. **2.** Left–right reversal of the orientation of symbols, e.g., reading *b* as *d*. The first meaning is the one usually intended. ➤➤ **reversals**.

stress 1. Generally, any force that when applied to a system causes some significant modification of its form, usually with the connotation that the modification is a deformation or a distortion. The term is used with respect to physical, psychological and social forces and pressures. Note that stress in this sense refers to a *cause*; stress is the antecedent of some effect. **2.** A state of psychological tension produced by the kinds of forces or pressures alluded to in 1 above. Note that stress in this sense is an *effect*; stress is the result of other pressures. When meaning 2 is intended, the term *stressor* is typically used for the causal agent. **3.** In linguistics, the emphasis placed on syllables and words. Here several levels of stress may be differentiated.

stress interview Quite literally, an interview in which the person being interviewed is deliberately put under considerable emotional stress to evaluate their ability to handle such tension in real-life situations. It is one form of ➤ **stress test**.

stressor ➤ **stress** (2).

stress reaction, gross A general label for a situational reaction brought on by extreme stress, such as that of combat in war or major civilian disasters like earthquake, fire, accident, etc. ➤➤ **post-traumatic stress disorder**.

stress test Generally, any test that is carried out under real-life or simulated real-life conditions of considerable stress. The term is used for both the psychologically stressful, such as a ➤ **stress interview**, and the physiologically stressful, such as a treadmill test for evaluating cardiovascular fitness.

stretch receptor A proprioceptor in muscle or tendons that is stimulated by pulling or stretching of tissue.

stretch reflex Reflexive muscle contraction to a pulling of the tendon of the responding muscle. Such reflexes are important in the maintenance of posture. Also called *myotactic reflex*.

stria atrophica The medical term for what are more commonly called *stretch marks*.

striate From the Latin for *striped*, marked by stripes or streaks. var., *striated*.

striate body ➤ **corpus striatum**.

striate cortex The primary visual cortex, the region surrounding the ➤ **calcarine fissure**. The term is applied because this area contains a layer of cells that show up as dark stripes under histological examination.

stria terminalis A fiber bundle that runs between the medial amygdala and various regions in the forebrain including the *medial* ➤ **preoptic area**.

striate muscle ➤ **muscle, striate**.

strident In phonetics, a ➤ **distinctive feature** (2) characterizing sounds produced with a distinct turbulence; e.g., /s/, /z/, /ch/.

string Generally, any concatenated series of stimuli. Thus, sentences are strings of words, written words are strings of letters, etc.

strip Goffman's term for any particular sequence of occurrences or actions in a larger ➤ **frame** (2) to which one wishes to draw attention.

striped muscle ➤ **muscle, striate**.

stroboscope Any device that presents a series of still pictures in rapid succession. When the time interval between the stills is appropriate, the viewer experiences motion. The standard motion-picture projector is, in effect, a stroboscope. ➤ **stroboscopic effect**.

stroboscopic effect 1. Generally, a type of ➤ **apparent *motion** perceived when two stationary stimuli are illuminated in rapid succession. The classic examples are motion pictures and advertising marquees. **2.** More specifically, the variations in the perception of real motion produced by changing the rate at which a flashing light illuminates it. The classic example here is changing the perceived rotation of a spoked wheel from forward to stationary to backward by changing the rate of the intermittent light.

stroboscopic motion ➤ **motion, stroboscopic**.

stroke 1. Generally, any sudden severe attack. **2.** More specifically, such an attack produced by a cerebrovascular accident such as the rupture of a blood vessel in the brain.

Strong-Campbell Interest Inventory The revision of the ➤ **Strong Vocational Interest Blank**. It reflects the many changes in vocational preferences that have taken place since 1927 when the original test was first published. It is based on a set of several hundred items including occupations, activities, amusements, school subjects and the like to which the test taker responds by indicating 'like,' 'indifferent' or 'dislike.'

strong law of effect ➤ **effect, strong law of**.

Strong Vocational Interest Blank A wide-ranging inventory designed to assess an individual's interests and preferences for a variety of vocations. It is based

on a set of norms established on the interests and preferences of persons who are acknowledged successes in various fields of endeavor. The subject's scores are compared with these norms and areas of similarity are identified.

Stroop test A procedure developed in 1935 by J. R. Stroop for studying verbal processes. The test consists of a series of color name words (*blue, red, green*) printed in non-matching colors. That is, the word *red* may be printed in blue ink. Most people find it extremely difficult to attend to the ink color alone when asked to name the color in which each word is printed, because of an automatic tendency to read the words, which produces interfering information.

structural Pertaining to ➤ **structure**. Compare with ➤ **functional**, ➤ **dynamic** and ➤ **behavioral**.

structuralism There are several theoretical and philosphical orientations that have been given or have assumed this label. All share a concern with the structure or organization of those phenomena that happen under consideration. However, since the phenomena that are and have been the focus of investigation as well as the presumed form of the underlying structure differ sharply from orientation to orientation, the term is found denoting approaches that differ, often dramatically, from each other. The following are those that have been most frequently designated as structuralist and which are of importance in the social sciences.

1. The system in experimental psychology closely associated with the writings and empirical findings of Edward B. Titchener. The approach was (the past tense is called for here since this particular approach effectively expired with Titchener) based on the presumption that all human mental experience, no matter how complex, could be viewed as blends or combinations of simple processes or elements. The experimental method used was ➤ **introspection** and the attempt was made to discover all of the basic elements of sensation and affection which went into making up mental life, and hence to reveal the underlying structure of mind. This approach was rather vigorously and effectively attacked by many: by behaviorists for its excessive mentalism, by Gestaltists for its unwarranted reductionism, by psychoanalysts for its insistence on studying only conscious awareness, by functionalists for its failure to appreciate the role and functions of mind and by various others for excluding the study of animals, children, the mentally disturbed, social groups and any other subject that could not use introspection. **2.** The theory of cognitive development of Jean Piaget. The focus here is very different from that in **1.** The structure presumed here is that of the mental representations which underlie intelligent, adaptive behaviors, and it is characterized as a sequence of quasi-logical and logical stages through which a child progresses to the end of a logically formal operatory level. ➤ **Piagetian** for more detail. **3.** Any of several sociological/anthropological approaches such as that of Claude Lévi-Strauss. Here the focus is on the social organization and societal structures and the manner in which they are learned and reacted to by members of the society under examination. The emphasis here is on the use of such organizational structures as the empirical basis for theoretical induction concerning the personal and group conceptualizations of the structure of their world, from both the psychological and the physical standpoints. There is, typically, strong emphasis on the analysis of religion, mythology and art.

Note that structuralism **1** is reductionistic and elemental while **2** and **3** are holistic and interactionist. Clearly there are many ways to approach the notion of a structured system.

structural psychology ➤ **structuralism** (1).

structure **1** n. An organized, patterned, relatively stable configuration. The term is certainly one of the most freely used in all of psychology and is found with reference to the purely physical (stimulus structure), the biological (brain structure), the

mental (the structure of memory), the social (group structure), the abstract (linguistic structure), etc. Generally, the term is used whenever one wishes to convey the notion that the entity being characterized, taken as a whole, has intrinsic organization and that this organization is, in fact, one of its most salient aspects. Frequently, structure is used as though the author intends it to be an antonym of ➤ **function**, ➤ **process** or even ➤ **behavior**. The difficulty here is that, more often than not, the functional, behavioral processes themselves have structure in that they too are organized, patterned and relatively stable. Approximate synonyms: ➤ **configuration**, ➤ **Gestalt**, ➤ **organization**, ➤ **system**; see each for details. **2** n. Any complex system that is regarded from the perspective of the whole, e.g. the structure of science. This use reflects the notion that the *structure* exists only when the totality is under consideration. **3** vb. To organize or construct a relatively stable configuration from many elements.

structured interview Any interview with a pre-set organization in which the topics, questions and their order of use are all determined in advance.

structured stimulus Generally, any stimulus with a salient, well-articulated and well-defined organization. The term appears most often in contrast with the so-called *unstructured stimuli*, of which the Rorschach ink blots are the classic example. However, the distinction here is not simply a matter of pure structure versus the lack of it; it has more to do with the extent to which the perceiver contributes to the structure. In the case of a simple, well-organized stimulus like a triangle, the primary source of structure can be regarded as the physical stimulus itself and there will be little interpersonal variation in what is perceived; in the case of a complex, ambiguously organized stimulus like an ink blot the perceiver invests the display with a great deal of interpreted structure, and there will be large individual differences in what is perceived. See also the discussion under ➤ **ambiguity**.

763

structure-of-intellect model J. P. Guilford's term for his three-dimensional model of intellectual functioning. It classifies intellectual traits along: (a) a set of *operations* – what a person *does*, including memory, cognition, divergent and convergent production, and evaluation; (b) a set of *contents* – the nature of the materials upon which operations are carried out, including those that are figural, semantic, symbolic and behavioral; and (c) a set of *products* – the forms in which information is processed, including units, classes, relations, systems, transformations and implications. The model predicts a total of 120 theoretically identifiable factors underlying intelligence.

STS Abbreviation for *short-term store*; ➤ short-term *memory.

Student's distribution The ➤ *t* *distribution. ➤➤ Student's test.

Student's test The ➤ *t* test. The name Student is a pseudonym. It was adopted in 1908 by its developer, William S. Gosset, a chemist for Guinness breweries, when the company would not allow him to publish his findings under his real name.

study 1 n. Generally, a field of investigation or a branch of science, e.g., the study of psychology. 2 n. More specifically, an experiment or investigation. Occasionally the term is used here somewhat more loosely, in that the strict controls assumed to be present in those investigations called *experiments* are not always present in those called *studies*. 3 n. Popularly, any attempt to learn material. 4 vb. To engage in or carry out any of the above.

stump hallucination ➤ phantom limb.

stupor 1. A general condition characterized by extreme unresponsiveness, lethargy and loss of orientation. 2 (obs.). Inability to speak, mutism.

stuttering A cover term for a number of ➤ speech disorders characterized by disruptions in the flow of speech. The most common of these disfluencies are blocking

or stammering, repetition of particular sounds and prolongation of certain sounds, syllables or words.

style of life Alfred Adler's term for the unique, pervasive manner of a person. He thought of it as being composed of the totality of one's motives, traits, interests and values, and as manifesting itself in all behavior.

sub- Combining form meaning *under, beneath, inferior, in small quantity*.

subception The use of information extracted from a stimulus exposed too rapidly or too faintly to be consciously perceived and reported. Needless to say, the evidence for this process must be indirect, such as an emotional reaction or an effect on the subject's reaction times or memory for the stimulus, etc. Contrast with ➤ perceptual defense, which is concerned with changes in threshold.

subclinical Referring to the period prior to the appearance of the symptoms of a disease or disorder.

subconscious 1 n. In psychoanalytic theory, a level of mind through which material passes on the way toward full consciousness. Note that, in fact, most purists eschew the term as overly popularized and imprecise, preferring the term ➤ preconscious. 2 n. In more general writings, an information store containing memories that are momentarily outside of awareness but which can easily be brought into consciousness. 3 adj. Characterizing information that is not part of one's momentary awareness but which can, given the proper circumstances, be made conscious. 4 adj. Descriptive of information or stimuli that are at the margins of attention, events that one is only vaguely aware of. It should not, in any circumstance, be used as a synonym for ➤ unconscious.

subcortical Pertaining to the neural structures and associated functions of cerebral tissue lying below the cortex.

subculture The culture of a well-defined segment within a larger society. It is assumed to reflect the dominant cultural patterns of the larger society but to have, in addition, special, different values, norms and customs. The term tends to be used rather subjectively since it is virtually impossible to determine just how distinct these cultural patterns must be before the label is applicable. Some authors restrict it to large, identifiable ethnic or religious groups but others use it for rather non-cohesive segments of a society.

subcutaneous Lit., under the skin. Commonly used to refer to the receptors found in and below the skin or to preparations introduced just under the skin.

subfornical organ An area of the brain just below the fornix. Involved in the control of drinking, it appears to function as the site of action of *angiotensin* (➤ **renin**) in that injections of it stimulate drinking while injections of *saralasin* (which blocks angiotensin receptors) inhibit drinking.

subgoal An intermediary goal selected as an aim toward which one works when directed, ultimately, toward a final goal.

subiculum A part of the *hippocampal formation* whose outputs project to the anterior thalamic nuclei and the mammillary bodies.

subitize To apprehend directly the number of dots or other small objects in an unstructured stimulus display without counting them. The limit on this process is about seven or eight.

subject **1** n. An organism (human or otherwise) who serves as a participant (willingly or otherwise) in an experiment. Several other terms are occasionally used interchangeably here, for which there are usually historical and/or traditional reasons. For example, *observer* was (and occasionally still is) used for the subject in an introspection experiment or a psychophysical investigation; *respondent* is often used in questionnaire or survey studies; *interviewee* in interviews; *testee* in testing; *patient* in medicine; *patient* and/or *client* in psychiatry and clinical psychology. By and large, one can use *subject* for the participant in any study; the other terms tend to be restricted to specific formats. **2** n. The topic of an investigation, the thing to which one refers or about which one speaks or writes. **3** adj. To be liable to or have a propensity for a particular disease or disorder. **4** vb. To influence, dominate, control.

subjective **1.** Loosely, characteristic of or dependent on an individual, a ➤ **subject** (1). Embedded in this core meaning of the term are three sub-themes, each reflecting a different sense of the dependency: (a) *private* – that which is subjective is internal, personal, not available for public scrutiny. This is found in meanings 2, 3 and 4 below. (b) *Mental* or *cognitive* – the subjective is experiential or psychic as opposed to physical or somatic. See here meanings 5, 6, 7 and 8. (c) *Individual* – the subjective is singular, only one person is involved. See sense 9. The following, more specialized usages are commonly found in the social sciences and can be seen as reflecting one or more of these senses of the term. **2.** Not directly public, not knowable to anyone else. The sense here is that the fundamental nature of an event can only be experienced internally, privately, and that the experience can never be publicly known but only inferred; e.g., weight is *objective*, heaviness is *subjective*; the acoustic wave form of a spoken sentence is *objective*, the meaning of the sentence is *subjective*. **3.** Not directly verifiable by others, not determinable by the public in any straightforward manner. This meaning is very close to *intuitive* or *implicit*; see the discussion under ➤ **clinical** *****prediction** for a classic example of the contrast between the *objective* and the *subjective* in this sense. **4.** By extension of 2 and 3, unreliable, biased, contaminated by personal, emotional evaluations. This meaning is primarily found as an epithet used against one whose subjective assessments in sense 3 differ from one's own; there is no *logical* reason why the subjective ought to be less reliable or trustworthy than the objective. Consider the nature of aesthetic judgements to appreciate this point. **5.** Of judgements made without the use of instruments or other devices. **6.** Internal to the body or, more commonly, to the mind. Here subjective is nearly synonymous with *mental* or *psychic*. **7.** By extension of 6, sensed or experienced as internally localized; e.g., experiences such as fatigue in which there is no simply determinable external stimulus are regarded as subjective. **8.** By still further extension, of experiences based on illusory or hallucinatory phenomena; imaginary. **9.** Personal, pertaining to a single individual, a specific person.

subjective attribute ➤ **attribute** (1).

subjective colors ➤ **Fechner's colors**.

subjective contour ➤ **contour, subjective**.

subjective error ➤ **error, subjective**.

subjective expected utility (SEU) The personal value of an event or an outcome to an individual. The SEU of any choice between alternatives is given by the sum of the person's *subjective probability estimates* of each alternative times the *utility* of each. An assumption of many theories of choice behavior and gambling is that people behave as if they maximized SEU.

subjective frequency ➤ **subjective probability**.

subjective idealism ➤ **idealism** (1).

subjective organization The grouping and classifying of words, pictures or events according to perceived similarities and interrelationships. For example, the set of animals *weasel, rabbit, lion, canary, cat* could be subjectively organized into predator v. prey categories or pet v. non-pet, or Old World v. New World, etc. ➤➤ **clustering**.

subjective probability (or **frequency**) The intuitive sense of the probability or frequency of occurrence of some event or events. The term is used with respect to judgements made without recourse to counting or other mathematical calculation.

subjective psychology An occasional label for introspective or phenomenological approaches to psychology. Compare with ➤ **objective psychology**.

subjective scoring Generally, any assessment of performance made by subjective means. The term is typically restricted to such scoring of tests as made by persons expert in the task. Projective tests like the Rorschach are scored subjectively, as are essay examinations in school.

subjective sensation Generally, any sensory experience that is produced internally and not as a direct result of physical energies impinging on one's receptors. The classic example is *tinnitus* (ringing in the ears).

subjective test Any test marked or scored using ➤ **subjective scoring**, i.e. a test for which there are no standardized, objective assessment procedures.

subjective vertigo ➤ **vertigo**.

subjectivism In ethics, the point of view that there are no absolutes in designation of right and wrong, that morality is derived from personal preferences and personal judgement. There are variations on this theme from the naïve '*X* is right because I like to do it' through '*X* is right because most people like to do it' to the more sophisticated, '*X* is right because it has properties *a, b, c,* all of which I have a preference for.' Contrast with ➤ **objectivism**.

subjectivity 1. The quality of dealing with objects and events as phenomenological, subjective experiences. **2.** An approach to phenomena characterized by internal interpretation. Contrast with ➤ **objectivity**.

subject–object differentiation ➤ **primary integration**.

sublimation 1. In classical psychoanalysis, the process whereby primitive, libidinous impulses are redirected and refined into new, learned, 'noninstinctive' behaviors. Typically, the term is used with the understanding that the learned behaviors are socially acceptable whereas the deep, primitive impulses would not be. Classical theory regarded creative and artistic tendencies as manifestations of sublimation. **2.** Generally, and more loosely, any redirection of energy from the socially unacceptable to the acceptable.

subliminal Lit., below the ➤ **limen**, below the absolute ➤ **threshold** (1). ➤➤ **subliminal** *perception and **subception** for further discussion of usage.

subliminal learning Learning of which one is not conscious. The term is often used with the connotation that the lack of consciousness is temporary and that when learning has proceeded sufficiently, the individual will be become aware of it. This seems fundamentally wrong, since extensive learning often takes place totally removed from awareness, e.g., learning the rules that enable one to speak a language. A better term here is ➤ **implicit** *learning.

subliminal perception ➤ **perception, subliminal**.

subliminal stimulus Any below-threshold stimulus.

submission 1. Generally, yielding to others, their demands, orders and needs, conformity. Compare here with ➤ **dominance** (4) and ➤ **ascendance**. **2.** In ethology, a pattern of behavior exhibited by the loser of a conflict that displays to the victor a clear sign that the vanquished animal submits and will withdraw from the arena. The victor permits the loser to leave without further harm. The classic example is in the wolf where the loser of a battle exposes his neck, his most vulnerable spot, and is allowed to withdraw unmolested. Also called *appeasement behavior*. Compare here with ➤ **dominance** (3).

submissiveness A tendency to yield to others, to conform to their orders and their leadership. ant., *dominance* (4).

subnormal Less than normal, below the average. ➤ **normal**.

subordination 1. Accepting orders, allowing oneself to be dominated. **2.** Classifying a thing into a lower subcategory or subclass.

subshock therapy Therapy using mild, nonconvulsive shock.

subsidiation A relationship occuring when one engages in any act that brings one to a subgoal.

substance 1. The heart of a matter, the central most meaningful aspect of a situation or a communication. **2.** In metaphysics, the essential nature of a thing or event. **3.** A drug.

substance abuse A ➤ **substance-related disorder** characterized by a maladaptive pattern of substance use to the point where the individual experiences clinically significant cognitive and behavioral impairment or emotional distress that has an impact on work, school, or the home. The term is only used in cases where there is no evidence of ➤ **substance dependence**. The drug or substance involved is typically specified, e.g., ➤ **alcohol abuse**. ➤➤ **drug abuse**.

substance dependence A ➤ **substance-related disorder** characterized by a maladaptive pattern of substance use to the point where the individual experiences clinically significant impairment or distress as manifested by the development of ➤ **drug** *tolerance and ➤ **withdrawal symptoms**. The drug or substance involved is typically specified, e.g., alcohol dependence. ➤➤ **drug** *dependence.

substance-induced disorders An umbrella term for any ➤ **organic mental disorder** that is intimately related to excessive and/or chronic consumption of a substance that has direct effects on the central nervous system. Most commonly these disorders are caused by psychoactive drugs taken nonmedically to alter mood or behavior, e.g., alcohol, barbiturates, amphetamines, cannabis, opiates, cocaine, etc.

substance P A polypeptide found in certain neurons of the dorsal-root ganglia, basal ganglia, hypothalamus and cerebral cortex. It is believed to act as a neurotransmitter and has been implicated in the functioning of primary afferent fibers of the dorsal-root ganglion cells that are involved in mediating pain.

substance-related delirium ➤ **delirium, substance related**.

substance-related delusion ➤ **delusion, substance-related**.

substance-related disorders An umbrella category for those disorders associated with chronic and/or inappropriate use of or exposure to drugs or other substances. Included are ➤ **substance abuse**, ➤ **substance dependence**, and ➤ **substance-induced disorders**. This term is preferred to *substance-use disorders* and *psychoactive substance abuse disorders* because these disorders may, on occasion, be caused by agents that are not psychoactive and not abused (e.g. some environmental toxins).

substance-use disorders ➤ **substance-related disorders**.

substantia gelatinosa The portion of the tip of the dorsal horn of the spinal cord gray matter that functions to integrate afferent information.

substantia nigra In the brain, a darkly pigmented layer of cells in the pons that is connected with the neostriatum by the nigrostriatal pathways. Dysfunctions in the dopamine projections from the substantia nigra are implicated in ➤ **Parkinson's disease**.

substantive universals ➤ **linguistic * universals**.

substitute In older writings, a synonym for *conditioned*.

substitute valence ➤ **valence, substitute**.

substitution 1. Generally, the replacing of one thing for another. Thus, more specifically: 2. Replacing one goal with another when the original has been blocked or removed. 3. In reading, writing or speaking, replacing a word, syllable, letter or phoneme for another. 4. In psychoanalysis, a defense mechanism whereby socially acceptable goals replace unacceptable ones.

substitution hypothesis The hypothesis that ➤ **symptom substitution** will occur if psychoneurotic symptoms are superficially treated without dealing with the underlying causes of the disorder. It is posed frequently by psychodynamically oriented clinicians as a criticism of any of the various forms of ➤ **behavior therapy** and ➤ **cognitive-behavioral therapy**.

substitution test Any test in which the subject must systematically replace each symbol in an array with another symbol, e.g., the ➤ **code test**.

subtest Any smaller division or part of a larger test or test battery.

subthalamic nucleus A group of cells lying below the thalamus and linked anatomically and functionally to the ➤ **basal ganglia**. Also called *nucleus of Luys*.

subtraction method Any of several methods for measuring the time it takes for particular psychological processes to occur. The best-known procedure is that developed by the Dutch physiologist F. C. Donders, who studied three kinds of tasks: (a) ➤ **simple *reaction time**; (b) ➤ **discrimination *reaction time**; and (c) ➤ **choice *reaction time**. By subtracting the time it took his subjects to carry out task (b) from the time it took to carry out (c) he obtained an estimate of how long it took to make a choice; by subtracting (a) from (b) he obtained an estimate of discrimination time.

subtractive mixing ➤ **color mixing**.

subvocalization The 'speech' that sometimes goes on while reading. Depending on one's theoretical biases the term could be used to refer to: (a) a nearly audible whisper; (b) subtle movements of the lips, tongue and jaw; (c) minute patterns of muscular tension in the larynx detectable only with electromyographic recording devices; or (d) purely implicit, covert, mental processes unobservable by physical means. A variety of synonyms exists, e.g., *subvocal speech*, *implicit speech*, *silent speech*, *covert speech*.

subvocal speech ➤ subvocalization.

success, fear of A term coined by Matina Horner for a fear of accomplishing one's goals or of succeeding in society's eyes. She originally argued that women displayed this fear more than men, since striving for success places a woman in a conflict between a general need for achievement and social values that tell her that she should not achieve 'too much.' More recent research seems to indicate that men are just as likely to show this hypothesized fear. It should be pointed out, however, that it is far from clear how thoroughly one can divorce this fear from a *fear of failure*, particularly when each new 'success' in life carries with it greater potential for greater failure.

successive approximations, conditioning by ➤ shaping.

successive contrast ➤ contrast.

successive reproductions, method of A procedure for investigating long-term memory for material in which the subject is required to reproduce the material on several widely spaced reproduction trials.

succinylcholine A muscle relaxant used in ➤ electroconvulsive therapy to minimize complications.

succorance need H. Murray's term for the need to receive aid, assistance and guidance from others.

succubus An evil spirit which has sexual intercourse with its victim during sleep. The female form is *succuba*. ➤➤ incubus.

succus Any bodily fluid or secretion.

sucking 1. Generally, any oral suction. **2.** More specifically, a reflex-like response observed in newborn and nursing mammals in which the nipple is grasped and milk drawn from it into the mouth.

sucking pad The fatty mass in the cheeks; it is particularly prominent in infants, where it aids in sucking.

suckling 1. The sequence of reflex-like behaviors in mammals including rooting,

grasping the nipple, sucking on it and swallowing the milk. **2.** The act of presenting the breast and nipple to the nursing newborn. **3.** Any newborn or young mammal still in the nursing period.

sudden infant death syndrome (SIDS) The term is used to cover any sudden and inexplicable death of an infant or a very young child. There are a number of hypotheses about the cause of such deaths, with sleep ➤ apnea being the most frequently cited, but what precipitates this drop in natural control over breathing is not completely understood. Particular classes of neonates are at risk including premature and low birth-weight infants. Also called *crib death* or *cot death*, it is one of the leading causes of death in the first few months of life.

sudoriferous Sweat-producing.

sufficient statistics ➤ statistic, sufficient.

suffix effect In the study of memory, the phenomenon that an extraneous stimulus (the 'suffix') presented just after the full list of to-be-recalled materials has the effect of depressing the recall of the materials.

suggestibility The condition of being readily responsive to suggestions from others.

suggestion 1. The process of inducing someone to behave in a particular way, accept a particular opinion or believe in something, by indirect methods. The term is only used when no force, argument, command or coercion is used to bring about the desired changes. **2.** The actual verbal or pictorial communication used in this process.

suicide 1. A person who intentionally kills himself or herself. **2.** The act of taking one's life. Émile Durkheim, the first to study suicide systematically, distinguished three different types, depending on what motivates the act of self-destruction: *altruistic*, *anomic* and *egoistic*; definitions of each are found below.

suicide, altruistic Durkheim's term for

suicide based on sacrificing oneself for the good of others. The soldier who hurls himself upon a grenade to save others, and the ritual suicide such as hara-kiri which is designed to save one's family from shame, are classic examples.

suicide, anomic Suicide that results, in Durkheim's analysis, from the sense that life no longer has meaning, from a sense of anomie, loneliness, isolation and loss of contact with the norms and values of society. Also called *normless suicide*.

suicide clusters ➤ **cluster suicides**.

suicide, egoistic In Durkheim's classification system, suicide resulting from a sense of deep personal failure, a feeling that one is personally responsible for not living up to societal and personal expectations.

sui generis Latin for *of its own particular kind*; a unique instance or example.

sulcus Generally, a shallow groove or furrow, especially on the surface of the brain. Sulci separate the elevated convolutions, the *gyri*. Occasionally used synonymously with ➤ **fissure**, but see that term for a distinction.

summation **1.** In statistics, the act of cumulating or totaling a series of numbers. See here ➤ Σ (under ➤ **sigma**). **2.** Generally, cumulative action, combination of effects. This sense of the term is typically found in combined phrases in which the specific properties of the summation are noted, e.g., ➤ **spatial *summation**, ➤ **temporal *summation**.

summation curve ➤ **ogive**.

summation, sensory Generally, an increase in experienced intensity or magnitude of sensory input as produced by either of two neurological processes: ➤ **spatial *summation** or ➤ **temporal *summation**.

summation, spatial The funneling of neurological impulses from two or more closely spaced loci of stimulation such that their net effect is greater than that of any of them taken separately.

summation, temporal The accumulating

neurological effect of stimulation occurring over time. For example, a subthreshold stimulus such as a very dim light will, because of the action of temporal summation, become visible if it is flashed very rapidly or if it is left on continuously for a period of time.

summation tone ➤ **combination tone**.

super- Combining form meaning *beyond*, *above*, *superior*.

superego In the Freudian tripartite model of the psyche, the hypothetical entity associated with ethical and moral conduct and conceptualized as responsible for self-imposed standards of behavior. The superego is frequently characterized as an internalized code or, more popularly, as a kind of *conscience*, punishing transgressions with feelings of guilt. In the classical psychoanalytic literature, the superego is assumed to develop in response to the punishments and rewards of significant persons (usually the parents), which results in the child becoming inculcated with the moral code of the community. Whereas the ➤ **id** is conceptualized as concerned with the pleasurable and the ➤ **ego** with the actual, the superego is viewed as being concerned with the ideal.

superego lacuna Lit., a gap in the superego, an area of conduct where one's internalized moral code fails to function.

superficial **1.** On or confined to the surface, particularly the surface of the body (the skin) or an organ, e.g., a superficial cut. **2.** Shallow, cursory, not thorough, dealing only with the trivial. **3.** Secondary or tangential. Here the reference is usually to personality characteristics that are regarded as rather unimportant in a person's overall make up.

superficial reflex A reflexive muscular contraction to a light gentle stimulus such as stroking the skin with a feather or a piece of cotton.

superior **1.** Above, higher, better. **2.** In charge of or in command of. **3.** In anatomical descriptions, particularly of brain structures, above (or dorsal) to an inferior (or ventral) structure.

superior colliculus ➤ **colliculus**.

superior intelligence An arbitrary designation usually taken to apply to those who score in the top 15% on an intelligence test.

superiority complex The conviction that one is better than or superior to others. Although there are (indeed, must be) persons who are in fact superior in various ways and who recognize their talents, the term is typically not used for them. Rather, it is reserved for those who have an exaggerated and unrealistic sense of themselves and is generally interpreted as a defense against deeper feelings of inferiority. Also known as *superiority feelings*. See and compare with ➤ **inferiority feelings** and ➤ **inferiority complex** and note that the problems of interpretation produced by the interchanging of the terms *feelings* and *complex* discussed there hold here as well.

superiority feelings ➤ **superiority complex**.

superior olivary nucleus ➤ **olivary nucleus, superior**.

superior temporal gyrus A *gyrus* on the upper part of the temporal lobe. The posterior portion is often called ➤ **Wernicke's area** and lesions in the dominant hemisphere have been implicated in various forms of aphasia.

supernatural Beyond or outside of the natural order. The term is typically used to refer to 'events' or 'phenomena' that are not explicable given the existing characterizations of nature. Occult phenomena and extrasensory perception are examples. ➤ **parapsychology** for further discussion.

supernormal Above or exceeding the normal. Distinguish from ➤ **supernatural**.

superordinate goals Goals that can only be achieved by cooperation among many individuals. Peace is a good example.

superordination Classifying in a higher or superior rank or category. The connota-

tion is that when a person is so categorized relative to others, the ranking carries with it the right to order or direct the actions of others of lower classifications. Compare with ➤ **subordination**.

supersonic 1. Characteristic of sound waves with a frequency beyond the normal range of the human ear, those above approximately 20,000 Hz. **2.** Pertaining to speeds in excess of that of sound, i.e. about 741 m.p.h. (1,192 k.p.h.) at sea level with air temperature of 32° F (0° C).

superstition Any notion or belief held in the absence of what one not holding that notion or belief would consider to be adequate evidence to substantiate or support it sufficiently to maintain such belief. Many superstitions have their roots in one or other theological system or religious tradition (indeed, some authors restrict the word to such cases), others exist uncritically as unexamined beliefs. Beliefs about the left side of the body (see here ➤ **sinister**) are examples of the former, the common practice of carrying 'good luck' charms of the latter. Some authorities treat superstitions as descendants of primitive attempts to understand the inexplicable, to make sense out of a complex and confusing world; others, notably behaviorists, see them as natural consequences of a failure to recognize the existence (or lack of existence) of cause-and-effect relationships between one's own behavior and subsequent occurrences in the world about us. For a case of this latter point of view, ➤ **superstitious behavior**.

superstitious behavior Behavior that results from and is maintained by adventious reinforcements which are, in reality, not specifically coordinated with it. The easiest way to demonstrate such behavior is to put an organism like a pigeon in a Skinner box and program the feeding mechanism to deliver reinforcements on a variable schedule independently of the behavior of the animal. When the first reinforcement occurs, the pigeon will be doing something, perhaps raising one of its wings. This wing-raising behavior is thus reinforced and will increase in frequency of occurrence and hence be more likely to be occurring when the next reinforcement arrives, which, of course, will even further strengthen the response. Over time the pigeon will display a highly developed superstitious wing-raising response, a response that has, in reality, no direct relationship to reinforcement received. The point of the demonstration is to show that the notion of a contingency between response and reinforcement is in the mind of the beholder and that a true assessment of cause and effect is not necessary for highly developed behavior. The argument is also made, not entirely convincingly, that such a demonstration reveals the ontogeny of sophisticated human superstitions; e.g., that rain dances don't 'cause' rain but are merely reinforced adventitiously on an irregular basis.

supervalent thought ➤ thought, supervalent.

supination 1. Lying flat on one's back, supine. 2. Turning one's arm (or leg) so that the palm (or sole) is upward. Opposite of ➤ pronation.

supplementary motor area ➤ motor area(s).

support 1. n. Generally, the furnishing of that which is needed or lacking, providing for well-being or improvement. In this broad sense, theories receive support from corroborative evidence, political positions receive support from large numbers of adherents, etc. 2. n. More specifically, the furnishing of comfort, recognition, approval, encouragement, etc. to another person. This is the meaning usually intended in the term ➤ supportive therapy. vb., *support*.

supportive therapy Very generally, any form of therapy or any therapeutic procedure in which direct help is provided. Such support may be largely psychological in nature, taking the form of ego-bolstering, compliments, encouragement, positive evaluations and the like, or it may be more direct and objective, such as in helping to plan specific courses of action, giving unambiguous advice with problems, working on behavior-modification programs, etc. Supportive therapy avoids probing the individual client's deeper conflicts and works with the more cognitive and behavioral aspects.

supposition A rough synonym for ➤ postulate.

suppression 1. In physiology, the complete cessation of some natural organic process; e.g., *amenorrhea* is often called 'suppression of the menses' if the woman has had one or more normal periods. 2. Broadly, conscious, voluntary elimination of some behavior. This sense can be found with respect to oneself (suppression of a bad habit) or to others (suppression of ideas, of a revolt, of a book). 3. In psychoanalysis, conscious exclusion of impulses, thoughts and desires that are felt to be unacceptable to the individual. The classic theory distinguishes suppression from ➤ repression in that the former is a conscious process and the latter, unconscious. Despite some nagging similarities in connotation, suppression should also be distinguished from both ➤ extinction and ➤ inhibition.

suppression, monocular Suppression of the information from one eye even though, physiologically, the mechanism functions properly. The condition typically occurs when there is a failure of normal binocular fusion and only the input from one eye is used.

suppressor variable A variable (or, more accurately, a test) which functions to improve the overall predictive validity of a battery of tests by suppressing irrelevant variance in another test. For example, a test battery for selecting industrial mechanics may include three tests: (a) a general background factors evaluation: (b) a mechanical-insight test: and (c) an academic-type test of mechanical principles. Now, suppose that the criterion of job success correlated zero with (c) but very highly with (b). By treating (c) as a suppressor variable and assigning it 'negative' weight, the overall validity of the test battery will be improved since those persons who might score highly on (b) purely through the application of academic principles, but lack the basic mechanical know-how, will be screened out.

supra- Combining form meaning *above, over, superior, in large quantities*.

suprachiasmatic nucleus A tightly packed nucleus of cells in the hypothalamus that appears to play a role in the monitoring of the light–dark cycle and is thought by many to be the primary biological clock – at least in the species that have been carefully studied such as the rat.

supraliminal Above ➤ **threshold**.

supraordinate stimulus In operant conditioning, a stimulus that serves to indicate to an organism which aspects of a complex environment are the relevant ones for a particular task.

suprarenal ➤ **adrenal**.

suprasegmental In linguistics, any of several phonemic elements which are conceptualized as superimposed on the consonant and vowel phonemes. Typically included here are ➤ **stress** (3), ➤ **juncture** and ➤ **pitch** (2). Note that these are usually treated as distinct from ➤ **prosodic features**, although some writers will use them interchangeably.

surdity Deafness.

surface color ➤ **color, surface**.

surface dyslexia ➤ **dyslexia, surface**.

surface pain ➤ **cutaneous *pain**.

surface structure In linguistics, the sequence of elements (phonemes, syllables, words, phrases, sentences) that comprise the actual message as written or spoken. Compare with ➤ **deep structure**.

surface trait ➤ **trait, surface**.

surgency A hypothesized personality trait characterized by ebullience, sociability, trustworthiness and the like.

surrogate 1. Generally, a person who takes on the role and function of another. A woman who carries to term the *in vitro* fertilized ovum of another woman is referred to as a *surrogate mother*. **2.** More specifically, a person who takes on the parental role and functions for another person's child. The classic example here is the teacher who becomes a student's parent surrogate. As used here, the connotation is that the child is unaware of the relationship. **3.** Loosely, any role substitute. Harry Harlow referred to the wire and/or cloth dolls he used in his studies of maternal attachment in monkeys as *surrogate mothers*.

surround 1. Broadly, the immediate environment within which one functions. It may include the internal and mental as well as the external and physical. **2.** In perception, the stimulus that literally surrounds another stimulus; the latter is called the ➤ **target**.

survey 1 n. A general evaluation, an inspection. **2** n. An examination or inspection carried out with specific aims in mind, a search for particular kinds of information. This sense is carried in a number of specific kinds of research designs in which questionnaires, inventories or interviews may be employed to gather information about attitudes, opinions or preferences in a society or some segment of it.

survey, normative A survey designed to determine the norms of some variable or test or the performance levels of some behavior in a large population. ➤ **normative**.

survey research Very broadly, the use of surveys typically carried out using questionnaires, polls or other sampling techniques to assess public opinion.

survey tests Tests constructed to yield general information about the distribution of levels of performance on some factor(s) in a group or population.

survival analysis An analysis of the history of specific cases or instances in terms of how long each persists in a particular state (i.e., how long they survive). Such analyses are common in medicine (how long illnesses last), in demography (life expectancies), in organizational psychology (the survival rate of small businesses), etc.

survival value The degree to which a particular biological structure or pattern of behavior contributes to the likelihood of survival. The term is used with respect to the survival of an individual organism and to the survival of a whole species.

survivor guilt A deep sense of guilt often experienced by those who have survived some catastrophe which took the lives of many others. It was first noted and subsequently studied in those who survived the Holocaust in the Second World War and has subsequently been seen in other circumstances including wars, famines, earthquakes, fires, etc. Part of the sense of guilt experienced by those who survived derives from a feeling that they somehow did not do enough to save others who perished; part of it comes from feelings of being unworthy relative to those who died.

survivor syndrome A term introduced by Lifton for a pattern of reactions frequently observed in those who have survived some terrible ordeal such as an earthquake, a flood or a war. Aspects of the syndrome include chronic anxiety, recurring dreams of the event, a general numbness, withdrawal from and loss of interest in the pleasures of life and, often, ➤ **survivor guilt**.

suspicion 1. A general attitude of doubt, a skeptical orientation, particularly with respect to the sincerity of other persons. 2. ➤ **suspiciousness**.

suspiciousness A hypothesized personality trait characterized by a general tendency to be untrustful and doubting and to withhold emotional commitment out of a fear of being hurt.

sustentacular cell Generally, a supporting cell. There are several kinds of cells that serve this kind of function, such as those found in the acoustic macula, the organ of Corti and the testes.

susto A ➤ **culture-specific syndrome** found in Latino cultures. The term means *soul loss* and the disorder is assumed to result from the loss of the soul owing to a frightening experience. Symptoms include general malaise, sadness, disturbed sleep, feelings of low esteem. It resembles a ➤ **major *depressive episode**.

Sutton's law A principle of diagnosis named after the notorious bank robber Willie Sutton who, when asked why he robbed banks, quipped, 'Because that's where the money is.' The principle, when applied to clinical diagnosis, states that one should look for a disorder where or in whom it is most likely to be found. It captures the generalization that all diseases and disorders have groups of predisposing factors.

sweet One of the four basic qualities of ➤ **taste**; see that entry for more detail.

Sydenham's chorea A childhood disease usually appearing between the ages of 5 and 15 and typically associated with rheumatic fever. Symptoms are spastic involuntary movements of muscles of limbs and trunk and occasional impairment of cognitive functions such as speech and memory. Recovery is usually complete in two or three months, but relapses may occur.

syl- ➤ **syn-**.

syllabary A form of writing in which the basic signs in the system correspond to the primary syllables in the spoken language. Modern Japanese is written (partly) using a syllabary. ➤ **orthography** for further discussion.

syllable A segment of speech consisting of a vowel or a continuant uttered alone or with one or more consonants and produced as part of a single pulse of air. Syllables are identified by a concentration of acoustic energy in the speech stream.

syllogism In logic, a valid deductive argument comprising three propositions, two serving as premises and the third as the conclusion. In the classic case, where there are only three terms, the syllogism is properly called a *categorical syllogism*; e.g., all dictionaries are boring, this book is a dictionary, therefore this book is boring. When at least one of the premises is a hypothetical proposition then one has a *hypothetical syllogism*; e.g., if poets ever lie to us we are in trouble, poets have been known to lie, therefore we are in trouble. When at least one proposition is a disjunction then one has a *disjunctive syllogism*; e.g., the mayor is either a crook or a fool, the mayor is honest, therefore the mayor is a fool. ➤ **valid**.

Sylvian fissure ➤ **lateral fissure**.

sym- ➤ **syn-**.

symbiosis 1. From the Greek, meaning *living together*, a relationship between members of different species who live together in a mutually beneficial manner. In the true symbiotic relationship, neither of the two could survive without the other; for example, the fig tree and the fig wasp where the wasp is dependent on the tree as a food source and the tree upon the wasp as its medium for fertilization. 2. Somewhat more loosely, any relationship between individuals where interdependencies exist. Sadomasochistic relationships are sometimes described as symbiotic, as are extremely interdependent parent–child relationships. When the term is used in this manner the connotation is that the relationship is pathological; this connotation is entirely absent in sense 1. Note also that some authors will use symbiosis to cover relationships which have nonmutual benefits, where one profits at the expense of the other. This practice is not recommended; such patterns of interaction are best described as *parasitic* and not symbiotic.

symbiotic psychosis An obsolescent term now largely replaced by ➤ **pervasive *developmental disorder**. The term was ill-advised on two counts: this category of childhood disorders bears little relationship to standard adult psychoses and the symbiotic relationship between parent and child hypothesized to play a causal role

has not been shown to be the primary factor in its etiology.

symbiotic stage ➤ **separation-individuation**.

symbol 1. Most generally, anything that represents, signifies or indicates something else. In the philosopher Charles Peirce's phrase, 'A symbol is a sign which is constituted a sign merely or mainly by the fact that it is used and understood as such.' In all of the following, more restrictive uses of the term this notion of symbol as arbitrary convention can be seen. 2. In linguistics, any language form (usually the *word* is the form under consideration) which can be used to represent a thing, event, person, etc. The word 'apple' is a symbol for the real apple. 3. In mathematics and (symbolic) logic, a mark or a ➤ **sign** (especially in sense 5 of that term) which is used to represent an operation; e.g., Σ is the symbol for summation. Note the interesting relationship between this meaning and 2 above. Whereas both are definitely referencing things that are *symbolic*, 2 denotes the idea of expression of things in words and 3 denotes the converting of words into 'symbols,' particularly those of mathematics and logic. 4. An action, event, device or utterance (particularly a verbal slogan) that is intended to signify ideas or principles beyond that specific action, event, device or utterance. Compare with the meaning of ➤ **sign** (1), which is used when the significance is limited to the thing itself. For example, fire as a *sign* of something burning as compared with fire as a *symbol* for life. 5. In Piaget's approach, an internal, private, endogenous representation. Here the term is clearly distinguished from ➤ **sign** (especially senses 1 and 2 of that term) in that Piagetians regard *signs* as arbitrary, publicly shared representations while *symbols* are conceptualized as internally produced by the individual.

In psychoanalytic theory several variations on the term are found. All depend on the notion that the symbol is an unconscious representation which disguises or distorts the thing represented such that what is perceived consciously is a misrepresentation of the 'real' meaning. In this fashion: **6.** A conscious image or idea that represents some deeper, repressed desire or impulse. This meaning is the one generally intended in the literature on dream symbols. **7.** An action or behavior that is representative of some unconscious wish or impulse. The classic example here is the so-called 'Freudian slip' (➤ **parapraxis**). **8.** Any object which, because of some measure of perceived similarity with one's unconscious needs, represents those needs and is taken as a symbol of one's deep conflicts. For example, a tower is interpreted as a phallic symbol. **9.** Any emotional symptom such as nervousness, or anxiety, which may be interpreted as representing a deeply repressed conflict.

symbol-digit test ➤ code test.

symbolic process Generally, any mental process based on the use of symbols, symbolization or symbolic representation. The term is found frequently in the writings of both cognitive psychologists and those with a psychoanalytic orientation. The former use it to refer to processes such as concept-formation, problem-solving, thinking, language, creativity and the like; the latter typically use it to denote psychodynamic operations whereby repressed needs and conflicts are dealt with in disguised forms. ➤ **symbol** for more detail on usage.

symbolic representation ➤ representation.

symbol, individual In psychoanalytic theory, a symbol whose repressed referent is specific to a particular individual and not presumed to represent any deep or universal symbolization. Compare with ➤ **universal *symbol**.

symbolism **1.** Generally, the act or the practice of using symbols. As in the case of the root term ➤ **symbol**, the manner in which the term is used will vary considerably, although this basic meaning will always be present. **2.** In essentially all forms of complex communication (e.g., language, art, music), the use of some

arbitrary 'thing' to represent or stand for some other thing. In the simplest case the word 'chair,' be it spoken or written, is symbolic of some prototypical, abstract *chair*. In more complex circumstances, the symbolism may be less direct. Metaphor and simile in language are based on such symbolisms; e.g., 'He has a mind like a sieve.' In esthetics, symbolism is the very heart of the communication in that emotion or affect is symbolically conveyed in artistic forms of painting, music, dance, etc. **3.** Within psychoanalytic theory, the unconscious process whereby repressed desires or wishes are transformed or disguised so as to be dealt with on a conscious level without psychic disturbance. Several theorists, notably Jung, have argued that this process forms the very foundations for all art, myth and religion. Note that meaning 3 here represents a *process* while 1 and 2 are *practices*. Some of the confusion produced by these different usages can be avoided by using, as many do, the term *symbolization* for 3, thereby freeing symbolism for the others.

symbolization ➤ symbolism (3).

symbol-substitution test ➤ code test.

symbol, universal In psychoanalytic theory, a symbol that is assumed to represent the same referent universally. The argument is made that such symbols reflect basic, primordial components of the human psyche. ➤ **universal** for a discussion of this issue from a general philosophical point of view. Compare with ➤ **individual *symbol**.

symmetric (or **symmetrical**) Having the property of ➤ **symmetry**.

symmetry **1.** The property of correspondence of the size, form, shape and overall arrangement of parts on both sides of some dividing line or plane or point. **2.** In mathematics, the property of a relation such that if it is valid for $x = y$ then it is also valid for $y = x$. **3.** By extension of 2, any general correspondence between polar terms such that their relationship is reversible, e.g., good–bad, black–white. **4.** Metaphorically, the property of being well pro-portioned, balanced. ants., *asymmetry*, ➤ **skewness** (used in statistics).

symmetry, bilateral Symmetry around a midline such that the left and right halves are mirror images of each other. The human body displays (roughly) such symmetry.

symmetry, radial Symmetry around a central point or axis such that all parts radiate from it equally. A wheel displays such symmetry.

sympathectomy A general term for any surgical excision of a portion of the sympathetic division of the autonomic nervous system.

sympathetic apraxia ➤ **apraxia, sympathetic**.

sympathetic chain The connected sequence of spinal sympathetic ganglia. ➤ **autonomic nervous system**.

sympathetic ganglion Generally, any of the ganglia of the sympathetic division of the ➤ **autonomic nervous system**.

sympathetic induction The process whereby the expression of affect by one person stimulates a corresponding emotion in another. ➤ **sympathy**.

sympathetic nervous system ➤ **autonomic nervous system**.

sympathetic vibration ➤ **resonance**.

sympathomimetic drug Any drug that imitates the effects of stimulation of the sympathetic nervous system.

sympathy 1. Lit., from the Greek roots (➤ **syn-** and ➤ **patho-**), feeling with. Hence, a set of circumstances in which one shares in the feelings of another. Typically, owing to the original Greek usage, the term is only used of painful or unpleasant emotions. **2.** A sense of compassion or understanding which allows one to interpret or justify the actions and/or feelings of another. In meaning 1 the clear connotation is that of a feeling *with* another, in 2 it is closer to a feeling *for*. The term is thus used in ways that can lead to real confusion. The difficulty derives from the tendency of English-speakers to use it in sense 1 and the French (where the word is a cognate) to use it in sense 2. In the technical psychological literature, 1 is usually what is intended; in popular writing or in literary criticism, 2 is more common. For further discussion on the general topic of shared affect, ➤ **empathy**.

symptom 1. From the Greek word for *occurrence*, any event or change in state in a system that tends to occur with another event or change of state and hence can be taken as an indicator or predictor of it. **2.** In medicine and clinical psychology, any such occurrence which can be used as an indicator of the existence of or changes in a pathological condition.

symptomatic act In psychoanalysis, any ordinary act that, under particular circumstances, can be interpreted as resulting from some unconscious process; e.g., ➤ **parapraxis**.

symptom bearer ➤ **symptom wearer**.

symptom cluster ➤ **syndrome** (2).

symptom formation In psychoanalysis, one of the complex processes through which neurotic symptoms are assumed to develop. The classic analysis is as follows: when substitute objects are found for unacceptable id impulses, occasionally the new object itself also turns out to be unacceptable but, because it permits some psychic satisfaction, the behavior associated with it persists and is manifested as a neurotic symptom.

symptom neurosis A loose term used descriptively for a neurosis that does not reflect any particular syndrome but in which clearly 'neurotic' patterns of behavior are present. The term *neurotic disorder* is used roughly equivalently – but see the extended discussion under ➤ **neurosis** for explication of meaning and usage.

symptom substitution (hypothesis) The hypothesis that if only the superficial behavioral manifestations of a neurosis are treated in psychotherapy the unresolved underlying conflict will 'erupt' elsewhere and new (and potentially more serious) symptoms will emerge. The hypothesis derives from the assumption that psychological disturbances are analogous to medical disturbances (see here ➤ **medical model**) and that they can only be treated by removal of the root cause of the disorder. The hypothesis is often invoked critically by classically trained psychotherapists as a warning against the dangers of a pure ➤ **behavior therapy**, which deals only with maladaptive behavior and does not concern itself with underlying psychic conflicts.

symptom-symbol hypothesis The hypothesis that a particular symptom may be viewed as a symbol of a particular underlying psychological conflict. The hypothesis is common among the psychoanalytically oriented but is regarded as highly questionable by clinicians of other persuasions.

symptom wearer (or **bearer**) An individual in a complexly structured group (like a family) who manifests the symptoms of a mental disorder while the other group members do not. A careful analysis sometimes shows that there is a complex pattern of interactive behavior in the group that is seriously maladaptive but that the psychic burden of it tends to fall mostly on one person.

syn- From the Greek, a combining form meaning *with, along with, together with, joined together.* vars., *syl-, sym-, sys-*.

synapse From the Greek for *juncture* or *point of contact*, the junction between the terminal button of the axon of one neuron and a part of the somatic or dendritic membrane of another neuron. The term itself was introduced at the turn of the century by the great English physiologist, Sir Charles Sherrington. A number of different types of synapses have been identified. They are usually denoted either by their anatomical characteristics (e.g., *axodendritic*) or by the neurotransmitter involved (e.g., *cholinergic*). They can be found in this volume under the qualifying term. adj., *synaptic*.

synaptic button ➤ **terminal button**.

synaptic cleft The small (roughly 20–30 nm) space between the terminal button of the presynaptic neuron and the membrane of the postsynaptic neuron across which the neurotransmitters flow.

synaptic transmission A general term used for the process of transmission of information from one (presynaptic) neuron to another (postsynaptic) neuron. For more details, ➤ **neurotransmitter, postsynaptic potential** and **synapse**.

synaptic vesicles Small capsule-like packages in the terminal buttons of presynaptic neurons that contain neurotransmitters.

syncope (*sin-co-pee*) A temporary loss of consciousness following a drop in blood flow to the brain, a fainting, a swoon.

syncretism **1.** Generally, a bringing together of various disparate aspects in a more or less coordinated manner so as to produce a more unified single system. As the term is used, the connotation is that the resulting system may lack coherence and contain contradictions and/or inconsistencies. **2.** In Piaget's developmental theory, a type of cognitive processing in which events are assimilated into global and largely unstructured schemas; that is, a rather nebulous classification system. Contrast this meaning with the Piagetian usage of ➤ **juxtaposition** (2). **3.** In sociological analyses, the union of disparate elements from different social systems into a new structure. **4.** In linguistics, the fusion of forms from different languages into a new form. **5.** In religion, the reconciliation (or attempts thereat) of opposing principles or practices into a novel, coherent system.

syndrome **1.** Generally, a number of characteristics, features, events or behaviors that seem to go with each other or are believed to be coordinated or interrelated in some way. **2.** More specifically, in medicine and clinical psychology, a cluster of symptoms that occur together and can be taken as indicative of a particular disease or other abnormality. Individual syndromes are listed in this volume under the qualifying term.

synergic ➤ **synergistic**.

synergistic 1. Generally, working together, cooperative. **2.** In physiology, characteristic of organs, muscles or the various elements of a large, coordinated system all of which function together in combination toward some unified aim. Synergistic muscles function together to effect a particular movement, synergistic drugs combine effects cooperatively, and so forth. Contrast with ➤ **antagonistic**. var., *synergic*.

synergistic drugs Any two drugs whose conjoint effects are greater than the sum of the effects of the two taken separately.

synesthesia The condition in which a sensory experience normally associated with one modality occurs when another modality is stimulated. To a certain extent such cross-modality experiences are perfectly normal; e.g., low-pitched tones give a sensation of softness or fullness while high-pitched tones feel brittle and sharp, the color blue feels cold while red feels warm. However, the term is usually restricted to the unusual cases in which regular and vivid cross-modality experiences occur, such as when particular sounds reliably produce particular color sensations. E.g., ➤ **chromesthesia**. var., *synaesthesia*.

synkinesis 1. Generally, an involuntary movement of one bodily part that occurs simultaneously with a voluntary movement of another part. **2.** Specifically, an involuntary movement in healthy muscle that accompanies an attempt to move a paralyzed muscle on the opposite side of the body.

synonym A word that has the same or very similar meaning as another word. Two words are said to be synonymous if one may be replaced by another in a sentence without modifying the meaning of the whole sentence. Although to some extent many such synonymous relationships exist between words and in this volume many pairs of technical terms

have been so labeled, it should be pointed out here that there are many compelling arguments suggesting that no two words or phrases can ever be truly regarded as synonyms in the sense that no semantic violence whatsoever is done by replacing one with the other.

syntactic aphasia ➤ **aphasia, syntactic**.

syntactic component In some contemporary linguistic theories, that aspect of a grammar that contains the formal rules and procedures for producing sequences of elements (usually morphemes or words). Contrast with ➤ **semantic component** (2).

syntagmatic association ➤ **paradigmatic * association**.

syntax That aspect of grammar that deals with the rules for combining morphemes and words into sentences. adj., *syntactic*. ➤➤ **grammar** and **semantic** and related terms.

syntaxis H. S. Sullivan's term for a mode of thinking and communicating in which the concepts used are objective and publicly observable. Syntaxic thinking is consensual, and thus open for inspection and validation, as opposed to parataxic, which is private and often distorted. See here ➤ **parataxis** (2) and ➤ **parataxic distortion**.

synthesis 1. The process of combining elements such that the resulting fusion, integration or organization results in a unified whole. **2.** The whole thus formed. Note that the connotation here is that the emergent whole has properties or qualities that are the result of the synthesis and not necessarily derivable from an analysis of the several elements. See here ➤ **creative synthesis**. adj., *synthetic*, which can also carry the additional connotation of artificiality. Contrast with ➤ **analysis**.

synthetic language 1. In linguistics, any language that tends to express grammatical relationships by the use of inflections. In synthetic languages, unlike ➤ **analytic languages**, word-order rules are relatively free. **2.** Any artificial language constructed for empirical investigation. Compare with ➤ **natural *language**.

synthetic speech Any speech produced by mechanical devices. Modern ➤ **speech synthesizers** produce remarkably human-sounding outputs.

synthetic trainer Any training device that simulates real-world conditions for the purpose of aiding the learning of a particular skill, a ➤ **simulator**.

synthetic validity ➤ **validity, synthetic**.

syntonia A general syndrome characterized by displays of a high degree of reactiveness to the surrounding environment. Some regard a syntonic as a well-adjusted person in harmony with the world, others hold onto the possibility that such reactiveness may be indicative of a proneness to bipolar disorder. With this kind of connotative conflict, this is a good term to avoid.

syphilis An infectious, chronic, venereal disease. It is caused by the spirochete *Treponema pallidum*, which enters the system through any break in the skin or a mucous membrane, most commonly during sexual intercourse. The disease has three stages. The primary stage is characterized by the tell-tale chancre that appears roughly two to four weeks after infection and some lymph-node enlargement. The secondary stage occurs about six weeks later and may be manifested in a number of symptoms including a rash, skin lesions, headaches, fever and lymph-node enlargement. Some, all or none of these may emerge in a given case. The tertiary stage occurs later, often years later, and is the dangerous stage. The heart, blood vessels and the entire central nervous system are frequently involved. Neural damage may be severe enough for a variety of psychotic behaviors to occur; see here ➤ **paresis**. The symptoms of syphilis in the secondary and tertiary stages are so varied that it has become known medically as 'the great imitator,' since without the proper tests it can easily be mistaken for any of a number of other diseases.

systaltic Alternately contracting and dilating; pulsating.

system 1. From the Greek, meaning *organized whole*. This sense of the term is carried along in all of the many specialized contexts in which it is found. Actually, because of the breadth and diversity of usage, the term is rarely found in isolation but is typically modified or qualified by other (one or more) terms or phrases, e.g., circulatory system, dynamic system, open system, nervous system, etc. **2.** A more or less well structured set of ideas, assumptions, concepts and interpretative tendencies which serves to structure the data of an area of science, e.g., the Copernican system in astronomy or any of the several schools of psychology such as behaviorism, structuralism, etc. **3.** Somewhat more restrictively, a particular arrangement of interconnected things (objects, machines, stimuli, etc.); a ➤ **configuration**.

system analysis ➤ **systems analysis**.

systematic 1. Characterized by reflecting the structure and organizational integrity of a ➤ **system** (1). **2.** Identified with a particular theoretical ➤ **system** (2). **3.** By extension, orderly, predictable, regular. Distinguish from ➤ **systemic**.

systematic desensitization Joseph Wolpe's term for the form of behavior therapy described under ➤ **desensitization procedure**.

systematic distortion Any regular change in the manner in which memories for preceding events or stimuli are modified. The term is quite general and is used by Gestalt psychologists for the filling in of gaps in incomplete pictures when they are recalled some time after presentation, by psychodynamically oriented theorists for the altering of memory for past events by defensive or repressive operations and by cognitive theorists for the constructive and interpretative processes that change the nature of material held in long-term memory.

systematic error ➤ **constant *error**.

systematic sampling ➤ **sampling, systematic**.

systematized delusion ➤ **delusion, systematized**.

systemic 1. Generally, pertaining to a ➤ **system** (1). **2.** More specifically, pertaining to the whole body rather than to any isolated part or organ. Distinguish from ➤ **systematic**.

systems analysis Generally and collectively, the processes and operations involved in the designing, implementing and coordinating of the various components of any complex system. The use of systematic analytical procedures derived from industrial/organizational psychology and assisted by the techniques of computer science to understand the workings of complex organizations, to identify problems and sources of error and to make recommendations for more efficient and effective structures.

systole The contracting phase of the heart cycle.

T

T 1. Temperature. 2. Time.

ₛTᵣ In Hull's notational system, *reaction time*. Elsewhere *RT* is used.

t 1. A symbol used for denoting the ratio between a statistic and the measure of its standard error. ➤ *t* **test** and ➤ *t* ***distribution**. 2. Abbrev. for *time*.

tabes 1. Generally, any progressive degeneration found in chronic disease. 2. More specifically, degeneration of the posterior columns of the spinal cord. syn., *tabes dorsalis* (for 2).

table A collection of scores or other data arranged in tabular form.

taboo 1. Any banned or prohibited act, object or behavior. 2. The act of prohibition. The term comes from the Polynesian *tabu* meaning *sacred, inviolable* and was originally associated with objects set aside for religious practices and customs and forbidden for general use. Contemporary image is much broader. adj., *taboo, tabooed*.

tabula rasa Latin meaning *blank tablet*. The term refers to the philosophical view that humans came into this world unencumbered (and unassisted) by particular innate ideas. Espoused strongly by the early British empiricists, it formed the basis of the theory that learning and experience are the critical factors in the human condition; the environment writes its message upon the pristine mind.

tach Laboratory slang for ➤ **tachistoscope**.

tachistoscope An instrument which, as the name suggests, presents visual materials under conditions of very brief exposures. A sophisticated variety may have up to three or four separate screens (the images from which may be superimposed upon each other in any combination), an extremely precise timing system that can present materials for extremely short dura-

tions (less than 1 millisecond) and illumination controls to adjust the brightness of the display. Also called *T-scope*, *tach*.

tach(y)- Combining form meaning *rapid, fast, swift*.

tachycardia A general term for any abnormally rapid heart action.

tachylalia Unusually rapid speech.

tachyphasia Very rapid or highly voluble speaking.

tachyphrenia Rapid mental functioning.

tachyphylaxis Rapid, acute development of tolerance to a particular drug resulting from frequent, repeated administration. ➤ **drug *tolerance**. syn., *acute tolerance*.

tacit 1. Unspoken or silent. 2. Inferred or understood. 3. Unconscious. ➤ **implicit**.

tact One of the main categories of verbal behavior suggested by Skinner in his operant analysis of language. A tact represents a large class of utterances all of which make contact in some sense with the physical world. That is, tacting is verbal behavior that is most clearly under the control of its antecedents; it results from or is linked with that which has gone before. Naming is the classic tact. Contrast with ➤ **mand**.

tactile ➤ **taxis**.

tactile Pertaining or relating to touch, tactual.

tactile agnosia ➤ **agnosia, tactile**.

tactile corpuscles ➤ **Meissner's corpuscles**.

tactile disks ➤ **Merkel's disks**.

tactile receptors ➤ **Meissner's corpuscles** and **Merkel's disks**.

tactoagnosia ➤ **tactile *agnosia**.

tactual ➤ **tactile**.

Tadoma method A method for communicating used by the deaf and the deafblind by placing the fingers on the speaker's lips and cheeks.

TAG An acronym for *talented and gifted*; TAG programs are educational programs designed specifically for the ➤ **gifted child**.

tag question Any interrogative formed by appending a 'tag' onto a declarative sentence. For example, in 'It's raining out, isn't it?' the 'isn't it?' is a *tag*. English has the interesting rule that the tag must be negative if the base sentence is affirmative and affirmative if the base is negative.

taijin kyofusho A ➤ **culture-specific syndrome** seen in Japan. It resembles a ➤ **social *phobia** marked by the distinctive sense that the individual's body or its parts or functions offend or displease others.

tail In statistics, the extended portion(s) of a distribution which, when presented graphically, appears as the part(s) of the curve that 'tail off.' Exactly where the tail(s) of a distribution begin and the body of the distribution leaves off is only subjectively determinable. ➤ **two-tailed test**.

Talbot brightness ➤ **Talbot-Plateau law**.

Talbot-Plateau law The generalization that when the rate of a flickering light is high enough so that a steady light is seen it will have a perceived brightness that is the mean of the periodic impressions. For example, if the flickering is composed of equally long on and off periods the steady state will have one-half the brightness of the on phase. This fused brightness is called *Talbot brightness*.

talent A high degree of ability for a particular skill. This term is particularly tricky in that it is used by many authors to connote a genetic basis for the skill. This genetic issue is theoretical and not lexical; properly the term is neutral with regard to issues of heredity v. environment. ➤➤ **ability**.

talion principle The principle of retribution, 'an eye for an eye and a tooth for a

tooth.' In psychoanalysis, the primitive fear that injury, real or intended, will be repaid in kind.

talk Speech, speaking, uttering. Talk is also used as a technical term to refer to normal, everyday speech by writers who wish to be clear that they are making reference to such 'ordinary' language as distinct from the often artificially constrained language and speech that is the focus of much of the laboratory-based research on language.

talking cure A half-joking term used to refer to psychoanalytic therapy in that the person's neuroses seem to be 'cured' by simply talking to the analyst. The usage has extended beyond pure psychoanalysis and is occasionally applied to other therapies based on having the individual talk through problems. The term was not coined by an analyst, but by a most famous patient, ➤ **Anna O**.

talking out The full and spontaneous discussion of one's emotional and behavioral problems. Usually the term is restricted to the therapeutic setting but it is flexible enough to be applied in other situations, e.g., with a counselor, a friend, a teacher.

talk turn ➤ **turn-taking**.

tandem reinforcement ➤ **schedules of *reinforcement**.

tangentiality A psychiatric term for a manner of speaking in which questions are answered in inappropriately oblique and irrelevant ways. Compare with ➤ **circumstantiality**.

tangential speech A style of speaking where one tends to drift off the topic.

tantrum A violent and uncontrolled display of anger.

tanyphonia A weak, thin, tinny-sounding voice.

tapetum A reflective layer of tissue behind the retina in the vertebrate eye. By reflecting light back onto the retina it increases the ability to see at low-illumination levels. It also causes the eye to 'shine' when viewed at the proper angle, an especially striking effect in some species such as cats.

tarantism The name for a disorder of the Middle Ages characterized by melancholy, stupor and, surprisingly, an uncontrollable desire to dance. The word derives from the mistaken early belief that the disorder was caused by the bite of a tarantula spider.

Tarasoff decision Named for a famous California case, the decision that a psychotherapist must warn appropriate persons upon becoming aware that his or her client likely presents a risk to another person or persons. Therapist–client ➤ **confidentiality** is broken in such cases.

Tarchanoff phenomenon ➤ **galvanic skin response**.

tardive Characterized by tardiness, lateness. Used of diseases and disorders in which the characteristic symptoms appear relatively late in the normal course of the disorder.

tardive dyskinesia Lit., a late-appearing abnormal movement, a disorder characterized by involuntary, stereotyped and rhythmic movements of the upper body and the face, most commonly tongue protrusion, rolling movements, chewing, lip-smacking, abnormal finger movements, leg-jiggling and neck, trunk and pelvis movements. It is a side effect of long-term use of ➤ **antipsychotic drugs**, and once it emerges is extremely resistant to treatment. The neuropathology of tardive dyskinesia has not been established, although there are indications that compensatory increases in the functioning of ➤ **dopamine** in the ➤ **basal ganglia** may be involved.

target 1. In studies of memory and decision-making, the item that the subject searches for in an array of items. If more than one item is searched for, the several are collectively called the *target set*. **2.** In perception, the specific stimulus the subject is to focus upon (the rest of the field is called the *background* or the *surround*).

3. In psychology, the cell or the type of cell that is affected by a particular chemical or nerve fiber; often called the *target cell*. **4.** Of research generally, the behavior or event that an investigator searches for.

target cell ➤ **target** (3).

target set ➤ **target** (1).

Tartini's tone ➤ **difference tone**. See the discussion under ➤ **combination tone**. The term honors an 18th-century Italian violinist who first noted the existence of difference tones during double-stopping of a violin string; he used them as a cue to assist in the tuning of his instrument.

task Generally, something that needs to be done, an act that one must accomplish. The term has enormous latitude in usage; it is used for simple physical movements as well as for life-goals, it covers personal tasks set by an individual or external demands established by others. It is, because of this generality of meaning, usually qualified to delimit the type of task under consideration.

task demands Those aspects of a particular task which, implicitly or explicitly, require of the individual the use of particular actions or particular patterns of thinking or feeling in order to accomplish the goal of the task. ➤➤ **demand characteristics** and **set** (2).

task-oriented A characteristic of persons who tend to focus their attention and energy toward the fulfillment of a given task. The task-oriented individual is goal-directed and less concerned with the affective or aesthetic aspects of a task than with its completion.

taste 1. Originally the meaning of taste was *to sense*, taken broadly, and it included any sense and any stimulus. Gradually the usage was narrowed, first to *touch* and the act of touching, with the connotation of appreciation of that touched (a meaning which still exists in many senses of the term), and finally to: **2.** The *gustatory* sense whereby information about the chemical composition of a soluble stimulus is conveyed via receptors (the ➤ **taste buds**) on the tongue and surface of the throat. There are four primary taste receptors, one for carbohydrates (sweet), one for acids (sour), one for salts (salty) and one for the variety of compounds that produce the sensation of bitter (bitter). Correspondingly the 'geography' of the tongue is roughly divisible into areas which are populated with specific taste receptors and which show specific sensitivity to the primary qualities; specifically, sweet in the tip and front, salty in the middle-front, sour along the side and bitter in the back. The sensations involved in taste are further complicated by the experiences of odors, pressures and textures, all of which play a role in gustatory experience. For example, to a person with total ➤ **anosmia**, an apple and an onion taste virtually the same. **3.** The ability to make well-reasoned and valid esthetic judgements concerning art, music, decoration, etc.

taste aversion A learned aversion to, and accompanying avoidance of, a particular food which has been associated with some painful outcome or toxic reaction. Also called *bait shyness*, *learned taste aversion*, and *learned taste avoidance*. ➤ **toxicosis** for more detail on the mechanism involved.

taste blindness The inability to taste particular substances at particular concentrations. The original work here suggested that some people are totally 'blind' to the taste of certain chemical compounds. It appears rather that they are not totally insensitive but simply have high thresholds for these compounds and can taste them if the concentration is increased sufficiently.

taste buds Individual sense organs clustered around small protuberances (*papillae*) and containing the receptor cells for mediating the sense of taste. Taste buds are found over the surface and sides of the tongue, on the soft palate and parts of the pharynx. Some taste buds contain only one kind of ➤ **taste cell** and respond to only a restricted class of chemical compounds;

others appear to contain several kinds of cells and hence respond to various compounds. The life of a taste bud is approximately 10 days.

taste cell The individual cell within each ➤ **taste bud** which functions as the receptor for the sense of taste.

taste tetrahedron A four-sided solid figure presented originally by Henning (➤ **Henning's prism** for smell) as a schematic model for the representation of the relations between taste qualities. Each of the four primary taste sensations (sweet, salty, sour, bitter) are placed at the corners and all other tastes are characterized as spatial locations assigned by combinations of these four.

TAT ➤ **Thematic Apperception Test**.

tau (τ) coefficient of correlation A measure of correlation developed by the statistician M. G. Kendall (and often called *Kendall's tau*) based upon comparisons between the rank order of each item (or subject) on each of two variables or tests.

taurine An amino acid suspected as being a neurotransmitter.

tautology 1. Generally, an unnecessary repetitiveness in language, e.g., 'As a rookie in his first year of play.' **2.** In logic, an expression wherein an argument is stated as equivalent to itself: $x = x$. **3.** By extension, a circular argument which proves nothing.

tautophone A projective device in which the subject listens to a recording of unintelligible sounds and is asked to elaborate on what they seem to be saying.

taxis 1. In older writings, ➤ **tropism**. In contemporary writing *taxis* is used for animals and *tropism* for plants. **2.** A response of an animate organism with respect to a particular stimulus. The response may be toward the stimulus (*positive taxis*) or away from it (*negative taxis*). Taxes are regarded as genetically controlled, species-specific reactions to particular stimulus events. adjs., *taxic*, *tactic*; pl., *taxes*.

-taxis A suffix used with words of Greek origin to denote specific taxes; e.g., *phototaxis* is a movement toward light, as displayed by moths.

taxonomic constraint The phenomenon that, in learning new word meanings, children assume that labels refer to objects of like kind rather than to those that are thematically related. That is, although children thematically relate dogs with bones they generalize taxonomically so that new instances of dogs are recognized as dogs and not bones.

taxonomy From the Greek, meaning *laws of arrangement*, any systematic set of principles for classification and arrangement.

Tay–Sach's disease An inherited disease characterized by severe neurological deterioration and accompanying mental and physical retardation. The deterioration, which is always fatal (usually within the first 18 months of life), results from a lack of a single enzyme necessary for proper metabolism. Also known as *infantile amauratic idiocy*, the disease occurs approximately 100 times more often in Jewish children, especially those of Ashkenazi ancestry, than among other racial and ethnic groups.

T data R. B. Cattell's shorthand term for any data based on the use of standardized testing procedures.

t distribution ➤ distribution, *t*.

teaching machine A general cover term for any device used in systematic programmed instruction. The term was first introduced by operant conditioners when they extended their research from simple learning to issues of pedagogy. ➤ computer-assisted instruction, programmed instruction.

tears Mildly saline solution secreted by the lacrimal glands which functions as lubrication.

teat The nipple of a mammary gland.

technique A fairly specific, learned procedure or set of procedures for accomplishing some specific goal. Typically the term is used with the connotation that these procedures are skilled and mastering them reflects a certain level of expertness. Usage is very broad and typically some qualifier is appended, e.g., statistical technique, experimental technique, etc. Compare with ➤ method and ➤ procedure.

technology That aspect of a culture which applies the findings, procedures and principles of systematic investigation into the identification and solution of problems. *Technology* is used more broadly than *science* and more generally than *engineering*.

technopsychology ➤ psychotechnology.

tectorial membrane A membrane that is part of the ➤ organ of Corti in the inner ear. It is a rather rigid structure in which the cilia of the hair cells are attached.

tectospinal tract One of the ➤ ventromedial pathways, it travels from the tectum to the spinal cord and coordinates movements of the head and trunk with those of the eyes.

tectum The dorsal portion of the midbrain, consisting of inferior and superior colliculi.

tegmentum The portion of the midbrain that contains the red nucleus, the substantia nigra and the nuclei and roots of the oculomotor nerve.

teknonymy The practice of referencing a parent through his or her offspring; e.g., 'She is Max's mother.'

telalgia Lit., distant pain. Used for any pain experienced away from the locus of the stimulus causing it, e.g., ➤ referred *pain.

tel(e)- Combining form meaning: **1.** *End* (from the Greek *telos*). **2.** *Far* or *distant* (from the Greek *tele*).

teleceptor A ➤ distance receptor. var., *teleoreceptor, telerecepter*.

telegnosis Lit., knowing at a distance; in ➤ parapsychology, knowledge of events by extrasensory means.

telegraphic speech Roger Brown's term for a highly reduced form of speech in which the unessential words are dropped out. This selective omission is similar to what one would leave out of a message to be sent as a telegram. It is observed in the early stages of language learning in children and occasionally in some forms of aphasia. Also called *telegraphese*.

telekinesis Lit., movement from afar; the hypothesized ability to manipulate objects mentally. ➤ **parapsychology**.

telencephalon A major subdivision of the forebrain. Its principal structures include the cerebral cortex, the basal ganglia and the limbic system. Also called the *end brain*.

teleo- Combining form meaning *perfect, complete*.

teleological Pertaining to ➤ **teleology**, to purposes, ends or goals.

teleological regression, principle of ➤ **progressive teleological-regression hypothesis**.

teleology Any of several theoretical and philosophical perspectives that share, in one form or another, a presumption that purpose and purposeful striving toward ends or goals is an essential component of all events. The term is most often associated with the doctrine that everything proceeds toward some divinely specified ultimate end, that all reality is infused with a *vitalist* spirit (➤ **vitalism**) that directs this process. This point of view is usually branded as a fallacy, on the grounds that, taken to its logical extreme, it entails the notion that the future has a causal impact on the present. Within psychology proper, at least two major theoretical positions have had teleological aspects, McDougall's ➤ **hormic psychology** and Tolman's ➤ **purposive psychology**. Neither ran foul of the teleological fallacy for both used the concept of purpose as a controlling or driving force behind behavior rather than a leading or enticing force. However, both positions suffered from other short-comings; see each for details. On occasion Piaget's theory of cognitive development has been called teleological. This is a mistake which comes from misreading his argument that the stage of formal operations is the end point of cognition toward which ontogeny strives. Actually, Piaget argued that his 'end point' is the result of modifications in cognition resulting from conflicts which more primitive cognitions of earlier stages produce. It is a natural outcome of unsatisfactory modes of thought and not a predetermined aim. ➤ **Piagetian**.

teleonomic Floyd Allport's term used to characterize the behaviors that can be viewed as resulting from some hypothesized purpose.

teleopsia A visual disorder in which objects are perceived as being further away than they are and the sense of depth generally is exaggerated.

teleoreceptor ➤ **distance receptor**, var., *teleceptor, telereceptor*.

teleotherapeutics The use of hypnotic suggestion in therapy.

telepathy The hypothesized ability for direct mental contact between two or more persons. ➤ **parapsychology** for a discussion of telepathic and other similar hypothesized paranormal abilities.

telephone scatalogia A ➤ **paraphilia** marked by recurrent and intense sexual urges involving the making of erotic or obscene telephone calls to nonconsenting individuals.

telephone theory (of hearing) ➤ **theories of *hearing**.

telereceptor ➤ **distance receptor**. var., *teleoreceptor, teleceptor*.

telesis The use of social and natural processes in a conscious and rational manner to achieve specified societal aims. Also called *social telesis*.

telestereoscope A ➤ **stereoscope** that produces an exaggerated sense of depth.

telesthesia A general term for those hypothesized paranormal abilities to perceive events, objects, thoughts, etc. without the use of normal sensory systems, e.g., *clairvoyance, telepathy.* ➤ **parapsychology** for a general discussion.

teletractor A device that augments sound waves and converts them into vibration patterns that can be felt on the skin. It is used as an aid in teaching speech and language skills to the deaf.

telic Pertaining to that which has purpose or can be viewed as goal-directed. ➤ **teleology**.

telic change Change, particularly social change, that has occurred because of systematic planning aimed at achieving some purpose or goal.

temper 1. Anger. 2. Mood or disposition, especially when conceived of as a personality trait, e.g., even-tempered.

temperament An aspect of an individual's general make-up characterized by dispositions toward particular patterns of emotional reactions, mood shifts and levels of sensitivity resulting from stimulation. There is a tendency to conceptualize temperament as a genetic disposition largely because fairly striking differences in reactivity to stimulation can be observed in neonates, especially to stimuli like loud noises, bright lights, sudden movements, touching, physical contact, etc. ➤ **personality** for a discussion of the general notions entailed here.

temperature regulation ➤ **thermoregulation**.

temperature sense The sensory system that responds to temperature and temperature changes. It includes the perception of stimuli below the adaptation level of the skin (➤ **cold**) and those above it (➤ **warm**). Also known as the *thermal sense* or *thermic sense.* ➤ **adaptation level** and **thermoregulation**.

temperature spots ➤ **cold spot** and **warm spot**.

temper tantrum ➤ **tantrum**.

template (matching) model A theory of ➤ **pattern recognition** which assumes that various internal representations (i.e. *templates*) of objects are stored in memory and new stimuli processed by comparing them with the templates until a match is found. Such a mechanism, incidentally, is widely used in computer-based systems such as those employed in banks, where the numbers of a check are 'read' and 'recognized' by a set of templates. However, as a theory of human pattern recognition, it is too simple; it cannot, for example, account for the ability to recognize that a, A, *A* and *a* are all examples of the same letter.

temporal Pertaining to: 1. Time. 2. The temple area of the head. 3. The area of the cortex under the temples.

temporal avoidance conditioning An operant-conditioning procedure in which an aversive stimulus (typically an electric shock) is presented at regular intervals (e.g., every 10 seconds). When the organism (usually a laboratory rat) makes the proper response (e.g., a bar press) the shock is delayed some fixed amount of time (e.g., 20 seconds). The procedure thus can be seen to have two independent variables, the *shock–shock (S–S) interval* and the *response–shock (R–S) interval.* Typically, good temporal avoidance conditioning develops and the animal learns to avoid the noxious events without the presence of any external stimulus. Since much of the original work with this procedure was carried out by M. Sidman, it is occasionally referred to in the literature as *Sidman avoidance conditioning* or *procedure.*

temporal lobe The lobe of the cerebrum located below the lateral fissure and in front of the occipital lobe.

temporal lobe amnesia ➤ **amnesia, temporal lobe**.

temporal lobe epilepsy ➤ **epilepsy, temporal lobe**.

temporal summation ➤ **summation, temporal**.

temporary threshold shift (TTS) Quite literally, the temporary (upward) shift in the threshold for a stimulus. An example of a TTS is that which occurs in hearing following exposure to high-intensity sounds.

temptation 1. A desire or urge to behave in a manner contradictory to what is socially accepted. **2.** The object or the circumstances which elicit this urge.

tendency 1. An internal state such that particular behaviors are likely to occur or can be learned relatively easily. This sense is intended when the object of discussion is an animate organism. ➤ **disposition** and **set**, both of which are used in similar ways. **2.** A directionality or focusing of a large number of scores or events. This meaning is applied very generally, particularly in statistics, e.g., *central tendency*.

tender-minded William James's term for a category of persons characterized by idealism, optimism, intellectualism, a tendency to be rational in thought and tendencies to be religious and to believe in free will. James contrasted such persons with the *tough-minded*, whom he characterized as being materialistic, realistic and pessimistic, and tending to be irreligious and fatalistic. Despite the intuitive sense that these groups of characteristics really do adhere in particular persons, factor-analytic studies have consistently failed to identify such personality types.

tendon Fibrous connective tissue by which muscles are attached to bones.

tendon reflex A reflexive muscular contraction elicited by a sudden stretching of a tendon. The ➤ **knee-jerk reflex** is the classic example.

tenet Any general principle, belief or dogma adhered to by a group or by a particular school of thought.

tense 1 adj. Generally, characterized by tautness, rigidity, stretched tight as in a muscle or fiber. **2** adj. Characterized by an emotional state of nervousness or strain, particularly a feeling of being pressured or stressed by events. **3** adj. In phonetics, a ➤ **distinctive feature** (2) descriptive of speech sounds produced by deformation of the vocal tract away from its resting position; the opposite of ➤ **lax**. **4** n. In linguistics, a verb-inflection category marking the time of action as past, present or future. **5** vb. To make or become tense, to create a state of ➤ **tension**.

tension 1. Generally, the act of straining or stretching or the state of being so strained or stretched. **2.** The sensation associated with contraction of a muscle, muscle group and/or the associated tendons, membranes and ligaments. **3.** An emotional state characterized by restlessness, anxiety, excitement and a general, diffuse preparedness to act. Note that this last usage is quite loose and that there is a variety of connotations which may be implied by its use depending on the preference of the writer. These variations come from the different presumptions about the causes of this state. Some, for example, assume that it results from the kind of *tension* referred to in 2 above, others view it as a result of the blocking or thwarting of attempts to achieve some goal or to fulfill some need, and still others treat it as an outcome of any strong, intense effort be it physical, emotional or intellectual. It is far from clear whether all of these entailments of the term are the same or even whether they share any underlying characteristics. In fact, in the technical literature the term *tension* is about as ill-defined as the popular term *nervous tension*. **4.** A state of strained mutual relations between members of a group, characterized by antagonism and a lack of cooperation; also called *social tension*.

tension reduction Lit., the lessening of tension. Occasionally used as a synonym for ➤ **drive reduction**.

tensor tympani A muscle in the tympanic membrane that controls the tension of the membrane and the amount of sound that will be passed to the middle ear.

tentorial notch The opening in the dura

mater through which the brain stem passes.

tentorium 1. Generally, any tent-like structure. **2.** Specifically, the fold of dura mater that separates the cerebellum from the cerebrum.

teratogen Anything that produces abnormalities in the developing fetus. *Physical teratogens* include such drugs as thalidomide which, when taken by the mother during early pregnancy, can produce a physically deformed infant. Those substances that do not produce gross physical abnormalities but may affect behavioral, emotional or cognitive processes are called *behavioral* or *psychological teratogens*.

teratology The study of birth defects, specifically the biochemical agents (➤ **teratogens**) that cause them.

terminal behavior In operant conditioning, the desired, final behavior being shaped. ➤ **shaping**.

terminal bulb ➤ **terminal button**.

terminal button The enlarged, button-like structure at the end of the branches of an axon containing neurotransmitter substances. Also called by various other named including: *terminal bulb, terminal knob; synaptic bulb, button* and *knob*; and *end bulb, button* and *knob*. ➤➤ **synapse** and related entries.

terminal factor ➤ **primary *factor**.

terminal insomnia ➤ **insomnia, terminal**.

terminal knob ➤ **terminal button**.

terminal reinforcement In circumstances in which reinforcements are received for partial completion of an extended task, the final reinforcement received at the end. Grades and credits are reinforcements for a student, but the degree or the diploma awarded at graduation is the terminal reinforcement.

terminal stimulus The maximum stimulus along some specified dimension that an organism is capable of responding to.

territorial aggression ➤ **aggression, territorial**.

territoriality The tendency to defend or protect one's space against invasion or incursion. The term is used broadly, so that the territory defended may be a real, physical one or a psychological or personal one; see here ➤ **personal space**. See also the following entries delineating the various kinds of territory that may be involved.

territory, primary A territory possessed and exclusively used by a particular organism or group. A home or a nest is such a territory, as is the area marked by an animal (usually by urinating around the perimeter). Encroachment is a serious affront and the possessor will generally defend against it vigorously.

territory, public (or free) Any territory to which almost anyone has free access. Generally the access to and occupancy of such territories is limited and constrained by social or legal convention. Examples are beaches, restaurants, parks, trains, etc.

territory, secondary A territory that is usually a blend of the private and the public. Such territories are not so clearly associated with the total control by one person of a ➤ **primary *territory**, but more control is exercised over access than in the ➤ **public *territory**. A private social club or a fraternal organization are examples.

tertiary circular reaction ➤ **circular reaction**.

test 1 n. Most generally, any procedure used to measure a factor or assess some ability. Included in this encompassing sense of the term are intelligence tests which yield IQ measures, medical tests which assess presence or absence of disease, aptitude tests which measure potential in some area, various personality tests which assess aspects of personal style, belief systems and attitudes, statistical tests which determine the significance of experimental results, etc. To prevent confusion in this plethora of assessment devices, one will usually append some qualifier to denote the type and form of test under consideration. The major forms of tests are presented in separate entries below; specialized tests are found elsewhere under the names they are commonly known by. **2** n. In logic, a criterion or critical operation that can be used to assess the validity of a proposition, the truth of a statement, the correctness of an argument, the accuracy of a theory, etc. **3** vb. To undertake to administer any of the assessment devices or procedures included in 1. **4** vb. To carry out the criterial operations outlined in 2.

testable Characterizing a hypothesis, proposition or theory that lends itself to some kind of systematic evaluation so as to assess its validity or applicability. Testability is a hallmark of a good scientific theory. ➤ **falsificationism**.

test age ➤ **age, test**.

test anxiety Quite literally, anxiety about taking a test. When high, such anxiety can depress scores.

test battery A collection of tests the results of which can be combined to produce a single score. Such batteries are used on the assumption that the errors inherent in each separate test will cancel each other out and the single score obtained will be maximally valid.

test bias ➤ **bias** (5).

testee One who takes a test.

testes pl. of ➤ **testis**.

test, group Any test that has been designed so that it can be administered to more than one person at a time.

testicle ➤ **testis**.

testicular Relating to ➤ **testis** or *testicle*.

testicular-feminizing syndrome ➤ **androgen-insensitivity syndrome**.

test, individual Any test designed to be administered to individuals one at a time.

testing effect The effect that taking a test has upon the attitudes or opinions that the test is designed to evaluate. It is a source of error in survey research, particularly where pretests are used which may alter attitudes independently of any experimental manipulation.

testis A male gonad or sex organ. One of two reproductive glands located in the scrotum which produce spermatozoa and the male hormone ➤ **testosterone**. syn., *testicle*.

test item Any specific question or specific component of a larger test.

test, mastery Generally, any test designed to determine whether a student has mastered a particular subject-matter.

test-operate-test-exit ➤ **TOTE**.

testosterone The most potent of the naturally occurring ➤ **androgens**. It is the primary testicular hormone in man, although small quantities are produced by the adrenal cortex of both males and females and by the ovaries in females. Testosterone accelerates tissue growth, causes maturation of the male genitals and the production of sperm, stimulates the development of the secondary sex characteristics including growth of facial, axillary and genital hair, voice changes, shifts in hairline (resulting in many cases in baldness), muscle development and the redistribution of body fat. It also plays an important role in aggression and dominance.

test, power of ➤ **power of a test, statistical**.

test–retest reliability ➤ **reliability, test–retest**.

tests and measurements A generic term used for the broad subfield within psychology that focuses on the development, design, administration, evaluation and application of psychological tests of all kinds.

test scaling The process of setting up a scale for a given test. The usual procedure is to administer the test to a sample group of persons and assign values to each item based on the scores obtained from the sample individuals.

test sophistication The extent to which a person has had experience with (psychological) tests and hence is aware of the general nature and procedures in use. In general, such *test-wise* individuals have an advantage over those who are naïve about tests and testing.

test, standardized Any test that has been subjected to a sufficiently thorough empirical analysis so that an adequate set of ➤ **norms** (1) has been developed and a reasonable assessment of its *reliability* and *validity* has been obtained.

test-wise ➤ test sophistication.

tetanizing shock Electric shock strong enough to cause ➤ **tetanus** (1). Such severe shocks have occasionally been used in experimental research (using animals) on the effects of punishment. Also called *traumatic shock*.

tetanus 1. Sustained tonic muscular spasms. **2.** An acute infectious disease caused by the tetanus bacillus, the primary symptom of which is a state of painful, persistent, tonic spasms of several voluntary muscles. The first affected are usually those controlling the jaw, hence the popular name, *lockjaw*.

tetany A condition marked by intermittent tonic muscular spasms, usually in the extremities. It is usually caused by changes in extracellular calcium resulting from parathyroid dysfunction. Prognosis is typically good, unlike that for ➤ tetanus (2), which is frequently fatal.

tetartanopia An extremely rare form of ➤ **dichromatism** in which reds and greens are seen normally but blues and yellows are poorly distinguished, with yellow (the so-called 'fourth' primary color) especially affected. The deficiency is so rare that its existence is in dispute.

tetra- Combining form meaning *four*.

tetrachoric correlation ➤ correlation, tetrachoric.

tetrachromatic theory ➤ opponent-process theory. ➤ theories of * color vision.

tetrahydrocannabinol ➤ THC.

textual In Skinner's behaviorist analysis of language, a class of verbal operants controlled by visual verbal stimuli like words or symbols.

texture gradient ➤ gradient of texture.

T-group ➤ sensitivity training.

thalamic Pertaining to the ➤ thalamus.

thalamic theory of emotion = *Cannon-Bard theory*. ➤ theories of emotion.

thalamotomy A form of psychosurgery in which thalamic fibers are severed. It has been used in a few cases with extremely violent patients or extremely hyperactive children. ➤ **psychosurgery** for a discussion of the ethics of such procedures.

thalamus The largest subdivision of the diencephalon of the forebrain. It is a complex, two-lobed structure with one lobe on each side of the massa intermedia that runs through the third ventricle. It functions as a kind of 'relay station' for afferent information in that all sensory stimuli (except olfactory) are received by it and projected to the cerebral cortex. A number of specific nuclei are found in the thalamus: some receive specific afferent inputs and project them to specific cortical *areas* (e.g., ➤ **lateral geniculate bodies,** ➤ **medial geniculate bodies**); other nuclei relay to the cortex but do not receive specific afferent inputs (e.g., ➤ **dorsomedial nucleus**); and others project diffusely to other thalamic nuclei as well as to the cortex (e.g., ➤ **midline nucleus,** ➤ **reticular nucleus**).

thanato- Combining form meaning death. ➤ **necro-** and related terms.

thanatology The study of the psychological and medical aspects surrounding death and dying.

thanatomania 1. A homicidal or suicidal mania. **2.** Wasting away and ultimate death following awareness that one has transgressed seriously some societal taboo or believing that one has been bewitched. Sense 2 is also called *voodoo death*.

thanatopsy An autopsy.

Thanatos The Greek god of death. In Freud's usage, Thanatos refers to the theoretical generalized instinct for death as expressed in such behaviors as denial, rejection and the turning away from pleasure. Compare with ➤ **Eros**.

that's-not-all technique A two-step device for obtaining compliance where the individual begins with a specific request and then lowers it. For example, sales go up when an object is sold for 'now $5 reduced from $7' compared with merely selling it for $5. Compare with ➤ **low-balling**.

THC The abbreviation for *tetrahydrocannabinol* which, for obvious reasons, tends to be used in place of the full scientific term. THC, the active ingredient in marijuana (➤ **cannabis** for details), is known to stimulate specific receptors in various locations in the brain including the *cerebellum*, the *caudate nucleus*, the *hippocampus*, and the *substantia nigra*. It has also been shown to have a variety of medical benefits, including the reduction of nausea caused by drugs used for cancer, lessening of the severity of asthma attacks, and decreasing the pressure on the eye caused by glaucoma. It also has side effects such as altering mood, disrupting concentration, interfering with memory, modifying visual and auditory perception, and distorting the sense of time. It is these 'side effects' that become the primary effects for those who use it as a recreational drug.

thelarche (*thelar'kee*) The onset of breast development at puberty.

thema H. Murray's term for a unit of behavior made of a ➤ **need** and a ➤ **press**. E.g., ➤ **Thematic Apperception Test**.

Thematic Apperception Test (TAT) A projective technique developed by Henry A. Murray and his co-workers. The person being tested is given a number of black-and-white pictures of various settings which are capable of being interpreted in any number of ways and is asked to tell a story about each. The stories are analyzed in terms of the *thema* which the person introduces into each narrative. The thema are, according to Murray's theory of personality, assumed to reflect deep needs, desires, fears, conflicts, etc. ➤ **projective technique** for further discussion.

theomania Delusionary condition in which the individual believes that he or she is God or has, more modestly, direct, divine inspiration for thoughts and actions.

theorem 1. A proposition that has been proved logically or a corollary thereof. **2.** A proposition that can be subjected to a logical proof (or disproof). Distinguish from ➤ **hypothesis**, ➤ **postulate**, ➤ **theory**.

theoretical equation ➤ **empirical *equation**.

theory This term has three distinct uses, ranging from the highly formal and precise of the philosophy of science to the loose and informal of popular language. To wit: **1.** A coherent set of formal expressions that provides a complete and consistent characterization of a well-articulated domain of investigation with explanations for all attendant facts and empirical data. Such a theory is ideally conceptualized as beginning with the induction of a set of primitive terms and ➤ **axioms**. These axioms are then used to deduce ➤ **theorems** which are then tested for their truth value, their ability to encompass known facts and, one hopes, their ability to predict new phenomena whose existence is not yet documented. Needless to say, such theories are rare indeed, even in the more developed natural sciences; in the social sciences there are few contenders and none of any generality. However, psychology abounds with 'theories'; they are usually of the following variety: **2.** A general principle or a collection of interrelated general principles that is put forward as an explanation of a set of known facts and empirical findings. This is the pragmatic sense of the term and is applied widely to proposed explanations which fall well short of the formal criteria for meaning 1. For example, Freud's theory of personality development fails the test of unambiguous deduction of theorems, which is one reason why many have argued that it cannot be rigorously tested; it is, still, called a 'theory.' To get some sense of how broad the coverage of this pragmatic meaning of the term is, consult the entries ➤ **theories of *color vision** and ➤ **stimulus-sampling theory** on one hand and the entry ➤ **personality** on the other. It will be clear from these that the term is 'awarded' to almost any honest attempt to provide an explanation of some body of fact or data. **3.** In popular parlance the term takes on exceedingly loose meanings. Here it even loses some of its explanatory connotations and becomes a kind of catch-word for any reasonable set of ideas or principles that are deemed dismissible or suspect. Hence, the common expression, 'Well, in *theory* that's a good proposal, but . . .'

theory-begging The device of giving a theoretical assumption the name of a well-established fact and thereby seeming to give credence to the theory.

theory-laden Of a term or concept whose reference can only be understood in the light of a particular theory. The notion of 'unresolved Oedipus complex' only makes sense within the context of classical psychoanalysis.

the others ➤ **significant other**.

therapeutic From the Greek, meaning *treatment*. **1.** Pertaining to the curative results of treatment. **2.** Having some curative properties. **3.** Characterizing any effective healing agent or procedure.

therapeutic community A social, cultural setting established for therapeutic reasons and within which those persons needing therapy live. The term is not used for just any psychiatric facility but for those established on the grounds that the whole social milieu, if properly controlled, can have a beneficial impact. ➤ **milieu therapy**.

therapeutics A generic label for any

branch of science or medicine concerned with treatment and cure of disease or other abnormal conditions.

therapeutic window In psychopharmacology, the range of plasma concentration of a drug that has significant therapeutic value. The lower limit is the base below which only placebo effects occur, the upper limit is that beyond which the drug's side-effects negate its therapeutic effects.

therapeutist ➤ **therapist** (1).

therapist **1.** A generic label for any individual trained in and practicing the treatment of diseases or other abnormal conditions. **2.** abbrev. of ➤ **psychotherapist**.

theraplay An occasional synonym for ➤ **play therapy**.

therapy An inclusive label for all manners and forms of treatment of disease or disorder. Because the term is so broad, both connotatively and denotatively, it is typically used with qualifiers to designate the form of therapy referenced. Some follow here, others are found throughout this volume under the alphabetic listing of the qualifying term.

therapy, active A general term for any therapeutic approach in which the therapist takes an active, directing role. E.g., ➤ **rational-emotive therapy**. Also called *directive therapy*. Contrast with ➤ **passive *therapy**.

therapy, didactic A kind of ➤ **directive therapy** in which the therapist instructs the client, explains things in detail and attempts to teach the client various specific ways to overcome his or her problems.

therapy, passive Generally, any therapy in which the therapist maintains a low profile and makes little or no attempt either to control the direction of therapy or to direct changes in the client. A good example is ➤ **client-centered therapy**. Contrast with ➤ **active *therapy**.

therapy, physical Generally, the use of any physical agent in a therapeutic fashion, e.g., massage, exercise, heat, etc.

therapy, preventive Any therapy that is designed to prevent a serious condition from developing.

therapy puppet A puppet used in ➤ **play therapy**.

theriomorphism The attribution to humans of nonhuman traits, characteristics and qualities. Typically used to refer to the invocation of explanatory mechanisms and principles derived from animal experimentation and observation for theoretical characterizations of human behavior. Contrast with ➤ **anthropomorphism**. syn., *zoomorphism*.

thermal 1. From the Greek, meaning *pertaining to heat*. 2. By extension, pertaining to temperature in a broad sense.

thermalgesia A condition of hypersensitivity to temperature in which relatively mildly warm stimuli are experienced as painful. var., *thermoalgesia*.

thermalgia A form of neuralgia characterized by intense burning sensations, pain and reddening of the skin. Also called *causalgia*.

thermal sense ➤ **temperature sense**.

thermanalgesia A pathological condition in which the normal painful reaction to hot stimuli is not experienced. var., *thermoanalgesia*.

thermanesthesia Insensitivity to temperature changes; an inability to experience normal warmth and cold. var., *thermoanesthesia*.

thermic sense ➤ **temperature sense**.

therm(o)- Combining form meaning *warmth, heat* or *hot* that is also used to refer to the full temperature range, including the experiencing of cold. The point is that there is only one physical dimension here, that of kinetic energy, and the subjective classifications of cold, warm, hot, etc. are dependent upon *adaptation levels* and *temperature gradients*.

thermoalgesia ➤ **thermalgesia**.

thermoanalgesia ➤ **thermanalagesia**.

thermoanesthesia ➤ **thermanesthesia**.

thermocouple A device for measuring temperature change.

thermoregulation The various adaptive processes in the body for regulating heat production and heat loss so that normal temperature is maintained. Centers in the hypothalamus have been identified which are critical parts within the general temperature-regulation system. They are stimulated by afferent cutaneous neural impulses and by the temperature of the blood; in turn, they regulate adaptive behaviors such as vasoconstriction or dilation, panting, sweating, etc.

thermotaxis ➤ **thermotropism**.

thermotropism An orienting response (➤ **tropism**) to a stimulus of a particular temperature. The term applies to such responses made to either warm or cold stimuli. *Thermotaxis* is used more or less synonymously although, strictly speaking the *-taxis* form is for animals and the *-tropism* for plants.

they-group ➤ **out-group**.

thinking As G. C. Oden phrased it recently, 'Thinking, broadly defined, is nearly all of psychology; narrowly defined, it seems to be none of it.' Given the subtle truth of this quip, we might be able to find a middle ground if we treat the term as denoting, most generally, any covert cognitive or mental manipulation of ideas, images, symbols, words, propositions, memories, concepts, percepts, beliefs or intentions. In short, a term used so that it encompasses all of the mental activities associated with concept-formation, problem-solving, intellectual functioning, creativity, complex learning, memory, symbolic processing, imagery, etc. Few terms in psychology cast such a broad net and few encompass such a rich array of connotations and entailments.

Certain components nonetheless lie at the core of all usages: (a) *Thinking* is reserved for symbolic processes; the term is not used for behaviors explicable by more modest processes such as that of rats learning a simple maze. (b) *Thinking* is treated as a covert or implicit process that is not directly observable. The existence of a thought process is inferred either from reports of the one who was doing the thinking or by observing behavioral acts that suggests that thinking was going on, e.g., a complex problem solved correctly. (c) *Thinking* is generally assumed to involved the manipulation of some, in theory identifiable, elements. Exactly what these 'elements of thought' are is anybody's (and sometimes it seems, everybody's) guess. Various theorists have proposed muscular components (Watson), words or language components (Whorf), ideas (Locke), images (Titchener), propositions (Anderson), operations and concepts (Piaget), scripts (Schank) and so forth. Note that some of these hypothesized entities are quite elemental and others quite holistic. No matter, all are serious proposals and all have at least some evidence to support their use in the process of thinking.

Because of the breadth and looseness of the term, qualifiers are often used to delimit the form of thinking under discussion. Some of these specialized terms follow, others are found under the alphabet listing of the qualifying term.

thinking, convergent Thinking which is characterized by a bringing together or synthesizing of information and knowledge focused on a solution to a problem. Such thinking is often associated with problem-solving, particularly with problems that have but a single correct solution. Compare with ➤ divergent *thinking.

thinking, critical A cognitive strategy consisting largely of continual checking and testing of possible solutions to guide one's work. Critical thinking is often contrasted with *creative thinking* (➤ creativity) in that the latter leads to new insights and solutions while the former functions to test existing ideas and solutions for flaws or errors.

thinking, divergent Thinking that is characterized by a process of 'moving away' in various directions, a diverging of ideas to encompass a variety of relevant aspects. Such thinking is frequently associated with creativity since it often yields novel ideas and solutions. Compare with ➤ convergent *thinking.

thinking type One of Jung's hypothesized personality types. ➤ function types.

thinning In operant conditioning, gradually shifting the contingencies of reinforcement from a schedule in which most or all responses are reinforced to a widely spread, intermittent schedule. ➤ schedules of *reinforcement.

thiopental An ultra-short-acting ➤ barbiturate.

thioridazine One of the ➤ phenothiazines used as an ➤ antipsychotic drug.

thioxanthines. A group of ➤ anti-psychotic drugs used in the alleviation of severe psychological disorders, primarily schizophrenia. The group includes *chloroprothixene* and *thiothixene*. Somewhat less potent than the ➤ phenothiazines, they are primarily used when an alternative is needed because of side-effects.

third ear Theodor Reik's metaphorical term for the intuitive perceptual 'processor' of the skilled clinician which, he argued, can and should be used as the primary instrument in gathering data for clinical, psychiatric diagnosis.

third moment The ➤ skewness of a distribution. ➤➤ moment (2).

thirst 1. An internal, physiological state that results from water deprivation. 2. A subjectively experienced internal state that results from water deprivation and is usually characterized by a dryness in the mouth, throat and mucous membranes of the pharynx. 3. A drive state resulting from water deprivation that produces a desire for fluids, specifically water, and motivates water-seeking behavior. 4. By extension, a desire or drive for something, e.g., a thirst for power, for knowledge, etc.

thirst, osmometric Thirst produced by increases in the relative osmotic pressure of extracellular fluids which results from loss of cellular fluids.

thirst, volumetric Thirst produced by decreases in the amount of extracellular fluid in the body.

thoracic Pertaining to the ➤ **thorax**.

thoracolumbar system Synonym for the *sympathetic nervous system*; ➤ **autonomic nervous system** for details.

thorax The part of the mammalian body between the neck and abdomen specifically demarcated by the diaphragm.

Thorndike-Lorge list A list of several tens of thousands of English words tabulated for frequency of usage as revealed in a variety of written materials, including children's books, novels, magazines, etc. The full compilation, published in 1944, was the first thorough word count in English; several more comprehensive and up-to-date ones have appeared since then.

Thorndike puzzle box One of the earliest (if not the earliest) pieces of laboratory apparatus specifically designed to study learning. It was invented by E. L. Thorndike in the 1830s and consisted of a box built of wooden slats into which an animal was locked. Through the bars the animal could see a food reward but could not obtain it until some mechanism was manipulated (usually a lever that was pushed) to open the box. Once in common use it has now been superseded by the ➤ **Skinner box** as the apparatus of choice for the study of operant behavior.

thought 1. A general term covering the cognitive processes discussed under ➤ **thinking**. **2.** A single but complex idea, proposition, etc.

thought broadcasting Experiencing one's thoughts as being broadcast from one's head out loud so that they can be heard by others. It is a common sympton of some forms of schizophrenia.

thought disorder An umbrella term for any disturbance in speech, communication, thinking, etc. Included here are delusions, flight of ideas, pathological perseveration and the like. When the disruption is in the form or structure of thinking rather than in the content, the term *formal thought disorder* is used.

thought disturbances A general term used to cover any erratic, disoriented, bizarre thinking. It is found primarily in the clinical literature, where it is cited as symptomatic of some neurotic and psychotic conditions.

thought experiment ➤ **mental *experiment**.

thought impulses A psychoanalytic term for those aspects of dreams hypothesized to result from the ordinary stresses and experiences of everyday life. The term is used to distinguish these mundane dream elements from those hypothesized to derive from deeper, unconscious conflicts. ➤➤ **day residue**.

thought insertion An experiencing of thoughts as though they were not one's own but rather were 'inserted' into one's mind. A common symptom of schizophrenia, it should be distinguished from auditory hallucinations where one hears voices that do not exist (which is also a symptom of schizophrenia).

thought-stopping Quite literally, the stopping of a train of thought. A technique used in behaviorally oriented therapies, such as rational emotive therapy, in which the therapist interrupts an undesirable thought process by the simple expedient of yelling 'Stop!' The client is then instructed on how to use the technique outside of the laboratory to interrupt counterproductive ways of thinking.

thought, supervalent A pattern of thinking which obsessively hovers around a particular topic. ➤ **obsession**.

thought withdrawal An experience that somehow one's thoughts have been taken away, removed as it were, from one's head. It is often accompanied by the sense that one has fewer thoughts left to use. It is a symptom of schizophrenia.

Thouless ratio The logarithmic transformation of the ➤ **Brunswik ratio**.

threat 1. Most generally, any action, gesture or response that indicates an intention to attack, harm or intimidate another. This meaning is found in various contexts; in lower animals it is usually manifested by overt and relatively stereotyped actions, in humans it may be similarly direct, but more often is elaborated by verbal and symbolic forms shaped by our culture. 2. A symbol or sign that portends future unpleasantness. 3. An idea or image (and the accompanying emotional experiences) concerning anticipated events.

threat to self-esteem model A generalization about how ➤ **helping behavior** is viewed by the one being helped. If the assistance is seen as self-supportive, it is appreciated, but if it is perceived as self-threatening, it tends to make the recipient feel inferior and dependent and it (and the helper) are viewed negatively.

three-color theory Another name for the *Young–Helmholtz theory*. ➤ **theories of *color vision**.

threshold 1. The statistically determined point along a stimulus continuum at which the energy level is just sufficient for one to detect the presence of the stimulus. This is the so-called *absolute* (or *detection*) *threshold*. 2. The statistically determined point in the magnitude of the difference between the energy levels of two stimuli which is sufficient for one to detect that the two are, in fact, different. This is the so-called *differential* (or *difference*) *threshold*. 3. The minimum stimulus energy sufficient to excite a neuron; see here ➤ **all-or-none law** (1).

These meanings derive from the vernacular meaning of the term (and its Latin form, ➤ **limen**, which see for details on usage) where the clear connotation is of a

point that separates one domain from another, just as the *threshold* of a house demarcates the interior from the exterior. In practice, however, psychological thresholds are only determinable through statistical procedures; they do not exist as unambiguous values. See here the discussions under ➤ **measurement of *threshold** and ➤ **signal-detection theory**. syn., *limen*; adj., *liminal*.

threshold, dual The term refers to the fact that some sensory dimensions seem to display two thresholds. For example, in the study of smell, there is one threshold at which the subject can just detect the presence of an odor and a second, higher one at which the subject can identify the odor.

threshold, measurement of Various psychophysical methods exist for determining the sensory ➤ **thresholds** (1, 2) for any sensory modality. The following three are the most basic and derive from the original work of Gustav Theodore Fechner. They are used for establishing both absolute and differential thresholds, since the same procedural principles apply in both: (a) *Method of limits* (also known as the *method of serial exploration* and the *method of minimal change*). For establishing a differential threshold a series of stimuli is presented in ascending and descending steps and the subject (or observer) reports whether each stimulus was larger, smaller or equal to a comparison stimulus. For absolute thresholds, there is no comparison stimulus and the subject simply reports whether the presence of the stimulus was detected or not. The usual convention is to take the 50% point as determining the threshold – the point at which the subject detects the stimulus half the time (for absolute thresholds) or determines that it is detectibly different from the comparison stimulus on half the trials (for differential thresholds). (b) *Method of constant stimuli* (also called the *method of right and wrong cases* and the *frequency method*). Similar to the method of limits except that rather than using a graded series of stimuli presented in ascending or descending fashion, a number of fixed stimuli are selected and each is presented many times in random order. (c) *Method of adjustment* (also called the *method of average error*, *method of reproduction* and *equation method*). Here the subject adjusts the stimulus directly. For the differential threshold it is adjusted relative to a comparison stimulus; for the absolute threshold the subject finds the weakest value detectable. ➤ **signal detection theory**. These represent the classical methods; not surprisingly, a number of variants exist but most are too arcane even for this volume.

threshold shift 1. Generally, any permanent or temporary shift in the threshold for a particular stimulus. **2.** In the study of audition, an *increase* in the threshold for a sound stimulus, a partial deafness.

Thurstone-type scales A number of scales, mainly ones constructed to measure attitudes, are collectively referred to by this label. All derive from the work of the American psychometrician, L. L. Thurstone, and are based on the general psychophysical technique known as the ➤ **method of *equal-appearing intervals**. The general procedure for constructing such scales is to take a number of statements reflecting particular attitudes with respect to some topic (e.g., capital punishment, abortion, apartheid) and have a large number of persons (called *raters* or *judges*) sort them in piles ranging from most strongly agreeing with the statement to most strongly disagreeing with it. The percentage of judges placing each statement in the various piles is calculated and forms the basis for determining the scale values assigned to each statement. Once such a scale has been constructed, a single score can be derived from any new person that reflects his or her attitudes on the issue. The technique here is simply to have each new subject indicate agreement or disagreement with each statement and then take the mean of the scale values of those with which agreement has been indicated.

-thymia, -thymic ➤ **-thymo-**.

thymine One of the four nucleotide bases that make up ➤ **deoxyribonucleic acid**. In ➤ **ribonucleic acid**, thymine is replaced by *uracil*.

-thymo- (-thymia, -thymic) 1. From the Greek meaning, *emotion, temper* or *soul*. Combining forms are used freely to connote a connection with emotionality, affect, mood, etc. **2.** Combining form for terms relating to the *thymus gland*.

thymus A gland located in the upper thorax anterior to and above the heart. Small at birth, it grows rapidly during the first two years of life, reaches its maximum size at puberty and undergoes involution after that. It produces the hormone *thymosin*, which plays a role in the development of immune responses. Removal during childhood is associated with increased susceptibility to infections and disease in later life.

thyroid (gland) An endocrine gland located at the base of the neck. It has two primary lobes lying on either side of the point where the larynx and trachea meet. The secretions of the thyroid control general metabolism and are important in the regulation of growth. ➤ **hypothyroidism** and **hyperthyroidism**.

thyroxin The thyroid hormone. Its main effect is an increase in metabolism. Excessive secretions lead to ➤ **hyperthyroidism**, deficiencies result in ➤ **hypothyroidism**. Untreated hypothyroidism in infancy leads to ➤ **cretinism**.

tic A stereotyped, involuntary, spasmodic, nonrhythmic movement or vocalization. Tics are experienced as virtually irresistible although mild forms can be suppressed to some extent. Stress and anxiety typically exacerbate the condition; concentrated activity and sleep ameliorate it. ➤ **tic disorders**.

tic disorders A class of disorders marked by movement or vocal ➤ **tics** and usually first manifested during childhood or adolescence. They are classified as either *chronic* or *transient* with a one-year duration being the distinguishing criterion. E.g., ➤ **Tourette's syndrome**.

tic douloureux ➤ **trigeminal neuralgia**.

tickle A rather peculiar sensation with accompanying reflex-like muscle movements produced most readily by light stroking of the skin. Tickle is a rather complex experience and dependent upon the location on the body stimulated, the amount of pressure applied, who is doing the tickling, whether or not it is anticipated and other factors. It is usually accompanied by emotional qualities, often strong, which are both slightly aversive in that there is often an attempt to avoid the stimulus and pleasurable in that it is sought out under the proper conditions. If one attempts to tickle oneself, it is possible to produce the reflex muscular reactions but the emotional 'tone' is missing.

tidal air The air that is inhaled and exhaled during normal breathing while at rest.

tilde (˜) **1.** In logic, the symbol for negation, ˜*A* means *not* A. **2.** In linguistics, a diacritical placed over a letter in writing to mark a modified pronunciation.

timbre Tonal quality, tonal character. The subjective experience associated with complex acoustic stimuli that results from the patterns of overtones, combination tones, harmonics and resonances.

time 1 n. A slippery concept indeed. As St Augustine puzzled it: when one asks him 'what is time?' he knows what it is, but no sooner is the question posed than the answer eludes him. The difficulty, he argued, lay in the problem of measurement and in the tendency to look for analogy between spatial and temporal measurements. These problems have received a certain, albeit not totally satisfactory, resolution in modern relational conceptions of time as an aspect of a four-dimensional space-time manifold. In this conception, time is not a separate 'thing' and it becomes metaphysically meaningless to talk of the 'flow' of time or the 'passage' of time. Rather, the full spatiotemporal structure of things is given by the changing distribution of matter.

The reason for going into this problem here is that this relational perspective is precisely the manner in which psychologists, perhaps without knowing it, speak of time and it is the only even marginally satisfactory way in which to conceptualize the psychological experiencing of time, duration, extension and the varied connotations of words like *past, present, future, now, then*, etc. Put simply, from a psychological point of view, time is always dealt with relativistically; time is marked and phenomenologically experienced as events occurring relative to other events. See, in this context, ➤ **psychological *time**, ➤ **social *time. 2** n. For those who find the above unrevealing it will do quite well to think of time as the interval between the beginning and the ending of a thing or event as measured by some arbitrarily selected marking device such as a stopwatch, a calendar, etc. **3** vb. To evaluate or measure the duration of an event.

time-and-motion analysis In industrial-organizational psychology, a study of the time that it takes for particular actions or operations to be carried out.

timed test Any test that has time constraints imposed on the person taking it. ➤➤ **speed test**.

time error ➤ **error, time**.

time out A period of time during which the behaviors under consideration are prevented from occurring or if they occur they go unreinforced. In experimental research of operant behavior a time out can be brought about by any number of techniques including removing the experimental subject, removing the manipulandum, introducing distracting stimuli or simply turning off all lights and plunging the experimental chamber into darkness. As a technique in behavior therapy it is used to weaken undesirable behavior, e.g., depositing a child throwing a temper tantrum gently but firmly in a room away from everyone else. abbrev., *TO*.

time perception The perception of the passage of time; the awareness of duration. The term is generally restricted to subjective time, the sense of the passage of time or the awareness of when an event occurred relative to other events. See here the extended discussion under ➤ **time** (especially 1).

time, psychological Experienced time, subjective time. The sense of duration independent of external markers like clocks, calendars, day/night cycles. It seems clear that this sense of time must be dependent upon internal, endogenous events. Some of these may be biological (➤ **biological clock, circadian rhythm**) and others may be mental or cognitive (➤ **cognitive marker**).

time sample ➤ **sample, time**.

time score Quite literally, a score based on how long it took to carry out a particular operation, solve a problem, identify a stimulus, etc.

time sense ➤ **time perception**.

time series The arranging or organizing of data along a time dimension, usually with constant temporal categories marked. For example, changes in some behavior may be coded along a temporal dimension in which observations are taken every day at noon, or once a week, etc. Time series are common modes of analysis for phenomena that show cyclical fluctuation, e.g., ➤ **circadian rhythm**.

time, social Time as marked and coded in accordance with significant events within a particular society or culture. The notions of astronomical time or clock time are not always present in this form of subjective time; the frame of reference becomes societal phenomena and, hence, concepts like 'before' or 'after' are relativistically marked but concepts like 'how long before (or after)' may not be. Social time scales may be very different from culture to culture.

time study ➤ **time-and-motion analysis**.

tinnitus A subjective sensation of a ringing or tinkling in the ears experienced in the absence of any external acoustic stimulus. It can be produced by a number of causes including diseases of the outer, middle or inner ear, nerve damage or as a reaction to some drugs such as quinine and aspirin.

tip-of-the-tongue (TOT) state A term coined by R. Brown and D. McNeill, albeit the concept that it denotes goes back to William James, who gave, in 1890, a most poetic characterization of this mental state in which one cannot quite recall a name or a word. As James put it. 'The rhythm of a lost word may be there without a sound to clothe it; the evanescent sense of something which is the initial vowel or consonant may mock us fitfully without growing more distinct. Everyone must know the tantalizing effect of the blank rhythm of some forgotten verse, restlessly dancing in one's mind, striving to be filled out with words.' In other words, the missing name or word is 'on the tip of the tongue.'

tissue Generally, any organic structure made up of cells with similar structures and common functions which are organized or bound together in some manner.

tissue need ➤ **need, tissue**.

titillate 1. To excite or arouse sexually. **2.** To tickle.

T-lymphocytes ➤ **immune reactions, specific**.

TM ➤ **transcendental meditation**

T-maze A maze shaped like a T, consisting of an approach alley and two arms, either one of which the subject may choose.

TMR ➤ **trainable mentally retarded**.

TO ➤ **time out**.

tobacco withdrawal ➤ **nicotine withdrawal**.

toilet training Simply, training an infant

801

to urinate and defecate in the socially accepted place and manner. Considerable fuss has been generated around this process, stimulated primarily by the notion derived from psychoanalytic theory that the manner in which toilet training is carried out may have a lasting impact on the individual's personality. Specifically, harsh or severe toilet training was hypothesized to lead to a neurotic perfectionism, stinginess and a generally ungiving and unforgiving personality. There is little (no?) evidence to support this presumed tie with toilet training other than the obvious – that harsh and severe parenting in any and all aspects of child-rearing may lead to a neurotic personal style in adulthood.

token **1.** An object taken to represent some thing or event, a ➤ **sign. 2.** A mark characteristic or indicative of some other thing or idea or principle, a ➤ **symbol. 3.** An object such as a coin that can be used as a medium of exchange. ➤ **token economy. 4.** A specific utterance or written form of a linguistic expression. In 'happiness begets happiness' there are three word tokens but only two word types. See here ➤ **type (4)** and **type–token ratio**.

token economy A form of behavior therapy in which a therapeutic environment is established based on the use of ➤ **tokens** (3) as secondary reinforcers. Derived from the premises of theories of conditioning and learning, such economies have been introduced into mental institutions, prisons, educational programs with problem children and the like. They operate according to three basic principles: (a) the patient (prisoner, child) is reinforced with tokens for appropriate behavior; (b) the number of tokens for a response is proportional to the requirements of the response (e.g., more work and more tokens); (c) the tokens may be cashed in for real, valued, rewards.

token-identity theory ➤ **identity theory**.

token reward A ➤ **token** (3).

tolerance **1.** An attitude of liberal accept-

ance of the behaviors, beliefs and values of others. The term is used by some with very positive connotations, in the sense that tolerance embodies vigorous defense of others' values and recognition of the worth of pluralism and that the truly tolerant person will resist any attempt to inhibit their free expression. Others, however, use it in a vaguely negative sense implying that tolerance is a kind of strained forbearance, a sort of gritting of one's teeth while putting up with the behavior, beliefs and values of others. This latter usage derives from: **2.** The ability to endure stress, strain, pain, etc., without serious harm. **3.** Shortened form of ➤ **drug *tolerance**.

tolerance, acute ➤ **Drug *tolerance** which develops very rapidly; on occasion a single dose may be sufficient. syn., *tachyphylaxis*.

tolerance, chronic ➤ **Drug *tolerance** which develops gradually over time with repeated doses. Two kinds of chronic tolerance usually distinguished are ➤ **drug-dispositional *tolerance** and **pharmacodynamic *tolerance**.

tolerance, cross ➤ **Drug *tolerance** for one pharmacological compound produced by chronic doses of another from the same family of drugs. For example, chronic use of heroin produces increased tolerance for all other opiates, even though they may never have actually been sampled.

tolerance, drug A condition of diminished responsiveness to a particular drug resulting from repeated exposure to it. Once tolerance has developed, increased doses are required to produce the effects achieved earlier with small doses. Various types of drug tolerance are distinguished; ➤ **acute *tolerance, chronic *tolerance, drug-dispositional *tolerance, pharmacodynamic *tolerance**.

tolerance, drug-dispositional ➤ **Chronic *tolerance** to a drug characterized by an increase in the speed and effectiveness with which the body can dispose of the substance. Alcohol illustrates this kind of tolerance whereby over time the body comes to metabolize it more and more rapidly. Compare with ➤ **pharmacodynamic *tolerance**.

tolerance level The acceptable limits of a substance that, if exceeded, would be potentially harmful.

tolerance of ambiguity ➤ ambiguity, tolerance of.

tolerance of anxiety ➤ anxiety, tolerance of.

tolerance, pharmacodynamic ➤ **Chronic *tolerance** of a drug, characterized by a gradual decrease in the effectiveness of the substance to act upon the bodily tissues. The barbiturates show this form of tolerance. Compare with ➤ **drug-dispositional *tolerance**.

Tolmanian The point of view associated with the work of the American psychologists Edward Chace Tolman (1886–1959). Tolman is probably best categorized as a neobehaviorist. Because of his strong affiliation with building a scientific psychology he embraced the core notion of ➤ **behaviorism** – that what an organism *does* is the source of legitimate data – but, because he eschewed the atomism of the Watsonian approach, he advocated the use of intervening variables and focused on a number of very non-behaviorist processes such as *purpose* (➤ **purposive psychology**), *expectation* (➤ **sign-Gestalt**), *belief* (➤ **belief-value matrix**) and *spatial representation* (➤ **cognitive map**).

-tome, -tomy Combining form meaning *cutting, slicing* or an *instrument for cutting*.

tomography An X-ray technique which enables one to obtain a picture of the three-dimensional structure of tissue.

tonal Pertaining to tones. Note that *tonal* and *auditory* are sometimes (but not, strictly speaking, correctly) used interchangeably – particularly in combined phrases. For entries not found below see those following ➤ **auditory**.

tonal attributes Generally, any of the

characteristics of auditory sensations that can be independently assessed. The standard analysis is that there are four such attributes: ➤ **pitch, loudness, volume** and **density**; see each for details. Also called *tonal dimensions* or, more generally, *auditory attributes* or *dimensions*.

tonal brightness A dimension of sensation accompanying auditory stimuli which seems, subjectively, to relate to a sense of the 'brightness' or 'dullness' of the sound. High-pitched tones are typically called bright or sharp and low-pitched ones dull or soft. syn., *tonal brilliance*.

tonal character ➤ timbre.

tonal color ➤ timbre.

tonal density ➤ density (3).

tonal dimension ➤ tonal attributes.

tonal gap Quite literally, a gap or hole in auditory perception, a region along the frequency dimension where, for any number of reasons, an individual shows reduced sensitivity. Compare with ➤ **tonal island**.

tonal interaction(s) Collectively, those interactions that occur between two or more tones sounded simultaneously and the properties of the cochlea of the inner ear. E.g., ➤ **combination tone**.

tonal intermittence ➤ auditory *flicker.

tonal island Quite literally, an island in auditory perception, a region along the frequency dimension where a person displays normal hearing but is surrounded by regions of reduced sensitivity. Compare with ➤ **tonal gap**.

tonality Loosely, an aspect of auditory sensation that refers to the perceived sense of 'intimacy' of any given tone to its various octaves. Tonality has been put toward as a possible additional ➤ **tonal attribute**.

tonal range ➤ tonal scale.

tonal scale The full range of frequencies perceivable in normal human hearing. In the young adult whose ears have not been assaulted by the outrages of factories, sub-ways, tubes and high-intensity rock music, the range is roughly 20–20,000 Hz. Also called *tonal range*.

tonal volume ➤ **volume**.

tone 1. Any sound produced by a regular or periodic vibrating source. Tones are *simple* or *pure* (➤ **tone, pure**) when the source vibrates with a single frequency and *compound* or *complex* (➤ **tone, compound (or complex)**) when more than one frequency is present. The term ➤ **noise** is reserved for auditory stimuli in which no regular periodic component exists. There are several different kinds of tones that can be identified; some follow this entry, others are found under the appropriate alphabetical listing. 2. In music, a standard unit that forms the basis for dividing up an octave. Different musical forms use different units; in the music of the Western world the whole tone corresponds to one-sixth of the octave, which yields 12 semitones. 3. A general body state in which organs, muscles, glands, etc. are functioning normally. 4. A state of normal muscular tension characterized by a slight stretching of muscle. Muscle tone is maintained by proprioceptive reflex and serves to keep the body in a general state of preparedness. syn., *tonus*, *tonicity*. 5. Loosely, emotional quality, mood or feeling. 6. In some languages (e.g., Chinese) a type of phoneme based on pitch and pitch contour. 7. Nontechnically, a characteristic quality of voice, as in the common admonishment, 'Don't you use that tone of voice with me.'

tone color ➤ **timbre**.

tone, compound (or **complex**) Any tone made up of two or more simple tones. Any complex tone can be analyzed into a number of pure, sinusoidal components by means of a ➤ **Fourier analysis**.

tone deafness Loosely, any poorer than normal ability to detect difference in pitch. The term does not carry the usual connotations of *deafness* in that thresholds for

individual tones may be normal. Also known as *asonia*.

tone, intermittence ➤ **interruption tone**.

tone, pure A tone produced by a single periodic vibration occurring at a fixed rate. Pure tones are approximated by good tuning forks, but the really pure tone is only heard when generated by sophisticated electronic equipment. Also called *simple tone*.

tone, summation ➤ **combination tone**.

tonic 1 adj. Pertaining to muscle ➤ **tone** (4) or *tonus*. 2 adj. Descriptive of languages that use ➤ **tone** (6) phonemes. 3 n. Any substance that increases bodily ➤ **tone** (3, 4). 4 n. The keynote of a scale or a chord founded on the keynote.

tonic immobility A condition of complete immobility resulting from contraction of muscle groups. It serves as a protective reaction against predators in many animals. Also called ➤ **freezing** and ➤ **death feigning**; see each for details on usage.

tonicity The state of possessing ➤ **tone** (3 or 4).

tonic spasm ➤ **spasm**.

tonoclonic Both *tonic* and *clonic*; used occasionally of severe muscle spasm.

tonometer 1. A device for measuring muscle tone. 2. A device for measuring the pitch of a tone.

tonotopic representation The point-by-point relationship between the basilar membrane and its representation along the auditory cortex.

tonotopy ➤ **tonotopic representation**.

tonus ➤ **tone** (3 and especially 4).

topagnosis A loss of the ability to localize the site of a tactile stimulus.

top-down processing Cognitive processing controlled by general principles, thoughts or ideas about the nature of the material being processed. The ➤ **word-superiority effect** is a good example of such processing. Compare with ➤ **bottom-up processing**.

topectomy A variation of the frontal lobotomy in which small cuts are made through the thalamofrontal tracts. ➤ **lobotomy**.

topography 1. A label used generally of any theoretical system in which the basic processes are characterized in terms of the regions or locales in which they are presumed to operate. The classic example here is Freud's vertical metaphor of the *conscious, preconscious* and *unconscious*. 2. The full characterization of the pertinent components of any response. For example, an operant response such as a bar press by a rat may occur in any one of many ways: with any paw, with its nose; it may be a forceful press, a weak press, a trembling press, etc. Each or all of these components may be selectively reinforced and thus modify the topography of the response.

topological psychology A descriptive term often used of Kurt Lewin's ➤ **field theory**. ➤➤ **topology**.

topology A branch of mathematics that deals with those properties of space which remain unchanged when the space is distorted. In psychology the principles have emerged in several areas, notably Lewin's ➤ **field theory** and Piaget's arguments concerning the infant's representation of space.

-topy Combining form meaning *place, location*.

torsion 1. Generally, the condition of being twisted or the act of twisting. 2. The minor rotation of the eye through the meridian (front to back) axis which occurs during normal eye movement. Also called (*ocular*) *torsional movement*.

total determination, coefficient of The square of the ➤ **multiple correlation coefficient**; hence, a number reflecting the proportion of total ➤ **variance** accounted for by all the independent variables in a multiple correlation.

total institution ➤ **institution, total**.

total recall Loosely, the ability to recall completely all information committed to memory. Such perfect storage and retrieval of memories is a myth. The closest thing to it is seen in some extremely accomplished mnemonists, who develop rich and elaborate schemes for remembering material (➤ **mnemonic device**) and in rare cases of people with eidetic imagery.

totem 1. An object or class of objects (usually but not always a species of animal or plant) which is viewed by members of a society or group as having a special, mystical and symbolic role in their community. 2. Any symbolic representation of the venerated object(s) in the above sense. In Freud's more speculative theorizing, the totem was taken as symbolic of the primal father.

TOTE (unit) An acronym for *test–operate–test–exit*. A hypothesized unit of planned, sensorimotor activity which is easiest to explain with an example. A person fills a bathtub and puts a hand in to check the temperature ('test'); finding it too hot, cold water is added ('operate'); finding it now satisfactory ('test') the water is turned off ('exit'). The TOTE unit was put forward as a model of behaviors in which actions to be taken are based on plans modified by feedback concerning actions already taken, a basic conceptualization borrowed from ➤ **cybernetics**.

TOT (state) ➤ **tip-of-the-tongue (TOT) state**.

touch Loosely and generally, the contact of some object with the body or the sensory experience which accompanies such contact. Since Aristotle we have been saddled with the notion that we possess a 'sense of touch,' and although the popular press (and even some technical literature) still refer to it as such, properly touch is not a unitary sensory system but an aspect of a complex group of ➤ **cutaneous senses** which includes pressure, pain (of at least two kinds), the temperature senses and tickle.

touch blends Sensations which are a mixture of other cutaneous experiences. The classic example is 'wetness,' which is produced by a blending of pressure and cold and can be experienced without any moisture at all as anyone who ever put on a rubber surgical glove can testify.

touch spot Loosely, any small local area of the skin that is highly sensitive to light touching.

tough-minded ➤ **tender-minded**.

Tourette's syndrome (or **disorder**) A neurological ➤ **tic disorder** characterized, in mild form, by involuntary tics and movements and, in advanced cases, by large involuntary bodily movements, noises like barks and whistles, and in many instances an uncontrollable urge to utter obscenities.

toxemia Any abnormal condition produced by toxic substances carried throughout the body by the bloodstream. var., *toxaemia*.

toxic Pertaining to poison, poisonous.

toxicosis 1. Any condition caused by poisoning. 2. An acquired syndrome in which an organism learns to avoid a particular food because of a conditioned aversion response to its smell or taste. The toxicosis reaction can be formed in a single trial during which consumption of a novel food is followed by nausea and sickness – even when the toxic reaction itself is not experienced for some hours after eating. The key to conditioning here is that the original association must be with an internal, digestively linked stimulus, either the smell or taste of the food substance, and the aversive outcome must be associated with an alimentary function such as nausea. Toxicosis is a particularly interesting phenomenon because it can be formed over such a long interval of time; in all other forms of classical conditioning the optimal interval is of the order of half a second. Also known by a virtual blizzard of other terms including *conditioned flavor* (or *food*, or *taste*) *aversion* (or *avoidance*), *learned flavor* (or *food*, or *taste*) *aversion* (or *avoidance*), any of the above without the '*conditioned*' or '*learned*' qualifier, *bait-shyness*, or simply the *Garcia effect* (after

the psychologist who did most of the early work).

toxic psychosis Any psychosis that results from organic damage produced by a toxic substance, e.g., *alcoholic psychosis*.

toxoplasmosis A syndrome caused by a congenital protozoan infection marked by head abnormalities, brain damage and resulting mental retardation, eye infections and visual impairment, and often seizures.

toy tests A general label for any psychological test utilizing toys. Not surprisingly such tests are used almost exclusively with children and frequently involve free play with common objects like puppets, dolls, blocks, etc. They are usually considered to be projective tests in that the child is assumed to reveal attitudes and feelings in the manner of play.

trace 1. The hypothesized modification of neural tissue resulting from any form of stimulation. 2. A minute amount of a substance. 3. A mark or sign.

trace conditioning An experimental conditioning procedure in which the onset of the unconditioned stimulus (US) does not occur until some time after the termination of the conditioned stimulus (CS). Thus, any conditioning that occurs depends upon a hypothetical trace that is left after the CS terminates. Trace conditioning, when it occurs, reveals the operation of a rather basic memory process. Compare with ➤ **delay conditioning**.

trace, perseverative Hull's term for neural firing that continued after the stimulus was removed. The more modern characterization of this general principle is found under ➤ **sensory information store**.

tracking 1. Following a target. 2. In education, the separating of each grade into levels and the assigning of each child to a particular level based on assessments of his or her (presumed) ability to master the material. Tracking may take place within a given school or separate schools may be established for different levels. Also called *streaming*.

tract 1. Generally, a pathway. 2. A bundle of nerve fibers that constitutes a particular functional and/or anatomical unit. 3. A group of organs that constitutes a continuous functioning pathway, e.g., digestive tract. 4. In sociology, a small division of a city or urban area.

tradition Any social custom or belief or a coordinated set of such customs and beliefs that are handed down through the generations.

traditional authority ➤ authority, traditional.

tradition-directed In the terminology of D. Riesman, a tendency to conform to and follow a society's traditions. As with his other terms, ➤ **inner-directed** and ➤ **outer-directed**, it is used for both the society which fosters such behavior patterns and the individual who displays them.

train Loosely, to direct activities and/or functions so as to produce some specified end state of condition. The term is used broadly; one can train plants, animals and people.

trainability The degree to which a particular individual can profit from training.

trainable mentally retarded (TMR) A label for a child who scores on a standardized IQ test within the range generally taken to represent ➤ **moderate *mental retardation**. ➤ **educable mentally retarded** for details on how the term is used.

training Generally, any specific instructional program or set of procedures designed to yield as an end product an organism capable of making some specific response(s) or engaging in some complex skilled activity. This broad definition encompasses essentially all contemporary usages of the term, from the programs of animal trainers in a circus (who use operant-conditioning procedures) to the physical regimen of an athlete or to a parent toilet-training a child.

training trial ➤ **learning *trial**.

trait Generally, any enduring characteristic of a person that can serve an explanatory role in accounting for the observed regularities and consistencies in behavior. This is the proper use of the term; it is incorrect and misleading to use it for the regularities themselves. The point is that a trait is a theoretical entity, a hypothesized, underlying component of the individual that is used to explain that person's behavioral consistencies and the differences between the behavioral consistencies of different persons. In this sense the term has wide applicability: (a) in biology it refers to a distinguishing anatomical feature; (b) in genetics it denotes an inherited characteristic; (c) in a larger sense it covers any aspect of an individual's personality. Note, also, that as one moves through these various domains of usage the referent of the term becomes more abstract and more difficult to assess. The problems become particularly serious here in the study of ➤ **personality**; see that entry, especially 2, and ➤ **personality trait** for details.

trait, acquired A trait that is the result of experience, a learned trait. Contrast with ➤ **inherited *trait**.

trait, compensatory Very loosely, any trait hypothesized to have become a significant part of an individual's make-up in order to compensate for some lack or reduced ability of some other function. ➤ **compensation** (1, 2) for the general theory here.

trait, inherited A trait due to genetic factors, one independent of learning or experience. Contrast with ➤ **acquired *trait**.

trait negativity bias A tendency to let negative information about an individual have a greater impact on impression formation than positive information. Put simply, one bad *trait* may destroy a person's reputation no matter how many good traits are present. Politicians and image makers are acutely aware of this bias.

trait organization A loose term generally taken to refer to some hypothesized set of interrelationships between an individual's various personality traits.

trait profile ➤ **profile analysis**.

trait, source A hypothetical 'deep' trait which is presumed to account for the fact that many ➤ **surface *traits** show relatively high mutual correlations.

trait, surface 1. An interrelated group of behaviors and manners observed to occur across various kinds of environment settings and constraints. 2. A hypothesized trait which is identified by factor analysis and presumed to be responsible for these correlated behaviors.

trait, unique 1. Interpersonally, a rare trait, one found in but a few. 2. Intrapersonally, a trait that shows essentially no correlation with others.

trait validity ➤ **validity, trait**.

trait variability Quite literally, the disperson of scatter of scores of an individual on several tests measuring traits.

trance 1. From the Latin for *passage*, trance originally referred to the state of passage from life into death. 2. A state in which consciousness is fragile or missing, voluntary action is poor or absent and normal bodily functions are reduced, perhaps to the degree that the individual appears to be in a deep sleep. This meaning carries some of the vestiges of the earlier meaning.

trance and possession disorder Temporary alteration in consciousness accompanied by a loss of sense of identity, a selective focusing on specific aspects of the environment, and stereotyped behaviors that are experienced as beyond one's control. These symptoms are accompanied by a belief that one is possessed by a spirit, power, or another person. The term is only used for conditions that result in distress and dysfunction and not for such states when they occur as normal components of religious and other cultural ceremonies. Recent evidence suggests that this disorder is the most common ➤ **dissociative disorder** reported in non-Western cultures.

trance disorder, dissociative An involuntary state of ➤ **trance** (2) that is not regarded as a normal aspect of the individual's religious or cultural traditions. It is the most common symptom of the various ➤ **culture-specific syndromes**.

trance, hypnotic Generally, a ➤ **trance** (2) induced by the use of hypnosis. Its most compelling feature is the high suggestibility of the subject, who tends to give up control over actions to the hypnotist. ➤ **hypnosis**.

trance, religious A trance induced by intense religious devotion. Actually the term *trance* here is slightly misleading, because this state typically does not show the reduced bodily function often associated with it but rather manifests an energetic, vigorous, even frenzied quality. Hence the term *ecstatic state* is preferred by some, although, to be sure, this has its problems with the connotations of ecstasy.

tranquilizers A generic label used for any of several classes of drugs all of which have one or more of the following properties: antianxiety, sedative, muscle-relaxant, anticonvulsant, antiagitation. The term is rarely used in the contemporary technical literature although it may still be found in some texts and in the popular press. When it is used, a distinction is often made between the 'minor' and the 'major' tranquilizers. The former are now classified as ➤ **antianxiety drugs** or *anxiolytics* and the latter as ➤ **antipsychotic drugs** or simply *antipsychotics*. See those terms for more details.

tranquilizers, major A general label for those drugs which are used primarily to improve the mood and behavior of patients with severe psychiatric disorders. The term is a connotative nightmare and is no longer used in the technical literature. Indeed, these drugs should really never have been called 'tranquilizers' since they have rather different actions than merely tranquilizing, and affixing the adjective 'major' suggests that these drugs are on a continuum with the ➤ **minor *tranquilizers**, which is pharmacologically incorrect. The preferred term is ➤ **antipsychotic drugs** because their most significant function is the alleviation of many of the symptoms of various psychoses.

tranquilizers, minor A general term for any of several classes of drugs that are used primarily in the treatment of anxiety and psychiatric disorders that have an anxiety-related component. The term is a misleading one in that it suggests that these drugs are on a continuum with the ➤ **major *tranquilizers**, which is pharmacologically incorrect. The preferred term is ➤ **antianxiety drugs** (see for details) or, simply, *anxiolytics*.

trans- Combining form meaning *across, beyond, over* or *through*.

transaction A behavioral event or aspect thereof whose essential nature is captured by interactions between the actor, other individuals involved and the environment. This very general meaning is carried into various areas of psychology: see the following entries for examples.

transactional analysis (TA) A form of psychotherapy originally developed by Eric Berne. It is practiced in a straightforward group setting in which the primary goal is to have the client achieve an adaptive, mature and realistic attitude toward life, to have, in Berne's words, 'the adult ego maintain hegemony over the impulsive child.'

transactional psychology An extension of the basic ideas of transactionalism from the study of perception (➤ **transactional theory**) to other areas of human behavior, notably social interaction.

transactional theory (of perception) A theory of perception based on the notion that what is perceived is dependent on knowledge gathered from interactive experiences with the environment. Perception, in this view, results from acquired but unconscious assumptions about the environment, represented as probabilities of transactions occurring within it. The real 'out-there' world and its perceptual properties are, it is argued, to be created in the transaction. The theory shares some of the principles of Egon Brunswik's theory, although the notion of ➤ **ecological validity** central to his arguments is down-played. The famous ➤ **Ames room** was used in many experiments of the transactionalists to reveal how one's expectations would lead one to make false perceptual inferences.

transcendental meditation (TM) A form of meditation and the techniques for practicing it developed and most effectively promulgated by the Maharishi Mahesh Yogi. ➤ **mysticotranscendent therapy** and **meditation**.

transcortical Lit., across the cortex. Typically used for neural pathways leading from one part of the cortex to another.

transcortical aphasia ➤ **aphasia, transcortical**.

transcortical motor aphasia ➤ **aphasia, transcortical motor**.

transcortical sensory aphasia ➤ **aphasia, transcortical sensory**.

transcription **1.** In general, an exact copy of something. **2.** In studies of language and communication, a complete record of what was said. When unqualified, it is assumed that normal orthographic forms are used, i.e. that the transcription is written in ordinary script; a *phonetic transcription* is one which has been rendered into the ➤ **International Phonetic Alphabet**; a *phonemic transcription* is one in which the text is presented in phonemic notation. **3.** In studies of nonverbal communication, a coded record of movements and gestures. Note that, in this usage, the copy is not nearly as exact as in 2. **4.** In the synthesis of genes and proteins, the process of duplication of information from aspects of deoxyribonucleic acid (DNA). Messenger ribonucleic acid (MRNA) is synthesized by transcription, the information being carried to ribosomes containing RNA.

transcutaneous electrical stimulation The use of electrical stimulation in ➤ **acupuncture**; see that term for details.

transducer Generally, any device that converts energy from one form to another. The term is used very broadly; ➤ **transduction** et seq.

transduction 1. Generally, the process by which some 'thing' is transformed. The 'thing' is usually specified, either by depending a qualifying term or by the context, hence: 2. In the study of sensory processes, the sequence of operations by which physical energy (e.g., sound waves, light) is transformed into patterns of neural impulses that give rise to sensory experiences. Often called *sensory transduction*. 3. In cognitive psychology, the operation of recoding information from one form into another. 4. In genetics, the transfer of genetic material from one cell to another through a vector.

transductive logic ➤ **transductive reasoning**.

transductive reasoning Piaget's term for the type of reasoning found in the preoperatory-stage child. Transductive reasoning tends to proceed from instance to instance, with the common thread that the child is centering on one particular aspect. Hence, it is neither deductive nor inductive. Occasionally it is called *transductive logic*, although its alogical quality makes this the nonpreferred term.

transection A cutting made across the long axis of tissue or a neural fiber; a cross- ➤ **section** (2).

transfer Loosely and generally, the process whereby experience on one task has an effect (either *positive* or *negative*) on performance on a different task subsequently undertaken. The underlying notion is that the knowledge or skill acquired in the first task either facilitates or interferes with carrying out the subsequent task. Since the term is so general,

qualifiers are often used to denote the specific type of transfer under consideration.

transfer appropriate processing Encoding of a stimulus or a set of stimuli in a manner that facilitates ➤ **positive *transfer** to a novel situation.

transferase An enzyme that catalyzes the transfer of particles from one chemical compound to another.

transfer, bilateral Transfer of performance to one side of the body following training of the opposite side, e.g., improved left-handed performance following right-handed training.

transference 1. Most generally, the passing on, displacing or 'transferring' of an emotion or affective attitude from one person onto another person or object. 2. Within psychoanalysis, the displacement of feelings and attitudes applicable toward other persons (usually one's parents but also siblings, a spouse, etc.) onto the analyst. 3. The emotional state that results from the process in 2. Transference here is often termed either *positive* or *negative*, depending upon whether the person develops pleasant or hostile attitudes toward the analyst. Note that many authorities regard transference as a state that is ubiquitous in human interaction. Its conspicuousness in psychoanalysis, they argue, is attributable simply to the calculated neutrality of the analyst, which allows it to be more unambiguously observed.

transference neurosis 1. Generally, a neurosis in which satisfaction is achieved by transforming one's libidinal investment from appropriate to inappropriate persons or objects. 2. Specifically, such a situation as it occurs during an ongoing psychoanalysis where the analyst becomes the inappropriate object.

transference resistance 1. Generally, the failure to recognize or acknowledge the process of ➤ **transference** (2) during psychoanalysis. 2. The use of transference during psychoanalysis as a defense against anxiety. Sense 1 here is a resistance *to* transference; 2 is the use *of* transference to resist something anxiety-provoking, for example, unearthing the past or the prospect of terminating analysis and being forced to do without the protection of the analyst. Sense 2 is often hyphenated to distinguish it from 1.

transfer function ➤ **modulation-transfer function**.

transfer, negative Transfer in which knowledge or skill acquired in one context or one task results in lessened performance in some other context or on some other task.

transfer, nonspecific Transfer in which general principles or rules learned in one situation are used in another even though there are few or no specific common elements. *Nonspecific* here is used to mean *abstract* or *rule-defined*. Compare with ➤ **specific *transfer**, which is used for more concrete cases.

transfer of training Transfer of learned skills from one situation to another. Some authors have used this term as a synonym of ➤ **transfer**. This is, however, not recommended, in that the *training* notion tends to be associated with motor acts and overtly displayed skills, whereas the term *transfer* itself is a much broader one which encompasses aspects that are symbolic and abstract. Put simply, *transfer of training* is best used only in behavioristic discourses.

transfer, positive Transfer in which knowledge or skills acquired in one context or on one task results in increased performance in another context or on another task.

transfer RNA ➤ **ribonucleic acid**.

transfer, specific Transfer in which there is a significant overlap in the specifics of the two tasks such that the knowledge or skill acquired in the learning of the first relates directly to performance on the second. *Specific* is generally used in the context to mean *concrete*. Compare with ➤ **non-specific *transfer**, where that which is transferred is more abstract.

transformation 1. Generally, modification or change in the form or structure of something. Clearly, a very rich conceptual notion and, not surprisingly, the term finds wide application in various specific domains. Hence: **2.** In mathematics and statistics, the modification of an equation or set of values that is made without altering the underlying 'meaning' or the set of quantitative relations entailed in the equation or set of values. See, e.g., ➤ **arcsine transformation. 3.** In logic, the systematic replacement of one set of symbols by another set according to rules which leave the two logically equivalent. Also called the *transformation rule* or *rule of inference*. **4.** In psychoanalysis, the altering of a repressed impulse or emotion so that in its disguised form it can be 'admitted' to consciousness. **5.** In linguistics, a rule that operates on a string of symbols (usually called a *phrase-marker* ➤ **tree** (2)) to convert it into a different string of symbols. For example, the phrase marker $NP_1 + V + NP_2$, which can be shown (with some technical refinements not needed here) to underlie a sentence like 'Max ate the soup,' can be converted by applying (with some even more technical refinements) the *passive transformation* into $NP_2 + $ 'was' $ + V + $ en $ + NP_1$, which underlies the sentence 'The soup was eaten by Max.' ➤ **transformational *grammar** for more details.

transformational (generative) grammar ➤ **transformational *grammar** and **generative *grammar**.

transformational rule ➤ **transformation** (5).

transformation rule ➤ **transformation** (3).

transformed score ➤ **score, transformed**.

transformism A term used occasionally to refer to evolutionary theory. That is, any theory that maintains that new species develop by gradual change induced in already existing species. Compare with ➤ **creationism**.

transient global amnesia ➤ **amnesia, transient global**.

transient ischemic attack Temporary interference with the blood supply to the brain in which no permanent damage is done to cortical tissue. Whatever neurological symptoms occur are temporary and last only a few minutes to several hours.

transient situational personality disorder A general rubric for a group of minor personality disturbances. The usual notion is that in dealing with particular environments, because of stress and attendant anxiety, some people adopt ways of coping that have negative consequences for them. These 'maladaptive' behaviors are not assumed to reflect necessarily any deeper problem and are usually alleviated with environment changes. Examples are emotional withdrawal from a tension-filled marriage, inability to cope in a new job in the ways expected and the like. ➤ **personality disorder**.

transient tic disorder ➤ **tic disorders**.

transition Movement from one area to another or change from one state to another. The term is used generally and freely.

transitional cortex A term used occasionally for those cortical cells that are intermediate in form and function between the phylogenetically older areas of the cortex and the newer areas.

transitional object ➤ **object, transitional**.

transitivity Lit., capable of passing over or through. Hence, a characteristic of a relation between elements x, y and z such that if x is related in a particular fashion to y and y in like fashion to z, then x is necessarily so related to z. 'Taller than' is such a relation and, in general, unidimensional relations will be transitive. 'Like better than' is not necessarily transitive; in general, multidimensional relations do not display transitivity. ➤ **intransitivity**.

translation 1. In genetics, the process through which information coded in messenger RNA (➤ **ribonucleic acid**) is used to produce a new protein molecule. The term derives from the fact that the original code is 'read' (from DNA) and 'translated' by messenger and transfer RNA into a ribosome. 2. In linguistics, the rendering of a message from one language into another. 3. By extension, interpretation of a message.

translocation ➤ **chromosomal alterations**.

translocation Down syndrome A rare form of ➤ **Down syndrome**.

translocation, reciprocal ➤ **chromosomal alterations**.

transmission 1. Generally, transferring or moving something from one location to another or the result of such a process. 2. In genetics, the passing of particular genes (and, by extension, their phenotypic manifestations as physical or behavioral traits) from one or both parents to the offspring. 3. In information theory, the passing of a message from the transmitter through some medium to the receiver. 4. In anthropology and sociology, the passing of traditions and customs to each succeeding generation. ➤ **cultural transmission**. 5. In physiology, the excitation of a neuron by another neuron. ➤ **neurotransmitter**.

transmitter 1. Generally, the source of a message; that aspect or component of any transmission system from which the information emanates. 2. In physiology, the substance that initiates the action of neural transmission whereby one neuron excites a neighboring neuron. Usually called a ➤ **neurotransmitter**, occasionally a *transmitter substance*.

transmitter substance ➤ **neurotransmitter**.

transmutation The act of transforming something with a particular nature, form or condition into another thing with a different nature, form or condition. Occasionally used to characterize the evolutionary emergence of one species from another.

transmutation of measures A relatively rare term for the process of transforming ➤ **raw *scores** into some set of ➤ **standard *scores**.

transmuted score ➤ transformed *score.

transneuronal degeneration Degeneration of a presynaptic or postsynaptic neuron that follows damage to the neuron with which it synapses. Such degeneration helps to explain why a lesion at one site in the central nervous system can have effects on a distant site. Also called *transsynaptic degeneration.*

transorbital lobotomy ➤ lobotomy, transorbital.

transparency 1. A property of an object such that light passes through it without significant distortion or significant reduction in its luminance. 2. A slide or piece of transparent film used to project an image which is drawn on it.

transpersonality An analytic feature of social behavior that is observed to occur across a variety of social settings and is not dependent on any one specific kind of social circumstance for its emergence.

transport Collectively, the mechanisms and processes involved in the movement of substances across a membrane. In physiological research, where the membrane is a biological one, the term *biotransport* is frequently used.

transposition 1. Generally, an exchange between some aspect(s) of two or more elements in a system. This sense of the term is used broadly and those things transposed may be temporal placements, logical relations, functional roles, spatial locations, etc. 2. In learning, a pattern of behavior where the subject selects a response to two or more stimuli based on relational factors and not upon the absolute physical characteristics of the stimuli. For example, a subject is first trained to choose a 4-inch-diameter circle over one with a 3-inch diameter. On a later 'transposition' test, the stimuli are a 4- and a 5-inch-diameter circle. Typically, the subject selects the 5-inch circle showing transposition of a relational concept, 'larger than.' 3. In music, shifting a composition to a

different key. 4. In reading and writing, a ➤ transposition error.

transposition behavior ➤ transposition (2).

transposition error 1. Generally, any error resulting from transposing two or more stimuli or elements of them 2. Specifically, in reading and writing, an error resulting from interchanging two or more letters, syllables or words.

transposition of affect Transferring one's feelings from one ➤ object to another. The term carries the connotation that the object upon which the affect is transposed is not a socially appropriate one. The term is used by some as a synonym of ➤ displacement.

transsexualism A condition characterized primarily by a belief that one is of the wrong sex. Several criteria have been proposed for identifying the true transsexual: (a) discomfort with one's sexual anatomy; (b) a persistent, deep desire to be a member of the other sex; (c) a wish to change one's genitalia; and (d) absence of other psychological disorders or genetic anatomical abnormalities such as hermaphroditism. Transsexualism is usually classified as a ➤ gender-identity disorder and is to be contrasted with ➤ homosexuality and ➤ transvestism. Also known as *sex-role inversion.*

transsituational Characterizing a pattern of social behavior that occurs across a number of social situations and is not dependent on a particular social context.

transsynaptic degeneration ➤ transneuronal degeneration.

transverse At right angles to the longitudinal axis of a body or organ.

transverse section ➤ section (2).

transvestic fetishism . A ➤ sexual disorder marked by intense and recurrent sexual urges and fantasies involving cross-dressing. The individual typically keeps a collection of women's clothes (the condition has only been described in males) and uses them to cross-dress when alone, usually masturbating to various fantasies. In many cases the cross-dressing progresses to public places and can even become the individual's standard mode of dress. Discomfort with one's gender (➤ **gender dysphoria**) may or may not be present. Male professional entertainers who work as female impersonators may or may not have the disorder; the terms are not synonymous. syn., *transvestism*. ➤ **paraphilia**.

transvestism ➤ **transvestic fetishism**.

tranylcypromine A ➤ **monoamine oxidase inhibitor** used as an antidepressant drug. Unlike most other drugs of this type, its effects last but a few hours after one stops taking it.

trapezoid body In the brain, a transverse neural pathway in the pons that arises from axons of cells in the cochlear nucleus. It carries fibers that eventually end up in the superior olivary complex on both sides of the brain stem and hence is an important pathway in the transmission of auditory information.

trauma From the Greek for *wound*, a term used freely either for physical injury caused by some direct external force or for psychological injury caused by some extreme emotional assault. pl., *traumas* or *traumata*.

traumatic aphasia ➤ **aphasia, traumatic**.

traumatic neurosis Loosely, any neurosis that develops as a result of some dramatic event such as severe fright, sudden serious injury and the like. ➤ **gross *stress reaction**.

traumatic psychosis A general term for any serious psychotic-like disorder that results from physical injury, usually a brain lesion.

traumatic shock ➤ **tetanizing shock**.

traumatophilia Unusual accident-proneness. Generally used of individuals who somehow seem to put themselves repeatedly into situations in which something goes seriously wrong, resulting in injury to themselves or to others. Also called *traumatophilic diathesis*.

traveling wave In the study of audition,

a term that describes nicely the mode of action of the basilar membrane when stimulated by a sound source above roughly 150 Hz. Specifically, with stimuli above this frequency there is a pattern of deflection of the membrane that begins at the stiffer, narrow end near the oval window and 'travels' down the membrane to the apex. The point of maximum deflection is given by the frequency of the stimulus, with low-pitched stimuli at the apex and high-pitched at the stapes. Note, if the stimulus is below roughly 150 Hz the whole membrane responds nearly in unison. ➤ **theories of *hearing**.

Treacher Collins syndrome A genetic disorder characterized by facial abnormalities including a misshapen jaw, a retracted chin, large nose, and malformed ears. Most cases have normal intelligence, although hearing and visual impairments may lead to an erroneous diagnosis of mental retardation.

treatment 1. Generally, and loosely, the subjecting of some person or some thing to some action, agent, substance or other influence. 2. Any specific procedure designed to cure or to lessen the severity of a disease or other abnormal condition. This meaning is also rather general and is used to cover medical, pharmacological, surgical or psychotherapeutic procedures. 3. In statistics, analyzing and interpreting data. 4. In experimental design, a particular experimental manipulation or procedure under which subjects are run. This sense is roughly synonymous with ➤ **independent *variable**.

treatment variable ➤ **independent *variable**.

tree (structure or **diagram)** 1. In anatomy and physiology, any structure with a tree-like branching pattern. Hence, dendrites are called tree structures, as are the bronchial tubes and their branches and terminal arborizations. 2. In linguistics, the schematic diagram of a sentence which reveals the underlying linguistic components of the sentence and the manner in which the words and morphemes are grouped together. A tree diagram of this kind is also called a *phrase-marker*, because the basic phrases that make up the sentence are clearly specified and their grammatical status marked.

tremograph Any instrument for recording and measuring tremors.

tremor Generally, any quivering or trembling of a part or parts of the body.

trend Generally, any directional tendency, a drift of events. Usage here is very broad and encompasses discernible patterns in one's data (e.g., ➤ **trend analysis**, **trend test**) and tendencies for persons to behave in particular ways (e.g., ➤ **neurotic trend**).

trend analysis Quite as it says, an analysis of trends, specifically with an eye toward predicting future events. The mathematical basis in all trend analyses is the same as that used in ➤ **interpolation**. ➤ **Delphi method** and **cross-impact matrix method** for some examples of trend analyses.

trend test Any of several statistical tests that assess whether two or more trends seen in the data can be said to be reliably different from each other.

trepan ➤ **trephine**.

trephine 1. To bore a small hole in the skull. 2. An instrument resembling a carpenter's circular saw for perforating the skull. var., *trepan*.

treppe The increasing in the contraction of a muscle when it is either stimulated constantly over a short period of time or stimulated at a rapid and regular rate. Also called *staircase phenomenon* (*treppe* is German for *staircase*).

tri- Combining form meaning *three*.

triads, method of An experimental procedure in which the subject is presented with three stimuli and must select the one that satisfies some criterion, e.g., the odd one, the middle one, etc.

triage The process of screening the sick, wounded or injured in times of crisis and classifying them into three groups: those who will likely recover eventually without therapy, those who are expected to die no matter what is done to assist them and those whose recovery is deemed to depend on their receiving adequate care. The last group is the *priority group* and the recipient of limited resources.

trial 1. Loosely, a try-out, a test, a single effort designed to accomplish something. 2. In experimental research, a single 'unit' where a stimulus is presented and some response is made. In this sense, each trial is generally assumed to be one component of an extended series of such 'units,' all of which taken together represent an experiment. 3. A large-scale plan for testing and evaluating the effectiveness of some drug or therapeutic procedure. Meaning 3 is also referred to as a *clinical trial* or a *clinical study*.

trial-and-error learning ➤ **learning, trial-and-error**.

trial, extinction In studies of conditioning, a ➤ **trial** (2) on which the reinforcing event is not presented or the unconditioned stimulus is omitted. ➤ **extinction**.

trial, learning In studies of conditioning, a ➤ **trial** (2) on which the reinforcement is delivered or the unconditioned stimulus is presented. Also called *training trial* and *acquisition trial*. ➤ **learning**.

tribadism Rubbing together of the genitals, specifically when both partners are female.

trichesthesia The tactile sensation experienced in the skin when a hair is touched or moved.

trichi-, tricho- Combining forms meaning *hair*.

trichomonas vaginalis A form of vaginitis characterized by itching, redness and burning, especially around the vulva. It is caused by the Trichomonas protozoa and, although it is not linked directly with sexual intercourse, it is often classified as a venereal disease because it can be communicated through intercourse.

trichotillomania Compulsive pulling of one's hair, often to the point of pulling it out.

trichotomy Division or classification into three, not necessarily equal, parts.

trichromacy Normal color vision. In operational terms, a trichromat can use three appropriately selected hues to match any other visual stimulus; hence, there are three color systems operating. Also occasionally called by a variety of similar terms including *trichromatism*, *trichromatopsia*, *trichromopsia*, *trichromia*, *trichromasy*. Compare with ➤ **dichromacy**.

trichromacy, anomalous A color-vision abnormality in which the individual can match any target color with a mixture of the three primary hues, but the mixtures are anomalous and quite different from those normally given. Such conditions are assumed to result from minor deficiencies in one pigment or another.

trichromasy ➤ **trichromacy**.

trichromat One with normal color vision; one with ➤ **trichromacy**. Contrast with ➤ **monochromat** and **dichromat**.

trichromatic theory = the *Young-Helmholtz theory*. ➤ **theories of *color vision**.

trichromatism ➤ **trichromacy**.

trichromatopsia ➤ **trichromacy**.

trichromia ➤ **trichromacy**.

tricyclic compounds A group of ➤ **antidepressant drugs** which function by preventing the re-uptake of amines in cholinergic synapses. The resulting increases in these stimulants are apparently the basis for their antidepressant effects. A host of these compounds is in use although the 'parent' drug *imipramine* is the most commonly prescribed. Tricyclics have a decided advantage over other drugs used for treatment of depression, such as monoamine oxidase inhibitors and the amphetamines, in that the side-effects are relatively minor and there is little tolerance or dependence.

tridimensional theory of feeling Wundt's theory that all feelings could be represented as being composed of three dimensions, pleasure–displeasure, excitement–depression and tension–relaxation.

trigeminal lemniscus ➤ **lemniscal system**.

trigeminal nerve The Vth ➤ **cranial nerve**. A mixed nerve with three afferent or sensory branches and one efferent or motor. The afferent branches are the major ones: the *ophthalmic* is from the forehead and scalp, mucosa of the nasal cavity and sinuses, cornea and conjunctiva, the *maxillary* from dura mater, gums and teeth of the upper jaw and upper lip, the *mandibular* is from the tongue, gums and teeth of the lower jaw, cheek, lower jaw and lip. The motor root is much smaller and carries fibers to the muscles of mastication.

trigeminal neuralgia A neuralgia of the ➤ **trigeminal nerve**. The primary symptom is a sudden stab of (often excruciating) pain typically beginning in the jaw and radiating along whichever branch of the nerve is affected. Also called *tic douloureux*.

trigger zone The area of a neuron, usually part of the axon, that has the lowest threshold for initiating an action potential.

triglycerides Complex molecules containing ➤ **glycerol** combined with the ➤ **fatty acids**. The body's reservoir of adipose or fatty tissue is filled with triglycerides.

trigram A three-letter sequence. Nonsense trigrams are often used in memory research.

trimmed mean ➤ **mean, trimmed**.

trip The period of time during which a person is under the influence of a psychedelic or hallucinogenic drug such as LSD. Often qualifiers such as 'bad' or 'good' are appended as needed.

triple-X syndrome A chromosomal anomaly in which three X chromosomes are present. Such individuals are phenotypically female, sexually normal and usually fertile, although menstrual problems and early menopause are common. Severe mental retardation is the single most striking feature.

trireceptor theory The theory of color vision based on the assumption that there are three types of receptors in the retina. ➤ theories of *color vision.

trisomy 18 A genetic disorder in which there is a third, anomalous 18th chromosome. The syndrome is characterized by mental retardation and various physical anomalies, the most common being low-set, malformed ears, flexion of the fingers, a small jaw, and heart defects.

trisomy 21 ➤ **Down syndrome**. This name is used occasionally because it identifies the genetic basis of the syndrome, namely a third, anomalous, 21st chromosome.

tritanopia An extremely rare form of inherited ➤ **dichromacy** characterized by a lowered sensitivity to blue light. The tri- prefix comes from the Greek for *third* and is used because the presumption is that the tritanope has a deficiency in the blue-light-absorbing pigment and blue is regarded as the third primary color. It is also seen, more commonly, as a result of retinal disease.

triune brain A term used by the psychologist Paul MacLean which captures the notion that the human brain can be conceptualized as three (more or less) independent aspects, each of which is viewed as having emerged at a different evolutionary time. The earliest to emerge was what he jokingly called the 'neural chassis,' including the spinal cord, hindbrain and midbrain, followed by the limbic system and the neocortex.

tRNA Abbrev. for *transfer* ➤ **ribonucleic acid**.

trocular nerve The IVth *cranial nerve*. A mixed nerve, it contains efferent or motor fibers to the superior oblique muscles of the eye and afferent or sensory fibers which convey proprioceptive information from the same muscles.

troilism A deep desire to have sexual relations in the presence of others.

troland A measure of illuminance that approximates that on the retina itself. Named after the physiologist L. T. Troland, it is, by definition, the illuminance of the retina that results when a surface luminance of 1 candle per square meter is incident through an apparent pupil of 1 square millimeter. Once the term *photon* was used for this measure but its commandeering by physics necessitated the change.

trophic hormones Anterior pituitary hormones with indirect action; that is, they affect secretions of other endocrine glands.

troph(o) Combining form meaning *food* or *nourishment*.

tropin Combining form used to indicate the stimulating effect of a substance (especially a hormone) on an organ or other site.

tropism A generic term for any unlearned orientation or movement of an organic unit as a whole toward a source of simulation. Typically used in compounds with the Greek word for the stimulus source, e.g., *phototropism* = turning toward light, *heliotropism* = movement toward the sun. Note that modern convention reserves *tropism* for plants and uses ➤ **taxis** for such automatic movements when made by animate organisms.

tropism, negative When unqualified *tropism* connotes movement toward a stimulus; the 'negative' is appended for cases in which the movement is away from the source.

Troxler's effect The generalization that when an observer maintains fixation on a point directly in front while attempting to view a stationary line off to one side this peripheral stimulus disappears. It is especially striking at low illumination levels but occurs at high levels as well where a sort of visual fog seems to creep in from the periphery, obscuring objects. A slight movement in the periphery will cause the peripheral stimuli to reappear.

true 1. In logic, a characteristic of a proposition which follows logically from the axioms in use and previous propositions whose truth is known. **2.** A characteristic of a proposition, statement or belief which corresponds with 'reality' as it is known. Note that what is true in sense 1 is not necessarily true in sense 2. **3.** In statistics, a characteristic of values which are based upon the full population of scores and not upon samples from that population, e.g., ➤ **true *mean.**

true value ➤ **true *score.**

true zero ➤ **absolute *zero.**

truncated distribution A distribution in which the extreme scores (at either or both ends) have been 'cut off.' The truncating may result from a decision to eliminate these scores from consideration or simply through a failure to collect data from the extreme(s). A classic example of a severely truncated distribution is the frequency distribution of IQ scores in universities, in which the lower part of the full population has been removed by entrance requirements.

tryptophan An amino acid required for normal growth and development. It functions as a precursor in the production of the inhibitory neurotransmitter *serotonin*. There is some evidence that it may function as an antidepressant.

T-scope Abbrev. for ➤ **tachistoscope.**

T score A type of score based on the transformation of normalized standard scores to a scale based on a mean of 50 and a standard deviation of 10.

TSD Abbrev. for *theory of signal detection*. ➤ **signal-detection theory.**

***t* test** Any of a number of statistical tests of significance based upon the *t* statistic. See the discussion under ➤ *t* ***distribution** for the principles involved.

TTR ➤ **type-token ratio.**

TTS ➤ **temporary threshold shift.**

818

tubectomy ➤ **salpingectomy.**

tubocurarine ➤ **curare.**

Tukey honestly significant difference test A ➤ *post hoc* test used after an analysis of variance or other test has shown overall significance. It enables one to compare all possible pairs of means while not changing one's criterion for a ➤ **Type I error** at a given level of significance. Also called *Tukey HSD test*.

tumescence A swelling of tissue or the condition of being swollen.

tuning fork A two-tined metal instrument constructed of highly tempered steel to reduce its overtones so that when struck it yields a nearly pure tone. A well-made set of tuning forks was once the pride of every experimental psychology laboratory; today they are hardly ever used, having been replaced by electronic tone generators.

tunnel vision A condition in which peripheral vision is severely reduced or lacking altogether and the individual can see only that which is projected onto the central area of the retina. The term is also used metaphorically to characterize the manner of thinking of the narrow-minded and the dogmatic.

Turing machine An abstract automaton (i.e. a computer or other finite, well-defined machine) characterized theoretically by the British mathematician Alan M. Turing in the 1930s. Basically, a Turing machine consists of a tape and reading head. The tape moves back and forth under the head, marking and changing the symbols on it one at a time based on information fed to it. In Turing's terminology, the machine is 'completely described' when every mark on the tape tells the machine: (a) the next symbol it should write: (b) the place on the tape it should go to; and (c) whether to move the tape forward or backward one step. Turing machines have fascinated computer scientists because, in the final analysis, when stripped of all of their sophisticated components a modern computer *is* a Turing machine. Workers in ➤ **artificial intelligence** and the ➤ **cognitive sciences** have been intrigued by the possibility that the human brain itself may be represented as a Turing machine.

Turing's test A 'test' of the adequacy of an artificial intelligence device on the question whether or not it can be said to think. As Alan Turing conceptualized it a human (A) is linked to another human (B) via a teletype through which they can converse without face-to-face interaction. At some point in time unknown to A, B is replaced with a computer. The test is whether this artificial device can so effectively simulate human responses that no matter what questions A poses to it, A cannot discern whether it is a computer or the original person B. According to Turing, any device capable of passing this test would have to be considered to be capable of human thought. ➤➤ **artificial intelligence**.

Turner's syndrome A chromosomal anomaly in phenotypic females. The basic genetic defect is a missing sex chromosome, so that the total count is 45, X. The syndrome is marked by short stature and absence of ovaries. With female sex hormones administered at the age of puberty normal secondary sex characteristics appear, although the sterility cannot be corrected. There is some evidence of minor intellectual impairment but it seems to be rather specific, showing up as a mild deficit in arithmetic skills and spatial organization.

turn-taking A pragmatic conversation principle usually (but, heaven knows, not always) respected in which each participant in a dialogue takes turns at speaking. The rules that govern turn-taking are rather complex and involve subtle factors like intonation, contour and pausing as well as the more straightforward invitations from the other person to speak, such as questions and partial lead-ins.

twilight sleep ➤ **sleep, twilight**.

twilight vision ➤ **scotopic vision**.

twin One of two offspring gestated in the same uterus and born at the same time.

twin control The use of twins in experimental studies as a way of controlling for genetic and environmental factors. When monozygotic twins are used the control over the genetic factors is complete; with dizygotic twins it is not, although the use of the latter has advantages over the use of regular siblings in that the environment within which they are raised is held roughly constant. ➤ **twin studies**.

twins, dizygotic Twins resulting from the (near) simultaneous fertilization of two ova by sperm cells. Since each twin develops from a separate zygote, they are no more alike genetically than any two siblings born at different times. Also called *fraternal twins*.

twins, monozygotic Twins resulting from the spontaneous fission of a single fertilized zygote. Such twins are genetically identical. Also called *identical, uniovular* or *monovular twins*.

twin studies The term twin studies refers collectively to a large number of studies carried out on monozygotic and dizygotic twins raised together or apart from each other. The focus of these studies is to sort out the relative contributions of heredity and environment to human behavior.

twitch A simple, spasmodic muscular contraction.

2AFC ➤ **two-alternative forced choice**.

two-alternative forced choice (2AFC) An experimental method used widely in studies of memory and learning in which the subject is presented with two alternative stimuli and must select one. For example, in studies of memory, one of the stimuli was seen before and one novel; the subject's task is to pick out the previously encountered stimulus. The procedure is preferred over simple choice techniques where, for example, the subject is shown a stimulus and asked whether it was seen before. This latter procedure is subject to bias owing to large individual differences in the tendency to respond 'yes' or 'no.'

two-point threshold The minimum distance on the skin between two point stimuli at which they are perceived as separate rather than as a single stimulus point.

two-tailed test In testing for the statistical significance of an observed difference (either between two samples or between a sample and a theoretical distribution) the question of the *direction* of the difference emerges. The standard statistical practice is as follows: If one anticipates the possibility that a particular manipulation may result in either extreme then a two-tailed test should be used, for example, in testing a new drug where it is not clear whether it should increase performance or depress it. In such a situation significance will result from data in either critical region of the distribution (i.e. in either of the two 'tails'). When one is utterly convinced that only differences in one direction could manifest themselves (e.g., the effects of practice on learning) then one could, in principle, run a *one-tailed test* that evaluates significance in one critical region (i.e. in only one 'tail'). One-tailed tests have the advantage that the entire critical region for concluding significance at a given level is contained in one tail and hence they are twice as likely to produce a significant result as is a two-tailed test. They will, of course, increase the likelihood of making a ➤ **Type 1 *error**. There are, however, good reasons for not recommending this rather standard statistical practice. Consider, for example, an experimenter who is running a study in which he or she is 'convinced' that only one directional outcome can occur (like the effects of practice on performance) and, hence, elects to use a one-tailed test. Suppose, however, that the experimental subjects are run with a large number of densely massed practice trials and consequently display dramatically poorer performance than control subjects who are run with fewer (but spaced) practice trials. In princi-

ple, since the experimenter had decided in advance to use a one-tailed test, the observed result is not significant and should not be reported in the literature. This, of course, is nonsensical in the extreme – no surprises would ever be publicly revealed. What would happen, of course, is that our experimenter would quickly reverse course and run a two-tailed test. One-tailed tests are, therefore, ill-advised. They increase the probability of Type I errors to an unacceptable level and, of course, will always be jettisoned in favor of two-tailed tests as soon as the scientist anticipates an interesting reversal of expectations.

tympanic Pertaining to the ear-drum, the ➤ **tympanic membrane**.

tympanic canal ➤ **cochlea**.

tympanic membrane The ear-drum, the flexible membrane stretched across the end of the external auditory meatus. It vibrates with the incoming stimulus and transmits the vibration pattern to the auditory ossicles. Also called *tympanum*.

type **1.** Generally, a class or group distinguished by possessing or displaying some particular characteristic. **2.** An individual or thing which embodies such 'typical' characteristics; a representative of a type in sense 1. See here ➤ **prototype**. **3.** A pattern of traits or other characteristics which can serve as criteria for classifying persons (or objects) into groups. See here the discussion of *type theories* under ➤ **personality**. **4.** A class of utterances or words defined so as to represent a coherent group for the purpose of determining a ➤ **type–token ratio**. ➤ **token** (4). When the term type is used by a particular author it is usually qualified with some other term or phrase to specify the reference; a few of these follow, the others are found under the alphabetical listing of the qualifier.

type A personality A temperament characterized by excessive drive and competitiveness, an unrealistic sense of time urgency, inappropriate ambition, a reluctance to provide self-evaluation, a tendency to emphasize quantity of output over quality and a need for control. Type A behavior is believed by many to be associated with coronary disease. Contrast with ➤ **type B personality**.

type, body ➤ somatotype.

type B personality A temperament characterized by a relaxed, easy-going approach to life, a focus on quality over quantity, low competitiveness and a tendency for self-reflection. Type B behavior is essentially the opposite of type A; ➤ **type A personality**.

type fallacy The tendency to encapsulate persons, concepts, categories, etc. and thus reify each type and treat it as distinct from others. Most psychological variables lie along dimensions and the dimensions often have identifiable poles. However, once these poles have been labeled as 'types,' it is easy to be seduced into treating them as if they were distinct from each other rather than as points along a continuum. Although most contemporary thinkers are aware of and sensitive to this problem as it pertains to dimensions like introversion and extraversion, they often fail to appreciate that it also pertains to dimensions like race (black–white) and even gender (male–female).

type-identity theory ➤ identity theory.

Type I error ➤ error, Type 1 (and Type II).

Type-R conditioning A term sometimes used to refer to ➤ **operant conditioning** and/or ➤ **instrumental conditioning**.

Type-S conditioning A term occasionally used for ➤ **classical conditioning**.

type–token ratio (TTR) In studies of language, the ratio of the number of ➤ **types** (4) to the number of ➤ **tokens** (4) in a corpus of language. In the most frequently used sense the count of tokens is the total number of words in the corpus and the count of types is the total number of different words. The closer to 1.0 the ratio is the greater the verbal diversity the person displays. Such ratios are often used in analysis of the verbal sophistication of children. Note, however, that what serves as a *type* is really quite arbitrary and various other forms of analysis are possible. For example; parts of speech could be used (noun, verb, etc.) and the ratio would then reflect flexibility of usage of grammatical forms.

Type II error ➤ error, Type I (and Type II).

typicality The degree to which a given example or a category can be said to be close to the abstract ➤ **prototype** of that category.

typing The process or operation of categorizing persons or objects.

typography The setting of type for printing. Many different type fonts or styles exist and there are good reasons for suspecting that they play a role in the ➤ **reading** process.

typology 1. Generally, the study of types and of the processes of classification into types. **2.** Any scheme of classification in which various instances are grouped together according to specifiable criteria.

tyrosine An amino acid that serves as a precursor for ➤ **dopamine, epinephrine, L-dopa** and ➤ **norepinephrine**.

U

UCR ➤ **unconditioned response**.

UCS ➤ **unconditioned stimulus**.

U curve ➤ **U-shaped curve**.

UG ➤ **universal *grammar**.

-ulous A suffix meaning *tending toward*.

ultimate explanation In evolutionary biology, an explanation of the behavior of a species in terms of the larger evolutionary factors that gave rise to the adaptive value of the behavior. An ultimate explanation of the mating behavior of the elephant seal, for example, would focus on the role of the size of the polygynous male in enabling it to defend his territory and his females from encroaching males and how these patterns of behavior promoted more offspring than other patterns. Compare with ➤ **proximate explanation**.

ultra- Combining form meaning *going beyond*, *extreme* or *excessive*.

ultradian rhythms Any of the many biologic rhythms that are shorter than one day.

ultrasonic Pertaining to sound waves whose frequency is beyond that of normal human hearing, e.g., roughly 20,000 Hz. Also called ➤ **supersonic** (2).

ultraviolet Pertaining to electromagnetic radiation the wavelength of which is shorter than that to which the normal human eye responds, e.g., below roughly 400 nm.

umbilical cord The cord that connects the fetus with the placenta.

Umweg ➤ **detour problem**.

Umwelt ➤ *Eigenwelt*.

un- A multifunctional prefix meaning *back*, *reversed* or *reversal of*, *negation of*, *annulment of*, *not*.

unambivalent Not ambivalent. Used in

psychoanalysis for any two motives that are in harmony.

unbalanced bilingual ➤ **bilingual, unbalanced**.

unbiased A term used in a variety of contexts to characterize operations or processes which display no bias, e.g., decision-making that reveals no prejudices, choice behavior that manifests no uneven or inappropriate tendency to select particular stimuli, sampling in which the samples selected are representative of the underlying population, tests that assess fairly the factors they have been designed to assess, etc. ➤ **bias** and related terms for a sense of the range and pattern of usage.

unbiased error ➤ **chance *error**.

unbiased estimate Any estimate made on the basis of representative sampling, i.e. sampling that is unbiased.

unbiased estimator Any statistic which, in principle, gives a value for any sample that is an unbiased estimate of the true value in the full population. The mean is an unbiased estimator.

unbiased sample ➤ **representative *sample**.

uncertainty 1. Generally, the state of belief when one does not fully believe, when one is unsure. **2.** In information theory, the degree to which there are no constraints upon the choices one has available or upon the possible outcomes of a situation. ➤ **entropy**.

uncomplicated Used loosely in psychiatric diagnosis to denote disorders that are not accompanied by any significant pathological features other than those that signal the existence of the primary disorder.

uncomplicated alcohol withdrawal ➤ **alcohol withdrawal**.

uncomplicated bereavement Normal reaction to the death of a loved one. It consists of various expressions of sadness, guilt, depression and the like that are deemed appropriate to one's experiences and interactions with the deceased while alive.

uncomplicated sedative, hypnotic, or anxiolytic withdrawal ➤ **sedative, hypnotic, or anxiolytic withdrawal**.

unconditional reflex This term is the proper translation of Pavlov's original term, which is now generally rendered as *conditioned response*. The condition*al* was converted to condition*ed* by a translator's error: the *reflex* was changed to *response* by theorists who wished to generalize the principles of conditioning beyond the domain of the reflexes which were the primary focus of Pavlov's research on ➤ **classical conditioning**.

unconditional response ➤ **unconditional reflex**.

unconditioned reflex ➤ **unconditioned response** and ➤ **unconditional reflex**.

unconditioned response (UCR, UR or **Ru)** Any response that is reliably elicited from an organism by a particular unconditioned stimulus. Such a well-established link between the unconditioned stimulus and the unconditioned response may be the result of previous learning or of the organism's innate behavioral repertoire, but in either case it is a prerequisite for the establishment of ➤ **classical conditioning**.

unconditioned stimulus (UCS, US or **Su)** Any stimulus that reliably elicits from an organism a particular unconditioned response. ➤ **classical conditioning**.

unconscious Three distinguishable patterns of usage exist for this term, each with noun and adjective forms; the first is more or less nontechnical, the second is broad and atheoretical, and the third is closely tied in with a particular point of view with respect to theories of the human condition. All three, however, make contact in some way with the general notion of a level of mind lacking in awareness. To wit: 1a n. A state characterized by a lack of awareness, unconsciousness. 1b adj. Characterizing an individual in such a state. These meanings when they occur in technical writings are roughly equivalent to those in everyday language. That is, they are used to refer to that pole of the dimension of mental arousal that is exemplified by coma, fainting, deep sleep or the result of general anesthesia. 2a n. A state characterized by a lack of awareness of ongoing internal processes. 2b adj. Characterizing those internal processes that proceed in an implicit manner outside of consciousness. While strictly speaking these two usages cover all processes occurring outside of an individual's awareness, the referents are typically the cognitive, emotional and/or motivational processes. Physiological processes, to be sure, take place largely without one's awareness but are rarely intended by users of the term.

Note that in both 1 and 2 above the term *unconscious* was actually never defined. In 1a, 1b it represented *loss* of consciousness; in 2a, 2b it represented that which was *not* conscious. This kind of lexicographic trickery never really solves problems; ➤ **conscious** and **consciousness** for more on this. ➤ **tacit, implicit** and **awareness** for further discussions of these semantic issues.

3a n. In the depth psychologies, especially psychoanalysis, a domain of the psyche encompassing the repressed id functions, the primitive impulses and desires, the memories, images and wishes that are too anxiety-provoking to be accepted into consciousness. 3b adj. Characterizing these primordial, repressed desires, memories and images. Note that the unconscious (3a) is assumed to be populated by two varieties of psychic entities, those that were once conscious but had been exiled from awareness and those that were never in consciousness. ➤ **repression** (1). Distinguish from ➤ **preconscious**, which is the domain of mind whose components are not momentarily a part of one's consciousness but which may be retrieved by a simple exercise of memory. Note that Freud referred to sense 3 here as the

UNCONSCIOUS COGNITIVE PROCESS

dynamic unconscious, owing to the actions of repression, and often used the term *descriptive unconscious* for the *preconscious* – causing no end of confusion.

unconscious cognitive process Generally, any process involving thinking, reasoning, judging, problem-solving, etc. which takes place without consciousness, without awareness. E.g., ➤ **implicit *learning**, ➤ **incubation** (3).

unconscious drive An id drive or need. ➤ **unconscious** (3a and 3b).

unconscious ideation ➤ **collective guilt**.

unconscious inference 1. Generally and literally, a judgement made on the basis of a limited amount of evidence or data and made without awareness. **2.** Specifically, a principle first articulated by the great German scientist Hermann von Helmholtz as an explanation for many perceptual phenomena. Helmholtz's principle is really only the specification of the general, literal meaning of the term with respect to the conditions under which such judgements are made. For example, things placed in front of other things block them from view, and everyone has had extended experience with such stimulus conditions. Hence, when two things (A and B) are arranged before us such that A is partially blocking B we 'unconsciously infer' that A must be closer to us than B.

unconscious knowledge Knowledge that a person is not aware of possessing, knowledge that is ➤ **tacit** (3).

unconscious memory ➤ **memory, unconscious**.

unconscious motivation ➤ **motivation, unconscious**.

unconsciousness The state of being ➤ **unconscious** (especially 1a).

uncontrolled 1. Unregulated, not controlled. **2.** Not measured, not assessed. The term is generally used of variables in an experiment that were neither systematically varied nor specifically held constant.

underachiever One whose actual perform- ance on a task or in some situation (most typically, in a school setting) is below what one would have predicted. Usually intelligence tests are the basis for the predictions, but the term is often used rather more loosely and assigned to persons on the basis of subjective feelings about their potential. See and contrast with ➤ **overachiever**.

underdetermined Of situations in which there is insufficient evidence, data or information to determine a value or the correct alternative in a set of choices, etc. ➤ **overdetermined**.

underextension ➤ **undergeneralization**.

undergeneralization The use of a word for a smaller and more specialized category of objects, events or circumstances than it is normally used for. Such *underextensions*, as they are also called, are common in young children, for example restricting the label 'kitty' to but one cat. Contrast with ➤ **overgeneralization**.

understand To comprehend, to appreciate the deep meaning of a thing or a process.

understanding 1. The process of comprehending something, of appreciating the meaning of a word, sentence, event, proposition, etc. **2.** An elusive intuitive process whereby one succeeds in apprehending the deep significant meaning of an event, a concept, an idea, etc. Note, some use ➤ **comprehension** as a synonym for both 1 and 2 here. **3.** A sympathetic appreciation for another person, particularly for their point of view on some matter or their belief on some issue. Here ➤ **sympathy** is a near-synonym. **4.** In older writings, a hypothesized mental faculty the function of which was to yield comprehension of the meanings of things.

underweight By convention, a condition in which body weight is 10% or more below the norms for a person's body type and age. Like ➤ **obesity**, this term is used rather loosely, since it is impossible to provide a definition that pertains uni-

824

formly to all persons – the 10% criterion is, of course, arbitrary and flexible.

undifferentiated Not differentiated. Used of wholes or of aggregates whose several components are not distinguished from each other. For example, in embryology, undifferentiated tissue is that which has not yet developed into its characteristic forms and structures, undifferentiated perceptions are those that are seen as unified wholes, mobs are undifferentiated groups of people, etc. ➤ **differentiation**.

undifferentiated schizophrenia ➤ **schizophrenia, undifferentiated**.

undifferentiated somatoform disorder ➤ **somatoform disorder, undifferentiated**.

undinism ➤ **urophilia**.

undistributed middle, fallacy of An argument that leads to an invalid conclusion because of the use of a premise that is not distributed. For example, given that 'All Communists are atheists' and 'Max is an atheist,' to conclude that 'Max is a Communist' would be to fall prey to the fallacy. To rescue the syllogism one would need to have an additional premise such as, 'All atheists are members of the Communist party.' The obviously fallacious aspects are shown if the syllogism takes a more blatant form such as: 'Max is a man,' 'Sam is a man,' therefore, 'Max is Sam.' Psychologists' interest in the fallacy stems from two observations: (a) some schizophrenics willingly accept these arguments, indeed find nothing wrong with concluding that, as in the above, Max and Sam are the same person; and (b) normal people are surprisingly susceptible to these invalid arguments and are open game for advertisers who exploit this; e.g., 'Distinguished people smoke Zonko cigars,' 'I smoke Zonko cigars,' therefore 'I am distinguished.' In both cases here the tendency is toward what is called ➤ **overgeneralization**.

undoing A defense mechanism, usually associated with children, in which one attempts to 'undo' the unpleasant outcome of some act by mentally replaying or in some cases ritualistically re-enacting the sequence of events but with a different, more acceptable ending. Some theorists have argued that this infantile operation lies behind later obsessive-compulsive behavior.

unfilled pause ➤ silent *pause.

unfolding A type of ➤ **multidimensional scaling** developed by Clyde Coombs. The technique is based on having a subject rank order a number of stimuli according to preference. The resulting preference ordering reflects an ideal point and the individual preferences are then 'unfolded' mathematically to display the locations of the scaled objects in any number of dimensions relative to the ideal point.

uni- Combining form meaning *one, singular*.

uniaural Pertaining to a single ear; ➤ **monaural** (preferred).

unicellular Single-celled.

unidextrous Preferring one hand over the other for most actions. Also called *handedness*.

unidimensional Descriptive of variables whose range of values can be expressed along a single dimension. Compare with ➤ **multidimensional**.

uniform distribution ➤ **distribution, uniform**.

uniformity 1. Generally, identity in all important respects. 2. In social psychology, a condition in which there is widespread ('uniform') agreement concerning some belief, practice or fact. The term is used loosely and relatively since there are probably few things which are truly uniformly believed by all members of a society. Compare with ➤ **conformity**.

unilateral Lit., pertaining to but one side. Hence: 1. Descriptive of actions or decisions made by one person or one group. 2. Pertaining to anatomical structures or processes on only one side of the body.

unimodal Having only one ➤ **mode**; used to characterize distributions with one 'peak.'

uniocular Pertaining to a single eye; ➤ **monocular** (preferred).

uniocular dichromat ➤ **dichromat, uniocular**.

uniovular twins ➤ **monozygotic *twins**.

unipolar cell (or **neuron**) A neuron with a single stalk leading from the soma. This neural process branches with the dendrites at one end and the axonal terminals at the other. In unipolar neurons, unlike neurons with more than one pole, the information is transmitted from dendrite to end button without passing through the somatic membrane. Compare with ➤ **bipolar** and ➤ **multipolar cell**.

unipolar depression ➤ **depression, unipolar**.

unipolar mania ➤ **mania, unipolar**.

unique factor ➤ **specific *factor**.

unique hues ➤ **primary *colors** (especially 2).

unique trait ➤ **trait, unique**.

unisexual Characteristic of a species in which each individual organism is either male or female but not both.

unit 1. One of something taken as a whole, a datum. **2.** A standard amount used as the basis of measurement. This meaning may convey: (a) something extremely precise and objectively well defined such as physical magnitude, e.g., a *second* as a unit of time, a *meter* as a unit of length; (b) something subjective but reasonably well defined, e.g., the *sone* as the unit for a scale of loudness; or (c) something quite loosely defined, e.g., an *utterance* as a unit of speech. adjs., *unitary* for 1, *unit* for 2.

unit character A characteristic or trait that is assumed to be genetically determined as a whole or as a unit. The notion is that there is no genetic parceling out of components; it is a case of all-or-nothing genetic transmission. Albinism is a good example, as is Down syndrome.

univariate Consisting of but one variable. An experiment using only one variable may be called a *univariate study*, although the term *single-factor study* (or *experiment*) is more common.

universal 1 adj. Pertaining to ➤ **universe** in any of that term's meanings. **2** adj. Pertaining to those underlying aspects or characteristics of human beings, their psychological make-up, their modes of thought, action and affect, that are presumed to be common among all despite the vast observed array of manifestations of them. Note that this meaning of the term is rarely used for the mundane or the obvious like simple anatomical features; it is generally reserved for the assertion of deeper, abstract components such as Jung's *archetypes*, Chomsky's *universal grammar*, Freud's *instincts* and the like. **3** n. Any one of those aspects that are assumed to be universal. **4** n. In logic, a proposition predicated of all members of a class.

universal complex In psychoanalytic theory, a complex hypothesized to have its roots in a fundamental instinct, one of those assumed to be ➤ **universal** (2), e.g., the *Oedipus complex*. Compare with ➤ **particular complex**.

universal grammar ➤ **grammar, universal**.

universalism In sociology, an approach to social theory in which standards of conduct are determined according to sets of principles assumed to reflect universal ethical standards. In this approach the tendency is to disregard mitigating circumstances or individual contexts. Contrast with the more relativistic approach of ➤ **particularism**.

universality The property of being ➤ **universal**, in any of that term's meanings.

universals A term used collectively for any of those aspects of the human condition that the user is asserting are ➤ **universal** (2).

universals, linguistic Those linguistic aspects that are common to all ➤ **natural**

*languages. These hypothesized universals are usually viewed as being of two types, *substantive universals*, which are common aspects of description of natural languages such as distinctive features, catalogs of word classes, sets of semantic features, etc., and *formal universals*, which represent the nature of generative rules found in natural languages, such as transformations.

universal symbol ➤ symbol, universal.

universe 1. Most generally, all things everywhere taken as a totality. 2. More specifically, a collection of things, taken together according to some defining feature(s) or characteristic(s). This meaning is close to that of ➤ set (1). 3. ➤ universe of discourse. 4. ➤ statistical *universe.

universe of discourse The full set of things under consideration in a given discussion, study or experiment.

universe, statistical The full population from which samples are drawn and about which inferences from the samples are made. For more detail ➤ population (2) and ➤ sample et seq.

unlearned A term used rather literally to refer to behaviors, acts, tendencies, dispositions and so forth that emerge in the life of an organism without any special training or instruction, in short, *without learning*. Unlearned behavior may be a simple reflex or a complex sequence of actions like walking upright. Note that labeling a behavior unlearned does not necessarily mean that experiential or maturational factors are not playing a role; even the most basic 'preprogrammed' behaviors like fixed-action patterns in lower organisms will not manifest themselves if the organism is deprived of the usual environmental experiences of its species.

unlearning A very general term used for any process or operation which leads to the elimination of previously learned behavior. Some use this term as though it were equivalent to ➤ extinction; others argue that one can only eliminate the effects of the previous learning by having

the organism acquire a new response that is incompatible with the old one, thus taking its place in the behavioral repertoire. For these latter theorists, unlearning is closer to ➤ counter conditioning.

unmarked adjective ➤ marked–unmarked adjectives.

unobtrusive procedure A general term for any research technique for gathering data without the individuals (persons or animals) being observed becoming aware of the procedures. It covers a large array of techniques, from the use of public and private records (e.g., census data, school reports, etc.), to hidden cameras and tape recorders and one-way mirrors for surreptitious observation of subjects, to hiding in the reeds beside a pond to record the natural behavior patterns of water fowl (➤ naturalistic observation).

unpack A term borrowed from the computer sciences where it refers to the recovery of original data that have been stored (or 'packed') with other data. It is used as a metaphor for the process of retrieval of specific memories from a large store of other memories and knowledge.

unpleasant 1. Characterizing an emotional experience that has negative, aversive or disagreeable qualities. In this sense the experience is usually conceptualized as the negative pole of a *pleasantness* dimension along which all emotional experiences can be located. 2. Characterizing any environmental state of affairs or stimulus conditions under which an organism will learn to make responses that result in its termination and not learn to make responses that result in its presentation. This is the behaviorist's use of the term, which attempts to avoid invoking the internal, subjective notions of 1 and relies, instead, on changes in behavior as criterial.

unpleasure The emotional experience that results from the exposure to stimuli that are *unpleasant*. This experience is usually treated as basic and primitive and resistant to conscious, introspective analysis. There is, admittedly, something strangely awkward about the term, although it serves well as the antonym of ➤ **pleasure**.

unreadiness, law of ➤ **law of *readiness**.

unreality, sense (or **feeling**) **of** Technical usage here is quite similar to common usage: a feeling that things experienced are somehow not 'real' or not 'right.' When it occurs occasionally in normal living it is usually interpreted as a failure to be able to integrate an experience with one's previous knowledge of things – and, indeed, the feeling occurs most often when encountering strange or novel situations. When it occurs frequently or continuously it is regarded as pathological.

unreflective Impulsive. With respect to cognitive style, ➤ **reflectivity–impulsivity**.

unreliability Ant. of ➤ **reliability** in any of the meanings of that term.

unresolved Generally, of conflicts or problems not yet worked out or 'resolved.' This meaning is found in cognitive psychology with respect to problems not solved or decisions not made and in psychotherapeutic discourse for psychological problems or conflicts with which the client has not yet come to grips.

unselected A term used occasionally to characterize a sample that was drawn from a population strictly at random. The connotation is that there were no pressures to select any particular elements and therefore the sample should display no bias. Note however that, while unselected sampling yields an approximately ➤ **representative *sample**, in actual practice most representative-sampling uses selected sampling techniques such as ➤ **area *sampling** or ➤ **stratified *sampling**.

unsociable ➤ **unsocial**.

unsocial Characterizing an individual who is lacking in *sociability*. The term is used both for those whose lack of socially interactive behavior is of their own choosing, i.e. those who are *unsociable*, and for those who are excluded from social interaction because their behavior violates social norms for acceptability, i.e. those who are *unsocialized*.

unsocialized ➤ **unsocial**.

unspaced practice ➤ **massed *practice**.

unspecified ➤ 'not otherwise specified'.

unstable Generally, characterizing that which is prone to change, that which is not stable. Hence: **1.** Of an individual who displays erratic and unpredictable behaviors and moods. **2.** Of an individual who is likely to display behaviors that are neurotic, psychotic or just plain dangerous to others. In this sense the term is used as a kind of informal psychiatric diagnosis. **3.** Of a statistic or a measure that has high variability. See here the discussion under ➤ **statistical stability**. **4.** Of an aspect of language likely to undergo variation over time. Phonetic aspects of languages are relatively unstable compared with syntactic. n., *instability*.

unstressed In linguistics, a syllable that receives minimal accentuation in a word, e.g., the *-er-* in *brotherhood*. ➤ **stress** (2).

unstructured interview An interview in which the topics to be covered are left unspecified at the outset and things are left to the unfolding interaction between the persons involved in the interview.

unstructured stimulus ➤ **structured stimulus**.

unvoiced ➤ **voicing**.

unweighted Characterizing scores which have not been subjected to any adjustments in terms of ➤ **weight** (2). Actually, this term is slightly misleading since unweighted scores are not really unweighted; rather, each has a nominal weight of 1.

up-and-down method In psychophysics, a variation on the *method of limits* (➤ **measurement of *threshold**) in which the ascending stimulus sequence is shifted to descending as soon as the subject changes response category and vice versa. Also called the *staircase method*.

'uppers' (or 'ups') Street slang for any drug that has stimulating, arousing effects. Most of these drugs are ➤ **amphetamines** or amphetamine-derived.

upper threshold The upper bound of sensitivity for a particular stimulus dimension. In some cases it can be empirically determined, e.g., the pitch of a tone, where the limit for the average, undamaged human ear is roughly 20,000 Hz. In other cases it cannot be so determined, because tissue damage occurs and obscures the empirical meaning of the term; e.g., loudness of a tone or brightness of a light.

UR ➤ **unconditioned response**.

ur- A prefix from the German, meaning *original* or *primitive*. Used roughly synonymously with ➤ **proto-**.

uracil One of the four nucleotide bases that make up ➤ **ribonucleic acid**. Uracil replaces the *thymine* in the *deoxyribonucleic acid* molecule.

urban ecology ➤ **ecology, urban**.

uresis Passing urine. ➤ **enuresis**.

urethra The tube from the bladder through which urine is passed.

urethral complex H. A. Murray's hypothesized syndrome involving urinal soiling, enuresis and urethral eroticism. Murray regarded it as a minor complex but theorized that it might be related to the ➤ **Icarus complex**.

urethral eroticism Sexual feelings associated with the urethral area. E.g., ➤ **urophilia**.

urge Nontechnical term for any strong desire.

urolagnia ➤ **urophilia**.

urophilia A ➤ **paraphilia** characterized by the deriving of erotic stimulation from the smell or taste of urine or from the viewing of a person urinating. Also called *urolagnia* and *undinism*.

US ➤ **unconditioned stimulus**.

use, law (or **principle**) **of** The not surprising generalization, first formalized around the turn of the century by E. L. Thorndike, that responses, functions, associations, etc., which are practiced, exercised or rehearsed (i.e. 'used') are strengthened relative to those which go unused.

user Lit., one who uses a thing. The most common reference is to one who takes a drug, with the connotation that it is taken excessively.

U-shaped curve Quite literally, any distribution which is shaped like the letter U, with high frequencies (or probabilities) for very low and very high values and low frequencies (or probabilities) for moderate values.

uterine Pertaining to the ➤ **uterus**.

uterine descent ➤ **matrilineal descent**.

uterine fantasy In psychoanalysis, any fantasy associated with the uterus, the most common being a fantasy about returning to the womb with its warmth and protection.

uterus The womb. In mammals, the female organ in which the embryo is contained and nourished during gestation. It is a muscular, pear-shaped structure consisting of an expanded upper part, a somewhat constricted central area and the cervix which joins the uterus with the vagina.

U test ➤ **Mann-Whitney U**.

utility 1. In biology, the degree to which a particular structure has value in promoting survival. 2. In statistics, the value of a test or a statistic. This meaning is rather loose and involves any of a number of factors including validity, reliability, robustness, etc. 3. As derived from economics, the value of a commodity or of money. This last meaning has been taken up in various psychological theories of choice behavior, decision-making, scaling, games, etc. Here, utility is taken as the value to an individual of making a particular choice, arriving at a particular decision, playing a game according to a particular strategy, etc. ➤➤ **value**, especially 1 and 3.

UTILIZATION

utilization **1.** Generally, the use to which something is put or its useful value. **2.** In studies of ➤ **feeding behavior**, the variety of physiological processes involved in the consumption of food, including digestion, absorption, metabolism and excretion.

utopia The ideal society. Taken from Thomas More's 1516 work of the same name, the term refers to any visionary system of social, political and personal perfection. Various persons since More have had their hand in utopian prescriptions, the American behaviorist, B. F. Skinner being among them. ➤ **Walden Two**.

utricle The larger of the two vestibular sacs in the inner ear. Like the ➤ **saccule**, it is roughly round in shape and has a layer of receptors on the bottom or 'floor' that respond to shifts in orientation of the head.

utterance Very generally, a unit of speech or of talk. An utterance may be anything from a single simple vocal sound ('uh-huh') to an extended, multisentence discourse. Determining exactly where a particular utterance begins and ends is no easy matter.

uvula The soft structure that hangs from the back of the soft palate in the midline of the mouth.

V

V **1.** Variable stimulus (also *v*). **2.** ➤ **Variance. 3.** *Photopic* ➤ **luminosity coefficient**; var. (3), *V*λ.

V′ *Scotopic* ➤ **luminosity coefficient**; var., *V′*λ.

V **1.** Variable stimulus (also *V*). **2.** Volume. **3.** Volt.

vaccinate To produce immunity to a disease by inoculation.

vacuum activity An ethological term referring to the occurrence of a ➤ **fixed action pattern** in the absence of its usual external stimulus (or *releaser*). The assumption is that *action-specific* energy builds up, breaks through the inhibitory function of the *innate releasing mechanism* and causes the fixed action pattern to occur spontaneously. A classic example is the darting, weaving flight of fly-catching swallows after they have been kept in an insect-free environment for some time. Also called *vacuum response* and, in keeping with the hydraulic metaphor that lies behind this and related concepts, *overflow activity*.

vacuum response ➤ **vacuum activity**.

vagina The muscular membranous canal from the uterus to the exterior.

vaginism ➤ **vaginismus**.

vaginismus Involuntary, painful spasms of the peri- and circumvaginal muscles of the vagina which make coitus either extremely painful or impossible. As a psychiatric label (➤ **sexual pain disorders**) it is only appropriate in cases where the condition causes marked distress or interpersonal difficulties.

vagitus The first crying of a newborn.

vagotomy A sectioning of the vagus nerve.

vagotonia Condition of vasomotor insta-

bility caused by overaction of the vagus nerve.

vagus nerve The Xth ➤ **cranial nerve**. A mixed nerve with widely distributed afferent and efferent branches, it innervates the external ear, pharynx, larynx, lungs, heart, kidneys, spleen, liver, stomach and intestines.

valence In Kurt Lewin's *field theory*, the psychological value of an object, event, person, goal, region, etc. in the *life space* of an individual. Lewin used the qualifiers *negative* and *positive* for the valences of things avoided and sought after respectively.

valence, substitute The valence associated with an object that has, for any number of possible reasons, come to serve as a substitute for an original but unreached object.

valid Denoting the circumstances in which, by the principles of logic, a statement is unambiguously implied by the premises. In this sense, the 'truth' of the argument or the accuracy with which it characterizes the real world are not issues. The validity of a proposition, conclusion, syllogism, etc. is given by formal adherence to proper reasoning; a perfectly valid conclusion can have no descriptive accuracy at all. ➤ **validity**, especially (2).

validation **1.** The process of determining the formal, logical correctness of some proposition or conclusion. Determination of ➤ **validity** (2). ➤ **valid. 2.** The process of assessing the degree to which a test or other instrument of measurement does indeed measure what it purports to measure. Determination of ➤ **validity** (3). On occasion the various combined forms of ➤ **validity** in sense (3) will be found using *validation*; however, in this volume, all such terms can be found under *validity*.

validity **1.** Generally and loosely, the property of being true, correct, in conformity with reality. This meaning, common in ordinary parlance, is typically *not* intended in the technical literature. **2.** In logic, the property of an argument or conclusion that it is deemed to be ➤ **valid** because it conforms with proper, logical principles. The fundamental notion here is that the reasoning process itself must be correct; an argument may have validity in this sense and not correspond with reality but the fault will lie with assumptions and not the reasoning process. ➤ **logic. 3.** In testing, the property of any measuring instrument, device or test that it measures what it purports to measure. Validity here is not a simple notion and it is not a simple 'either-or' property as in sense 2 and to some extent in sense 1. In the field of tests and measurements a large number of procedures has been developed to assess the validity of testing instruments, the most widely used of which are given below.

validity, a priori A kind of preliminary, intuitive estimate of the ➤ **content *validity** of a test. The degree to which the items on the test seem to have an intuitive, a priori relationship to the behaviors that are assumed to be being tested. Also called *common-sense validity*.

validity, coefficient of An index of a test's ➤ **validity** (3); the coefficient of correlation between the scores on the test and a set of ➤ **criterion scores** which are taken as reflective of the variable(s) the test is purported to measure. For example, for a test designed to assess scholastic aptitude the correlation would be between the test scores and academic performance as assessed by grade-point average (the criterion scores) and it would provide a measure of the test's validity.

validity, concurrent A kind of ➤ **criterion-related *validity** in which the relationship between the test scores and the criterion scores is established at the same time. Although similar in spirit to ➤ **predictive *validity**, the procedure really uses 'post-diction' rather than 'prediction.' For example, one way of evaluating the

validity of, say, a test for clerical skills would be to see how scores on the test correlate with the known clerical skills of a group of clerks whose performance has been evaluated in actual working conditions. Also called *status validity*.

validity, congruent A method of establishing the validity of a new test by correlating scores from it with scores from another test of established validity. The most typical case here is in intelligence testing, where newly developed tests are compared with the well-known tests like the Stanford-Binet or the Wechsler.

validity, consensual An informal procedure for assessing validity based upon the notion of consensus; that is, the more persons who concur in a proposition, the more likely it is to be valid or the more persons who agree on a perception the more probable that it is real. The term is rarely used in tests and measurements research; it is typically found in social psychology to characterize the principle that systematic support of a particular position grants it a greater acceptability to others. ➤ **consensual validation.**

validity, construct A set of procedures for evaluating the validity of a testing instrument based on the determination of the degree to which the test items capture the hypothetical quality or trait (i.e. *construct*) it was designed to measure. Thus, for example, if a test is supposed to provide a measure of intelligence one should ask: (a) What traits or qualities (constructs) actually characterize intelligence? And (b) do the test items actually tap such constructs? The initial stages of test construction are usually concerned with construct validity. Note that it provides neither a quantitative nor a static measure of validity. Unlike measures that depend on a ➤ **correlation of *validity**, there are no mathematical bases for determining validity and unlike measures that depend on known patterns of behavior (e.g., ➤ **criterion-related *validity**) the estimate of construct validity is always changing with the accumulation of further evidence about the traits and qualities that underlie the construct. ➤➤ content *validity, of which it is but one form.

validity, content An estimate of the validity of a testing instrument based on a detailed examination of the contents of the test items. By contents here is meant the actual constituent materials of the test items; the evaluation of them is carried out by reviewing each item to determine whether it is appropriate to the test and by assessing the overall cohesiveness of the several test items. For example, a test of mathematical abilities, in order to have a respectable level of content validity, should not phrase the items in such a way that verbal abilities are critical for the person taking the test to understand what is being asked. Further, the contents should be balanced so that all tested aspects are represented appropriately; the test should not be overloaded with, say, multiplication items to the neglect of addition items.

Establishing content validity is a largely subjective operation and relies on the judgements of 'experts' concerning the relevance of the materials used. It is also situation-specific and estimates made in one circumstance may not carry over to others. For example, a test of arithmetic skills developed and content-validated for a traditional school may have very low content validity if applied to a school using the so-called 'new math.'

validity, convergent and discriminant The degree to which any particular testing instrument has validity will reflect the extent to which scores on the test (a) correlate highly with factors that they, in principle, should correlate highly with, and (b) correlate poorly with factors that they, in principle, should correlate poorly with. *Convergent validity* is manifested by the former; *discriminant validity* by the latter.

validity, criterion The independent measure that a given test is designed to assess. ➤ criterion-related *validity.

validity, criterion-related Validity of a testing instrument assessed by determining the relationship between scores on the test and some independent, nontest criterion; ➤ concurrent *validity and ➤ predictive *validity are examples here. Also called *external validity*. ➤➤ empirical *validity.

validity, definitional In principle, validity of a test that is given by the fact that the items comprising it are, by definition, items that reflect the aspects being measured. A glance at the entry for ➤ definition(s) should alert one to the fact that, in practice, there is more to this notion than meets the eye. Compare with ➤ construct *validity.

validity, differential The validity of a test battery as assessed by its ability to predict differences in performance on two (or more) criteria.

validity, empirical The validity of a test as determined by empirical means; the degree to which the test actually works with real cases in a real sample of individual subjects. A common procedure here is to calculate a ➤ coefficient of *validity based on a set of criterion scores; ➤ criterion-related *validity.

validity, face Validity assessed by having 'experts' review the contents of a test to see if they seem appropriate 'on their face.' It really is a rather fuzzy procedure for validating a test, and, because of inherent subjectivity, is typically used only during the initial phases of test construction. While face validity seems superficially similar to ➤ content *validity, the procedures are quite different, the latter being a systematic procedure, the former closer to ➤ a priori *validity.

validity, factorial A type of ➤ construct *validity whereby several tests purported to measure the same underlying traits or constructs are factor-analyzed to determine whether they share common variance and thus can be said to be tapping the same underlying constructs.

validity, incremental With respect to various tests of personality, the amount of additional, valid information provided by a test beyond that obtained by other procedures.

validity, internal An informal procedure for determining the validity of a test by looking over each item and assessing the degree to which it is fulfilling its intended role in the test.

validity, intrinsic Validity of a testing instrument based on the items on the test manifestly displaying the fact that they are indeed evaluating the designated trait. For example, an item that asks the testee to spell a word is an intrinsically valid item on a test of spelling ability. ➤ **a priori *validity** and **face *validity**.

validity, nomological A variation of ➤ **construct *validity** that derives from the argument that construct validity actually involves two separate endeavors: one that focuses on validating the constructs or traits (often called ➤ **trait *validity**) and one that is concerned with validating the test within a larger theoretical framework – this latter is known as *nomological validity*.

validity, predictive A type of ➤ **empirical *validity** based on determining the extent to which the scores on a test are predictive of actual performance. A test designed to measure, say, clerical skills will have high predictive validity if it predicts who will and will not succeed in clerical jobs. Compare with ➤ **concurrent *validity**.

validity, sampling A variety of ➤ **content *validity** based on an assessment of the extent to which the various traits assumed to underlie what is being measured are represented in the test. It is, in practice, more of a control procedure to guard against introducing a bias into a test than a real measure of the test's validity.

validity, synthetic Validity of a complex testing instrument or of a full test battery based on the relationship between a composite score that is taken to represent the various factors that are represented on the test and actual performance. The term derives from the notion that one has syn-

thesized many elements or factors into a single value.

validity, trait A component of the larger process of establishing ➤ **construct *validity**, the determination of the extent to which the underlying traits the test is presumably measuring are indeed being measured. Compare with ➤ **nomological *validity**.

Valium ➤ **diazepam**.

value 1 n. The quality or property of a thing that makes it useful, desired or esteemed. Note the pragmatic aspect implied by this definition; the value of a thing is given by its role in a (social) transaction, the thing itself does not possess value. **2** n. An abstract and general principle concerning the patterns of behavior within a particular culture or society which, through the process of socialization, the members of that society hold in high regard. These *social values*, as they are often called, form central principles around which individual and societal goals can become integrated. Classic examples are freedom, justice, education, etc. **3** n. In economics, the net worth of a thing as determined by what it will bring in exchange, either in other goods or in some medium of exchange – usually money. This meaning, combined with 1 above, is very close to the meaning of the term ➤ **utility**, especially (3). **4** n. In mathematics, a quantity or magnitude as represented by a number. **5** n. In the Munsell system for classifying colors, the position along the brightness dimension. **6** vb. To assess the worth of a thing. **7** vb. To hold something in esteem based upon one's evaluation of it.

value, absolute A number or ➤ **value** (4) expressed without regard to its sign. The absolute value of -3 is the same as $+3$ and is denoted as $|3|$.

value analysis A type of ➤ **content analysis** which focuses on the tabulation of the frequency with which particular values are expressed in the message.

value judgement A perspective toward a person, object, principle, etc. based on how one values the properties or characteristics thereof.

values clarification A variation on moral education which emphasizes awareness and clarification of moral judgements and ethical considerations. Compare with ➤ **values education**.

values education An aspect of education focusing on specific instruction in moral and ethical values in society. The term is usually associated with the work of L. Kohlberg on ➤ **moral development**, which is based on the assumption that some moral positions are inherently better than others. Hence, the educational curriculum here is oriented toward raising the child's level of morality. Compare with ➤ **values clarification**.

value system Loosely, any reasonably coherent set of values. They may be treated as individual, societal or absolute.

Vandenbergh effect The acceleration of the onset of puberty in female mice caused by a *pheromone* in the urine of a mature male.

variability 1. In statistics, the degree to which the scores in a sample differ from each other or, as more commonly expressed, differ from the mean of the sample. ➤ **dispersion** for more detail. 2. In evolutionary biology, the degree to which changes are manifested from generation to generation in a species.

variable 1 n. That which changes, that which is subject to increases and/or decreases over time – in short, that which varies. Although for the most part a variable is taken as some 'thing' that undergoes changes, it is strictly speaking an abstraction, an amount, a quantity. If the variable as stated is intensity of a tone, it is the *intensity* that is the operative variable; if difficulty of a test is the variable in a study, the real variable is *difficulty*. The *tones* and the *tests* used are but ways in which to allow *intensity* and *difficulty* to manifest themselves. In mathematics and logic, this notion is captured more explicitly by treating a variable as a

symbol that represents, not any particular thing or value, but the class of things or the domain of values that satisfies the specified constraints. Compare here with ➤ **parameter**, especially (4). Within the social sciences various types of variables are distinguished as indicated in the following entries. 2 adj. Changing, varying, characterizing that which is subject to change or variation.

variable, autochthonous A variable that comes from within. ➤ **autochthonous**.

variable, control A variable which, in a particular experiment, is held constant or *controlled*. The term is semantically confusing and not recommended. Moreover, it is too easily confused with *controlled variable*, which is an occasional synonym for ➤ **independent *variable**.

variable, criterion The variable used to establish the criterion or standard against which other scores can be evaluated. E.g., ➤ **criterion-related *validity**.

variable, dependent 1. Any variable whose values are, in principle, the result of changes in the values of one or more ➤ **independent *variables**. In mathematics this notion of 'dependent' is readily represented by an expression of the kind, $y = f(x)$, where the values of y are dependent on the values of x. In psychology, the operative principle is that the behavior of the subject under consideration is (like y) dependent upon the manipulation of some other factors (the analog of x). ➤ **experiment**. 2. The variable(s) estimated from other, given values. This sense is found in studies using regression and correlation and the underlying sense of causality carried by 1 is absent here. One may estimate x from values of y if they are given or y from values of x if they are given, without concluding that either x or y is the direct cause of the other.

variable, independent 1. Any variable whose values are, in principle, independent of the changes in the values of other variables. In an experiment, any variable that is specifically manipulated so that its effects upon the ➤ **dependent *variable(s)** may be observed. Also called the *experimental variable*, the *controlled variable* and the *treatment variable*. See also the discussion under ➤ **experiment** for more on relevant terminology. **2.** In correlational analyses, the *criterion *variable*.

variable interval reinforcement ➤ **schedules of *reinforcement**.

variable, intervening An internal variable not directly assessable but whose properties can be inferred and interpreted on the basis of systematic manipulations in an ➤ **independent *variable** and observations of the concomitant changes in a ➤ **dependent *variable**. The hypothetical components of many theories in the social sciences are properly intervening variables, e.g., the psychodynamic notion of *ego strength* or Hull's concept of *habit strength* or the behaviorist's *bond* between a stimulus and a response. In such cases no direct measurement of these internal variables is possible; rather, they are interpreted as covert factors which 'intervene' between particular stimulus conditions (*independent variables*) and particular behaviors (*dependent variables*). ➤➤ **organic variable**.

variable, moderator Any variable that (statistically) links two or more other variables or in some way affects the relationship between them. That is, the action of the two primary variables is 'moderated' by the third.

variable, predictor Lit., the variable that one is attempting to predict. In test construction, for example, one way of assessing the validity of a testing instrument is to match the results of those who take the test against the performance they achieve in the real world; those who score high on a test of spelling aptitude should become good spellers in school. In this case, spelling performance in school is the predictor variable.

variable, proxy A variable used as an indirect measure of another variable when that second variable is difficult to measure

or directly observe. For example, the frequency of abuse of street drugs is difficult to measure but it can be studied through the *proxy variable* of hospitalizations for drug overdose.

variable ratio reinforcement ➤ **schedules of *reinforcement**.

variable stimulus In psychophysics, each of the set of stimuli which is compared with the ➤ **standard** (2).

variable time (VT) ➤ **schedules of *reinforcement**.

variance 1 n. The ➤ **standard deviation** squared. A measure of ➤ **dispersion** (or *variability*) of a set of scores, its most common use is in the statistical procedures known collectively as ➤ **analysis of variance**. **2.** Deviant human behavior.

variance, between-group The variance which results from the different groups or conditions in an experiment. In an analysis of variance the between-group variance is compared with the within-group variance.

variance, true The variance in a population of scores. The variance observed in a sample is an estimate of this 'true' population variance.

variance, within-group The variance within an experimental group or condition. In an analysis of variance, the within-group variance is compared with the between-group variance.

variant That which differs in significant ways from other things that are regarded as belonging to the same category or type. The term is applied to cases of diseases and syndromes that are uncharacteristic, to organisms that have features not typically found in that species, etc.

variate 1 n. A synonym of ➤ **variable** (1). **2** n. A particular value of any variable.

variation 1. Generally, change – especially change in the state or condition of something. **2.** In statistics, ➤ **dispersion**. **3.** In biology, differences between members of a species.

vary To change – with the connotation that such change is not so great that identity has been lost.

vas In anatomy generally, any vessel or duct through which liquids travel. pl., *vasa*.

vascular Pertaining to blood vessels or to tissue rich in blood vessels.

vascular dementia ➤ **dementia, vascular** and ➤ **multi-infarct *dementia**.

vas deferens The narrow, muscular duct from the testis to the prostatic urethra.

vasectomy Surgical procedure of cutting or tying off the vas deferens. Bilateral vasectomy is a common method for sterilization in the male since it only prevents movement of the sperm from the testes and does not affect hormonal balances or sexual experience. ➤ **salpingectomy**, the analogous procedure in the female. Distinguish from ➤ **castration**.

vaso- Combining form meaning *vessel* or, more commonly, *blood vessel*.

vasoconstriction The constriction of a blood vessel.

vasodepression Depression of the blood circulation.

vasodilation The expansion or dilation of a blood vessel. var., *vasodilatation*.

vasomotor 1. Pertaining to the nerves that have control over the muscular walls of the blood vessels. 2. Pertaining to the two forms of action of these nerves, namely, *vasoconstriction* and *vasodilation*.

vasopressin A hormone secreted by the posterior lobe of the pituitary gland that functions as part of the system maintaining water balance. It causes the kidneys to excrete a more concentrated urine, thereby retaining water in the body. Also called *antidiuretic hormone* (*ADH*).

vector 1. In mathematics and physics, a quantity with magnitude and direction. Schematically, a vector is represented as an arrow, a directed straight line in which magnitude is given by length and direction

by location of the tip. A number of physical quantities are vectors, such as force, momentum, velocity, etc. This rich and well-known mathematics has encouraged some psychologists to attempt to use vectors as a basis for modeling psychological performance. The most ambitious attempt was Kurt Lewin's theory of the ➤ **life space**, in which vectors represented forces producing directed movement. Other more modest applications have been made in *psychophysics*, *factor analysis* and *scaling*. 2. In statistics, a schematic representation of a particular score or value as a line of appropriate length and direction relative to other scores or values. 3. A disease carrier, an animal that transmits disease-producing organisms from the infected to the non-infected; e.g., the mosquito is the vector for malaria.

vector psychology See the discussion of Lewin's theory under ➤ **vector** (1).

veg The unit for perceived weight.

vegan A total vegetarian, one who has eliminated all animal protein from his or her diet.

vegetative 1 adj. Pertaining to plants. 2 adj. Pertaining to warts, moles, polyps or other outgrowths. 3 adj. Pertaining to the autonomic nervous system and the passive, involuntary functions of respiration, growth, digestion, etc. 4 adj. Generally, passive and quiescent. *Vegetate* is often used in this last sense to refer to the leading of an abnormally passive existence in which one does little more than maintain the *vegetative* (in sense 3 above) functions.

vegetative nervous system ➤ **autonomic nervous system**.

vegetative neurosis ➤ **vegetative** (4).

velar 1 adj. Pertaining to the ➤ **velum**. 2 n. In linguistics, a consonant produced by stopping or disturbing the air flow with the back of the tongue against the soft palate (the *velum*), e.g., the *k* in like, *g* in go.

velocity 1. Rate of motion with both

VELUM

speed and direction specified in either a straight line (*uniform velocity*) or in a curve (*angular velocity*). **2.** More loosely, speed, swiftness.

velum The soft ➤ **palate** of the roof of the mouth.

venereal **1.** (Archaic) Pertaining to Venus; Venusian is a corruption necessitated by the ascendance of the other meanings of venereal. **2.** Pertaining to sexual intercourse. **3.** Pertaining to conditions that arise from or are caused by sexual intercourse with an infected person; ➤ **venereal disease**.

venereal disease Generic term for any disease which is transmitted through sexual intercourse. The well-known classic cases are *syphilis* and *gonorrhea* but a number of other infections are also so classified such as *trichomonas vaginalis*, *lymphogranuloma venereum*, *granuloma inguinale*, *chancroid*, and, of course, *AIDS*.

ventilation **1.** In physiology, an estimate of the volume of air inhaled per day. **2.** Oxygenation of the blood. **3.** Refreshing the air by circulation and drawing off of foul air. **4.** Metaphorically, particularly in therapeutic discourse, the 'airing out' of one's problems, emotions, fears, etc. Compare this last with ➤ **catharsis**.

ventral From the Latin, meaning *pertaining to the belly*. Thus, in bipeds, toward the anterior or frontal part of the body; in quadrupeds, toward the lower, underside of the body. Compare with ➤ **dorsal**.

ventral amygdalofugal pathway A neural pathway between portions of the amygdala and the forebrain.

ventral anterior nucleus A thalamic nucleus that receives input from the globus pallidus and projects to the frontal cortex.

ventral corticospinal tract ➤ **corticospinal pathway**.

ventral lateral nucleus A thalamic nucleus that receives efferent input from the cerebellum and projects to the motor cortex.

ventral noradrenergic bundle ➤ **central tegmental tract**.

ventral posterior nucleus A thalamic nucleus that projects to the somatosensory cortex.

ventral root ➤ **spinal root**.

ventricle **1.** Generally, any small cavity in an organ. **2.** Either of the two lower chambers of the heart. **3.** Any of the four cavities in the brain. The two large lateral ventricles are in the cerebral hemispheres; they connect with the third ventricle, which in turn communicates with the fourth. The ventricular system is filled with cerebrospinal fluid.

ventricular folds The false vocal cords, folds of mucous membrane located just above the true vocal cords.

ventro- Combining form meaning *anterior*, *abdominal*; ➤ **ventral**.

ventromedial hypothalamic syndrome A behavior syndrome observed in experimental subjects (usually rats) following lesioning of the ventromedial hypothalamus (VMH). The syndrome typically exhibits two stages. In the initial *dynamic* stage the animal develops hyperphagia (overeating) and resulting obesity. As weight gradually stabilizes the animal enters the *static* stage, in which it shows little willingness to work for food, or to put up with any aversive conditions associated with food, and extreme finickiness, so that only easily obtainable, palatable food will be eaten. At first these characteristics led to the hypothesis that the VMH was a 'satiety' center that operated in a counterbalancing fashion with the lateral hypothalamus (➤ **lateral hypothalamic syndrome**). The current view, however, is that the VMH is not so much a *center* controlling feeding as it is part of a complex system and that the VMH syndrome itself results from the disruption of neural tracts that pass through the region (the ventral noradrenergic bundle).

ventromedial hypothalamus ➤ **hypothalamus**.

ventromedial pathways Collectively, the ➤ **reticulospinal tracts**, the ➤ **tectospinal tracts**, and the ➤ **vestibulospinal tracts**, all of which are involved in the control of movement.

verbal From the Latin for *word*, pertaining to, characterizing, characteristic of, concerned with, consisting of or expressed in words. Although there is a certain looseness in the manner of usage of the terms *verbal* and *oral*, the latter is derived from the Latin for *mouth* and, literally, should not be treated as a synonym. However, given that the human mouth's most notable products are its words, a certain synonymity in usage has proven hard to resist. ➤ **oral** for another distinction.

verbal behavior Lit., behavior that involves verbal responses, including speaking, reacting to words, memorization of verbal materials, etc. It is also the euphemism of choice for those with a behaviorist bent and who study the psychology of language but eschew the mentalistic cognitive assumptions of the discipline of ➤ **psycholinguistics**.

verbal conditioning 1. Generally, any conditioning in which verbal components are used as either stimuli or responses. 2. The operant conditioning of verbal behavior. Specifically, the shaping up of specific aspects of verbal behavior by reinforcement. ➤ **Greenspoon effect**.

verbal factor A factor found in many analyses of performance on intelligence tests or other tests of ability that emerges as a cluster of skills seemingly representative of a facility with language and verbal materials.

verbal generalization ➤ **generalization, verbal**.

verbal image 1. The recoding of a visual image into verbal form. 2. An echoic memory; ➤ **sensory-information store**.

verbal intelligence 1. Ability with language. 2. Intelligence as assessed by tests that rely upon ability with verbal materials. Meaning 2 is, of course, a theoretical induction from meaning 1, based on the premise that there is a deep relationship between intelligence and various linguistic

skills. ➤ **intelligence** and **performance test(s)** for more discussion.

verbalism 1. An utterance with form but no substance, a formal phrase used with little or no meaning. 2. The predominance of (mere) words over ideas.

verbalization 1. Generally, any verbal statement, an ➤ **utterance**. 2. The act of expressing oneself verbally. 3. Occasionally, verbosity. Compare with ➤ **vocalization**.

verbal learning Generally, the study of learning using verbal stimulus materials and verbal responses. 'Verbal' here is used rather inclusively and covers printed and written in addition to spoken materials. The study of verbal learning has historically embraced a number of procedures including paired-associate learning, serial learning and verbal problem solving. In recent years the term itself has lost currency, primarily because the area of research so labeled was developed by those with a behaviorist orientation. Such theorists tended to view the study of language as the study of ➤ **verbal behavior** and assumed that the general learning principles derived from their experiments could be used as the basis for a theoretical analysis of all linguistic phenomena. Few would defend such a position any longer and, as a result, the terms ➤ **psycholinguistics** and *psychology of language* are now preferred as labels for the general field. These terms carry distinct cognitive as opposed to behaviorist connotations.

verbal-loop hypothesis The theoretical principle that sensory/perceptual information is acquired and retained by translating what is perceived into words and remembering them.

verbal scale Frequently used synonymously with ➤ **verbal test**. However, the *scale* designation is reserved by some for a component of a larger test.

verbal summator A little used projective device in which low-intensity vowel-like sounds are presented and the subject is asked to report what is heard.

verbal test Generally, any test that is ultimately linked in some way with language knowledge, verbal skills, etc. Verbal tests may be *specifically* verbal, such as vocabulary tests, or they may be indirectly verbal, as with the early IQ tests where the verbal scale was only determined when the test battery was factor-analyzed. Contrast with ➤ **performance test**.

verbatim recall **1.** Memory for the exact words used in the original presentation of a message. **2.** A procedure for studying memory in which the subject's task is to attempt a word-for-word recall.

verbigeration Excessive, meaningless and repetitive speech.

verbomania ➤ **logorrhea**.

vergence Cover term for any turning of the eyes, specifically the turning of one eye relative to the other. E.g., ➤ **convergence**, ➤ **divergence**.

veridical Lit., truth-telling. Used primarily for statements that are true in the sense that they are substantiated by facts.

verification The process of determining the truth or correctness of a hypothesis. In scientific parlance it refers to the controlled process of collecting objective data to assess the truth of a theory or hypothesis. By extension, the term also refers to an everyday occurrence whereby one scans the environment in an informal manner to gather information about the appropriateness of one's perceptions, thoughts, suspicions, etc. vb., *verify*.

verificationism ➤ **falsificationism**.

verification time The time that it takes to determine the truth or falseness of a proposition. The measure is particularly useful in gauging the complexity of many cognitive processes since it is assumed that longer verification times imply more complex thought processes. ➤➤ **reaction time**, which is a more general measure.

vermis The part of the cerebellum located at the midline. Auditory and visual information arrive here from the *tectum*;

cutaneous and kinesthetic information from the spinal cord. It projects fibers via the *fastigial nucleus* and ultimately to the *vestibulospinal* and *reticulospinal tracts*.

vernacular The everyday, colloquial speech of a group of persons or in a circumscribed area.

vernier A small, finely graduated scale used as an auxiliary scale to give a measuring device greater adjustment accuracy.

vernier acuity ➤ **acuity, vernier**.

vertebra Any one of the 33 bony segments of the ➤ **spinal column**. pl., *vertebrae*; adj., *vertebral*.

vertex **1.** Generally, the top or summit of something. **2.** In anatomy, the uppermost peak of the head. **3.** In geometry the point furthest from the base, adj., *vertical*.

vertical **1.** Pertaining to the vertex, specifically the uppermost point of a thing. **2.** By extension, pertaining to the line or plane perpendicular to the ground or to the base of an object. **3.** Upright.

vertical décalage ➤ **décalage**.

vertical group ➤ **group, vertical**.

vertical growth ➤ **growth, vertical**.

vertical mobility Mobility between social or occupational classes. The term covers movement up or down in the social system, but it is most commonly used with the connotation of upward movement. Also called *vertical social mobility*.

vertical sampling ➤ **sampling, vertical**.

vertigo **1.** Loosely, dizziness. **2.** Technically, an inappropriate sensation of bodily movement (*subjective vertigo*) or object movement (*objective vertigo*) caused by disturbances of the sensory mechanism for equilibrium. Mostly it is a result of middle-ear disease but it also occurs in toxic conditions (e.g., excessive alcohol intake).

vesanic Loosely, pertaining to insanity, particularly to clearly marked psychoses.

vessel Generally, any duct, tube or canal through which flows some bodily fluid.

vestibular apparatus The bony cavity in the labyrinth of the inner ear, including the two vestibular sacs (the ➤ **utricle** and the ➤ **saccule**) and the three ➤ **semicircular canals**. See each for details on how the systems functions as the sensory mechanism for the perception of head position, acceleration and deceleration. ➤➤ **vestibule** (2), which is occasionally used as a synonym.

vestibular canal ➤ **cochlea**.

vestibular nerve ➤ **auditory nerve**.

vestibular nucleus A nucleus in the cerebellum that receives inputs from various other parts of the cerebellum, including the *fastigial nucleus* and the *flocculonodular lobe*, and projects its outputs to the spinal cord.

vestibular sacs Two small sacs in the inner ear that respond to gravity and provide information about the orientation of the head.

vestibule 1. Generally, any small cavity at the front of a canal. 2. Specifically, the middle part of the inner ear in front of the semicircular canals containing the utricle and saccule. Occasionally the term is used to include the whole of the ➤ **vestibular apparatus**, which see for details.

vestibulocochlear nerve ➤ **auditory nerve**.

vestibulo-ocular reflex The reflex-like adjustments in eye movements that compensate for head movement and permit the maintenance of a steady retinal image while moving about.

vestibulospinal tract One of the ➤ **ventromedial pathways**, it runs from the *vestibular nucleus* to the gray matter in the spinal cord and is involved in the control of posture in response to information that arises in the vestibular system.

vestige 1. Generally, a thing that in its present form is a degenerate or imperfect representation of a fully developed form which existed in the past. 2. Specifically, in biology, an organ or organ part showing such characteristics.

Vexierversuch The original German term for what is known as a ➤ **catch trial**.

VI Abbrev. for *variable interval*. ➤ **schedules of *reinforcement**.

viable 1. Of an organism, likely to live. 2. Of a seed or spore, likely to germinate. 3. Metaphorically, characterizing a theory or a hypothesis likely to stand up under stringent experimental test.

vibration Generally, periodic motion of matter. A full vibration cycle is from a given point through the full cycle and back to the original point, as in a sine wave. ➤➤ **vibration rate**.

vibration, forced (or **induced** or **sympathetic**) ➤ **resonance** (1).

vibration frequency ➤ **vibration rate**.

vibration rate The frequency of vibrations per unit of time (usually seconds). The years have witnessed several changes in the official notation used with respect to the rate of vibrating stimuli. Originally, a full vibration cycle was called a *double vibration* (or *d.v.*) and references to frequency of vibrations (as, for example, in the measurement of tones) were noted as *d.v.s.* (double vibrations per second). Later this rather cumbersome system was simplified to *cycle* and frequency was abbreviated as *cps* (cycles per second). Today the term of choice for vibrations per second is ➤ **Hertz**, abbreviated *Hz*.

vibratory sense A hypothesized sense that was assumed to have its own receptors and neural conduction system and which responded to a vibrating source. Most physiological psychologists now feel that it is not a separate sense but an aspect of other skin senses and is best thought of as rapidly moving *pressure* on the skin.

vicarious Substitute, pertaining to or functioning as a substitute.

vicarious brain process The assumption of cerebral function by another part of the brain following lesion to the original structure.

vicarious functioning Generally, the replacing of one psychological process for another which, for any number of reasons, has been thwarted, blocked, inhibited or repressed. The substituted process itself is often called a *vicarious function*.

vicarious pleasure 1. Loosely, pleasure derived from observing others enjoying themselves. **2.** Specifically, the enjoyment of a voyeur.

vicarious satisfaction 1. Loosely, satisfaction experienced by watching the success of others. **2.** Specifically, such satisfaction as experienced by a parent when an offspring succeeds where they did not.

vicarious trial and error (VTE) The covert or mental process of thinking through a sequence of tentative responses prior to (or instead of) making the overt responses. In board games like checkers, chess or go most players engage in a good deal of VTE behavior.

Vienna circle A collection of logicians and philosophers (notably Carnap, Reichenbach, Gödel and Feigl) who have had more than a passing influence on modern psychology. The essential focus of the circle was scientific philosophy, with an attendant empiricism and a deep trust in logical analysis. ➤ **logical positivism**, which embodies the tenets of the circle.

Viennese school Those psychoanalytic thinkers and practitioners who followed the classical tenets and theories of Sigmund Freud.

Vierordt's law The generalization that the ➤ **two-point threshold** is directly related to (a) the mobility of the part of the body and (b) the distance of the body part from the central axis.

viewing angle The angle between the surface being fixated on and the eye. Distinguish from ➤ **visual angle**.

viewing conditions A general term encompassing any and all of the factors present when a stimulus is viewed. Most writers restrict the use of the term to the physical factors involved (e.g., light level, stimulus size, nature of the display, viewing angle and the like); others, however, will include covert factors such as attentional focus, stress, emotionality, etc.

vigilance Alertness, watchfulness. The term is used broadly, with respect to processes that are intentional and conscious as well as those that are covert or unconscious. E.g., ➤ **perceptual vigilance**.

Vigotsky test ➤ **Vygotsky blocks**.

Vincent curve (or **method**) A procedure for analyzing data from experiments in which not all subjects took the same number of trials or the same amount of time to achieve a set criterion. The data from each subject are divided into fractions of trials or time and each fraction treated as equivalent to that from another subject. For example, using 1/10 as the fraction: for a subject who took 20 trials to learn the material the first data point is based on the average performance on the first two trials, the second on the next two trials and so forth; for a subject who took 100 trials to reach criterion, the first point would be the average of the first 10 trials and so on. The full *Vincent* or *Vincentized curve* for all subjects is then based on the averages of these averages.

Vineland Social Maturity Scale A scale of social maturity designed to assess capacity for independent functioning in a variety of social settings. The test is conducted by interview and the respondent's replies are matched against established norms for various ages.

violet The hue experienced when the human eye is exposed to short-wavelength light in the 400–440 nm range.

viraginity 1. Generally, the feeling in a woman that aspects of her have a male-like quality. **2.** Specifically, a condition in which a biological female feels that she should be male. ➤ **transsexualism**.

virgin 1. Generally, fresh, untouched,

unused. **2.** Specifically, a person who has not had sexual intercourse. The term is generally used only with those who have passed puberty and some authors restrict it to full adults, so that, strictly speaking, there are no 6-year-old but a goodly number of 16-year-old virgins. Note also that there is a tendency to apply the term only to females; while there is etymological justification for this limitation (*virgo* is Latin for *maiden*) modern usage includes males who fit the criteria.

virile Masculine, having the physical and biological characteristics of a mature male.

virilism The presence or development of male secondary sex characteristics in an anatomical female.

virtue A general tendency to behave in a manner that is in agreement with the moral code of a society. The term connotes that such behavior is voluntary; one who is impressed into obeying the code against his or her will is not considered virtuous. Some writers emphasize sex and sexual codes but this restriction is not necessary.

virulent Poisonous or dangerous, in the sense that a virulent substance is one capable of overcoming the body's natural defenses.

viscera Generally, the internal organs located in a body cavity; usually the reference is to the abdominal cavity and the abdominal organs. sing., *viscus*.

visceral **1.** Pertaining to the ➤ **viscera**. **2.** Emotional, nonmental, even nonthinking. This latter use is as common as it is misleading. It is seen reflected in the old distinction between the *viscerotonic* and the *cerebrotonic* components of temperament (➤ **constitutional theory**) and is manifested today in both the technical and nontechnical literatures by expressions like 'gut-level feeling' or 'gut reaction' to characterize an unanalyzed sense of rightness of action. In one sense such an extension of the term is not wholly wrong: emotional expression is often ac-

companied by visceral action; in another sense it confounds the semantics of the original term because the equating of emotionality with the viscera is a theoretical issue and not a lexicographic one.

visceral drive ➤ **viscerogenic drive**.

visceral learning ➤ **biofeedback**.

visceral sensations Sensations derived from receptors in the viscera. Although the motor fibers to the viscera are many compared with the sensory fibers from it, a variety of *visceral* (or *organic* as they are also called) sensations occur, including responses to distension, contraction, temperature changes and various chemicals. Pain in the viscera is often poorly localized, see here ➤ **referred *pain**.

viscero- Combining form meaning *pertaining to the viscera*.

visceroceptor An interoceptor in the viscera.

viscerogenic Lit., originating in the viscera.

viscerogenic drive Loosely, any drive based on physiological needs. Occasionally called *visceral drive*.

viscerotonia One of the three primary components of temperament assumed by ➤ **constitutional theory**.

viscus The rarely used singular form of *viscera*.

visible spectrum ➤ **spectrum, visual**.

visibility **1.** The property of a stimulus that makes it easy to see. **2.** The property of a stimulus such that the physical characteristics of of the energy radiating from it or reflected off of it are adequate for exciting a sufficient number of visual receptors for the experiencing of a visual sensation. ➤ **luminosity**.

visibility coefficient(s) ➤ **luminosity coefficient(s)**.

visibility curve(s) ➤ **luminosity curve(s)**.

visible speech An obsolescent term for the visual representation of an acoustic stimulus (specifically speech) as displayed by a sound ➤ **spectrograph**.

visile An individual with a preference for representing things in visual images and a sensitivity to visually presented material. In research on reading, such children are contrasted with ➤ **audiles**, who have a preference for auditory images and auditory stimuli.

vision 1. The sensory modality for seeing; the sense for which the stimulus is electromagnetic radiation (light) between approximately 380 and 740 nm in wavelength; the receptor for which is the eye or, more precisely, the photosensitive cells of the retina. 2. The process of seeing itself. 3. The perceptual experience of seeing. 4. A visual hallucination. 5. Clarity or foresight.

vision, achromatic Vision using the rods, black–white vision.

vision, alternating The alternate use of the two eyes.

vision, binocular Vision with both eyes, specifically with both fixated on the same point in the visual field. In normal binocular vision there is fusion of the images from the two eyes into a single percept.

vision, central Vision using the ➤ **fovea** and the ➤ **parafovea** of the retina.

vision, chromatic Color vision, vision using the cones.

vision, distance Defined arbitrarily as vision for objects that are 20 feet (approximately 6.1 meters) or more from the viewer.

vision, fovea Vision with the fovea. For details here, ➤ **fovea** and **photopic vision**.

vision, monocular Vision with one eye.

vision, near Defined arbitrarily as vision when the object viewed is approximately 2 feet (about 61 centimeters) or closer to the viewer.

vision, paracentral Vision using the area of the retina surrounding the fovea, the ➤ **parafovea**.

vision, perimacular Vision using the area of the retina surrounding the ➤ **macula lutea**.

vision, peripheral Vision using the ➤ **periphery of the retina**.

vision, persistence of ➤ **iconic** (2).

vision, stereoscopic Three-dimensional vision produced largely by the fusion of two slightly disparate views of a scene on each retina.

vision, theories of ➤ **theories of *color vision**.

visual Pertaining to vision.

visual acuity ➤ **acuity, visual**.

visual adaptation A general term covering several processes by which the visual system adapts itself to viewing conditions. E.g., ➤ **chromatic adaptation**, ➤ **dark adaptation**, ➤ **light adaptation**.

visual agnosia ➤ **agnosia, visual**.

visual angle A measure of the size of the projection of an object on the retina. In the figure, n is the *nodal point*, h the *height* of the object in the environment, d the *distance* of the object from n and α is the *visual angle*.

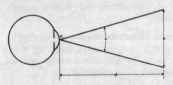

visual aphasia ➤ **alexia**.

visual axis A straight line from the external fixation point through the nodal point of the eye to the fovea of the retina.

visual capture The phenomenon that when one's kinesthetic information and visual information are discoordinate, the visual information tends to dominate. For example, while wearing prisms which displace the visual world slightly to one side one tends to 'feel' one's hand not as where it is physically but rather as where one sees it.

visual cliff An experimental apparatus designed to evaluate depth perception. It consists of a large box with a heavy glass top and a narrow board across the center of the glass. On one side of the board there appears to be a sharp drop-off (the 'visual cliff'); the other side appears shallow and safe. The subject (most commonly a newborn of a species) is placed on the board; consistent locomotion toward the safe side is taken to indicate an ability to perceive depth. Most species who can locomote at birth show an immediate avoidance of the 'cliff.' Human infants cannot be tested on the locomotor task for some months, but newborns placed face down directly over the 'cliff' side usually show considerable distress.

visual disparity ➤ retinal disparity.

visual dominance The phenomenon that if a light and a tone are presented simultaneously the light is usually perceived as having occurred first.

visual field 1. Objectively, all of the points in the physical environment that can be perceived by a stable eye at a given moment. **2.** The subjective, phenomenological perception of the space being viewed at a moment in time.

visual fixation ➤ fixation, visual.

visual image ➤ image, visual.

visual induction Generally, the induction of any visual perception resulting from another adjacent visual stimulus. A variety of phenomena has been reported, including induced-size effects, in which the perceived size of an object is altered by a neighboring stimulus, induced-color effects (➤ color contrast) and induced-brightness effects (see here ➤ Mach band). Also called *light induction*.

visualize To form a visual image.

visually evoked (cortical) potentials Quite literally, ➤ evoked potentials to visual stimuli measured at the cortex.

visually impaired Quite literally, characterizing a person with a relatively serious vision loss but not to the point of being blind. The term is preferred by many over ➤ blindness and its various qualified forms.

visual-motor Referring to or characterizing motor responses which are coordinated with visual stimulation. A special case of *sensorimotor* in which the sensory modality is vision. var., *visuomotor*.

visual-motor Gestalt test ➤ Bender Gestalt Test.

visual noise ➤ noise.

visual organization A general term derived from the Gestalt psychologists and used to refer to the basic notion that visual perception is inherently dependent upon the manner of organization of the manifold aspects of the visual field. The basic issues here are discussed under ➤ principle of *organization.

visual pigment(s) ➤ photopigment.

visual projection The attribution (i.e. *projection*) of a particular spatial location to a perceived object. It may not be equivalent to the ➤ optical projection (2), because of the various psychological factors that determine perceived location; ➤ perception (1).

visual purple ➤ rhodopsin.

visual righting reflex A reflex-like shift in head position to the fixation of different visual points.

visual space ➤ visual field (2).

visual span ➤ reading span.

visual type ➤ visile.

visual yellow ➤ xanthopsin.

visuomotor A variation on ➤ visual-motor.

visuotopy ➤ retinotopic representation.

vital 1. Characteristic of or pertaining to life. **2.** Making an essential contribution to life. **3.** By extension, critical, important.

4. In studies of personality, vigorous, enthusiastic.

vital capacity The volume of air that can be expelled after full inspiration.

vitalism A philosophical point of view which holds that a 'vital force' not explicable by mechanical, chemical or physical principles is responsible for life. It is a form of ➤ **pluralism**(1), involving the vital force in addition to the mind and body of ➤ **dualism**.

vitality **1.** Simply, that which differentiates the living from the nonliving. **2.** By extension, the capacity to remain alive. **3.** By further extension, movement, action or strength. **4.** In the study of personality, a behavior pattern marked by vigor, enthusiasm and endurance.

vital signs Generally, the indicators of life, e.g., respiration, pulse, normal body temperature, etc.

vital statistics **1.** Collectively, numerical data on information concerning births, deaths, marriages and the like in a given area. **2.** Specific numerical data on a particular individual such as height, weight, etc.

vitamin Any of a large number of extremely complex organic substances essential, in small quantities, for normal metabolism, growth and development. Vitamins are distinct from other essential substances like proteins, carbohydrates, fats, minerals and salts. Moreover, they supply no energy of their own and do not add significantly to bodily substance. Their primary roles are as regulators of metabolic processes and aids in the transformation of other substances into energy.

vitamin therapy ➤ **orthomolecular therapy**.

vitreous humor The transparent jelly filling the eye between the lens and the retina. Also called *vitreous body*.

vivi- Combining form meaning *alive*.

vivisection Experimental surgery on a living animal for the purpose of anatomi-

cal, physiological or pharmacological investigation. In many countries governmental policies exist which regulate experimentation on live animals and in some, e.g., the UK, a licence is required to perform such research work.

VMH Abbrev. for the *ventromedial nucleus* of the ➤ **hypothalamus**.

vocabulary **1.** The full compendium of words that an individual knows. **2.** The full list of words in use in a language. **3.** Any specifically circumscribed list of words. When this last meaning is intended, a qualifier is typically used to denote the conditions.

vocabulary, active Generally, the ➤ **vocabulary** (1) used 'actively,' i.e. in speaking and writing. Compare with ➤ **passive *vocabulary**.

vocabulary, passive Generally, the ➤ **vocabulary** (1) used 'passively,' i.e. in reading and listening. An individual's passive vocabulary is considerably larger than their ➤ **active *vocabulary**. Also called *recognition vocabulary*.

vocabulary, sight In early readers, the words that can be read quickly ('on sight') without having to engage in any explicit phonetic decoding. Children taught to read using the whole-word approach typically have large sight vocabularies.

vocabulary test Generally, any test for assessing an individual's vocabulary. There are a truly remarkable number of variations here; one can simply count the words recognized, insist on the subject providing a definition for each word, require that the words be used properly in sentences, ask for matching of words with given definitions and so forth. Each method will yield, of course, a different approximation of an individual's vocabulary.

vocal **1.** Pertaining to the voice. **2.** Outspoken.

vocal cords The two muscular folds of tissue in the larynx which, by rapidly opening and closing, set up the vibration patterns for voicing. The name 'cord' here is slightly misleading, suggesting, as it does, a 'string-like' affair; many authors prefer the term *vocal folds* or even *vocal flaps*, as anatomically more accurate.

vocal folds ➤ vocal cords.

vocality Generally, an aspect of an auditory sensation characterized as the extent to which it has 'vowel-like' properties.

vocalization 1. Generally, the use of the vocal apparatus to produce sounds. This meaning is rather inclusive and encompasses all manner of sounds, language-like and nonlanguage-like, made by humans (adult or infant) and those produced by other species. 2. Specifically, the production of sounds by *Homo sapiens* which are *not* part of true language, e.g., the babbling of infants. 3. The production of sounds by species other than *Homo sapiens*. Meaning 1 may be used as a synonym of ➤ **verbalization**, meanings 2 and 3 should not be.

vocal tract The whole sequence of structures utilized in the production of vocal sounds, including the larynx, the pharynx, the mouth and the nose and all other associated structures.

vocation 1. Etymologically, the role in life to which one has been 'called.' This meaning survives only in theological writings. 2. A job at which one works to earn a living.

vocational adjustment Quite literally, the degree to which one is suited, psychologically, to one's job.

vocational aptitude Potential for a particular vocation. The term is used with a connation of 'prediction.' That is, vocational aptitude generally refers to an assessment about how likely it is that an individual will be successful and satisfied in a particular job given what is known about his or her interests, abilities, training, education, etc.

vocational counseling Lit., counseling a person concerning the selection of a voca-

tion. The term is used broadly and encompasses specific testing of skills and abilities, psychological assessment of personality, motivation, life goals, etc. Generally, counseling (or *guidance*) is aimed at guiding an individual into an occupation for which a high aptitude has been displayed. Compare with ➤ **vocational selection**, where the focus is on finding the individual for the position.

vocational guidance ➤ vocational counseling.

vocational-interest blank ➤ Strong Vocational Interest Blank.

vocational selection The process of attempting to select the person(s) with the highest likelihood of success for a particular position. The skills and aptitudes needed for the particular vocation are presumably already known; the selection process is focused on finding the optimal individual(s) to be hired. Compare with *vocational counseling*, where the focus is on finding the job for the person.

voice 1. Sound produced by the vocal apparatus. 2. The vibration of the vocal cords when uttering a sound. ➤ **voicing**.

voice box A nontechnical term for the ➤ larynx.

voice disorders Abnormalities in the voice, e.g., excessive hoarseness, high-pitched, squeaky voice quality, etc.

voiced/voiceless ➤ voicing.

voice key A switch activated by a voice. The older, crude models were not really 'voice' keys since any sound would trigger them; more modern sophisticated models can be tuned to human voices.

voice onset time (VOT) The time between the beginning of the uttering of a sound and the vibration of the vocal cords. The easiest way to appreciate VOT is to say 'ba' and 'pa' with your fingers lightly touching your throat. The vocal cords vibrate at almost the same instant the lips are opened for 'ba' but there is a short lag (about 50–100 msec) in voicing for 'pa.' This lag time is the VOT.

voiceprint ➤ **spectrograph**.

voicing In phonetics, a ➤ **distinctive feature** (2) marked by the presence or absence of vibration of the vocal cords. In English all vowels are voiced and several consonants can be distinguished from each other purely by this feature, e.g., the voiceless *t* in 'ta' compared with the voiced *d* in 'da.'

vol The unit of measurement of the psychological continuum of perceived volume of an auditory stimulus. A vol is defined as the apparent volume of a 1,000-Hz tone at 40 db. ➤ **volume**.

volar ➤ **palmar**.

volition 1. Generally and loosely, conscious, voluntary selection of particular action or choice from many potential actions or choices. 2. In the writings of the early introspectionists, a complex arrangement of kinesthetic sensations and images that occurred along with a conceptualized goal or end of one's actions or thoughts.

volley The (near) simultaneous or synchronized firing of a number of neural impulses.

volley theory of hearing ➤ **theories of *hearing**.

volume In psychophysics, the sense of how much space a stimulus appears to take up; the psychological equivalent of the physicist's definition. Volume is experienced most clearly with sounds, where high-pitched tones are perceived as 'thin' and hence low in volume and low-pitched tones feel 'larger' or 'fuller' and hence as more voluminous. The unit for volume is the ➤ **vol**. The persistence of some radio and television manufacturers in mislabeling the *loudness* control *volume* (a confusing practice arising from a mislabeling of the control for compensating for the human ear's deficiencies at low- and high-pitched tones as *loudness*) has produced more than its share of confusion. Many olfactory sensations will also have a voluminous quality.

volume color ➤ **color, volume**.

volumetric thirst ➤ **thirst, volumetric**.

voluntarism The metaphysical doctrine that volition or free will is the prime force in reality. See, for more on this issue, ➤ **free will** and ➤ **determinism**.

voluntary 1. Characterizing that which is internally motivated, freely chosen, volitional. 2. Characterizing those psychological processes or behavior patterns that are under cortical control. Voluntary behaviors or processes are *emitted* by an organism and can be shaped using operant conditioning. Compare with ➤ **involuntary**.

voluntary admission Admission into a psychiatric institute or hospital undertaken voluntarily by the individual. While there are cases such as this, the term is also used as a euphemism for many borderline instances in which the individual may be told by the appropriate authorities that either they request 'voluntary' admission or a court order will be sought to impose admission. ➤ **commitment**.

voluntary muscle Any muscle under voluntary control; for the most part, ➤ **striate *muscles**.

voluntary parenthood ➤ **planned parenthood**.

volunteer bias A potential bias in any study where the subjects are volunteers rather than persons who have been selected from the population using sampling procedures that protect against non-representativeness. There is considerable evidence that volunteers are atypical; they are generally more highly motivated and tend to perform at a higher level on most tasks than control subjects who are selected at random.

vomeronasal organ A sensory organ that responds to various chemicals. In species that possess it (most but not all mammals) it mediates the effects of ➤ **pheromones**.

von Restorff effect The generalization that if, given a series of stimuli to be learned (e.g., a list of words), one of them is made physically distinctive in some way (e.g. printed in large type or in a different color from the others) it will be easier to learn and recall. Also called the *isolation effect*.

voodoo death ➤ **thanatomania**.

VOT ➤ **voice onset time**.

vowel A speech sound produced by vibrating the vocal cords without obstructing the passage of air through the vocal tract. Contrast with ➤ **consonant**.

voyeurism A ➤ **paraphilia** characterized by a pattern of sexual behavior in which one's preferred means of sexual arousal is the clandestine observing of others when they are disrobing, nude or actually engaged in sexual activity. Interestingly, a voyeur does not usually derive pleasure from strip-tease shows, public nudity or pornography; arousal is dependent upon the observed person(s) not being aware of their being observed. ➤ **scopophilia**.

VR Abbrev. for *variable ratio*. ➤ **schedules of *reinforcement***.

VT Abbrev. for *variable time*. ➤ **schedules of *reinforcement***.

VTE ➤ **vicarious trial and error**.

vulnerability marker ➤ **marker, vulnerability**.

vulnerable Easily injured. Used with respect to physical, psychological or sociological circumstances.

vulva The external parts of the female genitals, consisting of the major and minor labia and the outer part of the vagina.

Vygotsky blocks A set of 32 wooden blocks differing in shape, height, horizontal width and color. On the underside of each a nonsense word is written. In the standard design there are four nonsense words, one for all tall wide blocks, one for all low wide blocks, one for the tall thin ones and one for the low thin ones. Color and shape are irrelevant. The blocks have been used in a variety of concept-formation studies and experiments on thinking, primarily with children as subjects. Interestingly, although they are called Vygotsky blocks after the Russian philologist, psychologist and philosopher, L. S. Vygotsky, who used them extensively in his work, Vygotsky himself credited a colleague, L. S. Sakharov, with developing them. The use of the full set of blocks is occasionally called a *Vygotsky test*. var., *Vigotsky*.

Vygotsky test ➤ **Vygotsky blocks**.

W

W   1. ➤ Weber fraction. 2. ➤ Coefficient of *concordance. 3. *Weight or weighting factor* (also *w*).

WAIS   ➤ Wechsler Adult Intelligence Scale.

waking center   A term once applied first to an area of the hypothalamus and later to a part of the reticular formation, each of which was implicated as the primary locus of cells that functioned to waken an organism. It is now generally agreed that there is no single such brain center; brain stem and forebrain structures are known to exert control over the extremely complex sleep–waking cycle. See here ➤ sleep and related terms.

Walden Two   The title of a novel by the American behaviorist B. F. Skinner in which the principles of operant conditioning are applied to create a (or at least Skinner's characterization of a) utopia. ➤ Skinnerian.

Wald-Wolfowitz runs test   A nonparametric statistical test that evaluates whether two samples of data can be said to be drawn from the same population. The test analyzes the pattern of ➤ runs (3) in the two samples and reflects differences between them. ➤ runs test for a one-sample test.

Wallerian degeneration   The degeneration of an axon when it has been separated from its cell body. The myelin sheath degenerates into a chain of small lipoid drops which can be stained, a procedure that permits the tracing of the course of the injured fibers. The neurilemma, if left intact, forms a hollow tube through which the axon can regenerate.

walleye   1. An eye with abnormally light colored or white iris. 2. An eye with dense, opaque cornea. 3. Divergent ➤ strabismus.

ward   A large room in a hospital for the use of many patients.

warming-up period   ➤ warm-up period.

warm spot   A point on the skin where a punctate stimulus that is below adaptation level will evoke a sensation of warmth. It is not clear what specific sensory-receptor system is involved since examination of these warm spots reveals no special structures.

warmth   1. One of the skin senses. 2. The sensory experience resulting from a stimulus above the normal temperature of the skin (roughly 89° F or 32° C). However, the experiencing of warmth is dependent upon the adaptation level of the skin and after immersing one's hand in water of 95° F for a few minutes a stimulus of 92° F will be experienced as cool, not warm.

warm-up period   In many complex learning situations, a period of time during which movements and responses are tentative and inexact. var., *warming-up period*.

Wasserman test   A test for the presence of syphilis. It is based on the Wasserman reaction, in which the complement of fresh blood serum is fixated (rendered inactive or destroyed) by the presence of an antigen and its antibody.

waterfall illusion   A motion after-effect most easily demonstrated by viewing a set of horizontal stripes moving downward (as in a waterfall) for a time. When the objective movement is stopped, the stripes appear to move upward.

water-jar problem(s)   A set of problems involving three jars of varying capacity. In a typical problem there might be jars of say, 10, 19 and 45-oz capacity and the subject is asked how to obtain exactly 3 oz of water. The problems are usually presented as paper-and-pencil tests, although on occasion actual jars are used. They have been extensively used in the study of cognitive set in problem-solving.

850

Watsonian Referring to the psychological theory and philosophical point of view of the American behaviorist John Broadus Watson (1878–1958). The Watsonian approach was *pure* behaviorism; it was antimentalist to the extreme and regarded such cognitive experiences as thinking and feeling to be mere epiphenomena that accompanied peripheral behaviors such us sub-laryngeal movements or visceral and muscular responses. It also embodied a strict environmentalism in which genetic factors were assumed to be responsible for few (or none) of the observed differences between individuals. But as the term itself survives in contemporary writing, the strongest connotations are: (a) the advocacy of strictly objective methods in experimentation; and (b) the studied reliance upon only that which is publicly verifiable in attempts to theorize about, explain and predict behavior. ➤ **behaviorism**.

wave 1. An orderly, periodic motion of particles manifested as a moving crest (as on water or other liquid). 2. Any periodic vibration, as in, e.g., a *sine wave*. 3. Any oscillation, particularly as observed on some recording device such as an oscilloscope or a polygraph that reflects some measured activity. See here, e.g., ➤ **brain waves**.

wave amplitude A measure of the energy in a wave given as the height of the wave measured from the trough to the crest.

wave frequency The number of complete waves occurring per unit of time. Usually measured in full cycles per second or ➤ **Hertz**.

wavelength The distance between two equivalent points on adjacent waves. Usually measured as the distance between the crest, but any two points can be used.

wave of excitation 1. Generally, any neuronal impulse. 2. The propagation of an electrochemical charge along a neuron. 3. The excitatory impulses that travel through the conductile tissue of the ventri-

cles of the heart, resulting in the contraction of the chambers.

waxy flexibility ➤ catatonic waxy flexibility.

WB Scale ➤ Wechsler-Bellvue Scale.

weak law of effect ➤ empirical law of *effect.

weaning The gradual process of accustoming a mammalian offspring to do without its mother's milk (or substitute thereof).

weaning aggression ➤ aggression, weaning.

weaning, psychological 1. The process of gradually weakening and (one hopes) eventually breaking a child's psychological dependence upon the parents. 2. By extension, a client's gradual achievement of psychological independence from his or her psychotherapist; the process of dissolving ➤ **transference**.

weapon-focus effect The tendency for individuals witnessing a crime like an armed robbery to focus on the weapon. This typically impairs their ability to identify the culprit. ➤ **eyewitness testimony**.

Weber-Fechner law Since ➤ Fechner's law is derived from ➤ Weber's law, this combined term is occasionally used to encompass both generalizations. There is also some confusion in the older literature over whose law is called by which name, no little of it stemming from Fechner himself, in his generously referring to what we now call *Fechner's law* as *Weber's law* on the grounds that his general principle was a simple derivation from the law Weber had previously proposed.

Weber's law A psychophysical generalization due to the German physiologist Ernst Heinrich Weber. It states that the ➤ **just-noticeable differences** in stimuli are proportional to the magnitude of the original stimulus. Formally $\Delta I / I = k$ where I is the intensity of the comparison stimulus, ΔI is the increment in intensity just detectable and k is a constant. The law holds reasonably well for the mid-range of most stimulus dimensions but tends to break down when very low- or very high-intensity stimuli are used; e.g., for very low-intensity tones the Weber fraction is somewhat larger than it is for moderately loud tones. Note that the ratio is often rendered as $\Delta R/R$, where R stands for *Reiz* (German for *stimulus*) and as $\Delta S/S$, where S stands for *stimulus*. ➤➤ **Fechner's law**, which is derived from Weber's law.

Wechsler Adult Intelligence Scale (WAIS) One of the most frequently used tests of adult ➤ **intelligence**, it was derived from the earlier ➤ **Wechsler Bellevue Scale** and is based upon a series of subtests with two general categories of items, *verbal* and *performance*. Verbal items deal with general information, vocabulary, arithmetic tests, comprehension, similarities, analogies, etc.; performance items deal with picture arrangement and completion, block designs, spatial relations, and the like. The test was revised in 1981 and is familiarly known as the WAIS-R, pronounced 'waiss-are.'

Wechsler–Bellvue scale(s) The first of the intelligence tests to separate systematically *verbal* and *performance* abilities. The Wechsler–Bellvue I was published in 1929 and the revised Wechsler–Bellvue II appeared in 1946. In 1955 it was extensively revised, and is now generally known as the ➤ **Wechsler Adult Intelligence Scale (WAIS)**.

Wechsler Intelligence Scale for Children (WISC) An individually administered test of intelligence designed to be used with children ages 6 to 16. Like the Wechsler Adult Intelligence Scale from which it was developed, it has both *performance* and *verbal* components. It was revised in 1974 and is now known as the WISC-R.

Wechsler Preschool and Primary Scale of Intelligence (WPPSI) An intelligence test designed for use with children below the age of 6.

Wechsler scales A general label for the various Wechsler tests of intelligence, each of which is given above. Note that all the Wechsler scales are individually administered tests.

we-group ➤ **in-group**.

weight 1. Generally, the value of impact of an observation, event or piece of data. The connotation here is that of the degree to which that particular observation contributes to some overall conclusion or interpretation when measured against the impact or value of all other observed events or data. This meaning is paralleled in the standard legal language when one speaks of the 'weight of evidence' or of the 'weighing of testimony.' **2.** In statistics, a multiplicative factor which adjusts the relative impact of one (or more) selected score(s) upon the overall statistic. E.g., in calculating a grand mean from two separate means, each separate mean would be weighted to reflect the size of the sample from which it was calculated. Similarly, in psychological testing, the weight of subtests in a test battery is adjusted to improve overall predictive validity. The values by which each score is multiplied in such cases are called *weight coefficients*. **3.** The proportional contribution of each variable in a complex multivariate system to the total variance. See here ➤ **factor loading**, which reflects essentially the same concept. Meaning 2 is also called *nominal weight*; meaning 3, *effective weight*.

weight coefficient ➤ **weight** (2).

weighting Determining the ➤ **weight** (1) of the several scores under consideration so as to be able to assign the appropriate ➤ **weight** (2) to each.

Weigl-Goldstein-Scheerer Test A conceptual sorting task using a number of blocks of different color and shapes. They have been used to study concept learning and, like the ➤ **Goldstein-Scheerer tests**, to evaluate the disabilities that accompany various kinds of brain damage.

well-adjusted ➤ **adjustment**.

Weltanschauung A German term best

translated as *outlook on the world*; thus, one's overall philosophical perspective on all things.

Wernicke-Korsakoff syndrome Most cases of ➤ **Wernicke's syndrome** and ➤ **Korsakoff's syndrome** (see each entry for details on symptoms) are associated with severe alcoholism and are often observed in the same individual, for whom this hybrid term is used. Note, however, that the two syndromes are really different diseases; the former responds well to thiamine, the latter has no known cure.

Wernicke's aphasia ➤ **aphasia, Wernicke's.**

Wernicke's area A loosely circumscribed cortical area in the temporal region of the dominant hemisphere of the brain (i.e. the language hemisphere, which is the left for virtually all right-handed persons and the majority of left-handed persons). From a statistical point of view there is evidence that this general cortical region is involved in the reception and processing of *language*. However, it would be misleading to call it a *language-reception area* as some have done; there are extremely complex interrelationships between this area, the arcuate fasciculus that connects it with Broca's area, the neighboring regions of auditory cortex and the many interconnections with the frontal lobes. For some sense of the kinds of functions that may be involved here, ➤ **aphasia** et seq., especially ➤ **Wernicke's *aphasia.**

Wernicke's encephalopathy ➤ **Wernicke's syndrome.**

Wernicke's syndrome An acute brain disorder with eye-movement dysfunctions, ataxia, orientation problems and general mental confusion being the primary symptoms. It is related to severe alcoholism and is, in the classic case, followed by *alcoholic amnestic disorder* (or ➤ **Korsakoff's syndrome**), although this sequela can occasionally be prevented by large doses of thiamine. Also called *Wernicke's encephalopathy.*

Werther syndrome Named after the protagonist in Goethe's novel *The Sorrows of Young Werther*, the tendency for young people to attempt to take their own lives following a highly publicized suicide. The phenomenon, also called a ➤ **cluster suicide**, was identified when a rash of young male suicides followed the publication of Goethe's novel in which the hero takes his own life.

wet dream A dream accompanied by seminal emission. Since such dreams usually occur at night, they are also called *nocturnal emissions*, although this hardly seems an accurate term for the dream itself, more for the result.

Wever-Bray effect An aural potential that can be recorded using gross electrodes placed near the auditory nerve of an animal. It is made up of two separate potentials; one is the whole nerve-action potential, the other is the cochlear microphonic. What makes the Wever-Bray effect so startling is that if the changes in the electrical potentials are amplified and fed through an ordinary telephone receiver, one can actually understand words spoken through it into the experimental animal's ear.

WGTA ➤ **Wisconsin General Test Apparatus.**

white In vision, the visual sensation experienced when the eye is stimulated by a combination of wavelengths such that none dominates. White represents the extreme pole of the brightness dimension along the white–gray–black continuum. It may be produced by broad-spectrum light, as in normal daylight, or by careful balancing of complementary hues with high intensity. ➤➤ **white *noise** for the auditory analog.

white matter A general term for those parts of the spinal cord and the brain that contain a predominance of myelinated fibers. ➤ **Gray matter** reveals the predominance of cell bodies.

white noise ➤ **noise, white.**

Whitney extension ➤ **Mann-Whitney U.**

Whitten effect ➤ **Lee-Boot effect**.

whole-learning method Simply, learning material (usually verbal) in its entirety as opposed to learning it one small piece at a time – the so-called *part-learning method*.

whole object In psychoanalysis, an ➤ **object** that is responded to in a manner that makes it clear that the *whole* is the focus of the response and not any one aspect of it. Compare with ➤ **part object**.

whole-object assumption The phenomenon that in learning the meanings of new words the learner assumes that a new word pertains to the whole object and not to some part of it. For example, if during a visit to the zoo mother points and says, 'Look at the lemur,' the child assumes 'lemur' refers to the whole animal and not, say, its long, ringed tail. Compare with ➤ **mutual exclusivity assumption**.

whole-word method A method of reading instruction in which the focus is on the relationships between particular configurations of letters (the 'whole word') and its pronunciation. Often called the *look–say method*. Compare with ➤ **phonics method**.

wholism ➤ **holism**.

Whorfian hypothesis As put forward by the American linguist Benjamin Lee Whorf, the claim that language influences perception and thought. Actually, there are two forms of the hypothesis: a *weak form*, which argues that only perceptions are so influenced (e.g., the Eskimo, because of the many words in his language for snow, is hypothesized to distinguish variations in types of snow that would not be distinguished by a speaker of, say, English); and a *strong form*, which argues that abstract conceptual processes are so affected (e.g., the Hopi Indian language marks time in a relativistic fashion, compared with English's temporal breakdown into past, present and future, leading to the hypothesization that the very conceptualizations of time differ for the speakers of each language). Despite intensive research on the issues little or no convincing data have emerged to support the hypo-

thesis. It is likely that the complex interweaving between culture, social values, language and thought produces a rich representation of one's world knowledge which one's language can stretch or expand as necessary to encompass the perceptions and cognitions needed for effective verbal communication. From this view, language is an attempt to 'map' thought rather than its controller. The hypothesis is also known as the ➤ **Sapir-Whorf hypothesis**; see that term for reasons.

Wh-question In linguistics, any interrogative based on one of the 'wh-' words, *what*, *which*, *where*, *when*, *why*, *who*, *whose* and *(w)how*. Wh-questions are always 'information-seeking' as compared with ➤ **yes-no questions**.

wide-band procedures A term applied to the more subjective testing and evaluation procedures such as ➤ **projective techniques** and ➤ **interviews**. The term was borrowed from information theory and implies that a broad spectrum of coverage is provided but at the price of relatively poor accuracy and dependability, just as a wide-band receiver gives access to a broad range but with poor selectivity of information.

Wilcoxon test An extension of the ➤ **sign test**, which evaluates the magnitude of differences as well as their direction in assessing the significance of differences between matched pairs of scores. Also called the *matched-pairs signed-ranks test*.

Wild Boy of Aveyron One of the more famous case studies in psychology. Victor, a *feral child*, was found in the early 1800s near the town of Aveyron. Estimated to be about 7 years old at the time, he was trained and extensively studied by the French physician/educator Jean-Marc-Gaspard Itard. The growth and development of Victor intellectually, socially and, to a modest extent, verbally was described in loving detail by Itard over a period of many years and had a profound impact on educational theory and practice.

will 1. Generally, the internal, personal

capacity for free determination of choice or action. Usually conceptualized as a conscious function wherein one decides to engage in some behaviors and refrain from others. ➤ **free will** (2). **2.** The totality of the person. Sense 1 is somewhat archaic and rarely used in the technical literature these days, although the underlying notion lives on in any number of other terms, e.g. ➤ **purpose**, ➤ **volition**, ➤ **freedom** (1); sense 2 is captured largely by the term ➤ **self**.

willfulness A negative reactivity, a tendency to resist the suggestions and/or attempts at manipulation of others. The term generally carries a negative connotation, thus a willful person is not viewed as mature and independent.

Williams syndrome A genetic syndrome caused by a missing gene and surrounding DNA sequence on chromosome 7. Children with the disorder have abnormal calcium chemistry, various cardiac and circulatory defects, short stature with an 'elfinlike' face and mental retardation which can run from quite mild to moderate. Despite the mental retardation the typical Williams syndrome child has good language ability and is highly social and friendly. Also known as *hypercalcemia* and *William's syndrome.*

will power A nontechnical term for self-control or the ability to resist temptation.

will to power Adler's term for the desire to dominate others or the striving for superiority over them.

Wilson's disease A genetic disorder displayed as an error in copper metabolism. It is characterized by an open drooling mouth, contraction of the wrist, greenish-brown pigment of the corneas and brain damage which can cause a variety of motoric dysfunctions. Also called *hepato-lenticular degeneration.*

windigo A culture-specific syndrome observed in Algonquin Indians where a hunter imagines he is in the power of a flesh-eating supernatural monster.

win–shift lose–stay strategy The opposite of the ➤ **win–stay lose–shift strategy**. Here the subject shifts to an alternative choice following each correct response but remains with the previous choice when wrong.

win–stay lose–shift strategy A commonly observed strategy in two-alternative choice experiments whereby the subject continues to make the same response when correct ('win–stay') but abruptly switches to the other choice when wrong ('lose–shift'). Compare with ➤ **win–shift lose–stay strategy**.

WISC ➤ **Wechsler Intelligence Scale for Children**.

Wisconsin General Test Apparatus (WGTA) A piece of laboratory apparatus designed at the primate research lab at the University of Wisconsin. It houses a single monkey in a cage and has a fairly flexible set of trays and platforms which hold various stimulus items for presentation to the subject.

wish **1.** Generally, any longing or desire. Some authors use the term for either conscious or unconscious desires; others, however, prefer to limit it to one or the other. On some occasions it will be used so that it is clear that the individual makes no overt effort to gain the object(s) of the longing; here, ➤ **goal** or ➤ **aim** will be used for those things striven for. **2.** The object of the desire.

wish fulfillment **1.** In psychoanalysis, a complex process whereby id impulses are satisfied and, as a result, psychic tension is reduced. In the classical Freudian conception, dreams and parapraxes are vehicles for the action of wish fulfillment. In dreaming, for example, the primal id fails to distinguish between fantasies, images or hallucinations and reality and so the dreamer may represent as fulfilled in symbolic form wishes that would have otherwise disrupted sleep because of their unacceptability. **2.** More loosely and less technically, the satisfactory acceptance of any secondary goal following a thwarting of attempts to achieve the primary goal.

wishful thinking Thinking directed by, and along the lines of, one's wishes and desires rather than upon the objective constraints of reality. It is sometimes said that wishful thinking is not logical. This may be true in any given case but it is not a defining feature.

witchcraft The occult practice of sorcery. Beliefs concerning witchcraft and the role of its practitioners are found in many societies and with a wide range of variation ranging from evil or 'black' to beneficent or 'white' witches. There is no doubt that in a culture with the proper deep belief patterns a witch is an extraordinary and powerful person who can cure or maim another: there is also no doubt that occult powers have nothing to do with these capabilities. ➤ **faith healing, parapsychology, placebo effect**.

witch's milk An archaic term for the milk-like secretion occasionally exuded from an infant's breast. It is stimulated by lactating hormone from the mother.

withdrawal 1. A pattern of behavior characterized by the person removing him- or herself from normal day-to-day functioning – with all of its attendant frustrations, tensions and disappointments. Here the sense is of a neurotic removal of self from normal social discourse, accompanied by uncooperativeness, irresponsibility and often a reliance on drugs and alcohol to facilitate this social remoteness. 2. A conscious removing of oneself from particular situations. Here the connotation is very different from 1: in this sense the withdrawal is a calculated decision not to be involved for strategic, philosophical, political or other reasons. 3. In ethology a pattern of behaviour exhibited by the loser of a battle, who gives a display of ➤ **submission** and is allowed to leave the scene unmolested. 4. In psychopharmacology, the cessation of administration of a drug, especially one for which the individual has developed a dependence. ➤ **withdrawal symptoms**. 5. Eric Fromm's term for a neurotic lack of concern about the world to the point where the person's remoteness has self-destructive results. **6.** A method of birth control in which the penis is removed from the vagina prior to ejaculation.

withdrawal delirium Delirium caused by the withdrawal of a drug upon which one had built up a severe dependence. See, for some specifics, ➤ **alcohol withdrawal delirium** and ➤ **sedative, hypnotic, or anxiolytic withdrawal delirium**.

withdrawal symptoms A general term covering any of the effects of the cessation of administration of a substance upon which one has built up a dependence; ➤ **drug *dependence**. In older writings this term tends to be used only with respect to drugs with well-known 'addictive' properties, such as the opiates. Contemporary usage reflects the recognition that an array of post-administration effects occurs with many substances and the particular withdrawal symptoms under consideration are classified and keyed to the substance or class of substances for which the dependence has developed. E.g., ➤ **alcohol withdrawal, sedative, hypnotic, or anxiolyric withdrawal, tobacco withdrawal**. ➤➤ **tolerance**.

withdrawal syndrome, prolonged A syndrome in which the ➤ **withdrawal symptoms** associated with a drug continue for an extended period of time. ➤➤ **tolerance**.

within-group variance ➤ **variance, within-group**.

within-subjects design An experimental design in which each subject is used in all conditions. Compare with ➤ **between-subjects design**.

wolf child ➤ **feral child**.

Wolffian ducts The structures in the embryo that develop into the male internal sex organs.

Wolffian system In the developing embryo, the precursors of the internal male sex organs.

wolf-man The sobriquet of one of Freud's more famous patients, a man

WORKING THROUGH

whose dominant symptom was a recurring dream involving a marked fear of wolves. He was a Russian nobleman whom Freud analyzed intensely and from whom he gathered much of his 'evidence' for childhood sexuality and the *Oedipus complex*.

Woodworth Personal Data Sheet Although no longer in use, this self inventory rates an entry here as the first of the modern personality inventories. Developed during the First World War by Robert Sessions Woodworth, it was used to detect emotionally unstable soldiers.

word Surprisingly, linguists have a devilish time providing a precise definition here, despite the fact that essentially every literate person seems to know implicitly what this term refers to. Although there are problems with the following, it is certainly an acceptable working definition: the minimum free linguistic form. That is, the smallest ('minimum') unit ('form') of a language that can stand alone ('free') in a written and/or spoken format.

word blindness ➤ alexia.

word-building test A variation on an ➤ anagram task in which the subject is asked to construct as many words as possible from a given letter set.

word-completion task ➤ stem-completion task.

word configuration The overall shape of a word, its length, location of ascending and descending letters, placement of capital letters, etc. It is an important cue in the ➤ whole-word method of reading instruction.

word count A general term for any systematic assessment of the frequency of occurrence of words in written and/or spoken language. Often such counts are restricted to specific linguistic domains, e.g., first-year primers, parent–child interactions. However, several estimates of a full word count of a whole language have been made. Such counts are extremely useful research tools since they provide estimates of the familiarity which an average subject can be expected to have with

the words used in a particular experiment. E.g., ➤ **Thorndike-Lorge list**.

word deafness ➤ auditory *aphasia.

word-form dyslexia ➤ dyslexia, word-form.

word method An occasionally used shortened form of ➤ whole-word method.

word–nonword task ➤ lexical-decision task.

word salad An abnormal pattern of speaking in which the words seem as though they have been tossed randomly like a salad so that they come out in a discoordinated and uninterpretable jumble. It is seen occasionally in some forms of schizophrenia and aphasia.

word sentence ➤ holophrase.

word stem-completion task ➤ stem-completion task.

word-superiority effect (WSE) The phenomenon that a letter can be identified at a lower threshold and responded to more rapidly when it is part of a familiar word than if it is presented in isolation; e.g., the D in DOG is recognized more readily than a D presented alone. First reported by J. McKeen Cattell in the 1880s, the effect is an intriguing paradox since presumably one should have to be able to identify each of the separate letters in order to read the whole word. Several factors are known to play a role in the WSE, including the familiarity of the word, its orthography, its meaningfulness and the like.

working Assumed or used temporarily for the purpose of making further analyses, e.g., *working mean* (see here ➤ **assumed** *mean**) or ➤ **working hypothesis**.

working hypothesis An educated guess, a hypothesis about some issue that serves as the basis for further research until enough is learned about the phenomena to state a more formal hypothesis.

working mean ➤ assumed *mean.

working memory ➤ memory, working.

working through A general term often

used as characterizing the process of obtaining insight into one's problems during therapy.

work psychology A term preferred by many European psychologists to ➤ **industrial/organizational psychology**.

work sample Quite literally, a sample of work taken as representative of the work of an individual.

work-up The process of obtaining as much data as possible for diagnosing a disease or a psychological disorder.

world hypothesis Steven Pepper's term for a global, philosophical point of view toward theory, science, methodology, etc. In some important respects a world hypothesis is similar to Kuhn's notion of a ➤ **paradigm** (4).

wound 1. In medicine, any break or disruption in the integrity of tissue caused by physical trauma or violence. 2. By extension, in clinical psychology, a rent in the psychological fabric of a person caused by emotional trauma or violence.

WPPSI ➤ **Wechsler Preschool and Primary Scale of Intelligence**.

write As part of the accelerating 'spillover' of terms from the computer sciences this term can be seen not infrequently as a synonym for *remember*. That is, *to remember* is often phrased *to write into memory*.

writer's cramp A spasm of the muscles used in writing, usually considered to be a functional disorder.

writing disorder ➤ **expressive writing disorder, developmental**.

WSE ➤ **word-superiority effect**.

Würzburg school A group of researchers at Würzburg University led by Oswald Külpe, working around the turn of the century. Although they were *introspectionists* they extended their scope of research beyond that of the Titchnerian form of ➤ **structuralism** (1) and focused on the so-called 'higher mental processes' of thinking, problem-solving, cognitive set and the like. ➤➤ **imageless thought, set** (especially 2) and related entries.

X

X **1.** Any given raw score or, when the distinction needs to be made, a raw score of the *x*-distribution. **2.** Any given value of the independent variable.

$\overline{X}$ The arithmetic mean of a set of scores.

x A deviation from the mean of the *x*-variable.

xantho- Combining form meaning *yellow*.

xanthocyanopia A form of color blindness in which blues and yellows are distinguished, but reds and greens are not. var., *xanthocyanopsia*.

xanthopsia Characterizing vision in which the sensitivity to yellow is heightened and everything has a yellowish tinge. It occurs as a visual defect in some individuals but can be artificially induced by adapting the eye with blue light. Also called *yellow-sighted*.

xanthopsin Visual yellow, a visual pigment produced when ➤ **rhodopsin** is bleached by light.

x-axis ➤ **axis**.

X chromosome ➤ **chromosome**.

x coordinate ➤ **axis**.

xeno- Combining form from the Greek for *strange* or *foreign*. var., *zeno-*.

xenogenous Pertaining to that which is caused by a foreign body.

xenoglossophilia A tendency to use unnecessary words which are strange, unusual or have foreign origins. The neologist who coined this term sublimely condemned himself.

xenorexia A pathological condition characterized by the persistent swallowing of non-food objects. ➤ **pica**.

xero- Combining form meaning *dry*.

x value The value of a score on the *x-axis*; ➤ **axis**.

XX In genetics the shorthand notation for the normal genotypic pattern for a human female in which two sex chromosomes are present; ➤ **chromosome**.

XXX syndrome ➤ **triple-X syndrome**.

XXXY syndrome A variant of ➤ **Klinefelter's syndrome**.

XXY syndrome ➤ **Klinefelter's syndrome**.

XY In genetics, the shorthand notation for the normal genotypic pattern for a human male in which two sex chromosomes are present; ➤ **chromosome**.

XYY syndrome A ➤ **chromosomal anomaly** in which three sex chromosmes are present. Persons with the anomaly are phenotypically male, of above average height and with normal genital development, but their fertility may be low owing to reduced sperm production. Some years back there was a flurry of studies carried out that seemed to implicate this chromosomal pattern in aggressive and criminally violent behavior. Careful examination of large numbers of males, however, has failed to support any clear link between the XYY syndrome and aggression.

XYZ system A system of standard primaries taken as mathematical abstractions for a formal specification of color. Unlike the ➤ **RGB system** wherein the ➤ **color equation** is based on 'real' colors, the XYZ primaries are not real colors but exist only as mathematical expressions.

Y

Y **1.** Any given raw score of the *y* distribution. **2.** Any given value of the dependent variable.

y A deviation from the mean of the *y* variable.

YAVIS syndrome An acronym for *y*oung, *a*ttractive, *v*erbal, *i*ntelligent, *suc*cessful. A half-joking term used to describe the type of client that psychotherapists, in painfully simple terms, prefer to have in therapy. Persons displaying this syndrome make wonderful clients for a variety of reasons, not the least of which is that successful therapy is highly likely.

y-axis ➤ **axis**.

Y chromosome ➤ **chromosome**.

y coordinate ➤ **axis**.

yellow The hue experienced when the normal eye is exposed to light with wavelengths of approximately 575–585 nm, with a 'unique' yellow found, for most observers, at about 580 nm.

yellow-sighted ➤ **xanthopsia**.

yellow spot ➤ **macula lutea**.

Yerkes-Dodson law The generalization that task difficulty and arousal interact such that on difficult tasks low levels of arousal improve performance relative to high levels, but on easy tasks the reverse is true, with high arousal levels facilitating performance relative to low levels.

Yerkish The artificial language developed by D. Rumbaugh and co-workers for communication with chimpanzees. It consists of a set of arbitrary symbols that stand for words or concepts and some simple grammatical rules for ordering symbols to express meaning. The name derives from the Yerkes laboratory in Georgia,

USA, where the work was carried out.

yes–no question Any interrogative that takes either 'yes' or 'no' as the prescribed answer. There are three basic forms for such interrogatives: *auxiliary inversion* ('Did you do that?'), *tag questions* ('You did that, didn't you?') and a *rising-intonation contour* ('You did *that*?').

Y maze A ➤ **maze** shaped like a Y with a single approach alley and two arms, one of which the subject must choose.

yoga From the Sanskrit meaning *union*, a Hindu religious system of practices and beliefs whose objective is the attainment of spiritual union with the Supreme Being. There are a number of distinct branches of Yogic practice, some of which emphasize disciplined physical bodily control and others which are more cognitive or mental in orientation. ➤➤ **mysticotranscendent therapy**.

yoked control An umbrella term for a number of research techniques all of which share the feature that the experimental and control subjects are linked together (or 'yoked') in some fashion, although only the experimental subjects receive a critical treatment or experience a particular procedure. For example, in a learning study experimental and control subjects both receive reinforcements at the same time but delivery is contingent only on the behavior of the experimental subjects. Yoked subjects would therefore get the same number of reinforcements but independent of their behavior. Resist the temptation to spell the term with an '1.'

Young-Helmholtz theory ➤ **theories of** ***color vision**.

y value The value of a score on the *y-axis*; ➤ **axis**.

Z

Z ➤ **Z-transformation**.

z ➤ **z-score**.

zar A culture-specific syndrome found in north African and Middle Eastern societies marked by dissociative episodes that include odd behaviors like hitting one's head against a wall, singing, weeping and shouting. It is believed to be due to possession by a spirit with whom the individual may develop a close, on-going relationship.

Zeigarnik effect As first put forward by Bluma Zeigarnik in 1927, the generalization that unfulfilled tasks are retained better than fulfilled tasks. The term is generally taken today to refer to the principle that any task that is interrupted will be recalled better than a task that the individual is permitted to complete. Zeigarnik's original characterization, however, contained an important factor that often goes unmentioned in contemporary usage; specifically, that *fulfillment* is defined in terms of the individual's own sense of satisfaction; it is not simply completion of a task but satisfactory completion of it in terms of the goals of the person working on it.

Zeitgeber German for *time giver*. In the study of ➤ **circadian rhythms** it is used for whatever particular stimulus configuration provides the neural mechanisms of a particular species with information about temporal cycles. For most mammals, *light* is the *Zeitgeber*.

Zeitgeist German for *spirit of the times*. The term is used in a rather loose metaphysical manner to characterize the rich and varied matrix of ideas, trends, philosophies, economies, social structures, political climate, etc. that make up the tone of a culture during a given era. In historiographical work, the so-called *naturalistic approach* emphasizes the role of the *Zeitgeist* in directing and controlling events

and is usually balanced against the so-called *personalistic approach* which emphasizes the role of particular individuals. ➤ **great-man theory**.

Zen Buddhism A meditative school of Buddhism that focuses upon the 'stilling of the mind' with the aim of reaching the enlightened state (satori) in which one appreciates the true, mystical, unanalyzed nature of things beyond the normal, rational, conscious manner of 'ordinary' knowing. ➤ **mysticotranscendent therapy**.

Zener cards A deck of 25 cards used in research on extrasensory perception. Each card in the deck has one of five symbols (star, plus sign, wavy lines, circle, square) on it with each symbol appearing on five cards. Also called *ESP deck* (or *cards*) and *Rhine deck* (or *cards*) after J. B. Rhine, who used them extensively in his work in ➤ **parapsychology**.

zeno- ➤ **xeno-**.

zero, absolute The true zero point on any dimension; the point at which nothing of the variable under examination exists. The establishment of an absolute zero for a given variable is what permits measurement of that variable on a ➤ **ratio *scale** rather than on an ➤ **interval *scale**. The classic example here is temperature, where the establishment of an absolute zero at which all molecular action stops yielded the Kelvin scale by contrast with the Fahrenheit and Celsius scales on which the 'zero points' are arbitrary.

zero-order Referring to ordinary correlation coefficients, i.e. coefficients calculated from the original data where none of the variables have been held constant as is the case with ➤ **partial *correlations**.

zero population growth (ZPG) The demographic condition in which the number of deaths in a population approximates the number of viable births, so that the total population remains stable over a period of time.

zero sum-game ➤ **game, zero-sum**.

zeta (ζ) A measure of the degree to which a given regression is linear.

Zipf curve ➤ **Zipf's law**.

Zipf's law A generalization owed to George Kingsley Zipf (1903–50), a brilliant, dedicated scientist with a penchant for counting things. His law, in simplest terms, states that there exists an equilibrium between uniformity and diversity. This notion is best expressed in the so-called *Zipf curve*, which displays the relation between the frequency with which a particular event occurs (e.g., a word in a language) and the number of events which occur with that frequency. When exploring the statistical nature of natural languages, Zipf curves occur with remarkable uniformity of shape; that is, in any language and in any circumscribed corpus of that language (e.g., novels, newspapers, comic books, etc.) there are a very large number of very short words which occur with high frequency and progressively fewer longer words which occur with progressively lower frequency. Zipf hypothesized (wrongly, it turns out) that these uniformities were the result of a biological 'least effort' principle; they are now known to be merely the necessary result of particular stochastic processes. However, the basic principle codified in Zipf's name – the balance between uniformity and diversity – lives on.

Zöllner illusion The vertical lines in the diagram, above right, are all parallel.

zone of proximal development An unfortunately cumbersome term introduced by Vygotsky to refer to the conceptual space or zone between what a child is capable of doing on his or her own and what the child can acheive with assistance from an adult or more capable peer. As the term is used, it carries some of the notions of ➤ **readiness** (2), in that when the child is prepared to begin to undertake a task he or she can, through a process of ➤

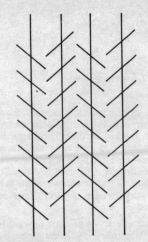

scaffolding, be moved to a qualitatively different and functionally more sophisticated level of performance.

zo(o)- Combining form meaning *animal*.

zooerasty Sexual intercourse with an animal; ➤ **paraphilia**.

zoomorphism ➤ **theriomorphism**.

zoophilla A ➤ **paraphilia** in which one's preferred means of sexual arousal and gratification is with animals.

zoosemiotics ➤ **semiotics**.

z-score A statistical score which has been standardized by being expressed in terms of its relative position in the full distribution of scores. A z-score is always expressed relative to the mean of the distribution and in standard deviation units, i.e. $z = (X - M)/SD$, where X = the individual score, M = the mean of the set of scores and SD = the standard deviation of the set of scores. Also known as the *standard score*, and in some older writings the *sigma score*.

Z-transformation A formula for transforming sample values of r (correlation coefficient) to make them correspond more closely to the normal distribution. Also called *Fisher's Z-transformation*.

Zürich school A term used to refer collectively to the followers of C. G. Jung; ➤ **Jungian** for details.

Zwaardemaker olfactometer A device for regulating the amount of gaseous materials delivered to the nose.

Zwaardemaker smell system A system for classifying smells. It is based on nine fundamental odors: ethereal (fruits), aromatic (spices), fragrant (flowers), ambrosiac (musk), alliaceous (garlic), empyreumatic (coffee), hircine (rancid), foul (bedbugs) and nauseous (feces). Compare with ➤ **Henning's prism**.

zygote The fertilized cell produced by the union of two gametes; in higher animals the two gametes are a sperm and an ovum.

Appendix A: Simple Phobias

Note. The term *phobia* comes originally from the Greek and to be etymologically correct the term for a specific phobia should use a Greek root; e.g., fear of being alone is properly *eremophobia* and not *autophobia* or *monophobia*, both of which use Latin roots. However, this nicety is not always followed and the following lists of ➤ **simple phobias** contain many that use Latin, English and French roots. The first part of this appendix gives definitions of phobias; the second part provides the technical term for a particular fear.

One big problem faced by a lexicographer compiling such a list is what phobias to include. From an etymological perspective, the number of phobias is limited only by the number of nouns in the language, and with a little creativity all manner of phobias can be generated. However, from a clinical point of view the number of objects which are the focus of documented phobias is not all that large; the vast majority of phobic disorders involve relatively few phobic objects and/or situations (➤ **phobia**, et seq.). In what follows I tried to include all those to which I could find some reference in the literature. Readers should feel free to generate their own at the slightest impulse; all you need is a Greek or Latin root and the suffix *-phobia*; e.g., *apiphobia* = bees, *aviophobia* = flying; *phasmophobia* = ghosts, etc., etc. . . .

Part I

acarophobia: 1. mites. **2.** by extension, small insects or animals.

acrophobia: heights.

agoraphobia: being alone in a public place (see entry in main body of dictionary).

aichmophobia: pointed instruments.

ailurophobia: cats.

algophobia: pain; that is, beyond the normal fear of pain.

amathophobia: dust.

amaxophobia: vehicles, riding in a vehicle.

androphobia: 1. man (i.e., the species, *Homo sapiens*). **2.** the male sex. Distinguish from ➤ **homophobia**.

anemophobia: 1. wind, drafts. **2.** by extension, air.

anginophobia: 1. generally, suffocation or being suffocated. **2.** specifically, an attack of ➤ **angina** (3).

anthrophobia: 1. man (singly). **2.** society (generally).

aphephobia: being touched by another person.

aquaphobia: 1. water. **2.** by extension, swimming.

arachn(e)ophobia: spiders.

astraphobia: 1. lightning. **2.** thunderstorms.

autophobia: oneself; being alone.

bacillophobia: bacilli (germs).

ballistophobia: 1. missiles. **2.** thrown objects. .

basiphobia: 1. generally, walking. **2.** in extreme cases, standing erect and walking.

bathophobia: 1. depth. **2.** occasionally, looking down from a high place.

belonephobia: sharp, pointed objects.

bibliophobia: books; also used for an irrational *hatred* of books.

brontophobia: thunder; not used for the mild form commonly found in children.

cainotophobia: 1. novelty. 2. new things. 3. new ideas. Also called *cenotophobia*.

cardiophobia: heart problems.

catotrophobia: 1. generally, mirrors. 2. specifically, breaking of a mirror.

cenotophobia: 1. novelty. 2. new things. 3. new ideas. Also called *cainotophobia*.

cherophobia: fun, gaiety.

claustrophobia: closed spaces.

computerphobia: computers or using them. Also called *cyberphobia*.

coprophobia: feces; by extension dirt, filth, contamination.

cyberphobia: computers or using them. Also called *computerphobia*.

cynophobia: dogs.

cypridophobia: 1. venereal disease. 2. sexual activity in general.

demophobia: crowds.

dysmorphophobia: imagined defects in appearance. However, ➤ **body dysmorphic disorder**.

enissophobia: criticism.

epistemophobia: knowledge.

eremophobia: solitude, being alone.

ereuthrophobia: blushing.

ergasiophobia: 1. work. 2. by extension, responsibility. Also spelled *ergophobia*.

ergophobia: 1. work. 2. by extension, responsibility. Also spelled *ergasiophobia*.

erotophobia: sex.

erythrophobia: 1. red objects. 2. by extension, blushing.

febriphobia: 1. fever. 2. a generalized fear of body dysfunction produced by a rise in body temperature.

gamophobia: marriage.

gatophobia: cats.

geumaphobia: tastes.

haphephobia: being touched by another person.

heliophobia: 1. the sun. 2. sunlight.

hematophobia: 1. the sight of blood (preferred). 2. blood. Also spelled *hemophobia*.

hemophobia: 1. the sight of blood (preferred). 2. blood. Also spelled *hematophobia*.

hierophobia: 1. religion. 2. sacred objects associated with religion. 3. religious rites.

homophobia: 1. when from the Latin root, man (i.e., the species *Homo sapiens*); a synonym of *androphobia*. 2. when from the Greek root, homosexuality.

hyalophobia: glass.

hydrophobia: 1. water. 2. rabies, the disease itself, not any fear of it. ➤ **hydrophobiaphobia**.

hydrophobiaphobia: contracting the disease rabies. ➤ **hydrophobia**.

hypertrichophobia: growth of bodily hair, particularly, excessive amounts.

hypnophobia: falling asleep.

iophobia: 1. being poisoned. 2. rusty objects.

kainophobia: new things, new experiences, new situations.

kenophobia: empty spaces.

keraunophobia: 1. lightning. 2. by extension, thunder.

kopophobia: becoming fatigued or exhausted.

lalophobia: 1. generally, speaking. 2. specifically, stammering or committing errors while speaking.

levophobia: things being on the left side of one's body.

macrophobia: large objects.

microphobia: small objects.

monophobia: being left alone.

mysophobia: 1. dirt. 2. contamination.

necrophobia: 1. generally, death. 2. more specifically, dead things. 3. most specifically, human corpses.

neophobia: 1. the new, the novel. 2. specifically, new foods. ➤ **dietary neophobia**.

nosophobia: 1. illness. 2. acquiring some specific illness.

nyctophobia: 1. night. 2. the dark, darkness. Not used for the common condition in children.

ochlophobia: crowds, crowded places.

odontophobia: 1. teeth. **2.** having one's teeth worked on by a dentist.

ombrophobia: rainstorms.

onomatophobia: a particular word or name.

ophidiophobia: snakes.

pan(t)ophobia: everything! (A most unpleasant disorder.)

parturiphobia: childbirth.

peccatophobia: committing a sin.

phobophobia: 1. fear. **2.** acquiring a phobia.

phonophobia: 1. generally, sound. **2.** specifically, the sound of one's own voice.

ponophobia: 1. pain. **2.** work, being overworked.

pyrophobia: fire.

rhypophobia: 1. defecation – the process. **2.** defecation – the product.

scopophobia: being seen by others.

scotophobia: the dark, darkness. Not used for the common condition in children.

stasibasiphobia: standing erect and walking.

stasiphobia: standing.

symbolophobia: 1. symbols. **2.** symbolic representations. It has been suggested, rather unkindly, that the disorder is caused mainly by long-term psychoanalysis.

taphophobia: 1. graves. **2.** being buried alive. var. *taphephobia*.

thalassophobia: the sea.

thanatophobia: 1. death. **2.** dead things, especially human corpses.

theophobia: 1. God. **2.** retribution from God for one's sins (real or imagined).

toxophobia: 1. poisons. **2.** being poisoned.

tremophobia: trembling.

trichopathophobia: in women, facial hair. ➤ **trichophobia**.

trichophobia: generally, hair.

triskaidekaphobia: The number that results from the operation of subtracting 1 from 14.

xenoglossophobia: 1. foreign languages. **2.** learning a foreign language.

xenophobia: 1. generally, foreigners or strangers. **2.** specifically, strange or foreign cultures or places.

zoophobia: animals.

Part II

air: anemophobia.

alone (being alone): autophobia, eremophobia, or monophobia.

alone in a public place: agoraphobia.

angina (or an angina attack): anginophobia.

animals: zoophobia.

books: bibliophobia.

blood (or sight of): hematophobia or hemophobia.

blushing: ereuthrophobia or erythrophobia (➤ **red**).

bugs: acarophobia.

buried alive: taphophobia.

cats: ailurophobia or gatophobia.

childbirth: parturiphobia.

closed spaces: claustrophobia.

computers: computerphobia or cyberphobia.

contamination: coprophobia or mysophobia.

corpses (especially human): necrophobia or thanatophobia.

criticism: enissophobia.

crowds: demophobia or ochlophobia.

darkness: nyctophobia or scotophobia.

death (generally), **dead things:** necrophobia or thanatophobia.

defecation (and its products): rhypophobia.

depth: bathophobia.

dirt: coprophobia or mysophobia.

dogs: cynophobia.

drafts: anemophobia.

dust: amathophobia.

erotica (sexuality): erotophobia.

empty spaces: kenophobia.

everything: panophobia or pantophobia.

exhaustion (becoming exhausted): kopophobia.

fatigue (becoming fatigued): kopophobia.

fear: phobophobia.

feces: coprophobia.

fever: febriphobia.

filth: coprophobia or mysophobia.

fire: pyrophobia.

foreigners: xenophobia.

foreign languages (or learning one): xenoglossophobia.

fun: cherophobia.

germs: bacillophobia.

glass: hyalophobia.

God: theophobia.

graves: taphophobia.

hair (generally): trichophobia.

hair (excess amounts of bodily): hypertrichophobia.

hair (facial – in women): trichopathophobia.

heart problems: cardiophobia (➤ angina).

heights: acrophobia.

homosexuality or homosexual persons: homophobia.

illness (or acquiring a specific illness): nosophobia.

knowledge: epistemophobia.

large objects: macrophobia.

left side (things being on the): levophobia.

lightning: astraphobia or keraunophobia.

males, the male sex: androphobia.

man (the species): androphobia, anthrophobia, or homophobia.

marriage: gamophobia.

mirrors, breaking a mirror: catotrophobia.

missiles: ballistophobia.

mites: acarophobia.

name (a particular): onomatophobia.

night: nyctophobia.

novelty, new things: cainotophobia, cenotophobia, kainophobia, or neophobia.

novel foods: neophobia (➤ dietary neophobia).

oneself: autophobia.

pain: algophobia or ponophobia.

phobia (acquiring one): phobophobia.

pointed instruments: aichmophobia or belonephobia.

poison (being poisoned): iophobia or toxophobia.

public places: agoraphobia.

rabies (catching the disease): hydrophobiaphobia.

rain, rainstorms: ombrophobia.

red (objects): erythrophobia.

religion: hierophobia.

responsibility: ergasiophobia.

retribution from God: theophobia.

riding in a vehicle: amaxophobia.

rusty objects: iophobia.

sacred (religious) objects: hierophobia.

sea: thalassophobia.

seen (by others): scopophobia.

sex: erotophobia.

sexual activity in general: cypridophobia.

sharp pointed instruments: belonephobia.

sin (committing one): peccatophobia.

sleep (falling asleep): hypnophobia.

small objects: microphobia.

snakes: ophidiophobia.

spaces (empty): kenophobia.

speaking (committing errors while): lalophobia.

society (generally): anthrophobia.

solitude: autophobia or eremophobia.

sound: phonophobia.

sound of one's own voice: phonophobia.

spiders: arachn(e)ophobia.

standing: stasiphobia.

standing erect and walking: stasibasiphobia.

strangers (strange cultures or places): xenophobia.

sun, sunlight: heliophobia.

swimming: aquaphobia.

symbols: symbolophobia.

tastes: geumaphobia.

teeth (having one's teeth worked on): odontophobia.

thirteen (the number): triskaidekaphobia.

thrown objects: ballistophobia.

thunder, thunderstorms: astraphobia, brontophobia, or keraunophobia.

touched by another person: aphephobia or haphephobia.

trembling: tremophobia.

vehicles: amaxophobia.

venereal disease: cypridophobia.

voice (one's own): phonophobia.

walking: basiphobia.

water: aquaphobia or hydrophobia.

wind: anemophobia.

word (a particular): onomatophobia.

work (being overworked): ponophobia.

work (responsibility): ergasiophobia.

working: ergophobia.

Appendix B: Authorities Cited

Note. An asterisk (*) before a name indicates that there is a separate entry on that person under an adjectival-form entry; e.g., Adler = Adlerian, Watson = Watsonian.

Abney, William de Wiveleslie (1843–1920), English chemist and physiologist.

*Adler, Alfred (1870–1937), Austrian psychiatrist.

Ainsworth, Mary (b. 1913), Canadian-born American developmental psychoologist.

Allport, Floyd (1890–?), American psychologist.

Allport, Gordon Willard (1897–1967), American psychologist.

Alzheimer, Alois (1864–1915), German physician and neurologist.

Ames, Adelbert Jr (1880–1955), American artist and educator.

Anderson, John Robert (b. 1947), Canadian-born American cognitive psychologist.

Anderson, Rose Gustava (1893–?), American psychologist.

Angell, James Rowland (1869–1949), American psychologist and educator.

Apgar, Virginia (1909–74), American physician, anesthesiologist.

Argyll-Robertson, Douglas M. C. L. (1837–1909), Scottish physician, ophthalmologist.

Arieti, Silvano (1914–82), Italian-born American psychiatrist.

*Aristotle (384–322 BC), Greek philosopher and educator.

Asch, Solomon E. (b. 1907), American psychologist.

Atkinson, John William (b. 1923), American social psychologist.

Aubert, Hermann (1826–92), German physician and psychologist.

Augustine, St (354–430), African-born philosopher and theologian.

Austin, John Langshaw (1911–60), English philosopher.

Babinski, Joseph F. F. (1857–1932), French neurologist.

Bandura, Albert (b. 1925), Canadian-born American psychologist.

Bárány, Robert (1876–1936), Austrian physician.

Bard, Philip (1898–1977), American psychologist.

Barnum, Phineas T. (1810–91), American showman, entrepreneur, charlatan.

Barr, Murray Llewellyn (b. 1908), Canadian anatomist.

Barron, Francis X. (b. 1922), American psychologist.

Bateson, Gregory (b. 1904), British/American philosopher and anthropologist.

Bayes, Thomas (1702–61), English mathematician and clergyman.

Bayley, Nancy (b. 1899), American developmental psychologist.

Beck, Aaron Temkin (b. 1921), American psychiatrist.

Becker, Ernst (1925–74), American anthropologist.

Bekhterev, Vladimir M. (1857–1927), Russian physiologist and neurologist.

Bell, Charles (1774–1842), Scottish anatomist.

Bem, Sandra (b. 1944), American psychologist.

Bender, Lauretta (b. 1897), American neurologist and psychiatrist.

Benham, C. E. (*fl.* 1890s), English scientist.

Bennett, George Kettner (b. 1904), American psychologist.

Berkeley, George, Bishop (1685–1753), Irish philosopher and theologian.

Berne, Eric (1910–70), Canadian-born American psychologist.

Bernheim, Hippolyte Marie (1837–1919), French physician and hypnotist.

Bernoulli, Daniel (1700–1782), Swiss mathematician and physician.

Bernreuter, Robert Gibbon (b. 1901), American psychologist.

Bernstein, Basil (b. 1924), British sociologist, linguist.

Bessel, Friedrich W. (1784–1846), German astronomer.

Betz, Vladimir A. (1834–94), Russian anatomist.

Bezold, Johann Friedrich W. (1837–1907), German physicist.

Bidwell, Shelford (1848–1909), English physicist.

Biederman, Irving (b. 1939), American perceptual and cognitive psychologist.

Bierce, Ambrose (1842–1913[?]), American satirist.

Binet, Alfred (1857–1911), French psychologist.

Binswanger, Ludwig (1881–1966), Swiss psychiatrist, existentialist.

Bleuler, Eugen (1857–1939), Swiss psychiatrist.

Boole, George (1815–64), English mathematician.

Boring, Edwin Garrigues (1886–1968), American psychologist and historian.

Braid, James (1795–1860), British writer, coiner of the term hypnotism.

Braille, Louis (1809–52), French educator.

Bray, Charles William (b. 1904), American physician.

Brazelton, Thomas Berry (b. 1918), American physician, pediatrician.

Brentano, Franz (1838–1917), German philosopher, psychologist and theologian.

Breuer, Joseph (1842–1925), Austrian physician.

Bridgeman, Percy (1882–1961), American physicist and philosopher of science.

Briquet, Pierre (1796–1881), French physician.

Broca, Paul (1824–80), French physiologist and surgeon.

Brodmann, Korbinian (1868–1918), German neurologist.

Brown, Roger (b. 1925), American psychologist.

Bruce, Hilda, English comparative psychologist.

Brücke, Ernst Wilhelm (1819–92), German physiologist.

Bruner, Jerome Seymour (b. 1915), American developmental psychologist.

Brunswik, Egon (b. 1903), American psychologist.

Bucy, Paul Clancy (b. 1904), American neurologist.

Bunsen, Robert Wilhelm (1811–1899), German chemist.

Cannon, Walter B. (1871–1945), American physiologist.

Capgras, Jean Marie Joseph (1873–1950), French psychiatrist.

Carnap, Rudolph (1891–1970), German-born, Austrian/American philosopher.

Carr, Harvey A. (1873–1954), American psychologist.

Carroll, Lewis (Charles Lutwidge Dodgson, 1832–98), English mathematician, cleric and fantasist.

Cattell, James McKeen (1860–1944), American psychologist and publisher.

Cattell, Raymond B. (b. 1905), British-born American psychologist.

Charcot, Jean Martin (1825–93), French physician, neurologist.

Charpentier, Pierre Marie Augustin (1852–1916), French physician.

Cherry, Colin (b. 1914), English communications scientist and psychologist.

Chomsky, Avram Noam (b. 1928), American linguist, philosopher and psychologist.

Christie, Richard (1918–92), American social psychologist.

Clérambault, G. G. de (1872–1934), French psychiatrist.

Comte, Auguste (1798–1857), French philosopher and sociologist.

Condillac, Étienne Bonnet de (1715–80), French philosopher.

Cooley, Charles Horton (1864–1929), American sociologist.

Coombs, Clyde (1912–88), American psychologist.

Corti, Alfonso Giacomo Gaspare (1822–76), Italian anatomist.

Coué, Émile (1857–1926), French pharmacist, therapist and phrasemaker.

Crespi, L. P. (*fl.* 1940s), American psychologist.

Cronbach, Lee J. (b. 1916), American psychometrician.

Dalton, John (1766–1844), English chemist.

*Darwin, Charles (1809–82), English naturalist.

Deiters, Otto Friedrich Karl (1834–63), German anatomist.

*Descartes, René (1596–1650), French philosopher and mathematician.

Dewey, John (1859–1952), American philosopher and educator.

Donders, Franciscus Cornelius (1818–89), Dutch physician.

Doppler, Johann Christian (1803–53), Austrian physicist.

Down, John Langdon Haydon (1828–96), English physician.

Drever, James (1873–1951), British psychologist and lexicographer.

Duncan, David Beattie (b. 1916), Australian-born American statistician.

Durkheim, Émile (1858–1917), French sociologist.

Ebbinghaus, Hermann von (1850–1909), German psychologist.

Edwards, Allen L. (b. 1914), American psychologist and statistician.

Ehrenfels, Christian von (1859–1932), Austrian philosopher and psychologist.

Ekman, Paul (b. 1934), American social and cognitive psychologist.

Ellis, Albert (b. 1913), American psychologist.

Emmert, Emil (1844–1911), Swiss ophthalmologist.

Engels, Friedrich (1820–95), German philosopher.

Erhard, Werner (b. 1935), American salesman.

Erikson, Erik Homburger (1902–94), German-born American psychoanalyst.

Estes, William Kaye (b. 1919), American psychologist.

Euclid (*fl. c.* 300 BC), Greek mathematician.

Ewald, Georg Heinrich August (1803–73), German semanticist.

Ewald, Julius Richard (1855–1921), German physiologist.

Eysenck, Hans Jürgen (b. 1916), German-born English psychologist.

Fant, Louis Judson (b. 1931), American educator.

Fechner, Gustav Theodor (1803–87), German physician, physicist, philosopher, psychologist, psychometrician and essayist.

Feigl, Herbert (b. 1902), Austrian-born American philosopher of science.

Féré, Charles (d. 1907), French neurologist.

Ferry, Edwin Sidney (1868–1956), American physicist.

Fisher, Ronald Aylmer (1890–1962), English geneticist and statistician.

Fitts, Paul Morris (1912–65), American psychologist.

Flesch, Rudolph F. (b. 1911), American philologist and psychologist.

Fodor, Jerry (b. 1935), American philosopher.

Fourier, Jean Baptiste Joseph (1768–1830), French mathematician.

Frank, Jerome David (b. 1909), American psychiatrist.

Frankl, Viktor (b. 1905), German-born American psychiatrist.

Freud, Anna (1895–1982), Austrian-born British psychoanalyst.

*Freud, Sigmund (1856–1939), Austrian neurologist and psychoanalyst.

Frisch, Karl von (1886–?), Austrian zoologist, ethologist.

Fromm, Erich (1900–1980), German-born American psychoanalyst.

Fromm-Reichmann, Frieda (1889–1957), American psychoanalyst.

Frostig, Marianne B. (b. 1906), Austrian-born American psychologist.

Fullerton, George Stuart (1859–1925), American psychologist.

Galen (129-c. 199), Greek physician and philosopher.

Galileo Galilei (1564–1642), Italian astronomer and physicist.

Gall, Franz Joseph (1758–1828), German physician and phrenologist.

Galton, Francis (1822–1911), English natural scientist and psychologist.

Ganser, Sigbert (1853–1931), German psychiatrist.

Garcia, John (b. 1917), American psychologist.

Gauss, Carl Friedrich (1777–1855), German mathematician.

Gesell, Arnold Lucius (1880–1961), American psychologist.

Gibson, James Jerome (1904–80), American psychologist.

Goddard, Henry Herbert (1866–1957), American psychologist.

Gödel, Kurt (1906–78), Czech-born American mathematician and logician.

Goffman, Erving (1922–82), Canadian-born American sociologist.

Goldenhar, M. (b. 1912), American physician.

Goldstein, Kurt (1878–1965), German-born American psychologist.

Golgi, Camillo (1843–1926), Italian physiologist, histologist.

Goodenough, Florence Laura (1886–?), American psychologist.

Gossett, William Sealy (Student) (1867–1947), British statistician.

Gottschaldt, K. (b. 1902), German psychologist.

Gould, Stephen Jay (b. 1941), American zoologist, paleontologist and essayist.

Grassmann, H. (fl. 1850s), German scientist.

Greenspoon, Joel (b. 1921), American psychologist.

Gregory, Richard Langton (b. 1923), English psychologist.

Grice, H. Paul (b. 1913), American philosopher.

Guilford, Joy Paul (b. 1897), American psychologist.

Guthrie, Edwin Ray (1886–1959), American psychologist.

Guttman, Louis (b. 1916), American psychologist.

Haab, Otto (1850–1931), Swiss physician, ophthalmologist.

Hall, Granville Stanley (1844–1924), American psychologist.

Harlow, Harry (1905–81), American psychologist.

Hartley, David (1705–57), English physician and philosopher.

Harvey, O. J. (b. 1927), American psychologist.

Head, Henry (1861–1940), English neurologist.

Hebb, Donald Olding (1904–85), Canadian psychologist.

Hegel, Georg Wilhelm Friedrich (1770–1831), German philosopher.

Heider, Fritz (1896–1988), Austrian-born American psychologist.

Helmholtz, Hermann Ludwig Ferdinand (1821–94), German physiologist, psychologist.

Helson, Harry (b. 1898), American psychologist.

Henning, Hans (*fl.* 1910s–1920s), German psychologist.

Heraclitus (*c.* 540–*c.* 480 BC), Greek philosopher.

Herbart, Johann Friedrich (1776–1841), German philosopher and educator.

Hering, Heinrich Ewald (1866–1948), German physiologist.

Hering, Karl Ewald Constantin (1834–1918), German physiologist.

Hertz, Heinrich Rudolph (1857–94), German physicist.

Hess, Eckardt H. (b. 1916), American psychologist.

Hick, W. E. (*fl.* 1950s), American psychologist.

Hilgard, Ernest R. (b. 1904), American experimental psychologist.

Hippocrates (*c.* 460–*c.* 377 BC), Greek physician.

Hiskey, Marshall S. (b. 1908), American psychologist.

Hobbes, Thomas (1588–1679), English philosopher.

Höffding, Harald (1843–1931), German philosopher, psychologist.

Holmgren, Alarik Frithiof (1831–97), Swedish physiologist.

Horner, Matina Souretis (b. 1939), American psychologist.

Horney, Karen (1885–1952), German-born American psychiatrist.

Hovland, Carl (1912–61), American psychologist.

*Hull, Clark Leonard (1884–1952), American psychologist.

Hume, David (1711–76), Scottish philosopher and historian.

Hunt, Howard Francis (b. 1918), American psychologist.

Hunter, Walter S. (1889–1953), American psychologist.

Huntington, George (1850–1916), American neurologist.

Husserl, Edmund (1859–1938), German philosopher.

Hyman, Ray (b. 1928), American psychologist.

Ishihara, Shinobu (1879–1963), Japanese ophthalmologist.

Itard, Jean Marc Gaspard (1774–1838), French physician and educator.

Jackson, John Hughlings (1835–1911), English neurologist.

Jacobson, Edmund (1888–?), American physician.

*James, William (1842–1910), American psychologist and philosopher.

Janet, Pierre Marie Félix (1859–1947), French physician, psychiatrist.

Johnson, Marcia K. (b. 1943), American cognitive psychologist.

Jones, Alfred Ernest (1879–1958), British psychoanalyst, biographer.

Jost, Adolf (1874–?), German psychologist.

*Jung, Carl Gustav (1875–1961), Swiss psychiatrist, psychoanalyst.

Kahn, Eugen (1887–?), German psychologist.

Kahneman, Daniel (b. 1934), Israeli-American cognitive psychologist.

Kanner, Leo (1894–?), Austrian-born American psychiatrist.

Kant, Emanuel (1724–1804), German philosopher.

Kantor, Jacob Robert (1888–?), American psychologist.

Katz, David (1884–1953), German-born Swedish psychologist.

Katz, Jerrold J. (b. 1932), American philosopher and linguist.

Keller, Frederick (b. 1899), American psychologist and educator.

Kelly, George (1905–66), American psychologist.

Kendall, Maurice George (b. 1907), English statistician.

Kent, Grace Helen (1875–?), American psychologist.

Kimble, Gregory Adams (b. 1917), American psychologist.

Klein, Melanie (1882–1960), Austrian psychoanalyst.

Kleine, Willi (*fl.* 1920s), German psychiatrist.

Kleinfelter, Harry Fitch (b. 1912), American physician, geneticist.

Klüver, Heinrich (1898–1979), German-born American neurologist.

Koffka, Kurt (1886–1941), German-born American psychologist.

Kohlberg, Lawrence (1927–87), American psychologist.

Köhler, Wolfgang (1887–1967), German-born American psychologist.

Kohs, Samuel Calmin (1890–?), American psychologist.

Kolomogorov, Andrei Nikolaevich (b. 1903), Russian mathematician.

König, Karl Rudolph (1832–1901), German-born French physicist.

Korsakoff, Sergei Sergeievich (1854–1900), Russian neurologist.

Korte, A. (*fl.* 1910s), German psychologist.

Krause, Wilhelm (1833–1910), German anatomist.

Kretschmer, Ernst (1888–1964), German psychiatrist.

Kruskal, William Henry (b. 1919), American mathematician, statistician.

Kuder, George Frederic (b. 1903), American psychologist.

Kuhlman, Frederick (1876–1941), American psychologist.

Kuhn, Thomas S. (b. 1922), American physicist, philosopher of science.

Külpe, Oswald (1862–1915), German psychologist.

Ladd-Franklin, Christine (1847–1930), American psychologist.

Laing, Ronald David (b. 1927), Scottish-born psychiatrist.

Lamarck, Jean-Baptist Pierre Antoine (1744–1829), French naturalist, evolutionist.

Lamaze, Fernand (1890–1957), French obstetrician.

Lambert, Johann Heinrich (1728–77), German mathematician, astronomer.

Land, Edwin Herbert (b. 1909), American sensory psychologist and inventor.

Landolt, Edmund (1846–1926), French ophthalmologist.

Lange, Carl Georg (1834–1900), Danish physiologist.

Lange, Cornelia de (1871–1950), Dutch physician.

Langer, Ellen (b. 1947), American social psychologist.

Lashley, Karl Spencer (1890–1958), American psychologist.

Leboyer, Frédéric (b. 1918), French obstetrician.

Leibniz, Gottfried Wilhelm von (1646–1716), German philosopher, mathematician.

Leiter, Russell Graydon (b. 1901), American psychologist.

Lesch, M. (b. 1939), American physician.

Levin, Max (b. 1901), Russian-born American neurologist.

Lévi-Strauss, Claude (b. 1908), French anthropologist.

Lewin, Kurt (1890–1947), German-born American psychologist.

Liberman, Alvin M. (b. 1917), American psychologist and linguist.

Lifton, Robert Jay (b. 1926), American psychiatrist.

Likert, Rensis (1903–81), American social scientist.

Lippitt, Ronald (b. 1920), American psychologist.

Lissajou, Jules Antoine (1822–80), French physicist.

Lloyd Morgan, Conway, *see* Morgan, Conway Lloyd.

Locke, John (1632–1704), British philosopher

Lombroso, Cesare (1836–1909), Italian criminologist.

Lorenz, Konrad Zacharis (b. 1902), Austrian ethologist.

Lorge, Irving Daniel (1905–61), American psychologist.

Lotze, Rudolph Hermann (1817–81), German physiologist and psychologist.

Luria, Alexander Romanovich (1902–77), Russian psychologist.

Luria, Salvatore Edward (b. 1912), Italian-born American biologist.

Mach, Ernst (1838–1916), Austrian physicist and philosopher.

Machiavelli, Niccolò (1469–1527), Florentine statesman and political theorist.

Machover, Karen Alper (b. 1902), American psychologist.

MacLean, Paul Donald (b. 1913), American physician.

Magendie, François (1783–1855), French physiologist.

Maharishi Mahesh Yogi (b. *c.* 1920), Indian mystic.

Maier, Norman R. F. (b. 1900), American psychologist.

Malthus, Thomas Robert (1766–1834), English economist and demographer.

Mandler, George (b. 1924), Austrian-born American cognitive psychologist.

Mann, Henry Berthold (b. 1905), Austrian-born American mathematician.

Marfan, Antoine Bernard Jean (1858–1942), French physician.

Markov, Andrei Andreievich (1856–1922), Russian mathematician.

Marx, Karl (1818–83), German social philosopher.

Maslow, Abraham Harold (1908–70), American psychologist.

Masoch, *see* Sacher-Masoch

Maxwell, James Clerk (1831–79), Scottish physicist.

May, Rollo (b. 1909), American psychoanalyst, existentialist.

McCarthy, Dorothea (1906–74), American developmental psychologist.

McClelland, David (b. 1917), American psychologist.

McConnell, James Vernon (b. 1925), American psychologist.

McCullough, C. (*fl.* 1960s), American psychologist.

McDougall, William (1871–1938), British-born American psychologist.

McNeill, David (b. 1933), American cognitive psychologist.

McNemar, Quinn (b. 1900), American psychologist and statistician.

Mead, George Herbert (1863–1931), American social philosopher.

Mead, Margaret (1901–78), American anthropologist.

Meissner, Georg (1829–1905), German physiologist and anatomist.

*Mendel, Gregor Johann (1822–84), Austrian monk and geneticist.

Merkel, Friedrich Siegmund (1845–1919), German anatomist.

Merrill, Maud Amanda (1888–?), American psychologist.

Merton, Robert King (b. 1910), American sociologist.

Mesmer, Franz Anton (1733–1815), German physician and hypnotist.

Meyer, Adolf (1866–1950), Swiss-born American psychiatrist.

Meyer, Max F. (1873–?), American psychologist.

Mill, James Stuart (1773–1836), Scottish philosopher.

Mill, John Stuart (1806–73), English philosopher and economist.

Miller, George Armitage (b. 1920), American cognitive psychologist.

Miller, Wilfred Stanton (1883–?), American psychologist.

Mills, C. Wright (1916–62), American sociologist.

Minsky, Marvin Lee (b. 1927), American computer scientist and philosopher.

Mischel, Walter (b. 1930), American psychologist.

Molyneux, William (1656–98), Irish lawyer, political and philosopher.

Moniz, Antonio Egas (1874–1955), Portuguese neurosurgeon.

More, Thomas (1477–1535), English lawyer, writer, saint.

Moreno, Jacob L. (1890–1974), Austrian-born American psychiatrist.

Morgan, Conway Lloyd (1852–1936), English zoologist and psychologist.

Moro, Ernst (1874–1951), Austrian pediatrician.

Morton, John (b. 1933), English cognitive psychologist.

Mowrer, Orval Hobart (1907–82), American psychologist.

Müller, Georg Elias (1850–1934), German psychologist.

Müller, Johannes Peter (1801–58), German physiologist.

Müller-Lyer, Franz Karl (1857–1916), German psychiatrist and psychologist.

Munsell, Albert Henry (1858–1918), American artist.

Murphy, Gardner (1895–1979), American psychologist.

Murray, Henry Alexander (b. 1893), American psychologist.

Necker, Louis (1730–1804), Swiss mathematician and physicist.

Neill, Alexander Sutherland (1883–1973), British educator.

Neisser, Ulric Richard Gustav (b. 1928), American cognitive psychologist.

Newell, Allen (1927–92), American cognitive psychologist and computer scientist.

Newport, Elissa (b. 1947), American developmental psychologist.

Newton, Isaac (1642–1727), English physicist, mathematician, philosopher.

Nissl, Franz (1860–1919), German neurologist.

Nyhan, W. L. (b. 1926), American physician.

Occam, William of (c. 1280–1349), English philosopher.

Oden, Gregg (b. 1948), American cognitive psychologist.

Ohm, Georg Simon (1787–1854), German physicist.

Olds, James (1922–79), American physiological psychologist.

Oden, Gregg (b. 1948), American cognitive psychologist.

Ohm, Georg Simon (1787–1854), German physicist.

Olds, James (1922–79), American physiological psychologist.

Orbison, W. D. (fl. 1940s), American psychologist.

Ornstein, Robert E. (b. 1942), American psychologist.

Osgood, Charles Egerton (b. 1916), American psychologist.

Osten, Wilhelm von (fl. 1900s), German animal trainer.

Ostwald, Wilhelm (1853–1932), German physicist, chemist.

Pacini, Filippo (1812–83), Italian anatomist.

Paivio, Allan U. (b. 1925), Canadian cognitive psychologist.

Panum, Peter Ludwig (1820–85), Danish physiologist.

Papez, James Wenceslas (1883–1958), American anatomist, physiologist.

Parkinson, James (1755–1824), English physician.

*Pavlov, Ivan Petrovich (1849–1936), Russian physiologist.

APPENDIX B: AUTHORITIES CITED

Peale, Norman Vincent (b. 1898), American preacher.

Pearson, Karl (1857–1936), English statistician.

Peirce, Charles Sanders (1839–1914), American philosopher.

Pepper, Steven (1891–?), American philosopher.

Perky, C. W. (*fl.* 1910s), American psychologist.

Perls, Frederick (Fritz) S. (1893–1970), German-born American psychiatrist.

Pfungst, Oskar (*fl.* 1910s–1920s), German psychologist.

*Piaget, Jean (1896–1980), Swiss psychologist.

Pick, Arnold (1851–1924), Prague psychiatrist.

Pinel, Philippe (1745–1826), French physician, psychiatrist.

Piper, Hans Edmund (1877–1915), German physiologist.

Plateau, Joseph Antoine Ferdinand (1801–83), Belgian physicist.

Plato (*c.* 427–*c.* 347 BC), Greek philosopher.

Poetzl, Otto (1877–?), Austrian psychiatrist.

Poggendorff, Johann Christian (1796–1877), German physicist.

Poisson, Siméon Denis (1781–1840), French mathematician.

Polanyi, Michael (1891–1976), Hungarian-British scientist and philosopher.

Popper, Karl Raimund (1902–94), Austrian-born English philosopher.

Porter, Thomas Cunningham (*fl.* 1890s–1900s), English scientist.

Porteus, Stanley David (1883–?), Australian-born American psychologist.

Praeder, Andrea (*fl.* 1960s), Swiss pediatrician.

Premack, David (b. 1925), American psychologist.

Pribram, Karl Harry (b. 1919), Austrian-born American physician, psychologist.

Prince, Morton (1854–1929), American psychiatrist, psychologist.

Pulfrich, Karl P. (1858–1927), German physicist.

Purkinje (Purkyně), Jan Evangelista (1787–1869), Czech physiologist.

Rank, Otto (1884–1939), Austrian psychoanalyst.

Ranvier, Louis Antoine (1835–1922), French physiologist.

Rayleigh, John William Stuart (1842–1919), English mathematician, physiologist.

Reber, Arthur Samuel (b. 1940), American cognitive psychologist and lexicographer.

Reich, Wilhelm (1897–1957), Austrian-born American psychoanalyst.

Reichenbach, Hans (1891–1953), German-born American philosopher.

Reid, Thomas (1710–96), Scottish philosopher.

Reik, Theodor (1888–1970), Austrian-born American psychoanalyst.

Reil, Johann Christian (1759–1813), German physician.

Reissner, Ernst (1824–78), German anatomist.

Rescorla, Robert (b. 1940), American experimental psychologist.

Restorff, *see* von Restorff.

Rett, Andreas (*fl.* 1960's), Austrian neurologist.

Reynolds, George Stanley (b. 1936), American psychologist.

Rhine, Joseph Banks (1895–1980), American parapsychologist.

Ribot, Théodule A. (1839–1916), French psychologist.

Ricco, Annibele (1844–1919), Italian astronomer.

Richardson, Marion Webster (1891–?), American psychologist.

Riesman, David (b. 1909), American sociologist.

Robin, Pierre (1867–1950), French dental surgeon.

Robinson, Edward Stevens (*fl.* 1910s–1930s), American psychologist.

Rogers, Carl (b. 1902), American psychologist.

Rolando, Luigi (1773–1831), Italian anatomist.

Romberg, Moritz Heinrich von (1795–1873), German neurologist.

Rorschach, Hermann (1884–1922), Swiss psychiatrist.

Rosanoff, Aaron Joshua (1878–1943), American psychologist.

Roscoe, Henry Enfield (1833–1915), English chemist.

Rosenthal, Robert (b. 1933), American psychologist.

Rosenzweig, Saul (b. 1907), American psychologist.

Rotter, Julian Bernard (b. 1916), American psychologist.

Rozin, Paul (b. 1936), American cognitive and physiological psychologist.

Rubin, Edgar J. (1886–1951), Danish philosopher.

Rubin, Zick (b. 1944), American social psychologist.

Ruffini, Angelo (1864–1929), Italian anatomist.

Rumbaugh, Duane (b. 1929), American psychologist.

Russell, Bertrand Arthur William (1872–1970), British philosopher, mathematician.

Rycroft, Charles (b. 1914), British psychoanalyst and lexicographer.

Ryle, Gilbert (1900–1976), British philosopher.

Sacher-Masoch, Leopold von (1836–95), Austrian lawyer and writer.

Sachs, Bernard Parney (1858–1944), American neurologist.

Sade, Donatien Alphonse François de (1740–1814), French essayist, novelist, revolutionary.

Sanson, Louis Joseph (1790–1841), French surgeon.

Sapir, Edward (1884–1939), American linguist.

Schacter, Daniel (b. 1952), American neurocognitive psychologist.

Schachter, Stanley (b. 1922), American psychologist.

Schank, Roger (b. 1946), American linguist, cognitive scientist.

Scheerer, Martin (1900–1961), German-born American psychologist.

Scheffé, Henry (b. 1907), American mathematician.

Schwann, Theodor (1810–82), German anatomist.

Searle, John (b. 1932), American philosopher.

Seashore, Carl Emil (1866–1949), Swedish-born American psychologist.

Sebeok, Thomas Albert (b. 1920), Hungarian-born American linguist.

Sechenov, Ivan Mikhailovich (1829–1905), Russian physiologist.

Seligman, Martin E. P. (b. 1942), American psychologist.

Selye, Hans (1907–82), Austrian-born Canadian endocrinologist and psychologist.

Semon, Richard (1859–1918), German biologist.

Shannon, Claude Elwood (b. 1916), American applied mathematician.

Shaw, George Bernard (1856–1950), Irish playwright and critic.

Sheldon, William H. (1898–1970), American psychologist.

Shepard, Roger Newland (b. 1929), American psychologist.

Sherrington, Charles Scott (1861–1952), English physiologist.

Sidman, Murray (b. 1923), American psychologist.

Simon, Herbert Alexander (b. 1916), American economist, philosopher, psychologist.

Simon, Théodore (1873–1961), French psychologist.

Skaggs, Ernest Burton (*fl.* 1920s–1940s), American psychologist.

*Skinner, Burrhus Frederic (1904–90), American psychologist.

Smirnov, Nikolai Vasilevich (b. 1900), Russian mathematician.

Snellen, Hermann (1834–1908), Dutch ophthalmologist.

Solomon, Richard L. (b. 1918), American behavioral psychologist.

Spearman, Charles Edward (1863–1945), English psychologist and psychometrician.

Spence, Janet Taylor (b. 1923), American psychologist.

Spencer, Herbert (1820–1903), English philosopher.

Spitz; René A. (1887–1974), Austrian-born American psychologist.

Spooner, William A. (1844–1930), English cleric.

Steele, Richard (1672–1729), English essayist and playwright.

Stern, Wilhelm (1871–1938), German psychologist.

Sternberg, Saul (b. 1933), American psychologist.

Stevens, Stanley Smith (1906–73), American psychologist, psychophysicist.

Stilling, Jakob (1842–1915), German ophthalmologist.

Stratton, George Malcolm (1865–1957), American psychologist.

Strong, Edward Kellogg, Jr (1884–1963), American psychologist.

Stroop, J. R. (*fl.* 1930s), American (?) psychologist.

Student, *see* Gossett, William S.

Sullivan, Harry Stack (1892–1949), American psychiatrist.

Sutton, Willie (b. 1901), American bank robber.

Sydenham, Thomas (1624–89), English physician.

Sylvius, Franciscus (1614–72), Dutch anatomist.

Szasz, Thomas Stephen (b. 1920), Hungarian-born American psychiatrist.

Talbot, William Henry Fox (1800–1877), English physicist and photographer.

Tarchanoff, Ivan Romanovich (1846–1908), Russian physiologist.

Tartini, Giuseppe (1692–1770), Italian violinist.

Tay, Warren (1843–1927), American physician.

Terman, Lewis Madison (1877–1956), American psychologist and psychometrician.

Teuber, Hans L. (1916–77), German-American physiological psychologist.

Thorndike, Edward Lee (1874–1949), American psychologist and lexicographer.

Thorpe, William Homan (b. 1902), English ethologist.

Thurstone, Louis Leon (1887–1955), American psychologist and psychometrician.

Tinbergen, Nikolaas (b. 1907), Dutch ethologist.

Titchener, Edward Bradford (1867–1927), English-born American psychologist.

Toffler, Alan (b. 1928), American writer, social commentator.

*Tolman, Edward Chace (1886–1959), American psychologist.

Tourette, Georges Gilles de la (1857–1904), French psychiatrist.

Treacher Collins, Edward (1862–1932), British neurologist.

Trivers, Robert (b. 1943), American evolutionary biologist.

Troland, L. T. (*fl.* 1920s–1930s), American psychologist.

Troxler, D. (*fl.* 1800s), German scientist.

Tukey, John Wilder (b. 1915), American statistician.

Turing, Alan Mathison (1912–54), English

mathematician, philosopher, computer scientist.

Turner, Henry Herbert (1892–1970), American endocrinologist.

Tversky, Amos (b. 1937), Israeli-American cognitive psychologist.

Twitmeyer, Edwin B. (1873–1943), American psychologist.

Urban, Frank M. (*fl.* 1910s–1920s), American (?) psychologist.

Vierordt, Karl (1818–84), German physiologist.

von Restorff, Hedwig (*fl.* 1930s), German psychologist.

Vygotsky, Lev Semionovich (1896–1934), Russian developmental psychologist.

Wagner, Allan (b. 1934), American experimental psychologist.

Wallach, Hans (b. 1904), German-born American psychologist.

Waller, August Volney (1816–70), English physiologist.

Wallis, Wilson Allen (b. 1912), American economist and statistician.

Walters, Richard (1918–68), Canadian-American psychologist.

Wassermann, August Paul von (1866–1925), German bacteriologist.

*Watson, John Broadus (1878–1958), American behavioral psychologist.

Weber, Ernst Heinrich (1795–1878), German physiologist and psychophysicist.

Wechsler, David (1896–1981), Romanian-born American psychologist.

Weigl, Egon (*fl.* 1920s–1960s), Romanian-born psychologist.

Weiskrantz, Lawrence (b. 1926), British neuropsychologist.

Wernicke, Carl (1848–1905), German neurologist.

Wertheimer, Max (1880–1943), Czech-born American psychologist.

Wever, Ernest Glen (b. 1902), American psychologist.

Whitney, Donald Ransom (b. 1915), American mathematician and statistician.

Whorf, Benjamin Lee (1897–1941), American linguist and chemical engineer.

Wiener, Norbert (1894–1964), American mathematician.

Wilcoxon, Frank (1892–?), Irish-born American chemist and statistician.

Willi, H. (*fl.* 1960's), Swiss pediatrician.

Williams, J. C. P. (*fl.* 1960), New Zealand physician.

Wilson, Edward O. (b. 1929), American entomologist and sociobiologist.

Wilson, Samuel A. K. (1878–1937), British neurologist.

Wolff, Kaspar Friedrich (1733–94), German anatomist.

Wolpe, Joseph (b. 1915), South African-born American psychiatrist.

Woodworth, Robert Sessions (1869–1962), American psychologist.

Wulf, F. (*fl.* 1920s), German psychologist.

Wundt, Wilhelm Max (1832–1920), German physiologist, psychologist, philosopher.

Yerkes, Robert Mearns (1876–1956), American psychologist.

Young, Thomas (1773–1829), English physician and physicist.

Zajonc, Robert (b. 1923), American social psychologist.

Zeigarnik, Bluma (b. 1900), Russian psychologist.

Zipf, George Kingsley (1903–50), American philologist.

Zöllner, Johann Karl Friedrich (1834–82), German physicist.

Zwaardemaker, Hendrik (1857–1930), Dutch physiologist.